CHARLESWORTH

COMPANY LAW

D0892842

AUSTRALIA
Law Book Co.
Sydney

CANADA and USA
Carswell
Toronto

HONG KONG
Sweet & Maxwell Asia

NEW ZEALAND
Brookers
Wellington

SINGAPORE and MALAYSIA
Sweet & Maxwell Asia
Singapore and Kuala Lumpur

CHARLESWORTH

COMPANY LAW

SEVENTEENTH EDITION

By

Geoffrey Morse, LL.B.
Barrister, Professor of Corporate and Tax Law
at the University of Birmingham

and

Stephen Girvin, PhD, LL.B., LL.M.
Associate Professor of Law
at the National University of Singapore

Accounting Editor

Richard Morris, B.A., M.Sc., F.C.A.
Professor Emeritus of Accounting
at the University of Liverpool

Insolvency Editor

Sandra Frisby, PhD
Lecturer in Corporate and Financial Law
at the University of Nottingham

Markets Regulation Editor

Alastair Hudson, LL.B., LL.M., PhD
Professor of Equity and Law
at Queen Mary, University of London

LONDON
SWEET & MAXWELL
2005

First Edition	(1932)	By His Honour Judge Charlesworth
Second Edition	(1938)	,, ,, ,, ,,
Third Edition	(1940)	,, ,, ,, ,,
Fourth Edition	(1946)	,, ,, ,, ,,
Second Impression	(1947)	
Third Impression	(1948)	
Fifth Edition	(1949)	,, ,, ,, ,,
Second Impression revised	(1950)	,, ,, ,, ,,
Sixth Edition	(1954)	,, ,, ,, ,,
Second Impression revised	(1956)	,, ,, ,, ,,
Seventh Edition	(1960)	By T. E. Cain
Second Impression	(1962)	
Eighth Edition	(1965)	,, ,, ,, ,,
Ninth Edition	(1968)	,, ,, ,, ,,
Tenth Edition	(1972)	,, ,, ,, ,,
Eleventh Edition	(1977)	,, ,, ,, ,,
Second Impression	(1980)	
Twelfth Edition	(1983)	By Geoffrey Morse
Thirteenth Edition	(1987)	,, ,, ,, ,,
Fourteenth Edition	(1991)	,, ,, ,, ,,
Fifteenth Edition	(1995)	,, ,, ,, ,,
Second Impression	(1997)	
Sixteenth Edition	(1999)	,, ,, ,, ,,
Seventeenth Edition	(2005)	,, ,, ,, ,,

Published by
Sweet & Maxwell Limited of
100 Avenue Road
Swiss Cottage
London NW3 3PF
(*www.sweetandmaxwell.co.uk*)
Phototypeset by LBJ Typesetting Ltd
of Kingsclere
Printed in England by MPG Books Ltd, Bodmin, Cornwall

No natural forests were destroyed to make this product; only farmed timber was used and replanted

A CIP catalogue record for this book is available from the British library

ISBN 0421–887907

PREFACE

In the five years which have elapsed since the last edition of this book, there have been a number of changes to the statutory framework regulating companies in Great Britain. But the major issue, that of a substantial new Companies Act following the official Company Law Review's Final Report presented to the DTI in 2002, is still in the future. That Review, set up by the DTI, produced a number of very thoughtful and thorough documents, although its Final Report was somewhat less radical than might have been supposed. The Government did respond in 2003 with a White Paper and a draft bill, accepting many of the Review's proposals. That, however, only covered part of the Review's ambit. A further White Paper and draft bill were published in March 2005, and a bill was included in the Queen's Speech in May 2005. This may become law some time in 2006, but may not come into effect until some time thereafter. In any event, this edition includes the major recommendations of the Review and the draft bills at appropriate places in the text. One other recommendation which appeared too late for the text was the Government's Draft Bill on the reform of the law of corporate manslaughter (March 2005).

The most important of the changes which have actually been enacted have been in the field of corporate insolvency. The combined effect of the Insolvency Act 2000 and Enterprise Act 2002 has been to streamline administration orders, abolish the concept of an administrative receiver, change the priority of payment of debts, strengthen the voluntary arrangement procedure and allow a disqualification undertaking to be agreed between the Secretary of State and a director as an alternative to lengthy and costly disqualification proceedings following a corporate insolvency. Insofar as companies have securities which are dealt with on the various markets, the laws regulating those markets have been radically changed by the Financial Markets and Services Act 2000. That is really part of a wide and complex area of regulation of the finance industry and the capital markets, but its impact on companies is the subject of Chapter 7.

In terms of the general structure of company law, the domestically inspired statutory changes have been relatively modest. There have been measures allowing for the introduction of treasury shares into British law (these are its own shares which a company purchases and retains—often reallocating them to employee share schemes) and allowing anonymity of addresses for directors of companies subject to harassment as a result of the company's business, the strengthening of DTI investigation powers and further regulation of auditors, who seem to have taken the blame for the major corporate collapses in recent years. To that end, the Stock Exchange has also revised its rules on the corporate governance of listed companies. Auditors have also been subject to increased EU-based regulations. Finally, we have also seen the introduction of a new business form, the Limited Liability Partnership (LLP), which is part company and part partnership, and a new corporate form, the Community Interest Company, which appears at the moment to be a form in search of a user.

It is from the EC that the most interesting legislative developments have come. After 30 years, the European Company (or *Societas Europaea*—SE) has become a reality. This is now part of British law and, in theory at least, enables companies to form themselves into a company which to some extent (although nowhere near the amount originally envisaged) transcends the internal boundary requirements of the EC. But tax and employee participation problems may well prove to be real stumbling blocks. The SE also raises general questions as to the ability of companies to move their operations within the EC and/or to merge across frontiers. Those questions (and the SE) are the subject of a new chapter, 32, at the end of the book. In addition, the EC has also finally agreed the text of the 13th Directive on Takeovers, which must be implemented by May 2006. Although this will have a limited effect on the actual rules which regulate the conduct of takeovers, it will put the current self-regulatory Takeover Panel and the City Code on a statutory footing for the first time.

This change is, according to the Government's Consultative Document, to be effected by primary legislation which will also include the recommendations of the Company Law Review on the statutory right of a successful bidder to acquire a dissenting minority's shares (the so-called squeeze out provisions). Given that the DTI will have to be given parliamentary time to comply with the EC timetable for the Directive's implementation, it may well be that the bill will also include some or even several of the Company Law Review's proposals accepted by the Government in its White Paper, as a first stage in the implementation of the Review. These could include the ill-advised move to codify directors' duties and, more hopefully, the proposals to abolish the financial assistance and court-based reduction of capital rules for private companies. There are several recent precedents for companies bills to increase exponentially whilst proceeding through Parliament.

The Courts have also been occupied with a number of cases in the field of company law. Whilst no single case has the effect of an *Ebrahimi* or an *O'Neill v Phillips*, there have been important clarifying decisions on such areas as corporate contracts, the ambit of a director's duty of loyalty, the defences to and remedies for breaches of that duty, classes and procedure for schemes of arrangement, de facto and shadow directors, the tariffs for and exceptions to directors' disqualification orders, pre-emption clauses, the relationship between s.122(g) of the Insolvency Act and s.459 of the Companies Act, and the relationship between the concept of unfairly prejudicial conduct in the latter and derivative actions. In other areas, it has to be said that the courts have to some extent compounded the existing confusion. It is increasingly difficult to reconcile the cases decided regularly on the vexed topic of financial assistance given by a company for the acquisition of its own shares. In addition, the precise ambit of s.35A, the endless attempts to delineate between fixed and floating charges, establishing the exceptions if any to the principle of no-reflective loss, the long-running problem of the consequences of non-disclosure of an interest by a director in a corporate contract and the relationship between agency and breaches of duty by the directors are all matters it seems for judicial debate rather than resolution.

In preparing this edition, due to pressures of time, I have had the invaluable help of Dr Stephen Girvin, currently at the National University of Singapore, who took over responsibility for Chapters 1 to 6 and 16 to 19, as well as keeping an eye on developments in Scotland. He has done a thorough and professional job, totally in keeping with the style of the book, and I am much in his debt. The insolvency chapters (23 to 29) have passed to Dr Sandra Frisby of the University of Nottingham. I am grateful that someone with her acknowledged expertise on insolvency was on hand to cover this ever-important and much-changed area. To Professor Richard Morris, who continued to look after the accountancy chapters (20 to 22), I can only add my usual amazement as to his ability to provide a coherent and understandable path through what appears to be an ever moving forest. Finally I am also indebted to Professor Alastair Hudson who, as an expert, undertook to rewrite Chapter 7 on the impact of market regulation on companies. That is now a vast and important subject in its own right and daunting for anyone not familiar with all its nuances. Alastair has also produced the magician's trick of making something so complex so understandable.

To each of the above, the book and I owe a great deal. This is a unique book which I have come to cherish and which benefits enormously from new blood, provided it is, of course, compatible. My fellow editors are that and much more. The rest of the book is of course still my responsibility as is the whole in its overall coverage. We have all worked to the law as we understood it to be as on the February 1, 2005.

Geoffrey Morse

Bromsgrove, Worcestershire
May 2005

CONTENTS

TABLE OF CASES

TABLE OF STATUTES

TABLE OF STATUTORY INSTRUMENTS

TABLE OF RULES OF THE SUPREME COURT (SI 1965/1776)

REFERENCES TO CITY CODE ON TAKEOVERS/MERGERS

Chapter 1

NATURE OF REGISTERED COMPANIES

THIS book is mainly concerned with registered companies, whether public or private, limited by shares.[1] The term "registered company" means a company incorporated or formed by registration under the Companies Acts. The major Act is the Companies Act 1985, which consolidated a series of Acts passed between 1948 and 1983, latterly in response to the UK's obligations as a member of what was then the EC. This Act has now been amended on several occasions,[2] starting with the Companies Act 1989, but for all intents and purposes it may still be regarded as the principal Act. In this book, unless otherwise stated, or if the context otherwise requires, references to sections and schedules are to those of the Companies Act 1985. References to "the Act" are to the Companies Act 1985. In many instances, changes made by the 1989 Act and other amendments in subsequent legislation have been effected by the substitution of sections into the Act.

The Act provides[3] that for the purpose of the registration of companies under the Act, there shall be offices (Companies Registration Offices in England and Scotland) at such places as the Secretary of State (for Trade and Industry) thinks fit, and that he may appoint such registrars, assistant registrars, clerks and servants as he thinks necessary for the registration of companies and may make regulations with respect to their duties.

Section 1(1) enables two or more persons associated for any lawful purpose[4] to form an incorporated company with or without limited liability, by complying with the requirements of the Act in respect of registration. As is explained later in this chapter, the requirements are that certain documents be delivered to the appropriate Registrar of Companies and certain fees paid. Under s.10, for example, a memorandum of association and articles of association must be delivered to the Registrar, who must retain and register them.

The rest of this chapter attempts first of all to give a simple answer to the question "what is a registered company?" and then to trace briefly the history of the registered company. After that there is a note on the current legislation applicable to companies in particular, including the relevant measures of the European Union. Finally, the following topics are dealt with: the procedure to obtain the registration of a company; the effect of the registration of a

---

[1] In general terms commercial companies.
[2] For the details of some of these changes, see p.8, below.
[3] s.704.
[4] A private company may be formed by one person only: s.1(3A). *cf.* the Draft Companies Bill 2002, which recommends permitting public companies to be so formed (cl.2): *Modernising Company Law* (Cm 5553-II, 2002).

company—this is that the company is a corporation with a legal existence separate from that of its members, who usually have limited personal liability; the liability of a registered company, *i.e.* of this separate artificial legal person; and the contrast between registered companies and partnerships—a partnership is not a corporation and the partners do not have limited liability.

What is a Registered Company?

A registered company, *i.e.* a company incorporated by registration under the Companies Acts, is regarded by the law as a person, just as a human being is a person. This artificial or juristic person can own land and other property, enter into contracts, sue and be sued, have a bank account in its own name, owe money to others and be a creditor of other people and other companies, and employ people to work for it. The company's money and property belong to the company and not to the members or shareholders, although the members or shareholders may be said to own the company. Similarly, the company's debts are the debts of the company and the shareholders cannot be compelled to pay them, although if, for example, the company is being wound up and its assets do not realise a sum sufficient to pay its debts, a shareholder whose liability is limited by shares is liable to contribute to the assets up to the amount, if any, unpaid on his shares. A company, of course, can only act through human agents, and those who manage its business are called directors. The directors are agents of the company and transact business, etc., on behalf of the company. They may authorise other agents to act on the company's behalf, *e.g.* the company secretary. The company will be bound by any transaction entered into on its behalf if the agent is acting within his authority. The company is also liable for torts[5] and crimes committed by its servants and agents within the scope of their employment or authority. This concept of the company as a corporation, *i.e.* a person separate and distinct from the other persons who are its members and directors, is the fundamental principle of company law.

A company must have members, otherwise it would never exist at all, and in the case of a company with a share capital these members are called shareholders. A shareholder's position with regard to the company itself and to other shareholders is regulated by the Act, by the memorandum and the articles of association and by any agreement between the shareholders, and also by the principle that controlling shareholders, *i.e.* those with sufficient votes to pass a resolution in general meeting, must act bona fide for the benefit of the company as a whole. The memorandum and articles vary considerably among different companies, but in every case the shareholder's position is that of the owner of one or more shares in the company, which shares usually carry a right to vote at general meetings, and, if profits are made, a right to receive dividends, if declared, on his shares. His shares are something which he has bought—perhaps from the company, or perhaps from somebody else—and something which he can sell or give away, either in his lifetime or by his will.

The general rule is that a shareholder cannot get his money back from the company so long as the company is in existence, because the position is not that

---

[5] Or, in Scots law, delict.

of a person who has lent money to the company or has deposited his money as with a bank or a building society—it is that of the owner of property, namely, the shares, which can only be turned into money if a buyer can be found to pay for them. Shares may be fully paid or partly paid. When the shares are only partly paid, the shareholder can be compelled to pay them up fully if called upon by the company or, if the company is being wound up and its debts exceed its assets, by the liquidator. In any event, it is the general policy of the Act to see that the issued share capital is maintained intact, except for losses in the way of business, so that it may be available to satisfy the company's debts. Accordingly, while the company is a going concern the general rule is that no part of the paid-up capital may be returned to the shareholders without the consent of the court, or by following strict procedures intended to protect creditors.

A company may be formed to acquire and carry on an existing business, which may or may not belong to the promoters, or to start some new business. However, a company is commonly formed as a private company to acquire the promoters' business. In this case, a price is put on the business and paid by the issue to the promoters of shares credited as fully or partly paid in the company. Most of the price will be left owing to the promoters so that if the company is later wound up they will rank for repayment of it as unsecured creditors; otherwise if they take the whole price in the form of shares credited as fully paid they will rank for repayment of capital after the unsecured creditors. If a company is formed to acquire a business which does not belong to the promoters they may provide the necessary funds for the company by taking shares in the company for cash.

A company can also raise money by borrowing.[6] Persons who lend money to a company may be issued with debentures to show that they have lent money and are entitled to interest on their loans. Unlike shareholders, they are not members of the company and they have no right to vote at general meetings. Creditors may take a charge over the company's property by way of security for repayment of their debt. Such charges must be registered with the Registrar of Companies.

Shares in, and debentures of, public companies are extensively bought as investments by people who wish to derive an income from their capital and/or achieve capital growth. In order to facilitate transactions in such securities, the companies involved will be quoted on the Stock Exchange and are known as quoted companies. To protect investors from dishonest or incompetent people who form companies in which the investors are likely to lose their money, disclosure of such things as the company's past financial record and the benefits of being a director, is required in the document on the strength of which the public is invited to subscribe for shares or debentures of the company. Provision is also made for a company's accounts and the balance sheet and profit and loss account to be audited every year by auditors appointed by the shareholders and for the balance sheet and the profit and loss account and certain other documents to be circulated to every shareholder and debenture holder. With the

---

[6] Money borrowed by a company is sometimes called "loan capital". It should not be confused with "share capital": Ch.9.

exception of unlimited companies, a copy of the balance sheet and the other documents must also be lodged with the Registrar of Companies. The Stock Exchange itself also provides detailed rules regulating the affairs of quoted companies.

The directors of a company, who are usually appointed by the members at their annual general meeting, have wide powers to manage the company's business conferred upon them by the articles. The members cannot control the exercise of these powers, although they can, *e.g.* alter the articles. The directors, in turn, owe certain duties of good faith and care to the company.

The Acts have increasingly required disclosure by companies, their directors and substantial shareholders of many financial and other particulars. Usually this will be to the Registrar who will keep the information on the company's file. Such information is then available to anyone who makes a search of that file and is seen as one of the prices of incorporation. There is no constructive notice of such information, however.

A registered company is capable of perpetual succession but it may become insolvent or it may decide to retire from business. In such a case it is wound up, *i.e.* it is put, or it goes, into liquidation, and a person, called a liquidator, is appointed to wind up its affairs. He sells the company's property and pays as much of its debts as he can do out of the proceeds of sale. If there is a surplus, he distributes it among the shareholders. When the liquidation is completed the company is dissolved and ceases to exist.

THE DEVELOPMENT OF MODERN COMPANY LAW

The modern commercial company, incorporated by registration under the Act, is the result of the fusion of two different legal principles. A registered company, like a statutory company or a chartered company, is a "corporation",[7] *i.e.* in the eyes of the law it is a person, capable of perpetual succession and quite distinct from the natural persons who are its members at any given moment.[8] However, the expression "company" is not confined to a corporation but can include a partnership, which is not a corporation but, at least in the case of an English partnership,[9] is merely the relationship between the individual partners. The present-day registered company represents the fusion of the principle of incorporation with that of partnership.

At common law, the Crown has always had the right of granting charters of incorporation.[10] Non-trading companies, such as the Law Society and the Institute of Chartered Accountants, are the kind of company now incorporated by charter but trading companies have in the past been formed in this way. The right was first used for creating commercial corporations at the end of the sixteenth and the beginning of the seventeenth centuries, when such companies as the Levant Company, the East India Company, the Hudson's Bay Company

---

[7] s.13(3), below, p.25.

[8] *Salomon v Salomon & Co. Ltd* [1897] A.C. 22, below, p.25.

[9] A Scottish partnership, although not a corporation, is a legal person distinct from the partners of whom it is composed: Partnership Act 1890, s.4(2).

[10] A chartered company is sometimes referred to as "a common law corporation".

and the notorious South Sea Company (afterwards incorporated by special Act of Parliament) were incorporated. As these corporations were legal entities quite distinct from their members, it followed that at common law the members were not liable for the debts of the corporation, and, indeed, the Crown had no power to incorporate persons so as to make them liable for the debts of the corporation.[11] In a partnership, on the other hand, the partners were always liable for all the debts of the firm and their liability was unlimited.

In England, trading companies were originally regulated companies, that is, companies in which each member traded with his own stock subject to the rules of the company, but towards the end of the seventeenth century the joint-stock company emerged,[12] and this is the form of the company in common use today. In a joint-stock company, the company trades as a single person with a stock which is jointly contributed by its members. Such companies could only be formed by special Act of Parliament or by charter but, as the advantages of the joint-stock form of trading became better known, these methods proved too expensive and dilatory to meet the growing commercial needs of the nation. Accordingly, there grew up a new type of company based upon contract. This contract took the form of an elaborate deed of settlement containing provisions regulating the relations of the members among themselves and providing for the transfer of shares. A body formed in this way was only a partnership in the eyes of the law and the liability of the members was unlimited. This type of unincorporated company fell into disfavour with the legislature, largely owing to the activities of fraudulent promoters and unscrupulous share dealers, and in 1720 the Bubble Act was passed to deal with it. Unfortunately, that Act had the effect of suppressing unincorporated companies without satisfying the want which had given rise to their existence, so that "joint-stock" enterprises had to wait till the middle of the nineteenth century before incorporation "for any lawful purpose" could be obtained by the simple process of registration, and personal liability be limited by "one magic word".[13]

The origins of company law in Scotland were distinct from those in England, although regulated companies and joint-stock companies did exist from at least the later years of the seventeenth century. The common law of Scotland sanctioned formation of companies with transferable shares and under the management of directors, and recognised such companies as having a personality separate from that of their members.[14] In Scotland, common law companies constituted under contracts of co-partnership corresponded to the English deed of settlement companies. The 1720 Bubble Act extended to Scotland but, because of the common law companies, probably had no legal effect there.[15]

In 1825, by the Bubble Companies, etc., Act, the 1720 Bubble Act was repealed and the Crown was empowered in grants of future charters to provide

---

[11] *per* Lindley L.J. in *Elve v Boyton* [1891] 1 Ch.501 at p.507, CA.

[12] Holdsworth, *History of English Law*, Vol.8, pp.206–222.

[13] Carr, *Select Charters of Trading Companies*, Selden Society, Vol.28.

[14] The decision in *Stevenson & Co. v Macnair and others* (1757) M. 14,560 and 14,667; 5 Brown's Supp. 340 suggests that Scottish courts might even, under continental influence, have developed a principle of limited liability in relation to these companies.

[15] An Act of 1825 (6 Geo. 4, c. 131) mentioned with approval the practice which had prevailed in Scotland of forming joint-stock companies with transferable shares.

that the members of the corporation should be personally liable for the debts of the corporation to such extent as the Crown should think proper. This was the beginning of "limited liability." By the Chartered Companies Act 1837, the Crown was empowered to grant letters patent, *i.e.* to grant the advantages of incorporation *without* granting a charter, to a body of persons associated together for trading purposes. The persons in question had to register a deed of partnership dividing the capital into shares and providing for transfers, and satisfy the other requirements of the Act; limited liability was then granted to them. The association to which the letters patent were granted did not become a body corporate and the grant of limited liability was an advantage to which they would otherwise not have been entitled.

By the Joint Stock Companies Registration, etc., Act 1844, provision was made in England for the incorporation of companies by registration without the necessity of obtaining a Royal Charter or a special Act of Parliament. The peculiarity of this statute, however, was that, instead of allowing the usual common law consequences of incorporation to follow, it proceeded on the lines of the Chartered Companies Act 1837 and merely gave a corporate existence to a body which it still evidently regarded as a partnership, because it imposed much the same liability on the members for the debts of the company as they would have had for the debts of a parternship. This Act also made it compulsory to register as companies all partnerships with more than 25 members[16] Liability limited by shares, *i.e.* where a member's liability is limited to the amount, if any, unpaid on his shares, was introduced in the case of registered companies by the Limited Liability Act 1855, and the Joint Stock Companies Act 1856 substituted two documents, the memorandum of association and articles of association, for the deed of settlement.

In Scotland, the registered company was not introduced until the Act of 1856: neither the 1844 Act nor the 1855 Act applied to Scotland.

The Companies Act 1862 repealed and consolidated the previous Acts. It also established liability limited by guarantee and, in general, prohibited any alteration in the objects clause[17] of the memorandum of association. This prohibition remained until the Companies (Memorandum of Association) Act 1890 enabled the objects to be altered for some purposes with the leave of the court, after a special resolution[18] had been passed by the members in general meeting. The Companies Act 1867 contained a power to reduce share capital. The Directors' Liability Act 1890 introduced the principle of the liability of the directors to pay compensation to persons who have been induced to take shares on the strength of false statements in a prospectus. The Companies Act 1900 contained the first provisions relating to the contents of prospectuses, the compulsory audit of the company's accounts and the registration of charges with the Registrar. The Companies Act 1907 made provision for the private (as opposed to the public) company, *i.e.* a company which is prohibited from inviting the public to subscribe for its shares or debentures.[19] Modern company law was taking shape.

---

[16] The maximum number of members for a partnership used to be 20, with exceptions for most professional firms (s.716), but that provision was repealed by the Regulatory Reform (Removal of 20 Member Limit in Partnerships etc) Order 2002, SI 2002/3203.

[17] Dealt with below, p.63.

[18] *ibid.*

[19] Below, p.42.

The 1948 Act and its successors

The 1948 Companies Act made far-reaching changes in the law relating to company accounts. As the Cohen Report[20] (on which the 1948 Act was based) said, "The history of company legislation shows the increasing importance attached to publicity in connection with accounts. The Act of 1862 contained no compulsory provisions with regard to audit or accounts, though Table A[21] to that Act did include certain clauses dealing with both matters. In 1879, provision was made for the audit of the accounts of banking companies, but it was not until 1900 that any such provision was made generally applicable. It was only on July 1, 1908, when the Companies Act 1907 came into force, that provision was made for including a statement in the form of a balance sheet in the annual return to the Registrar of Companies, and that provision exempted private companies from this requirement." The Companies Act 1929 required a balance sheet and a profit and loss account to be laid before the company every year, while the present Acts set out in great detail the contents of those accounts, with stringent provisions for their audit. The 1948 Act also for the first time required the auditor of a public or a private company to have a professional qualification.[22]

A number of the recommendations contained in the Jenkins Report[23] were given effect in the 1967 Act which amended the 1948 Act in a number of respects, including new provisions in connection with a company's accounts. 1972 saw the European Communities Act, s.9 of which related solely to company law since the UK was obliged on accession to comply with an existing EC Directive of 1968 on the harmonisation of company law.[24] This section's principal change was to modify the law relating to *ultra vires* and the problems of agency in relation to companies.[25] In Scotland, the Companies (Floating Charges and Receivers) (Scotland) Act 1972 modified the law of Scotland in relation to floating charges and made provision for the appointment of receivers.

The Companies Act 1976 enacted, amongst other things, some but not all of the clauses and Schedules of the abortive Companies Bill 1973. The 1976 Act amended the law relating to the filing of company accounts and the keeping of accounting records. It provided, amongst other things, for the disqualification of persons taking part in the management of companies if they were persistently in default in complying with the requirements to deliver documents to the Registrar.

The Companies Act 1980 was inspired by an EC Directive of 1976 regulating the control of public companies. It provided for the first time a major distinction between public and private companies, including minimum financial require-

---

[20] (1945) Cmd. 6659, para.96.
[21] A model set of articles of association.
[22] For a fuller treatment of the history of company law, see Gower, *Modern Company Law* 6th ed. (1997), Chs 2 and 3.
[23] (1962) Cmnd. 1749. This report has never been implemented in full or dealt with in any consistent manner although certain of its recommendations were implemented by the 1989 Act after a gap of 27 years.
[24] The impact of EC Directives on company law is one of the modern features of the law. See p.15, below.
[25] This worked along the lines of the Jenkins Committee recommendations in para.42 of the Report. It proved to be defective in many ways, however, and was rewritten by the 1989 Act.

ments for the former. It also contained new provisions relating to the issuing of shares and the payment for them. Payment of dividends became the subject of statutory rules. Tighter restrictions on directors were imposed following the many "unacceptable faces of capitalism" which manifested themselves in the 1970s. Insider dealing,[26] one of the most obvious of those, became a criminal offence.

The 1981 Companies Act was likewise prompted by an EC Directive, this time of 1978, on company accounts. It provided a new format for accounts and for the public disclosure of them. In addition, however, new rules for company names, the purchase and redemption by a company of its own shares and for more stringent disclosure of shareholders were included. Various other reforms were also appended. The technical nature of much of this legislation was so complex that mistakes were made. One particularly embarrassing one, the accidental prohibition of many employee share and pension trusts had to be corrected, in haste, by the Companies (Beneficial Interests) Act 1983.

The 1985 consolidation and after

In 1981 proposals were made for a consolidation of the various Acts from 1948 onwards. There were two joint Reports of the Law Commission and the Scottish Law Commission[27] which recommended many technical amendments to the existing law in order to assist consolidation. These amendments were effected by the Companies Acts (Pre-Consolidation Amendments) Order 1984[28] and the Companies Acts (Pre-Consolidation Amendments) (No. 2) Order 1984[29] which, by virtue of s.116 of the Companies Act 1981, only took effect on the consolidation itself coming into force. After consultation it was decided to produce a single main Act, the Companies Act 1985, with 747 sections and 25 Schedules (up to seven separate Acts had been canvassed) with three small satellite Acts. The 1981 Act provisions relating to the use of business names by all traders, including companies, were separated into the Business Names Act 1985, and those of the 1980 Act relating to insider dealing were also hived off into a separate Act, the Company Securities (Insider Dealing) Act 1985, since those rules applied to securities other than those belonging to companies. The fourth Act, the Companies Consolidation (Consequential Provisions) Act 1985, dealt with transitional matters, savings provisions, repeals and consequential amendments to other Acts. In one area, however, it was not consequential: s.28 repealed, rather than consolidated, the existing provisions on cost book companies.

Whilst the consolidation was proceeding through Parliament, the Companies (Accounts and Audit) Regulations 1984 and the Companies (Share Premium Account) Regulations 1984 were passed and had to be taken into account. The resulting consolidation, taking into account the various amendments referred to above and the need to harmonise legislative styles and phrases over a 30-year period, was by no means a "scissors and paste" consolidation. In the main, it

---

[26] See Ch.19.
[27] (1983) Cmnd. 9114, (1984) Cmnd. 9272.
[28] SI 1984/134.
[29] SI 1984/1169.

used short subsections and many of the pre-existing sections were divided. It was a triumph of draftsmanship in what was then the largest consolidation ever undertaken. By way of departure from previous practice, Tables A to F, the model forms of memorandum and articles etc., are now contained in separate regulations, the Companies (Tables A to F) Regulations 1985,[30] rather than in a Schedule to the Act. Table A itself was redrafted for this purpose. The whole consolidation came into effect on July 1, 1985.

But it proved to be a short-lived oasis of calm as a unified source of company legislation. Two more EC Directives, the third (on mergers)[31] and the sixth (on divisions),[32] were implemented by the Companies (Mergers and Divisions) Regulations 1987,[33] which added a new section and Schedule to the 1985 Act in the area of schemes of arrangement.[34] More importantly, the Insolvency Act 1985, implementing some of the recommendations of the Cork Committee (Insolvency Law and Practice—Report of the Review Committee)[35] repealed many of the sections of the 1985 Act relating to liquidation and other aspects of corporate insolvency and replaced them with several new concepts, *e.g.* administration orders, as well as making several amendments to the rules governing insolvent liquidations. The Act was based on a White Paper,[36] itself based on the Cork Report. The resulting *pot pourri* of legislation on corporate liquidation and insolvency was itself consolidated into the Insolvency Act 1986, apart from the provisions relating to directors' disqualification which were consolidated into the Company Directors Disqualification Act 1986. The result is that some of the 1948 Act winding up provisions were consolidated in 1985, amended in that year and re-consolidated in 1986.

In addition the reform of the law governing the investment industry, prompted by a report by Professor Gower commissioned by the Department of Trade and Industry, was suggested by a White Paper, "Financial Services in the United Kingdom: A New Framework for Investor Protection"[37] and implemented by the Financial Services Act 1986. Whilst this Act is largely concerned with regulating the City and the investment industry generally, it has had a double impact on company law. The first was indirect in that company securities are investments for this purpose and those who deal in them were, therefore, subject to the Act's new regulatory system. The second was direct. The Financial Services Act provided new rules for the public issue of shares whether listed on the Stock Exchange or otherwise. It also recast the provisions in the Companies Act 1985 relating to the compulsory acquistion of shares on a take-over and amended the rules relating to insider dealing in the Company Securities (Insider Dealing) Act 1985. The Financial Services Act thus repealed many of the 1985 Act sections relating to the public issue of shares and the Stock Exchange (Listing) Regulations 1984.[38] (The latter were passed to implement yet another set of EC

---

[30] SI 1985/805.
[31] Dir. 78/855/E.C.
[32] Dir. 82/89/E.C.
[33] SI 1987/1991.
[34] See Chap. 30, below.
[35] (1982) Cmnd. 8558.
[36] (1984) Cmnd. 9175.
[37] (1985) Cmnd. 9432.
[38] SI 1984/716.

directives, on listing particulars, the admission of securities to listing and the continuing disclosure of information by listed companies,[39] These lay alongside the 1985 Act provisions in a totally obscure manner and may usefully be consigned to history).

Companies Act 1989

More substantial changes were made by the Companies Act 1989 which was occasioned by the need to implement two further E.C. directives, the seventh on group accounts[39a] and the eighth on the qualification of auditors.[39b] The opportunity was also taken to amend and extend the 1985 Act provisions relating to investigations (together with investigations under the Insolvency Act 1986 and the Financial Services Act 1986), the doctrine of *ultra vires* and application of the agency law to corporate transactions[39c] and in several other largely unrelated areas, some of which were recommended by the Jenkins Committee in 1962. Finally, several amendments to other Acts were made, most importantly to the Financial Services Act 1986. Most of the 1989 Act changes were effected by adding, substituting or amending sections in the earlier Acts.

Parts of the 1989 Act have not actually been brought into force, despite the time which has elapsed since they were enacted. One important example of this is Pt IV of the 1989 Act, on the registration of company charges. Although certain of the interim recommendations of the Diamond Committee on Security Interests over Personal Property[40] were implemented in the 1989 Act, a more radical proposal which would have involved a US-style notice filing system, was not acted upon then. Indeed, the Department of Trade and Industry (the DTI) in 1996 advised that it was not intending to implement Pt IV. Most recently, the Law Commission[41] has published two consultation papers on this.[42] Another example of non-implementation has been in relation to the abolition of the doctrine of constructive notice, provided for in s.142 of that Act, which would have added s.711A to the principal Act.

Post-1989 developments

A number of important company law developments have occurred since 1989 which have necessitated changes and additions to the 1985 Act. One of the principal sources of these changes, as ever, have been new EC directives on company law, with the changes implemented by statutory instrument, under powers to amend legislation in this way given by s.2(2) of the European Communities Act.[43]

---

[39] Dir. 80/390/EC, Dir. 79/279/EC, and Dir. 82/121/EC.
[39a] Dir. 83/349/EC.
[39b] Dir 84/253/EC.
[39c] See p.92, below.
[40] *A Review of Security Interests in Personal Property* (DTI, November 1988). For discussion see Michael Bridge, "Form, substance and innovation in personal property security law", [1992] J.B.L. 1.
[41] See too "Registration of rights in security by companies", Scot. Law. Com. Report No.197 (2004).
[42] *Registration of Security Interests: Company Charges and Property other than Land*, L.C.C.P. No. 164 (2002); *Company Security Interests: A Consultative Report*, L.C.C.P. No. 176 (2004). See to below, p.527.
[43] As to these, see p.15, below.

These include the directive amending the fourth and seventh directives on company accounts[44]; the eleventh directive on disclosure requirements for branches of oversea companies[45]; and the major shareholdings directive relating to disclosure of such interests in listed companies.[46] The most fundamental of these changes, however, has been the introduction of the single member company, *i.e.* whereby one person may form a private company, as the result of the implementation of the twelfth directive on single member private limited companies[47] by the Companies (Single Member Private Limited Companies) Regulations 1992.[48] Other changes to the 1985 Act have come from other sources, including the Welsh Language Act 1993.

One directive has led to primary legislation, however. Implementation of the directive co-ordinating regulations on insider dealing[49] led to the repeal of the Company Securities (Insider Dealing) Act 1985, part of the 1985 consolidation, and its replacement by Part V of the Criminal Justice Act 1993. Further, as part of a deregulation policy, there are wide powers to remove statutory burdens from small businesses, including companies, under section 1 of the Deregulation and Contracting Out Act 1994, by delegated legislation. One example is the Deregulation (Resolutions of Private Companies) Order 1996.[50] That Act also amended the 1985 Act in relation to the removal of non-trading private companies from the register of companies.

Reform of company law legislation

The Law Commission

The mandate of the Law Commission of England and Wales,[51] which was set up in 1965,[52] is to keep the law of England and Wales under review and to recommend reform, when needed.[53] There have been a number of instances since 1989 when the Commission has undertaken work in the company law area.[54] Most notably, this has included a report on *Shareholder Remedies*[55] and a report on *Company Directors: Regulating Conflicts of Interests and Formulating a Statement of Duties,*[56] both of which, to some extent, fed into the work of the Company Law Review (CLR).[57] As we have seen, recent work has been on the

---

[44] Dir. 90/604.
[45] Dir. 89/666.
[46] Dir. 88/629.
[47] Dir. 89/667.
[48] SI 1992/1699.
[49] Dir. 89/592.
[50] SI 1996/1471. See p.263, below.
[51] See *www.lawcom.gov.uk*. And also of its Scottish equivalent. The Scottish Law Commission: see *www.scotlawcom.gov.uk*.
[52] See Mr Justice Scarman, "The Work of the Law Commission for England and Wales", (1969) 33 Western Ontario L.R. 33.
[53] See s.3 of the Law Commissions Act 1965.
[54] Often in conjunction with the Scottish Law Commission.
[55] Law Comm. Rep. No.246 (1997).
[56] Law Comm. Rep. No.261 (1999). Undertaken jointly with the Scottish Law Commission: see Scot. Law. Comm. Rep. No. 173.
[57] Below, p.12.

registration of company charges.[58] In the related area of partnership law, the Law Commission also produced a Report on *Partnership Law*.[59]

The Company Law Review (CLR)

On March 4, 1998, the Department of Trade and Industry (DTI) published a consultative document entitled *Modern Company Law for a Competitive Economy*. This marked out a fundamental review of modern company law with terms of reference to make recommendations having:

(1) Considered how core company law could be modernised in order to provide a simple, efficient and cost-effective framework for carrying out business activity which provided the maximum freedom and flexibility while protecting those involved in the enterprise and was drafted in clear, concise and unambiguous language that can be readily understood by those involved in business.

(2) Considered whether company law, partnership law and other legislation together provided an adequate choice of legal vehicle for business at all levels.

(3) Considered the proper relationship between company law and non-statutory standards of corporate behaviour.[60]

(4) Reviewed the extent to which foreign companies operated in Great Britain should be regulated under British company law.

In the ensuing years, virtually no aspect of company law was left unscrutinised by those responsible for conducting the Review. In all, the Review produced a significant amount of work in consultation and other documents,[61] culminating in *Modern Company Law for a Competitive Economy—Final Report*, in two volumes.[62] The government then published a response to the Review in a White Paper, *Modernising Company Law*,[63] published in July 2002, also in two volumes.[64] This White Paper set out the government's policy on modernizing company law including draft clauses.

There was little progress on this until 2004, when the DTI published a further consultation document, *Company Law: Flexibility and Accessibility*.[65] Patricia Hewitt, the then Secretary of State, stated there that:

[58] Above, p.10.
[59] Law Com. Report No.283 (2003). Jointly with the Scottish Law Commission: see Scot. Law. Comm. Rep. No.192.
[60] Para.5.3.
[61] *Company Law Review: The Strategic Framework* URN 99/654; *Company General Meetings and Shareholder Communication* URN 99/1144; *Company Formation and Capital maintenance* URN 99/1145; *Reforming the Law Concerning Overseas Companies* URN 99/1146; *Company Law Review—Developing the Framework* URN 00/656; *Company law Review—Capital Maintenance: Other Issues* URN 00/880; *Company Law Review—Registration of Company Charges* URN 00/1213; *Company Law Review—Completing the Structure* URN 00/1335; *Company Law Review—Trading Disclosures, a Consultation paper* URN 01/542.
[62] Presented to the Secretary of State on July 26, 2001.
[63] Cm. 5553.
[64] See Robert Goddard, "'Modernising Company Law': The Government's White Paper" (2003) 66 Modern L.R. 402.
[65] May 2004.

"[The Government] will be following the route-map that the Company Law Review (CLR) provided except where there are compelling reasons to depart from it. We will legislate as soon as parliamentary time allows and will publish beforehand a draft Bill for consultation."[66]

The document clearly recognises, however, that parliamentary time is at a premium and outlines, in effect, a new system of legislating for company law via a special form of secondary legislation[67] "making it easier to keep the legislation updated over time".[68] This proposal amounts to a significant contraction of the intentions which were declared at the time of the institution of the CLR and, if it proceeds, will see an already difficult piece of primary legislation, the Companies Act 1985, increasingly subject to amendments, instead of a new state-of-the-art Companies Bill.[69]

The Companies (Audit, Investigations and Community Enterprise) Act 2004

This new Act made was passed in 2004 and has been brought into force, in stages, during 2005.[70] The Act makes changes to both the Companies Act 1985 and the Companies Act of 1989 in three main areas and is part of the Government's strategy to restore investor confidence in the wake of major corporate scandals such as those involving Enron and Worldcom.[71] Thus, a key objective is to strengthen audit practice and corporate governance. Part I of the Act therefore contains provisions which strengthen the independence of the system of supervising auditors (sections 1–7), and enforces accounting and reporting requirements (sections 8–18). Other important provisions in Part I are those which amend the company investigations regime (sections 21–24),[72] and those relaxing the prohibition on provisions made by companies to indemnify directors against liability to third parties (sections 19–20).[73]

Much of the Act is concerned with making provision for the establishment of a new corporate vehicle, the *Community Interest Company (CIC)*,[74] which is intended to make it simpler and more convenient to establish a business whose profits and assets are to be used for the benefit of the community. Companies wishing to become a CIC are required to pass a community interest test and to produce an annual report showing that they have contributed to community interest aims.[75] There will be a statutory "lock" on the profits and financial assets

---

[66] At p.4.

[67] The Regulatory Reform Order procedure, as established by the Regulatory Reform Act 2001.

[68] And see the response of the House of Commons Trade and Industry Committee's Ninth Report, *Updating Company Law: the Government's consultation document on "Company Law: Flexibility and Accessibility"* (September 21, 2004).

[69] For an extremely critical reaction to this consultation paper, see Len Sealy, "The reform of company law: selling British business short". (2004) Sweet & Maxwell's Company Law Newsletter 1.

[70] See The Companies (Audit, Investigations and Community Enterprise) Act 2004 (Commencement) and Companies Act 1989 (Commencement No. 18) Order 2004. SI 2004/3322. The whole Act will be in force by October 1, 2005.

[71] Discussed, below, Chapter 00.

[72] See p.380, below.

[73] See p.314, below.

[74] See *www.dti.gov.uk/cics/*.

[75] See ss 37–38.

of CICs and, where a CIC is limited by shares, there is a power to impose a "cap" on any dividend.[76] A new, independent Regulator is responsible for approving the registration of CICs and ensuring they comply with their legal requirements,[77] as well as having a whole range of other powers, such as suspending or removing CIC directors.[78]

Other legislative changes

There have in the past few years been other changes which have had an impact in ancillary areas of company law and should be noted here. Chief among these is the Financial Services and Markets Act 2000,[79] which creates the Financial Services Authority (FSA), a "super-" or "mega-" regulator which covers a wide regulatory scope and embraces not only investment business but also banking and insurance. Under this Act, the Treasury and the FSA are given extensive delegated powers. One important impact of this is that the FSA is now the "competent authority" for the purposes of listed securities.[80]

In the field of insolvency law, there have been a number of important changes. The Insolvency Act 2000 makes a number of changes to the law on company voluntary arrangements (CVAs)[81] and also introduces a new deregulated procedure for the disqualification of unfit directors.[82] These changes are integrated into the Insolvency Act 1986 and the Company Directors Disqualification Act 1986, respectively. The Enterprise Act 2002 has made further changes to personal and corporate insolvency law, to competition law, and to consumer protection law. In relation to corporate insolvency, the objective has been to introduce measures which encourage the use of collective insolvency procedures, increase the prospects of recovery for unsecured creditors, and promote a culture of rescuing ailing companies.[83]

Other statutes have also effected changes to the law. Among the most important of these is the Electronic Communications Act 2000, the relevant delegated legislation[84] for which permits communications between companies and their shareholders and debenture holders to be via electronic modes. This has introduced many changes to the Companies Act 1985.[85]

Other important changes have been implemented by the delegated legislation. Thus, treasury shares were introduced into UK law in December 2003[86] and a number of further important changes are made to the Companies Act 1985.[87]

---

[76] See s.30.

[77] s.27.

[78] s.46.

[79] The Financial Services Act 1986 is repealed. See the Financial Services and Markets Act 2000 (Consequential Amendments and Repeals) Order 2001, SI 2001/3649, reg.3(1)(c).

[80] The Stock Exchange, which has been demutualised, plays a less prominent regulatory function.

[81] ss 1–4.

[82] ss 5–8. As to disqualification, see below, p.321.

[83] See Sandra Frisby, "In search of a rescue regime: the Enterprise Act 2002", (2004) 67 Modern L.R. 247.

[84] See The Companies Act 1985 (Electronic Communications) Order 2000, SI 2000/3373.

[85] See too the Companies House website: *www.companieshouse.gov.uk.*

[86] The Companies (Acquisition of Own Shares)(Treasury Shares) Regulations 2003, SI 2003/1116 and the Companies (Acquisition of Own Shares) (Treasury Shares) No.2 Regulations 2003 SI 2003/3031.

[87] In particular, ss 162A–162G are inserted into the Companies Act 1985.

The principal purpose is to allow certain companies to purchase their own shares to hold such shares "in treasury" rather than cancel them as was originally required under the pre-existing provisions of the Companies Act 1985.

Current UK company law

To sum up, current UK company law is to be found partly in the 1985 Act, which is still the principal Act, and in five major Acts: the Insolvency Act 1986, the Company Directors Disqualification Act 1986, the Companies Act 1989, the Criminal Justice Act 1993 and the Financial Services and Markets Act 2000. However, company law as reflected in these Acts has also been amended or modified by several statutory instruments as well as by the Insolvency Act 2000, the Electronic Communications Act 2000, the Enterprise Act 2002, and the Companies (Audit, Investigations and Community Enterprise) Act 2004.

No attempt has been made to codify company law, *i.e.* to reduce to a code all the statute law and common law on the topic, unlike Acts such as the Partnership Act 1890, the Sale of Goods Act 1893 (now 1979, as amended), and the Marine Insurance Act 1906. The various Companies Acts, as we have seen, have largely consolidated provisions contained in previous Acts. Although there was some hope, at least in the period 1998 to 2001 when the CLR was at work, that there would be a major initiative to produce a new Companies Act for the UK, it is still not certain that this will occur. Accordingly, the legislation, which is often technical and complex, looks set to continue in complexity and difficulty. The legislation, unlike the case law, applies to both England and Scotland and, in some cases, the legislation has replaced case law decisions, often of long standing. Nevertheless, a significant part of company law is based on decided cases[88] and this aspect of company law jurisprudence has shown no signs of diminishing in either volume or importance.[89] Finally, attention should be drawn to the City Panel on Takeovers and Mergers, which operates a Code without the force of law, but which is of great significance in the public company sphere.[90]

Impact of the European Union

In General

From the preceding discussion[91] it will have become clear that it is not enough for the UK company lawyer merely to absorb legislative changes emanating from Westminster. Since joining what was then the European Economic Community (EEC) in 1972, it has become necessary for every company lawyer to take cognisance of the harmonisation programme of the company laws of the Member States. The source for this programme is what is now Art.44 of the Consolidated

---

[88] As the volumes in Butterworths Company Law Cases (B.C.L.C.) and British Company Cases (B.C.C.) provide more than ample testimony.

[89] See David Milman, "The Courts and the Companies Acts: The Judicial Contribution to Company Law" [1990] L.M.C.L.Q. 401.

[90] See below, Ch.31.

[91] Above, pp.7–11.

Treaty of the European Union and of the Treaty Establishing the European Community, which enjoins the Council of Ministers to "act by means of directives"[92] and then goes on to specify that the Council and the Commission are to coordinate safeguards for "companies and firms".[93] National legislatures are required to give effect to these and to amend their law, if necessary, to comply with them.[94]

Within the UK steps have, in the past, been taken to implement a whole range of directives.[95] Implementation of these directives by primary legislation does not present any real difficulty in domestic law, but the trend of implementing such changes by means of delegated legislation can lead to problems connected with whether the changes go further than was needed. Further, the difficulty of adapting the changes to existing law may apply to a wider spectrum of companies than those covered by the directive, in effect creating a two-tier system of law.

Problems can arise when either the directive has not been implemented by the due date or the implementing legislation does not properly comply with the terms of the directive. In such a case, the European Court of Justice has held that directives have *vertical direct effect*, meaning that as between the Member State and an individual or company, the provisions of the directive must be given precedence over the national law.[96] Although this is said not to apply as between two companies and/or individuals (so-called *horizontal direct effect*), the European Court has stated that, in applying national law, whether passed before or after the date for implementing the directive, the national court must interpret its law so far as possible in the light of the wording and purpose of the directive in order to achieve the result required by the directive.[97] In another area of law, the same court has allowed a claim for damages against a Member State for non-implementation of a directive.[98]

Of importance too, perhaps more so than directives on company law, have been arguments which arise under Art.43 of the Treaty, as to rights of establishment. This provides that restrictions on the freedom of establishment of nationals in the territory of another Member State "shall be prohibited" and goes on to say that such rights of freedom of establishment "shall include . . . companies or firms". This right of corporate mobility was accepted by the court in *Centros Ltd v Erhverus-og Selkabsstyrelsen*,[99] and has been followed subsequently.[1]

Directives implemented in UK law

For ease of reference, the following are the main directives which have been implemented in UK law[2]:

[92] Art.249.
[93] Art.44(2)(g).
[94] Whether or not other Member States have done so: see *Ministère Public v Blanguernon* [1991] B.C.L.C. 635, ECJ.
[95] See below, p.17.
[96] See *Karella v Greek Ministry for Industry, Energy and Technology* [1994] 1 B.C.L.C. 774, ECJ.
[97] See *Marleasing SA v La Comercial Internacional de Alimentacion SA* [1993] B.C.C. 421, ECJ.
[98] *Andrea Francovich v The Republic (Italy)* [1993] 2 C.M.L.R. 66.
[99] [2000] Ch.446, ECJ.
[1] *Überseering BV v Nordic Construction Company Baumanagement GmbH* [2005] 1 C.M.L.R. 1, ECJ. See also *Kamer van Koophandel en Fabrieken voor Amsterdam v Inspire Art Ltd* Case C-167/01, ECJ.
[2] For detailed analysis, see *Palmer's Company Law* 25th ed. (1992-), Part 16.

(1) The First Company Law Directive 68/151/EEC, which *inter alia* provided for relief against the doctrine of *ultra vires* and limits on directors' authority, was implemented in s.9 of the European Community Act 1972.[3]

(2) The Second Company Law Directive 77/91/EEC provided minimum requirements on the formation of companies, and the maintenance, increase and reduction of capital and this was implemented in the Companies Act 1980 and amended in the Companies Act 1981.

(3) The Third Company Law Directive 78/855/EEC was directed at the co-ordination of mergers within a Member State and was implemented in the UK via the Companies (Mergers and Divisions) Regulations 1987[4] and by inserting s.427A and Sch.15A into the Companies Act 1985.

(4) The Fourth Company Law Directive 78/660/EEC, on the disclosure of financial information and the contents of the company's annual accounts, was implemented in the Companies Act 1981.

(5) The Sixth Company Law Directive 82/991/EEC, on the division of public companies, was implemented in the UK in the Companies (Mergers and Divisions) Regulations 1987.[5]

(6) The Seventh Company Law Directive 83/349/EEC on consolidated accounts, supplementing the Fourth Directive, was implemented in the Companies Act 1989.

(7) The Eighth Company Law Directive 84/253/EEC on the qualification and independence of auditors in both private and public companies was implemented in the Companies Act 1989.

(8) The Eleventh Company Law Directive 89/666/EEC, on disclosure requirements for branches opened in a Member State, was implemented by the Oversea Companies and Credit and Financial Institutions (Branch) Disclosure Regulations 1992.[6]

(9) The Major Shareholdings Directive 88/629/EEC, relating to the disclosure of such interests in listed companies was implemented by the Disclosure of Interests in Shares (Amendment) Regulations 1993.[7]

(10) The Twelfth Company Law Directive 89/556/EEC, on the formation of private companies with one member, was implemented by the Companies (Single Member Private Limited Companies) Regulations 1992.[8]

(11) The Directive Co-ordinating Regulations on Insider Dealing 89/592/EEC was implemented in the Criminal Justice Act 1993.[9]

---

[3] See the discussion of these provisions, which are now to be found in ss 35–36C of the Companies Act 1985, at p.94, below.
[4] SI 1987/1991.
[5] SI 1987/1991.
[6] SI 1992/3179.
[7] SI 1993/1819.
[8] SI 1992/1699.
[9] See Chapter 19, below.

(12) The Directive amending the Fourth and Seventh Directives on Company Accounts 90/604/EEC was implemented in the Companies Act 1985 (Accounts of Small and Medium-Sized Enterprises and Publication of Accounts in ECUS) Regulations.[10]

The Council Regulation 2001/2157/EC,[11] on the statute for a European company (SE), and Council Directive 2001/86/EC supplementing the statute for a European Company (SE) with regard to the involvement of employees,[12] were most recently implemented in The European Public Limited Liability Company Regulations 2004.[13] Also implemented were a number of Regulations and Directives in relation to accountancy standards, which were implemented in the Companies Act 1985 (International Accounting Standards and Other Accounting Amendments) Regulations 2004, and Directive 2003/6/EC of the European Parliament and Council on insider dealing and market manipulation[13a] in the Financial Services and Markets Act 2000 (Market Abuse) Regulations 2005.[13b] [14]

New directives and other legislation

A full consideration of the fast moving and changing face of European company law is beyond the scope of this book.[15] However, attention may be drawn to a new Directive 2004/25/EC on takeover bids,[16] and the proposal of the European Commission for a Directive on cross-border mergers,[17] to which the Council has now agreed.[18]

Other developments

In September 2001, the European Commission set up a Group of High Level Company Law Experts with the objective of initiating a discussion on the need for the modernisation of company law in Europe.[19] The Group was given a dual mandate, which included providing the Commission with recommendations for a modern regulatory European company law framework. The Group duly presented its Final Report of the High Level Group of Company Law Experts on November 4, 2002 and this focused on corporate governance in the EU and the modernisation of European Company Law.

The European Commission responded with *Modernising Company Law and Enhancing Corporate Governance in the European—A Plan to Move Forward* on May 21, 2003. This set out a comprehensive plan of action for company law

---

[10] SI 1992/2452.
[11] [2001] O.J. L294/1.
[12] [2001] O.J. L294/22. See Chapter 32, below.
[13] SI 2004/2326.
[13a] [2003] O.J. L96/16.
[13b] SI 2005/381.
[14] SI 2004/2947.
[15] For detailed analysis see *Palmer's Company Law* 25th ed. (1992-), Part 16.
[16] O.J. L142, 30/04/2004 P. 0012–0023.
[17] Press release IP/03/1564, November 18, 2003.
[18] See press release IP/04/1405, November 25, 2004.
[19] See, generally, *http://europa.eu.int/comm/internal_market/company/index_en.htm*.

reform throughout the EU and the issue which still has to be determined in the likely impact of this on UK company law. Indeed, these proposals raise real questions about the interaction of the plan with existing UK reform initiatives.

During 2004, the Commission consulted on:

(1) Directors, remuneration;

(2) Cross border transfer of companies' registered offices;

(3) Board responsibilities and improving financial and corporate governance information;

(4) Shareholder rights;

(5) Independent directors and Board Committees;

(6) Corporate governance; and

(7) Companies' capital.

In relation to these consultations, the Commission has, through a Commission Recommendation, invited Member States to reinforce the presence and role of independent non-executive directors on listed companies' boards.[20-21] Simultaneously, the Commission has adopted a Recommendation on directors' remuneration.[22]

Two other developments should be highlighted. The first of these was the establishment in October 2004 of a European Corporate Governance Forum to examine best practices in Member States with a view to enhancing the convergence of national corporate governance codes and providing advice to the Commission.[23] In January 2005, the Commission announced that it intended to set up a consultative committee, the Advisory Committee on Corporate Governance and Company Law, in order to enable it to obtain technical advice on the implementation of the 2003 Plan.[24]

The European Economic Interest Grouping

The E.E.I.G. was created by an EC regulation (*i.e.* a document which has direct legislative effect in the UK unlike a directive which must in general terms be implemented by the UK Parliament to be effective), Council Regulation 2173/85,[25] as supplemented by the European Economic Grouping Regulations 1989.[26] The intention behind this Regulation was to allow the creation of a separate legal entity for cross-border co-operation between businesses in different Member States. These may or may not be companies. Formation is by contract, registered with the registrar of companies. This contract must include

---

[20-21] Press release IP/04/1182, October 6, 2004.
[22] Press release IP/04/1183, October 6, 2004.
[23] Press release IP/04/1241, October 18, 2004. This forum held its first meeting on January 20, 2005.
[24] To this end, it has invited applications from interested parties (January 7, 2005).
[25] [1985] O.J. L199/1.
[26] SI 1989/638.

the objects of the E.E.I.G.—since making profits in its own right is not allowed, these must require the E.E.I.G. to enhance the activities of its members, *e.g.* by joint research or development. The members of the E.E.I.G. will have unlimited liability for its debts, no public investment is allowed and the maximum number of employees is limited to 500. An E.E.I.G. can be formed in any Member State and is subject to some aspects of the national law in which it is registered, *e.g.* as to the use of name, certain winding-up rules etc. UK law must equally recognise an E.E.I.G. registered in another Member State.

The European Company (SE)

The idea of a cross-border European Company (or *Societas Europaea*—SE),[27] to facilitate mergers of companies, has now, after a long parturition, become reality. Although first mooted in 1970, interest in the idea revived in 2001, with a Council Regulation on the Statute for a European Company,[28] supplemented by a directive on the involvement of employees.[29] Now in force in the EU,[30] the initiative is aimed at large multinational companies and is organised on the basis of supranational law, rather than the law of just one Member State. Nevertheless, much of the applicable law will be the public company law of the Member State. The SE is brought into force in the UK by the European Public Limited-Liability Company Regulations 2004.[31]

The Human Rights Act

In 1998, the Human Rights Act was passed by Parliament and came into force on October 2, 2000.[32] The main effect of the Act has been to implement into UK law the provisions of the European Convention on Human Rights. Although it may not seem that this Act would have an impact on company law decisions, certain decisions have indicated that it could have potential. One area is in relation to Art.6.1 of the Convention, which provides that in the determination of any civil rights and obligations or any criminal charge, everyone is entitled to a fair hearing by an independent and impartial tribunal. The impact of this Article has been felt in relation to DTI investigations,[33] but was dismissed in relation to the Company Directors Disqualification Act.[34] Similarly, the Provisions of Protocol I, Art.1,[35] which were raised by a petitioner in relation to a scheme of arrangement under s.425,[36] was rejected by the court on the basis that it was established that a

[27] For detailed consideration see below, Ch.32.
[28] 2157/2001/EC, [2001] O.J. L294/1.
[29] Directive 2001/86/EC.
[30] Press release IP/04/1195, October 8, 2004.
[31] As from October 8, 2004: SI 2004/2326.
[32] The Human Rights Act 1998 (Commencement No. 2) Order 1998, SI 2000/1851.
[33] See *Saunders v United Kingdom* [1998] 1 B.C.L.C. 362, ECHR; *I.J.L., G.M.R., and A.K.P. v United Kingdom* [2002] B.C.C. 380, ECHR.
[34] See *Secretary of State for Trade and Industry v Eastaway* [2001] 1 B.C.L.C. 653.
[35] This *inter alia* provides that every natural or legal person is entitled to the peaceful enjoyment of his possessions and that no one shall be deprived of his possessions except in the public interest and subject to the conditions provided for by law and by the general principles of international law.
[36] See, below, p.660.

scheme which were purely financial did not infringe Protocol I.[37] However, yet other cases have shown that the Convention is capable of protecting corporate rights, for example in relation to Art.8 of the Convention, which lays down the basic principle that everyone has the right to respect for his private and family life, his home and his correspondence.[38]

PROCEDURE TO OBTAIN REGISTRATION OF A COMPANY

To obtain the registration of a company certain documents must be delivered to the appropriate Registrar of Companies and certain fees must be paid. If the registered office is to be situate in England or in Wales,[39] the appropriate registrar is the Registrar of Companies for England,[40] and the address is Companies Registration Office, Crown Way, Maindy, Cardiff CF14 3UZ.[41] If the registered office is to be situate in Scotland[42] the appropriate registrar is the Registrar of Companies for Scotland[43] and the address is Companies House, 37 Castle Terrace, Edinburgh EH1 2EB.

Documents which must be delivered to the Registrar

The following documents must be delivered to the Registrar of Companies:

(1) A memorandum of association[44] stating, *inter alia*, the objects of the company and if, as is common, the company is a limited company with a share capital, the amount of share capital with which the company proposes to be registered and its division into shares of a fixed amount,[45] *e.g.* £10,000 divided into 10,000 shares of a nominal amount of £1 each. If the company is a public company this figure must be not less than the authorised minimum,[46] currently £50,000.[47]

(2) Usually, printed articles of association[48] providing for such matters as the transfer of shares in the company, the holding of general meetings, *i.e.* meetings of the members or shareholders, the directors' powers of management and the extent to which they can delegate their powers to a managing director, and the payment of dividends.

(3) If the memorandum states that the registered office is to be situated in Wales and the memorandum and articles are in Welsh, a certified translation in English.[49]

---

[37] *Re Waste Recycling Group plc* [2003] E.W.H.C. 2065; [2004] 1 B.C.L.C. 352.
[38] See *R. v Broadcasting Standards Commission ex parte British Broadcasting Corporation* [2001] Q.B. 885, CA.
[39] See below, p.59.
[40] s.10(1)(a).
[41] There is also an Information Centre in London at Companies House Executive Agency, 21 Bloomsbury Street, London WCIB 3XD.
[42] Below, p.47.
[43] s.10(1)(b).
[44] s.10. The memorandum is dealt with in Ch.3, below.
[45] s.2(5).
[46] s.11.
[47] s.118(1).
[48] s.7. Articles are dealt with in Ch.4, below.
[49] s.710B(2). For the meaning of a certified translation see the Companies (Welsh Language Forms and Documents) Regulations 1994 (SI 1994/117).

(4) A statement in the prescribed form[50] of the names of the intended first director or directors, and first secretary or joint secretaries, and the particulars specified in Sch.1.[51] Such statement must be signed by or on behalf of the subscribers of the memorandum and must contain a consent to act signed by each of the persons named in it.[52] Where the memorandum is delivered for registration by an agent for the subscribers, such statement must specify that fact and the name and address of that person.[53] The statement must also specify the intended situation of the company's registered office.[54]

(5) A statutory declaration,[55] by a solicitor engaged in the formation of the company or by a person named as director or secretary of the company in the statement delivered under (4) above, of compliance with the requirements of the Acts in respect of registration.[56] In place of the statutory declaration, there may now be delivered to the registrar, a statement, using electronic communications, that the requirements have been complied with. The registrar may accept such a statement as evidence of compliance.[57] The penalty for making a false statement is imprisonment or a fine "or both".[58]

(6) A statement of capital,[59] unless the company is to have no share capital.

For the purpose of ensuring that documents delivered to the Registrar are of standard size, durable and easily legible, the Secretary of State may prescribe such requirements as he considers appropriate. If a document delivered to the Registrar does not, in his opinion, comply with such requirements, he may serve a notice on the person or persons by whom the document was required to be delivered, whereupon, for the purposes of any enactment which enables a penalty to be imposed in respect of an omission to deliver a document to the Registrar, the duty to deliver is not discharged but the person subject to the duty has 14 days after the date of service of the notice in which to discharge it.[60]

Following the implementation of the Companies Act 1985 (Electronic Communications) Order 2000,[61] it is now possible for electronic communications to be used for the delivery of "any document" to the Registrar, provided that such delivery is in the form and manner directed by her.[62] Since July 23, 2001, it has

---

[50] Form 10.
[51] Below, pp.271, 334.
[52] s.10(3).
[53] s.10(4).
[54] s.10(6).
[55] Form 12.
[56] s.12(3).
[57] s.12(3A), inserted by the Companies Act 1985 (Electronic Communications) Order 2000, SI 2000/3373.
[58] s.12(3B).
[59] Form 117.
[60] s.706.
[61] SI 2000/3373.
[62] s.707B(1).

been possible, on payment of the relevant fee,[63] for incorporations to be effected electronically by agents and professional intermediaries.[64]

The duty of the Registrar on receiving the above-mentioned documents is to examine them to see whether the statutory requirements have been complied with, but in exercising his duty he has no power to hold a judicial inquiry on evidence.[65] Among the statutory requirements to be observed are:

(1) That the memorandum is signed by either one or two persons, and, if the memorandum is accompanied by articles, that the articles are signed by the same person(s).[66]

(2) That the company is being formed for a lawful purpose.[67]

If the company is being formed for a purpose prohibited by law,[68] the Registrar will decline to register it. If the Registrar does register a company with illegal objects the court will cancel the registration on an application by the Attorney General.[69]

(3) That the other requirements of the Act, *e.g.* as to the contents of the memorandum and articles, are complied with.[70]

(4) That the proposed name is not one which is absolutely, or conditionally, prohibited.[71]

(5) That the memorandum and articles are in the statutory form.[72]

Any person may inspect a copy[73] of the documents or other material kept by the Registrar relative to individual companies on payment of a fee, and may require a copy or extract of them on payment of the current fee.[74] Such copies may be furnished in an electronic form.[75]

Registration fees

Section 708 empowers the Secretary of State, by regulations made by statutory instrument, to require payment to the Registrar of such fees as may be specified in the regulations in respect of the performance by the Registrar of such functions under the Companies Acts as may be specified, including the receipt by

---

[63] For electronic incorporations this is £15 (£30 for same day): see the Companies (Fees) Regulations 2004, SI 2004/2621, Sch.4.

[64] In 2003–2004, this accounted for some 67 per cent of the new companies incorporated. See *Companies in 2003–2004* (DTI, 2004), p.26.

[65] *R. v Registrar of Companies, ex p. Bowen* [1914] 3 K.B. 1161.

[66] ss 1(1)(3A), 2, 7, below, pp.50, 72.

[67] s.1(1).

[68] *R. v Registrar of Companies, ex p. More* [1931] 2 K.B. 197 CA.

[69] *R. v Registrar of Companies, ex p. Attorney General* [1991] B.C.L.C. 476.

[70] ss 1(1)(3A), 2, 7, 11.

[71] s.26, below, p.51.

[72] ss 3, 8 below, pp.50, 72.

[73] s.709.

[74] As to which, see the Companies (Fees) Regulations 2004, SI 2004/2621, Sch.4.

[75] s.710A.

him of any notice or other document which the Acts require to be given or delivered to him.[76]

CERTIFICATE OF INCORPORATION

On the registration of a company the Registrar gives a certificate, either authenticated by a seal prepared under s.704(4) or under his hand, that the company is incorporated, in the case of a limited company that it is limited and, if it is a public company, that the company is a public company: s.13. The certificate of incorporation, which may be described as the company's birth certificate, is in the following form for private companies.[77]

Certificate of Incorporation

I HEREBY CERTIFY that   , Limited, is this day Incorporated under the Companies Act 1985, and that the Company is Limited.
    Given under my hand at Cardiff this   day of .

Section 711(1)(a) requires the Registrar to publish in the appropriate *Gazette*[78] notice of the issue of a certificate of incorporation.

Section 13(7) provides that the certificate is conclusive evidence that all the requirements of the Act in respect of registration and of matters precedent and incidental thereto have been complied with, and that the association is a company authorised to be registered and duly registered. If the certificate states that the company is a public company, it is conclusive evidence that it is such a company.

It is thought that the subsection means that it cannot be argued that a company is not validly incorporated except where a statutory provision as to substance invalidates the registration.[79]

The certificate of incorporation has also been held to be conclusive as to the date of incorporation.[80] The reason for this section is that once a company is registered and has begun business and entered into contracts, it would be disastrous if any person could allege that the company was not duly registered.[81]

The certificate will not, however, be conclusive if a trade union should be registered as a company[82] as the registration of a trade union under the Companies Acts is void by statute.[83] Again, the certificate is not conclusive as to

---

[76] The fee for incorporation (other than electronic) is £50, for same day registration, and £20, otherwise. See the Companies (Fees) Regulations 2004, above.

[77] Public companies would have a different name and the additional declaration that it is a public limited company.

[78] This amounts to official notification. The appropriate Gazette is either the *London* or the *Edinburgh Gazette* depending upon the company's domicile. See *www.gazettes-online.co.uk.*

[79] *Per* Megarry J. in *Gaiman v National Association for Mental Health* [1971] Ch. 317, at p. 329. See also the speech of Lord Wrenbury in *Cotman v Brougham* [1918] A.C. 514, at p.523.

[80] *Jubilee Cotton Mills Ltd v Lewis* [1924] A.C. 958, where it was also held that "From the date of incorporation" in s.[13(3)] included any portion of the day on which the company was incorporated.

[81] *Per* Lord Cairns in *Peel's Case* (1867) L.R. 2 Ch.App. at p.682.

[82] *British Association of Glass Bottle Manufacturers Ltd v Nettlefold* (1911) 27 T.L.R. 527.

[83] Trade Union and Labour Relations (Consolidation) Act 1992, s.10(3)(a).

the legality of a company's objects—proceedings may be brought to have the registration cancelled where objects are illegal.[84]

The Registrar will allocate each registered company a registered number, *i.e.* a sequence of letters and numbers, which must be disclosed on all its business letters and order forms.[85]

EFFECT OF REGISTRATION OF A COMPANY

From the date of incorporation mentioned in the certificate of incorporation, the subscribers of the memorandum, together with such other persons as may from time to time become members of the company, form a body corporate by the name contained in the memorandum, capable forthwith of exercising all the functions of an incorporated company, but with such liability on the part of the members to contribute to the assets of the company as is mentioned in the Act: s.13(3).

The registered company is a body corporate, *i.e.* a legal person separate and distinct from its members.

S had for many years carried on business as a boot manufacturer. His business was solvent when it was converted into a company, *i.e.* a company limited by shares was formed, the subscribers to the memorandum of which were S and his wife, daughter and four sons (for one share each), and the business was sold to the company at a price of £39,000. The terms of sale were approved by all the shareholders. £9,000 was paid in cash. £20,000 fully paid shares of £1 each were allotted to S so that S's wife and children held one share each and S. held 20,001 shares. S left the rest of the price on loan to the company and for this sum of £10,000 he was given debentures secured by a charge on the company's assets. It seems that the directors were S and his sons and that S was appointed managing director. After a depression the company went into liquidation. The assets were sufficient to satisfy the debentures, but the unsecured creditors, with debts amounting to £7,000, received nothing. *Held*, that the proceedings were not contrary to the true intent and meaning of the Companies Act; that the company was duly registered and was not a mere "alias" or agent of or trustee for the vendor; that S was not liable to indemnify the company against creditors' claims; that there was no fraud upon creditors (or shareholders); that the company (or the liquidator) was not entitled to rescission of the contract of purchase: *Salomon v Salomon & Co. Ltd* [1897] A.C. 22.[86]

"The company is at law a different person altogether from the subscribers to the memorandum; and, though it may be that after incorporation the business is precisely the same as it was before, and the same persons are managers, and the same hands receive the profits, the company is not in law the agent of the subscribers or trustee for them. Nor are the subscribers as members liable, in any shape or form, except to the extent and in the manner provided by the Act"; *per* Lord Macnaghten at p. 51.[87]

One effect of this is that the property of the company belongs to the company itself and not to the individual members,[88] so that even the largest shareholder

---

[84] *R. v Registrar of Companies, ex p. Attorney General* [1991] B.C.L.C. 476, adopting the words of Lord Parker of Waddington in *Bowman v Secular Society Ltd* [1917] A.C. 406, at p.439.

[85] ss 705; 351(1)(a).

[86] Although *Salomon's* case is now generally accepted in Scots law, the Scottish courts were, about the same time and independently of that authority, giving effect to the same principle, *e.g. Henderson v Stubbs' Ltd* (1894) 22 R. 51, *Grierson, Oldham & Co. Ltd v Forbes, Maxwell & Co. Ltd* (1895) 22 R. 812 and *John Wilson & Son Ltd v Inland Revenue* (1895) 23 R. 18.

[87] *cf. Broderip v Saloman* [1895] 2 Ch.323, CA.

[88] See *Bowman v Secular Society Ltd* [1917] A.C. 406.

has no insurable interest in the property of the company.[89] The managing director, even if he owns all the shares except one, cannot lawfully pay cheques to the company into his own banking account or draw cheques for his own purposes upon the company's banking account,[90] and two sole shareholder/directors can be convicted of theft from "their" company.[91]

This principle of the independent corporate existence of a registered company is of the greatest importance in company law. As we shall see, it is this which mainly distinguishes a registered company from a partnership, which is the relation which subsists between persons carrying on a business in common with a view of profit. A partnership is not a corporation and, at least in the case of an English partnership,[92] is only a description of the relationship between the partners, *i.e.* a partnership has no legal existence but is merely the association of two or more persons carrying on business together. The property of the firm belongs to the partners and the firm's debts are the debts of the partners, *i.e.* the partners are personally liable for the firm's debts, whereas in a registered company the assets and liabilities are those of the corporation and not of the members.[93]

This separation of the corporation and its members so that the members are not liable for the company's debts was reaffirmed by the House of Lords in *J. H. Rayner (Mincing Lane) Ltd v Department of Trade and Industry.*[94] This case arose out of the collapse of the International Tin Council in 1985 which left it owing millions of pounds to a number of metal traders and banks. The Council had been formed by several states and the Council's creditors sought to recover its debts from those member states. The House of Lords first decided that the Council was a body corporate with its own separate legal personality distinct from its members and it followed therefore that only the Council and not its members could be liable for the debts. Under English law only the party to a contract can be liable on that contract and the only contracting party here was the Council. It would be for Parliament to provide otherwise in any given case.[95]

Lord Oliver expressed the decision thus:

> "Once given the existence of the I.T.C. as a separate legal person and given that it was the contracting party in the transactions upon which the appellants claim . . . there is no room for any further inquiry as to what type of legal person the contracting party is. The person who can enforce contracts and the persons against whom they can be enforced in English law and the parties to the contract and in identifying the parties to the contract there are no gradations of legal personality."[96]

The liability of a member of a company limited by shares to contribute to the company's assets (for the purpose of enabling its debts to be paid) is limited to

---

[89] *Macaura v Northern Assurance Co. Ltd* [1925] A.C. 619.
[90] *A. L. Underwood Ltd v Bank of Liverpool & Marine Ltd* [1924] 1 K.B. 775, CA.
[91] *Att.-Gen.'s Reference (No. 2 of 1982)* [1984] Q.B. 624; *R. v Phillipou* (1989) 5 B.C.C. 33.
[92] A Scottish partnership or firm has a separate legal existence and is not merely the association of two or more persons. The property of the firm belongs to the firm, and the firm's debts are primarily those of the firm, although each partner may ultimately be made personally liable for the firm's debts. See, however, *Major v Brodie* [1998] S.T.C. 491.
[93] See *Ferguson v Wilson* (1866) L.R. 2 Ch. App. 77, at p.89.
[94] [1990] 2 A.C. 418.
[95] See, *e.g.* n.92, above.
[96] [1990] 2 A.C. 418, at p.508.

the amount, if any, unpaid on his shares.[97] Thus if he has taken one thousand shares of £1 each in the company and the shares are fully paid up he is normally under no further liability to contribute to the assets. In the case of a partnership every partner is jointly liable with the other partners for all the firm's debts.[98]

A registered company is capable forthwith of exercising all the functions of an incorporated company, *e.g.* it can hold land and other property, and it can sue and be sued.[99] If the company is a public company it cannot commence business until the requirements of s.117 have been complied with.[1]

The veil of incorporation

It was established in *Salomon v Salomon & Co. Ltd*, above, that a registered company is a legal person separate from its members. This principle may be referred to as "the veil of incorporation". In general, the law will not go behind the separate personality of the company to the members, so that, *e.g.* in *Macaura v Northern Assurance Co. Ltd*,[2] it was held that the largest shareholder had no insurable interest in the property of the company. However, there are exceptions to the principle in *Salomon's* case, where the veil is lifted, or pierced, and the law disregards the corporate entity and pays regard instead to the economic realities behind the legal facade; *i.e.* where the facts supersede form. These exceptions may be classified into those expressly provided by statute and those under judicial interpretation.[3]

One example of a case where "the veil is lifted" by statute[4] is where a public company carries on business for more than six months with less than the statutory minimum of members (two), in which event every person who is a member during any part of the time that business is so carried on after the end of the six-month period and who knows that business is being so carried on, is jointly and severally liable for all the company's debts contracted during such time and may be severally sued therefore (s.24, intended to ensure that the number of members for such companies does not fall below the statutory minimum). This is exceptional because the general rule is that the company's debts cannot be enforced against the members.

Again, where an officer of a company signs, on behalf of the company, a bill of exchange, promissory note, cheque or order for money or goods in which the company's name is not mentioned correctly, the officer is personally liable to the holder of the bill of exchange, etc., for the amount thereof unless it is paid by the company (s.349(4)).[5]

---

[97] s.1(2).

[98] Further differences between registered companies and partnerships are dealt with later in this chapter.

[99] See *Foss v Harbottle* (1843) 2 Hare 461, at pp.490–491. See the discussion, below, at p.341.

[1] Below, p.137.

[2] [1925] A.C. 619.

[3] See also Ruthven, "Lifting the Veil of Incorporation in Scotland", 1969 *Juridicial Review*, p.1 and *Glasgow City Council v Caststop Ltd* (2003) S.L.T. 526, ED.

[4] But see *R. v Warrington Crown Court* [2002] UKHL 24; [2002] 1 W.L.R. 1954, HL, where the House of Lords held that withholding information as to the identity of the members of the company was not indicative of the lack of fitness or bona fides of the members for the purpose of the Licensing Act 1964.

[5] Below, p.56. Other examples include liability for fraudulent and wrongful trading: see below, p.317.

The grounds upon which the courts will lift the corporate veil are more difficult to define. Initially there were a number of fairly random examples. Thus, a company registered in England was held to be an alien enemy if its agents or the persons in *de facto* control of its affairs were alien enemies, and in determining whether alien enemies have such control, the number of alien enemy shareholders and the value of their holdings were material.[6] Another example was that in cases such as *Re Express Engineering Works Ltd*,[7] the decision of all the shareholders was held to be the decision of the company, *e.g.* something less formal than a resolution, even a special resolution, duly passed at a general meeting was regarded as the act of the company. Further, it was held in *Re Bugle Press Ltd*[8] that if A Ltd makes an offer for the shares in B Ltd and in substance A Ltd is the same as the majority shareholding in B Ltd, A Ltd will not be able to invoke section 429[9] and compel the minority shareholders in B Ltd to sell their shares to A Ltd. In these circumstances the law goes behind the corporate personality of A Ltd to the individual members. The court will not allow that section to be invoked for an improper purpose.

The case of *Gilford Motor Co. Ltd v Horne*[10] shows that the courts will not allow a company to be used as a device to mask the carrying on of a business by a former employee of another person and to enable the former employee to break a valid covenant in restraint of trade contained in the contract under which he was formerly employed. In that case the employee convenanted that after the termination of the employment he would not solicit his employer's customers. Soon after the termination of his employment he formed a company of which the two directors and shareholders were his wife and one other person and which sent out circulars to customers of his former employer. An injunction was granted against the ex-employee and the company.[11]

Some judges in the past adopted a more general approach based on the interests of justice as being the guiding light. Thus, Lord Denning M.R. was prepared to lift the veil in *Wallersteiner v Moir*[12]—he said that in that case the plaintiff was also in breach of what is now s.330 (which in general prohibits a company making a loan to a director) because the company of which he was a director made a loan to another company which was his puppet, so that the loan should be treated as made to him. In 1985, the Court of Appeal lifted the veil when a defendant in a company fraud case took elaborate steps to conceal his assets by a complex network of companies and trusts. The court allowed the veil to be lifted in order to establish exactly what he owned and where it was located. They stated that this could be done in the interests of justice irrespective of the legal efficacy of the corporate structure provided he either substantially or effectively controlled the company concerned. The network of companies had been set up in an attempt to confuse and conceal.[13]

[6] *Daimler Co. Ltd v Continental Tyre etc. Ltd* [1916] 2 A.C. 307.
[7] [1920] 1 Ch. 466, CA, below, p.247.
[8] [1961] Ch. 270, CA, below, p.699.
[9] Ch.31, below.
[10] [1933] Ch. 935, CA.
[11] See also *Jones v Lipman* [1962] 1 W.L.R. 832. These cases are said to be examples of the veil being pierced where the situation is a "sham". They are equally explicable on the basis that extending the injunction to the companies was simply necessary for its enforcement.
[12] [1974] 1 W.L.R. 991, CA.
[13] *Re A Company* [1985] B.C.L.C. 333, CA.

The interests of justice approach was also applied in *Creasey v Breachwood Motors Ltd*[14] where an employee who had a claim for unfair dismissal against a company found that, after that claim had arisen, all the assets of the company had been transferred to another company owned by the same individuals and the first company had been dissolved. The second company was added as a defendant to the action. In doing so the judge had to distinguish the decision of the Court of Appeal in *Adams v Cape Industries plc*[15] where that court refused to pierce the veil of incorporation with respect to an action brought against one company in a group with respect to liability for another company in that group in another country. He did so on the basis that the cause of action had not accrued at the time in that case whereas it had done so at the time of the actions of the defendants in the present case.

Instead of relying on the interests of justice approach,[16] the Court of Appeal in *Adams* had applied the test as stated by Lord Keith in the Scottish case of *Woolfson v Strathclyde Regional Council*[17] that the veil would only be pierced where special circumstances exist indicating that it is a mere facade concealing the true facts. That case, like *Adams*, concerned the question as to whether a group of companies could be regarded as a single entity for legal purposes. In *Woolfson*, the issue was whether a subsidiary and parent company could be regarded as a single entity in order to enable them to claim compensation for disturbance on a compulsory purchase. The issue had previously arisen in *D.H.N. Food Distributors Ltd v Tower Hamlets London Borough Council*[18] where the Court of Appeal in England allowed the claim on the basis that D.H.N. was in a position to control its subsidiaries in every respect. The House of Lords in *Woolfson* distinguished the *D.H.N.* case on its facts but also doubted whether it was a correct application of the general principle, stated above, that the veil should only be pierced where special circumstances exist indicating that it is a mere façade concealing the true facts. In *City of Glasgow DC v Hamlet Textiles Ltd*,[19] the Scottish Court of Session allowed inquiry as to the true ownership of property in Glasgow where the formal title was held by an English wholly-owned subsidiary of a Scottish company and whose sole function was the holding of that formal title.

The approach taken by the House of Lords in the *Woolfson* case (above) was also applied in *National Dock Labour Board v Pinn & Wheeler Ltd*.[20] The judge refused to regard three related companies as being a single entity for the purposes of a demarcation dispute. Only where there was a mere façade concealing the true facts would the corporate veil be pierced. In this case the companies had been retained for good commercial reasons. The test was also applied by Lightman J. in *Acatos & Hutcheson plc v Watson*[21] in relation to the

---

[14] [1993] B.C.L.C. 480. See below, p.30.
[15] [1990] Ch. 433, CA.
[16] Which it expressly rejected: at p.536.
[17] 1978 S.C. HL 90. See too *Tough v S.P.S. (Holdings) Ltd*, 2000 G.W.D. 9–319 I.H.
[18] [1976] 1 W.L.R. 852, CA.
[19] 1986 S.L.T. 415.
[20] (1989) 5 B.C.C. 75.
[21] [1995] 1 B.C.L.C. 218.

purchase by a company of another company whose principal asset was shares in the purchaser. Since this was neither a facade nor a sham he regarded the purchaser as having acquired shares in the second company and not its own shares.

The position is therefore becoming clearer. There must be some evidence of impropriety or fraud[22] before the corporate veil can be pierced. Thus the Court of Appeal in *Re H*,[23] upheld an order made against the assets of two companies controlled by two individuals accused of excise fraud, rejecting the argument that the assets of the companies and those of the individuals were separate. Basing their judgment on *Adams v Cape Industries*, the Court of Appeal held that this was an "appropriate case" in which to lift the veil:

> "As to the evidence, it provides a prima facie case that the defendants control these companies; that the companies have been used for fraud, in particular the evasion of excise duties on a large scale; that the defendants regard the companies as carrying on a family business, and that company cash has benefitted the defendants in substantial amounts."[24]

In the case of *Trustor AB v Smallbone (No.3)*,[25] the Chancery Division confirmed this general approach, holding that where the defendant, a managing director, had transferred substantial sums to another company, the court was entitled to pierce the veil and recognise the receipt of that company as that of the individual in control, because it was used as a device or façade to conceal the true facts.[26]

On the other hand, in the absence of such impropriety or fraud, the courts will not pierce the corporate veil. This approach was taken by Toulson J. in *Yukong Line Ltd v Rendsburg Investments Corporation*.[27] An individual signed a charter-party on behalf of one company. That company was in breach of the agreement and the other party obtained an injunction against that company's assets. It then discovered that that company had closed its account and transferred it to another company. The individual controlled both companies. The judge refused either to regard the individual as therefore being a party to the agreement or to make the second company liable in damages for the breach.

A similar approach was also taken by the Court of Appeal in *Ord v Belhaven Pubs Ltd*.[28] On facts similar to *Creasey v Beachwood Motors Ltd*,[29] the Court of Appeal refused to pierce the corporate veil. They rejected any idea that a group of companies could be regarded as a single entity except in very limited circumstances where there was some impropriety or the company was a façade concealing the true facts.[30] Even in that situation it was suggested that the

---

[22] See, *e.g.*, *R. v Omar* [2004] EWCA Civ 2320, at para. [18]; *DPP v Compton* [2002] EWCA Civ 1720.
[23] [1996] 2 B.C.L.C. 500.
[24] [1996] 2 B.C.L.C. 500, at 511. See also *Gencor ACP Ltd v Dalby* [2002] 2 B.C.L.C. 734, at p.744.
[25] [2001] 1 W.L.R. 1177. Applied in *Buckinghamshire County Council v Briar* [2002] EWHC 2821; [2003] Envir. L.R. 25.
[26] At p.1185.
[27] [1998] 1 W.L.R. 294. See also *Ringway Road Marking v Adbruf Ltd* [1998] 2 B.C.L.C. 625, *Tough v SPS (Holdings) Ltd*, 2000 G.W.D. 9–319 I.H.
[28] [1998] 2 B.C.L.C. 447, CA.
[29] Above, p.29.
[30] See also *Skjevesland v Geveran Trading Co Ltd* [2000] B.P.I.R. 523.

situation was best dealt with by applying the insolvency laws. The Court also expressly stated that the decision in *Creasey* should no longer be regarded as authorative.[31]

LIABILITY OF REGISTERED COMPANIES

One consequence of the concept of a company's separate personality is that it can be liable for breaches of contract, torts (in Scots law, delicts), crimes, etc. But for obvious reasons, it can only act through human agents or employees, so that, as a general principle, a company can only be liable either where a principal would be liable for the acts of an agent or an employer liable for the acts of an employee. In Chapter 6 the concept of agency, which is central to an understanding of company commercial transactions, is discussed but sometimes the law only imposes obligations or affords benefits to those who actually do the act, or who have a particular state of mind, and since a company cannot physically do anything, or think anything, there can be a problem assimilating companies into the general law. The answer is that in certain circumstances the acts and mind of the governing body of the company are regarded as the acts and mind of the company—thus, for example, if they intend to defraud, so does the company. Sometimes known as the *alter ego* doctrine, this is the antithesis of the doctrine of separate corporate personality.

The doctrine was first laid down by the House of Lords in *Lennards Carrying Co. v Asiatic Petroleum*[32] where the major shareholder's negligence in navigating the company's ship was held to be the negligence of the company for the purposes of assessing liability. Viscount Haldane L.C. said: "For if Mr Lennard was the directing mind of the company, then his action must, unless a corporation is not to be liable at all, have been an action which was the action of the company itself."[33] This doctrine has been applied in various areas of the law[34] but for some years it remained unclear as to exactly whose acts and intentions could be attributed to the company. In *Bolton (Engineering) Co. Ltd v Graham & Son*,[35] Lord Denning drew a distinction between the acts of those directors and managers who control what the company actually does and the acts of mere servants who simply carry out the course of action prescribed by those in control.

The doctrine was developed in *Tesco Supermarkets Ltd v Nattrass*,[36] where the supermarket chain was prosecuted under s.11(2) of the Trade Descriptions Act 1968 for carrying an incorrect advertisement as to the availability of a brand of washing powder at a reduced price. Their defence was that provided by s.24(1) of the 1968 Act, *i.e.* that the commission of the offence was due to the act or default of another person and that they had taken all reasonable care, etc., to avoid the

---

[31] The Court of Appeal also doubted the decision in the *DHN* case, above, p.29.

[32] [1915] A.C. 705, HL.

[33] *ibid.* p. 717. That test was applied in *El Ajou v Dollar Land Holdings plc* [1994] 1 B.C.L.C. 464, CA. See also *Woodhouse v Walsall MBC* [1994] 1 B.C.L.C. 435.

[34] See, *e.g.* *Green v Green* [1993] 1 F.L.R. 326 for an example in family law and *Re Tecnion Investments, Ltd* [1985] B.C.L.C. 434, CA on a procedural issue.

[35] [1957] 1 Q.B. 159, CA.

[36] [1972] A.C. 153, HL. As to the position in Scotland, see *Purcell Meats (Scotland) Ltd v McLeod*, 1987 S.L.T. 528; *Transco plc v Her Majesty's Advocate* [2005] B.C.C. 296; 2004 S.L.T. 41.

commission of the offence. The relevant question was whether the manager of the particular branch, who had failed to check the stock, was "another person" for this purpose, or whether his default was that of the company. The House of Lords held that he was "another person"; a branch manager of his type was not sufficiently senior to be the *alter ego* of the company. Such an *ego* would be found amongst the directors, managers, secretary or other officers of the company, or someone to whom they had delegated control and management, with full discretionary powers, of some sections of the company's business.

On the other hand, the House of Lords in *Re Supply of Ready Mixed Concrete*[37] held that the acts of local managers of the company which were in breach of an order made against the company under the Restrictive Trade Practices Act 1976, were to be regarded as the acts of the company. This was so despite the fact that senior managers of the company had issued orders to prevent this. The acts of an employee acting within the course of his employment were the acts of the company for this purpose. Companies should be judged by what they had done rather than by what they have said.[38]

The apparent conflict between these two decisions of the House of Lords was explained by Lord Hoffmann in the subsequent case of *Meridian Global Funds Management Asia Ltd v Securities Commission*.[39] That case, a decision of the Privy Council on appeal from New Zealand, concerned the failure of the company to disclose an interest in shares in another company as required by legislation when that interest was known. The actual failure to disclose was the fault of two senior investment managers of the company who worked without supervision and who were aware of the facts. The question was whether their default was also that of the company.

Lord Hoffmann stated that whether a person's acts or mind could be attributed to the company so as to make it liable in situations where agency or vicarious liability would not solve the issue was a matter of construction of the particular provision under which liability was sought. It was a question of construction and not of metaphysics involving *alter egos*, etc. Thus the *Tesco* and *Ready Concrete* cases could be explained. Applying that approach to the facts in *Meridian*, the Privy Council held that the policy of the Act requiring disclosure was for immediate disclosure by those who knew they had a disclosable interest. For a company that must be by those who had, with the authority of the company, acquired that interest. Any other construction would render the Act inoperative.

On the other hand this attribution doctrine does not apply to misappropriations *from* the company by those in control of its affairs. Such misappropriations are not the act of the company as there is no consensus between the controller and the company.[40] It is also clear that where the company is the victim of fraud it will not be fixed with any knowledge of an employee or officer who is defrauding it. Conversely the application of the doctrine to determine whether a company has been defrauded requires that an employee or officer whose mind is that of the company has been deceived.[41]

[37] [1995] 1 B.C.L.C. 613, HL.
[39] See also *National Rivers Authority v Alfred McAlpine Homes East Ltd* [1994] 4 All E.R. 286.
[39] [1995] 2 A.C. 500, PC. See also *Crown Dilmun v Sutton* [2004] EWHC 52; [2004] 1 B.C.L.C. 468.
[40] *Stephens v T. Pittas Ltd* [1983] S.T.C. 576; *Att.-Gen.'s Reference (No. 2 of 1982)* [1984] Q.B. 624; *R. v Phillipou* (1989) 5 B.C.C. 33.
[41] *R. v Rozeik* [1996] 1 B.C.L.C. 380, CA.

In recent years, a particular focus of the alter ego doctrine has centered around the liability of companies for corporate manslaughter,[42] following a number of high-profile rail accidents and other disasters. One of the cases to explore the issue was *Attorney-General's Reference (No.2 of 1999)*,[43] which arose out of the rail disaster at Southall. At first instance, the court ruled that it was a condition precedent to a conviction for manslaughter by gross negligence for a guilty mind to be proved and, where a human defendant was prosecuted, it might only be convicted via the guilty mind of a human being with whom it might be identified. One of the two questions referred by the Attorney-General was whether a non-human defendant could be convicted of the crime of manslaughter by gross negligence in the absence of evidence establishing the guilt of an identified human individual for the same crime. The Court of Appeal answered in the negative; unless an identified individual's conduct, characterisable as gross criminal negligence, could be attributable to the company, the company was not liable for manslaughter.[44] There was no evidence that the courts had started a process of moving from identification to personal liability as a basis for corporate liability; indeed, as the Meridian case had showed,[45] the primary "directing mind and will" rule still applied.[46]

REGISTERED COMPANIES AND PARTNERSHIPS CONTRASTED

Advantages of a registered company

A registered company has many advantages over a partnership, which is defined in the Partnership Act 1890[47] as the relationship which subsists between persons carrying on a business in common with a view of profit, and which is not, *e.g.* the relation between members of a company registered under the Companies Acts or incorporated by or in pursuance of any other Act of Parliament or Royal Charter. A registered company has the same advantages over an individual trader. These advantages include the following:

(1) A registered company is a corporation,[48] *i.e.* a separate legal person distinct from the members, whereas an English partnership is merely the aggregate of the partners (although a Scottish partnership has one of the attributes of a corporation in that it is "a legal person distinct from the partners of whom it is composed").[49] Consequently:

(a) The debts and contracts of a registered company are those of the company and not those of the members, whereas in the case of an

---

[42] The subject also of work by the Law Commission: see *Legislating the Criminal Code: Involuntary Manslaughter* (Law Commission Rep. No.237, 1996). See to Celia Wells, *Corporations and Criminal Responsibility* 2nd ed. (2001).

[43] [2000] Q.B. 796, CA.

[44] At p.815.

[45] Above, p.32.

[46] [2000] Q.B. 796, CA, at p.816. See too *Crown Dilmun v Sutton* [2004] EWHC 52; [2004] 1 B.C.L.C. 468.

[47] s.1. See generally on partnerships, Morse, *Partnership Law* 5th ed. (2001).

[48] s.13(3); *Salomon v Salomon & Co. Ltd* [1897] A.C. 22, above, p.17.

[49] Partnerships Act 1980, s.4(2). See *Major v Brodie* [1998] S.T.C. 491.

English firm every partner is jointly and severally liable with the other partners for all the firm's debts and obligations incurred while he is a partner.[50] (In Scotland the firm's debts are those of the firm but, if the firm fails to pay, each individual partner may be made liable. Again, the firm's contracts are those of the firm but the individual partners may be made liable for them.)

(b) Unless it is dissolved, a registered company continues in existence[51] so that it is not affected by the death, bankruptcy, mental disorder or retirement of any of its members. In the case of a partnership, on the other hand, on the death or bankruptcy of a partner, subject to any agreement between the partners the partnership is dissolved as regards all the partners.[52] In practice the share of a partner who dies or retires has to be found out of the business or provided for by the other partners, and this may cause serious financial embarrassment to the firm.

(c) The property of a registered company belongs to and is vested in the company, so that there is no change in the ownership of, or in the formal title to, the property on a change in the ownership of shares in the company. In an English partnership, the property belongs to the partners and is vested in them. Consequently there are changes in the ownership of, and in the formal title to, the firm's property from time to time on the death or retirement of a partner or trustee. (In a Scottish partnership, while the partnership property belongs to the firm as a separate *persona*, the formal title to that property may be, and in the case of heritable property must be, in the names of the partners or of other persons in trust for the firm.)

(d) A registered company can contract with its members and can sue and be sued on such contracts. In England, a partner probably cannot contract with the firm. (In Scotland, by virtue of the firm's separate personality, a partner can contract with the firm and can sue and be sued on such contracts.)

(e) Each partner is normally an agent for the firm for the purpose of the business of the partnership[53] and, subject to any agreement to the contrary between the parties, may take part in the management of the partnership business.[54] The members of a registered company as such are not its agents and have no power to manage its affairs—the directors are agents and managers, *i.e.* they have the powers given to them by the articles.

(f) Subject to any restrictions in the articles, which there may be in the articles of a private company,[55] shares in a registered company can

---

[50] *ibid.*, s.9.

[51] See above, p.4.

[52] Partnership Act 1890, s.33(1). As to dissolution by the court in the event of the mental disorder of a partner, see 1890 Act, s.35, and Mental Health Act 1959, s.103 (the latter is not applicable to Scotland). As to dissolution by notice by a retiring partner, see 1890 Act, s.32.

[53] Partnership Act 1890, s.5.

[54] *ibid.*, s.24(5).

[55] These have not been compulsory for private companies since 1980.

be transferred or mortgaged[56] without the consent of the other share-holders. Subject to any agreement to the contrary, a person cannot be introduced as a partner without the consent of all the existing partners[57] and if in England a partner charges his share of the partnership for his separate debt the other partners normally have the option to dissolve the partnership.[58]

(2) The liability of a member of a registered company to contribute to its assets may be, and usually is, limited, *e.g.* limited, in the case of a company limited by shares, to the amount unpaid on his shares[59] (although the person controlling a private company may have to give a personal guarantee of the company's bank overdraft) but the members of a partnership are jointly and severally liable for all the debts of the firm.[60] This advantage can be secured in a partnership by a person's being a limited partner in a limited partnership formed under the Limited Partnerships Act 1907, but relatively few such partnerships have been formed,[61] owing to the superior advantages of the private limited company.

(3) There is no limit to the number of members of a company, but, except in the case of, *e.g.*, certain professional partnerships such as solicitors, a partnership with more than 20 members for the purpose of carrying on any business which has for its object the acquisition of gain is prohibited.[62]

(4) A registered company has greater facilities for borrowing than a partnership, *e.g.* the company may borrow on debentures.[63]

(5) Floating charges can be created by a registered company but not by a partnership.[64]

Advantages of a partnership

A partnership or an individual trader has certain advantages over a registered company:

(1) There are fewer formalities to be observed, and therefore there is less publicity and less expense involved in forming a partnership, *e.g.* there is no need to be registered, or to file a memorandum and articles, with the Registrar, and therefore there are no registration fees, and legal

---

[56] In Scots law "transferred in security".
[57] Partnership Act 1890, s.24(7).
[58] *ibid.*, s.33(2) (not applicable to Scotland: see s.23(5)).
[59] s.1.
[60] Partnership Act 1890, s.9.
[61] There has, over the past five years, been a steady growth in the numbers. In 2003–2004, there were 11,287 of them (compared with 7,587 in 1999–2000). See *Companies in 2003–2004* (DTI, 2004), at p.49.
[62] s.716.
[63] Below, Ch.23.
[64] *ibid.*

costs are less. A partnership agreement may be oral or even inferred from conduct.

(2) There are fewer formalities and therefore more flexibility and less publicity and less expense in running a partnership, *e.g.* returns do not have to be delivered to a Registrar. The internal management structure is fluid—there are no requirements for directors or general meetings, etc.

(3) A partnership's accounts are never open to public inspection. Except in the case of certain unlimited companies,[65] those of a registered company are, as are the other documents which any registered company must lodge with the Registrar.[66]

(4) A partnership is not subject to the rules in connection with raising and maintenance of share capital, to which a registered company which is not an unlimited company is subject.[67]

LIMITED LIABILITY PARTNERSHIPS AND COMPANIES

In the last few years, another business form has made its appearance on the UK scene, after a remarkably swift gestation.[68] This is the Limited Liability Partnership (LLP),[69] which came into being with effect from April 6, 2001, following the passing of the Limited Liability Partnership Act 2000.[70] Of great importance, besides the relatively short provisions of the Act, is delegated legislation which has been passed inter alia to extend provisions of the Companies Act 1985 to LLPs.[71] This smorgasbord approach of legislating by reference creates difficulties of nightmarish proportions for those seeking to interpret the legislation.[72] Nevertheless, notwithstanding this and comments to the effect that the LLP is premised on an "ungainly mixture of company law and partnership law", the LLP appears to have achieved a measure of success in its relatively young life.[73] The principal features, compared with companies and ordinary partnerships, are as follows:

(1) Unlike an ordinary partnership, but like companies, the LLP is a body corporate with a legal personality which is separate to that of its members.[74]

---

[65] Below, Ch.20.

[66] s.426.

[67] Below, Ch.9.

[68] The antecedents were two DTI consultation papers: *Limited Liability Partnership—A New Form of Business Association for Professionals* (Consultation Paper, URN 97/597, 1997); *Limitation Liability Partnerships—Draft Bill* (Consultation Paper, URN 98/874, 1998).

[69] Available too in Scotland. See the Limited Liability Partnerships (Scotland) Regulations 2001, SI 2001/128.

[70] For detailed treatment, see Geoffrey Morse (ed.), *Palmer's Limited Liability Partnership Law* (2002).

[71] See the Limited Liability Partnerships Regulations 2001, SI 2001/1090 and the Limited Liability Partnerships (No.2) Regulations 2002, SI 2002/913.

[72] See, *e.g.*, Geoffrey Morse, "Partnerships for the 21st century—Limited Liability Partnerships and Partnership Law Reform in the United Kingdom", [2002] Singapore Journal of Legal Studies 455, at p.464.

[73] In 2003–2004 there were 7,396 registered LLPs in the UK. See *Companies in 2003–2004* (DTI, 2004), p.50.

[74] s.1(2).

(2) Unlike private companies, which may be formed by one person,[75] LLPs, rather like partnerships, can only be formed by two or more persons.[76]

(3) Rather like companies, LLPs must go through a process of registration with the Registrar of Companies[77] and must lodge with her an "incorporation document"[78] before the granting of an certificate of registration which, once issued, is conclusive evidence that the requirements for registration have been satisfied.[79]

(4) Again, rather like companies, the members of the LLP are agents for the LLP and not for one another,[80] and so there will be no liability for members for one another's wrongdoing.

(5) Unlike an ordinary partnership, but like (most) companies, the members of an LLP have limited liability, *viz.* they have such liability to contribute to its assets in the event of its being wound up.[81]

(6) Internally, LLPs reflect a compromise between the principles of ordinary partnership law and companies, with some provisions, *e.g.* equality of participation in capital, profits, and management, being derived from ordinary partnership law, while others, *e.g.* the availability of the remedy for unfair prejudice, are derived from company law.

(7) LLPs, like companies, but unlike ordinary partnerships, are obliged to file with the Registrar information regarding its members, designated members and registered office.[82] Furthermore, LLPs must publish annual accounts and, in general are subject to the regime for accounting and audit of the Companies Act 1985.[83]

(8) For tax purposes, LLPs are like partnerships, not corporate entities.[84]

(9) Finally, for the purposes of insolvency, LLPs are treated in the much the same way as corporate insolvencies.[85]

---

[75] See p.43, below.
[76] s.2(1)(a).
[77] s.3(1).
[78] See s.2(1)(b) and s.2(2).
[79] s.3(4).
[80] s.6(1); *cf.* PA 1890, s.5.
[81] s.1(4).
[82] s.9.
[83] As to this, see the Limited Liability Partnership Regulations 2001, SI 2001/1090.
[84] s.10.
[85] s.14.

Chapter 2

CLASSIFICATION OF REGISTERED COMPANIES

COMPANIES LIMITED BY SHARES, COMPANIES LIMITED BY GUARANTEE AND UNLIMITED COMPANIES

A registered company may be[1]:

(1) a company limited by shares, in which case the liability of a member to contribute to the company's assets is limited to the amount, if any, unpaid on his shares; or

(2) a company limited by guarantee, in which case the liability of a member is limited to the amount which he has undertaken to contribute *in the event of its being wound up*; or

(3) an unlimited company, in which case the liability of a member is unlimited: s.1(2).[2]

The vast majority of registered companies are companies limited by shares. Such companies must have a share capital, whereas unlimited companies may or may not have a share capital. Companies limited by guarantee cannot have a share capital if they were formed after December 22, 1980 and are instead supported by subscriptions or fees paid by the members: s.1(4).

Companies limited by guarantee

A company limited by guarantee is a registered company in which the liability of members is limited to such amount as they respectively undertake to contribute to the assets of the company in the event of its being wound up: s.1(2)(b).[3] The members are not required to contribute whilst the company is a going concern. The memorandum of a company limited by guarantee, in addition to containing the clauses normally contained in a memorandum,[4] must state that each member undertakes to contribute to the assets of the company in the event of its being wound up while he is a member, or within one year after he ceases to be a member, for payment of its debts contracted before he ceases to be a member,

---

[1] See too the Government's draft Bill, *Modernising Company Law*, above, cl. 1.
[2] This section provides the statutory rules for the liability of the members of a company for its debts. The common law position is that there is otherwise no liability at all: see *J. H. Rayner (Mincing Lane) v DTI* [1990] 2 A.C. 418, HL, p.26, above.
[3] See the Government's draft Bill, *Modernising Company Law*, above, cl. 3.
[4] Below, p.50.

and of the costs of winding up, and for adjustment of the rights of the contributories, such sum as may be required, not exceeding a specified amount: s.2(4). The sum specified in Table C, below, is £100. Whatever the amount of the guarantee specified in the memorandum, it cannot be increased or reduced.

The amounts which the members have agreed to contribute in a winding up cannot be mortgaged or charged by the company whilst it is a going concern.[5] They are not assets of the company whilst it is a going concern.

Prior to the 1980 Act, a company limited by guarantee could be formed either with or without a share capital, but was usually formed without a share capital, in which event money to acquire such things as premises may be raised by loans from the members. Since the 1980 Act, no such company can be formed with, or acquire, a share capital: s.1(4). The majority of companies limited by guarantee are formed to incorporate professional, trade and research associations, or clubs supported by annual subscriptions. Many will be able to take advantage of s.30 and omit the word "Limited' ' from their names.[6]

Every company limited by guarantee is obliged to register articles of association with the memorandum: s.7(1). If the company has no share capital, the memorandum and articles must be in the form set out in Table C, or as near thereto as circumstances admit: s.3 and 8(4). Table C is a model form of memorandum and articles for such a company and is set out in the Companies (Tables A to F) Regulations 1985.

An article of a company limited by guarantee with no share capital is not invalid just because it is not contained in Table C. Section 8 is concerned with the form of the articles of such a company and the word "form' ' here does not embrace contents. Provided that the draftsman of such articles follows the general form of Table C he is free to add, subtract or vary as the needs of the case suggest.[7]

Every provision in the memorandum or articles of a company limited by guarantee and not having a share capital, or in any resolution of the company, purporting to give any person a right to participate in the divisible profits of the company otherwise than as a member is void, and every provision in the memorandum or articles, or in any resolution, purporting to divide the undertaking of the company into shares or interests is treated as a provision for share capital notwithstanding that the nominal amount or number of the shares or interests is not specified: s.15. The object of this section is to prevent the registration of companies with shares of no par value.[8]

Because of the strict régime applied to public companies, few companies limited by guarantee can be registered as such companies. In practice they will be private companies.[9]

Apart from what has been said in this chapter, most of what is said elsewhere in this work applies to companies limited by guarantee as it does to companies limited by shares.

---

[5] *Re Irish Club* [1906] W.N. 127; *Robertson v British Linen Co.* (1890) 18 R., 1225 (O.H.), approved *obiter* in *Lloyds Bank Ltd v Morrison & Son*, 1927 S.C. 571.
[6] Below, p.43.
[7] *Gaiman v National Association for Mental Health* [1971] Ch. 317.
[8] Companies of the kind involved in *Malleson v General Mineral Patents Syndicate Ltd.* [1894] 3 Ch. 538.
[9] Below, p.43.

Unlimited companies

A company may be registered as an unlimited company, in which case there is no limit on the members' liability to contribute to the assets: s.1(2)(c).[10] In the years immediately preceding 1967, comparatively few such companies were formed, although they are the oldest class of registered company, but the exemption from publication of accounts[11] given by the 1967 Act, made them more popular.

The memorandum and articles of an unlimited company with a share capital must be in the form set out in Table E, or as near thereto as circumstances admit: ss 3(1)(f) and 8(4)(c). Table E is a model form of memorandum and articles set out in the Companies (Tables A to F) Regulations 1985. The company is obliged to register articles with the memorandum: s.7(1). The articles must state, if the company is to have a share capital, the amount of the share capital: s.7(2). There is no requirement that the division of the share capital into shares of a fixed amount be stated. The name will not, of course, include the word "Limited", and there will be no limitation of liability clause in the memorandum. Since 1980 unlimited companies cannot be public companies: s.1(3).

An unlimited company is exceptional in that its members may be associated on the terms that they may withdraw in the mode pointed out by the memorandum and articles, so as to be free from liability in the event of a winding up,[12] and it seems that such a company may validly provide by its memorandum and articles for a return of capital to its members, *i.e.* without the consent of the court. Similarly an unlimited company may purchase its own shares if its constituent documents authorise it to do so.[13]

Re-registration of unlimited company as limited private company

Section 51 provides that an unlimited company (not already re-registered by virtue of s.49, below) may be re-registered as a private company limited either by shares or by guarantee if a special resolution to that effect and complying with the requirements set out below is passed, and the application for re-registration is in the prescribed form, signed by a director or the secretary and lodged with the Registrar, together with certain documents, not earlier than the day on which the copy of the resolution filed under s.380 is received by him.

The resolution—

(1) must state the manner in which the liability of members is to be limited and the share capital if the company is to be limited by shares;

(2) must provide for the appropriate alterations in and additions to the memorandum and articles according to whether the company is to be limited by shares or by guarantee and so with or without a share capital.

---

[10] See the Government's draft Bill, *Modernising Company Law*, above, cl. 4.
[11] Below, Ch.20.
[12] *Re Borough Commercial and Building Socy.* [1893] 2 Ch. 242.
[13] See, *e.g. Nelson Mitchell v City of Glasgow Bank* (1879) 6 R. (H.L.) 66; (1878) 6 R. 420. See Ch.10, below.

The documents which must also be lodged are printed copies of the memorandum and articles as altered.

The Registrar must issue an appropriate certificate of incorporation, whereupon the status of the company is changed and the alterations in and additions to the memorandum and articles take effect.[14] Such a certificate is conclusive evidence of compliance with the requirements of the section with respect to re-registration and of re-registration.[15]

Re-registration of unlimited company as a public company

No unlimited company can be a public company: s.1(3). Since such a company is therefore a private company, conversion of an unlimited company to a public company requires two steps. First, the acquisition of limited liability and a share capital and second, the acquisition of public company status. Both steps may be achieved in one process under ss 43 to 48. The procedure for re-registration of a private company as a public company is modified to include the appropriate requirements for the acquisition of limited liability; *i.e.* a special resolution similar to that required by s.51: s.48. Following a pre-consolidation amendment[16] it is no longer possible to re-register a company which has already been re-registered as an unlimited company as a public company under s.43.[17]

The Registrar must issue a certificate stating that the company has been incorporated as a company limited by shares and is a public company. Such a certificate is conclusive evidence of the fact that it is a public company: ss 47(5), 48(3)(b).

Re-registration of limited company as unlimited

Section 49 enables a limited private company (not previously re-registered in pursuance of s.51, above) to be re-registered as unlimited with the unanimous consent of its members.[18] The application for re-registration must be in the prescribed form, signed by a director or the secretary and lodged with the Registrar together with certain documents. A public company cannot be re-registered as an unlimited company—it must attain private company status first; nor can a company which has previously been re-registered or unlimited: s.49(3).

The application must set out the appropriate alterations in and additions to the memorandum and, if articles have been registered, the articles according to whether or not the company is to have a share capital. If articles have not been registered, the application must have annexed to it, and request the registration of, appropriate printed articles.

The Registrar must issue an appropriate certificate of incorporation, which will be conclusive evidence of proper re-registration: s.50(3).[19]

---

[14] s.52(2).
[15] s.52(3). As to the meaning of conclusive evidence, see p.24, above.
[16] The Companies Acts (Pre-Consolidation Amendments) Order 1984 SI 1984/134, para. 39.
[17] s.43(1).
[18] A community interest company is, however, excluded from doing so: Companies (Audit, Investigations and Community Enterprise) Act 2004, s.52(1).
[19] For the meaning of conclusive evidence, see p.24, above.

Open-ended investment companies

In 1996, a new type of company, the open-ended investment company (or "oeic"), by now rather well-known in the EU, became possible also under UK company law.[20] Initially, oeics were subject to the scrutiny of the Securities and Investment Board (SIB), but with the enactment of the Financial Services and Markets Act in 2000,[21] oeics became subject to the Financial Services Authority (FSA)[22] and new regulations were passed to reflect this change.[23]

Oeics are specialised investment companies which, in effect, allow for an incorporated form of unit trust. The investors in such a company purchase and sell shares—rather like units in a unit trust—in the company, reflecting the underlying value of the investments held by the company, but do not acquire any proprietary rights in the company's property. Participants in an oeic are able to redeem any part of their shareholding and, because this means that such companies must buy back their own shares, oeics are permitted to buy back their own shares in a way not currently permitted for other types of company.[24] Shareholders in an oeic are not liable for the debts of the company. The detailed rules applicable to these companies are, however, beyond the scope of this book.[25]

PUBLIC AND PRIVATE COMPANIES

A registered limited company may be a public company or a private company. By s.1(3), a public company is a limited company with a share capital which has a memorandum stating that it is a public company and which has been registered or re-registered as such.

A company which is not a public company is, by default, a private company. Thus the private company is the residual class of companies, without any special requirements.[26] This is a complete reversal of the position prior to 1980, whereby all companies were public companies unless their articles contained certain restrictions, *e.g.* as to the transferability of shares. The vast majority of registered companies are private companies.[27]

There are three requirements for the registration of a company as a public company:

    (1) it must state that it is a public company both in its memorandum and by its name. There must be a clause to that effect in the memorandum[28] and its name must end with the words "public limited company",

---

[20] See the Open-Ended Investment Companies (Companies with Variable Capital) Regulations 1996, SI 1996/2827.

[21] See s.236.

[22] As to which, see above, p.14.

[23] The Open-Ended Investment Companies Regulations 2001, SI 2001/1228, revoking 1996, SI 1996/2827, above.

[24] See p.163, below.

[25] But see, for a detailed account, *Palmer's Company Law*, Part 5A.

[26] This may be contrasted with the position of the private company under the CLR, where the law relating to companies has been emphasised.

[27] In 2003–2004, there were 11,700 public companies on the register, compared with 1,831,100 private companies: see *Companies in 2003–2004* (DTI, 2004), at p.34.

[28] s.1(3)(a).

(frequently abbreviated to "plc").[29] A private company uses the traditional "Limited" or "Ltd" at the end of its name;

(2) the memorandum must be in the form specified in Table F of the
Companies (Tables A to F) Regulations 1985[30];

(3) the company must have an authorised capital figure (the amount of
shares it may issue to the public) of at least the *authorised minimum*,
currently £50,000[31]: s.11.[32]

There are substantial differences in the capital requirements as applied to
public and private companies. In particular a public company cannot commence
business or exercise any borrowing powers unless it has actually allotted shares
up to the authorised minimum and has received at least one quarter of that
amount: ss 101(1) and 117(2).[33]

Since 1980, private companies are no longer required either to restrict the
transferability of their shares or to limit the number of members involved,
although most private companies do have such restrictions and are small in size.
Under Part VI of the Financial Services and Markets Act 2000 they would not be
able to apply to be quoted[34] on the Stock Exchange and, under s.81 of the
Companies Act 1985, it is a criminal offence for a private company to make an
offer to the public of its shares.

The minimum number of members for a public company is two[35] but one will
suffice for a private company[36] and a public company must have at least two
directors[37] whereas a private company need only have one.[38]

A private company needs no minimum capital either for registration or the
commencement of business.

A private company with only one member is known as a **single-member
company**. The fact that it only has one member must be recorded in the
company's register of members, but not on the public register.[39] In general terms,
the provisions of the Act are to apply to single member companies in the same
way as to other companies, with such modifications as are necessary.[40] There are,
however, of necessity, special provisions for meetings and resolutions of such
companies.[41]

---

[29] Below, p.17.
[30] s.3(1)(a)(b).
[31] s.118(1).
[32] This has been retained in the Government's draft Bill: *Modernising Company Law*, above, cl. 16.
[33] Below, p.132.
[34] *i.e.*, "listed", to use the terminology of the 2000 Act.
[35] The CLR has recommended that the ability of a single person to form a private company should be
extended to a public company: *Final Report* Vol 1 (2002) para.9.2. This was accepted by the
government. See *Modernising Company Law* above, cl. 2.
[36] ss 1(3A).
[37] s.282(1).
[38] s.282(3).
[39] s.352A.
[40] The Companies (Single Member Private Limited Companies) Regulations 1992 (SI 1992/1699),
Art.2(1).
[41] See Ch.14, below.

Disadvantages of a private company

The effective embargo on access to the capital markets preserved by Part VI of the Financial Services and Markets Act 2000 and s.81 of the Companies Act 1985 may be regarded as the only disadvantage of a private company as compared with a public company.

Advantages of a private company

A private company has a number of advantages over a public company. These advantages include the following:

(1) A private company need not issue subsequent issues of shares by way of a rights issue: sections 89 and 91.[42]

(2) A private company does not need an authorised minimum capital either for registration or to commence business under ss 11 and 117. It may commence business (and make binding contracts and exercise its borrowing powers) immediately on incorporation.[43]

(3) A private company is not subject to the majority of the provisions relating to the payment for shares. This enables a private company to issue shares in return for assets other than cash without lengthy and complex valuations: ss 101–116.[44]

(4) A private company need not convene an extraordinary general meeting in the event of a serious loss of capital: s.142.[45]

(5) A private company may give itself wider charges on its own shares to recover debts owed to it by its members. Public companies are restricted in this respect: s.150.[46]

(6) A private company need not make provision for unrealised capital losses when distributing a dividend: s.264.[47]

(7) Directors of private companies are much less restricted in their financial dealings with their company and need disclose far less information about such arrangements in the accounts: ss 330–344.[48]

(8) The company secretary does not need to be specially qualified or experienced: s.286.[49]

(9) Private companies may be excused from publication of some or all of their accounts, depending on their size: ss 247–252.[50]

---

[42] Below, p.134.
[43] Below, p.137.
[44] Below, p.142.
[45] Below, p.158.
[46] Below, pp.234, 236.
[47] Below, Ch.22.
[48] Below, p.291.
[49] Below, p.334.
[50] Below, Ch.20.

(10) Private companies may provide financial assistance for the purchase of their own shares by following the statutory procedure: ss 155–158.[51]

(11) Private companies may purchase or redeem their own shares out of capital: ss 171–177.[52]

(12) There is no obligation to disclose the true ownership of private company shares, however substantial the holding: ss 198–211.[53]

(13) Private companies can use the written resolution procedure instead of holding a formal meeting: ss 381A–381C.[54]

(14) Private companies may by passing elective resolutions dispense with the need to comply with certain internal requirements of the Act: s.379A.[55]

(15) Private companies may have only one member: s.1(3A).[56]

Other differences between a private company and a public company are:

(1) At a general meeting of a private company a motion for the appointment of two or more directors may be made by a single resolution: section 292(1).[57]

(2) A proxy can speak at a meeting of a private company: section 372(1).[58]

Re-registration of a private company as a public company

A private company[59] may be re-registered as a public company if it complies with the three conditions set out in ss 43 to 48.

(1) It must pass a special resolution that it be so re-registered and that its memorandum and articles be amended accordingly (*e.g.* to provide for a change of name): s.43(1)(2).

(2) It must send an application in the prescribed form signed by a director or secretary of the company to the Registrar together with a printed copy of the amended memorandum and articles, a copy of the latest balance sheet and an unqualified report by the auditors on that balance sheet, a copy of another report by the auditors that the company's net assets are not less than its capital as stated in that balance sheet, and a declaration of compliance by a director or secretary[60] and that the

---

[51] Below, Ch.11.
[52] Below, Ch.10.
[53] Below, p.197.
[54] Below, p.263.
[55] Below, p.260.
[56] Above, p.42.
[57] Below, p.270.
[58] Below, p.256.
[59] Other than one without a share capital or one that has previously been re-registered as a private company.
[60] Subject to s.43(3A), which now permits the statutory declaration to be substituted, using electronic communications, by a statement made by a director or secretary of the company. This was inserted by the Companies Act 1985 (EC) Order 2001, SI 2001/3373.

company's position *vis-à-vis* its net assets is unchanged since the last balance sheet: s.43(3).

(3) It must comply with the necessary financial criteria both for a public company to be able to commence business[61] and as to the payment for shares in public companies: ss 44 and 45.[62]

This applies equally to shares issued since the last balance sheet and before the application; in particular it must have the *authorised minimum* capital.[63]

If the Registrar is satisfied he must issue a certificate of incorporation stating that the company is a public company.[64] This is conclusive evidence that the company is a public company and that all the procedures as to re-registration have been complied with.[65]

Re-registration of a public company as a private company

A public company may be re-registered as a private company if it complies with the conditions in ss 53 to 55.

(1) It must pass a special resolution that it be so re-registered and that its memorandum and articles be amended accordingly (*e.g.* to remove the statement in the memorandum that it is a public company): s.53(1)(2).

(2) It must send an application in the prescribed form signed by a director or secretary of the company to the Registrar together with a printed copy of the amended memorandum and articles: s.53(1)(b).

(3) 28 days must have elapsed from the passing of the resolution and, either, no application has been brought under s.54 to have the resolution set aside, or the court has confirmed the resolution despite such an application. Such an application may be brought for the cancellation of the resolution to re-register by, either, the holders of five per cent. or more of the issued share capital or any class of capital, or not less than 50 members, within 28 days of the passing of the resolution. No-one who voted for the resolution can make such an application.[66] The court has extensive powers on hearing such an application including confirming or cancelling the resolution, adjourning the proceedings for an arrangement to be made, altering the memorandum and articles, and, if necessary, providing for the purchase

---

[61] Below, p.137.
[62] Below, p.142.
[63] See s.45(2).
[64] s.47(1). See too Companies (Audit Investigations and Community Enterprise) Act 2004, s.52(2)— for community interest companies.
[65] For the meaning of "conclusive evidence", see p.24, above.
[66] s.54(2).

by the company of the shares of the dissentient members.[67] This is one of several minority protection sections which occur throughout the Act.

If the Registrar is satisfied he must issue a certificate of incorporation "appropriate to a private company."[68] This is conclusive evidence that the requirements as to re-registration have been complied with and that the company is a private company.[69]

Re-registration of public companies by law

If a public company reduces its capital under s.135[70] so that its allotted share capital is less than the *authorised minimum* the court is empowered to order that the company be re-registered as a private company and that its memorandum and articles be amended accordingly. In such a case no special resolution is necessary and no application by a minority is possible: s.139.

HOLDING AND SUBSIDIARY COMPANIES

It is sometimes important to know whether a registered company is a subsidiary or a holding company. One reason is that s.23[71] generally prevents a subsidiary from being a member of its holding company. Another reason is that the financial assistance regulations apply as between holding and subsidiary companies.[72] The meaning of the terms "subsidiary" and "holding company" is given in ss 736 and 736A, and it is convenient to deal with those definitions here.

Sections 736 and 736A were introduced by the 1989 Act to provide a redefinition of holding and subsidiary companies for company law purposes. The 1989 Act introduced another, additional definition of a group purely for the purposes of the group accounting requirements introduced by that Act, as required by the seventh EC directive.[73] The need to redefine the general concept of a group of companies was made more imperative by the planned programme of EU legislation specifically aimed at groups.

Under s.736, there are three ways of establishing that a company (B) is a subsidiary of another company (A):

(i) where A holds a majority of the voting rights in B (this may be called *voting control*);

(ii) where A is a member of B and can appoint or dismiss a majority of its directors (this may be called *director control*);

---

[67] s.54(5)(6).
[68] s.55(1). See too the Companies (Audit, Investigations and Community Enterprises) Act 2004, s.52(2)—for community interest companies.
[69] s.55(3).
[70] Below, Ch.9.
[71] Below, p.190.
[72] Below, Ch.11.
[73] Below, Ch.20.

(iii) where A is a member of B and controls alone or under an agreement with others a majority of the voting rights in B (this may be called *contract control*).

If C is a subsidiary of B and B is a subsidiary of A, then C is also regarded as being a subsidiary of A.

A wholly-owned subsidiary is one whose shares are all owned by one company, its wholly-owned subsidiaries and their and its nominees.

Section 736A expands upon this basic framework. When calculating the voting rights (for voting control or contract control) it is the rights attached to the shares which count.[74] For the purposes of calculating a majority of the board (for director control) it is the majority of the voting rights on the board on all, or substantially all, matters which must be taken into account and not a numerical majority.[75] A company is deemed to be able to control the appointment or dismissal of the director of another company if either that director's appointment follows necessarily from his appointment as a director of the first company or the directorship is held by the first company itself. Rights to appoint or dismiss a director which require another's consent do not count unless there is no-one else who has those rights under the new criteria.[76]

The final aspect of the definition is to discover which *rights*, either as to voting or as to the appointment or dismissal of directors, should be attributed to whom for the purpose of establishing any of the three methods of control. The following rules will apply:

(a) rights which are applicable at all times will count. Restricted rights, *i.e.* ones which only apply in certain circumstances, will only count if they are in fact exercisable at the relevant time. On the other hand a general right which is in a temporary abeyance will still count[77];

(b) fiduciary rights (*i.e.* held only as a trustee) do not count against the trustee[78];

(c) nominee rights (*i.e.* those exercisable only on instructions or with consent) are to be attributed to the beneficial owner[79];

(d) where shares are mortgaged, the rights attached to those shares count as those of the lender and not the borrower only if, apart from normal creditor protection rights, they are exercisable only by or with the lender's, or the lender's subsidiaries', instructions[80];

(e) the rights of a subsidiary count as those of its holding company and rules (c) and (d) above must not be read as applying to the contrary[81];

---

[74] s.736A(2).
[75] s.736A(3).
[76] s.736A(3)(a)(b).
[77] s.736A(4).
[78] s.736A(5). Further, where the shares are held in a fiduciary capacity only because the transferor retains them under a contract to transfer them at a future date, the voting rights remain with the transferor: *Michaels v Harley House (Marylebone) Ltd* [2000] Ch. 104, CA.
[79] s.736A(6).
[80] s.736A(7).
[81] s.736A(8).

(f) any voting rights held by a company in itself must be discounted when making the calculation[82]; and

(g) rights held under (b)–(f) are cumulative if necessary.[83]

The above, complex, definition may be amended by regulations made by the Secretary of State under s.736B of the Act.

---

[82] s.736A(10).
[83] s.736A(11).

Chapter 3

MEMORANDUM OF ASSOCIATION

EVERY registered company must have a memorandum of association, which is the registered company's charter.[1] In general, the memorandum regulates the company's external affairs, whilst the articles regulate its internal affairs.[2] The purpose of the memorandum is to enable persons who invest in or deal with the company to ascertain what its name is, whether it is a public company or community interest company, whether it is an English or a Scottish company, what its objects are, whether the liability of its members is limited and what share capital it is authorised to issue. The memorandum may contain other matters apart from those just referred to. It must also contain an association clause and be properly subscribed. The provisions of the memorandum can be altered in certain specified cases.

Section 2 provides that the memorandum of every company must state:

(1) The name of the company: s.2(1)(a).

(2) Whether the registered office of the company is to be situated in England, Wales or Scotland: s.2(1)(b).

(3) The objects of the company: s.2(1)(c).

(4) That the liability of the members is limited, if the company is limited by shares or by guarantee: s.2(3).

(5) In the case of a limited company having a share capital, the amount of share capital with which the company proposes to be registered and the division thereof into shares of a fixed amount: s.2(5).

Section 1(3)(a) provides that the memorandum of a public company must state, in addition, the fact that the company is a public company. Similarly, the memorandum of a community interest company (CIC) must state that the company is to be a community interest company.[3]

In the case of a company limited by guarantee the memorandum must also state that each member undertakes to contribute to the assets of the company in the event of its being wound up while he is a member, or within one year after he

---

[1] See *per* Lord Cairns, L.C., in *Ashbury Railway Carriage Co. Ltd v Riche* (1875) L.R. 7 H.L. 653, at pp.667, 668.

[2] The CLR recommended that both the memorandum and articles be replaced with a single document constitution: see *Final Report* Vol 1 (2002) para.9.4. This was accepted by the government in its draft Bill: see *Modernising Company Law* (Cm 5553-II, 2002), cl.5.

[3] Companies (Audit, Investigations and Community Enterprise) Act 2004, s.32(1).

ceases to be a member, such amount as may be required, not exceeding a specified amount.

Where the memorandum states that the registered office is to be in Wales, the memorandum and the articles may be in Welsh but, if they are, they must be accompanied by a certified translation into English: s.710B(2).[4]

Subscription of the memorandum

The memorandum must state the desire of the subscribers to be formed into a company and the agreement of each to take a specified number of shares in the company. Two or more persons must subscribe their names to the memorandum: s.1(1), unless the company is being formed as a single member private limited company: s.1(3A).[5] The form of a memorandum of association of a private company must be that set out in Table B, and, for a public company, that set out in Table F, of the Companies (Tables A to F) Regulations 1985 or as near to those forms as circumstances admit: s.3(1).[6]

No subscriber may take less than one share and each subscriber must write opposite to his name the number of shares he takes.[7] Each subscriber must sign the memorandum in the presence of at least one witness, who must attest the signature: s.2(6). However, where the memorandum is delivered to the Registrar otherwise than in legible form and is authenticated by each subscriber in the manner directed by the Registrar, the requirements for signature in the presence of one witness and attestation do not apply: s.2(6A).[8]

THE NAME

The memorandum must state the name of the company: s.2(1)(a). The general rule is that any name may be selected. However, a company cannot be registered by a name which is prohibited, either absolutely or conditionally: s.26.[9] Further, the last word of the name of a private limited company must be the word "Limited" (s.25(2)), unless the company is able to comply with the criteria for exemption in s.30 and dispenses with the word. The last words of a public company must be "public limited company" (s.25(1)).[10] Where the memorandum of a limited company states that its registered office is to be in Wales, the last word of the name of the company may be "Cyfyngedig" if the company is a private company,[11] or "Cwmni cyfyngedig cyhoeddus" if it is a public company.[12] In all cases the appropriate abbreviations may be used: s.27.[13] These are Ltd, plc,

---

[4] See also the Companies (Welsh Language Forms and Documents) Regulations 1994 (SI 1994/117).
[5] See p.43, above.
[6] The Government's draft Bill makes provision for the Secretary of State to prescribe model constitutions: *Modernising Company Law*, above cl.11.
[7] s.2(5)(b)(c).
[8] Inserted by the Companies Act 1985 (Electronic Communications) Order 2000, SI 2000/3373.
[9] Below p.52.
[10] The requirements in s.25 do not apply to community interest companies: the Companies (Audit, Investigations and Community Enterprise) Act 2004, s.33(5).
[11] s.25(2)(b).
[12] s.25(1).
[13] There are similar requirements for community interest companies: see the Companies (Audit, Investigations and Community Enterprise) Act 2004, s.33. See also Sch.6, para.3.

cyf, and ccc, respectively.[14] In selecting a name, it is not necessary to use the word "Company", and the modern tendency is to omit it. A short name is an obvious practical convenience.

The word "Limited" is a misnomer. The company's liability for its own debts is not limited, but it is the members of the company who are not liable for the company's debts (except to the limited extent for public companies provided by s.24),[15] because the company is a legal entity separate and distinct from its shareholders. The important thing about the name is that it should show to others that the company is a body corporate, and not a mere unincorporated partnership. It is too late now to reserve the word "Company" for the exclusive use of incorporated companies, because that is in common use by persons who are not incorporated, *e.g.* by partnerships. The American term "Incorporated" expresses the true idea, and that or some synonymous word is to be preferred to "Limited."

The use of the word "Limited" or "Cyfyngedig," or any contraction or imitation of it, as the last word of the name under which any person carries on business without being incorporated with limited liability, is prohibited: s.34. Similarly, the use of the words "public limited company" or its Welsh equivalent or any abbreviation of it by any person who is not a public limited company is an offence: s.33.

Prohibited and controlled names

Section 26(1) provides seven grounds upon which the registration of a name or change of name is absolutely prohibited.[16]

    (1) A name including "limited," "unlimited", "community interest company, or "community interest public limited company,"[17] "public limited company," or their Welsh equivalents otherwise than at the end of the name;

    (2) A name including any abbreviation of those words otherwise than at the end of the name;

    (3) which includes, at any place in the name, the expressions "investment company with variable capital" or "open-ended investment company" or their Welsh equivalents[18];

    (4) which includes, at any place in the name, the expression "limited liability partnership" or its Welsh equivalent[19];

    (5) A name which is *the same as* a name appearing in the index of registered names kept by the Registrar;

---

[14] s.27(4).
[15] Above p.27.
[16] See too the government's draft Bill, *Modernising Company Law*, above, cl.198.
[17] Inserted by the Companies (Audit, Investigations and Community Enterprise) Act 2004, Sch.6, para.2.
[18] "Cwmni buddsoddi â chyfalaf newidiol" and "cwmni buddsoddiant penagored", respectively. Introduced by the Open-Ended Investment Companies Regulations 2001, SI 2001/1228.
[19] "Partneriaeth atebolrqydd cyfyngedig".

(6) A name, the use of which would, in the opinion of the Secretary of State, constitute a criminal offence;

(7) A name which in the opinion of the Secretary of State is offensive.

The important prohibition is (5)—a name which is *the same as* one already on the index of registered names kept by the Registrar under s.714. This includes the names of all registered companies, limited partnerships, limited liability partnerships, and industrial and provident societies, and so registration of a company name confers a partial monopoly of the use of that name. The onus of checking the index is on those who wish to register the name. There is no pre-registration control on registration of names similar or "too like" those already on the index but such a name may be compulsorily altered within one year of registration under s.28(2)—so called "post registration control."[20] When deciding whether one name is *the same as* another minor differences are to be disregarded under s.26(3). Accents, type and case of letters and the word "the" if it is the first word of the name, are examples of such minor differences.

Section 26(2) provides for the controlled use of certain words and expressions either on the registration of a company or a change of name. The use of any name which in the opinion of the Secretary of State would be likely to give the impression that the company is connected in any way with Her Majesty's Government or with any local authority or includes any name or expression specified in the appropriate regulations cannot be registered without his consent. The appropriate regulations are the Company and Business Names Regulations 1981.[21] These regulations specify many separate words or expression, including their plural and possessive forms, which require consent before use. These include: "Abortion", "Chamber (or Chambers) of Commerce", "Duke", "English", "Health Visitor", "National", "Royal", "Stock Exchange", "Trade Union", "Trust", and "Windsor".

When a company wishes to use such an expression it must request the "relevant body", if one is specified, to indicate whether (and if so why) it has any objections to the proposal. Relevant bodies include the Home Office and the Scottish Ministers. The reply of the relevant body must be sent to the Registrar by the applicant when registration or the change of name is applied for: s.29(2). The Secretary of State will then make his decision.

Since similar names can be registered, there is a possibility of passing-off actions being brought against registered companies, even though such names can be compulsorily changed within one year of registration.[22] Under the general law, the court has jurisdiction to grant an injunction[23] to restrain a company from using a trade name colourably resembling that of the plaintiff if the defendant's trade name, though innocently adopted, is calculated, *i.e.* likely,[24] to deceive,

---

[20] Below, p.57.
[21] SI 1981/1685. As amended by the Company and Business Names (Amendment) Regulations 1982 (SI 1982/1653), 1992 (SI 1992/1196), 1995 (SI 1995/3022), and 2001 (SI 2001/259).
[22] Below, p.57.
[23] The Scottish equivalent is interdict.
[24] *Per* Earl of Halsbury L.C. in *The N. Cheshire and Manchester Brewery Co. Ltd v The Manchester Brewery Co. Ltd* [1899] A.C. at p.84.

either by diverting customers from the plaintiff to the defendant or by occasioning confusion between the two businesses, *e.g.* by suggesting that the defendant's business is in some way connected with that of the plaintiff.

In *Ewing v Buttercup Margarine Co. Ltd*,[25] the plaintiff, who carried on business under the trade name of the Buttercup Dairy Company, was held entitled to restrain a newly registered company from carrying on business under the name of the Buttercup Margarine Company Ltd on the ground that the public might reasonably think that the registered company was connected with his business.

However, if the company's business is or will be different from that of the complaining party, confusion is not likely to arise, and an injunction will not be granted.[26]

A company having a word in ordinary use as part of its name cannot prevent another company from using the same word.

So, Aerators Ltd were unable to prevent the registration of Automatic Aerators Patents, Ltd because the word "aerator" was a word in common use in the English language and Aerators Ltd had no monopoly of it: *Aerators Ltd v Tollitt* [1902] 2 Ch. 319.

Exemption from using the word "Limited"

Under s.30 a private company limited by guarantee has a right to exclude the word "Limited" from the end of its name if certain criteria are met and certified. Prior to the 1981 Act such exemption was available to all private companies if they were so licensed by the Department of Trade and Industry. Such licensed companies continue to enjoy their exemption under the present section.

The present criteria are that the company is to be formed for the promotion of commerce, art, science, education, religion, charity or any profession and anything incidental or conducive to any of those objects; that by its memorandum or articles it must apply its income solely for the promotion of those objects, prohibit the payment of dividends to its members, and require all its surplus assets on a winding up to be transferred to a similar body rather than to its members.[27] A statutory declaration either by the solicitor engaged in the formation, or by a director or secretary of the company, that the company is one to which the section applies will suffice to obtain the exemption: s.30(4), (5). However, in place of the statutory declaration, the Registrar may accept a statement which uses electronic communications, made by a person falling within s.30(5), which states that the company complies with the requirements of s.30(3): s.30(5A).[28] The Registrar can refuse to register unless a statutory declaration has been delivered to him: s.30(5B). There are also penalties for persons making false statements under s.30(5A): s.30(5C).[29]

---

[25] [1917] 2 Ch. 1, CA.
[26] *Dunlop Pneumatic Tyre Co. Ltd v Dunlop Motor Co. Ltd*, 1907 S.C. HL 15, where the respondents carried on a motor-repairing company; similarly an interdict was refused in *The Scottish Union and National Insurance Co. v The Scottish National Insurance Co. Ltd*, 1909 S.C. 318.
[27] s.30(3). This requirement was always insisted on under the previous system.
[28] Inserted by the Companies Act 1985 (Electronic Communications) Order 2000, SI 2000/3373.
[29] *ibid*. The penalties are to "imprisonment or a fine, or both".

There is an absolute ban on any alterations of such a company's memorandum or articles so as to breach the criteria—there are fines in default: section 31(1), (5). Any purported alteration will thus be void. If there is a breach of any of the criteria without any such change the Secretary of State can require the addition of the word "Limited" to the company's name and a resolution of the directors to that effect will suffice for the change of name: s.31(2). Such a company cannot again acquire the exemption without the express approval of the Secretary of State: s.31(3).

Any company which obtains exemption under s.30 is relieved of the necessity of (1) having "Limited" as part of its name, (2) publishing its name[30] and (3) sending lists of members to the Registrar,[31] although s.351 requires the fact that it is a limited company to be mentioned in its business letters and order forms.

Associations taking advantage of this exemption are typically chambers of commerce, schools and colleges, research associations, learned societies, professional qualifying bodies and charitable bodies doing social work.

Publication of name by company

The Act provides that every company must:

(1) paint or affix its name on the outside of every office or place in which its business is carried on, in a conspicuous position, in letters easily legible: s.348(1);

(2) mention its name in legible characters in all business letters of the company and in all notices and other official publications, and in all bills of exchange, promissory notes, endorsements, cheques and orders for money or goods, bills of parcels, invoices, receipts and letters of credit: s.349(1),[32]

(3) engrave its name in legible characters on its seal, if it has one: section 350(1).[33]

An exception is that by s.30(7) a company entitled to dispense with the word "Limited" as part of its name[33a] is excepted from the provisions of the Act relating to the publishing of its name, although as noted above, s.351 requires the fact that it is a limited company to be mentioned in legible characters in all its business letters and order forms.

Fines are imposed on the company and its officers for non-compliance with the above requirements.[34]

---

[30] Under ss 348, 349, 350, below.

[31] Under s.363, below.

[32] There are additional requirements for charitable companies: Charities Act 1993, s.68, in England and by s.112(6) C.A. 1989 for Scotland.

[33] Where a company entered into a bond by way of deed and used a seal engraved with its trading name rather than its registered name, in breach of s.350, it was held that this did not render the bond a nullity or enforceable by a third party beneficiary against a surety: *OTV Birwelco Ltd v Technical and General Guarantee Co. Ltd* [2002] EWHC 2240 (TCC); [2002] 2 B.C.L.C. 723.

[33a] Above, p.54.

[34] See, *e.g.*, s.348(2); s.350(2).

Company names and company cheques, etc.

If an officer of the company or any person on its behalf, signs or authorises to be signed on behalf of the company any bill of exchange, cheque or order for money or goods in which the company's name is not correctly mentioned,[35] he is liable to a fine and, in addition, he is personally liable to the holder of the bill of exchange, cheque or order, for its amount, unless it is paid by the company: s.349(4).[36] Such personal liability is a secondary liability, arising only if the company itself fails to pay, *e.g.* because of liquidation.

The courts have long established that liability under s.349(4) will be imposed upon such an officer when the words "limited" or "plc" are not included on the face of the bill or cheque.[37] The original intention was that third parties should not be misled into thinking that they were dealing with an unlimited organisation when they were dealing with a limited company. There need be no element of deceit involved, however, and the courts will not order rectification of the cheque simply on the basis that "everybody was aware of what the situation was". Rectification cannot be used by an individual simply to avoid a statutory liability.[38]

The situation is less clear where there is a mistake as to the spelling of the name of the company. In one case, *Durham Fancy Goods Ltd v Michael Jackson (Fancy Goods) Ltd,*[39] where the third party had prepared and specified the form of acceptance of the bill which it required and which misdescribed the company's name as "M. Jackson (Fancy Goods) Ltd," the court refused to allow the third party to enforce the personal liability of the officer who signed the bill on the basis of estoppel. The authority of this decision has since been doubted,[40] however, and it has been distinguished in subsequent cases where the third party had not actually prepared the bill or cheque involved,[41] and more recently where although the third party had prepared the bill it had not *prescribed* the form of wording, but had simply put forward bills which it used for the officer to accept in the proper form.[42] Until recently it was assumed therefore that any mistake in the spelling of the name gave rise to personal liability,[43] but in *Jenice Ltd v Dan,*[44] it was held that since the purpose of the section was to ensure that third parties knew they were dealing with a limited company, a minor spelling mistake on the printed cheque in which one letter of the company's name was omitted did not give rise to any liability on the part of the person signing it.

---

[35] Abbreviation of "Company" to "Co." is not a breach of the section, however: *Banque de l'Indochine et de Seuz S.A. v Euroseas Finance Co. Ltd* [1981] 3 All ER 198.

[36] In one case, the company's name did not appear at all on a bill of exchange and the directors were held liable: *Novaknit Hellas SA v Kumar Bros International Ltd* [1998] C.L.C. 971.

[37] *Penrose v Martyr* (1858) 120 E.R. 595, *Atkin v Wardle* (1889) 5 T.L.R., 734, *British Airways Board v Parish* [1979] 2 Lloyds Rep. 361, CA.

[38] *Blum v O.C.P. Repartition SA* [1988] B.C.L.C. 170, CA; *Rafsanjan Pistachio Producers Co-operative v Reiss* [1990] B.C.L.C. 352.

[39] [1968] 2 Q.B. 839.

[40] *Blum v O.C.P. Repartition SA, above.*

[41] *Barber & Nicholls v R. & G. Associates (London) Ltd* (1982) 132 N.L.J. 1076.

[42] *Lindholst A/S v Fowler* [1988] B.C.L.C. 166, CA.

[43] See the cases cited above, and *Bondina Ltd v Rolloway Shower Blinds* [1986] B.C.L.C. 177; *John Wilkes (Footwear) Ltd v Lee International (Footwear) Ltd* [1985] B.C.L.C. 444.

[44] [1993] B.C.L.C. 1349.

An officer cannot be liable for authorising a signature, as distinct from the signature itself, unless he authorises the making of the order, etc., on an incorrectly named document.

A company, Lee International (Footwear) Ltd, ordered several moccasins from the plaintiffs on an old order form which gave the company's former name. The order was signed by one director. The other director, being unaware of the fact that an old order form was being used, was held not to be liable under the section: *John Wilkes (Footwear) Ltd v Lee International (Footwear) Ltd* [1985] B.C.L.C. 444.

What amounts to a signature may vary according to the context. It is possible that a signature in the company's name alone will suffice, but there must be an individual affixation of that name in confirmation of the order concerned by the officer for him to authorise that signature and so be liable under the section. Merely authorising the filling up of a form with an incorrect name printed on it will not suffice.[45]

Change of name

Companies may change their registered names voluntarily or under compulsion. The latter gives the Department of Trade and Industry control over names similar to those already registered even though they cannot prevent registration of such names.

(1) A company may change its name at any time by a special resolution which takes effect from the issue of a new certificate of incorporation by the Registrar: s.28(1).[46] Such a change of name is subject to the same restrictions as are applicable to the choice of name for a new company registering a name for the first time.[47] The only exception to this freedom to change a name applies where it is proposed to remove the word "limited" from a company's name and there has been a direction of the Secretary of State to the contrary.[48]

(2) If a name has been registered which is *the same as* one already on the index of registered names or one that ought to have appeared on the index at the time of registration or is in the opinion of the Secretary of State *too like* any such name, the name must be changed on the direction of the Secretary of State: s.28(2). Such a direction must be given within 12 months of the original registration and must be complied with within such period as is specified.

Names are *the same* as existing ones as defined by s.26(3).[49] The Registrar has published notes for guidance as to what will be considered *too like* names, *e.g.* phonetically identical names or where two

---

[45] *Oshkosh B'Gosh Incorporated v Dan Marbel Incorporated Ltd* [1989] B.C.L.C. 507.
[46] This requirement cannot be varied by the court: see *Halifax plc v Halifax Repossessions Ltd* [2004] EWCA Civ. 331; [2004] 2 B.C.L.C. 455, CA, at p.461.
[47] Above, p.51.
[48] s.31(3). See above, p.54.
[49] Above, p.53.

names have a distinctive element in common, or where because of a similarity of the name and operations of two companies there is likely to be some confusion. These are not conclusive criteria however.

(3) When a company has applied to have a controlled name or expression as part of its name it will furnish information to the relevant body and the Department in order to obtain permission under s.26(2).[50] If misleading information has been given or undertakings or assurances have not been fulfilled the Secretary of State may by direction require the company to change its name: s.28(3). Such a direction may be given up to five years from the original registration and must be complied with within such period as is specified.

(4) If the Secretary of State considers that a name gives a misleading indication of the nature of the company's activities so as to be likely to cause harm to the public, he may direct a change. A direction must normally be complied with within six weeks. Within three weeks the company may apply to the court to have the direction set aside: s.32. In *Association of Certified Public Accountants of Britain v Secretary of State for Trade and Industry*,[51] the court held that on such an application the burden of proof was on the Secretary of State to show that the company's name is so misleading that it is likely to cause harm to the public.

When a company changes its name a new certificate of incorporation will be issued by the Registrar (ss 28(6), 32(5)) and the new name takes effect from the date of issue of the new certificate.[52]

A change of name does not affect any rights or obligations of the company or any legal proceedings by or against the company: ss 28(7), 32(6).

Business names

If a company which has a place of business in Great Britain, whether or not incorporated here, carries on business in Great Britain under a business name which does not consist of its corporate name without any addition other than one which indicates that the business is being carried on in succession to the former owner, it becomes subject to the Business Names Act 1985.

The first consequence of this is that the company's business name may not without permission of the Secretary of State include any of the words or expressions subject to control on registration of a corporate name; *i.e.* those within s.26(2) and its regulations: Business Names Act, s.2. An identical procedure to obtain permission must be followed: Business Names Act, s.3. There is a 12-month period of grace where a business has been transferred to a company which then uses the previous permitted business name.

---

[50] Above p.52.
[51] [1997] 2 B.C.L.C. 307.
[52] The old name continues until then. See *Shackleford, Ford & Co. Ltd v Dangerfield* (1868) L.R. 3 C.P. 407. In *Lin Pac Containers (Scotland) Ltd v Kelly,* 1982 S.L.T. 50 (O.H.), a contract entered into in the new name was held valid even though the new certificate was issued three days later.

The second consequence is that a company using a business name distinct from its corporate name must disclose its corporate name and an address for the service of any document on all its business letters, written orders for goods or services, invoices and receipts, and written demands for payment arising in the course of the business, and display a statutory notice of such particulars in each of its business premises (to which either its customers or suppliers have access). Further it must supply such particulars to anyone who asks for them and with whom anything is done or discussed in the course of the business. This must be done by giving him notice "immediately" on request: Business Names Act, s.4.

In default of these obligations the company and its officers may be liable to fines. In addition, failure to comply with the disclosure provisions is subject to some civil consequences under s.5 of the Business Names Act 1985. If a company seeks to enforce any action arising out of a contract made at a time when it was in breach of the disclosure obligations, the court must dismiss the action if the other party can show that he either has a course of action against the company which he was unable to pursue because of the breach or has suffered some financial loss in respect of that contract by reason of the company's breach. The section however has no application either to proceedings brought by such a company on counter-claim or to the right of set-off if it is sued by the other party.

THE REGISTERED OFFICE

A company must at all times have a registered office to which communications and notices may be addressed: s.287(1).[53] The memorandum must state whether the registered office is to be in England and Wales, Wales or Scotland: section 2(1)(b).[54] The actual address of the registered office need not be set out in the memorandum, but notice of the address must be given to the Registrar in the statement which, under s.10, above,[55] must be delivered for registration with the memorandum. That address is thus the initial address on incorporation of the company: s.287(2).

The statement as to the registered office in the memorandum fixes the company's nationality and domicile, *e.g.* if the memorandum states that the office is to be in England the company is an English company with British nationality and an English domicile. A corporation is domiciled where it is incorporated and cannot change this domicile,[56] except by Act of Parliament, and the law of a corporation's domicile governs all questions of its status, *e.g.* is it duly incorporated, what are its powers, has it been dissolved? The nationality of a corporation,

---

[53] This is so even where the company ceases trading. *In Re Oakwood Storage Services Ltd* ([2003] EWHC 2807 (Ch); [2004] 2 B.C.L.C. 404) a company ceased trading when Customs and Excise took over its bonded premises, which was also its registered office. The Court held that, in such circumstances, the directors must put in place arrangements to ensure that documents served on the company at its registered office came to their notice.

[54] The CLR recommended that a company registered in Wales should, by special resolution, be able to change this to "England and Wales": *Final Report*, above, para.9.8. This, and the reverse scenario, was accepted by the Government: *Modernising Company Law*, above, cl.196 and 197.

[55] Above, p.21.

[56] *Gasque v I.R.C.* [1940] 2 K.B. 80.

seldom relevant in private international law, also depends on the place of incorporation.

The reason for requiring a company to have a specific registered office is that, since the company has a legal existence but does not have a physical existence, it is necessary to know where the company can be found, where the communications and notices may be addressed and where documents can be served on it. A company need not, and very frequently does not, carry on its business at its registered office. There is nothing, for example, to prevent a company with a registered office in England from carrying on its business abroad.

A document can be served on a company by leaving it at or sending it by post to the registered office of the company: s.725(1). It is not necessary to send it by registered post.[57]

If a company registered in Scotland carries on business in England, the process of any court in England can be served at the principal place of the company's business in England, a copy being posted at the same time to the registered office: s.725(2), (3).

Section 351(1) requires every company to mention its place of registration and registered number, and the address of its registered office, in legible characters on all its business letters and order forms. A company which fails to comply with the subsection, or an officer of a company or other person on its behalf who issues or authorises the issue of a letter or form which does not comply, is liable to a fine.[57a] The phrase "order forms" means forms which the company makes available for other persons to order goods or services from the company and includes, *e.g.* coupons in newspapers which the public fill in when asking for goods to be supplied.

Change of address of the registered office

A company may change the address of its registered office on giving proper notice to the registrar. The new address takes effect on the entry of that address on the register but the company has 14 days after giving due notice in which to use the new address and to transfer the registers, etc., required to be kept there before it commits any offences for using the wrong address, etc. This is because the company will not be able to discover the actual date of registration without making a specific search of the register: s.287(3)(4)(5).

Persons dealing with the company may, on the other hand, validly serve any document on the company at the old address within 14 days of the registration of the new address: s.287(4). This is because the new address will in practice appear on the company's registered file a few days after registration.

If a company is unavoidably unable to keep its registers, etc., at its registered office in circumstances in which it was impracticable to give the registrar prior notice, the company and its officers will not be liable if it can show that it resumed performance of that duty at other premises as soon as practicable and notified the registrar of that new address within 14 days of doing so: s.287(6)(7).

---

[57] *T.O. Supplies (London) Ltd v Jerry Creighton Ltd* [1952] 1 K.B. 42.
[57a] s.351(5).

Section 711 provides that the Registrar must publish in the *Gazette* notice of the receipt by him of notice of a change in the situation of a company's registered office; *i.e.* he must officially notify it. The point being that s.42 provides that a company cannot then rely against other persons (as regards service of any document on the company) on any change in the situation of the company's registered office if either it was not officially notified (under s.711) at the material time and is not shown by the company to have been known at that time to the person concerned, or if the material time is less than 16 days after official notification and it is shown that the person concerned was unavoidably prevented from knowing of the event at that time.[58]

Items which must be kept at the registered office

The following must be kept at the registered office of a company:

(1) The register of members and, if the company has one, the index of members, unless the register is made up at another office of the company, when they may be kept at that office, or is made up by an agent, when they may be kept at the agent's office: ss 352–354.

(2) The minute books of general meetings: s.383(1).

(3) The register of interests in the notifiable percentage or more of the shares carrying unrestricted voting rights and, if there is one, the index of names, unless the register of directors' interests is not kept at the registered office, when it must be kept where the register of directors' interests is kept: ss 211(8), 213.

(4) The register of directors and secretaries: s.288(1).

(5) The register of directors' interests in shares in, or debentures of, the company or associated companies, together with, if the company has one, the index of names in the register, unless the register of members is not kept at its registered office, when they may be kept where the register of members is kept: s.325.

(6) A copy of each director's contract of service or a memorandum thereof, unless kept where the register of members is kept or kept at the company's principal place of business: s.318.

(7) If the company has one, the register of debenture holders, unless the register is made up at another office, when it may be kept where it is made up, or is made up by an agent, when it may be kept at the agent's office: section 190.

(8) A copy of every instrument creating or evidencing any charge requiring registration under Pt XII of the Act: s.407.

(9) The company's register of charges affecting property of the company: s.407.

---

[58] On the other hand official notification does not constitute notice of such a change to anyone: *Official Custodian of Charities v Parway Estates* [1985] Ch. 151, CA.

(10) Any proposed contract or option for an off-market purchase by a company of its own shares, for 15 days prior to the resolution to approve it: ss 164(6), 165(2).

(11) Any proposed release by a company of its rights under an off-market purchase contract or option to purchase its own shares: s.167(2).

(12) Any contract for the purchase by a company of its own shares approved by the company must be kept at the registered office for 10 years from the purchase of the shares or the determination of the contract: s.169(4).

(13) The requisite statutory declaration of solvency and auditors' report where a private company intends to purchase or redeem its own shares out of capital: s.175(6).

Under s.723A the Secretary of State is empowered to make provision by regulations for the inspection and copying of these documents kept at the company's registered office. Under the current regulations[59] companies must make the documents available for inspection for not less than two hours between 9am and 5pm on each business day (excluding weekends and bank holidays) and allow anyone making such an inspection to copy the information by the taking of notes or the transcription of the information (but are not obliged to provide any other facilities).[60] Inspection of all documents is free to members of the company and the fees for non-members are fixed at a maximum of £2.50 per hour.[61] The register of charges and documents creating a charge may also be inspected free by debenture holders: s.423(1).

THE OBJECTS

The memorandum must state the objects of the company: s.2(1)(c).[62] As Lord Parker of Waddington said in *Cotman v Brougham*,[63] the statement of the objects in the memorandum was originally intended to serve a double purpose:

(1) to protect the subscribers who learn from it the purposes to which their money can be applied[64];

(2) to protect persons dealing with the company, who can discover from it[65] the extent of the company's powers.

At common law, a corporation has the same legal capacity as a human being[66] but, in order to protect the shareholders and those who deal with the company,

---

[59] The Companies (Inspection and Copying of Registers, Indices and Documents) Regulations 1991 (SI 1991/1998).

[60] reg.3(2).

[61] Sch.2.

[62] The CLR recommended that this requirement be abolished: see *Final Report*, above, para.9.10. This was accepted by the Government in its draft Bill, cl.1(5) of which (*Modernising Company Law*, above) provides that "a company formed under this Act has unlimited capacity."

[63] [1918] A.C. 514 at p. 520. See also *per* Lord Wrenbury at pp.522, 523.

[64] A member can require the company to send him a copy of the memorandum on payment of a fee: s.19(1).

[65] They can inspect the memorandum and the other documents kept by the Registrar, s.709(1).

[66] *Case of Sutton's Hospital* (1612) 10 Co.Rep. 23a; Blackstone Comm. 1, 593; *University of Glasgow v Faculty of Physicians and Surgeons* (1834) 13 S. 9; (1835) 2 S. & M. 275: (1837) 15 S. 736; (1840) 1 Rob. 397.

the courts evolved the *ultra vires* doctrine to the effect that since a registered company is an artificial person incorporated by Parliament for the objects stated in the memorandum, it has power only to carry out such objects together with anything incidental thereto. Anything done which is outside the scope of the objects clause was therefore *ultra vires* and void. The result of this doctrine was that objects clauses became very lengthy because companies took all the objects they could conceivably require and the original short form envisaged by the model memorandum in the Companies (Tables A to F) Regulations was rarely used. Nevertheless the *ultra vires* doctrine continually caused unnecessary hardship for innocent third parties and introduced extreme complexity into the law. An additional "protection" for shareholders and third parties was provided by the original rule that the objects clause could not be altered except by a special Act of Parliament or a reconstruction. Later, the objects could be altered but only for specified purposes, initially with the court's consent.

The first EC directive required a change in the law of *ultra vires* and this was implemented by s.9(1) of the European Communities Act 1972 which became s.35 of the Companies Act 1985. That section proved to have serious defects, however, and in 1985 Professor Dan Prentice, of Oxford University, was commissioned by the DTI to write a report on the *ultra vires* rule. This report led to major reforms by the 1989 Act. These reforms have effectively abolished the *ultra vires* rule so far as third parties are concerned, allowed for a catch-all short-form objects clause, given companies a general power of alteration of all such clauses, and limited even their internal effects. Most of the old law has been swept away and readers are referred to the thirteenth edition of this work for a detailed analysis of the *ultra vires* rule, etc., prior to 1991. In this edition, only a summary of the pre-1991 position is given.

Form and alteration of the objects clause

Companies are still required to have an objects clause: s.2(1)(c). As the result of the legacy of the *ultra vires* doctrine contemporary objects clauses are, as stated above, usually very long and have general clauses at the end, *e.g.* that every object is a separate main object[67] or that the company may do, in addition to the objects listed, anything which the directors consider can be carried on in conjunction with its other objects.[68] Such clauses, developed in response to the court's attempts to limit long objects clauses by discovering main objects and winding up a company for failure of that main object, are perfectly valid.

The first change in the law relating to the objects clause introduced by the 1989 Act is contained in s.3A of the 1985 Act. This section relates to the form of the objects clause and provides that where the memorandum states that the object of the company is to carry on business as a general commercial company, that company is deemed to be able to carry on any trade or business whatsoever and have the power to do anything which is incidental or conducive to the conduct of any trade or business by it. This new short form of objects clause is therefore

---

[67] See, *e.g. Cotman v Brougham* [1918] A.C. 514.
[68] See, *e.g. Bell Houses Ltd v City Wall Properties Ltd* [1966] 2 Q.B. 656.

available to any commercial company and if used will considerably shorten company memoranda. It is not clear, however, whether companies may adopt the wording of s.3A as part of a wider objects clause and still retain the benefit of that section. The section speaks only of *the* object of the company being set out as stated and not of one of the objects, etc.

The 1989 Act also substantially changed the power of a company to alter its objects. Section 4(1) of the 1985 Act now allows a company to alter its objects clause by a special resolution at any time and for any reason.[69] Previously any alteration had to be for a specified purpose. The important point to note, however, is that any such change must be effected by a special resolution. This has consequences for the effects of the objects clause both on third parties[70] and internally on the directors and shareholders.[71]

The new general right of alteration remains, however, subject to s.5 of the 1985 Act. That section provides that certain dissentients may, within 21 days after the passing of the special resolution, apply to the court for an alteration of the objects to be cancelled, and then the alteration is of no effect unless it is confirmed by the court. The application for cancellation can be made by the holders of not less than 15 per cent in nominal value of the company's issued share capital or any class thereof or, if the company is not limited by shares, not less than 15 per cent of the members.[72] An application cannot be made by a person who consented to or voted for the alteration.[73]

Section 5 also provides that on an application for cancellation the court may confirm the alteration of objects wholly or in part and on such terms as it thinks fit, and may adjourn the proceedings to enable an arrangement to be made for the purchase, other than by the company, of the interests of dissentient members.[74] Alternatively, the court may provide for the purchase of the dissentient members' shares by the company or make any alterations to the memorandum or articles of the company.[75] Such alterations have the same effect as one duly authorised by the company.[76] If the court orders that no specified or general alterations be made to the memorandum or articles this overrides any power in the Act to the contrary.[77]

A company exempt from using the word "Limited" at the end of its name cannot alter its objects so as to take them outside the conditions for such exemption: s.31(1).

When the objects are altered, a printed copy of the special resolution, or a copy in some other form approved by him, must be delivered to the Registrar within 15 days: s.30(1). If no application is made for cancellation of the alteration, section 6(1) requires that a printed copy of the memorandum as

---

[69] The Companies (Audit, Investigations and Community Enterprise) Act 2004 makes provision for regulations to be made restricting community interest companies from altering their objects (s.32(6)).
[70] Below, p.65.
[71] Below, p.67.
[72] s.5(2).
[73] *ibid.*
[74] s.5(4).
[75] s.5(5).
[76] s.5(7).
[77] s.5(6).

altered must be delivered to the Registrar between 21 and 36 days after the date of the resolution. If an application for cancellation is made to the court, the company must forthwith give notice in the prescribed form thereof to the Registrar and, on the alteration being cancelled or confirmed, an office copy of the court order must be delivered within 15 days.[78] In the case of confirmation, a printed copy of the memorandum as altered must also be delivered: s.6(1)(a).

Effect of the objects clause on corporate transactions—corporate capacity

As has been explained above the objects clause by virtue of the doctrine of *ultra vires* severely restricted the capacity of a company to make contracts, donations, etc. Any act which was outside the objects clause was *ultra vires* and void. A company could not be sued on any such act[79] and probably could not enforce it.[80] A company was, however, allowed to do things which were reasonably incidental to its stated objects.[81] Above all an *ultra vires* act could not be ratified even by all the members.[82] A further restriction on third parties was that they were deemed to have constructive notice of the contents of the objects clause. An example of the potential injustice caused by a combination of these restrictions is *Re Jon Beauforte Ltd.*[83]

> A company, authorised by its memorandum to carry on business as costumiers and gown makers, started the business of making veneered panels. This was *ultra vires*. They ordered and received coke for this business from coke merchants. Correspondence showed that the coke suppliers had actual notice that the coke was required for the business of veneered panel manufacturers, and since they had constructive notice of the objects clause that this was an *ultra vires* activity. *Held*, they could not prove for their debts in the company's liquidation. Nor in practice could they recover the coke, which legally remained theirs, since it had been consumed.

It would have been different if the coke merchant had not known that the coke was to be used for an *ultra vires* purpose because he could have assumed that it was for an *intra vires* business.

The *ultra vires* doctrine therefore proved to be both unduly restrictive on shareholders and a trap for unwary third parties. In 1986, however, its operation was restricted by the Court of Appeal in *Rolled Steel Products Ltd v British Steel Corporation,*[84] so that it only applied to the capacity of the company strictly construed. Earlier cases had decided that a company had no capacity to exercise any of its powers, *e.g.* to borrow or lend money, otherwise than for the authorised objects of the company. This approach was rejected in the *Rolled Steel* case. If the company has a power in its objects clause, *e.g.* to give guarantees, then it has the capacity to give a guarantee for any purpose. Thus, the common law doctrine of

---

[78] s.6(1)(b).
[79] *Ashbury Railway Carriage Co. Ltd v Riche* (1875) L.R. 7 H.L. 653.
[80] *Bell Houses Ltd v City Wall Properties Ltd* [1966] 2 Q.B. 656; *Cabaret Holdings Ltd v Meeance Sports & Radio Club Inc.* [1982] N.Z.L.R. 673.
[81] *A.G. v Great Eastern Railway Co.* (1880) 5 App.Cas. 473.
[82] See n.79, above.
[83] [1953] Ch. 131.
[84] [1986] Ch. 246, CA. See also *James Finlay Corporation Ltd v R. & R.S. Mearns* 1988 S.L.T. 302 (O.H.).

ultra vires was finally refined so that a transaction or act would only be void for lack of corporate capacity if it was not capable of falling within the terms of the objects clause either as an object or as a power.[85]

It is important to note that the objects clause is also important in relation to corporate transactions outside the area of corporate capacity because it could limit the authority of the company's agents to bind the company even though the company itself has capacity. Questions of agency are dealt with in Chapter 6, below. In this chapter we are concerned only with the company's own capacity.

Statutory amendments to the ultra vires doctrine

Section 9(1) of the European Communities Act 1972, which became the original s.35 of the 1985 Act, provided that in favour of a person dealing with a company in good faith any transaction decided upon by the directors was deemed to be within the capacity of the company. Good faith was presumed in the absence of evidence to the contrary and the third party was not bound to enquire as to the company's capacity (thus reversing the concept of constructive notice). This section proved to be defective in several areas—it did not protect the company, it was limited to dealings and so arguably not to gratuitous transactions,[86] it required a transaction decided on by the directors (all of them?) and finally no definition was provided of good faith. In *International Sales & Agencies Ltd v Marcus*[87] it was suggested that good faith would be destroyed if the third party had actual knowledge that the transaction was *ultra vires* or could not in all the circumstances have been unaware of the *ultra vires* nature of the transaction. It was also suggested that a decision by a sole director or managing director would suffice if the full board had properly delegated the appropriate powers to him.[88]

As a result of the general dissatisfaction with the *ultra vires* concept and the perceived inadequacies of s.35, the 1989 Act substituted a new s.35 into the 1985 Act. Section 35(1) now reads:

> "The validity of an act done by a company shall not be called into question on the ground of lack of capacity by reason of anything in the company's memorandum."

This subsection effectively abolishes the *ultra vires* doctrine insofar as it affects the capacity of the company. It is actually framed so as to exclude any limits on corporate capacity in the whole memorandum but for practical purposes this will mean the objects clause.[89] Unlike its predecessor the new s.35 applies to all acts and for all purposes whatever the status of the third party. An argument that the section is defective because any lack of corporate capacity is caused by what is *not* in the memorandum rather than what is included, must presumably fail on the basis that since this section is implementing an EC directive it must be construed so as to give effect to that directive's purpose.[90] However, the section

---

[85] For a modern example of this approach see *Halifax Building Society v Meridian Housing Association Ltd* [1994] 2 B.C.L.C. 540.

[86] See, *e.g. Re Halt Garage (1964) Ltd* [1982] 3 All E.R. 1016, 1024, *per* Oliver J.

[87] [1982] 3 All E.R. 551.

[88] Agreement by all the directors individually would also suffice: *T.C.B. Ltd v Gray* [1987] Ch. 458.

[89] It is possible that the capital clause could be infringed by a corporate transaction.

[90] Following the European Court's ruling in *Marleasing S.A. v La Comercial Internacional de Alimentacion S.A.* [1993] B.C.C. 421; above p.16.

only applies to an act done by a company. It begs the question therefore as to whether those acting on the company's behalf have the power to bind the company to an act in question; *i.e.* have they the authority to act on the company's behalf so that it is an act of the company? The fact that the company has the necessary capacity is therefore only the first element in deciding whether the company is bound by an act. All these and other issues relating to corporate transactions and third parties are discussed in Chapter 6. One consequence is, however, that the company will now always have the ability to ratify any act which is contrary to its objects clause. Since such a ratification would amount to a *de facto* alteration of the objects clause it must be effected by a special resolution (new s.35(3), below) in the same way as any actual alteration of the clause under s.4.

Section 35 is subject to s.322A of the Companies Act 1985 where the third party is a director of the company concerned. That section is dealt with in Chapter 6, below.

Effect of the objects clause on shareholders' rights and directors' duties

A company's objects clause has, in addition to its effects on corporate transactions *vis-à-vis* third parties, always fulfilled a role in the internal aspects of company law. The memorandum binds the company and its members to the same extent as if it had been signed and sealed by each member, and contained covenants on the part of each member to observe all the provisions of the memorandum, especially the objects clause: s.14(1). The effect of this section is that generally there is a contract between the company and its members that the memorandum will be complied with.[91] One consequence of this is that any member has a personal right to seek an injunction to prevent the commission of any act which is outside the objects clause,[92] *i.e.* the investor is entitled to see that the objects for which he invested are adhered to. Since this is a personal right no question of a derivative action arises.[93]

The 1989 Act reforms expressly preserved this right to seek an injunction but it is now subject to two major limitations, one express and one implied.

New s.35(2) of the 1985 Act provides:

> "A member of a company may bring proceedings to restrain the doing of an act which but for subsection (1) would be beyond the company's capacity; but no such proceedings shall lie in respect of an act to be done in fulfilment of a legal obligation arising from a previous act of the company."

Thus there can be no right to an injunction if the company is legally bound to the act complained of, *i.e.* if the third party can rely on the validity of the act. In deciding that, the new rules as to corporate capacity (set out above) and corporate agency (see Chapter 6, below) will operate. It follows that if the directors have effectively bound the company to an act outside its objects clause

---

[91] Section 14 also applies to the articles of association. For a detailed analysis of this contract and its effects see p.73, below, where what is said applies equally to the memorandum.

[92] *Colman v Eastern Counties Railway* (1846) 10 Beav. 1.

[93] Below, p.343.

no action for an injunction will lie. Since, in practice, members will probably only discover the existence of the act or transaction after it has been concluded, it is unlikely, as the result of s.35(2), that they will be able to prevent it happening by an injunction.

The second, implied, limitation on the granting of injunctions stems from the fact that the objects clause is now freely alterable by a special resolution under s.4 and any action outside the objects clause can be ratified by such a resolution under s.35(3). Since an injunction is a discretionary remedy it is unlikely that one would be granted if either of the above were imminent or likely. One alternative possibility for an aggrieved minority shareholder may be to petition under s.459 of the Act on the basis of unfairly prejudicial conduct. It is likely that acting outside the objects clause would still be seen to be in breach of a shareholder's legitimate expectations.[94] Alternatively, in certain cases, such a shareholder could petition under s.122(1)(g) of the Insolvency Act 1986 for a winding up on the just and equitable ground.[95]

There remains, however, a second internal consequence of the objects clause. The directors, acting in the exercise of their powers, are under a duty to act both within the limits of the objects clause and bona fide for the benefit of the company.[96] These duties are owed to the company and not to individual members *per se* so the rules as to derivative actions will apply and in general only the company may enforce them. In this connection s.35(3) provides that, notwithstanding the new rules as to corporate capacity:

> "It remains the duty of the directors to observe any limitations on their powers flowing from the company's memorandum."

Since the duties of the directors are owed to the company, the company may ratify such a breach and accordingly s.35(3) allows ratification of any act which would otherwise be contrary to the limitations imposed by the memorandum by a special resolution. However, such ratification is not to affect the liability of the directors, *e.g.* to make good any losses incurred as the result of the act, unless there is a separate resolution to that effect. Special resolutions are required since such ratification will amount to a *de facto* alteration of the objects clause.[97]

If the directors act in breach of their duties in this respect, other persons involved in the breach may well become liable to the company as constructive trustees, if they have the requisite knowledge of the situation. Again the company may only excuse their liability by a special resolution: s.35(3).[98]

THE LIMITATION OF LIABILITY

Whether the liability of the members is limited by shares or by guarantee it is enough if the memorandum merely states that the liability of the members is limited: s.2(3).

---

[94] But see now *O'Neill v Phillips* [1999] 1 W.L.R. 1092, HL. See below, p.366.
[95] Below, p.353.
[96] See generally, Ch.15, below.
[97] Such a breach may give further support to a petition under s.459. See note 94, above.
[98] The position of such third parties is discussed in Ch.6, below.

Even though a company is exempted under s.30 from using the word "Limited" as part of its name, the memorandum must contain a statement that the liability of the members is limited.

We saw earlier that under s.24[99] a member who knows that a public company is carrying on business with less than the statutory minimum of members may become severally liable for its debts and may be sued therefor, *i.e.* not only does he lose the privilege of limited liability but the veil of incorporation is lifted and he can be sued by the creditors of the company.

THE SHARE CAPITAL

In the case of a limited company with a share capital, s.2(5) provides that the memorandum must state the amount of share capital with which the company proposes to be registered and its division into shares of a fixed amount, *e.g.* £ 100,000 divided into 100,000 shares of £1 each.[1] This capital, called the "nominal capital" or the "authorised capital," is that which the company is authorised to raise by the issue of shares. This figure is, however, purely nominal. It is important only in that it represents the aggregate amount of shares which the company may issue. The actual or allotted capital will depend on how many shares are issued. The stated amount of each share is called its nominal amount or par value. Today it is usual to have shares of a nominal amount of £1 or less each because of their marketability.[2]

It is perfectly legal to have an authorised capital expressed in more than one currency, *e.g.* £3 million and US$3 million. There is no requirement to state the cumulative total. Similarly, individual shares can be expressed in any currency, although only one currency per share is allowed. The shares will still be of a fixed amount for the purposes of the Act, even though they may fluctuate in value owing to the exchange rates.[3]

A public company, however, cannot be registered unless its memorandum has an authorised capital figure of not less than the *authorised minimum*: s.11. This is currently £50,000 (s.118), which is a low figure in practical terms. Other financial requirements must be met by public companies before they commence business.[4] The present requirement merely relates to the shares it *may* issue.

The shares into which the nominal capital is divided may be divided into classes, *e.g.* preference and ordinary shares, but it is usual to do this in the articles rather than in the memorandum.[5]

OTHER CLAUSES

The matters set out above must be stated in the memorandum: s.2. The contents

---

[99] Above, p.27.
[1] The CLR recommended that the requirement as to authorised share capital fall away, to be replaced by a statement as to the share capital to be allotted to members on formation. See *Final Report*, above, para.9.4. This was accepted by the Government: see *Modernising Company Law*, above, cl.6.
[2] The 1985 Tables B and F use the figure of £1. The former Table B used the figure of £200.
[3] *Re Scandinavian Bank Group plc* [1988] Ch. 87. There are in fact several multi-currency companies on the register. Since the adoption of the Euro by some members of the EU, some companies will fix their shares in Euros.
[4] Below, p.137.
[5] See *Andrews v Gas Meter Co.* [1897] Ch. 361, CA.

of the memorandum, however, are not restricted to these and may include any other provisions which the framers desire to insert. Sometimes the memorandum contains provisions dealing with the rights attaching to particular classes of shares such as preference shares, *e.g.* dividend and voting rights and the right to participate in the assets on a winding up. When this is so, the articles cannot be referred to for the purposes of ascertaining the rights of the shareholders, unless there is some ambiguity to be explained or some omission to be supplemented.[6] However, the rights of the holders of particular classes of shares are now usually contained in the articles.

THE ASSOCIATION CLAUSE AND SUBSCRIPTION

The association clause is the clause by which the subscribers (or subscriber in the case of a single member private company) to the memorandum declare that they desire to be formed into a company in pursuance of the memorandum and agree to take the number of shares set opposite their respective names.[7] The subscription contains their names, addresses and descriptions and the number of shares which each subscribes for.[8] The subscribers must take at least one share each.[9] Each subscriber must write opposite his name the number of shares he takes and must sign in the presence of at least one witness. The signatures must be attested but one witness may attest all or both signatures: s.2. The Registrar requires the date of execution to be given. Note, however, that s.2(6) is now subject to s.2(6A), which provides that where a memorandum is delivered to the Registrar, otherwise than in legible form, and is authenticated by each subscriber in such manner as he directs, the requirements for signature in the presence of at least one witness and for attestation of the signature do not apply.[10]

In England, a minor[11] may sign the memorandum because, the contract being voidable and not void, any subsequent avoidance by him will not invalidate the registration.[12]

ALTERATION OF THE MEMORANDUM GENERALLY

A company may alter its memorandum of association only in the cases, in the mode and to the extent for which express provision is made in the Act: s.2(7).[13] It

---

[6] *Re Duncan Gilmour & Co. Ltd* [1952] 2 All E.R. 871.
[7] The CLR recommended that this be replaced by a formal statement by a director or secretary that the material delivered met the legal requirements: *Final Report*, above, para.9.5. See *Modernising Company Law*, above, cl.7.
[8] s.2(5)(c).
[9] s.2(5)(b).
[10] Inserted by the Companies Act 1985 (Electronic Communications) Order 2000, SI 2000/3373.
[11] *i.e.* a person under the age of 18. In Scotland, a person over 16 has full contractual capacity; see below, p.187.
[12] *Re Laxon & Co. (No. 2)* [1892] 3 Ch. 555. And see s.13, above, p.24.
[13] The CLR recommended that the model constitution should be freely alterable by special resolution, but that the members should be able to agree to "entrench" certain provisions (*e.g.*, by requiring unanimity, or a higher than 75 per cent threshold, for changes). See *Final Report*, above, para.9.8. This was accepted by the Government. See *Modernising Company Law*, above, cl.20 and cl.21.

has been seen that the name and objects clauses may be altered under s.28 and 4 of the Act respectively, above. The capital clause can be altered under ss 121 and 135.[14] In addition, by s.17, subject to the provisions of ss 16 and 459, above, any condition in the memorandum which could have been in the articles (*i.e.* not such things as the name, the objects or the share capital, which must be in the memorandum) can be altered by special resolution, unless the memorandum itself provides for or prohibits the alteration of the condition, or it relates to class rights, *i.e.* the special rights of any class of members.

Since provisions concerning class rights are the only important provisions which may be in either the memorandum or the articles, and they cannot be altered under s.17 if they are in the memorandum, it follows that the section is unimportant in practice. Further, as was stated earlier, class rights are normally contained in the articles. The methods of varying class rights are explained later.[15]

Section 17 contains the same provisions as to application to the court for cancellation of an alteration as ss 5 and 6,[16] except that there is no equivalent of s.6(4).

Section 16 provides that neither the memorandum nor the articles can be altered so as to require a member to take up more shares, or in any way increase his liability to contribute to the share capital or otherwise pay money to the company, unless he consents in writing. Section 16 is, therefore, a "minority section," *i.e.* a section intended to prevent the minority of the members being oppressed by the majority.[17] Under s.459 the court can make an order to relieve any part of the members who are being unfairly prejudiced and such an order may alter the memorandum or the articles, in which event the company cannot make a further alteration, inconsistent with the order, without the leave of the court: s.461(3).

Section 18(2) provides that where a company is required to send to the Registrar any document making or evidencing an alteration in the company's memorandum or articles (other than a special resolution under s.4) the company must send with it a printed copy of the memorandum or articles as altered.

Section 711(1)(b) requires the Registrar to publish in the *Gazette* notice of the receipt by him of any document making or evidencing an alteration in the memorandum or articles of a company. Section 42(1) provides that a company cannot rely against other persons on any alteration to the memorandum or articles if it had not been officially notified (under s.711) at the material time and is not shown by the company to have been known at that time to the person concerned, or if the material time is less than 16 days after official notification and it is shown that the person concerned was unavoidably prevented from knowing of the event at that time.[18]

---

[14] See Ch.9, below.

[15] Below, p.209.

[16] Above, p.64.

[17] Below, Ch.17.

[18] Official notification does not, however, constitute notice to anyone; *Official Custodian of Charities v Parway Estates Ltd* [1985] Ch. 151, CA.

Chapter 4

ARTICLES OF ASSOCIATION

WHEREAS the memorandum is the company's charter, indicating its nationality, the nature of its business and its capital, the articles of association are the regulations for the internal arrangements and the management of the company.[1] The articles deal with the issue of shares, transfer of shares, alteration of share capital, general meetings, voting rights, directors (including their appointment and powers), managing director, secretary, dividends, accounts, audit of accounts, winding up and various other matters which will be referred to later.

As between the memorandum and the articles, the memorandum is the dominant instrument so that in so far as their provisions conflict, the memorandum prevails,[2] although, apart from matters which by statute must be in the memorandum, reference may be made to the articles to explain an ambiguity in the memorandum or to supplement it where it is silent.[3] Section 7 provides that articles *may*, in the case of a company limited by shares, and *must* in the case of a company limited by guarantee[4] or an unlimited company, be registered with the memorandum.

Table A in the Companies (Table A to F) Regulations 1985 is a model form of articles for a public company limited by shares. Any company limited by shares however may (1) adopt Table A in full, (2) adopt Table A subject to modifications, or (3) register its own articles and exclude Table A: s.8(1).[5]

In the case of a company limited by shares, if articles are not registered, or, if articles are registered, in so far as they do not modify or exclude Table A, Table A will automatically be the company's articles: s.8(2).

A private company should register its own articles adopting all or any of the regulations in Table A as are appropriate. Minimum requirements for the articles of a private company were abolished in 1980,[6] although it may still be thought desirable to indicate whether and how the transfer of shares is restricted.[7] Articles must:

(1) be printed (typewriting is not admissible);

(2) be divided into paragraphs numbered consecutively;

(3) be signed by each subscriber to the memorandum of association in the presence of at least one witness, who must attest the signature: s.7(3).

[1] See the earlier comments as to model constitutions, above, p.51.
[2] *Re Duncan Gilmour & Co. Ltd* [1952] 2 All E.R. 871.
[3] *Liquidator of The Humboldt Redwood Co. Ltd v Coats*, 1908 S.C. 751.
[4] Above, p.38.
[5] And see *Modernising Company Law* (Cm 5553-II, 2002), cl.11.
[6] s.28 of the 1948 Act was repealed by the 1980 Act.
[7] This was formerly one of the minimum requirements for forming a private company.

Note, however, that s.7(3) is now subject to s.7(3A), which provides that where the articles are delivered to the Registrar, otherwise than in legible form, and are authenticated by each subscriber in such manner as he directs, the requirements for signature in the presence of at least one witness and for attestation of the signature do not apply.[8]

If the memorandum states that the registered office is to be situated in Wales, the memorandum and articles to be delivered for registration under s.10 may be in Welsh but, if they are, they must be accompanied by a certified translation into English: s.710B(2).

Effect of memorandum and articles

Subject to the provisions of the Act, the memorandum and articles, when registered, bind the company and the members as if they had been signed and sealed by each member, and contained convenants on the part of each member to observe their provisions: s.14. The result is:

(1) The articles (and the memorandum) form a contract binding the members to the company.[8a] A shareholder may therefore bring an action to enforce any personal rights contained in the articles but is otherwise limited to bringing a derivative action or a petition for unfairly prejudicial conduct.[9]

The articles provided for the reference of differences between the company and any of the members to arbitration. H, a shareholder, brought an action against the company in connection with a dispute as to his expulsion from the company, *i.e.* a dispute between the company and him in his capacity, as a member. *Held*, the company was entitled to have the action stayed, as the articles constituted a contract between the company and its members in respect of their ordinary rights as members: *Hickman v Kent or Romney Marsh Sheep-Breeders' Assocn.* [1915] 1 Ch. 881.[10]

> ". . . articles regulating the rights and obligations of the members generally as such do create rights and obligations between them and the company respectively": *per* Astbury J. at p.900.

A dispute as to a director's right to inspect the company's books, and accounts, including minutes of board meetings, i.e. a dispute between the company and the director in his capacity as director, is not within the terms of articles like those in Hickman's case supra, even though the director is also a member. The plaintiff sued for, inter alia, a declaration in a representative capacity as a shareholder. It was then claimed that a director had recieved remuneration to which he was not entitled. He asked for a stay but was refused it: Beattie v E. & F Beattie Ltd [1938] Ch. 708, CA.

(2) Although s.14 does *not* provide that the memorandum and articles shall bind the company and the members as if they had been signed and sealed *by the*

---

[8] Inserted by the Companies Act 1985 (Electronic Communications) Order 2000, SI 2000/3373.

[8a] As to the special nature of the c.14 contract, see *Bratton Seymour Service Company Ltd v Oxburgh* [1992] B.C.L.C. 693, CA, at p.698.

[9] Ch.17, below.

[10] An article prohibiting any member from taking legal proceedings against his company is contrary to public policy and not binding: *St. Johnstone Football Club Ltd v Scottish Football Assocn. Ltd*, 1965 S.L.T. 171 (O.H.).

company, and contained convenants *on the part of the company* to observe their provisions, the articles constitute a contract binding the company to members.

A company declared a dividend and passed a resolution to pay it by giving to the shareholders debenture bonds bearing interest and redeemable at par, by an annual drawing, over 30 years. The articles empowered the company to declare a dividend "to be paid" to the shareholders. *Held*, the words "to be paid" meant paid in cash, and a shareholder could restrain the company from acting on the resolution on the ground that it contravened the articles: *Wood v Odessa Waterworks Co.* (1889) 42 Ch.D. 636.

On the other hand the fact that the articles are not so executed by the company limits the time for enforcing such a contract against the company to six years and not the 12 years allowed for contracts under seal: *Re Compania de Electricidad de la Provincia de Buenos Aires Ltd.*[11]

The courts will imply two terms into this contract insofar as it relates to the powers of the directors: (a) they must be exercised in good faith and in the interests of the company; and (b) they must be exercised fairly as between shareholders (which does not mean identically).[12]

(3) Members are only bound by and entitled on the above mentioned contract *qua* members, *i.e.* in their capacity as members: *Beattie v E. & F. Beattie Ltd*, above; *Eley v Positive Life Assurance Co. Ltd*, below.

(4) The articles (and the memorandum) constitute a contract between each individual member and every other member but in most cases the court will not enforce the contract as between individual members,[13] it is enforceable only through the company or, if the company is being wound up, the liquidator.

> "It is quite true that . . . there is no contract in terms between the individual members of the company; but the articles . . . regulate their rights *inter se*. Such rights can only be enforced by or against a member through the company, or through the liquidator representing the company; but . . . no member has, as between himself and another member, any right beyond that which the contract with the company gives": *per* Lord Herschell in *Welton v Saffery* [1897] A.C 299 at p. 315.

It seems that it is the rule in *Foss v Harbottle*[14] which prevents an individual member enforcing the contract. However, the rule is irrelevant where the articles give a member a personal right. In such a case the contract is directly enforceable by one member against another *without* the aid of the company.

Articles of a private company provided that if a member intending to transfer his shares should inform the directors, the *directors* "will take the said shares equally between them at a fair value." *Held*, the articles bound the defendant directors to buy the plaintiff's shares and related to the relationship between the plaintiff as a member and the defendant, not as directors, but as members of the company,[15] and it was not necessary for the company to be a party to the action: *Rayfield v Hands* [1960] Ch. 1.

---

[11] [1978] 3 All E.R. 668. Scots law does not recognise any distinction between contracts under seal and other contracts.

[12] *Mutual Life Insurance Co. of New York v The Rank Organisation Ltd* [1985] B.C.L.C. 11.

[13] *Per* Farwell L.J. in *Salmon v Quin and Axtens Ltd* [1909] 1 Ch. 311, CA.

[14] Below, Ch.17.

[15] As is usual, the directors had shares in the company and so were members.

(5) The provisions of the articles and the memorandum do not constitute a contract binding the company or any member to an outsider,[16] *i.e.* a person who is not a member of the company,[17] or to a member in a capacity other than that of member, *e.g.* that of solicitor, promoter or director of the company.[18]

This is on the general principle that a person who is not a party to a contract has neither rights nor liabilities under it.

The articles provided that E should be the solicitor to the company. He was employed as such for a time but subsequently the company ceased to employ him. *Held*, E was not entitled to damages for breach of contract against the company. The articles did not create a contract between E and the company: *Eley v Positive Life Assurance Co. Ltd* (1876) 1 Ex.D. 88, CA.[19]

However, if a director takes office on the footing of an article providing for remuneration for the director, although the article is not in itself a contract between the company and the director, its terms may be implied into the contract between the company and the director.

An article provided that the remuneration of the directors should be the annual sum of £1,000. The directors were employed and accepted office on the footing of the article. For some time the directors, who were also members, acted as directors but were not paid. The company went into liquidation. *Held*, the article was embodied in the contract between the company and the directors and they were entitled to recover the arrears of remuneration: *Re New British Iron Co*. [1898] 1 Ch. 324.[20]

(6) Because of the words "Subject to the provisions of this Act" in s.14, the contract constituted by the memorandum and articles can be varied to the extent that those documents can be altered in accordance with the provisions of the Act. The extent to which the memorandum may be altered has been dealt with already.[21] It will be seen shortly that, subject to a number of restrictions, the company may always alter the articles by special resolution.

Alteration of articles

Subject to the provisions of the Act and to the conditions in its memorandum, a company may by special resolution alter or add to its articles.[22] An alteration or addition so made is as valid and can be altered in the same way as if originally

---

[16] See *per* Astbury J. in *Hickman's* case, above p.73, at p.900. A prospective purchaser of shares, being an outsider, cannot found on a breach of a restriction on transfer contained in the articles so as to obtain reduction of his purchase and repayment of the price: *Williams v MacPherson*, 1990 S.L.T. 279 (O.H.).

[17] A Scots illustration is *National Bank of Scotland Glasgow Nominees Ltd v Adamson*, 1932 S.L.T. 492 (O.H.); see also *Scottish Fishermen's Organisation Ltd v McLean*, 1980 S.L.T.(Sh.Ct.) 76.

[18] *Globalink Telecommunications Ltd v Wilmbury Ltd* [2002] EWHC 1988; [2003] 1 B.C.L.C. 145.

[19] A comparable Scottish case is *Muirhead v Forth etc. Steamboat Mutual Insce. Assocn.* (1893) 21 R., HL 1; (1893) 20 R. 442.

[20] In *Globalink Telecommunications Ltd*, above, there was insufficient evidence to support an incorporation of article provisions into an external contract.

[21] Above, p.70.

[22] See the comments made above, p.70, as to alterations and "entrenching" provisions.

contained in the articles: s.9(1). Thus a provision in the articles purporting to deprive the company of its power to alter them is void,[23] *e.g.* a provision that no alteration of the articles shall be effective without the consent of X, or that on a proposed alteration only the shares of those opposed shall have a vote.[24]

(1) By s.9(1) the power to alter articles is subject to the provisions of the Act, *e.g.* ss 16, 459[25] and 127.[26]

If, as is common, special rights are attached to a class of shares by the articles then the "modification of rights clause" which is either express or implied by the Act[27] (which provides for alteration of the class rights only with the consent of a specified proportion or the sanction of a specified resolution of the shareholders of the class), ensure that those class rights can only be altered with such consent or sanction.[28] Further, by s.127 dissentient holders of not less than 15 per cent of the issued shares of the class may, within 21 days after the consent was given, apply to the court to have the variation cancelled.[29] This restriction on the alteration of the articles has been held in one case to apply not only to rights actually attached to a specific class of shares, *e.g.* preference shares, but also to rights given by the articles to certain members in their capacity as members. This means that a group of shareholders can enjoy the protection of the variation of a class rights procedure if they *qua* shareholders enjoy different rights, *e.g.* of pre-emption of other shares, even though the shares they own are in no way distinguished from other shares; *i.e.* if their class rights attach to them as shareholders and not specifically to the shares themselves.[30]

(2) A company's power to alter its articles is subject to the conditions in the memorandum: s.9(1). Consequently an alteration of articles must not conflict with the memorandum.

(3) Under the general law the power to alter articles must be exercised bona fide for the benefit of the company as a whole.

Articles gave the company a lien on partly paid shares for all debts and liabilities of a member to the company. Z, on his death, owed money to the company (arrears of calls on partly paid shares), and was the only holder of fully paid shares. The articles were altered so as to give the company a lien on fully paid shares. *Held*, the alteration was valid and, as from the date of the alteration, gave the company a lien on Z's fully paid shares in respect of the debts contracted before the date of the alteration: *Allen v Gold Reefs of West Africa Ltd* [1900] 1 Ch. 656, CA.[31]

---

[23] *Malleson v National Insurance Corporation* [1894] 1 Ch. 200.
[24] *Per* Russell L.J. in *Bushell v Faith* [1969] 2 Ch. 438, CA at p.448.
[25] Below, Ch.17.
[26] Below, p.211.
[27] Below, p.210.
[28] Below, p.211.
[29] s.127(2)(3).
[30] *Cumbrian Newspapers Group Ltd v Cumberland and Westmorland Herald Newspaper & Printing Co. Ltd* [1987] Ch. 1. See also *Harman v BML Group Ltd* [1994] 2 B.C.L.C. 674.
[31] *cf. Liquidator of W. & A. M'Arthur Ltd v Gulf Line Ltd*, 1909 S.C. 732. For comments on *Allen's* case, see *Moir v Thomas Duff & Co. Ltd* (1900) 2 F. 1265.

The power conferred on companies to alter articles "must, like all other powers, be exercised subject to those general principles of law and equity which are applicable to all powers conferred on majorities and enabling them to bind minorities. It must be exercised, not only in the manner required by law, but also bona fide for the benefit of the company as a whole, and it must not be exceeded. These conditions are always implied, and are seldom, if ever expressed": *per* Lord Lindley M.R. at p.671. "The fact that Zuccani's executors were the only persons practically affected at the time by the alterations made in the articles excites suspicion as to the bona fides of the company. But, although the executors were the only person who were actually affected at the time, that was because Zuccani was the only holder of paid-up shares who at the time was in arrear of calls. The altered articles applied to all holders of fully paid shares, and made no distinction between them. The directors cannot be charged with bad faith": *Per* Lord Lindley M.R. at p.675.[32]

It is for the shareholders, and not for the court to say whether an alteration of articles is for the benefit of the company, unless no reasonable man could so regard it.

The articles provided that S and four others should be permanent directors of the company, unless they should become disqualified by any one of six specified events. None of the six events had occurred. S on 22 occasions within 12 months failed to account for the company's money he had received, and the articles were accordingly altered by adding a seventh event disqualifying a director, namely, a request in writing signed by all the other directors that he should resign. Such a request was made to S who was also a shareholder. *Held*, the contract, if any, between the plaintiff and the company contained in the original articles was subject to the statutory power of alteration, and the alteration was bona fide for the benefit of the company as a whole and valid: *Shuttleworth v Cox Bros. & Co. (Maidenhead) Ltd* [1927] 2 K.B. 9, CA.

"Then the first thing to be considered is whether, in formulating the test I have mentioned, Lindley M.R. [in *Allen's* case *supra*] had in mind two separate and distinct matters; first, bona fides, the state of mind of the persons whose act is complained of, and secondly, whether the alteration is for the benefit of the company, apart altogether from the state of mind of those who procured it. In my opinion this view of the test has been negatived by this Court in *Sidebotham's* case.[33] So the test is whether the alteration of the articles was in the opinion of the shareholders for the benefit of the company.[34] By what criterion is the Court to ascertain the opinion of the shareholders upon this question? The alteration may be so oppressive as to cast suspicion on the honesty of the persons responsible for it, or so extravagant that no reasonable man could really consider it for the benefit of the company": *per* Bankes L.J. at p.18. See also *per* Scrutton L.J. at p.23.

In particular an alteration of articles is liable to be impeached if its effect is to discriminate between the majority shareholders and the minority so as to give the former an advantage of which the latter are deprived. It is not necessary that persons voting for an alteration of articles should dissociate themselves altogether from their own prospects.[35]

---

[32] On this point see also *Mutual Life Insurance Co. of New York v The Rank Organisation* [1985] B.C.L.C. 11.

[33] Below, p.78.

[34] This has been said to include both present and future members of the company: *per* Megarry J. in *Gaiman v National Association of Mental Health* [1971] 1 Ch. 317 at p.338.

[35] *Per* Lord Evershed M.R. in *Greenhalgh v Arderne Cinemas* [1951] Ch. 286, CA at p.291.

If an alteration of articles is bona fide for the benefit of the company, it is immaterial that it prejudices a minority of the members.

A private company, in which the directors held a majority of the shares, altered its articles so as to give the directors power to require any shareholder who competed with the company's business to transfer his shares, at their fair value to nominees of the directors. S who had a minority of the shares and was in competiton with the company, brought an action for a declaration that the special resolution was invalid. *Held*, (1) as a power to expel a shareholder by buying him out was valid in the case of original articles it could be introduced in altered articles, provided that the alteration was made bona fide for the benefit of the company as a whole; (2) the alteration was so made and was valid: *Sidebottom v Kershaw, Leese & Co.* [1920] 1 Ch. 154, CA.[36]

> "I think . . . that it is for the benefit of the company that they should not be obliged to have amongst them as members persons who are competing with them in business and who may get knowledge from their membership which would enable them to compete better": *per* Lord Sterndale M.R. at p.166.

The principles of natural justice are not applicable in this field.[37]

It has been held that the members of a company, acting in accordance with the Act and the constitution of the company, and subject to any necessary consent on the part of the class affected, can alter the relative voting powers attached by the articles to various classes of shares, provided that the special resolution is passed in good faith for the benefit of the company as a whole.

The issued capital of S Ltd comprised 400,000 management shares, which under the articles carried eight votes each, and 3,600,000 ordinary shares. On the acquisition by S Ltd of the shares in B Ltd in consideration of the issue of 8,400,000 ordinary shares in S Ltd, the articles were altered so as to double the votes carried by management shares in order to ensure continuity of management. The special resolution was passed by a large majority at an extraordinary general meeting of the company. The holders of management shares, directors of S Ltd, did not vote in respect of these shares or their ordinary shares. Nor did they vote at a separate class meeting of the ordinary shareholders which sanctioned the special resolution. *Held*, the alteration was valid: *Rights and Issues Investment Trust Ltd v Stylo Shoes Ltd* [1965] Ch. 250.[38]

In the absence of a prohibition in the memorandum the articles can be altered so as to authorise the issue of preference shares taking priority over existing shares although no power to issue preference shares is conferred by the memorandum or the original articles.[39]

(4) A company cannot agree not to alter its articles.[40] The members can, however, as between themselves agree not to vote in favour of an alteration unless they all consent, provided that this does not bind future members.[41]

---

[36] See also *Crookston v Lindsay, Crookston & Co. Ltd*, 1922 S.L.T. 62 (O.H.).

[37] *Per* Megarry J. in *Gaiman's case*, above p.73, at p.335.

[38] A comparable Scottish case is *Caledonian Insurance Co. v Scottish American Invest. Co. Ltd* 1951 S.L.T. 23 (O.H.).

[39] *Andrews v Gas Meter Co.* [1897] 1 Ch. 361, CA.

[40] *Southern Foundries (1926) Ltd v Shirlaw* [1940] A.C. 701, at p.739, *per* Lord Porter; *Allen v Gold Reefs of West Africa Ltd* [1900] 1 Ch. 656, at p.671, *per* Lindley M.R.

[41] *Welton v Saffery* [1987] A.C. 299, at p.331, *per* Lord Davey.

In *Russell v Northern Bank Development Corp. Ltd*,[42] the House of Lords upheld an agreement between the four shareholders of a company not to vote in favour of an increase in the company's share capital unless they and the company agreed in writing. In doing so they emphasised that the company could not be bound by this agreement and only allowed the agreement to stand because it was valid as between the shareholders without the company's involvement. An agreement involving the company would have been void if it had been included in the company's articles and an extraneous agreement such as this would involve the company effectively fettering its statutory power. The agreement between the shareholders was personal to them and did not bind their successors.

(5) If a company alters its articles in breach of a contract to which it is a party, such an alteration is valid but it may give rise to an action for damages against the company for breach of contract.

Although there were earlier decisions which suggested that a third party could obtain an injunction to prevent a company altering its articles in breach of a contract,[43] the above statement was made by Lord Porter in *Southern Foundries (1926) Ltd v Shirlaw*[44] and approved by Scott J. in *Cumbrian Newspaper Group Ltd v Cumberland and Westmorland Herald Newspaper and Printing Co. Ltd.*[45] It is perfectly possible for a contract to incorporate the articles as a term in the contract but any such clause is subject to alteration in the normal way.

It is clear that any alteration of the articles under s.9(1) may, in an appropriate case, be used as the basis for bringing a petition under s.459 of the Act.[46] A recent example of this was in *Re Smiths of Smithfield Ltd*,[47] which arose in connection with an alteration of the articles which was alleged to exclude the petitioner from his pre-emption rights and constituted a variation of his class rights.[48] One of the issues was whether the alteration could be challenged as constituting unfairly prejudicial conduct under s.459. The judge agreed that it could[49] but confirmed that such allegation had to be specifically pleaded, which they had not been on the facts of the case.

Inspection of articles

A company is required to furnish a copy of its memorandum (embodying any alterations) and of its articles to its members on request, on payment of not more than five pence a copy: ss.19, 20.

Any person, whether a member of the company or not, may inspect a copy of the memorandum and articles of association of any company at the office of the

---

[42] [1992] B.C.L.C. 1016, HL.
[43] *Bailey v British Equitable Assurance Co.* [1904] 1 Ch. 374; *British Murac Syndicate v Alperton Rubber Co.* [1915] 2 Ch.186.
[44] [1940] A.C. 701, at p.740.
[45] [1987] Ch. 1.
[46] See below, Ch.17.
[47] [2003] EWHC 568 (Ch); [2003] B.C.C. 769.
[48] It was argued that the variation was therefore in breach of s.125. See below, p.209.
[49] [2003] B.C.C. 769, at p.782.

Registrar of Companies. He may also have a copy or extract of them: ss 709, 710A.

Interpretation of the articles

As a general proposition, the articles (and the memorandum) will be construed in accordance with the established rules for the interpretation of contracts, *viz.* giving the words used their ordinary meaning derived from the context in which they appear.[50] The court will exclude from the admissible background the previous negotiations of the parties and their declarations of subjective intent.[51] It will not imply any terms into the articles other then those which are needed to give effect to the language of the articles, for questions of business efficacy or otherwise.[52] Nevertheless, the interpretation of the contract is not carried out in vacuum and has to be conducted against the background knowledge which would reasonably have been available to the contracting parties at the time of the contract.[53] Accordingly, as part of the relevant background, it has been held to be legitimate to have regard to the original form of the articles of association of a plc.[54]

Rectification of articles

The court has no inherent jurisdiction to rectify the articles, even if it is proved that they were not in accordance with the intention of the original signatories.[55]

---

[50] See *Towcester Racecourse Co Ltd v The Racecourse Association Ltd* [2002] EWHC 2141 (Ch); [2003] 1 B.C.L.C. 260, at p.268.
[51] See *Investors Compensation Scheme Ltd v West Bromwich Building Society* [1998] 1 W.L.R. 896, at p.913, applied in *Folkes Group plc v Alexander* [2002] EWHC 51 (Ch); [2002] 2 B.C.L.C. 254, at p.257.
[52] See *Bratton Seymour Service Co Ltd v Oxborough* [1992] B.C.L.C. 693; *Towcester Racecourse Co Ltd v The Racecourse Association Ltd*, above.
[53] *Investors Compensation Scheme Ltd v West Bromwich Building Society*, above, at p.912, applied in *Folkes Group plc v Alexander*, above, at p.257.
[54] *Folkes Group plc v Alexander*, above.
[55] *Scott v Frank F. Scott (London) Ltd* [1940] Ch. 794, CA.

Chapter 5

PROMOTERS

BEFORE a company can be formed, there must be some persons who have an intention to form a company, and who take the necessary steps to carry that intention into operation. Such persons are called "promoters." Promoters stand in a fiduciary position towards the company and, as a result, they owe certain duties.

MEANING OF TERM "PROMOTER"

The term promoter was originally defined in the Act by reference to the preparation of a prospectus to accompany a public offer of shares only for the purposes of liability for a misstatement in a prospectus. That part of the Act was repealed by the Financial Services Act 1986,[1] which uses the term "promoter" but does not define it.[2] However, a promoter has been described judicially, for example, as "one who undertakes to form a company with reference to a given project and to set it going, and who takes the necessary steps to accomplish that purpose."[3]

A company may have several promoters and, as is shown by cases such as the *Leeds Theatres* case, below, one existing company may promote another new company. Persons who give instructions for the preparation and registration of the memorandum and articles of association are promoters. So, too, are persons who obtain the directors (very often a promoter is himself a prospective director), issue a prospectus, negotiate underwriting contracts or a contract for the purchase of property by the company, or procure capital.

A person may become a promoter after the company is incorporated, *e.g.* by issuing a prospectus or preparing listing particulars, or by procuring capital to enable the company to carry out a preliminary agreement. Whether a person is actually a promoter and, if so, the date when he became one and whether he is still one, are questions of fact.

A person who has taken no active part in the formation of a company and the raising of the necessary share capital but has left it to others to set up the company on the understanding that he will profit from the operation is a promoter.[4]

---

[1] Itself now repealed. See the Financial Services and Markets Act 2000 (Consequential Amendments and Repeals) Order 2001, SI 2001/3649, Art.3(1)(c).
[2] Financial Services and Markets Act 2000, s.90(8). The former definition was in s.67(2)(c) of the 1985 Act, repealed by s.150(6) of the Financial Services Act 1986.
[3] *Per* Cockburn C.J. in *Twycross v Grant* (1877) 2 C.P.D. 469, CA at p.541.
[4] See *per* Lindley J. in *Emma Silver Mining Co. Ltd v Lewis* (1879) 4 C.P.D. 396, at p.408, and *Tracy v Mandalay Pty. Ltd* (1952–53) 88 C.L.R. 215.

Anyone who acts merely as the employee or agent of a promoter is not himself a promoter. A solicitor, therefore, who merely does the legal work necessary to the formation of a company is not as such a promoter.[5]

At one time, the business of a company promoter was almost a separate business in itself, but this is not so today. Further, the increasingly strict provisions of successive Companies Acts, culminating in the Financial Services and Markets Act 2000, in relation to the issue and contents of listing particulars or a prospectus have almost eliminated the fraudulent company promoter.

POSITION AND DUTIES OF PROMOTERS

A promoter is not an agent for the company which he is forming because a company cannot have an agent before it comes into existence.[6] Furthermore, he is usually not treated as a trustee for the future company.[7] However, from the moment he acts with the company in mind, a promoter stands in a fiduciary position[8] towards the company and therefore he must not make any secret profit out of the promotion, *e.g.* a profit on a sale of property to the company. These liabilities are independent of any liability for misstatements, etc. in listing particulars or a prospectus (see Chapter 7).

A promoter must disclose a profit which he is making out of the promotion to either:

(1) an *independent* board of directors,[9] or

(2) the existing and intended shareholders, *e.g.* by making disclosure in a prospectus.[10]

The requirement of an independent board of directors is one which, in most cases, cannot be complied with, as the promoters, or some of them, are usually the first directors of the company. In the formation of a private company, the promoter usually sells his business to a company, of which he is managing director, and in which he is the largest shareholder, but, nevertheless, the transaction cannot be impeached on the ground that there is no independent board of directors.[11]

"After *Salomon's Case* I think it is impossible to hold that it is the duty of the promoters of a company to provide it with an independent board of directors, if the

[5] *Re Great Wheal Polgooth Ltd* (1883) 53 L.J.Ch.42.
[6] *Kelner v Baxter* (1866) L.R. 2 C.P. 174, below, p.74; *Tinnevelly Sugar Refining Co. Ltd v Mirrlees, Watson & Yaryan Co Ltd*(1894) 21 R. 1009.
[7] *Omnium Electric Palaces Ltd v Baines* [1914] 1 Ch. 332, below; *Edinburgh Northern Tramways Co. v Mann* (1896) 23 R. 1056, below.
[8] *Henderson v The Huntington Copper etc. Co. Ltd* (1877) 5 R. HL 1; (1877) 4 R. 294; the fiduciary relationship was regarded as arising from agency rather than from trust in *Edinburgh Northern Tramways Co. v Mann* (1896) 23 R. 1056.
[9] *Erlanger v New Sombrero Phosphate Co.* (1878) 3 App.Cas. 1218, PC *post*; *Tracy v Mandalay Pt. Ltd*, above.
[10] *Lagunas Nitrate Co. v Lagunas Syndicate* [1899] 2 Ch. 392, CA; *Scottish Pacific Coast Mining Co. Ltd v Falkner, Bell & Co.* (1888) 15 R. 290.
[11] *Salomon v Salomon Co. Ltd* [1897] A.C. 22, at p.17. See above, p.25.

real truth is disclosed to those who are induced by the promoters to join the company."[12]

Remedies for breach of duty

If a promoter fails to make full disclosure of a profit made by him out of the promotion the following remedies may be open to the company. Since the promoter's duties are owed to the company the rule in *Foss v Harbottle*[13] is relevant to their enforcement.

(1) Where the promoter has, *e.g.* sold his own property to the company, the company may rescind the contract and recover the purchase-money paid.

A syndicate, of which E. was the head, purchased an island in the West Indies said to contain valuable mines of phosphates for £55,000. E. formed a company to buy this island, and a contract was made between X., a nominee of the syndicate, and the company for its purchase at £110,000. *Held,* as there had been no disclosure by the promoters of the profit they were making, the company was entitled to rescind the contract and recover the purchase-money from E. and the other members of the syndicate: *Erlanger v New Sombrero Phosphate Co.* (1878) 3 App.Cas. 1218, PC.

The right of rescission may be lost in a number of ways. For example, it will be lost if the parties cannot be restored to their original positions, as where the property has been worked so that its character has been altered.[14] However, even if restitution is strictly not possible, rescission may be allowed if restitution is substantially possible. The right to rescind will also be lost if third parties have acquired rights for value, by mortgage or otherwise, under the contract.[15]

(2) The company may compel the promoter to account for any profit he has made.

Intending to buy property and to form a company and resell the property to the company or another purchaser, a syndicate of four persons bought charges on the property at a discount. They afterwards bought the property for £140,000, formed a company of which they were the first directors and resold the property to the company for £180,000. As a result of this, they made a profit of £40,000 on the property and one of £20,000 on the charges which were paid off in full with the £140,000 received for the property. A prospectus was issued, disclosing the profit of £40,000 but not that of £20,000. It appears that rescission had become impossible. *Held,* the £20,000 was a secret profit made by a syndicate as promoters of the company and they were bound to pay it to the company: *Gluckstein v Barnes* [1900] A.C. 240.

(3) The company may sue the promoter for damages for breach of his fiduciary duty.

The F Co. contracted to purchase two music-halls for £24,000 and had the property conveyed to its nominee, R, intending to sell it to the T Co. when formed. The F Co. then

---

[12] *Per* Lindley M.R. in the *Lagunas* case, above, at p.426.
[13] Below, Ch.17.
[14] As in *Lagunas Nitrate Co. v Lagunas Syndicate* [1899] 2 Ch. 392, CA.
[15] As in *Re Leeds and Hanley Theatres of Varieties Ltd* [1902] 2 Ch. 809, below, where the mortgagee of the property had sold it.

promoted the T Co. and agreed to sell the music-halls to it for £75,000 and directed R to convey them. The board of directors of T Co. was not an independent board. A prospectus was issued to the public by the T Co., giving R as the vendor, and not disclosing the interest of F Co. or the profit it was making. *Held,* the prospectus should have disclosed that F Co. was the real vendor and the amount of profit it was making. For breach of their fiduciary duty to those invited to take shares the promoters were liable in damages to the company and the measure of damages was the promoters' profit: *Re Leeds and Hanley Theatres of Varieties Ltd* [1902] 2 Ch. 809, CA.

Where promoters sell their own property to the company, the company cannot affirm the contract and at the same time ask for an account of profits or for damages as this would be, in effect, asking the court to vary the contract of sale and order the defendants to sell their assets at a lower price.[16]

PAYMENT FOR PROMOTION SERVICES

A promoter has no right against the company to payment for his promotion services in the absence of an express contract with the company. In England such a contract will normally have to be under seal since the company cannot make a valid contract before incorporation and when the contract can be made the consideration by the promoter will normally be past.[17] In the absence of such a contract he cannot even recover from the company payments he has made in connection with the formation of the company.

The rule that consideration must not be past is not part of Scots law, and the promoter of a Scottish company might be entitled to found on a suitably worded provision in the memorandum or articles to the effect of recovering from the company payments made by him in connection with the formation of the company.[18] The success of a promoter's claim against the company seems to depend on his establishing that the relevant provision creates a *jus quaesitum tertio* in his favour. Where such a right is established, a promoter is entitled to remuneration for professional services rendered.[19] If no such right is established, neither promoters nor experts employed by them have a right to remuneration from the new company; such experts have no claim except against the persons who employed them, namely the promoters.[20]

Any amount or benefit paid or given within the two preceding years, or intended to be paid or given, to a promoter must normally be disclosed in a prospectus or listing particulars.[21]

SUSPENSION OF PROMOTERS

A person who has been convicted on indictment of any offence in connection

---

[16] *Re Cape Breton Co.* (1885) 29 Ch.D. 795, CA; *Jacobus Marler Estates Ltd v Evatt* [1971] A.C. 793, PC.
[17] *Clinton's Claim* [1908] 2 Ch. 515, CA.
[18] *Scott v Money Order Co. etc. Ltd* (1870) 42 Sc. Jur. 212.
[19] See, *e.g. Edinburgh Northern Tramways Co. v Mann* (1896) 23 R. 1056.
[20] *Per* Lord M'Laren in *J. M. & J. H. Robertson v Beatson, M'Leod & Co. Ltd*, 1908, S.C. 921 at p.928.
[21] See Ch.7, below.

with the promotion or formation of a company may have an order made against him by the court that he shall not, without leave of the court, be a director, liquidator, receiver or take part in the management of a company for a period of up to 15 years: Company Directors Disqualification Act 1986, s.2.[22]

[22] Below, p.321.

Chapter 6

CORPORATE TRANSACTIONS

THIS chapter deals, first, with contracts and other transactions made on behalf of a company before it is formed, and secondly, with those made after the company has been formed. Since a company is an artificial person, it cannot physically enter into a transaction but must always do so either through a human agent or in writing under its common seal. This chapter is therefore also concerned with the impact of company law on the rules of agency as to the making of such transactions and the law relating to contracts under seal involving companies. Finally, the chapter concludes with a note on a procedural rule which may prevent a company from enforcing its contracts if it is unable to provide security against having to pay the defendant's costs if the action is unsuccessful.

CONTRACTS MADE BEFORE INCORPORATION OF COMPANY

Effect on company

If, before the formation of a company, some person purports to make a contract on its behalf, or as trustee for it, *e.g.* a contract for the sale of property to the company, the contract, or "preliminary agreement" as it is sometimes called, is not binding on the company when it is formed, even if the company takes the benefit of the contract. Before incorporation the company lacks capacity to make the contract[1] and an agent cannot contract on behalf of a principal who is not in existence.[2]

Solicitors, on the instructions of persons who afterwards became directors of the company, prepared the memorandum and articles of association of the company, and paid the registration fees. *Held*, the company was not liable to pay their costs: *Re English and Colonial Produce Co. Ltd* [1906] 2 Ch. 435, CA.[3]

Similarly, a company cannot, after incorporation, enforce a contract made in its name before incorporation, or sue for damages for breach of such a contract since it was not a party to that contract.

---

[1] "If somebody does not exist they cannot contract," *per* Harman J. in *Rover International Ltd v Cannon Film Sales Ltd* [1987] 1 W.L.R. 1597, at p.1599.

[2] This does not apply to a company which contracts in a new name prior to the change of name becoming operative. Such a company is at all times in existence: *Oshkosh B'Gosh Incorporated Ltd v Dan Marbel Inc. Ltd* [1989] B.C.L.C. 507; *Vic Spence Associates v Balchin*, 1990 S.L.T. 10 (O.H.).

[3] For Scots law *cf.* Lord President Dunedin in *Welsh & Forbes v Johnston* (1906) 8 F. 453 at p.457, and Lord M'Laren in *J. M. & J. H. Robertson v Beatson, M'Leod & Co. Ltd,* 1908 S.C. 921 at p.928 above p.71. See also *F. J. Neale (Glasgow) Ltd v Vickery,* 1971 S.L.T. (Sh.Ct.) 88.

N. Co. agreed with a person acting on behalf of a future company, P. Co., that N. Co. would grant a mining lease to P. Co. P. Co. discovered coal whereupon N. Co. refused to grant the lease. *Held*, P. Co. could not compel N. Co. to grant the lease: *Natal Land etc. Co. Ltd v Pauline Colliery Syndicate Ltd* [1904] A.C. 120 PC.[4]

Further, such a contract cannot be ratified by the company after it is incorporated[5]—the company was not a principal with contractual capacity at the time when the contract was made—although, as is explained later, the contract may be novated.

The Gravesend Royal Alexandra Hotel Company Ltd was being formed to buy an hotel from K. At a time when all concerned knew that the company had not been formed, a written contract was made "on behalf of" the proposed company by A, B and C for the purchase of £900 worth of wine from K. The company was formed, and the wine handed over to it and consumed, but before payment was made the company went into liquidation. *Held*, A, B and C were personally liable on the contract, and no ratification could release them from their liability: *Kelner v Baxter* (1866) L.R. 2 C.P. 174.

"Where a contract is signed by one who professes to be signing 'as agent,' but who has no principal existing at the time, and the contract would be altogether inoperative unless binding on the person who signed it, he is bound thereby; and a stranger cannot by a subsequent ratification relieve him from that responsibility": *per* Erle C.J. at p.183.

This situation cannot be remedied either by the operation of the doctrine of estoppel by convention. That requires an assumption of fact, *i.e.* that the company would be bound, by both parties to a contract prior to the "agreement". Since the company was not then in existence it could make no such assumptions.[6]

Effect on individuals

At common law, if an individual contracts as "agent"[7] for a future company, whether there is a contract between him and the other person involved depends upon whether the agent was intended to be a party to the contract.[8] That is a question of construing the terms of the written contract and does not depend simply upon the way that the individual signed the contract.[9]

In *Kelner v Baxter*, above, it was intended that A, B and C should contract personally. In the *Newborne* case, the intention was that only the future company should contract.

Tinned ham was sold to S. Ltd. The contract was "We have this day sold to you . . . (Signed) Leopold Newborne (London) Ltd." The signature was typed and underneath was written "Leopold Newborne." The market price of ham fell and S. Ltd. refused to take

---

[4] *Molleson and Grigor v Fraser's Trustees* (1881) 8 R. 630 is a Scottish authority.
[5] *Kelner v Baxter*, below; *Tinnevelly Sugar Refining Co. Ltd v Mirrlees, Watson & Yaryan Co. Ltd* (1894) 21 R. 1009. See also *Cumming v Quartzag Ltd*, 1980 S.C. 276, in which, following the *Tinnevelly* case, the Court of Session held that an agreement made on behalf of a company to be incorporated could not give rise to a *jus quaesitum tertio* in favour of the company when incorporated; Hector L. MacQueen, *Promoters' Contracts, Agency and the Jus Quaesitum Tertio*, 1982 S.L.T. (News) 257.
[6] *Rover International Ltd v Cannon Film Sales Ltd* [1987] 1 W.L.R. 1597.
[7] Strictly, one cannot be agent for a principal not yet in existence.
[8] *Phonogram Ltd v Lane* [1982] Q.B. 938 at p.945, *per* Oliver L.J. Approved in *Cotronic (UK) Ltd v Dezonie* [1991] B.C.L.C. 721, CA and *Badgerhill Properties Ltd v Cottrell* [1991] B.C.L.C. 805, CA.
[9] *e.g.* whether he signs "per pro" the company or "for and on behalf of the company".

delivery. When an action was brought it was found that Leopold Newborne (London) Ltd had not been incorporated at the time of the contract and Leopold Newborne tried to enforce the contract in his own name. *Held*, neither Leopold Newborne (London) Ltd nor Leopold Newborne could enforce the contract. It was not a case of an agent undertaking to do certain things himself as agent for somebody else. It was a contract in which a company purported to sell. Leopold Newborne did not purport to contract as principal or agent—the contract purported to be made by Leopold Newborne (London) Ltd, on whose behalf it was signed by a future director. "This company was not in existence and . . . the signature on that document, and indeed, the document itself . . . is a complete nullity": *Newborne v Sensolid (Great Britain) Ltd* [1954] 1 Q.B. 45.[10]

The position of the individual was, however, changed substantially by s.9(2) of the European Communities Act 1972, which became s.36(4) of the 1985 Act.[11] That section was repealed by the 1989 Act and replaced by s.36C of the 1985 Act.[12] The latest section retains, however, the same concepts as its predecessor.

Section 36C(1) provides:

> "A contract which purports to be made by or on behalf of a company at a time when the company has not been formed has effect, subject to any agreement to the contrary, as one made with the person purporting to act for the company or as agent for it, and he is personally liable on the contract accordingly."[13]

This means that in circumstances like those in *Newborne's* case, above, today, unless there is an agreement to the contrary, there will be a contract between the individual who purports to act for the company and the other person involved. The words "subject to any agreement to the contrary" allow for the case where there is a novation.

In *Phonogram Ltd v Lane*,[14] the Court of Appeal considered the effect of the old s.36(4) which was identical in all relevant respects to s.36C. They held that it rendered the individual "agent" liable even though the company was not at the time in the course of formation.[15] Further, a contract can be "purported" to be made by a company even though both parties to the contract knew that the company had not then been formed. They also considered that signing the contract as an agent, or as in the *Newborne* case, above, would not amount to an agreement to the contrary so as to avoid personal liability. Lord Denning M.R. considered that only a clear exclusion of personal liability would suffice.[16]

It used to be thought that individuals contracting on behalf of an unformed company might not be entitled to sue on the contact,[17] but this has now been

---

[10] See also *Cotronic (UK) Ltd v Denozie* [1991] B.C.L.C. 721, CA and *Badgerhill Properties Ltd v Cottrell* [1991] B.C.L.C. 805, CA.

[11] See the discussion in *Braymist Ltd v The Wise Finance Co Ltd* [2002] EWCA Civ 127; [2002] Ch. 273, CA, at pp.283–285.

[12] Introduced by s.130(4) C.A. 1989.

[13] Subs.36C(2) extends this liability to deeds in England and obligations in Scotland. The section applies equally to companies incorporated outside Great Britain: the Foreign Companies (Execution of Documents) Regulations 1994 (SI 1994/950) and the Foreign Companies (Execution of Documents) (Amendment) Regulations 1995 (SI 1995/1729).

[14] [1982] Q.B. 938.

[15] A contrary argument based on the French text of the Directive implemented by the 1972 Act was rejected.

[16] But signing the contract in the *Newborne* manner prevents the individual enforcing the contract: *Cotronic (UK) Ltd v Denozie* [1991] B.C.L.C. 721.

[17] See *Cotronic (UK) Ltd v Denozie* [1991] B.C.L.C. 721; *Badgerhill Properties Ltd v Cottrell* [1991] B.C.L.C. 805.

resolved in the latest case on s.36C(1), *Braymist Ltd v The Wise Finance Co Ltd.*[18] W entered into an agreement with an unformed company for the purchase of a piece of land and this was signed on behalf of the company by its solicitors. Subsequently, when W refused to complete the purchase, the solicitors rescinded the agreement and brought an action for breach of contract. At first instance,[19] the judge held that the solicitors, as agents, could enforce the contract under s.36C(1). This was confirmed by the Court of Appeal, the majority[20] of whom were of the view that s.36C(1) not only made a party who entered into a contract as agent for an unformed company personally liable on the contract, it also entitled the agent to enforce the contract himself.[21] In so far as there were any further difficulties arising from this, such as the identity of the contracting party,[22] this could be dealt with on ordinary common law principles.[23] On the facts, as it was clear that the identity of the seller of the land had been of no importance to W, the solicitors could enforce the agreement.[24]

Section 36C only applies, however, to a contract made on behalf of a company which has not been formed. Thus it has been held not to apply to a contract made on behalf of a company which no longer existed[25] or on behalf of a company which had been formed but was not properly named in the contract.[26]

New contract after incorporation—novation

Of course, a company may, after incorporation enter into a new contract with the other party to the same effect as a contract made on its behalf before incorporation, in which event there is a novation, *i.e.* the old contract is discharged and replaced by the new. Such a new contract may be inferred from the acts of the parties after incorporation.

J had agreed with W, acting on behalf of a company about to be formed, to sell certain property to the company. After the company's incorporation, the directors resolved to adopt the agreement, and to accept J's offer to take part of the purchase-money in debentures instead of cash. *Held*, a contract was entered into by the company with J to the effect of the previous agreement as subsequently modified: *Howard v Patent Ivory Mfg. Co.* (1888) 38 Ch.D. 156.[27]

However, such a new contract will not be inferred if the acts of the company after incorporation are due to the mistaken belief that it is bound by the contract made before incorporation.

[18] [2002] EWCA Civ 127; [2002] Ch. 273, CA.
[19] *The Times*, March 27, 2001.
[20] Arden L.J. considered that parliament had not intended s.36C to determine the rules which should apply where an agent made a contract as agent on behalf of a principal then claimed to enforce the contract: [2002] Ch. 273, CA, at p.289.
[21] At p.291.
[22] See, *e.g.* at p.293.
[23] The case law is referred to in the judgment of Arden L.J.: at pp.286–288.
[24] Judge L.J. confirmed that the normal incidents appropriate to any contract applied equally to deemed or statutory contracts, such as that created by s.36C(1): at p.293.
[25] *Cotronic (UK) Ltd v Denozie* [1991] B.C.L.C. 721.
[26] *Badgerhill Properties Ltd v Cottrell* [1991] B.C.L.C. 805.
[27] *cf. James Young & Sons Ltd and Liquidator v Gowans (James Young & Sons' Trustee)* (1902) 10 S.L.T. 85 (O.H.) and *Park Business Interiors Ltd v Park*, 1991 S.L.T. 818 (O.H.) (shares allotted for pre-incorporation expenses where company after incorporation had accepted liability to pay those expenses).

A contract was made between W and D, who was acting on behalf of an intended company, for the grant of a lease to the company. The company, on its formation, entered on the land the subject of the lease and began to erect buildings on it but did not make any fresh agreement with respect to the lease. *Held*, the agreement, being made before the formation of the company, was not binding on the company, and was incapable of ratification; and the acts of the company were done in the erroneous belief that the agreement was binding on the company and not evidence of a fresh agreement between W and the company: *Re Northumberland Avenue Hotel Co.* [1886] 33 Ch.D. 16, CA.

Modern practice

Agreements to sell property to a company about to be formed are not now, as a rule, made with a person expressed to be acting on behalf of the company, because of the liability incurred by such person, and the absence of liability incurred by the company unless there is a novation. Although the other party will not be bound before the company is formed, the modern practice is for the promoters[28] to have prepared, before the company is incorporated, a draft agreement to which the company is expressed to be a party, and for the agreement to be executed by the other party and on behalf of the company after incorporation, pursuant to a clause in the company's memorandum to that effect. If, as is common, a company is being formed to acquire the promoters' business,[29] it does not matter that the promoters are not bound.

CONTRACTS MADE PRIOR TO COMMENCEMENT OF BUSINESS

Any contract made by a public company after it is incorporated but before it is entitled to commence business[30] is nevertheless valid, but in such cases if the company fails to comply with its obligations within 21 days of being asked to do so the directors are liable to compensate the other party for any loss or damage consequent on its inability to commence business: s.117(8).

FORM OF CONTRACTS

A company may make contracts either in writing under its common seal or by an agent acting within his authority, express or implied, on the company's behalf: s.36.[31] The rules as to the form of contracts for companies are the same as those for individuals, *e.g.* as to whether the contract needs to be in writing or under seal or can be made orally.

Execution of documents—England and Wales

A company may execute any document by affixing its common seal in accordance with the articles (see below).[32] However, a company is not required to have a

---

[28] Above, Ch.5.

[29] Above, p.82.

[30] See below, p.137.

[31] This section together with s.36A, below, applies with modifications to overseas companies: the Foreign Companies (Execution of Documents) Regulations (SI 1994/950) as amended by the Foreign Companies (Execution of Documents) (Amendment) Regulations 1995 (SI 1995/1729).

[32] It has been held, however, that there is nothing in s.36A which requires a company to use its registered name rather then its trading name in the body of a deed or bond. Accordingly, on the facts, a contractor was held entitled to enforce the bond against a surety: *OTV Birwelco Ltd v Technical and General Guarantee Co Ltd* [2002] EWHC 2240 (TTC); [2002] 2 B.C.L.C. 723.

common seal and whether it has one or not it may execute a document in such a way that it will have the same effect as one made under the seal: s.36A. That section provides that any document signed by a director and the company secretary or by two directors, and expressed, in either case, to be executed by the company (by any form of words) will be treated as if the seal had been affixed.[33]

Further, it they intend the document to be a deed and that is made clear on the face of the document, it will take effect as a deed upon delivery.[34] Such delivery will also be execution of the deed unless a contrary intention is proved.[35]

To protect third parties acting in good faith for valuable consideration,[36] a document which *purports* to be signed by a director and secretary or two directors will be as valid as if it was signed by actual directors and/or the actual secretary provided the other conditions are fulfilled.[37] Thus third parties need not investigate the validity of the appointment of those signing the document.[38]

Execution of documents—Scotland

The law relating to the execution of documents in Scotland was radically reformed by the Requirements of Writing (Scotland) Act 1995.

The general rule is that a written document signed by the granter is required for certain purposes, principally for contracts relating to land.

The Act (s.7(7) and Sch.2) has special provisions on companies. It provides that where a granter of a document is a company, the document is signed by the company if it is signed on its behalf by:

(a) a director; or

(b) the secretary; or

(c) a person authorised to sign the document on its behalf.

Such a signature gives the document formal validity.

Separate provision is made for self-evidencing status (or "probativity"). In order to be probative, the document must, under the Act, also be "attested" (signed) by one witness. Alternatively, resort may be had to the pre-1995 rule, which is preserved by the Act of 1995: the document is probative if it is subscribed on behalf of the company by:

(a) two of the directors; or

(b) a director and the secretary; or

(c) two persons authorised to subscribe the document on behalf of the company.

---

[33] s.36A(4).

[34] s.36A(5).

[35] Similar provisions apply to deeds executed by individuals: see s.1 of the Law of Property (Miscellaneous Amendments) Act 1989.

[36] Including lessees and mortgagees.

[37] s.36A(6).

[38] This is similar to the general protection given to conveyancers generally in s.74 Law of Property Act 1925.

In that case the document need not be witnessed or sealed with the company's seal (which a company is no longer required to have): s.36B as substituted by the Requirements of Writing (Scotland) Act 1995, Sch.4).

Use of the seal

Table A, Art.101 provides: "The seal shall only be used by the authority of the directors or of a committee of directors authorised by the directors. The directors may determine who shall sign any instrument to which the seal is affixed and unless otherwise so determined it shall be signed by a director and by the secretary or by a second director."

A company which continues to have a common seal and whose objects comprise the transaction of business in foreign countries may, if authorised by its articles, have for use in any place outside the UK, an official seal. The official seal must be a facsimile of the company's common seal, with the addition on its face of the name of every place where it is to be used: s.39.

Section 40[38a] allows a company which continues to have a common seal to have an official seal for use in sealing securities issued by the company and for sealing documents creating or evidencing securities issued by the company. This official seal must be a facsimile of the common seal of the company with the addition on its face of the word "Securities".

A document requiring *authentication* by a company is sufficiently authenticated by the signature of a director, secretary or other authorised officer, and need not be under seal: s.41.

Bills of exchange

Bills of exchange and promissory notes can be drawn, accepted or indorsed on behalf of a company by any person acting under the company's authority: s.37. Officers who sign their own names without making it clear that they are signing on behalf of the company may incur personal liability.[39] But when a director signs the modern form of company cheque with the company name and account number printed on it, he has been held to be signing only as an agent and is not personally liable on the cheque, even though he has not expressly signed on behalf of the company or as its agent.[40]

TRANSACTIONS BY AGENCY

Unless a company contracts in writing using its common seal, or the equivalent procedures discussed in the previous section, it can only enter into a transaction through the medium of agency, *i.e.* by a transaction made by an agent acting on behalf of the company who either has authority to bind the company to that transaction at the time or whose actions are subsequently validly ratified by the

---

[38a] Amended by the addition of s.40(2) by the Requirements of Writing (Scotland) Act 1995, Sch.4.

[39] *Brebner v Henderson*, 1925 S.C. 643; contrast *McLean v Stuart and Others*, 1970 S.L.T. (Notes) 77 (O.H.).

[40] *Bondina Ltd v Rollaway Shower Blinds* [1986] 1 W.L.R. 517, CA.

company. In general, therefore, the central question is whether the agent has the requisite authority to bind the company (his principal), and in this respect companies are in many ways no different from individuals—the ordinary rules of agency apply as to establishing authority. But companies are artificial persons with a constitution laid down by the memorandum and articles. We have already seen, in Chapter 3, that the objects clause in the memorandum used to restrict the capacity of the company itself to enter into transactions which were outside that clause and a company clearly cannot authorise an agent to do what it itself had no capacity to effect. s.35 of the Act has removed any such constitutional restrictions based solely on corporate capacity[41] but the memorandum and articles may equally restrict the authority of a company's agents to act on its behalf. In such a case any person dealing with the company would not be able to rely on an agent having authority if the transaction was contrary to the company's constitution, *e.g.* if it was contrary to a restriction in either the memorandum or articles.

Limitations under the company's constitution—the position prior to 1991

The effect of company law on the general law of agency therefore has been that even if an agent is otherwise acting within his authority to bind the company, a third party will not be able to enforce the transaction if the agent was acting contrary to the company's constitution. Since a third party was deemed to have constructive notice of all the company's registered documents, including the memorandum and articles, he could not rely on the agent having authority where the act was contrary to such documents. This doctrine was, however, subject to an exception, known as the rule in *Royal British Bank v Turquand*,[42] whereby if an agent was acting apparently consistently with the company's constitution, the third party was not affected by any internal irregularity, *e.g.* the lack of disclosure of a director's interest in a contract to the board as required by the articles, since he could not have discovered whether such disclosure had or had not been made.[43] Third parties did not have constructive notice of matters not on the register.[44] Only actual notice of such an irregularity would affect the transaction.[45]

This situation was substantially changed, however, in 1972 by s.9(1) of the European Communities Act 1972, which became s.35 of the 1985 Act. That section, which attempted to remove the limits on corporate capacity,[46] also restricted the effect of limitations on the authority of the company's agents arising from the company's constitution. It suffered from serious defects, however, which have already been noted in Chapter 3, and was repealed by the 1989 Act. That Act substituted a new s.35 and added new ss 35A and 35B into the 1985 Act. These new sections apply as to the effects of the company's

---

[41] Above, p.66.
[42] (1856) 6 El. & Bl. 327.
[43] *Cowan de Groot Properties Ltd v Eagle Trust plc* [1991] B.C.L.C. 1045.
[44] Thus whether or not an ordinary resolution had been passed would not matter since there is no requirement to register an ordinary resolution, whereas the lack of a required special resolution authorising the deal would destroy the agent's authority—special resolutions must be registered.
[45] But see p.102, below.
[46] Above, p.65.

constitution on the authority of a company's agents as from 1991 onwards. For a detailed discussion of the position prior to 1991, readers are referred to the 13th edition of this work.

Limitations under the company's constitution—the position from 1991

We have already seen in Chapter 3 that, from 1991 onwards, nothing in a company's memorandum can affect the capacity of a company to enter into a transaction, following the new s.35. In addition, new s.35A removes any constitutional limitations on the powers of the board of directors and those authorised by them to act on behalf of the company so far as bona fide third parties are concerned, whilst preserving the existing internal rights of members to control the directors if they do act contrary to the company's constitution. The position is substantially different, however, if the third party is himself a director of the company concerned (see below).

Section 35A(1) provides that:

> "In favour of a person dealing with a company in good faith, the power of the board of directors to bind the company, or authorise others to do so, shall be deemed to be free of any limitation under the company's constitution."

The policy of the section was recently described as follows by Carnwath L.J.: "The general policy seems to be that, if a document is put forward as a decision of the board by someone appearing to act on behalf of the company, in circumstances where there is no reason to doubt its authenticity, a person dealing with the company in good faith should be able to take it at face value".[47] Putting this another way, s.35(A)(1) removes any restrictions imposed upon the authority of the board of directors, either to act themselves or to empower others to act, by the company's constitution if the third party is dealing in good faith. If s.35A(1) applies then the sole question is whether the agent was acting within his authority irrespective of the company's constitution. What amounts to authority is considered below.

It is necessary to analyse s.35A(1). First, the section only applies in favour of a third party. While this does not include the company and its members,[48] it seems that a third party could include a director of a company.[49] Of course, the company, like any other principal, may always ratify any agent's acts, unless they are illegal, and then enforce the transaction. Such ratification will need to be by special resolution only if the transaction is contrary either to a provision in the memorandum or articles since a special resolution would be required to alter such a provision.[50]

---

[47] *Smith v Henniker-Major & Co* [2002] EWHC Civ 762; [2003] Ch. 182, CA, at p.213, citing *Friedrich Haagga GmbH* [1974] E.C.R. 1201, at p.1210 (per Advocate General Mayras).

[48] It has been held, overruling the court below (see [2003] EWHC 1507; [2003] 1 W.L.R. 2360), that a member receiving a bonus share issue is not a "person": *EIC Services Ltd v Phipps* [2004] EWCA Civ 1069, [2004] 2 B.C.L.C. 589, CA.

[49] See *Smith v Henniker-Major & Co* [2002] EWCA Civ 762; [2003] Ch. 132, CA, at p.213. But *cf.* Schiemann L.J., at.215.

[50] Under ss 4 and 9 respectively. Section 35(3) makes the position clear with respect to the memorandum, but it must equally apply to the articles. Ratification of a breach of the articles cannot be by anything less than a special resolution which must be registered s.38D(1).

Secondly, that person must be "dealing with a company" and s.35(2)(a) provides that anyone who is a party to any transaction[51] or other act to which the company is a party is dealing with that company.[52] The use of the words "transaction" and "act" seem to indicate that gratuitous acts will be included. However, it has been established that a third-party non-member will not "deal with" a company for the purposes of the section merely because the company receives and registers a transfer of shares.[53]

Thirdly, the person dealing with a company must be acting in good faith. s.35A(2)(b) provides that bad faith is not to be assumed simply because the third party knew that the act was contrary to the directors' powers under the constitution. This was intended to reverse the judicial interpretation of the phrase in the previous s.35 that good faith would be defeated if the third party actually knew or could not in all the circumstances have been unaware of the defect.[54] Something more than mere awareness is now required, presumably understanding, although it is unclear whether this is to be subjectively or objectively tested. What was intended no doubt was a distinction between notice and knowledge, with only the latter counting, as it does for liability for receipt of trust property under constructive trusts.[55] The wording of the section is such, however, that a third party may on the one hand be able to plead the validity of the transaction against the company under s.35A on the basis that, although he has objective but not subjective knowledge of the defect, that is not enough to defeat a presumption of good faith, whilst on the other hand he may be liable to the company as a constructive trustee under the knowing receipt category because he has such objective knowledge of the defect.

The position of the third party with respect to good faith is further strengthened by s.35A(2)(c) which requires a presumption of good faith until the contrary is proved, and s.35B which provides that the third party is not bound to enquire whether a transaction[56] is either contrary to the memorandum or is subject to any constitutional limitations on the powers of the directors.

Fourthly, in favour of such a third party, the powers of the board of directors to bind the company or authorise others to do so are to be free of any limitations under the company's constitution. A company's constitution includes its memorandum and articles and under s.35A(3) any resolution of the company or of a class of shareholders and any shareholder agreement.[57] The freedom given by

---

[51] See *T.C.B. Ltd v Gray* [1986] Ch. 621 for the court's views as to what constitutes a transaction in this context.

[52] See, *e.g. International Sales and Agencies Ltd v Marcus* [1982] 3 All E.R. 551, *Re Halt Garage (1964) Ltd* [1982] 3 All E.R. 1016, *International Factors (N.I.) Ltd v Streeve Construction Ltd* [1984] N.I.J.B.

[53] In such a case, it was doubted whether the company was in any "meaningful sense" a party to the transaction or act, which had taken place between a notional transferor and the claimant: *Cottrell v King* [2004] EWHC 397 (Ch); [2004] 2 B.C.L.C. 413, at p.421.

[54] *International Sales and Agencies Ltd v Marcus*, above p.66, approved in *International Factors (N.I.) Ltd v Streeve Construction Ltd.*

[55] *El Ajou v Dollar Land Holdings plc* [1994] 1 B.C.L.C. 464, CA; *Brown v Bennett* [1999] 1 B.C.L.C. 649, CA; *Crown Dilmun v Sutton* [2004] EWHC 52; [2004] 1 B.C.L.C. 468. It may be that the criteria for liability as a constructive trustee for "knowing receipt" will be whether dishonesty can be shown. That test has been applied to the related liability for "knowing assistance": *Royal Brunei Airlines v Tan* [1995] 2 A.C. 378, PC; *Twinsectra Ltd v Yardley* [2002] UKHL 12; [2002] 2 A.C. 164.

[56] But not in this case an act.

[57] All but special resolutions were covered by the rule in *Turquand's* case (above, p.93) which is still valid, in any event.

s.35A(1) thus applies to any acts of the directors as a whole or of any agent to whom they have delegated the transaction expressly or impliedly. It would not appear, however, to apply to the powers of a single director without authorisation from the board.[58] The section is not intended to extend the authority of an agent, simply to remove fetters if he would otherwise have authority to bind the company. It is possible, however, that in one respect at least it has extended the ordinary rules of agency.[59]

If the third party is not acting in good faith, the company may always ratify the transaction either by an ordinary resolution, or by special resolution if the defect relates to the memorandum or articles.[60]

Directors as third parties

The general rule, discussed above, that if the third party dealing with the company is in good faith no restrictions imposed upon the company's directors by the company's constitution will affect him, is modified where that third party is himself a director of that company or of its holding company.[61] This is emphasised again by s.35A(6) which, *inter alia*, provides that s.322A "has effect notwithstanding this section". There are two issued to be considered. The first is whether, so far as s.35A(1) is concerned, a director can be person "dealing with a company". This question arose on the peculiar facts of the case of *Smith v Henniker-Major & Co.*[62] The issue here was whether the chairman of the board of a company, S, who purported to act as an inquorate board[63-64] meeting to assign the company's rights of action to himself, could rely on the protection afforded by s.35A(1). Although the transaction was one in which S clearly had a self-interest, he was seeking to combat the misconduct of two of his fellow directors from making off with a corporate opportunity. At first instance,[65] the judge concluded that s.35A only applied to a properly constituted board, which was a pre-condition to the exercise of board power, and so the section was not available to S. Although agreeing with the outcome and dismissing the appeal, the Court of Appeal was nevertheless divided. All the judges concluded that the phrase "person dealing with a company" was wide enough to include a director,[66] but differed as to the impact of this on S.[67] The majority thought that, because S was not simply a director dealing with the company, but the chairman of the board, he was under a duty to ensure that the company's constitution was properly applied. He could not seek to turn a decision which

---

[58] By analogy with the decision in *Mitchell & Hobbs (UK) Ltd v Mill* [1996] 2 B.C.L.C. 102 on directors' powers under the articles; below, p.282.

[59] See p.101, below.

[60] See p.94, above.

[61] This modification also applies to persons connected with such a director or an associated company of such a director, as defined in s.346.

[62] [2002] EWCA Civ 762; [2003] Ch.182, CA. Carnwath L.J. described the facts as "quite exceptional" (at p.214).

[63-64] The board meeting was attended by S only.

[65] [2002] B.C.C. 544.

[66] [2002] EWCA Civ 762; [2003] Ch. 182, CA, at p.213 and p.216 *per* Carnwath L.J. and Schiemann L.J. respectively).

[67] Robert Walker L.J. dissenting. See especially at p.198.

had no validity under the company's constitution into one of the board of directors properly convened.

The second issue concerns the scope of s.322A This provides that, where a director is a third party and the board exceeds any limitation on their powers under the company's constitution, then the transaction[68] is voidable at the instance of the company, whether or not the director is dealing in good faith: s.322A(1)(2). The transaction remains valid, however, until it is avoided by the company, unless it is void for some reason (*e.g.* if it is illegal under the Act): s.322A(4). The purpose of s.322A was interpreted as follows by one judge:

> ". . it seems to me that the purpose of Section 322A is to protect a company in circumstances where its directors exceed their powers in connection with transactions entered into by the Company with one or more of their number (or their associates) to the disadvantage of the Company and to the advantage of one or more of the directors (or associates). It is true that the effect of the section is wider than that, and that it may well have been intended to ensure that directors are penalized if they fail to behave with particular propriety in connection with transactions between the company and themselves. However, I do not think that detracts from the main mischief at which the Section is directed.[69]

The company will lose the right to rescind (avoid) the transaction in any of the following circumstances:[70–71]

(i) restitution of property supplied is no longer possible;

(ii) the company is indemnified against any loss or damage arising from the transaction;

(iii) bona fide purchasers without actual notice of the defect have acquired rights which would be affected by the avoidance, *e.g.* if the subject matter has been deposited as security with a bank; or

(iv) the transaction is ratified by the company either by an ordinary or special resolution[72] as necessary.

It is important to remember that to be valid the transaction does not need to be ratified in this way, it is valid unless avoided by the company. The right to rescind or avoid a transaction may be limited under the general law, *e.g.* by undue delay.

Where there are two (or more) persons dealing with a company, one of whom is a director and the other is neither a director nor connected with one, and where that second person is dealing in good faith then he may continue to rely on the protection given by s.35A, above, although the director will be subject to s.322A. To avoid the difficult situation of a transaction which is valid for one person under s.35A but voidable against another (the director) under s.322A,

---

[68] Defined so as to include any "act": see s.322A(8).
[69] *per* Neuberger J. in *Re Torvale Group Ltd* [1999] 2 B.C.L.C. 605, at p.622. See too *Smith v Henniker-Major & Co* [2002] EWCA Civ 762; [2003] Ch.182, CA, at p.216 (*per* Schiemann L.J.).
[70–71] s.322A(5).
[72] A special resolution will be needed if the defect arises from limitations in the memorandum or articles. See p.94 above.

either the third party or the company may apply to the court to settle the matter. The court may then affirm the transaction as a whole, set it aside on just terms or sever it: s.322A(6)(7).[73]

Finally, s.322A provides that whether or not the transaction is avoided the director who deals with the company and any director of the company who authorised the transaction must account to the company for any gain arising from the transaction and indemnify the company against any loss.[74] The company may, however, waive this right by the appropriate resolution.

Internal consequences

Just as with the memorandum, any limitations on the powers of the directors, etc., contained in the company's constitution remain binding on the directors as a limitation on their powers and a contractual right for the members.[75] The liberalisation of the effects of such limitations on third parties under s.35A does not affect any right of the members to petition for an injunction preventing any breach of their powers by the directors or the liability of the directors and others for such breaches: s.35A(4)(5). No injunction can be granted, however, if the company is already legally obliged to carry out the transactions. This is identical to the equivalent provision in s.35 and what has been said on that section applies equally here.[76]

Agency—persons acting in good faith

If the outsider is dealing with the company in good faith, as defined in s.35A, above, he will be able to enforce any contract made by an agent on the company's behalf if that agent was acting within his authority, irrespective of any limitations on his powers under the company's constitution. If the outsider is not acting in good faith, the position is different.[77] An agent may bind his principal (in this case the company) if he has acted within his actual, implied or apparent authority.

As to actual authority, an individual director or committee of the board may be specifically authorised by the board of directors to make a particular contract on behalf of the company.[78] Alternatively, this may be defined in the individual director's contract of employment.[79] In *Rolled Steel Products (Holdings) Ltd v B.S.C.*[80] Slade L.J. stated that the directors had no actual authority to exercise any express or implied power of the company other than for the purposes of the company as set out in the memorandum; although if the shareholders

---

[73] See *Re Torvale Group Ltd* [1999] 2 B.C.L.C. 605, where the court validated certain scheme debentures.
[74] s.322A(3).
[75] See the discussion at p.65, above.
[76] Above, p.66.
[77] Below, p.102.
[78] Or a board of directors may pass a resolution authorising two of their number to sign cheques: *per* Lord Denning M.R. in *Hely-Hutchinson v Brayhead Ltd* [1968] 1 Q.B. 549, CA, at p.583.
[79] As in *SMC Electronics Ltd v Akhter Computers Ltd* [2001] 1 B.C.L.C. 433, CA.
[80] [1986] Ch. 246, CA.

unanimously consented this might not be so. Browne-Wilkinson L.J. expressed no opinion on this point and it would seem that on agency principles a simple majority will suffice to give the directors such actual authority. Whether the directors are then acting in breach of their fiduciary duties is a separate question which does not *per se* affect the outsider.[81]

As to implied authority, a director may, under a power in the articles, be appointed to an office, *e.g.* that of managing director, whch carries with it authority to make certain contracts on behalf of the company.[82] However, the question of implication does not stop there and authority may be implied from the conduct of the parties and the circumstances of the case.[83] A person with actual authority to obtain quotations of prices has no implied authority to communicate acceptance of such quotes where no decision to purchase has been made by his principal—at most such a person may have apparent authority.[84] On the other hand, a director will have implied authority to enter into transactions where these are ordinarily incidental to his duties. Thus, where the terms of a director's contract of employment were potentially ambiguous, a director was nevertheless still held to have implied authority to enter into commission agreements generally, such that his company was held liable on profits on sales to another company.[85]

A company is also bound by the acts of an agent acting within his apparent authority[86] where he lacks actual authority (although actual authority and apparent authority are not mutually exclusive and may often co-exist). It has been said that apparent authority is a form of estoppel by implied representation.[87] Thus an outsider may be protected where an individual director acts on behalf of the company without actual authority but with apparent authority, which apparent authority may arise from a representation that he has authority made by the board of directors or such a representation contained in the company's public documents. In *Rolled Steel Products (Holdings) Ltd v B.S.C.*,[88] Slade L.J. thought that the directors would have such authority in relation to any transaction which falls within the company's express or implied powers.

In such a case the company will be bound if the other party can prove:

(1) that he was induced to make the contract by the agent being held out as occupying a certain position in the company;

---

[81] Below, Ch.15.

[82] *per* Willmer L.J. in *Freeman & Lockyer v Buckhurst Park Properties (Mangal) Ltd* [1964] 2 Q.B. 480, CA at pp.488, 489. Diplock L.J. agreed. And see *Paterson's Trustees v Caledonian Heritable Security Co. Ltd* (1885) 13 R. 369 (manager borrowed money for purposes of company, and used money to purchase heritable property the title to which was taken in his own name).

[83] As in *Hely-Hutchinson v Brayhead Ltd* [1968] 1 Q.B. 549, CA, below, p.100.

[84] *Crabree-Vickers Pty. Ltd v Australia Direct Mail Advertising Co. Pty. Ltd* (1976) 50 A.L.J.R. 203, following the *Freeman & Lockyer* case and *Turquand's* case.

[85] *SMC Electronics Ltd v Akhter Computers Ltd* [2001] B.C.L.C. 433, CA.

[86] *Panorama Developments (Guildford) Ltd v Fidelis Furnishing Fabrics Ltd* [1971] 2 Q.B. 711, CA, below, p.335, where the secretary had apparent authority to hire cars on behalf of the company.

[87] *Freeman & Lockyer*, above, at pp.498, 503 (*per* Pearson L.J. and Diplock L.J., respectively).

[88] [1986] Ch. 246.

(2) that the representation, which is usually by conduct, was made by the person with actual authority to manage the company, generally or in respect of the matters to which the contract relates, who are usually the board of directors[89]; and

(3) that the contract was either one which a person in the position which the agent was held out as occupying would usually have actual authority to make or one which the company had by its conduct as a whole represented that he had authority to make.[90]

Condition (2) is due to the fact that the principal, the company, is not a natural person. It follows from the condition that the outsider cannot, as a rule,[91] rely on the agent's own representation that he has authority.[92]

R, the chairman of the directors of the defendant company, B Ltd, acted as its *de facto* managing director. The board knew of and acquiesced in that and the articles of B Ltd empowered the board to appoint a managing director. H was the chairman and managing director of a public company, P Ltd, which needed financial assistance. B Ltd was prepared to help and accordingly in January, 1965 B Ltd bought shares in P Ltd from H for £100,000 and proposed to inject £150,000 into P Ltd. H became a director of B Ltd but never saw its memorandum and articles and did not attend board meetings until May 19, 1965. After that meeting, R and H agreed that H would put more money into P Ltd if B Ltd would secure his position. R, on behalf of B Ltd, signed letters to H in which B Ltd purported to indemnify H against loss on his guarantee of a bank loan of £50,000 to P Ltd and to guarantee a loan by H to P Ltd. H then advanced £45,000 to P Ltd. When P Ltd went into liquidation, H had to honour his guarantee and he claimed the £50,000 and the £45,000 from B Ltd. B Ltd denied liability and said that R had no authority to sign the letters (and that the contracts were unenforceable for non-disclosure of H's interest in accordance with s.317). *Held*, that on the facts R had actual authority implied from the conduct of the parties and the circumstances of the case to enter into the contracts with H (and that it was too late to avoid them for non-disclosure of H's interest as required by the articles): *Hely-Hutchinson v Brayhead Ltd* [1968] 1 Q.B. 549, CA,[93] applying the *Freeman & Lockyer* case, below.

The articles of a company formed to purchase and resell an estate empowered the directors to appoint one of their body managing director. K, a director, was never appointed managing director but, to the knowledge of the board, he acted as such. On behalf of the company he instructed architects to do certain work in connection with the estate. *Held*, the company was bound by the contract and liable for the architects' fees. K had apparent authority because he had been held out by the board as managing director and, therefore, as having authority to do what a managing director would usually be authorised to do on behalf of the company, and this act was within the usual authority of a managing director. Accordingly, the plaintiffs could assume that he had been properly appointed: *Freeman & Lockyer v Buckhurst Park Properties (Mangal) Ltd* [1964] 2 Q.B. 480, CA.[94]

---

[89] But occasionally the shareholders: *Mahony v East Holyford Mining Co.* (1875) L.R. 7 H.L. 869, below, p.107.

[90] *Ebeed v Soplex Wholesale Supplies Ltd* [1985] B.C.L.C. 404, CA. Usually these will be the same.

[91] See the *Crabtree-Vickers* case, above, p.99.

[92] *Per* Diplock L.J. in the *Freeman & Lockyer* case, at p.505 and Lord Pearson in the *Hely-Hutchinson* case, at p.593.

[93] And see below, p.308. A corresponding Scots case is *Allison v Scotia Motor etc. Co. Ltd* (1906) 14 S.L.T. 9 (O.H.), where a *de facto* managing director engaged a works manager of the company for a period of five years. See below, p.267.

[94] Applying *Biggerstaff v Rowatt's Wharf Ltd* [1896] 2 Ch. 93, CA and *British Thomson-Houston Co. v Federated European Bank Ltd* [1932] 2 K.B. 176, CA. See also *Clay Hill Brick Co. Ltd v Rawlings* [1938] 4 All E.R. 100; *Rhodian River Shipping Co. S.A. v Halla Maritime Corp.* [1984] B.C.L.C. 139.

The persons who signed the articles of a company, and who under the articles were entitled to appoint directors, treated some of themselves as directors although there was no proper appointment. The articles provided that cheques should be signed as directed by the board. The person acting as secretary informed the company's bank that the "board" had resolved that cheques should be signed by two of three named directors and countersigned by the secretary. The bank acted on the communication and honoured cheques so signed. *Held*, the bank was entitled to honour the cheques and was not liable to refund the money paid. The rule in *Turquand's* case applied; *Mahony v East Holyford Mining Co.* (1875) L.R. 7 H.L. 869.

The requirement appears to be that the representation was made by a person with "actual" authority to manage the business. Thus if the representation is made by someone with no such authority the outsider cannot rely on it.

A sales representative, with the title of "unit manager," purported to bind his company to repay sums advanced by the bank to another company. He had no actual or apparent authority to do so. The bank sought confirmation from the company's "general manager" of its City branch. He confirmed the "unit manager's" authority, but he himself had no authority to make loans. *Held*, the bank could not rely on the general manager's statements as to the unit manager's authority: *British Bank of the Middle East v Sun Life Assurance of Canada (UK) Ltd* [1983] B.C.L.C. 78, HL.[95]

Where the outsider relies on a representation by the board of directors it is of course not necessary that he should actually have inspected the company's public documents but where he is seeking to rely on a representation in the public documents it is essential that he inspected them. A party seeking to set up an estoppel (or, in Scots law, a personal bar) must show that he relied on the representation which he alleges, be it a representation in words or a representation by conduct.

A director purported to make, on behalf of the company, an agreement whereby an outsider was to sell on commission goods imported by the company and to retain the proceeds as security for a debt due from another company. The outsider had not inspected the company's public documents and did not know of the power of delegation contained in the articles. Further, the agreement was so unusual as to put the outsider upon inquiry to ascertain whether the director had authority in fact. *Held*, the company was not bound: *Houghton & Co. v Nothard, Lowe and Wills Ltd* [1927] 1 K.B. 246, CA; affirmed on other grounds [1928] A.C. 1.

R. Co., by their principal director, A, purported to enter into an oral contract with B, who was a director of and purported to act for P. Co. but had no actual authority. The alleged contract was that the two companies should finance the sale of a telephone directory holder produced by a third company. R. Co. claimed repayment of money paid by them to B as agent for P. Co. in pursuance of the contract. R. Co. alleged that P. Co. were estopped from denying B's authority because the P. Co.'s articles provided that the directors could delegate their powers to a committee of one or more directors. However, A had not inspected the articles until after the action began (and even if A had inspected the articles a single director would not normally have authority to act for the company). *Held*, because A had not inspected the articles when the contract was made, they could not be relied on as conferring ostensible or apparent authority on B, and the action failed: *Rama Corporation Ltd v Proved Tin, etc., Ltd* [1952] 2 Q.B. 147.

---

[95] *Quaere* the effect of the wording of s.35A on this situation? Now the power of the director to authorise others to act on behalf of the company is free of any limitation under the company's constitution. Does this allow any representation to bind the company in such situations?

Ratification

There is another issue, which has already been mentioned in the context of s.35A(1),[96] and that is, as a matter of general agency law, that a company may adopt, expressly or impliedly,[96a] a transaction purportedly entered into in its name, but not, in fact, authorized at the time. The form that the ratification takes, in the company context, will be special resolution only where the transaction is contrary to a provision of the memorandum or articles.[97]

The doctrine of ratification, which is "equivalent to an antecedent authority",[98] has retrospective effect and the transaction in question must be adopted in its entirety.[99] Ratification will not be permitted where, to do so, would prejudice a third party. In particular, an act which has to be done within a certain time cannot be ratified after the expiration of that time[1] and the ratification must be reasonable in all circumstances.[2] A party wishing to reply on retrospective ratification would not succeed in such a bid where they were serious allegations involved and where there was clear prejudice to them caused by delay in bringing proceedings.[3]

Agency—persons acting otherwise than in good faith

If the third party is not acting in good faith, he cannot rely on s.35A and will by definition have subjective knowledge of the express limitation in the company's constitution. Unless the transaction is ratified therefore the company will not be bound. In addition, the rule in *Turquand's* case has never applied in four situations, which in effect provide that an outsider acting in bad faith will be bound by internal irregularities as well. In such cases even if the agent is otherwise acting within his implied or apparent authority the outsider will be bound by the irregularity and the company will not be liable.

The rule in *Turquand's* case does not apply, *i.e.* the company is not bound and the outsider is not protected, in the following cases:

(1) Where the outsider knows of the irregularity or lack of actual authority.[4]

Under the articles the directors had power to borrow up to £1,000 on behalf of the company without the consent of a general meeting and to borrow further money with such consent. The directors themselves lent £3,500 to the company without such consent, and

---

[96] Above, p.96.

[96a] It has been held that, where a managing director had acted outside his implied authority delegated to him by the board, its failure to intervene, in full knowledge of his actions, constituted an implied ratification of it: *Macari v Celtic Football and Athletic Co Ltd* 1999 S.L.T. 138, O.H.

[97] Pursuant to s.491) and s.9(1).

[98] See *Koenigsblatt v Sweet* [1923] 2 Ch.314, at p.325 (*per* Lord Sterndale M.R.).

[99] See *Smith v Henniker-Major & Co* [2002] EWCA Civ 762; [2003] Ch. 182, CA, at p.203. There is authority which suggests that the adoption of part of a transaction may amount to a ratification of the whole: see *Re Mawcon Ltd* [1969] 1 W.L.R. 78.

[1] See *Presentaciones Musicales SA v Secunda* [1994] Ch. 271, CA.

[2] As to this point, see *Re Portuguese Consolidated Copper Mines Ltd* (1890) 45 Ch.D. 16, CA.

[3] See *Smith v Henniker-Major & Co* [2002] EWCA Civ 762; [2003] Ch. 182, CA, at p.207.

[4] See *Criterion Properties plc v Stratford UK Properties LLC* [2004] UKHL 28; [2004] 1 W.L.R. 1846, at p.1856.

took debentures. *Held*, the company was liable, and the debentures were valid, only to the extent of £1,000: *Howard v Patent Ivory Manufacturing Co.* (1888) 83 Ch.D. 156.

(2) Where the outsider purported to act as a director in the transaction, *i.e.* to act for and on behalf of the company in the transaction. On the other hand, if a director, acting in his private capacity, contracts with his company, acting by another director, the former director is not automatically to be treated as having constructive knowledge of any defect in the latter's authority, so as to exclude the rule.[5]

(3) Where there are suspicious circumstances putting the outsider on inquiry.

The sole director of and main shareholder in a company paid cheques, drawn in favour of the company, into his own account. *Held*, the bank was put upon inquiry and not entitled to rely on his ostensible authority, and could not rely on the rule: *A. L. Underwood Ltd v Bank of Liverpool & Martins* [1924] 1 K.B. 775, CA.[6]

The articles of a company carrying on business as forwarding agents empowered the directors to determine who should have authority to draw bills of exchange on the company's behalf. C, the company's Manchester manager, drew bills on the company's behalf in favour of K, who took them, believing C to be authorised to draw them. C had no such authority, and it was unusual for a branch manager to have such authority. *Held*, the company was not liable to the holders on the bills because (1) K did not know of the power of delegation in the articles and therefore could not rely on its supposed exercise; (2) the bills were forgeries; (3) even if K had known of the power of delegation, he was not entitled to assume that a branch manager had ostensible authority to draw bills on behalf of his company: *Kreditbank Cassel GmbH v Schenkers Ltd* [1927] 1 K.B. 826, CA.

(4) Where a document is forged so as to purport to be the company's document, unless, perhaps, it is held out as genuine by an officer of the company acting within the scope of his authority.[7]

Validity of acts of directors—procedural defects in appointment

Where there is a defect in the appointment of a director who has acted for the company, the outsider may be protected by s.285 and an article like Table A, reg.92. The section provides that the acts of a director or manager are valid notwithstanding any defect that may afterwards be discovered in his appointment or qualification. Table A, reg.92, provides that all acts done by any meeting of the directors or of a committee of directors or by any person acting as a director shall, notwithstanding that it be afterwards discovered that there was some defect in the appointment of any such director or person acting as aforesaid, or that they or any of them were disqualified, be as valid as if every such person had been duly appointed and was qualified and had continued to be a director.

The effect of these provisions is to validate the acts of a director who has not been validly appointed because there was some procedural slip or irregularity in his appointment. Thus, an outsider dealing with the company, *or a member*, is

---

[5] *Morris v Kanssen* [1946] A.C. 459; *Hely-Hutchinson v Brayhead Ltd* [1968] 1 Q.B. 549 (Roskill J.).
[6] Followed in *Rolled Steel Products (Holdings) Ltd v B.S.C.* [1986] Ch. 246, CA.
[7] *Ruben v Great Fingall Consolidated* [1906] A.C. 439, *post*, p.194, particularly *per* Lord Loreburn L.C. at p.443.

entitled to assume that a person who appears to be a duly appointed and qualified director is so in fact.

The articles included an article like Table A, Art.92. T, N and S, *de facto* directors, made a call, payment of which was resisted by some shareholders on the ground that T, N and S were not *de jure* directors. For example, unknown to his co-directors, N had vacated office by parting with his qualification shares, although he later acquired a share qualification and continued to act as a director. *Held*, the article operated not only as between the company and outsiders but also as between the company and its members, and covered the irregularities alleged, so that the call was valid: *Dawson v African Consolidated Land etc. Co.* [1898] 1 Ch. 6, CA.

It is immaterial that it is clear from the company's public documents that a director is not duly qualified to act.[8]

The provisions do not validate acts where there has been no appointment at all.[9] Thus they have no effect on substantive rather than procedural defects. So they cannot validate acts which could not have been done even by a properly qualified director. In *Craven-Ellis v Canons Ltd*,[10] for example, what is now s.285 did not empower improperly qualified directors to do what properly qualified directors could not do, namely, appoint an improperly qualified director as managing director.

SECURITY FOR COSTS

In the last resort a company can only enforce a contract by taking legal proceedings. Since it is the general practice for the loser in legal proceedings to pay the costs of the winner, a defendant who successfully defends an action brought by a company which is in doubtful financial circumstances may find that it is unable to recover its costs from that company. s.726(1) therefore provides that:

> "Where in England and Wales,[11] a limited company is plaintiff in an action or other legal proceedings, the court . . . may, if it appears by credible testimony that there is reason to believe that the company will be unable to pay the defendant's costs if successful in his defence, require sufficient security to be given for those costs, and may stay all proceedings until the security is given."[12]

There are two questions for the court in such cases. First, does it have the power to make such an order for security for costs. The section applies to any

---

[8] *per* Farwell J. in *British Asbestos Co. Ltd v Boyd* [1903] 2 Ch. 439, at p.444. In this case a director vacated office on becoming secretary.

[9] *Morris v Kanssen* [1946] A.C. 459, applied in *Grant v John Grant & Sons Pty. Ltd* (1950) 82 C.L.R. 1.

[10] [1936] 2 K.B. 403, CA, below, p.293.

[11] The position in Scotland is governed by a similar rule in s.726(2). See *Merrick Homes Ltd v Duff*, 1996 S.L.T. 932; *Balfour Beatty Ltd v Brinmoor Ltd*, 1997 S.L.T. 888 (O.H.); *Assuranceforeningen Skuld v International Oil Pollution Compensation Fund (No.3)* 2000 S.L.T. 1352, O.H.

[12] The court had a similar power under RSC Ord. 23 (now CPR, part 25.13) where the plaintiff company is ordinarily resident outside the jurisdiction: see *Longstaff International Ltd v Baker & McKenzic* [2004] EWHC 1852 (Ch); [2004] 1 W.L.R. 2917. For the meaning of ordinary residence see *Re Little Olympian Each Ways Ltd* (No. 2) [1995] 1 B.C.L.C. 48. Such an order would not be discriminatory under E.C. law: *Chequepoint SARL v McClelland* [1997] 1 B.C.L.C. 117.

legal proceedings and these have been held to apply to a petition under s.459 of the Act[13] and where the company is bringing a counterclaim when it is itself the defendant in the main action.[14] To make such an order the court has to be satisfied on the evidence that the company would, and not merely might, be unable to pay the defendant's costs. This would be established if the company had a deficit on its current account even though it had a small balance sheet surplus.[15]

The second question relates to the amount of the required security. The cases establish that the court has a complete discretion in this area and that there are no set rules.[16] This must be done in relation to all the facts of the case, including the conduct of the company and the defendant. The court must achieve a balance between protecting the defendant and preventing the abandonment of a genuine claim by the company.[17] In *Keary Developments Ltd v Tarmac Construction Ltd*[18] the Court of Appeal said that the courts will not refuse an order simply because that would stifle the claim. It will equally, however, not allow the section to be used as an instrument of oppression. The courts will have regard to the company's prospects of success, but whether or not the claim would be stifled is a matter for the company to prove. The court must award a sufficient security which in the circumstances is just, and not necessarily a complete security.[19] The wealth of the defendant and whether or not he has indemnity insurance are in most cases irrelevant to this equation.[20]

[13] *Re Unisoft Group Ltd (No. 1)* [1993] B.C.L.C. 1292, CA.
[14] *Hutchison Telephone (UK) Ltd v Ultimate Response Ltd* [1993] B.C.L.C. 307, CA. But it does not apply to an interlocutory application by a defendant: *C.T. Bowring & Co. (Insurance) Ltd v Corsi & Partners Ltd* [1995] 1 B.C.L.C. 148.
[15] *Europa Holdings Ltd v Circle Industries (UK) plc* [1993] B.C.L.C. 320, CA.
[16] *Roburn Construction Ltd v William Irwin (South) & Co. Ltd* [1991] B.C.C. 726, CA, applying the majority reasoning in *Sir Lindsay Parkinson & Co. Ltd v Triplan Ltd* [1973] Q.B. 609.
[17] *ibid.*
[18] [1995] 2 B.C.L.C. 395 CA. See also *Paper Properties Ltd v Jay Benning & Co.* [1995] 1 B.C.L.C. 172, and *Turberville Smith Ltd v Turberville Smith* [1998] 1 B.C.L.C. 134.
[19] *Innovare Displays plc v Corporate Broking Services Ltd* [1991] B.C.C. 174, CA.
[20] *Croft Leisure Ltd v Gravestock & Owen* [1993] B.C.L.C. 1273.

Chapter 7

PUBLIC OFFERS OF SHARES

INTRODUCTION

This chapter deals with the legal responsibilities incumbent on a company when it issues shares to the public and the liabilities that may attach to that company or to its advisors for any misfeasance committed during that share issue.[1] This chapter is concerned with public offers of shares as opposed to private placements of shares, and therefore is concerned with share offers in public companies as opposed to private companies, whether those shares are entered on the Official List or not. The underlying policy behind the regulation of shares issues which are marketed to the public is a combination of the protection of the integrity of the marketplace and the maintenance of investor confidence in that marketplace. This thread has run through the nineteenth-century cases concerned with false statements in prospectuses, and is still at the forefront of the Financial Services Authority's regulation of the admission of securities to the Official List in the twenty-first century.

There are three types of shares which are of importance to us. The most significant for our purposes are shares in public companies which are to be traded on the London Stock Exchange and which are to be admitted to the Official List for this purpose. Shares will only be admitted to the Official List if they comply with the Listing Rules and must continue to comply with the Listing Rules throughout their listing. The second category of shares are shares in public companies which are not admitted to the Official List but which are marketed to the public nevertheless. The marketing of these shares must comply with the Public Offers of Securities Regulations rather than the Listing Rules. The third category of shares are shares in private companies which are not marketed to the public and which are therefore not considered in this chapter. These nature of these various bodies and regulations are considered in the next section.

The first section of this chapter will explain the various sources of the law which govern share issues: a combination of EC Directives, statutory obligations relating to share issues contained in the Financial Services and Markets Act 2000, formal regulation by the Financial Services Authority, ordinary criminal and civil law liabilities for misfeasance in relation to issues of shares to the public, and general market practice. The second section of this chapter will focus on shares which are to be marketed to the public and listed on the Official List maintained by the Financial Services Authority,[2] and the Listing Rules which govern such

---

[1] For a more detailed account of these principles, the reader is referred *Palmer's Company Law*, Part 5—"Capital Issues".

[2] While published by the London Stock Exchange, the functioning of the Official List is regulated by the Financial Services Authority in its role as the "UK Listing Authority".

share issues. This type of share issue is governed by Financial Services Authority regulation. Also considered, in the third section of this chapter, are share issues which are not intended to be listed on the Official List and which are regulated separately. Having considered those two regimes for regulating share issues, we will consider the statutory principles governing compensation for misstatement in a prospectus in the fourth section of this chapter and then the general law dealing with the liabilities of issuing companies and their advisors in the fifth and final section.

THE SOURCES OF THE LAW ON THE PUBLIC ISSUE OF SHARES

The fundamentals relating to the public issue of shares

There are two principal means by which companies can acquire capital: either by borrowing it or by issuing shares. Borrowing can take the form of ordinary loans or it can take the form of debt securities, such as bonds. Both debt securities and shares are forms of security which can be listed on the London Stock Exchange. This chapter will focus on shares issued by public companies having been marketed to the public. There are restrictions on the ability of private companies issuing shares to the public.

There are a number of sources of the law relating to the public issue of shares. The governing statutes are the two principal EC Directives dealing variously with the requirements for a valid prospectus and the regulations which member states of the EU must create to govern the issue of shares to the public. The domestic legislation dealing with the implementation of the requirements of those Directives is then found in Financial Services and Markets Act 2000 (FSMA 2000) and in the Listing Rules.

EC Directives concerning the public offers of securities

The underpinnings of law and the regulation of public offers of securities are to be found in the relevant EC Directives. The original sources of the law relating to the public offer of shares were the three founding directives: the Admission Directive,[3] the Listing Particulars Directive[4] and the Interim Reports Directive,[5] as supplemented by the Public Offers Directive.[6] These directives were repealed in 2001 by the Consolidated Admission and Reporting Directive of 2001[7] and then replaced by the Prospectus Directive of 2003[8] and supplemented by the Treasury Directive 2004.[8a]

The principal goal of the EC directives in this area is to harmonise the treatment of the public issue of securities across the European Union. Consequently, those directives have sought to establish minimum requirements for the

---

[3] Council Dir. No. 79/279/EEC.
[4] Council Dir. No. 80/390/EEC.
[5] Council Dir. No. 82/121/EEC.
[6] Council Dir. No. 88/627/EEC.
[7] Council Dir. No. 2001/34/EC.
[8] Council Dir. No. 2003/71/EC.
[8a] Council Dir. No. 2004/109/EC.

publication of prospectuses and minimum requirements for domestic regulation dealing with the marketing and issue of securities to the public. It has been the case that the regulation of these activities in the UK has been more stringent than the standards set out in the EC directives, reflecting the detailed governance of these markets in the UK historically.

The introduction of recent directives with a focus on harmonisation of municipal regulation in each member state would seem to mean, *prima facie*, that the UK's regulation of these markets will not be able to establish regulations which are more detailed or materially different from the EC directives or the regulations of other Member States. Harmonisation requires an equalisation of regulation. Yet, despite the growing harmonisation, the directives do permit Member States to determine the extent to which some of their provisions apply. Moreover, the Financial Services Authority (FSA) has indicated, as a result of public consultation, that it will continue to impose more stringent requirements on applicants seeking admission to the Official List because that will "contribute to deep and liquid markets" for securities on the UK based on investors' confidence in the integrity of the Official List regime.[9] The subsidiary objectives of the directives include the provision of equivalent protection for investors and greater inter-penetration of national securities markets across the EU so that an issue of securities in one member state can be effected more easily in other member states.

Rather than consider the terms of these directives in detail, we shall instead consider the manner in which the general principles established in the directives have been implemented in the UK in principal legislation and by FSA regulation.

The role of the Financial Services and Markets Act 2000

There has been a transformation in the regulation of public offers of shares from self-regulation and regulation by the London Stock Exchange under its own Listing Rules with the enactment of FSMA 2000 in relation to financial services generally. Rather than relying on the development of regulations by the Stock Exchange itself, the FSA now functions as a external regulator of the most of the financial services industry in the UK, acting on the basis of the statutory principles set out in Pt VI of FSMA 2000, comprising ss 72–103 which contains the statutory regime for the official listing of securities under the heading "Official Listing". The most significant provisions relating to the public issue of shares are considered below.

FSMA 2000 had two principal distinctions from its predecessor, the Financial Services Act 1986 (which it repealed). The first distinction relates to the establishment of the FSA which acts as the principal regulator for financial services activity in the UK. The previous system had been a series of different self-regulatory organisations, established to regulate different market sectors according to their own regulations, rather than a single regulator able to scrutinise the whole spread of financial services markets. The FSA was granted a range of sanctions by FSMA 2000, some of which are considered below, which

---

[9] FSA, *The Listing Review and implementation of the Prospectus Directive*, CP04/16, p.5.

gave it a more formidable standing in the regulation of financial markets. The second distinction from the previous legislation was the establishment of a set of general objectives for the FSA to meet when carrying out its functions: these objectives were focused not only on the preservation of the integrity of financial markets but also on the enhancement of the UK economy and the education of the investing public. These active obligations imposed on the FSA were of a very different order from ordinary obligations to regulate financial markets. Their impact on the regulation of the issue of share capital is considered below.

Regulation by the UK Listing Authority

The "Official List" is maintained by the FSA, acting in its capacity as the UK Listing Authority (referred to in this chapter as "UKLA"), discharging the obligations of the "competent authority" as required by the relevant EC Directives relating to the supervision of the securities markets in the UK. In terms of the sources of the law on the public issue of securities we have to think beyond the EC Directives and FSMA 2000 and also consider the regulations created by the UKLA in the form of its *UKLA Guidance Manual* which indicate its practices in relation to the administration of the Listing Rules.[10] These practices are of great significance because they govern the manner in which UKLA will grant and revoke regulatory authorisations, as envisaged by the EC Directives.

The powers and duties of the UKLA divide into four main types: maintenance of the official list; the preparation of those regulations which make up the Listing Rules; censure and punishment for infraction of any of the Listing Rules; and the broader context of its obligations as the Financial Services Authority within FSMA 2000. It is then left to the UKLA to admit to the official list "such securities and other things it considers appropriate".[11] In framing these regulations, the FSA is acting both in its role as the UK Listing Authority, replacing the Council of the London Stock Exchange, and also in the broader role defined in Pt I of FSMA 2000 to protect the competitive position of the UK economy,[12] to promote awareness of financial matters among all categories of investor,[13] to protect consumers,[14] and to act proportionately in the discharge of its regulatory functions.[15] Taken together with the power to create listing rules, the UKLA is at liberty to decide what it considers to be appropriate. However, under EU law these powers are to be exercised in line with the EC Directives considered above.

The objectives which are set for the UKLA by s.73(1) of FSMA 2000 are as follows:

(1) "to promote investor confidence in standards of disclosure, in the conduct of issuers' affairs and in the market as a whole by the listing rules, and in particular the continuing obligations regime";

---

[10] As provided for by the Official Listing of Securities (Change of Competent Authority) Regulations 2000 enacted further to Financial Services and Markets Act 2000, s.73.
[11] Financial Services and Markets Act 2000, s.74(2).
[12] Financial Services and Markets Act 2000, s.2(3)(e).
[13] Financial Services and Markets Act 2000, s.4(1).
[14] Financial Services and Markets Act 2000, s.5(2).
[15] Financial Services and Markets Act 2000, s.2(3)(c).

(2) "to ensure that listed securities should be brought to the market in a way that is appropriate to their nature and number and which will facilitate an open and efficient market for trading in those listed securities"; and

(3) "to ensure that an issuer makes full and timely disclosure about itself and its listed securities, at the time of listing and subsequently".

As we consider the Listing Rules we shall see that the requirement imposed on issuers of making full disclosure of all relevant information to the investing public is a central part of the regulation of that market.

Liabilities under the general law

There are two general kinds of liability considered below: first, liability to compensate anyone who suffers loss as a result of some misstatement in the listing particulars under s.90 of FSMA 2000 and, secondly, liability under common law or equity for damages or rescission of the contract for the acquisition of shares on grounds of negligence or fraud.

References in this chapter to provisions of a statute are references to the Financial Services and Markets Act 2000 (referred to as "FSMA 2000"), unless expressed to the contrary. Similarly, references to the "Listing Rules" are references to the listing rules created by the FSA, in its capacity as the UK Listing Authority further to FSMA 2000, in force at the time of writing. The Listing Rules are modified from time to time and a new edition is Scheduled to publish in July 2005.

THE ADMISSION OF SHARES TO THE OFFICIAL LIST

The scope of public offers of securities

The principal advantage of admission of securities to the Official List is the confidence which this process inculcates in investors that the issuing company has complied with the procedures, considered in this section, which are set down by the Listing Rules. However, admission to the Official List also has important consequences for the issuer, principally because the issuer will be subject to the continuing obligations contained in the Listing Rules which are imposed on issuers whose securities are listed. An application for listing must be made in accordance with s.75 of FSMA 2000. That means, the application must be made to the competent authority in such a manner as the Listing Rules may require.[16] While the Listing Rules set out these requirements in detail, the UKLA is nevertheless empowered to make admission to listing subject to any special condition which it considers appropriate.

An offer is deemed to be made to the public if any member of the public may acquire that investment, even if the offer is made to a section of the public or even to existing shareholders of a public company, as opposed to a private placement which can be demonstrated to have been made to a strictly limited

---

[16] Financial Services and Markets Act 2000, s.75(1).

class of people. A person is said to offer securities if, and only if, that person makes an offer as principal, which if accepted, would give rise to a contract for their issue, or, alternatively, if that person invites another person to make an offer to him.[17] Alternatively, an offer is considered to have been made where any offer is made to the public which is not defined as being an exempt offer within the regulations.[18]

The core principles of the Listing Rules

The UKLA's general principles

The objectives which the UKLA sets out in its *Guidance Manual* are to formulate and enforce listing rules which:

(1) provide an appropriate level of protection for investors in listed securities;

(2) facilitate access to listed markets for a broad range of enterprises; and

(3) seek to maintain the integrity and competitiveness of UK markets for listed securities.[19]

Therefore, the UKLA in its practices applying the terms of formal regulation and their powers under FSMA 2000 considers itself to be bound both by the ordinary regulatory principle of protecting investors and securing a viable market in securities, and also by its economic role to preserve the competitiveness of UK markets as against markets in other jurisdictions.

In the implementation of its powers, particularly in relation to censure and to the grant of authorisations as considered below, these general principles are of great significance to the UKLA's decisions. Indeed, as will emerge from the discussion to follow, the Listing Rules are generally expressed in very general language even when dealing with apparently detailed matters: such as the required contents for prospectuses and listing particulars. A company wishing to make an offer of shares to the public, and its professional advisors, are therefore required to consider whether the detail of the share issue complies with the standards expressed in these general principles and not simply to comply with a list of detailed rules. The former, more general approach, it is suggested, requires a more subtle understanding of UKLA practice than the latter approach would.

Conditions for admission to listing

The first category of requirements relate to the company's capacity and composition. In effect, they concern the company's status and activities, and are contained in Chapter 3 of the *Listing Rules*. The company must be validly incorporated and must have published or filed audited accounts for three years

---

[17] Financial Services and Markets Act 2000, s.103(4).
[18] Financial Services and Markets Act 2000, Sch.11, para.1(1).
[19] UKLA, *Guidance Manual*, para 1.3.7.

before the date of the listing particulars. The company must also be conducting "an independent business" which is revenue earning for the period covered by the accounts (*Listing Rules*, Ch.3, rule 3.6) and must also have "sufficient working capital" (*Listing Rules*, Ch.3, paras 3.10-3.11). Furthermore, the company's directors must have "collectively appropriate expertise and experience for the management of its business" (*Listing Rules*, Ch.3, paras 3.8) and be free of conflicts of interest between their fiduciary and personal capacities.

The second category of requirements relate to the securities themselves. The expected aggregate market value of all securities to be listed must be at least £700,000 for shares and £200,000 for debt securities (*Listing Rules*, Ch.3, paras 3.16). However, UKLA may admit securities of lower value if satisfied that there will be an adequate market for those securities (*Listing Rules*, Ch.3, paras 3.17).

The requirement for a sponsor

The applicant company will not be permitted to apply entirely by itself. Rather, the company must have a sponsor to assist the listing. The sponsor is required to be approved to act as such by the UKLA and will be a professional or a financial institution capable of assisting the company to bring an issue of shares before the market. The sponsor is required to conduct a "due and careful enquiry of the issuer and its advisors" and therefore does not act entirely as the agent of the company. The sponsor's role is to supply information to the UKLA and as such to certify that the issuing company has complied with the requirements of the Listing Rules during the application process and thereafter. The sponsor's principal duty to the issuing company is "to ensure that the issuer is properly guided and advised as to the application or interpretation of the relevant listing rules" (*Listing Rules*, Ch.2, para.2.10(a)). The sponsor is at risk of sanction by UKLA if it fails to perform its duties adequately and thus the market can have confidence in the scrutiny which has been conducted into the issuer and the securities which are being issued.

Listing particulars and prospectuses

The requirement for listing particulars and prospectuses

Listing particulars have two different purposes. The first is to fulfil the function of a prospectus or offering document in providing investors with suitable and sufficient information about the securities which are being issued and about the company which is issuing them. The second is to act as marketing material which seeks to induce investors to subscribe for securities either from the company or from an intermediary. The philosophy behind the regulation of the official listing of securities is that of promoting minimum levels of disclosure of prescribed information both to UKLA and to the public. Offers of securities will be made by means of a prospectus which gives potential investors detailed financial and other information both about the terms of the securities and also about the issuer.

When new securities are admitted to the Official List then there must be a prospectus approved by UKLA and published by the issuer (s.84(1)). The listing particulars which are required to be lodged with UKLA for approval will usually include a prospectus, although there will be situations in which a prospectus will not be required among the listing particulars: for example where there are no new securities being issued to the public beyond the current membership of the company. It is unlawful for any securities to be offered to the public in the UK before the required prospectus or listing particulars, as appropriate, have been published (*Listing Rules*, Ch.5, rule 5.1(b)). Contravention of this prohibition of publication before approval constitutes a criminal offence (*ibid*).

The general duty of disclosure in listing particulars

As mentioned above, the basis of the regulation of public offers of securities is to ensure that investors and their professional advisors have sufficient information to be able to make informed investment decisions when seeking to buy listed securities. The core guidance on what sort of information is to be provided in the listing particulars is contained in the principle that the issuer is required to disclose all information which investors and their professional advisors would reasonably require when making an informed assessment both as to the financial condition of the issuing company and as to the rights attaching to the securities to be issued (s.80(1)). This is referred to in this chapter as the "general duty of disclosure". In all cases, the general duty of disclosure in s.80 must be complied with and supplementary listing particulars may be necessary in certain circumstances.

There is no definitive, statutory or regulatory list of the material which is to be included in the listing particulars: rather, the people preparing the listing particulars must consider the general duty of disclosure and decide what sort of information is required by the context. Section 80(4) provides that when deciding what information to include in the listing particulars, those people preparing the listing particulars must have regard to:

"(a) the nature of the securities and their issuer;
 (b) the nature of the persons likely to consider acquiring them;
 (c) the fact that certain matters may reasonably be expected to be within the knowledge of professional advisers of a kind which persons likely to acquire the securities may reasonably be expected to consult; and
 (d) any information available to investors or their professional advisers as a result of requirements imposed on the issuer of the securities by a recognised investment exchange, by listing rules or by or under any other enactment."

Therefore, the listing particulars would be required to consider the type of information necessary from the perspective of the likely investors, the nature of the securities and the broad range of professional advisers who might be called upon in relation to those securities. These listing particulars must then be submitted to UKLA for approval before any admission to listing or offer of the securities to the public can be conducted.

The requirement for supplementary listing particulars

After the listing particulars have been prepared there may nevertheless be supplementary listing particulars required if there has been some "significant change" relating to the material contained in the original listing particulars (s.81). This provision applies if there has been a significant change "at any time after the preparation of listing particulars which have been submitted to the competent authority under section 79 and before the commencement of dealings in the securities concerned following their admission to the official list" (s.81(1)). Alternatively, supplementary listing particulars may be required in circumstances in which "a significant new matter arises, the inclusion of information in respect of which would have been so required if it had arisen when the particulars were prepared" (s.81(1)(b). A change or new matter is important if it is significant for the purpose of making an informed assessment of matters concerning the issuer and the securities to which the general duty of disclosure relates (s.81(2)).

Exemptions from the obligation to make full disclosure in published listing particulars

There are three principal exceptions to the obligation to publish listing particulars (*Listing Rules*, Ch.5). First, such a dispensation might be available where the securities have already been the subject of a public issue, or if the securities are being issued in connection with a takeover offer or a merger. In that situation, it is required that a document has been published within the previous 12 months which satisfies UKLA that sufficient information is in the public domain. The second exception arises when the securities have been listed in another member state for not less than three years before the application. The third exception arises if the shares have been traded on the Alternative Investment Market[20] for a continuous period of two years before the application. The circumstances supporting the absence of listing particulars are then to be published in an exempt listing document.

Alternatively, UKLA may authorise the omission of information from listing particulars, if its disclosure would be contrary to the public interest, or if its disclosure would be seriously detrimental to the issuer; or if its disclosure is considered unnecessary for the type of people who are normally expected to invest in securities of this kind (s.82).

Persons responsible for the contents of listing particulars

Persons responsible under statute

It is important to know which people will be considered to be responsible for the contents of the listing particulars, because it is those people who will bear an obligation to compensate investors for any loss suffered as a result of any misstatement in the terms of the listing particulars (under s.90). The information

---

[20] The Alternative Investment Market (known generally as AIM) is the listed market for smaller companies than those which appear on the Official List.

contained in the listing particulars will have been prepared by the issuing company's directors and their professional advisors, and will also incorporate the advice of any relevant experts where appropriate. From the company's perspective, the prospectus is marketing material through which it seeks to represent to potential investors the benefits of the securities at issue. This marketing material is required to contain a range of accounting and other information on which investors will rely when making investment decisions, as considered above. Consequently, any errors in the prospectus will constitute misrepresentations made to investors, attracting those forms of liability considered below.

The persons who are considered to be legally responsible for the contents of the listing particulars or supplementary listing particulars are described in the Financial Services and Markets Act (Official Listing of Securities) Regulations 2001, reg.6.[21] (All references in this section are to those Regulations, except where indicated to the contrary). Regulation 6(1) provides that the following categories of person are to be taken as being responsible for the contents of the listing particulars:

(a) the company which issues the securities;

(b) the directors of the issuing company at the time when the particulars are submitted to UKLA;

(c) everyone who has authorized himself to be named, and is named, in the listing particulars as a director or who has agreed to become a director of that body either immediately or at a future time;

(d) everyone who accepts, and is stated in the particulars as accepting, responsibility for the listing particulars; and

(e) anyone else who has authorized the contents of the listing particulars.

In relation to the liability of individual directors, reg.6 provides that a person is not to be treated as responsible for the listing particulars if they are published without that person's knowledge or consent, provided that he gives reasonable public notice that they were published without his knowledge or consent as soon as he becomes aware of the fact (reg. 6(2)).

It is a requirement of the Listing Rules that each director of the issuing company accept responsibility for listing particulars relating to certificates representing shares or in relation to securities issued as part of takeover of a listed or an AIM company (*Listing Rules*, Ch.5, para.5.3). If someone accepts responsibility for a part only of the listing particulars, then that person will be liable only for statements made in that part of the particulars if they state their liabilities to be so limited in the particulars (reg.6(3)). Therefore, it is possible for individuals, advisers or companies to limit their liabilities by refusing to accept responsibility for part or all of the particulars. This possibility of the exemption from liability could be said to subvert the policy that listing particulars promote

---

[21] SI 2001/2956. These provisions are paralleled, in relation to unlisted securities, by the Public Offers of Securities Regulations 1995, SI 1995/1537, reg.13.

transparency in the process of disclosure and of responsibility for such disclosure. Alternatively, it could be said to be unjust to impose a liability on someone participating in the preparation of the listing particulars when they have not consented to accept that liability.

The liability of professional advisors

In considering the liability of professional advisers for any statement made in or omission from the listing particulars, a distinction is to be made between advisers giving professional advice generally and thereby opening themselves up to general liability at common law, and those advisers whose advice is partly in the form of statements reproduced in the listing particulars. It is in relation to that latter category that the legislation refers. Regulation 6(4) provides that:

> "Nothing in this regulation is to be construed as making a person responsible for any particulars by reason of giving advice as to their contents in a professional capacity."

The question as to whether or not a person is to be held liable for the contents of listing particulars, on the basis that they advised as to the suitability of their contents in a professional capacity, is left open. What reg.6(4) does is to remove any presumption that a professional adviser should necessarily be held to be liable for the contents of those particulars in all circumstances. Consequently, it is suggested, the adviser would be liable if he had advised that the contents of the listing particulars were acceptable when those listing particulars were not; whereas he would not be liable if he had either advised that the contents of the listing particulars were unacceptable or advised only on matters unrelated to the defects in the listing particulars.

Continuing obligations imposed by the Listing Rules

There are *continuing obligations* on the issuer of securities, meaning that the issuer bears obligations even after authorisation for admission of the securities to the Official List has been granted. The principal continuing obligation is to warn UKLA and the market of any significant changes in the issuer's affairs which would affect the value or rights attached to the securities. So, under Ch.9 of the *Listing Rules*, a company must notify a Regulatory Information Service "without delay" of "any major new developments in its sphere of activity which are not public knowledge" which would lead to a "substantial movement in its price" by virtue of affecting its assets or liabilities, or would lead to a substantial movement in the price of its listed securities (*Listing Rules*, Ch.9, para.9.1).

Financial promotion and advertisements

It is not only the sale of investments to the general public without authorisation which is restricted, but also the advertisement of investments to the public. In FSMA 2000, the financial promotion code provides that no person shall "in the course of business, communicate an invitation or inducement to engage in investment activity" (s.21(1)). Section 98(1) of the FSMA 2000 provides that no advertisement may be issued in the United Kingdom unless the contents of the advertisement have been submitted to UKLA and that authority has either approved those contents or authorised the issue of the advertisement without such approval. The publication of an advertisement before listing particulars have been approved by the UKLA is a criminal offence (s.98(2)).

Suspension of securities and cancellation of listing

There are two principal responses available to the UKLA if the listing or trading in securities is considered to be a threat to the market in securities in general terms. First, the *Listing Rules* provide that, "where the smooth operation of the market is, or may be temporarily jeopardised or where protection of investors so requires, the UKLA may suspend . . . the listing of securities at any time and in such circumstances as it thinks fit" (*Listing Rules*, Ch.1, rule 1.15). Second, the *Listing Rules* provide that the authority may cancel the listing of securities "if it is satisfied that there are special circumstances which preclude normal regular dealings in them" (*Listing Rules*, Ch.1, rule 1.19).

Offers of Unlisted Securities

Offers of unlisted securities, *i.e.* those where no application is to be made for listing on the Stock Exchange, are subject to Pt II of the Public Offers of Securities Regulations 1995.[22] However, if the offeror wishes to take advantage of the Mutual Recognition of Prospectuses Directive to facilitate an application for listing in another Member State, he will need to follow a different course of having the prospectus pre-vetted by the Stock Exchange. That procedure is set out in the next part of this chapter. The following provisions apply therefore only to offers of unlisted securities where that facility is not required.

The prospectus requirement—publication and registration

The Regulations impose three requirements on offerors of unlisted securities relating to the need for a prospectus relating to the offer. The first is that when such securities are offered to the public for the first time, a prospectus complying with the Regulations must be published by the offeror by making it available to the public, free of charge, at an address in the UK during the whole of the period during which the offer is open: reg.4(1). The meaning of offered to the public is considered below. The second requirement is that before publishing such a prospectus it must be registered with the registrar: reg.4(2). Finally, any advertisement, notice, poster or other document, other than the prospectus itself, announcing a public offer of securities where a prospectus is required under the Regulations must state that a prospectus is or will be published, giving an address

---

[22] These include securities traded on the Alternative Investment Market.

in the UK from which it can be obtained: reg.12. Breach of any of these provisions is a criminal offence and can also give rise to civil liability, *e.g.* for breach of statutory duty: reg.16.[23]

Offered to the public

A prospectus is not required to be published, etc., under the Regulations unless the securities are being offered to the public. This concept is defined in the Regulations, which then go on to provide a large number of exceptions where, even if there is an offer of securities to the public, there need be no prospectus. An offer, and thereby an offeror, is defined by reg.5 so as to mean either an offer, which if accepted, would give rise to a binding contract to issue or sell the securities (a contractual offer) or an invitation to a person to make such an offer (an invitation to treat).

Such an offer is made to the public if it is made to any section of the public, whether selected as members or debenture holders of a company, or as clients of the person issuing the prospectus or in any manner, and not just to the public at large: reg.6. This wording was used in the Companies Act under the previous regime which then excluded only two types of such offers. The new regime, however, taking advantage of the exceptions allowed for in the directive, specifies no less than 20 such exceptions. Cases decided under the old law must therefore be treated with some care before applying them to the new rules.[24]

Exceptions to the prospectus requirement

Because of the wide definition of an offer to the public, reg.7 sets out 20 situations where there is no need to publish or register a prospectus under the Regulations. These exceptions, which are cumulative, are as follows:

(i)   offers to persons in connection with their trades, professions or occupations;

(ii) offers to no more than 50 persons (including any previous offers of the same securities in the previous 12 months);

(iii) offers to members of a club or association where they have a common interest in its affairs and to what is to be done with the proceeds of the offer;

(iv) offers to a restricted circle of people whom the offeror reasonably believes to be sufficiently knowledgable to understand the risks involved;

---

[23] If the breach is as to the content of the prospectus rather than as to its being published, etc., then there is no contravention of reg.16. Instead there are specific remedies which are set out at p.121 *et seq.*

[24] For such cases see the 13th edition of this work.

(v)   offers made in connection with a bona fide underwriting agreement[25];

(vi) offers by private companies to existing members, employees or their families,[26] or debenture holders of the company;

(vii) offers to the government or a local or public authority;

(viii) offers of a total value of less than 40,000 ecus (including any previous offers of the same securities in the past 12 months);

(ix) offers whereby each person acquiring the securities must pay at least 40,000 ecus or equivalent;

(x) offers of securities with a value of at least 40,000 ecus each;

(xi) offers made in connection with a takeover offer[27];

(xii) offers made in connection with a merger[28];

(xiii) shares offered free of charge to existing shareholders (bonus shares)[29];

(xiv) shares offered in exchange for shares in the same company if there is no increase in the company's share capital[30];

(xv) offers limited to employees, former employees and their spouses and children (under the age of 18);

(xvi) offers arising from the conversion of convertible debentures or warrants where the original issues were accompanied by a prospectus or listing particulars;

(xvii) offers by charities and certain other non-profit making bodies;

(xviii) certain shares issued by building societies and industrial and provident societies;

(xix) offers of Euro-securities (within s.207 of the Act);

(xx) offers of securities which are of the same class and were issued at the same time as securities which were accompanied by a prospectus in accordance with the regulations.

Form and content of a prospectus

A prospectus published under the Regulations must contain all the information specified in Sch.1 to the Regulations presented in as easily analysable and comprehensible form as possible: regs 8(1)(3). This requirement is subject to a dispensation in reg.8(2) whereby if a particular item in the Schedule is inappropriate to the issuer's business the prospectus must contain equivalent

---

[25] See below, p.131.
[26] Defined as to include spouses, children and their decendants and certain trustees for those people.
[27] As defined in s.428 C.A. 1985. See Ch.31, below.
[28] See Ch.30, below.
[29] See below, Ch.22.
[30] See Ch.9, below.

information if that is appropriate. The Schedule provides detailed requirements relating to the issuer and the persons responsible for the prospectus, if different, and the securities on offer. The prospectus must be dated and give the names and functions of the directors of the issuing company.

In addition, reg.9 imposes a general duty of disclosure over and above that required by the Schedule. This is similar to that imposed by s.146 of the Act for listed securities. Thus the prospectus must disclose all the information with respect to the assets and liabilities, financial position, profits and losses, prospects of the issuer of the securities and the rights attaching to the securities as an investor would reasonably require in order to make an informed assessment, having regard to the nature of both the issuer and the securities.

This general duty of disclosure is limited by reg.9(2) to the information which the persons responsible for the prospectus (not necessarily the issuer) either knew about or could reasonably have discovered by making enquiries.

The Regulations contain various derogations from the need to publish a prospectus in accordance with the Schedule. Where the shares are to be admitted to an approved exchange (*e.g.* the Alternative Investment Market) on a pre-emptive basis[31] certain information can be omitted by the governing body of the exchange if it is available as a result of the disclosure requirements of that exchange; reg.8(4). Similarly, where an offer relates to shares of a class which are already admitted to an approved exchange, the governing body of that exchange may allow the offer to proceed without a prospectus if they amount to no more than a 10 per cent increase in the shares already admitted and the disclosure rules of the exchange provide the necessary information: reg.8(5).

Reg.8(6) provides that where the same issuer makes an offer of securities within twelve months of a previous offer of different securities for which a prospectus was issued, the issuer may simply append a copy of that first prospectus with a second prospectus detailing the changes which have taken place since the first offer. Finally, reg.11(1) empowers the Treasury or the Secretary of State to authorise the omission of material which if disclosed would be contrary to the public interest, and reg.11(2) applies a relaxation in the case of a genuine secondary offer, *i.e.* one not by the issuer of the securities or anyone acting on his behalf. Where the secondary offeror does not have the specified information available and has not been able to obtain it by making reasonable efforts to do so, then there is no obligation to include it.

Supplementary prospectus

If, during the currency of an offer, there is any significant change in any material in the prospectus, or a significant inaccuracy in the prospectus is discovered, or if a significant new matter arises which would have been included in the prospectus either under the Schedule or the general duty of disclosure had it arisen when that was prepared, a supplementary prospectus must be published and registered at the same time but otherwise in the same way as the prospectus: reg.10. A significant matter, change or error is one which would affect an informed

---

[31] See below, p.120.

assessment by a prospective purchaser. Where the person who delivered the prospectus for registration is unaware of the change, etc., there is no duty on him to issue a supplementary prospectus unless he was notified of it by a person responsible for the prospectus who is under a duty to notify him of any such change, etc. Failure to comply with these requirements may lead to civil liability.[32]

Misrepresentations and omissions

Civil and criminal liability for misrepresentations and omissions in a prospectus and supplementary prospectus are dealt with later in this chapter.[33]

LIABILITIES FOR ISSUES OF SECURITIES UNDER STATUTE

There are two, general categories of liability: first, statutory liabilities and secondly liabilities arising on the basis of common law. The defendants may be the company itself or, in relation to the preparation of listing particulars, the directors and advisors of the company too. The question of who will be responsible for the contents of the listing particulars was considered above.

Compensation for defective listing particulars under statute

The basis for a claim for compensation under s.90

Any person responsible for the preparation of the listing particulars will be liable to pay compensation to any person who suffers loss as a result of "any untrue or misleading statement in the particulars" or as a result of the omission from the listing particulars of anything which would otherwise have been required by the general duty of disclosure under s.80 (s.90). There are therefore three heads of liability.

The first head of liability relates to untrue or misleading statements. It is not a requirement of the statutory language that there have been fraud or any other intention to deceive: rather, the statement made must have misled the claimant. Equally, the concept of "untrue" would seem to include statements which are "incorrect" and not necessarily to require that they be untrue as a result of some lie or deceit. The second head of liability relates to the omission of material which would otherwise be required by the duty of disclosure in s.80, as considered above.

The third head of liability relates to situations in which "listing particulars are required to include information about the absence of a particular matter, the omission from the particulars of that information is to be treated as a statement in the listing particulars that there is no such matter" (s.90(3)). Therefore, the liability for compensation is not limited to active errors in the listing particulars but rather they also include omissions of material which are required by the

[32] See below, p.122.
[33] Below, p.122.

listing particulars. Liability is then owed to persons who have "acquired securities of the kind in question and suffered loss in respect of them as a result of the failure" (s.90(4)).

Defences to a statutory claim for compensation under s.90

There are five possible defences to a claim for compensation under s.90(1), set out in Sch.10 to FSMA 2000.

(1) The first defence is based upon the *defendant's belief* at the time when the listing particulars or any prospectus was submitted for approval to UKLA (Sch.10, para.1(3)(a)). The defendant must have reasonably believed that any statement made in the listing particulars was not untrue nor misleading, or that anything omitted had been omitted properly. The defendant must have continued to hold to that belief at the time when the securities were acquired by the claimant; or it must not have been reasonably practicable to bring any relevant matter to the claimant's attention (Sch.10, para.1(3)(b)); or that the defendant had taken reasonable steps to bring those matters to the claimant's attention ((Sch.10, para.1(3)(c)). The defendant must establish one of four alternatives. The first is that the defendant continued in his original belief until the time when the securities were acquired. The three other alternatives contemplate the defendant having ceased to hold that belief.

(2) The second defence relates to a *statement by an expert* which is included in the listing particulars or in a prospectus (Sch.10, para.2(1)). That statement must have been reproduced in the listing particulars with the expert's consent. An "expert" is anyone whose profession, qualifications or experience give authority to a statement made by him (Sch.10, para.8); although the defence is not a defence to the expert's own negligence but rather only to some third person reproducing that expert's statement. The statement must have been considered to have been validly included in the documentation at the time when that documentation was published, or otherwise as in relation to the first defence.

(3) The third defence is based upon the *publication of a correction* or the taking of reasonable steps to secure publication of such a correction (Sch.10, para.3). The defendant must show either that a correction had been published before the securities were acquired by the claimant, in such a way that the correction could reasonably be expected to have come to the claimant's attention, or that the defendant took all reasonable steps to secure publication of such a correction.

(4) The fourth defence relates to a *statement made by a public official* which is included in the listing particulars, prospectus, supplementary listing particulars or supplementary prospectuses, provided always that the defendant satisfies the court that the statement was accurately and fairly reproduced (Sch.10, para.5).

(5) The fifth defence applies if the defendant satisfies the court that the *claimant knew the statement was false or misleading*, or knew of any matter which had been omitted (Sch.10, para.6). An example would be if the claimant knew that a particular piece of financial information in the prospectus was incorrect in which case it would not be open to a claimant to claim that the incorrect nature of the information caused a fall in the value of the security and in consequence

the claimant's own loss. At common law, also, if the claimant had a full appreciation of the true position at the time of making an investment, regardless of any misstatement in or omission from the prospectus, then he will not be able to recover compensation for any loss which resulted from the investment.[34]

LIABILITIES UNDER COMMON LAW AND IN EQUITY

Since a company is liable for the misrepresentations of its directors and other agents acting within the scope of their authority, a person induced to subscribe for shares or debentures by a misrepresentation in a prospectus or listing particulars may have other remedies under the general law against the individual or the individuals responsible, *e.g.* promoters, directors or experts.[35] In this section we will consider the possibility of recovery of damages at common law or rescission of a contract of allotment contracted further to a negligent or a fraudulent misrepresentation.

Negligent misrepresentation

Negligent misrepresentation under statute

Damages in lieu of rescission may be recovered in England and Wales under s.2(2) of the Misrepresentation Act 1967. That provision states that, where a person has entered into a contract after a misrepresentation made to him *otherwise than fraudulently*, and he would be entitled to rescind that contract, then the court may award damages in lieu of rescission if it appears to the court that it would be equitable so to do. Damages for *negligent* misrepresentation may be recovered from the company under s.2(1) of the Misrepresentation Act 1967, which provides that where a person has entered into a contract after a misrepresentation made to him by another party thereto and as a result has suffered loss, then the representor is liable in damages unless he proves that on reasonable grounds he believed up to the time when the contract was made that the representation was true.[36]

Negligent misstatement at common law

It may also be possible to claim damages for negligent misrepresentation under the principle in *Hedley Byrne & Co. Ltd v Heller & Partners Ltd*.[37] Under that principle, tortious damages will be available for any financial loss which is caused by a negligent misrepresentation. It does not matter whether that misrepresentation was spoken or written, nor does it matter that the misrepresentation was honestly, though negligently, made. The principle in *Hedley Byrne v Heller*

---

[34] *Watts v Bucknall* [1903] 1 Ch. 766. See also *JEB Fasteners Ltd v Marks, Bloom and Co. (a firm)* [1981] 3 All E.R. 289.

[35] As in *Frankenburg v Great Horseless Carriage Co* [1900] 1 Q.B. 504, CA.

[36] A similar provision to s.(1) applies in Scotland under s.10(1) of the Law Reform (Miscellaneous Provisions)(Scotland) Act 1985.

[37] [1964] A.C. 465.

imposes liability under a duty of care in the following circumstances. First, one party must seek information or advice from another party in circumstances in which the party seeking advice relies on that other party to exercise due care. It must be reasonable for the party seeking advice to rely on the other party to exercise such care and it must also be the case that the party giving the advice knows or ought to know that reliance is being placed on his skill, judgment or ability to make careful inquiry. Furthermore, the party giving the advice must not expressly disclaim responsibility for his representation.[38]

The restrictive nature of this form of liability was affirmed by the House of Lords in *Caparo Industries plc v Dickman*[39] in which case their Lordships stressed that the defendant's liability was limited to those whom he knew would receive the statement and would rely upon it for the purposes of a particular transaction. For that reason it was held that there was no liability in tort to purchasers of shares in the after market[40] because the prospectus had been issued in respect of the original purchase only.[41]

Caparo Industries plc v Dickman related to a claim brought by a claimant which had acquired shares in a target company, Fidelity plc, as part of a takeover. The claimant contended that it had relied on Fidelity's accounts for the accounting year 1983–84, which had been audited by the accountants Touche Ross and which showed a pre-tax profit of £1.3 million. After acquiring a controlling shareholding in the target company, the claimant discovered that the company's true financial position demonstrated a loss of £0.4 million. Consequently, the claimant sought to establish a breach of a duty of care in negligence on the part of the accountants when acting as the auditors of the company. The claimant argued that, as a person intending to acquire a controlling shareholding in the company, the accountants owed it a duty of care when auditing the company's accounts. Lord Bridge held that "[i]f a duty of care were owed so widely, it is difficult to see any reason why it should not equally extend to all who rely on the accounts in relating to other dealings with a company as lenders or merchants extending credit to the company".[42] Therefore, it was held that on policy grounds a general duty of care ought not to be imposed on auditors in such situations.[43]

As to the circumstances in which there may be liability for misstatements when making offers to the public, Lord Bridge suggested that general statements as to the condition of company would generally be unlikely to attract liability in tort on the basis that:

> "The situation is entirely different where a statement is put into more or less general circulation and may foreseeably be relied on by strangers to the maker of the

---

[38] See now *Caparo v Dickman* [1990] 2 A.C. 605 at 638, *per* Lord Oliver reiterating this principle. See also Lord Bridge at 620–21 and Lord Jauncey at 659–60 (especially at 660E "the fundamental question of the purpose"). Also see *James MccNaughton Papers Group Ltd v Hicks Anderson & Co. (a firm)* [1991] 1 All E.R. 135 But *cf: Morgan Crucible Co. plc v Hill Samuel Bank Ltd* [1991] 1 All E.R. 148.

[39] [1990] 1 A.C. 605, HL.

[40] That is, purchasers of the securities who were not original subscribers for the shares but who acquired them subsequently in the open market.

[41] *Al-Nakib Investments (Jersey) Ltd v Longcroft* [1991] B.C.L.C. 7. See also *Morgan Crucible Co. v Hill Samuel Bank Ltd* [1991] B.C.L.C. 178.

[42] [1990] 2 A.C. 605.

[43] Approving *Al Saudi Banque v Clark Pixley* [1990] Ch. 313.

statement for any one of a variety of different purposes which the maker of the statement has no specific reason to anticipate."[44]

Therefore, his lordship's view was that statements put into general circulation would be less likely to attract liability in tort because the maker of that statement could not ordinarily know the purposes to which his statement would be put to use by the claimant. On the facts of *Caparo Industries plc v Dickman* it was recognised that an auditor's role is primarily to verify for the benefit of shareholders that the accounts constitute a true and fair view of the financial position of the company. It was therefore held that an auditor cannot also be said to be liable for the reliance which a person, even if a current shareholder, might choose to put on that auditor's report in deciding whether or not to acquire a controlling stake in the company.

Similarly, in *Al-Nakib Investments (Jersey) Ltd v Longcroft*[45] the claimants, who had acquired shares in the after-market, alleged that the prospectus and two interim reports issued by M Ltd contained misrepresentations as to the identity of the person who would be manufacturing the company's products. The defendants successfully applied to have these claims struck out, in so far as they related to purchases of the company's securities in the after-market, on the basis that they disclosed no reasonable cause of action. As to the prospectus, it was held by Mervyn Davies J. that it had been issued for a particular purpose, namely to encourage subscription for shares by a limited class of subscribers and that any duty of care in relation to its issue was directed to that specific purpose only. It had not been directed at purchases in the after-market and therefore any misrepresentation therein could not found a claim based on the tort of negligence.[46]

There are, however, two cases which have taken a different approach on the facts in front of them from the cases considered above. First, in *Morgan Crucible Co plc v Hill Samuel Bank Ltd*,[47] the directors and financial advisors of the target company had made express representations in the course of a contested takeover forecasting a 38 per cent increase in pre-tax profits at a time when an identified bidder for the company had emerged. The purpose behind these and other representations had been to induce the bidder to make a higher bid because the bidder had relied on those statements. The Court of Appeal held that there was therefore a relationship of sufficient proximity between the bidder and those who had been responsible for the statements to found a duty of care in negligence.

Secondly, in *Possfund Custodian Trustee Ltd v Diamond*[48] there had been a placement of shares on the Unlisted Securities Market[49] and subsequent pur-

---

[44] [1990] 2 A.C. 605, [1990] 1 All E.R. 568, 576. Approving *Scott Group v Macfarlane* [1978] 1 N.Z.L.R. 553, 566, *per* Richmond P.

[45] [1990] 3 All E.R. 321.

[46] Reliance was placed on *Peek v Gurney* (1873) L.R. 6 H.L. 377 in which similar conclusion was reached. In this regard, Mervyn Davies J relied, *inter alia*, on dicta of Lord Jauncey in *Caparo Industries plc v Dickman* [1990] 2 A.C. 605, [1990] 1 All E.R. 568, 607. His lordship also placed reliance on dicta of Lord Griffiths in *Smith v Eric S. Bush* [1989] 2 All E.R. 514, 536, to similar effect.

[47] [1991] 1 All E.R. 148.

[48] [1996] 2 All E.R. 774.

[49] The forerunner of the Alternative Investment Market.

chases of those shares after the placement in the after-market. The prospectus prepared in relation to the initial placement greatly understated the issuer's liabilities to pay extra premiums to syndicates at Lloyds. The company subsequently went into receivership due, in no small measure, to the burden of paying those extra premiums. Purchasers of those shares in the after-market contended that they had relied on those statements made in the prospectus, that it had been reasonable for them to rely on the prospectus in that way in making their purchases, and that those responsible for the prospectus had breached a duty of care owed to purchasers of the shares. Lightman J. held that the purpose of a prospectus at common law and under statute in English law had always been[50]:

". . . to provide the necessary information to enable an investor to make an informed decision whether to accept the offer thereby made to take share on the proposed allotment, but not a decision whether to make after-market purchases."

Lightman J. refused to strike out this claim on the basis that in these circumstances the investors had been justified in relying on the statements made in the prospectus when making their investment decisions. It was held that such a duty of care would exist if the subsequent purchaser could show the following things: that he relied reasonably on the prospectus; that he reasonably believed that the defendant intended him to act on them; and that there was a sufficiently direct connection between the parties to make such a duty fair, just and reasonable.

Fraudulent misrepresentation

The basis of the liability for fraudulent misrepresentation

Fraud is difficult to prove. Nevertheless, promoters, directors, experts or the persons making an offer for sale, are liable for fraud if it can be shown that they signed, or authorised the issue of, a prospectus containing a false statement which they did not honestly believe to be true[51] with the intention that another person should act upon it, and that he acted on it to his detriment. The test is subjective, *i.e.* did they honestly believe the statement to be true according to its meaning as understood *by them*, albeit erroneously, when it was made.[52] If they cannot be proved to have made a false representation knowingly, or without belief in its truth, or recklessly, careless whether it be true or false, they may have to pay compensation under the statutory provisions, above, the predecessor of which[53] was first enacted as a result of the decision in *Derry v Peek*.[54]

The case of *Derry v Peek* itself concerned a company which asserted in its prospectus that the company had the right to operate trams by steam power rather than by horses, whereas in fact it was only able to use steam power if the

---

[50] [1996] 2 All E.R. 774, 787.
[51] *per* Lord Herschell in *Derry v Peek* (1889) 14 App. Cas. 337 at p.374.
[52] *Akerhielm v De Mare* [1959] A.C. 789, PC.
[53] Directors' Liability Act 1890.
[54] (1889) 14 App. Cas. 337. See also *Lees v Tod* (1882) 9 R. 807; *Boyd & Forrest v Glasgow etc. Ry. Co.*, 1912 S.C. HL 93.

Board of Trade authorised it so to do. In the event, the Board of Trade refused its permission. The plaintiff shareholder brought an action for fraud against the directors on the basis that the statement in the prospectus had formed the basis of the contract for purchase of the shares. It was held that the directors were not liable for fraud because they had made the statement in the prospectus to the effect that the company could use steam power in the honest belief that it was true.

The measure of damages for fraudulent misrepresentation

The measure of damages for fraud is *prima facie* the difference between the actual value of the shares at the time of allotment and the sum paid for them.[55] The plaintiff is entitled to recover all the actual damage directly flowing from the fraudulent misrepresentation.[56] This principle means that in some cases the value as at the date of allotment will not be applied, *e.g.* where the plaintiff is locked into the shares by reason of the fraud.[57] It is not an action for breach of contract, however, and therefore no damages in respect of prospective gains can be recovered, merely the out-of-pocket loss.

The House of Lords in *Smith New Court Securities Ltd v Scrimgeour Vickers (Asset Management) Ltd*[58] was required to consider the measure of damages available for fraudulent misrepresentation, and particularly the extent to which the size of the loss suffered by the claimant had been foreseeable. In that case there had been two entirely unrelated frauds. The first fraud related to deliberately misleading information given to the claimant by the defendant concerning the number of bids already acquired for those shares. The second fraud was unrelated to the first, although the discovery of the second fraud brought the first fraud to light. The value of the shares had fallen sharply on the discovery of the second fraud. The question arose whether the quantum of damages should reflect the value after the discovery of the second fraud or irrespective of that fraud. Lord Browne-Wilkinson set out seven principles which are to inform decisions in this area[59]:

"(1) The defendant is bound to make reparation for all the damage directly flowing from the transaction.

(2) Although such damage need not have been foreseeable, it must have been directly caused by the transaction.

(3) In assessing such damage, the plaintiff is entitled to recover by way of damages the full price paid by him, but he must give credit for any benefits which he has received as a result of the transaction.

(4) As a general rule, the benefits received by him include the market value of the property acquired as at the date of acquisition; but such general

---

[55] *McConnel v Wright* (1903) 1 Ch. 546, CA; *Davidson v Tulloch* (1860) 3 Macq. 783; 22 D. HL 7.

[56] *Doyle v Olby (Ironmongers) Ltd* [1969] 2 Q.B. 158, CA.

[57] *Smith New Court Securities Ltd v Scrimgeour Vickers (Asset Management) Ltd* [1997] 1 B.C.L.C. 350, HL.

[58] [1996] 4 All E.R. 769.

[59] *per* Lord Browne-Wilkinson in [1996] 4 All E.R. 769, 778–779.

rule is not to be inflexibly applied where to do so would prevent him obtaining full compensation for the wrong suffered.

(5) Although the circumstances in which the general rule should not apply cannot be comprehensively stated, it will normally not apply where either (a) the misrepresentation has continued to operate after the date of the acquisition of the asset so as to induce the plaintiff to retain the asset or (b) the circumstances of the case are such that the plaintiff is, by reason of the fraud, locked into the property.

(6) In addition, the plaintiff is entitled to recover consequential losses caused by the transaction.

(7) The plaintiff must take all reasonable steps to mitigate his loss once he has discovered the fraud."

It was held that, while there was a duty on the claimant to mitigate his loss, where the investments had been acquired in this case as part of a long-term investment strategy there was no obligation on the claimant to sell the shares immediately where that would not have been a sensible strategy because of the low price which could have been acquired for those shares after the second fraud had been discovered. In any event, the claimant is entitled to recover the difference between the price at which the shares were acquired and the real value of those shares. Therefore, the claimant was entitled to recover the loss suffered even though the added loss caused by the discovery of the second fraud had not been foreseeable.

Rescission on grounds of misrepresentation

In order to obtain rescission of a contract of allotment of shares on the ground that it was induced by misrepresentation, the allottee must prove, first, a material false statement of fact which, secondly, induced him to subscribe.

Material false statement of fact

It is not sufficient to claim rescission of a contract of allotment to demonstrate that there was some mistake made in the listing particulars or in some other statement. First, then, the statement must have been an assertion of a fact and not merely a statement of opinion.[60] Therefore, a statement that the property of the company is worth a certain sum of money, or that the profits are expected to reach a certain figure, is only opinion and gives no right to rescission, except where it can be proved that the maker of the statement did not hold the opinion. Statements, on the other hand, such as "the surplus assets, as appear by the last balance sheet, amount to upwards of £10,000"[61] and that certain persons have agreed to be directors,[62] are all assertions of fact and, if false, will give rise to a

---

[60] *Liverpool Palace of Varieties Ltd v Miller* (1896) 4 S.L.T. 153(O.H.).
[61] *Re London and Staffordshire Fire Insurance Co.* (1883) 25 Ch.D. 149.
[62] *Re Scottish Petroleum Co.* (1883) 23 Ch.D. 413, CA; *Blakiston v London and Scottish Banking etc. Corpn. Ltd* (1894) 21 R. 417; contract *Chambers v Edinburgh etc. Aerated Bread Co. Ltd* (1891) 18 R. 1039.

right to rescission. The second requirement is that the statement be material to the investor's decision to investment and not a statement as to a peripheral matter. On the authorities it has been held that a representation in a prospectus to the effect that the members of the company were comprised of "a large number of gentlemen in the trade and others", when only a dozen out of a total membership of 55 were in fact in the trade, was not a material misrepresentation.[63] Statements as to the company's assets or the condition of its accounts would be material representations.[64]

Where the facts are not equally well known to both sides, a statement of opinion by one who should know the facts often implies a statement of fact, *i.e.* that there are reasonable grounds for his opinion, and if it can be proved that he could not as a reasonable man honestly have had the opinion, there is misrepresentation of fact.[65] Again, a statement of intention does not amount to a representation of fact unless it can be proved that the alleged intention never existed.[66]

If a prospectus refers to a report which contains inaccurate statements of fact, the contract can be rescinded if the company has vouched for the accuracy of the report, but otherwise it cannot. Thus, if the company employs an accountant to go through the books and make a report, and then sets out the report in a prospectus, it will not be liable for an inaccuracy in the report.[67] But if the company makes statements of its own, although they are expressed to be based upon a report, it will be liable for an inaccuracy unless in clear and unambiguous terms it has warned intending applicants that it does not vouch for the accuracy of the report, or of any statement based on it. So, in *Re Pacaya Rubber and Produce Co. Ltd*[68] the prospectus contained extracts from a report of a Peruvian expert as to the condition of rubber estate which the company sought to acquire. It was held that these extracts from the report contained in the prospectus formed the basis of the contract. On the basis that the company had not distanced itself from the report nor suggested that it did not vouch for the accuracy of the report, the company was taken to have contracted on the basis of the contents of the report. Therefore, the contracts of allotment could be rescinded.

Non-disclosure of a material fact amounts to misrepresentation if the omission renders that which is stated misleading. It has been said[69] that "[i]t is not that the omission of material facts is an independent ground for rescission, but the omission must be of such a nature as to make the statement actually made misleading."[70]

The allottee must have been induced to subscribe by the false statement

Whether or not an allottee was induced to subscribe by reason of the misrepresentation is a question of fact depending on the circumstances of each case. It is

---

[63] *City of Edinburgh Brewery Co. Ltd v Gibson's Trustee* (1869) 7 M. 886.
[64] *Re London and Staffordshire Fire Insurance Co.* (1883) 25 Ch.D. 149.
[65] per Bowen L.J. in *Smith v Land, etc., Corpn.* (1884) 28 Ch.D. 7, CA at p.15.
[66] *Edgington v Fitzmaurice* (1885) 29 Ch.D. 459, CA.
[67] *Bentley & Co. v Black* (1893) 9 T.L.R. 580, CA.
[68] [1914] 1 Ch. 542. See also *Mair v Rio Grande Rubber Estates Ltd* (1913) S.C. HL 74.
[69] per Rigby L.J. in *McKeown v Boudard Peveril Gear Co. Ltd* (1896) 74 L.T. 712 at p.713.
[70] *Coles v White City (Manchester) Greyhound Assn. Ltd* (1929) 48 T.L.R. 230, CA.

not sufficient that the prospectus has been widely advertised in the locality if there is proof that the applicant relied, not on the prospectus, but on independent advice.[71] He is entitled to rely upon the prospectus, however, and is not bound to verify the statements it contains. Where, therefore, a prospectus simply gave information as to the dates of and parties to contracts, and stated where they could be inspected, without indicating that they were material contracts, the omission of the applicant to inspect them did not fix him with notice of their contents.[72] The false statement need not have been the decisive inducing cause of the contract. It is enough that it was one of the contributory causes.[73] Rescission enables the allottee to recover what he paid for the shares or debentures, plus interest.

Loss of the right to rescind

The right to rescind is lost:

(1) if, after discovering the misrepresentation, the allottee does an act which shows that he elects to retain the shares and so affirms the contract (for example, if he attends and votes at general meetings)[74];

(2) if he fails to act within a reasonable time of discovering the true facts. The right to rescind must be exercised promptly if the company is a going concern, and even a delay of a fortnight has been held to be too long in such a case[75];

(3) if restitution is impossible,[76] *e.g.* because he sells the shares; or

(4) if the company goes into liquidation.[77]

DIRECT INVITATIONS, OFFERS FOR SALE, PLACINGS

Shares or debentures may be offered to the public by means of:

(1) a direct invitation to the public; or

(2) an offer for sale; or

(3) a "placing".

Offers for sale

An offer for sale is the usual way in which shares or debentures are offered to the public. It occurs when an issuing house (either a specialised concern or a

---

[71] *M'Morland's Trustees v Fraser* (1896) 24 R. 65.
[72] *Aaron's Reefs Ltd v Twiss* [1896] A.C. 273.
[73] *Edgington v Fitzmaurice* (1885) 29 Ch.D. 459, CA.
[74] *Sharpley v South and East Coast Ry. Co.* (1876) 2 Ch.D. 663, CA.
[75] See *Re Scottish Petroleum Co.* (1883) 23 Ch.D. 413, CA.
[76] *Western Bank v Addie* (1867) 5 M. HL 80.
[77] *Oakes v Turquand* (1867) L.R. 2 HL 325; *Western Bank v Addie* (1867) 5 M. HL 80; *Houldsworth v City of Glasgow Bank* (1880) 7 R. HL 53; (1880) 5 App Cas 317.

department of a merchant bank) subscribes for an issue of shares or debentures and then invites the public to purchase from it at a higher price.

Where it is difficult to fix the issue price of the shares or debentures being offered to the public, because it is uncertain what the public response to the offer will be, an offer for sale by tender may be made. In this event, a minimum price is fixed and the issue price is determined by the prices tendered in the applications. Thus, where 250,000,000 ordinary 25p shares are offered, a minimum price of 80p a share may be fixed. The prices tendered may range from 80p to £2 and the shares may all be sold at 87p. The object is to ensure that the company receives what the shares are worth to the public, and to defeat stags who, by taking shares and then immediately selling them at a higher price, would otherwise receive the difference between the issue price of a share and its worth to the public.

Placings

An issue of shares or debentures may be placed in one of two ways. An issuing house may subscribe for the issue and then invite its clients (*e.g.* insurance companies and pension funds) to purchase from it at a higher price.

Alternatively, an issuing house or stockbrokers or a bank may, without subscribing, act as agents for the company or issuing house and invite their clients to take from the company. In this case the agents will be paid a commission called "brokerage" for their services.

COMMISSIONS AND DISCOUNTS

In order to procure capital a company frequently desires to pay a commission or discount to a person introducing capital.

Section 97(1) of the Companies Act 1985 allows a company to pay a commission to a person in consideration of his subscribing or agreeing to subscribe, absolutely or conditionally, or procuring or agreeing to procure subscriptions, for *shares* in the company if:

(1) the payment is authorised by the articles (authority in the memorandum is insufficient[78]);

(2) the commission does not exceed either (a) any limit imposed by such rules or, if there are no such limits, 10 per cent. of the price at which the shares are issued, or (b) the amount or rate authorised by the articles, whichever is the less.

This subsection applies as well to private as to public companies.[79] It enables a company to pay underwriting commission or brokerage, which commissions are dealt with below.

Section 98 of the 1985 Act provides that, except as allowed by s.97, no company shall apply any of its shares or capital money, either directly or

---

[78] *Re Republic of Bolivia Exploration Syndicate Ltd* [1914] 1 Ch. 139.
[79] *Dominion of Canada General Trading Syndicate v Brigstocke* [1911] 2. K.B. 648.

indirectly, in payment of any commission, discount or allowance to any person in consideration of his subscribing or agreeing to subscribe, whether absolutely or conditionally, or procuring or agreeing to procure subscriptions, absolute or conditional, for any *shares* in the company.

Underwriting

Before an issue of shares is made to the public, it is usual to insure the success of the issue by having it underwritten. Underwriting means "agreeing to take so many shares, more or less in number, as are specified in the underwriting letter if the public do not subscribe for them."[80] Another definition is, an agreement "to take up by way of subscription in a new company or new issue a certain number of shares if and so far as not applied for by the public.[81] An underwriter does not guarantee that the public will take up the shares; he agrees with the company to subscribe for them himself on the happening of an event, *i.e.* the failure of the public to subscribe them fully. The underwriter may be, for example, a broker, a bank or an issuing house.

The consideration for underwriting usually takes the form of an underwriting commission which the underwriter receives whether or not the public take up all the shares underwritten. The commission may be in the form of shares or it may be a payment out of the money derived from the issue of shares underwritten. Again, it is thought that it may be a payment out of the company's profits, if the company has profits in hand and they have not been capitalised. In any case, s.97 of the 1985 Act, above, must be complied with.

Brokerage

Brokerage is a payment made to an issuing house or brokers in return for their placing shares or debentures without subscribing.[82] It differs from underwriting commission in that it is a payment made to a person for placing shares or debentures without involving him in any risk of having to take them. Section 98(3) of the Companies Act 1985 provides that nothing in the section affects the power of any company to pay such brokerage as was previously lawful. It was previously held in *Metropolitan Coal Consumers' Association v Scrimgeour*[83] that brokerage of a reasonable amount payable in the ordinary course of business was legal.

A payment is brokerage only if it is paid to "stockbrokers, bankers and the like, who exhibit prospectuses and send them to their customers, and by whose mediation the customers are induced to subscribe."[84]

---

[80] *per* Lindley L.J. in *Re Licensed Victuallers' Mutual Trading Association* (1889) 42 Ch.D. 1, CA, at p. 7.
[81] *per* Lord Tomlin in *Australian Investment Trust Ltd v Strand and Pitt Street Properties Ltd* [1932] A.C. 735, PC at p.745.
[82] *Re Olympic etc. Reinsurance Co. Ltd* [1920] 2 Ch. 341, CA; *cf. Premier Briquette Co. Ltd v Gray*, 1922 S.C. 329.
[83] [1885] 2 Q.B. 604, CA.
[84] *per* Bailhache J. in *Andreae v Zinc Mines of Great Britain Ltd* [1918] 2 K.B. 454, at p.458.

Chapter 8

ALLOTMENT AND COMMENCEMENT OF BUSINESS

THIS chapter deals first with the powers of the directors and the company to allot shares, then with the contract of allotment under which shares are allotted by a company to a person who has applied for them, certain statutory restrictions on allotment by a public company, and the return which the company usually must deliver to the Registrar after it has allotted shares. Finally, the chapter deals with certain statutory restrictions on the commencement of business by a public company.

Authority to allot shares

Prior to the 1980 Act, directors generally had the power to allot shares up to the limit of the authorised capital.[1] This led to several abuses by directors allotting shares to their allies in order to forestall takeover bids.[2] Under what is now s.80 of the 1985 Act, however, the directors of any company may not allot shares, or any right to acquire shares, without express authority being given either in the articles or by a resolution in general meeting.

Such authority may be given for a specific allotment or generally and must state the maximum amount of the shares which may be issued. Even if the authority is given by the articles it cannot last for more than five years, and, in any case, it can be varied, revoked or renewed by an ordinary resolution. Thus the articles may actually be altered, on this one occasion, by an ordinary resolution.[3] A copy of any resolution either conferring, revoking, varying or renewing the authority must, however, be registered with the Registrar as if it were a special resolution, under s.380,[4] and notice of it must be put in the appropriate Gazette under s.711.[5]

A private company may by elective resolution[6] decide that s.80A shall apply. In such a case the directors can be given either an indefinite authority to allot shares or one for any fixed period, rather than for the five year maximum period. The only restrictions are that the authority must state the maximum amount of shares which may be allotted under it and, if it is for a fixed period, the date on which it is to expire. Such authority may still be varied or revoked by an ordinary resolution. If the election itself is revoked (by an ordinary resolution) then the

---

[1] Above, p.69.
[2] See, *e.g. Hogg v Cramphorn* [1967] Ch. 254; *Bamford v Bamford* [1970] Ch. 212; below, p.300.
[3] *cf.* s.9; above, p.76.
[4] Below, p.261.
[5] Above, p.72.
[6] Elective resolutions must be unanimous. See p.260, below.

authority under s.80A will be construed as one for five years only. Thus for example if it has been in existence for six years it will cease immediately. The Company Law Review recommended that s.80 should no longer apply to private companies having only one class of shares.[7]

Nothing in s.80 affects the validity of any allotment, but any director who knowingly and wilfully contravenes it may be prosecuted and fined. It has no application to employee share schemes.

Pre-emption rights

The 1980 Act introduced further restrictions on the allotment of ordinary, "equity", shares by companies for cash other than those subject to employee share schemes. This basic restriction is, however, subject to wide exemptions.

Under s.89 of the 1985 Act, ordinary shares issued for cash[8] must first be offered to existing,[9] ordinary shareholders in proportion to the nominal value of their existing holdings. The articles may go further and provide for such pre-emption rights to apply with each class of ordinary shares. Such rights are not given by the Act to the holders of preference shares or shares to be paid for, in whole or in part, otherwise than by cash. Any offer must be open for 21 days.[10] Any shares not taken up on the *pro rata* basis must then be offered to the ordinary shareholders generally. Any contravention of the statutory or other pre-emption rights renders the company and any officer in default liable to compensate any existing shareholders who have suffered a loss as a result.

Private companies may exclude the effects of s.89[11] by a provision to that effect in their articles: s.91. Such exclusions must be clear, however, and where the articles can be read consistently with the sections, the latter will apply.[12] In addition, both public and private companies may qualify or exclude pre-emption rights if their directors have the authority to issue shares under s.80.[13] If the directors have a general authority to allot shares under that section, the company, either by its articles, or by a special resolution, may vary or exclude s.89 altogether. On the other hand, if the directors only have authority to make a specific allotment, s.89 can only be modified or excluded by a special resolution recommended by the directors and supported by a circular sent out with the notices of the meeting, setting out the directors' reasons for making the recommendation, the amount to be paid to the company on the allotment, and the directors' justification for that amount. Directors who issue a misleading, false or deceptive circular in support of such a resolution may be convicted and fined or imprisoned. The exclusion or modification of pre-emption rights in this way may be renewed or revoked by a special resolution: s.95.[14]

---

[7] Final report, Vol 1 (2001) para.4.5.
[8] Including the re-sale of treasury shares, see p.167, below.
[9] Including those who held shares 28 days before the offer was made, but excluding any shares held by the company in treasury: see p.167, below.
[10] s.90.
[11] Both on issues for cash and the re-sale of treasury shares.
[12] *Re Thundercrest Ltd* [1995] 1 B.C.L.C. 117.
[13] Above, Ch.7.
[14] This procedure is modified by Sch.15A, para.3 if the written resolution procedure is used by a private company (see below, p.233). The circular must be sent to each member prior to his signature. The Company Law Review suggested no changes to the pre-emption regime: Final Report, Vol 1 (2001) para.3.160.

AGREEMENT FOR ALLOTMENT

The ordinary law of contract, which usually requires an offer and an acceptance if there is to be an agreement, applies to agreements to take shares in a company. An offer is made by the applicant in sending a form of application for shares to the company or issuing house and it is accepted by the allotment of shares to the applicant.

As provided for in s.80, the power to allot shares is normally vested in the board of directors. Shares will be allotted when the board passes the appropriate resolution. They will not actually be issued, however, until they are entered into the register of members.[15]

An acceptance must be unconditional[16] and correspond with the terms of the offer. If, therefore, the application was for 100 shares and only 25 were allotted, the allotment would be a counter-offer and the applicant could refuse to take any shares. An issue may be over-subscribed, and the company unable to make an allotment in full to every applicant. In order to obviate these difficulties the form of the application usually runs, "I agree to accept such shares or any smaller number that may be allotted to me."

To constitute a binding contract, an acceptance must be communicated to the offeror.[17] If the parties must have contemplated that the post might be used to communicate acceptance, the posting of a letter of allotment is sufficient communication to the applicant.

> G applied for shares in the H company. A letter of allotment was posted, but never reached G. *Held*, G was a shareholder in the company: *Household Fire Insurance Co. v Grant* (1879) 4 Ex.D. 216, CA.[18]

Communication, however, may be made in any way which shows the applicant that the company has accepted his offer,[19] *e.g.* by a letter demanding payment of an instalment on the shares,[20] or by receipt of a notice calling a general meeting and notification given orally by the secretary that shares have been allotted.[21] The applicant must, however, have *agreed* to take shares and not merely have expressed a "willingness" to take them.[22] The sending to a person who has not so agreed of notices of meetings and of letters making calls on the shares does not of itself make the recipient a shareholder.[23]

An offer can be revoked at any time before acceptance is communicated.

> H applied for shares in a company. Shares were allotted to him, and the letter of allotment sent to the *company's* agent to deliver by hand to H. Before the letter was

---

[15] *National Westminster Bank plc v I.R.C.* [1994] 2 B.C.L.C. 239, HL.
[16] *Liquidator of the Consolidated Copper Co. etc. Ltd v Peddie* (1877) 5 R. 393.
[17] See *Entores Ltd v Miles Far East Corporation* [1955] 2 Q.B. 327, CA.
[18] Doubted in Scotland: *Mason v Benhar Coal Co. Ltd* (1882) 9 R. 883, *per* Lord Shand at p.890.
[19] *Chapman v Sulphite Pulp Co. Ltd* (1892) 19 R. 837.
[20] *Forget v Cement Products Co. of Canada* [1916] W.N. 259, PC.
[21] *Chapman v Sulphite Pulp Co. Ltd* (1892) 19 R. 837; see also *Curror's Trustee v Caledonian Heritable Security Co. Ltd* (1880) 7 R. 479 and *Nelson v Fraser* (1906) 14 S.L.T. 513 (O.H.).
[22] *Mason v Benhar Coal Co. Ltd* (1882) 9 R. 883.
[23] *Goldie v Torrance* (1882) 10 R. 174; and see *Liquidator of the Florida etc. Co. Ltd v Bayley* (1890) 17 R. 525.

delivered H withdrew his application. *Held,* H was not a shareholder in the company: *Re National Savings Bank Association* (1867) L.R. 4 Eq. 9.

To be effective, revocation of an offer must be communicated to the offeree. Thus notice of the revocation of an application must reach the company before the letter of allotment is posted.[24] If the revocation is communicated by post, it is not effective until the letter is received by the company.

An offer lapses if it is not accepted within the time prescribed or, if none is prescribed, within a reasonable time. Thus an allotment must be made within a reasonable time after the application, otherwise the application will lapse and the applicant will be entitled to refuse to take the shares.

On June 8 M offered to take shares in the R company. He heard nothing until November 23, when he received a letter of acceptance. M refused to take the shares, *Held,* M was entitled to refuse, as his offer had lapsed: *Ramsgate Victoria Hotel Co. Ltd v Montefiore* (1866) L.R. 1 Ex. 109.

An offer is also terminated by the failure of a condition subject to which it was made. Thus if an application for shares is conditional, *e.g.* on the applicant having a contract to supply goods to the company,[25] or on all capital being subscribed,[26] and the condition is not fulfilled when shares are allotted to him, the applicant is under no liability to take the shares.

A conditional application must be distinguished from an application for shares coupled with a collateral agreement, *e.g.* where £10 shares are to be paid up to the extent of £1.50 in cash on allotment, that the balance is to be set-off against goods to be supplied to the company by the allottee. In the latter case, when shares are allotted the applicant becomes a shareholder with the right merely of suing the company on the collateral agreement.[27]

RESTRICTIONS ON ALLOTMENT

Sections 84, 85, and 101 contain restrictions on allotment by *public* companies. s.84 provides that no allotment can be made unless either the capital is subscribed for in full or the offer states that if it is not so subscribed the allotment will nevertheless take place subject to any specified conditions.

If any of the above conditions are not satisfied within 40 days of the first issue of the prospectus, all money received must be forthwith returned to the applicants without interest. If it is not returned within 48 days of the issue of the prospectus, the directors are jointly and severally liable to repay it with interest at five per cent. per annum. A director is not liable, however, if he proves that the default in repayment was not due to any misconduct or negligence on his part.

No allotment unless minimum payment paid up

Under s.101 no share may be allotted unless one quarter of the nominal value and the whole of any premium on the share has been paid up. In breach the

---

[24] *Byrne v Van Tienhoven* (1880) 5 C.P.D. 344; *Thomson v James* (1855) 18 D. 1.
[25] *Shackelford's Case* (1866) L.R. 1 Ch.App. 567.
[26] *Swedish Match Co. Ltd v Seivwright* (1889) 16 R. 989.
[27] *Elkington's Case* (1867) L.R. 2 Ch.App. 511; *cf. Liquidator of the Pelican etc. Insurance Co. Ltd v Bruce* (1904) 11 S.L.T. 658 (O.H.), and see opinions in *National House etc. Investment Co. Ltd v Watson,* 1908 S.C. 88.

share will be regarded as having been so paid up but the allottee and any subsequent holder will be liable to pay that amount together with interest. A bona fide purchaser without actual notice of the breach is not liable nor any successor to such a person. In addition the court may grant relief under s.113.[28] Contravention by the company and any officer in default is a criminal offence: s.114.

Effect of irregular allotment

When an allotment is made which does not satisfy the provisions of s.84, above, s.85 gives the applicant two remedies, one against the company and the other against the directors.

As against the *company*, the allotment is *voidable* by the allottee within one month after allotment, even if the company is being wound up. Legal proceedings need not be taken within a month. Notice of avoidance within the month, followed by prompt legal proceedings after the month, is sufficient.[29]

As against the *directors*, the allottee can sue such of them as have knowingly contravened or authorised the contravention of the provisions for any loss, damages or costs he may have sustained or incurred thereby. Any such proceedings against directors must be brought within two years after allotment. The company has a similar remedy against the directors for any loss, damages or costs sustained or incurred by it.

RETURN AS TO ALLOTMENTS

Section 88 provides that whenever a limited company with a share capital makes any allotment of its *shares*, it must, within a month, deliver to the Registrar—

(1) A return of the allotments, stating the number and nominal amount of the shares, the names, addresses and descriptions of the allottees and the amount paid or payable on each share, whether on account of the nominal value of the share or by way of premium.

(2) In the case of shares allotted *otherwise than for cash*, a contract constituting the title of the allottee to the allotment, together with any contract of sale or for services or other consideration for the allotment, and a return stating the number and nominal amount of shares so allotted, the extent to which they are to be treated as paid up, and the consideration for the allotment.

RESTRICTIONS ON COMMENCEMENT OF BUSINESS

A private company can commence business, exercise any borrowing power[30] which it has and make binding contracts immediately on incorporation.

---

[28] See generally Ch.9, below.
[29] *Re National Motor Mail-Coach Co. Ltd* [1908] 2 Ch. 228.
[30] Below, Ch.23.

By s.117, a public company must do none of these things until it has either obtained a certificate from the Registrar that it may do so or is re-registered as a private company.

To obtain a certificate under this section, the company must make a declaration to the Registrar in the prescribed form[31] signed by a director or secretary of the company:

(1) Stating that the nominal value of the company's *allotted* share capital is not less than the authorised minimum (£50,000)[32];

(2) Disclosing the amount of such allotted share capital actually paid up at that time (at least 25 per cent of the nominal value and the whole of any premium is necessary)[33];

(3) Stating the amount, or estimated amount, of the preliminary expenses of the company and the persons by whom any of those expenses have been paid or are payable; and

(4) Detailing any amount or benefit paid or given or intended to be paid or given to any promoter of the company, and the consideration for the payment or benefit.

This declaration may be accepted by the Registrar as sufficient evidence of the matters stated therein.

If the Registrar issues a certificate under this section, it is conclusive evidence that the company is entitled to do business and exercise any borrowing powers.

If a public company enters into a transaction without a certificate under s.117, the transaction remains valid, but if the company fails to comply with any obligations under it within 21 days of being called upon to do so, the directors are liable to indemnify the other party for any loss suffered as a result. In addition, the company and any officer in default will be guilty of a criminal offence.

Finally, if more than a year after the incorporation of a public company it has not been issued with a s.117 certificate, the Secretary of State may petition the court for the company to be wound up under s.122 of the Insolvency Act 1986.[34]

---

[31] Or by way of an electronic communication as defined in s.15 of the Electronic Communications Act 2000.

[32] s.118.

[33] s.101.

[34] Below, Ch.27.

Chapter 9

SHARE CAPITAL

THE topics dealt with in this chapter are the rules that a company's share or equity capital must be raised and, once raised, must be maintained for the benefit of creditors, and the consequent need to control the reduction of share capital. These rules, long established, were amplified by the Second EC Directive. The current trend, however, is to regard them as antiquated, and that they should be replaced by solvency and liquidity criteria (see end of the chapter).

MEANING OF "CAPITAL"

The word "capital" used in connection with a company has several different meanings, thus it may mean the nominal or authorised share capital, the issued or allotted share capital, the paid-up share capital or the reserve share capital of the company.

The *nominal* or *authorised capital* is merely the amount of share capital which the company is authorised to issue, not what it has actually issued. As we have seen,[1] in the case of a limited company the amount of potential share capital with which it proposes to be registered, and the division thereof into shares of a fixed amount (the nominal amount), must be set out in the memorandum of association, but this amount may be increased or reduced as explained later.[2] Companies may fix on any figure, which is large enough for its potential requirements. In earlier times, stamp duty was payable on this figure which had the effect of keeping it as low as possible, but that no longer applies. It must be remembered that public companies must have at least £50,000 authorised capital: ss 11 and 118.

The *issued* or *allotted capital* is that part of the company's nominal capital which has been issued or allotted to the shareholders. The company is not bound to allot all its capital at once, although a public company must allot at least £50,000 nominal value of shares before it may commence business (s.117). Allotments of capital are made as they are needed by the directors, if properly authorised under the Act,[3] up to the amount allowed by the authorised capital figure. The restrictions and controls imposed by the Act relate in general to the *allotted* shares. In certain cases, such as taxation, it may be important to distinguish between the allotment and issue of shares. In *National Westminster Bank plc v I.R.C.*,[4] the House of Lords by a majority decided that a share is

---

[1] Above, p.69. The Company Law Review recommended that this requirement should be abolished: Final Report, Vol 1 para.10.6.
[2] Below, pp.147, 151.
[3] Above, Ch.7.
[4] [1994] 2 B.C.L.C. 239, HL.

allotted when the company and shareholder are contractually bound and it is only issued when the shareholder is registered as such on the register of members.[5]

The *paid-up capital* is that part of the issued capital which has been paid up by the shareholders. The company may, for example, have a nominal capital of £500,000 divided into 500,000 shares of a nominal amount of £1 each, of which £400,000 is issued, *i.e.* 400,000 of the shares have been issued, but only £100,000 has been paid up, *i.e.* the company has so far required only 25p. to be paid up on each share. The *uncalled capital* is the remainder of the issued capital and can be called up at any time by the company from the shareholders in accordance with the provisions of the articles. Section 101 requires public companies to call up at least one quarter of the nominal value of a share and all the premium on allotment. Uncalled capital is rare today.[6]

The paid-up share capital includes the nominal value of the shares paid-up and any premium on such shares.[7] For example, if 10,000 £1 shares are sold for £2 each the paid up capital will be £20,000. This will however be expressed as £10,000 share capital and £10,000 share premium account in the balance sheet. It has even been held that where the shareholders agree to increase a company's capital without any formal allocation of shares, that increase will be treated like a share premium and so subject to the capital maintenance rules.[8]

Section 351 provides that if, in the case of a company having a share capital, there is on the stationery used for any business letters, or on the order forms of the company, a reference to the amount of the share capital, the reference must be to paid-up share capital.

RAISING OF SHARE CAPITAL

The issued share capital of a company is the fund to which creditors of the company can look for payment of their debts, and so, to protect the creditors, it has been held that the issued share capital must actually be raised. This means that shares can be treated as paid up only to the extent of the amount actually received by the company in cash or in kind, and must not be issued at a discount, *i.e.* must not be issued as fully paid for a consideration less than payment or the promise of payment of the nominal amount of each share,[9] although the company may not necessarily require payment in full of the nominal amount on allotment. There is no objection to shares being issued at a premium, *i.e.* at more than the nominal value.[10] The rule that the share capital must be raised is intended to ensure that money or assets equal in amount or value to the paid-up capital on paper is or are received by the company.

In one particular case, no additional funds will be received by the company on an issue of shares. This is where a company makes an issues of *bonus shares*. This involves the capitalisation (*i.e.* the creation of issed share capital) of distributable

---

[5] Below, p.191.
[6] So too is the part of that uncalled capital designated a reserve capital under s.120. That was a fund only to be called up on a winding-up.
[7] *Post*, p.145.
[8] *Kellar v Williams* [2002] 2 B.C.L.C. 390 (PC).
[9] *Ooregum Gold Mining Co. v Roper* [1892] A.C. 125, codified by s.100, below, p.119.
[10] Below, p.145.

profits[11] and appropriating to each existing shareholder, out of the profits to be capitalised, what is needed in paying up in full the unissued shares which are to be allotted as bonus shares.[12] Thus the shareholders receive additional shares but the overall value of the company is unchanged; there are simply more shares reflecting that value, although distributable profits have become issued share capital. The issuing process has been described as being analogous to a contract.[13] Article 110 of Table A requires an ordinary resolution authorising the directors to issue bonus shares and there must be sufficient distributable profits.[14]

ISSUE OF SHARES AT A DISCOUNT

The general rule has always been that shares must *not* be issued at a discount, *i.e.* must not be issued as fully paid for a consideration less than the nominal amount.[15] This is now expressly stated in s.100. The shareholder must pay the full nominal value of his shares, whether he pays in cash or in kind, together with interest on the discount. Any subsequent holder of the shares may also be held liable for the discount unless he is a bona fide purchaser for value without actual notice of the discount issue or a subsequent transferee of the shares from such a person. The court may grant relief in appropriate circumstances under s.113. Contravention of s.100 is a criminal offence by the company and any officer in default (s.114). The general principle was first established in England by the House of Lords in 1892.

> The market value of the £1 ordinary shares of a company was 2s 6d. The company thereupon issued preference shares of £1 each with 15s. credited as paid, leaving a liability of only 5s. a share. A contract to this effect was registered under what is now s.52. *Held*, the issue was *ultra vires*, and allottees were liable to pay for the shares in full: *Ooregum Gold Mining Co. of India Ltd v Roper* [1892] A.C. 125.[16]
>
> "The dominant and cardinal principle of [the Companies] Acts is that the investor shall purchase immunity from liability beyond a certain limit on the terms that there shall be and remain a liability up to that limit": *per* Lord Macnaghten at p.145.

There is no issue at a discount where shares are issued at par, *e.g.* after the exercise of an option to take them up at par, even though they could otherwise be issued at a premium,[17] or where shares are issued at a lesser premium than that at which they might have been paid.[18]

---

[11] Which are not subject to the capital maintenance rules. See Ch.22, below. Bonus share can also be used to convert other capital funds, such as the share premium account, into issued shares. That will simply increase the number of shares but leave the overall amount of share capital unaffected.

[12] If this has not been done then the shareholders have no rights to the shares: *Topham v Charles Topham Group Ltd* [2003] 1 BCLC 123.

[13] *Re Cleveland Trust plc* [1991] BCLC 424.

[14] For the consequences of a defect in the procedure see *EIC Services Ltd v Phipps* [2004] BCC 814 CA. The error cannot be validated under s.35A since a shareholder is not a person dealing with a company: see p.94, above.

[15] The Company Law Review ultimately recommended that the nominal value of shares be retained, although the requirement, enshrined in the Second EC Directive, is under review by the EC Commission. *Final Report*, Vol 1, para.10.7.

[16] An earlier Scottish case to the same effect is *Klenck v East India Co. etc. Ltd* (1888) 16 R. 271, where the memorandum contained a power to issue shares at a discount.

[17] *Hilder v Dexter* [1902] A.C., below, p.145.

[18] *Cameron v Glenmorangie Distillery Co. Ltd* (1896) 23 R. 1092.

There is nothing to prevent debentures being issued at a discount. However, in the case of convertible debentures, *i.e.* those convertible into shares, if the debentures are issued at a discount, with a right to exchange them for fully paid shares equal in nominal amount to the par value of the debentures, the right has been held void as being a right to an issue of shares at a discount.[19] The right will be valid if it is a right to fully paid shares equal in nominal amount to the issue price of the debentures—the shares will not then be issued at a discount.

The general rule is subject to the following exceptions:

(1) There is in effect a discount when shares are issued by a private company for an overvalued non-monetary consideration, as in *Re Wragg Ltd*, below.[20]

(2) Similarly where, under s.97, above[21] commission is paid to a person who agrees to subscribe, or to procure subscriptions, for shares in a company.

CONSIDERATION FOR ALLOTMENT

The general rule is therefore that an allottee must pay for his shares in full. Under s.99(1) shares are only treated as paid up to the extent that the company has received money or money's worth (including goodwill and know-how) in return for them. Section 99(2) further prohibits a public company from accepting an undertaking by any person to do work or perform services in return for shares. Such an undertaking may nevertheless be enforced by the company (s.115), and the holder of shares issued in return for such undertaking becomes liable to pay any shortfall in the value for the shares (s.99(3)).

Any subsequent holder of shares not regarded as fully paid up as a result of a breach of s.99, may be liable for the amount due, unless he is either a bona fide purchaser of the shares without actual notice of the defect, or an immediate subsequent transferee from such a person (s.112). The court may grant relief in appropriate circumstances (s.113). Contravention of s.99 by a company and any officer in default is a criminal offence (s.114).

Shares taken by any subscriber to the memorandum of a public company in pursuance of an undertaking of his in the memorandum must be paid up in cash (s.106).

Payment of non-cash consideration—public companies

Section 102 prohibits a public company[22] from accepting as consideration for shares any undertaking, *e.g.* to transfer property, which is to be or may be performed more than five years after the date of the allotment. Any variation of a valid undertaking (*i.e.* within five years) taking it outside the five year period is

---

[19] *Mosely v Koffyfontien Mines Ltd* [1904] 2 Ch. 108, CA.
[20] p.144.
[21] p.131.
[22] The 2nd EC Directive which instigated these sections does not apply to private companies.

void. Any allotment in contravention of this requirement, or a failure by the purchaser to fulfil a valid undertaking within the contract period, renders the allottee liable to pay the company the amount owed on the shares, together with interest. Any subsequent holder of the shares is also liable, subject to the bona fide purchaser exemption noted above.[23]

Section 103 provides that a public company, and not just a quoted company, may not allot shares for any non-cash consideration unless a report on the value of the consideration had been made by an independent person qualified to be an auditor of the company. His report must be sent to the company within six months prior to the allotment and to the proposed allottee. He may accept another's valuation if it is reasonable to do so, provided that that person is also independent and appears to be qualified and such facts are disclosed in the report. The company's auditor may be so used: s.108.

The report must state the amount payable on the shares, a description of the consideration and the valuation methods used, the date of valuation and the extent to which the shares are to be treated as paid up by the consideration and in cash. It must be filed with the Registrar: s.111.

In making his report, the expert may require from the officers of the company such information and explanation as he thinks necessary to enable him to carry out the valuation or to make the report. False, misleading or deceptive statements made in this context constitute criminal offences: s.110.

There is a general exemption for shares issued generally to shareholders in another company on a take-over or merger with the other company: s.103(5). Such issues are, however, subject to the extra-statutory rules on takeovers: see Chapter 31, below. There is also an exemption for shares issued in return for the transfer of shares in another company under an arrangement which is open to all the shareholders at that company[24]: s.103(2)(4). Such issues are, however, subject to other controls: see Chapter 30, below.[25]

In default of such a report, the allottee will be liable to pay any amount owed on the shares in cash if either he did not receive a copy of the report or he knew or ought to have known of the breach: s.103(6). Subsequent holders may also be liable subject to the bona fide purchaser exemption. Relief may again be given by the court if it is just and equitable to do so, taking into account the actual amount received for the shares and other liabilities of the allottee under the contract: s.113.[26] It is for the allottee to show that the company has actually received assets to the value of the nominal value and premium of the shares in order to obtain this relief.[27]

These provisions only apply if the shares are issued "otherwise than for cash." Issues for cash are defined in s.738(2) so as to include payment by a cheque

---

[23] s.112.

[24] Excluding treasury shares.

[25] There is a proposal to amend the Second Directive to provide to further exemptions where there is a value based on market price and where the asset has been valued in accordance with audited accounts: COM (2004) Oct. 2004.

[26] See, *e.g. Re Ossory Estates plc* (1988) 4 B.C.C. 460. In *Re Bradford Investments plc* [1991] B.C.L.C. 224 the failure to obtain a report led to the shareholders losing their right to vote under the articles.

[27] *Re Bradford Investments plc (No.2)* [1991] B.C.L.C. 688.

received by the company in good faith, or the release of liability of the company for a defined sum (*i.e.* a set-off)[28] or an undertaking to pay cash at a future date. This may be thought to cover a multitude of sins although it does not include the assignment of a debt.[29]

It is convenient to note here that similar provisions apply, by virtue of ss 104 and 109, to the acquisitions by public companies of non-cash assets from any subscriber of the memorandum, within two years of the issue of the certificate entitling it to commence business, if the consideration to be given by the company is not less than 10 per cent of the nominal value of the company's issued shares at that time.

Payment of non-cash consideration—private companies

Sections 102–112 do not apply to private companies, but where shares are allotted as fully or partly paid up otherwise than in cash, a contract constituting the title of the allottee to the allotment together with any contract of sale, or for services or other consideration for the allotment, or, if such a contract is not in writing, particulars of the contract, must, with the return as to allotments, be delivered to the Registrar, usually within a month after the allotment: s.88.[30] Default renders the officers of the company liable to penalties but does not make the allotment void.

Any such contract must be supported by consideration. Provided there is some consideration, however, the courts will not inquire into the adequacy of that consideration unless it is merely colourable or manifestly inadequate. Thus provided property is transferred to the company in return for shares the court will not examine whether that property is actually worth the value of the shares.[31]

The goodwill, stock-in-trade and property of a business was sold to a company for £46,000, of which £20,000 was to be paid in fully paid shares. The stock-in-trade was shown in the company's books at a figure of £11,000 less than the sum allocated to it in the agreement. On the company's going into liquidation, a misfeasance summons was taken out to obtain payment for the shares. *Held*, since the agreement could not be impeached, the adequacy of the consideration could not be gone into: *Re Wragg Ltd* [1897] 1 Ch. 796, CA.

In England, however, past consideration is no consideration.[32]

A private company decided to turn itself into a public company. Before doing so it resolved to allot £6,000 of fully paid shares to the existing directors and shareholders, and a contract was made agreeing to allot the shares in consideration of their past services and expenses in forming the company and establishing the business. The contract was registered and the shares were allotted. The company afterwards went into liquidation. *Held*, the director and shareholders were liable to pay for the shares, as there was no consideration in money or money's worth for the allotment, past services being no consideration: *Re Eddystone Marine Insurance Co.* [1893] 3 Ch. 9, CA.

---

[28] Thus preserving the decision in *Spargo's Case* (1873) L.R. 8 Ch.App. 407.
[29] *Systems Control plc v Munro Corporate* [1990] B.C.C. 386.
[30] Above, p.137.
[31] *Re Wragg Ltd* [1897] Ch. 796; *Park Business Interiors Ltd v Park* [1992] B.C.L.C. 1034.
[32] In Scotland past consideration is valid consideration so that, *e.g.*, shares can be issued in return for the past services of the company's promoters: *Park Business Interiors Ltd v Park* [1992] B.C.L.C. 1034.

An agreement by a private company to allot shares in consideration of services to be performed in the future also renders the allottee liable to pay for the shares.[33] "It is not open to a company to agree with the holder or proposed holder of its shares to replace the statutory liability by a special contract sounding in damages only".[34] However, a private company may agree to pay a fixed sum immediately for services to be performed in the future, *e.g.* for the erection of a building, and to satisfy that debt by the allotment of shares.[35]

Where the contract is fraudulent or shows on the face of it that the consideration is illusory, the allottee is liable to pay for the shares.

G agreed to sell a concession to a company which agreed to allot him as fully paid 400 shares forthwith and also one-fifth of any future increase of capital. *Held*, the agreement was good so far as it obliged the company to allot one-fifth of any future increase of capital but void so far as it relieved G from paying for the shares. It was apparent that the value of the concession bore no relation to the amount of the shares: *Hong Kong and China Gas Co. Ltd v Glen* [1914] 1 Ch. 527.

"If the agreement were that the property to be purchased should be valued, and that against this property shares should be issued as fully paid to an extent exceeding the amount of the valuation by one-third, the arrangement would ... be bad as to this excess of one-third. It would to this extent be apparent on the face of the contract that the attempted discharge of a part of the liability was illusory": *per* Sargant J., at p.539.

ISSUE OF SHARES AT A PREMIUM

Where a company's issued shares have a market value greater than the amount paid up on them, then, when further shares are being issued, the company may require applicants to agree to pay more than the nominal amount of the new shares, *i.e.* to pay a premium.

A company may, without any special power in its articles, issue its shares at a premium, *i.e.* for a consideration in cash or in kind which exceeds the nominal amount of the shares, although there is no law which obliges a company to issue its shares above par because they are saleable at a premium in the market.[36] However, by s.130, where shares are issued at a premium, whether for cash or otherwise, a sum equal to the aggregate amount or value of the premiums must be transferred to the "share premium account".

As will be seen later, s.130 extends the principle that the share capital of a company must be maintained[37] to a share premium account, because the section fees on to provide that the provisions of the Act relating to reduction of capital apply to this account, *i.e.* it cannot be reduced without leave of the court except where it is applied in:

(1) paying up unissued shares of the company to be issued to members as fully paid bonus shares[38]; or

---

[33] *National House etc. Investment Co. Ltd v Watson*, 1908 S.C. 888.
[34] *Per* Parker J. in *Gardner v Iredale* [1912] 1 Ch. 700, at p.716.
[35] *Gardner v Iredale*, above.
[36] *Per* Lord Davey in *Hilder v Dexter* [1902] A.C. 474, at p.480, *Cameron's* case, above.
[37] *Re Moorgate Mercantile Holdings Ltd* [1980] 1 All E.R. below, p.149.
[38] Other ways in which bonus shares can be paid for are dealt with, below, Ch.22.

(2) writing off (a) the preliminary expenses, or (b) the expenses of, or the commission paid or discount allowed on, an issue of shares or debentures of the company; or

(3) providing for the premium payable by the company on the redemption of shares[39] or debentures.[40]

Although share premiums are regarded as capital, it is not capital belonging to any individual shareholder. The shareholder paying the premium has no dividend rights in respect of it and has no automatic right to repayment of it in a winding up.

The issue of shares at a premium accentuates the unreality of the nominal or par value of a share. The capital in the share premium account is an anomalous form of capital because it is capital on which no dividend is paid, which is not attributable to the ownership of any class of shares, which is not part of the company's nominal capital, and which the ordinary investor may not realise is part of the company's actual capital.

Share premium account and issues other than for cash

Shares can be issued at a premium not only for cash but also for consideration other than cash. If, in the latter case, the value of the consideration received, *e.g.* of land, exceeds the nominal value of the shares issued there is an issue of shares at a premium and s.130 applies.

In *Head (Henry) & Co. Ltd v Ropner Holdings Ltd*[41] this principle was applied where a company acquired a majority of the shares in another company by virtue of an exchange of shares, and the value of the shares acquired exceeded the value of the shares issued. The excess had to be transferred to the share premium account, with the result that the pre-acquisition profits of the acquired company, reflected in the value of its shares, were frozen and could not be distributed as dividends by the acquiring company. This decision was regarded as fallacious by many lawyers and accountants, with the result that few such transfers to share premium accounts were made. The principle was, however, confirmed in *Shearer v Bercain*,[42] and, following that decision, the Act provides two forms of relief from the obligations of s.130 in certain defined circumstances.[43]

Merger relief

Where the issuing company acquires a 90 per cent holding in another company[44] by way of a share for share exchange no transfer to the share premium account

---

[39] Below, Ch.10.

[40] Below, Ch.23.

[41] [1952] Ch.124.

[42] [1980] 3 All E.R. 295.

[43] These reliefs can be extended or varied by subsequent regulations: s.134. In fact this has been done with respect to the second relief—see the following note below. A general amnesty for pre-February 1981 mergers can be found in s.12 of the Companies Consolidation (Consequential Provisions) Act 1985.

[44] This is 90 per cent of the nominal value of the equity share capital excluding any shares held as treasury shares (see Chap. 10, below).

need be made: s.131. In fact this is a wide relief as it applies whether or not the issuing company owned any shares in the other company, *e.g.* it applies to a company owning 60 per cent of the shares of a subsidiary acquiring another 30 per cent. There is no obligation in such cases to disclose any "premiums" in the balance sheet. It also applies if the consideration provided by the acquired company is a cancellation of its issued shares rather than an issue—a frequent practice in schemes of reconstruction.

Group Reconstruction Relief

Where a wholly-owned subsidiary acquires a shareholding (not necessarily 100 per cent) in a fellow subsidiary (not necessarily wholly-owned) in return for an allotment of its own shares or other non-cash assets to its holding company or another of its wholly-owned subsidiaries, relief from s.130 is available: s.132.[44a] Only the lower of the cost or book value to the issuing company of the acquired shares need be taken into account.

Where both ss 131 and 132 could apply only the latter relief can be claimed.[45]

ALTERATION OF SHARE CAPITAL

Section 121 provides that a limited company with a share capital, if so authorised by its articles, may alter the conditions of its memorandum relating to share capital by:

(1) increasing its [authorised] share capital; or

(2) consolidating and dividing all or any of its share capital into shares of larger amount than its existing shares; or

(3) converting all or any of its paid-up shares into stock, or reconverting stock into paid-up shares of any denomination; or

(4) subdividing all or any of its shares into shares of smaller amount than is fixed by the memorandum; or

(5) cancelling shares which have not been taken or agreed to be taken by any person. (This is called "diminution of capital" and it should not be confused with reduction of capital which will be explained later.[46])

All these powers require for their exercise a resolution of the company in general meeting.

Increase of capital

Every increase of the nominal or authorised capital figure in the memorandum, must be effected by the company in general meeting: s.121. If the articles

---

[44a] The present form of this relief originates from the Companies (Share Premium Account) Regulations 1984 (SI 1984/2007), which substituted the new section into the 1981 Act and so the 1985 Act. The original form of the relief, which operated until December 1984, can be found in Sch.25 to the 1985 Act.

[45] For the effect on group accounts see Chap. 20, below.

[46] s.121(5). See below, p.151.

authorise the increase of capital, whether an ordinary or a special resolution is required depends on the articles.

Table A, reg.32, provides: "The company may by ordinary resolution—(a) increase its share capital by new shares of such amount as the resolution prescribes; . . ."

If the articles do not give authority to increase capital, the articles must be altered by special resolution so that they do give authority but the one special resolution can both authorise and effect an increase.[47]

The notice convening the meeting must specify the amount of the proposed increase.[48] Within 15 days after the passing of the resolution effecting the increase, a notice in the prescribed form of the amount of the increase must be filed with the Registrar. A printed copy of the resolution effecting the increase, or a copy in some other form approved by him, must also be filed with the Registrar (s.123).

Consolidation of shares

This takes place when several shares are consolidated into one, *e.g.* when 20 5p shares are consolidated into one £1 share. Consolidation is effected in the same way as an increase of capital under s.121, *i.e.* if the articles authorise consolidation, the resolution specified in the articles must be passed. If the articles are silent, a special resolution to give authority and to effect the consolidation is necessary. Table A, reg.32(b), requires an ordinary resolution. Notice must be given to the Registrar within a month of the consolidation (s.122).

Conversion of shares into stock

The difference between stock and shares was described by Lord Hatherley as follows: "Shares in a company, as shares, cannot be bought in small fractions of any amount, fractions of less than [the nominal value] but the consolidated stock of a company can be bought just in the same way as the stock of the public debt can be bought, split up in as many portions as you like, and subdivided into as small fractions as you please." He also referred to stock as "simply a set of shares put together in a bundle.[49]

A company *cannot issue stock directly* but can only convert shares into stock under s.121, although there seems to be no reason for this rule today. The conversion can only be made if the shares are fully paid. The conversion of shares into stock (or a reconversion of stock into shares) is effected in the same way as an increase of capital under s.121. Notice must be given to the Registrar within a month (s.122).

Although in theory stock can be transferred in fractional amounts, in practice the articles usually confer on the directors power to fix the minimum amount transferable.

---

[47] *Campbell's Case* (1873) I.R. 9 Ch.App. 1. Remember that the Company Law Review recommended the abolition of this figure.

[48] *MacConnell v E. Prill & Co. Ltd* [1916] 2 Ch. 57.

[49] In *Morrice v Aylmer* (1875) L.R. 7 HL 717 at pp.724, 725.

The advantage of converting shares into stock was that the work caused by the fact that each share had a separate number was obviated. However, this advantage is now minimised by the proviso to s.182(2), under which shares need not have a distinguishing number.[50] In practice stock is now rare and Table A no longer contains any reference to it.

Subdivision of shares

This is the division of shares into shares of smaller amount, *e.g.* the division of one £1 share into 20 5p shares, and it is often resorted to for the purpose of improving the marketability of expensive shares. Subdivision is effected in the same way as an increase of capital: s.121. Table A, reg.32(c), requires an ordinary resolution. If the shares are not fully paid up, the proportion between the amount paid and the amount unpaid on each reduced share must be the same as it was in the case of the share from which the reduced share is derived (s.121(3)). The subdivision of shares must be registered with the Registrar within a month (s.122).

Cancellation of unissued shares

A company can cancel shares which have not been taken or agreed to be taken[51] by any person, and *diminish* the amount of its nominal share capital by the amount of the shares so cancelled. This is not to be deemed a reduction of share capital (s.121(5)). Cancellation is effected in the same way as an increase of capital: s.121. Table A, reg.32(d), requires an ordinary resolution. Notice of cancellation must be registered with the Registrar within a month (s.122).

MAINTENANCE OF SHARE CAPITAL

It is currently a fundamental principle of company law that the share capital must be maintained. It has been said that "a company cannot, without the leave of the court or the adoption of a special procedure, return its capital to its shareholders. It follows that a transaction which amounts to an unauthorised return of capital is *ultra vires* and cannot be validated by shareholder ratification or approval."[52] This is not affected by s.35 of the Act since it is not derived from the company's memorandum.[53] Capital may be lost as a result of ordinary business risks and, as we shall see, it may be returned to the shareholders with the consent of the court under s.135, but otherwise, subject to the certain carefully controlled exceptions,[54] it must be maintained since it is said to be the fund to which creditors of the company look for payment of their debts.[55] This position is now under review, as discussed at the end of this chapter.

---

[50] Below, p.205.
[51] Where a person offers to take unissued shares but that has not been accepted, there is no agreement to take shares for this purpose: *Re Swindon Town Football Co. Ltd* [1990] B.C.L.C. 467.
[52] *per* Hoffmann J. in *Aveling Barford Ltd v Perion Ltd* [1989] 1 W.L.R. 360 at p. 364; approved by Harman J. in *Barclays Bank plc v British Commonwealth Holdings plc* [1996] 1 B.C.L.C 1.
[53] See Ch.3, above.
[54] See Chs 10 and 11, below.
[55] See, *e.g. Jenkins v Harbour View Courts Ltd* [1966] N.Z.L.R. 1, CA.

The principle that the share capital of a company must be maintained boils down to this—paid up share capital must not be returned to its members, apparently even indirectly,[56] and their liability in respect of capital not paid up on shares must not be reduced.

The principle has the following consequences:

(1) A company generally must not purchase its own shares unless it follows the strict procedures laid down by the Act.[57]

(2) A subsidiary company generally must not be a member of its holding company and any allotment or transfer of shares in a holding company to its subsidiary is void: s.23.[58]

(3) It is generally unlawful for a company to give any kind of financial assistance for the acquisition by any person of its own shares or those of its holding company. There are, however, exceptions to this rule: ss 151–158.[59]

(4) Dividends must not be paid to the shareholders except out of distributable profits as defined by the Act, *i.e.* in general not out of capital.[60]

(5) Where a public company suffers a serious loss of capital, *i.e.* of more than half the subscribed capital, a meeting of the company must be called to discuss the issue.[61]

There are certain exceptions to the principle:

(1) A company may reduce its share capital with the consent of the court under s.135, below[62]

(2) A company may purchase or redeem its shares under the Act.[63]

(3) A company may purchase its own shares under a court order made either under s.459 to relieve an unfairly prejudiced minority[64] or s.54 to relieve a minority on the conversion of a public company to a private company.

(4) Capital may be returned to the members, after the company's debts have been paid, in a winding up.

Other apparent exceptions are forfeiture of shares and surrender to avoid a forfeiture, although here the amount paid on the shares remains with the

---

[56] *Barclays Bank plc v British Commonwealth Holdings plc* [1996] 1 B.C.L.C. 1, *per* Harman J. The CA did not express a view on this issue.
[57] Below, Ch.10.
[58] Below, p.190.
[59] Below, Ch.11.
[60] Below, Ch.22.
[61] Below, p.158.
[62] p.151.
[63] Below, Ch.10.
[64] Below, Ch.18.

company when the shareholder unable to pay a call is relieved of liability for future calls, and the shares revert to the company, bear no dividend and must either be reissued or cancelled.[65]

Finally, the principle as to maintenance of share capital has been extended—

(1) By s.170, to a capital redemption reserve set up when redeemable shares are redeemed or other shares purchased by the company out of profits.[66]

(2) By s.130, to a share premium account.[67]

REDUCTION OF CAPITAL

The share capital of the company must be subscribed in money or money's worth. This capital may be lost or diminished according to the fluctuations of the business, but otherwise, subject to the Act,[68] it cannot be reduced without the sanction of the court.[69] Thus any agreement which has the effect of returning capital to a shareholder is void, however indirect that effect might be.[70] The object of requiring the court's sanction is threefold—(1) to protect persons dealing with the company, so that the fund available for satisfying their claims shall not be diminished except by ordinary business risks; (2) to ensure that the reduction is equitable as between the various classes of shareholders in the company; (3) to protect the interests of the public.[71]

Reduction procedure

Section 135 provides that, subject to the confirmation by the court, a limited company with a share capital may, if authorised by its articles, by *special resolution*, reduce its share capital and, if and so far as is necessary, alter its memorandum by reducing the amount of its share capital and of its shares.

"The court," in relation to a company, means the court with jurisdiction to wind up the company: s.744. The courts with jurisdiction to wind up a company are set out in ss 117 and 120 of the Insolvency Act 1986 and will be dealt with later.[72]

Power to reduce must be given in the articles; power in the memorandum is not effective.[73] The power must be a specific power to reduce.[74]

Table A, reg.34, provides: "subject to the provisions of the Act, the company may by special resolution reduce its share capital, any capital redemption reserve and any share premium account in any way."

---

[65] *per* Lord Herschell at p.417, and Lord Watson at p.424, in *Trevor v Whitworth* (1887) 12 App. Cas. 409.

[66] Below, p.166.

[67] Above, p.145.

[68] See Chs 11 and 12, below.

[69] This is generally known as the rule in *Trevor v Whitworth* (1887) 12 App.Cas. 409, HL.

[70] For a complex agreement which had this effect see *Barclays Bank plc v British & Commonwealth Holdings plc* [1996] 1 B.C.L.C. 1.

[71] *per* Lord Watson in *Trevor v Whitworth* (1887) 12 App.Cas. 409, at p. 423; *per* Lord MacNaghten in *British and American Finance Corporation Ltd v Couper* [1894] A.C. 399 at p.411.

[72] Below, Ch.27.

[73] *Re Dexine Rubber Co.* [1903] W.N. 82.

[74] *John Avery & Co. Ltd, Petitioners* (1890) 17 R. 1101.

If the articles do not authorise the reduction of capital, *two* special resolutions—one to alter the articles so as to give authority and the other to effect the reduction—will be necessary, in addition to the consent of the court.[75]

The court cannot condone a reduction which has been carried out without its prior approval.[76] The resolution must be in the correct form and comply with the requirements of s.378 as to the exact notice required.[77]

Cases of reduction

The power to reduce capital given by s.135 is general, *i.e.* if the proper procedure is adopted a company can reduce its share capital in any case. However, the section specifies three particular cases of reduction:

(1)   the extinction or reduction on shares in respect of capital not paid up;

(2)   with or without the extinction or reduction of liability on shares, the cancellation of paid-up share capital which is lost or unrepresented by available assets;

(3)   with or without the extinction or reduction of liability on shares, the payment off of any paid-up share capital which is in excess of the wants of the company.

For example, if a company has more than enough capital, it may reduce the nominal amount of shares by repaying paid-up capital, as where fully paid shares of a nominal amount of £5 each are reduced to £2 fully paid shares and £3 is paid back on each share. This would reduce the company's nominal, issued and paid-up capital and, so far as the nominal capital and the nominal amount of the shares are concerned, alter the memorandum. In one case, 10 per cent of the capital was returned on the footing that the amount returned could be called up again.[78]

A return of capital may be at a premium.

A reduction of capital involved repaying the capital paid-up on each of the company's preference shares of 50p each plus a premium of 25p per share. The court confirmed the reduction: *Re Saltdean Estate Co. Ltd* [1968] 1 W.L.R. 1844.

A reduction may involve the company paying off part of its share capital not with money but by transferring to its shareholders shares of another company.[79] Alternatively it can be used to create a reserve out of the share premium account

[75] *Re Patent Invert Sugar Co.* (1885) 31 Ch.D. 166, CA; *Oregon Mortgage Co. Ltd, Petitioners,* 1910 S.C. 964.

[76] *Alexander Henderson Ltd, Petitioners,* 1967 S.L.T. (Notes) 17.

[77] *Re Moorgate Mercantile Holdings Ltd,* [1980] 1 All E.R. 40. However, if there is an error in the actual resolution as passed which is so insignificant that no one would be prejudiced by its correction the court will allow the reduction to proceed: *Re Willaire Systems plc* [1987] B.C.L.C. 67. See also *Re European Homes Products plc* (1988) 4 B.C.C. 779.

[78] *Scottish Vulcanite Co. Ltd, Petitioners* (1894) 21 R. 792; *cf. William Brown Sons & Co. Ltd, Petitioners,* 1931 S.C. 701, and *Stevensons, Anderson & Co. Ltd, Petitioners,* 1951 S.C. 346.

[79] *Westburn Sugar Refineries Ltd, Petitioners,* 1951 S.C. HL 57; [1951] A.C. 625.

arising on an acquisition which will then be available to set off against that "surplus" on consolidated account.[80]

Moneys withdrawn from the capital and set free by the reduction can be employed in the purchase of the company's own shares which it is intended to extinguish. The procedure can also be used to convert ordinary shares into redeemable shares, at least where there is a specific date for the redemption.[81]

The reduction procedure cannot be used as a device to raise new capital to replace capital which has disappeared, *e.g.* by the conversion of £1 fully paid shares into £1 shares with only 75p paid, thus imposing an additional liability on shareholders.[82] On the other hand it can be used as a method of varying the type or denomination of capital. In such cases the reduction resolution will be contingent on the corresponding increase of capital taking place. This practice was approved in *Re TIP-Europe Ltd*[83] provided the increase has taken place prior to the court's approval being given. In this way shares may be converted into a different currency, *e.g.* from sterling into dollars, by cancelling the sterling shares and immediately issuing dollar shares.[84]

Questions for the court on reduction

Subject to the discretion conferred on the court by s.135 and the statutory provisions for the protection of creditors, below, the question whether there should be a reduction of capital and, if so, how it should be effected, is a domestic question for the prescribed majority of the shareholders to decide.[85] The court should sanction a reduction unless what is proposed to be done is unfair or inequitable in the interests of (1) the creditors, (2) the shareholders or (3) the public who may have dealings with the company or may invest in its securities.[86] The court has to decide, on the evidence as a whole, whether to approve the reduction. Since many applications[87] are unopened there is a duty on the company of full and frank disclosure to the court.[88]

Reductions due to over capitalisation

When creditors are not concerned (because the reduction does not involve the diminution of any liability in respect of unpaid capital or the payment to any shareholder of any paid-up capital) the questions to be considered by the court are:

---

[80] *Per* Lord Macnaghten in *British and American Finance Corporation v Couper* [1894] A.C. 399 at p. 414.

[81] *Forth Wines Ltd, Petitioners*, 1993 S.L.T. 170.

[82] See s.16 and also *W. Morrison & Co. Ltd, Petitioners* (1892) 19 R. 1049.

[83] (1987) 3 B.C.C. 647. See also *Re M.B. Group plc* (1989) 5 B.C.C. 684 and *Re B.A.T. Industries plc*, September 3, 1998.

[84] *Re Anglo-American Insurance Co. Ltd* [1991] B.C.L.C. 564.

[85] *British and American Finance Corpn. v Couper* [1894] A.C. 399. See Lord President Inglis in *Hoggan v Tharsis Sulpher etc. Co. Ltd* (1882) 9 R. 1191 at p.1212.

[86] *Westburn Sugar Refineries Ltd, Petitioners*, 1951 S.C. HL 57; [1951] A.C. 625. *Re Ratners Group plc* [1988] BCLC 685.

[87] These are not normal adversarial proceedings.

[88] *Re Ransomes plc* [1999] 2 BCLC 591.

(1)   ought the court to refuse its sanction to the reduction out of regard to the interest of those members of the public who may be induced to take shares in the company?

(2)   is the reduction fair and equitable as between the different classes of shareholders?[89]

When capital is being returned as surplus to the company's requirements, it should normally[90] be returned first to the class of shareholders with priority as to capital in a winding up,[91] at any rate where preference shares are not entitled to participate in surplus assets.[92]

> A coal company with a capital of £400,000, half of which was in ordinary shares and half in 6 per cent preference shares, had a surplus of capital as a result of nationalisation. A special resolution was passed reducing the capital by paying off the preference shares. By the articles, the preference shareholders in the event of a winding up had a right to priority of repayment of capital *but no further right to participate in the surplus assets*. *Held*, the reduction should be confirmed as fair and equitable, the preference shareholders having no right to a continuance of their rate of dividend during the life of the company if the company desired and had the means to pay them off. The preference shareholders were being treated in accordance with their rights and it was immaterial that the elimination of their shares extinguished any hopes which they had of obtaining some additional advantage as a result of regulations to be made under the Coal Industry Nationalisation Act 1946, s.25: *Prudential Assurance Co. Ltd v Chatterley-Whitfield Collieries Ltd* [1949] A.C. 512.[93]

It is not necessary for the company to show by how much its capital is surplus to its requirements. "Public policy" is not a ground for the court's refusing to confirm a reduction which is otherwise unobjectionable, *e.g.* reduction may be confirmed although the motive for it may have been avoidance of the consequences of possible future nationalisation,[94] or minimisation of tax liability.[95]

A modification of rights clause in the articles has no application to a cancellation of shares on a reduction of capital which is in accord with the rights attached to the shares under the articles.[96] It follows, therefore, that if the reduction of capital of a class of share is itself made a class right by the articles, any reduction will be subject to the modification procedure, usually approval by three quarters of that class, before it can be confirmed by the court.[97]

If the necessary approval has been obtained, the reduction will be approved unless it is unfair or has been sanctioned by the influence of some improper or

---

[89] *Poole v National Bank of China Ltd* [1907] A.C. 229. See Lord Parker of Waddington in *Caldwell & Co. Ltd v Caldwell*, 1916 S.C. HL 120 at p.121. *Re Ratner Group*, above, *Re Ransomes plc*, above.

[90] But not always: see *William Dixon Ltd, Petitioners*, 1948 S.C. 511.

[91] *Wilsons and Clyde Coal Co. Ltd v Scottish Insurance Corporation Ltd*, 1949 S.C. HL 90; 1948 S.C. 360; *Prudential Assurance Co. Ltd v Chatterley-Whitfield Collieries Ltd* [1949] A.C. 512.

[92] *per* Lord Greene M.R. in the *Prudential* case, above, in the Court of Appeal [1948] 2 All E.R. 593 at pp.596, 600.

[93] See Chap. 12, below, on preference shares generally.

[94] See n.79, above.

[95] *David Bell Ltd, Petitioners*, 1954 S.C. 33.

[96] *Re Saltdean Estate Co. Ltd* [1968] 1 W.L.R. 1844; *House of Fraser v A.C.G.E. Investments Ltd* [1987] A.C. 387; 1987 S.C. HL 125; *cf. Re Old Silkstone Collieries Ltd* [1954] Ch. 169, CA.

[97] *Re Northern Engineering Industries plc.* [1994] 2 B.C.L.C. 704, CA.

extraneous consideration.[98] There is a duty on the company to explain the reduction to its shareholders. The court will also consider the financial risk to the remaining shareholders.[99]

In one case, where there were special circumstances, a reduction involving a variation of class rights was confirmed although no class meeting of the class of shareholders (the preference shareholders) had been held—no one objected, there was no prospect of liquidation (when the preference shareholders had the right to participate in surplus assets after repayment of capital), and the preference shareholders received more than they would have received by selling.[1]

When one part of a class of equity shareholders is treated differently from another, the usual practice is to proceed by a scheme of arrangement under s.425, under which the interests of the minority are better protected.[2]

Reductions due to loss of capital

In England, where reduction is sought on the ground that capital has been lost or is not represented by available assets, evidence of the loss or that the available assets do not represent the capital must be given.[3] A reduction may be confirmed where capital has been lost but it is still represented by available assets.

A company had built up a reserve fund. It had incurred a loss arising from the depreciation in the value of its public-houses below the amount stated in the balance sheet, and it proposed to reduce its capital by apportioning the loss between its capital account and the reserve. *Held*, the loss ought to be rateably apportioned between the capital account and the reserve, and the company was not bound to apply the whole of its reserve to wipe out the loss: *Re Hoare & Co. Ltd* [1904] 2 Ch. 208 CA.

Capital is not lost unless it is permanently lost.[4] If the evidence is therefore that the loss might not be permanent the courts will not allow a reduction unless the company gives an undertaking to protect the creditors in the event of the loss being made good. In one case[5] the judge required an undertaking to place any sums recovered in respect of the loss (by way of compensation) into capital reserve so that it could not be distributed as dividend. But in a subsequent case[6] Nourse J. refused to accept that such an undertaking must always require a reserve to be set aside indefinitely to safeguard the interests of future creditors and shareholders. The undertaking in most cases need only safeguard the interests of creditors at the time of the reduction.

---

[98] *Re Welsbach Incandescent Gas Light Co. Ltd* [1904] Ch. 87, CA. A scheme of arrangement is not necessary: *Oban and Aultmore-Glenlivet Distilleries Ltd, Petitioners* (1903) 5 F. 1140, and *Marshall, Fleming & Co. Ltd, Petitioners*, 1938 S.C. 873 (O.H.).

[99] See *Re Ransomes plc* [1999] 2 B.C.L.C. 591.

[1] *Re William Jones & Sons Ltd* [1969] 1 W.L.R. 146.

[2] *Re Robert Stephen Holdings Ltd* [1968] 1 W.L.R. 522.

[3] *Per* Lord Parker of Waddington in *Caldwell & Co. Ltd v Caldwell*, 1916 S.C. HL 120 at p.121. Scottish courts dispense with such evidence where there is no reason to suspect the bona fides of the parties: *Caldwell's* case.

[4] *Re Haematite Steel Co.* [1901] 2 Ch. 746 at 749 *per* Romer L. J.; *Re Walsbach Incandescent Gas Light Co. Ltd* [1904] 1 Ch. 87.

[5] *Re Jupiter House Investments (Cambridge) Ltd* [1985] 1 W.L.R. 975.

[6] *Re Grosvenor Press plc* [1985] 1 W.L.R. 980.

This approach was followed in *Quayle Munro Ltd, Petitioners*,[7] where the court confirmed a petition to cancel the share premium account to allow for past losses leaving a credit balance as a special reserve fund. Undertakings were only needed for present creditors with respect to that reserve, and could allow for the writing off of future losses irrespective of any creditors.

Creditors' rights to object to reduction

If a proposed reduction of share capital involves either (1) diminution of liability in respect of unpaid share capital, or (2) payment to any shareholder of any paid-up capital,[8] and (3) in any other case where the court so directs, creditors who, if the company were being wound up, would be able to prove against it, are entitled to object to the reduction. For this purpose the court must settle a list of creditors, with the nature and amount of their claims, and may publish notices fixing a day by which creditors not entered on the list are to claim to be entered. Such of the creditors as do not consent to the reduction must be paid off or the company must secure payment of their claims by appropriating such amount as the court directs: s.136. In special circumstances the court may dispense with these requirements: s.136(6).

Before dispensing with a list of creditors under s.136(6) the court must be satisfied that no creditor who might be entitled to object to the reduction would be prejudiced by it.[9]

If there is no overall diminution in the company's issued and paid up share capital, *e.g.* where the cancelled shares are to be replaced by equivalent shares, the creditors cannot in practice object to the proposed reduction of capital, because no asset out of which their claims could be satisfied is being given up or returned to the shareholder.[10]

A company had a paid-up share capital of £1,000,000, and had also issued £1,000,000 debentures secured by a trust deed constituting a floating charge. In 1904, losses to the extent of £800,000 were incurred and no dividends had since been paid, any profits being applied in reduction of the deficiency. By 1917 the deficiency had been reduced to £640,000, and the company proposed to reduce its capital to £360,000 by writing off the lost capital. The latest balance sheet showed assets worth £1,500,000. The debenture holders objected. *Held*, as the reduction involved no diminution of unpaid capital or repayment to shareholders of paid-up capital, creditors were not entitled to object unless a strong case was made out, and the debenture holders had not made out any such case: *Re Meux's Brewery Co. Ltd* [1919] Ch. 28.

It is not clear whether creditors may object to such a reduction of capital which is intended to be followed by a distribution of assets; but in *Re B.A.T. Industries plc*[11] Neuberger J. was of the opinion that they could not.

[7] 1992 S.C. 24; [1994] 1 B.C.L.C. 410.
[8] Replacement of preference shares with loan stock, which became a common practice for the purposes of reducing liability to corporation tax, counts as such payment, although the loan stock does not fall to be repaid by the company until a future date: *Lawrie & Symington Ltd, Petitioners*, 1969 S.L.T. 221.
[9] *Re Lucania Temperance Billiard Halls (London) Ltd* [1966] Ch. 98.
[10] *Re B.A.T. Industries plc*, September 3, 1998.
[11] *ibid.*

The object of reducing capital, where capital has been lost or is not represented by available assets, is to enable the accounts to present a realistic picture of the company's financial position, which may permit the company to pay dividends. To safeguard the creditors in the case of an application by a company to write off capital not lost or unrepresented by available assets, thereby setting free capital which might be distributed among the shareholders, the court is empowered by s.136 to give effect to a creditor's objection "in any other case".

Order for reduction; Minute of reduction

Confirmation by the court must precede the actual reduction of capital.[12] On making an order confirming the reduction, the court may direct:

(1) for special reasons, that the company add the words "and reduced" to its name for a specified time.

(2) that the reasons for reduction and the causes leading to the reduction be published, with a view to giving proper information to the public (s.137).

Section 138 provides that a copy of the order for reduction and a minute approved by the court showing the amount of the share capital, the number of shares into which it is divided, the amount of each share and the amount, if any, deemed to be paid up on each share, must be registered with the Registrar.[13] The Registrar then grants a certificate of registration, which is conclusive evidence of the reduction and that all the requirements of the Act with respect to reduction have been complied with—even if it is afterwards discovered that the special resolution for a reduction was not properly passed,[14] or that there was no power in the articles to reduce capital.[15] The reduction takes effect as from the date of registration. By s.380,[16] a copy of the special resolution must be forwarded to the Registrar within 15 days.

Reduction below authorised minimum capital

Where the court confirms a reduction of capital of a public company which has the effect of bringing the nominal value of the company's allotted share capital below the authorised minimum capital[17] this will only be registered (and so will only be effective) if the company is first re-registered as a private company: s.139.

To ease this process the court may authorise the company to re-register as a private company under s.53[18] without passing a special resolution and will also

---

[12] *Alexander Henderson Ltd, Petitioners,* 1967 S.L.T. (Notes) 17.

[13] Where the reduction takes the share capital to nil for a split second and new shares are then issued, this fact can be included in the minute of reduction: *Re Anglo-American Insurance Co. Ltd* [1991] B.C.L.C. 564.

[14] *Ladies' Dress Association v Pullbrook* [1900] 2 Q.B. 376, CA.

[15] *Re Walker and Smith Ltd* [1903] W.N. 82.

[16] Below, p.261.

[17] £50,000: s.118.

[18] Above, p.46.

specify the necessary alterations to the company's memorandum and articles. In practice many public companies prohibit any reduction of capital below the authorised minimum in their articles.[19]

SERIOUS LOSS OF CAPITAL

Following the EC Second Directive,[20] under s.142 the directors of a *public* company are obliged to call an extraordinary meeting of the company within 28 days from the earliest date on which any director knew that the company had suffered a serious loss of capital.

A serious loss of capital occurs where the net assets of the company are half or less of the amount of the company's called up share capital. In other words if it has lost half or more of its called up share capital.

The meeting must be fixed for a date not later than 56 days from when the obligation arose. It is to consider whether any, and if so what, measures should be taken to deal with the situation. Directors who knowingly and wilfully authorise or permit a failure to convene such a meeting are liable on conviction to a fine.

There is some ambiguity as to what may actually be discussed. s.142(3) provides that the meeting may not be used to discuss anything "which could not have been considered at that meeting apart from this section." Does this include a resolution to dismiss or censure the directors? Such a resolution may fall within the ambit of the section.

PROPOSALS FOR REFORM

In recent times, mainly as a result of the Company Law Review, the whole concept of the raising and maintenance of a company's share capital has been called into question as an effective means of protecting creditors, both in the UK[21] and the European Community. The Second EC Directive enshrines many of the existing principles[22] so far as public companies are concerned and this, and other practical considerations, led the Review to recommend the retention of the nominal value of a share. With regard to the reduction of capital procedure, the Review ultimately proposed that for private companies, the existing court approval procedure would remain but that there would be an alternative procedure involving a declaration of solvency by the directors and a special resolution by the members. For a public company, this alternative procedure would also allow any creditor to be able to challenge the proposed reduction in court[23] on the basis of lack of necessary and adequate safeguards or security for repayment of the debts.[24]

---

[19] But see *Re M.B. Group plc* (1989) 5 B.C.C. 684; *Re Anglo-American Insurance Co. Ltd*, [1991] B.C.L.C. 564.

[20] Art.17.

[21] See *e.g.* Armour, *Share capital and creditor protection: Efficiency Rules for a Modern Company Law* (2000) 63 MLR 355 and Ferran. *Creditors' Interests and 'Core' Company Law* (1999) 20 Co Law 314.

[22] This is currently under review by the Commission, which has published a draft amending the Directive. The Government in consulting on the proposals therein (March 2005).

[23] Access to the courts is a requirement of the Second Directive.

[24] This would put the onus of proof onto the creditor/applicant rather than the full and frank requirement imposed at present on the company.

Ultimately the capital maintenance rules for all companies will be replaced by a solvency and liquidity requirement. For private companies, that may be sooner rather than later. Those requirements are actually used in some of the recent statutory exceptions to the rule, discussed in the following two chapters.

Chapter 10

THE ACQUISITION AND REDEMPTION BY A
COMPANY OF ITS OWN SHARES: TREASURY SHARES

THE principle that a company cannot reduce its capital except in accordance with the Act, discussed in the previous chapter, means that it is unlawful for a company to buy or redeem its own shares without statutory authorisation, irrespective of how far such a purchase is in the interests of the company or its shareholders as a whole.[1] This rule does not, however, prevent a company from buying the shares of another company even if that second company's assets consist entirely of a holding of shares in the purchaser—the court will not pierce the corporate veil. The purchaser is buying shares in the second company and not its own shares.[2] Companies were, however, able to issue redeemable preference shares under s.58 of the 1948 Act; *i.e.* preference shares which were expressly redeemable at a future date. The 1981 Act replaced that narrow power with a general power to issue redeemable shares of any type and gave companies the additional power for the first time to purchase their own shares. Changes made in 2003 allow public companies to retain and re-issue such shares. These are known as treasury shares.

This chapter is concerned with these powers of purchase and redemption, covering a company's ability to do so, the mechanisms involved, the funds available and the capital consequences of so doing. The powers were originally part of a "package" designed to assist small companies in finding outside investors who might wish to be able to withdraw such investment at will. To this end it will be seen that private companies may in some cases fund the acquisition or redemption out of capital. The effect is that subject to certain procedures and authority all shares are now potentially redeemable either by the terms of their issue or by subsequent agreement.

ACQUISITIONS—THE GENERAL RULE

Section 143 now codifies the rule prohibiting a company from acquiring its own shares. However, this does not apply in the following cases:

    (i)   shares acquired otherwise than for valuable consideration, *e.g.* gifts[3];

---

[1] See *Trevor v Whitworth* (1887) 12 A.C. 409.

[2] *Acatos & Hutcheson plc v Watson* [1995] 1 B.C.L.C. 218. The judge suggested that it might be different if the second company was formed expressly for the purpose of avoiding the rule. Under s.23, *post*, p.190, the purchaser's own shares so acquired can be retained by the newly acquired subsidiary although the voting rights attached to them are suspended.

[3] Following *Re Castiglione's W.T.* [1958] Ch.549. In *Vision Express (UK) Ltd v Wilson (No. 1)* [1995] 2 B.C.L.C. 419, it was held that the prohibition applied to an agreed settlement of litigation whereby the company agreed to buy its own shares, albeit for a much reduced price. It was in essence still a purchase transaction.

(ii) acquisitions on a reduction of capital under s.135[4];

(iii) the redemption or purchase of its shares under the Act (discussed below);

(iv) purchases authorised by the court under ss 54[5], 461[6] or 5[7];

(v) the forfeiture of shares or acceptance of any shares surrendered in lieu for failure to pay for them.[8]

(vi) the acquisition of a company which owns shares in the acquiring company.[9]

All other acquisitions are void and cannot be cured retrospectively once they have taken place.[10]

Acquisitions by nominees

Section 144 provides that if a person subscribes for shares in a company or buys them for a third party partly-paid up, apparently in his own name, but in reality as a nominee for the company, he is to be regarded as the full owner of the shares to the exclusion of the company. He thus becomes personally liable for the amount owed on the shares. If he fails to pay within 21 days of being asked to do so the other subscribers, or the directors, whichever is appropriate, will be liable to pay, subject to a defence that they acted honestly and reasonably and ought fairly to be excused.

Section 145, however, provides that the company retains the ownership of such shares in two cases:

(i) if a public company provides financial assistance for the purchase of such shares. This topic is dealt with in the following chapter. Here we are only concerned with assistance given to a nominee. Such shares must be cancelled or disposed of within one year under s.146;

(ii) where the company is a trustee only of the shares and has no beneficial interest in them. Thus a company acting as a trustee may accept shares issued by itself in the name of a nominee on behalf of a trust fund. Beneficial interests for this purpose do not include certain residential interests commonly found in trust deeds, corporate pension funds or employee share schemes, as defined in Sch.2.

Of course the company retains the beneficial ownership of shares to which s.144 does not apply—*e.g.* fully paid up shares acquired from a third party.

---

[4] Above, Ch.9.
[5] Above, p.46.
[6] Below, p.372.
[7] Above, p.64.
[8] Below, p.236.
[9] *Acatos & Hutcheson plc v Watson* [1995] 1 B.C.L.C. 218.
[10] *Re R. W. Peak (Kings Lynn) Ltd* [1998] 1 B.C.L.C. 193. This does not apply where the irregularity relates only to the number of treasury shares exceeding the maximum allowed under s.162B. See below, p.167.

Consequences of an acquisition

Apart from purchases and redemptions under the Act, shares acquired by a company or its nominee must be treated as follows:

(i) shares acquired by the company as gifts, or by forfeiture or surrender for non-payment of calls, shares acquired by a nominee without financial assistance from the company and in which the company has a beneficial interest (*e.g.* gifts of fully paid up shares to a company's nominee)—disposal or cancellation of the shares within three years: s.146;

(ii) shares acquired by a nominee of a public company with financial assistance from the company—disposal or cancellation of the shares within one year: s.146. Cancellation may be achieved by a resolution of the directors reducing the capital by the nominal amount of the shares acquired without complying with s.135: s.147. If necessary a public company must apply to be re-registered as a private company.[11]

REDEMPTION AND PURCHASE OF SHARES

Redeemable shares

Section 159 allows companies to issue redeemable shares of any class, *i.e.* shares which are specifically redeemable under the terms of their issue.

To issue redeemable shares, a company must have power to do so by its articles. No company may issue only redeemable shares[12] but one non-redeemable share will technically be enough. Shares issued under s.159 may be issued either as redeemable at a fixed date or event, or as redeemable at the option of the company or the shareholder; but any shares redeemed must be fully paid up at the date of redemption—there must be no incidental reduction of capital, and the terms of redemption must provide for payment on redemption. This has been interpreted as meaning payment in full and not by instalments.[13] In one case, the court allowed a company to issue redeemable shares on a reduction of capital as a replacement for ordinary shares which were cancelled under the scheme.[14]

Apart from those basic requirements, the terms and conditions of redemption are to be as specified in the company's articles. Further restrictions, set out in s.159A, contained in the 1989 Act, never came into force and were repealed in 2003.[15]

When redeemable shares are redeemed they must be cancelled at once and the issued share capital figure reduced accordingly: s.160(4). Holding the shares in treasury is not an option for redeemed shares.

---

[11] *i.e.* because it ceases to comply with the authorised minimum capital under s.118.
[12] Nor can a company purchase its own shares if that would leave only redeemable shares in existence: s.162. See below.
[13] *Peña v Dale* [2004] 2 BCLC 508.
[14] *Forth Wines Ltd, Petitioners*, 1993 S.L.T. 170.
[15] By the Companies (Acquisition of Own Shares) (Treasury Shares) Regulations 2003, SI 2003/1116.

Replacement issues of shares can be made prior to the redemption without any increase in the authorised capital figure being necessary, so that if the new issue would take the nominal capital temporarily above the authorised figure, s.121 will not apply: s.160(5).[16]

The funds available for redemption of shares are discussed below.

Purchase by a company of its own shares

Section 162 allows companies to purchase their own shares by following one of three procedures contained in ss 164 to 166 of the Act. The power to purchase must be included in the articles—it can include the purchase of redeemable shares, *e.g.* if the date for redemption has not been reached. There is nothing in the Act which either allows or prohibits the *compulsory* purchase by a company of its own shares. It is doubtful whether a majority of the shareholders can be given a general power to do this because of the doctrine of a fraud on the minority[17] but the point remains open *vis-à-vis* the company itself.

Subject to the rules that a company cannot buy itself out completely or leave only redeemable shares, and that the purchase price must be paid in full on purchase,[17a] the terms and manner of the purchase can be framed as desired.[18]

The funds available to a company for the purchase of its own shares are dealt with below. The power to purchase its own shares, and the treatment of purchased shares, can only be implemented, however, by one of the following three procedures:

Off-market purchases. A purchase of unquoted shares,[19] *i.e.* in general, those of private companies, is governed by s.164. Such a purchase requires a special resolution of the company authorising it to make the contract to purchase (*N.B.* not the purchase itself). In *Re R. W. Peak (Kings Lynn) Ltd*[20] it was said that since such approval must take place prior to the contract it cannot be given informally[21] by the terms of the contract itself. In the event of a public company buying its own unquoted shares such approval must then be limited to a contract made within a period of no more than 18 months from the granting of approval.[22]

Such authority to contract may be varied, renewed or revoked by a special resolution.

The proposed contract, or a memorandum of its terms, must be available for inspection for at least 15 days ending with the date of the meeting at the company's registered office and at the meeting itself.[23] The name of the proposed

---

[16] Above, p.147.

[17] *Brown v British Abrasive Wheel Co.* [1919] 2 Ch.290; *Dafen Tinplate Co. Ltd v Llanelly Steel Co.* [1920] 2 Ch.124; *cf. Sidebotham v Kershaw, Leese and Co.* [1920] 1 Ch.154.

[17a] *Peña v Dale* [2004] 2 B.C.L.C. 508.

[18] They need not be determined by the articles, as for redeemed shares: s.162(2A).

[19] *i.e.* shares which are not traded on a recognised investment exchange or if so purchased are not subject to a marketing arrangement, in either case within the meaning of Pt XVIII of the FSMA 2002.

[20] [1998] 1 B.C.L.C. 193.

[21] Below, p.262.

[22] This time-limit stems from the Second Directive. There is a proposal to amend the directive to allow a five-year period: Com (2004) October 2004.

[23] The documents must be sent to each member prior to his signature if the written resolution procedure is being used: Sch.15A, para.5, see below, p.263.

vendor(s) must be made clear. That is because such vendors may not vote with the shares concerned on the resolution if such a vote would affect the result. In such circumstances failure to abstain with those votes will invalidate the resolution.[24] The vendor(s) can however vote with any other shares owned and can demand a poll[25] to exercise those votes.

It is not clear whether a breach of the various procedural requirements will make the purchase void under s.143. It has been said that failure to pass the required resolution prior to the contract being made and a breach of the voting restrictions will have that effect.[26] On the other hand, a breach of the rule requiring a memorandum of the contract to be available for 15 days prior to the meeting was said not to invalidate the purchase, at least where all the shareholders were aware of the terms of the contract.[27] The answer may well be that if the requirement can be seen as protecting only the shareholders and they all in effect waive that protection then the purchase will be valid.

Any variation of the contract itself, as distinct from the authority to enter into it, must be authorised in the same way as the original contract except that both contracts must be available for inspection.

It has also been decided in Scotland that a contract to purchase shares which has not complied with the statutory requirements for approval cannot be enforced.[28] In *Vision Express (UK) Ltd v Wilson (No. 2)*,[29] however, it was held that an agreement by the company to acquire its own shares as part of an agreed settlement of litigation and which was as such illegal under s.143, could be cured by the introduction of an implied term that the acquisition should comply with the statutory provisions, *i.e.* the off-market procedure under s.164.[30] Thus, since the company had in fact passed the necessary resolution, specific performance of the agreement would be ordered. But in the ordinary case where the transaction has already been completed the transaction cannot be validated in this way.[31]

Contingent purchase contracts. Companies may purchase options to acquire their own shares under the terms of s.165. The procedure involved is that for an off-market purchase, *i.e.* a special resolution authorising each such option. Such a procedure means that listed companies cannot purchase traded options to acquire their own listed shares so as to speculate against the value of such shares.

Market purchases. Public companies may, however, purchase their quoted shares under the procedure laid down by s.166. In essence the company needs the prior approval of an ordinary resolution[32] for the purchase of a number of shares

---

[24] In the case of a written resolution the vendor's signature is irrelevant provided all the other shareholders sign the resolution: Sch.15A, para.5. See p.263 below.

[25] Below, p.255.

[26] *Re R W Peak (Kings Lynn Ltd* [1998] 1 BCLC 193 at 198–205; *Wright v Atlas Wright (Europe) Ltd* [1999] 2 BCLC 301 at 310–315.

[27] *BDG Roof-Bond v Douglas* [2000] 1 BCLC 401.

[28] *Western v Rigblast Holdings Ltd*, 1989 G.W.D. 23–950 (Sh.Ct.).

[29] [1998] B.C.C. 173.

[30] On the basis that where an agreement can be performed in a lawful or unlawful manner there was a presumption that the parties intended to carry it out in the lawful manner. See *e.g. Brady v Brady* [1989] A.C. 755, below, p.178.

[31] *Re R. W. Peak (Kings Lynn) Ltd* [1998] 1 B.C.L.C. 193.

[32] This resolution must, however, be registered as if it was a special resolution.

within a specified price band and within a specified time, not greater than 18 months.[33] The maximum and minimum figures in the price band may be settled by reference to a formula.

The need for a general rather than a specific authority to purchase is dictated by the Stock Exchange rules on trading. It is difficult to see, however, why only an ordinary resolution should be required.

The Stock Exchange has its own rules covering such purchases.

Disclosure of purchases

Under s.169 details of all purchases which either cannot or do not lead to the company exercising the treasury share option must be registered within 28 days. A purchase may be effected by a surrender of shares so that no transfer document will be necessary. Under s.169A, where the company is able, and intends to, retain some or all of the shares as treasury shares (see below), their acquisition and subsequent disposal must be notified to the Registrar within 28 days of the relevant event.

All contracts of purchase or options to purchase must also be kept at the company's registered office for 10 years from the date of completion of the purchase or expiry of the options, as appropriate. These must be open to inspection. Option contracts need only be registered if activated.

Assignment and release of a company's rights to purchase

Under s.167 any assignment by a company of its rights under a contract to purchase its own shares is totally prohibited. Companies are not allowed to speculate against their own share price by buying and selling rights to purchase.

Companies with rights under an off-market purchase or option, however, may release such rights if such a release is approved by a special resolution. The vendor shareholders are, however, prohibited from voting with those shares if it would affect the result.

Funds available for redemption or purchase

The rules relating to the funding of a redemption or purchase of a company's own shares are the same. They are set out in ss 160(1) and (2).

The nominal value of the redeemed or purchased shares may be paid for either out of the company's distributable profits[34] or the proceeds of a specific fresh issue of shares made for the purpose. In the event there will be no reduction of capital—in the latter case a fresh amount of capital will replace that used.

The premium on any such shares may, however, only be paid for out of distributable profits unless the shares themselves were originally issued at a

---

[33] This time limit in the Second Directive as subject to a proposal by the EC Commission to extend it to 5 years: Com (2004) Oct. 2004.

[34] Below, Ch.22. These include a non-capital reserve created on a reduction of capital: *Quayle Munro Ltd, Petitioners*, 1992 S.C. 24; [1994] 1 B.C.L.C. 410. Payment in kind rather than in cash is allowed: *BDG Roof-Bond Ltd v Douglas* [2000] 1 BCLC 401.

premium. In that case the proceeds of a fresh issue may be used up to the amount of the company's share premium account at the time. In effect the share premium account may be used to fund the purchase or redemption and then be replaced by a fresh issue of shares.

Under s.168, any payment to acquire an option to purchase shares, or to obtain any variation or release from a contract to purchase, as distinct from the purchase itself, must be found from distributable profits.

In so far as the company uses distributable profits for such payments the funds available for dividends[35] are thereby reduced: s.274. Further, in such a case an amount equal to the amount of profits used must be transferred on the company's balance sheet to a fund known as the *capital redemption reserve*: s.170. This is a capital fund to which the rules relating to reduction of capital apply. The object of this section is to prevent the balance sheet showing a paper profit which might be distributed by way of dividend. That profit would otherwise arise through the current assets being reduced once by the amount necessary to redeem or purchase the shares, whereas both the share capital[36] and the revenue reserve would be reduced by that amount.

Failure by a company to redeem or purchase its own shares

If a company has issued redeemable shares under s.159 and fails to redeem them, or agrees to purchase its own shares and fails to honour that agreement, the shareholder has a right of action for breach of contract under s.178.

Section 178(2), however, provides that the company shall not be "liable in damages for any failure on its part to redeem or purchase the shares".[37] In *Barclays Bank plc v. British and Commonwealth Holdings plc*,[38] the Court of Appeal held that this restriction was limited to a claim for damages in respect of the company's breach of its actual agreement to purchase or redeem its shares. It did not apply to an action by a party other than the shareholder for breach of a covenant by the company, even though the breach of that covenant, failure to maintain its assets value, caused the failure to redeem and the damages for breach of covenant were measurable by the failure to redeem. The Court of Appeal also indicated that in any event the prohibition was probably restricted to actions by shareholders.[39] A shareholder may apply for an order of specific performance,[40] but this will only be made if the company is able to fulfil its obligations out of distributable profits.

If the company goes into liquidation after the obligation to redeem or purchase has arisen the shares are regarded as being cancelled on the liquidation but the vendor/shareholder may prove (apply for) any loss suffered as a creditor in the liquidation unless the company could not have fulfilled its obligations out

---

[35] Below, Ch.22.

[36] Because of the need to cancel the redeemed or purchased shares.

[37] Such a claim if made by a shareholder would gain priority over other shareholders' rights against the company in the event of a liquidation since it would in effect turn the right for a repayment of capital into a creditor's claim for damages.

[38] [1996] 1 B.C.L.C. 1, CA.

[39] For the reasons given in n.37 above.

[40] S.178(3). See *Vision Express (UK) Ltd v Wilson (No. 2)* [1998] B.C.C. 419.

of distributable profits at any time between the date of redemption or purchase and the date of liquidation. Such a vendor/shareholder is a deferred creditor[41] and, as such, will be paid after all the other creditors but before the shareholders.

Treatment of purchased shares—treasury shares

In general, s.160(4) applies to purchased shares as it does to redeemed shares, so that they must be cancelled. But changes made in 2003 by two Regulations[42] allow some companies the option to retain and, if desired, reissue their purchased shares.[43] These are known as treasury shares, *i.e.* they are held by the company in treasury, pending disposal or cancellation. The ability to diminish or increase the number of its shares owned by shareholders is seen as an advantage to companies in managing their capital structures, *i.e.* their debt/equity ratios. In addition to introducing this new regime, the 2003 Regulations made numerous amendments to other sections of the Act to deal with the new situation whereby a company could be the owner of its own shares. These are mentioned throughout the book, but the general theme is to discount them from all calculations of percentage holdings and thresholds etc. There were also knock on effects for the Stock Exchange and the Takeover Panel.[44]

The treasury share option is in fact a very limited one. It only applies if three requirements are met. First, the shares (referred to as qualifying shares) must either be listed or traded on the Alternative Investment Market.[45] That excludes all private companies at a stroke.[46] Second, the shares must have been purchased out of distributable profits,[47] and third, they cannot exceed in total more than ten per cent of the nominal value of the shares or of the shares of the class concerned.[48] Shares above that limit are known as excess shares and must be either disposed of or cancelled (under the procedure set out in s.162D—see below) within 12 months.[49]

If those three conditions are met, then under s.162A, the company may hold some or all of them and/or deal with all or any of them[50] either by sales for cash[51] or pursuant to an employee share scheme.[52] It may of course cancel them at any

---

[41] Below, Ch.29.

[42] Companies (Acquisition of Own Shares) (Treasury Shares) Regs 2003, SI 2993.1116; Companies (Acquisition of Own Shares) (Treasury Shares) (No 2) Regs. SI 2003/3031.

[43] These are allowed under the terms of the Second EC Directive.

[44] See generally Morse, *The Introduction of Treasury Shares into English Law and Practice* [2004] JBL 303.

[45] s.162(4).

[46] If the shares cease to be qualifying shares they must be calcelled immediately: s.162E(1).

[47] s.162(2B).

[48] s.162B. This is the maximum currently permitted by the Second EC Directive but there is a proposal from the EC Commission to amend that directive to allow purchases in total up to the level of a company's distributable reserves: COM 04, Oct 2004.

[49] Here are penalties in default under s.162G. s.143 does not apply to contraventions of the numerical limit.

[50] Under s.162D.

[51] This does not apply where there has been a takeover offer and the offeror has achieved a 90 per cent acceptance rate and wishes to invoke ss 429–430F of the Act to acquire the rest. In such a case the company cannot dispose of its hares to anyone else. See Ch.31 below.

[52] In practice, assenting shares to such a scheme may be one of the most useful aspects of treasury shares.

time. If the shares are resold for cash, s.162E provides that insofar as the proceeds are equal to or less than the price paid by the company to acquire them, they are to be regarded as distributable profits.[53] Any excess of receipts over the purchase price is, however, regarded as capital and an equivalent amount must be transferred to the share premium account.

The company is to be registered as the owner of treasury shares in the register of members, but this is a purely nominal ownership as no rights such as voting or attending meetings can be exercised by the company in respect of such shares: s.162C. The exceptions to this are: (i) the company may keep any bonus shares issued in respect of the treasury shares, but such bonus shares will themselves become treasury shares; and (ii) since the company may acquire redeemable shares as treasury shares, it may redeem them and make any payment due on them.

REDEMPTION OR PURCHASE OF SHARES OUT OF CAPITAL

Sections 171 to 177 allow private companies to purchase or redeem their own shares out of capital. These sections do not increase the powers of redemption or purchase themselves—ss 159 to 166 must first be complied with[54]—but they extend the funds available beyond distributable profits and proceeds of a fresh issue of shares. In essence, if those funds prove to be insufficient, *private* companies may resort to "capital." If the alternative procedure for the reduction of capital for private companies recommended by the Company Law Review is introduced, the review recommended that this procedure would be redundant and should be repealed.[55]

"Capital" in this context is any fund other than distributable profits and the proceeds of a fresh issue, whether or not it is technically capital for the rules relating to reduction of capital, etc.[56] Thus undistributable profits[57] may be used. s.171 however, makes it clear that private companies must first utilise distributable profits before resorting to "capital".

To use the power a private company must have authority to do so in its articles. Secondly, there must be a shortfall in the funds available to all companies (distributable profits and issue proceeds). In reality, this means distributable profits as there is no obligation to make a special issue of shares to provide any proceeds: s.171.

To ascertain whether there is a genuine shortfall the company must calculate its available distributable profits under s.263[58] by reference to accounts drawn up at any date within the three months immediately preceding the date on which the directors make the required declaration of solvency, which initiates the procedure. The accounts must enable a reasonable judgment to be made: s.172. The shortfall between available profits and the amount needed for purchase or redemption is known as the *permissible capital payment* (P.C.P.).

---

[53] Thus they are available for distribution on the basis that they are replacing the profits used to acquire the shares.
[54] Above, p.162.
[55] *Final Report*, Vol. 1 para.10.6.
[56] Above, p.150. See also *Quayle Munro Ltd, Petitioners*, 1992 S.C. 24.
[57] *e.g.* the revaluation reserve.
[58] Below, Ch.22.

If the P.C.P. and the proceeds of any issue used for the redemption or purchase are together less than the nominal value of the shares redeemed or purchased, the remainder must have come from distributable profits. In that case s.171(4) provides that an equivalent amount to those profits must be transferred to the *capital redemption reserve* as in the general funding power and for the same reasons.

However, if the P.C.P. and the proceeds of any issue used for the redemption or purchase amount to more than the nominal value of the shares redeemed or purchased, part of those capital funds must have been used to cover the redemption or purchase of the premium on those shares. In such a case s.171(5) provides that the excess must be deducted either from the capital redemption reserve, the share premium account, share capital figure or unrealised profits of the company. If such profits are subsequently realised they cannot then be used for dividends.

Exercise of the power

Section 173 makes it unlawful for a company to use its *permissible capital payment* (P.C.P.) unless the procedure laid down in that section is followed. This procedure is in addition to that required for the approval of the purchase; it is to approve the redemption or purchase *out of capital.*

Just as a specific off-market purchase requires the prior authority of a special resolution so does the use of capital. However in this case it must be preceded not by details of the contract but by a statutory declaration of solvency by the directors. This declaration must relate both to the company's immediate ability to pay its debts after using its P.C.P. and its ability to do so for the following year, taking into account the company's resources and the directors' management intentions.[59] It must be accompanied by an auditors' report that the P.C.P. has been properly ascertained and that the declaration of solvency itself is not unreasonable: s.173.

That declaration must be followed on the same day or within one week by the necessary special resolution.[60] After it has been passed no payment can be made for five weeks. (This is to enable any objection to the payment to be made to the court—see below.) The resolution must then be implemented within two further weeks: s.174.

The proposed vendor will invalidate the resolution if he votes with the shares in question in such a way as to affect the result.[61]

The requirement of a special resolution will put the shareholders on notice as to what is intended. But since this involves "capital," the company's creditors need to know. It may affect their guarantee fund. Accordingly s.175 requires the company to place a notice both in either the London or the Edinburgh Gazette,

---

[59] A similar procedure applies to the rules allowing financial assistance to be given by private companies for the purchase by others of these shares. See Ch.13, below.

[60] The written resolution procedure may be used (below, p.232). In such a case the documents must be supplied to each member prior to his signature of the resolution: Sch.15A, para.6.

[61] If the resolution is a written resolution the signature, or otherwise, of the vendor is irrelevant: Sch.15A, para.6.

as appropriate,[62] and in a national newspaper.[63] The latter can, theoretically, be avoided by giving a notice to each creditor of the company.

The notice must state that the resolution has been passed and what its effect is. It must also specify the P.C.P. and the date of the resolution and state first that the statutory declaration of solvency and auditors' report are available for inspection at the company's registered office and second that a creditor may apply to the court, within five weeks of the date of the resolution, to have the resolution set aside.

The declaration of solvency and the auditors' report must be available both for shareholders at the meeting, and subsequently, for either shareholders and creditors at the registered office during the five week holding period: s.174. Further, they must be registered with the Registrar by the first notice date—*i.e.* the date of publication in the Gazette or the newspaper, whichever is earlier.

Objections by members and creditors

Under s.176, any member who did not vote for the special resolution authorising the use of capital, or any creditor[64] may petition the court to have the resolution set aside within five weeks of the date of the resolution. For a creditor the effective time limit may be four weeks since the advertisements putting him on notice can be put in up to a week after the resolution.

On such a petition the court has all the powers available to it as on a petition to prevent a public company re-registering as a private company under s.54. Thus it may order a compulsory purchase of the shareholder's shares by the company, alter the company's constitution, cancel, amend or confirm the resolution or impose new time scales for its implementation: s.177.

If either there are no objections, or the court overrides them, the P.C.P. may be used by the company for the purchase or redemption as appropriate.

Liability of shareholders and directors

Where a private company which has made a payment out of capital under s.173 for the purchase or redemption of its own shares is wound up as being unable to pay its debts within one year of the payments being made, s.76 of the Insolvency Act 1986 applies.

In such a case the recipient of the payment, known as the relevant payment, and any director who signed the statutory declaration of solvency without having reasonable grounds for doing so, are liable to repay the amount of the relevant payment up to the amount needed to cover the company's insolvency.

This liability is linked to the amount of the relevant payments needed to cover the company's outstanding debts. Liability is joint and several so that any of the recipients or directors may be sued for the whole amount leaving him to recover a contribution from the others.

---

[62] Depending on the location of the company's registered office.
[63] In England and Wales, or Scotland as appropriate.
[64] There appears to be no minimum debt required.

By way of protection anyone who might be liable to make payment under this section may petition to wind up the company on the grounds of its insolvency or on the just and equitable ground under s.122(1)(f) or (g) of the Insolvency Act 1986.[65]

---

[65] Below, Chs 27 and 18 respectively.

Chapter 11

FINANCIAL ASSISTANCE BY A COMPANY FOR THE PURCHASE OF ITS OWN SHARES

UNDER s.54 of the 1948 Act (which replaced s.45 of the 1929 Act), it was unlawful for a company to give any person financial assistance for the purchase of, or subscription for, its own shares or those of its holding company. The motives were originally to preserve the share capital, but later to prevent the misuse of assets by those in control of a company[1] and to prevent the creation of a false market in that company's shares—*i.e.* by artificially stimulating demand for the shares at a time when the share price may be particularly important, *e.g.* in a take-over situation.[2]

Section 54 of the 1948 Act was itself repealed by the 1981 Act and replaced by what are now ss 151 to 158 of the 1985 Act. Section 151 re-enacts the basic prohibition in a much modified form and applies to all companies. Section 153 contains many exceptions to that prohibition. Private companies are, however, allowed to give such assistance generally, subject to safeguards for creditors and minority shareholders, under what are known as the "whitewash provisions", ss 154 to 158.[3] The prohibition has been much criticised and calls for its repeal or modification are frequently made. It is seen as outdated and as a barrier to innocent transactions. The proposal for reform are set out at the end of this chapter.

The basic prohibitions

Section 151 applies two basic prohibitions on the giving of financial assistance—one when the assistance precedes the acquisition and the other when it follows it. In both cases a breach is a criminal offence, both for the company and any officer in default, which can lead to a term of imprisonment, or a fine, or both.[4] There are differences from the original 1948 prohibition brought about by the apparently very wide scope of the earlier section.

(1) Financial assistance given before or at the time of the acquisition. It is unlawful[5] for a company or any of its subsidiaries to give financial assistance

---

[1] By using corporate funds to assist a takeover bidder in the acquisition of the controlling interest by way of a loan, see, *e.g. Selangor United Rubber Estates Ltd v Cradock (No. 3)* [1968] 1 W.L.R. 1555. It is suggested that this above is better covered by controls on directors' activities: see Ch.16 below.

[2] Other provisions are now aimed at controlling this—see FSMA 2000, which renders this part of the rationale redundant.

[3] Art. 23 of the Second Directive which requires some restrictions does not apply to private companies.

[4] Originally under s.54 of the 1948 Act the only sanction was a £100 fine. For the civil consequences see below.

[5] Subject to the exemptions set out below.

directly or indirectly for the purpose of an acquisition or proposed acquisition by any person of its own shares or those of its holding company, either before or at the same time as the acquisition took place: s.151(1).

Thus assistance may be direct or indirect. It applies to all acquisitions of shares so that it includes all transfers of shares.

(2) *Financial assistance given after the acquisition.* It is also unlawful for a company or any of its subsidiaries to give financial assistance directly or indirectly for the purpose of reducing or discharging any liability incurred by any person for the purpose of an acquisition of that company's own shares or those of its holding company, provided that the acquisition took place prior to the assistance being given: s.151(2).

For this prohibition a person incurs a liability if he changes his financial position by making any agreement of any type: s.152(3)(a). That liability is reduced or discharged by the company if the financial assistance is given wholly or partly for the purpose of restoring that person's financial position to what it was before the acquisition took place: s.152(3)(b).

Subsidiaries

The prohibitions apply equally to a subsidiary providing financial assistance for the acquisition of shares in its holding company. In *Arab Bank plc v Mercantile Holdings Ltd*[6] it was held that the mere fact that a subsidiary provides such assistance does not mean that the assistance has been provided by the holding company, although there may be circumstances, *e.g.* where the holding company transfers an asset to the subsidiary which the latter then uses to provide the assistance, where the holding company may do so indirectly. That case also decided that the prohibitions do not apply to foreign subsidiaries providing assistance in relation to the shares of a UK holding company.

The key criteria

The potential width of the prohibitions means that they may well strike down transactions which in no way threaten any of the original reasons for their existence. It is essential, however, to realise that the prohibitions will only apply if (i) there is *assistance* given by the company *for the purpose of the acquisition* of its shares[7] and (ii) that assistance is *financial*. It is not enough to show either that there is a financial transaction involving a company and a person acquiring its shares if there was no assistance, or that there was the necessary assistance if it is not also financial. It is helpful to take these two requirements in reverse order.

Financial assistance

Financial assistance for both the prohibitions is inclusively defined in s.152(2). If the transaction does not fall within this definition then the sections cannot apply.

---

[6] [1994] 1 B.C.L.C. 330.
[7] Or for reducing the liability in the case of post-acquisition assistance.

It includes gifts,[8] the giving of a guarantee,[9] security[10] or indemnity,[11] loans and other forms of credit agreements, and releases and waivers—and any "other financial assistance" which reduces the net assets of the company "to a material extent"[12] or which has no net assets.[13] Only in the last of these is there any requirement that the company has actually lost assets. The others need no such element and so can hardly be said to be part of the maintenance of capital regime.

In *Parlett v Guppys (Bridport) Ltd*,[14] the Court of Appeal held that where a number of independent companies had agreed to pay the plaintiff a salary and bonus if he transferred his shares in one of them, the net assets of that company had not been reduced since there were sufficient distributable profits to pay the sums due. They did not therefore have to decide as to whether they were reduced by "a material extent" but rejected the idea, put to them by both counsel, that 5 per cent would be the relevant criteria. It would be a question of degree.

Assistance for the purpose

The financial assistance must be also be given for the purpose of the acquisition of the shares. The difficulties of this requirement were highlighted initially by the decision of the Court of Appeal in *Belmont Finance Corporation v Williams Furniture Ltd (No 2)*[15] on the different wording of the former s.54 of the 1948 Act. The case was concerned with the situation where a company enters into a commercial transaction, *e.g.* buying goods from a supplier, and at the same time that supplier uses the proceeds to buy shares in the company. Buckley L.J. was of the opinion that in such a case it would not have amounted to a breach of the old section if the company had a genuine need for the goods but that it would have been if the purpose of the supply had been to provide the supplier with funds to acquire the shares, even if the company paid the full value for them. He left open the middle case, *i.e.* where the purpose of the transaction was partly to put the supplier in funds and partly to obtain the goods.

In another case on the former s.54, *Charterhouse Investment Trust Ltd v Tempest Diesels Ltd*,[16] Hoffmann J. suggested an alternative approach in such

---

[8] Which may well include overpayments made by a company: see *Plat v Steiner* (1989) 5 B.C.C. 352.

[9] This has been defined in *Yeoman Credit Ltd v Latter* [1961] 1 W.L.R. 828 at p.831 as: "a contract to answer for the debt, default or miscarriage of another who is to be primarily liable to the promisee."

[10] For the definition of a security see *Singer v Williams* [1921] 1 A.C. 41, HL.

[11] This has been given its strict legal meaning, *i.e.* "a contract by one party to keep the other harmless against loss": *Barclays Bank plc v British and Commonwealth Holdings plc* [1996] 1 B.C.L.C. 1, CA. Thus it was held in that case not to apply to a contract whereby the damages recoverable for its breach were the same as would have been recovered under an indemnity.

[12] Net assets for this purpose are defined by reference to the company's assets and liabilities.

[13] *In MT Realisations Ltd v Digital Equipment Co Ltd* [2002] 2 B.C.L.C. 688, Laddie J said that this meant that if a company had net assets there must be a material reduction but that if it did not, any reduction would suffice—the concept was otherwise the same. But this was doubted by the CA in *Chaston v SWP Group plc* [2003] 1 BCLC 675 where the two were said to be alternatives—either a material reduction in net assets, or no assets.

[14] [1996] 2 B.C.L.C. 34, CA.

[15] [1980] 1 All E.R. 393.

[16] [1986] 1 B.C.L.C. 1.

difficult cases. The question, he said, was whether there had been a net transfer of value by the company to the acquirer. Since, in that case, that could not be shown, there was no financial assistance. The test should be applied by looking at the *commercial realities* of the transaction as a whole and not be strained to cover transactions not fairly within it.

When the sections were redrafted into their present form an attempt was made to solve the *Belmont* problem by reference to the principal purpose or main purpose of the company. Before turning to these ill-fated and largely irrelevant "purpose exceptions", however, it is necessary to consider the interpretation of the reworded s.151. The initial consideration was given by the Court of Appeal in *Barclays Bank plc v British and Commonwealth Holdings plc*[17] as to the approach to be adopted in deciding whether, assuming there was *financial* assistance, there has been a breach of either of the prohibitions in s.151.

Aldous L.J., with whose judgment the other members of the Court of Appeal agreed, adopted the following approach of Mahoney J. in *Burton v Palmer*[18] to the equivalent provision in the New South Wales legislation.

> "There may, of course, be circumstances in which the obligations entered into by a company are entered into for a collateral purpose: in such circumstances it may be that the company will, in the particular case, be giving financial assistance. But, collateral purpose aside, if [s.151] is to be relevant, there must be more than the incurring, in connection with the transfer of shares, of an obligation which may involve the company in the payment of money. The obligation must be such that it is properly to be categorised as financial assistance. . . . I do not mean by this that the relevance of [s.151] is to be determined by a schematic analysis of the obligation undertaken. The words "financial assistance" are words of a commercial rather than a conveyancing kind and the form of the obligation or transaction will not be conclusive."

On that basis, assuming always that the assistance is financial within the meaning of the section, the primary test to establish whether there has been a breach of s.151 is whether the obligation on the company can properly be categorised as financial assistance in a commercial sense.[19] That clearly mirrors the "commercial reality" approach to the former section applied by Hoffmann J. in *Charterhouse*. If, in reality, that obligation involves the collateral purpose of giving such assistance, then the section will apply. An example of that, given by Mahoney J. in *Burton v Palmer*, is where a company gives a warranty with the intention that it will have to pay damages in order to provide the funds for an acquisition of its shares. If there is no such obvious collateral purpose, however, then applying the commercial reality test has proved to be more difficult.[20]

An example is the Court of Appeal's view in *MacPherson v European Strategic Bureau Ltd*.[21] That case concerned an agreement whereby, as part of an exit

---

[17] [1986] 1 B.C.L.C. 1, CA.

[18] [1980] 2 N.S.W.L.R. 878 at pp. 889–890.

[19] If so, then it seems that the section will apply if the assistance is given to the vendor rather than to the purchaser of the shares: *Armour Hick Northern Ltd v Whitehouse* [1980] 3 All E.R. 833; *Partlett v Guppy's (Bridport) Ltd* [1996] 2 B.C.L.C. 34 CA.

[20] The absence of any such collateral purpose meant that the Court of Appeal in the *Barclays Bank* case were able to validate a covenant entered into by a company as part of a complex deal to persuade another to take shares in the company even though breach of that covenant gave rise to an action for damages against the company.

[21] [2000] 2 B.C.L.C. 683, disagreeing with the judge below, [1999] 2 B.C.L.C. 203.

package, two of the three active shareholders agreed to sell their shares to the other for a nominal value and a share of the future profits accruing to the company from a contract they had helped to set up. The Court indicated that in their provisional view this was in breach of s.151. Without referring to any previous decisions, the Court said that the agreement provided a strong incentive for the sale of the shares and that it was inconceivable that the vendors would have transferred their shares for a nominal value unless they had also had the benefit of the future profits share agreement. That obligation was therefore the financial assistance involved.[22]

In *MT Realisations Ltd v Digital Equipment Co Ltd*,[23] Laddie J., in a clear attempt to limit the scope of the section, said that in the absence of a collateral purpose there was a distinction between a company giving financial incentives for another to enter into an agreement or concurrent benefits (outside the section) and financial assistance for the actual acquisition of the shares. There was a difference between assistance given in connection with a transfer and assistance given for the actual transfer.[24] This approach was, however, roundly criticised by the Court of Appeal in *Chaston v SWP Group Ltd.*[25] The company had paid the fees for the drawing up of a report on its parent company for the benefit of a prospective purchaser of the parent company's shares. Rejecting Laddie J.'s approach,[26] the Court of Appeal said that this payment had assisted the purchaser, helped smooth the course of the acquisition and was to further it. It must therefore have been for the purpose of the acquisition. Arden L.J. also made the following points: (i) there was no need for the company to suffer a detriment (except for a loss to the net assets if required to establish that the assistance was financial);[27] (ii) it was sufficient if the assistance was an inducement; (iii) there was no need to establish any impact on the company's share price; and (iv) the assistance need only be one of the purposes of the obligation.[28]

But the Court of Appeal also stressed the commercial reality test first stated by Hoffman J. in *Charterhouse* and this has been applied in the cases since *Chaston*. In *Dyment v Boyden*,[29] for example, two shareholders jointly owned a nursing home and the company which ran it. One of them, Mr Boyden, was disqualified from running a nursing home and agreed to transfer his shares to Mrs Dyment in return for the other surrendering her interest in the property. He then negotiated

---

[22] It could be argued that they were therefore in fact finding that here was a collateral purpose. The judge took a different view, that the profit share agreement was in reality compensation for unpaid work the shareholders had performed for the company and not for the shares. The case was actually decided on different issues.

[23] [2002] 2 B.C.L.C. 688.

[24] The CA upheld this actual decision but on other grounds based on a complex analysis of the facts which in their view did not establish that there had been any financial assistance by the company concerned. They did also stress the commercial reality test; [2003] 2 B.C.L.C. 117.

[25] [2003] 1 B.C.L.C. 675. The CA in *MT Realisations* refused to be drawn into this dispute.

[26] And explaining the *Barclays Bank* case on the curious basis that there was no intention that the covenant would ever be used (but it was).

[27] Under s.152(1)(iv), above.

[28] Given the very narrow interpretation applied to the purpose exceptions, below, which might have been expected to have come into play in this situation, this is not surprising. And, in fact, Arden L.J. used s.153 to come to this conclusion. It is hard to see, however, the mischief in the facts of *Chaston* which would have made it a criminal offence.

[29] [2004] 2 B.C.L.C. 427; affmd [2005] B.C.C. 79, CA.

a rental from the company in excess of the market rate. Hart J. and the Court of Appeal held that the excess rental agreement was not post-acquisition unlawful financial assistance for the transfer because although it was connected with the sale of the shares it was not for the purpose of that sale in a commercial sense. The clear purpose of the company (as inferred from Mrs Dyment's acts) was to enter into an agreement which would allow its business to continue. The purpose of Mr Boyden may well have been to make up for his loss of income from the company, but that was not the company's purpose.

Similarly in *Harlow v Loveday*,[30] commercial reality dictated that a charge given by the company to A as security for a loan made by A to B, which was used by B to purchase shares in the company, was given for the purpose of the acquisition. Although B was not bound to use the loan monies to purchase the shares, each of the parties knew what the loan and security were for.

The purpose exceptions

For the reasons already stated, two new exceptions were introduced by the 1981 Act. They can be found in s.153(1) in relation to financial assistance given before or at the same time as the acquisition and s.153(2) for post-acquisition assistance. However, both contain the same two exceptions based on the purpose, for which the assistance was given.

(1) *Where the principal purpose of giving the financial assistance was not for the purpose of the acquisition and was given in good faith in the interests of the company.* The exception was designed to protect groups of companies with relevance to the post-acquisition assistance prohibition. For example, where, following the acquisition of a new subsidiary company, the acquiring company has to charge the assets of that subsidiary to comply with a prior debenture which requires all the assets of the group to be charged on security. In such a case, the security would not be given for the principal purpose of reducing a liability incurred for the purpose of acquiring the subsidiary.

(2) *Where even if the principal purpose of giving the financial assistance was for the acquisition of shares it was an incidental part of some larger purpose and was given in good faith in the interests of the company.* This exception was also defined with reference to post-acquisition financial assistance within a group of companies. For example, when a subsidiary company provides funds to its parent company some years after it has been acquired to effect a more efficient deployment of assets within the group, the proviso may relieve the parent company of indebtedness incurred for the purpose of acquiring the subsidiary but if the larger purpose can be established it will be exempt.

These two purpose exceptions contain an inherent difficulty. They could be interpreted very widely so that if there is any overall scheme, *e.g.* a takeover bid, which involves financial assistance being given for the purpose of the acquisition of shares, the overall scheme will serve as the principal or larger purpose for the

[30] [2004] B.C.C. 732.

exceptions to apply, even though the narrow purpose of giving the assistance was the acquisition (the latter is, as we have seen, necessary for the prohibition to apply in the first place). On the other hand if the purpose of giving the assistance is the acquisition of shares (as above, the starting point) how can the giving of that assistance (as distinct from the acquisition of the shares) ever be part of a larger or principal purpose? In either extent what is meant by good faith in this context?

In *Brady v Brady*,[31] a group of private companies, which ran two businesses, was controlled by two brothers who quarrelled, with a resulting deadlock. The proposed solution was a division of the businesses between them, but one was more valuable than the other. To equalise the division, a complex series of transactions followed, one of which involved the transfer of a large proportion of one company's assets to pay off loan stock which had been issued as the purchase price of that company's shares. This was clearly a breach of s.151 since at least part of the purpose was to assist[32] the acquisition of the shares. The question arose as to whether the transaction could be saved under either of the purpose exceptions. The Court of Appeal was prepared to allow that the division of the group was a larger purpose of which the giving of the financial assistance was but an incidental part, but refused to apply the exception on the grounds that it was not given in good faith in the interests of the company, apparently on the basis that in the context of financial assistance the company includes the creditors as well as the shareholders, and the former had never been taken into consideration.

The House of Lords reversed the Court of Appeal on that point. Without deciding whether the interests of the creditors had to be considered, since at all times the group was solvent so that the creditors were not at risk and, in other respects, since the division of the group had prevented deadlock and expensive winding up petitions, it was in the interests of the company.

But on the main issue, the House decided that the assistance had not been given either as subsidiary to a principal purpose or incidental to a larger purpose. The key, according to Lord Oliver, was to distinguish between motive and purpose. The reason or motive was the division of the group but the only purpose of the assistance was to allow the shares to be acquired. "Larger" is not the same as "more important" nor is "reason" the same as "purpose". Thus the House of Lords came down on the restrictive interpretation of the purpose exceptions.

Following that decision the purpose exceptions will be of little use where as the result of a transaction a company provides financial assistance to a person acquiring its shares. Whether that is a collateral purpose of an otherwise innocent-looking transaction or whether the transaction itself can properly be categorised as financial assistance in a commercial sense so that s.151 applies, any reference to a larger or main purpose will be regarded as one of motive or reason. The situation will be best resolved on the issue as to whether the whole

---

[31] [1989] A.C. 755, HL; [1988] B.C.L.C. 20, CA. See also *Plaut v Steiner* (1989) 5 B.C.C. 352, where it was held that it could never be in the interests of the company if it became insolvent as a result of giving the assistance.

[32] *cf. Dyment v Boyden*, where on not dissimilar facts there was held to be no financial assistance in a commercial sense. Section 153 was not in issue in that case.

transaction can properly be categorised as financial assistance within s.151, rather than on the wording of s.153(1) and (2).[33]

There is, however, a suggested alternative application of the purpose exceptions. The test would be whether there was some overall corporate purpose, *i.e.* one for the benefit of the company itself, which would then remove a transaction otherwise in breach of s.151 (under either the collateral purpose or proper categorisation test). In *Brady v Brady* after all the transaction was for the benefit of solving the shareholders' dispute and not for the company as such.

There are also a number of specific types of transaction which are excluded from the ambit of s.151.

Authorised transaction exceptions

Section 153(3) sets out nine specific transactions permitted under company law which are not to be subject to the prohibition. These are as follows:

   (i) the distribution of lawful dividends.[34] The rules relating to the funds available for dividends are considered strong enough to protect companies. One of the old abuses was to extract unusually large dividends from a company to repay a loan used by the borrower to gain control of the company.

   (ii) distributions made in the course of a winding-up[35];

   (iii) the allotment of bonus shares[36];

   (iv) anything done under a court order under s.425[37];

   (v) anything done under an arrangement between a company and its creditors under s.1 of the Insolvency Act 1986[38];

   (vi) anything done under an arrangement made in pursuance of s.110 of the Insolvency Act 1986[39];

   (vii) any reduction of capital confirmed by the court under s.137[40];

   (viii) a redemption of shares under s.159[41];

   (ix) a purchase of its own shares by a company under ss 162–178.[42]

Loans and employee share scheme exceptions

The following three exceptions were, in general, available in the former s.54. They are only available to public companies if the book value of the net assets is

---

[33] This seems to have happened in the not dissimilar case of *Dyment v Boyden* [2005] B.C.C. 79 CA, above.
[34] Below, Ch.22.
[35] Below, Ch.29.
[36] Below, Ch.22.
[37] Below, Ch.30.
[38] Below, Ch.24.
[39] Below, Ch.30.
[40] Above, Ch.9.
[41] Above, Ch.10.
[42] *ibid.*

not reduced as a result, or, if it is, the assistance is paid out of distributable profits[43]: s.154.

(1) *Lending as part of the ordinary course of business.* If the lending of the money is in the company's course of business *and* the loan itself is within the ordinary course of that business s.151 does not apply. Banks may use this exception but an unusual loan will not qualify for exception[44]: s.153(4)(a).

(2) *Employee share schemes.* There is no prohibition on the provision of financial assistance by a company for the purposes of an employees' share scheme[45] if it is given in good faith in the interests of the company: s.153(4)(b). This exception was widened by the 1989 Act to allow companies, for example, to guarantee loans made to such schemes. Before, assistance was limited to the provision of money for the acquisition of such shares. The good faith criteria was added, however, and as we have seen this is by no means easy to define in such a context.[46] Directors can be included. This exception also applies to the provision of assistance by the company or another company in the same group to allow beneficiaries under a scheme and their families to trade between themselves: s.153(4)(bb)(5).

(3) *Loans to employees to purchase shares.* A company may lend money to those employed in good faith by the company in order for them to purchase shares in that company or its holding company for their own benefit. It does not apply to directors: s.153(4)(c).

Civil consequences of a breach

Section 151, like its predecessor, provides that financial assistance given in breach of the section is unlawful but provides only a criminal sanction. The question arises therefore as to the civil consequences of such a breach.

After some initial hestitation,[47] the courts have held that the actual financial assistance provided by the company, such as security for a loan[48] or guaranteeing an illegal security,[49] is void. It is clear that no such unlawful financial assistance may be enforced against the company. There is still some doubt, however, as to whether the company may enforce a loan against the borrower even if it constitutes financial assistance on the basis that the prohibitions are designed to protect the company.[50] In any event, the further question then arises as to

---

[43] Below, Ch.22.
[44] *Steen v Law* [1964] A.C. 287. A loan deliberately made by a bank with the purpose of an acquisition in mind is unlikely to be regarded as a usual loan.
[45] Defined in s.743.
[46] Above, p.178.
[47] *Victor Battery Co. Ltd v Curry's Ltd* [1946] Ch.242.
[48] *Selangor United Rubber Estates Ltd v Cradock (No. 3)* [1968] 1 W.L.R. 497; *Carney v Herbert* [1985] A.C. 301, PC; *Harlow v Loveday* [2004] B.C.C. 723.
[49] *Heald v O'Connor* [1971] 1 W.L.R. 497.
[50] See the statements of Lord Denning M.R. and Scarman L.J. in *Wallersteiner v Moir* [1974] 1 W.L.R. 991 at 1014, 1033, and of Buckley L.J. and Goff L.J. in *Belmont Finance Corp. Ltd v Williams Furniture Ltd* [1979] Ch.250 at 261, 271.

whether the whole transaction for the acquisition of shares is also void. This question arises in two different situations, where the financial assistance has actually been given and where it might potentially be given.

Validity of the transaction—actual financial assistance

In *South Western Mineral Water Co. v Ashmore*[51] Cross J. suggested that the agreement might be saved if the parties proceeded with the acquisition of the shares in a manner dissociating the purchase from the invalid security—*e.g.* by the seller/lender waiving his rights in the security or by the buyer paying the price at once. In the absence of this, however, the whole agreement to acquire the shares was in his opinion void.

In *Carney v Herbert*,[52] however, the Privy Council decided that if the unlawful elements in the transaction could be severed from the overall transaction and their elimination would leave the basic contract of sale of the shares unchanged, the remainder of the agreement could be enforced. Only the unlawful elements would be void. The fact that the vendor might have refused to enter into the transaction unless the unlawful elements had been included was *not* a relevant factor in determining their severability. The effect of this is to allow a contract of sale to be enforced where there is no damage to the company.

> H, A and J were directors of A Ltd and of its subsidiary N Ltd C was the fourth director of these companies and he decided to buy the shares of the other directors. They agreed to sell their shares to I Ltd, a company controlled by C, the purchase price to be payable in three instalments by I Ltd. C guaranteed I Ltd's payments, which were also secured by mortgages executed over N Ltd's property. I Ltd failed to pay for the shares and H, A and J sued C on his guarantee. C alleged that the whole transaction was void for unlawful financial assistance. The Privy Council held that the only unlawful financial assistance was the mortgage over N Ltd's property and that this could be severed so as to leave the sale and guarantee intact and enforceable: *Carney v Herbert* [1985] A.C. 301, PC.[53]

Validity of the transaction—potential financial assistance

In *Carney v Herbert*, above, two further allegations of financial assistance were made. First, it was said that payment for the shares had been made by means of a cheque drawn on the company's account. The Privy Council held that since there were a number of ways that such payment could have been effected without breaching the section it would not be assumed that it was in breach. Secondly, it was shown that the vendor/directors had been released from liability on their loan accounts with the company as part of the agreement with a consequent reduction in the purchase price of the shares. That was again held not to be necessarily financial assistance since it was more than offset by a credit balance in the purchaser/director's loan account. Since that could be reduced to the extent of the release it would leave the company in an identical position as before.

---

[51] [1967] 1 W.L.R. 1110.
[52] [1985] A.C. 301, PC. This decision was approved in *Neilson v Stewart*, 1991 S.C. HL 22. See also *Motor & General Insurance Co. Ltd v Gobin* (1987) 3 B.C.C. 61.
[53] But where the guarantee is of an illegal security it cannot be severed from the illegality and cannot therefore be enforced: *Heald v O'Connor* [1971] 1 W.L.R. 497.

That part of the decision illustrates the courts' desire to preserve the validity of a transaction if there is only potential financial assistance. Thus where there is a contract for the acquisition of shares which could be performed in a number of ways, only one of which would contravene s.151, the courts will assume that it was intended to perform the contract in a lawful manner, consistent with the benefit of the company, and order specific performance accordingly. In *Parlett v Guppys (Bridport) Ltd*,[54] therefore the Court of Appeal held that even assuming that the agreement to pay the vendor's salary would have amounted to financial assistance if it had been paid by the company whose shares were being acquired, it was reasonable to assume that in reality it would be paid by the other companies involved in the agreement. Such a solution would be beneficial to the companies as a whole.[55]

Liability of those participating in the breach

It was held that s.54 of the 1948 Act was passed to protect the company from having its assets misused and not merely to protect its creditors[56] and this will also apply to s.151. Thus any director who is knowingly a party to a breach of this section will be in breach of duty as a trustee of company funds to the company and liable to repay the loss.[57]

In addition anyone who receives the funds of the company so misapplied is liable to it as a constructive trustee if his knowledge makes it unconscionable for him to retain the benefit. Dishonesty is not essential.[58] Anyone who assists in the breach is also liable as an accessory but only if he acted dishonestly.[59]

It appears from the *Belmont* case that the company may also recover in the tort of conspiracy[60] if it can prove: (1) that the conspirators combined to participate in a common agreement with a common purpose; (2) that the combination was to carry out an unlawful purpose; *i.e.* the provision of financial assistance contrary to s.151; and (3) that the company suffered damages as a consequence. Damage must be proved.

General exemption for private companies—THE WHITEWASH PROCEDURE

Private companies may obtain complete exemption from the prohibitions regarding the provision of financial assistance for the acquisition of their own shares provided that they comply with a set procedure and timetable under ss 154 to

---

[54] [1996] 2 B.C.L.C. 34, CA.
[55] See also *Lawlor v Gray* [1984] 3 All E.R. 345; *Grant v Cigman* [1996] 2 B.C.L.C. 24. Such a solution cannot apply, however, if the transaction has been completed and no order for specific performance is sought: see *Re R. W. Peak (Kings Lynn) Ltd* [1998] 1 B.C.L.C. 198.
[56] *Wallersteiner v Moir* [1974] 1 W.L.R. 991, 1014, *per* Lord Denning M.R.
[57] *Belmont Finance Corp. v Williams Furniture Ltd (No. 2)* [1980] 1 All E.R. 393; *Wallersteiner v Moir*, above; *Karak Rubber Co. v Burden (No. 2)* [1972] 1 W.L.R. 602.
[58] *See Bank of Credit and Commerce International (overseas) Ltd v Akindele* [2000] 4 All E.R. 221, CA.
[59] *Royal Brunei Airlines v Tan* [1995] 2 A.C. 378. In *Twinsectra Ltd v Yardley* [2002] A.C. 164, it was held that the dishonesty required was both objective (dishonest by reasonable standards) and subjective (he was aware of his dishonesty).
[60] Or in Scots law under the general law of delict.

158. This general exemption is in addition to the exceptions already mentioned which are applicable to all companies. It is not available, however, for the acquisition of shares in a holding company unless that is itself a private company: s.155.

A general restriction on the use of this exemption is that the assistance must either leave the book value net assets of the company untouched[61] or be made out of distributable profits, s.155(2).[62] The idea is to protect creditors by ensuring that only funds available under s.263 for distribution as dividend are used.[63] That section, however, does not require companies to make provision for unrealised losses, so s.155(6) requires the directors to make a statutory declaration of the company's solvency prior to giving the assistance. If the shares to be acquired are in the company's holding company the directors of that company must also make a declaration.

Statutory declaration. Section 156 prescribes the form of the declaration. First, it must set out the assistance to be given,[64] the business of the company and the identity of the recipient. Secondly the directors must state that *in their opinion* the company will be able to pay its debts both immediately after giving the assistance and as they fall due during the following year.[65]

Attached to the declaration must be an auditors' report to the effect that they are not aware of anything to indicate that the opinion of the directors is unreasonable.[66] The declaration must be made by all the directors and will be invalid if they have not made sufficient enquiries into the financial affairs of the company, such that they can honestly make the required statements. Similarly, the auditor can only properly sign the report if his inquiries are sufficient that he can honestly make the required statement.[67] However, it will not be invalidated by errors if, taken as a whole, it is reasonably clear to an intelligent reader what the true position is. The court is mindful of the consequences of non-compliance with the procedure.[68]

Special resolution. To protect shareholders rather than creditors the financial assistance must be approved by a special resolution of each of the companies (holding, subsidiary) involved: s.155(4).

The statutory declaration and auditors' report must be available at the meeting at which the special resolution is passed. The meeting must take place on the

---

[61] A loan which is never going to be repaid will reduce the net assets: *Re In A Flap Envelop Co Ltd* [2004] 1 B.C.L.C. 64; but in that case it could not be shown that it could not be borne by distributable profits.

[62] This has been said to be for the protection of creditors *Harlow v Loveday* [2004] B.C.C. 372.

[63] Below, Ch.22.

[64] The obligation is to provide particulars of the form and principal terms of the financial assistance so that an omission of the identity of property to be charged and the kind of charge taken did not invalidate the declaration. The solvency declaration is, however, regarded as the more important: *Re S.H. & Co. (Realisations) 1990 Ltd* [1993] B.C.C. 60.

[65] If it is intended to wind up the company during this time the declaration must state that the company will be able to pay its debts within 12 months of the winding up.

[66] Provided that the relevant particulars are provided it is not necessary to use the official form: *Re N.L. Electrical Ltd* [1994] 1 B.C.L.C. 22.

[67] *Re In A Flap Envelope Co Ltd* [2004] 1 B.C.C.C. 64.

[68] *Harlow v Loveday* [2004] B.C.C. 732.

same day as, or within one week of, the date on which the declaration is made: s.157.[69] The declaration, auditors' report and resolution must be registered with the Registrar within 15 days of the passing of the resolution: s.156(5).[70]

After passing the resolution the company may not act upon it for four weeks unless all the members voted in favour. This allows a dissenting minority to petition the court to have the resolution set aside (see below). If more than one company is involved the period runs from the date of the last resolution to be passed: s.158.

Assuming that there are no minority shareholder objections the company must then implement the authority within eight weeks of the making of the declaration of solvency. In general therefore companies will have between three and four weeks to implement the authority after the four week delay, depending on how soon the resolution followed the declaration: s.158.

Minority protection. Holders of at least 10 per cent of the nominal share capital of any class, who did not vote for the authorising resolution, may apply to the court to have the resolution set aside. Such applications must be made within 28 days of the passing of the resolution—which corresponds to the waiting period for the company: s.157(2)(3).

The court has wide powers on such an application—those which are available to it on a petition under s.54[71] to prevent the re-registration of a public company as a private one. One of these powers is to order that the minority be bought out. The court may otherwise cancel, confirm or vary the resolution. Whilst the petition is being considered the resolution cannot be implemented unless the court orders otherwise: s.158(3).

The existence of this exemption procedure persuaded the House of Lords in *Brady v Brady*,[72] to allow the company to adopt the procedure and so rectify the illegality.

Proposals for reform

Given the facts that, as we have seen, the parameters of the prohibitions are far from clear[73]; that the mischief they are intended to prevent is either mainly illusory (share capital maintenance) or covered by other provisions (market rigging and abuse of company funds); and that they have the potential to upset (and in theory at least criminalise) a multiplicity of the ever increasingly complex and basically beneficial corporate transactions,[74] it is not surprising that proposals for the reform of the sections have been made on a regular basis since 1993.[75]

---

[69] If the written resolution procedure (below, p.263) is used then the relevant documents must be sent to each member prior to his signature: Sch.15A, para.4.

[70] Breach of this obligation does not, however, invalidate the procedure: *Re N.L. Electrical Ltd* [1994] 1 B.C.L.C. 22.

[71] Above, p.46.

[72] [1989] A.C. 755, HL, above.

[73] The width of the CA's interpretation in the *Chaston* case has not eased the situation.

[74] The Company Law Review noted that legal advice connected with the possibility of a breach of s. 151 costs companies at least £320m a year: *Strategic Framework* (1999) para.5.4.22.

[75] The DTI published various proposals in 1993, 1996 and 1997. The Law Society also published proposals in 1997.

Such proposals are, however, currently restricted by the fact that the Second EC Directive as yet requires the UK to prohibit a public company from making loans, advancing funds or providing security for the acquisition of its shares.[76]

The Company Law Review, for the reasons given above, recommended that the prohibitions should be repealed so far as private companies are concerned, and that the purpose exceptions for public companies should be redrafted so as to apply only where the acquisition of the shares is not the *predominant* reason for the transaction.[77] It is doubtful whether such redrafting will in fact make things easier. What, for example, was the predominant reason in *Chaston*?

Further, the European Commission has put forward a proposal to amend the Second Directive to allow a public company to give financial assistance in total up to the limit of its distributable reserves if it follows a prescribed procedure, not dissimilar to the British whitewash procedure for private companies, designed to maintain minority shareholder and creditor protection.[78] The company's liquidity and solvency must not be put at risk for at least five years after the transaction[79] and the board must ensure that adequate fees and interest are paid by the third party and tat adequate security is given. The assistance must be approved by a special resolution of the general meeting which has been given details and reasons for the assistance. Finally the acquisition must take place in fair market conditions and at a fair price. There will be the right for a dissentient minority to petition the court and a need to prevent any conflict of interest arising where a director is the third party being assisted.[80]

---

[76] That is, however, a narrower requirement than ss 151 and 152 currently impose.
[77] *Final Report*, Vol 1 (2001) para 2.30. The DTI has accepted these proposals.
[78] COM 04, Oct 2004.
[79] Taking the credit standing of the potential purchaser and the properly projected cash flows of the company into account.
[80] The Government is consulting on this proposal (March 2005).

Chapter 12

MEMBERSHIP

THIS chapter is concerned with the members of a company, *i.e.* in the case of a company limited by shares, the shareholders. In addition to the ways in which a person can become a member and the persons who can become members, the following topics are dealt with: the register of members which every company must keep, disclosure of substantial shareholdings in public companies, and the annual return which every company must make to the Registrar.

WAYS OF BECOMING A MEMBER

The members of a company consist of:

(1) The subscribers to the memorandum.[1] These are deemed to have agreed to become members, and on the registration of the company they must be entered as members in its register of members: s.22(1).

(2) Directors who have signed and delivered to the Registrar an undertaking to take and pay for their qualification shares.[2]

(3) All other persons who have agreed to become members of the company *and* whose names are entered in the register of members: s.22(2).[3]

Subscribers to the memorandum

A subscriber to the memorandum becomes a member on registration of the company, and an entry in the register of members is not necessary to make him a member of the company. It is the duty of the directors to enter his name at once in the register, but their failure to do this will not enable him to escape liability for calls on the shares for which he has signed the memorandum.[4]

A subscriber's obligation to take the shares for which he has subscribed is not satisfied by the (later) allotment of shares credited as fully paid and to which someone else is entitled.

M signed the memorandum for five shares. The company had agreed to allot paid up shares to C, as the purchase price of property sold to the company, and C directed the

---

[1] Above, p.70.
[2] Below, p.272.
[3] s.22 is not conclusive as to membership for voting purposes if the entry on the register is wrongly made, *e.g.* if those who have agreed to become members and who have been put on the register have failed to comply with other requirements for membership under the articles: *POW Services Ltd v Clare* [1995] 2 B.C.L.C. 435.
[4] *Evans's Case* (1867) L.R. 2 Ch.App. 427.

company to allot five of these shares to M. This was done and the company was afterwards wound up. *Held*, M was liable to pay for the five shares for which he had signed the memorandum: *Migotti's Case* (1867) L.R. 4 Eq. 238.

If, however, the entire share capital has been allotted to others, the subscriber is under no liability to take shares.[5]

A subscriber to the memorandum cannot rescind the contract to take shares on the ground of a misrepresentation made by a promoter, because (a) the company could not appoint an agent before it came into existence and it is therefore not liable for the promoter's acts, and (b) by signing the memorandum the subscriber became bound, on the registration of the company, not only as between himself and the company, but also as between himself and the other persons who should become members on the footing that the contract existed.[6]

In Scotland, specific implement is available as a remedy to enforce an undertaking to subscribe for shares.[7]

Other members

A person, other than those mentioned above, who has agreed to become a member of the company does not actually become one until his name is entered in the register of members. Section 22 "makes the placing of the name of a shareholder on the register a condition precedent to membership."[8] Registration is essential for membership[9] but it does not necessarily make the person a member[10] so far as the company is concerned. A member agrees to become a member, however, if he consents to do so even though there is no contract between him and the company that he should be entered on the register: *Re Nuneaton Borough A.F.C. Ltd.*[11]

Such a person may take an allotment of his shares direct from the company,[12] or may purchase shares from an existing member,[13] or he may succeed to shares on the death or bankruptcy of a member.[14]

WHO CAN BE MEMBERS

Minors

In English law a minor, *i.e.* a person under the age of 18,[15] may be a member unless this is forbidden by the articles. However, a minor's contract to take shares

---

[5] *Mackley's Case* (1875) 1 Ch.D. 247.
[6] *Lord Lurgan's Case* [1902] 1 Ch. 707.
[7] *Beardmore & Co. v Barry*, 1928 S.C. 101; affirmed 1928 S.C. HL 47.
[8] *Per* Fry L.J. in *Nicol's Case* (1885) 29 Ch.D. 421, CA, at p.447; *per* Lord Deas in *Macdonald v City of Glasgow Bank* (1879) 6 R. 621 at p.633.
[9] See *Re Baku Consolidated Oilfields Ltd* [1994] 1 B.C.L.C. 173.
[10] *POW Services Ltd v Clare* [1995] 2 B.C.L.C. 435; below, p.192.
[11] [1989] B.C.L.C. 454.
[12] Above, p.133.
[13] Below, p.213.
[14] Below, p.229.
[15] Family Law Reform Act 1969, s.1.

is voidable by him before or within a reasonable time after he attains the age of 18. If he avoids he cannot recover the money paid for the shares unless there has been a total failure of the consideration for which the money was paid.

S, an infant,[16] agreed to take 500 £1 shares from a company, and paid 10s. on each share. She received no dividend on the shares. While still an infant she repudiated the shares, and brought an action (a) for a declaration that she was entitled to avoid the contract, and (b) to recover the money she had paid. *Held*, (a) S was entitled to rescind and so was not liable for future calls, but (b) there was no total failure of consideration and S could not recover money already paid because she had got the thing for which the money was paid, a thing of value: *Steinberg v Scala (Leeds) Ltd* [1923] 2 Ch.452, CA.

If the company is wound up the minor member loses his right to avoid unless the liquidator agrees.[17]

In Scotland the capacity of young persons is governed by the Age of Legal Capacity (Scotland) Act 1991. The general rules are:

(1) A person under the age of 16 years has no legal capacity to enter into any transaction; his guardian may act on his behalf.

(2) A person of or over 16 years but under 18 years has legal capacity to enter into any transaction, but such a person is entitled up to the age of 21 to apply to the court to have the transaction set aside if it is "prejudicial", *i.e.* if it is a transaction which:

   (a) an adult, exercising prudence, would not have entered into in the circumstances, and

   (b) has caused, or is likely to cause, substantial prejudice to the young person.

This provision might make another party reluctant to enter into a transaction with a person between 16 and 18, and so the Act provides that all the parties to a proposed transaction may make a joint application to the court to have the transaction ratified by the court. The court must not grant such an application if it considers that an adult, exercising reasonable prudence and in the circumstances, would not enter into the transaction. If a proposed transaction is ratified by the court, the transaction cannot afterwards be set aside as a prejudicial transaction.

A person of 18 years of age or over has full legal capacity.

Personal representatives

Ownership of the shares of a deceased member is transmitted to his executors[18] or administrators. They must produce to the company the grant of probate of the will, or of letters of administration of the estate, or, in Scotland, of confirmation and, notwithstanding anything in the articles, such document must be accepted by

---

[16] The age of majority was formerly 21 and persons under that age were called "infants".

[17] *Symons' Case* (1870) L.R. 5 Ch. 298.

[18] In Scots law the term "executors" is used whether there is a will or not, and "confirmation" is the equivalent of both probate and letters of administration.

the company as sufficient evidence of the grant: s.187.[19] Production to the company does *not*, however, make the representatives members of the company.[20] The deceased member's estate is the member for some purposes, such as an article providing that on an increase of capital the new shares are to be divided among the existing members in proportion to their existing shareholdings.[21]

The personal representatives are liable for calls[22] on partly paid shares only to the extent of the deceased's assets in their hands, and if in England the personal representatives default on a winding up in paying sums due from the deceased, the company can obtain an order for administration of the estate of the deceased member: s.81(3) of the Insolvency Act 1986.

The personal representatives are entitled to transfer the shares without being registered as members (s.183(3)),[23] and to receive all dividends, bonuses or other benefits from the shares, but the articles usually prevent them from voting at general meetings.

Table A, reg. 31, provides: "A person becoming entitled to a share in consequence of the death or bankruptcy of a member shall have the rights to which he would be entitled if he were the holder of the share, except that he shall not, before being registered as the holder of the share, be entitled in respect of it to attend or vote at any meeting of the company or at any separate meeting of the holders of any class of shares in the company."

Personal representatives may, however, be entitled to be given notice of general meetings, even though they have no right to attend and vote at the meetings. Table A, reg. 38, gives them a right to be given notice of general meetings.

Personal representatives are entitled, if they so choose and there is no contrary provision in the articles, to be registered as members.[24] The articles may give the directors, the same power to decline to register personal representatives as members as the directors would have had in the case of a transfer by the deceased shareholder before his death.[25]

If personal representatives are registered as members, they become personally liable for calls, although they have a right of indemnity against the deceased's estate.[26]

Trustees in bankruptcy

A bankrupt may be a member of a company, although the beneficial interest in his shares will be vested in his trustee in bankruptcy as from the time when he is adjudged bankrupt.[27] Unless the articles provide to the contrary, a shareholder

---

[19] For foreign personal representatives, see *Re Baku Consolidated Oilfields Ltd* [1994] 1 B.C.L.C. 173.

[20] *Macdonald v City of Glasgow Bank* (1879) 6 R. 621.

[21] *per* Lord Herschell in *James v Buena Ventura Nitrate Grounds Syndicate Ltd* [1896] 1 Ch. 456, CA, at p.464.

[22] Below, p.233.

[23] See *Buchan v City of Glasgow Bank* (1879) 6 R. HL 44; (1879) 6 R. 567; *Safeguard Industrial Investments Ltd v National Westminster Bank Ltd* (1982) 1 WLR 589, CA.

[24] *Edwards v Ransomes and Rapier Ltd* [1930] W.N. 180.

[25] See, *e.g.*, *Shepherd's Trustees v Shepherd*, 1950 S.C. HL 60. See also below, p.228.

[26] *per* Cotton L.J. in *Duff's Executors' Case* (1886) 32 Ch.D. 301, CA, at p.309.

[27] Insolvency Act 1986, s.306(1). In Scots law, a debtor's estate vests as at the date of sequestration in the permanent trustee: Bankruptcy (Scotland) Act 1985, s.31.

does not cease to be a member of the company on becoming bankrupt. Accordingly, as long as he is on the register he is entitled to exercise any vote conferred by his shares at the meetings of the company, even though the articles provide—as does reg. 38 of Table A—that notice of meetings is to be sent to the trustee in bankruptcy and not to the bankrupt.[28] The bankrupt must vote in accordance with the directions of the trustee.

Other companies

1. A company may, if authorised by its memorandum, take shares in and be a member of another company. It attends meetings of the other by a representative authorised by resolution of its directors: s.375(1)(a).[29]

2. In general a company cannot be a member of itself, either directly or through a nominee (s.143). This was designed to re-inforce the share capital rules. A company may, however, in certain circumstances purchase or acquire its own shares. Under the Act companies may redeem or purchase their own shares but they must cancel the shares so acquired unless they retain them as treasury shares. Such shares are registered in the name of the company itself, but it cannot exercise any of the rights of membership in respect of them. This topic was covered in Chapter 10. Companies may also forfeit or accept the surrender of their shares. (See Chapter 13).

3. Section 23[30] provides that, for similar reasons, subject to certain exceptions, a subsidiary company[31] cannot be a member of its holding company and any allotment or transfer of shares in a holding company to its subsidiary is void.[32] This prohibition cannot be evaded by having a nominee for the subsidiary. There are exceptions where the subsidiary is concerned (a) as a personal representative, or (b) as a trustee, unless the holding company or a subsidiary of it is beneficially interested under the trust otherwise than by way of security for the purposes of a transaction entered into in the ordinary course of a business which includes the lending of money.

For example, as regards (a), Y, who holds shares in X Bank Ltd, appoints its subsidiary, X Bank (Executor & Trustee) Ltd, as his executor and on Y's death the subsidiary is registered in respect of the shares.

As to (b), Y transfers his shares to the subsidiary on trust for a beneficiary, Z, who borrows money from X Bank Ltd and secures repayment by mortgaging his interest in the shares to X Bank Ltd.

The definition of beneficial interest for this purpose excludes those detailed in Sch.2. These are minor and residual interests under company pension and employee shares schemes. Otherwise a subsidiary's pension fund could not invest in its parent company.

---

[28] *Morgan v Gray* [1953] Ch. 83.
[29] Below, p.257.
[30] This section was redrafted and expanded by s.129 CA 1989.
[31] Above, p.47.
[32] In Scotland this does not prevent a company from arresting its subsidiary's shares to found jurisdiction, at least where the shares are marketable: *Stenhouse London Ltd v Allwright*, 1972 S.L.T. 255.

There are further exceptions where the subsidiary holds the shares as part of its business as a securities dealer and where, after October 20, 1997, it holds shares in another company and *subsequently* becomes a subsidiary of that company. It may retain the shares but cannot vote in respect of them.

REGISTER OF MEMBERS

Section 352 provides that every company[33] must keep a register of its members containing;

(1) the names and addresses[34] of the members, and, if the company has a share capital, a statement of the shares held by each member, distinguishing each share by its number[35] so long as it has one and by its class if there is more than one class of shares, and the amount paid or agreed to be considered as paid on the shares of each member. If the company has converted shares into stock, the register must show the amount of stock held by each member. In any other case where the company has more than one class of members the register must show the class to which each member belongs.[36]

(2) the date at which each person was entered in the register as a member;

(3) the date at which any person ceased to be a member.

In addition, s.352A(1) provides that where a private company's number of members falls to one then, in addition to the name and address of the sole member, the register must state: (a) that the company only has one member; and (b) the date on which the company became a single member company. If the number of members subsequently increases to two or more the register must state both the fact that the company has ceased to have only one member and the date of the change.[37] Default renders the company and every officer in default liable to a fine: s.352A(3).

The register may be kept by making entries in a bound book or by recording the required information in any other manner, including a computer, so long as adequate precautions are taken to guard against falsification: ss 722 and 723. Any entry relating to a former member may be removed from the register after 20 years from the date on which he ceased to be a member: s.352(6).

A company with more than 50 members must, unless the register of members constitutes an index, keep an index (which may be a card index) of the names of its members, and must alter the index within 14 days after any alteration in the register. The index must be kept at the same place as the register and must

---

[33] There are special rules for those listed companies with shares held in an electronic form. In essence the following provisions only apply with some amendments to the shares held in certificated form.

[34] This means the address given by the member and not an address substituted by someone else: *POW Services Ltd v Clare* [1995] 2 B.C.L.C. 435.

[35] Below, p.205.

[36] This applies therefore to guarantee companies without a share capital. It was added by 1981 Act, s.101 and reverses the decision in *Re Performing Right Society Ltd* [1978] 3 All E.R. 972, CA.

[37] s.352A(2). This is the only formal requirement as to a single member company's existence as such.

contain sufficient information to enable the account of each member in the register to be readily found: s.354.

The register of members is *prima facie* evidence of any matters directed by the Act to be inserted in it: s.361. This does not mean, however, that a person so included is a member for the purpose of attending meetings, etc.[38]

Inspection of register

The register is to be kept at the company's registered office, but if the register is made up at another office of the company, it may be kept there, and if it is made up by an agent, it may be kept at his office. If the company is registered in England, the register must not be kept outside England, and it the company is registered in Scotland, the register must not be kept outside Scotland. When the register has not always been kept at the registered office, notice must be given to the Registrar of the place where it is kept: s.353.

The register and index are to be open to the inspection of any member without charge, and of any other person on payment of the appropriate fee.[39] Within 10 days after being required to do so, the company is bound to furnish, either to a member or to any other person, a copy of any part of the register on payment of the appropriate charge[40]: s.356(3). The court can compel access to the register if the company refuses access.[41] The right of inspection terminates on the company going into liquidation.[42]

The company may, on giving notice by advertisement in some newspaper circulating in the district in which its registered office is situate, close the register for any time or times not exceeding 30 days in each year: s.358. This is to enable the company to prepare a list of members entitled to payment of a dividend.

Importance of register

The importance of the register as a public representation of who the members are and what their liability is has often been emphasised, and a company has no power to create a right of pledge or lien over the register, since that would deprive the public of their statutory right of access and inspection.[43] The register and not the share certificate is the document of title to shares, the share certificate being merely an acknowledgement on the part of the company that, at the time of its issue, the name of the person mentioned in it is duly recorded in the register.[44] There is a distinction, however, between the liability of the company and the individuals on the register to third parties as a result of that representation on the one hand, and the internal question as to whether the individual is actually a member for voting purposes, etc., on the other.[45]

---

[38] *POW Services Ltd v Clare* [1995] 2 B.C.L.C. 438.

[39] See Companies (Inspection of Registers, Indices and Documents) Regulations 1991, SI 1991/1998.

[40] *Re Kent Coalfields Syndicate Ltd* [1898] 1 Q.B. 754, CA. There is concern about having to do this for outsiders seeking to make mailshots to the members. See *e.g.* Company Law Review, *Final Report Vol 1* (2001) para. 11.44.

[41] *Pelling v Families Need Fathers Ltd* [2002] 1 B.C.L.C. 645.

[42] *e.g.* per Lord Curriehill in *Liquidator of the Garpel etc. Co. Ltd v Andrew* (1866) 4 M. 617 at p.623.

[43] *Liquidator of the Garpel etc. Co. Ltd v Andrew* (1866) 4 M. 617.

[44] *Re Baku Consolidated Oilfields Ltd* [1994] 1 B.C.L.C. 173.

[45] *POW Services Ltd v Clare* [1995] 2 B.C.L.C. 438.

Any liability incurred by a company as the result of making or deleting an entry in its register, or failing to do either, cannot be enforced against it more than 20 years after the date of first default: s.352(7). This is a final limitation provision; earlier ones may well apply.

Power of court to rectify register

Section 359(1) gives the court a discretion to rectify the register of members in two cases, namely—

(1) if the name of any person is, without sufficient cause, entered in or omitted from the register;

(2) if default is made or unnecessary delay takes place in entering on the register the fact of any person having ceased to be a member.

Application to the court for rectification may be made by the person aggrieved, [46] by any member of the company, or the company itself. The main criterion is that there must be a legitimate interest[47] and if rectification of the register would directly affect the legal rights of another person, then the court may not order rectification without hearing that other person.[48] It has recently been confirmed that the court's discretion under s.359 is the same as its discretion to grant or refuse specific performance and, as such, would be affected by delay and prejudice.[49]

The court may order rectification of the register by deleting a reference to some only of the registered shareholder's shares. It need not delete his name entirely. Thus when an existing shareholder was registered as the holder of an additional number of shares issued in breach of the then Exchange Control Regulations the court deleted the reference to those shares only: *Re Transatlantic Life Assurance Co. Ltd.*[50]

Where the person on the register has been wrongly included, the court will examine, for the purposes of voting, etc., whether that person is properly a member without rectification of the register.[51] The court has exclusive jurisdiction as to the rectification of the registers of British registered companies, irrespective of the nationality of the parties.[52]

Section 359(3) provides that:

"On such application the court may decide any question relating to the title of a person who is a party to the application to have his name entered in or omitted from

---

[46] This includes a person who is alleging that the shares ought to have been allotted to him and that another has been registered in respect of those shares, even though he does not yet have a right to be registered: *Re Thundercrust Ltd* [1995] 1 B.C.L.C. 177.

[47] See *Re New Millennium Experience Co Ltd* [2003] EWHC 1823 (Ch); [2004] 1 B.C.L.C. 19, where no legitimate interest was shown.

[48] *Sitchell's Case* (1867) 3 L.R. Ch. App. 119.

[49] See *Re ISIS Factors plc* [2003] EWHC 1653 (Ch); [2003] 2 B.C.L.C. 411.

[50] [1979] 3 All E.R. 357.

[51] See n.45 above.

[52] *Re Fagin's Bookshop plc* [1992] B.C.L.C. 118; *International Credit and Investment Co. (Overseas) Ltd v Adham* [1994] 1 B.C.L.C. 66.

the register, whether the question arises between members or alleged members, or between members or alleged members on the one hand and the company on the other hand, and generally may decide any question necessary or expedient to be decided for rectification of the register."

There is older authority to the effect that rectification of the register is the only method of resolving disputes as to legal title to shares.[53] Some doubt was cast on this at first instance in *Re Hoicrest Ltd*,[54] when the court was asked to rectify the register in relation to a number of shares alleged to be held by K. The judge decided that the court had no jurisdiction to entertain K's application under s.359 because he could not produce a legal transfer of the shares alleged to be held by him[55] and, until he could do so, there was sufficient cause for omitting his name from the register. The judge also gave a restricted interpretation to s.359(3), suggesting that this section related only to incidental matters under subss (1) and (2) of s.359. However, the Court of Appeal[56] has reversed this decision and emphasised that subs (3) confers on the court a general discretionary power to resolve a dispute on title, although it would not follow that the power of determination should always be exercised.[57] While true that the court would not make an order which required the company or its board to act in contravention of the Companies Act[58] or the articles, this did not prevent the court from resolving, prior to deciding whether or not to make an order for rectification, relevant disputes about entitlement to shares.[59]

The court may order not only rectification of the register but also payment by the company of any damages sustained by any party aggrieved. However, the applicant must show for subs (1) that he was improperly entered in or omitted from the register. If the true complaint is that he was never allotted any shares at all and if instead they were validly allotted to a third party, the applicant will only be entitled to an action for damages for breach of contract. The applicant has never been entitled to be on the register and so has no remedy under s.359.[60]

If an order is made in the case of a company required to send a list of members to the Registrar[61] notice of the rectification must be given to the Registrar: s.359(4).

Where the directors have power in the articles to refuse to register a transfer of shares, their failure to act may be challenged under s.359.[62]

An order for rectification may be made even if the company is being wound up.

B, a transferee of shares in a company, sent in his transfer for registration but, by mistake, registration of the transfer was omitted. The company then went into liquidation

---

[53] Based on *Shaw, Ex p. Re Diamond Rock Boring Co Ltd* (1877) 2 Q.B.D. 463.
[54] [1998] 2 B.C.L.C. 175.
[55] In reliance on s.183(1) of the 1985 Act. See below, p.213.
[56] [2001] W.L.R. 414, CA.
[57] At p.419. And so, on the facts of the case, Mummery L.J. made directions for the trial of a preliminary issue on whether the parties had agreed that the shares should be transferred to K: at p.420.
[58] *i.e.* under s.183. See below, p.213.
[59] [2001] W.L.R. 414, CA , at p.419.
[60] *Re BTR plc* (1988) 4 B.C.C. 45.
[61] See below, p.203.
[62] *Re Swaledale Cleaners Ltd* [1968] 1 W.L.R. 1710, CA, below, p.228.

with a view to reconstruction and B, thinking that he was on the register of members, served the liquidator with notice of dissent to the scheme. The liquidator disregarded the notice on the ground that B was not a member. *Held*, there was such "default or unnecessary delay" in registration as entitled B to rectification of the register: *Re Sussex Brick Co.* [1904] 1 Ch.598, CA.[63]

Section 359 does not exhaust the court's power to order rectification and does not prevent the court from altering the register in cases other than those specified. Accordingly where shares were registered in the names of two joint holders, and under the articles the first alone could vote and if the first was ill or absent the second could not vote or be appointed a proxy, an order was made to have the holding split into two holdings with the names of the shareholders in different order.[64] Rectification is, however, always a discretionary remedy and not one available as of right.[65]

Trusts not to be entered on register in England

Section 360 provides that no notice of any trust shall be entered on the register, or be received by the Registrar, in the case of companies registered in England (which, for this purpose, includes Wales). This means that, subject as below, the company is entitled to treat every person on the register of members as the beneficial owner of shares, even if in fact he holds them on trust for another, *i.e.* the company need not take notice of equitable interests in shares. Partly as a result of s.360, nominee shareholdings are common. The potential abuses (tax evasion, etc.) are legion but the only current anti-avoidance provisions concern substantial shareholding disclosure rules, set out below.[66] Under current law, therefore, if the company registers a transfer of the shares held by a person as trustee, it is under no liability to the beneficiaries even if the sale was a breach of trust and in fraud of the beneficiaries.

X's shares were, on his death, registered in the name of his executors. They subsequently transferred the shares to Y in breach of the terms of X's will, and the transfer was registered by the company. The company had a copy of the will in its possession, and its president was one of X's executors. *Held*, the company did not act wrongfully, as it was only bound to satisfy itself from the will that the executors were executors, and was not concerned with the disposition by X of his property: *Simpson v Molson's Bank* [1895] A.C. 270.

A further result is that the company is not a trustee for persons claiming the shares under an equitable interest. For example, if A, the owner of shares, makes an equitable mortgage of his shares by depositing his share certificate and a blank transfer with B as security for a debt and afterwards makes another equitable mortgage of the same shares by depositing another blank transfer of them with C

---

[63] See also *Stocker v Liqdrs. of the Coustonholm Paper Mills Co. Ltd* (1891) 19 R. 17; *Barbor v Middleton*, 1988 S.L.T. 288 (O.H.) (petitioner declared never to have been a member).

[64] *Burns v Siemens Brothers Dynamo Works Ltd* [1919] 1 Ch. 225.

[65] *Re Piccadilly Radio plc* [1989] B.C.L.C. 683.

[66] The DTI consulted on the disclosure of beneficial interests in unlisted companies in 2002, but no response has yet been published.

as security for another debt, saying that he has lost his share certificate, C cannot by giving notice to the company affect the company with notice of his interest in the shares or gain any priority of B.[67] As will be seen later,[68] the proper way to protect the interest of a beneficiary in shares is to serve a stop notice. As a rule, if a company receives notice of an equitable claim it should allow the person giving the notice to apply for a restraining order, if he makes a request to that effect, before registering a transfer to his prejudice.[69]

The articles frequently deal with notice of trusts, as does Table A, reg. 5:

> Except as required by law, no person shall be recognised . . . as holding any share upon any trust, and (except as otherwise provided by the articles or by law) the company shall not be bound by or recognise any interest in any share except an absolute right to the entirety thereof in the holder."

It is doubtful whether this adds anything to the effect of s.360, although the section deals only with entries on the register while the article is not limited to entries on the register.[70] The Company Law Review were undecided as to whether beneficial owners should be given rights, *e.g.* to vote, but did recommend that s.360 should be amended to allow companies to recognise the rights of beneficial owners if they wish, but to retain the right of transfer solely in the trustee.[71]

A trustee of shares who is entered on the register is entitled to exercise any vote conferred by the shares although he may be bound to vote in accordance with the directions of the beneficiary. The trustee is personally liable to the company for any calls or other obligations attaching to the shares but is entitled to an indemnity from the beneficiary, not only out of the trust property but to the full extent of his indebtedness in respect of the shares.[72] The company cannot put the beneficiary on the list of contributories but it can, through the trustee, enforce the trustee's right to an indemnity.[73]

A purchase of shares in the name of a nominee, even if a minor or a man of straw, is legal. In such a case the company cannot go behind the nominee to the beneficial owner.

M and G, a firm of stockbrokers, bought shares which were registered in the name of L, their clerk. L was an infant. On the company's going into liquidation, the liquidator applied that M and G's names might be substituted for that of L in the register of members and the list of contributories. *Held*, the application failed, as there was no contractual relation between the company and M and G: *Re National Bank of Wales Ltd* [1907] 1 Ch.582.

If a person applies for shares in a fictitious name, or in the name of a person who has never agreed to accept the shares, rectification of the register can be obtained so as to place the name of the real owner upon the register.[74]

---

[67] *Société Générale de Paris v Walker* [1885] 11 App. Cas.20.

[68] Below, p.231.

[69] *per* Lindley L.J. in *Société Générale de Paris v Tramways Union Co.* (1884) 14 Q.B.D. 424, CA at p.453.

[70] See below, p.235.

[71] *Final Report, Vol 1* para.3.51. The DTI has indicated approval of this.

[72] *Hardoon v Belilios* [1901] A.C. 118, PC.

[73] *Per* James L.J. in *Re European Society Arbitration Acts* (1878) 8 Ch.D. 679, CA at p.708.

[74] *Pugh and Sharman's Case* (1872) L.R. 13 Eq. 566; *Richardson's Case* (1875) L.R. 19 Eq. 588.

Trusts may be entered on register in Scotland

It has always been competent for companies registered in Scotland to enter notices of trusts on their registers.[75]

Entry of a notice of trust does *not* have the effect of limiting the liability of the trustees to the amount of the trust estate in their hands.[76]

The legal position of trustees is distinct from that of executors.[77]

On the assumption of a new trustee by deed of assumption his name may be entered on the register without any transfer being executed, and the trustee will then be a member and liable as such.[78] A trustee who duly resigns his office by minute registered in the Books of Council and Session, and intimated to his co-trustees and to the company, is entitled to have his name removed from the register; no deed of transfer is necessary.[79] When one of several trustees dies, shares registered in the names of the trustees vest in the surviving trustees, and the executors of the deceased trustee are not liable as members even though no intimation of the death has been given to the company.[80] The last surviving trustee, however, is in a different position from the other trustees in that his death does not automatically terminate his liability as a member.[81]

The liability of trustees to the company is *in solidum*, not *pro rata, i.e.* the company may hold any one of the several trustees liable for the full amount due on shares.[82]

Trustees who have been made liable for calls in respect of shares forming part of the trust estate are entitled to full relief from the trust estate without reference to their own payments or ability to pay; the trust estate may be made liable beyond what the trustees can personally pay, and the company may by diligence compel the trustees to make the right of relief available to the company.[83]

The persons for whom shares are held in trust are *not* members of the company, although their names may appear on the register.[84]

DISCLOSURE OF SUBSTANTIAL SHAREHOLDINGS

Sections 198–220 contain provisions for securing the disclosure and registration of substantial individual interests in share capital carrying unrestricted voting rights. The aim is to ensure that despite the nominee-friendly rules relating to the register of members, directors, shareholders and employees of a *public* company may ascertain the identity of, for instance, any person who may be in the process

---

[75] As to the purpose of such entry, see, *per* Cairns L.C. in *Muir v City of Glasgow Bank* (1879) 6 R. HL 21 at p.26.

[76] *Muir v City of Glasgow Bank* (1879) 6 R. HL 21 (1878) 6 R. 392, following *Lumsden v Buchanan* (1865) 3 M. HL 89.

[77] *Per* Lord Selborne in *Buchan v City of Glasgow Bank* (1879) 6 R. HL 44 at p.50.

[78] Trusts (Scotland) Act 1921, s.21; *Bell v City of Glasgow Bank* (1879) 6 R. HL 55; (1879) 6 R. 548.

[79] 1921 Act, s.19(1); *Dalgleish v Land Feuing Co. Ltd* (1885) 13 R. 223.

[80] *Oswald's Trustees v City of Glasgow Bank* (1879) 6 R. 461.

[81] *Low's Executors v City of Glasgow Bank* (1879) 6 R. 830.

[82] *Cuninghame v City of Glasgow Bank* (1879) 6 R. 98; (1879) 6 R. 679.

[83] *Cuninghame v Montgomerie* (1879) 6 R. 1333; contrast *Brownlie v Brownlie's Trustees* (1879) 6 R. 1233.

[84] *Gillespie & Paterson v City of Glasgow Bank* (1879) 6 R. HL 104; (1879) 6 R. 714.

of buying shares in the company through nominees whose name will only appear on the register, to gain control of it or of any person who is in a position to veto a special resolution of the company not only at the date of the request but also in respect of the previous three years.[85] In addition they allow companies to carry out their own investigations into such matters without necessitating intervention by the Secretary of State under ss 442–444.[86] These provisions have been subjected to amendment by various statutory instruments, including the implementation of Directive 88/27/EEC which applies only to listed and so, not all, public companies.[87]

Disclosure obligations—public companies

Section 198 requires any person who acquires or disposes of a notifiable interest in shares to inform the company of that and of any significant change in the number of shares in which he is or was interested. A notifiable interest is currently defined[88] either as a material interest in "relevant share capital" amounting to three per cent or more, or any interests in shares amounting to ten per cent or more of the "relevant share capital". A material interest includes any interest in shares other than an interest as the manager of a UK investment scheme an EC collective investment scheme, an open-ended investment company or unit trust.[89] "Relevant share capital" is defined as the voting shares of any public company excluding treasury shares: s.198(2). On adding up any individual's interest to ascertain whether he has passed the disclosure threshold, ss 204–208 provide for the attribution to individuals of interests in shares. These attributed interests are added to those already clearly held by the person to ascertain whether or not he is obliged to make disclosure of his interest in shares under this part of the Act.

Under s.202(1) any person obliged to disclose must within two days of the date upon which the obligation arose make the appropriate disclosure of his interest, material or otherwise as relevant, in writing to the company specifying the share capital to which it relates. He must also state either the number of shares in that public company in which he knows he was interested immediately after the time his obligation to notify arose together with the names of the registered holder(s) of those shares and the number of shares for each registered holder,[90] or state that he no longer has a notifiable interest if that is the case: s.202. Any known changes in those particulars must be subsequently notified by him to the company within two days of the day upon which he became aware of them and this obligation continues until he notifies the company that he has no longer any interest in those shares: s.202(4).

[85] *Re Geers Gross* [1987] 1 W.L.R. 837.
[86] Below, p.337.
[87] See the Disclosure of Interests in Shares (Amendment) Regulations 1993 (SI 1993/1819); the Disclosure of Interests in Shares (Amendment) (No. 2) Regulations 1993 (SI 1993/2689); the Financial Services and Markets Act 2000 (Consequential Amendments and Repeals) Order 2001 (SI 2001/3649) and the Collective Investment Schemes (Miscellaneous Amendments) Regulations 2003 (SI 2003/2066).
[88] The figure may be changed by statutory instrument: s.210A.
[89] This includes any interest at a person who can lawfully manage investments belonging to another.
[90] This is defined so as to include options held by nominees.

Section 198(4) states that the time an obligation arises is either the time the event or change of circumstances occurred or the time when the person becomes aware of those facts.

Sections 203 and 208 aim to make subject to the disclosure provisions interests in shares which arise indirectly. The notifiable interests in shares defined in s.208 include interests in shares on which a person has an option or a right to call for delivery or to acquire an interest in them. Section 203 specifies various instances where a person is attributed with the interests which are ostensibly held by other persons and which are to be taken into account in ascertaining whether or not he is obliged to make notification under ss 198–202.

Concert parties

Further important attributions of interests in shares are contained in ss 206 and 207 which deal with so-called "concert parties,"[91] *i.e.* those combinations of persons with agreements for the purpose of acquiring interests in shares. The aim is to prevent control in concert, in other words avoidance of the disclosure provisions by groups of persons secretly agreeing that while each acquires openly less than the disclosure threshold level they will secretly use the combined interests to gain control or to ensure a takeover or a special resolution at the meeting of the company. Sections 204 and 205 provide that each person involved in any such agreement is to be attributed with the interests of all the other parties to it even though some of those persons' interests may have been acquired before or outside of the so-called "concert party" agreement. The effect is that in ascertaining the obligation of each member of a concert party individually to notify his interests, the interests of all the other members are added to his interest or interests and if the total exceeds three per cent or ten per cent, as appropriate, he must make notification in accordance with s.204. In addition, under s.205 that person shall state that he is a party to such an agreement, the names and if known to him, the addresses of the other parties to the agreement, which, if any, of the shares to which the notification relates are shares in which he is interested by reason of attribution under s.204 and if that is the case, he must also notify the number of those shares.

In addition to the obligation to notify the company, s.206 obliges all the persons involved in a concert party to keep each other informed of facts relevant to their shareholding. This provision aims to give each and every member of a concert party the ability to know whether or not the interests attributed to him under s.204 (alone or together with any other interest he might have) are such as to necessitate his making a notification under ss 198–201. To do this he must know all the interests attributable to him and any changes in those interests.

Section 204, for example, may impose an obligation to disclose where two or more persons agree that one or more of them acquire interests in relevant shares of a particular "target" company. Once such interests have been acquired the obligation to disclose is not affected by any further acquisition under it or by a variation of or alteration in the membership of, the agreement. Section 205 states

---

[91] *cf.* the City Code on Take-overs and Mergers, below, p.675.

that each party to the agreement is deemed interested in all the shares in the target company held by any other party to the agreement irrespective of whether or not they were acquired pursuant to the agreement.

Therefore all the concert party members must inform every other member of their existing interests, acquisitions and disposals of shares in that company and this obligation comes into being with the first acquisition of shares in that company in pursuance of the "concert party" agreement: s.206(2). Each party to the agreement has three days from the day on which the obligation arose within which to notify the other parties in writing of his interests in target company shares and of his current address: s.206(8). Failure to meet these obligations is made a criminal offence by s.210(3)(c).

Notifiable interests

Section 208 defines for the purpose of the duty to disclose the interests to be notified. Most significant is that a person is deemed to have an interest in shares if he enters into a contract for their purchase or where, even though he is not the registered holder, he is entitled to exercise or control the exercise of any right conferred by holding those shares or (trust aside) he has a right to call for delivery of the shares to himself or his order or he has a right to acquire an interest in shares or is under an obligation to take an interest in shares whether or not in any case that right or obligation is conditional or absolute. Joint interests are attributed equally to each person who has an interest and it is immaterial that the shares in which a person has an interest are unidentifiable. In this way contingent agreements which otherwise might be used to conceal an interest requiring disclosure are exposed.

Section 209 lists various interests in shares which do not give rise to the disclosure obligation under ss 198–202, for example an interest in shares as a security is an exempt security interest and disregarded if it is held by specified bodies which lend money in the course of business.[91a] Criminal liability for failure to meet the obligations imposed under this part of the Act is contained in s.210. Under s.210(3) failure to comply with ss 198–202 is made a criminal offence.

The Secretary of State may by regulations amend the notifiable percentage, the definition of relevant share capital, the time limits for notification and the definition of and exclusions from notifiable interests: s.210A.

Shares which are the subject of an offence may have imposed on them by the Secretary of State all the restrictions of Pt XV of the Act.[92]

Register of substantial shareholders

By s.211, every public company must maintain a register of interests in shares notified to it in accordance with ss 198–202. It must record the relevant information against the name of the person obliged to provide such information together with the date of the entry and where the company is notified that a

---

[91a] As amended by the Financial Services and Markets Act 2000 (Consequential Amendments and Repeals) Order 2001, SI 2001/3649.
[92] Below, p.174.

person has ceased to be party to an agreement to which s.204 applies it must record that fact against that person's name wherever his name appears in the register as a party to that agreement. These obligations must be fulfilled by the company within three days of notification. Section 211(5) and (6) prescribe the form that the register and the index to the register are to take and specifies that the company must make any necessary alterations in the index within 10 days of a name being entered on the register.

Company's power to require information

Under s.212, a public company can require information from existing members about the capacity in which they hold their shares, and it is further empowered to make enquiries of any person who it has been informed is or who its investigations reveal to be, interested in shares in the company. Members may be asked whether or not any voting rights on their shares are controlled by another person under some agreement and if that is the case, particulars of the parties and terms of the agreement may be required. Members and persons who also indicated that they were interested in shares during the three years prior to the date of notice under this section must disclose details of their present interests or any past interests in shares held within the previous three years or of any other past or present interest not referred to in a notice issued under this section. Such information, known to a member, must be disclosed to the company. Likewise the company may require similar information from any person named or revealed as a party to such an agreement as will enable it to cross check the information it receives concerning interests in shares. Section 212 is subject to change by regulations made by the Secretary of State under s.210A.

A public company is entitled to use s.212 to probe and discover the true beneficial owner, of its shares.[93] It is a failure to comply with the section if the person required fails to give a full and truthful answer so far as it lies within his knowledge, and this can include failure to disclose the precise nature of his interest in the shares.[94]

However, such a person must be given time not only to collect the information but to take legal advice to ensure that it is complete. In the case of UK residents the same day ought to suffice but two days would be needed for non-residents.[95]

The company, in turn, is obliged by s.213 to register the information received in response to an inquiry under s.212 including an indication of the fact and date of the requirement imposed by the company under s.212. Thus not only the company but the public has a right to know of the true owners of the shares.

Furthermore the company may be compelled to investigate and, under the power given in s.212, report on persons who hold the controlling interest in the company. This power of compulsion is provided by s.214 to a 10 per cent minority of shareholders at the date of making the requisition provided they comply with the procedures laid down in the section, such as specifying the manner in which the company is to exercise its power and the giving of

---

[93] *Re Lonrho plc (No. 2)* (1988) 4 B.C.C. 234.
[94] *Re TR Technology Trust plc* [1988] B.C.L.C. 256.
[95] *Lonrho plc v Edelman* (1989) 5 B.C.C. 68.

reasonable grounds for their request. There is, however, nothing to stop the members making the request, applying to the court if the company is slow in responding to a good request or to the Department of Trade and Industry in terms of ss 442–445, 454–457 and 732. Also if the company fails to comply with a valid requisition to exercise its powers of investigation then both it and every officer of it who is in default is liable to a fine specified in Sch.24 to the Act. Likewise should any person validly[96] requested by the company fail to provide the requisite information in terms of s.212 he becomes subject to the penalties imposed by s.216. Under this provision the company can ask the court to impose restrictions set out in Pt XV of the Act, including putting a stop on dividend payments to or the exercise of voting rights by that person. Also persons who fail to comply or who knowingly or recklessly give false information are liable to imprisonment and/or a fine as shown in Sch.24. But no offence justifying such an order or such other penalties would be committed if the person can prove that the notice seeking information is frivolous or vexatious.

Section 217(2) imposes on the company the obligation to notify within 15 days any person whose name has been provided to it as a member and state what entries in consequence have been made against his name on the register of interests in shares and inform him of his right to apply to have the entry removed in accordance with the procedures in s.217. A person whose name appears in the register of share interests as a party to an agreement to which s.204 applies and who ceases to be a party to that agreement may apply in writing to the company to record that fact (if satisfied) in every place where his name appears as a party to the agreement in the register. If a company refuses such a request the applicant may apply to the court for an order to remove the entry or to enter the fact that it is incorrect or that he has ceased to be a party to any such agreement. The company having removed any name from the register on request or under an order to do so must within 14 days make the necessary alterations to any associated index. Failure to comply with any of the obligations imposed by this section exposes the company and officers in default to a fine and a daily default fine for a continued contravention as set out in Sch.24. According to s.218 the same applies where any deletion not authorised by s.217 occurs and in addition it requires the company to restore any improperly removed name to the register as soon as reasonably practicable.

Both the s.211 register of interests and the s.215 report on investigation must by virtue of s.219 be kept available for inspection without charge to members and non-members at either the company's registered office or the place where the register of members is kept. Again, failure to do so makes both the company and any officer in default criminally liable[97] and the court may by order compel an immediate inspection or order that a copy be sent to the person requiring it.[97a]

Restrictions for non-disclosure of interests in shares

If there is a breach of the compulsory notification provisions under ss 198 to 202 the Secretary of State may order that all or any of the restrictions on transfer,

---

[96] An invalid notice will have no effect: *Malaga Investments Ltd, Petitioners*, 1987 S.L.T. 603 (O.H.)
[97] s.219(3).
[97a] s.219(4).

voting receipt of dividends and rights issues, set out in Pt XV of the Act (ss 454 to 457)[98] shall apply to those shares: s.210. Similarly if there is a failure to provide information as requested by a company under s.212, the company may go to court to ask for such restrictions to be imposed upon the shares: s.216. In either case, the Secretary of State or the court may protect third parties who might be unfairly affected by the restrictions, by providing that certain acts by those parties shall not constitute a breach of Pt XV or by otherwise varying the order.

Subject to the protection of third parties who have been unfairly affected by the restrictions, who may seek an order from the court exempting them from the restrictions, the restrictions may only be lifted by the Secretary of State or the court as appropriate if either:

(i) the relevant facts about the shares have been disclosed and no unfair advantage has accrued to anyone as the result of non-disclosure,[99] or

(ii) the shares are transferred for valuable consideration, under a transfer approved or ordered by the court, in which case the court may pay the proceeds to those beneficially interested in the shares: ss 456, 457.

Under (ii) the transfer, *i.e.* a sale or exchange, must be approved by the court: it is not enough that the applicant is proposing to sell the shares at arm's length. It is always a matter for the court's discretion, but if the relevant facts have not been disclosed it is less likely to be exercised.[1]

Similarly, in any case the question of costs is a matter for the court's discretion. In general the court will consider each party upon whom a notice has been served, or against whom an obligation has arisen, and ascertain whether that party has provided full information within its power and whether its default has caused or contributed to the costs incurred.[2]

ANNUAL RETURN

Further details as to shareholders must also be disclosed in the company's annual return. Every company must make such a return to the Registrar each year made up to a date not later than the company's "return date." That date is fixed initially at one year from the date of the company's incorporation, and subsequently it is one year from the date when the last return was made up. Because the only restriction is that an annual return must not be made up to a period of more than 12 months from the previous one, the return date may be brought forward so as to harmonise return dates within a group of companies. The return date concept allows a "shuttle system" for annual returns. Under this system the Registrar sends out a completed annual return based on last year's information to the company in advance of its return date. The company need only amend it, have it signed by a director or the secretary and return it to the

---

[98] See also p.386, below.
[99] See, *e.g. Re Ricardo Group plc* (1989) 5 B.C.C. 388.
[1] *Re Geers Gross plc* [1987] 1 W.L.R. 837.
[2] *Re The Bestwood plc* [1989] B.C.L.C. 606; *Re Ricardo Group plc (No. 2)* [1989] B.C.L.C. 766.

Registrar within 28 days of the return date. It is an offence for any director or officer of the company to fail to comply with these obligations: s.363.

The contents of the annual return for all companies are specified by s.364. The following information is required:

(a) address of the registered office;

(b) the type of company it is, according to a classification scheme laid down by the Registrar;

(c) its principal business activities, according to a prescribed classification[3];

(d) the name and address of the company secretary (if that is a firm, the name and principal officer of the firm may be used; if it is a company its corporate name and registered office will suffice);

(e) the name and address[4] of all directors, including shadow directors[5];

(f) details of nationality, date of birth, and business occupation;

(g) location of the register of members[6] if it is not at the registered office;

(h) location of the register of debenture holders if it is not at the registered office; and

(i) notification of any election by a private company to dispense with the laying of accounts[7] or the holding of an annual general meeting.[8]

In addition, if the company has a share capital, s.364A requires the annual return to contain details of shares allotted or subscribed for, of each class of share, of current shareholders and those who have ceased to be shareholders since the previous return was made up, including details as to which class of share is so held or has ceased to be held. Once a list of such shareholders has been given, a full list is only required every three years, intervening returns need only specify any changes.

The required contents of an annual return can be amended by regulations made by the Secretary of State: s.365.[9]

---

[3] For this purpose the Standard Industrial Classification of Economic Activities 2003 is used: The Companies (Principal Business Activities) (Amendment) Regs 2002 (SI 2002/3081).

[4] Unless the director has obtained a confidentiality order under ss 723B–723F on the basis of protection from intimidation. A service address can be substituted. See Companies (Particulars of Usual Residential Address) (Confidentiality Orders) Regs 2002 SI 2002/912.

[5] See s.365(3). For shadow directors, see below, p.269.

[6] Above, p.191.

[7] Below, Ch.22.

[8] Below, p.242.

[9] The Company Law Review recommended retaining the annual return, even for small companies: *Final Report, Vol 1* para.11.45.

Chapter 13

SHARES

A share has been defined as "the interest of a shareholder in the company measured by a sum of money, for the purpose of liability in the first place, and of interest in the second, but also consisting of a series of mutual covenants entered into by all the shareholders *inter se* in accordance with [the Companies Act, s.14[1]]. The contract contained in the articles of association is one of the original incidents of the share."[2] The share is measured by a sum of money, namely, the nominal amount of the share, and also by the rights and obligations belonging to it as defined by the Companies Acts and by the memorandum and articles of the company. The undivided profits form an integral part of the shares to which they appertain.[3]

Each share in a company must be distinguished by its appropriate number, provided that it need not have a number if all the issued shares, or all the issued shares of a particular class, are fully paid up and rank *pari passu* for all purposes: s.182(2). Numbers are usually dispensed with today.

A share certificate, which specifies the shares held by the member and which is *prima facie* evidence[4] of his title to the shares (s.186), is usually issued to a shareholder except where the share is held in a de-materialised form.[5]

Shares in a company are personal estate, transferable in the manner provided by the articles of the company or under the provisions of the Stock Transfer Act 1963: s.182(1).[6] Shares are intangibles, *i.e.* choses in action,[7] and are located in the country in which the register of members is kept.[8]

A shareholder may borrow money on the security of his shares, *i.e.* in England, he may give the lender a mortgage over the shares to secure the payment of interest and repayment of the principal sum.[9]

Classes of Shares

A company is not bound to issue all its shares with the same rights but may

---

[1] Above, Ch.4.

[2] *Per* Farwell J. in *Borland's Trustee v Steel Bros. & Co. Ltd* [1901] 1 Ch. 279 at p.288. See also *Whittome v Whittome (No. 1)* 1994 S.L.T. 114 (O.H.).

[3] *Carron Co. v Hunter* (1868) 6 M HL 106.

[4] Or in Scotland, sufficient evidence unless the contrary is shown.

[5] Below, p.217.

[6] Different transfer procedures apply to de-materialised (or uncertificated) shares: see below.

[7] In Scotland shares are incorporeal moveable property. See *Whittome v Whittome (No. 1)*, 1994 S.L.T. 114 O.H.

[8] *International Credit and Investment Co. (Overseas) Ltd v Adham* [1994] 1 B.C.L.C. 66. If, unusually, the shares are negotiable instruments it is the place where the paper constituting the negotiable instrument is kept: *Re Harvard Securities Ltd* [1997] 2 B.C.L.C. 369.

[9] See below. In Scotland shares may be assigned in security.

confer different rights on different classes of shares.[10] Such classes may be described as ordinary shares and preference shares but the name by which a class of shares is called gives only an indication of the rights attaching to it in any particular company, and to ascertain the rights reference must be made to the articles or the terms of issue of the shares.

Although the memorandum of association is required to set out the division of the nominal capital into shares of a fixed amount, it is not required to set out, and in practice it will not usually set out, the different classes of shares into which the capital is divided. However, the articles will normally give the company power to issue different classes of shares.

Table A, reg. 2, provides: "Subject to the provisions of the Act and without prejudice to any rights attached to any existing shares, any share may be issued with such rights or restrictions as the company may by ordinary resolution determine."

Where a company issues shares with rights which are not stated in its memorandum or articles or in any resolution or document which must be registered with the Registrar,[11] or varies the rights attached to shares otherwise than by amendment of its memorandum or articles or by resolution or document requiring registration, s.128 requires the company to deliver particulars to the Registrar within one month unless the shares are uniform with shares previously issued.

Preference shares

Preference shares are shares the issue of which was authorised by the memorandum or the articles and which are entitled to some priority over the other shares in the company. They usually carry a right to preference in payment of dividend (if a dividend is declared) at a fixed rate, and a right to preference in the repayment of capital in a winding up. There may be several classes of preference shares, first, second and third, ranking one after the other.

The rights attached to preference shares are always a question of construction of the memorandum, the articles or the terms of issue of the shares. However, unless the articles, etc., otherwise provide, the rights which attach to preference shares are as described below. These *prima facie* rights differ according to whether the company is a going concern or in liquidation.

When the company is a going concern

1. When a right to a preferential dividend is given without more, it is a right to a *cumulative* dividend, *i.e.* if no preference dividend is declared in any year the arrears of dividend are carried forward and must be paid before a dividend is paid on the other shares.[12] If, however, the shares are declared to be non-

---

[10] The Company Law review recommended continuation of such variable rights, e.g. voting: *Final Report*, Vol.1, para.7.29.

[11] See s.380.

[12] *Webb v Earle* (1875) L.R. 20 Eq. 556; *Ferguson & Forrester Ltd v Buchanan*, 1920 S.C. 154. Interest is not payable on the arrears: *Partick etc. Gas Co. Ltd v Taylor* (1888) 15 R. 711.

cumulative preference shares, or the preferential dividend is to be paid out of the yearly profits,[13] or out of the net profits of each year,[14] the dividend will not be cumulative.

2. Preference shares are *non-participating, i.e.* they do not confer any right to a participation in the surplus profits of the company, after payment of a specified rate of dividend on the ordinary shares, in the absence of anything to that effect in the articles, etc. Where a special resolution that the holders of preference shares were entitled to a cumulative preference dividend at the rate of 10 per cent per annum and that such shares should rank, both as regards capital and dividend in priority to the other shares, the holders were only entitled to a 10 per cent dividend in the distribution of profits—the provision defined the whole terms of the bargain between the shareholders and the company.[15] Sometimes, however, cumulative and participating preference shares are created, conferring a right to participate in surplus profits up to a fixed percentage, *e.g.* a right to a preferential dividend of seven per cent may be given, together with a further right, after seven per cent has been paid on the ordinary shares, to participate in the surplus profits equally with the ordinary shares until an additional seven per cent has been paid, but no more.

3. Unless the articles, etc., otherwise provide, preference shares carry the *same voting rights* at general meetings as the other shares.[16] However if, as is common, the preference shareholders are expressly given a right to vote in certain specified circumstances, *e.g.* when their preference dividend is in arrears[17] or the rights attached to the preference shares are being varied, *prima facie* they have no right to vote in other circumstances.

When the company is being wound up

1. In the absence of a provision in the articles, etc., arrears of cumulative preference dividend are not payable out of the assets in a liquidation, unless the dividend has been declared.[18] If, however, as is usual, the articles provide for the payment of arrears, such arrears are payable out of the surplus assets after payment of the company's debts, whether or not any undistributed profits are included in the assets.[19] If the articles provide only for payment of all arrears "due" at the date of winding up, no arrears will be payable unless dividends have been declared, because a dividend is not due until it has been declared.[20]

---

[13] *Adair v Old Bushmills Distillery* [1908] W.N. 24.
[14] *Staples v Eastman Photographic Materials Co.* [1896] 2 Ch. 303, CA; contrast *Miln v Arizona Copper Co. Ltd* (1899) 1 F. 935.
[15] *Will v United Plantations Co. Ltd* [1914] A.C. 11.
[16] See s.370(6), below, Ch.14.
[17] Preference dividend is in arrears if it has not been paid even though that is because there are no available profits: *Re Bradford Investments plc* [1991] B.C.L.C. 224.
[18] *Re Crichton's Oil Co.* [1902] 2 Ch. 86, CA; *Re Catalinas Warehouses & Mole Co. Ltd* [1947] 1 All E.R. 51; *Robertson-Durham v Inches*, 1917, 1 S.L.T. 267 (O.H.).
[19] *Re Springbok Agricultural Estates Ltd* [1920] 1 Ch. 563; *Re Wharfedale Brewery Co. Ltd* [1952] Ch. 913. The rules as to the payment of dividends (below, Chap. 22) have no application to the surplus assets in a winding up.
[20] *Re Roberts and Cooper Ltd* [1992] 2 Ch. 383.

2. *Prima facie*, preference shares have no priority in the repayment of capital in a winding up. However, such a right may be, and usually is, given by the articles, and its effect is that after the company's debts and liabilities, and any arrears of preference dividend which are payable, have been paid, the preference shareholders are entitled to repayment of their capital in full before the ordinary shareholders are repaid their capital.[21]

3. Where there are surplus assets available after the discharge of all the company's liabilities and the repayment of the capital to the shareholders, such surplus assets are divisible rateably among all classes of shareholders in the absence of any provision in the articles, etc., to the contrary.[22] But, if, as is common, the articles set out the rights attached to a class of shares to participate in profits while the company is a going concern or to share in the property of the company in liquidation, *prima facie* those rights are exhaustive. Thus, articles giving preference shareholders priority in the repayment of capital in a liquidation but containing no reference to any further rights in the capital do not entitle the preference shareholders to participate in such surplus assets.[23]

The colliery assets of a coal mining company had been transferred to the National Coal Board under the Coal Industry Nationalisation Act 1946 and the company was to go into voluntary liquidation. Meanwhile the company proposed to reduce its capital by returning their capital to the holders of the preference stock. The articles provided that in the event of a winding up the preference stock ranked before the ordinary stock to the extent of repayment of the amounts, called up and paid thereon. *Held*, the proposed reduction was not unfair or inequitable. Even without it, the preference shareholders would not be entitled in a winding up to share in the surplus assets or to receive more than a return of their paid up capital. Accordingly, they could not object to being paid, by means of the reduction, the amount which they would receive in the proposed liquidation: *Wilsons and Clyde Coal Co. Ltd v Scottish Insurance Corpn. Ltd*, 1949 S.C. HL 90; [1949] A.C. 462.

It follows from this decision that where the preference shareholders have priority as to repayment of capital on a winding up they should also be paid off first on a reduction of capital due to over-capitalisation,[24] and have no right to complain about any variation of their class rights,[25] since it is in accord with their rights[26] unless the articles expressly make such a reduction as such a class right, in which case the variation of class rights procedure must be used.[27]

If articles expressly give preference shareholders a right to share in surplus assets after the repayment of capital, they are entitled to share in accumulated profits in a liquidation even if the articles give the ordinary shareholders a right to exclusive enjoyment of accumulated profits not required for the preference

---

[21] See, *e.g. Re Walter Symons Ltd* [1934] Ch. 308; *Re E. W. Savory Ltd* [1951] 2 All E.R. 1036.

[22] *Monkland Iron etc. Co. Ltd v Henderson* (1883) 10 R. 494; *Liquidators of Williamson-Buchanan Steamers Ltd, Petitioners*, 1936 S.L.T. 106 (O.H.).; *Town and Gown Assocn. Ltd, Liquidator, Petitioner*, 1948 S.L.T. (Notes) 71 (O.H.).

[23] *Wilsons and Clyde Coal Co. Ltd v Scottish Insurance Corpn. Ltd*, 1949 S.C. HL 90; 1948 S.C. 360; *Re The Isle of Thanet Electricity Supply Co. Ltd* [1950] Ch. 161, CA.

[24] Above, Ch.9.

[25] *Prudential Assurance Co. Ltd v Chatterley-Whitfield Collieries Ltd* [1949] A.C. 512 HC. See below.

[26] *Re Saltdean Estate Co. Ltd* [1968] 1 W.L.R. 1844; *House of Fraser plc v A.C.G.E. Investments Ltd* [1987] A.C. 387 HL, 1987 S.C. HL 125.

[27] *Re Northern Engineering Industries plc* [1994] 2 B.C.L.C. 704, CA.

dividend—the right of the ordinary shareholders depends on the appropriate resolutions being passed before a winding up.[28]

Variation of class rights

1. Where a company's shares are divided into classes, "class rights" are special rights of a class of shares, *e.g.* a preferential right as to dividend attached to preference shares where a company's shares are divided into preference shares and ordinary shares.

Section 125 clearly applies to alterations governing the rights attaching to any class of shares in a company whose share capital is divided into shares of different classes. It has, however, been held that it is not necessary for those rights to be attached to particular types of shares as long as they are given to a class of members in their capacity as members or shareholders, *e.g.* a right of pre-emption over other shares. For the purposes of s.125 therefore the share capital of a company is to be regarded as being divided into different classes, if shareholders, *qua* shareholders, enjoy different rights. It follows that the shares could come into or go out of a particular class on their acquisition or disposal by a particular individual.[29] Where a quorum right has been held to be a class right, it cannot be overridden by an order under s.371 to hold a general meeting with a reduced quorum.[30]

Class rights are usually given to preference shareholders and if the articles give the *ordinary* shareholders a right to the distributable profits after payment of a dividend on the preference shares, and a right to surplus assets on a liquidation, these are *not* class rights—they are no more than would be implied if the articles did not refer to them.[31] However, it seems that the original ordinary shares in *Greenhalgh v Arderne Cinemas*,[32] *post*, formed a class of shares within the meaning of an article providing for variation of the rights attached to a class of shares. Again, in *Lord St. David's v Union-Castle Mail Steamship Co. Ltd*,[33] where under the articles the large number of preference shares carried a right to vote when the preference dividend was in arrears and, such dividend being in arrears, the preference shareholders proposed to alter the articles so as to give themselves a right to vote on all resolutions, it was held that the proposed resolution would not affect the rights of the small number of ordinary shares unless the ordinary shareholders approved it in accordance with an article providing for variation of class rights, *i.e.* class rights were attached to the ordinary shares.[34]

2. If class rights are set out in the memorandum, or incorporated therein by reference to the articles,[35] they are only alterable if all the members of the

---

[28] *Dimbula Valley (Ceylon) Tea Co. Ltd v Laurie* [1961] Ch. 353.

[29] *Cumbrian Newspaper Group Ltd v Cumberland and Westmorland Newspaper and Printing Co. Ltd* [1987] Ch. 1; *Harman v BML Group Ltd* [1994] 2 B.C.L.C. 674, CA.

[30] *Harman v BML Group Ltd* [1994] 2 B.C.L.C. 674, CA. See p.244, below.

[31] *Hodge v James Howel & Co., The Times*, December 13, 1958, CA.

[32] [1946] 1 All E.R. 512, CA.

[33] *The Times*, November 24, 1934.

[34] See too, *Rights and Issues Investment Trust Ltd v Stylo Shoes Ltd* [1965] Ch. 250, above, p.66.

[35] *Dimbula Valley (Ceylon) Tea Co. Ltd v Laurie* [1961] Ch. 353.

company agree[36] unless the memorandum itself provides a method of alteration which must be complied with, or a method of alteration is provided by articles which were included at the time of the original incorporation of the company,[37] or the consent of the court is obtained to a scheme of arrangement under s.425.[38]

The power to alter the memorandum conferred by s.17[39] does not authorise any variation or abrogation of the special rights of any class of members.

3. The rights of different classes of shares are, however, usually set out in the articles[40] and the articles often provide for the variation of class rights. In any event s.125 now implies such a variation procedure.

If the articles attach class rights to a class of shares and contain a "modification of rights clause" the class rights may in general be varied, with the consent of the specified proportion or resolution of the holders of shares of the class, by a valid alteration of the articles by a special resolution of the company in general meeting.[41] In two cases, *viz.* a variation relating to the directors' powers to issue shares[42] and one connected with a reduction of capital,[43] the required majority is three quarters whatever the articles may say: s.125(3).

Such modification of rights clauses must be complied with: s.125(4). Any meeting held must comply with the Act as to the notice and conduct of meetings with a minimum quorum of the holders of at least one third in nominal value of the class (excluding treasury shares) being at least two in number: s.125(6).

If the articles do not set out a modification of rights clause, the rights can nevertheless be varied either by the written consent of the holders of three quarters of the issued shares of that class (excluding treasury shares) or by an extraordinary resolution to that effect passed at a separate meeting of that class: s.125(2). Again the meetings provisions in the Act must be complied with: s.125(6). The Company Law Review recommended that s.125 be simplified so as to apply the 75 per cent majority rule to all alteration of class rights.[42]

There is no effective compliance with a modification of class rights unless those holding a sufficient majority of the shares of the class vote in favour of the modification in the bona fide belief that they are acting in the interests of the general body of members of the class, *i.e.* at the class meeting the majority shareholders must consider what is best for the shareholders as a class, not what is best in their own interests.

A reduction of capital was to be effected by cancelling the five per cent £1 cumulative preference shares and allotting the holders an equivalent amount of six per cent unsecured loan stock repayable 1985/90. The majority of the preference shareholders, who supported the reduction, were also holders of 52 per cent of the company's ordinary stock and non-

---

[36] s.125(5).
[37] s.125(4).
[38] Below, Ch.58.
[39] Above, p.70.
[40] Class rights set out in a shareholders' agreement have the same affect as if they were contained in the articles: *Harman v BML Group Ltd* [1994] 2 B.C.L.C. 674, CA.
[41] Above, p.75.
[42] Above, Ch.7.
[43] Above, Ch.9.
[42a] Unless a higher figure is entrenched in the articles by unanimous decision of the members: Final Report, Vol 1, para.7.28.

voting ordinary shares. Minority preference shareholders opposed the reduction. The court refused to confirm it. The majority preference shareholders had considered what was best in their own interests, based on their large equity shareholding, without considering what was best for preference shareholders as a class. Further, the reduction was unfair[44]— the advantages of the exchange into unsecured stock did not compensate for the disadvantages: *Re Holders Investment Trust Ltd* [1971] 1 W.L.R. 582.

4. Where there is in the articles (or the memorandum) an express or implied power to vary class rights, the exercise of that power is subject to s.127. This section provides that if, in the case of a company with a share capital divided into different classes of shares, provision is made by the articles (or memorandum) for the variation or abrogation of the rights attached to any class of shares, subject to the consent of a specified proportion of the holders of the shares of the class or the sanction of a resolution passed at a separate meeting of the holders of such shares, and in pursuance of such provision the rights attached to any such class of shares are varied, an application can be made to the court to have the variation cancelled, whereupon it has no effect unless and until it is confirmed by the court. The section also applies to variations under the procedure implied by s.125(2): s.127(1)(b).

Those who can apply are the holders of not less than 15 per cent of the issued shares of the class, discounting treasury shares, and who did not consent to or vote for the variation. The application must be made within 21 days after the giving of the consent or the passing of the resolution.

The court may disallow the variation if, after hearing the various parties interested, it is satisfied that the variation would unfairly prejudice the shareholders of the class in question. If the court is not so satisfied it must confirm the variation.

The company must, within 15 days, send a copy of the order made by the court to the Registrar of Companies: s.127(5).

The object of the section is to protect shareholders from being prejudiced by the voting of other shareholders who hold shares of another class in addition to those of the class affected by the variation.

For example, if a variation reduces the dividend on preference shares from seven per cent to six per cent per annum, and 80 per cent of the preference shareholders are also ordinary shareholders, the requisite consent of the preference shareholders is likely to be obtained, since the variation will leave more profits for a dividend on the ordinary shares. This would be unfair to the 20 per cent of the preference shareholders who are not ordinary shareholders and they could apply under s.127.

5. A variation of class rights, includes an abrogation of those rights: s.125(8).[45] However, it has been held that class rights are *not* "varied" by the subdivision of other shares, under a power in the articles, which results in the holders of the shares with the class rights being outvoted by the holders of the other shares.

---

[44] Above, Ch.9.
[45] Preference shareholders' rights are not abrogated by being repaid first on a reduction of capital: *House of Fraser plc v A.C.G.E. Investments plc* [1987] A.C. 387; 1987 S.C. HL 125, unless such a reduction is made a specific class right: *Re Northern Engineering Industries plc* [1994] 2 B.C.L.C. 704, CA.

2s. ordinary shares, as regards voting, ranked *pari passu* with the 10s. ordinary shares. Each 10s. share was sub-divided into five 2s. ordinary shares. *Held*, the voting rights of the original 2s. shares had not been varied. The only voting right attached to that class was one vote per share, and that right remained: *Greenhalgh v Arderne Cinemas Ltd* [1946] 1 All E.R. 512 CA.[46]

Again, class rights are *not* "affected" by the creation or issue of new shares of the class ranking equally with the old.

Capital was being increased by the issue of 600,000 £1 preference shares ranking *pari passu* with the existing 600,000 £1 preference stock, and 2,640,000 ordinary shares of 10s. each ranking *pari passu* with the existing £3,300,00 ordinary stock. The new shares were to be issued to the ordinary stockholders and paid for out of the reserve fund. *Held*, the proposed issue of new capital did not "affect" the rights of the existing preference shareholders. Only the enjoyment of the rights was affected, the rights themselves were not: *White v Bristol Aeroplane Co. Ltd* [1953] Ch.65, CA.[47]

A modification of rights clause in the articles cannot be altered by special resolution without the appropriate consent of shareholders of the class under that procedure: s.125(7).

Deferred shares

Deferred shares, which are sometimes called founders' or management shares, are usually of small nominal amount with a right to take the whole or a proportion of the profits after a fixed dividend has been paid on the ordinary shares. The rights of the holders of deferred shares depend on the articles or the terms of issue.

Deferred shares are rarely issued now and the modern tendency is to convert existing deferred shares into ordinary shares.

Non-voting ordinary shares

In recent years some companies have issued non-voting ordinary shares. The purpose of such issues is to enable the companies concerned to raise money and at the same time enable those with the majority of the existing voting shares to retain control. However, with the idea of ensuring that the public is not misled, the Stock Exchange requires non-voting shares to be designated as such. This is usually done by describing the shares as A Ordinary shares, etc.

Employees' shares

Some companies issue special shares to their employees. Modern tax legislation, however, in general only provides tax incentives for companies who provide their employees with ordinary shares, *i.e.* those not specifically available only to employees.

---

[46] And see the *Dimbula* case, above, p.209.
[47] And see *Re John Smith's Tadcaster Brewery Co. Ltd* [1953] Ch. 308, CA.

Transfer of Shares

There is a distinction between a transfer of shares and a transmission of shares. A transfer is by the act of the member, while a transmission occurs by operation of law on the death or the bankruptcy of a member. The procedure on transfer is set out below, but it requires at least a valid contractual agreement or gift.[48] In *Harvela Investments Ltd v Royal Trust Company of Canada (C.I.) Ltd*[49] the House of Lords held that the holder of shares in a private company could not validly invite other parties to submit sealed bids for those shares and then accept a bid which is referential, *i.e.* one which is given as an amount above that submitted by the other bidder. If such bids were allowed one party could not lose and the other party could not win.

The following account as to the form and procedure of transfers of shares does not apply to transfers of shares held in electronic or uncertified form under the CREST system which operates in respect of some listed companies. A note on that system is included at the end of this section.

Form of transfer

Section 183(1), which was passed to make sure that there is an instrument which can be stamped with stamp duty, provides that it is unlawful for a company to register a transfer of shares, and so complete the legal title, unless a "proper instrument of transfer" has been delivered to the company. Consequently it is illegal to have an article that upon the death of a shareholder his shares shall be deemed to have passed to his widow, without any transfer.[50]

The form of the transfer may be that prescribed by the articles but a "proper instrument" for the purposes of s.183(1) does not necessarily mean an instrument complying with the formalities prescribed by the articles—it means an instrument such as will attract stamp duty.[51] Thus a transfer document which failed to state the consideration for the transfer was held to be valid since it was still appropriate for stamping purposes—the Revenue could go behind the form to ascertain that amount.[52]

> Table A, reg. 23, provides: "The instrument of transfer of a share may be in any usual form or in any other form which the directors may approve and shall be executed by or on behalf of the transferor and, unless the share is fully paid, by or on behalf of the transferee."

Where the shares are only partly-paid it is essential that the transferee signs the transfer document to accept the liability on the shares.[53]

---

[48] If the full transfer formalities are not complied with, there will still be an equitable transfer or assignment under the contract or gift. See p.215, below.
[49] [1986] A.C. 207, HL.
[50] *Re Greene* [1949] Ch. 333.
[51] *Re Paradise Motor Co. Ltd* [1968] 1 W.L.R. 1125, CA; *Dempsey v Celtic Football and Athletic Co. Ltd* [1993] B.C.C. 514; *Nisbet v Shepherd* [1994] 1 B.C.L.C. 300.
[52] *Nisbet v Shepherd* [1994] 1 B.C.L.C. 300.
[53] *Dempsey v Celtic Football and Athletic Co. Ltd* [1993] B.C.C. 514.

In the case of a company limited by shares, if shares are fully paid they may be transferred by a simplified form of transfer, namely a stock transfer under hand in the form set out in Sch.1 to the Stock Transfer Act 1963.[53a] Such a transfer need be executed only by the transferor and need not be attested: 1963 Act, s.1.

Procedure on transfer

If a shareholder has sold or given all his shares comprised in one share certificate[54] to one person,[55] the transfer is effected as follows:

(1) the transferor sends the transferee the "proper instrument of transfer" required by s.183(1) and executed by the transferor,[56] together with the share certificate relating to the shares comprised in the transfer;

(2) the transferee then executes the transfer[57] if it is in accordance with the articles, and forwards it, with the share certificate[58] and the registration fee, to the company for registration;

(3) within two months after the transfer is lodged the company must either issue a new share certificate to the transferee or, where the directors are exercising a power to refuse registration, send *him* notice of its refusal to register the transfer: ss 183(5), 185(1).

A transfer may also be registered, at the request of the transferor, in the same manner and subject to the same conditions as if registration were applied for by the transferee: s.183(4).

Certification of transfer

If a holder of shares sells or gives some only of his shares comprised in a share certificate, *e.g.* 250 shares out of 1,000, it will be unsafe for him to deliver his share certificate for 1,000 shares to the purchaser. Similarly if he sells some of the shares to one person and the rest to another. The usual procedure in such cases is, therefore:

(1) the transferor executes the transfer and sends it, with the share certificate, to the company;

(2) the secretary indorses on the transfer the words "certificate lodged" or similar words, and returns the transfer so certificated to the transferor;

(3) the transferor hands over this certificated transfer to the transferee against payment of the price;

[53a] As amended by the Stock Transfer (Amendment of Forms) Order 1974 (SI 1974/1214).

[54] As to shares comprised in a share warrant, see below, p.238.

[55] As to the procedure when, *e.g.* part only of the holding is being sold, see Certification of transfer, below.

[56] Where there is a dispute as to whether the transferor signed the transfer form the burden of proof is on the transferee to show that it was so signed: *Elliott v The Hollies Ltd* [1998] 1 B.C.L.C. 627.

[57] If he is required to do so under the articles and see *Dempsey v Celtic Football and Athletic Co. Ltd* [1998] B.C.C. 514.

[58] See below, p.219.

(4) the transferee executes the transfer[59] if it is in the form prescribed by the articles, and forwards it to the company for registration;

(5) within two months the company either issues new share certificates or, where a power to refuse registration is being exercised, informs the *transferee* of its refusal to register him: ss 183(5), 185(1), above

The certification of a transfer by the company is a representation by the company to any person acting on the faith of the certification that there have been produced to the company such documents as show a *prima facie* title to the shares in the transferor, but it is not a representation that the transferor has any title: s.184(1). However, if a company *fraudulently or negligently* makes a false certification the company is liable in damages to a person who acts on the faith of it to his detriment: s.184(2).

Suppose that P transferred all his shares to X and his certificate was lodged by X with the company. Before registration was completed, P executed a transfer of some of the shares to Y, who sold them to B. Y's transfer to B was negligently certificated by the company and, on the strength of this, B paid Y. The company registered X and refused to register B. The company is liable in damages to B.

A certification is deemed to be made by the company if it is made by a person, such as the secretary, authorised to issue certificated transfers on the company's behalf, and if it is signed by a person authorised to certificate transfers on the company's behalf: s.184(3).

When a transfer is certificated the company destroys the original certificate and issues new certificates. But if it *negligently* returns the original certificate with the certified transfer to the transferor and the transferor then fraudulently deals with the original certificate so as to inflict loss on a third party, *e.g.* the transferor purports to transfer *all* the shares comprised in the original certificate to the third party, the company is not liable to the third party. The reason is that the share certificate is neither a negotiable instrument nor a statement that the transferor is still the owner on the part of the company issuing it[60] and the company owes no duty to the public as to the custody of the certificate. Further, the company is not estopped from denying the validity of the transferor's title to the shares *previously* transferred, because the proximate cause of the third party's loss is the fraud of the transferor and not the negligence of the company.[61]

Rights as between transferor and transferee

On a sale of shares the ordinary contract between the parties is that the vendor shall give to the purchaser a valid transfer and do all that is required to enable the purchaser to be registered as a member in respect of the shares, the

---

[59] If required to do so by the articles.
[60] See below, p.220.
[61] *Longman v Bath Electric Tramways Ltd* [1905] 1 Ch. 646. The Scottish equivalent of "estoppel" is personal bar, but, in the absence of Scottish authority on certification, it seems doubtful whether a company would be entitled to deny the validity of a share certificate in the circumstances mentioned: *cf. Clavering, Son & Co. v Goodwins, Jardine & Co. Ltd* (1891) 18 R. 652.

purchaser's duty being to get himself registered.[62] The vendor's duty is not only to give a genuine transfer but also, where the vendor is not the transferor, one which is signed by a transferor willing that the transfer shall be registered.

Solicitors instructed stockbrokers to sell stock and enclosed the certificate and a blank transfer (*i.e.* a transfer in which the transferee's name had still to be inserted) signed by the stockholder. The stockbrokers sold the stock but the stockholder repudiated the contract and the company, on her instructions, refused to register the transfer. The stockbrokers replaced the stock by a purchase on the Stock Exchange and sued the solicitors for an indemnity. *Held*, (1) the solicitors were principals of the stockbrokers as regards the sale, (2) it was the solicitor's duty to deliver a transfer executed by a transferor willing that it should be registered, and (3) the solicitors were liable. *Hichens, Harrison, Woolston & Co. v Jackson & Sons* [1943] A.C. 266.

If the directors, in pursuance of a power in the articles,[63] decline to register the transfer, the purchaser, unless he bought "with registration guaranteed", will be unable to sue the vendor for damages or rescind and recover the price from the vendor—there is no implied condition subsequent to such effect.[64] In such a case the vendor will be a trustee of the shares for the purchaser.[65] The vendor is, of course, under a duty to the purchaser not to prevent or delay the registration of the transfer.[66]

As from the time of the contract of sale the equitable or beneficial interest in the shares passes to the purchaser, and the vendor holds the legal title as quasi-trustee for the purchaser.[67] No transferee can obtain the legal or complete title until his name is entered on the register of members.[68] In the case of a gift, delivery of the share transfer form is usually required to effect on equitable assignment of the shares.[69] That may not always be required if, in the circumstances, it would be unconscionable for the donor to recall the gift.[70]

Until the transfer is registered, the vendor will receive any dividends or other benefits declared on the shares and, in the case of partly paid shares, calls may be made on him. As between the vendor and the purchaser the rights and liabilities depend on the terms of the contract. The shares may be bought "cum" or "ex" dividends or rights, or with a specified sum paid. In the absence of any such agreement, the purchaser is entitled to dividends or other benefits declared after the *date of the contract*.[71]

In September 1935, R sold shares privately to W. In April 1936, the company declared a dividend for the year ending December 31, 1935. *Held*, the sale being by

---

[62] *Skinner v City of London Marine Insce. Corpn.* (1885) 14 Q.B.D. 882, CA.

[63] See below, p.227.

[64] *London Founders Assocn. Ltd v Clarke* (1888) 20 Q.B.D. 576, CA.

[65] *Stevenson v Wilson*, 1907 S.C. 445; this quasi-trust would not, however, defeat a subsequent arrestment of the shares by a creditor of the transferor: *per* Lord Moncrieff (Ordinary) in *National Bank of Scotland Glasgow Nominees Ltd v Adamson*, 1932 S.L.T. 492 (O.H.) at p.495.

[66] *Hooper v Herts* [1906] 1 Ch. 549, CA

[67] *Hawks v McArthur* [1951] 1 All R 22

[68] See *per* Lord Gifford in *Morrison v Harrison* (1876) 3 R. 406 at p.411; see also *Tennant's Trustees v Tennant*, 1946 S.C. 420.

[69] Since equity will not assist a volunteer, the donor must have done everything required of him to effect the gift: *Re Rose* [1952] Ch. 499, CA.

[70] *Pennington v Waine* [2002] 2 B.C.L.C. 448, CA.

[71] *Black v Homersham* (1878) 4 Ex.D. 24; *Re Kidner* [1929] 2 Ch. 121.

private bargain and not governed by Stock Exchange rules, W was entitled to the whole dividend and it was not apportionable between W and R: *Re Wimbush* [1940] Ch.92.

Subject to contrary agreement, the purchaser must indemnify the vendor against calls made after the date of the contract.[72]

Again, until the transfer is registered, the vendor is entitled to exercise any vote conferred by the shares but he must vote as directed by the purchaser.[73]

An unpaid vendor of shares who remains on the register of members after the contract of sale retains *vis-à-vis* the purchaser the right to vote in respect of those shares. Where the contract expressly provides for delay in payment and makes alternative arrangements as to voting then the unpaid vendor will lose his right to vote,[74] but not where the purchaser defaults in payment even though the voting rights have passed to the purchaser under the contract.[75]

Shares held in electronic form

Where shares are listed on the Stock Exchange transfers are effected through members of the Exchange who may also act as principal traders and market makers and there is no direct link between a buyer and seller. They will sell and buy shares to their clients' instructions but there still has to be payment by the buyer and transfer of the legal title to the buyer. This process is known as settlement. In order to speed up this process an optional new form of electronic transfer was introduced in 1996, known as CREST. Under this system, where the company, the operator of the system and the shareholder all agree, transfers are effected without the need for either a written instrument of transfer or a share certificate.

The system is governed by the Uncertificated Securities Regulations 2001.[76] The shares are said to have been dematerialised and transfers are effected by computer instructions through the operator of the system. In essence, the stock and cash accounts of the buyer and seller are debited and credited. The major difference is that legal title passes at that point and not on the later registration with the company. Such companies must now keep a *register* of its certificated shares and a *record* of its uncertified shares. The actual register of those is kept by CREST. Both registers are *prima facie* evidence of what is on them, but the CREST register will have priority. CREST remains optional but in an increasingly electronic age, a paperless market is a distinct future possibility. The regulations provide detailed rules for such transfers and some safeguards where the system breaks down.

Priorities

English law

The general rules are:

---

[72] *Spencer v Ashworth, Partington & Co.* [1925] 1 K.B. 589, CA.
[73] *Dempsey v Celtic Football and Athletic Co. Ltd* [1993] B.C.C. 514.
[74] *Musselwhite v C.H. Musselwhite & Son Ltd* [1962] Ch. 964, where a contract for the sale of shares provided that the transfer and share certificate should be held by a third party until the price was paid by instalments over a period of years.
[75] *JRRT (Investments) Ltd v Haycroft* [1993] B.C.L.C. 401.
[76] SI 2001/3755.

(1) The party who is on the register of members and therefore has the legal title has priority.

(2) If neither party is on the register, the party whose equitable title is first in time has priority.

For example, if X, the registered owner, is trustee of the shares for Y and, in breach of trust sells the shares to Z, who buys without notice of the trust and becomes registered as owner before the company knows of the trust, Z will have priority over Y. Nor can Y bring an action for conversion against Z. Y only has an equitable interest in the shares whereas Z is a bona fide purchaser of the shares without notice of Y's interest. Y's interest has therefore been extinguished.[77] A company, however, is entitled to a reasonable time for the consideration of every transfer before it registers the transfer, and therefore if Y, in the example just given, had given notice of his claim to the company before Z was actually registered as owner, he would have been entitled to priority over Z, as his equitable title would have been first in time.

C assigned all his property to P as trustee for C's creditors. The property included some shares. P asked for the share certificates but was unable to obtain them from C; he then gave notice of the assignment to the company. C, after the date of the assignment to P, sold the shares to X, who applied for registration. *Held*, P, having an equitable title which was prior in time, was entitled to registration: *Peat v Clayton* [1906] 1 Ch.659.

Entry on the register after notice of a prior equitable claim will not give priority.

In 1893 X transferred debentures of a private company to Y on trust for X for life with remainder to X's sons. The transfer was not registered. In 1894 one son sold his share of the debentures to Z. In 1911 X deposited the debentures with the bank as security for the company's overdraft. In 1914 the bank, on learning of the settlement and transfer to Y, took a transfer of the debentures from X, and were registered as owners. *Held*, Z was entitled to priority over the bank: *Coleman v London County and Westminster Bank Ltd* [1916] 2 Ch.353.

It has been said[78] that even if a complete legal title has not been obtained, a person who has, as between himself and the company, a present, absolute, unconditional right to registration before the company learns of a better title, has the same priority as if he were actually registered. It is doubtful, however, whether anything short of registration will give priority, except perhaps in very special circumstances. Directors should refuse to register a transfer after receiving notice of an adverse equitable claim to the shares, unless the transfer has already been passed for registration.[79]

Delay in obtaining registration is dangerous to a transferee for two reasons: a later transferee may gain priority by obtaining registration first, or an earlier equity may come to light.

---

[77] *M.C.C. Proceeds Inc. v Lehman Bros. Int. (Europe)* [1998] 2 B.C.L.C. 659.
[78] *Per* Romer J. in *Moore v North Western Bank* [1891] 2 Ch. 599 at pp.602, 603.
[79] *Per* Joyce J. in *Ireland v Hart* [1902] 1 Ch. 522 at p.529.

A husband mortgaged shares of which he was trustee for his wife. Before the mortgagee was registered the wife successfully claimed that her equitable title prevailed over that of the mortgagee: *Ireland v Hart* [1902] 1 Ch.522.

To protect himself such a transferee should issue a stop notice.[80]

Scots law

If there are competing claims for membership of a company, the person preferred is the one who first completes his title to the shares by having his name entered on the register; a mere assignation of shares, even though intimated to the company, does not make the assignee a member.[81] Where a competition arises between a transferee and an arrester, the transferee is preferred to the arrester as soon as the transfer has been registered.[82] In a question between a transferee whose transfer has been duly intimated to the company but not registered and a subsequent arrester, the intimation of the transfer has been held to cut out the arrestment.[83]

Directors may delay registration where they suspect that a transfer is effected by fraud or dishonesty[84] but, if they receive intimation of a competing interest in the shares from some party other than the transferee, they are entitled to register the transfer unless the intimation is followed up by a legal measure such as interdict.[85] The company must be made a party to any such interdict process, and interdict has been refused where it was alleged that share transfers, bearing that the beneficial interest remained in the transferors, had been executed by a body of trustees to certain of their own number and another person in order to give the transferees a qualification to act as directors; the possibility that the shares had been transferred in breach of trust was not, the court held, a matter which concerned the company or which made the registration of the transferees invalid.[86]

SHARE CERTIFICATES

Every company must complete the share certificates and have them ready for delivery within two months[87] after the allotment of any of its shares or after the date on which a transfer of its shares is lodged for registration, unless the conditions of issue otherwise provide, under a penalty of a default fine: s.185. The form of the certificate is governed by the articles. Table A, reg. 6, gives the right to a certificate without payment and provides that it shall be under the seal of the company,[88] and shall specify the shares to which it relates and the amount paid up thereon.

---

[80] See p.202, below.
[81] *Morrison v Harrison* (1876) 3 R. 406.
[82] *National Bank of Scotland Glasgow Nominees Ltd v Adamson*, 1932 S.L.T. 492 (O.H.).
[83] *Jackson v Elphick* (1902) 10 S.L.T. 146 (O.H.).
[84] *Property Investment Co. of Scotland Ltd v Duncan* (1887) 14 R. 299.
[85] *Per* Lord M'Laren in *Shaw v Caledonian Rlwy. Co.* (1890) 17 R. 466 at p.482.
[86] *Elliot v J. W. Mackie & Sons Ltd*, 1935 S.C. 81.
[87] Except for shares held in electronic form.
[88] This can include the official seal for this purpose authorised under s.40.

The certificate is a formal statement by the company under its common seal if it has one, or its official seal under s.40, or is otherwise signed in accordance with s.36A, that the person named therein is the holder of the number of shares in the company specified in the certificate at the date of issue. It is *prima facie* evidence[89] of the title of that person to the shares: s.186.[90] It is not, however, a document of title (as the register of members is), but wrongful interference with the right to possession of it can be the subject of a claim in the tort of conversion for which full damages are recoverable and not just for its value as a piece of paper).[91] The object of the certificate is to facilitate dealings with the shares, whether by way of sale or security, and so make them more valuable to their owner. On the other hand, a share certificate is not a negotiable instrument, so that its accidental loss or destruction is not a matter of great moment. The articles usually make provision for the granting of a new certificate in such a case.

Table A, reg. 7, provides: "If a share certificate is defaced, worn out, lost or destroyed, it may be renewed on such terms (if any) as to evidence and indemnity and payment of the expenses reasonably incurred by the company in investigating evidence as the directors may determine but otherwise free of charge, and (in the case of defacement or wearing out) on delivery up of the old certificate."

Estoppel[92] as to statements in a certificate

The issue of a share certificate may give rise to an estoppel against the company. The company cannot deny the truth of the certificate against a person who has relied on the certificate and in consequence has changed his position.

T, the registered holder of shares, left the share certificate with her broker. T's signature was forged to a transfer in favour of S. T did not reply to notice of the transfer sent to her by the company and a new certificate in the name of S was issued by the company. A bought from S and paid for the shares on delivery of the share certificate and a new share certificate was issued to A. The fraud was subsequently discovered and T's name was restored to the register. *Held*, the company was liable to indemnify A. The giving of the certificate to S amounted to a statement by the company, intended to be acted upon by purchasers of shares in the market, that S was entitled to the shares, and A having acted on the statement, the company was estopped from denying it. A was entitled to recover from the company as damages the value of the shares at the time when the company first refused to recognise him as a shareholder, with interest: *Re Bahia and San Francisco Rlwy. Co.* (1868) L.R. 3 Q.B. 584.

There is no estoppel in favour of a person, such as S in the above case, who procures the granting of a certificate on a forged transfer[93] or forged power of attorney,[94] even if he has acted in good faith. In fact the company may be able to

---

[89] In Scotland it is sufficient evidence: s.186, as amended by the Requirements of Writing (Scotland) Act 1995.

[90] See *Re Baku Consolidated Oilfields Ltd* [1994] 1 B.C.L.C. 173.

[91] *M.C.C. Proceeds Inc. v Lehman Brothers International (Europe)* [1998] 2 B.C.L.C. 659, CA; see also *International Credit and Investment (Overseas) Co. Ltd v Adham* [1994] 1 B.C.L.C. 66; and see above, p.191.

[92] Personal bar is the Scottish equivalent of "estoppel". See Lord Kyllachy (Ordinary) in *Clavering, Son & Co. v Goodwins, Jardine & Co. Ltd* (1891) 18 R. 652 at p.657.

[93] *Sheffield Corporation v Barclay* [1905] A.C. 392, below, p.222.

[94] *Starkey v Bank of England* [1903] A.C. 114.

claim an indemnity from such a person.[95] There is no estoppel either in favour of a person who relies on the certificate either to establish that the person named is still the owner or that the person in possession is in fact the owner. It applies only to someone relying on the fact that the person named was the owner at the date of issue.[96]

The company may be estopped from denying the title to shares of the person to whom it has issued a share certificate.[97]

D bought 30 shares through a broker, L, who was also secretary of the company, and paid L She received and returned to L a transfer of shares executed to L's direction by his clerk, P, who was never a man of substance and who did not hold any shares. The transfer, which did not specify the numbers of the shares, was put before the board by L and passed without production of P's certificate being required, and a new certificate prepared by L was issued to the effect that D held 30 shares, numbers 115—144 inclusive. The chairman, who did not sign the certificate, did not notice that the shares were part of his holding (numbers 1–133). The board properly relied on the secretary to check transfers and certificates with the register. Two years later the board notified D that P's transfer was invalid and declined to recognise her as a shareholder. L was bankrupt by then and the company could not prove that he could not have reimbursed D if, when the certificate was issued, the company had refused to issue it. *Held*, D was entitled to damages: *Dixon v Kennaway & Co.* [1900] 1 Ch.833.

The company may also be estopped from denying the amount stated to be paid up on shares.

B lent money to a company on the security of fully paid shares in the company and was handed by the company share certificates for 10,000 shares of £1 each which the certificates stated to be fully paid up. No money had been paid on the shares, which had been issued direct by the company to B, but B did not know this. On the company's going into liquidation, B was placed on the list of contributories in respect of these shares. *Held*, the company was estopped by the certificate from denying that the shares were fully paid up and B was entitled to have his name removed from the list of contributories: *Bloomenthal v Ford* [1897] A.C. 156.[98]

The company may be made liable in damages to the person who has relied on the statement in the share certificate.[99]

If B, in the *Bloomenthal* case, had known that the shares were not fully paid up, there would have been no estoppel—there is no estoppel in favour of a person who knows the untruth of statements in a share certificate.[1] An original allottee, therefore, will seldom be in a position to benefit from the principle.[2]

---

[95] Below, p.194.
[96] *Longman v Bath Electric Tramways Ltd* [1905] 1 Ch. 646; *International Credit and Investment Co. (Overseas) Ltd v Adham* [1994] 1 B.C.L.C. 66; *Royal Bank of Scotland plc v Sandstone Properties Ltd* [1998] 2 B.C.L.C. 429.
[97] *Balkis Consolidated Co. Ltd v Tomkinson* [1893] A.C. 396.
[98] *cf. Waterhouse v Jamieson* (1870) 8 M HL 88, in which it was held that statements in the memorandum and articles, which also appeared in share certificates, as to the amount paid up on shares could not be contradicted by the liquidator.
[99] *Clavering, Son & Co. v Goodwins, Jardine & Co. Ltd* (1891) 18 R. 652.
[1] See *Crickmer's Case* (1875) L.R. 10. Ch.App. 614. In England, if the shares had been transferred to a purchaser without notice that they were not fully paid up he could give a good title to a purchaser from him without notice: *Barrow's Case* (1880) 14 Ch.D. 432, CA.
[2] *Liquidator of Scottish Heritages Co. Ltd* (1898) 5 S.L.T. 336 (O.H.): contrast *Penang Foundry Co. Ltd v Gardiner*, 1913 S.C. 1203 (O.H.).

The company is not estopped where a certificate is a forgery.

R lent money to the secretary of a company for his own purposes on the security of a share certificate issued to R by the secretary and certifying that R was registered as transferee of the shares. The secretary issued the share certificate without authority, affixed the common seal and forged the signatures of two directors, so that the certificate apparently complied with the articles. R sued the company for damages for refusal to register him. *Held*, in the absence of evidence that the company had held out the secretary as having authority to do more than the mere ministerial act of delivering share certificates, when duly made, to those entitled to them, the company was not estopped from disputing the claim or responsible for the secretary's act: *Ruben v Great Fingall Consolidated* [1906] A.C. 439.

Forged transfers

A forged transfer of shares is a nullity and cannot affect the title of the shareholder whose signature is forged. If the company, therefore, has registered the forged transfer and removed the true owner of the shares from the register, it can be compelled to replace him.[3] It can then claim an indemnity from the person who sent the forged transfer for registration, *e.g.* either the transferor or his broker, if it has sustained loss through acting thereon. No estoppel in favour of such a person arises from a share certificate issued to him even though he knows nothing of the forgery—he has not relied on the act of the company in issuing the certificate.

B sent to the corporation for registration a transfer of stock which stood in the names of T and H. The transfer was a forgery, T having forged H's signature to the transfer, but B was ignorant of this. The corporation registered the transfer. B transferred the stock to third parties to whom certificates were issued. The corporation was estopped from denying that those registered were the stockholders entitled. H subsequently discovered the forgery and compelled the corporation to buy him an equivalent amount of stock and to pay him the missing dividends with interest. *Held*, B was bound to indemnify the corporation upon an implied contract that the transfer was genuine: *Sheffield Corporation v Barclay* [1905] A.C. 392.[4]

It has been suggested that the company may not, however, be able to claim a complete indemnity if it is guilty of negligence in failing to spot the forgery, by virtue of s.2(1) of the Civil Liability (Contribution) Act 1978.[5] This was doubted, however, in *Royal Bank of Scotland plc v Sandstone Properties Ltd*,[6] on the basis that the whole principle of the right to an indemnity would be affected by such a claim for contribution.

In an effort to prevent the registration of a forged transfer, companies usually, on a transfer being lodged for registration, write to the shareholder informing

---

[3] *Barton v N. Staffordshire Rlwy. Co.* (1888) 38 Ch.D. 458.

[4] In *Royal Bank of Scotland plc v Sandstone Properties Ltd* [1998] 2 B.C.L.C. 429, this principle was applied even where the company had issued the fraudster with a duplicate share certificate which was then used in the forged transfer. The duplicate certificate was not the proximate cause of the loss. That was the request for the transfer; *cf.* Lord Kyllachy (Ordinary) in *Clavering, Son & Co. v Goodwins, Jardine & Co. Ltd* (1891) 18 R. 652 at p.657.

[5] *Yeung v Honk Kong and Shanghai Bank Ltd* [1980] 2 All E.R. 599 PC. In Scotland see Law Reform (Miscellaneous Provisions) (Scotland) Act 1940, s.3.

[6] [1998] 2 B.C.L.C. 429. That case equally suggests there is no joint liability as joint tortfeasors.

him of the transfer and of their intention to register it unless by return of post they hear that he objects. The neglect of the shareholder to reply to this communication does not estop him from proving that the transfer is a forgery.[7]

RESTRICTIONS ON TRANSFER

Every shareholder has a right to transfer his shares to whom he likes, unless the articles provide to the contrary.[8]

By the Companies Acts "it is provided that the shares in a company under these Acts shall be capable of being transferred in manner provided by the regulations of the company. The regulations of the company may impose fetters upon the right of transfer. In the absence of restrictions in the articles the shareholder has by virtue of the statute the right to transfer his shares without the consent of anybody to any transferee, even though he be a man of straw, provided it is a bona fide transaction in the sense that it is an out-and-out disposal of the property without retaining any interest in the shares—that the transferor bona fide divests himself of all benefit. . . . In the absence of restrictions it is competent to a transferor, notwithstanding that the company is *in extremis* to compel registration of a transfer to a transferee notwithstanding that the latter is a person not competent to meet the unpaid liability upon the shares. Even if the transfer be executed for the express purpose of relieving the transferor from liability, the directors cannot upon that ground refuse to register it unless there is in the articles some provision so enabling them": *per* Buckley L.J. in *Lindlar's Case* [1910] 1 Ch.312 CA at p. 316.[9]

In the case of a private company, the articles may, and usually do, restrict the right to transfer its shares.[10] In the case of a public company, shares must normally be free from restrictions on the right of transfer if a stock exchange quotation is to be obtained.[11]

Any restrictions on the transfer of shares are a derogation from the common law right of free transfer. It follows that: any rights conferred by the articles will not be extended to situations not covered by them,[12] the procedure laid down in the articles for the exercise of the rights must be strictly followed,[13] and if the rights are not actively exercised the right of free transfer will revive.[14]

If there has been a registered transfer in breach of the articles the only remedy available to an aggrieved shareholder is rectification of the register. This is a discretionary remedy, however, and will not be granted to third parties for extraneous purposes.[15]

---

[7] *Re Bahia and San Francisco Rlwy Co.* (1868) L.R. 3 Q.B. 584, above, p.220, *Barton v L. & N.W. Rlwy Co.* (1890) 24 Q.B.D. 77, CA.

[8] *Weston's Case* (1868) L.R. 4 Ch.App. 20: *O'Meara v The El Palmar Rubber Estates Ltd.*, 1913, 1 S.L.T. 383 (O.H.). It is otherwise, *e.g.*, where the company is being wound up and a transfer is prevented by I.A. 1986, s.127, below, Ch.27.

[9] See also *Borland's Trustee v Steel Bros. & Co. Ltd* [1901] 1 Ch. 279. For Scottish authority to the same effect, see, *e.g.*, Lord Kincairney (Ordinary) in *Stewart v James Keiller & Sons Ltd* (1902) 4 F. 657 at p.667.

[10] Until the 1980 Act such restrictions were obligatory for private companies.

[11] Admission of Securities to Listing. The main advantage of a stock exchange quotation is that it makes the securities more marketable.

[12] *Furness & Co. v Liquidators of "Cynthiana" Steamship Co. Ltd* (1893) 21 R. 239.

[13] *Neilson v Ayr Race Meetings Syndicate Ltd*, 1918, 1 S.L.T. 63 (O.H.).

[14] *Shepherd's Trustees v Shepherd*, 1950 S.C. HL 60 (application for registration granted, the two directors having failed to agree to refuse registration); *Re New Cedos Engineering Co. Ltd* [1994] 1 B.C.L.C. 797.

[15] *Re Piccadilly Radio plc* [1988] B.C.L.C. 683. For rectification of the register, see p.193, above.

Such restrictions usually fall within one of two categories: pre-emption clauses and refusal clauses.

Pre-emption clauses

The articles of a private company usually contain a pre-emption clause, *e.g.* to the effect that no shares shall be transferred to any person not being an existing member of the company so long as a member can be found to purchase them at a fair price to be determined in accordance with the articles.[16] Such a pre-emption clause does not entitle the company to refuse to register a transfer of shares from one member to another member of the company.[17] Where the value of shares for the purpose of such a clause falls to be fixed by the directors, the court will not review the directors' valuation provided that they have acted fairly and honestly.[18]

Sometimes the clause provides that a member desiring to sell any of his shares must inform the directors of the number of shares, the price and the name of the proposed transferee, and the directors must first offer the shares at that price to the other shareholders. In such a case, any member to whom the shares are offered cannot buy part only of the shares, and if none of the members is willing to buy all the shares the proposed transfer can be carried out.[19] Many pre-emption clauses also provide the machinery whereby the shares may be offered to the existing members, *e.g.* by making the company secretary agent for their sale. In *Tett v Phoenix Property and Investment Co.*[20] the articles simply provided that there should be no transfer if any member indicated that he was willing to purchase the shares. The Court of Appeal, reversing Vinelott J., implied a term into the articles requiring a transferor to take reasonable steps to give the other members a reasonable opportunity to offer to purchase the shares at a fair value. Strictly speaking such a clause is not a pre-emption clause since it simply forbids a transfer to outsiders where a member has indicated his willingness to buy.

A member whose shares have been offered to other members under a pre-emption clause has been held entitled to withdraw his offer at any time before its acceptance.[21]

Application to transfers of beneficial interests

Most disputes centre around the question as to whether transfers of beneficial interests in shares will be caught by a pre-emption clause or whether it will only operate on transfers of the legal title. The issue was brought into focus by the decision of the Court of Appeal in *Safeguard Industrial Investments Ltd v National Westminster Bank plc.*[22] In that case, an executor was registered as such as a member and so held the legal title to the shares on trust for the beneficiaries

---

[16] Valued as at the date of the transfer under the clause, unless the contrary is expressed: *Pennington v Crampton* [2004] BCC 611. For valuation methods see p.240, below.

[17] *Delavenne v Broadhurst* [1931] Ch. 234.

[18] *Stewart v James Keiller & Sons Ltd* (1902) 4 F. 657.

[19] *The Ocean Coal Co. Ltd v The Powell Duffryn Steam Coal Co. Ltd* [1932] 1 Ch. 654.

[20] [1986] B.C.L.C. 149, CA.

[21] *J. M. Smith Ltd v Colquhoun's Trustees* (1901) 3 F. 981.

[22] [1982] 1 WLR 62.

under the will. On their instructions, it did not intend to transfer the shares into the beneficiaries' names. It was held that this did not invoke the pre-emption clause.[23] That clause only operated against a proposed transfer of the *legal* title and that was not proposed.[24] The Court distinguished the earlier case of *Lyle & Scott Ltd v Scott's Trustees*,[25] where the shareholders had given the outside purchaser (making a bid for the company) general voting proxies and had also agreed to execute transfers and to deliver up their share certificates when asked to do so. They were held to be desirous of transferring their shares and so invoked the pre-emption clause. The difference was said to be that in *Lyle* the shareholders had done everything they had to do to transfer the shares and were bound to transfer them on request. In *Safeguard*, although the beneficiaries could ask for transfer of the legal title they had no intention of doing so.

A different aspect of the distinction between legal and equitable interests in this context arose in *Theakston v London Trust plc.*[26] One member agreed to sell his shares to another member but in fact the purchase price was paid by a non-member, in whose name the shares were charged and according to whose instructions the "purchaser" was to vote. Harman J. held that this was a transfer from one member to another and so outside the pre-emption clause. The fact that the transferee had equitable obligations to an outsider did not affect the position.

But in general the position is that if the transferor, as in *Lyle*, has put himself into a position whereby he must transfer the legal title to his shares on request he will be caught by the pre-emption clause.[27] The trick is to somehow give the intending purchaser the benefits and security of a transfer without becoming bound to transfer the shares on request. An ingenious solution was found in *Re Sedgefield Steeplechase (1927) Ltd.*[28] The company had a pre-emption clause applying to those intending to transfer their shares to an outsider. An outside buyer for the company had entered into agreements with about 80 per cent of the members to the effect that they were bound to vote and otherwise comply with any instructions given to them by the bidder and to use their best endeavours to alter the articles to remove the pre-emption clause. But these agreements were specifically subject to an obligation on the part of the members not to do anything contrary to the pre-emption clause. When the other member sought to invoke the pre-emption clause her application was rejected, first by Lord Hoffmann[29] and then by the Court of Appeal. Lord Hoffmann said that since the

---

[23] The beneficiaries were not existing members so that a transfer of the legal title to them would have invoked the clause.

[24] It would have been different if the company had adopted regs 31 and 32 of Table A which applies the pre-emption provisions to the registration of the executors as shareholders in the first place. The reasoning in *Safeguard* was followed in similar circumstances in *Pennington v Crampton* [2004] B.C.C. 611, where the main issue was whether the company's articles had impliedly overruled regs 31 and 31 which were supposedly incorporated into them. That case also decided that the particular clause would not operate on a change of executor.

[25] [1959] A.C. 763.

[26] [1984] B.C.L.C. 390.

[27] *Re Macro (Ipswich) Ltd* [1994] 2 BCLC 354; *Hurst v Crampton Bros (Coopers) Ltd* [2003] BCLC 304.

[28] [2003] B.C.C. 889.

[29] Sitting as a first instance judge and not for a short time in the House of Lords.

members were not under an obligation to transfer the shares in violation of the clause the clause could not apply.

> "The general principle which I would derive from the cases is that a shareholder who has done nothing inconsistent with an intention to comply, at the appropriate moment, with the subsisting provisions of the articles, cannot be required to serve a transfer notice at an earlier stage. The obligation attaches only when the shareholder has entered into arrangements . . . which place him under a contractual obligation to execute and deliver a transfer in violation of the rights of pre-emption."[30]

The Court of Appeal were dismissive of any such principle but upheld the decision as a matter of construction of the particular clause.

It is true that each clause has to be considered individually and they have become more complex as a result of the case law. Many now seek to cover transfers of beneficial interests as well as the legal title. That difficulties of construction remain can be seen from the pre-action case of *Rose v Lynx Express Ltd*.[31] The pre-emption clause in question applied to the transfer of the legal or beneficial ownership of the shares and to any sale or disposition of any legal or equitable interest in a share whether or not by the registered owner. The registered owner was the nominee for two limited partnerships. The question was whether the pre-emption clause applied where there was a change in the membership of those limited partnerships. On one construction whereby the clause would not apply, any member could easily circumvent the clause by transferring his shares to a nominee and then assigning his beneficial interest. The other construction, however, whereby the clause would apply, would arguably require the nominee to give a transfer notice in respect of the entire holding even where there was no proposed purchaser of that holding. In the circumstances the Court of Appeal felt unable to resolve the point without a full trial.

Transfers in breach of the clause

If the provision in the articles relating to the offer of the shares to the existing shareholders before a transfer is made is disregarded, the directors cannot validly register the transfer since it is a transfer in breach of the articles.[32] In England the same is true in the case of a sale, in disregard of the articles, by a mortgagee under his power of sale.[33] However, a transfer by a shareholder, in breach of the pre-emptive rights given by the articles, to a person who has paid for the shares operates as a transfer of the *beneficial interest* in the shares, so that the transferee takes priority over a judgment creditor who subsequently obtains a charging order[34] on the shares.[35] But if the transferee is not a purchaser for value he takes

---

[30] [2003] B.C.C. 889 at 996E.

[31] [2004] 1 B.C.L.C. 455.

[32] *Tett v Phoenix Property and Investment Co. Ltd* [1986] B.C.L.C. 149, CA.

[33] *Hunter v Hunter* [1936] A.C. 222.

[34] Below, p.231.

[35] *Hawks v McArthur* [1951] 1 All E.R. 22. In *Tett v Phoenix Investment and Property Co. Ltd* above, Vinelott J. upheld *Hawks v McArthur* and rejected any general argument to the contrary based on *Hunter v Hunter*, above. This part of his judgment was not challenged in the Court of Appeal.

Similarly, in Scotland, in a competition between a transferee and an arrester, the arrester was held not to be entitled to found on an alleged failure on the part of the company to observe the proper procedure relating to pre-emption and registration of transfers, with the result that the court declared that the shares had vested in the transferee: *National Bank of Scotland Glasgow Nominees Ltd v Adamson*, 1932 S.L.T. 492 (O.H.).

subject to the equitable interests arising under the option given by the pre-emptors clause to the other shareholders.[36] There must be substantial compliance with the pre-emption procedure before a transfer outside its terms can be effective. If there is no such compliance the court can award an injunction to prevent such transfer.[37]

It has also been held that a company enforcing a power of sale under a lien on its own shares must itself comply with the pre-emption clause in its articles in effecting that sale: *Champagne Perrier-Jouet S.A. v H. H. Finch Ltd.*[38]

Note what is said later as to the duty of care owed by an auditor who values shares in the knowledge that his valuation will determine the price to be paid under a contract.[39]

Directors' powers to refuse transfers

In addition to containing a pre-emption clause, the articles of a private company often contain an article that the directors may, in their absolute discretion and without assigning any reason therefor, refuse to register any transfer of any share.

Where the directors have a discretionary power of refusal they must, as with all their other fiduciary powers, (i) act within the terms of the power and (ii) act bona fide in what they consider to be the interests of the company and not for a collateral purpose. Where the power is unrestricted (the normal case) the courts, in considering whether the directors have so acted bona fide for the benefit of the company use the presumption that the directors have been acting in good faith and the onus of proving the contrary is therefore on those challenging the decision.[40] Thus the courts will not impugn the decision simply because the directors disliked the transferor or transferee. Personal relationships are a fact of life in small companies. Private views of the directors would only affect the issue if they overcame the view as to what was in the best interests of the company.[41]

Articles gave the directors "an absolute and uncontrolled discretion" to refuse to register any transfer of shares. The two directors each held 4,001 of the 8,002 ordinary shares. F died and his son, as the executor, applied for the shares to be registered in his name. S refused, but offered to register 2,001 shares if 2,000 were sold to him at a fixed price. F's son applied for rectification of the register but failed. There was nothing to show that the director's power was not exercised bona fide in the company's interest: *Re Smith and Fawcett Ltd* [1942] Ch.304 CA.

If the articles empower the directors to decline to register transfers on certain grounds, *e.g.* on the ground that the transferor is indebted to the company, or that the transferee is a person of whom they do not approve, they can be interrogated as to the ground on which they have refused registration, although

---

[36] *Cuttrell v King* [2004] 2 B.C.L.C. 814.
[37] *Curtis v J.J. Curtis & Co. Ltd* [1986] B.C.L.C. 86 NZ.
[38] [1982] 1 W.L.R. 1359.
[39] Below, p.240.
[40] *Village Cay Marina Ltd v Acland* [1998] 2 B.C.L.C. 327, PC; *Charles Forte Investments Ltd v Amanda* [1964] Ch. 240, CA, *per* Willmer L.J. at pp.252–254 and *per* Danckwerts L.J. at pp.260–261.
[41] *Popely v Planarrive Ltd* [1997] 1 B.C.L.C. 8.

not as to the reasons for their refusal, unless the articles provide that they shall not be bound to specify the grounds for their refusal, in which case they cannot be interrogated at all.[42]

If the directors give reasons for their refusal, the court can decide whether they are sufficient to justify the refusal.

The articles empowered the directors to refuse to register a transfer if they certified that "in their opinion it is contrary to the interests of the company that the proposed transferee should be a member thereof." The directors declined to register transfers of single shares, stating that it was contrary to the interests of the company that shares should be transferred singly or in small amounts to outside persons with no interest in, or knowledge of, shipping. *Held*, this was a bad reason for refusing—refusal should have been on grounds personal to the transferee—and the transfers were directed to be registered: *Re Bede S.S. Co. Ltd* [1917] 1 Ch.123 CA.

The directors are not, however, confined to the reasons they have given, at least in the normal case where they are not bound by the articles to make a certification as to their opinion. It is for the court to decide whether the directors were acting bona fide in the interests of the company, and the reasons given are merely evidence of that.[43]

A formal active exercise of the right of refusal to register is required before the company is authorised to refuse to register shares in the names of the transferees. Where directors are equally divided and so come to no decision to decline to register, the transfer must be registered.[44]

Where the articles provided that no share should be transferred to a person not already a member of the company without the consent of the directors and, to prevent a particular transfer from being registered, a director purposely abstained from attending board meetings so that a quorum could not be obtained, it was held that the transferee was entitled to an order directing the company to register the transfer.[45]

In one case the board lost their right to veto a transfer because they were guilty of an unreasonable delay of four months in deciding whether or not to exercise the veto—the period of two months specified in s.183(5) for giving a transferee notice of the company's refusal to register a transfer was considered to be the outside limit after which there is unnecessary delay for this purpose, unless in an exceptional case it is impossible to constitute a board.[46] No such rule applies, however, where the directors come to a decision within the two month period but fail to communicate that to the transferee within that period.[47] Where there are no properly appointed directors to constitute a quorum to decide whether to exercise the right of refusal any refusal to register is a nullity,[48] but the transferee has no right to registration until the end of the period within which a

---

[42] *Berry and Stewart v Tottenham Hotspur Football Club Co. Ltd* [1935] Ch. 718.
[43] *Village Cay Marina Ltd v Acland* [1998] 2 B.C.L.C. 327, PC.
[44] *Shepherd's Trustees v Shepherd*, 1950 S.C. HL 60, *per* Lord Porter at p.66; *Re Hackney Pavilion Ltd* [1924] 1 Ch. 276.
[45] *Re Copal Varnish Co. Ltd* [1917] 2 Ch. 349.
[46] *Re Swaledale Cleaners Ltd* [1968] 1 W.L.R. 1710, CA; *Re Inverdeck Ltd* [1998] 2 B.C.L.C. 242.
[47] *Popely v Planarrive Ltd* [1997] 1 B.C.L.C. 8.
[48] *Re New Cedos Engineering Co. Ltd* [1994] 1 B.C.L.C. 797.

properly constituted board could have exercised the power, *i.e.* two months. It follows that any purported registration during that period is invalid.[49]

In a rare case, the remedy of the transferee, or of the transferor, on a refusal to register a transfer is to apply to the court to rectify the register of members by substituting his name for that of the transferor under s.359. Unnecessary delay in registering a transfer does not in itself constitute a ground for rectification, and a transferor applying for rectification must be able to show that he has been prejudiced by the delay.[50] A winding-up petition is not the proper remedy for the transferor where registration of a transfer is refused.[51]

TRANSMISSION OF SHARES

Section 183(2) provides that s.183(1) above,[52] does not prejudice any power of a company to register as shareholder any person to whom the right to any shares in the company has been transmitted by operation of law. Transmission of shares occurs on the death or the bankruptcy of a member, or, if the member is a company, on its going into liquidation.

On the death of a sole shareholder the shares vest in his personal representative,[53] *i.e.* his executor or administrator.[54] The company is bound to accept production of the probate of the will or, in the case of an intestacy, letters of administration of the estate, or, in Scotland, the confirmation as executor, as sufficient evidence of the grant: s.187.[55] Subject to any restrictions in the articles, the personal representative may be registered as a member or transfer the shares without himself becoming a member: s.183(3).[56]

Table A, reg. 30, provides: "Any person becoming entitled to a share in consequence of the death or bankruptcy of a member may, upon such evidence being produced as the directors may properly require, elect either to become the holder of the share or to have some person nominated by him registered as the transferee. If he elects to become the holder he shall give notice to the company to that effect. If he elects to have another person registered he shall execute an instrument of transfer of the share to that person. All the articles relating to the transfer of shares shall apply to the notice or instrument of transfer as if it were an instrument of transfer executed by the member and the death or bankruptcy of the member had not occurred."

When shares are jointly held, the surviving holder becomes the sole holder. Under Table A, reg. 29, the estate of the deceased joint holder is not released from any liability in respect of the shares.

MORTGAGE OF SHARES (ENGLISH LAW)

In England, a shareholder who borrows money on the security of his shares may give the lender either a legal mortgage or an equitable mortgage over the shares.

---

[49] *Re Zinotty Properties Ltd* [1984] 1 W.L.R. 1249.
[50] *Property Investment Co. of Scotland Ltd v Duncan* (1887) 14 R. 299.
[51] *Charles Forte Investments Ltd v Amanda* [1964] Ch. 240, CA.
[52] p.185.
[53] *Re Greene* [1949] Ch. 333.
[54] Executor in Scots law: see p.188, above.
[55] See, *e.g. Re Baku Consolidated Oilfields Ltd* [1994] 1 B.C.L.C. 173.
[56] Regs 31 and 32 of Table A apply any pre-emption or refusal powers in the articles to the executor or administrator becoming the registered member. If these are disapplied then the executor is not subject to them unless or until he transfers the legal title: *Safeguard Industrial Investments Ltd v National Westminsters Bank Ltd* [1982] 1 W.L.R. 589, CA, See p.224 above.

Legal mortgage

A legal mortgage of shares is effected by transfer of the shares to the lender (the mortgagee) followed by registration of the transfer by the company. There should also be a document setting out the terms of the loan and containing an agreement to retransfer the shares on repayment of the amount borrowed with interest. The document will empower the lender to sell the shares in the event of default by the borrower (the mortgagor). When exercising a power of sale the lender is under a duty to take reasonable care to obtain a proper price for the shares. He does not have to wait for a higher price but he must obtain the true market value of the shares. Any clause in the deed which purports to exclude this liability for negligence must be expressly worded to that effect.[57]

This form of mortgage gives the lender complete security up to the value of the shares. He will be entitled to dividends and to exercise any voting rights in respect of the shares, unless it is agreed that the dividends shall be paid to the borrower and that he shall exercise the voting rights as the borrower directs.[58]

However, restrictions on the transfer of shares contained in the articles[59] may prevent this kind of mortgage being made. Further, it might not be advisable where the shares are not fully paid because the lender on the register would be personally liable for calls.

Equitable mortgage

1. An equitable mortgage of shares may be made by depositing the share certificate with the lender as security for such a loan. In such a case the lender can enforce his security by applying to the court for a sale of the shares or for an order for transfer and foreclosure.[60]

2. A method more commonly adopted is for the borrower to deposit with the lender the share certificate together with a blank transfer, i.e. a transfer signed by the borrower with the transferee's name left blank. In such a case the lender has an *implied* power to sell the shares if default is made by the borrower in making repayment at the agreed time or, if no time for repayment is agreed, within a reasonable time after notice.[61] The implied power of sale includes power to insert the name of the buyer in the blank transfer if, as is usual, the articles provide for transfers to be in writing. The borrower is under an implied obligation not to delay registration of the transfer so filled up.[62]

No equitable mortgage is in itself absolutely secure because the borrower remains on the register and may sell the shares and procure the registration of the purchaser with priority over the lender, who would have no remedy against the company.

C deposited his share certificate and a blank transfer with R as a security for a loan. Upon the certificate was printed: "Without the production of this certificate no transfer of

[57] *Bishop v Bonham* [1988] B.C.L.C. 656, CA.
[58] *Siemens Brothers & Co. Ltd v Burns* [1918] 2 Ch. 324.
[59] Above, p.223.
[60] *Harrold v Plenty* [1901] 2 Ch. 314.
[61] *Hooper v Herts* [1906] 1 Ch. 549.
[62] *Powell v London and Provincial Bank* [1893] 2 Ch. 555, CA.

the shares mentioned therein can be registered." C sold the shares to Y and induced the company to register Y as owner of the shares without the production of the share certificate. R sued the company for wrongfully registering the shares in Y's name. *Held*, the company was not liable as it owed no duty of care to R, and the statement on the certificate was only a warning to the owner of the shares to take care of the certificate and not a statement of fact giving rise to an estoppel: *Rainford v James Keith & Blackman Co. Ltd* [1905] 1 Ch.296.[63]

However, the mortgagor must exercise any voting rights as directed by the mortgagee.[64]

Stop notice

To obtain complete protection, an equitable mortgagee of shares should serve a stop notice. This is done by filing an affidavit setting out the facts, and a notice in the prescribed form, in the Central Office of the Supreme Court or in a District Registry and serving an office copy of the affidavit and a duplicate notice on the company. The effect of the notice is that, whilst it continues in force, if the company receives any request to register a transfer of the shares in question it must give notice in writing to the person who has served the notice. Within eight days, such person must apply for an injunction restraining the transfer or the company will be at liberty to register the transfer.[65]

Charging order

A judgment creditor of the registered owner of shares may obtain an order charging the shares with payment of the judgment debt,[66] after which, until the order is discharged, the company cannot permit a transfer except with the authority of the court. A charging order will not have priority over a mortgage created by deposit of the share certificate and a blank transfer before the date of the charging order, as the judgment creditor can be in no better position than the judgment debtor at the time when the order was made.

ASSIGNATION OF SHARES IN SECURITY (SCOTS LAW)

The only effective way of assigning shares in security is by the execution and registration of a transfer in favour of the lender. See the section headed "Legal mortgage," above.

No form of the equitable mortgage recognised by English law gives the lender any real security in competition with the general creditors of the borrower.[67] Accordingly, where a borrower delivers the share certificate to the lender and

---

[63] Reversed on the facts [1905] 2 Ch. 147, CA. On the facts the company was affected with notice of R's charge and he was able to recover the price of the shares which had been paid to the company in repayment of a loan made by the company to C.

[64] *Wise v Lansell* [1921] 1 Ch. 420.

[65] RSC, Ord. 50, rr.11–15. See also the Charging Orders Act 1979.

[66] RSC, Ord. 50, rr.2–7.

[67] *Gourlay v Mackie* (1887) 14 R. 403; *per* Lord Gifford in *Morrison v Harrison* (1876) 3 R. 406 at p. 411; *cf. Guild v Young* (1884) 22 S.L.R. 520 (O.H.).

undertakes to transfer the shares to the lender when requested to do so, a transfer executed within six months before the borrower's sequestration or his granting of a protected trust deed is reducible as an unfair preference under s.36 of the Bankruptcy (Scotland) Act 1985.[68] For the purposes of that section the day on which a preference was created is the day on which the preference became "completely effectual",[69] and that would only be so when the transfer had been registered. It may be, however, that where a completed transfer has been delivered to the lender along with the share certificate so that the lender is in a position to have himself registered as a member without further interposition of the borrower, registration of the transfer on the eve of the borrower's sequestration is not open to challenge as an unfair preference provided the delivery of the documents to the lender was made more than six months before the borrower's sequestration.[70]

Stop notices and charging orders are not part of Scots law. When a company called on to register a transfer receives intimation from some person other than the transferee that that other person has an interest in the shares, the company is entitled to proceed to register the transfer unless the intimation is followed up by an application for interdict or other legal measure.[71]

Shares are subject to arrestment at the instance of the creditors of the shareholder, whether the arrestment is in execution,[72] or merely to found jurisdiction.[73] Where competition arises between a transferee and an arrester the transferee has the preferable right to the shares as soon as his transfer has been lodged, even although it is not registered before the lodging of the arrestment.

In January, S transferred 200 shares to M and 1,000 shares to F, and the transfers were received by the secretary of the company on January 19, and February 2, respectively. Because of an arrestment lodged the previous November against S at the instance of a bank, the transfers were not registered. On March 30, arrestments were executed at the instance of D against S. *Held*, the transfers to M and F were preferable to D's arrestments: *Harvey's Yoker Distillery Ltd v Singleton* (1901) 8 S.L.T. 369 (O.H.).

> "An arrestment can only attach property belonging truly and in substance to the common debtor. Now these shares did not belong in substance to Singleton at the time of the arrestment, because he had by that time done all in his power to dispose of them by executing the transfers": *per* Lord Stormonth Darling (Ordinary) at p.370.

An arrester is not entitled to found on any irregularity in the registration procedure to the effect of defeating the transferee's title.[74] Intimation to the

---

[68] This provision is the successor to the repealed Bankruptcy Act 1696 (Scots Act 1696, c.5) which made fraudulent preferences reducible on the ground of notour bankruptcy.

[69] Bankruptcy (Scotland) Act 1985, s.36(3).

[70] *Guild v Young* (1884) 22 S.L.R. 520 (O.H.), decided under the 1696 Act, can give at best slender support to the proposition. Whereas the 1696 Act affected only *voluntary* preferences conferred by the bankrupt on favoured creditors, s.36 of the 1985 Act applies to any *transaction entered into* by the debtor. Although s.36 is not restricted to the challenge of voluntary preferences, it is submitted that the registration by the creditor of an already executed transfer in circumstances such as arose in *Guild v Young* would not be classed as a *transaction entered into* by the debtor.

[71] *Per* Lord M'Laren in *Shaw v Caledonian Rlwy Co.* (1890) 17 R. 466 at p.482.

[72] *Sinclair v Staples* (1860) 22 D. 600.

[73] *American Mortgage Co. of Scotland Ltd v Sidway*, 1908 S.C. 500.

[74] *National Bank of Scotland Glasgow Nominees Ltd v Adamson*, 1932 S.L.T. 492 (O.H.); for an arrestment made effective by the granting by the court of a warrant to sell the shares, see *Valentine v Grangemouth Coal Co. Ltd* (1897) 35 S.L.R. 12 (O.H.).

company of a transfer, even without registration, has the effect, in a question between the transferee and a subsequent arrester of cutting out the arrestment.[75]

CALLS ON SHARES

A call on shares is a demand by the directors that a member pay to the company money which is unpaid on his shares, whether on account of the nominal value of the shares or by way of premium.[76] If, when shares are issued, the full amount of each share is not payable at once as in the privatisation issues, the terms of issue will provide that part is payable on application, part on allotment and the remainder by instalments at fixed dates, in which case the instalments are not calls,[77] as the obligation of the shareholder to pay is not dependent on a call from the company. However, in a rare case, the company may not require all the nominal amount of a share, or the full amount of a premium on a share, to be paid at or soon after allotment but may leave part to be called up in accordance with the provisions of the articles as and when required by the company or, in the event of a winding up, by the liquidator. If so, a shareholder is bound to pay the whole or part of the balance unpaid on his shares "as and when called on", in accordance with the provisions of the articles. Calls, including communication of the call notice, must be made in the manner laid down in the articles.[78]

In England, a call creates a specialty debt due from the shareholder to the company (s.14(2)), and so the period within which an action can be brought for payment of it is 12 years.[79] In Scotland a call remains enforceable until the expiry of 20 years.[80] Table A, reg. 15, provides for payment of interest from the date fixed for payment until actual payment.

If authorised by the articles, a company may make arrangements on the issue of shares for a difference between the shareholders in the amounts and times of payment of calls: s.119(a). Table A, reg. 17, authorises such an arrangement. Such a power does not entitle directors to make calls on all the shareholders except themselves,[81] at any rate without the knowledge and sanction of the other shareholders—the directors' power to make calls must be exercised bona fide for the benefit of the company as a whole, and not so as to give themselves an advantage over other shareholders. The usual proper purpose will be to raise the money for the company, but there may be other valid reasons.[82]

Any arrangement made under s.119(a) must be made at the time of the issue of shares. If no such arrangement is made, the rule is that *"prima facie* it is entirely improper for the directors to make a call on some members of a class of shareholders who stand in the same relation to the company as the other members of the class without making a similar call on all the other members of that class."[83]

---

[75] *Jackson v Elphick* (1902) 10 S.L.T. 146 (O.H.).
[76] For Scots *dicta* on the nature of a call see Lord President M'Neill in *Wryght v Lindsay* (1856) 19 D. 55 at p.63; affd. (1860) 22 D. HL 5.
[77] But articles may provide that they shall be *deemed* to be calls: see Table A, reg. 16.
[78] See e.g. *Hunter v Senate Support Services Ltd* [2004] E.W.H.C. Ch. 1085.
[79] Limitation Act 1980, s.8(1).
[80] Prescription and Limitation (Scotland) Act 1973, s.7.
[81] *Alexander v Automatic Telephone Co.* [1900] 2 Ch. 56, CA.
[82] *Hunter v Senate Support Services Ltd* [2004] E.W.H.C. Ch. 1085.
[83] *Per* Sargeant J. in *Galloway v Hallé Concerts Society* [1915] 2 Ch. 233 at p.239.

Table A, regs 18 to 22, provides for forfeiture for non-payment of a call or an instalment.[84]

LIEN ON SHARES (ENGLISH LAW)

The articles of a private company may give the company a lien on the shares held by a member for his unpaid call or instalment, or for some other debt due from him to the company. Public companies however may only have a lien on such shares for an unpaid call or instalment on those shares: s.150. By way of exception a money-lending or credit company may have a lien on any of its shares for non-payment of a debt owed by the shareholder in the ordinary course of the company's business.

Such a lien is an equitable charge upon the shares, and gives rise to the same rights as if the shares had been expressly charged by the member in favour of the company.[85]

Table A, reg. 8, provides: "The company shall have a first and paramount lien on every share (not being a fully paid share) for all moneys (whether presently payable or not) payable at a fixed time or called in respect of that share. The directors may at any time declare any share to be wholly or in part exempt from the provisions of this regulation. The company's lien on a share shall extend to any amount payable in respect of it."

The articles of a private company may extend regulation 8 to include any debt owed by a member to the company. Where a director had incurred a debt by virtue of the company paying bills on his behalf, the company was held to have a lien on his shares even though it was also, by virtue of another article, prohibited from making a loan to that director on security of its shares. The company had not made a loan to the director; he had simply become indebted to the company: *Champagne Perrier-Jouet S.A. v H. H. Finch Ltd* [1982] 1 W.L.R. 1359.

The articles may grant a lien on shares which are fully paid but in such a case an official quotation on the Stock Exchange cannot be obtained.[86] If the lien given by the articles extends only to shares not fully paid, the company can alter its articles so as to give a lien on all shares, even if only one member will be affected by the alteration.[87]

Table A, reg. 24, empowers the directors to decline to register the transfer of a share on which the company has a lien.

A shareholder against whom a lien is to be enforced can compel the company to assign its lien to his nominee who is willing to pay off the amount of the lien.[88]

How a lien is enforced

A lien is enforced, like any other equitable charge, by a sale.

---

[84] Below, p.236.
[85] *Everitt v Automatic Weighing Machine Co.* [1892] 3 Ch. 506.
[86] Admission of Securities to Listing.
[87] *Allen v Gold Reefs of West Africa Ltd* [1900] 1 Ch. 656, CA, above, p.76.
[88] See n.85, *above*.

Table A provides: "9. The company may sell in such manner as the directors determine any shares on which the company has a lien if a sum in respect of which the lien exists is presently payable and is not paid within 14 clear days after notice has been given to the holder of the share or the person entitled to it in consequence of the death or bankruptcy of the holder demanding payment and stating that if the notice is not complied with the shares may be sold."

Further, articles usually give the company power to nominate someone to execute the transfer.

However the sale of the shares is subject to any restrictions on the transferability of those shares contained in the articles of a private company, *e.g.* a pre-emption clause requiring them to be offered to existing shareholders.[89]

A lien cannot be enforced by forfeiture even if power to forfeit is contained in the articles.

The articles of a company provided that the company should have a lien on shares for the debts of the shareholder, and also provided that the lien could be enforced by forfeiture. *Held*, (1) forfeiture for debts generally, as distinct from debts due from the shareholder as a contributory, amounted to an illegal reduction of capital; (2) power to forfeit on failure to redeem after notice amounted to a clog on the shareholder's equity of redemption, and was invalid and *ultra vires: Hopkinson v Mortimer, Harley & Co. Ltd* [1917] 1 Ch.646.

Priority of lien

When a third party advances money on the security of shares, a question may arise as to whether the third party has priority over the company's lien. In such a case, if the third party gives notice of his security to the company before the company's lien arises, the third party will have priority, but otherwise not.

The articles of a company gave "a first and paramount lien and charge" on shares for debts due from the shareholder. A shareholder created an equitable mortgage of his shares by depositing the share certificate with a bank as security for an overdraft and the bank gave notice of the deposit to the company. The shareholder subsequently became indebted to the company whereupon a lien arose in favour of the company. *Held*, the bank had priority as the company's lien arose after notice of their equitable mortgage. The notice was not notice of a trust contrary to what is now s.360 but notice affecting the company, in its character of trader, with knowledge of the bank's interest: *Bradford Banking Co. v Briggs & Co.* (1886) 12 App.Cas.29.[90]

Similarly, where the shareholder is a trustee, the company's lien will prevail over the claims of the beneficial owners unless the company is given notice, before the lien arises, that the shareholder is a trustee.

A trustee held shares in a company, the articles of which gave the company a lien on shares standing either in a single name or in joint names for any debt due from any of the holders, either separately or jointly with any other person. There was also an article like Table A, reg. 5. Long after the registration of the shares in the trustee's names, one of the trustees incurred a liability to the company. It was *not* alleged that the company had notice

---

[89] *Champagne Perrier-Jouet S.A. v H. H. Finch Ltd* [1982] 1 W.L.R. 1359.
[90] *cf. Champagne Perrier-Jouet S.A. v H. H., Finch Ltd* [1982], above.

of the trust before the lien arose. *Held*, the company's lien prevailed over the title of the *cestuis que trust: New London and Brazilian Bank v Brocklebank* (1882) 21 Ch.D. 302 CA.

The title of the beneficial owners, however, will have priority if the company has notice, before the lien arises, that the shareholder is a trustee of the shares.[91]

The company has no lien on the shares registered in the name of a trustee for debts due to it from the beneficial owner.[92]

If a lien in favour of the company has arisen and the shareholder sells part only of his shares, the purchaser can require the company to discharge the lien primarily out of the shares not sold.[93]

A lien does not cease on the shareholder's death, but may be enforced against his executors.[94]

LIEN ON SHARES (SCOTS LAW)

A company has at common law and independently of any provision in its articles a lien on shares held by a member for debts due by the member to the company.[95] Articles, however, usually make express provision to the same effect. The lien enables the company to refuse to register any transfer of the shares until the transferor's debt to the company has been satisfied.

A company whose articles expressly limit the lien to partly paid shares may alter the articles so as to extend the lien to all shares, but if such an alteration is not made until after a transfer of fully paid shares has been presented for registration the transferee's right to be registered is not affected by that alteration.[96]

A lien can be enforced by a sale only if the power of sale has been conferred by the articles, or a warrant is obtained from the court. A lien in respect of debts other than calls or instalments could not be enforced by forfeiture, since that would be an illegal reduction of capital.

Where X, a shareholder, has assigned his shares in security to Y who has completed his title to the shares by being registered as the holder of them, the company is no longer entitled to a lien on the shares in respect of debts due to it by X, since X is not the registered holder.[97]

For the provisions of s.150 and of Table A on lien, see "Lien (English Law)", above.

FORFEITURE OF SHARES

Although a forfeiture of a member's shares by the company is recognised by the Act, the directors may forfeit shares only if expressly authorised to do so by the articles and only for non-payment of a call or an instalment: s.143(3)(d).

---

[91] *Mackereth v Wigan Coal Co. Ltd* [1916] 2 Ch. 293.
[92] *Re Perkins* (1890) 24 Q.B.D. 613, CA.
[93] *Gray v Stone* (1893) 69 L.T. 282.
[94] *Allen v Gold Reefs of West Africa Ltd* [1900] 1 Ch. 656, CA.
[95] *Hotchkis v Royal Bank* (1797) 3 Paton 618; (1797) M. 2673; *Burns v Lawrie's Trustees* (1840) 2 D. 1348; *Bell's Trustee v Coatbridge Tinplate Co. Ltd* (1886) 14 R. 246.
[96] *Liquidator of W & A M'Arthur Ltd v Gulf Line Ltd*, 1909 S.C. 732.
[97] *Paul's Trustee v Thomas Justice & Sons Ltd*, 1912 S.C. 1303.

Table A provides:

Regulation 18 "If a call remains unpaid after it has become due and payable the directors may give to the person from whom it is due not less than 14 clear days' notice requiring payment of the amount unpaid together with any interest which may have accrued. The notice shall name the place where payment is to be made and shall state that if the notice is not complied with the shares in respect of which the call was made will be liable to be forfeited."

Regulation 19 "If the notice is not complied with any share in respect of which it was given may, before the payment required by the notice has been made, be forfeited by a resolution of the directors and the forfeiture shall include dividends or other monies payable in respect of the forfeited shares and not paid before the forfeiture."

Forfeiture, being in the nature of a penal proceeding, is valid only if the provisions of the articles, *e.g.* as to notice, are strictly followed. Any irregularity will avoid the forfeiture.[98] The forfeiture will also be voidable if the directors fail to take into consideration a material fact, such as the alternative possibilities.[99] To protect purchasers of the forfeited shares against possible irregularities in the forfeiture, the articles usually provide, as does Table A, reg. 22, that the title of the purchaser shall not be affected by any invalidity in the proceedings in reference to the forfeiture. But where the purchaser took the shares with full knowledge of the material facts giving rise to the irregularity it was held to be bound by the irregularity.[1]

Forfeited shares may be sold or reissued by a private company according to the provisions of the articles. A public company however must cancel the forfeited shares unless they are disposed of within three years. In the interim period the company may not vote with the shares. If this cancellation takes the public company below the authorised minimum capital it must re-register as a private company: s.146.

Forfeited shares can be reissued at less than the amount which has been paid on them.

A company had forfeited a number of shares of £5.25 each, £2 25 paid, and proposed to reissue them at the price of £1.50. a share. *Held*, the company could do so, as it was not bound to treat the forfeited shares as if nothing had been paid upon them: *Morrison v Trustees, etc., Corpn. Ltd* (1898) 68 L.J.Ch.11 CA.

The purchaser of the reissued shares is liable for the payment of all future calls duly made, including one for the amount of the call which occasioned the forfeiture.[2] Consequently, there is no issue of shares at a discount, as the company has already received the amount paid up. The purchaser should be credited with any subsequent payments made by the ex-owner.[3]

The effect of the forfeiture on the former owner of the shares is to discharge him from his liability on the shares.[4] To prevent this position from arising, the articles usually preserve the liability of the former owner.[5]

---

[98] *Johnson v Lyttle's Iron Agency* (1877) 5 Ch.D. 687, CA.

[99] *Hunter v Senate Support Services Ltd* [2004] E.W.H.C. Ch. 1085.

[1] *ibid.*

[2] *New Balkis Eersteling Ltd v Randt Gold Mining Co.* [1904] A.C. 165, where the purchaser was to hold the shares "discharging from all calls due prior to such purchase".

[3] *Re Randt Gold Mining Co.* [1904] 2 Ch. 468. *Re Bolton*, below, shows that the converse is true.

[4] *Stocken's Case* (1868) L.R. 3 Ch.App. 412; in *Goldsmith v Colonial Finance etc. Corpn. Ltd* [1909] 8 C.L.R. 241, Griffith C.J., at p.249, and Barton J., at p.253, thought that what Lord Cairns L.J. said in *Stocken* was founded on the particular article there in question.

[5] Table A, reg.21.

The company cannot recover more than the difference between the calls due and the amount received on reissue.

B underwrote two blocks of shares in a company. The issue to the public was a failure and B was consequently allotted (*inter alia*) 8,200 £1 shares in the company. He was unable to pay the calls on these shares, which were forfeited. They were then reissued so that the company received the balance of the calls in full, but to obtain the new allottees the company had to pay £1,018 by way of commission. B became bankrupt. The articles provided that the holder of forfeited shares should remain liable for calls notwithstanding the forfeiture and the company attempted to prove for the balance of calls due from B. *Held*, the company could not receive payment of the calls twice over and could only prove for the actual loss sustained *viz.* the £1,018 commission: *Re Bolton* [1930] 2 Ch.48.

Surrender of Shares

The Act does not give a company any express power to accept a surrender of his shares by a member. A company's articles, however, frequently give power to the directors to accept a surrender of shares where they are in a position to forfeit such shares, *i.e.* for non-payment of calls or instalments on those shares: s.143(3)(d).

Surrender in these circumstances has been described as an "apparent exception" only to the principle of maintenance of capital,[6] since "the extinction of the obligation of a bankrupt shareholder can injure nobody."[7]

Following s.143, a company may only acquire its own shares in a few cases in addition to a surrender in lieu of forfeiture. These have been considered above.[8] It appears that in all those cases, *e.g.* a purchase by the company, a surrender of shares may be used as the method of acquisition. No other forms of surrender appear to be valid.

In particular, a surrender of partly paid shares, not liable to forfeiture, is unlawful, as it (a) releases the shareholder from further liability in respect of the shares, (b) amounts to a purchase by the company of its own shares, and (c) is a reduction of capital without the sanction of the court.

A company sustained a loss of £4,000 and the directors agreed to share the loss between themselves. They therefore surrendered shares to the amount of £4,000. The shares were £11 each, £10 paid, and the intention was that the directors should be released from the remaining £1 a share unpaid. The company subsequently became more prosperous and the directors took proceedings to have the surrender declared invalid. *Held*, the surrender was invalid as amounting to a purchase by the company of its own shares: *Bellerby v Rowland & Marwood, Steamship Co. Ltd* [1902] 2 Ch.14 CA.

Shares which have been validly surrendered can be reissued in the same way as forfeited shares, if the articles authorise their reissue.

Share Warrants

A share warrant is a document issued by a company either under its common seal

---

[6] Above, p.149.
[7] *Per* Lord M'Laren in *Gill v Arizona Copper Co. Ltd* (1900) 2 F. 843 at p.860.
[8] Above, Chap.10.

or otherwise in compliance with s.36A[9] stating that the bearer of the warrant is entitled to the shares specified therein: s.188.

Before share warrants can be issued the following conditions must be satisfied:

(1) the company must be a company and limited by shares;

(2) there must be authority in the articles (Table A does not authorise the issue of share warrants);

(3) the shares must be fully paid up: s.188.

When the issue of share warrants is authorised, the articles usually provide for such matters as the deposit of the share warrant with the company a certain number of days before any right is exercised, and for the giving of notices of meetings by advertisement.

On issuing a share warrant, the company must strike out of its register of members the name of the holder of the shares as if he had ceased to be a member and make the following entries in the register:

(1) the fact of the issue of a warrant;

(2) a statement of shares included in the warrant, distinguishing each share by its number, so long as the share has a number;

(3) the date of issue of the warrant: s.355(1).

The bearer of a share warrant may, however, if the articles so provide, be deemed to be a member of the company either to the full extent or for any purposes defined in the articles: s.355(5).

A share warrant can, subject to the articles, be surrendered for cancellation, whereupon the holder is entitled to be entered in the register of members: s.355(2).

A share warrant differs from a share certificate in the following respects:

(1) the bearer of a warrant is not entered in a register: s.355;

(2) he is entitled to the shares specified in the warrant: s.188(1);

(3) the shares are transferable by delivery of the warrant: s.188(2);

(4) a warrant is a negotiable instrument and if it is stolen and afterwards gets into the hands of a bona fide purchaser for value without notice of the fraud, he can enforce against the company payment of coupons for dividends due in respect of such share warrant[10];

(5) coupons for dividends may be attached to a warrant: s.188(3).

Dividends are advertised, and then collected upon the handing over of the appropriate coupon. This procedure is necessary because the company does not know to whom to send the dividend:

[9] Or in Scotland with the Requirements of Writing (Scotland) Act 1995.
[10] *Webb Hale & Co. v Alexandria Water Co. Ltd* (1905) 93 L.T. 339.

(6) holding a share warrant is not enough where the articles require a director to hold a specified share qualification: s.291(2).[11]

Share warrants are not very common. This is because until 1979, they could only be issued with Treasury consent and had to be deposited with an authorised depository, because of the serious consequences of loss or theft, and also because of the heavy stamp duty. Another reason is that the company has to advertise in newspapers to get in touch with the shareholders. With the abolition of exchange controls in 1979 there are fewer restrictions on their use.

Section 189 makes special provision for certain offences in connection with share warrants in Scotland.

CHALLENGING THE VALUATION OF SHARES

Articles of private companies often provide that a member who wants to sell his shares must first offer them to the existing members at a price to be fixed by the auditors. Similar provisions are often applicable in the case of a member's death.[12] Many orders under s.46 also require valuation of such shares. The various methods of valuation are discovered in relation to that section in Ch.17. But when the auditor or other expert makes a valuation the question may arise as to whether either side may validly challenge that valuation. Originally it was held that the valuation could be set aside on the grounds of mistake by the valuer,[13] but later that it could only be so set aside if the valuer had given reasons (a "speaking certificate") but not if no reasons were given ("a non-speaking certificate").[14] Such a distinction has now been rejected by the Court of Appeal in *Jones v Sherwood Computer Services plc*.[15] On principle they decided that any valuation could only be set aside if the valuer had departed from his instructions in a material respect, *e.g.* if he valued the wrong number of shares or failed to employ an expert valuer for a specific item which he was required to do,[16] or valued shares by reference to assets otherwise than those specified in his instructions.[17] and not on the basis of mistake *e.g.*as to what those assets were. The reason for this change in the courts' approach has been the possibility of the aggrieved party suing the valuer in negligence, which did not exist at the time of the original decisions.

A valuer may now therefore be liable in negligence to either party even though the valuation may not be liable to be set aside. To be liable in this way a valuer must be acting as a valuer and not as an arbitrator, *i.e.* settling a dispute between at least two parties which was sent to him to resolve in such a way that he had to exercise a judicial discretion.[18] An auditor of a private company who, on request,

---

[11] Below, p.272.
[12] Above, pp. 229, *et seq.*
[13] *Dean v Prince* [1954] CH. 409, CA.
[14] *Burgess v Purchase and Son (Farms) Ltd* [1983] Ch. 216; analysing *Campbell v Edwards* [1976] 1 W.L.R. 403, CA and *Baber v Kenwood Manufacturing Co. Ltd* [1978] 1 Lloyd's Rep. 175, CA.
[15] [1992] 1 W.L.R. 277.
[16] *Jones (M.) v Jones (R.R.)* [1971] 1 W.L.R. 840.
[17] *Macro v Thompson* (No. 2) [1997] 1 B.C.L.C. 626.
[18] *Sutcliffe v Thackrah* [1974] A.C. 727.

values its shares in the knowledge that this valuation will determine the price to be paid under a contract owes a duty of care to both the vendor and the purchaser. An agreement for valuation is not generally one for an arbitration. The function of a valuer is usually to settle a price so that no differences arise between the parties. His function is not to make an award after a difference has arisen. Only in the latter case will no duty of care arise.[19]

Even if a duty of care does arise, the standard of care expected of an ordinary auditor is not that of a specialist valuer. This "auditor standard" will only be displaced by express contrary intention.[20]

---

[19] See *Leigh v English Property Corporation* [1976] 2 Lloyd's Rep. 298.
[20] *Whiteoak v Walker* (1988) 4 B.C.C. 122.

Chapter 14

GENERAL MEETINGS

THIS chapter is concerned with general meetings, *i.e.* meetings of the members or shareholders of a company and certain other persons (the auditors, the personal representatives of a deceased member and the trustee in bankruptcy of a bankrupt member). The various kinds of general meeting are dealt with first, including who may call such meetings. Then the procedure for calling meetings, including the notice that the members must be given is explained. Thirdly, proceedings at general meetings are dealt with—how many members must be present to constitute a meeting and enable it to transact business, who takes the chair, how a vote is taken and so on. Fourthly, the various kinds of resolution that may be passed at a meeting, including elective resolutions, are explained. Finally, the effects of formal or informal written resolutions which do not require a meeting at all are discussed. In general the Company Law Review made detailed rather then sweeping proposals in relation to meetings.[1]

For obvious reasons, special provisions have to be made for single member private companies. In general, it is possible for the single member either to constitute a meeting or to decide on an issue which requires a resolution, in which case a written record of the decision must be kept.

If a company has more than one class of shares, class meetings, *i.e.* meetings of the holders of the shares of a certain class, may be held. Some of the sections referred to below, *e.g.* s.369 with regard to the length of notice for calling meetings, also apply to meetings of any class of members of a company as they apply to general meetings of the company. Section 125(6) provides that the provisions of the Act and the articles relating to general meetings apply to class meetings, except that a quorum shall be two persons at least holding or representing by proxy one-third of the issued shares of the class and that any holder of shares of the class present in person or by proxy may demand a poll.

KINDS OF GENERAL MEETING

Annual general meeting

By s.366 the general rule is that, subject to an election by a private company to the contrary under s.366A, every company must hold an annual general meeting, specified as such in the notice calling it, every year, with an interval of not more than 15 months between one annual general meeting of the company and the next. The word "year" means calendar year, *i.e.* the period January 1 to

---

[1] *Final Report, Vol. 1* paras 7.5–7.16.

December 31.[2] A limited exception is that as long as a company holds its first annual general meeting within 18 months of incorporation it need not hold it in the year of incorporation or, sometimes in the following year, *e.g.* a company incorporated on October 1, 2005, might hold its first annual general meeting in March 2006.

The directors must call the annual general meeting. The object of s.366 was to ensure that those members who wish to do so can meet together and confront the directors at least once a year. The usual business at an annual general meeting can include: the declaration of a dividend, the consideration of the accounts, balance sheets and the reports of the directors and auditors, the election of directors in place of those retiring, and the appointment of, and the fixing of the remuneration of, the auditors, although in modern practice some of these will be considered at other meetings rather than at the annual general meeting.

If default is made in holding an annual general meeting, the Secretary of State may, on the application of any member of the company, call or direct the calling of a meeting and give such ancillary directions as he thinks expedient, including a direction that one member present in person or by proxy shall be deemed to constitute the meeting: s.367.

Under s.366A a private company may, by an elective resolution,[3] dispense with the holding of an annual general meeting. It may also by such a resolution elect not to lay its annual accounts at the meeting,[4] and not to appoint its auditors annually,[5] which dispenses with a large part of its annual business. Any member may, despite a s.366A election being in force, require an AGM to be held by giving notice[6] to that effect to the company at least three months before the end of the year in question, and s.366 will then apply. If the election is revoked no meeting need be held in that year, however, if there are less than three months of the year remaining.[7]

Extraordinary general meetings

Any general meeting of a company, other than an annual general meeting, is an extraordinary general meeting. Table A, reg. 36, so provides and reg. 37 provides that the directors *may*, whenever they think fit, convene an extraordinary general meeting.[8]

Further, by s.368, despite anything in the articles, the directors are *bound* to convene an extraordinary general meeting on the valid requisition of the holders

[2] *Gibson v Barton* (1875) L.R. 10 Q.B. 329.
[3] Below, p.260.
[4] Below, Ch.22.
[5] Below, Ch.23.
[6] This may be electronic communication within the meaning of s.15 of the Electronic Communications Act 2000.
[7] Under Government proposals, the position will be reversed so that private companies will have to opt into holding an AGM (by ordinary resolution). Public companies could opt out by unanimous vote of all the members (*e.g.* a subsidiary company): *Modernising Company Law*, Cm 5553–1, paras 2.10–2.19.
[8] In the unlikely absence of anything in the articles, any two members holding at least one-tenth of the issued share capital (excluding treasury shares) may call a meeting: s.370(3).

of not less than one-tenth of the paid-up capital of the company carrying the right of voting at general meetings[9] or, if the company has no share capital, of members representing not less than one-tenth of the total voting rights. If the directors do not, within 21 days of the deposit of the requisition at the registered office of the company, proceed to convene the meeting fixed for a date within 28 days of its being summoned, the requisitionists, or the holders of more than half their voting rights, may convene it themselves so long as it is held within three months after such deposit.[10] The reasonable expenses of the requisitionists in convening the meeting must be repaid by the company, which must retain them out of any remuneration of the directors in default.

The section imposes three requirements for a valid requisition: a deposit: a statement of the objects: and the signature of the requisitionists. In *PNC Telecom plc v Thomas*,[11] the requisition was made by sending a fax to the company. This was held to be a valid means of depositing the requisition. It was argued that since no amendments had been made to s.368 under the Electronic Communication Act 2000, as there had been to many other sections concerning meetings, only delivery of hard copy would suffice. That argument was rejected. The fax predated the internet and email and had been allowed as a means of communication in many official contexts. With regard to the objects, it has long been established that only if the requisition states an object which is incapable of being effectively achieved that the directors can ignore it.[12] This was the situation in *Rose v McGivern*,[13] where the single resolution proposed (to appoint a number of directors) was contrary to the formal requirements of the Act.[14]

Section 142 requires the directors of a public company to call a general meeting in the event of a serious loss of capital. In such a case the meeting must be convened within 28 days for a date not later than 28 days after the notice convening the meeting.

Meetings convened by the court

By s.371, if for any reason it is impracticable to call a meeting in any manner in which meetings may be called, or to conduct a meeting in the manner prescribed by the articles or the Act, the court may, either of its own motion or on application by any director or any member entitled to vote at the meeting, order a meeting to be called, held and conducted in such manner as the court thinks fit, and may give such ancillary directions as it thinks expedient, including a direction that one member present in person or by proxy shall be deemed to constitute the meeting. The question for the court is whether it is impracticable to call a meeting not whether it is impossible.[15]

---

[9] Excluding treasury shares.

[10] This right may be abrogated if the requisitionists are themselves directors who have, by failing to attend board meetings, been the cause of the directors' default: *Thyne v Lauder*, 1925 S.C. 123 (O.H.).

[11] [2004] 1 B.C.L.C. 88.

[12] *Isle of Wight Rly Co v Tahourdin* (1883) 25 Ch.D. 320.

[13] [1998] 2 B.C.L.C. 593.

[14] But see *PNC Telecom plc v Thomas*, above, where no such specifics as to the number of resolutions were included in the notice.

[15] *Re El Sombrero Ltd* [1958] Ch. 900.

In recent times the courts have used this power to prevent a minority shareholder using the quorum provisions as a weapon in a dispute, *i.e.* by refusing to attend meetings so that no quorum under the articles or shareholders agreement can be obtained.[16] The section is designed to enable companies to conduct their business. The company must be able to manage its affairs and a majority shareholder to exercise his rights without being subject to a veto. But since it is a procedural section this will not apply, if the right of a member to be present for a quorum to be obtained is a class right of that member.[17]

> E. Ltd had three members, A, B and C. A and B were directors and held five per cent of the shares each. C, who was not a director, held 90 per cent of the shares. No general meetings were held. The articles provided that a quorum at a meeting should be two members. A and B frustrated C's efforts to call a meeting under s.368 by refusing to attend. C gave special notice of his intention to move ordinary resolutions to remove the directors at the next extraordinary general meeting, and asked the court to call a meeting under s.371 and to direct that one member should be a quorum. C's application was opposed by the directors. *Held*, the application should be granted because (1) otherwise C would be deprived of his right to remove the directors under s.303, (2) the directors were in breach of their statutory duty by not holding an annual general meeting: *Re El Sombrero Ltd* [1958] Ch.900.[18]
>
> O Ltd had two members, A and B, who were the sole directors. A owned 51 per cent of the votes and B the remainder. They fell out and A called a meeting to dismiss B as a director. B refused to attend so that the quorum provisions for meetings (two) could not be complied with. On A's application under s.371, the court ordered a meeting with a quorum of one, otherwise there would be a deadlock situation. The quorum provisions did not give B a veto. A's conduct in dismissing B was a matter for other proceedings: *Re Opera Photographic Ltd* [1989] 1 W.L.R. 634.

The jurisdiction of the court under the section is very wide and will apply whenever "as a practical matter the desired meeting of the company cannot be conducted." Thus it has been used to order a meeting restricted to a few members to be followed by a postal ballot of all the members, where it was feared that a normal meeting would lead to a riot, even though there was no problem with obtaining a quorum or otherwise complying with the articles.[19]

Where there is a dispute between the shareholders which is the subject of other proceedings[20] and one of the parties seeks an order under s.371 because the other party refuses to attend meetings, the court has a discretion whether to make an order under the section. If the application under s.371 is made prior to the other proceedings it is more likely to be granted then if the application is made after the other proceedings have commenced.[21] A s.371 application is not the appropriate forum to discuss allegations relevant to s.459.[22] But it is a

---

[16] *Re Opera Photographic Ltd* [1989] W.L.R. 684. *Re Woven Rugs Ltd* [2002] 1 B.C.L.C. 324; *Vectone Entertainment Holding Ltd v South Entertainment Ltd* [2004] 2 B.C.L.C. 224.

[17] *Harman v BML Group Ltd* [1994] 2 B.C.L.C. 704, CA.

[18] For a Scottish instance, see *Edinburgh Workmen's Houses Improvement Co. Ltd, Petitioners*, 1935 S.C. 56.

[19] *Re the British Union for the Abolition of Vivisection* [1995] 2 B.C.L.C. 1. The court may impose conditions on any order it makes. *Re Woven Rugs Ltd* [2002] 1 B.C.L.C. 324.

[20] Usually a petition under s.459. See below, p.321.

[21] *Re Sticky Fingers Restaurant Ltd* [1992] B.C.L.C. 84; *Re Whitchurch Insurance Consultants Ltd* [1993] B.C.L.C. 1359; *Re Opera Photographic Group Ltd* [1989] 1 W.L.R. 634.

[22] *Re Woven Rugs Ltd* [2002] 1 B.C.L.C. 324; *Vectone Entertainment Holding Ltd v South Entertainment Ltd* [2004] 2 B.C.L.C. 224.

procedural section and so, where the company is "deadlocked", *e.g.* where there are two shareholders, each with equal voting rights, so that either can prevent a resolution being passed, the Court of Appeal held that s.371 could not be used by one of them to break the deadlock by ordering a meeting of the applicant alone. The section was not designed to shift the balance of power in a case where the shareholders have specifically agreed that it be shared equally.[23]

Section 371 is concerned with ensuring that the company's business can be carried on—it is not as such a minority protection section. Thus in *Union Music Ltd v Watson.*[24] The company was the singer Russell Watson's manager. It owned 51 per cent of the shares in Arias Ltd. Watson owned the other 49 per cent. They were also the only directors. Under the articles, a quorum for any meeting was two and under a shareholders' agreement the consent of both shareholders was needed for a meeting to be held. The two parties fell out on a grand scale and the company became deadlocked at both board and meeting level. Union wanted to call a meeting with a quorum of one solely to appoint another director so as to enable the company to function. The judge refused to do so on the basis that it would be wrong to interfere with the situation as agreed by the parties. The Court of Appeal reversed this decision. Subject to not interfering with class rights or the case where there are two equal shareholders, the court could make the order if the majority shareholder was being improperly prevented from exercising its rights and the company was not able to manage its affairs properly. The quorum agreement in this case was not a class right and Union, as majority shareholder, could properly appoint another director under normal circumstances. By way of contrast, in *Might SA v Redbus Interhouse plc,*[25] the court refused to make an order under the section to restrain any of the directors of the company from chairing the meeting. It had been argued that each of them would have a conflict of interest in doing so. That did not make it impractical to call the meeting. There were other remedies available to the minority shareholders if the chairman actually abused his position.

CALLING GENERAL MEETINGS

To be validly held a meeting must be called in accordance with the Act and the company's articles. Thus all members entitled to attend must be given notice. In one case, where a number of persons attending a meeting were subsequently found not to be members of the company because of an irregularity in their membership the meeting was declared to be invalid: *POW Services Ltd v Clare.*[26] The judge in that case also said that the meeting was invalid because the addresses of the members were not correctly entered on the register of members. That omission prevented free communication between members, without which "a meeting cannot be valid."[27]

---

[23] *Ross v Telford* [1998] 1 B.C.L.C. 82, CA. In such cases it is unlikely that s.459 will assist, so that deadlocked companies really are so.
[24] [2003] 1 B.C.L.C. 453.
[25] [2004] 2 B.C.L.C. 449.
[26] [1995] 2 B.C.L.C. 435.
[27] *Ibid.* at p.451, *per* Jacob J.

Length of notice for calling meetings

The effect of s.369 is that notwithstanding a provision in the articles providing for shorter notice:

(1) an annual general meeting must be called by not less that 21 days' written notice:[28]

(2) any other general meeting of a limited company must be called by not less than 14 days' written notice,[29] unless a special resolution is to be proposed, in which case, by s.378, not less than 21 days' such notice is required.[30]

Table A, regulation 38, provides that the notice shall be clear notice, *i.e.* exclusive of the day on which it is served or deemed to be served and of the day for which it is given.[31]

In addition to using electronic communication, a company can use its website or the internet as a means of giving notices provided the individual member has agreed to this. This right may be exercised despite anything to the contrary in the company's articles.[32]

A meeting may be called by shorter notice than that specified above or in the articles if that is agreed to by—(1) all the members entitled to attend and vote in the case of an annual general meeting or a meeting where an elective resolution is being proposed; or (2) a majority in number of the members holding not less than 95 per cent of the shares giving the right to attend and vote[33] or, in the case of a company without a share capital, representing not less than 95 per cent of the total voting rights, in the case of any other meeting. A private company may by an elective resolution[34] reduce the percentage of members required to sanction short notice to 90 per cent: ss 369(3), (4); 378(3); 379A(2A).

If a resolution is to be passed on short notice, it must be appreciated that the resolution is being so passed.[35]

Sections 369(3), (4), 378(3) and 379A(2A) are derived from cases like *Re Express Engineering Works Ltd*[36] and *Re Oxted Motor Co. Ltd*[37] which established that it is competent for all the shareholders to waive formalities as regards notice of meetings, etc.

In the *Express Engineering* case five persons formed a private company in which they were the sole shareholders. They sold to the company for £15,000 a property which they

---

[28] Or by electronic communication.

[29] *ibid.*

[30] The Government has proposed 14 days as the period for all meetings. *Modernising Company Law*, Cmn 5553–I, para. 2.17.

[31] In Scotland, articles may be so worded as not to require *clear* notice, *e.g.* a provision that "days shall be reckoned, excluding the first and including the last of such days," allows the day of the meeting to be counted: *The Aberdeen Comb Works Co. Ltd, Petitioners* (1902) 10 S.L.T. 210.

[32] The Electronics Communications Act also provides for the situation where the web crashes: See s.369(4B)–(4G).

[33] Excluding treasury shares.

[34] Below, p.260.

[35] *Re Pearce Duff & Co. Ltd* [1960] 1 W.L.R. 1014.

[36] [1920] 1 Ch. 466, CA.

[37] [1921] 3 K.B. 32.

had just bought for £7,000. The price was to be paid by the issue of debentures for £15,000 by the company. The transaction was carried out at a "board" meeting of the five individuals who appointed themselves the directors. The articles forbade a director to vote in respect of a contract in which he was interested. It was held that there was no fraud and the company was bound in the matter by the unanimous agreement of the members. Consequently the debentures were valid.

In the *Oxted Motor* case both members of a company waived the normal length of notice of a meeting at which an extraordinary resolution for voluntary winding up was validly passed.

The *Express Engineering* case was applied in *Re Bailey, Hay & Co. Ltd*[38] where short notice was given of a meeting to pass an extraordinary resolution for voluntary winding up but all five corporators attended and the resolution was passed by the votes of two shareholders, the other shareholders abstaining from voting. The resolution was deemed to have been passed with the unanimous agreement of all the corporators and those who abstained were treated as having acquiesced in the winding-up.

Service of notice of meetings

Section 370 provides that, unless the articles provide to the contrary, notice of the meeting of a company is to be served[39] on every member of the company as required by Table A. Section 387(1) requires that notice of every general meeting be given to the auditors.

If notice of a meeting is not given to every person entitled to notice, any resolution passed at the meeting will be of no effect.

A committee of a club met and passed a resolution expelling Y from the club. X, a member of the committee, was not summoned to the meeting, as she had previously informed the chairman that she would be unable to attend meetings. *Held*, the omission to summon X invalidated the proceedings of the committee: *Young v Ladies' Imperial Club Ltd* [1920] 2 K.B. 523, CA.

To obviate this result it is usually provided in the articles, as in Table A, reg. 39, that the accidental omission to give notice to, or the non-receipt of notice by, any person entitled to receive notice shall not invalidate the proceedings at that meeting. The onus of proof is on those claiming that the meeting was valid to show that the omission was accidental and not deliberate.[40]

In *Re West Canadian Collieries Ltd* [1962] Ch.370, the omission to give notice of a meeting to a few members, because the plates for these members were inadvertently kept out of the machine when the envelopes for the notices were being addressographed, was an accidental omission within an article like Table A, Art. 39.

However, in *Musselwhite v C. H. Musselwhite & Sons Ltd* [1962] Ch.964, the omission to give notice of a general meeting to the unpaid vendors of shares who remained on the register of members because the directors erroneously believed the vendors were no longer members, was due to an error of law and was not an accidental omission within such an article.

---

[38] [1971] 1 W.L.R. 1357.
[39] See Table A, reg. 112 for the methods of service.
[40] *POW Services Ltd v Clare* [1995] 2 B.C.L.C. 435, at p.450 *per* Jacob J.

Nature of notice of meetings

The articles of a company will contain provisions dealing with the nature of the notice to be given of meetings. Table A, reg. 38, provides that the notice of a meeting shall state the time and place of the meeting and the general nature of the business to be transacted.

Notice of an annual general meeting was in common form and included in the business was "to elect directors." C, the retiring director, offered himself for re-election, but was not elected. A motion was proposed for the election of three new directors to fill up the places of the retiring director and two vacancies, but the chairman refused to accept it. *Held*, the refusal was wrong, as the notice sufficiently specified the general nature of the business to bring it within the competence of the meeting to elect directors up to the number permitted by the articles: *Choppington Collieries Ltd v Johnson* [1944] 1 All E.R. 762, CA.

Notice of the business to be transacted must "state the resolution to be passed in such way as fairly to state the purpose for which the meeting is convened, so that every shareholder may make up his mind whether he will or will not attend with knowledge of the result of his act."[41]

Directors of a holding company had from 1907 to 1914 been receiving remuneration as directors of a subsidiary company without the knowledge of the shareholders of the holding company. Special resolutions, authorising the directors to retain the remuneration and altering the articles to allow the directors to receive remuneration as directors of subsidiary companies, were proposed and an extraordinary general meeting summoned to pass them. The notice did not specify the amount of the remuneration, which was £44,876. The resolution was passed. A shareholder brought an action on behalf of himself and all other shareholders of the company against the company and its directors claiming, *inter alia*, a declaration that the resolution was not binding upon the company. *Held*, the resolution was not binding as the notice was insufficient: *Baillie v Oriental Telephone etc. Co. Ltd* [1915] 1 Ch.503, CA.[42]

The notice of a general meeting at which an elective resolution, a special resolution or an extraordinary resolution is to be proposed must specify the intention to propose the resolution as a special resolution or an extraordinary resolution[43] as the case may be: ss 378, 379A. There must be complete identity between the substance of the resolution as passed and the substance of the resolution set out in the notice. Thus in a resolution for a reduction of capital a change in the amount proposed to be reduced of £321 out of a total of £1,356,900 as shown in the notice was held to invalidate the notice. Changes because of grammatical or clerical errors or the use of more formal language might however be allowed.[44]

Where a meeting has been requisitioned under s.371, above, it may competently deal with business proposed by the board[45] additional to that specified in

---

[41] Stiebel's *Company Law* (3rd. ed.), p.335.

[42] Benefits to directors particularly must be disclosed. See e.g. *Kaye v Croyden Tramway Company* [1898] 1 Ch. 355.

[43] Strictly interpreted in *Rennie v Crichton's (Strichen) Ltd*, 1927 S.L.T. 459 (O.H.), in which a notice of a resolution for voluntary winding up was held invalid because it did not specify the intention to propose the resolution *as an extraordinary resolution*; for *obiter dicta* to the contrary see *North of Scotland etc. Steam Navigation Co. Ltd, Petitioners*, 1920 S.C. 94.

[44] *Re Moorgate Mercantile Holdings Ltd* [1980] 1 All E.R. 40.

[45] *Rose v McGivern* [1998] 2 B.C.L.C. 593.

the requisition, provided adequate notice of the additional business has been duly given.[46]

Every notice calling a meeting of a company with a share capital must contain a statement, given reasonable prominence, that a member entitled to attend and vote may appoint a proxy to attend and vote instead of him, and that the proxy need not be a member of the company: s.372(3).

Notice of members' resolutions and statements

If some of the members of a company themselves wish to move a resolution at an *annual general meeting*, or to circulate to members a statement relating to any proposed resolution or the business to be dealt with at *any general meeting*, they can do so under s.376. The section provides that on the written requisition of members holding not less than one-twentieth of the voting rights of the members entitled to vote at the relevant meeting,[47] or of one hundred members on whose shares there has been paid up an average sum of not less than £100 a member, the company must:

(1) give notice to every member entitled to receive notice of the annual general meeting of any resolution which may properly be moved and is intended to be moved at that meeting;

(2) circulate to every member entitled to receive notice of any general meeting any statement, of not more than 1,000 words, relating to any proposed resolution or the business to be dealt with at the meeting.

The notice of the resolution must be given, and any statement must be circulated, with the notice of the meeting or, if that is impracticable, as soon as possible afterwards. The company is not bound to circulate a statement if, on the application of the company or any aggrieved person, the court is satisfied that the rights given by the section are being abused to secure needless publicity for defamatory matter: s.377(3).

The requisition must be signed by the requisitionists and deposited at the registered office: (1) at least six weeks before the meeting when notice of a resolution is required; and (2) at least one week before the meeting in any other case. A sum reasonably sufficient to meet the company's expenses must be deposited or tendered: s.377(1).[48]

If the directors call an annual general meeting for a date six weeks or less after deposit of the requisition, the requisition is deemed to have been properly deposited.

Special notice

Section 379 provides that where under the Act special notice is required of a resolution, notice of the intention to move it must be given *to the company* not

---

[46] *per* Lord Hill Watson (Ordinary), in *Ball v Metal Industries Ltd*, 1957 S.C. 315 (O.H.) at p.316.

[47] Excluding treasury sharers.

[48] The Government intends that the company shall bear the expense. *Modernising Company Law* Cmn 5553–I, para. 2.24.

less than 28 days before the meeting at which it is to be moved, and the company must give notice of the resolution *to the members* when it gives them notice of the meeting (or, if that is not practicable, either by advertisement in a newspaper having an appropriate circulation or in any other mode allowed by the articles, not less than 21 days before the meeting). To close a loophole which would otherwise allow directors to avoid the provision by claiming that the notice had not been given in time, the section also provides that if the directors call a meeting for a date 28 days or less after the notice has been given to the company, the notice is deemed to have been properly given. The notice to the company may be left at or sent by post to the registered office: s.725.

Special notice is only required by ss 293, 303 and 388 (appointment of a director who has attained the age of 70, removal of directors and the appointment and removal of auditors respectively).

Section 379 does not confer any rights on a shareholder to have a resolution to which it applies circulated if he cannot fulfil the requirements of s.376, above. It simply confers a right to receive notice in a special way if the resolution is being proposed in due form.[49]

PROCEEDINGS AT GENERAL MEETINGS

Quorum

Under Table A, reg. 40, no business is to be transacted at a general meeting unless a quorum of members is present. Formerly this article only required a quorum when the meeting proceeded to business and so in England was satisfied if a quorum was present at the beginning of the meeting.[50] This was not the law in Scotland, however,[51] and the new wording agrees with that law.

The quorum must be an effective quorum, *i.e.* it must consist of members qualified to take part in and decide upon questions before the meeting,[52] and where articles require a quorum of members to be "present" (without any such addition as "personally or by proxy") that word means "present in person."[53]

By s.370, unless the articles otherwise provide, a quorum, except for a single member private company, is two members present in person for any company. Table A, regulation 40, also fixes two members present in person or by proxy as a quorum. Under s.370A, one member present in person or by proxy is a quorum for a single member private company despite any contrary provision in the articles. As to a quorum at a class meeting, see s.125(6), above.[54]

Strictly, since the word "meeting" *prima facie* means a coming together of more than one person, one person cannot constitute a meeting,[55] even where he

[49] *Pedley v Inland Waterways Association Ltd*, [1977] 1 All E.R. 209.
[50] *Re Hartley Baird Ltd* [1955] Ch. 143, distinguished in *Re London Flats Ltd* [1969] W.L.R. 711.
[51] *Henderson v Louttit & Co. Ltd* (1894) 21 R. 674.
[52] *POW Services Ltd v Clare* [1995] 2 B.C.L.C. 435.
[53] *M. Harris Ltd, Petitioners*, 1956 S.C. 207, in which a member represented by an attorney was held not to be "present".
[54] p.210.
[55] *Sharp v Dawes* (1876) 2 Q.B.D. 26, CA, applied in *Re London Flats*, above; *cf. Souter, Petitioner*, 1981 S.L.T. (Sh. Ct.) 89, in which a single creditor was held not to constitute a committee of inspection.

attends in more than one capacity or holds proxies for the other persons.[56] However, in *East v Bennett Bros. Ltd*[57] it was held that one member, who held all the shares of a class, constituted a class meeting. Further, under ss 367[58] and 371,[59] the Secretary of State and the court, respectively, may direct that one member shall be deemed to constitute a meeting and the sole member of a single member company may clearly constitute a meeting given the quorum provision in s.370A.

If a quorum is not present within half an hour of the time appointed for the meeting, Table A, reg. 41, provides that the meeting shall stand adjourned to the same day in the next week at the same time and place, or to such time and place as the directors may determine, and if at the adjourned meeting a quorum is not present within half an hour, the members present shall form a quorum. It is thought that a single member can constitute a quorum at an adjourned meeting.[60]

Chairman

Section 370 provides that, unless the articles otherwise provide, the members present at a meeting may elect any member as a chairman. However, the articles usually provide who is to be chairman. Table A, reg. 42, states that the chairman of the board of directors shall preside at every general meeting of the company, or if there is no such chairman, or if he is not present within 15 minutes after the time appointed for the meeting or is unwilling to act, the directors present shall elect one of themselves to be chairman. Regulation 43 provides that if no director is willing to act as chairman or if no director is present within 15 minutes, the members present may elect one of their number to be chairman of the meeting.[61]

It is the duty of the chairman:

(1) to preserve order,

(2) to see that the proceedings are regularly conducted,[62]

(3) to take care that the sense of the meeting is properly ascertained with regard to any question properly before it,[63]

(4) to decide incidental questions arising for decision during the meeting, *e.g.* whether proxies are valid.[64]

---

[56] *James Prain & Sons Ltd, Petitioners*, 1947 S.C. 325. This case was distinguished in *Neil M'Leod & Sons Ltd, Petitioners*, 1967 S.C. 16, in which the requisite quorum of three *members* personally present was held to be constituted by two individuals, one of whom attended in two capacities (*i.e.* as a member holding shares in his own right and as a member entitled to vote in respect of a trust holding).

[57] [1911] 1 Ch. 163.

[58] Above, p.243.

[59] Above, p.244.

[60] See *Jarvis Motors (Harrow) Ltd v Carabott* [1964] 1 W.L.R. 1101.

[61] In *Re Bradford Investments plc* [1991] B.C.L.C. 224 it was held that where no directors are present and there is a dispute as to who may vote then any member may appoint a chairman. This could later be challenged only if the voting rights were themselves subject to challenge.

[62] *Byng v London Life Association Ltd* [1990] Ch. 170, CA.

[63] *National Dwellings Society v Sykes* [1894] 3 Ch. 159.

[64] Below, p.256.

He must allow the minority of the shareholders to have a reasonable time to put forward their arguments, but at the expiration of that time he is entitled, if he thinks fit, to put a motion to the meeting that the discussion be terminated.[65]

The chairman has no casting vote unless expressly given one by the articles.[66] Table A reg. 50, gives him a casting vote.

Adjournment

A chairman can only adjourn a meeting at his own will in cases of disorder, or where owing to inadequacy of space it is impossible for all those entitled to take part in the debate or vote. In such a case he need not put a motion for an adjournment. If the chairman exercises this common law power of adjournment he must act not only in good faith but also reasonably in deciding when to reconvene the meeting, so that adjourning to another location for the afternoon of a morning meeting was held not to be reasonable since it did not give all members a reasonable opportunity for attending.[67] If, in any other case, he purports to so adjourn the meeting it may elect another chairman and proceed with the business.[68]

The chairman is not bound to adjourn a meeting, even if the majority desire him to do so,[69] unless the articles otherwise provide.

Table A, reg. 45, provides:
"The chairman may, with the consent of a meeting at which a quorum is present (and shall if so directed by the meeting), adjourn the meeting from time to time and from place to place, but no business shall be transacted at any adjourned meeting other than the business which might properly have been transacted had the adjournment not taken place. When a meeting is adjourned for fourteen days or more, at least seven clear days' notice shall be given specifying the time and place of the adjourned meeting and the general nature of the business to be transacted. Otherwise it shall not be necessary to give any such notice."

Conduct of a meeting

In *Byng v London Life Association Ltd*,[70] it was held that a meeting could be properly held in more than one room provided that all the rooms are properly provided with audio-visual links so that those in all the rooms can see and hear what is going on in the other rooms and that all due steps are taken to direct to the overflow rooms those unable to get into the main meeting.

Where there are insufficient audio-visual links, as in that case, the main meeting may still constitute a meeting although it will be incapable of proceeding to business. The chairman may therefore validly adjourn this "meeting". There is no rule of law that a meeting at which members are validly excluded is a nullity for that purpose.[71]

---

[65] *Wall v London and Northern Assets Corporation* [1898] 2 Ch. 469, CA.
[66] *Nell v Longbottom* [1894] 1 Q.B. 767.
[67] *Byng v London Life Association Ltd* [1990] Ch. 170, CA.
[68] *East v Bennett Bros Ltd* [1911] 1 Ch. 163.
[69] *Salisbury Gold Mining Co. Ltd v Hathorn* [1897] A.C. 268.
[70] [1990] Ch. 170, CA.
[71] Mustill L.J. dissented on this point.

Subject to provisions of the Companies Act and the articles, the way in which the business at a meeting is to be conducted is decided by the meeting itself.

"There are many matters relating to the conduct of a meeting which lie entirely in the hands of those persons who are present and constitute the meeting. Thus it rests with the meeting to decide whether notices, resolutions, minutes, accounts, and such like shall be read to the meeting or be taken as read; whether representatives of the Press, or any other persons not qualified to be summoned to the meeting, shall be permitted to be present, or if present shall be permitted to remain; whether and when discussion shall be terminated and a vote taken; whether the meeting shall be adjourned. In all these matters, and they are only instances, the meeting decides, and if necessary a vote must be taken to ascertain the wishes of the majority. If no objection is taken by any constituent of the meeting, the meeting must be taken to be assenting to the course adopted": *per* Lord Russell of Killowen in *Carruth v I.C.I. Ltd* [1937] A.C. 707 at p.761.

Voting

1. *A show of hands*

The common law rule is that, unless the articles otherwise provide, a resolution put to a meeting is normally decided in the first instance by a show of hands.[72] Further, on a show of hands each member entitled to vote and present in person has one vote only, *i.e.* proxies[73] are not counted. In practice articles do not provide otherwise, *e.g.* Table A, reg. 46, below, provides that a vote shall be by a show of hands unless a poll is demanded and reg. 54 provides that subject to any rights or restrictions attached to any class of shares, every member present in person shall have one vote on a show of hands, *i.e.* proxies cannot vote.

Table A provides:
Regulation 57 "No member shall vote at any general meeting or at any separate meeting of the holders of any class of shares in the company, either in person or by proxy, in respect of any share held by him unless all moneys presently payable by him in respect of that share have been paid."
Regulation 58 "No objection shall be raised to the qualification of any voter except at the meeting or adjourned meeting at which the vote objected to is tendered, and every vote not disallowed at the meeting shall be valid. Any objection made in due time shall be referred to the chairman whose decision shall be final and conclusive."

In *Marx v Estates & General Investments Ltd*,[74] Brightman J. said that there is much to be said for an article like reg. 58. In that case a proxy form, which was liable to stamp duty because it authorised a proxy to vote at more than one meeting but which was unstamped, was not void but a valid authority capable of being stamped, and since the company had accepted it without objection at the meeting the votes cast by the proxy were valid. Further, by virtue of reg. 58 the objection taken several days after the meeting was made too late.

A bankrupt shareholder may vote if he is still on the register.[75] A shareholder, even if he is a director, can vote although he has an interest in the question to be

[72] *Re Horbury Bridge Coal Co.* (1879) 11 Ch.D. 109, CA.
[73] Below, p.256.
[74] [1976] 1 W.L.R. 380.
[75] *Morgan v Gray* [1953] Ch. 83.

voted on, provided that the majority of the members do not unfairly oppress the minority.[76]

> "The shareholder's vote is a right of property, and prima facie may be exercised by a shareholder as he thinks fit in his own interest": *per* Lord Maugham in *Carruth v I.C.I. Ltd* [1937] A.C. 707 at p.765.

Table A, reg. 47, provides that, unless a poll is demanded, a declaration by the chairman that a resolution has on a show of hands been carried, or carried by a particular majority, or lost, and an entry to that effect in the minutes, is conclusive evidence of the fact without proof of the number or proportion of the votes recorded for or against.[77]

2. *A poll*

Although a show of hands can be taken quickly, it is not an accurate method of ascertaining the wishes of the members of a company because the votes of those voting by proxy are not counted. Further, it does not pay due regard to the wishes of a member holding a large number of shares since he has only one vote on a show of hands. Consequently, although the right to demand a poll exists at common law, s.378(4) gives a statutory right to demand a poll in the case of a special or an extraordinary resolution and articles always make provision for taking a poll. The effect of Table A, reg. 46, is that a poll may be demanded before, or on the declaration of the result of, a show of hands, *i.e.* it is not necessary to have a show of hands before a poll is taken.[78] A proper demand for a poll does away with the need for, or the result of, a show of hands.

The number of votes which a member has on a poll depends upon the articles. Section 370(6) states that unless the articles otherwise provide a member shall have one vote in respect of each share or each £10 of stock held by him, and regs 54 and 59 of Table A provide that, subject to any rights or restrictions attached to any class of shares, on a poll every member present in person or proxy shall have one vote for each share of which he is the holder, *i.e.* proxies can be counted.

A poll is complete when the result is ascertained, not on an earlier day when the votes are cast.[79]

Section 373 provides that, on any question other than the election of the chairman or the adjournment of the meeting, any article is void in so far as it excludes the right to demand a poll or requires more persons to demand a poll than (a) five members entitled to vote at the meeting,[80] or (b) members representing one-tenth of the voting rights, or (c) members holding one-tenth of the paid-up capital conferring a right to vote.[81] Further, a proxy has the same

---

[76] Below, Ch.18.

[77] Where a show of hands has been taken and the minutes record the passing of the resolution but omit any mention of the show of hands, further evidence may be required to establish the validity of the procedure: *Fraserburgh Commercial Co. Ltd, Petitioners*, 1946 S.C. 444.

[78] *per* Jenkins L.J. in *Holmes v Keyes* [1959] Ch. 199, CA at p.212, although see *per* Lord Blanesburgh in *Carruth's* case, above, at p.755.

[79] *Holmes v Keyes*, below, p.271.

[80] Excluding rights countered on treasury shares.

[81] *ibid.*

right to demand a poll as the member he represents. If articles could require a considerable number of members to demand a poll the right would be worthless. It is essential that a proxy be able to demand a poll—he has no vote on a show of hands.

Table A, reg. 46, provides that in addition to the members in (b) or (c), above, a poll may be demanded by the chairman or by two members having the right to vote at the meeting, and, by article 48, that the demand for a poll may be withdrawn, but only with the consent of the chairman.

The poll is taken as laid down in the articles. Table A, reg. 51, provides that a poll demanded on the election of a chairman or on a question of adjournment shall be taken forthwith. If demanded on any other question, it shall be taken at such time as the chairman directs. Where, under articles similar to Table A, a poll was demanded on a question of adjournment and taken, but the scrutineers informed the chairman that the result could not be announced within the time during which the meeting hall was available, it was held that the meeting subsequently convened to hear the result was a continuation of the original meeting, with the result that no proxies deposited between the date of the original meeting and the date of the continuation meeting were valid, as the articles required proxies to be deposited 48 hours before the meeting.[82]

On a poll, a member entitled to more than one vote need not cast all his votes or cast them all in the same way: s.374. This provision was introduced to meet the difficulties of a large trust corporation which might hold shares in a company on behalf of two or more different trusts, whose respective interests might well require different exercises of its votes.[83]

The Government has proposed that members will be able to demand a poll in advance of the meeting and to vote on that poll without either attending or appointing a proxy.[84]

Proxies

Although there is no common law right to vote by proxy,[85] s.372 gives such a right.

The section provides that any member entitled to attend and vote at a company meeting may appoint another person, whether a member of the company or not, to attend and vote as his proxy, and if the company is a private company, to speak as his proxy. Every notice calling a meeting must state this right of a member to appoint a proxy. Unless the articles otherwise provide, a proxy can only vote on a poll, a member of a private company cannot appoint more than one proxy to attend on the same occasion, and a member of a company without a share capital cannot appoint a proxy. The Government has proposed that proxies should have full speaking and voting rights, and be able to demand a poll.[86] Articles cannot require the instrument appointing a proxy to be

---

[82] *Jackson v Hamlyn* [1953] Ch. 577, applying *Shaw v Tati Concessions Ltd* [1913] 1 Ch. 292.
[83] *Per* Walton J. in *Northern Counties Securities Ltd v Jackson & Steeple Ltd* [1974] 1 W.L.R. 1133, at p.1147.
[84] *Modernising Company Law* Cmn 5553-I, paras 2.18–2.19.
[85] *Per* Lord Hanworth M.R. in *Cousins International Brick Co. Ltd* [1931] 2 Ch. 90, CA at p.100.
[86] *Modernising Company Law* Cmn 5553-I, para. 2.18–2.19.

deposited with the company more than 48 hours before a meeting or an adjourned meeting. If articles could require the instrument to be deposited a considerable time before a meeting the right to appoint a proxy would be worthless.

A proxy is appointed by an instrument in writing or by electronic communication in accordance with the articles or to an electronic address as notified by the company. There are two forms of proxy in use—a general proxy appointing a person to vote as he thinks fit, having regard to what is said at the meeting, and a special proxy appointing a person to vote for or against a particular resolution. A special proxy is often called "a two-way proxy." The Stock Exchange requires two-way proxy forms to be sent to shareholders.[87] The articles usually provide for the form and proof of proxies.[88]

Section 372(6) provides that if invitations to appoint a proxy by a person or one of a number of persons specified in the invitations are issued at the company's expense to some only of the members entitled to vote at a meeting, every officer of the company who knowingly and wilfully authorises or permits their issue is liable to a fine, although an officer is not liable by reason only of the issue to a member, at his written request, of a form of appointment naming the proxy or of a list of persons willing to act as proxy, if the form or list is available to every member entitled to vote. If this were not so the directors might send the proxy papers to friendly shareholders only.

It is the duty of the chairman to decide on the validity of proxies. If the articles provide, as does Table A, reg. 58, that votes tendered at a meeting and not disallowed shall be deemed to be valid, the court will not review the chairman's decision, even if it is wrong, in the absence of fraud or bad faith on his part.[89] Where articles do not incorporate Table A, a mere misprint or some quite palpable mistake on the face of a proxy form does not entitle the company to refuse to accept the proxy.[90]

A shareholder who has given a proxy is free to attend the meeting and vote in person, in which case the vote tendered by the proxy may properly be rejected.[91] He does not thereby revoke the proxy, however, and the proxy may, e.g. vote on a second resolution on which the shareholder does not vote.[92]

A corporation, whether a company within the meaning of the Act or not, may, if it is a member of another corporation which is such a company, by resolution of its directors or other governing body[93] authorise such person as it thinks fit to act as its representative at any meeting of the company or any class of members of the company. The representative is entitled to exercise on behalf of the

---

[87] Admission of Securities to Listing.

[88] See Table A, regs.59 to 63. Electronic communication may be void despite anything to the contrary in the articles.

[89] *Wall v Exchange Investment Corporation* [1926] Ch. 143, CA. And see *Marx v Estates and General Investments Ltd* [1976] 1 W.L.R. 380, above, p.254.

[90] *Oliver v Dalgleish* [1963] 1 W.L.R. 1274, where the proxies referred to the "annual general meeting" instead of the "extraordinary general meeting" and there was no other meeting which could be confused with the date which was stated in the proxies.

[91] *Cousins v International Brick Co. Ltd*, above, where the proxy had not been revoked under Table A, art. 63. above.

[92] *Ansett v Butley Air Transport Ltd* (No. 2.) (1958) 75 W.N. NSW 306.

[93] See, *e.g. Hillman v Crystal Bowl Amusements Ltd* [1973] 1 W.L.R. 162, CA.

corporation the powers which the corporation could exercise if it were an individual shareholder of the company: s.375. Such a representative is *not* a proxy and may vote on a show of hands as well as on a poll, and may address the meeting even if the company is not a private company.

Minutes

Every company must keep minutes of all proceedings of general meetings. Such minutes, signed by the chairman of the meeting at which the proceedings were held or of the next succeeding meeting, are evidence of the proceedings: s.382(1), (2). Unless the articles so provide, they are not conclusive evidence, and so, if a resolution has been passed, but is not entered in the minutes, other evidence to prove it will be admitted.[94] However, when the articles provide that the minutes, signed by the chairman, shall be "conclusive evidence without any further proof of the facts therein stated," as between those bound by the articles, namely the company and the members *qua* members,[95] evidence cannot be called to contradict the minutes unless they have been fraudulently written up.[96]

When minutes have been duly made, there is a presumption that all the proceedings were in order, and all appointments of directors, managers or liquidators are deemed to be valid: s.382(4).

The books containing minutes of general meetings are to be kept at the registered office and open to the inspection of any member without charge. A member is entitled to be furnished, within seven days, with a copy on payment of the prescribed fee. If inspection is refused or copies are not sent, the court can compel immediate inspection of the books[97] or direct that copies be sent to those requiring them: s.383. The minute books may be bound, or loose-leaf provided that adequate precautions are taken for guarding against falsification: s.722. Section 723, above, enables the company to use a computer to keep the minutes.

Written resolutions[98] must be recorded in the same way as minutes of proceedings of meetings and, if signed by a director or the company secretary, such a record will be evidence of the agreement proceedings. It is also evidence that the requirements of the Act have been complied with, unless the contrary is proved. Section 383 (above) applies to such a record: s.382A.

Where the sole member of a single member private company takes a decision which has the effect of a resolution of a general meeting, he must provide the company with a written record of that decision. Failure to do so may lead to a fine being imposed but does not invalidate the decision: s.382B.

RESOLUTIONS

Kinds of resolution

In the absence of a contrary provision in the Act or in the memorandum or the

---

[94] *Re Fireproof Doors* [1916] 2 Ch. 142; *cf. Fraserburgh Commercial Co. Ltd, Petitioners*, 1946 S.C. 444.
[95] Above, p.75.
[96] *Kerr v Mottram* [1940] Ch. 657.
[97] By the member himself or by a named expert on his behalf; *McCusker v McRae*, 1966 S.C. 253.
[98] Below, p.263.

articles the company in general meeting acts by ordinary resolution. Sometimes, however, the Act or the memorandum or articles require a special resolution or an extraordinary resolution. Elective resolutions are required for private companies to elect out of a few internal requirements of the Act and are discussed below. Any of these types of resolution may be effected by the written resolution procedure, below.

An *ordinary resolution*, which is not defined in the Act, is a resolution passed by a simple majority of the votes of the members entitled to vote[99] and voting in person or, where allowed, by proxy, at a meeting of which notice has been duly given. The length of the notice depends upon a number of factors including the kind of meeting at which the resolution is passed.[1]

Section 378 defines an *extraordinary resolution* as a resolution passed by at least a three-fourths' majority of [the votes of] the members entitled to vote and voting, in person or, where allowed, by proxy, at a general meeting of which notice specifying the intention to propose the resolution as an extraordinary resolution has been duly given. Again the length of the notice depends upon a number of factors including the kind of meeting at which the resolution is passed.

A *special resolution* is defined as a resolution passed by a majority of at least three-fourths of [the votes of] the members entitled to vote and voting, in person or, where allowed, by proxy, at a general meeting of which at least 21 days' notice specifying the intention to propose the resolution as a special resolution has been given: s.378(2).

The words in brackets must be read into s.378 because voting may be on a show of hands, in which case each member will usually have one vote, or on a poll, in which case each member will usually have one vote for each of his shares.

In England a provision in the articles that the day of service is to be included in the number of days' notice to be given does not apply to notice of a special resolution, *i.e.* the period of not less than 21 days prescribed by s.378 is a period of not less than 21 clear days, exclusive of the day of service of the notice and of the day on which the meeting is to be held. Articles cannot curtail the length of time which Parliament has said must elapse between the date on which the notice is served and the date on which the meeting is held.[2] In Scotland the requisite notice under s.378(2) means a notice of not less than 21 days computed by excluding the day on which the notice is received by the shareholder but including the day on which the meeting is to be held.[3] We have seen that less than 21 days' notice of a special resolution may be given if it is so agreed by a majority in number of the members holding not less than 95 per cent. of the shares giving the right to attend and vote at the meeting:[4] s.378(3).

At a meeting at which a special resolution or an extraordinary resolution is submitted to be passed, a declaration of the chairman that the resolution is carried is, unless a poll is demanded, conclusive evidence of the fact without

[99] *Bushell v Faith* [1970] A.C. 1099. A shareholders' agreement may, however, prevent a member voting in a particular way on a particular resolution: *Russell v Northern Bank Development Corp Ltd* [1992] B.C.L.C. 1016.
[1] Above, p.247.
[2] *Re Hector Whaling Ltd* [1936] Ch. 208, applied in *Thompson v Stimpson* [1961] 1 Q.B. 195.
[3] *Neil McLeod & Sons Ltd, Petitioners*, 1967 S.C. 16, *per* Lord President Clyde at p.20.
[4] Excluding treasury shares.

proof of the number or proportion of the votes recorded in favour of or against the resolution: s.378(4). This provision prevents a resolution from being challenged on the ground, *e.g.* that certain shareholders were not qualified to vote.[5] If, however, the declaration of the chairman is fraudulent, or shows on the face of it that the proper majority has not been obtained, it is not conclusive.

> A special resolution was put to the meeting. The chairman then said: "Those in favour 6; those against 23; but there are 200 voting by proxy,[6] and I declare the resolution carried." *Held*, the declaration was not conclusive, and the resolution was not passed: *Re Caratal (New) Mines Ltd* [1902] 2 Ch.498.[7]

Further, the chairman's declaration is not conclusive where the resolution has not been effectively submitted to the meeting, *e.g.* if a show of hands has not been taken as required by the articles.[8]

The chairman can put a resolution to the meeting without its being seconded, unless the articles prohibit it.

Elective resolutions

Section 379A provides for an elective resolution which a private company may use to elect out of any of five internal requirements of the Acts. The Secretary of State has the power to add additional areas of election by regulations: 1989 Act, s.117.

An elective resolution may be made by a private company for any one of the following purposes:

    (i)   to apply s.80A in relation to the authority of directors to allot shares,[9]

   (ii)   to dispense with the laying of accounts and reports before a general meeting,[10]

  (iii)   to apply s.366A to dispense with the holding of an annual general meeting,[11]

  (iv)   to reduce the percentage required for sanctioning short notice of meetings or special resolutions,[12]

   (v)   to dispense with the annual appointment of auditors.[13]

An elective resolution requires at least 21 days' notice in writing or by electronic communication[14] both of the terms of the resolution and of the

---

[5] *Grahams' Morocco Co. Ltd, Petitioners*, 1932 S.C. 269.

[6] Those "voting" by proxy could not vote on a show of hands.

[7] A corresponding Scottish case is *Cowan v Scottish Publishing Co. Ltd* (1892) 19 R. 437.

[8] *Citizens Theatre Ltd, Petitioners*, 1946 S.C. 14; *cf. Fraserburgh Commercial Co. Ltd, Petitioners*, 1946 S.C. 444.

[9] Above, Ch.7.

[10] Below, Ch.20.

[11] Above, p.243.

[12] Above, p.246.

[13] Below, Ch.21.

[14] Within the meaning of s.15 of the Electronic Communication Act 2000.

meeting although shorter notice will suffice if all those entitled to attend and vote at the meeting so agree. It must then have the unanimous consent of all those entitled to attend and vote at the meeting—one shareholder can therefore prevent it being pursued. The election can be revoked at any time by an ordinary resolution and is automatically revoked if the company is re-registered as a public company. No company may contract out of this elective regime by its articles: s.379A.

An elective resolution and one revoking an elective resolution must be registered in the same way as a special resolution: s.380. Both may be effected by the written resolution procedure, below.

Amendments

If a positive amendment, pertinent to the subject-matter of the resolution, is proposed, it must be voted upon first. If the chairman refuses to put a proper amendment to the meeting, the resolution, if passed, is not binding.[15]

An amendment cannot be moved if it goes beyond the notice convening the meeting. Because notice of special business must state the resolution to be passed in such a way as fairly to state the purpose for which the meeting is convened, there is little scope for amendment where a resolution is special business. Where a notice of a meeting stated that it was to pass, with such amendments as should be determined, a resolution that three named persons be appointed directors, an amendment to elect two other directors as well was held valid.[16] Again, there is little scope for amendment of special, extraordinary and elective resolutions since, as we have seen, the notice of such resolutions must set out the exact wording of the resolution.[17] However, where a notice of a meeting stated that it was to pass special resolutions to wind up voluntarily and to appoint X as liquidator, and the second resolution was dropped and a new one to appoint Y as liquidator was passed, it was held that Y's appointment was valid because as soon as the resolution to wind up was passed a liquidator could be appointed, without notice, under the Act.[18]

Registration and copies of certain resolutions

A printed copy of certain resolutions and agreements, or a copy in some other form approved by him, must be forwarded to the Registrar within 15 days after they are passed or made and, where articles have been registered, a copy must be annexed to every copy of the articles issued subsequently: s.380(1), (2).

Section 380 applies to, *inter alia*, special and extraordinary resolutions, elective resolutions, written resolutions and other resolutions agreed to by all the members[19] which would otherwise not have been effective unless passed as special resolutions or extraordinary resolutions, and resolutions agreed by all the

---

[15] *Henderson v Bank of Australasia* (1890) 45 Ch.D. 330, CA.
[16] *Betts & Co. Ltd v Macnaghten* [1910] 1 Ch. 430.
[17] *Re Swindon Town Football Co. Ltd* [1990] B.C.L.C. 467, 468, *per* Harman J.
[18] *Re Trench Tubeless Tyre Co.* [1990] 1 Ch. 408, CA.
[19] A company holding treasury shares is not a member for this purpose s.380(4A).

members[20] of a class of shareholders. This section also applies to certain ordinary resolutions, *e.g.* one to vary or revoke the authority of the directors to issue shares under s.80, or to revoke an elective resolution: s.380(4).

A resolution passed at an adjourned meeting is treated as having been passed on the date on which it was in fact passed, and is not deemed to have been passed on the date of the original meeting: s.381.

It will be remembered that a printed copy of a resolution effecting an increase of capital, or a copy in some other form approved by the Registrar, must also be filed within 15 days: s.123.

INFORMAL AND WRITTEN RESOLUTIONS

Informal resolutions: the duomatic principle

The courts have evolved a principle known as the *Duomatic* principle,[21] that if all the members who have the right to attend and vote at a general meeting assent to a transaction which the meeting could carry into effect, that assent is as binding as a resolution of the meeting would be. It is not necessary that they should hold a meeting in one room or one place to express that assent simultaneously.[22] In one case,[23] it was held that this principle could apply where the four apparent shareholders assented, even though, unknown to everyone involved, there was another shareholder.

This principle has been applied to an assent to vary the articles of a company even though no formal special resolution to that effect had been passed: *Cane v Jones*.[24] It has also been applied to override shareholders' agreements,[25] and to meetings of a class of shareholders,[26] on the basis that those who have agreed to procedural restrictions can agree to waive them. The principle cannot apply where the assentors could not validly have passed the resolution at a formal meeting,[27] or where, although the members have been informed, their assent has not been sought.[28] It is not clear whether the assent must be given by the registered owner or whether it can be given by the beneficial owner.[29] But it must be given by all the members, a majority will not suffice.[30]

A more complex question is whether the principle can override a statutory requirement for a resolution. In *R. W. Peak (Kings Lynn) Ltd*, the judge left open the question whether it could be used in cases where the Act required a specific procedure to be followed, *e.g.* the requirements for a company validly to purchase its own shares, on the basis that the matter involved more than protection of the

---

[20] *ibid.*
[21] Formulated in *re Duomatic Ltd* [1969] 2 Ch 365 from earlier cases by Buckley J.
[22] *Parker & Cooper Ltd v Reading* [1926] Ch 975.
[23] Re *Peña v Dale* [2004] 2 B.C.C.C. 508.
[24] [1981] 1 All E.R. 533. See also *Re Bailey, Hay & Co Ltd* [1971] 1 W.C.R. 1357.
[25] *Euro Brokers Holdings Ltd v Monecor (London) Ltd* [2003] 1 B.C.L.C. 506, CA.
[26] *Re Torvale Group Ltd* [1999] 2 B.C.L.C. 605.
[27] *Re New Cedos Engineering Co. Ltd* [1994] 1 B.C.L.C. 797.
[28] *EIC Services Ltd v Phipps* [2003] B.C.C. 931 (the CA was not concerned with this point).
[29] *Domoney v Godinho* [2004] 2 B.C.L.C. 15; *Shahar v Tsitsekkos* [2004] EWHC 2659.
[30] *Extrasure Travel Insurance Ltd v Scattergood* [2003] 1 B.C.L.C. 598.

shareholders. The earlier cases suggest that all lack of formalities can be cured by the relevant assents but they were not faced with such procedures. Similarly in *Demite Ltd v Protec Health Ltd*[31] another judge expressed doubts as to whether the principle could apply to the necessary approval of a transaction between a director and his or her company under s.320.

This issue was considered by the Court of Appeal in *Atlas Wright (Europe) Ltd v Wright*.[32] The Court applied the *Duomatic* principle in the context of the approval of a director's service contract under s.319 which requires an ordinary resolution. The answer is to be found by looking at the purpose of the statutory requirement in question. Section 319 was passed purely for the protection of the shareholders and so they could properly waive its formalities, assuming that they were properly informed. The purpose of some aspects of the share purchase legislation[33] and the substantial transactions legislation[34] was to protect a wider constituency, *e.g.* the creditors, and so the shareholders alone could not waive the formalities. That dichotomy has since been applied to prevent the principle applying to the rules for financial assistance and distributable profits, again on the basis of creditor protection.[35]

Further, Table A, reg. 53, provides that a written resolution signed by all the members entitled to attend and vote at general meetings shall be as effectual as if passed at a general meeting of the company duly convened and held. However, Nourse J. in *Re Barry Artist Ltd*,[36] whilst approving the use of such an informal resolution as a special resolution for a reduction of capital, stated that he would not do so again since the reduction of capital procedure requires confirmation by the court.[37] This decision cast doubt on the exact parameters of reg. 53 similar to those concerning the *Duomatic* principle.

Written resolutions under the Act

As a result of those doubts, the 1989 Companies Act introduced a new statutory procedure to allow private companies to pass any resolution without holding a meeting, provided all those who could have attended the meeting and voted sign the resolution instead. The clear intention is that this procedure will be available even where the resolution is part of a wider process such as those mentioned above.

To effect this, the 1989 Act introduced four new s.s, 381A, 381B, 381C and 382A, and one new Schedule, 15A, into the 1985 Act. The original provisions proved, however, to be unduly complex in so far as they involved the company's auditors having to respond to the proposed resolution before it could take effect

---

[31] [1998] B.C.C. 637, at p.648.
[32] [1999] 2 B.C.L.C. 301, CA.
[33] *R. W Peak (Kings Lynn) Ltd*, above. Other aspects of the share purchase procedures have been said to be for the protection of the shareholders only and so susceptible to the principle: *BDG Roof-Bond Ltdv Douglas* [2000] 1BCLC 401.
[34] As in *Demite Ltd*, above.
[35] *Bairstow v Queens Moat Houses plc* [2001] 2 B.C.L.C. 531. This flexibility has persuaded the Government not to adopt the Company Law Review's proposal to codify the *Duomatic* principle: *Modernising Company Law*, Cmn 5553–1 paras 2.31–2.35.
[36] [1985] B.C.L.C. 283.
[37] Above, p.151.

in such a way that it was difficult for the auditors to frame their response, and defective in that it was unclear whether it had also invalidated written resolutions under an article such as reg. 53. As a result the provisions were amended in 1996[38] to provide a simpler relationship with the auditors and to preserve written resolutions framed under the articles.

The basic procedure is set out in s.381A. No notice requirements apply and, provided all the relevant members sign a document which accurately states the resolution, it need not be the same document or even identical wording. Moreover, a signature can be delegated to another. Thus several letters can be sent for signature.

Under s.381A(3) the date of the resolution is the date when the last relevant member signs it; until then the resolution has no validity at all and so is subject to a veto by any member. The date of the resolution is also the date of the passing of the resolution for the relevant provisions of the Act. A written resolution under this procedure can be used to effect all types of resolution and is to be deemed to be duly passed for all purposes. Under Sch.15A, however, the procedure cannot be used to dismiss a director under s.303 or an auditor under s.391.

Section 381B requires any director or secretary who knows both that it is proposed to seek agreement for a resolution and the terms of that resolution to secure that the company's auditors are notified of the contents of the resolution before it is sent to the members for signature. Failure to do so will lead to a fine[39] but has no affect on the validity of the resolution.

Under s.382A, written resolutions must be recorded in the same way as ordinary resolutions. If the procedure is being used to effect a special, extraordinary or elective resolution it must be registered as such.

Section 381C makes it clear that nothing in the statutory procedure invalidates any resolution validly passed under either the *Duomatic* principle or a written resolution procedure under the articles. The statutory procedure is an alternative. That section also prevents companies restricting the statutory procedure by their articles.

The new written resolution procedure is available even on those occasions where a resolution is required as part of a complex authorisation procedure, by adapting that procedure to the written resolution process: Sch.15A. The six areas affected are: a disapplication of pre-emption rights,[40] exemption by a private company from the financial assistance provisions,[41] approval of off-market purchase contracts and contingent purchase contracts by a company in relation to its own shares,[42] approval by a company for the redemption or purchase of its own shares out of capital,[43] approval of directors' service contracts,[44] and funding

---

[38] By the Deregulation (Resolutions of Private Companies) Order 1996, SI 1996/1471.

[39] There are defences available under s.381B(3) based on impracticability or reasonable belief that the auditors have been notified.

[40] Above, Ch.7.

[41] Above, Ch.11.

[42] Above, p.140. See *Re R. W. Peak (Kings Lynn) Ltd* [1998] 1 B.C.L.C. 193 for problems of the timing of such a resolution.

[43] *ibid.*

[44] Below, Ch.15.

of directors' expenditure.[45] These variations are dealt with in relation to their subject area but in general any voting prohibition is lifted in such a way that it becomes irrelevant whether the restricted person signs the resolution or not, and any necessary documents are required to be sent to each relevant member in advance of his signing rather than in advance of the meeting.

The Government has proposed that the requirement for unanimity should be replaced by a requirement for the signatures of those holding the necessary percentage of the votes, depending upon the type of resolution. Information must still be sent to all the shareholders, even if the requisite majority (often a single person) has been obtained.[46]

[45] *ibid.*
[46] *Modernising Company Law*, Cmn 5553–I paras 2.26–2.30.

Chapter 15

DIRECTORS

THE management of a company is usually entrusted to a body of persons called "directors." It will be seen later that the Act requires a public company to have at least two directors and a private company to have at least one. Among other things, this chapter deals with the appointment, remuneration and vacation of office of directors. It also shows that the directors of a company act as a board, that normal articles (*e.g.* Table A, reg. 70) give the directors extensive powers to manage the company's business (and that so long as the directors act within their powers, the company in general meeting cannot overrule them), and that articles can empower the directors to appoint a managing director and delegate any of their powers to him.

The most important topics dealt with in the chapter are the consequent fiduciary duties and duties of care which a director owes to his company in exercising these powers. Statutory developments have imposed further restrictions and obligations on the directors and provide for disclosure by them of many transactions involving themselves and the company. Additional restrictions imposed by the Stock Exchange in respect of directors of listed companies are set out in Chapter 18. *This chapter is concerned with the restrictions imposed by law.* The chapter concludes with the impact of corporate insolvency on the liability of directors for their conduct prior to the insolvency. The Company Law Review made several proposals on the law relating to directors and the Government has also been much exercised by such matters as executive pay.

It should be noted that in a private company the directors are usually substantial shareholders. In a public company, the directors normally have few shares, their fees and other emoluments, rather than their dividends, being their main source of profit from the company, with the result that management and ownership of the company are divorced. Further, in practice, such companies will have different grades of director, full-time or executive directors and part-time or non-executive directors.

WHO IS A DIRECTOR?

The exact name by which a person occupying the position of director is called, is immaterial as, under s.741(1) in the Act, the expression "director" includes any person occupying the position of director by whatever name called. Although there is some dispute, the current view is that this provision only applies to persons properly appointed as "directors" but who operate under a different title, *e.g.* as a "governor".[1] Such persons are known as "*de jure*" directors, *i.e.* they

[1] *Re Lo-Line Electric Motors Ltd* [1988] B.C.L.C. 698 at 706 *per* Browne-Wilkinson V.-C.; *cf. Re Eurostem Maritime Ltd* [1987] P.C.C. 190, *per* Mervyn Davies J.

are directors because they have been properly appointed as such. But the definition in s.741(1) is inclusive only and allows for others, not properly appointed, to be regarded as directors. There are two such categories: *"de facto"* directors and "shadow" directors.

De facto directors

The courts have long accepted that a person who has never been properly appointed as a director may nevertheless be regarded as being a director for the purposes of imposing some liability or restriction on him, usually in the context of imposing a disqualification order. Such persons are those who have acted as if they were directors although they have never been appointed as such. They are known as *"de facto"* directors. The essential element is that they are openly acting as directors and, as such, should be contrasted with the statutory category of "shadow" directors, dealt with below, who work behind the scenes. In most cases, these categories are mutually exclusive since one claims to be a director whilst the other claims not to be one.[2] But in both cases they have exercised an influence on the governance of the company.

The question is exactly what does a person have to do to become a *de facto* director? Two judges initially attempted to provide an answer.

In *Re Hydrodan (Corby) Ltd*, Millett J. said[3]:

"A *de facto* director is a person who assumes to act as a director. He is held out as a director by the company, and claims and purports to be a director, although never actually or validly appointed as such. To establish that a person was a *de facto* director of a company, it is necessary to plead and prove that he undertook functions in relation to the company which could properly be discharged only by a director. It is not sufficient to show that he was concerned in the management of a company's affairs or undertook tasks in relation to his business which cannot properly be performed by a manager below board level."

Although that definition was applied in *Secretary of State for Trade and Industry v Morrell*,[4] it was criticised by Lloyd J. in *Re Richborough Furniture Ltd*,[5] principally as to the need for any element of holding out. Instead he substituted a revised version of the other element in Millett J.'s definition, *i.e.* as to the necessary acts:

"It seems to me that for someone to be made liable . . . as a *de facto* director, the court would have to have clear evidence that he had either been the sole person directing the affairs of the company . . . or, if there were others who were true directors, that he was acting on an equal footing with the others in directing the affairs of the company. It also seems to me that, if it is unclear whether the acts of the person in question are referable to an assumed directorship, or to some other capacity such as a shareholder or, as here, a consultant, the person in question must be entitled to the benefit of the doubt."[6]

---

[2] See *Re Kaytech International plc* [1999] 2 B.C.L.C. 351 at 422 *per* Robert Walker L.J.
[3] [1994] 2 B.C.L.C. 180, 183.
[4] [1996] B.C.C. 229.
[5] [1996] 1 B.C.L.C. 507.
[6] *ibid.* at p.524.

That test was approved and applied in *Secretary of State for Trade and Industry v Laing*[7] with the gloss that even if one particular act could be regarded as amounting to a *de facto* directorship, that does not mean that the person is still acting as such. One can cease to be a *de facto* director simply by ceasing to act as such. The idea that if the acts could be attributable to acting in a capacity other than a director, the person should be given the benefit of the doubt, was also approved in *Secretary of State for Trade and Industry v Hickling*[8] and *Re Sykes (Butchers) Ltd.*[9]

In *Secretary of State for Trade and Industry v Tjolle*,[10] Jacob J. considered both the tests set out above. He said that it may be difficult to formulate a single test, and that it would not be sufficient to make a person a *de facto* director simply on the basis that he was held out as a director, or even used the title. That would, however, be a factor to be taken into account and may require the person to rebut a presumption of directorship. What was required was evidence of activities which could only be discharged as a director and/or either that the person was the sole person directing the affairs of the company, in the sense of taking major decisions on proper financial information, or was acting on an equal footing with others in so directing. With regard to the idea of an equal footing, Jacob J. pointed out that this meant the right to participate in management decisions and not necessarily equal power in coming to those decisions. After all, that is the reality in most boardrooms.

It seems, therefore, that there is no one decisive factor and that those above are not exhaustive. In *Re Kaytech International plc*, the Court of Appeal[11] said that overall the court must be satisfied that the individual had assumed the status and functions of a director, so as to have openly exercised real influence in the corporate governance of the company. In that case, the individual had been the moving spirit in setting up the company, had pretended to raise the capital and variously described himself as a director and as chief executive. Even though he apparently did not consider himself to be one, the court had little difficulty in finding that he was a *de facto* director. Likewise in *Secretary of State for Trade and Industry v Jones*,[12] a similar finding was made against a substantial shareholder in a small company who had taken an active part in running the company in order to protect his investment and had signed a letter as "joint managing director".

On the other hand no such finding was made against the defendant in *Re Red Label Fashions Ltd*.[13] There was no clear indication that she had acted as a director rather than as a manager or "a compliant and dutiful wife willing to perform any role which [her husband] wanted her to perform in the hope that this might lead to the saving of their marriage and further their jointly owned company". Again, in *Secretary of State v Becker*,[14] there was found to be no

---

[7] [1996] 2 B.C.L.C. 324.
[8] [1996] B.C.C. 678.
[9] [1998] 1 B.C.L.C. 110.
[10] [1998] 1 B.C.L.C. 333.
[11] [1999] 2 B.C.L.C. 351.
[12] [1999] B.C.C. 336.
[13] [1999] B.C.C. 308. This was so even though the defendant had consistently lied about her role and functions.
[14] [2003] 1 B.C.L.C. 555.

evidence of the defendant undertaking functions in relation to the company which could properly only be discharged by a director.

Shadow directors

Several of the statutory provisions in both the Companies Act and the Insolvency Act relating to directors also apply to "shadow directors".[15] Section 741(2)[16] provides that these are persons in accordance with whose instructions the directors are accustomed to act, excluding purely professional advice. These are different from *de facto* directors because they do not purport to act as directors, on the contrary they claim not to be directors but hide behind those who are. They "lurk in the shadows". In *Re Hydrodam (Corby) Ltd*,[17] the question arose as to whether two directors of a parent company could be regarded as shadow directors of a subsidiary company. It was said that for someone to be a shadow director four things must be shown: (1) those who are the proper or de facto directors of the company; (2) that the person directed those directors as to how to act in relation to the company;[18] (3) that those directors acted in accordance with such directions;[19] and (4) that they were accustomed so to act. The judge was prepared to accept that the parent company may have been a shadow director of its subsidiary[20] but the two directors of the parent company could not be liable as shadow directors of the subsidiary simply because they took part in board meetings of the parent company. Further, if they acted in implementing board decisions with respect to the subsidiary, they were only acting as agents of the parent company. It would have been different if they had acted individually with respect to the subsidiary company.

The definition was expanded on by Morritt L.J. in *Secretary of State for Trade and Industry v Deverell*.[21] He set out the following propositions, noting that "lurking in the shadows" was not an essential part of the definition:

(1) the definition should be construed in the normal way to give intention to Parliament's intention ascertainable from the mischief to be dealt with and the words used, especially the protection of the public, even though the provision may be quasi-penal[22];

(2) the purpose of the definition is to identify those, other than professional advisers, with a real influence on corporate affairs; *but it is not necessary that the influence should be exercised over the whole field of its corporate activities;*

---

[15] Fiduciary duties could also apply to such persons: see *Yukong Line Ltd v Rendsburg Investments Corporation of Liberia (No. 2)* [1978] 1 W.L.R. 294, 311.

[16] See also s.251 of the IA 1986.

[17] [1994] 2 B.C.L.C. 180.

[18] Directing, only one or two out of several directors will not be enough: *Kuwait Asia Bank E.C. v National Mutual Life Nominees Ltd* [1990] B.C.L.C. 868, *Re Unisoft Group Ltd* (No. 2) [1994] B.C.C. 766.

[19] But not if it is rescue plan initiated by a creditor in return for extending credit. The directors had a choice to "take it or leave it". *Re PFTZM Ltd* [1995] 2 B.C.L.C. 354.

[20] This depends upon the wording of the particular statutory provision, many of which negate this possibility.

[21] [2000] 2 B.C.L.C. 133.

[22] Such as wrongful trading or disqualification proceedings.

(3) whether a communication is a direction or instruction must be construed in the light of the evidence and not the label used, but it is not necessary to prove the understanding of either party—communication and its consequences will suffice in most cases;

(4) advice given in a non-professional capacity may well come within the category of direction or instruction;

(5) although sufficient, there is no need to show in all cases that the properly appointed directors cast themselves in a subservient role or surrendered their respective discretions—that would be to put a gloss on the phrase "accustomed to act".[23]

NUMBER AND APPOINTMENT OF DIRECTORS

Every public company registered on or after November 1, 1929, must have at least two directors. Companies registered before that date, and every private company, must have at least one director: s.282. Apart from s.282, the number of directors is regulated by the articles.

As to the *first directors*, s.13(5) provides that the persons named in the statement of first directors and secretary, which must be delivered for registration with the memorandum, shall, on the incorporation of the company, be deemed to have been appointed as the first directors and secretary, and any appointment by any articles delivered with the memorandum shall be void unless the person concerned is named as a director or secretary in the statement. This is the only provision in the Act which deems someone to be a director. In all other cases whether a person is registered as a director has nothing to do with the question of whether or not that person is a director in fact:

"It is the company, acting by the procedures under the articles which makes or sacks a director."[24]

Subsequent directors are thus appointed in the way laid down in the articles, *e.g.* by the company in annual general meeting.

Table A provides:

"Regulation 73. At the first annual general meeting all the directors shall retire from office, and at every subsequent annual general meeting one-third of the directors who are subject to retirement by rotation or, if their number is not three or a multiple of three, the number nearest to one-third shall retire from office; but, if there is only one director who is subject to retirement by rotation, he shall retire."

"Regulation 74. Subject to the provisions of the Act, the directors to retire by rotation shall be those who have been longest in office since their last appointment or re-appointment, but as between persons who became or were last re-appointed directors on the same day those to retire shall (unless they otherwise agree among themselves) be determined by lot."

The articles also usually contain a clause, as does Table A in reg. 78, providing that casual vacancies, *i.e.* vacancies occurring between two annual general

---

[23] Millet J in *Hydrodam* suggested otherwise. But those words do require some pattern and a single instruction, however significant, will not suffice: *Secretary of State v Becker* [2003] 1 B.C.L.C. 555.

[24] *per* Jacob J. in *POW Services Ltd v Clare* [1995] 2 B.C.L.C. 435, 440.

meetings, may be filled by the directors. Regulation 79 also provides that the directors may appoint additional directors to hold office until the next annual general meeting but so that the total number of directors fixed in accordance with the articles is not exceeded.[25] Where there are articles similar to regs 78 and 79 the power of appointing additional directors has not been delegated to the directors so as to exclude the inherent power of the company in general meeting to appoint directors.[26]

The appointment of directors at a general meeting, except in the case of a private company, must be voted on individually unless a resolution to the contrary has first been agreed to by the meeting without any vote being given against it. A motion for the appointment of two or more persons as directors of a public company by a single resolution is void (although the operation of s.285, by which the acts of the "directors" are valid, is not excluded and no provision in the articles for the automatic reappointment of retiring directors in default of another appointment applies): s.292.

Table A, reg. 75, provides that if the company at the meeting at which a director retires by rotation does not fill the vacancy, the retiring director, if offering himself for re-election, is deemed to have been re-elected unless (a) another person is elected, (b) a resolution not to fill the vacancy is passed, or (c) a resolution for his re-election is lost. In the absence of a provision like (c), a retiring director will be deemed to be re-elected even though a resolution that he be re-elected is lost.[27] It is also provided, by reg. 76, that no person, other than the retiring director or a person recommended by the directors, is eligible for election as a director unless notice of intention to propose him, signed by a member entitled to vote, is left at the registered office not less than 14 nor more than 35 days before the meeting, together with a signed notice of his willingness to act.

Assignment of office by directors

If the articles or any agreement contains power for a director to assign his office to another person, an assignment is of no effect unless and until it is approved by a special resolution of the company: s.308.

Persons Who Cannot be Directors

Currently there is no ban on companies being appointed as directors of other companies, but the Government has indicated that this will change and that, over a period of time, such corporate directorship will be outlawed.[28] But there are certain persons who cannot be appointed or act as directors.

Age

A person who has reached the age of 70 cannot be *appointed* director *unless* the company is private and not the subsidiary of a public company, *or* the articles

---

[25] Any such appointments must be made at a valid meeting of the board. See *POW Services Ltd v Clare* [1995] 2 B.C.L.C. 435.
[26] *Worcester Corsetry Ltd v Witting* [1936] Ch. 640.
[27] *Grundt v Great Boulder Proprietary Mines Ltd* [1948] Ch. 145, CA.
[28] *Modernising Company law*, Cmn 5553-I, paras 3.32–3.34.

otherwise provide, *or* he is appointed or approved by a resolution of which special notice, stating his age, has been given: s.293.[29] The exceptions are such as to make this section ineffective.

A person who is *first* appointed a director of a company, other than a private company which is not the subsidiary of a public company, after he has reached the age at which the directors retire under the Act or the articles, must give notice of his age to the company: s.294.

Bankruptcy

An undischarged bankrupt must not act as director of, or be concerned in the promotion, formation or management of, a company without the leave of the court by which he was adjudged bankrupt,[30] under penalty of imprisonment or a fine or both: Company Directors Disqualification Act 1986, s.11. Such a person may be personally liable if he acts whilst disqualified—see below.[31]

Disqualification

A director who has been disqualified from acting as a director under the Company Directors Disqualification Act 1986 cannot be a director whilst so disqualified. This topic is dealt with at the end of this chapter.

SHARE QUALIFICATION OF DIRECTORS

A share qualification is a specified number of shares which a person must hold in the company to qualify him for appointment as a director of it. There is, however, no share qualification unless the articles otherwise provide, although there is no such requirement in Table A. It should be remembered that in the case of a private company a director will in any event usually be a substantial shareholder.

When a qualification is imposed, a director not already qualified must obtain his qualification within two months of his appointment or the shorter time fixed by the articles: s.291(1).[32] If a director fails to obtain his qualification within the appropriate period, or if he thereafter ceases to hold it, his office is vacated and he is liable to a fine until he ceases to act as director: s.291(3).[33]

REGISTER OF DIRECTORS AND SECRETARIES

Section 288(1) provides that a company must keep at its registered office a register of its directors and secretaries. In the case of an individual director, s.289

---

[29] The Company Law Review recommended removal of the age limit in favour of the disclosure of the age of all directors: *Completing the Structure*, para. 4.43.

[30] For Scotland, substitute "sequestration of his estates was awarded" for "he was adjudged bankrupt."

[31] Below, p.333.

[32] See *Holmes v Keyes* [1959] Ch. 199, CA.

[33] The Company Law review recommended that this offence be repealed as obsolete: *Developing the Framework* para.3.111.

provides that the register must contain his name[34] and any former name,[35] address,[36] nationality and business occupation, together with particulars of any other present or past directorships held by him (except directorships of companies of which the company is the wholly owned subsidiary, or which are wholly owned subsidiaries either of the company or of another company of which the company is the wholly owned subsidiary) and the date of his birth. The obligation relating to past directorships only relates to the previous five years and does not apply to dormant companies (below). The register is open to inspection by members without fee and by others on payment of the prescribed fee.

Within 14 days of any change in the directors or secretary or in the particulars contained in the register, the company must notify the Registrar of the change and the date when it occurred. A notification of a person having become a director or secretary must contain his signed consent to act as such: s.288(2). Registration of a person as a director does not of itself make that person a director—there must be a valid appointment. It may, however, prevent the company denying that that person is a director against someone who has relied on that registration.[37]

Section 711 requires the Registrar to publish in the *Gazette* notice of the receipt by him of any notification of a change among the directors of a company. Further, s.42 provides that a company cannot rely against other persons on any change among its directors if it had not been officially notified at the material time and is not shown by the company to have been known at that time to the person concerned, or if the material time is less than 16 days after official notification and it is shown that the person concerned was unavoidably prevented from knowing of the event at that time. Such official notification does not constitute notice to anyone—s.42 has a purely negative effect.[38]

PARTICULARS OF DIRECTORS ON BUSINESS LETTERS

No company may state, in any form, the name of any of its directors[39] in a business letter, either in the text or as a signatory, unless it states in legible characters the name of every director of the company: s.305. Initials or recognised abbreviations of forenames may be used.

DISCLOSURE OF DIRECTORS' SHAREHOLDINGS, ETC.

Obligation of director to notify company of his interests in shares in, or debentures of, it or associated companies

Subject to any exceptions made by the Secretary of State,[40] a person who

---

[34] A corporate director will use its corporate name. An LLP and a Scottish partnership can use its firm name.

[35] This does not include the maiden name of a married woman, the previous name of a peer or a name changed before the director was 18 or more than 20 years ago.

[36] If the director obtains a confidentiality order under ss 723B-723F, this may be a service rather than an actual address. This is intended to protect directors from harassment from intimidatory pressure groups. See the Companies (Particulars of Usual Residential Address) (Confidentiality Orders) Regulations 2002, SI 2002/912. Applications are made to Companies House.

[37] *POW Services Ltd v Clare* [1995] 2 B.C.L.C. 435, 440.

[38] *Official Custodian of Charities v Parway Estates Ltd* [1985] Ch. 151.

[39] This includes shadow directors.

[40] See the Companies (Disclosure of Directors' Interests) (Exceptions) Regulations 1985. (SI 1985/802).

becomes a director[41] when he is interested in shares in or debentures of the company or its subsidiary, holding company or co-subsidiary, must, within five days[42] (or, if he does not know of the interest, within five days after it comes to his knowledge), give the company written notice of his interests and of the number of shares of each class in, and the amount of debentures of each class of, the company and each of the associated companies: s.324(1).

A director must (within five days, if he knows of the event and that its occurrence gives rise to the obligation; otherwise within five days after he becomes aware that the occurrence of the event gives rise to the obligation) give the company written notice if, while he is a director:

   (i)   an event occurs in consequence of which he becomes or ceases to be interested in shares in or debentures of the company or an associated company; or

   (ii) he contracts to sell any such shares or debentures; or

   (iii) he assigns a right given to him by the company to subscribe for shares in or debentures of the company; or

   (iv) he is granted by an associated company a right to subscribe for shares in or debentures of that other company, or he exercises or assigns such a right;

stating the number or amount, and class, of shares or debentures involved: s.324(2). Certain other matters such as the price or other form of consideration must be stated too.

Schedule 13 provides detailed rules for determining what amounts to an interest in shares and debentures for the purposes of s.324. These include restricted rights of ownership, rights of control over shares or debentures, interests under a trust but not as a trustee, joint interests and the right to acquire any shares or debentures.

Contravention of s.324, or making to the company a statement known to be false or recklessly making a false statement, gives rise to liability to two years' imprisonment or a fine or both. Proceedings can, in England or Wales, be instituted only by or with the consent of the Secretary of State or the Director of Public Prosecutions.

If it appears that s.324 has been contravened the Secretary of State may order an investigation: s.446.[43]

Extension of obligation to disclose to interests of spouses and children

For the purposes of s.324, above, an interest of the spouse of, or of a child under the age of majority of, a director (not being himself or herself a director) in shares or debentures is treated as the director's interest, and a contract,

---

[41] Including shadow directors: s.324(6).
[42] Excluding Saturdays, Sundays and bank holidays.
[43] Below, p.386.

assignment or right of subscription entered into, exercised or made by, or a grant made to, such a spouse or child is treated as that of the director: s.328(1)(2).

Within five days after the event in question comes to his knowledge, a director must notify the company in writing if, while he or she is a director:

(a) the company grants the director's spouse or child a right to subscribe for shares in or debentures of the company; or

(b) such spouse or child exercises such a right: s.328(3).

In each case the like information as is required by s.324, above, must be stated: s.328(4). If s.328(4) appears to have been contravened the Secretary of State may order an investigation: s.446.[44]

In s.328, "son" includes step-son and adopted son, and "daughter" includes a step-daughter and adopted daughter.

Register of directors' shareholdings, etc.

Section 325 contains provisions for securing that information furnished under s.324, and certain other information about directors' interests,[45] is recorded and made available.

Every company must keep a register for the purposes of s.324 and whenever it receives information from a director in consequence of that section, within three days[46] thereafter it must inscribe in the register, against his name, the information and the date of inscription.

When a company grants a director a right to subscribe for shares or debentures it must, within a similar time, inscribe against his name the date of the grant, the period during or time at which it is exercisable, the consideration for the grant, the description of the shares or debentures and the number or amount thereof, and the price to be paid. When such a right is exercised there must be inscribed that fact (identifying the right), the number or amount of shares or debentures involved, the fact that they were registered in his name or the names of the persons in whose names they were registered, together with the number or amount registered in the name of each person.

The entries against the names in the register must appear in chronological order. If a director requires it, the nature and extent of his interest in shares or debentures must also be recorded.

The company is not, by virtue of anything done for the purposes of s.325, affected with notice of, or put upon inquiry as to, the rights of any person in relation to shares or debentures.[47]

Index of names

Unless the register is in the form of an index the company must also keep an index of the names inscribed therein. The index must give a sufficient indication

[44] *ibid.*
[45] Including shadow directors.
[46] Excluding Saturdays, Sundays and bank holidays.
[47] For inspection of the register see above, p.50.

to enable the information against each name to be readily found and must be altered within 14 days after the date on which a name is entered in the register.

Contravention of s.325

There are default fines[48] and other fines for contravention of s.325, and the court is empowered to order inspection of the register and delivery of a copy: s.326.

Duty of company to notify recognised investment exchange of acquisition of its securities by director

Section 329 provides that when a company, whose shares or debentures are listed on a recognised investment exchange,[49] is notified of any matter by a director under s.324 or s.328 above, and that matter relates to shares or debentures listed on an investment exchange, the company must notify that exchange of the matter before the end of the following day (Saturdays, Sundays and Bank Holidays in any part of Great Britain being disregarded).

If there is default in complying with the section the company and every officer in default is guilty of an offence and liable on summary conviction to a fine and further to a default fine, although proceedings in England and Wales cannot be instituted except by, or with the consent of, the Secretary of State or the Director of Public Prosecutions.

DEALING BY DIRECTORS IN CERTAIN OPTIONS

To prevent directors from speculating against the value of their company's shares, s.323, as extended by s.327, penalises the dealing by directors,[50] their spouses or children, in options to buy or sell quoted shares in, or quoted debentures of, the company or associated companies. A director who buys a right to call for delivery, or a right to make delivery, or, at his election, a right either to call for or to make delivery, at a specified price and within a specified time of a specified number of relevant shares or a specified amount of relevant debentures, is liable to two years' imprisonment or a fine or both: s.323.

"Relevant shares" and "relevant debentures" mean, respectively, shares in, or debentures of, the company or its subsidiary, holding company or co-subsidiary, as respects which a stock exchange listing has been granted in Great Britain or elsewhere.

Buying a right to subscribe for shares or debentures is not penalised, nor is buying debentures which carry a right to subscribe for or convert into shares.

Section 327 extends s.323 to the spouse of, or child under the age of majority of, a director, not being herself or himself a director of the company, except that it is a defence for such a spouse or child, charged with an offence under s.323, to prove that he had no reason to believe that his spouse or parent was a director of the company in question. "Child" includes step-child and adopted child.

---

[48] Sch.24.
[49] As defined in Pt XVIII of the FSMA 2000.
[50] Including shadow directors.

If it appears that s.323 has been contravened the Secretary of State may order an investigation: s.446.[51]

VACATION OF OFFICE BY DIRECTORS

A director may cease to be such for various reasons, *e.g.* death, dissolution of the company, retirement by rotation under articles like Table A, regs 73 and 74, above,[52] retirement under an age limit, retirement in accordance with the terms of the articles,[53] removal under s.303, or because they are subject to a disqualification order by a court or by the terms of the articles.[54]

Retirement of directors under age limit

A director must retire at the end of the first annual general meeting after he reaches 70 *unless*:

(1) the company is a private company which is not the subsidiary of a public company; or

(2) the articles otherwise provide; or

(3) he was appointed or approved by the company in general meeting by a resolution, *i.e.* an ordinary resolution, of which special notice, stating his age, was given: s.293.

If a director should have to retire under this section he may be reappointed by an ordinary resolution of which special notice,[55] stating his age, has been given. The result is that the section is a weak one and unimportant in practice. In particular, the articles may alter the age limit or provide that directors shall not be obliged to retire on reaching any age.[56]

Vacation of office by directors under the articles

The articles usually provide for the vacation of office by directors either voluntarily by resignation or involuntarily on the happening of certain events, *e.g.* bankruptcy or resignation.[57] Whether a director has in fact resigned in accordance with the articles is a question of fact, *e.g.* whether the company has notice of the resignation.[58]

When the articles provide that a director shall vacate his office if he absents himself from board meetings for a certain time,[59] the office will not be vacated if

---

[51] Below, p.386.
[52] p.239.
[53] See e.g. *Damoney v Godinho* [2004] 2 B.C.L.C. 15.
[54] Below, p.321.
[55] Above, p.250.
[56] The Company Law Review recommended the repeal of all age limits in favour of disclosure of the age of all directors: *Completing the Structure*, para.4.43.
[57] These grounds are distinct from those who cease to be directors because they are subject to a disqualification order made by the court; below, p.286.
[58] *POW Services Ltd v Clare* [1995] 2 B.C.L.C. 435; *Damoney v Godinho* [2004] 2 B.C.L.C. 15.
[59] See, *e.g.* Table A, reg.81.

the absence is involuntary, as where the director is ill and unable to travel.[60] On the other hand, if the director is absent because his doctor has advised that his health will be benefited by going abroad, the office will be vacated.[61]

On the happening of any of the events mentioned in the articles, the vacation of office is automatic and the board of directors has no power to waive the offence or condone the act.[62] Similarly, on the resignation of a director the office is automatically vacated, so that the resignation cannot be withdrawn without the consent of the company.[63]

In *Lee v Chou Wen Hsien*[64] the articles provided that a director should vacate his office if he was "requested in writing by all his co-directors to resign." The Privy Council held that a notice in the correct form validly removed the recipient from his directorship even if it was made with an ulterior motive. Any challenge had to be made on the basis that the other directors had acted in breach of their fiduciary duty which was in any event owed to the company and not to an individual director.[65] The clause was so drafted that the dismissal was automatic on the giving of the correct notice.

Removal of directors by the members

By s.303, a company may by ordinary resolution[66] remove a director before the expiration of his period of office, *notwithstanding* anything in the articles or in any agreement between him and the company. Special notice must be given of any resolution to remove a director or to appoint another person in place of a removed director at the meeting at which he is removed. On receipt of notice of an intended resolution to remove a director the company must send a copy to the director concerned, who is entitled to have his representations in writing of a reasonable length sent to the members of the company or read out at the meeting and also to be heard on the resolution at the meeting. The director may be deprived of the former right if the court is satisfied that it is being abused to secure needless publicity for defamatory matter.

It has been held that nothing in the Act prevents the articles giving a director's shares special voting rights, *e.g.* three votes per share on a poll, on a resolution to remove him.[67] On the other hand, it appears that the company cannot validly contract not to remove a director although the shareholders may do so as between themselves.[68]

Subsection (5) provides that nothing in s.303 deprives a removed director of any compensation[69] or damages payable to him in respect of the termination of

---

[60] *Mack's Claim* [1900] W.N. 114.
[61] *McConnell's Claim* [1901] 1 Ch. 728.
[62] *Re The Bodega Co. Ltd* [1904] 1 Ch. 276.
[63] *Glossop v Glossop* [1907] 2 Ch. 370; *OBC Caspian Ltd v Thorp*, 1998 S.L.T. 653 (O.H.). For the position where the "director" resigns prior to the formation of the company, see *POW Services Ltd v Clare* [1995] 2 B.C.L.C. 435.
[64] [1985] B.C.L.C. 45 PC.
[65] Below, p.299.
[66] This is a rare case where the Act *expressly* provides for an ordinary resolution. The written resolution procedure is not available for such a purpose: Sch.15A para.1.
[67] *Bushell v Faith* [1970] A.C. 1099.
[68] *Russell v Northern Bank Development Corp. Ltd* [1992] B.C.L.C. 1016.
[69] *e.g.* for unfair dismissal. See *Parsons v Parsons Ltd* [1978] I.C.R. 456.

his appointment as director or of any appointment, *e.g.* as managing director, terminating with that as director; and nothing in the section derogates from any power of removal which may exist apart from the section, *e.g.* a power of removal given by the articles of the company. For example, as will be explained later,[70] he will be entitled to damages if he has a contract of service, outside the articles, appointing him managing director for a specified period which has not yet expired, and his removal is inconsistent with such contract. Section 318, below,[71] enables members to inspect the service contract and thus ascertain how much it will cost to remove a director.

A director validly removed from office may, if he is a member, in appropriate circumstances be entitled to an order under s.459 where the affairs of the company have been conducted in an unfairly prejudicial manner,[72] or an order that the company be wound up by the court on the ground that winding up is just and equitable.[73]

PROCEEDINGS OF DIRECTORS

Table A, reg. 88, provides that subject to the articles, the directors may regulate their proceedings as they think fit.[74]

Regulation 88 further provides that a director may, and the secretary on the requisition of a director must, at any time summon a board meeting.

Every director is entitled to have reasonable notice of a meeting except that reg. 88, above, provides that notice need not be given to a director who is absent from the United Kingdom. What is reasonable notice depends on the practice of the company, but if a director wishes to complain of the shortness of the notice he should act promptly, otherwise the court will not interfere.[75]

If notice is not properly given, the proceedings at the meeting are void.

Application was invited for 106,000 shares, and the directors resolved not to allot until 14,000 shares were applied for. A subsequent meeting was held at which two directors, a quorum, were present, when a resolution was passed to allot the shares applied for, about 3,000. The meeting was held at a few hours' notice at 2 o'clock. This was much shorter notice than had ever been given before. One director did not receive notice until next day, and another gave notice that he could not attend until 3 o'clock. *Held*, the allotment was void: *Re Homer District Gold Mines* (1888) 39 Ch.D. 546.

A quorum is that number of directors which must be present to make the proceedings of the board valid. The articles usually fix a quorum. Table A, reg. 89, provides: "The quorum for the transaction of the business of the directors may be fixed by the directors and unless so fixed at any other number shall be two." If the number of directors sinks below the quorum, the directors cannot act unless the articles provide, as they usually do, that the continuing directors can act.

[70] p.283.
[71] p.285.
[72] Below, p.359.
[73] *Re Westbourne Galleries Ltd* [1973] A.C. 360, below, p.353.
[74] See *Hunter v Senate Support Services Ltd* [2004] EWHC Ch 1089 at para.127.
[75] See *Browne v La Trinidad* (1887) 37 Ch.D. 1, CA.

Table A, reg. 90, provides that if the number of directors is less than the number fixed as the quorum, the continuing directors or director may act only for the purpose of filling vacancies or of calling a general meeting.

In ascertaining whether a quorum is present, those directors who are incompentent to vote on the matter under discussion must not be counted.[76] Directors, however, can attend the meeting even if they are unable to vote.[77] One transaction cannot be split up into two resolutions so as to qualify directors to vote.

Y and D, two directors of a company, had made advances to the company in consideration of receiving debentures. The company had four directors, three of whom were a quorum. A resolution was passed granting a debenture to Y. Y did not vote on this resolution. Another resolution was then passed granting a debenture to D, on which D did not vote. The two debentures ranked equally among themselves. *Held*, the issue of the two debentures formed one transaction in which Y and D were equally interested and that the two resolutions were invalid for want of a quorum: *Re North Eastern Insurance Co. Ltd* [1919] 1 Ch.198.[78]

The articles deal with the election of a chairman. By Table A, reg. 91, the directors may elect a chairman of their meetings and determine the period for which he is to hold office.

Table A, reg. 93, provides that a resolution in writing, signed by all the directors entitled to receive notice of a meeting of the directors, shall be as valid as if it had been passed at a board meeting duly convened and held.[79] Similarly where the directors unanimously assent without either a formal or written resolution that will suffice.[80] But there must be unanimity so that the abstention of one or more of the directors will negate such a "resolution".[81] One problem which has arisen is where the company has two directors, one of whom is abroad and so not entitled to receive notices of a meeting under reg. 88, above, and the other signs a resolution under reg. 93. The quorum for a meeting is two (reg. 89). Is the written resolution valid? Despite the wording of reg. 93 it has been held in both England and Scotland[82] that the answer is no. Regulation 93 is not intended to oust the quorum requirements for a board meeting.

Section 382 provides that minutes of proceedings at directors' meetings must be entered in books kept for the purpose, and such minutes signed by the chairman of the meeting at which the proceedings were had, or by the chairman of the next succeeding meeting, are evidence of the proceedings.[83] Where

---

[76] *Re Greymouth Point Elizabeth Ry., etc. Co. Ltd* [1904] 1 Ch. 32. See also Table A, reg.89 as to alternate directors, and reg.95.

[77] *Grimwade v B.P.S. Syndicate Ltd* (1915) 31 T.L.R. 531.

[78] See also *Ireland Alloys Ltd v Buchanon* 1998 G.W.D. 13–365.

[79] Regulation 93 is subject to the regulations as a whole including reg.89 at to quorum: *Davidson & Begg Antiques Ltd v Davidson*, 1997 S.L.T. 301 (O.H.).

[80] *Re Bonelli's Telegraph Co.* (1871) L.R. 12 Eq. 246; *Runciman v Walter Runciman plc* [1992] B.C.L.C. 1084; *Hunter v Senate Support Services Ltd* [2004] EWHC Ch 1089

[81] *Municipal Mutual Insurance Ltd v Harrop* [1998] 2 B.C.L.C. 540.

[82] *Hood Sailmakers Ltd v Axford* [1997] 1 B.C.L.C. 721 and *Davidson & Begg Antiques Ltd v Davidson* [1997] S.L.T. 301 (O.H.), respectively.

[83] This is not conclusive evidence, however. Further it must be clear that the minutes were signed by the chairman and kept in the minute book: *POW Services Ltd v Clare* [1995] 2 B.C.L.C. 435.

minutes have been duly made there is a presumption that the relevant meeting was duly held and convened, that all proceedings were duly had and that all appointments of directors and managers were valid. Thus where the board duly authorises the chairman to sign the minutes of a previous invalid meeting or of one at which an invalid resolution has been "passed", the effect is to ratify the defect, *e.g.* where not all directors agreed to an informal resolution.[84]

By s.722 the minutes may be kept in a bound book, or in a loose-leaf book provided that adequate precautions are taken for guarding against falsification. Minutes may also be kept on a computer under s.723. If the minutes are incomplete, a resolution duly passed can be proved by other evidence.[85]

POWERS OF DIRECTORS

The powers of the directors depend on the articles since, apart from requiring that certain things, *e.g.* alterations to the articles (s.9) or the capital (ss 121, 135) or the delegating of authority to issue shares (s.80), must be done by the members in general meeting, the Act leaves the distribution of powers between the general meeting and the board to the articles, which in practice always give the directors extensive powers.

Table A provides:
Regulation 70: "Subject to the provisions of the Act, the memorandum and the articles and to any directions given by special resolution, the business of the company shall be managed by the directors who may exercise all the powers of the company. No alteration of the memorandum or articles and no such direction shall invalidate any prior act of the directors which would have been valid if that alteration had not been made or that direction had not been given. The powers given by this regulation shall not be limited by any special power given to the directors by the articles and a meeting of directors at which a quorum is present may exercise all powers exercisable by the directors."

If they act within the very wide powers of management given to them by such an article, directors are not bound to obey resolutions passed by the shareholders at a general meeting; such resolutions cannot override a decision of the directors or control the exercise of their powers in the future.[86] Only by altering the articles or passing a special resolution can the members interfere.

The articles of a company contained an article like the predecessor of Table A, reg. 70, except that it was stated to be "subject to such regulations as might be made by the company by extraordinary resolution." The majority of the shareholders arranged a sale of the company's undertaking and requisitioned a meeting at which an ordinary resolution requiring the directors to seal the contract was passed. *Held*, the directors were not bound to obey the resolution: *Automatic Self-Cleansing Filter Syndicate Co. Ltd v Cuninghame* [1906] 2 Ch.34, CA.

The articles contained an article like the predecessor of Table A, reg. 70, and also provided that no resolution of the directors to acquire or dispose of premises was to be

---

[84] *Municipal Mutual Insurance Ltd v Harrop* [1998] 2 B.C.L.C. 540.
[85] *Re Fireproof Doors Ltd* [1916] 2 Ch. 142.
[86] *Automatic Self-Cleansing Filter Syndicate Co. Ltd v Cuninghame* [1906] 2 Ch. 34, CA; *Salmon v Quin and Axtens Ltd* [1909] 1 Ch. 311, CA; [1909] A.C. 442; *Breckland Group Holdings Ltd v London and Suffolk Properties Ltd* [1989] B.C.L.C. 100; *Rose v McGivern* [1998] 2 B.C.L.C. 593; *cf. Marshall's Valve Gear Co. Ltd v Manning Wardle & Co. Ltd* [1909] 1 Ch. 267.

valid unless neither A nor B dissented. (A and B were the managing directors.) The directors resolved to acquire premises. B dissented. An ordinary resolution to the same effect as the board resolution was passed at an extraordinary general meeting of the company. *Held*, the ordinary resolution was inconsistent with the articles and the company was restrained from acting on it: *Salmon v Quin & Axtens Ltd* [1909] 1 Ch.311, CA; [1909] A.C. 442.

> "This Court decided not long since, in [the *Automatic Self-Cleansing* case], that even a resolution of a numerical majority at a general meeting of the company cannot impose its will upon the directors when the articles have confided to them the control of the company's affairs": *per* Farwell L.J. in [1909] 1 Ch.311 at p. 319, quoting Buckley L.J. in *Gramophone & Typewriter Ltd v Stanley* [1908] 2 K.B. 89, CA.

"Thus, as it seems to me, there is little doubt that the law is that, where matters are confided by articles such as article [70] to the conduct of the business by the directors, it is not a matter where the general meeting can intervene": *per* Harman J. in *Breckland Group Holdings Ltd v London & Suffolk Properties Ltd* [1989] B.C.L.C. 100 at p. 106.

In accordance with the principle set out above, a resolution passed by a company in general meeting that the directors should make an advance of money to the shareholders pending the declaration of a dividend was held to be inoperative.[87]

The powers thus granted to the directors under reg. 70 can only be effected by the board of directors, however, and not by an individual director acting without reference to the board.[88]

The powers of the board may also be regulated by a shareholders' agreement. In *Breckland Group Holdings Ltd v London and Suffolk Properties Ltd*,[89] the company had adopted reg. 70 of Table A and also had a shareholders' agreement that no litigation could be brought without the approval of a director appointed by each of the two shareholders. Harman J. decided that a combination of reg. 70 and the agreement precluded any interference by the general meeting in a decision whether to bring proceedings on behalf of the company.

There is a limited residual power in the general meeting if directors are unable to exercise one of their powers because of deadlock on the board or because their number has fallen below the number required for a quorum, the company in general meeting may exercise the power.[90]

The position is similar if a company has no directors.[91] Where a company has no directors and two individuals, acting without the authority of the company, commence an action in the company's name the company in general meeting or, if the company is being wound up, the liquidator can ratify the proceedings.[92]

On the other hand, if the directors exceed or improperly exercise their powers,[93] their action is voidable and so can be ratified by an ordinary resolution

---

[87] *Scott v Scott* [1943] 1 All E.R. 582.

[88] *Mitchell & Hobbs (UK) Ltd v Mill* [1996] 2 B.C.L.C. 102.

[89] Above.

[90] *Barron v Potter* [1914] 1 Ch. 895, where the articles gave the board of directors power to appoint an additional director and, owing to differences between the directors, no board meeting could be held for the purpose. *Held*, the company retained power to appoint additional directors in general meeting. See also *Foster v Foster* [1916] 1 Ch. 532.

[91] *per* Lord Hailsham of St. Marylebone in *Alexander Ward & Co. Ltd v Samyang Navigation Co. Ltd*, 1975 S.C. (H.L.) 26 at p.47.

[92] *Alexander Ward* case, above.

[93] As to improper exercises see p.299, below.

of the company in general meeting.[94] If they act contrary to the company's articles or memorandum it must be ratified by a special resolution.[95]

By way of defence to a take-over bid directors allotted 500,000 shares at par for cash to a third company which was the principal distributor of the products of the company to be taken over. The articles provided that the unissued shares were to be at the directors' disposal. Two shareholders brought an action against the three directors, the third company, and the company, claiming a declaration that the allotment was invalid in that the directors had not acted bona fide in the interests of the company. *Held*, assuming that the allotment was *intra vires* the company and the directors but not bona fide in the interests of the company and therefore voidable, it could after full disclosure be ratified by an ordinary resolution at a general meeting: *Bamford v Bamford* [1970] Ch.212, CA.

If the directors fail to take into account a material consideration, the exercise of the power is similarly voidable, although it is not clear whether to decide whether it should be set aside if they might or only if they would have decided differently.[96]

Power to manage the business of the company does not as such give directors power to fix their own remuneration.[97] The articles, however, usually empower them, or a committee of the board, to do so.[98]

The directors cannot delegate their powers unless empowered to do so by the articles. It will be seen later[99] that the articles usually provide for delegation to a managing director. They may also provide for delegation to a committee of directors.[1] However, such a delegation must be validly authorised by the articles or such a committee will have no authority to enter into the transaction. In *Guinness plc v Saunders*,[2] a committee of the directors set up to conduct a take-over bid had no authority under the articles to authorise special payments to the directors involved. Such payments could only be authorised by the full board. It followed that the payments were unauthorised, and therefore reclaimable from the directors concerned.

REMUNERATION OF DIRECTORS

Where the director does not have a service contract

Directors as such are not employees of the company, but managers or controllers of the company's affairs and, in that capacity, are regarded as fiduciaries.[3] Accordingly, like trustees, they have no claim to payment for their services unless, as is usual, there is a provision for payment in the articles.[4]

---

[94] *Grant v United Kingdom Switchback Rlwys. Co.* (1888) 40 Ch.D. 135, CA; *Hugg v Cromphorn* [1967] Ch. 245.
[95] ss 35, 35A; see Chs 3 and 6.
[96] *Hunter v Senate Support Services Ltd* [2000] EWHC Ch. 1089.
[97] *Foster v Foster* [1916] 1 Ch. 532.
[98] See below.
[99] p.292.
[1] See Table A, reg.72.
[2] [1990] 2 A.C. 663, HL.
[3] Below, p.299.
[4] *per* McCardie J. in *Moriarty v Regent's Garage Co. Ltd* [1921] 1 K.B. 423, at p.446; *cf.* Lord President Inglis in *M'Naughtan v Brunton* (1882) 10 R. 111 at p.113. See Ch. 18, below.

If there is no authorisation, either in the articles or elsewhere, for payment a director cannot make a claim for payment by way of quantum meruit or in equity for special work performed. Thus in *Guinness plc v Saunders*, above, the House of Lords refused such a claim by a director who had successfully negotiated a take over bid for the company but whose remuneration was not properly authorised either by the directors or the company.[5]

Table A provides:
Regulation 82: "The directors shall be entitled to such remuneration as the company may by ordinary resolution determine and, unless the resolution provides otherwise, the remuneration shall be deemed to accrue from day to day."
Regulation 83: "The directors may be paid all travelling, hotel and other expenses properly incurred by them in connection with their attendance at meetings of directors or committees of directors or general meetings or separate metings of the holders of any class of shares or of debentures of the company or otherwise in connection with the discharge of their duties."

If remuneration is voted to the directors, it constitutes a debt due from the company and is consequently payable not only out of profits but also out of capital.[6]

A director who is entitled to remuneration for his services is not entitled to his travelling and other expenses in attending board and other meetings unless the articles expressly so provide.[7]

Unless authorised by the articles, directors cannot vote remuneration to one of themselves or appoint one of their number to a salaried position with the company. It has been said that "Directors have no right to be paid for their services, and cannot pay themselves or each other, or make presents to themselves out of the company's assets, unless authorised so to do by the instrument which regulates the company or by the shareholders at a properly convened meeting."[8]

The article governing directors' remuneration was the same as the predecessor of reg. 82.[9] The *directors* passed a resolution appointing K, one of the directors, "overseas director" at a salary of £1,800 a year. In pursuance of this appointment K was obliged to go, and did go, to Australia. He sued for arrears of salary. *Held*, the appointment was *ultra vires* the board, so that K could not recover the arrears of salary and was liable to refund salary already received: *Kerr v Marine Products Ltd* (1928) 44 T.L.R. 292.

On the other hand, where the articles do allow a director's fees to be fixed by the board, or a committee of the board, the board (or committee) must act bona fide in the interests of the company in fixing the remuneration. In breach the authorisation for the payment will be invalid.[10] Provided all the board or committee acquiesce in the payments being authorised then no formal meeting

---

[5] See also *Zemco Ltd v Jerrom-Pugh* [1993] B.C.C. 275.
[6] *Re Lundy Granite Co.* (1872) 26 L.T. 673.
[7] *Young v Naval and Military Society* [1905] 1 K.B. 687.
[8] *per* Lindley L.J. in *Re George Newman & Co.* [1895] 1 Ch. 674, CA at p.686.
[9] *See above.*
[10] *Zemco Ltd v Jerrom-Pugh* [1993] B.C.C. 275.

need be held.[11] The court will not interfere with the amount payable unless it is a sham.[12] The position is, however, different on an insolvency.[13]

A resolution of the directors to forgo fees to which they are entitled is binding on them and on the company if the company is a party to the agreement.[14] Otherwise the directors may rescind the resolution and claim for fees.[15]

When a director ceases to be a director during a year of office, a question arises as to whether he is entitled to have his remuneration apportioned. If, *e.g.* the articles say that he is to be paid "at the rate of" so much a year, he is entitled to be paid for the period during which he was a director.[16] On the other hand, if he is to be paid £10,000 a year, or in a way other than at the rate of so much a year, it has been held that he is entitled to be paid only for each complete year he serves, and not for any broken period.[17]

Directors' Service Contracts—Executive Pay

In addition to being a director a person may be appointed to a post within the company, such as the managing or finance director, in which case he will be given a service contract as an employee of the company. Such persons are often referred to as the executive directors as opposed to the non-executive directors. It is usual for the articles to provide that the terms of such contracts be fixed by the board or a committee of the board, and they must act bona fide in the interests of the company in exercising this power.[18] Similar rules apply to the variation or renewal of such contracts.[19] It appears that since the director concerned has an obvious interest in such a contract he must still disclose that interest under s.317, although, in the absence of any impropriety, the consequences of not doing so are unlikely to be severe.[20]

Where a director has been paid fees out of the company without proper authorisation he cannot claim a set-off against money owed to him under a service contract. He must repay the money improperly paid, since he is a constructive trustee of it, and sue under his contract for damages.[21]

The level of executive directors' pay and severance benefits has been the subject of some controversy in recent times and is one of the central issues in the corporate governance debate highlighted in Chapter 18. It will be seen there that for the larger companies for which this is an issue, the solution is to rely on the

---

[11] *Runciman v Walter Runciman plc* [1992] B.C.L.C. 1084. The position is different if the board is unaware of the payments as in *Guinness plc v Saunders* [1990] 2 A.C. 663, HL.
[12] *Re Halt Garage (1964) Ltd* [1982] 3 All ER 1016; *Currencies Direct Ltd v Ellis* [2002] 2 B.C.L.C. 482.
[13] See below.
[14] *West Yorkshire Darracq Agency Ltd v Coleridge* [1911] 2 K.B. 326.
[15] *Re Consolidated Nickel Mines Ltd* [1914] 1 Ch. 883.
[16] *Swabey v Port Darwin Gold Mining Co.* (1889) 1 Meg. 385, although despite the report, the articles did not contain the words "at the rate of," as pointed out in *Inman's* case, below.
[17] *Salton v New Beeston Cycle Co.* [1899] 1 Ch. 775; *Inman v Ackroyd & Best Ltd* [1901] 1 Q.B. 613, CA, followed in *Liquidator of the Fife Linoleum etc. Co. Ltd v Lornie* (1905) 13 S.L.T. 670 (O.H.).
[18] The contract will not be binding on the company if it has been issued otherwise than as required by the articles: *UK Safety Group Ltd v Heane* [1998] 2 B.C.L.C. 208.
[19] *Runciman v Walter Runciman plc* [1992] B.C.L.C. 1084.
[20] See below, p.273.
[21] *Zemco Ltd v Jerrom-Pugh* [1993] B.C.C. 275.

non-executive directors to modify pay and severance levels. The Government has fought shy of imposing any legal limits on pay or benefits, but as a result of a consultation exercise in 1999 and 2001,[22] it introduced a disclosure measure, the Directors Remuneration Report.[23] In 2003, it also introduced a further consultation exercise covering the contracts, performance and severance pay of directors, under the leading title "Rewards for Failure".[24] The resulting responses again showed little inclination for legislation, although they pointed to some success with the Remuneration Report, preferring to rely on best practice under the corporate governance codes as set out in Chapter 18.

The Act imposes some controls on directors' service contracts. Section 318 provides that, subject as below, every company must keep a copy of each director's contract of service[25] or of any variation thereof, or a memorandum thereof setting out its terms if it is not in writing, at one place. This obligation extends to the directors of its subsidiary companies, if any. The place may be:

(1) the company's registered office; or

(2) the other place where the register of members is kept; or

(3) its principal place of business in England, if the company is registered in England, or in Scotland if the company is registered in Scotland.

Notice of such place and of any changes in it must be given to the Registrar except where the documents have always been kept at the registered office.

Contracts requiring a director to work wholly or mainly outside the United Kingdom are excluded although a memorandum of the duration of the contract, and, if appropriate, the name and place of the subsidiary company, must be kept. Also excluded are those where the unexpired term of the contract is less then 12 months or the contract can be terminated by the company without payment of compensation within 12 months.

There are default fines[26] for contravention of s.318 and the court is empowered to order an inspection.

To prevent possible abuse by directors granting themselves long-term service contracts in order to obtain large compensation payments in the event of a dismissal, s.319 seeks to limit the length of such contracts without the approval of a general meeting at which a copy of the proposed contract is available, and where such a copy has been available for inspection at the registered office for the previous 15 days.[27] Any term in such a contract which entitles a director[28] to employment with the company for longer than five years must be approved by the company in general meeting.

Any term in breach of this section is void and replaced by one which enables the company to terminate the contract at any time, subject to reasonable notice.

---

[22] URN 01/1400
[23] See p.287, below.
[24] URN 03/652.
[25] This applies also to shadow directors.
[26] Sch.24.
[27] Such a resolution may be passed using the written resolution procedure provided the agreement, etc., is supplied to each relevant member prior to his signature: Sch.15A, para.7.
[28] This includes a shadow director.

This requirement cannot be avoided by negotiating several consecutive five year agreements, since no second contract may succeed the first if that contract has more than six months left to run. It is not difficult to avoid the impact of s.319. However, one way is for contracts to be five year "rolling" contracts, *i.e.* which at any time have five years to run. Various proposals for reform have been made, the current consensus being that five years is too long.[29]

Directors Remuneration Report

Companies must disclose specified aggregate amounts paid to the directors in their accounts under s.232 and Sch.6. In addition, as a result of public disquiet over the levels of executive pay and severance benefits, often associated with an under-performing company, the Government introduced the Directors Remuneration Report Regulations in 2002.[30] Quoted companies must publish a report on their directors' remuneration. In particular, the report must set out details of each director's remuneration package, the company's remuneration policy and the role of the remuneration committee, the board and the members in the remuneration process. A further interesting item is that where, as is usual, there is a performance-linked package, the company must produce at least one performance graph comparing the company's performance over the previous five years with that of its comparator(s) or an index.[31]

Whilst this report must be submitted to the general meeting for approval by an ordinary resolution,[32] the vote is only on the report as a whole and even then is only advisory in the sense that the board need not act upon a rejection. In practice, such an adverse vote is unlikely since the board will wish to avoid such an embarrassing situation. But there is some evidence that the report's existence is concentrating the minds of both boards and shareholders and their have been some notable no votes and abstentions.

Compensation for loss of office

It is unlawful for a company to make to a director any payment by way of compensation for loss of office, or as consideration for or in connection with retirement, unless particulars of the proposed payment, including the amount, are disclosed to the members and the proposal is approved by the company: s.312. It was held in *Re Duomatic Ltd*[33] that disclosure must be made to *all* members, even those with no right to attend and vote at general meetings, whilst the payment is still a proposed payment, although in *Wallersteiner v Moir*[34] Lord Denning M.R. said that he imagined that payment could be later approved by the company in general meeting. The section does not apply, however, to compensa-

---

[29] The Law Commission originally suggested three years. The Company Law Review suggested three years on appointment and one year thereafter, with the meeting able to extend this to five years. *Final Report*, vol 1, paras.6.12–6.14.

[30] SI 2002/1986. This issue is also part of the corporate governance debate discussed in Ch. 18.

[31] S. 234B and Sch 7A.

[32] S. 241A.

[33] [1969] 2 Ch. 365.

[34] [1974] 1 W.L.R. 991, CA at p.1016.

tion for breach of a service contract or other payments which the company is contractually bound to make.[35] As a result the section has little effect. It was also said that the section does not apply, even to gratuity payments, in relation to a position other then as a director.[36]

It is unlawful for anyone to make to a director a payment by way of compensation for loss of office, etc., in connection with the transfer of the whole or part of the company's undertaking or property unless particulars are disclosed and approved. If such a payment is not disclosed the director holds it upon trust for the company: s.313.

When, in connection with a transfer of all or any of the shares in the company resulting from (a) an offer made to the general body of shareholders, (b) an offer made with a view to the company becoming the subsidiary of another, (c) an offer made with a view to an individual obtaining control of not less than one-third of the voting power at a general meeting, or (d) any other offer conditional on acceptance to a given extent, a payment is to be made to a director as compensation for loss of or retirement from office, he must take reasonable steps to see that particulars of the proposed payment, including the amount, are sent with any notice of the offer for their shares given to the shareholders. If this is not done, or the payment is not, before the transfer of the shares, approved by a meeting of the shareholders summoned for the purpose, the director holds the payment on trust for the persons who have sold their shares as a result of the offer: ss 314 and 315.

Sections 313, 314 and 315 cannot be avoided, *e.g.* by paying more than the market value for a director's shares, because s.316 provides that, in connection with ss 313 and 315, the price paid to a director for any of his shares in the company in excess of the price which could have been obtained by other shareholders, or the money value of any valuable consideration given to him, is deemed to have been a payment to him of compensation for loss of office. References in ss 313 to 315 to payments of compensation for loss of office exclude bona fide payments of damages for breach of contract or of pensions in respect of past services. But these provisions have been held not to protect an *ex gratia* payment in lieu of pension made on the eve of liquidation in the case of a company whose directors had no power to make such payments.[37]

SUBSTANTIAL PROPERTY TRANSACTIONS INVOLVING DIRECTORS

Section 320 was introduced to provide a check on dealings between a company and its directors. It provides that no arrangement may be made without the approval of the general meeting between a director[38-39] and his company

---

[35] *Taupo Totara Timber Co. Ltd v Rowe* [1978] A.C. 537 PC; *Lander v Premier Pict Petroleum Ltd*, 1997 S.L.T 1361 (O.H.); [1998] B.C.C. 248; *Mercer v Heart of Midlothian plc* 2002 S.L.T. 945, O.H.
[36] But these will have to be disclosed in the Director's Remuneration Report.
[37] *Gibson's Executor v Gibson*, 1978 S.C. 197 (O.H.).
[38-39] Including a shadow director.

involving the transfer, either way,[40] of a non-cash asset,[41] if its value exceeds £100,000 or 10 per cent of the company's net assets, provided it is not less than £2,000.[42] Where the asset has a special value to the director that can be used instead of the market value.[43] The section applies equally to dealings between a company and one of its shadow directors[44] and between a company and a person connected with one of its directors.[45] If the arrangement is with a director of the company's holding company, that company must also approve it by an ordinary resolution.

The purpose of the section has been said to be:

> "The thinking behind that section is that if the directors enter into a substantial commercial transaction with one of their number, there is a danger that their judgment may be distorted by conflicts of interest and loyalties, even in cases where there is no actual dishonesty. The section is designed to protect a company against such distortions. It enables members to provide a check. Of course that does not necessarily mean that the members will exercise a better commercial judgment; but it does make it likely that the matter will be more widely ventilated and a more objective decision reached."[46]

The mischief aimed at by the section is the acquisition of an asset by the company at an inflated price or a disposal at an undervalue. Thus it has been said[47] that the necessary approval of the arrangement, although not requiring approval of every last detail, must cover the central aspects of the arrangement, e.g. the price involved, or at least a minimum price or a yardstick by reference to which the price is to be fixed. Further what has been approved must actually be what happens in practice. Section 322 provides that any arrangement in breach of s.320 is voidable by the company unless restitution of the status quo is impossible.[48] If the company cannot avoid the transaction or chooses not to do so, the director concerned,[49] and any director who authorised the transaction, are

---

[40] Thus applying both to sales to the company by a director, e.g. Pavlides v Jensen [1956] Ch. 565; and sales to a director by the company, e.g. Daniels v Daniels [1978] Ch. 406. But a disposal to a corporate body, as opposed to one which is to a person connected only with the directors, would not be caught by s.320: see Clydebank Football Club v Steadman 2002 S.L.T. 109, O.H.

[41] As defined in s.739. This can include the benefit of a contract or a beneficial interest in property: Re Duckwari plc (No. 1) [1997] 2 B.C.L.C. 713 CA. It does not, however, include the right of a director to compensation in cash for termination of his service contract. That was not an asset since it could not be assigned and in any event it was a right to cash: Lander v Premier Pict Petroleum Ltd [1998] B.C.C. 248.

[42] The burden of proof is on those alleging that the monetary limits have been exceeded: Receivers of Niltan Carlton Ltd v Hawthorne [1998] 2 B.C.L.C. 298. The time for valuing the asset is the time of the agreement: Lander v Premier Pict Petroleum Ltd [1998] B.C.C. 248.

[43] Micro Leisure Ltd v County Properties and Developments Ltd [2000] B.C.C. 872 (Ct. Sess.); 1999 S.L.T. 1428 O.H.

[44] s.320(3).

[45] These are defined in s.346. They include a director's minor children, spouse, partners and any company in which the director and his associates control 20 per cent of the equity share capital.

[46] per Carnwath J. in British Racing Drivers' Club Ltd v Hextall Erskine & Co. [1997] 1 B.C.L.C. 182, 198. For those reasons failure by a firm of solicitors to advise the directors of the need to comply with the section with consequent loss to the company was held to be negligence giving rise to liability for such losses.

[47] Demite Ltd v Protec Health Ltd [1998] B.C.C. 638 at p.649 per Park J.

[48] Mere passage of time does not affect the right to avoid the transaction: Demite Ltd v Protec Health Ltd [1998] B.C.C. 638.

[49] Including shadow directors and persons connected with the director. If the agreement is between a company and a connected person then the director will not have to account if he took all reasonable steps to ensure compliance s.322(5).

liable to account for any gains and/or indemnify the company against any loss. A connected person and any director who authorised the transaction will not be liable if they can show that they did not know the relevant facts which constituted the breach.[50]

If the company avoids the transaction such loss is limited to the expenses of the transaction plus interest and any expenses of maintaining the asset. In other cases, however, the loss would include not only the difference between the market value of the asset at the date of the transaction and the price paid or received by the company, but also any subsequent loss of value after the date of the transaction, *e.g.* due to a subsequent fall in the value of the asset, together with maintenance expenses and interest on the total amount. This is because the liability of those in breach of the section is regarded as a liability for breach of a fiduciary obligation and not for damages for breach of contract.[51]

O Ltd agreed to purchase some land for £495,000 and paid a deposit of £49,500 to stakeholders. O Ltd then made an agreement with D Ltd whereby the property was actually conveyed to D Ltd, D Ltd paying £49,500 to O Ltd. C was a director of D Ltd and a 20 per cent shareholder in O Ltd. D Ltd completed the purchase, partly by raising a loan at a substantial rate of interest. Subsequently the value of the land fell. D Ltd spent £24,000 on obtaining planning permission but even then only sold the land for £178,000. D Ltd claimed that the transaction was in breach of s.320 and that O Ltd was liable to indemnify D Ltd against the loss arising on the sale, the costs of obtaining the planning permission, the costs of financing the bank loan, the costs of maintaining the land and interest on the whole amount. It was held that s.320 applied because: (i) this was the transfer of a non-cash asset (the right under the contract of purchase or the beneficial ownership of the land); (ii) it was between a company, D Ltd, and a person connected with one of its directors, O Ltd, (C owned 20 per cent of O Ltd); and (iii) the value of the asset, £49,500, was more than 10 per cent of the net assets of D Ltd. Having sold the land, D Ltd could not, however, avoid the transaction. Although there was no evidence that the price paid by D Ltd was more than the market value at the time, it was held to be entitled to recover the loss caused by the subsequent fall in value of the property, the costs of the planning permission and the maintenance costs, together with interest on the whole amount. All those liabilities flowed from the transaction itself. The planning permission costs had in fact increased the resale price and so reduced the overall loss on the sale. But D Ltd could not recover the costs of the bank loan because those did not flow from the transaction itself. There was no liability for the means by which the requisition was made. *Re Duckwari plc (No. 1)* [1997] 2 B.C.L.C. 713, CA; *Re Duckwari plc (No. 2)* [1998] 2 B.C.L.C. 315, CA; *Re Duckwari plc (No. 3)* [1999] 1 B.C.L.C. 168, CA.

The section does not apply if the director concerned received the assets solely by virtue of being a member (*e.g.* on a general reduction of capital), or the transaction was entered into by the liquidator during the course of the compulsory winding up of an insolvent company. However, in *Demite Ltd v Protec Health Ltd*,[52] it was held, somewhat unrealistically, that there was no implied exception for a sale by a receiver acting as the company's agent,[53] so that the prior approval of the transaction by the general meeting was required. Most transactions within a group of companies are also excluded, as are transactions

---

[50] S. 322(6).
[51] *Re Duckwari plc (No. 2)* [1998] 2 B.C.L.C. 315, CA.
[52] [1998] B.C.C. 638.
[53] For alternative ways around this see [1998] B.C.C. 638 at p.647.

on a recognised investment exchange made through an independent broker by a director of a group which includes the market maker concerned and transactions whereby a person requires an asset from the company in his capacity as a member of that company:[54] s.321.

Disclosure of such arrangements in the accounts is required by s.232.[55]

LOANS TO DIRECTORS

Section 330 prohibits various categories of loans and other credit transactions between a company and its directors, "shadow directors" and "persons connected with its directors." A subsidiary is equally restrained as regards its holding company.[56] Sometimes there is a dispute as to whether the payment was a loan or an advance on remuneration.[57]

All companies are prohibited from making loans to, giving guarantees for and security for loans to, their directors or "shadow directors." The strength of this provision appears, however, to be somewhat weakened by the decision of Walton J. in *Champagne Perrier-Jouet S.A. v H. H. Finch Ltd*,[58] that where a company paid a great many bills for one of its directors it had not made a loan to that director. "Money paid to B at the request of A is quite definitely not a loan."[59] This would seem to be an obvious loophole in the general embargo on loans.

In addition, however, public companies, and companies forming part of a group which includes a public company, may not make loans, give guarantees or securities to persons connected with such directors. Further, public companies may not make "quasi-loans" to their directors, etc., nor may they provide credit facilities for such persons. A "quasi-loan" is defined (s.331(3)) to include the provision of credit card facilities, *e.g.* where the company is the cardholder and the card is used by the director. A credit transaction is one where goods or services are provided on the undertaking that payment will be made later.

These prohibitions cannot be avoided by directors assigning their liabilities to their company or by "back to back" deals, *i.e.* where two companies each make what appear to be separate provisions for each other's directors.

Sections 332 to 338 provide certain exceptions to the prohibitions of s.330. The effect is to allow all loans up to a total of £5,000 outstanding for each director; to allow all credit transactions, if they are on normal commercial terms; to provide an exemption for loans to cover expenses incurred by a director for company purposes, provided the transaction has the prior approval of the general meeting[60] or is ratified within six months, subject to a maximum of £20,000 for directors of public companies; to allow quasi-loans up to £5,000 outstanding at

---

[54] But not an acquisition by the company from a director/member.

[55] It is possible that a director may be excused from liability under s.727, below p.280, but not if he has a personal interest in the transaction and benefits from it: *Re Duckwari plc (No. 2)* [1998] 2 B.C.L.C. 315, CA.

[56] This includes a wholly-owned subsidiary, unlike s.320 above.

[57] *Currencies Direct Ltd v Ellis* [2002] 2 B.C.L.C. 482.

[58] [1982] 1 W.L.R. 1359.

[59] *ibid.*, p.1364.

[60] The various amounts and purposes must be disclosed at the relevant meeting: s.337. If the written resolution procedure is used such disclosures must be made to each relevant member before he signs the resolution: Sch.15A.

any one time if the terms require repayment within two months; to allow loans for defending any criminal or civil proceedings conditional on repayment if the director is convicted or judgement is given against him; and to allow credit transactions up to £10,000 outstanding at any one time per director.

In addition moneylending companies[61] may make loans and quasi-loans to directors on normal commercial terms but, banking companies excepted, the amount outstanding must not exceed £100,000. Directors of such companies may also be allowed to participate in subsidised house purchase schemes up to a limit of £100,000.

The various sums used in ss 334 to 338, *i.e.* £5,000, £10,000, £20,000 and £100,000, are sums outstanding at any time and are calculated in accordance with s.339.

Section 341 provides civil consequences for a breach of s.330 which are virtually the same as those for a breach of s.320 (substantial property trans-actions), above.[62] In *Re Ciro Citterio Menswear plc*,[63] it was held that a director acting in breach of s.336 does not thereby become a constructive trustee of the money. It could not therefore be followed into property bought with the money. The only liability is to account. This decision was based on the premise that the loan was voidable, which is contrary to the idea of constructive trusteeship. However, this is difficult to reconcile with the decision of the Court of Appeal in *Re Duckwari plc (No. 2)*[64] on s.320, which imposed full liability as on a misappropriation of assets by a director. Where a loan in breach of s.330 is thus voidable under s.341 by the company, it has been held that a demand for repayment of a loan which on its terms is not due for repayment amounts to an avoidance.[65] In addition, s.342 provides for a series of criminal offences for public companies and their directors who know or have reasonable cause to believe that s.330 has been breached.

Sections 232 to 237 require particulars of all loans, etc., whether prohibited or not, to be disclosed in the accounts unless they are less than £2,000 in total. This includes disclosure of the principal terms of the transaction and the true beneficiary. Banking companies are subject to special rules. Auditors must disclose any breach of the disclosure requirements in their report.

MANAGING DIRECTOR

Unless the directors are empowered to appoint a managing director[66] by the articles, the directors cannot appoint a managing director.[67] When the articles empower the directors to appoint a managing director, the company in general

---

[61] s.338(2).
[62] s.338(4).
[63] [2001] 1 B.C.C.C. 672.
[64] [1998] 2 B.C.C.C. 315.
[65] *Tait Consibee (Oxford) Ltd v Tait* [1997] 2 B.C.L.C. 349, CA.
[66] For discussion of the general nature of the post of managing director, see *Anderson v James Sutherland (Peterhead) Ltd*, 1941 S.C. 203, also *Hindle v John Cotton Ltd* (1919) 56 S.L.R. 625, (H.L.) (managing director held to be an "employee" within the meaning of the articles) and opinions in *Kerr v Walker*, 1933 S.C. 458.
[67] *per* Swinfen Eady J. in *Boschoek Proprietary Co. Ltd v Fuke* [1906] 1 Ch. 148 at p.159.

meeting cannot itself make such an appointment without first altering the articles.[68]

Table A, reg. 84, provides that the directors may appoint *one or more of their number* to the office of managing director for such period and on such terms as they think fit, and, *subject to the terms of any contract of service*, may revoke such appointment; that a director so appointed shall not, whilst holding that office, retire by rotation, but that the appointment shall be automatically determined if he ceases to be a director.

Subject to the articles, the powers and duties of a managing director depend upon his contract of service with the company.

C was appointed a managing director of H Co. His service agreement provided that he should perform the duties and exercise the powers in relation to the business of H Co. and the businesses of its existing subsidiary companies which might from time to time be assigned to or vested in him by the directors. Later the directors resolved that C should confine his attention to a particular subsidiary company. C sued for damages for breach of contract. C's action was dismissed: *Caddies v Harold Holdsworth & Co. (Wakefield) Ltd*, 1955 S.C. (H.L.) 27; [1955] 1 All E.R. 725 HL.

The board may delegate any of their very extensive collective powers of management to the managing director.[69] On the other hand, without such delegation the implied authority of a managing director is not limitless. He has no such implied power to act contrary to the articles and resolutions of the company and/or the board,[70] or to bring proceedings in the company's name,[71] or to use the company's money to bribe someone for the benefit of the company.[72]

Where directors have a discretionary power to dismiss a managing director, this power must be exercised in good faith in the interests of the company and not for some ulterior purpose such as appropriation of the managing director's shares.[73]

If, where the appointment of a managing director is in fact void, he performs services which are accepted by the company, it has been held that he is entitled to reasonable remuneration.

The articles authorised the directors to appoint one of their number managing director. By contract under the company's seal, C was appointed managing director at a salary. The seal was affixed to the contract by a resolution of the board of directors but none of the directors had acquired his qualification shares. C himself acted as managing director, but also failed to acquire his qualification shares. *Held*, C's contract was void and C was not properly appointed managing director. His claim for remuneration in contract failed but the alternative claim in quasi-contract succeeded, *i.e.* he was entitled to payment on a *quantum meruit* basis arising from the performance of his services and their acceptance by the company: *Craven-Ellis v Canons Ltd* [1936] 2 K.B. 403 (C.A.).[74]

---

[68] *Thomas Logan Ltd v Davis* (1911) 104 L.T. 914; 105 L.T. 419.
[69] Table A, reg.72.
[70] *Guinness plc v Saunders* [1990] 2 A.C. 663, HL.
[71] *Mitchell & Hobbs (UK) Ltd v Mill* [1996] 2 B.C.L.C. 102.
[72] *E. Hannibal & Co. Ltd v Frost* (1988) 4 B.C.C. 3.
[73] *John Cotton Ltd* (1919) 56 S.L.R. 625, HL.
[74] In *Guinness plc v Saunders* [1990] 2 A.C. 663 the House of Lords refused a *quantum meruit* claim by a director, but in rather different circumstances, where there was no doubt as to the lack of validity of the appointment.

POSITION OF DIRECTORS

As a company has no physical but only a legal existence, the management of its affairs, as we have seen, is entrusted to the directors whose exact position in relation to the company is, however, has proved rather hard to define.[75] Directors as such are not employees of the company,[76] but are rather managers who may be said to be (1) fiduciaries, and (2) agents for the company. The result is that they owe fiduciary duties and duties of care to the company, as will be explained later.

"The Directors are a body to whom is delegated the duty of managing the general affairs of the Company. A corporate body can only act by agents, and it is of course the duty of those agents so to act as best to promote the interests of the corporation whose affairs they are conducting. Such agents have duties to discharge of a fiduciary nature towards their principal. And it is a rule of universal application that no one, having such duties to discharge, shall be allowed to enter into engagements in which he has, or can have, a personal interest conflicting, or which possibly may conflict, with the interests of those whom he is bound to protect": *per* Lord Cranworth L.C. in *Aberdeen Rlwy. Co. v Blaikie Bros.* (1854) 1 Macq. 461 at p. 471.

Directors as trustees/fiduciaries

Even though the company is clearly the legal owner, directors have long been regarded as the equivalent of trustees of the company's property and money under their control[77] and as being in a fiduciary position in relation to the exercise of their powers of management of the company.[78]

Thus in their dealings with the company's assets, etc., the directors will be liable for breach of trust if they misapply them, giving rise to an action against them for damages or equitable compensation for any loss caused to the company or, even if there is no loss, to account for any gain they may have made as a result of the breach.[79] Similarly, such liability to compensate or to account will attach to the directors if they act in breach of any of their fiduciary duties in the exercise of their powers of management. In certain cases the company may also recover its property (or its loss) from third parties who have either received the property or assisted in the breach.[80]

Where a person has improperly profited from his fiduciary position the court has equitable jurisdiction to award interest on the judgment for damages for misfeasance or breach of duty as a director.[81]

---

[75] *Quaere* whether there is any contract between a company and its directors arising out of the appointment alone: *Newtherapeutics Ltd v Katz* [1990] B.C.L.C. 700.

[76] See *e.g. Buchan v Secretary of State for Employment* [1997] B.C.C. 145.

[77] See *e.g. per* Lord Selborne L.C. in *Great Eastern Rlwy. Co. v Turner* (1872) L.R. 8 Ch. 149 at p.152. Sometimes they are referred to as constructive trustees but more properly they are treated as being equivalent to a trustee: *JJ Harrison (Properties) Ltd v Harrison* [2002] 1 B.C.L.C. 174.

[78] See below.

[79] *Selangor United Rubber Estates Ltd v Cradock (No. 3)* [1968] 1 W.L.R. 1555, below p.295; *Bishopsgate Investment Management v Maxwell (No. 1)* [1993] B.C.L.C. 1282; *Gwembe Valley Development Co Ltd v Koshy (No. 3)* [2004] 1 B.C.L.C. 131.

[80] See below.

[81] *Wallersteiner v Moir (No. 2)* [1975] Q.B. 373, CA, where the interest awarded was compound interest at one per cent per annum above the official bank rate or minimum lending rate in operation at the time.

Because directors are regarded as being trustees, or as having trustee-like responsibilities, it has now been accepted that actions against them for breach of fiduciary duty are subject to s.21 of the Limitation Act 1980. That requires any action by a beneficiary to recover trust property or in respect of any trust to be brought within six years, after which it is said to be time barred. There is no such limitation, however, if either the action is in respect of fraud or for a fraudulent breach of trust,[82] or to recover trust property or its proceeds from the trustee or property previously received by the trustee and converted to his own use.[83]

The fiduciary position of a director means that they must not put themselves in a position where their duties of good faith and their personal interest may conflict. Thus they are not entitled to any remuneration from the company or to make any profit out of a corporate transaction without authorisation. Further they are under a duty to disclose all material circumstances to the company when contracting with the company or where they have an interest in a corporate transaction.[84]

The extent of the directors' fiduciary position is constantly being explored in the courts.[85] The Court of Appeal has held that there is no rule that directors cannot bind themselves as to the future exercise of their powers in a particular manner if the contract as a whole is substantially for the benefit of the company, e.g. where money is paid to a company by a developer and the directors agree to support the latter's application for planning permission,[86] despite strong earlier decisions that in such cases the directors' duty to the company must override any such agreement where the two subsequently became irreconcilable.[87] Again in *Elliot v Wheeldon*,[88] it was held that it was at least arguable that where there was a joint venture agreement between two people operating through the medium of a company of which they both became directors, and one director continued his pre-existing personal guarantee of that company's debts, the other director owed a duty to his fellow director not to act as a director so as to increase the latter's liability under the guarantee. The questions as to whether a director can owe fiduciary duties to a shareholder as distinct from the company and who exactly is the company for this purpose are dealt with below.[89]

It has now been widely accepted, however, that directors' duties should be codified so that the current equitable flexibility will be replaced by a definitive list. This point is dealt with below.[90]

Third party liability

Since directors are, equivalent to trustees of the company's assets it follows that if there is a breach of trust and company property is misapplied, anyone who

[82] See *Gwembe Valley Development Co Ltd (No 3) v Koshy* [2004] 1 B.C.L.C. 131 CA.
[83] See *JJ Harrison Properties Ltd v Harrison* [2002] 1 B.C.L.C. 162.
[84] All these duties are discussed later at pp. 267 *et seq.*
[85] See eg *Bhullar v Bhullar* [2003] 2 B.C.C.C. 241 CA.
[86] *Fulham Football Club Ltd v Cabra Estates plc* [1994] 1 B.C.L.C. 363, CA.
[87] *Rackham v Peek Foods Ltd* [1990] B.C.L.C. 895; *John Crowther Group plc v Carpets International plc* [1990] B.C.L.C. 460; *Dawson International plc v Coats Patons plc*, 1988 S.L.T. 854 (O.H.).
[88] [1993] B.C.L.C. 53.
[89] See below, p.297 below.
[90] See below p.305.

receives such property with knowledge of the breach on duty will be liable to the company as a constructive trustee. This is commonly referred to as "knowing receipt". That does not require actual dishonesty on the part of the third party but simply that his knowledge makes it unconscionable for him to retain the benefit.[91]

There is an additional liability on anyone who dishonestly procures or assists the directors in such a breach of trust. Originally classified as "knowing assistance" with various complex definitions of knowledge, this liability is now based on dishonesty, to be decided in the light of the person's knowledge, experience, intelligence and motives. It is also clear that liability under this head does not, however, require a fraudulent or dishonest breach of trust by the directors.[92]

There may be a further, proprietary, remedy against a third party. This is known as "tracing" and allows the company to recover directly against either the property or its proceeds in the hands of the third party.[93]

If there is no breach of trust involving actual misapplication of corporate assets but a breach of fiduciary duty by the directors in the exercise of their powers, it has been held that there can be no liability for "knowing receipt" of trust property.[94] There may, however, be liability for "knowing assistance" if the requisite dishonesty and assistance can be shown.[95]

Directors as agents

Directors are agents through whom a company acts,[96] and it is largely because they are agents that they were originally regarded as owing fiduciary duties and certain duties of care to the company.

> "Directors of a company are fiduciary agents, and a power conferred upon them cannot be exercised in order to obtain some private advantage or for any purpose foreign to the power": *per* Dixon J. in *Mills v Mills* (1938) 60 C.L.R. 150 at p. 186.

Like other agents, directors incur no personal liability on contracts made by them on behalf of the company, within the scope of their authority.[97]

E contracted to supply goods to a company of which H was chairman of directors, payment to be made by the issue of £600 of the company's debentures. The contract was made at a board meeting at which H was chairman. E constantly pressed for the debentures, but none was issued, and eventually the company was wound up. *Held*, H was not liable to an action at the suit of E: *Elkington & Co. v Hürter* [1892] 2 Ch.452.

If, however, directors exceed the powers given to them by the memorandum and articles they will be liable for breach of warranty of authority.[98] Their actions

---

[91] *Bank of Credit and Commerce International (Overseas) Ltd v Akindele* [2001] Ch. 437.
[92] *Royal Brunei Airlines v Tan* [1995] 2 A.C. 378.
[93] See *Bracken Partners Ltd v Gutteridge* [2003] 2 B.C.L.C. 84; *Clark v Cutland* [2003] 2 B.C.L.C. 393, CA.
[94] *Brown v Bennett* [1998] 2 B.C.L.C. 97.
[95] *ibid. per* Rattee J. at p.105. On the facts of that case it was held that no assistance was shown in the case of one defendant and no knowledge in the case of another.
[96] See, *e.g. per* Lord Selborne L.C. in *Great Eastern Rlwy. Co. v Turner* (1872) L.R. 8 Ch. 149 at p.152. See Ch.6.
[97] Directors may be personally liable under s.349(4), above, p.44.
[98] *Firbank's Exors. v Humphreys* (1886) 18 Q.B.D. 54, CA.

may be ratified by the company in general meeting even if they have acted contrary to the company's constitution.[99]

Directors may be *specifically appointed* agents for the shareholders to negotiate a sale of the company's shares. If so, the shareholders are liable for their fraud.

R, managing director of N Ltd, by frauds of which the other directors were ignorant, made N Ltd profitable, and negotiated with E Ltd for the sale of the shares in N Ltd without disclosing that the profits were based on dishonest trading. The negotiations were reported to the shareholders who, in ignorance of R's fraud, authorised R to complete the sale on the basis of his negotiations. The fraud was subsequently discovered and the shareholders were sued for damages. *Held*, they were liable as R was their agent to negotiate the sale of their shares, and they were liable for his fraud even though it preceded his appointment as agent: *Briess v Woolley* [1954] A.C. 333.

Further, directors may *hold themselves out* to the shareholders as agents for the shareholders, in which case the directors must disclose any profit made by them to the shareholders.

Directors entered into negotiations for the amalgamation of the company with other companies. Before the negotiations were completed they induced a number of shareholders to give them options on their shares at par, representing that this was necessary to effect the amalgamation. The directors then exercised the option and thereby made a handsome profit. *Held*, they had to account for this profit to the shareholders: *Allen v Hyatt* (1914) 30 T.L.R. 444,[1] distinguishing *Percival v Wright*, below.

DUTIES OF DIRECTORS

To whom are the duties owed?

In general, directors owe their fiduciary duties[2] and duties of care[3] to the company. Traditionally this meant the members as a body to the exclusion of the interests of other stakeholders in the company, such as employees, creditors or individual shareholders. However, the position has changed slightly. The Act itself, in s.309, first introduced in 1980, provides that directors must also have regard to the interests of the employees as a whole. That section has two weaknesses, however. First it makes no attempt to resolve the position where the interests of the members and those of the employees conflict and second it provides the employees with no means of enforcing this duty. As we shall see in Chapter 17, since the duties of directors are owed to the company only the company may enforce them and this means either a majority of the shareholders or, in exceptional cases, a minority shareholder but not the employees. It follows that in most cases the majority shareholders can ratify a breach of duty.

The courts have also now accepted that the traditional concept of the members' interests being paramount in considering directors' duties may be displaced by the interests of the creditors where the company has been operating

[99] See Ch.6.
[1] See also *Munro v Bogie* [1994] 1 B.C.L.C. 415 CS (O.H.)
[2] *per* Lord Cranworth L.C. in *Aberdeen Railway Co. v Blaikie Bros.* (1854) 1 Macq. 461 at p.471.
[3] *per* Romer J. in *Re City Equitable Fire Insurance Co. Ltd* [1925] Ch. 407 at p.428.

under doubtful solvency.[4] In *Liquidator of West Mercia Safetywear Ltd v Dodd*,[5] the Court of Appeal adopted the following statement of Street C.J. in the Australian case of *Kinsela v Russell Kinsela Pty Ltd*[6]:

> "In a solvent company the proprietary interests of the shareholders entitle them as a general body to be regarded as the company when questions of the duty of directors arise . . . But where a company is insolvent the interests of the creditors intrude. They become prospectively entitled, through the mechanism of liquidation, to displace the power of the shareholders and directors to deal with the company's assets. It is in a practical sense their assets and not the shareholders' assets that, through the medium of the company, are under the management of the directors pending liquidation, return to solvency, or the imposition of some alternative administration."

The importance of this is that in such cases the members would not be able to ratify the acts of the directors so as to excuse them from liability which, as we have seen, they could otherwise do if the company was solvent.[7] It also negates any resolution of the directors or executive of their powers.[8] But directors are only required to act in good faith for the creditors as a whole in such situations; they are not to be regarded as liquidators,[9] so that they will not be liable if they have made bona fide commercial judgments in the circumstances of the case.[10] It has also been held that directors owe no duty of care to individual creditors for economic loss.[11] But in *Brady v Brady*,[12] the House of Lords left open the question as to whether the interests of the creditors were relevant to the issue of whether financial assistance for the acquisition of its own shares by a company had been given in good faith in the interests of the company.[13]

With regard to individual shareholders the traditional view has been that the directors are not trustees for them so that they may, for example, purchase shares from an individual shareholder without disclosing any information which they may have which affects the value of the shares, such as negotiations for the sale of the company. This is based on the decision to that effect in *Percival v Wright*[14] but this case has been doubted as creating an absolute rule in both New Zealand[15] and England[16] and distinguished by the Privy Council where there has been a specific finding that the directors were acting as agents for the shareholder in question.[17] The general rule was, however, confirmed recently by

---

[4] An alternative phrase is "where the company is in such financial difficulties that its creditors are at risk": *Re MDA Investment Management Ltd* [2004] 1 B.C.L.C. 217 at 245, *per* Park J.

[5] [1988] B.C.L.C. 250, CA. See also *Nicholson v Permakraft (N.Z.) Ltd* [1985] N.Z.L.R. 242.

[6] [1986] 4 N.S.W.L.R. 722 at p.730.

[7] *Re DKG Contractors Ltd* [1990] B.C.C. 903; *cf. Multinational Gas & Petrochemical Co. Ltd v Multinational Gas & Petrochemical Services Ltd* [1983] Ch. 258 CA. The position will be limited in practice because of the statutory liability of directors for wrongful trading, below, p.317.

[8] *Colin Gwyer & Associates Ltd v London Wharf (Limehouse) Ltd* [2003] 2 B.C.L.C. 153.

[9] *Re Welfab Engineers Ltd* [1990] B.C.L.C. 833.

[10] *Facia Footwear Ltd v Hinchliffe* [1998] 1 B.C.L.C. 218.

[11] *Nordic Oil Services Ltd v Berman*, 1993 S.L.T. 1168 (O.H.); *Yukong Line Ltd v Rendsburg Investments Corporation of Liberia* [1998] 1 W.L.R. 294; *Re Pantone 485 Ltd* [2002] 1 B.C.L.C. 266.

[12] [1989] A.C. 755, HL.

[13] Above, p.178.

[14] [1902] 2 Ch. 421.

[15] *Coleman v Myers* [1977] 2 N.Z.L.R. 225, CA.

[16] *Re Chez Nico (Restaurants) Ltd* [1992] B.C.L.C. 192.

[17] *Allen v Hyatt* (1914) 30 T.L.R. 444 PC.

the Court of Appeal in *Peskin v Anderson*.[18] The position is perhaps best
expressed by Browne-Wilkinson V.-C. in *Re Chez Nico (Restaurants) Ltd.*[19]

> "Like the Court of Appeal in New Zealand, I consider the law to be that in
> general, directors do not owe fiduciary duties to shareholders but owe them to the
> company: however, in certain special circumstances fiduciary duties, carrying with
> them a duty of disclosure, can arise which place directors in a fiduciary capacity *vis-
> à-vis* the shareholders."

As the law develops it will become clearer as to what these special circumstances may be. In *Dawson International plc v Coats Patons plc*,[20] it was said that
if the directors chose to give shareholders advice about a take-over offer they
must act in good faith but that this was a fiduciary duty owed to the company, *i.e.*
the present and future members and not to the current members as vendors of
their shares. In *Munro v Bogie*,[21] the articles, by appointing the directors as agents
for shareholders wishing to sell their shares with a duty to find purchasers for
those shares, were held to create a duty of disclosure on the directors to the
shareholders as to factors affecting the value of those shares, even though the
valuation was to be by the auditors. In *Peskin v Anderson*,[22] the Court of Appeal,
having accepted that special circumstances could give rise to a fiduciary
relationship, found that the dealings between the directors and the shareholders
had not caused the shareholders to leave and that there was no specific
information they should have been told.

Fiduciary duties

The fiduciary duties, usually expressed as the duty of loyalty, of directors are:

(1) to exercise their powers within the company's constitution, bona fide
for the benefit of the company as a whole,[23] as defined above, and for
their "proper purpose";

(2) not to put themselves in a position in which their duties to the company
and their personal interests may conflict.[24] This means that they cannot
take any unauthorised benefits from a corporate transaction; must
disclose all interests in such transactions; and must not compete with
the company.

Exercise of powers

With regard to the exercise of their wide powers of management it is clear that
directors must act bona fide for the benefit of the company and not for any

---

[18] [2001] 1 B.C.L.C. 372, CA.
[19] [1992] B.C.L.C. 192 at p.208.
[20] 1988 S.L.T. 854 (O.H.), affirmed on other grounds 1989 S.L.T. 655; *cf. Re A Company* [1986]
B.C.L.C. 382.
[21] [2001] 1 B.C.L.C. 372, CA.
[22] [2001] 1 B.C.L.C. 372, CA.
[23] And not, *e.g.* for his fellow directors: *Lee v Chou When Hsien* [1985] B.C.L.C. 45, PC; above, p.278.
[24] *Guinness plc v Saunders* [1990] 2 A.C. 633, HL.

collateral purpose such as to benefit or protect themselves. But this test is effectively a subjective one, so that if the directors honestly believe that they are acting in the best interests of the company there can be no breach of duty, whether the court thinks that it was in the company's best interests or not. The issue is one of honesty.[25] The position was clearly spelt out by Jonathan Parker J in *Regentcrest Ltd v Cohen*:

> "The duty imposed on directors to act bona fide in the interests of the company is a subjective one...The question is not whether, viewed objectively by the court, the particular act or omission which is challenged was in fact in the interests of the company; still less is the question whether the court, had it been in the position of the director at the relevant time, might have acted differently. Rather, the question is whether the director honestly believed that his act or omission was in the interests of the company. The issue is as to the director's state of mind. No doubt, where it is clear that the act or omission under challenge resulted in substantial detriment to the company, the director will have a harder task persuading the court that he honestly believed it to be in the company's interest; but that does not detract from the subjective nature of the test."[26]

The final sentence of that quote allows the court in effect to import some basic reasonableness test in the sense that the alleged honest belief must be credible.[27] Thus in *Colin Gwyer & Associates v London Wharf (Limehouse) Ltd*,[28] it was said that where the directors had failed to separate their own interests from those of the company, their assertion that they had acted in the best interests of the company should be examined with particular care. Would an intelligent and honest man in the directors' position have reasonably believed that it was for the benefit of the company.

But it is not enough just to exercise a power for the benefit of what the directors honestly believe is in the best interests of the company. They must also exercise their powers for their proper purpose; *i.e.* for the purpose for which it was granted. An example of this is the power to allot new shares, which is a fiduciary power, even though now subject to controls in s.80, above. The purpose of that power is to raise capital for the company and for no other purpose, (*i.e.* the prevention of a take-over bid).[29]

> Directors, in an endeavour to secure control in order to forestall a take-over bid, issued unissued shares in the company to trustees to be held for the benefit of employees, the shares being paid for by the trustees out of an interest-free loan from the company. *Held*, the issue exceeded the directors' fiduciary power, it being immaterial that it was made in the bona fide belief that it was in the interests of the company. Since the directors did not hold the majority of the shares before the new issue, the issue could be ratified by the company in general meeting, the votes carried by the shares issued to the trustees not being exercised: *Hogg v Cramphorn Ltd* [1967] Ch.254.

The reasoning in *Hogg v Cramphorn* was criticised and distinguished in Canada in the case of *Teck Corporation Ltd v Millar*[30] on the basis that it was an exception

---

[25] If there is no honest belief then there will be a breach: see *e.g. Extrasure Travel Insurances Ltd v Scattergood* [2003] 1 B.C.L.C. 598.

[26] [2001] 1 B.C.L.C. 80 at 105b. See also *Re Smith and Fawcett Ltd* [1942] Ch. 304.

[27] Sometimes the word is actually used: see e.g. *Re Pantone 485 Ltd* [2002] 1 B.C.L.C. 266.

[28] [2003] 2 B.C.L.C. 153.

[29] *Piercy v S. Mills & Co. Ltd* [1920] 1 Ch. 77; *Hogg v Cramphorn Ltd* [1967] Ch. 254; *Bamford v Bamford* [1970] Ch. 212, CA.

[30] (1972) 33 D.L.R. (3d) 288.

to the general rule that directors must act bona fide in what they consider to be the best interests of the company. It was not correct to say that issuing shares otherwise than to raise capital was always a breach of duty. Directors were entitled to consider the reputation, experience and policies of anyone seeking to take-over the company. If they decided on reasonable grounds that the take-over would cause substantial damage to the company's interests they were entitled to use their powers to protect the company.

This divergence of view was considered by the Privy Council in the case of *Howard Smith Ltd v Ampol Petroleum Ltd*[31] where, on similar facts to *Hogg v Cramphorn*, the judge had established (i) that the primary purpose of the allotment was not to raise money but to destroy the existing majority block of shares and (ii) that the directors were not motivated by self-interest. The Privy Council rejected both extreme arguments—*i.e.* that once no self-interest is discovered there can be no breach of duty, and that an allotment of shares can only be made to raise capital—any other purpose being wrong. Instead they considered that no limitation can be placed in advance on the exercise of the directors' powers. The court must examine the substantial purpose for which the power was exercised and whether that purpose was proper or not. The court must respect the directors' opinion on questions of management but in other cases it is a question for decision in each case. Although *Teck's* case was concerned with an area of management this was not—it was a question of altering an existing majority shareholding into a minority one. In *Mutual Life Insurance v The Rank Organisation*,[32] Goulding J. applied this distinction between areas of management and others in upholding a rights issue which was not available to certain U.S. shareholders. Unlike the *Howard Smith* case it did not upset the status quo but maintained the investment policy of the company.

In the *Howard Smith* case it was said that it was unconstitutional for the directors to exercise their powers purely for the purpose of destroying an existing majority or creating a new majority which had not previously existed and as such it was not an area of management. The company's constitution is separate and distinct from the powers themselves. Thus it would be a breach of duty for the directors to operate contrary to the memorandum or articles of the company[33] or to enter into a contract on behalf of the company whereby they remained in post as directors so that the shareholders could not exercise their constitutional rights to appoint new directors.[34] Similarly, using company funds other than for the commercial purposes of the company is contrary to the concept of management which has been delegated to the board.[35] In other cases which are regarded as being management areas, however, the courts will simply apply the bona fide test to decide whether the directors have acted in breach of their duty in exercising a power under the articles, *e.g.* to vary the terms of the managing director's service contract.[36]

---

[31] [1974] A.C. 821, PC.
[32] [1985] B.C.L.C. 11.
[33] See Chs 3 and 6.
[34] *Lee Panavision Ltd v Lee Lighting Ltd* [1992] B.C.L.C. 22, CA.
[35] *Extrasur Travel Insurances Ltd v Scattergood* [2003] 1 B.C.L.C. 598.
[36] *Runciman v Walter Runciman plc.* [1992] B.C.L.C. 1084. See also *CAS (Nominees) Ltd v Nottingham Forest FC plc* [2002] B.C.L.C. 613, where a statutory provision was not regarded as being mandatory.

If the directors act in breach of their duty, then they will be liable to account for any profits made and to compensate the company for any loss incurred. If the director actually obtains corporate assets for himself, he becomes liable as a constructive trustee and the company will be able to recover the property or its proceeds from him. These various remedies, together with any defences, are discussed later in this section. But there is one further issue. If the directors, in abuse of their powers, have entered into a contract with a third party, clearly the members can ratify it, but in what circumstances can that third party nonetheless enforce the contract against the company?

The issue arose in *Criterion Properties Ltd v Stratford UK Properties LLC.*[37] The alleged abuse of power was an agreement entered into by the then managing director of the company which allowed for the sale of certain assets to S if another party obtained control of Criterion. This is known as a "poison pill" in the world of takeovers, since it makes the company less attractive to outside predators.[38] Since there was evidence that this contract would damage the company more than an outsider gaining control of the company, the Court of Appeal held that it was an abuse of power.[39] The question, however, was whether the contract could be enforced by S. The Court of Appeal held that it was a question of whether it would be unconscionable for S to retain the benefit of the contractual right. The House of Lords disagreed on that issue. In their view the situation was purely one of agency—did the managing director have authority to make that contract?[40] If he did, it was enforceable; if he did not, it was not.[41]

A nominee director, *e.g.* a director appointed by a shareholder, owes the same duties to the company as any other director.[42]

Conflict of interest and duty—the no-profit rule

Because a director is in a fiduciary position, he must not make an undisclosed or secret profit by reason of that position. If he does, he must account for it to the company. It is immaterial that the company itself could not have obtained the profit.[43] The company in general meeting may, however, consent to such a profit being made or kept.

A was a director of B Co. and, on the company's behalf, contracted for the building of fishing smacks. Unknown to the company, he was paid a commission on the contract by

[37] [2004] 1 WLR 1846 (HL) cf. [2003] 2 B.C.L.C. 129 CA.
[38] See Ch.32, below.
[39] But they did not hold that all poison pills would be so categorised.
[40] Under the principles set out in Ch.6, above.
[41] The difference may not be that great. If the third party knew or ought to have known of the abuse of power how can he have understood the director to have had any authority?
[42] *per* Lord Denning in *Meyer v Scottish C.W.S. Ltd*, 1958 S.C. (H.L.) 40 at pp.67, 68; [1959] A.C. 324 at pp.366, 367; *per* Ungoed-Thomas J. in *Selangor United Rubber Estates Ltd v Cradock (No. 3)* [1968] 1 W.L.R. 1555, at pp.1613, 1614; *cf., e.g. per* Jacobs J. in *Re Broadcasting Station 2 GB Pty. Ltd* [1964–65] N.S.W.R. 1648; at p.1663, where he said that so long as the nominee directors believed that the interests of the shareholder who nominated them were identical with those of the company, they could follow the wishes of the shareholder without a close personal analysis of the issues.
[43] See e.g. *Gencor ACP Ltd v Dolby* [2000] 2 B.C.L.C. 734; *Industrial Development Consultants Ltd v Cooley* [1972] 1 WLR 443.

the shipbuilders. A was also a shareholder in an ice company which, in addition to dividends, paid bonuses to shareholders who were owners of fishing smacks and who employed the ice company in supplying ice to the fishing smacks. A employed the ice company in respect of B Co.'s fishing smacks and received the bonus. *Held*, A must account to B Co. for both the commission and the bonus, although the bonus could never have been received by B Co. as it was not a shareholder in the ice company: *Boston Deep Sea Fishing Co. v Ansell* (1888) 39 Ch.D. 339, CA.

R Ltd owned one cinema and wanted to buy two others with a view to selling the three together. R Ltd formed a subsidiary company to buy the two cinemas, but was unable to provide all the capital required; so all the directors of R Ltd except one subscribed for some of the shares in the subsidiary themselves. The cinemas were acquired and the shares in R Ltd and the subsidiary sold at a profit. *Held*, the former directors who subscribed for shares in the subsidiary themselves must account to R Ltd for the profit they made, because it was only through the knowledge and opportunity they gained as directors of R Ltd that they were able to obtain the shares. The one former director who did not himself subscribe but merely found someone else to do so was under no liability nor was a solicitor who was invited to subscribe by the directors: *Regal (Hastings) Ltd v Gulliver*.[44]

> "The rule of equity which insists on those, who by use of a fiduciary position make a profit, being liable to account for that profit, in no way depends on fraud, or absence of bona fides; or upon such questions or considerations as whether the profit would or should otherwise have gone to the plaintiff [*i.e.* the company], or whether the profiteer was under a duty to obtain the source of the profit for the plaintiff, or whether he took a risk or acted as he did for the benefit of the plaintiff, or whether the plaintiff has in fact been damaged or benefited by his action. The liability arises from the mere fact of a profit having, in the stated circumstances, been made. The profiteer, however honest and well-intentioned, cannot escape the risk of being called upon to account": *per* Lord Russell of Killowen in the *Regal* case at p. 144.

A director must not divert to his own use any corporate property[45] or any "maturing business opportunity" that his company is pursuing even after his resignation, at least if his resignation is prompted by that desire.[46] There is no breach of duty, however, if a director, whilst still a director, investigates the possibility of setting up his own future business after he ceases to be a director.[47] He must not go beyond the preliminary steps,[48] however. He may resign and then seek to solicit the workforce, but if another director knows of this and does not alert the other directors to that, that will itself be a breach of duty.[49] He may not use confidential information, *e.g.* trade secrets, obtained in his capacity as a director for his own use, but this does not apply to general information gained from his directorship, *e.g.* as to a particular market.[50]

This strict, but quite sophisticated, principle was further explained by the Court of Appeal in *Bhullar v Bhullar*.[51] The concept of a maturing business

---

[44] [1967] 2 A.C. 134 (Note), applied in *Phipps v Boardman* [1967] 2 A.C. 46.
[45] *Ball v Eden Project Ltd* [2002] 1 B.C.L.C. 313.
[46] *Industrial Development Consultants Ltd v Cooley* [1972] 1 W.L.R. 443; *Island Export Finance Ltd v Umunna* [1986] B.C.L.C. 460; *CMS Dolphin Ltd v Simonet* [2001] 2 B.C.L.C. 704.
[47] *Balston Ltd v Headline Filters Ltd* [1990] F.S.R. 385; *Framlington Group plc v Anderson* [1995] 1 B.C.L.C. 475.
[48] *Coleman Taymer Ltd v Oakes* [2001] 2 B.C.L.C. 749.
[49] *British Midland Tool Ltd v International Tooling Ltd.* [2003] 2 B.C.L.C. 523.
[50] *Island Export Finance Ltd v Umunna (ante)*; *Dranez Anstalt v Hayek* [2002] 1 B.C.L.C. 693.
[51] [2003] 2 B.C.L.C. 241, CA.

opportunity is not limited in the sense that the company must be already interested in or aware of the contract/property which the director has appropriated. The basic question is always whether the director has allowed his personal interest to conflict with his duty to the company. Thus a director was held liable for buying a property that would have been worthwhile for the company to have acquired, since it was adjacent to its existing property. The company was not aware of this opportunity but its existence was something the company should have been made aware of as part of the director's duties. The test, more akin to a potential business opportunity test, was whether a reasonable man looking at the facts would think there was information which it was relevant for the company to know and so it should be disclosed to the company.

In that respect, it is also a breach of the same duty of loyalty for a director to fail to disclose to the company his own misconduct or that of another director (or former director) in seeking to appropriate a maturing or other business opportunity.[52] Thus where a director does not actually appropriate a contract to himself but is interested in so doing, and persuades the company to seek better terms so that it loses the contract, he is liable in damages to the company. Failing to disclose his misconduct is simply part of failing to act bona fide for the benefit of the company.

In the *Regal* case the directors could have protected themselves by a resolution (either antecedent or subsequent) of the Regal shareholders in general meeting,[53] and the case was distinguished in *Lindgren v L. & P. Estates Ltd*[54] where the directors were released from liability by the company retaining them on the board, after it had knowledge of the facts (the alleged breach of duty was that the directors had merely "rubber-stamped" the decision of other persons).

In a case before the Privy Council, the managing director of a company obtained licences for the company to develop a mine but it was unable to proceed owing to financial problems. He resigned and with the knowledge of the directors, he developed the mine himself. The Privy Council held that he was not liable to account for his profits since the rejection by the company and the knowledge of the board excused him: *Queensland Mines Ltd v Hudson*.[55] This decision also has some Canadian support,[56] but seems to be out of line with the established UK position as established by the *Regal* and subsequent cases.[57]

---

[52] *Item Software (UK) Ltd v Fassihi* [2004] B.C.C. 994 CA; *British Midland Tool Ltd v Midland International Tooling Ltd* [2003] 2 B.C.L.C. 523; *Crown Dilmun v Sutton* [2004] 1 B.C.L.C. 468.

[53] *per* Lord Russell of Killowen ar p.150.

[54] [1968] Ch. 572, CA, in which it was also held that the prospective directors of a company owe no duty to it and that directors of a parent company owe no duty to, and are not debarred from contracting with, a subsidiary with an independent board; *cf Gwembe Valley Development Co Ltd v Koshy*, [1998] 2 B.C.L.C. 613 where a general understanding by the other directors coupled with a knowledge of the transaction was held to be insufficient to indicate consent.

[55] (1978) 18 A.L.R. 1, PC.

[56] *Peso Silver Mines Ltd v Cropper* (1966) 58 D.L.R. (2d) 1.

[57] For Scotland see Lord Young in *Great North of Scotland Railway Co. v Urquhart* (1884) 21 S.L.R. 377, 382, and *Laughland v Millar, Laughland & Co.* (1904) 6 F. 413 (contract for indirect secret benefit of director held unenforceable).

The first remedy for any breach available to the company is to seek an account of profits. This can take into account expenses incurred in connection with those profits and a reasonable allowance for overheads; but also a sum to take into account other benefits which might have been derived from the contracts/property (*e.g.* from increased cash flow) provided there was a reasonable connection between them.[58] This right can extend against a company or partnership used by the director to receive the benefit—the liability applies both to the company/partnership, if it is unconscionable for it to retain the benefit, and the director.[59] There are also the remedies of damages or equitable compensation (which could include loss of opportunity).[60] If the property actually becomes vested in the director, he is liable as a trustee and subject to the additional remedy of full recovery of the property or its proceeds.[61] There may well also be remedies against third parties for knowing receipt or assistance and the proprietary remedy of tracing (dealt with above).

Codification of directors' duties

Despite the complexities and subtleties of the equitable duties imposed upon directors, the current thinking is that they are too obscure and difficult for directors to understand. Accordingly, first the Law Commission[62] and then the Company Law Review[63] proposed a statutory list of duties to replace the equitable ones. The government has indicated its acceptance of most of their recommendations and has produced draft clauses to that effect.[64]

Under these draft clauses a director must:

(i) act in accordance with the company's constitution and exercise his powers for their proper purpose;

(ii) act in the way, he decides in good faith, would be most likely to promote the success of the company for the benefit of its members as a whole, taking into account all the material factors that it is practicable in the circumstances for him to identify;[65]

(iii) not use for his own benefit any property or information of the company, or any opportunity of the company which he became aware of in the performance of his function as a director, unless the company has consented to it by a resolution; or, in the case of a private company, its use has been authorised by the board (ignoring the director involved) and the articles do not forbid it; or in the case of a public company, the articles allow the board to authorise it and it has done so.

---

[58] *CMS Dolphin Ltd v Simonet* [2001] 2 B.C.L.C. 704.
[59] *ibid*; *Crown Dilmun v Sutton* [2004] 1 B.C.L.C. 468; *cf Gencor ACF Ltd v Dolby* [2000] 2 B.C.L.C. 734.
[60] *Gidman v Barron* [2003] EWHC 153 (Ch).
[61] *JJ Harrison (Properties) Ltd v Harrison* [2002] 1 B.C.L.C. 162, CA.
[62] Law Comm No 261, Cm 4436 (1999).
[63] *Final Report*, Vol. 1 (2001) paras 3.7–3.10.
[64] *Modernising Company law—Draft Clauses* (2002) Cm 5553-II. Adopted also in (2005) Cm 6456.
[65] These are the interests of the company's business relationships, impact on the environment and the community; business standards and fairness between the members. This is all that is left of an original intention to widen considerably the potential beneficiaries of directors' duties.

Since these may not become law in their current form, it is not yet appropriate to dissect them. But a few comments may be made. First, they seem particularly rigid, especially as to the no profit rule. The current rules are quite sophisticated. Equity has survived as a UK institution because of its ability to develop general principles (see *e.g.* the *Bhullar* case above). Codification is a stultifying exercise and prevents such organic growth. Second, the concept of material factors seems simply a counsel of perfection, designed to appease the stakeholder lobby. Third, the proper purpose rule is far too rigid and does not take into account the current subtleties. Finally, the idea that a private company board can authorise a profit provided the director involved is no guarantee of impartiality and may well lead to many more minority shareholder actions.

Disclosure of directors' interests in corporate transactions—the self-dealing rule

It soon became established that the application of fiduciary principles to directors allowed a company to automatically avoid any contract which the board entered into on its behalf in which one or more of the directors had an interest, unless that interest had been disclosed to the company and approved by the general meeting.[66] This was so, whether or not the director was acting bona fide for the benefit of the company. Any benefit derived by the director from such a contract could also be recovered.[67] This need to disclose an interest was extended to include not only contracts made directly with a director, *e.g.* a service contract, but also those in which he had an interest, *e.g.* as a shareholder[68] or partner[69] of the other contracting party. It does not apply to interests of a director's spouse or other personal contacts. In such a case only the usual fiduciary duty will apply but it has been suggested that the burden at proving good faith etc should be on the directors.[70]

It is not surprising that this strict rule, known as the self-dealing rule, was unacceptable to the business community and companies began to modify the application of the principle by clauses in their articles so as to avoid the embarrassment and delay involved in disclosure to and approval by the general meeting. Such articles are now common-place in modern company constitutions.[71] Regulation 85 of Table A provides:

> "Subject to the provisions of the Act, and provided that he has disclosed to the directors the nature and extent of any material interest of his, a director notwithstanding his office:
>
> (a)   may be a party to, or otherwise interested in, any transactions or arrangement with the company or in which the company is otherwise interested;

---

[66] *Aberdeen Ry. Co. v Blaikie Bros.* (1854) 1 Macq. 461. The right to avoid a contract for non-disclosure is not affected by the provisions of the first E.C. directive or s.35A: *Coöperative Rabobank 'Vecht en Plassengerbeid' BA v Minderhoud* [1998] 2 B.C.L.C. 507, ECJ.

[67] *per* Lord Cairns L.C. in *Parker v McKenna* (1874) L.R. 10 Ch.App. 96 at p.118.

[68] *Transvaal Lands Co. v New Belgium (Transvaal) Land, Co.* [1914] 2 Ch. 488, CA.

[69] *Costa Rica Ry. v Forwood* [1901] 1 Ch. 746, CA.

[70] *Newgate Stud Company v Penfold* [2004] EWHC 2993 (Ch).

[71] As in *Ireland Alloys Ltd v Dingwall* 1999 S.L.T. 267, O.H., where the disclosure requirements in the articles were not followed and this invalidated decisions taken at a meeting of the directors of the company.

(b) may be a director or other officer of, or employed by, or a party to any transaction or arrangement with, or otherwise interested in, any body corporate promoted by the company or in which the company is otherwise interested; and

(c) shall not, by reason of his office, be accountable to the company for any benefit which he derives from any such office or employment or from any such transaction or arrangement or from any interest in any such body corporate and no such transaction or arrangement shall be liable to be avoided on the grounds of any such interest or benefit."

Regulation 86 provides:

"For the purposes of reg. 85—

(a) a general notice given to the directors that a director is to be regarded as having an interest of the nature and extent specified in the notice in any transaction or arrangement in which a specified person or class of person is interested shall be deemed to be a disclosure that the director has an interest in any such transaction of the nature and extent so specified; and

(b) an interest of which a director has no knowledge and of which it is unreasonable to expect him to have knowledge shall not be treated as an interest of his."[72]

Parliament intervened in the 1929 Act to prevent some of the more excessive clauses in the articles of companies. The modern provision, in s.317 of the 1985 Act, provides a statutory duty on a director who is in any way, directly or indirectly, interested in any actual or proposed contract, transaction or arrangement with the company to declare the nature of that interest at a meeting of the board of directors. Loans and other credit transactions involving directors or connected persons are specifically included in this.

Disclosure must be made to the board of the nature of the director's interest, however slight, but the section does not require any other information.[73] Disclosure under the section must be made at the first meeting of the board at which the transaction is discussed or, if the director was not present, at the next meeting held after he became so interested. If a director subsequently becomes interested in a transaction after it is made, disclosure must be made at the next meeting of the board, whether or not it would be on the agenda. Alternatively a director may give a general notice to the board to the effect that he is a member of a specific company or firm and is interested in any transaction made with that company or firm or that he is interested in any transaction made with a specific person with whom the director is connected.

The immediate question which arises is how the statutory duty of disclosure to the board relates both to the equitable duty of disclosure to the company and provisions in the articles which seek to modify that equitable duty such as Art. 85 above. The section itself merely imposes a fine on the director for non-compliance but also provides that nothing in the section "prejudices the operation of any rule of law restricting directors from having an interest" in corporate transactions.

---

[72] Other articles allowing self-dealing, etc., have been held to be subject to disclosure under regs 85 and 86: *Gwembe Valley Development Co Ltd v Koshy* (No 3) [2004] 1 B.C.L.C. 131, CA.

[73] Regulation 85 requires a director to disclose the nature and extent of his interest. The Company Law Review recommended disclosure be limited to material interests of which the director is aware; *Completing the Structure* (2001), paras 4.11–4.16.

It is reasonably clear that if a director discloses his interest in accordance with both the section and Art. 85, or equivalent, then he will be liable neither to a fine nor to the effects of the basic equitable doctrine. The validity of Art. 85 to avoid the latter has always been assumed under the general equitable principle that the beneficiary may waive or modify a breach of fiduciary obligations.[74] But such disclosure does not of itself absolve a director from liability for breach of a fiduciary duty other than non-disclosure, *e.g.* if the action disclosed amounts to acting otherwise than bona fide for the benefit of the company. Only the company in general meeting could ratify that.[75]

It is also clear that if a director fails to disclose his interest at all, either under the section or Art. 85, then not only is he liable to a fine under the section but the company may avoid the contract and recover any benefits accruing to the director under the conflict of interest and duty principle, since he will not be able to take advantage of the modification clause in the articles.[76] This was the decision both of the Court of Appeal in *Hely-Hutchinson v Brayhead*[77] and the House of Lords in *Guinness v Saunders*,[78] although in both cases the company was held for other reasons not to be able to rescind the contract.[79]

A more complex situation arises where there is no disclosure of an interest by a director, under the section but either the articles do not require disclosure, or provide a different procedure which has been complied with. Does non-disclosure under s.317, by itself, allow the company to rescind the contract? All three members of the Court of Appeal in *Hely-Hutchinson v Brayhead Ltd* stated that the fact of non-disclosure under the section simply brought the normal principles of equity into play. The emphasis of each judge was, however, different. It is arguable that Lord Denning M.R. thought that the contract would be voidable since the articles could not allow the directors to contract out of their statutory duty to disclose. This was also the opinion of Lord Templeman in *Guinness v Saunders.*[80]

Lord Pearson and, arguably, Lord Wilberforce in *Hely-Hutchinson*, on the other hand, were more inclined to the view that non-disclosure under the section had no effect on the equitable principles which therefore became a matter for the articles alone to decide. The section merely imposed a fine in default. That was also the firm opinion of Lord Goff in *Guinness v Saunders*, and of two judges in subsequent cases.[81] On that basis it must be assumed that non-disclosure under the section would not invalidate the contract where the articles absolve the director from disclosing his interest. But it has to be said that in no case has the issue arisen directly since the articles have always required disclosure and that, if directly confronted with the issue, a different conclusion might be reached. The

---

[74] *Movitex Ltd v Bulfield* [1988] B.C.L.C. 104; see below, p.315.

[75] *Re Neptune (Vehicle Washing Equipment) Ltd (No. 2)* [1995] B.C.C. 1000.

[76] The right of recovery flows from the breach of duty and not the failure to disclose: *Coleman Taymor Ltd v Oakes* [2001] 2 B.C.L.C. 749.

[77] [1968] 1 Q.B. 549, CA.

[78] [1990] 2 A.C. 663, HL.

[79] It was impossible to restore the parties to their original position.

[80] [1990] 2 A.C. 663 at p.695.

[81] *per* Harman J. in *Lee Panavision Ltd v Lee Lighting Ltd* [1991] B.C.L.C. 575 at p.583; and *per* Knox J. in *Cowan de Groot Properties Ltd v Eagle Trust plc.* [1991] B.C.L.C. 1045 at p.1113.

Court of Appeal in *Lee Panavision Ltd v Lee Lighting Ltd*,[82] expressly refused to discuss the issue. More recently it has been said in two cases that breach of s.317 makes the contract voidable, but in neither case were the articles discussed.[83]

In addition, there are other difficulties in this area which also await a solution. Art. 85 requires disclosure to the board but, unlike s.317, does not specify any method of disclosure. In the *Lee Lighting Ltd* case,[84] Harman J. decided that since Art. 85 was expressly "subject to the provisions of the Act" the disclosure procedures in s.317 must be read into the article. The Court of Appeal in that case again expressed no opinion on this matter. This solution would give a neater result since it would not then be possible to comply with the Act but not Art. 85 or vice versa. The alternative would reopen the effect of non-compliance with one provision on the other which raises similar issues to those just discussed. It may, however, depend upon the wording of the particular article in question.

Another difficult area is what amounts to an interest which must be disclosed. In *Cowan de Groot Properties Ltd v Eagle Trust*,[85] the question arose as to whether in a contract of sale between A Ltd and B Ltd a director of A who was either a creditor of B, or of shareholders of B, had a disclosable interest. The judge was of the opinion that in most cases that would not amount to a disclosable interest but that circumstances could exist where the director would have an interest in B making that contract. He did, however, state that a director who was a bare trustee for another would not have a disclosable interest. On the other hand, it is clear that s.317 applies both to the granting and variation of directors' service contracts. In *Runciman v Walter Runciman plc*,[86] this was expressly decided despite the "apparent absurdity" of requiring such a disclosure where it is patently obvious that the director has an interest.

Such situations, however, raise the further question of whether there can ever be implied disclosure to the board under s.317. This issue arose in the *Lee Lighting* case where the directors all knew of each others' interest in the agreement being discussed by the board. The Court of Appeal, unlike Harman J. at first instance, were reluctant to regard this as a breach of s.317 but that approach might seem to miss the point that a formal declaration would not only require the other directors to expressly consider the conflict of interest position, it would also be recorded in the minutes of the directors and there could be no suspicion of secret dealings. For those reasons, and the possible abuses concerning shadow directors, Lightman J. in *Re Neptune (Vehicle Washing Equipment) Ltd*[87] held that a single director was obliged to disclose a redundancy payment he authorised for himself to a 'meeting' of the board and record that fact in the

---

[82] [1992] B.C.L.C. 22, CA.
[83] *Craven Textile Engineers Ltd v Batley Football Club Ltd* [2001] B.C.C. 679; *re MDA Investment Management Ltd* [2004] 1 B.C.L.C. 217.
[84] [1991] B.C.L.C. 575.
[85] [1991] B.C.L.C. 1045.
[86] [1992] B.C.L.C. 1084. See also *Re Neptune (Vehicle Washing Equipment) Ltd (No. 1)* [1995] 1 B.C.L.C. 352.
[87] [1995] 1 B.C.L.C. 352.

minutes. It remains, however, to be decided what the penalty might be for such a technical non-disclosure.[88]

That issue was left open by Lightman J. in the *Neptune* case. In the *Runciman* case, Simon Brown J. also declined to give any definitive view but he did refuse to allow the company to rescind the contract. Rescission is a discretionary remedy which the courts may refuse to allow even where it has not been lost by acquiesence or delay. In *Re Dominion International Group plc*,[89] Knox J. said that where there was genuine informed consent by all the directors, a failure to make a declaration under s.317 would be a technical and not a substantive default, although he did not say what, if any, consequences would follow. Other cases have also stressed the need for a formal rather than an informal disclosure; "piecemeal and informal" information gathered by the directors would not suffice.[90] But in one case the lack of a formal minute as to disclosure was held not to be decisive of the matter.[91]

Directors competing with company

Under the general law, apart from the case where a director has a service agreement with the company which requires him to serve only the company, there is somewhat surprising authority to the effect that, despite the conflict of interest and duty principle, he may become a director of a rival company, *i.e.* that in this way he may compete with the first company, provided that he does not disclose to the second company any confidential information obtained by him as a director of the first company, and that what he may do for a rival company he may do for himself[92] or a rival firm. However, it has been said that he must not subordinate the interests of the first company to those of the second and that if he does so it is at the risk of an application under s.459.[93] In the more recent case of *In Plus Group Ltd v Pyke*,[94] the Court of Appeal allowed a director to be a director at a rival company but only in the very unusual circumstances of that case.[95] It is clear that all three judges were concerned by the width of the previous decisions.

---

[88] At a subsequent full trial the non-disclosure in that case was held to be substantive and not technical and further that the director had no authority anyway to authorise the payment: *Re Neptune (Vehicle Washing Equipment) Ltd (No. 2)* [1995] B.C.C. 1000. The Company Law Review recommended that there should be no need to disclose interests, the material provisions of which were known to the board: *Completing the Structure* (2000) paras 4.11–4.16

[89] [1996] 1 B.C.L.C. 572.

[90] *Gwembe Valley Development Co Ltd v Koshy (No 3)* [2004] 1 B.C.L.C. 131, CA; *Re MDA Investment Management Ltd* [2004] 1 B.C.L.C. 217.

[91] *Re Marini Ltd* [2004] B.C.C. 172.

[92] *London & Mashonaland Exploration Co. v New Mashonaland Exploration Co.* [1891] W.N. 165; *per* Lord Blanesburgh in *Bell v Lever Bros. Ltd* [1932] A.C. 161 at p.195.

[93] *per* Lord Denning in *Meyer v Scottish C.W.S. Ltd*, 1958 S.C. HL 40 at p.68; [1959] A.C. 324 at p.368. Below Ch.19.

[94] [2002] 2 B.C.L.C. 201, CA.

[95] The director had effectively been excluded from the first company for some time and to so owed only nominal duties to it.

Duties of care

Directors' duties of care towards the company were, for many years, defined in three propositions laid down by Romer J. in *Re City Equitable Fire Insurance Co. Ltd.*[96] These were:

(1) A director need not exhibit in the performance of his duties (*i.e.* his functions) a greater degree of skill than may reasonably be expected from a person of his knowledge and experience (*i.e.* the particular director's own knowledge and experience) and not that of the reasonable man. He must take such care, however, in the performance of his duties as an ordinary man might be expected to take on his own behalf.

(2) A director is not bound to give continuous attention to the affairs of his company. His duties are of an intermittent nature to be performed at periodical board meetings.

(3) In respect of all duties that, having regard to the exigencies of business, and the articles of association, may properly be left to some other official, a director is, in the absence of grounds for suspicion, justified in trusting that official to perform such duties honestly.

All three of these propositions have, however, been substantially qualified by later cases. The standard of care as laid down in proposition (1) was first modified in respect of an executive director, *i.e.* one who has a service contract with the company. There is an implied term in such a contract that he will use reasonable skill in the performance of the duties of the office based on what might reasonably be expected from a person in his position.[97] But, more significantly, the general standard of care for all directors has been restated by Hoffmann L.J. in two cases, with virtually no discussion, as being the same as the test for establishing wrongful trading under s.214(4) of the Insolvency Act 1986.[98] In *Norman v Theodore Goddard*,[99] this was stated as being that of a reasonably diligent person having the knowledge, skill and experience both of a person carrying out that director's functions and of that person himself. Thus the test is both objective and subjective. This test was also applied by Hoffmann L.J. in *Re D'Jan of London Ltd*[1] to establish the negligence of a director in signing an inaccurate fire insurance proposal form to insure the company's property. Since it is now accepted that the wrongful trading standard is the standard of care for negligence,[2] the cases on wrongful trading (and disqualification), on what is expected of a director, set out later in this chapter, will be of great significance in any negligence action.

The attendance duty under proposition (2) has also been tightened up. In *Dorchester Finance Co. Ltd v Stebbing*,[3] two non-executive directors were held to

---

[96] [1925] Ch. 407, at p.428.
[97] *Lister v Romford Ice and Cold Storage Co. Ltd* [1957] A.C. 555.
[98] Below, p.317.
[99] [1991] B.C.L.C. 1028. The director was excused liability on the basis of reasonable reliance on another under the third of Romer J.'s propositions.
[1] [1994] 1 B.C.L.C. 561, CA, see also *Cohen v Selby* [2001] 1 BCLC 176, CA.
[2] See e.g. the Government's position as set out in *Modernising Company Law*, Cmn 5553–1, paras. 3.2–3.7, accepting the suggestions of the Company Law Review.
[3] [1989] B.C.L.C. 498.

be negligent in not attending board meetings of a subsidiary company even though it was shown that it was not commercial practice to do so.

The third proposition (delegation of responsibility) is of particular relevance to the supervisory role of the non-executive directors in the larger companies.[4] In *Equitable Life Assurance Society v Bowley*,[5] it was said, without a detailed examination of the issue since it was a summary application, that the law in this area is developing and that the third proposition no longer represents the modern law. It was plainly arguable that a company may look to its non-executive directors for independence of judgement and supervision of the executive management. An alternative formulation to the third proposition is that set out by Jonathan Parker J. and approved by the Court of Appeal in the disqualification case of *Re Barings plc (No. 5)*:

> "(i) Directors have, both collectively and individually, a continuing duty to acquire and maintain a sufficient knowledge and understanding of the company's business to enable them properly to discharge their duties as directors. (ii) Whilst directors are entitled (subject to the articles of association of the company) to delegate particular functions to those below them in the management chain, and to trust their competence and integrity to a reasonable extent, the exercise of the power of delegation does not absolve a director from the duty to supervise the discharge of the delegated functions. (iii) No rule of universal application can be formulated as to the duty referred to in (ii) above. The extent of the duty, and he question whether it has been discharged, must depend on the facts of each particular case, including the director's role in the management of the company."[6]

That formula was concerned with delegation by all directors down the chain of management but it could equally well apply to supervision of those above the non-executive directors in that chain.

Duties of care, as is the case with fiduciary duties, can always be ratified by the company.[7]

Personal liability of directors in tort to third parties

In certain cases a director may be personally liable for some wrong connected with his company. In *C. Evans and Sons Ltd v Spritebrand Ltd*,[8] the Court of Appeal discussed a director's liability for torts committed by his company. They decided that a director is not automatically liable for such torts even if it is a small company over which he exercised total control. It is necessary to examine the role he played in regard to the commission of the tort. On the other hand it would not always be necessary to prove that the director had acted recklessly or knowing that the company's acts were tortious. If the tort itself required negligence or recklessness then the director's state of mind might well be relevant, but for torts of strict liability different considerations could apply.

---

[4] For the situation of a non-active director of a small company see the sections on wrongful trading and disqualification, below.
[5] [2004] 1 B.C.L.C. 180.
[6] [1999] 1 B.C.L.C. 433 at 489, approved [2000] 1 B.C.L.C. 523 at 535–536, CA.
[7] *Pavlides v Jensen* [1956] Ch. 565.
[8] [1985] 1 W.L.R. 317.

But in *Williams v Natural Health Foods Ltd*,[9] the House of Lords held that the controller of a small company which had made negligent misstatements to its franchisees, was not personally liable for the tort of negligent misstatement. There was no evidence of personal dealings or conduct which would have led the franchisees to assume that the director was willing to assume personal responsibility to them. Nor was he a joint tortfeasor with the company—the only relationship giving rise to liability was that between the company and the franchisees.

It is clear, however, that the decision in *Williams* was largely based on the peculiarities of the tort of negligent misstatement, which requires a specific finding of the assumption of personal responsibility for the statement by the tortfeasor. The director, acting as an agent, on the facts had not assumed that personal responsibility. As such it had nothing to do with the concept of the company as a separate legal person—the decision would have been the same if the principal had been an individual. That analysis enabled the House of Lords in the subsequent case of *Standard Chartered Bank v Pakistan National Shipping Corporation*,[10] to hold a director personally liable in the tort of deceit and to set aside his defence that he had made the fraudulent misstatement on behalf of the company. Although that may make the company liable, it did not absolve him from liability for his own tort. Deceit does not require any assumption of personal responsibility so it was no defence to say that he made the statement on behalf of another (which happened to be a company).

The principles governing the liability of a director as a joint tortfeasor with the company have been set out in two cases relating to intellectual property. In *MCA Records Inc v Charly Records Ltd*,[11] Chadwick L.J. said that: (i) a director will not be liable as a joint tortfeasor if all he is doing is carrying out his constitutional role as a director, *e.g.* by voting at board meetings; (ii) but he will be liable if he participates or is involved in committing the tort in ways which go beyond the exercise of constitutional control, even though he could have procured the same acts through the exercise of such control. In the cases, the test was whether the director "intends and procures and shares a common design" that the infringement takes place.

Contribution between directors

The liability of directors for breaches of duty is joint and several,[12] so that where the directors have misapplied the company's funds, as by paying dividends out of capital or advancing money for an unauthorised purpose, a director who has been sued for the misapplication is entitled to contribution from the other directors who were parties to it.[13] If, however, the money misappropriated has been applied for the sole benefit of one of the directors, that director is not entitled to obtain contribution.[14]

---

[9] [2003] 1 B.C.L.C. 244, HL.

[10] [2003] 1 B.C.L.C. 93, CA. These propositions were used by Pumfrey J in *Koninklijke Philips Electronics NV v Princo Digital Disc GmbH* [2004] 2 B.C.L.C. 50.

[11] [1998] 2 All E.R. 577, HL. See also *Partco Group Ltd v Wragg* [2004] B.C.C. 782, CA.

[12] *Bishopsgate Investment Management Ltd v Maxwell (No. 2)* [1993] B.C.L.C. 1282.

[13] *Ramskill v Edwards* (1886) 31 Ch.D. 100; see also (for England) Civil Liability (Contribution) Act 1978, and (for Scotland) Law Reform (Miscellaneous Provisions) (Scotland) Act 1940, s.3.

[14] *Walsh v Bardsley* (1931) 47 T.L.R. 564.

Relief of directors from liability for breach of duty

By a resolution in general meeting

Since directors' fiduciary duties are owed to the members as a body, the majority of the members in general meeting may, at least while the company is solvent, after full disclosure of all material circumstances, waive a breach of fiduciary duty by a director.[15] If the breach involves acting contrary to the company's memorandum or articles such ratification must be by a special resolution.[16] In any case, however, if he is a member, the director may vote in favour of waiver, provided that there is no fraud on the minority of the members.

> The directors of a company contracted to buy a ship from a vendor who was a director. (This was a breach of duty by him since the articles contained no clause authorising a director to contract with the company. At a general meeting a resolution affirming the contract was carried, against the wishes of the minority shareholders, by reason of the fact that the vendor held the majority of the shares in the company. *Held*, the resolution was valid. As a shareholder, the vendor was merely using his voting power to his own advantage, and there was no question of a fraud on the minority—there was no unfairness or impropriety: *N.-W. Transportation Co. v Beatty* (1887) 12 App.Cas.589, PC.
>
> Two directors of a construction company negotiated for a construction contract in the usual way in which the company's business was carried on, and then took the contract in their own names. A meeting of the company was called, and by their votes as holders of three-quarters of the shares a resolution was passed declaring that the company had no interest in the contract. *Held*, the benefit of the contract belonged to the company and the directors must account to the company for it, and the purported ratification was a fraud on the minority and ineffective: *Cook v Deeks* [1916] 1 A.C. 554, PC.

The position will be different if the company is operating under doubtful solvency since the duties may then be owed to the creditors rather than the members of the company.[17]

Not by a provision in the articles, etc.

Under the general law a director can be exempted from liability for breach of duty by a provision in the articles of the company. However, this is now limited by ss 309A to C, introduced in 2004[18] and which replaced, for directors, the previous limitations set out in s.310.[19] Section 309A(1),(2) states that, subject to what is said below, any provision[20] for exempting a director from liability for negligence, default, breach of duty or breach of trust in relation to the company is void. Section 309A(3) applies a similar rule to any indemnity against any such liability, provided, directly or indirectly, for a director by his company.[21]

---

[15] *Bamford v Bamford* [1970] Ch. 212, CA; *Gencor ACP Ltd v Dolby* [2000] 2 B.C.L.C. 734. 269.

[16] ss 35(3), 35A(5). See Ch.6, above.

[17] *Re DKG Contractors Ltd* [1990] B.C.C. 903.

[18] By the Companies (Audit, Investigations and Community Enterprise) Act 2004, following the recommendations of the Company Law Review: *Final Report, Vol 1* (2001) paras 6.2–6.4.

[19] That section, introduced in 1929, still applies to auditors. It no longer applies to officers, however, and neither do the new sections.

[20] Defined in all the sections as a provision of any nature whether contained in the company's articles or any contract; s.309A(6).

[21] Or for a director of an associated company—see s.309A(6). This is any holding or subsidiary company or another subsidiary company in the same group.

This ban on indemnities does not prevent the company taking out an indemnity insurance policy as cover against such liability[22] or from providing what is called a qualifying third-party indemnity provision.[23] Under s.309B, such an indemnity provision will only be a qualifying one if it does not apply to any liability to the company, or with regard to the payment of any criminal fine or regulatory penalty, or the payment of costs in any proceedings in which he is convicted, or where judgment is given against him on in favour of the company. The latter includes any application under s.727 (see below) in which relief is not granted by the court. The existence of such qualifying third-party indemnity provisions must be disclosed in the Directors' Report and as part of a directors service contract disclosure requirements.[24]

One problem with the revamped sections, is that they still appear to be inconsistent with reg. 85 of Table A (and similar articles) which allow a director to have an interest in a transaction, etc., subject to disclosure to the board. Insofar as this is an attempt to relieve the director from the conflict of interest rule (above) is it not exempting him from a breach of duty or trust and so void under s.310? In *Movitex Ltd v Bulfield*,[25] Vinelott J. resolved the difficulty by deciding that the conflict of interest rule was a disability imposed by equity and not a duty owed by the director. Thus by modifying the rule the articles are removing a disability and not exempting a breach of duty under s.309A.[26]

By the court

Section 727 provides that if, in proceedings for negligence, default, breach of duty or breach of trust against a director or other officer or auditor of a company, it appears that he has acted honestly and reasonably, and that, having regard to all the circumstances, including those connected with his appointment, he ought fairly to be excused, the court may relieve him, wholly or partly, from liability on such terms as it thinks fit.[27]

The court has to decide both that the director acted honestly and reasonably and that he ought to be excused. Whilst "honestly" might be subjective, "reasonably" would seem to be objective. In negligence cases this might appear to be difficult to establish.

B and G, two of the directors of a company were present at a finance committee in June at which it was resolved to sell £60,000 War Bonds and to reinvest the proceeds at B's discretion. In September, G inquired about the reinvestment of the proceeds and was told that they had been temporarily invested on the Stock Exchange. B misappropriated the proceeds of sale. *Held*, (1) G was negligent in allowing the money to remain in B's hands longer than was reasonable and in not making inquiries as to its permanent investment,

---

[22] See s.309A(5).

[23] See s.309A(4)

[24] Under s.309C. See p.283, above and Ch.20 below. Loans may also be made by a company to a director to defend criminal and civil actions but the loan must be repayable on conviction or where judgment is given in favour of the company.

[25] [1988] B.C.L.C. 104.

[26] See also the analysis in *Re Neptune (Vehicle Washing Equipment) Ltd (No. 2)* [1995] B.C.C. 1000.

[27] This defence can be raised for the first time at the trial: *Re Kirby's Coaches Ltd* [1991] B.C.L.C. 414. See also *Clydebank Football Club Ltd v Steadman* 2002 S.L.T. 109, O.H.

and (2) though G. had acted honestly, he had not acted reasonably and ought not to be granted relief: *Re City of London Insurance Co.* (1925) 41 T.L.R. 521.

In *Selangor United Rubber Estates Ltd v Cradock (No. 3)*[28] directors of a public company who disposed of virtually all its assets without regard for minority shareholders, and without consideration, but blindly at the behest of the majority shareholder who nominated them to the board, did not act reasonably and could not be relieved. In *Re Duomatic Ltd*[29] a director dealing with payment to another director of compensation for loss of office, who did not seek legal advice but dealt with the matter himself without a proper exploration of what should be done on the company's behalf, did not act reasonably.

But in *Re D'Jan of London Ltd*,[30] Hoffmann L.J. held that a director who had acted negligently but "understandably" and who would have suffered a personal loss through his shareholding in the company at the time of the negligence could be excused under the section.

The most recent cases have involved the improper declaration of dividends. In *Bairstow v Queens Moat Houses plc*,[31] the Court of Appeal emphasised that the burden of proof to establish honesty and reasonableness was on the defendant, and that a finding of dishonesty was total. In *Re Marini Ltd*,[32] it was doubted whether a director who had received an unlawful dividend to the prejudice of creditors could ever be said to have acted reasonably, however honest he had been.

Section 727 only applies to proceedings against a director for breach of duty by, on behalf of, or for the benefit of, the company as a whole.[33] It does not apply to claims against a director by a third party to enforce a debt, *e.g.* arrears of general betting duty.[34] It has no relevance either to a claim by a company for recovery of money paid to a director under an unauthorised and void contract, since that is not founded on a breach of duty,[35] or to a claim for wrongful trading.[36] But in *Re Duckwari plc (No. 2)*,[37] the Court of Appeal considered that s.727 could apply to a liability to indemnify the company under s.322, although it would not avail a director who had a personal interest in the transaction and who has benefitted from it.

DIRECTORS AND INSOLVENCY

When a company becomes insolvent its directors may face additional liabilities and consequences to those in operation whilst the company is a going concern. In addition to those detailed in Chapter 29 which apply generally, the Insolvency Act 1986 imposes specific liabilities on directors under the headings of wrongful

[28] [1968] 1 W.L.R. 1555.
[29] [1969] 2 Ch. 365.
[30] [1994] 1 B.C.L.C. 561; *cf. Re Brian D. Pierson (Contractors) Ltd* [1997] B.C.C. 26.
[31] [2001] 2 B.C.L.C. 531, CA. See also *Inn Spirit Ltd v Burns* [2002] 2 B.C.L.C. 780.
[32] [2004] B.C.C. 172. Reliance on financial advice might also not be enough.
[33] Whatever remedy is sought: *Colemen Taymor Ltd v Oakes* [2002] 2 B.C.L.C. 749.
[34] *Customs and Excise Commissioners v Hedon Alpha* [1981] 2 All E.R. 697, CA.
[35] *Guinness plc v Saunders* [1990] 2 A.C. 633, HL.
[36] *Re Produce Marketing Consortium Ltd* [1989] B.C.L.C. 513; below, p.318.
[37] [1998] 2 B.C.L.C. 315, CA.

trading; liability for setting up successive companies under the same name, the so-called "Phoenix Syndrome"; and liability for misfeasance. Corporate insolvency may also lead to the directors being disqualified.

Liability for wrongful trading

One of the principal aims of the Insolvency Act 1986 was to encourage directors to put their company into liquidation when all reasonable expectation of saving it has gone. Before 1986 the only remedy available to a liquidator against a director who had allowed his company to incur debts after all reasonable hope had gone was to institute proceedings for fraudulent trading. This remedy still exists and can give rise to both civil and criminal consequences.[38] But it requires proof of intent to defraud creditors and in practice that is often difficult to establish. Under s.214 of the Insolvency Act 1986 there is now an additional liability on directors and shadow directors[39] for those guilty of wrongful trading in such circumstances.[40]

To establish wrongful trading the liquidator of a company must show that the company has gone into an insolvent liquidation,[41] that the director, prior to the liquidation, knew or ought to have concluded that there was no reasonable prospect that the company could avoid going into insolvent liquidation, and that he took insufficient steps in the circumstances to minimise the potential loss to the company's creditors: Insolvency Act 1986, s.214(2)(3).[42] Note that no dishonesty need be involved, simply unreasonable behaviour or negligence.[43] Where the directors have addressed the reality of the situation and have prepared revised business plans and forecasts that may be taken as evidence of a reasonable belief that the company will survive.[44] But a superficial belief that the situation was due to "temporary cash flow shortages," the ignoring of losses in the accounts and an unreasonable failure to realise that many of the company's assets were worth less was held to be clear evidence of wrongful trading.[45]

To decide whether a director ought to have concluded that an insolvent liquidation was unavoidable the court must ask whether that would have been the conclusion of a reasonably diligent person having both the general knowledge, skill and experience that might reasonably be expected of a person carrying out that particular director's duties with regard to the company (including those entrusted to him even if he does not actually carry them out) and the general

---

[38] Below, Ch.27.

[39] And also for *de facto* directors, above p.267.

[40] No defence under s.727 is available against a claim for wrongful trading: *Re Produce Marketing Consortium Ltd* [1989] B.C.L.C. 513; above, p.315.

[41] This is defined as where, at the time of the winding up, its assets are insufficient for the payment of its debts and other liabilities and the expenses of winding up. This is known as balance sheet insolvent.

[42] Any such action must be brought by the liquidator within six years of the insolvent liquidation and the court may strike out the claim if there is inordinate and inexcusable delay by the liquidator in actually commencing the proceedings: *Re Farmizer (Products) Ltd* [1997] 1 B.C.L.C. 589, CA.

[43] Becoming aware of pressing creditors will suffice: *Re DKG Contractors Ltd* [1990] B.C.C. 903.

[44] *Re Sherborne Associates Ltd* [1995] B.C.C. 40.

[45] *Re Brian D Pierson (Contractors) Ltd* [2001] 1 B.C.L.C. 275; see also *Rubin v Gunncer* [2004] B.C.C. 684.

knowledge, skill and experience which that director actually has: Insolvency Act 1986, s.214(4)(5).[46]

In construing these provisions Knox J. in *Re Produce Marketing Consortium Ltd (No. 2)*,[47] held that each director had to be judged by what might reasonably be expected of a person fulfilling his functions in a reasonably diligent way, always bearing in mind certain minimum standards such as the preparation of annual accounts and a basic awareness of the company's financial position, etc. Further such a director must be judged not only on the facts as known to him but those which he would have known had the company complied with its obligations under the Act, *e.g.* as to the publication of accounts, so as to establish when the wrongful trading began. These minimum standards are expected of all directors, even one who takes no part in running the business. There is no such thing as a "sleeping director".[48] Where the liquidator specifies a specific date as to when the wrongful trading began he cannot subsequently ask the court to make such a finding as at a later date instead.[49]

Many companies actually begin life as balance sheet insolvent but in *Re Cubelock Ltd*[50] it was held that that was not enough to constitute wrongful trading, unless perhaps the company was formed with totally insufficient capital. The liability would only arise if the directors allowed the company to continue to trade when they knew or ought to have known that there was no reasonable prospect of the creditors ever being paid. A reasonable, if mistaken, belief that the company could trade into profit was not enough.

Although all directors must be aware of the company's financial situation, where the non-executive directors questioned that position and actively considered whether to allow the company to continue trading it was held that they had acted reasonably. They had reasonably relied on the accounts and the opinions of the finance director and auditor that the company was insolvent. They were not expected to show: "the sort of intricate appreciation of recondite accounting details possessed by a specialist in the field."[51]

If wrongful trading is established the court may require the director to make a contribution to the company's assets: Insolvency Act 1986, s.214(1).[52] Such an order is to be compensatory, *i.e.* to provide an amount equal to that by which the company's assets were depleted by the directors' conduct from that date, and not penal.[53] There must be a connection between the wrongful trading and the loss to the company's net assets. A loss caused, *e.g.* by bad weather would not be included.[54] The absence of fraudulent intent can be taken into account but is not

---

[46] This test has also been applied as to the standard of care of directors generally: above, p.310.

[47] [1989] B.C.L.C. 520.

[48] *Re Brian D Pierson Ltd* [2001] 1 B.C.L.C. 275 at 302.

[49] *Re Sherborne Associates Ltd* [1995] B.C.C. 40.

[50] [2001] B.C.C. 523.

[51] *Re Continental Assurance of London plc* [1996] B.C.C. 888.

[52] The liquidator cannot assign that sum to a third party in return for the third party funding the action: *Re Oasis Merchandising Services Ltd* [1997] 1 B.C.L.C. 689.

[53] For this reason the liability survives the death of the director: *Re Sherborne Associates Ltd* [1995] B.C.C. 40. That case also suggested that responsibility for the wrongful trading could be reduced by a defence of reasonable reliance on another. If there was no diminution in the company's assets during the wrongful trading, there is no liability: *Re Marini Ltd* [2004] B.C.C. 17.

[54] *Re Continental Assurance of London Ltd* [1996] B.C.C. 888.

in itself a reason for fixing a low or nominal figure. Any amount is payable with interest from the date of winding up.[55] If the company has failed to keep any records the court can use its discretion in calculating the period of wrongful trading for this purpose.[56] Following such an order the court may also make a disqualification order against the director: Company Directors Disqualification Act 1986, s.10.[57]

Liability for use of insolvent company's name

Another abuse prior to 1986 was the so-called "Phoenix" company operation. The liquidator would dispose of the company, its name and assets to the existing directors, who would purchase it with other funds and then continue to trade in exactly the same way as before the insolvent liquidation leaving the creditors of the old company stranded. To prevent this happening, ss 216 and 217 of the Insolvency Act 1986 provide that where a company goes into insolvent liquidation,[58] anyone who was a director (or shadow director[59]) of that company at any time in the previous year and who becomes a director of a company using the name[60] or trading name of the insolvent company within five years commits an offence, unless he either has leave of the court or comes within limited exceptions under the Insolvency Rules 1986.[61] This prohibition extends to being concerned in the promotion, formation, management or taking part in the business of a company using the insolvent company's name. The offence is one of strict liability.[62]

In deciding whether a name is so similar to suggest an association with the first company, the courts will adopt an objective test and a purposive approach. Merely using different stationery etc. will not be enough.[63] The mater will be looked at in the context of all the circumstances in which the two names were actually used or likely to be used. These would include the types of product, location, type of customers and the persons involved in the two companies.[64]

The Insolvency Rules allow, *inter alia*, the director to act as such in respect of the new company where the business of the old company has been acquired by the new company[65] under arrangements made with an insolvency practitioner[66] provided notice is given to all the creditors of the old company within 28 days of the completion of the acquisition. The court's residual discretion may allow the director to act as such with respect to the new company but may require certain undertakings as to future conduct of the management of that company.[67] In

[55] *Re Produce Marketing Consortium Ltd (No. 2)* [1989] B.C.L.C. 520.

[56] *Re Purpoint Ltd* [1991] B.C.L.C. 491.

[57] Below, p.321.

[58] See n.31, above.

[59] Including a *de facto* director? above p.267.

[60] Or any name which is so similar as to suggest an association with the previous company; see below.

[61] S.216.

[62] *R v Cole* [1998] 2 B.C.L.C. 234, CA.

[63] *Archer Structures Ltd v Griffiths* [2004] B.C.C. 156.

[64] *Ricketts v Ad Valorem Factors Ltd* [2004] 1 B.C.L.C. 1, CA.

[65] This does not have to include the old company's liabilities: *Re Bonus Breaks Ltd* [1991] B.C.C. 546.

[66] See Ch.25, below.

[67] *Re Bonus Breaks Ltd* [1991] B.C.C. 491.

deciding whether to grant such leave, however, the court will only be concerned with the risk to creditors of the old and new companies. In the absence of any evidence to the contrary it is not a question as to the director's fitness to act as such, that is relevant only to the separate question of disqualification. Nor is there any general rule that undertakings must be given as to the new company.[68]

In addition to the criminal offence under s.216, s.217 imposes personal liability on a director who acts either as such or in the management of a company in breach of s.216, for all debts incurred by that company whilst he is in breach. In *Thorne v Silverleaf*,[69] the Court of Appeal upheld a director's liability under this section to an investor in the second company, despite the fact that it was alleged that the latter was fully aware of the breach and had encouraged it. Public policy demanded that the liability under s.217 be strict. A similar view was taken in *Ricketts v Ad Valorem Factors Ltd*,[70] where the liability was imposed, even though the second company was not Phoenix company.

Personal liability of delinquent directors, etc.

Section 212 of the Insolvency Act 1986 provides that if in a winding up it appears that any person who is or has been an officer[71] of the company, or a promoter, or manager, liquidator, or administrative receiver of a company, has misapplied or retained or became accountable for any money or other property of the company, or has been guilty of any misfeasance or breach of trust or other duty to the company the court may on the application of the Official Receiver,[72] the liquidator or any creditor or contributory,[73] examine his conduct and order him to repay or restore the assets or to contribute to the assets of the company as the court thinks just. A contributory can only bring such an action with the leave of the court.

This section replaced s.631 of the Companies Act 1985 which had established a similar summary procedure whereby directors and others could be called to account swiftly for any breach of duty or misfeasance prior to the liquidation. In many ways it is identical with s.631 and many of the cases on that section will still apply. The main differences are that s.212 applies to administrative receivers and includes breaches of duty other than breaches of trust, *i.e.* negligence.[74] Although "misfeasance" is not a Scots law term, the section does apply to Scotland.

Section 631 was held to be procedural only. It gave a summary remedy, not a new cause of action.[75] It has been said that it "did not create any new liability, any new right, but only provides a summary mode of enforcing rights which must

---

[68] *Penrose v Official Receiver* [1996] 1 B.C.L.C. 389; *Re Lighting Electrical Contractors Ltd* [1996] 2 B.C.L.C. 302.

[69] [1994] 1 B.C.L.C. 637.

[70] [2004] 1 B.C.L.C. 1.

[71] This includes a director, manager or secretary.

[72] Not applicable in Scotland.

[73] Below, Ch.29.

[74] Thus overriding the earlier case law on s.631—see *Re B. Johnson & Co. (Builders) Ltd* [1955] Ch. 634.

[75] *Coventry and Dixon's Case* (1880) 14 Ch.D. 660, CA. See Lord President Inglis in *Liquidators of City of Glasgow Bank v Mackinnon* (1881) 9 R. 535 at p. 564 and Lord Guest (Ordinary) in *Lord Advocate v Liquidators of Purvis Industries Ltd*, 1958 S.C. 338 (O.H.), at p.342.

otherwise have been enforced by the ordinary procedure of the Courts." Also, that the applicant "must shew something which would have been the ground of an action by the company if it had not been wound up." There seems no reason why this should not apply equally to s.212 of the Insolvency Act 1986.

A summons was taken out by the liquidator against the secretary of a company for sums overdrawn by him on account of his salary on the instructions of the managing director. *Held*, as this was a claim for repayment of an ordinary debt due from the secretary without any wrongful conduct on his part, no order on the summons ought to be made: *Re Etic Ltd* [1928] Ch.861.

Instances of misfeasance under s.631 were the improper receipt by a director of his qualification shares from a promoter,[76] the overpayment of a director when he knew the company was insolvent,[77] and of an *ex gratia* payment in lieu of pension on the eve of liquidation.[78] No set-off was allowed to a claim for misfeasance under that section.[79] In relation to s.212 it has been held to include transfer of the company's business without requiring payment for goodwill and a non-genuine redundancy payment.[80]

The court has a discretion as to the amount to be ordered to be paid on an application under s.212 of the Insolvency Act 1986.

A liquidator negligently admitted a proof, which he should have disallowed, and as a result the company paid £30,000 to a creditor. An attempt to recover this failed, as there was no mistake of fact on the liquidator's part. *Held*, the liquidator was liable for misfeasance under s.631, but the court, in the exercise of its discretion, ordered him to pay only such a sum as would enable the creditors to be paid in full with interest at five per cent: *Re Home and Colonial Insce. Co. Ltd* [1930] 1 Ch.102.

Further, the court's power under s.631 was not merely to specify a sum by way of compensation but to apportion it between co-defendants in such a way and with such priority of liability as the court thought fit.[81] Again there is no reason to suppose that s.212 of the Insolvency Act 1986 has altered this.

An application under s.212 has been held irrelevant where it was an attempt to gain information rather than to obtain a remedy on information already known.[82]

DISQUALIFICATION OF DIRECTORS

The law relating to disqualification orders was consolidated from the Companies Act 1985 and the Insolvency Act 1985 into the Company Directors Disqualification Act 1986, as amended by the Insolvency Act 2000.

Disqualification orders other than on insolvency

Conviction of indictable offence or fraud in a winding up

Under s.2 of the Company Directors Disqualification Act 1986 the court may make a disqualification order that a person may not be a director of or be

---

[76] Which occurred in *Eden v Ridsdales Railway Lamp Co. Ltd* (1889) 23 Q.B.D. 368, CA.
[77] *Blin v Johnstone*, 1988 S.L.T. 335.
[78] *Gibson's Executor v Gibson*, 1978 S.C. 197 (O.H.).
[79] *Ex p. Pelly* (1882) 21 Ch.D. 492, CA.
[80] *Re Brian D. Pierson (Contractors) Ltd*, [2001] 1 B.C.L.C. 275. The latter payment was, however, excused under s.727, see p.315 above.
[81] *Re Morcambe Bowling Ltd* [1969] 1 W.L.R. 133.
[82] *Gray v Davidson*, 1991 S.L.T. (Sh.Ct.) 61.

concerned in any way, whether directly or indirectly, in the management of a company if he has been convicted of an indictable offence in connection with the promotion, formation, management or liquidation of a company, or with the receivership or management of a company. Such an order may also be made under s.4 of the 1986 Act if in a winding up it has appeared that a person has been guilty of fraudulent trading[83] or that he or she has been guilty, while an officer, of fraud or breach of duty in relation to the company. An offence is committed in connection with the management of a company if it has some factual connection with the management of a company; it does not have to be committed in the actual management of the company. Thus it includes insider dealing in the relevant company's shares[84] and carrying on an unlawful business through the medium of a company.[85] The maximum length of the order is 15 years.[86]

The period of disqualification must date from conviction, not, *e.g.* from the convicted person's release from prison.[87] The restriction on taking part in the management of the company is very wide. In particular the words "be concerned in" the management do not mean "take part in," and so include acting as a management consultant.[88]

In *R. v Young*,[89] the director had had a three and a half year record of successful business after committing the offence before the matter came to court. On the offence he was given a conditional discharge but disqualified for two years. This was quashed by the Court of Appeal (Criminal Division) on the basis of the intolerable delay and his recent record. Disqualification was a punishment which should be linked to the conditional discharge.

Persistent default

Section 3 of the 1986 Act provides that a person may alternatively be disqualified from being a director of or being concerned in the management of a company if he has been persistently in default in relation to any provision of the Companies Acts which requires any document to be delivered, or notice of any matter to be given, to the Registrar.[90]

The fact that a person has been persistently in default in relation to any provision of the Companies Acts may be conclusively proved by showing that in the five years ending with the date of the application he has been adjudged guilty (whether or not on the same occasion) of three or more defaults. A person is to be treated as being adjudged guilty of a default if:

    (a) he is convicted of any offence by virtue of any contravention of or failure to comply with any provision of the Companies Acts (whether on his own part or on the part of the company); or

[83] Below, Ch.27. This applies whether or not he is actually convicted of the offence.
[84] *R. v Goodman* [1994] 1 B.C.L.C. 349.
[85] *R. v Georgiou* (1988) 4 B.C.C., CA. See also *R. v Austen* (1985) 1 B.C.C. 99 528.
[86] Disqualification orders may run concurrently. For the width of the disqualification, see p.287, below.
[87] *R. v Bradley* [1961] 1 W.L.R. 398, CCA.
[88] *R. v Campbell* [1984] B.C.L.C. 83, CA. See also *Drew v H.M. Advocate*, 1996 S.L.T. 1062.
[89] [1990] B.C.C. 549.
[90] The conditions for application for, and breach of, an order are set out above.

(b)   a default order is made against him under ss 242 and 713 or ss 41, 170 of the Insolvency Act 1986, below.

However, it is not necessary to show three such convictions. In *Re Arctic Engineering Ltd*,[91] failure to send 35 required returns to the Registrar was held to be sufficient evidence for the making of an order.

An order made on this basis may only last for five and not 15 years.

Successive convictions or default orders

Alternatively, under s.5 of the 1986 Act a disqualification order may be made if a person is convicted of any offence by virtue of or failure to comply with any provision of the Act and in the five year period up to that conviction he has been convicted of other such offences or received default orders (see above), totalling three in number. In this case the court making the conviction can impose the disqualification order which may last for five years.

In *Re Civica Investments Ltd*,[92] the judge said that deciding the length of the disqualification was similar to the passing of a sentence in a criminal case. Elaborate reasoning was therefore unnecessary for, as more of the cases arose, it would be undesirable for the judge to be taken through the facts of previous cases. The five year period was a maximum and should be reserved for serious cases. In the case before him, since most of the defaults had been remedied the judge imposed a one year disqualification only.

Following an investigation by the DTI

The Secretary of State may apply for a disqualification order against a person if it appears to him to be expedient in the public interest following a report by inspectors,[93] or from the production of books and papers[94] or the entry and search of premises.[95] The decision of the Secretary of State not to apply may be challenged by way of judicial review by a person with sufficient interest but only if the decision was perverse or that the only lawful and proper decision would have been to make an application.[96] The court may make an order if it is satisfied that the person's conduct makes him unfit to be concerned in the management of a company: Company Directors Disqualification Act 1986, s.8. This is the same test as is applied in relation to orders made following a corporate insolvency[97] and the courts apply similar criteria both as to unfitness and as to the length of the period imposed,[98] although there is no mandatory minimum period. Evidence which the defendant has been compelled to give to the inspectors may be used in the disqualification proceedings,[99] but not the inspectors' own notes or drafts.[1]

---

[91] [1986] 1 W.L.R. 686.
[92] [1983] B.C.L.C. 458.
[93] Under s.437.
[94] Under s.447.
[95] Under s.448.
[96] *R. v Secretary of State, ex p. Lonrho plc* [1992] B.C.C. 325.
[97] See below.
[98] *Re Samuel Sherman plc.* [1991] 1 W.L.R. 1070; *Re Looe Fish Ltd* [1993] B.C.L.C. 1160 (improper allotment of shares to maintain control).
[99] *R. v Secretary of State, ex parte McCormick* [1998] B.C.C. 379, CA.
[1] *Re Astra Holdings plc* [1998] 2 B.C.L.C. 44. But in that case a side letter to the report expressing the view that the directors should not be disqualified had to be produced by the Secretary of State.

Disqualification orders following corporate insolvency

If the court is satisfied that a person is or has been a director[2] of a company which has become insolvent[3] within the past two years,[4] and that his conduct as such makes him unfit to be concerned in the management of a company,[5] it must make a disqualification order against him for at least two years: Company Directors Disqualification Act, s.6.[6] The order may be stayed pending an appeal.[7] The conduct may relate to one or more companies as specified, provided it tends to show unfitness. There may be evidence relating to a "lead" company (or companies)[8] and collateral companies. However, there is no requirement that the conduct in relation to a collateral company should be the same as, similar to, or explanatory or confirmatory of the conduct relied on in relation to the lead company. The only connection required is that the defendant was a director of both companies and the conduct shows unfitness.[9]

The application for such an order must be made by the Secretary of State (i.e. in practice, the Disqualification Unit of the DTI), if it appears to him to be in the public interest, as the result of information received from a liquidator, administrator, or administrative receiver. Those officials are under a duty to report information about a director's conduct in such matters to the Secretary of State: Company Directors Disqualification Act 1986, s.7.[10] Although the proceedings are civil, involving the civil standard of proof,[11] and not criminal they do involve penal consequences for the director. However, the European Court of Human Rights has held that only Art.6(1) of the European Convention on Human Rights applies (right to a fair trial within reasonable time) and not Arts 6(2) and (3) (presumption of innocence and specific right of defence in criminal trials).[12] It has therefore been held that natural justice requires that he should know the substance of the charges he has to meet,[13] so that a different charge cannot be introduced during the trial,[14] although the defendant's conduct during the proceedings may be used as an additional ground of unfitness.[15] The proceedings will not be automatically stayed because there are criminal charges also actually being brought,[16] or because they are taking places after other proceedings.[17] A company becomes insolvent for the purpose of such orders: (a) when it goes into liquidation at a time when its assets are insufficient to pay its debts, etc.[18]; (b)

---

[2] Including a shadow director and de facto director.
[3] See below.
[4] See below.
[5] See below.
[6] This section applies equally to non-residents and to conduct which occurred outside the UK: Re Seagull Manufacturing Co. Ltd (No. 2) [1994] 1 B.C.L.C. 273.
[7] Secretary of State v Bannister [1995] 2 B.C.L.C. 271.
[8] Re Surrey Leisure Ltd [1999] 2 B.C.L.C. 457, CA.
[9] Secretary of State v Ivens [1997] B.C.C. 801, CA.
[10] See the Insolvent Companies (Reports on Conduct of Directors) Rules 1996, SI 1996/1909.
[11] Re Living Images Ltd [1996] 1 B.C.L.C. 348.
[12] DC v United Kingdom [2000] B.C.C. 710, ECHR.
[13] See e.g. Re Sutton Glassworks Ltd [1997] 1 B.C.L.C. 26.
[14] Secretary of State for Trade and Industry v Crane [2001] 2 B.C.L.C. 222.
[15] Secretary of State for Trade and Industry v Ragna [2001] 2 B.C.L.C. 48.
[16] Re Cubelock Ltd [2001] B.C.C. 523.
[17] Secretary of State for Trade and Industry v Reynard [2002] 2 B.C.L.C. 625, CA.
[18] The effective date here is the making of the winding-up order: Re Walter L. Jacob & Co. Ltd [1993] B.C.C. 512. "Debts" in this context includes the liquidator's remuneration: Re Gower Enterprises Ltd [1995] 2 B.C.L.C. 107.

when an administration order is made in respect of the company[19]; (c) when an administrative receiver is appointed[20]: Company Directors Disqualification Act, s.6(2).

Time limit for applications

The director must be given ten days clear notice before the institution of proceedings. Failure to do so may make the proceedings invalid under s.16(1) of the Company Directors Disqualification Act.

However, failure to give such notice will not invalidate proceedings commenced without it unless there has been substantial prejudice caused to the defendant.[21]

More importantly s.7(2) of the Act provides that no application for a disqualification may be made after the end of the period of two years beginning with the day when the relevant company first became insolvent unless the court gives leave or the defendant consents to the delay.[22] This means the earliest of the insolvent acts set out above.[23] In deciding whether to give leave for an application out of time the court must take into account all the circumstances of the case, including the purpose for which the discretion was given and the public interest.[24] Among the factors to be considered are[25]: (i) the length of the delay; (ii) the reasons for the delay[26]; (iii) the strength of the case against the director; and (iv) the degree of prejudice caused to the director by the delay. In assessing the third of those factors the courts have allowed hearsay evidence to be used.[27] In general they will not go into the merits of the case in the same way as in a full trial. If there is a conflict of evidence then the courts must decide on the supporting evidence but if there is no conflict but an explanation by the defendant, these can be taken together.[28]

Striking out the application

As in all civil litigation an application to disqualify a director may be struck out by the courts for want of prosecution once the original application has been made. The Court of Appeal in *Re Manlon Trading Ltd*[29] said that the fact that the

---

[19] But not an interim order: *Secretary of State for Trade and Industry v Palmer* [1993] B.C.C. 650; 1994 S.C. 707.

[20] Whether or not that appointment was valid: *Secretary of State for Trade and Industry v Jabble* [1998] 1 B.C.L.C., CA.

[21] *Secretary of State for Trade and Industry v Langridge* [1991] B.C.L.C. 543; followed in *Secretary of State for Trade and Industry v Lovat*, 1996 S.C. 32.

[22] *Re New Technology Systems Ltd* [1997] B.C.C. 810.

[23] *Re Tasbian Ltd* [1990] B.C.C. 318; *Secretary of State for Trade and Industry v Normand*, 1994 S.L.T. 1249 (O.H.); *Secretary of State for Trade and Industry v Campleman 1999* S.L.T. 787, O.H.

[24] *Secretary of State for Trade and Industry v Davies* [1997] 2 B.C.L.C. 317, CA.

[25] *Re Probe Data Systems Ltd (No. 3)* [1992] B.C.L.C. 405, CA; *Re Polly Peck International plc (No. 2)* [1994] 1 B.C.L.C. 574; *Re Packaging Direct Ltd* [1994] B.C.C. 213; *Secretary of State for Trade and Industry v Cleland* [1997] 1 B.C.L.C. 437.

[26] See *e.g. Re Noble Trees Ltd* [1993] B.C.L.C. 1185; *Re Copecrest Ltd* [1994] 2 B.C.L.C. 284, CA; *Re Cedar Developments Ltd* [1994] 2 B.C.L.C. 714.

[27] *Re Polly Peck International plc (No. 2)* [1994] 1 B.C.L.C. 574.

[28] *Re Packaging Direct Ltd* [1994] B.C.C. 213.

[29] [1995] 1 B.C.L.C. 578, CA.

proceedings were brought in the public interest had to be balanced against the prejudice caused to the defendant by an inordinate or inexcusable delay. That could include consideration of delay in bringing the proceedings, *i.e.* at the end of the two-year time limit as well as delay after such commencement. Prejudice which might be caused by such delay would include the fact that the defendant would not be able to obtain other directorships during the delay. The European Court of Human Rights has held that such prejudice together with the impact on the defendant's reputation requires special diligence and expedition so that a delay of four and a half years after proceedings had been started was found to be a breach of Art. 6(1) of the European Convention on Human Rights which requires all civil proceedings to be heard within a reasonable time.[30]

An action may also be struck out for reasons other than delay such as the loss of documents by the applicant. In such a case the question is whether or not that loss can be compensated for at the substantive hearing.[31] Other reasons for striking out include a situation where it is plain and obvious that the case will fail,[32] or where the defendant has already been subject to proceedings on the same facts.[33] But it is not the courts' role to decide whether the Secretary of State has been over zealous in bringing the action.[34]

Disqualification undertakings

The sheer volume of proceedings for disqualification orders following an insolvency put great pressure on the system. To help alleviate this, a summary procedure, known as the *Carecraft* procedure,[35] was adopted for non-contentious cases. In essence this involved an agreed statement by the parties of the facts and the appropriate period of disqualification. But this still involved going to court and the court was not bound by the agreement.

Under changes made by the Insolvency Act 2000, however, the Secretary of State may now accept a disqualification undertaking from the defendant that he will not act as a director, receiver, promoter or manager of a company or as an insolvency practitioner for a stated period of between two and 15 years.[36] The legal effect of such an undertaking is the same as a disqualification order made by the court. The Secretary of State must be satisfied both that the disqualification is justified and that it is expedient in the public interest to accept an undertaking. In *Re Blackspur Group plc (No. 3)*,[37] the Court of Appeal held that in delegating this matter to the Secretary of State, Parliament had intended her to have a better appreciation of what was expedient in the public interest than the courts, so that she was quite entitled to refuse to accept an undertaking which did not have a schedule of the grounds of unfitness attached. Whilst the use of such undertakings will save much unnecessary expense, there is a danger that it

---

[30] *EDC v United Kingdom* [1998] B.C.C. 370, E.C.H.R..
[31] *Re Dexmaster Ltd* [1995] 2 B.C.L.C. 430.
[32] *Re Barings plc (No. 3)* [1998] 1 B.C.L.C. 590, C.A.
[33] *Secretary of State for Trade and Industry v Baker (No. 4)* [1999] 1 B.C.L.C. 226, CA.
[34] *ibid.*
[35] First used in *Re Carecraft Construction Co Ltd* [1993] B.C.L.C. 1259
[36] CDDA s.1(1A) and 7(2A).
[37] [2002] 2 B.C.L.C. 263 CA.

may be seen as a way of avoiding the possibility of having to pay the substantial costs involved in defending any formal proceedings.

Unfitness to be concerned in the management

In deciding whether a person's conduct makes him unfit to be concerned in the management of a company, s.9 of the Company Directors Disqualification Act 1986 requires the court to have regard to the matters specified in Sch.1 to that Act. These are: (a) any misfeasance, breach of duty or misapplication of assets[38]; (b) failure to comply with the requirements under the Companies Act relating to books and records, returns and accounts[39]; and, where the company has become insolvent; (c) responsibility for the cause of insolvency or for losses of customers who furnished advance payments and involvement in any transaction (or preference) which can be set aside[40]; and (d) failure to comply with the statutory requirements relating to insolvency.

In addition to such specific criteria the judges have laid down various tests to determine whether a director's conduct is deserving of disqualification. In *Re Dawson Print Group Ltd*[41] Hoffmann J. said:

"There must, I think, be something about the case, some conduct which if not dishonest is at any rate in breach of standards of commercial morality, or some really gross incompetence which persuades the court that it would be a danger to the public if he were allowed to continue to be involved in the management of companies, before a disqualification order is made."

In *Re Churchill Hotel (Plymouth) Ltd*[42] Peter Gibson J. construed this to mean that gross incompetence without a breach of commercial morality would suffice for a disqualification, whilst the statement was approved by Browne-Wilkinson V.-C. in *Re McNulty's Interchange Ltd*[43] together with his own test in *Re Lo-Line Electric Motors Ltd*[44] that:

"Ordinary commercial misjudgment is in itself not sufficient to justify disqualification. In the normal case, the conduct complained of must display a lack of commercial probity although I have no doubt that in an extreme case of gross negligence or total incompetence disqualification could be appropriate."

However, the Court of Appeal in *Re Sevenoaks Stationers (Retail) Ltd*[45] although describing such statements as helpful in identifying particular circum-

[38] See *e.g Re Keypak Homecare Ltd (No. 2)* [1990] B.C.C. 117; *Re T. & D. Services Ltd* [1990] B.C.C. 592; *Re Tansoft Ltd* [1991] B.C.L.C. 339; *Re Dominion International Group plc (No. 2)* [1996] 1 B.C.L.C. 572; *Re Ward Sherrard Ltd* [1996] B.C.C. 418.
[39] See, *e.g. Re Rolus Properties Ltd* (1988) 4 B.C.C. 446; *Re T. & D. Services Ltd, ante; Re New Generation Engineers Ltd* [1993] B.C.L.C. 435 and *Re Firedart Ltd* [1994] 2 B.C.L.C. 340.
[40] See *Secretary of State for Trade and Industry v Gray*, [1995] 1 B.C.L.C. 276 CA; *Re Living Images Ltd* [1996] 1 B.C.L.C. 348 *Secretary of State for Trade and Industry v Creegan* [2002] 1 B.C.L.C. 99, CA and Chap. 29, below.
[41] (1987) 3 B.C.C. 322, 324.
[42] (1988) 4 B.C.C. 112, 117.
[43] (1988) 4 B.C.C. 533, 536.
[44] [1988] Ch. 477, 479. See also *Re Chartmore Ltd* [1990] B.C.L.C. 673; *Re Tansoft Ltd* [1991] B.C.L.C. 339; *Re Austinsuite Furniture Ltd* [1992] B.C.L.C. 1047.
[45] [1991] B.C.L.C. 325.

stances in which a person would clearly be unfit warned against treating them as paraphrases of the wording of the section. It is a question of whether particular conduct makes a director unfit to be concerned in the management of a company. They added that incompetence to a marked degree would be sufficient, it need not be total, although it must amount to more than a simple commercial misjudgment, involving some form of lack of probity or abuse of the system. In *Secretary of State v Goldberg,*[46] after reviewing the cases, Lewison J. held that the question of unfitness required a broad-brush approach and rejected an argument that it was based on three criteria: competence, discipline and honesty.[47] But he did say that it would require a high standard before the court would disqualify someone who had acted honestly and had not broken any duty to anyone. The judge continued:

> "In considering whether a director is unfit, it is important to consider the cumulative effect of such of the allegations as are proved against him."

The clearest case where the courts regard the conduct as amounting to unfitness is where successive companies are formed which each become insolvent in turn, often transferring the business from one to the other.[48]

The general intention is to protect the public from abuse of the limited liability given by a company. However, the Court of Appeal, including Hoffmann L.J., in *Secretary of State for Trade and Industry v Gray*[49] made it quite clear that no such requirement is needed for an order to be made. It was irrelevant that the judge had decided that the director was no longer such a danger. The intention is also to raise standards of those who act as directors. The same idea is sometimes phrased by reference to the test being whether the director has forfeited the right to enjoy the privileges of limited liability by failing to perform the attendant duties.[50] A similar view was taken by Lord Woolf M.R., giving the judgment of the Court of Appeal in *Secretary of State for Trade and Industry v Griffiths.*[51] The fact that between the time of the acts complained of and the date of the hearing the defendant has shown that he has mended his ways and is no longer a danger to the public does not mean that no order should be made. There is a deterrent element involved in the procedure. Lord Woolf M.R. also said that the question for the court as to unfitness should be answered by the use of common sense and by adopting a practical and flexible approach so as to confine the evidence to that which is probative. Detailed or repetitive evidence should not be allowed. Over-elaboration in the preparing and hearing of cases and a technical approach to evidence simply leads to delay.

[46] [2004] 1 B.C.L.C. 597.
[47] See to *Secretary of State for Trade and Industry v Mitchell* 2002 S.L.T. 658, O.H., where Lord Carloway confirmed that unfitness had to be looked at in the context of the circumstances at the time, including the director's mental state, but disregarding improvement in conduct and expressions of remorse afterwards.
[48] *Re Travel Mondial Ltd* [1991] B.C.C. 224; *Re Linvale Ltd* [1993] B.C.L.C. 654; *Re Swift 736 Ltd* [1993] B.C.L.C. 896, CA.
[49] [1995] 1 B.C.L.C. 276, CA.
[50] This test was used by Vinelott J. in *Re Stanford Services Ltd* (1987) 3 B.C.C. 326, Peter Gibson J. in *Re Bath Glass Ltd, ante,* Mervyn Davies J. in *Re Majestic Recording Studios Ltd* (1988) 4 B.C.C. 519, and Hoffmann J. in *Re Ipcon Fashions Ltd* (1989) 5 B.C.C. 773 and Nicholls V.-C. in *Re Swift 736 Ltd* [1993] B.C.L.C. 896.
[51] [1998] 2 B.C.L.C. 646, CA.

Disqualification orders have been refused where the director's conduct was only imprudent and improper[52] and where there was a reasonable reliance on advice which indicated that the director had none of the badges of a man who had exploited limited liability in a cynical way, with disregard for proper responsibility, or by incompetence.[53] Allegations of incompetence alone have been said to require a high standard. The order should not be made out of sympathy for the creditors or to appease them.[54]

On the other hand, it has been held that there are minimum standards which can be expected of all directors. In small companies, directors have been disqualified even where they have taken no active part in the management of the company. A director cannot simply abrogate his responsibilities as a director to others[55]; he has to keep himself informed and will be unfit otherwise.[56] Even reliance on professional advice may be insufficient where the director has asked no questions and done exactly as he was told to do.[57] As applied to larger companies, this has been stated in the context of responsibility to supervise others, whether as executive directors supervising senior employees or non-executive directors supervising the executives. The leading case is *Re Barings plc (No.5)*,[58] following the spectacular collapse of that bank as a result of the activities of a single trader in Singapore. Failure by the directors to control the trader's activities, in particular failure to implement internal audit requirements, rendered the directors unfit. The existing controls were described as crass and an absolute failure. There was incompetence to a high degree in a management role and that was enough. Errors of judgment could amount to unfitness.

Failure to resign as a director is not fatal, however. If the director protests against further trading and stays on to use his influence,[59] he will not be unfit unless he has also been directly involved in the breaches of statutory duty, *e.g.* as to the production of accounts.[60]

One area of dispute has been the relevance of a director allowing his company to run up arrears of money which it ought to have paid over to the tax authorities. The significant point is that these debts are not trading debts in the ordinary sense since they arise out of the use for other purposes of money which the company actually receives on behalf of the Crown, *e.g.* VAT collected from suppliers, income tax deducted at source from employees' wages under the Pay As You Earn system and national insurance contributions similarly deducted and not handed over to the correct authorities. In *Re Dawson Print Group Ltd*[61]

---

[52] *Re Bath Glass Ltd, ibid.* See also *Re ECM (Europe) Electronics Ltd* [1991] B.C.C. 268 and *Re Wimbledon Village Restaurant Ltd* [1994] B.C.C. 753; *Secretary of State for Trade and Industry v Blackwood* 2003 S.L.T. 12, I.H.

[53] *Re Douglas Construction Services Ltd* (1988) 4 B.C.C. 553.

[54] *Re Cubelock Ltd* [2001] B.C.C. 523.

[55] *Official Receiver v Vass* [1999] B.C.C. 516 (the defendant was named as a director of a large number of companies registered in Sark in the Channel Islands—this is known as the "Sark Lark").

[56] Even if he has an honest but unreasonable belief that he is not a director: *Re Kaytech International Ltd* [1999] 2 B.C.L.C. 351 CA.

[57] *Re Bradcrown Ltd* [2001] 1 B.C.L.C. 547.

[58] [2000] 1 B.C.L.C. 521 CA, upholding [1999] 1 B.C.L.C. 433.

[59] Unless he has no realistic chance of doing so and is staying on for his fees: *Secretary of State for Trade and Industry v Gash* [1997] 1 B.C.L.C. 341.

[60] *Re C S Holdings Ltd* [1997] B.C.C. 172; *Secretary of State v Arif* [1997] 1 B.C.L.C. 34.

[61] (1987) 3 B.C.C. 322. See also *Re CV Fittings Ltd* (1989) 5 B.C.C. 210; *Re Keypak Homecare Ltd (No. 2)* [1990] B.C.C. 117.

Hoffmann J. rejected the idea that in some way these sums amounted to quasi-trust moneys so that misappropriation was a serious matter. Failure to pay such debts was not a sufficient breach of commercial morality as to justify a disqualification. In *Re Stanford Services Ltd*,[62] Vinelott J., whilst deciding that failure to set aside sums to cover those debts was not in itself a breach of commercial morality, stated that the Crown was nevertheless an involuntary creditor and if a company went into liquidation with such sums owing and irrecoverable the directors would be regarded as either being improperly informed as to the company's financial position or as acting improperly in using the money to finance the company's current trade.

In *Re Sevenoaks Stationers (Retail) Ltd*[63] the Court of Appeal agreeing with Hoffmann J.'s statement, regarded non-payment of Crown debts as important, not because of the fact that they were such debts, but because their non-payment indicated that the director was only paying those creditors who were pressing for their debts at the time to the detriment of other creditors, including the Crown. Viewed in that light such non-payment was a factor to be taken into account when deciding whether a director was unfit to be concerned in the management of a company. This approach has since been adopted by the judges.[64]

Period of disqualification

If the court finds that a director is unfit to be concerned in the management of a company under s.6 of the Company Directors Disqualification Act 1986, it has no choice but to impose a period of disqualification of between two and 15 years.[65] This is the only area where a disqualification order must be imposed; the court has no discretion except as to the length of the order. This was criticised by Vinelott J. in *Re Pamstock Ltd*[66] as being unduly rigid, especially as no minimum period is required in other areas such as fraudulent trading. There is no equivalent of a conditional discharge.

The Court of Appeal in *Re Sevenoaks Stationers (Retail) Ltd*[67] laid down what, in effect, amounts to sentencing guidelines, which have been adopted in all the cases decided thereafter. The 15-year ambit should be divided into three bands. The band over 10 years should be used only for very serious cases such as a second disqualification[68]; that between six and 10 years for serious cases involving some form of breach of duty such as misappropriation of assets or deliberate misuse of the corporate form to prejudice creditors, and that from two to five years for less serious cases such as gross negligence or incompetence. The length

---

[62] (1987) 3 B.C.C. 326. This approach was followed in other cases, *e.g.* in *Re Lo-Line Motors Ltd* [1988] Ch. 477.

[63] [1991] B.C.L.C. 325.

[64] See *e.g. Re City Investment Centres Ltd* [1992] B.C.L.C. 956; *Re New Generation Engineers Ltd* [1993] B.C.L.C. 435; *Re Park House Properties Ltd* [1997] 2 B.C.L.C. 530; *Re Verby Print for Advertising Ltd* [1998] 2 B.C.L.C. 23; *Re Amaron Ltd* [2001] 1 B.C.L.C. 562 (where an attempt to negotiate with the Inland Revenue failed).

[65] Section 6(4).

[66] [1994] 1 B.C.L.C. 716.

[67] [1991] B.C.L.C. 325, CA.

[68] For examples of such a serious case see *Secretary of State for Trade and Industry v McTigue* [1996] 2 B.C.L.C. 477, CA. *Re Sever Ltd* [1999] B.C.C. 221; *Official Receiver v Vass* (1999) B.C.C. 316.

of the period is a matter for the court and not for agreement between the parties.[69]

In *Secretary of State for Trade and Industry v Griffiths*,[70] the Court of Appeal, approved its earlier decision in *Secretary of State for Trade and Industry v McTigue*,[71] that fixing the appropriate period was a matter for the judge in accordance with the *Sevenoaks* principles. The Court of Appeal also said that although imposing a disqualification period is not technically a "punishment", in reality it is a sentencing exercise and must contain a deterrent element. "Plea bargaining" as such is not allowed but credit may be given for admission of facts which would otherwise have taken a great deal of time and expense to prove. There should be no need to be over-elaborate in deciding this question and the citation of previous cases as to the period of disqualification will usually be unnecessary and inappropriate. The best approach would be to fix the period on the basis of the gravity of the offence and then take into account any mitigating factors such as the age and health of the defendant, delay in proceedings and admission, etc.

There are many reported examples of this system operating in practice, two may suffice by way of illustration. In *Re A & C Group Services Ltd*[72] the allegations against three directors included not only responsibility for the company's failure by ineffective stewardship of its affairs such as defective accounting procedures, failure to take into account excessive trading losses and non payment of Crown debts, but also more serious allegations of improper use of company funds, making misleading statements, taking excessive remuneration and illegal use of directors' loan accounts. One of the directors was identified as being responsible for all of these and was disqualified within the middle band, for six years. That took into account the delay in bringing the proceedings and the fact that he had admitted the charges. The other two directors were held not to be primarily responsible for the more serious allegations and to have been influenced by the other at a time of ill health. Nevertheless they were responsible for the poor management and should be disqualified for the minimum period of two years. In *Official Receiver v Stern*,[73] a 12-year penalty was imposed where the defendant had taken money out of the company and allowed it to trade at a time when he knew it was insolvent, had financed the business out of monies owed to the Crown and been party to the Phoenix syndrome. This was a particularly serious case.

Both parties can appeal against the length of the disqualification period and it is possible for the period to be increased on appeal if the judge is found to have erred in principle rather than simply as to the exercise of his discretion. In *Re Swift 736 Ltd*[74] the defendant had been a director of sixteen insolvent companies. In respect of six of these, which had carried on the same business in succession as the previous one failed, he had not been the principal director. The other

---

[69] *Re Barings plc* [1998] B.C.C. 583.
[70] [1998] 2 B.C.L.C. 646, CA.
[71] [1996] 2 B.C.L.C. 477, CA.
[72] [1993] B.C.L.C. 1297.
[73] [2002] 1 B.C.L.C. 119 CA.
[74] [1993] B.C.L.C. 312, CA.

directors had already been disqualified for five years in separate proceedings. With regard to the other 10 companies the complaints were of failure to keep proper accounts and to file returns, etc. The judge disqualified him for three years. The Court of Appeal decided that the judge had been over-concerned with the periods given to the other directors and had failed to take into account the other 10 companies. Taken together this was serious misconduct and justified a six-year period.

The court has the power under s.17 of the 1986 Act when making a disqualification order to make an exception for a particular company. It may also hear applications for exceptions to a disqualification undertaking. The Court of Appeal in *Secretary of State for Trade and Industry v Griffiths*,[75] said that whether such a discretion is likely to be exercised is not a relevant factor in determining the period of disqualification. The principles for exercising this discretion were set out in *Secretary of State for Trade and Industry v Collins*.[76] The company must be shown to need the defendant's services; there must be no risk to the public; and there must be no subversion of the order, even if only of its deterrent effect. The burden of proof is on the defendant.

The court may impose conditions on the granting of leave.[77] Failure to observe these conditions may lead to such leave being withdrawn. It could also mean acting as a director contrary to the order, which could involve criminal penalties and personal liability.[78]

Costs

The normal rule is that costs are awarded against the losing party but the court has a discretion. There has been some dispute as to the basis upon which costs are to be awarded against a disqualified director. Some judges have awarded costs on an indemnity basis, (*i.e.* full costs unless the defendant can prove that they are unreasonable) rather than the normal standard basis (where costs have to be justified) on the grounds that these are public interest proceedings.[79] Others have used the standard basis unless the defendant has acted unreasonably.[80] The matter appears to have been resolved by the Court of Appeal in *Re Dicetrade Ltd*,[81] in favour of the latter approach. These are civil proceedings and the Secretary of State must take his chance. Cases where the indemnity basis would be appropriate include where the defendant makes extravagant claims or a wholly false and futile defence, or defends claims with no conceivable defence. With regard to orders for costs made against the Secretary of State the court again has a complete discretion as to the basis used.[82] An indemnity basis was used where the allegations were misconceived and no explanation had ever been sought from the defendants.[83]

[75] [1998] 2 B.C.L.C. 646, CA.
[76] [2000] B.C.L.C. 233.
[77] *Re Chartmore Ltd* [1990] B.C.L.C. 673; *Secretary of State for Trade and Industry v Palfreman*, 1995 S.L.T. 156 (O.H.); [1995] 2 B.C.L.C. 301.
[78] *Re Brian Sheridan Cars Ltd* [1996] 1 B.C.L.C. 327.
[79] See *e.g. Re Brooks Transport (Purfleet) Ltd* [1993] B.C.C. 766.
[80] See *e.g. Re Synthetic Technology Ltd* [1993] B.C.C. 549.
[81] [1994] 2 B.C.L.C. 113, CA. See also *Re Godwin Warren Ltd* [1993] B.C.L.C. 80, CA.
[82] *Re Southbourne Sheet Metal Co. Ltd (No. 2)* [1993] B.C.L.C. 135.
[83] *Secretary of State for Trade and Industry v Blake* [1997] 1 B.C.L.C. 728.

Personal liability of persons acting whilst disqualified through bankruptcy or by a disqualification order or undertaking

Any person disqualified by reason of his personal bankruptcy under s.11 of the Company Directors Disqualification Act 1986 or by a disqualification order or undertaking and who becomes involved in the management of the company,[84] or acts in breach of a condition attached to leave to act as a director of a specific company under s.17 is personally liable for all debts incurred whilst he was so involved. This liability extends to those who although not disqualified themselves act or are willing to act on the orders of someone who is so disqualified and whom he knows is so disqualified. Anyone who has so acted is presumed to be willing to act in the future. The liability extends to debts incurred whilst they were so acting or willing to act: Company Directors Disqualification Act 1986, s.15. Liability under this head can also lead to a criminal offence under s.13 of the Act. The offence is one of strict liability so that it is no defence that the defendant thought that he was no longer bankrupt.[85]

Register of disqualification orders and undertakings

Section 18 of the Company Directors Disqualification Act provides that the prescribed officer of any court which makes an order that a person shall not, without the leave of the court, be a director of or be concerned in the management of a company for a specified period or grants leave in relation to such an order, must furnish the Secretary of State with particulars of the order or the grant of leave where the order is made under that Act.

The Secretary of State must maintain a register of such orders, undertakings accepted by her, and grants of leave, which register is open to inspection on payment of such fee as may be specified by the Secretary of State in regulations made by statutory instrument.[86]

---

[84] This includes acting as a director or directly or indirectly taking part in the management of the company: C.D.D.A. 1986 s.15(4). See *R. v Campbell, above.*

[85] *R. v Brockley* [1994] 1 B.C.L.C. 606.

[86] See the Companies (Disqualification Orders) Regulations 2001 (SI 2001/967).

Chapter 16

THE SECRETARY

EVERY company must have secretary and a sole director cannot also be secretary: s.283(1), (2). The secretary may be an individual or a Scottish firm or a corporation, but a corporation cannot be the secretary if its sole director is also the sole director of the company: s.283(4). A company may have all the partners of a firm as joint secretaries: see s.290. That section also requires disclosure of the identity of the secretary in the register of directors and secretaries to be kept by the company under s.288.[1]

Section 286, first introduced in 1980, requires the directors of a public company to secure that the secretary is a person who appears to them to have the requisite knowledge and experience to be a secretary. In addition a public company secretary must have either been a public company secretary for three out of the five years before his present appointment, or be a barrister, advocate or solicitor, or a member of one of the professional accountancy bodies or of the Institute of Chartered Secretaries and Administrators, or be someone who because of his position or qualifications appears to the directors to be capable of discharging the duties of a public company secretary. A private company secretary need have no such qualifications.

The secretary is usually appointed by the directors, but sometimes he is named in the articles.[2]

Table A, reg. 99, provides: "Subject to the provisions of the Act, the secretary shall be appointed by the directors for such term, at such renumeration and upon such conditions as they may think fit; and any secretary so appointed may be removed by them."

The position of a company's secretary has changed a great deal in the last 100 years. In 1887 it was said that: "a secretary is a mere servant; his position is that he is to do what he is told, and no person can assume that he has any authority to represent anything at all; nor can anyone assume that statements made by him are necessarily to be accepted as trustworthy without further inquiry."[3] Accordingly, it has in the past been held that a company is not liable for the acts of its secretary in fraudulently making representations to induce persons to take shares in the company,[4] or in issuing a forged share certificate.[5] The secretary is,

---

[1] Subject to the new provisions as to confidentiality orders: see ss 723B–723F, inserted by the Criminal Justice and Police Act 2001.

[2] As to which see *Eley v Positive Life Assurance Co. Ltd* (1876) 1 Ex.D. 88, CA, above, p.75.

[3] *per* Lord Esher M.R. in *Barnett, Hoares & Co. v South London Tramways Co.* (1887) 18 Q.B.D. 815, CA, at p.817.

[4] *Barnett, Hoares & Co. v South London Tramway Co.*, above.

[5] *Ruben v Great Fingall Consolidated* [1906] A.C. 439, above, p.222.

however, the proper official to issue share certificates, and so the company is estopped or barred from denying the truth of genuine share certificates issued by him without the authority of the company.[6] He may also, with a director, validly excute a deed on behalf of the company whether or not that company has a common seal.[7]

It has also been held under the old cases that the secretary has no implied authority to bind the company by contract.[8]

Thus, it has been held that he has no implied authority[9] to borrow money on behalf of the company,[10] issue a writ in the company's name[11] or lodge defences in the company's name,[12] and it is not his duty as secretary to instruct the company as to its legal rights.[13]

The secretary of a company is not "an official who *virtute officii* can manage all its affairs with or without the help of servants, in the absence of a regular directorate": *per* Lord Parker in *Daimler Co. Ltd v Continental Tyre Co. Ltd* [1916] 2 A.C. 307 at p.377.

However, the modern status of the company secretary was taken into account in *Panorama Developments (Guildford) Ltd v Fidelis Furnishing Fabrics Ltd*[14] where it was said[15] that a company secretary is a much more important person now than he was in the past. He is the chief administrative officer of the company with extensive duties and responsibilities. This appears not only in the modern Companies Acts but in the role which he plays in the day-to-day business of the company. He is no longer a mere clerk. He regularly makes representations on behalf of the company and enters into contracts on its behalf which come within the day-to-day running of its business. So much so that he may be regarded as held out as having authority to do such things on behalf of the company. He is certainly entitled to sign contracts connected with the administrative side of a company's affairs, such as employing staff and ordering cars. All such matters come within the implied or apparent authority of a company's secretary.

The secretary, purportedly on behalf of the company, fraudulently hired cars, ostensibly for the purpose of meeting customers, and used the cars for his own private purposes. *Held*, the secretary had implied authority to enter into contracts for the hire of cars on behalf of the company and the company was liable to pay the hire charges: *Panorama Developments (Guildford) Ltd v Fidelis Furnishing Fabrics Ltd* [1971] 2 Q.B. 711, CA.

On the other hand it appears that he still has no implied authority to make representations about the company in relation to a commercial transaction, *e.g.* a syndicated loan.[16]

[6] *Clavering, Son & Co. v Goodwins, Jardine & Co. Ltd* (1891) 18 R. 652.
[7] S.36A(4). Above, p.91.
[8] *Houghton & Co. v Nothard, Lowe & Wills Ltd* [1928] A.C. 1. He may of course be given actual authority to do anything: see *UBAF Ltd v European Banking Corp.* [1984] Q.B. 713.
[9] Above, p.99.
[10] *Re Cleadon Trust Ltd* [1939] Ch. 286, CA.
[11] *Daimler Co. Ltd v Continental Tyre, etc., Co. Ltd* [1916] 2 A.C. 307.
[12] *Edington v Dunbar Steam Laundry Co.* (1903) 11 S.L.T. 117 (O.H.).
[13] *Niven v Collins Patent Lever Gear Co. Ltd* (1900) 7 S.L.T. 476 (O.H.).
[14] [1971] 2 Q.B. 711, CA.
[15] *Per* Lord Denning M.R. and Salmon L.J., at pp. 716, 717.
[16] *UBAF Ltd v European American Banking Corp.* [1984] Q.B. 713.

The duties of the secretary depend on the size and nature of the company, and on the arrangement made with him. In any case he will be present at all meetings of the company, and of the directors, and will make proper minutes of the proceedings. He will issue, under the direction of the board, all notices to members and others. In practice he will usually countersign every instrument to which the seal of the company is affixed. Alternatively, he is one of those whose signature will validate a document as a document under seal by virtue of s.36A (Ch.6, above). He or his department will conduct all correspondence with shareholders in regard to transfers and otherwise, will certify transfers, and will keep the books of the company, or such of them as relate to the internal business of the company, *e.g.* the register of members, the share ledger, the transfer book, the register of charges, etc. He will also make all necessary returns to the Registrar, *e.g.* the annual return, notices, etc.

If a provision requires or authorises a thing to be done by or to a director and the secretary it is not satisfied by the thing being done by or to the same person acting both as director and as secretary: s.284.

If a person is secretary of two companies, a fact which comes to his knowledge as secretary of one company is not notice to him as secretary of another company, unless it was his duty to the first company to communicate his knowledge to the second company.

H was secretary to two companies, A Co. and B Co. B. Co. drew a bill on a third company, C Co., and indorsed it in favour of A Co. The bill was dishonoured by C Co. and no notice of dishonour was given to B Co. It was claimed that as H, in his capacity of secretary, knew of the dishonour, no notice was necessary. *Held*, notice to H, as secretary of A Co., was not notice to B Co.: *Re Fenwick, Stobart & Co.* [1902] 1 Ch.507.

In England, a full-time secretary has been held to be an employee so as to be entitled to preferential payment of his salary on a winding up but a part-time secretary is not.[17]

The secretary is an officer of the company: s.744. In some instances therefore he is in the same position as a director so that a provision in the articles or in any contract for relieving him from liability is void: s.309a.[18] In addition it is perfectly possible for the secretary to be liable following a breach of trust or fiduciary duty by the directors under the "knowing assistance" head of liability, or under the tort of conspiracy, provided, in either case that the requisite criteria are satisfied.[19] Again, the court can relieve him from liability in certain cases: s.727.[20]

A secretary has been held to have no lien over the books of the company coming into his possession in the course of his duties.[21]

---

[17] *Cairney v Back* [1906] 2 K.B. 746 below, p.581. Scottish cases in which a secretary was held not be a "clerk or servant" for this purpose are *Scottish Poultry Journal Co.* (1896) 4 S.L.T. 167 (O.H.), *Clyde Football etc. Co. Ltd* (1900) 8 S.L.T. 328 (O.H.) and *Laing v Gowans* (1902) 10 S.L.T. 461 (O.H.).

[18] Above, p.314.

[19] See, *e.g. Brown v Bennett* [1998] 2 B.C.L.C. 97.

[20] As amended by the Companies (Audit, Investigations and Community Enterprise) Act 2004, s.19(2). Above, p.315.

[21] *Gladstone v M'Callum* (1896) 23 R. 783 (minute book); *Barnton Hotel Co. Ltd v Cook* (1899) 1 F. 1190 (register of members and other books and documents at secretary's own premises).

Chapter 17

MAJORITY RULE AND MINORITY PROTECTION

Majority Rule

The members of a company can express their wishes at general meetings by voting for or against the resolutions proposed. As such, the will of the majority of the members usually prevails and if the appropriate majority is obtained a resolution binds all the members, including those who voted against it. Sometimes the majority is a simple majority and sometimes it is a three-quarters majority—for example, an ordinary resolution is a resolution passed by a simple majority of the votes of the members entitled to vote and voting; a special resolution is a resolution passed by a three-quarters majority of the votes of such members.[1] This can be said to be the first example of what is called "majority rule".

Further, it should be remembered that, subject to a few restrictions, the articles of a company, which constitute a contract binding the company and the members, can be altered by special resolution.[2]

Another example of majority rule, as we shall see, is the rule in *Foss v Harbottle*, by which, subject to certain exceptions, if a wrong to a company is alleged, or if there is an alleged irregularity in its internal management which is capable of confirmation by a simple majority of the members, the court will not interfere at the suit of a minority of the members.

Exercising Majority Control

We have seen that under the principle of majority rule the company in general meeting may waive a breach of fiduciary duty by a director who contracts with the company as in the *N.W. Transportation* case,[3] or by one who makes a secret profit out of his position as in *Regal (Hastings) Ltd v Gulliver*,[4] or may waive a breach of a director's duty of care, as in *Pavlides v Jensen*.[5] It has often been stated that although the directors of a company owe fiduciary duties[6] to the company, as such, shareholders do not: "When voting, a shareholder may consult his own interests."[7]

---

[1] Above, p.258.
[2] Above, p.75.
[3] (1987) 12 App. Cas.589, PC.
[4] [1967] 2 A.C. 134.
[5] [1956] Ch.656.
[6] Above, p.294.
[7] *Per* Megarry V.-C. in *Estmanco (Kilner House) Ltd v G.L.C.* [1982] 1 W.L.R. 2 at p.11.

Until recently it has thus been accepted that a share is a piece of property which is to be enjoyed and exercised for the owner's personal advantage.[8] Thus a shareholder may bind himself by contract to vote in a particular way:

"When a director votes as a director for or against any particular resolution in a directors' meeting he is voting as a person under a fiduciary duty to the company for the proposition that the company should take a certain course of action. When a shareholder is voting for or against a particular resolution he is voting as a person owing no fiduciary duty to the company and who is exercising his own right of property, to vote as he thinks fit. The fact that the result of the voting at the meeting (or at a subsequent poll) will bind the company cannot affect the position that, in voting, he is voting simply in exercise of his own property rights . . . a director is an agent, who casts his vote to decide in what manner his principal shall act through the collective agency of the board of directors; a shareholder who casts his vote in general meeting is not casting it as an agent of the company in any shape or form. His act therefore, in voting as he pleases, cannot in any way be regarded as an act of the company": per Walton J. in Northern Countries Securities Ltd v Jackson and Steeple Ltd [1974] 1 W.L.R. 1133, at p.1144.

In Greenwell v Porter,[9] where executors and trustees of a will who held shares agreed to sell some to G., who stipulated that he should nominate X as a director and that the executors should, when X retired by rotation, vote for his re-election, it was held that the executors were bound by the agreement. It may be mentioned that there was a voting agreement in Greenhalgh v Mallard[10] but it was held that the shareholders who agreed to vote in a certain way were under no obligation to retain their shares and there was no continuing obligation running with the shares.

This right to vote has, however, always been subject to the doctrine of fraud on the minority so that the majority cannot waive a breach of a director's fiduciary duty by approving a misappropriation by him of the company's property which would be a fraud on the minority. That is what the majority tried to do in Cook v Deeks.[11]

Members cannot, by resolution in general meeting, expropriate the company's property.

The shareholders in E Co., which was formed with the object of constructing a submarine telegraph, were H Co. with 3,000 shares, M with 2,000 and 13 other persons with 325 between them. H Co. was to make and lay cables for E Co. The directors of E Co., who were nominees of H Co., and H Co. decided not to pursue an action in which E Co. was claiming a concession to construct the telegraph, procured the passing of a resolution in general meeting to put E Co. into voluntary winding up and concealed the fact that they had agreed to end the agreement between E Co. and H Co. so that H Co. could sell the cable to a third company. M brought an action on behalf of himself and the other shareholders, except those who were defendants, in which he joined E Co. as a defendant. He claimed, inter alia, a declaration that H Co. was a trustee of the resulting profit for M and the other shareholders in E Co. Held, M succeeded. The majority shareholder had obtained certain advantages by dealing with something which was the property of the whole company: Menier v Hooper's Telegraph Works (1874) L.R. 9 Ch.App. 350.

---

[8] See, e.g. N.W. Transportation v Beatty, above, p.337.
[9] [1902] 1 Ch. 530. See also Puddephat v Leith [1916] 1 Ch. 200.
[10] [1943] 2 All E.R. 234, CA.
[11] [1916] 1 A.C. 554, below, p.345.

As regards the property of other members of the company, we saw in Chapter 4 that, on the authority of *Sidebottom v Kershaw, Leese & Co.*,[12] an alteration of the articles by special resolution in general meeting in order to enable some members to acquire the shares of other members must be bona fide for the benefit of the company as a whole.

Further, we saw that cases such as *Greenhalgh v Arderne Cinemas Ltd*,[13] and *Shuttleworth v Cox Bros. Ltd*,[14] established the rule that in making any alternation to the articles the general meeting must act bona fide for the benefit of the company as a whole. Similarly, a class meeting of preference shareholders sanctioning a modification of the special rights of the preference shares must act bona fide for the benefit of the class as a whole.[15]

It was said in a Scottish case[16] that: "Prima facie, the shareholders are the best judges of their own affairs, and it is only where it appears that some sinister motive has operated, or that interests other than the interest of the company have plainly prevailed, that the Court will entertain a complaint. The test always is, Is the thing complained of a thing done in the interest of the company?—or, to put it perhaps more accurately. Is the action of the majority irreconcilable with their having proceeded upon any reasonable view of the company's interest?" In the case in question a resolution of a general meeting to issue unissued shares to the managing director at a lower premium than would have been obtained on the market was valid. In another Scottish case it was said that "The question . . . is whether the resolution complained of . . . can be held to be so oppressive and extravagant that no reasonable man could consider it to be for the benefit of the Company."[17]

Thus controlling members do owe a duty to the company, *i.e.* the corporators as a body, to act bona fide for the benefit of the company as a whole and not to commit a fraud on the minority.

It has been said in one case, however, that the controlling members may in fact be subject to more stringent controls than the accepted doctrine of a fraud on the minority, although not being subject to the full fiduciary duties of a director.

In *Clemens v Clemens Bros. Ltd*[18] the defendant owned 55 per cent of the issued shares of a family company. She was one of five directors and proposed to give the other directors shares and to set up a trust for long-service employees. The plaintiff, who was the defendant's niece, held 40 per cent of the shares and was not a director. The defendant proposed resolutions to increase the capital so that the plaintiff's shares would fall below 25 per cent of the total and her right to veto special resolutions would be lost. It was also clear that she would never now obtain control of the company. The judge held that the defendant was not entitled to exercise her majority votes as an ordinary shareholder in any way she pleased. That right was subject to equitable considerations which could make it unjust to exercise them in a particular way. In this case such considerations applied and the resolutions would be set aside.

---

[12] [1920] 1 Ch. 154, CA, above, p.78.
[13] [1951] Ch. 286, CA, above, p.77.
[14] [1927] 2 K.B. 9, CA above, p.77.
[15] *Re Holders Investment Trust Ltd* [1971] 1 W.L.R. 583, at p.182.
[16] *per* Lord Kyllachy (Ordinary) in *Cameron v Glenmorangie Distillery Co. Ltd* (1896) 23 R. 1092 at p.1095.
[17] *per* Lord Wark (Ordinary) in *Harris v A. Harris Ltd*, 1936 S.C. 183 at p.192.
[18] [1976] 2 All E.R. 268.

One interpretation of this case is that it shows that the majority do not have unrestricted voting rights if it is "unjust" in the particular circumstances.

In *Estmanco (Kilner House) Ltd v Greater London Council*[19] Megarry V.-C., however, accepted the general proposition that the shareholders do not owe any fiduciary duties but affirmed that in altering the articles they are subject to the doctrine of fraud on the minority, *i.e.* they must act in what they believe to be in the best interests of the company as a whole. In that case the majority shareholder wished to deprive the company of a right of action under a contract and proposed, and carried, a resolution to that effect. A minority shareholder sought to bring an action on behalf of the company[20] to prevent this. Megarry V.-C. considered the situation thus[21]:

> "Plainly there must be some limit to the power of the majority to pass resolutions which they believe to be in the best interests of the company and yet remain immune from interference by the courts. It may be in the best interests of the company to deprive the minority of some of their rights or some of their property, yet I do not think that this gives the majority an unrestricted right to do this, however unjust it may be, and however much it may harm shareholders whose rights as a class differ from those of the majority."

More recently, however, in *Re Swindon Town Football Club Ltd*,[22] Harman J. said that the general rule that shareholders are entitled to vote in their own interest remains the law and is the correct proposition, even though it has not been followed on every modern occasion, notably in *Clemens v Clemens Bros Ltd* (above). The judge also accepted the proposition that: "The company is entitled to consider lawful resolutions, however silly, and, if thought fit, to pass them, and it is not for the court to tell the company that it should not be silly."[23]

On the other hand, the courts do retain an inherent power to grant an injunction to prevent a shareholder from voting with his shares if there would otherwise be substantial injury to the company, or to protect secured creditors from destruction of the secured assets.[24]

Minority protection

Both under the general law and under the Companies and other Acts there is some protection of the minority.[25]

Examples of minority protection are:

(1) Under the general law, the doctrine that the majority of the members must not commit a fraud on the minority but must act bona fide for the benefit of the company as a whole.[26]

---

[19] [1982] 1 All E.R. 437.
[20] Below, p.343.
[21] [1982] 1 W.L.R. 2, at pp.11–12.
[22] [1990] B.C.L.C. 467.
[23] *ibid.*, at p.469.
[24] *Standard Chartered Bank v Walker* [1992] B.C.L.C. 603.
[25] The CLR made a number of recommendations in this area, but these have not, so far, been taken up by the government. See the CLR, *Final Report* Vol 1 (2002), paras 7.33–7.62.
[26] Above, p.338.

(2) The exceptions to the rule in *Foss v Harbottle*, in which case an individual member may bring what is known as a derivative action on behalf of the company.

(3) The various sections intended to protect a minority of members. Some apply on a general basis; thus under ss 122 and 124 of the Insolvency Act 1986[27] a member can petition the court to wind up the company on the ground that it is just and equitable that the company be wound up. Further, under s.459[28] of the Companies Act a member can petition the court for other relief where the company's affairs are being conducted in an unfairly prejudicial manner to some or all of the members, including himself.

Other minority sections enable a number of shareholders to challenge the majority on specific issues. For example, under s.5(2), dissentient holders of 15 per cent of the issued shares can apply to the court for cancellation of an alteration of objects.[29] Again, under s.127(2), where class rights are varied in pursuance of a clause in the articles, dissentient holders of 15 per cent of the issued shares of the class can apply for cancellation of the variation.[30] Finally, under ss 431(2) and 442(3),[31] 200 members or the holders of one-tenth of the issued shares can apply to the Department of Trade and Industry for an investigation of the company's affairs or of the ownership of the company.

THE RULE IN *FOSS V HARBOTTLE*[32]

The rule is that, as one would expect, the proper plaintiff[33] in an action to redress an alleged wrong to a company on the part of anyone, whether director, member or outsider, or to recover money or damages alleged to be due to it, is prima facie the company and, where the alleged wrong is any irregularity which might be made binding on the company by a simple majority of members, no individual member can bring an action in respect of it.[34]

In other words, the company is normally the proper plaintiff in an action to recover loss or to enforce a duty owed to the company by directors or controlling members, and where the breach of duty can be condoned by an ordinary resolution of the members in general meeting, no individual member or minority of members may sue. In particular an individual shareholder cannot bring an action alleging that the loss suffered by the company has consequently diminished the value of his or her shares.[35]

---

[27] Below, p.353.
[28] Below, p.359.
[29] Above, p.641.
[30] Above, p.211.
[31] Below, p.381.
[32] "It is common ground between the parties, and those familiar with the complications of the rule in *Foss v Harbottle* will not find this a matter of surprise, that difficult questions do arise," *per* Knox J. in *Smith v Croft (No. 2)* [1987] B.C.L.C. 206, 208.
[33] The Scots term is "pursuer."
[34] See *per* Lord Davey delivering the judgment of the court in *Burland v Earle* [1902] A.C. 82 (P.C. at pp.93, 94.
[35] *Prudential Assurance Co. Ltd v Newman Industries Ltd* [1982] Ch. 204, CA; *Stein v Blake (No. 2)* [1998] 1 B.C.L.C. 573, CA. See p.350, below.

A general meeting may be held so that the members may by ordinary resolution decide whether to sue or not. If such a meeting has been held and the breach of duty condoned not only does this prevent a single shareholder from bringing an action it may, depending on the circumstances also prevent the liquidator from subsequently doing so.[36] It also follows that where the wrong may be ratified by a special resolution, and such a resolution is passed, no action will lie.[37] It is for this reason also that the employees of a company to whom the directors now owe a duty following s.309,[38] first introduced in 1980, may find it impossible to enforce such a right. Only the members have the right to enforce it.

The rule is therefore a combination of two principles:

(1) the proper plaintiff principle,

(2) the majority rule principle.

Two members took proceedings on behalf of themselves and all other members except those who were defendants against the directors of a company to compel them to make good losses sustained by the company owing to the directors buying their own land for the company's use and paying themselves a price greater than its value. *Held*, as there was nothing to prevent the company from taking the proceedings, if it thought fit to do so, the action failed: *Foss v Harbottle* (1843) 2 Ha. 461; 67 E.R. 189.[39]

A minority shareholder sought to bring an action on behalf of himself and to all other shareholders, save three who were directors, against those directors and the company for damages, alleging that the directors had been negligent in selling an asset of the company for less than its market value. Most of the shares in the company were held by another company, the directors of which were also directors of the first company. *Held*, since the sale of the mine was *intra vires* the company, and there was no allegation of fraud by the directors or appropriation of assets of the company by the majority shareholders in fraud of the minority, the action was not maintainable. It was open to the company, on the resolution of a majority of the shareholders, to sell the mine at a price decided by the company in that manner, and it was open to the company by a vote of the majority to decide that, if the directors by their negligence had sold the mine at an undervalue, proceedings should not be taken by the company against the directors. *Semble*, it is sometimes admissible to go behind the apparent ownership of shares to discover whether a company is in fact controlled by wrongdoers, *e.g.* where the shares are held by nominees: *Pavlides v Jensen* [1956] Ch. 565.[40]

The rule not only avoids multiplicity of suits; it also recognises that litigation at the suit of a minority of the members is futile if the majority do not wish it.

"If the thing complained of is a thing which in substance the majority of the company are entitled to do, or if something has been done irregularly which the

---

[36] Above, p.341.

[37] See s.35(3); p.68, above.

[38] Above, p.297.

[39] Applied in *Hawkesbury Development Co. Ltd v Landmark Finance Pty. Ltd* [1969] 2 N.S.W.R. 782. See too *Rixon v Edinburgh Northern Tramways Co.* (1889) 16 R. 653 at p.656.

[40] Scottish illustrations are *Lee v Crawford* (1890) 17 R. 1094 (action against director for payment to the company of funds alleged to have been illegally lent to officials of the company), *Cameron v Glenmorangie Distillery Co. Ltd.* (1896) 23 R. 1092 (directors carrying out shareholders' resolution to allot to managing director unissued shares at a premium considered by a shareholder to be inadequate) and *Brown v Stewart* (1898) 1 F. 316 (claim for damages against directors on ground that they had acted recklessly in commencing business when so few shares had been applied for).

majority of the company are entitled to do regularly, or if something has been done illegally which the majority of the company are entitled to do legally, there can be no use in having litigation about it, the ultimate end of which is only that a meeting has to be called, and then ultimately the majority gets its wishes": *per* Mellish, L.J. in *MacDougall v Gardiner* (1875) 1 Ch.D. 13, CA at p.25.[41]

Thus the rule prevents the company being subjected to a long and expensive litigation to no ultimate purpose if an independent majority of the company do not wish to pursue the claim. As a result the application of the rule is dealt with as a preliminary issue before any full trial is held.[42]

Under this rule, the court will not, for example, interfere with irregularities at meetings at the instance of a shareholder.

The articles empowered the chairman, with the consent of the meeting, to adjourn a meeting, and also provided for taking a poll if demanded by five shareholders. The adjournment was moved, and declared by the chairman to be carried; a poll was then demanded and refused by the chairman. A shareholder suing on behalf of himself and all other shareholders except those who were directors brought an action against the directors and the company for a declaration that the chairman's conduct was illegal and an injunction to restrain the directors from carrying out certain arrangements without the shareholders' approval. *Held*, the action could not be brought by a shareholder; if the chairman was wrong, the company alone could sue: *MacDougall v Gardiner* (1875) 1 Ch.D. 13, CA.

Nor will the court grant a declaration that the accounts are not in the correct form at the instance of a shareholder: *Devlin v Slough Estates Ltd.* [1983] B.C.L.C. 497.

Derivative actions—exceptions to the rule in *Foss v Harbottle*

The rule is subject to a number of exceptions, in which case a minority of shareholders, or even an individual shareholder, may bring a minority shareholders' action, under CPR,[43] Part 19.9[44]; *i.e.* the minority shareholders sue on behalf of themselves and all other shareholders except those who are defendants, and must join the company as a defendant.[45] The directors or majority shareholders are usually defendants. This action is brought instead of an action in the name of the company.

"The form of the action is always" A.B. (a minority shareholder) on behalf of himself and all other shareholders of the company' against the wrongdoing directors and the company": *per* Lord Denning M.R. in *Wallersteiner v Moir (No. 2)* [1975] Q.B. 373, CA at p.390.

This type of action is a *derivative action, i.e.* the right to sue derives from that of the company.[46] The shareholders as such have no such right. If their own personal rights are being infringed they may bring a *representative* action, below.

---

[41] *cf.* Lord Hunter in *Harris v A. Harris Ltd*, 1936 S.C. 183 at p.198.

[42] *Prudential Assurance Co. Ltd v Newman Industries (No. 2) Ltd* [1982] Ch. 204, CA; *Smith v Croft (No. 3)* [1987] B.C.L.C. 355; below, p.346.

[43] Formerly under RSC, Ord.15, rr 12 and 12A.

[44] Not applicable to Scotland. Although there is no special form for a "derivative action" in Scots law, the competency of the derivative action is vouched in Scottish authority. The minority shareholder would require to proceed in his own name and the court will apply the normal tests and procedures to a preliminary issue of the competency or title to sue: *Wilson v Inverness Retail and Business Park Ltd* 2003 S.L.T. 301, O.H.

[45] CPR, Pt 19.9(2). As such it is separate and distinct from any personal action being brought by the minority shareholder: *Cooke v Cooke* [1997] 2 B.C.L.C. 28.

[46] See the CLR's recommendations: *Final Report*, above, paras 7.46–7.51.

The nature of the derivative action is that it is a "procedural device for enabling the court to do justice to a company controlled by miscreant directors or shareholders."[47] It follows that the court is entitled to examine the conduct of whoever intends to start such proceedings—the person must be doing so for the benefit of the company and not for some other purpose; *i.e.* he or she must be a proper person to bring a derivative action. A particular person might not be a proper person because his or her conduct is tainted in some way which under the rules of equity may bar relief; *e.g.* he or she might not come with "clean hands" (*e.g.* having participated in the wrong), or have been guilty of delay,[48] or be motivated by purely personal motives which are not bona fide for the benefit of the company.[49]

A husband was the majority shareholder and his wife the minority shareholder of a company. The husband had appropriated money belonging to the company for his own use, but the wife had previously brought matrimonial proceedings and had been awarded a sum in respect of that money by the court. The Court of Appeal decided that she was not a proper person to bring a derivative action on behalf of the company since she had, with knowledge of the facts, elected to pursue the matrimonial claim, and it would be inequitable to allow a double claim. A defendant to a derivative action can raise any defence which he could have raised had the action been brought by the shareholder personally: *Nurcombe v Nurcombe* [1985] 1 W.L.R. 370, CA.

There is therefore no right to bring a derivative action, the court has a discretion whether to allow an action to be brought. Thus an action has been dismissed where there was another viable remedy[50] and where an independent group of shareholders were opposed to the action.[51]

It also follows from the nature of a derivative action that if the company, either through its directors or majority shareholders has no right to bring an action then no derivative action can be allowed.[52] A minority shareholder[53] cannot have a larger right to relief than the company itself would have if it were the plaintiff. If therefore there is a valid reason why the company, acting through its directors or majority shareholders, should not sue, it will equally prevent a minority shareholder suing on its behalf.[54] For that reason Hart J. refused to allow a derivative action against a director based on the allegation that he had paid one creditor in preference to another. Such matters were to be resolved by the creditors through the medium of liquidation.[55]

---

[47] *Nurcombe v Nurcombe* [1985] 1 W.L.R. 370, *per* Lawton L.J. at p.376. See also *Wallersteiner v Moir (No. 2)* [1975] Q.B. 373, *per* Lord Denning M.R. at p.390.

[48] *Towers v African Tug Co.* [1904] 1 Ch. 588.

[49] *Barrett v Duckett* [1995] 1 B.C.L.C. 243, CA. But *cf. Wilson v Inverness Retail and Business Park Ltd* 2003 S.L.T. 301, O.H., where Lord Eassie suggested (at p.307) that there was nothing in the Companies Act which removed the derivative action from the aggrieved minority shareholders' forensic arsenal or subjected the use of the material in that arsenal to some prior judicial pass or permission.

[50] *ibid.*

[51] *Smith v Croft (No. 3)* [1987] B.C.L.C. 355. See p.346, below.

[52] See *Watts v Midland Bank plc* [1986] B.C.L.C. 15, 20, *per* Peter Gibson J.

[53] This may include a 50 per cent shareholder: *Barrett v Duckett*, above, but *cf. Halle v Trax BW Ltd* [2000] B.C.C. 1020, which seems to contradict this point.

[54] *Smith v Croft (No. 3)* [1987] B.C.L.C. 355.

[55] *Knight v Frost* [1999] 1 B.C.L.C. 364.

Subject to those constraints, a derivative action may be brought in the following cases:

(1) Where the wrong complained of is a fraud by the majority of the members on the minority and the wrongdoers are in control of the company in general meeting, *i.e.* they control the majority of the shares in the company, and they will not permit an action to be brought in the name of the company. If the aggrieved minority could not bring a minority shareholders' action in this case their grievance would never reach the courts. Where an action is brought under this exception the wrongdoers are usually both directors and controlling shareholders.

In *Cook v Deeks*[56] a shareholder brought a minority shareholders' action to compel the directors to account to the company for the profits made out of the construction contract which they took in their own names.[57]

In Scotland it has been held that the minority must have first made a definite attempt to obtain the company's co-operation: it is not sufficient for them to plead that the majority had the power to outvote them; *per* Lord Kyllachy (Ordinary) in *Lee v Crawford* (1890) 17 R. 1094 at p. 1096; *Brown v Stewart* (1898) 1 F. 316.

Later cases have widened this exception to the rule in two ways and, possibly, narrowed it in others. First as to the meaning of "fraud" in this context:

In *Daniels v Daniels*[58] the minority shareholders of a company were allowed to bring an action where the directors had authorised the sale of company land to one of them at a price alleged to be well below its market value. The directors objected that since fraud had not been alleged the action should not be allowed.

Templeman J. laid down a wider definition of "fraud" for this purpose: "If minority shareholders can sue if there is fraud, I see no reason why they cannot sue where the action of the majority and the directors, though without fraud, confers some benefit on those directors and majority shareholders themselves."[59] The judge distinguished *Pavlides v Jensen*, above, on the grounds that in that case the directors had not benefited by their "negligence". It follows from this that there is no exception where the allegation is simply that the directors were acting with a collateral purpose with no benefit to themselves.[60]

In *Estmanco (Kilner House) Ltd v Greater London Council*[61] the majority shareholder proposed to alter a contract it had with the company in order to deprive the minority shareholders of certain rights. The majority shareholder then proposed a resolution whereby the company should not sue for breach of contract. When a minority shareholder sought to sue on the company's behalf the majority shareholder argued that since it had acted bona fide for the benefit of the company there was no fraud on the minority to allow such an action.

Megarry V.-C, refused to accept that test of fraud on the minority as applicable for the purposes of bringing an action. It only related to the alteration of the company's articles.

---

[56] [1916] 1 A.C. 554.
[57] See also *Menier v Hooper's Telegraph Works* (1874) L.R. 9 Ch.App. 350. For Scotland see also *Rixon v Edinburgh Northern Tramways* (1889) 16 R. 653 and *Hannay v Muir* (1898) 1 F. 306.
[58] [1978] Ch. 406.
[59] *ibid.*
[60] *Re Downs Wine Bar Ltd* [1990] B.C.L.C. 839.
[61] [1982] 1 W.L.R. 2.

In this case the action of the majority shareholder injured one category of shareholder to the benefit of another. Fraud in this sense is abuse of a power.

The second development concerns the requisite element of "control" by the majority. It has always been accepted, as stated above, that this means actual voting control. But in *Prudential Assurance Co. Ltd v Newman Industries Ltd (No. 2)*[62] Vinelott J. was prepared to extend the exception when the alleged fraud was committed by directors who did not exercise actual voting control but who exercised control in *practice*.[63] It was suggested that control could be established by the votes controlled by the defendants together with those voting with them as a result of apathy or influence. Large public companies, such as *Newman*, are in fact controlled by holders of less than 50 per cent of the votes. The Court of Appeal in that case did not express any opinion on this point.

(2) Where the act is one which is illegal or *ultra vires* the company's powers.[64]

The members cannot ratify an illegal or *ultra vires*[65] act. However, if the act is merely contrary to the company's written constitution it may now be condoned, and any action against the directors waived, by separate special resolutions under s.35(3).[66] An individual shareholder still has the right to seek an injunction to prevent such an act, which is not subject to the rule in *Foss v Harbottle*, and this is preserved by ss 35(2) and 35A(4)[67] unless the company is already bound. It follows that an act contrary to the company's written constitution is better regarded as falling within (3) below following the changes made by the 1989 Act, rather than under this head.

Even if the act is illegal, *e.g.* under the Companies Act, however, the majority may validly resolve to take no action to remedy the wrong done and if that resolution is made in good faith and in what the majority consider to be for the benefit of the company, it will bind the minority.[68]

In *Smith v Croft (No. 3)*,[69] the action involved alleged payments by the directors in breach of s.151, *i.e.* the financial assistance rules,[70] which if proved would have been illegal. The judge held that an individual shareholder did not have an absolute right to bring a derivative action on that basis to recover the money so spent, as distinct from preventing it beforehand. Such a right of recovery would only be available if the company had such a right. In that case a majority of the independent shareholders[71] did not wish the action for recovery to be brought and the judge regarded that as a sufficient reason to disallow the action.

> "Ultimately the question which has to be answered . . . is: 'Is the plaintiff being prevented improperly from bringing these proceedings on behalf of the company?' If

---

[62] [1981] Ch. 257.
[63] There was no such control in *Halle v Trax BW Ltd* [2000] B.C.C. 1020.
[64] *Flitcroft's Case* (1882) 21 Ch.D. 519, CA. That case involved paying dividends out of capital.
[65] *ibid.*
[66] Above, p.68.
[67] Above, p.98.
[68] *Taylor v National Union of Mineworkers (Derbyshire Area)* [1985] B.C.L.C. 237.
[69] [1987] B.C.L.C. 355.
[70] Above, Ch. 11.
[71] That is a question of fact in each case.

it is an expression of the corporate will of the company by an appropriate independent organ that is preventing the plaintiff from prosecuting the action he is not improperly but properly prevented and so the answer to the question is No. The appropriate independent organ will vary according to the constitution of the company concerned and the identity of the defendants, who will in most cases be disqualified from participating by voting in expressing the corporate will"; *per* Knox J. [1987] B.C.L.C. 355, 403.

(3) Where the matter is one which can be validly done or sanctioned, not by a simple majority, but only by some special majority, *e.g.* a special resolution, which has not been obtained. If an action could not be brought in this case the company could, in breach of the memorandum or articles, do de facto by ordinary resolution that which according to its regulations can only be done by a special resolution.

Thus in *Baillie v Oriental Telephone Co. Ltd*,[72] a shareholder was able to bring a minority shareholders' action to restrain the company from acting on a special resolution of which insufficient notice had been given.[73]

Acts contrary to the company's written constitution may be ratified by a special resolution, so that the above rule applies in that case. However, it may be that in all such cases, where an action is for recovery of loss to the company, a majority of the independent shareholders may be able to prevent such an action being brought, following the decision in *Smith v Croft (No. 3)*, above.

(4) It was assumed, although not decided, in *Heyting v Dupont*[74] that there may be a further exception to the rule in *Foss v Harbottle*—namely where justice demands that an action be brought, *e.g.* where all that is alleged is damage to the company arising from a director's misfeasance in withholding an asset of the company without fraud or *ultra vires.*

The company was to exploit an invention of the defendant's consisting of a machine for making plastic pipes and the defendant withheld the company's patent application. However, the company could not have exploited the invention because it was in a state of paralysis owing to discord, so there was no damage to the company and therefore justice did not require that exception be made.

In the *Prudential* case[75] Vinelott J. based his decision on the derivative action against the directors on the doctrine that a minority action could be allowed if "the interests of justice require that a minority action should be permitted."[76] The Court of Appeal did not need to discuss the rule in *Foss v Harbottle* because the company had actually adopted the case, but expressed the firm opinion that any exception based on the justice of the case was not a practical one. This was also the opinion of the Court of Appeal in *Baggs v Hampshire Technology Organisation Ltd*,[77] where the Court expressly rejected any exception based on the

[72] [1915] 1 Ch. 503, CA, above, p.249.
[73] And see *Dunn v Banknock Coal Co. Ltd* (1901) 9 S.L.T. 51 (O.H.).
[74] [1964] 1 W.L.R. 843, CA, *per* Russell and Harman L.JJ. at pp.851, 854.
[75] Above, p.345.
[76] [1980] 2 All E.R. 841 at p.877.
[77] November 20, 1997, CA.

fact that the company concerned could not afford to bring the action and the controlling shareholder sought to do so instead.

Procedure

The real difficulty is that the question of whether a minority shareholder should be allowed to bring a derivative action must be a preliminary issue tried before the merits of the case, *e.g.* alleged fraud, are debated. For that reason the Court of Appeal rejected any exception based on the demands of justice since it will in effect need a full trial of the issues to decide whether justice would be served by allowing the action to brought. The Court of Appeal in that case thought that in such a preliminary action the minority shareholder should be required to establish at least a prima facie case that (a) the company is entitled to the relief claimed, and (b) the action falls within the proper boundaries of the rule restricting members' actions on behalf of the company.

This preliminary procedure was approved by Knox J. in *Smith v Croft (No. 2)*[78] as a half way house between assuming for procedural purposes either that all allegations are true or requiring the plaintiff to prove everything as a preliminary issue, as happened in the *Prudential* case. The CPR[79] implements these decisions by requiring a minority shareholder to apply for leave to continue the action and for the defendant to be served with the claim form.[80]

It has recently been emphasised that the requirement for permission to continue cannot be dismissed as a mere technicality; the provisions of CPR Part 19.9 underline the need for the court to retain control over all the stages of a derivative action.[81]

On the other hand, the court may now authorise civil proceedings to be brought on behalf of the company by such persons and on such terms as it shall direct, as the result of a petition under s.459, below.

The minority shareholders' action is called a derivative action[82] to indicate that the right being enforced is that of the company. If the company is in liquidation such an action should be taken over by the liquidator if he is willing to do so.[83]

In relation to the jurisdiction of an English court to entertain a derivative claim brought by shareholders on behalf of a foreign company, it has recently been held that the court would have such a power and that such a claim could be served out of the jurisdiction on the foreign company.[84] On the facts of the case, however,[85] which involved the bringing of a derivative claim by the minority shareholders of a company incorporated in India, the claimants had not shown that England was the appropriate forum for the claim,[86] and so the court set aside an earlier order by the master permitting such service.

---

[78] [1987] B.C.L.C. 206.

[79] Formerly 15, r.12A of the RSC.

[80] Pt 19.9(3).

[81] *Portfolios of Distinction Ltd v Laird* [2004] EWHC 2071 (Ch); [2004] 2 B.C.L.C. 741, at p.760, citing *Barrett v Duckett*, above p.344.

[82] *Per* Lord Denning M.R. at p.390 and Scarman L.J. at p.406 in *Wallersteiner v Moir (No. 2)* [1975] Q.B. 373, CA. Scarman L.J. said that the American description of a minority shareholders' action brought to obtain redress for the company, as a stockholders' derivative action, is apt.

[83] *Fargo Ltd v Godfroy* [1986] B.C.L.C. 370.

[84] Pursuant to CPR, Pt 19.9(3).

[85] *Konamaneni v Rolls Royce Industrial Power (India) Ltd* [2002] 1 W.L.R. 1269.

[86] In accordance with the principles laid down in the case of *Spiliada Maritime Corp v Cansulex Ltd* [1987] A.C. 460.

The Legal Aid Act 1988 makes no provision for legal aid in a minority shareholders' action since it is regarded as being the company's action and companies are not entitled to legal aid, unless they are acting purely on behalf of an individual.[87] But it is open to the court in such an action to order the company to indemnify the plaintiff against the costs of the action.[88] The minority shareholder should apply for the sanction of the court soon after issuing his claim form. If granted he will be given such indemnity.[89]

It has been held that applications for indemnity should be made *inter partes* and that the court will apply the same criteria as when deciding whether there is a triable case.[90] Further it has been held that costs should not be awarded unless financially necessary. This contradicts an earlier case,[91] where an indemnity order was granted on the basis of whether an honest, independent and impartial board would have authorised the action and the fact that the minority shareholder was not impecunious was held not be a ground for refusing the indemnity order. No order for an indemnity will be made, however, where neither the petitioner nor the defendant is a minority shareholder and the defendant is not in control of a company.[92]

It would be unlawful as being contrary to public policy for a solicitor to accept a retainer for the plaintiff(s) to conduct the action on a contingency fee basis (*i.e.* he is paid the fee if he wins but not if he loses).[93]

Representative actions

In *Hogg v Cramphorn*[94] the plaintiff was held to be justified in suing in a representative capacity in respect of the alleged wrongful disposition of the company's money by the directors which could be condoned by a resolution in general meeting, so that the action should have been dismissed unless it was not a *derivative* representative action but an individual rights *representative* action.

A member of a company may enjoy a right alone or in common with other members of the company and the rule in *Foss v Harbottle* has no application where individual members sue, not in right of the company, but in their own right to protect their *individual* rights as members[95]—in such a case a member can bring an action in his own name and may sue on behalf of himself and other members, and the breach of duty owed to an individual shareholder cannot be ratified by a majority of shareholders. Thus in *Pender v Lushington*[96] a shareholder was able to enforce the article giving him a right to vote at meetings and

---

[87] *R. v Chester and North Wales Legal Aid Area Office, ex p. Floods of Queenferry* [1998] 2 B.C.L.C. 436, CA.
[88] CPR, Pt. 19.9(7).
[89] However, it has been held that such is not secured by a lien for unrecovered costs on the company's assets, or assets recovered as a result of the action: *Qayoumi v Oakhouse Property Holdings plc* [2002] EWHC 2547(Ch); [2003] 1 B.C.L.C. 352.
[90] *Smith v Croft* [1986] 1 W.L.R. 580.
[91] *Jaybird Group Ltd v Greenwood* [1986] B.C.L.C. 319.
[92] *Halle v Trax BW Ltd* [2000] B.C.C. 1020.
[93] *Wallersteiner* case, above.
[94] [1967] Ch. 254, above, p.269.
[95] *Per* Sir George. Jessel M.R. in *Pender v Lushington* (1877) 6 Ch.D. 70 at pp.80, 81.
[96] (1877) 6 Ch.D. 70.

compel the directors to record his vote. Similarly, actions for damages by shareholders in their own right do not come within the rule. Thus where the defendant owes a duty to the shareholder personally, no restrictions apply.[97]

Circumstances in which an individual member can sue in his own name include actions to prevent:

(1) the company from acting illegally or contrary to the memorandum[98];

(2) proposed acts where a special majority is required and has not been obtained[99];

(3) the company from acting contrary to its articles;

(4) asserting a statutory right, *e.g.* to rectify the register of members under s.359.

Reflective losses

At one time it was thought that where the wrong was a breach of duty to the company *and* also damaged the rights of individual members, in the sense of lowering the value of their shares, individual members could sue for the damage to themselves as plaintiffs, in their own right.[1] One member could thus sue on behalf of the others by way of a so-called *representative action*.

In *Prudential Assurance Co Ltd v Newman Industries Ltd (No. 2)*,[2] the minority shareholder used this form of action in addition to a derivative action. The basis for the claim was the loss suffered by the shareholders as a result of the directors' alleged fraud on the company and the shareholders argument was that because the company had lost money their own personal profit expectations been diminished. The Court of Appeal *inter alia* held that, where a company suffered loss caused by a breach of duty owed to it and a shareholder, the latter's loss, in so far as this was measured by the diminution in value of his shareholding, or the loss of dividends, merely reflected the loss[3] suffered by the company in respect of which the company had its own cause of action and the shareholder, in such a case, could not recover damages.[4] The *Prudential* approach was subsequently followed by the Court of Appeal in *Stein v Blake (No. 2)*,[5] where loss was sustained by a shareholder by reason of a misappropriation of the company's assets and primarily involved a diminution in the value of his shares. The Court of Appeal held that such a loss was fully reflected in the loss suffered by the

---

[97] *R.P. Howard Ltd v Woodman, Matthews & Co.* [1983] Com.L.R. 100.

[98] *Per* Lord Campbell L.C. in *Simpson v Westminster Palace Hotel* (1860) 8 H.L.C. 712, 11 E.R. 608 at p.610; *Russell v Wakefield Waterworks Co.* (1875) L.R. 20 Eq. 474, at p.481. See also ss 35(3) and 35A(4), above, pp.68 and 98.

[99] *Edwards v Halliwell* [1950] 2 All E.R. 1064, CA.

[1] *i.e.* thereby avoiding the rule in *Foss v Harbottle*.

[2] [1982] 1 Ch. 204, CA.

[3] See Charles Mitchell, "Shareholders' claims for reflective loss", (2004) 120 L.Q.R. 457.

[4] [1982] 1 Ch. 204, CA, at pp.222–223. As it was subsequently put, by Arden L.J., "the company's claim, if it exists, will always trump that of the shareholder": *Day v Cook* [2001] EWCA Civ 592; [2002] 1 B.C.L.C. 1, CA, at p.15.

[5] [1998] 1 B.C.L.C. 573, CA.

company and fully compensated by restitution to the company.[6] However, this must be distinguished from the situation where the loss is caused directly to the shareholders who, as a result of a breach of duty by the directors to advise them, have parted with their shares at an undervalue.[7]

In the last few decades, a clutch of important cases have revisited what has become known as the "*Prudential* principle" and have sought to exploit the personal rights exception in *Foss v Harbottle*. The Court of Appeal has confirmed that the onus will be on the defendant to establish the applicability of the reflective loss principle.[8]

The principle was the subject of comprehensive review by the House of Lords in the case of *Johnson v Gore Wood & Co*.[9]

J, a businessman, held shares in W Ltd and on its behalf instructed a firm of solicitors, G to act for it in connection with a purchase of land. In particular, G was instructed to serve a notice exercising an option to purchase this land, but this was subsequently followed by a dispute as to its validity. In the end, W Ltd suffered substantial losses and brought proceedings for professional negligence against G. At the same time, solicitors acting for W Ltd informed G that J also had a personal claim against them. The claim by W Ltd was eventually settled, but J proceeded with his action, which G sought to strike out as an abuse of process of the court. *Held*: that J was, in principle, entitled to recover in respect of any loss that he had himself suffered that was not merely a reflection of the loss suffered by W Ltd. However, he would not be allowed to recover in respect of the diminution in value of his pension and in respect of his majority shareholding in W Ltd. His other heads of claim in respect of his own quantifiable damage would not be struck out.

The House of Lords has therefore affirmed the following essential principles:[10]

(1) Where a company suffers loss caused by a breach of duty owed to it, only the company may sue in respect of that loss and no action lies at the suit of a shareholder suing in that capacity to make good a diminution in the value of the shareholder's shareholding where that merely reflects the loss suffered by the company.

(2) A claim will not lie by a shareholder to make good a loss which would be made good if the company's assets were replenished through action against the party responsible for the loss, even if the company, acting through its constitutional organs, has declined or failed to make good that loss.

(3) Where a company suffers loss but has no cause of action to sue to recover that loss, the shareholder may sue in respect of it if he has a cause of action so to do, even though the loss is a diminution in the value of the shareholding.

---

[6] At p.579.
[7] See *Heron International Ltd v Lord Grade* [1983] B.C.L.C. 244, CA, where Lawton L.J. explained (at p.262) that: "*Foss v Harbottle* has nothing whatever to do with a shareholder's right of action for a direct loss caused to his own pocket as distinct from a loss caused to the coffers of a company in which he holds shares."
[8] *Shaker v Al-Bedrawi* [2002] EWCA Civ 1452; [2003] Ch. 350, CA, at p.378.
[9] [2002] 2 A.C. 1.
[10] At pp.35–36 (*per* Lord Bingham).

(4) Where a company suffers loss caused by a breach of duty to it, and a shareholder suffers a loss separate and distinct from that suffered by the company caused by breach of a duty independently owed to the shareholder, each may sue to recover the loss caused to it by breach of the duty owed to it, but neither may recover loss caused to the other by breach of the duty owed to that other.

A number of recent cases have since followed these principles and rejected a number of shareholder claims. Thus, where a claimant sought to recover from his solicitor for the diminution in value of his shares following various disastrous investments made through companies which he owned or set up for the purpose, the Court of Appeal held that he could not so claim as these were reflective losses which were primarily company losses and not personal losses.[11] By a majority, the Court of Appeal held, however,[12] that the claimant did have a claim in relation to a sum invested in an estate agency business as this sum was part of a personal obligation owed to the claimant by his solicitor.

Likewise, in a case where claimant property developers sought to recover against a firm of surveyors for negligent or fraudulent misrepresentation in valuing certain property, the losses suffered by them were held to be reflected losses and not recoverable by them personally.[13] The principle has also been upheld in circumstances where a defendant had a defence to a company's claim[14] and in a recent case where the court held that the fact that a claim was brought for breach of fiduciary duty did not prevent the claim being barred by the application of the rule against reflective loss.[15]

But in two further cases, the *Prudential* principle has been distinguished. In the first case, *Shaker v Al-Bedrawi*,[16] the claimant alleged that he was beneficially entitled to a substantial proportion of the company's shares, held on trust for him by the company's sole director. He brought proceedings on the basis that his case was a claim for the director, as trustee, to account to him, as beneficiary, for a due proportion of a sum deriving from the use of the trust property. The Court of Appeal held that the reflective loss principle would preclude the claim only if the defendant could show that the whole of the claimed profit reflected what the company had lost and which it had a cause of action to recover. Further, it would not be right to bar the action unless the defendants could establish not merely that the company had a claim to recover a loss reflected by the profit, but that such was available on the facts.[17] Peter Gibson L.J. concluded by pointing out that

"In circumstances where the *Prudential* principle applies to bar a viable claim on the footing of the company's cause of action which it does not assert, the application of the principle can work hardship. Moreover in this case the application of the

---

[11] *Day v Cook* [2001] EWCA Civ 592; [2002] 1 B.C.L.C. 1, at p.51.
[12] Arden L.J. dissenting.
[13] *Ellis v Property Leeds (UK) Ltd* [2002] EWCA Civ 32; [2002] 2 B.C.L.C. 175, CA.
[14] See *Barings plc v Coopers & Lybrand (No. 4)* [2002] 2 B.C.L.C. 364.
[15] *Gardner v Parker* [2004] EWHC Civ 781; [2004] 2 B.C.L.C. 554.
[16] [2002] EWCA Civ 1452; [2003] Ch. 350, CA.
[17] At pp.377–378.

principle might serve to leave the trustee holding a profit without being accountable for it to his beneficiary, and that may run counter to a basic equitable principle."[18]

The second case, *Giles v Rhind*,[19] involved a claim by one director against another director who, on leaving the company, had diverted his former company's most lucrative contract to another company in which he had an interest. The action by the company against the defendant had had to be discontinued when the latter was unable to put security for his costs.[20] The claimant now alleged breaches of a shareholders' agreement and claimed damages for the loss of value of his shares in his company and loss of remuneration which he would otherwise have earned. The Court of Appeal confirmed that there were no reasons of principle or policy to prevent a shareholder from recovering damages where the wrong done to the company had made it impossible for it to pursue its own remedy against the wrongdoer by reason of impecuniosity attributable to the wrong which had been done to it.

It has also been held that the reflective loss principle would not prevent a bar to relief being sought under s.459.[21] Thus, the fact that conduct might give rise to a cause of action at the suit of the company, did not mean that it was incapable of also giving rise to unfair prejudice and preclude the court from awarding financial compensation to the petitioners.[22]

WINDING UP BY THE COURT ON THE "JUST AND EQUITABLE" GROUND

Under ss 122 and 124 of the Insolvency Act 1986 a contributory may petition that a company be wound up by the court and where the court is of opinion that it is just and equitable that the company should be wound up, the court may order winding up.[23]

Who may bring a petition

A member of a company is a contributory, and it has been held that a holder of fully paid-up shares is a contributory.[24] Thus in appropriate circumstances even a single member can petition for a winding up.[25] We shall see[26] that s.124(2)(b) of the 1986 Act generally prevents a contributory from petitioning unless he has held his shares for at least six months.

---

[18] *ibid.*
[19] [2002] EWCA Civ 1428; [2003] Ch. 618, CA.
[20] The company went into receivership. Chadwick L.J. stated (at p.642) that: "The paradigm case in which, by reason of the wrong done to it, the company is unable, in practice, to pursue its claim against the wrongdoer is one in which the company is obliged to abandon its claim because the wrong has deprived it of the funds needed for that purpose."
[21] Below, p.359.
[22] *Atlasview Ltd v Brightview Ltd* [2004] EWHC 1056 (Ch); [2004] 2 B.C.L.C. 191, at p.208.
[23] In certain cases a creditor may also petition for a winding up on this ground. See *e.g. Morrice v Brae Hotel (Shetland) Ltd* [1997] B.C.C. 670.
[24] *Re National Savings Bank Assocn.* (1866) L.R. 1 Ch.App. 547; *Walker and Others, Petitioners* (1894) 2 S.L.T. 230 and 397 (O.H.).
[25] A petitioner must establish his *locus standi* to be a contributory, although the court has a discretion in all cases: *Re A Company* [1996] 2 B.C.L.C. 409.
[26] Below, Ch.27.

In petitioning for a winding up on the just and equitable ground a member is not confined to such circumstances as affect him as a shareholder, *i.e.* he is not confined to cases where his position as a shareholder has been worsened by the action of which he complains; he is entitled to rely on any circumstances of justice or equity which affect him in his relations with the company or with the other shareholders,[27] although it may be otherwise on a petition under s.459. The relationship between petitions for winding up and those under s.459 is dealt with below.[28]

The court will not, as a rule, order a winding up on a contributory's petition unless he alleges in the petition, and proves at the hearing, at least to the extent of a *prima facie* case, that there will be assets for distribution among the shareholders or that some disadvantage would accrue to him by virtue of his membership which could be avoided or minimised,[29] a purely private advantage will not suffice.[30] The reason is that unless there are such assets the contributory has no interest in a winding up. The courts will not normally strike out a petition before the hearing on that basis, however, unless it has no doubts about the matter. Thus even where the company's only asset was a non-assignable lease with no clear market value the judge let the petition go to trial since it might have been of some value to the company.[31] Similarly, where the petition is based on the fact that there has been a failure to provide accounts and information so that it is impossible for the petitioner to be able to tell whether or not there will be a surplus available to the contributories, the courts will allow the petition to proceed.[32]

Further, a contributory's petition which is opposed by the majority of the contributories will usually not be granted except where the conduct of the majority is something of which the minority have a right to complain,[33] or the main object of the company has failed.[34] The petitioner need not establish that the other members have not acted bona fide in the interests of the company.[35] If the directors who are not contributories wish to bring a petition they must be acting unanimously.[36]

Meaning of just and equitable

An order for winding up on the just and equitable ground will be made in the following circumstances, some of which do not involve oppression of the minority:

[27] *Ebrahimi v Westbourne Galleries Ltd* [1973] A.C. 360.
[28] p.379.
[29] *Re Rica Gold Washing Co.* (1879) 11 Ch.D. 36, CA; *Re Martin Coulter Enterprises Ltd.* [1988] B.C.L.C. 12; *Re Instrumentation Electrical Services Ltd* (1988) 4 B.C.C. 301.
[30] *Re Chesterfield Catering Co. Ltd* [1976] 3 All E.R. 294. If the petitioner is also a creditor and the company is insolvent the petition may be amended to one seeking a winding up on the grounds of insolvency: *Re Commercial and Industrial Insulations Ltd* [1986] B.C.L.C. 19.
[31] *Re Martin Coulter Enterprises Ltd* [1988] B.C.L.C. 12.
[32] *Re Wessex Computer Stationers Ltd* [1992] B.C.L.C. 366.
[33] *Re Middlesborough Assembly Rooms Co.* (1880) 14 Ch.D. 104, CA; *Re Tivoli Freeholds Ltd* [1972] V.R. 445.
[34] *Re German Date Coffee Co.* (1882) 20 Ch.D. 169; *Pirie v Stewart* (1904) 6 F. 847; *Re Perfectair Holdings Ltd* (1989) 5 B.C.C. 837; contrast *Cox v "Gosford" Ship Co. Ltd.* (1894) 21 R. 334 and *Galbraith v Merito Shipping Co. Ltd*, 1947 S.C. 446.
[35] See n.27.
[36] *Re Instrumentation Electrical Services Ltd* (1988) 4 B.C.C. 301.

(1) Where the main object of the company has failed or the company is engaging in acts which are entirely outside what can fairly be regarded as having been within the general intention or common understanding of the members when they became members.

A company was formed to acquire the English portion of the aircraft business of M. Blériot, a well-known airman. M. Blériot refused to carry out the contract. *Held*, the company should be wound up because its substratum had gone: *Re Blériot Aircraft Co.* (1916) 32 T.L.R. 253.

A company formed to purchase, charter and work ships and to carry on the business of shipowners lost its only vessel. Its remaining asset was a balance of £363 in the bank. A majority in number and value of shareholders petitioned for compulsory winding up, but a minority of shareholders desired to carry on the business as charterers. *Held*, it was just and equitable that the company should be wound up: *Pirie v Stewart* (1904) 6 F. 847.

(2) If the company is a "bubble," *i.e.* there is no bona fide intent on the part of the directors to carry on business in a proper manner.[37]

The court will not order a solvent company to be wound up merely because it is making a loss or is deeply indebted if the majority of the shareholders are against a winding up,[38] or if no meeting of shareholders has been held to consider winding up.[39] A company was wound up, however, where it had a contract damages claim against it to which it was defenceless and which the petitioner could have invoked at any time.[40]

(3) Where the company was formed to carry out a fraud, or to carry on an illegal business.

T.E.B. and his sons were relatives of, and had been employed by, persons who carried on the business of piano manufacturers under the name of J. B. & Sons. They left J. B. & Sons and formed a company called T. E. B. & Sons Ltd for carrying on a similar business. A prospectus was issued which stated that the price paid for the business was £76,650, when it was really only £1,000 in cash together with £5,000 in shares in the company. Money was subscribed by the public and most of this money found its way into the hands of the persons who were the real, though not the ostensible, promoters. J. B. & Sons obtained an injunction restraining the company from using the name B, and it was found that the company was formed to filch as much trade as possible from J. B. & Sons. Numerous actions were brought against the company for fraud in the prospectus. *Held*, the company should be wound up: *Re Thomas Edward Brinsmead & Sons* [1897] 1 Ch. 45; 406, CA.[41]

Fraudulent misrepresentation in the listing particulars or prospectus[42] or fraud in the course of business with the outside world[43] are not, by themselves, grounds

[37] *Re London and County Coal Co.* (1866) L.R. 3 Eq. 355.
[38] *Re Suburban Hotel Co.* (1867) L.R. 2 Ch.App. 737 (company making a loss), *Black v United Collieries Ltd* (1904) 7 F. 18 (company deeply indebted). See also *Galbraith v Merito Shipping Co. Ltd*, 1947 S.C. 446, *per* Lord Mackay, at p.458.
[39] *Cox v "Gosford" Ship Co. Ltd* (1894) 21 R. 334; *Scobie v Atlas Steel Works Ltd* (1906) 8 F. 1052.
[40] *Re Dollar Land Holdings plc* [1994] 1 B.C.L.C. 404.
[41] See also *Secretary of State for Trade and Industry v Hasta International Ltd*, 1998 S.L.T. 73 (O.H.).
[42] *Re Haven Gold Mining Co.* (1882) 20 Ch.D. 151, CA.
[43] *Re Medical Battery Co.* [1894] 1 Ch. 444.

for winding up the company, as the majority of the shareholders may waive the fraud, or there may be a change of management; but fraud in the real, though not the ostensible, object of the company will be such a ground.

(4) Where the mutual rights of the members are not exhaustively defined in the articles, *e.g.* where they entered into membership on the basis of a personal relationship involving mutual confidence or an understanding as to the extent to which each is to participate in the management of the company's business, and that confidence is not maintained or the petitioner is excluded from the management.

From about 1945, E and N were partners in a carpet dealing business with an equal share in the management and profits. In 1958 they formed a private company to take the business over. E and N were the first directors and each held 500 £1 shares. The articles provided that shares could not be transferred without the directors' consent. Later, N's son, G, was appointed a director and E and N each transferred 100 shares to him. The company made good profits which were all distributed by way of directors' remuneration, *i.e.* no dividends were paid. After a disagreement between E and N, with whom G sided, N and G at a general meeting removed E as director by ordinary resolution under s. [303], and thereafter excluded him from the conduct of the company's business. E petitioned for an order under s. [122(1)(g) of the Insolvency Act 1986] that the company be wound up on the ground that it was just and equitable. *Held*, (by the House of Lords) that it was just and equitable that the company be wound up. After a long association in partnership, during which he had had an equal share in the management and profits, E had joined in the formation of the company; the inference was indisputable that he and N had done so on the basis that the character of the association would, as a mater of personal faith, remain the same; and E had established that N and G were not entitled, in justice and equity, to make use of their legal powers of expulsion. Furthermore E was unable to dispose of his interest in the company without the consent of N and G: *Ebrahimi v Westbourne Galleries Ltd* [1973] A.C. 360.

Per Lord Wilberforce at pp. 374, 375: "... there has been a tendency to create categories or headings under which cases must be brought if the [just and equitable] clause is to apply. This is wrong. Illustrations may arise but general words should remain general and not be reduced to the sum of particular instances."

And at p.379: "The words [just and equitable] are a recognition of the fact that a limited company is more than a mere legal entity, with a personality in law of its own: that there is room in company law for recognition of the fact that behind it, or amongst it, there are individuals, with rights, expectations and obligations *inter se* which are not necessarily submerged in the company structure. That structure is defined by the Companies Act and by the articles of association by which shareholders agree to be bound. In most companies and in most contexts, this definition is sufficient and exhaustive, equally so whether the company is large or small. The 'just and equitable' provision does not ... entitle one party to disregard the obligation he assumes by entering a company, nor the court to dispense him from it. It does, as equity always does, enable the court to subject the exercise of legal rights to equitable considerations; considerations, that is, of a personal character arising between one individual and another, which may make it unjust, or inequitable, to insist on legal rights, or to exercise them in a particular way.

It would be impossible, and wholly undesirable, to define the circumstances in which these considerations may arise. Certainly the fact that the company is a small one, or a private company, is not enough. There are very many of these where the association is a purely commercial one, of which it can safely be said that the basis of association is adequately and exhaustively laid down in the articles. The superimposition of equitable considerations requires something more [than the fact that the company is a small one, or a private company], which typically may include one, or probably more, of the following elements: (i) an association formed or continued on the basis of a personal relationship, involving mutual confidence—this element will often be found where a pre-existing partnership has been converted into a limited company; (ii) an agreement, or understanding, that all, or some (for there may be 'sleeping members'), of the shareholders shall participate in the conduct of the business; (iii) restriction on the transfer of the members' interest in the company—so that if confidence is lost, or one member removed from management, he cannot take out his stake and go elsewhere."

Ebrahimi v Westbourne Galleries was applied in *Re A. & B.C. Chewing Gum Ltd*,[44] where the petitioners held one-third of the company's shares on the basis that they should have equal control with the two individual respondents, who were brothers and directors of the company and owned the other two-thirds of the shares. To achieve equality of control, the articles were altered so as to provide, *inter alia*, that the petitioners could appoint and remove a director representing them, and that decisions at board meetings should be unanimous. The petitioners, the respondents and the company also signed and sealed a shareholders' agreement setting out the way in which the day to day business was to be conducted. The respondents refused to recognise the petitioner's removal of their director and the appointment of another in his place. This was not a case of one side making use of its legal rights to the prejudice of another—the petitioners were excluded from their legal and contractual rights. Their right to management participation was repudiated.

Weinberg and Rothman were the sole shareholders in and directors of a company, with equal rights of management and voting power. After a time they became bitterly hostile to one another and disagreed about the appointment of important servants of the company. All communications between them were made through the secretary. The company made large profits in spite of the disagreement. *Held*, mutual confidence had been lost between W and R and the company should be wound up: *Re Yenidje Tobacco Co. Ltd* [1916] 2 Ch. 426, CA.[45]

Whether it is just and equitable to wind up a company depends on facts which exist at the time of the hearing and a petitioner is confined to heads of complaint set out in his petition.[46]

It is a matter therefore for the petitioner to establish mutual confidence and/or entitlement to management participation. If he can establish neither, then the matter will be left to be dealt with under the company's articles,[47] or possibly by a petition under s.459,[48] below. Such confidence or entitlement may be shown either by the very nature of the company and the relationship between the member/directors, as in a quasi-partnership company similar to that in the *Ebrahimi* case,[49] above, or by representations being made to the petitioner to a similar effect.[50] There is no necessary requirement of establishing equal rights of

[44] [1975] 1 W.L.R. 579.
[45] See also *Re Worldhams Park Golf Course Ltd* [1998] 1 B.C.L.C. 554; *Re Phoneer Ltd* [2002] 2 B.C.L.C. 241.
[46] *Re Fildes Bros. Ltd* [1970] 1 All E.R. 923.
[47] *Re A Company* (1988) 4 B.C.C. 80.
[48] *Re A Company, ex p. Estate Acquisition and Development Ltd.* [1991] B.C.L.C. 154.
[49] Such a relationship may be destroyed by agreed changes in the relationship between the parties: *Third v North East Ice & Cold Storage Co. Ltd* [1998] B.C.C. 242.
[50] *Tay Bok Choon v Tachansan Sdn. Bhd.* (1987) 3 B.C.C. 132, PC.

management. Thus in *Quinlan v Essex Hinge Co. Ltd*[51] the remedy was extended to a petitioner who had joined the company as a director and minority shareholder, on the basis that he was akin to a junior partner. The remedy is even available to someone who is part contingent creditor and part contingent shareholder, *i.e.* a co-venturer with capital at stake who has a right to take shares, and who has been wrongfully excluded from the management he was intended to have, although it will not be available if he is pursuing a separate action for damages based on the same facts.[52] There is no bar to a petition by a shareholder who is guilty of misconduct if that is not the cause of the breakdown in confidence.[53]

If the petitioner can establish that the affairs of the company are not being managed in a proper manner then if the petition is not due to be heard for some time, the court will appoint a receiver[54] to manage the company's affairs to preserve the status quo and avoid any prejudice to either side. That jurisdiction is exercised by analogy with partnership law.[55]

Alternative remedies

If, in the case of a contributories' petition, the court is of opinion that it is just and equitable that the company should be wound up and some other remedy, *e.g.* accepting an offer to purchase his shares, or seeking an order under ss 459–461, below, is available to the petitioners,[56] the court *must* nevertheless make a winding up order unless it is of the opinion that the petitioners are acting unreasonably in not pursuing the other remedy: Insolvency Act 1986 s.125(2).

In *Re A Company*,[57] Warner J. decided that where the petitioner had a potential claim under s.459, that did not make it unreasonable for him to maintain a claim for a winding up order since it was not plain and obvious that the relief that he would get at the hearing would be relief under s.459. The question would be resolved by the judge at the hearing. Even if the winding-up petition was damaging to the company it did not follow that a petitioner claiming his rights as a quasi-partner was being unreasonable in preventing a petition. Similarly the Court of Appeal in *Re Copeland & Craddock Ltd*[58] held that it was not inevitably unreasonable if a petition under s.459 for shares to be bought by the majority has a winding up petition in the alternative. One result of such a winding up would be to effect a sale of the business as a going concern in the open market and the petitioner could bid for it. The position is even clearer where the court has already refused an application under s.459.[59]

With regard to a bona fide offer being made by the other members under the articles for the petitioner's shares, *i.e.* at a valuation by an independent valuer,

---

[51] [1996] 2 B.C.L.C. 417.
[52] *Re A Company* (1987) 3 B.C.C. 575.
[53] *Vujnovich v Vujnovich* (1989) 5 B.C.C. 740, PC.
[54] Under s.37 of the Supreme Court Act 1981.
[55] *Re A Company* [1987] B.C.L.C. 133.
[56] See *CVC/Opportunity Equity Partners Ltd v Demarco Almedia* [2002] UKPL 16; [2002 2 B.C.L.C. 108, PC, where no remedy, other than one for winding up was possible, there being no s.459 equivalent in the Cayman Islands.
[57] (1989) 5 B.C.C. 18.
[58] [1997] B.C.C. 294, CA.
[59] *Vujnovich v Vujnovich* (1989) 5 B.C.C. 740.

the Court of Appeal in *Virdi v Abbey Leisure Ltd*,[60] overruling the judge below and other earlier decisions, decided that this was not an automatic reason for striking out the winding up petition. There was nothing unreasonable in the petitioner refusing to accept the risk that a valuer's decision might apply a discount for his minority shareholding, since the machinery in a winding up to determine claims against the company was preferable to their worth being estimated by an accountant. Winding up of necessity effects a full assets valuation of the petitioner's shares. If the essence of the decision to allow petitions based on equitable considerations in *Ebrahimi v Westbourne Galleries Ltd*[61] was that the company's constitution, *e.g.* as to dismissal of a director, might be overriden, then it could be likewise equitable to ignore the share valuation provisions in the articles. Equally, where there are no proper accounts to enable the share valuation provisions to operate, an offer to purchase the petitioner's shares will not be a bar to the petition being brought.[62]

Each case is, however, dependent on its facts. In *Re A Company*,[63] the judge struck out the winding up petition on the basis that it was a remedy of last resort, there was no realistic possibility of it succeeding, and that an order under s.459 for the purchase of the petitioner's shares would be at a fair price taking into account the allegations of unreasonably low dividend payments.

This case and others have shown a marked degree of reluctance on the part of the courts to grant the remedy. Thus in *Fuller v Cyracuse Ltd*,[64] the court held that it was an abuse of process for a minority shareholder to persist with a winding up petition under s.122(1)(g) when he had been offered a buyout at a price fixed by an independent valuer.[65] In these circumstances, there was another remedy available to the petitioner within the meaning of s.125(2) and so the petition would be struck out. It is also clear that the jurisdiction to make a winding-up order is not any wider than the jurisdiction to grant relief under s.459. Accordingly, it has been held that if the conduct relied on by the petition is not unfair for the purposes of that section, it could not found a case for a winding-up order on the just and equitable ground.[66]

ALTERNATIVE REMEDY FOR UNFAIRLY PREJUDICIAL CONDUCT

Section 210 of the 1948 Act, now repealed, provided that any member who complained that the affairs of the company were being conducted in a manner oppressive to some part of the members, including himself, could petition for an order under that section. That section suffered from several drawbacks however,[67] and was repealed in 1980 and replaced by what are now ss 459 to 461 of the 1985 Act.

Under s.459[68-69] any member of the company can petition the court for an order on the ground that the affairs of a company are being or have been

---

[60] [1990] B.C.L.C. 342. See also *Re Copeland & Craddock Ltd* [1997] B.C.C. 294, CA.
[61] [1973] A.C. 360, above p.356.
[62] *Re Wessex Computer Stationers plc* [1992] B.C.L.C. 366.
[63] [1997] 1 B.C.L.C. 479.
[64] [2001] 1 B.C.L.C. 187.
[65] See further, p.375, below.
[66] *Re Guidezone Ltd* [2000] 2 B.C.L.C. 321.
[67] For details see the twelfth edition of this work.
[68-69] Below, p.361

conducted in a manner which is unfairly prejudicial to the interests of its members generally or of some part of the members (including at least himself) or that any actual or proposed act or omission of the company (including an act or omission on its behalf) is or would be so prejudicial.[70]

The reference to all of the members being affected, as distinct from some part of the members, was added by a 1989 Act amendment, to avoid confusion caused by conflicting decisions on whether if all the members were affected a petition would lie.[71]

If the company is a small private company all the members should be joined as respondents since they may well be affected by the petition.[72] This might not be the case in a larger company, however. Unlike a derivative action the petitioner cannot ask for an indemnity against costs[73] although legal aid is available.[74] The court may in appropriate circumstances either appoint a receiver[75] or grant an interim injunction to protect the petitioner,[76] pending a full hearing of the petition.

A majority shareholder can bring a petition if the board and the minority shareholders act together to prejudice him, but not if the board have been dismissed.[77]

The conduct must relate to the affairs of the company

The section only applies if the unfairly prejudicial conduct relates to the affairs of the company.[78] Thus a petition was refused where the allegation was that a major shareholder had paid off the company's bank loan and had taken a transfer of the bank's security over the company's assets. It was held to have been an act by the respondent in her personal capacity and had not affected the company's position as mortgagor.[79] It is a question of fact whether the actions of a parent company can amount to the conduct of the affairs of a subsidiary.[80]

This arose in *Gross v Rackind*[81] where the Court of Appeal was asked to consider whether it would have the power to make an order in relation to a holding company where it was the affairs of its wholly-owned subsidiary that were being or had been conducted in an unfairly prejudicial manner. The Court of

---

[70] This remedy is not available to an employee but only to members: *Re A Company* [1986] B.C.L.C. 391.
[71] *Re A Company* [1988] 1 W.L.R. 1068, *cf. Re Sam Weller Ltd* (1989) 5 B.C.C. 810.
[72] *Re A Company (No. 007281 of 1986)* [1987] B.C.L.C. 593. Although *cf. Re Ravenhart Service (Holdings) Ltd* [2004] EWHC 76 (Ch); [2004] 2 B.C.L.C. 376, which suggests that it is not necessary for all the other culpable shareholders to be joined as respondents (at p.396).
[73] Above, p.349. *Re A Company* [1987] B.C.L.C. 82.
[74] Thus making it an attractive alternative action: See *Lowe v Fahey* [1996] 1 B.C.L.C. 262.
[75] *Re A Company* [1987] B.C.L.C. 133; *Wilton-Davies v Kirk* [1998] 1 B.C.L.C. 274. The costs of the receiver are payable out of the assets of the company but the court may direct that they are ultimately born by the respondent: *Re Worldhams Park Golf Course Ltd* [1998] 1 B.C.L.C. 554.
[76] *Safinia v Comet Enterprises Ltd* [1994] B.C.C. 883; *Rutherford, Petitioner* [1994] B.C.C. 867; *cf. Wright, Petitioners* [1997] B.C.C. 198.
[77] *Re Baltic Real Estate Ltd* [1993] B.C.L.C. 498.
[78] As defined by the company's constitution: *Re Legal Costs Negotiators Ltd*, [1998] 2 B.C.L.C. 171, CA. See p.325, below.
[79] *Re A Company* [1987] B.C.L.C. 141.
[80] *Nicholas v Soundcraft Electronics Ltd* [1993] B.C.L.C. 360.
[81] [2004] EWCA Civ 815; [2004] 4 All E.R. 735, CA.

Appeal held that the expression "the affairs of the company" in s.459 is "one of the widest import" which could include the affairs of a subsidiary of a holding company.[82]

In *Re Astec (BSR) plc*,[83] Jonathan Parker J. held that, whilst the acts of the board of directors as a whole would relate to the affairs of the company, the acts of a minority of the board acting as nominees of a major shareholder in a public company did not amount to such conduct. The judge was also prepared to accept that a resolution passed by the general meeting amounted to conduct relating to the affairs of the company. Shareholder and other agreements may be relevant but it depends upon the context.[84] Where the subject of the dispute is in an agreement (*e.g.* such as the terms upon which the company was formed) there are divergent authorities, with an earlier case suggesting that the petition will not be allowed to proceed.[85] However this has not been followed in a more recent case, which has held that the statutory right conferred on members of a company to apply for s.459 relief is inalienable and could not be diminished or removed by contract and that s.9 of the Arbitration Act 1996 did not compel the court to stay the proceedings.[86] Where the petitioners had also obtained a freezing order[87] against the respondent directors, the court held that this would be discharged in view of the s.459 petition, unless the allegations were sufficient to constitute a relevant cause of action against them.[88]

The interests affected must be those of the petitioner as a member

Under s.459, the right to petition under the section is given to "members". The primary reference point for this is the definition of "member" in s.22 of the Act.[89] Additionally, the Secretary of State may petition under s.459,[90] and this includes a case where a report has been made to him pursuant to s.437, following an investigation under the relevant provisions of the Act,[91] and also where the Financial Services Authority has exercised its powers under the Financial Services and Markets Act 2000.[92]

It has been held that a "member"[93] includes registered shareholders[94] and those with a perfect transfer of shares to them in equity.[95] It has also been held

---

[82] At p.741. The Court of Appeal also held that the affairs of the subsidiary could also be the affairs of its holding company, especially where, as on the facts, the directors of the holding company also represented a majority of the directors of the subsidiary.

[83] [1998] 2 B.C.L.C. 556.

[84] *Re A Company* [1997] 2 B.C.L.C. 1; *c.f. Re Unisoft Group Ltd (No. 3)* [1994] 1 B.C.L.C. 609; *Re Leeds United Holdings plc* [1996] 2 B.C.L.C. 545.

[85] *Re Vocam Europe Ltd* [1998] B.C.C. 396.

[86] *Exeter City Association Football Club Ltd v Football Conference Ltd* [2004] EWHC 2304 (Ch); [2004] 1 W.L.R. 2910.

[87] Formerly known as a "Mareva injunction", as developed in England in the case of *Nippon Yusen Kaisha v Karageorgis* [1975] 1 W.L.R. 1093, CA.

[88] *Re Premier Electronics (GB) Ltd* [2002] 2 B.C.L.C. 634.

[89] As to which, see p.186 above.

[90] Under s.460(1).

[91] See p.383 below.

[92] s.460(1A), as substituted by the Financial Services and Markets Act 2000 (Consequential Amendments and Repeals) Order 2001, SI 2001/3649.

[93] Executors of members may bring such a petition: see s.459(2).

[94] So a person who has assented to registration as a shareholder is a member for the purpose of presenting a petition: *Re Nuneaton Borough Association Football Club Ltd* [1989] B.C.L.C. 454, CA.

[95] See *Re Quickdome Ltd* [1988] 1 B.C.L.C. 370.

that a s.459 petition may be founded on conduct which pre-dated a petitioner's registration as shareholder, so long as the petitioner is a member at the time of presentation of the petition.[96] On the other hand, a beneficiary under a trust[97] would not have standing. In *Atlasview Ltd v Brightview Ltd*,[98] the court struck out as petitioners B and his wife, on the basis that neither were members or those to whom shares had been transferred by operation of law.[99] On the other hand, in the same case it was held that a company as a member would not be struck out as a petitioner, although a bare nominee; the interests of such a nominee shareholder were "capable of including the economic and contractual interests of the beneficial owners of the shares".[1]

More recently, it has been confirmed in *O'Neill v Phillips*[2] that the requirement of prejudice having been suffered by a member should not be too narrowly or technically construed.[3] The judge at first instance in that case had dismissed the petition because the prejudice suffered was in the petitioner's capacity as an employee rather than as a shareholder.[4] Although this was overturned by the Court of Appeal,[5] the House of Lords emphasised that it was the terms, agreement, or understanding on which the petitioner became associated as a member which would generate any restraint on a power of expulsion against him.[6]

Section 459 has no application if the interests of the member which are affected by the unfairly prejudicial conduct are not those which he enjoys *qua*[7] member. In *Re a Company*, a petition was rejected where it was brought by petitioners holding shares as executors for two minors, because the conduct affected them *qua* executors and not members.[8] Likewise, in *Re J.E. Cade & Son Ltd*,[9] a petition was rejected where it related to the petitioner's position as the landlord of a farm, farmed rent-free by his family company on the basis that no tenancy would be created. The petition failed because the petitioner was pursuing his interests as a freeholder and not as a member.[9a]

In *R & H Electrical Ltd v Haden*,[10] a petition was allowed even though the petitioner was alleging that his interests as a creditor in relation to a loan he made to the company had been affected by his dismissal as a director. The fact that a creditor is also a member will not normally suffice, but here the petitioner

---

[96] *Lloyd v Casey* [2002] 1 B.C.L.C. 454, at p.465.
[97] *Re a Company* [1986] B.C.L.C. 39.
[98] [2004] EWHC 1056 (Ch); [2004] 2 B.C.L.C. 191.
[99] There was also no basis under which CPR Pt 19.2(2)(a) could be invoked to support a non-member as a party, since that rule was confined to cases where it was desirable "so that the court can resolve all matters in dispute in the proceedings": at p.202.
[1] At p.203 (*per* Jonathan Crow).
[2] Below, p.366.
[3] [1999] 1 W.L.R. 1092, HL, at p.1105.
[4] Reported as *Re a Company (No 00709 of 1992)* [1997] 2 B.C.L.C. 739, at p.758. See too *Re a Company* [1986] B.C.L.C. 391.
[5] Also reported at [1997] 2 B.C.L.C. 739.
[6] [1999] 1 W.L.R. 1092, HL, at p.1105.
[7] *i.e.* "in the capacity of" member.
[8] [1983] B.C.L.C. 126. See too *Re Alchemea Ltd* [1998] B.C.C. 964 where, on the unusual facts of the case, it was held that the petitioners were affected as employees only.
[9] [1992] B.C.L.C. 213.
[9a] See also *Brown v Scottish Border Springs Ltd* 2002 S.L.T. 1213, O.H.
[10] [1995] 2 B.C.L.C. 280.

had, in effect, provided all the venture capital for the business and so his right to remain in management of the company while that capital was at risk could amount to an interest as a member. Similarly, in *Re a Company*,[11] the right of the members to sell their shares at the best price was held to be subject to protection under s.459 because it did not relate simply to their interests as vendors.

Meaning of unfairly prejudicial conduct

Section 459(1) will be applicable to cases where the petitioner can show that the company's affairs "are being" or "have been" conducted in a manner which is unfairly prejudicial. There is, however, no statutory definition of what constitutes "unfairly prejudicial" conduct. It will be sufficient that a prejudicial act has been proposed[12] or that there has been prejudicial conduct of the company in the past.[13] Thus, the alleged conduct may be past, present or future. The test of unfair prejudice is objective and does not depend on the subjective intention of the respondent[14] and, within certain constraints,[15] the court is given a wide discretion to determine the matter.[16] As always, a balance has to be struck between the breadth of the discretion given to the court and the principle of legal certainty.[17]

Unfairness—earlier cases

An important group of cases on s.459 has been concerned with whether or not particular actions concerning the conduct of the company's business could be regarded as being both unfair and prejudicial. As one judge pointed out, it was not enough for conduct to be unfair without being prejudicial or prejudicial without being unfair.[18] Thus, in *Re D.R. Chemicals Ltd*,[19] the action of a majority shareholder and director in allotting shares to himself to increase his shareholding from 60 per cent to 96 per cent was held not only to be a breach of the pre-emption rules of the Companies Act[20] but was also a "blatant case" of unfairly prejudicial conduct. On the other hand, the fact that, after that date, the minority shareholder/director was paid no remuneration was not since he had taken no further part in the running of the company. Similarly, in *Re Ringtower Holdings plc*,[21] the late presentation of accounts was regarded as non-prejudicial. Where pre-emption provisions in the articles were deleted and the company re-

---

[11] [1986] B.C.L.C. 382.
[12] A mere fear of future actions will not suffice, however: see *Re Astec (BSR) plc* [1998] 2 B.C.L.C. 556.
[13] See, *e.g.*, *Re Kenyon Swansea Ltd* [1987] B.C.L.C. 514.
[14] *Re Sam Weller & Sons Ltd* [1990] B.C.L.C. 80, at p.85; *Anderson v Hogg* [2002] B.C.C. 923 (Ct. Sess.), at p.931.
[15] Notably those laid down in *O'Neill v Phillips* [1999] 1 W.L.R. 1092, HL, below, p.366.
[16] See, *e.g.*, *In Re J.E. Cade & Son Ltd*, where Warner J. said that "the court . . . has a very wide discretion, but it does not sit under a palm tree": [1992] B.C.L.C. 213, at p.227.
[17] *per* Lord Hoffmann in *O'Neill v Phillips* [1999] 1 W.L.R. 1092, HL, at p.1099.
[18] *per* Peter Gibson J. in *Re a Company (No 005685 of 1988)* [1989] B.C.L.C. 427, at p.437. See too *Re Legal Costs Negotiators Ltd* [1999] 2 B.C.L.C. 171, CA, at p.197.
[19] (1989) 5 B.C.C. 39.
[20] Above, p.224.
[21] (1989) 5 B.C.C. 82. See also *Re a Company* (1989) 5 B.C.C. 792.

registered as a private company as part of a management buy-out by the majority, this was not unfair to the minority, since the offer was available to them even though it might be prejudicial since they might be locked into the company if they refused the offer.

Further guidance as to the meaning of unfair prejudice was given by the Court of Appeal in *Re Saul D Harrison & Sons plc*.[22] Hoffmann L.J. stressed there that fairness was being used "in the context of a commercial relationship".[23] Thus, the starting point should be whether or not the conduct complained of was in accordance with the contractual terms which governed the relationships of the shareholder with the company and each other, *i.e.* whether or not the conduct complained of was in accordance with the articles.[24] If the board stepped outside their fiduciary duties, *e.g.* by exercising their powers for an ulterior purpose, they had stepped outside the bargain between the shareholders and the company. In Hoffmann L.J.'s opinion, trivial breaches of the articles would not suffice.[25] However, in cases where the letter of the articles did not reflect fully the understandings on which the shareholders were associated—as, for example in companies such as those in *Ebrahimi v Westbourne Galleries Ltd*, above—there might be additional equitable rights, arising out of the fundamental understanding between the shareholders, which formed the basis of their association but was not put into contractual form.[26]

In the same case, Neill L.J. sought to extract some guidelines from the earlier decisions. In his view the words "unfairly prejudicial" were general words to be applied flexibly to meet the circumstances of the particular case. Thus, in construing the word "unfairly", it would be necessary to take account not only the legal rights of the petitioner, but also any equitable considerations.[27]

Unfairness after Saul D. Harrison

Following the guidelines laid down in *Re Saul D. Harrison Ltd*, Neuberger J. in *Re Marchday Group plc*[28] held that an allegation against the directors which involved no breach of the articles and nothing unlawful or underhand on the part of the directors could not found a petition. It would be different if the allegations had raised the issue of the directors acting *ultra vires, e.g.* by issuing shares at a discount. In *Re Astec (BSR) plc*,[29] Jonathan Parker J. held that the concept of wider rights outside the articles, etc., had no part to play in a public quoted company. The shareholders had no legitimate expectations based on alleged breaches of the Stock Exchange Listing Rules,[30] the City Code on Take-overs and

---

[22] [1995] 1 B.C.L.C. 14, CA.
[23] At p.17.
[24] And other collateral agreements between shareholders.
[25] [1995] 1 B.C.L.C. 14, CA, at p.18. He took as his starting point for this Lord Cooper's understanding of "oppression" in *Elder v Elder & Watson* 1952 S.C. 49, *viz.* "a visible departure from the standards of fair dealing and a violation of the conditions of fair play on which every shareholder who entrusts his money to the company is entitled to rely".
[26] At p.19. See *Hall v Gamut Technologies Ltd* 1999 S.L.T. 1276, O.H.
[27] At p.31.
[28] [1998] B.C.C. 800.
[29] [1998] 2 B.C.L.C. 556.
[30] Above, Ch.7.

Mergers[31] or the Combined Code on Corporate Governance.[32] A majority shareholder could exercise its powers under the articles and the board was to be judged by the articles and the Act. To decide otherwise would be a recipe for chaos.

The particular issue in *Re Saul D. Harrison* was the extent to which mismanagement of the company could amount to unfairly prejudicial conduct. In *Re Elgindata Ltd*[33] it was said that serious mismanagement causing economic harm to the business could be unfairly prejudicial conduct but that in most cases simply mismanagement would not suffice. The Court of Appeal in *Re Saul D. Harrison* emphasised that there would have to be a breach of duty involving abuse of power by the directors or ulterior motives, but in *Re Macro Ipswich Ltd (No. 1)*,[34] Arden J. allowed a petition based on serious mismanagement which had caused economic loss to the company and would continue to do so into the foreseeable future. In *Re BSB Holdings Ltd (No. 2)*,[35] the same judge said that what was needed was unfairly prejudicial conduct in a commercial context. She rejected the idea that only an abuse of power or an ulterior motive would suffice and suggested that acting otherwise than for the benefit of the company could suffice.

In *Re Blackwood Hodge plc*,[36] Jonathan Parker J. said that not all breaches of fiduciary duty would suffice, finding no evidence of prejudice on the facts of the case. Harman J., however, has held that failure to implement a business plan was not just negligent mismanagement but abandonment of a structure which was the foundation of the petitioner's involvement with the company, so that if it had not been done bona fide in the interests of the company it could amount to unfairly prejudicial conduct.

It is clear that whatever the exact scope of petitions based on mismanagement, there is a real possibility of their being used as an alternative to a derivative action for a breach of fiduciary duty so avoiding the complexities of such actions.[37]

If the conduct of the controller is *prima facie* "above board" it may still, because of surrounding circumstances, be "unfairly prejudicial" for the purposes of s.459.

L owned one-third of the shares of a company and was a director. He was removed from his directorship by the other two shareholders and presented a petition under s.459. An emergency general meeting of the company was then called to increase the company's capital and to give the directors power to allot the new shares. The majority shareholders only intended to issue the shares pro rata by way of a rights issue. L sued for an injunction to prevent this rights issue. Harman J. granted the injunction. Although the proposed rights issue was prima facie fair since it would not alter the balance, it might in certain circumstances amount to unfairly prejudicial conduct *e.g.* (i) if it was known that the dissenting shareholder could not afford to take up the offer and this was the reason for

---

[31] Below, Ch.31.
[32] Now the Revised Combined Code. Below, p.393.
[33] [1991] B.C.L.C. 959.
[34] [1994] 2 B.C.L.C. 354.
[35] [1996] 1 B.C.L.C. 155.
[36] *Trace v European Healthcare Group plc*, February 4, 1998.
[37] See *Lowe v Fahey* [1996] 1 B.C.L.C. 262.

making it, or (ii) if the dissenting shareholder was engaged in litigation and the offer was designed to deplete his available funds. The judge also said that when a s.459 petition had been presented the status quo between the parties should be preserved until the hearing except where a change was absolutely essential: *Re A Company*.[38]

Unfairness: O'Neill v Phillips

The leading case on s.459 is now *O'Neill v Phillips*,[39] which was the first case to go all the way to the House of Lords on this provision of the Act. Lord Hoffmann stated that

> "In s.459 Parliament has chosen fairness as the criterion by which the court must decide whether it has jurisdiction to grant relief. It is clear .. that it chose this concept to free the court from technical considerations of legal right and to confer a wide power to do what appeared just and equitable. But this does not mean that the court can do whatever the individual judge happens to think fair. The concept of fairness must be applied judicially and the content which is given by the courts must be based upon rational principles."[40]

O, a manual worker, was employed by P Ltd, which was owned by P, who held the entire issued share capital of 100 £1 shares. Subsequently, P gave O 25 shares and appointed him as a director of P Ltd, with the declared intention that he should eventually take over the running of the company and be allowed to draw 50 per cent of the profits. This duly occurred, together with an indication that O's shareholding would be increased to 50 per cent once certain targets were reached. This never materialised; during a recession, P resumed personal command of the company, becoming MD. Subsequently, O's entitlement to 50 per cent of the profits was withdrawn, although he continued to receive his salary and any dividends payable on his 25 per cent shareholding. O brought a petition under s.459, founded on P's termination of equal profit-sharing and his repudiation of the alleged agreement for the allotment of more shares. This was dismissed at first instance but an appeal was successful, the Court of Appeal[41] ordering P to purchase O's shares, and holding that O had suffered unfair prejudice. In allowing the appeal, Lord Hoffmann held that: (1) unfairness to a member ordinarily required some breach of the terms on which he had agreed that the company's affairs should be conducted and since P had not agreed unconditionally to give O more shares or to share equally in the profits, he had not acted unfairly in withdrawing this; (2) a member of a company who had not been dismissed or excluded from participation in its management was not entitled to demand the purchase of his shares simply because of a breakdown in trust and confidence between the parties.

The important principles to emerge from this case may be stated as follows. First, confirming a line of reasoning espoused by him in *Re Saul D. Harrison Ltd*, above, a member of a company will not ordinarily be entitled to complain of unfairness unless there has been some breach of the terms[42] on which he agreed that the affairs of the company should be conducted.[43] Second, there will be cases

---

[38] [1985] B.C.L.C. 80.

[39] [1999] 1 W.L.R. 1092, HL.

[40] At p.1098.

[41] [1997] 2 B.C.L.C. 739, CA.

[42] Such terms are commonly contained in the articles of association and sometimes in collateral agreements (*i.e.* shareholder agreements) as between the shareholders: [1999] 1 W.L.R. 1092, HL, at p.1098.

[43] At pp.1098–1099. Lord Hoffmann went on to say that he did not suggest that such was the only form of conduct which would be regarded as unfair for the purposes of s.459: see p.1101.

in which equitable considerations will make it unfair for those conducting the affairs of the company to rely upon their strict legal powers, and "unfairness" may therefore consist "in a breach of the rules or in using the rules in a manner which equity would regard as contrary to good faith".[44]

This restatement of principle by Lord Hoffmann has not slowed down the numbers of cases brought before the courts under s.459. Thus, it has been held that the conduct of a respondent majority shareholder of a company who arranged, without the petitioner's knowledge, for a substantially increased service charge to be paid and for payments to a pension fund, largely for his own benefit, amounted to unfairly prejudicial conduct.[45] In *Brownlow v G H Marshall Ltd*,[46] the petitioner, a member and director of a family company, was removed from office without any reasonable offer having been made for her shares. Her claim for an order that her shares be purchased was upheld on the basis that the company was one in which considerations of a personal character arising out of the relationships between family shareholders, which gave rise to equitable considerations.[47] In *Pettie v Thomson Pettie Tube Products Ltd* 2001 S.L.T. 473, O.H., minority shareholders successfully brought a s.459 petition after alleging that a company's actions in allotting shares at par and substantially below their value to other shareholders was unfairly prejudicial to their interests because it reduced the value of prior shareholdings.

But s.459 petitions have also failed on many occasions where unfair prejudice could not be shown. Thus, where the petitioner was unable to show, either singly or collectively, that there was unfair conduct for the purposes of s.459, the court declined the petition.[48] In particular, Jonathan Parker J. concluded that "there was nothing . . . which equity would regard as being contrary to good faith".[49] Similarly, where the board of a company had acted in accordance with its powers of general management conferred by the articles in relation to an issue of new shares which altered the control of the company, the court concluded that there was no unfair prejudice to the petitioner.[50]

In a later case, conduct which required a petitioner, who was a director and minority shareholder, to sign certain conditions coupled with a threat to dismiss him if he did not sign did not amount to unfair prejudice.[51] Nor, for that matter, was a minority shareholder successful in alleging that he had suffered unfair prejudice because of the sale of property at an undervalue. The Court of Appeal[52] held that there had been no harm done and no damage or prejudice

---

[44] At p.1099, by analogy with *Ebrahimi v Westbourne Galleries Ltd* [1973] A.C. 360, above p.356. See too *Re Guidezone Ltd* [2000] 2 B.C.L.C. 321, at pp.355–356; *Anderson v Hogg* [2002] B.C.C. 923 (Ct. Sess.), at p.931.

[45] *Lloyd v Casey* [2002] 1 B.C.L.C. 454. See too *Anderson v Hogg* [2002] B.C.C. 923 (Ct. Sess.), where a majority of the Court of Session confirmed that it was unfairly prejudicial to the petitioner when the respondent paid himself a sum, described as a redundancy payment, from the company.

[46] [2000] 2 B.C.L.C. 655.

[47] At p.674. The court held that the existence of service agreements did not change the position.

[48] *Re Guidezone Ltd* [2000] 2 B.C.L.C. 321.

[49] At p.359.

[50] CAS *(Nominees) Ltd v Nottingham Forest FC plc* [2002] 1 B.C.L.C. 613.

[51] Nor, in the same case, was conduct requiring him to sign a share transfer: *Re John Reid & Sons (Strucsteel) Ltd* [2003] EWHC 2329 (Ch); [2003] 2 B.C.L.C. 319.

[52] Affirming the decision at first instance.

caused to the appellant as a minority shareholder because the evidence showed that the price obtained was the best price reasonably available.[53] Also unsuccessful was the case involving a forced departure of a director from the board of a company, alleged to be unfair because another director had not been asked to resign and because of the company's refusal to provide relevant financial information to the potential purchaser of his shares.[54]

Exclusion from management and "legitimate expectations"

A number of earlier cases on s.459 dealt with the position of directors excluded from management in the case of companies formed on the basis of management participation. In *Re a Company (No. 002567 of 1982)*, Vinelott J. said that he thought that it was unlikely that such persons were intended to be excluded from s.459, even though it would not strictly affect his rights as a shareholder.[55] In a leading case of this earlier period, *Re R.A. Noble & Sons (Clothing) Ltd*,[56] Nourse J. accepted that exclusion from management participation could amount to unfairly prejudicial conduct in cases such as *Re Westbourne Galleries*, above, even though the value of the petitioner's shareholding would not have been seriously diminished. A number of subsequent cases accepted that if the company was a quasi-partnership company, dismissal from management would suffice to found an petition under s.459,[57] but in *Re a Company (No 00709 of 1992)*, it was said that, in such cases, unless another capacity could be attributed, any unfairly prejudicial conduct must affect the petitioner qua member.[58]

However, it was in the case of *Re a Company*,[59] that Hoffmann J. first considered that exclusion from a legitimate expectation of taking part in a company's long-term management would be unfairly prejudicial. In another case in the same year, he said that in each such case the question was whether the terms on which the relationship came to an end were unfairly prejudicial to any of the participants.[60] Similarly, in *Re Ringtower Holdings plc*,[61] Peter Gibson J. accepted that if management participation was a legitimate expectation then its demise could found an petition on the basis of unfair prejudice. Thus, in *Re Kenyon Swansea Ltd*,[62] attempts by the majority shareholders to alter the articles to regain control was held to be contrary to the legitimate expectations of the petitioner as to control.

In *Re Regional Airports Ltd* the petitioners complained that, as a quasi-partnership company in which all the shareholders were entitled to participate as directors and to be consulted about all major issues affecting their interests as shareholders, their removal as directors, an excessive claim to remuneration of a

---

[53] *Rock Nominees Ltd v RCO (Holdings) plc* [2004] EWCA Civ 118; [2004] 1 B.C.L.C. 439, CA.
[54] *Mears v R Mears & Co (Holdings) Ltd* [2002] 2 B.C.L.C. 1.
[55] [1983] 1 W.L.R. 927, at p.933.
[56] [1983] B.C.L.C. 273.
[57] See, *e.g.*, *Quinlan v Essex Hinge Co Ltd* [1996] 2 B.C.L.C. 417.
[58] [1997] 2 B.C.L.C. 739.
[59] [1986] B.C.L.C. 376.
[60] *Re a Company* [1986] B.C.L.C. 362.
[61] (1989) 5 B.C.C. 82.
[62] [1987] B.C.L.C. 514.

50 per cent shareholder, and a proposed rights issue were unfairly prejudicial to their interests. The court upheld the petition on the basis that, in the context of their legitimate expectations, they were entitled to be dealt with on the basis of mutual trust and confidence.[63] In *Richards v Lundy*[64] the court upheld the petition on the basis that the petitioner had been unfairly excluded from the management of the company and from his position as a director. Additionally, the conduct of the respondents was unfair because there had been a failure to satisfy the petitioner's legitimate expectation that the value of his 10 per cent shareholding should reflect the fact that no dividends were to be declared on the shares and that the shares should be regarded as his pension.

Reliance on arguments as to legitimate expectations have not, however, always been successful. Thus, in *Re Blue Arrow plc*,[65] Vinelott J., although taking into consideration the wider equitable rights of the petitioner, rejected a petition by the president of a company when the articles were altered to allow her to be removed by a majority of the directors since she had no legitimate expectation that this would not happen on the company becoming a public company. Similarly, in *Re Posgate & Denby (Agencies) Ltd*,[66] the non-voting shareholders were held to have no legitimate expectation as to a resolution to sell off some of the company's assets and in *Jaber v Science and Information Technology Ltd*,[67] one shareholder was held to have no such interest in the voting rights of others. A variation on this was applied in *Re Tottenham Hotspur plc*,[68] where there was a dispute between a minority shareholder and the controlling shareholder of a quoted public company as to the former's dismissal as chief executive of the company. The dismissed chief executive was held to have no legitimate expectation of remaining in control since there was nothing which indicated to the other shareholders that the company was to be governed by anything other than its constitution, so that the board could dismiss him.

The majority in a quasi-partnership company, having forced the dismissal of a director, cannot complain if that individual refuses to sell his shares in the company to them. A complaint that he is no longer working for the benefit of all does not relate to the affairs of the company.[69] In *Re a Company, Ex p. Estate Acquisition and Development Ltd*,[70] Mummery J. considered that the dismissal of a director, alteration of the company's constitution and lack of information was sufficient even in a company which was not a quasi-partnership company.

Legitimate expectations after O'Neill v Phillips

In *Re Saul D Harrison & Sons plc*, above, Hoffmann L.J. confirmed that he had in the past borrowed from public law the term "legitimate expectation" to describe

[63] [1999] 2 B.C.L.C. 30.
[64] [2001] 1 B.C.L.C. 376.
[65] [1987] B.C.L.C. 585.
[66] [1987] B.C.L.C. 28.
[67] [1992] B.C.L.C. 764.
[68] [1994] 1 B.C.L.C. 655. See also *Astec (BSR) plc* [1998] B.C.L.C. 556 as to the position vis-à-vis public quoted companies generally.
[69] *Re Legal Costs Negotiators Ltd* [1999] 2 B.C.L.C. 171, CA.
[70] [1991] B.C.L.C. 154. But for public quoted companies, see *Re Astec (BSR) plc* [1998] 2 B.C.L.C. 556.

the personal relationship between a shareholder and those controlling the company which would entitled him to say that it would, in certain circumstances, be unfair for them to exercise a power conferred by the articles upon the board or the company in general meeting.[71] In *O'Neill v Phillips*, Lord Hoffmann (as he now was) recanted from this position and said that such a legitimate expectation could exist only when equitable principles would make it unfair for a party to exercise rights under the articles. He concluded that

> "The concept of a legitimate expectation should not be allowed to lead a life of its own, capable of giving rise to equitable restraints in circumstances to which the traditional equitable principles have no application."[72]

Thus, applying this approach, the court in the case of *Parkinson v Eurofinance Group Ltd*[73] found that the exclusion of the petitioner from the management of a company was not justified. In particular, the grounds which had been advanced for his immediate exclusion did not justify summary dismissal, and his dismissal without an offer to purchase his interest was unfairly prejudicial to him.[74]

Exit at will or "No-fault divorce"

One of the arguments in *O'Neill v Phillips*, above, was that it was of no consequence that the respondent had done anything unfair and that because trust and confidence had broken down between the parties the petition ought to be granted. In effect, this would mean that one member of the company ought to be entitled at will to require the others to buy his shares at a fair value.[75] This was flatly rejected by Lord Hoffmann, however, on the basis that there was no support in the authorities for such a right of unilateral withdrawal.[76] Further, he noted the views of the Law Commission's Report on *Shareholder Remedies*[77] on such a right of exit at will, which was that:

> "In our view there are strong economic arguments against allowing shareholders to exit at will. Also, as a matter of principle, such a right would fundamentally contravene the sanctity of a contract binding the members and the company which we considered should guide our approach to shareholder remedies."[78]

This approach was followed in *Re Phoenix Office Supplies Ltd*,[79] where the Court of Appeal held that the petitioner had not shown, albeit as a member of a quasi-partnership company, that he had been unfairly prejudiced. A member of a company who wished voluntarily to sever his connection with the company for personal reasons, was not by s.459 given the means of forcing the other members to purchase his shareholding, when he had no contractual right so to do.

---

[71] [1995] 1 B.C.L.C. 14, CA, at p.19.
[72] [1999] 1 W.L.R. 1092, HL.
[73] [2001] 1 B.C.L.C. 720.
[74] At p.750.
[75] As to which, see below, p.377.
[76] [1999] 1 W.L.R. 1092, HL, at p.1104.
[77] Law. Com. No. 246 (1997).
[78] [1997] 1 W.L.R. at p.1105.
[79] [2002] EWCA Civ 1740; [2003] 1 B.C.L.C. 76, CA.

Similarly, in *Re Jayflex Construction Ltd*[80] the court held that it was not sufficient to found a petition for relief to show that trust and confidence between members of a quasi-partnership company had broken down, regardless of whether that breakdown could be said to be the result of the conduct of the respondent. Further, the court said that a refusal by one 50 per cent shareholder to agree to a sealed bids procedure for the compulsory sale of shares did not constitute relevant unfairness.

Conduct of the petitioner

In deciding whether to grant a petition under s.459 the conduct of the petitioner is relevant only to the extent either that it might make the conduct of the controllers although prejudicial not unfair, or that it might affect the remedy which the court may make. There is no general rule, as with the old s.210, that the petitioner must come "with clean hands."[81]

X owned 250 and Y Ltd 750 shares in a company which ran degree courses. Y Ltd appropriated the students to its own courses and X was dismissed as a director and teacher. He set up another college and took several intending students with him. Nourse J. held that such an act was not a bar to his petition—on the facts there was no justification for Y Ltd's action: *Re London School of Electronics.*[82]

Further there is no rule that knowledge by the petitioner of any illegality in the company's business will bar a petition. It may be a consideration in deciding the case, however.[83]

Procedural aspects

It has been held that a petition can be brought against a former controller of a company for unfairly prejudicial conduct whilst he was a member.[84] Nor is it a bar that some of the shares are the subject of disputed ownership.[85] On the other hand a single petition covering a group of companies has been rejected on the basis that a separate petition must be brought for each company.[86]

A petitioner is not entitled to an indemnity against costs as in a derivative action[87] and in general costs will follow the result of the petition, although a reduction may be made on a successful petition if some heads prove to have been unsuccessful.[88] In general, no order will be made if the company is under the control of an administrative receiver unless the complaint relates to prevention of the petitioner selling his shares prior to the appointment.[89] A company other

---

[80] [2003] EWHC 2008 (Ch); [2004] 2 B.C.L.C. 145.
[81] *cf.* derivative actions, above, p.343.
[82] [1986] Ch. 211. See also *Re Pectel Ltd* [1998] B.C.C. 405.
[83] *Bermuda Cablevision Ltd v Colica Trust Co. Ltd* [1998] 1 B.C.L.C. 1, PC.
[84] *A Company* [1986] 1 W.L.R. 281.
[85] *Re Garage Door Associates Ltd* [1984] 1 W.L.R. 35.
[86] *Re A Company* [1984] B.C.L.C. 307.
[87] *Re A Company* [1987] B.C.L.C. 82, see above p.349. See, however, *Clark v Cutland* [2003] EWCA Civ 810; [2004] 1 W.L.R. 783, CA, at p.794.
[88] *Re Elgindata Ltd (No. 2)* [1993] B.C.L.C. 119.
[89] *Re Hailey Group Ltd* [1993] B.C.L.C. 459.

than the one directly involved may be joined as a party if it is directly involved in the transactions complained of,[90] but this is a matter for the court's discretion.[91]

Interface with s.371 orders

In general, the courts will act to prevent changes to the company's constitution or assets pending the hearing of the petition[92] but the ordinary business of the company must be allowed to proceed. In this context a question can arise whereby during the existence of a s.459 petition the court is asked to order a meeting under s.371 because the necessary quorum for a meeting cannot be obtained, usually due to the dispute. This is particularly difficult if the purpose of the meeting is to appoint new directors of the company. In *Re Opera Photographic Ltd*,[93] the existence of a s.459 petition was held not to be a bar on the court making a s.371 order and this was followed in *Re Whitchurch Insurance Consultants Ltd*.[94] In that case the s.459 petition was presented on the eve of the hearing of the s.371 petition and the position may be different if the s.371 petition is presented some time after that under s.459. Thus in *Re Sticky Fingers Restaurant Ltd*[95] the court in those circumstances made the order under s.371 on the proviso that any director appointed by the meeting should undertake not to interfere with the s.459 petitioner's management rights pending the outcome of that petition. In *Harman v BML Group plc*,[96] the existence of a s.459 petition was regarded as a factor to be taken into account and the Court of Appeal took notice of the fact that the allegations related to misappropriations by those in control who were petitioning under s.371.

Involvement of the company

The courts may also grant an injunction against the company being involved in the petition. This is designed to prevent the majority/respondents from dissipating the company's assets in what is essentially a shareholder dispute.[97] This rule may be relaxed to allow the company to be represented at the time when the judgment is given so as to have an input into the consequential orders which may be made[98]; but no other costs should be charged to the company and, if they are, an assets valuation will be amended to protect the petitioner.[99] It follows that individual respondents cannot use corporate assets to fund their involvement if the company has not authorised those payments.[1] The company may apply to the court for permission to be involved but in *Re A Company*[2] the court held that

---

[90] *Re BSB Holdings Ltd* [1993] B.C.L.C. 915.
[91] *Re Little Olympian Each-Ways Ltd* [1994] 2 B.C.L.C. 420.
[92] See, *e.g. Re Mountforest Ltd* [1993] B.C.C. 565; *Corbett v Corbett* [1998] B.C.C. 93.
[93] [1989] 1 W.L.R. 634.
[94] [1993] B.C.L.C. 1359.
[95] [1992] B.C.L.C. 84.
[96] [1994] 2 B.C.L.C. 674.
[97] *Re Milgate Developments Ltd* [1993] B.C.L.C. 291.
[98] *Re A Company, ex p. Johnson* [1992] B.C.L.C. 701.
[99] *Re Elgindata Ltd* [1991] B.C.L.C. 959.
[1] *Corbett v Corbett* [1998] B.C.C. 93.
[2] [1994] 2 B.C.L.C. 146.

there was a rebuttable presumption that the company should not be involved and it would have to show that it was necessary or expedient in the company's interests to do so. Advance approval would require the most cogent evidence of compelling circumstances although it was not an automatic bar that the majority and the board were the same people.

Available remedies—s.461

If the court is satisfied it may make such order as it thinks fit.[3] No specific request need be made in advance.[4] However, the section provides five possible orders[5] which the court may make.[6]

(1) an order regulating the affairs of the company in the future[7];

(2) an order to restrain the doing or continuing of an act or to rectify any omission[8];

(3) an order authorising civil proceedings to be brought in the name and on behalf of the company by such persons and on such terms as the court may direct[9];

The respondent to a petition argued that the petitioner was too emotionally involved and vindictive to be given control of any litigation. The Court of Appeal still authorised proceedings to be brought but subject to certain conditions: (i) protection of creditors; (ii) the control of the litigation to be solely the affair of the petitioner's solicitor to the entire exclusion of the petitioner; (iii) no other legal proceedings to be commenced without legal opinion in support; and (iv) no direct communication between the petitioner and respondent: *Re Cyplon Developments Ltd.*[10]

(4) an order altering the company's memorandum or articles. This will have automatic effect without any resolution of the company usually required for such alterations.[11] Such alterations may not be re-altered without the court's consent.[12]

(5) an order providing for the purchase of any member's shares by other members or a purchase of such shares by the company itself.[13] In the latter case it will arrange for the reduction of capital accordingly.

---

[3] s.461(1). This can include refusing the specific relief sought where that is inappropriate or there is a preferred alternative: *Antoniades v Wong* [1997] 2 B.C.L.C. 419, CA; or where the wrong has already been remedied by other means: *Re Legal Costs Negotiators Ltd* [1999] 2 B.C.L.C. 171, CA.

[4] This was required under the former s.210.

[5] For interim orders see p.374, below.

[6] s.461(2).

[7] This order could be made under the old s.210: see *Re H.R. Harmer Ltd* [1959] 1 W.L.R. 62, CA. In practice such orders usually now merge with those under (5) below to provide a solution: see, *e.g. Re A Company* (1989) 5 B.C.C. 792; but see also *McGuinness v Bremner plc*, 1988 S.L.T. 891 (O.H.) where such an order was made under this head alone.

[8] This was new in 1980. An instance occurred in *Whyte, Petitioner*, 1984 S.L.T. 330, in which the court pronounced orders restraining a company from holding a meeting, and from passing a resolution removing a director and replacing him with another, and restraining two shareholders from moving or voting in favour of such resolutions.

[9] This was new and intended to alleviate the rule in *Foss v Harbottle*, above, p.341.

[10] Unreported, March 3, 1982.

[11] s.461(4). A copy of the order must instead be filed with the Registrar within 14 days: s.461(5).

[12] s.461(3).

[13] This is an exception to s.143, above, p.160.

In making an order as to the purchase of shares the court has very wide powers. In certain situations the court will order that the petitioner buy out the controller's shares,[14] but that is unusual. Usually the issue is one of the purchase of a minority shareholder's shares. Such an order will usually be made against the controlling shareholders but it can also be made against another company controlled by those shareholders which has been used as a vehicle to deprive the first company of its assets.[15]

Such purchases raise several questions. By what method are those shares to be valued and at what date? As to the former it appears that when the shareholding is in a quasi-partnership company (*i.e.* an incorporated partnership such as that in *Re Westbourne Galleries Ltd*[16]) so that the shares were taken up initially and are still held by the shareholder as part of the management agreement, then the sale is in effect one from an unwilling vendor. The shares should therefore be valued pro rata according to the value of the shares as a whole.[17] On the other hand where the shareholding has simply been acquired as a minority shareholding it should be valued at a discounted value as a minority shareholding.[18] Similarly where the petitioner has chosen to accept the ending of the management participation agreement and to remain as a minority shareholder his shares will be valued at the discounted price.[19] Preference shareholders, particularly those who have brought upon themselves the buy-out of their shares, will be treated the same way.[20] The court will adopt special valuation rules where the company is in a special positon, *e.g.* a football club where the valuation depends upon prestige rather than profits.[21] In general, the shares should be valued taking the most up to date valuation available.[22]

Where the court orders that the shares be purchased under the pre-emption rules in the articles, *i.e.* by a valuer, the court will only subsequently interfere in the valuation if the instructions given to the valuer were wrong or not complied with.[23] If the valuation on that basis subsequently proves to be impossible the court will substitute its own valuation machinery.[24]

In some cases, the court will determine the valuation at trial, especially where the parties are in basic disagreement on the basis of the valuation.[25] Pumfrey J. has provided the following guidance:

---

[14] *Re Bovey Hotel Ventures Ltd*, Unrep. June 10, 1982, CA; *Re Nuneaton Borough AFC Ltd (No. 2)* [1991] B.C.C. 44; *Re Brenfield Squash Racquets Club Ltd* [1996] 2 B.C.L.C. 184.
[15] *Re Little Olympian Each-Ways Ltd (No. 3)* [1995] 1 B.C.L.C. 636.
[16] Above, p.356.
[17] *Virdi v Abbey Leisure Ltd* [1990] B.C.L.C. 342, at p.350; *Brownlow v G.H. Marshall Ltd* [2000] 2 B.C.L.C. 655.
[18] *Re Bird Precision Bellows Ltd* [1986] Ch. 658, CA; *Re London School of Electronics* [1986] Ch. 211; *Re Ghyll Beck Driving Range Ltd* [1993] B.C.L.C. 1126; *Re Macro (Ipswich) Ltd* [1994] 2 B.C.L.C. 354.
[19] *Re D.R. Chemicals Ltd* (1989) 5 B.C.C. 39.
[20] *Re Planet Organic Ltd* [2000] 1 B.C.L.C. 366. In this case, the appropriate discount was assessed to be 30 per cent.
[21] *Re A Company* (1989) 5 B.C.C. 792.
[22] *Re Regional Airports Ltd* [1999] 2 B.C.L.C. 30.
[23] *Macro v Thompson (No. 2)* [1997] 1 B.C.L.C. 626, CA; *Kranidites v Paschali* [2001] EWCA Civ 357; [2003] B.C.C. 353, CA.
[24] *Macro v Thompson (No. 3)* [1997] 2 B.C.L.C. 36.
[25] See, *e.g.*, *Parkinson v Eurofinance Group Ltd* [2001] 1 B.C.L.C. 720.

"I think that when arriving at a 'fair value' in the absence of a market it is necessary to assume that the notional sale is taking place between the active participants in the transaction, since the whole purpose of the valuation is to be fair as between the parties. There is no market to provide an objective external criterion. The actual parties must be taken to participate in the sale as willing participants."[26]

Although the date of valuation is prima facie the date of the purchase order[27] this is not a general rule and if the value of the shareholding has been affected by the unfairly prejudicial conduct, the valuation date can be the date when the conduct began,[28] the date of the bringing of the petition,[29] or, in the case of an appeal, the agreed value as at the time of the first instance hearing.[30] The court has no power to make an interim order for payment pending an order for the purchase of the shares except where the only dispute is as to the valuation and the interim order is on the lowest possible contended valuation.[31]

In the case of an order for an interest, it has been held that such is not beyond the powers of the court under s.461.[32] Thus, in *Re Planet Organic Ltd*,[33] the court found that there was nothing upon which interest should run, Jacob J. concluding that a forced sale was not like a case where damages had been caused and interest ran on the damages and so no interest element would be included in the amount payable to the petitioner.[34] It has been stated that such a power has to be exercised with extreme caution; Robert Walker L.J. has advised that

"If a petitioner seeking an order for the purchase of his shares contends . . . that they should be valued at a relatively early date but then augmented by the equivalent of interest, he must put forward that claim clearly and persuade the court by evidence that it is the only way, or the best way, to a fair result. It should not be a last-minute afterthought . . . Unless a petitioner is asking for no more than simple interest at a normal rate he should also put before the court evidence on which the court can decide that amount (if any) to allow."[35]

Effect of offer to buy out the petitioner

If there is a breakdown in relations between director/shareholders so that one of them brings a petition under s.459 on the basis of unfairly prejudicial conduct, the most likely order that the court will make is that one side, usually the majority shareholders, buy out the other. As we have seen,[36] such an order will provide for the method and date of the valuation of the shares. In several cases,

---

[26] At p.753. On the facts of the case, he concluded that the company should be valued on a going concern basis, on the usual principles (at p.754).

[27] *Re D.R. Chemicals Ltd.*, above; *Richards v Lundy* [2000] 1 B.C.L.C. 376.

[28] *Re OC (Transport) Services Ltd* [1984] B.C.L.C. 251.

[29] *Re London School of Electronics*, above; *Re Cumana Ltd* [1986] B.C.L.C. 430, CA.

[30] *Profinance Trust SA v Gladstone* [2002] EWCA Civ 1031; [2002] 1 W.L.R. 1024, CA, at p.1042. See too *Bilkus v King* [2003] EWHC 2516.

[31] *Re A Company* (1987) 3 B.C.C. 41; *Ferguson v Maclennan Salmon Co. Ltd*, 1990 S.L.T. 658.

[32] See *Re Bird Precision Bellows Ltd* [1986] Ch. 658, CA, where the Court of Appeal rejected any claim to interest.

[33] [2000] 1 B.C.L.C. 366.

[34] At p.375.

[35] *Profinance Trust SA v Gladstone* [2001] EWCA Civ 1031; [2002] 1 W.L.R. 1024, CA, at p.1035.

[36] Above, p.373.

however, the majority will have already made an offer to purchase the peti-tioner's shares under the terms of the company's articles and the court is then faced with the problem as to whether such an offer, providing usually for valuation by an independent valuer such as the company's auditors, in effect settles the matter and accordingly no court order is necessary.[37]

In *Re Benfield Greig Group plc*,[38] the executors of a 30 per cent shareholding brought a petition under s.459 on the basis that they had been unfairly prejudiced, *inter alia*, by a failure on the part of the auditors to ascertain the true market value of the shares and that their valuation was one which no reasonable valuer could have arrived at, there being *prima facie* evidence that they had made a mistake. The evidence revealed that, prior to being appointed, the auditors had been engaged by the company to negotiate and agree with the Inland Revenue the value of incentive shares to be issued by the company to its employees. The Court of Appeal reversed the judge at first instance[39] and concluded that it was clearly arguable that the auditors had compromised their ability to be an independent valuer and that the executors had a real prospect of success in establishing a case under s.459.[40]

In *Re A Company*[41] the articles actually required the dismissed director to offer his shares to the other shareholders. The majority intended to invoke this provision and on that basis Hoffmann J. refused to allow a s.459 petition based on that dismissal to continue. The articles had made provision in advance for what was to happen if there was a breakdown in relations. As in all such cases it was clear that one party had to leave and on the facts that had to be the petitioner on the terms of the articles. The judge did not, however, confine this principle to cases where the petitioner was obliged to sell his shares, but extended it to all cases where there is a dispute leading to a s.459 petition except where the majority have been guilty of bad faith or plain impropriety or the articles provide an arbitrary or artificial method of valuation.

> "It is almost always clear from the outset that one party will have to buy the other's shares and it is usually equally clear who that party will be. The only real issue is the price of the shares . . . . Not many such petitions go to full hearing. They are usually settled by purchase of the petitioner's shares at a negotiated price. But the presentation of such a petition is a powerful negotiating tactic . . . . In these circumstances it seems to me that if the articles provide a method for determining the fair value of a party's shares, a member seeking to sell his shares upon a breakdown of relations with other shareholders should not ordinarily be entitled to complain of unfair conduct if he has made no attempt to use the machinery provided by the articles . . . . I therefore do not consider that in the normal case of breakdown of a corporate quasi-partnership there should ordinarily be any 'legitimate expectation' that a member wishing to have his shares purchased should be entitled to have them valued by the court rather than the auditors pursuant to the articles.[42]

This approach was initially followed in several cases. In *Re A Company*,[43] such an offer was held to render the s.459 petition inappropriate, and the exact words

---

[37] No interest is payable on such an agreement unless expressly agreed: *Harrison v Thompson* [1992] B.C.L.C. 833.
[38] [2001] EWCA Civ 397; [2002] 1 B.C.L.C. 65, CA.
[39] [2000] 2 B.C.L.C. 488.
[40] [2001] EWCA Civ 397; [2002] 1 B.C.L.C. 65, CA, at p.75.
[41] [1987] 1 W.L.R. 102.
[42] [1987] 1 W.L.R. 102, at p.110.
[43] (1987) 3 B.C.C. 624.

of Hoffmann J. quoted above were applied by Peter Gibson J. in *Re A Company*,[44] by Hoffmann J. again, *Re A Company*[45] and Judge Paul Baker Q.C. in *Re Castleburn Ltd*.[46] In the latter case it was also said that if the valuers make a mistake the petitioner has a remedy to attack the valuation without resorting to a s.459 petition.

On the other hand, the court ordered a valuation under s.461 if the valuer under the articles could not be seen to be wholly independent of the directors and to have no connection with the unfairly prejudicial conduct.[47] Nor did an offer to purchase some shares prevent a petition where the petitioner claimed to be entitled to other shares in the company.[48]

However, the Court of Appeal in *Virdi v Abbey Leisure Ltd*,[49] in rejecting the idea that an offer under the articles would automatically bar a winding-up petition on the just and equitable ground[50] and reversing Hoffmann J. on that point, refused either to confirm or reject the idea that it would automatically bar an unfairly prejudicial petition. Following that decision, Harman J. in *Re A Company ex parte Holden*[51] decided that an offer to purchase was no bar where the s.459 petition was a management exclusion case, even though the articles included a compulsory share purchase procedure. The petitioner, he said, has no real right to challenge the auditors' valuation or to make representations to him.

However, in *Re A Company*,[52] a petition was again stayed in a non-exclusion case following an offer by the majority shareholder. The respondent was held to have minimised the risk inherent in a valuation under the articles and the petitioner would receive a fair value for his shares. In *West v Blanchet*[52a] the petition was stayed when the court found that the respondents, in making an offer, had funds readily available to do so.

Lord Hoffmann has laid down the following guidelines as to what would count as a reasonable[53] offer:

(1) The offer must be to purchase the shares at a fair value, ordinarily a value representing an equivalent proportion of the total issued share capital, without a discount for its being a minority holding.

(2) The value, if not agreed, should be determined by a competent expert.

(3) The offer should be to have the value determined by the expert as an expert, with the objective of economy and expedition.

(4) The offer should provide for equality of arms between the parties and both should have the same right of access to information about the company which bears on the value of the shares and both should have the right to make submissions to the expert.

[44] (1988) 4 B.C.C. 80.
[45] (1989) 5 B.C.C. 218.
[46] [1991] B.C.L.C. 89.
[47] *Re Boswell & Co. (Steels) Ltd* (1989) 5 B.C.C. 145.
[48] *Re A Company* (1989) 5 B.C.C. 18.
[49] [1990] B.C.L.C. 342, CA.
[50] Above, p.353.
[51] [1991] B.C.L.C. 597.
[52] [1996] 2 B.C.L.C. 192.
[52a] [2001] 1 B.C.L.C. 795.
[53] See *West v Blanchet*, above, where the court had to consider the reasonableness of competing offers made by two equal shareholders.

(5) As to costs, these need not always be offered. If there is a breakdown between the parties, the majority shareholder should be given a reasonable opportunity to make an offer before he becomes obliged to pay costs. The mere fact that the petitioner has presented his petition before the offer did not mean that the respondent must offer to pay the costs if he was not given a reasonable time.[54]

Furthermore, he has also stated that

". . . parties ought to be encouraged, where at all possible, to avoid the expense of money and spirit inevitably involved in such litigation by making an offer to purchase at an early stage."[55]

Applications to strike-out

In certain circumstances proceedings under s.459 may be struck out on the basis that the petition fails to disclose a reasonable cause of action.[56] The discretion to do so is now contained in the CPR Part 3.4.[57]

In certain cases, the strike out proceedings may be invoked because a reasonable offer has been made to purchase the petitioner's shares. As a matter of principle, in *Re Saul D. Harrison*, Hoffmann L.J. stated that

"I accept that the notoriously burdensome nature of s.459 proceedings does not lighten the burden on the respondent who applies to have the petition struck out. He must still satisfy the court that the petitioner's case is plainly and obviously unsustainable. But I think that the consequences for the company mean that a court should be willing to scrutinise with care the allegations in a s.459 petition and, if necessary, the evidence proposed to be adduced in support, in order to see whether the petitioner really does have an arguable case."[58]

Thus, in *Re Oriental Gas Co Ltd*, the judge accepted that it was appropriate for him, in considering whether to strike out a petition, to ask whether it was "plain and obvious" that the relief sought would never be granted.[59] In allowing the application to strike out, he warned that litigants should be encouraged to make an application "sooner rather than later".[60] It is clear that the court will strike out the application where there has been an intentional delay, such that it is no

---

[54] *O'Neill v Phillips* [1999] 1 W.L.R. 1092, HL, at pp.1107–1108.

[55] At p.1106.

[56] As to the arguments for staying an action in Chancery, pending a s.459 petition, see *Jones v Jones* [2002] EWCA Civ 961; [2003] B.C.C. 226. It was alleged in that case that the Chancery action was being funded out of corporate funds, giving the respondents to the s.459 petition financial support for their defence. The Court of Appeal ordered that the Chancery proceedings be adjourned pending the resolution of the s.459 petition.

[57] Formerly RSC, Ord 18, r.19(1). Generally, see *Lawrance v Lord Norreys* (1890) 15 App. Cas.210, at p.220; *Wenlock v Maloney* [1965] 1 W.L.R. 1239, CA.

[58] [1995] 1 B.C.L.C. 14, CA, at p.22. In this case the petition was struck out because the court was satisfied that the claim of unfairness by the minority shareholder was not reasonably arguable. See too *Re Astec (BSR) plc* [1998] 2 B.C.L.C. 556, where a petition was struck out where it was being used as a tactical ploy to exert pressure to achieve a collateral purpose (in forcing a takeover bid).

[59] [1999] B.C.C. 237, at p.245.

[60] *ibid.*

longer possible to have a fair trial. Thus, on the unusual facts of *Re Vitara Foods Ltd* the court found that there had not merely been delay, but the proceedings had become meaningless at law and, in the face of such an inordinate and inexcusable delay, the petition would be struck out.[61]

Subsequent cases have considered striking out in the context of the Woolf Reforms to Civil Procedure (the CPR). In *North Holdings Ltd v Southern Tropics Ltd*, the Court of Appeal has emphasised the need, in striking out applications, for active case management, so as to reduce the time and expense involved in ascertaining the fair price to be paid for the petitioner's shares.[62] In *Arrow Nominees Inc v Blackledge*[63] the Court of Appeal found, on the facts, which included forged documents, that there had been a "flagrant and continuing affront to the court" and that striking out was not a disproportionate remedy for such an abuse.[64] A petition to strike out would, however, not follow where, for example, there have been countervailing offers for the purchase of shares by the parties and where "who should buy whose shares had become the battleground of the petition".[65]

In relation to striking out for delay, the authorities establish that any sanction by the court in relation to a particular case of delay has to be proportionate and requires a degree of flexibility by the court. So, in *Hateley v Morris*[66] the court decided not to strike out a petition under s.459 for delay because to do so would not be fair or proportionate. On the facts, both parties were at fault and striking out the petition would not dispose of their dispute.

In declining to strike out an application for abuse of process, Jonathan Crow provided the following succinct summary of the principles in *Atlasview Ltd v Brightview Ltd*:[67]

(1) The court had an inherent jurisdiction to prevent its process being abused.

(2) The public policy underlying the exercise of the court's discretion was to discourage stale claims and multiple proceedings by encouraging disputes to be brought to a timely conclusion.

(3) The question whether or not a particular action was an abuse of process would depend on all the circumstances, taking into account both the public policy issues and the private rights and interests of the particular parties.

(4) The circumstances in which proceedings may be held to represent an abuse of process could not be exhaustively defined.

(5) It was too dogmatic to suggest that, because an issue could have been raised in earlier proceedings, it should have been so raised.

---

[61] [1999] B.C.C. 315. But *cf. Guinness Peat Group plc v British Land Co plc* [1999] 2 B.C.L.C. 243, CA, which the Court of Appeal decided was not an appropriate case to strike out the petition.
[62] [1999] B.C.C. 746, CA, at p.770. See too *Re Rotadata Ltd* [2000] 1 B.C.L.C. 122, at p.127.
[63] [2000] 2 B.C.L.C. 167, CA.
[64] At p.202.
[65] *Apcar v Aftab* [2003] B.C.C. 510, at p.519.
[66] [2004] EWHC 252 (Ch); [2004] 1 B.C.L.C. 582.
[67] [2004] EWHC 1056 (Ch); [2004] 2 B.C.L.C. 191, at pp.200–201.

(6) A collateral attack on an earlier decision of a court of competent jurisdiction may be, but was not necessarily, an abuse of process.

(7) If an earlier decision was of a court exercising civil jurisdiction, that was binding on the parties and their privies in any later civil proceedings.

(8) If the parties bringing the collateral attack were not parties to the earlier decision or their privies, it would only be an abuse if the attack would produce obvious unfairness to another party, or bring the administration of justice into disrepute.[68]

Joint petitions for a just and equitable winding up and the alternative remedy

In the past, many petitions based on management exclusion cases sought either a just and equitable winding up under s.122 of the Insolvency Act 1986 (above) or relief under ss 459 to 461, as alternatives. Prior to 1980, it was generally easier to obtain a winding-up order (*e.g.* Re *Westbourne Galleries Ltd*, above). Thus in *Re R.A. Noble and Sons*,[69] Nourse J. refused to grant a petition under s.459 on the grounds that objectively the management exclusion had not been unfair since it was partly due to the petitioner's disinterest. The judge did, however, make a winding-up order since the exclusion had been the substantial cause of the breakdown in mutual confidence. Thus for a winding up the question is whether the management exclusion was a substantial cause of the subjective breakdown of the underlying equitable obligation of mutual trust whereas for an alternative remedy petition the exclusion must amount to unfairly prejudicial conduct affecting the petitioner *qua* member.[70] Similarly in *Jesner v Jarrad Properties Ltd*,[71] conduct by the controller of two companies in using the assets of one to fund the other was held not to be unfair to the minority shareholders since both companies were owned by the same people, but a winding-up order was granted on the basis of breach of underlying management rights.

The Chancery Division warned in a Practice Direction[72] that a petition under s.122(1)g should only be used as an alternative to a s.459 petition if that is either the preferred relief or possibly the only relief available.

The court has a discretion whether to allow one or both of the petitions to proceed. Thus in *Re Copeland Craddock Ltd*,[73] a joint petition was allowed to proceed because the relief sought under s.459 was to buy out the respondent and the winding up provided an alternative way of buying back into the company, from which he had been excluded, on a purchase from the liquidator. On the other hand, in *Re A Company*[74] the judge struck out the winding-up petition since

---

[68] On the facts of the case, the judge held that the application should not be struck out because it was not possible to conclude that the petition represented an abuse of process.

[69] [1983] B.C.L.C. 273. See also *Coulson Sanderson & Ward Ltd v Ward, The Financial Times*, October 18, 1985; *Teague, Petitioner*, 1985 S.L.T. 469 (O.H.) (provisional liquidator appointed) and *Re A Company* (1989) 5 B.C.C. 18.

[70] *Re A Company* [1990] B.C.C. 221.

[71] [1993] B.C.L.C. 1032; 1993 S.C. 34.

[72] Chancery 1/90 [1990] B.C.L.C. 452.

[73] [1997] B.C.C. 294.

[74] [1997] 1 B.C.L.C. 479.

the winding up was a remedy of last resort, the company was prosperous, and there was no reasonable chance of such an order being made.

It remains to be seen, however, given the seminal decision in *O'Neill v Phillips*, above, whether such joint petitions will still be resorted to, particularly in view of cases such as *Re Guidezone Ltd*[75] which have indicated that if the conduct relied on by the petitioner is not unfair for the purposes of that section, it could not found a case for a winding-up order on the just and equitable ground.[76]

Investigations and Powers to Obtain Information

Statutory provision is made for a number of forms of inspection.[77] These comprise investigation of a company's affairs, investigation of the ownership of a company, investigation of share dealings, and inspection of companies' books and papers.

Investigations of a company's affairs

Appointment of inspectors

1.   In the case of a company with a share capital, *on the application of not less than 200 members or of members holding not less than one-tenth of the shares issued, or on the application of the company*, the Secretary of State *may* appoint one or more inspectors to investigate the affairs of the company and to report on them. The application must be supported by evidence showing that the applicant or applicants have good reason for requiring investigation. Security, not exceeding £5,000, for the costs of the inquiry, may be required by the Secretary of State (for Trade and Industry): s.431.

An inspector is usually a Queen's Counsel, a Chartered Accountant or an official of the Department of Trade and Industry. In serious cases two inspectors will be appointed.

2.   The Secretary of State *shall* appoint an inspector or inspectors *if the court by order, declares that an investigation ought to be made*: s.432(1).

3.   The Secretary of State *may on his own initiative*[78] appoint inspectors if it appears:

   (i)   that a company's affairs are being or have been conducted with intent to defraud its creditors or the creditors of any other person or otherwise for a fraudulent or unlawful purpose or in a manner which is unfairly prejudicial to part of its members, or that any actual or proposed act or omission of the company is or would be so prejudicial or that it was formed for a fraudulent or unlawful purpose; or

   (ii)   that the promoters or the person managing its affairs have been guilty of fraud, misfeasance or other misconduct towards the company or its members; or

---

[75] [2000] 2 B.C.L.C. 321.
[76] See too, above, p.359.
[77] *e.g.* the investigation into the affairs of Mirror Group Newspapers plc.
[78] It is not improper for inspectors to be appointed where criminal investigations are proceeding at the same time: *Re London United Investments plc* [1992] B.C.L.C. 285.

(iii)   that the members have not been given all the information as to the company's affairs which they might reasonably expect: s.432(2).

Inspectors appointed under this head may be appointed on the basis that any report they may make is not to be for publication. In such a case the usual rules as to availability and publication (below) will not apply: s.432(2A).[79]

If the Secretary of State appoints inspectors under these heads the company has no right to state its case before the inspectors are appointed. The only requirement is that the decision to appoint is made in good faith.[80]

Powers of inspectors

1.   An inspector may, if he thinks it necessary, investigate any other body corporate which is or has been either the company's subsidiary or holding company[81] or a subsidiary of its holding company or a holding company of its subsidiary: s.433(1).

2.   He may call for the production of documents[82] by past or present officers and agents (including bankers, solicitors and auditors) of the company or a related company, whose duty it is to produce to the inspector all documents of or relating to the company or related companies which are in their custody or power, to attend before the inspector when required and to give the inspector all reasonable assistance. These powers extend to persons other than officers or agents if the inspectors consider that they are or may be in possession of any information which they believe to be relevant to the investigation[83]: s.434(1)(2).

3.   The inspector may examine any person on oath for the purposes of an investigation: s.434(3).

If an officer or agent refuses to perform his duties under s.434 the inspectors may certify that refusal to the court which may punish him as if he were in contempt of court: s.436. The privilege against self-incrimination does not apply and the officer or agent must answer the questions of the inspectors unless their questioning becomes unfair or oppressive.[84]

A solicitor or barrister need not disclose a privileged communication made to him, except as regards the name and address of his client, and a banker need not disclose any information which is confidential by virtue of banking business relating to his customers other than the company unless either the customer consents or the Secretary of State authorises the disclosure: s.452.

---

[79] This is intended to speed up investigations to decide whether any offences have been committed. It is also a result of the House of Fraser Holdings plc investigation, and the unsuccessful attempt by Lonrho plc to have the report published before the Secretary of State was willing to do so: see [1989 1 W.L.R. 525, HL.
[80] *Norwest Holst Ltd v Department of Trade* [1978] 3 All E.R. 280.
[81] Above, p.47.
[82] Documents include information held in an electronic form, *e.g.* on a computer, and the inspectors may require such information in a legible form: s.434(6).
[83] This could include partners and members of unincorporated associations not covered by s.433, above.
[84] *Re London United Investments plc* [1992] B.C.L.C. 285. See also, particularly, *Re an inquiry into Mirror Group Newspapers plc* [2000] Ch. 194.

An answer given by a person to a question put under powers given by s.434 (or s.446) may according to the Act be used in evidence against him: s.434(5).[85] There is no breach of Art. 6(1) of the European Convention on Human Rights in the case of the use of that evidence in civil proceedings, *e.g.* a petition to disqualify a person from being a director.[86]

4.   An inspector may at any time, and, if directed to do so, must inform the Secretary of State of any matters coming to his knowledge as a result of their investigation: s.437(1A). If matters have come to light which have led to the affairs being placed in the hands of the appropriate prosecuting authority the Secretary of State may direct the inspector either to take no further steps or to proceed only as directed by him.[87] In such a case no final report will be made unless either the inspectors were appointed by a court order or the Secretary of State so directs: s.437(1C).

It has been held that the inspectors' function is investigatory and not judicial but they must, in view of the consequences which may follow from their report, act fairly and, before they condemn or criticise a person, give him a fair opportunity to answer what is alleged against him.[88] It is sufficient for the inspectors to put to witnesses what has been said against them by other persons or in documents to enable them to deal with those criticisms in the course of the inquiry; it is not necessary for the inspectors to put their tentative conclusions to the witnesses in order to give them an opportunity to refute them.[89]

It has been said[90] that the considerations which are to be borne in mind in respect of an inquiry under the Companies Act are:

(a)   it is a very special kind of inquiry. It is not a trial. There is no accused, prosecutor, no charge. It is simply an investigation;

(b)   there is no one to present a case to the inspector. There is no "counsel for the Commission." The inspector has to do it all himself;

(c)   the investigation is in private. This is necessary because witnesses may say something defamatory of someone else, and it would be quite wrong for it to be published without the party affected being able to challenge it;

(d)   the inspectors have to make their report. They should state their findings on the evidence and their opinions on the matters referred to them. They should make it with courage and frankness, keeping

[85] And subject to s.434(5A)(5B), inserted following the decision of the European Court of Human Rights in *Saunders v UK* [1998] 1 B.C.L.C. 362. See too *I.J.L., G.M.R. & A.K.P. v United Kingdom* [2002] B.C.C. 380, ECHR

[86] *R. v Secretary of State for Trade and Industry, ex p. McCormick* [1998] 2 B.C.L.C. 18. See also *R. v Lyons*, [2002] UKHL 44; [2003] 1 A.C. 976.

[87] s.437(1B).

[88] *Re Pergamon Press Ltd* [1971] Ch. 388, CA, where the persons who were required to give evidence were not entitled to see the transcripts of evidence of witnesses. In *Testro Bros. Pty. Ltd v Tait* (1963) 109 C.L.R. 353, the majority of the High Court of Australia held that the inspector need not, before making a report on the company's affairs, give the company an opportunity of answering or explaining matters which, if unanswered or unexplained, might give rise to adverse findings or comment in the report.

[89] *Maxwell v Department of Trade and Industry* [1974] 1 Q.B. 523, CA.

[90] *Per* Lord Denning M.R., at p.533.

nothing back. Before they condemn or criticise a person they must act fairly by them.

Inspectors' report

The inspectors may make interim reports, and on the conclusion of the investigation they must make a final report to the Secretary of State.

The Secretary of State may send a copy of a report to the company's registered office, and, if he thinks fit, may furnish a copy on request and on payment of the prescribed fee to any member of the company or other company dealt with in the report, or to any person whose conduct is referred to in the report, or to the auditors of the company, or to the applicants for the investigation, or to any other person whose financial interests appear to be affected by it, *e.g.* creditors. He may also order the report to be printed and published.[90a] Where the appointment was under s.432 in pursuance of a court order, a copy *must* be furnished to the court: s.437(2). Section 437 has no application where the inspectors were appointed under s.432 on the basis that their report would not be published.[91]

In exercising his decision as to publication the Secretary of State must act reasonably and according to relevant considerations. He is entitled to withhold publication in the public interest if publication would inhibit a criminal investigation and/or prejudice the fair trial of anyone subject to such investigation.[92]

Proceedings on inspectors' report

Section 124A of the Insolvency Act 1986 provides that if it appears to the Secretary of State from the inspectors' report, or from any information obtained under an investigation,[93] that it is expedient in the public interest that the company be wound up, he may present a petition that it be wound up by the court if the court thinks it just and equitable that the company be wound up.[94] No evidence of fraud or misfeasance is necessary.

In addition a minority shareholder may use an inspector's report to support his own petition to wind up the company on the just and equitable ground under s.122(1)(g) of the 1986 Act.[95]

If from the report, etc., it appears that civil proceedings ought in the public interest to be brought by any company, s.438 empowers the Secretary of State to bring such proceedings in the name and on behalf of the company. The Secretary of State must indemnify the company against costs or expenses incurred by it in connection with any such proceedings.[96] If civil proceedings are properly brought under this section and there is no evidence to show that the company will be able to pay the defendant's costs if the defence is successful, the defendant is fully

---

[90a] s.437(3).
[91] Above, p.381.
[92] *R. v Secretary of State for Trade and Industry, ex p. Lonrho plc* [1989] 1 W.L.R. 525, HL.
[93] Below, p.385.
[94] Above, p.353.
[95] *Re St. Piran Ltd* [1981] 1 W.L.R. 1300.
[96] s.438(2).

protected by the indemnity provision in the section and security cannot be ordered under s.726.[97]

Under s.460(1), the Secretary of State may bring a petition for an alternative remedy consequent on a report.

Investigation of the ownership of a company[98]

Appointment of inspectors

1.   Where he considers that there is good reason to do so, the Secretary of State (for Trade and Industry) *may* appoint one or more inspectors to investigate and report on the membership of a company, for the purpose of determining the true persons who are, or have been, financially interested in the success or failure of the company, or able to control or materially influence its policy: s.442(1). The scope of the investigation may be defined either as to time or as to the matters to be investigated: s.442(2).

2.   Unless the application is vexatious, the Secretary of State *must* appoint an inspector, on the application, with regard to particular shares or debentures, of those members who can apply under s.431[99] for an investigation of the company's affairs provided the applicants give security as to costs not greater than £5,000.[1] The appointment shall not exclude from the scope of the investigation any matter stated by the applicants unless the Secretary of State is satisfied that it would be unreasonable to investigate it. The Secretary of State may, however, refuse to appoint inspectors if the powers to require information as to persons interested in shares (below) will be sufficient: s.442(3).

Powers of inspectors. Inspectors' report

An inspector appointed under s.442, above, has the same powers as an inspector appointed to investigate the affairs of a company under ss 431 and 432. Section 437 applies to the report of inspectors appointed under s.442.[2]

In addition, the sections apply in relation to all persons whom the inspector reasonably believes to be or to have been financially interested in the success or failure of the company or related company, or able to control or materially influence its policy. However, the Secretary of State may furnish the company or any person with an abbreviated copy of the report if he is of the opinion that there is good reason for not divulging part of it: s.443(3).[3]

Power to require information as to persons interested in shares, etc.

Where it appears that there is good reason to investigate the ownership of any shares or debentures of a company, and that it is unnecessary to appoint an

---

[97] *Selangor United Rubber Estates Ltd v Cradock* [1967] 1 W.L.R. 1168.
[98] *e.g.* the investigation, by Mr J. B. Lindon Q.C. of the membership of the Savoy Hotel Limited, June 14, 1954.
[99] Above, p.381.
[1] s.442(3B).
[2] Above, p.383.
[3] See *Clegg v Secretary of State of Trade and Industry* [2002] EWCA Civ 519; [2003] B.C.C. 128.

inspector for the purpose, the Secretary of State (for Trade and Industry) may require any person whom he reasonably believes to have or to be able to obtain any information as to the present and past interests in the shares or debentures and the names and addresses of the persons interested therein and of any persons who act or have acted for them in relation to the shares of debentures to give them such information: s.444(1).

A person is deemed to have an interest in a share or debenture if he has a right to acquire or dispose of it or any interest therein, or to vote in respect thereof, or if his consent is necessary for the exercise of any right of other persons interested therein, or if such other persons can be required or are accustomed to exercise their rights in accordance with his instructions: s.444(2).

Failure to give information required under this section, or making a statement known to be false in a material particular, or recklessly making a statement false in a material particular, is punishable by imprisonment or a fine or both: s.444(3).

Powers to impose restrictions on shares, etc.

If the Secretary of State has difficulty in finding out the relevant facts about any shares or debentures, he may direct that the shares or debentures shall be subject to restrictions: s.445(1).[4] The restrictions prevent transfers and agreements to transfer, the exercise of voting rights, the issue of further shares or debentures in right of the shares or debentures or to the holder thereof, including an agreement to transfer such rights, and, except in a liquidation, payment or agreement to transfer payment of any sums due from the company on the shares or debentures, whether in respect of capital or otherwise, *e.g.* payment of a dividend: s.454(1).[5]

If an order is made, any person aggrieved may appeal to the court for the order to be lifted. The court may only lift an order if it is satisfied: (i) that all the relevant facts about the shares have been disclosed and that no unfair advantage has accrued to anyone by the earlier failure to disclose; (ii) the shares are to be transferred for a valuable consideration[6] and the court approves the transfer; or (iii) if the restrictions unfairly affect the rights of third parties, when a partial exemption can be given: s.456(1A), (3).

Where an order has been made, either the Secretary of State or the company may apply to the court for a further order that the shares be compulsorily transferred free from some or all of the restrictions.[7] The proceeds of a compulsory transfer are to be paid into a separate fund against which the owners can claim, subject to the payment of costs: s.457(1).

Contravention of such restrictions renders the person or company concerned liable to penalties, although a prosecution in England can be instituted only by or with the consent of the Secretary of State: ss 455 and 732.

---

[4] Exceptions can be made to protect third party rights: s.445(1A).
[5] This includes payment on a take-over bid: *Re Ashbourne Investments Ltd* [1978] 2 All E.R. 418.
[6] This will include, *e.g.* accepting a take-over offer of shares in the offeror company. It is no longer restricted to sales for cash.
[7] s.456(5).

Investigation of share dealings

Section 446(1) provides that if it appears to the Secretary of State (for Trade and Industry) that ss 323[8] or 324[9] or 328(3)–(5)[10] (these sections being concerned with penalisation of dealing in options by, and notification of interests of, directors or their spouses or children) may have been contravened, he may appoint one or more competent inspectors to investigate and report to him.

Sections 434 to 437,[11] which impose on officers and agents the duty to assist inspectors, apply with one or two modifications.[12] Thus s.446 applies, *e.g.* to any individual who is, or an officer of a company which is, an authorised person under the Financial Service and Markets Act 2000 (see Chapter 19, below).

Inspection of a company's books and papers

This is dealt with in ss 447 to 451A as follows—[13]

Power of Secretary of State to require production of documents

Section 447(2) provides that the Secretary of State (for Trade and Industry) may, if he thinks there is good reason to do so, require a company to produce such documents[14] and provide such information as may be specified.

Without prejudice to any lien he may have,[15] production of documents may be required from any person who appears to be in possession of them to any investigator.[16] Copies of or extracts may be taken from a document produced under the section.[17] If the documents are not produced or the information is not provided, the investigator may certify this fact in writing to the court and if, after hearing any witnesses and any statement offered in defence, the court is satisfied that the offender failed without reasonable excuse to comply with the requirement, it may deal with him as if he had been guilty of contempt of court: s.453C.[18]

Nothing in that section compels a lawyer to produce a document containing a privileged communication made to him: s.452(2).[19]

If a person provides information which he knows to be false in a material particular, or recklessly provides information which is false in a material particular, he is liable to imprisonment or a fine or both: s.451(1)(2).[20]

---

[8] Above, p.276.
[9] Above, p.273.
[10] Above, p.274.
[11] Above, p.382.
[12] s.446(3).
[13] As amended by the Companies (Audit, Investigations and Community Enterprise) Act 2004, ss 21–24 and Sch. 2, Pt. 3. These changes came into force on April 6, 2005 (see the Companies (Audit, Investigations and Community Enterprise) Act 2004 (Commencement) Order 2004, SI 2004/3322).
[14] Documents include information stored on computers and any copies required must be given in a legible form.
[15] s.447(6).
[16] Thus such low-key investigations may be undertaken by private firms.
[17] s.447(7). See too s.447(9) as to information recorded otherwise than in legible form.
[18] This section was inserted into the Companies Act 1985 by the Companies (Audit, Investigations and Community Enterprise) Act 2004, s.24.
[19] See too s.448A.
[20] Substituted by Sch. 2, para. 19 of the Companies (Audit, Investigations and Community Enterprise) Act 2004.

Information provided: evidence

Section 447A[21] provides that any statement made by a person under s.447 may be used in evidence against him,[22] except that in criminal proceedings in which the person is charged with a relevant offence[23] no evidence relating to the statement may be adduced by or on behalf of the prosecution, and no question relating to it may be asked by or on behalf of the prosecution unless evidence relating to it is adduced or a question relating to it is asked in the proceedings by or on behalf of that person.[24]

Power to enter and remain on premises

Section 453A[25] provides that an inspector[26] or investigator[27] may at all reasonable times require entry to relevant premises[28] and remain there for such period as he thinks necessary, if he is authorised to do so by the Secretary of State and he thinks that to do so will materially assist him in the exercise of his functions.[29] The inspector or investigator may be accompanied by such other persons as he thinks appropriate.[30] Any person who intentionally obstructs a person under the section is guilty of an offence and is liable on conviction to a fine.[31] Section 453B then details a number of procedural requirements for the purposes of the preceding section. These include the investigator or inspector producing evidence of his identity and of his appointment or authorisation[32] and, as soon as practicable after obtaining entry, giving to an appropriate recipient[33] a written statement as to his powers and the rights and obligations of those present on the premises.[34] If there is no person present who appears to be an appropriate recipient for these purposes, then there must be sent to the company a notice of the fact and time of the visit as well as the statement which would have been presented to an appropriate person.[35] As soon as practicable after the visit, a written record of the visit must be prepared and, if requested to do so by the company, it must be given a copy of the record.[36] In the case where the company

---

[21] Inserted by the Companies (Audit, Investigations and Community Enterprise) Act 2004, Sch.2, para.17.

[22] s.447A(1).

[23] *i.e.*, any offence, other than those enumerated in s.447A(3).

[24] s.447A(2).

[25] Inserted by the Companies (Audit, Investigations and Community Enterprise) Act 2004, s.23.

[26] *i.e.*, someone appointed under ss 431, 432, or 442: s.453A(7).

[27] *i.e.*, a person authorised for the purposes of s.447: s.453A(8).

[28] This is defined as premises which the investigator believes are used (wholly or partly) for the purposes of the company's business: s.453A(3).

[29] s.453A(1)(2).

[30] s.453A(4).

[31] s.453A(5).

[32] s.453B(3)—and this extends also to any person accompanying him who is required to produce evidence of his identity.

[33] As defined in s.453B(8).

[34] s.453B(4).

[35] s.453B(5). See too the Companies Act 1985 (Power to Enter and Remain on Premises: Procedural) Regulations 2005 (SI 2005/684) reg.2.

[36] s.453B(6)(a). See too the Companies Act 1985 (Power to Remain on Premises: Procedural) Regulations 2005, above, reg.3.

is not the sole occupier of the premises, the inspector or investigator must, if requested to do so by the occupier, give the occupier a copy of the record.[37]

As was the case also in respect of s.447, above, if the documents are not produced or the information is not provided, the investigator may certify this fact in writing to the court and if, after hearing any witnesses and any statement offered in defence, the court is satisfied that the offender failed without reasonable excuse to comply with the requirement, it may deal with him as if he had been guilty of contempt of court: s.453C.[38]

Entry and search of premises

If a justice of the peace, or in Scotland a justice of the peace or a sheriff, is satisfied, on information on oath, or in Scotland on evidence on oath, laid by or on behalf of the Secretary of State or anyone authorised, that there are reasonable grounds for suspecting that there are on any premises any documents, in any form, of which production has been required under any investigation provision, and which have not been produced, he may issue a warrant authorising any constable and any other named person and other constables to enter and search the premises and take possession of any documents either appearing to be such or relevant to the investigation or to take steps to preserve them, or to take copies of them or to require any person named in the warrant to provide an explanation of them or state where they may be found: s.448(1)(3).

A similar warrant may also be issued if the justice of the peace, etc., is satisfied on information under oath that there are reasonable grounds for believing that an offence has been committed (punishable with at least two years' imprisonment), that there are premises on which documents relevant to that offence are kept, that the Secretary of State could require such documents and that such documents might not be produced but might be tampered with: s.448(2).

Any documents of which possession is taken may be retained for three months or, if within that period there are commenced criminal proceedings (being proceedings to which the documents are relevant), until the conclusion of the proceedings: s.448(6).

Penalties are imposed for obstructing the exercise of a right of entry or search, or of a right to take possession of documents s.448(7).

Provision for security of information

Under s.449(1),[39] no information or document obtained under ss 447 and s.453A, above,[40] may be disclosed unless the disclosure is made to a person specified in Sch. 15C or is of a description specified in Sch. 15D.[41] The specified persons in

---

[37] s.453B(6)(b).
[38] Inserted into the Companies Act 1985 by the Companies (Audit, Investigations and Community Enterprise) Act 2004, s.24.
[39] Substituted by the Companies (Audit, Investigations and Community Enterprise) Act 2004, Sch.2, para.18.
[40] See also s.449(10).
[41] Inserted by the Companies (Audit, Investigations and Community Enterprise) Act 2004, Sch.2, para.25.

Sch. 15C include the Secretary of State, the Lord Advocate, the Director of Public Prosecutions, the Financial Services Authority, and a constable.[42] Schedule 15D contains a list of some 49 disclosures. Among the more relevant of these are:

(1) a disclosure made for the purpose of enabling or assisting an inspector appointed under Pt XIV of the Companies Act;

(2) a disclosure for the purpose of enabling or assisting a person authorised under s.447, above, to exercise his functions;

(3) a disclosure for the purpose or enabling or assisting the Secretary of State or Treasury to exercise any of their functions *inter alia* under the Companies Act 1985, the insider dealing legislation, the Insolvency Act 1986, and the Company Directors Disqualification Act 1986;

(4) a disclosure for the purpose of enabling or assisting the Bank of England to exercise its functions;

(5) a disclosure for the purpose of enabling or assisting the Panel on Takeovers and Mergers to exercise its functions;

(6) a disclosure for the purpose of enabling or assisting the Financial Services Authority;

(7) a disclosure with a view to the institution of proceedings under ss 6 to 8 of the Company Directors Disqualification Act 1986.

Any person who discloses any information in contravention is guilty of an offence and is liable on conviction to imprisonment or a fine or to both.[43] Disclosure of information is not prohibited if it is or has been available to the public from any other source.[44]

The Secretary of State may disclose any information obtained under any of the investigation sections to certain other bodies concerned in financial regulation, *e.g.* the Financial Services Authority and overseas regulatory authorities; and in any other case where it is not restricted by the section concerned: s.451A.

Penalisation of destruction, etc., of company documents

Section 450(1) provides that an officer of a company, who destroys, mutilates or falsifies, or is privy to the destruction, etc., of a document affecting or relating to the property or affairs of the company is guilty of an offence unless he proves that he did not intend to conceal the state of affairs of the company or to defeat the law. Similarly if he fraudulently parts with, alters or makes an omission in, any such document.[45] The penalty is imprisonment or a fine or both.[46]

---

[42] And, for Scotland, a procurator fiscal and the Scottish Ministers. This includes any officer or employee of the person: s.449(8).

[43] s.449(6).

[44] s.449(9).

[45] s.450(2)

[46] s.450(3)

Investigation to assist overseas regulatory authorities

The Companies Act 1989 introduced new powers to allow the Secretary of State to compel the divulging of information and documents "for the purpose of assisting an overseas regulatory authority which has requested his assistance in connection with inquiries being carried out by it or on its behalf": s.82(1) C.A. 1989. These powers are designed to enable the UK to comply with its obligations under various conventions on the mutual co-operation between countries relating to financial markets. As such they apply equally to the investigations into insider dealing set out in Chapter 19.

An overseas regulatory authority is one which is concerned with functions similar to those of the Secretary of State with regard to companies, financial services, or any other UK regulatory authority, or to the control of insider dealing, companies or financial services: s.82(2) C.A. 1989.

The Secretary of State, or his agent or other competent person, cannot exercise these powers unless he is satisfied that the assistance requested is for the purposes of its regulatory functions,[47] and may take into account when making his decision whether he would be given reciprocal help of this nature, the seriousness of the matter, the public interest and above all whether the alleged breach relates to a law which has no close parallel in the UK or to an asserted jurisdiction which is not recognised by the UK.[48] Finally, the Secretary of State may require the overseas authority to contribute towards the costs incurred.[49]

The powers exercisable by the Secretary of State are similar to those given to inspectors appointed under s.432 (company investigation) and 442 (company ownership). Thus they include powers to require the production of documents, the giving of evidence on oath and to require such assistance as the person concerned is reasonably able to give: s.83 C.A. 1989. The standard exemptions for professional privilege are included by s.84, and s.85 imposes criminal sanctions for failure to comply or the giving of false or misleading information.

The restrictions on the disclosure of information so obtained are broadly similar to those relating to domestic investigations under s.449: ss 86 and 87 C.A. 1989.

---

[47] s.82(3) C.A. 1989.
[48] s.82(4) C.A. 1989.
[49] s.82(6) C.A. 1989.

Chapter 18

CORPORATE GOVERNANCE

As we have seen in Chapter 15, the powers of management of companies are vested in the board of directors to the extent that the general meeting may not interfere with their exercise, except by removing the board or by enforcing the fiduciary and other duties which are imposed on directors. We have further seen in Chapter 14 that in respect of listed companies the machinery available for the general meeting to exercise any realistic control on the boards of such companies is inadequate and in Chapter 17 that the possibilities for a minority shareholder to exercise such control, especially in listed companies, are extremely limited both by the rule in *Foss v Harbottle* and the decision in *Re Astec (BSR) plc*[1] that the concept of "legitimate expectation" has no role in petitions under s.459 in the case of listed companies. Thus, despite the existence of all the legal controls on directors, a number of concerns have arisen with respect to the control of such companies. Perceived excessive remuneration packages awarded to directors of some companies, together with other so called scandals such as the *Guinness* affair and, further afield, Enron and WorldCom, have led to additional structural controls on listed companies. These additional controls are collectively known as corporate governance.

The question of the corporate governance of listed companies has been the subject of three specific reports prepared for the Stock Exchange, initially those of the Cadbury Committee[2] and the Greenbury Committee.[3] Those reports were then considered by the Hempel Committee which produced a final report[4] and in June 1998 consolidated that and the earlier ones into a Combined Code.[5] The Combined Code contains a set of principles, followed by detailed provisions reflecting best practice to attain those principles, combining the work of the three committees.

Despite all the changes effected by the work of the three committees, however, renewed attention had to be given to the UK position following the downfall of Enron and WorldCom abroad. The corporate governance weaknesses which these widely publicised corporate events highlighted revolved mainly around the effectiveness of non-executive directors and the audit function. In the United States, predictably, the response was heavy-handed, with the passing of the so-called Sarbanes-Oxley Act 2002,[6] aimed at quashing further corporate

---

[1] [1998] 2 B.C.L.C. 556. By the very nature of such companies the just and equitable winding-up remedy cannot apply to them. Generally, on "legitimate expectations", see p.367, above.
[2] Report of the Committee on the Financial Aspects of Corporate Governance 1992.
[3] Directors' Remuneration: Report of a Study Group 1995.
[4] *Committee on Corporate Governance: Final Report*, January 1998.
[5] *Committee on Corporate Governance: The Combined Code*, June 1998.
[6] Pub. L. No. 107–204.

governance failures.[7] In the UK, the response has been a more measured one. In April 2002, the Secretary of State in the Department of Trade and Industry and the Chancellor of the Exchequer commissioned Derek Higgs to prepare a review on the role of independent directors (or non-executive directors) and to make recommendations for changes to the Combined Code.[8] The Higgs Report,[9] as it is known, was duly published in January 2003. In September 2002, Sir Robert Smith was charged by the Financial Reporting Council (FRC),[10] the guardians of the Combined Code, to undertake a review of audit committees. His Report[11] was also published in January 2003.[12] The Revised Combined Code[13] was approved by the FRC in July 2003 and came into effect on November 1, 2003. It supersedes and replaces the 1998 Combined Code[14] and one commentator has remarked that it is "the biggest shake-up of boardroom culture in more than a decade".[15] Although the Code builds upon the earlier versions, it also retains the flavour of the Higgs Report and many of the recommendations contained in that Report find a place in the Code. Thus, although the Code contains many provisions which will not seem too unfamiliar, it does contains provisions which now emphasise the role of the non-executive director (NED),[16-17] and in particular, the relationship with shareholders and representation of shareholder interests at board level. The Code has also enhanced the role of the audit committee.

Formerly, the Stock Exchange required all listed companies, as part of the requirements for listing, to make a disclosure statement addressing matters contained in the Code.[18] Now, however, Chapter 12.43A of the Listing Rules provides that the following items *must* be provided in a company's annual report and accounts:[19]

(1) A narrative statement of how it has applied the principles set out in s.1 of the Code, providing explanations which enables its shareholders to evaluate how the principles have been applied.[20]

(2) A statement[21] as to whether or not it has complied throughout the accounting period with the Code provisions set out in s.1 of the Code. A company which has not complied, or complied with only some of the

---

[7] See John Paul Lucci, "Enron—The bankruptcy heard around the world and the international ricochet of Sarbanes-Oxley", (2003) 67 Albany L.R. 211.

[8] See, generally, *www.dti.gov.uk/cld/non-exec-review/*.

[9] *Review of the role and effectiveness of non-executive directors.*

[10] See *www.frc.org.uk.*

[11] *Audit Committees—Combined Code Guidance.*

[12] See the joint DTI and Treasury News Release P/2003/31, which followed the publication of these two reports.

[13] All references to "the Code" hereafter are to the Revised Combined Code, unless otherwise indicated.

[14] Preamble to the Code, para.1.

[15] Tony Tassel, "Investors urged to adopt Higgs Standards", *Financial Times*, July 24, 2003.

[16-17] As they will be referred to hereafter.

[18] For the discussion, see the 16th ed., pp.343–344.

[19] See too Schedule C of the Code itself, which provides for "Disclosure of corporate governance arrangements".

[20] Para.12.43A(a).

[21] This must be reviewed by auditors, before publication, but only insofar as certain provisions of the Code are concerned.

provisions, must specify those Code provisions with which it has not complied and for what part of the period such non-compliance continued, and give reasons for any non-compliance.[22]

(3) A report to the shareholders by the Board, containing, *inter alia*, a statement of the company's policy on executive directors' remuneration.[23]

The consequence of these requirements is that listed companies will have to explain their governance policies as defined in the Code.

THE REVISED COMBINED CODE ON CORPORATE GOVERNANCE

The Code of Best Practice

The Code contains 17 principles of good corporate governance.[24] The Preamble, *inter alia* states that:

> "While it is expected that listed companies will comply with the Code's provisions most of the time, it is recognised that departure from the provisions of the Code may be justified in particular circumstances. Every company must review each provision carefully and give a considered explanation if it departs from the Code provisions."[25]

Apart from its main provisions, the Code is supplemented by three schedules, as well as Guidance on Internal Control (The Turnbull Guidance), Guidance on Audit Committee (The Smith Guidance), and Suggestions for Good Practice from the Higgs Report. The principles and their amplification are contained under five headings which reflect their areas of concern. The principles consist of a "Main Principle", followed by "Supporting Principles" and "Code provisions", although some provisions do not include one or other of the Supporting Principle or Code Provisions.[26]

Directors

Principle A.1,"The Board", provides that the company must be headed by an effective board which is collectively responsible for the success of the company. The Supporting Principles are to the effect that the board's role is to provide entrepreneurial leadership within a framework of prudent and effective controls which enables risk to be assessed and managed. Thus, it should set strategic aims, ensure necessary financial and human resources and review management performance. In particular, NEDs[27] should constructively challenge and help develop proposals on strategy, scrutinise performance of management, satisfy themselves

---

[22] Para.12.43A(b).
[23] Para.12.43A(c). Much other detailed information is required in sub-paras (i)–(x).
[24] The original Combined Code of 1998 contained 14 such principles.
[25] Preamble, para.5.
[26] As indicated in the discussion, below.
[27] See too Sch. B of the Code, which is headed, "Guidance on liability of non-executive directors: care, skill and diligence". For general discussion, see p.310, above.

on integrity of financial information, determine remuneration and have a prime role in succession planning. The Code Provisions then provide that the board should meet sufficiently regularly to discharge its duties, including a formal schedule of matters reserved for its decision. So that all the shareholders are fully informed, the annual report should include a statement of how the board operates and should identify the chairman and other company officials, such as the chairman and the members of the nomination, audit and remuneration committees. Further, the chairman should hold meetings with an NEDs, without the executives present, and the NEDs should meet, without the chairman, at least annually. If the directors have concerns, which cannot be resolved, about the running of the company or any proposed action, they should ensure that this is recorded in the board minutes. On resignation, an NED should provide a written statement to the chairman, for circulation to the board, if they have any such concerns. Finally, the company should arrange appropriate insurance cover in respect of legal action against its directors.

Principle A.2, "Chairman and chief executive", provides that there should be a clear division of responsibilities at the head of the company between the running of the board and the executive responsibility for the running of the company's business. No one individual should have unfettered powers of decision. The Supporting Principles provide that the chairman is responsible for leadership of the board and for ensuring that all directors receive accurate, timely and clear information. He is also responsible for ensuring effective communication with shareholders and for facilitating the contribution of NEDs. Thus, he should ensure that executive directors and NEDs maintain a good relationship. The Code Provisions then provide that the roles of chairman and chief executive should not be exercised by the same person and the exact division of responsibilities should be set out in writing and agreed to by the board. The chairman should, on appointment, meet the independence criteria set out in principle A.3, below. In particular, a chief executive should not go on to be chairman, but exceptionally, if this does happen, the board should consult major shareholders and set out the reasons in their next annual report.

Principle A.3, "Board balance and independence", provides that the board should include a balance of executive and NEDs (and in particular independent NEDs), such that no individual or small group of individuals can dominate the board's decision taking. The Supporting Principles are to the effect that the board should not be unwieldy. It should have a balance of skills and experience, should ensure power and information are not concentrated, be regularly refreshed, not place undue reliance on individuals, and ensure that only members should attend audit, nomination and remuneration committee meetings. The Code Provisions are that the board should identify each NED which it considers to be independent. A list of indicative independence criteria are then set out. Except for smaller companies,[28] at least half the board, excluding the chairman, should be independent NEDs. The board should appoint a senior independent NED, who should be available to shareholders if they have concerns which

---

[28] This is defined as one that is below the FTSE 350 throughout the year immediately prior to the reporting year.

contact through the normal channels has failed to resolve or for which such contact is inappropriate.

Principle A.4, "Appointments to the Board", provides that there should be a formal, rigorous and transparent procedure for the appointment of new directors to the board. The Supporting Principles state that appointments should be on merit and against objective criteria, that appointees should have enough time available to devote to the job, and that the board should satisfy itself that plans are in place for an orderly succession. The Code Provisions then state that there should be a nomination committee consisting of a majority of members who are independent NEDs and that the chairman or an NED should chair the committee except when choosing a new chairman. The committee should make available its terms of reference and should prepare a description of the role and capabilities required. For the appointment of a chairman, a job specification should be prepared, which includes an assessment of the time commitment expected. The terms and conditions of the appointment of NEDs should also be made available for inspection. A chairman's other significant commitments should be disclosed to the board before appointment and included in the annual report. Changes to external commitments should be reported as they arise and included in the annual report. No individual should chair more than one FTSE 100 company. Further, other significant appointments of NEDs should be disclosed and the board informed of subsequent changes. An executive director should not be allowed to become an NED of more than one FTSE 100 company nor the chair of such a company. A separate section of the annual report should set out the work of the nomination committee and an explanation given if neither an external search consultancy nor open advertising has been used in the appointment of a chairman of NED.

Principle A.5, "Information and professional development", provides that the board should be supplied in a timely manner with information in a form and of a quality appropriate to enable it to discharge its duties. Further, all directors should receive induction on joining the board and should regularly update and refresh their skills and knowledge. The Supporting Principles are that the chairman is responsible for ensuring that directors receive accurate, timely and clear information. He should ensure that directors continually update their skills and knowledge and the company should provide the necessary resources for them to do so. Under the direction of the chairman, the company secretary's responsibilities include facilitating information flows to and from the board and advising the board on governance matters. The Code Provisions provide that the chairman should ensure that new directors receive a full formal induction, including an offer to major shareholders to meet a new NED. There should also be access to independent professional advice at the company's expense. Finally, it is stated that all directors should have access to the advice and services of the company secretary, who is responsible for ensuring that board procedures are complied with. Both the appointment and removal of the company secretary should be a matter for the board as a whole.

Principle A.6, "Performance evaluation", provides that the board should undertake a formal and rigorous annual evaluation of its own performance and that of its committees and individual directors. The Support Principle states that evaluation should ensure that each director contributes effectively and demonstrates commitment to the role. In particular, the chairman should seek appointments and resignations on the basis of strengths and weaknesses of the board. The Code Provisions provide that the board should state in the annual report how performance evaluation of the board, its committees and its individual directors has been conducted. The NEDs, led by the senior independent director, should be responsible for a performance evaluation of the chairman, taking into account the views of the executive directors.

Principle A.7, "Re-election", provides that all directors should be submitted for re-election at regular intervals, subject to continued satisfactory performance and that the board should ensure planned and progressive refreshing of the board. There is no Supporting Principle, but the Code Provisions state that all directors should be subject to election confirmed at the first AGM and then re-elected at intervals of no more than three years. NEDs should be appointed for specified terms and the board should set out why they believe that such an individual should be elected. Any term over six years should be subject to rigorous review and should take into account the need for progressive refreshing of the board and serving more than nine years could be relevant to the determination of a NED's independence.[29-30]

Remuneration[31]

Principle B.1, "The Level and Make-up of Remuneration", provides that levels of remuneration should be sufficient to attract, retain and motivate quality directors, but that the company should avoid paying more than is necessary for this purpose. A significant portion of executive director's remuneration should be structured so as to link rewards to corporate and individual performance. The Supporting Principle states that the remuneration committee should judge the position of the company relative to other companies, albeit using such comparisons with caution. They should also be sensitive to pay and employment conditions elsewhere in the group, especially when determining annual salary increases. The Code Provisions are then broken down into (1) remuneration policy and (2) service contracts and compensation. In relation to (1), remuneration policy, it is provided that performance related elements should form a significant portion of the total package and should be designed to align the interests of executive directors with those of the shareholders and to give the directors keen incentives to perform at the highest levels. In designing such schemes, the remuneration committee should, in this respect, follow the provisions attached to Sch. A of the Code.[32] Executive share options should not be offered at a discount, save as permitted under the Listing Rules. On the other hand, levels of remuneration for NEDs should reflect the time commitment and responsibilities of the role, but should not include share options. Where, exceptionally, these are granted, shareholder approval should be sought in advance. Where external NED posts are held by executive directors, the

---

[29-30] As set out in Code Provision A.3.1, above.
[31] As to this, see too The Directors' Remuneration Report Regulations 2002, SI 2002/1986.
[32] "Provisions on the design of performance related remuneration".

remuneration report should state whether the earnings are retained as well as the amount. As to (2), service contracts and compensation, the remuneration committee should aim to avoid rewarding poor performance and should take a robust line on reducing compensation to reflect departing director's obligations to mitigate loss. Notice or contract periods should be set at one year or less.

Principle B.2, "Procedure", provides that there should be a formal and transparent procedure for developing policy on executive remuneration and for fixing the remuneration packages of individual directors. No director should be involved in deciding his or her own remuneration. The Support Principles provide that the remuneration committee should consult the chairman and or chief executive about their proposals relating to the remuneration of the other executive directors and should be responsible for appointing external consultants in respect of executive director remuneration. Potential conflicts of interest should be recognized and avoided and the chairman should ensure communication with shareholders with regards to remuneration. The Code Provisions are to the effect that the board should establish a remuneration committee, who should all be independent NEDs and that the remuneration committee should make available its terms of reference. Where remuneration consultants are used, there should be a statement as to whether they have any connection with the company. The committee should have delegated responsibility for all remuneration for all executive directors and the chairman, including pension and compensation payments. It should also monitor remuneration for senior management (the first layer of management below board level). The board itself (or the shareholders, if required by the articles) should set the NEDs remuneration and shareholders should be invited to approve all long-term incentive schemes, as defined in the Listing Rules.

Audit Committee and Auditors

Principle C.1, "Financial Reporting", provides that the board should present a balanced and understandable assessment of the company's position and prospects. The Supporting Principle states that responsibility extends to interim and other price-sensitive public reports and reports to regulators as well as to information required to be presented by statutory requirements. The Code Provisions then go on to state that the directors should explain in the annual report their responsibility for preparing the accounts and there should be a statement by the auditors about their accounting responsibilities. The directors should report that the business is a going concern statement, with supporting assumptions or qualifications as necessary.

Principle C.2, "Internal Control", provides that the board should maintain a sound system of internal control to safeguard shareholders' investments and the company's assets. There is no Supporting Principle, but the Code Provisions are that there should be an annual review by the board of the system of internal controls which should be reported to the shareholders. This should cover all material controls, including financial, operational and compliance controls and risk management systems.

Principle C.3, "Audit Committee and Auditors", provides that the board should establish formal and transparent arrangements for considering how they should apply the financial reporting and internal control principles and for maintaining an appropriate relationship with the company's auditors. There are no Supporting Principles, but the Code Provisions are that the board should establish an audit committee consisting of independent NEDs with at least one member with recent and relevant financial experience. The main role and responsibilities of the audit committee should be set out and should include monitoring, review, recommendations, and the development and implementation of an external auditor to supply non-audit services. The terms of reference of the audit committee should be made available and a separate section in the annual report should describe work done in discharging their responsibilities. The audit committee should review arrangements in place for staff concerns to be raised in confidence and should also review internal audit activities and the reasons for an absence of an internal audit function, if applicable. It should have primary responsibility for making a recommendation on the appointment, reappointment and removal of external auditors. The annual report should explain to shareholders how, if the auditor provides non-audit services, auditor objectivity and independence is safeguarded.

Relations with shareholders

Principle D.1, "Dialogue with Institutional Shareholders", provides that there should be a dialogue with shareholders based on mutual understanding of objectives. The board as a whole has responsibility for ensuring that a satisfactory dialogue with shareholders takes place. The Supporting Principles provide that the chairman should ensure that sufficient contact is maintained, whilst recognising that most contact will be through the chief executive and finance director. The board is encouraged to keep in touch with shareholder opinion in whatever ways are most practical and efficient. The Code Provisions are to the effect that the chairman should ensure that the views of shareholders are communicated to the board and that he should discuss governance and strategy with major shareholders. Further, NEDs should be offered the opportunity to meet major shareholders and the senior independent director should attend sufficient meetings with a range of major shareholders for a balanced view. There should be a statement in the annual report by the board as to the steps taken to develop an understanding of the views of major shareholders, for example through face-to-face contact, analyst's or broker's briefings, and surveys of shareholder opinion.

Principle D.2, "Constructive Use of the AGM", provides that the board should use the AGM to communicate with investors and to encourage their participation. There is no Supporting Principle, but the Code Provisions elaborate that the company should count all proxy votes and ensure that votes cast are properly recorded. In particular, there should be a separate resolution for each substantially separate issue and there should be a resolution relating to the report and accounts. The chairman should arrange for the chairmen of the audit, remuneration and nomination committees to be available to answer questions and for all directors to attend. Finally, the company should arrange for the notice and working papers for AGM to be sent to shareholders at least 20 working days before the meeting.

Institutional shareholders

The provisions of this part contain no Code Provisions.

Principle E.1, "Dialogue with companies", provides that institutional share-holders should enter into a dialogue with companies based on the mutual understanding of objectives. The Supporting Principle states that institutional shareholders should apply the principles set out in the Institutional Shareholders' Committee's "The Responsibilities of Institutional Shareholders and Agents—Statement of Principles".

Principle E.2, "Evaluation of Governance Disclosures" provides that when evaluating companies' governance arrangements, particularly those relating to board structure and composition, due weight should be given to all relevant factors drawn to their attention. The Support Principle states that institutional shareholders should carefully consider explanations given for departure from the Code and communicate in writing where appropriate. They should avoid a box-ticking exercise in assessing the company's corporate governance and should bear in mind the size and complexity of the organisation and the nature of the risks and challenges it faces.

Principle E.3, "Shareholder Voting", provides that institutional shareholders have a responsibility to make considered use of their votes. The Supporting Principles are to the effect that institutional shareholders should take steps to ensure voting intentions are being translated into practice. They should, on request, make available to their clients information on the proportion of resolutions on which votes were cast and non-discretionary proxies lodged. Finally, major shareholders should attend AGMs where appropriate and practicable and this should be facilitated by companies and registrars.

Effect of the Code

It is too early to determine how effective the Revised Combined Code will be. If it eventually proves to be as successful as the City Code on Take-overs and Mergers,[33] then it will be extremely beneficial. There are competing reports as to whether this will indeed be so.[34] Many of the principles are of a very general nature and heavily reliant on NEDs and also institutional investors. Nevertheless, there may be some scope for the courts having regard to it in such areas as directors' duties of care as a guide to good practice.

European developments

Finally, it should be mentioned that this is also an area in which the European Commission has begun to take an interest and was heralded in *Modernising Company Law and Enhancing Corporate Governance in the European—A Plan to Move Forward*.[35] During 2004, following a consultation on the matter, the

---

[33] See Chapter 31, below.
[34] See, *e.g.*, Kit Bingham, "UK boards adapt to new environment", *eFinancial News.com*, October 10, 2004; Sundeep Tucker, "Patchy performance on Higgs standards", *Financial Times*, July 26, 2004.
[35] May 2003. See the discussion, above, p.18.

Commission formally invited Member States, through a Commission Recommendation, to reinforce the presence and role of independent non-executive directors on listed companies' boards. The protection of shareholders, employees and the public against potential conflicts of interest, by an independent check on management decisions, was seen to be particularly important to restore confidence in financial markets after recent scandals.[36-37] Commissioner McCreevy has recently stated, in relation to corporate governance, that:

> "Europe has a role to play. That role is to co-ordinate where possible Member States' efforts to improve corporate governance practices, through changes in their national company law, securities law or in corporate governance codes. There are different traditions in different Member States and those should be respected, but we must avoid unnecessary divergences which distort the single market and make life difficult for investors. Member States want and need to learn from each other's experience. The Corporate Governance Forum brings together a vast amount of high-level experience and expertise. It has a key strategic role to play".[38]

It remains, of course, to be seen what impact these developments are likely to have on the future development of UK company law in this area.

In that respect the Cadbury Code was considered by Jonathan Parker J. in *Re Astec (BSR) plc*[39] in connection with a petition under s.459.[40] The judge gave the following analysis:

> "So far as corporate governance is concerned, members of the public buying shares in listed companies may well expect that all relevant rules and codes of best practice will be complied with in relation to the company. But that expectation cannot, in my judgment, give rise to an equitable constraint on the exercise of legal rights conferred by the company's constitution (of which . . . the Cadbury Code form[s] no part) so as to found a petition under s.459. It is in essence little more than an expectation that the company's affairs will not be conducted in a manner which is unfairly prejudicial to the interests of the members generally, or of some part of its members, an expectation which one would expect to be present in every case."[41]

[36-37] See Press Release IP/04/1182, October 6, 2004.
[38] See Press Release IP/05/78, January 20, 2005.
[39] [1998] 2 B.C.L.C. 556.
[40] Above, p.364.
[41] [1998] 2 B.C.L.C. 556, at p.590.

Chapter 19

INSIDER DEALING

Introduction

Part V of the Criminal Justice Act 1993 deals with certain forms of insider trading and makes them criminal offences.[1] Provisions to regulate dealings in a company's shares came about because of widespread concern prior to 1980 about the misuse of confidential information by officers of the company, in particular, but also by their associates, their families and friends to whom information about the company had been relayed by them, or the misuse by others outside the company such as accountants, auditors and bankers who might equally have access to restricted information about the company which would affect the value of its shares on the market.

Insider dealing occurs where an individual or organisation buys or sells securities while knowingly in possession of some piece of confidential information which is not generally available and which is likely, if made available to the general public, to materially affect the price of these securities. So, for example, there is insider trading where a company director knows that the company is in a bad financial state and sells his shares in it knowing that in a few days' time this news will be made public together with an announcement of a cut in dividend payment. Likewise, the director would be insider dealing if, on being informed, before it was generally known by the public, that the company has discovered oil or gold on its own land, he bought more shares in the company in the not unrealistic expectation of an increase in their market value as a result of the subsequent public announcement.

Ethical and legal objections

The moral or ethical reasons[2] for prohibiting such activities is that the use of insider information is clearly unfair to those who deal with the insider. One of the difficulties, however, is that in many cases it is seen as a victimless crime in that it is difficult to identify those who have lost by the insider dealing where, as the law currently requires, it takes place on a Stock Exchange dealing.

From the point of view of company law, perhaps a more significant reason for attempting to regulate insider trading by law is that the insider with access to confidential information is thereby in a potential conflict-of-interest situation.

---

[1] This Act replaced the provisions first introduced in ss 68–73 of the Companies Act 1980 and consolidated into the Company Securities (Insider Dealing) Act 1985.

[2] There are some economic arguments in favour of the practice.

For example, he may be in such a position within the company as to be able to dictate or at least influence when the public disclosure of price-sensitive information is to be made. In that situation his decision and his own desire to trade advantageously in the company's shares may conflict; in other words the best interests of the company may wrongly take second place to his own self interest. Directors are duty bound, subject to the considerations contained in s.309 of the Companies Act 1985 and s.187 of the Insolvency Act 1986,[3] only to act bona fide in the best interests of the company as a whole.[4]

Furthermore, such unethical conduct is likely to bring not only the reputation of the company concerned but also that of the securities market in this country into disrepute with the possible risk of a consequent adverse investment effect. For this reason in particular, the Financial Services Act 1986[4a] extended the scope of the provision aimed at preventing the abuse of information obtained by persons in their official capacity in connection with the new regulation of the securities and investment industry, and provided the innovation of investigations into suspected insider dealing. The Companies Act 1989 allowed for investigations at the request of overseas regulators since insider dealing may well take place on an international scale.

Since then, the Financial Services and Markets Act 2000 has been brought into force, effecting very significant changes to financial services regulation in the UK. Although the Act does not specifically deal with insider dealing, it does contain a complex new provision termed "market abuse" in Pt VIII. Market abuse is defined as behaviour *inter alia* "which is based on information which is not generally available to those using the market but which, if available to a regular user of the market, would or would be likely to be regarded by him as relevant when deciding the terms on which transactions in investments of the kind in question should be effected".[5] This is very similar to, but not entirely on all fours with, the equivalent definition in the Criminal Justice Act 1993.[6] The Financial Services Authority (FSA) is given a number of sanctions which it may invoke against persons who engage in such market abuse.[7] It remains to be seen whether the FSA does, in fact, invoke these provisions in respect of insider dealing.

Methods of control

Given that it is recognised as wrong for a director or another to deal in a company's shares knowing of some development which will affect the price of the

---

[3] The first of these enjoins directors in the performance of their functions to have regard to the interests of the company's employees as well as those of its members (but without providing employees with any legal sanction for failure to do so). The latter section now permits a company to make provision for the benefit of its employees or ex-employees on the cessation or transfer of the whole or part of its business even if it is not in the best interests of the company and permits a liquidator to make over assets to employees in satisfaction of the amount decided to be provided to them in such circumstances.

[4] *Hutton v W. Cork Rly.* (1883) 23 Ch.D. 654, CA; *Re Lee Behrens & Co.* [1932] Ch. 46; *Evans v Brunner Mond & Co.* [1921] 1 Ch. 359; *Parke v Daily News* [1962] Ch. 927; and *Re Roith* [1967] 1 W.L.R. 479.

[4a] Since repealed.

[5] s.118(2)(a). *cf.* now the amendments introduced by the Financial Services and Markets Act 2000 (Market Abuse) Regulations 2005, SI 2005/381.

[6] Below, p.405.

[7] See s.123.

shares and to which other members or the public generally are not privy, then the question arises how to put an end to such unethical activity. The universal condemnation of this malpractice has produced differing solutions for its eradication.

In the United States of America, which has been in the forefront of the attack on insider trading, the solution adopted is to make the insider disgorge his ill-gotten gains to the company itself or to the individual with whom he dealt.

In the United Kingdom on the other hand the approach has been to progress from a few disparate provisions of the Companies Act and prohibitions contained in various self-regulatory codes to making certain instances of insider dealing a criminal offence. These offences were first created in 1980 partly at the request of the Take-over Panel who acknowledged that their self-regulatory code was inadequate to control the practice. The current provisions are set out in Pt V of the Criminal Justice Act 1993, incorporating changes required by the EU insider dealing directive.[8] These are dealt with in detail below but two general points should be noted at this stage. First, the offences do not apply to private share deals and, second, there are no civil consequences of a transaction being a criminal offence. The option for that in the directive was not adopted in this country.

Prior to the creation of the criminal offences by the 1980 Companies Act, the only statutory restrictions on insider trading by company officers were the prohibitions on option dealings by directors and the requirement that a register of their share dealings and the dealings of their spouses and children be maintained and available for inspection by an interested person.[9] These 1967 statutory provisions were ineffective because although they purported to create a legal duty or obligation to disclose share dealings, yet they provided no remedy for failure to comply with the Act's requirements.

Also by that time there were sanctions conceived and imposed by the Stock Exchange Authorities and the City Panel under the City Code on Take-overs and Mergers.[10] These, however, are only an extra-statutory form of self-regulation and open to criticism because they have no legal backing.[11] Despite that, these bodies have devised strict rules, for example, relating to the disclosure of director's personal interests in shares in relation to certain profitable transactions such as take-over bids; for absolute secrecy before any significant announcement is made, and for regulating dealings by insiders in the shares while negotiations continue.[12] In theory any breach of the rules, at the Panel's direction will be investigated by it or the Financial Services Authority (FSA), and improprieties chastised or corrected by appropriate action.

Civil liability

At common law officers of a company have always been freely permitted to hold and deal in the shares of their company. The only sanction which the common

---

[8] Dir. 89/592/EC [1989] O.J. L334/30.

[9] See Ch.15, above.

[10] See Ch.31, below.

[11] They rely on private reprimand, public censure or the withdrawal of access to the facilities of the securities market.

[12] The City Code on Takeovers and Mergers.

law imposed was to make actionable the use of certain confidential information belonging to the company. Such information included industrial or trade secrets and details concerning customers.[13] The misuse of such information by directors, whether it occurred during the course of, or after the termination of, corporate office, was actionable.

The reason why the common law imposed no clear prohibition on the use of insider information in share dealings stems largely from the decision in *Percival v Wright*.[14] In this case where directors had purchased a member's shares in the knowledge that there was a ready buyer for all the shares of the company at a higher price than they paid him, it was held that the transaction could not be set aside for the director's failure to disclose the negotiations which were already taking place at a higher price. There was said to be no duty to disclosure because there was no fiduciary relationship between the directors and individual share-holders. The directors' duty was owed by the company alone. It followed that the ordinary rules of contract applied. Subsequently in the case of *Allen v Hyatt*[15] the courts did recognise special but very limited circumstances in which a duty might be owed by directors to individual shareholders. In that particular case the directors had profited through share purchases from members and were held accountable to them because they had purported to act as agents for the members by inducing the latter to give them purchase options over each member's shares supposedly to facilitate a proposed amalgamation. Unless some special relationship of this type could be shown so as to establish a legal duty to disclose all relevant information, the officer retained his profit without adverse legal consequences.[16]

PART V OF THE CRIMINAL JUSTICE ACT 1993

The criminal offences concerned with insider dealing are contained in Pt V of the Criminal Justice Act 1993. These replace the former offences contained in the Company Securities (Insider Dealing) Act 1985[17] which was repealed by the 1993 Act. The current provisions incorporate the requirement to implement the EU directive on insider dealing,[18] together with other changes in the light of experience with the former provisions.

The three offences

Section 52 creates three separate offences, each of which may only be committed by an individual and within the United Kingdom.[19]

---

[13] See *British Industrial Plastics v Ferguson* [1938] 4 All E.R. 504; *Cranleigh Precision Engineering Ltd v Bryant* [1965] 1 W.L.R. 1293; *Measure Bros v Measures* [1910] 1 Ch. 336, [1910] 2 Ch. 248; *Printers & Finishers Ltd v Holloway* [1965] 1 W.L.R. 1.

[14] [1902] 2 Ch. 421.

[15] (1914) 30 T.L.R. 444.

[16] See, *e.g. Munro v Bogie* [1994] 1 B.C.L.C. 415.

[17] See the 14th edition of this work.

[18] Dir. 89/592/EC [1989] O.J. L334/30.

[19] S.62 requires either that the person committing the offence be within the UK at the relevant time or that the transaction takes place in the UK Where the offence is communicating information to another it is sufficient that the recipient be within the UK at the relevant time.

The offences, which must be proved by the prosecution beyond all reasonable doubt, are:

(i)   where an insider[20] deals in securities[21] to which the inside information relates (the dealing offence): s.52(1);

(ii) where an insider[22] encourages another person[23-24] to deal in such securities, knowing or having reasonable cause to believe that the other would do so (the encouraging offence): s.52(2)(a);

(iii) where an insider[25] discloses the inside information to another person, otherwise than in the proper performance of the functions of his employment, office or profession (the disclosure offence): s.52(2)(b). There is no definition of what is meant by "proper" in this context and as with many other areas this will have to be settled by a judge and jury at the trial.

The dealing and encouraging offences can only be committed if the dealing actually takes place on a regulated market[26] or the person dealing is either a professional intermediary or relying on such a person. A professional intermediary is defined in s.59(1) to mean a person carrying on a business of dealing in securities and who holds himself out to the public as such. The effect of these restrictions is that private off-market transactions are not covered by the Act.

No offence can be committed by a person who is acting on behalf of a public sector body[27] in pursuit of monetary policies or policies with respect to exchange rates or the management of the public debt: s.63(1).

The penalties and civil consequences

On conviction of any of the three offences an individual can be sentenced to a maximum of seven years' imprisonment on indictment or six months on a summary conviction, together with a fine.[28] No prosecution can be brought without the consent of either the Secretary of State for Trade and Industry or the Director of Public Prosecutions: s.61(2).[29]

Section 63(2) provides, however, that no contract shall be void or unenforceable simply because of the fact that an offence was committed. Thus there are to

---

[20] Defined below.

[21] *ibid.*

[22] *ibid.*

[23-24] Not necessarily an individual.

[25] *ibid.*

[26] These are defined in Art.9 of the Insider Dealing (Securities and Regulated Markets) Order 1994 (SI 1994/187) as amended by The Insider Dealing (Securities and Regulated Markets) (Amendment) Order 2002 (SI 2002/1874) including all the relevant stock exchanges and investment exchanges in the EU and Austria, Finland, Iceland, Norway, Sweden and Liechtenstein. Those regulated by the UK, for jurisdictional purposes are set out in Art. 10 of the Order, principally the London Stock Exchange.

[27] As defined in s.60(3)(b).

[28] s.61(1).

[29] In 2002–2004, there were 27 prosecutions under s.52: see *Companies in 2003–2004* (HMSO, 2004), at p.45.

be no civil consequences of an offence of insider dealing. This is intended to protect market transactions and the option to provide a civil remedy allowed for in the directive has not been adopted. The wording of s.63 is different from its predecessor in the 1985 Act which provided that no contract was to be void or voidable as a consequence of an offence. Thus the courts were able to hold that a contract was nevertheless unenforceable by the insider.[30] That is no longer possible so that in theory at least a criminal will be able to enforce a contract which was the subject of his crime.

The three offences each involve consideration of one or more of four concepts: securities, dealing, insider and inside information. It is necessary, therefore, to examine each of these in turn.

Securities

The dealing or information being communicated must relate to securities which are covered by the Act. These are defined in s.54(1) as those within Sch. 2 to the Act subject to any conditions for specific types of security as the Treasury may prescribe.[31] Schedule 2 includes shares and debentures issued by companies. The condition required for these to be securities to which the Act applies is that they must be officially listed within the European Economic Area[32-33] or to be admitted to, quoted on, or regulated by a regulated market within that area.

Dealing

The dealing and encouraging offences require a definition of what amounts to dealing. Section 55(1) therefore provides that a person deals in securities if he acquires or disposes of them either as principal or agent, or if he procures their acquisition or disposal by another person who may, but does not need to be under his control. Agreements to acquire or dispose of securities, to create securities or ending an agreement which created a security are all caught by the section.

Insiders

All three offences can only be committed by individuals who are insiders. These are called by the Act "persons who have information as insiders". Under s.57(1) an individual can only be in that position if the information he has is inside information and he knows both that it is inside information and that he has it from an inside source. The concept of inside information is discussed below. The information will be deemed to have come from an inside source in relation to corporate securities in any of three situations. In other words those within these situations are potential insiders, who may or may not be actual insiders depending upon their knowledge. No one else can be an insider. The situations are specified in s.57(2):

---

[30] *Chase Manhattan Equities Ltd v Goodman* [1991] B.C.L.C. 897.
[31] See the Insider Dealing (Securities and Regulated Markets) Order 1994 (SI 1994/187, SI 1996/1561, SI 2000/1923 as amended, and SI 2002/1874).
[32-33] The EU and certain other European countries, including Norway.

   (i)   information gained by being a director, employee or shareholder[34] of
        the company (issuer of securities) which has issued the shares or
        debentures in question;

  (ii) information gained by access to it through the individual's employment,
        profession or office. Note that there is no requirement, as previously,
        that the person be connected with the relevant company through his
        employment, *etc.* Thus individuals, such as financial journalists, can now
        be temporary potential insiders;

 (iii) information which an individual has obtained directly or indirectly from
        a person within (i) or (ii) above. These people are known as "tippees"
        from primary insiders. Because of the word "indirectly", this liability
        can extend to sub-tippees, *i.e.* a tippee's tippee, although of course in all
        cases the requisite degree of knowledge must also be proved. Under the
        previous law the House of Lords held that a tippee could be regarded
        as obtaining information even if he did not actively seek the informa-
        tion but was merely a passive recipient of it.[35]

Thus potential insiders are those directly connected with the company in
question, those who come across the information professionally and tippees from
any of those. To make them actual insiders, and so liable for any of the three
offences, it must be shown that the potential insider knows both that it is inside
information and came from an inside source.

Inside information

The concept of inside information is therefore crucial to the definition of an
insider and thus to the offences themselves. The definition, which is largely taken
from the directive, is in s.56. There are four requirements specified in s.56(1):

   (i)   the information must relate to particular securities or to a particular
        company or its business but not to securities generally or companies
        generally;

  (ii) it must be specific or precise;

 (iii) it must not have been made public; and

 (iv) it must be such that if it were made public it would be likely to have a
        significant effect on the price or value of any securities, which are then
        known as price affected securities.

Many of these concepts are undefined and will have to be decided on by a jury
after judicial guidance in each case. When, for example, does a rumour cease to
be rumour and become specific or precise?

The only factor which is defined, non-exhaustively, in the Act is when
information is deemed to have been made public and so is no longer insider

---

[34] Shareholders as such were not potential insiders under the previous Act.
[35] *Attorney-General's Reference (No. 1 of 1988)* [1989] A.C. 971.

information. Section 58(2) states that inclusion of the information on records to which the public have access and publication of it in accordance with the rules of a regulated market,[36] such as the information service of the Stock Exchange, will be sufficient. Since the section also makes it clear that such information is to be treated as being made public even if it is communicated to a section of the public for a fee and can only be accessed by observation, it is thought that this will include computer-linked market information systems. If that is correct, the position is different from the previous law where it was agreed that time had to be allowed for the market to digest the information before it could be regarded as being in the public domain.

The defences

Section 53 provides specific defences to the three offences. With regard to the dealing and encouraging offences there are three defences which must all be proved by the defendant on the balance of probabilities.[37] The specified defences are set out in section 53(1) and (2):

(i)   that the defendant did not at the time expect the dealing, by himself or another, to result in a profit or the avoidance of a loss. It is not for the prosecution therefore to show a profit motive but for the defence to show that there was none;

(ii)   that at the time the defendant reasonably believed that the information was widely enough known (although not made public) so as not to prejudice the other parties to the dealing. This is intended to save certain City transactions such as underwriting, etc.;

(iii)   that the defendant would have dealt (or encouraged another to deal) in the securities even if he had not had the inside information. This may protect, *e.g.* a takeover bidder or possibly a trustee who under his duty as a trustee to do the best he can for the beneficiaries was obliged under trust law to deal. There is no specific defence for such conflict of duty situations,[38] however, as under the previous law.

Section 53(3) provides for two defences, again to be proved on the balance of probabilities by the defendant, for the disclosure offence:

(i)   that the defendant did not expect that any person (the tippee) would deal as a result of such disclosure; and

(ii)   that, even if the defendant did expect another to deal, he did not expect a profit or avoidance of a loss to arise from such a dealing using inside information.

---

[36] See p.406, above.

[37] Thus it is not for the prosecution to prove that the defence is not applicable if the defendant simply raises the matter. This confirms the decision in *R. v Cross* [1991] B.C.L.C. 125 on the previous, different, wording.

[38] These could include liquidators, executors and administrators among others.

Schedule 1 to the Act also contains three general defences, available in respect of all three offences: for market makers; those acting reasonably with market information; and those involved in price-stabilisation transactions under s.144(1) of the Financial Services and Markets 2000.[38a] These defences are outside the scope of company law.

Investigations into insider dealing

When the offence of insider dealing was first made law by the Companies Act 1980 no provision was made or mechanism included whereby alleged or suspected abuse of insider information might be investigated by a regulatory body other than the police. Despite the fact that this was a serious drawback to any effectiveness that the legislation might have had, no amendment was made to rectify that weakness until the Financial Services Act 1986 empowered the Secretary of State to appoint investigators into what appears to him to be a contravention of Part V of the Criminal Justice Act 1993. In investigating alleged insider dealing the investigators were provided with wide powers[39] similar to those vested in an inspector appointed under the Companies Act 1985.[40]

Since the repeal of the 1986 Act,[41] however, these powers have been vested in the Financial Services Authority (FSA) which may appoint one or more competent persons to conduct an investigation on its behalf.[42] If an investigator considers that any person is or may be able to give information which is or may be relevant to the investigation, he can require this person to attend before him at a specified time and place and answer questions or otherwise to provide such information as he may require for the purposes of the investigation.[43]

The investigator can also require the person to produce, at a specified time and place, any specified documents or documents of a specified description which appear to the investigator to relate to any matter relevant to the investigation.[44] Finally, the investigator may also otherwise require the person to give him all assistance in connection with the investigation which the person is reasonably able to give.[45] Failure to comply can lead to the investigator certifying that fact in writing to a court.[46] If the court is satisfied that the person in default failed, without reasonable excuse to comply, it may deal with the defaulter as if he were in contempt.[47]

The Secretary of State may vary the terms of the investigation and direct the inspectors to take no further steps. Any person convicted of an offence as a result of an inquiry may be required to contribute towards the costs of the inquiry.

[38a] As substituted by the Financial Services and Markets Act 2000 (Consequential Amendments and Repeals) Order 2001, SI 2001/3649.

[39] Financial Services Act 1986, s.177.

[40] Companies Act 1985, Part XIV, ss 431–453, above, p.380.

[41] See the Financial Services and Markets Act 2000 (Consequential Amendments and Repeals) Order 2001 SI 2001/3649, Art. 3(1)(c).

[42] s.168(2)(a) and s.168(3) of the Financial Services and Markets Act 2000.

[43] s.173(2).

[44] s.173(3). A journalist would not be exempt from this requirement: see *Re an Inquiry under the Company Securities (Insider Dealing) Act 1985* [1988] A.C. 660.

[45] s.173(4).

[46] s.177(1).

[47] s.177(2).

Chapter 20

ACCOUNTS

INTRODUCTION

For 50 years after legislation was enacted permitting limited liability companies to be set up by registration, there were very few regulations concerning financial disclosures and the preparation of accounts. Such matters were perceived as being domestic matters to be determined by a company's shareholders,[1] the assumption being that they would decide how much information (independently attested or not) the business should publish in order to help lower its financing costs. This non-interventionist philosophy was also reflected in a number of decisions concerning the payment of dividends, the view being that the courts should not in general interfere in the business decision-making process unless there were good grounds for believing that the rights of creditors and share-holders were being prejudiced.[2]

Towards the end of the nineteenth century, attitudes began to change as the effects of inequalities of information between parties and of manipulation of data became apparent. Moreover, with a third of new companies failing shortly after incorporation, there was increasing support for the view that unsecured creditors had insufficient information on which to base their decisions. The result was that the statutory audit was introduced in 1900, and in 1908 the 10,000 businesses in the newly created "public" class of company were required to file their balance sheets. However, the 30,000 or so "private" concerns were still exempt from this provision.

By 1925, the numbers of companies registered had risen to around 95,000 (of which some 85,000 were private), but the 1929 Companies Act nevertheless did not extend the duty to file accounts to private companies, nor did it substantially expand the disclosure requirements for company financial statements. It was only following the report of the Cohen Committee in 1945 that the central role of the modern corporation in the economy and in society was recognised. As a result, the 1948 Companies Act outlawed reserve accounting (which had made it extremely easy to manipulate reported earnings) and required the preparation of group accounts and slightly more elaborate (although still truncated) profit and loss accounts. By that time, there were some 200,000 registered companies, of which over 90 per cent enjoyed private status, and the Act required some of these (a small proportion, described as "non-exempt") to file their annual accounts for the first time.

---

[1] See, for example, *Re Spanish Prospecting Co. Ltd.* [1911] 1 Ch. 92.
[2] See Ch.22.

The Jenkins Committee, reporting in 1962, favoured further compulsory disclosure, and it proposed that exempt private companies (which comprised some 75 per cent of the 400,000 or so companies then registered) should also be made to file their financial statements, the purpose being to benefit unsecured creditors. A requirement to this effect was included in the 1967 Companies Act, and this led to a rapid increase in the annual number of company searches, which rose from 600,000 in 1960 to 3.1 million in 1985 and to over 4 million by the 1990s.[3] The 1967 Companies Act also greatly extended the disclosures which had to be made in the income statement, in notes to the accounts, and in the directors' report (*e.g.* turnover, hire charges, movements in fixed assets and segmental analyses of activities).

Companies and unincorporated businesses had effectively been required to prepare annual accounts for income tax purposes since the latter half of the nineteenth century. But the 1960s and the 1970s witnessed an upsurge in activity aimed at regulating the ways in which companies publicly reported their financial affairs, most of it of a quasi-legal nature (*e.g.* in order to control inflation between 1965 and 1979; for monitoring monopolies; and from 1973 for assessing VAT). But by the 1960s and 1970s the business community was becoming ever more concerned about the "signalling properties" of accounting numbers. On the one hand, this related to the 2,000 or so British listed companies, for which it was important to try to indicate to investment analysts the trend in permanently sustainable earnings; and on the other, for credit suppliers and bank lenders dealing with the much larger number of unlisted public and private companies.[4]

With conflicts of interest becoming more prevalent in relation to financial disclosures, the leading accountancy bodies set up the Accounting Standards Committee (ASC) in 1969, and over the next 20 years it issued a number of mandatory statements concerning the preparation and publication of companies' annual accounts. The ASC's efforts were reinforced by statements of the International Accounting Standards Committee (IASC), set up in 1973, and the London Stock Exchange's *Listing Agreement*, published in 1972.[5] In the meantime, attempts to harmonise accounting regulations within the Common Market countries led to the introduction of new rules in the Companies Acts of 1980, 1981 and 1989,[6] the avowed aim being to encourage the efficient allocation of capital within the European Union.

The opportunity was also taken when framing the 1989 Act to reform the institutional framework for setting accounting standards. The process is now supervised by a broadly based Financial Reporting Council (FRC), which guides the work of three subsidiary bodies: the Accounting Standards Board (ASB), the Urgent Issues Task Force (UITF), and the Financial Reporting Review Panel (FRRP). The ASB is recognised by SI 1990/1667 as the delegated authority

---

[3] Annual searches in the year to March 31, 2004, totalled nearly 40m, of which well over 90 per cent were by computer.

[4] For a discussion of the economic case for mandatory financial disclosures, see M. Bromwich, *Financial Reporting, Information and Capital Markets* (Pitman, London, 1992).

[5] From 1993 these became the *Listing Rules*. Since 2000 these rules have been published by the Financial Services Authority (FSA) rather than by the London Stock Exchange.

[6] The 1980 and 1981 Acts were consolidated in the Companies Act 1985, some of whose sections and Schedules have been substituted by the 1989 Act and various SIs.

empowered to establish accounting standards under s.256 of the 1985 Act. It publishes Financial Reporting Standards (FRSs), which have to be applied by companies when preparing their statutory accounts.[7] For its part, the UITF publishes brief "abstracts" which deal with matters of immediate concern but which are not covered by accounting standards. As for the monitoring role, the FRRP is recognised by SI 1991/13 as the delegated authority empowered to examine *prima facie* defective accounts and require their amendment.

Since the early 1970s, there have been various initiatives to introduce global accounting and auditing standards, but in recent years added impetus has come from the European Commission. This culminated in 2002 with the Commission requiring that from 2005 onwards, listed companies within the EU would have to prepare their consolidated accounts in accordance with International Financial Reporting Standards (IFRSs)[8] and have them audited in accordance with international auditing standards.

IFRSs are published by the International Accounting Standards Board (IASB), which has endorsed many of the International Accounting Standards (IASs) published by its predecessor body, the International Accounting Standards Committee (IASC). IFRSs and endorsed IASs are now collectively referred to as "international accounting standards" (IASs). Individual EU states are permitted to extend the application of these standards to unlisted companies and individual company accounts. This led in November 2004 to the release of SI 2004/2947. "The Companies Act 1985 (International Accounting Standards and Other Accounting Amendments) Regulations 2004", which implements these changes by altering the 1985 Act.[9]

While it is intended that ultimately all British companies will have to comply with a single set of financial reporting rules, the situation at the moment is that there will be different reporting requirements for listed and unlisted companies. The current position is that from 2005 onwards:

● The consolidated accounts of listed companies[10] will have to be prepared in accordance with "international accounting standards" (lASs).

● The individual accounts of companies in a group where the parent is listed will have to be prepared in accordance *either* with IASs *or* with UK accounting standards. However, for administrative convenience, it seems likely that such statements will normally be prepared in accordance with IASs.[11]

---

[7] The ASB has adopted the standards established by its predecessor body, the ASC, until such time as it issues new standards to supersede them.

[8] Regulation 1606/2002 of the European Parliament and of the Council of July 19, 2002 (known as "The International Accounting Standards (IAS) Regulation"). See O.J. L 243, September 11, 2002.

[9] The SI substitutes new ss 226, 226A, 226B, 227, 227A, 227B, 227C and 228A into the 1985 Act, with amendments to various other sections and Schedules. It also inserts new material on accounting for financial instruments and the application of "fair value accounting" into Schs 4, 5, 6 and 8 to the Act.

[10] Companies listed on the Alternative Investment Market (AIM) will not have to apply IASs until 2007.

[11] s.227C in fact requires subsidiary undertakings should normally apply accounting principles consistent with those of their parent company.

- The financial statements of unlisted companies and their subsidiaries will have to be prepared in accordance *either* with IASs *or* with UK accounting standards. However, for administrative convenience, it seems likely that in the immediate future such statements will normally be prepared in accordance with national accounting standards published by the ASB.

In the meantime, the ASB's strategy is to minimize differences between UK FRSs and IASs. Consequently, where appropriate it is reissuing IASs as FRSs with minor amendments to ensure compliance with British company law. Thereafter, the ASB will initiate a series of "step changes", replacing one or more existing UK standards with standards based on IASs as IASB projects are completed.

One result of the changes over the past 25 years is that no less than a third of the texts of the Companies Acts 1985 and 1989 are concerned with accounting and auditing regulations. These in turn are supported by over 4,000 pages of supplementary material dealing with accounting standards and guidance for auditors. It is therefore not possible here to do more than outline the key features of the legislation and rules. However, the decision table on p.415 may help the reader as it indicates the pages where each main issue is dealt with.

ACCOUNTING RECORDS

Section 221 of the Companies Act 1985 requires every company to ensure that adequate accounting records are kept, sufficient to show and explain its transactions. Moreover, they must be such as to disclose with reasonable accuracy at any time the financial position of the company, and also enable a balance sheet and profit and loss account to be prepared so as to give a true and fair view of the company's financial position and profit or loss. Parent companies are equally required in relation to subsidiaries to which the provisions of s.221 do not apply to take reasonable steps to ensure such undertakings keep sufficient accounting records so that the group accounts give a true and fair view.

In particular, the accounting records must contain:

(a) entries from day to day of all monies received and expended, with details of transactions, and

(b) a record of assets and liabilities.

In addition, a company dealing in goods must keep statements of stock held at the end of each financial year and of stocktakings from which the year-end statements are made up, as well as records of all goods sold and purchased (other than in ordinary retail trade transactions), showing goods, buyers and sellers so as to allow identification. However, there is no requirement to keep statements of work in progress.

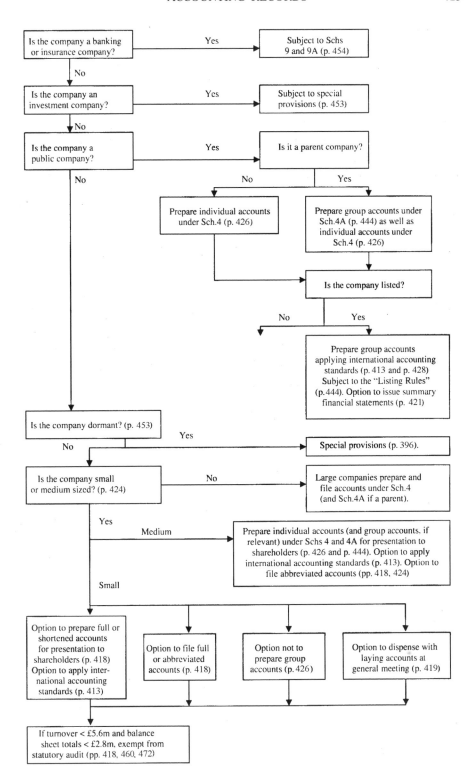

Is the company a banking or insurance company? — **Yes** → Subject to Schs 9 and 9A (p. 454)

No ↓

Is the company an investment company? — **Yes** → Subject to special provisions (p. 453)

No ↓

Is the company a public company? — **Yes** → Is it a parent company?

No ↓

Is it a parent company? — **No** → Prepare individual accounts under Sch.4 (p. 426)

Is it a parent company? — **Yes** → Prepare group accounts under Sch.4A (p. 444) as well as individual accounts under Sch.4 (p. 426)

Is the company listed?

No / **Yes** → Prepare group accounts applying international accounting standards (p. 413 and p. 428) Subject to the "Listing Rules" (p.444). Option to issue summary financial statements (p. 421)

Is the company dormant? (p. 453) — **Yes** → Special provisions (p. 396).

No ↓

Is the company small or medium sized? (p. 424) — **No** → Large companies prepare and file accounts under Sch.4 (and Sch.4A if a parent).

Medium → Prepare individual accounts (and group accounts, if relevant) under Schs 4 and 4A for presentation to shareholders (p. 426 and p. 444). Option to apply international accounting standards (p. 413). Option to file abbreviated accounts (pp. 418, 424)

Small ↓

Option to prepare full or shortened accounts for presentation to shareholders (p. 418) Option to apply international accounting standards (p. 413)

Option to file full or abbreviated accounts (p. 418)

Option not to prepare group accounts (p. 426)

Option to dispense with laying accounts at general meeting (p. 419)

If turnover < £5.6m and balance sheet totals < £2.8m, exempt from statutory audit (pp. 418, 460, 472)

Section 222 requires that the accounting records must be open for inspection by the officers of the company at all times, but there is no express statutory provision authorising the court to compel inspection. However, it was held in *M'Cusker v M'Rae*[12] that the Court of Session may, on the petition of a director, order a company to make the accounting records available for inspection by the director and by a named accountant on his behalf. A shareholder has no right to inspect the books of account of the company unless one is given to him by the articles.

If the accounting records are kept outside Great Britain, such accounts and returns must be kept in Britain as will disclose the position of the business at intervals not exceeding six months and will enable the directors to ensure that any balance sheet or profit and loss account prepared by them gives a true and fair view of the company's financial position and profit or loss.

For the purposes of the Companies Act, accounting records need not be kept in bound books, so long as adequate safeguards are taken to prevent their falsification and the records are capable of being reproduced in a legible form (ss 722–723; SI 1985/724). The records must normally be kept for a minimum period of three years for a private company, or six years for a public company. However, the Taxes Management Act 1970 effectively requires a six-year retention period, and in order to cover against possible actions for negligence under the Limitation Act 1980 (as amended) the retention period would have to be as long as 15 years. Failure to keep accounting records as required is an offence for which officers of the company are liable, the penalty being imprisonment and/or a fine.

ACCOUNTING REFERENCE PERIODS

Sections 223(1)–(2) and (for overseas companies) 700–701 of the Companies Act 1985 provide that the directors of a company must prepare accounts based on an *accounting reference period* for its *financial year*. This commences on the day after the date to which the last accounts were prepared and ends on the last day of the company's normal financial year. However, in order to accommodate natural week ends, the directors may at their discretion move such reference date to up to seven days before or after the last day of the company's normal financial year.

Under s.224(1) the accounting reference period is determined by the *accounting reference date*. For companies incorporated before April 1, 1996, this could either be chosen by the company itself, giving notice to the Registrar of Companies (s.224(2)); or, failing that, it would be March 31 for companies incorporated before April 1, 1990, while for those incorporated thereafter it would be the end of the month in which the anniversary of its incorporation would fall (s.224(3)) Where the company opted to choose the date, notice had to be given within nine months of incorporation (s.224(2)).

The accounting reference date of a company incorporated after April 1, 1996, will be the last day of the month in which the anniversary of its incorporation falls (s.224(3A)). More generally, a reference period must be not less than six nor more than 18 months (s.224(2)(4)), while the period covered by the profit and

---

[12] 1966 S.C. 253. See also *Conway v Petronius Clothing Co. Ltd.* [1978] 1 W.L.R. 72.

loss account must begin with the first day of that accounting reference period and end not more than seven days before or more than seven days after the reference period (s.223(2)).[13] Notice may be given to the Registrar specifying a new accounting reference date, the effect of which will be to alter (a) the current and subsequent or (b) the previous and subsequent accounting reference periods of the company (s.225(1)). However, the change cannot be made in respect of a previous accounting reference period if the permitted interval allowed for laying and delivering accounts for such a period has expired.

Notice under s.225 must state whether the new period is to be shorter or longer than the current reference period, and in any case extension is not possible if a current period plus the extension is more than 18 months in duration, except where an administrative order under Part II of the Insolvency Act 1986 is in force. Moreover, not more than one extension will generally be allowed within a period of five years, except to bring the reference periods of holding and subsidiary companies into line.

LAYING THE ACCOUNTS BEFORE THE COMPANY IN GENERAL MEETING AND FILING THEM WITH THE REGISTRAR

Except where advantage is taken of the provisions in ss 252–253 of the 1985 Act (below, pp.419–420), a company's directors must lay before the company in general meeting in respect of each financial year copies of its accounts and the directors' and auditors' reports (s.241).[14] They are also required to deliver copies of the accounts and directors' and auditors' reports to the Registrar of Companies within the time intervals specified in s.244. Failure to comply with these provisions renders the directors liable to a fine. Moreover, if the accounts and reports are still not filed within 14 days of receipt of a notice requiring them to do so, the court may make a direction ordering them to make good the default within a specified time (s.242).[15] A civil penalty can also be imposed on the company for not filing accounts, the size depending on whether the company is public or private and the length of the delay (s.242A).

Where a parent company has an unconsolidated subsidiary which is registered and operates outside Great Britain, or is an unincorporated business, copies of its latest individual and/or group accounts have to be filed, together with the auditors' report (s.243).

The periods allowed for laying and delivering a company's accounts and the directors' and auditors' reports are normally 10 months after the reference period

---

[13] Companies House returns for the year ended March 31, 2004, show some 22 per cent of companies have March 31 year ends and another 17.5 per cent December 31 year ends. However, for listed companies about 40 per cent have December 31 year ends and 20 per cent March 31 year ends; and some 15 per cent avail themselves of the concession to vary the year end date by up to 7 days.

[14] If a company is exempt from having to have a statutory audit under s.249A (below, pp.418–419, 460, 472), it need not present or file an auditor's report: s.249E(1)(b). The government's White Paper on "Modernising Company Law", published in July 2002, proposes that listed companies should be required to publish their accounts on their websites within four months of their year ends.

[15] In May 1984, no fewer than 58 per cent of active companies were failing to file their accounts on time. Following an advertising campaign and the introduction of a tougher enforcement policy, whereby over 85,000 defaulting companies were fined in the year to March 31, 1997, the compliance rate has subsequently risen to over 95 per cent.

for a private company and seven months for a public company.[16] Certain modifications are allowed where companies are in their first accounting reference period or where they shorten their accounting reference periods. Thus for a company in its first reference period, where such a period is greater than 12 months, the accounts must be laid and delivered within 22 months of its date of incorporation if it is a private company, or 19 months if it is a public company. However, this is subject to the proviso that there should always be a minimum allowed period of three months between the end of the reference period and the last date for laying and delivering accounts. Where a company's reference period is shortened under s.225,[17] the period allowed for laying and delivering the accounts is that which expires later of:

(a) the period normally allowed, and

(b) three months from the date of the notice of the change in the accounting reference period given under s.225 (s.244).

Quoted companies are required by the *Listing Rules* to issue their annual reports and accounts within six months of the end of the financial period to which they relate.

Abbreviated and shortened accounts

Sections 246 and 246A of the Companies Act 1985 offer concessions to medium and small-sized private companies or groups, as defined in ss 247, 247A, 248 and 249 of the Act, permitting them to file *abbreviated* financial statements with the Registrar of Companies in compliance with the provisions of s.246A or Sch. 8A to the Act.[18] In addition, under ss 249A and 249B, any company (other than a charitable company) which qualifies as small under ss 247 and 249, and whose annual turnover and balance sheet totals respectively do not exceed £5.6m and £2.8m, is exempt from the *statutory audit requirement* (below, pp.460, 472).

It is estimated that some 90 per cent of all registered companies qualify as small companies, but around 174,000 of the 2,016,700 companies registered at March 31, 2004 can be regarded as "inactive". Nevertheless, in the year ending on that date, 1,271,300 had filed financial statements, of which 12.9 per cent submitted full accounts, 7.8 per cent abbreviated small sized company accounts, 0.9 per cent abbreviated medium sized company accounts, and 1.3 per cent group accounts. A further 56.9 per cent were exempt from the statutory audit, and 16.0 per cent were classified as dormant.

These statistics show the impact of extending the audit exemption provisions (see below, pp.460, 472) under SI 2000/1430, raising the annual turnover threshold from £350,000 to £1m, as the annual percentages of companies filing full accounts for years prior to 2001–2002 was around 40 per cent, with a similar

---

[16] The July 2002 white paper on "Modernising Company Law" proposes reducing the intervals to seven months for private companies and six months for public companies.

[17] Above, pp.416–417.

[18] Below, pp.421, 424–426, 437, 450, 453.

proportion filing abbreviated financial statements. The DTI estimates that a further 31,000 small companies will be eligible to file small company accounts with the increase in the turnover and doubling of the balance sheet total criteria in SI 2004/16. This is significant, given that only 99,700 companies filed "small" abbreviated accounts in the year to March 31, 2004, although the number of companies filing such accounts was 444,800 as recently as 2000–2001. The number of medium-sized companies filing abbreviated accounts in the year to March 31, 2004, was 11,000, and the DTI estimates that a further 16,000 will be eligible to do so with the increase in the qualifying size criteria. Another 69,000 companies should quality for the "audit exemption", in addition to the 723,700 that benefited in 2003–2004, saving them around £94 million annually.

The concessions relating to the *filing* of abbreviated accounts do not directly affect the information to be provided to members of a company, except with respect to the provision of group accounts (below, p.426). However, s.246 of the 1985 Act permits companies qualifying as small to lay a slightly simplified set of "shortened" financial statements before members in general meeting, amalgamating some of the more detailed balance sheet headings and removing various requirements that small companies should disclose certain information in notes to their accounts and in their directors' reports (Sch. 8 to the 1985 Act).

Approval by directors

A company's annual accounts have to be approved by its board of directors, and the balance sheet and the copy delivered to the Registrar must be signed on their behalf by one of their number. Moreover, every copy of the balance sheet that is laid before the company in general meeting or which is otherwise circulated and published must state the name of the signatory. Failure to observe these requirements renders the company and its defaulting officers liable to a fine. Equally, directors who approve the accounts without taking reasonable steps to ensure they comply with the requirements of the Companies Acts or to prevent their being approved are liable to a fine (s.233). Special provisions apply where "shortened" accounts are presented to shareholders and where "abbreviated" accounts are delivered to the Registrar (above, p.418 and below, pp.424–425).

The Registrar must publish in the Gazette notice of the receipt by him of any document delivered by a company in pursuance of s.242, *i.e.* its annual accounts, including the directors' report and (where relevant) the group accounts and/or the auditors' report (s.711).

Directors of an unlimited company are not required to deliver accounts and annexed reports to the Registrar unless a connected company has limited liability (s.254).

Dispensing with the obligation to lay accounts

A private company may, by elective resolution in accordance with s.379A, dispense with presenting before the company in general meeting its annual accounts and the directors' report, together with (where relevant) the auditors' report. Such a resolution relates to the financial statements for the year in which it is made, and the election carries over to subsequent financial years. However, the financial statements still have to be circulated to members, and references in the Act to the laying of accounts are therefore to be interpreted as referring to the documents so circulated (s.252).

Where an election is in force dispensing with the requirement to lay before a company in general meeting its annual accounts and the directors' report, together with (where relevant) the auditors' report, copies of these statements must be sent to members at least 28 days before the period allowed for laying and delivering accounts, together with a notice of their rights to require the laying of accounts and annexed reports before a general meeting. Failure to do so renders the company and its officers liable to fines. An objecting member or auditor must then inform the company within 28 days of the accounts being circulated, and the directors must then convene a general meeting within 21 days, failing which the objecting party may do so himself. Such a meeting must be held within three months. Where an objecting party has to convene a meeting, he may recover reasonable expenses from the company (s.253).

Revision of defective accounts and reports

Where a company's annual accounts, summary financial statement, directors' report and/or directors' remuneration report do not comply with the provisions of the Companies Acts, the directors may voluntarily revise them (s.245). The Secretary of State may also give notice to a company's directors indicating how he believes the financial statements and/or reports laid before the company or delivered to the Registrar may not comply with the Act's requirements. The directors must within a specified period of up to a month give satisfactory explanations or prepare revised financial statements and/or reports, failing which the Secretary of State may apply to the court (s.245A).

Procedures to be followed are given in SI 1990/2570 concerning the revision of defective accounts under s.245. Sections 245B and 245C and SI 1991/13 empower the Financial Reporting Review Panel (FRRP) to apply to the court for a declaration that the accounts are in breach of the Acts and for an order requiring directors to prepare revised financial statements. In undertaking its enquiries, information held by the Inland Revenue may be disclosed under restricted circumstances to the FRRP (ss 245D and 245E).[19] The investigating party may also require the company or its officers, employees or auditor to provide information and explanations under restricted circumstances to facilitate its enquiries (ss 245F and 245G and Sch.7B).[20]

The right to receive accounts

Under s.238, a copy of a company's annual accounts and directors' report, together with (where relevant) a copy of the auditors' report, must be sent to every member, debenture holder, and other person entitled to receive notice of

[19] Inserted by the Companies (Audit, Investigations and Community Enterprise) Act 2004, which also amended s.245C.
[20] Inserted by the Companies (Audit, Investigations and Community Enterprise) Act 2004.

general meetings at least 21 days before the date of the meeting at which they will be laid. If all the members entitled to attend and vote so agree, a shorter time will suffice. Failure to comply renders the company and every officer in default liable to a fine. Under s.239, any member or debenture holder is entitled to a copy on demand without charge. Failure to comply within seven days with such a demand renders the company and every officer in default liable to a fine.

Publication of financial statements

Section 240 distinguishes between a company's "statutory" and "non-statutory" accounts, the former being defined as the full individual or group accounts (including "abbreviated" accounts[21]) properly delivered to the Registrar. Such statutory accounts must, where appropriate, be accompanied by the relevant auditors' report.

Where non-statutory accounts[22] are published, they must not be accompanied by the auditors' report relating to the statutory accounts, but rather with a statement indicating:

(a) that they are not the statutory accounts;

(b) whether statutory accounts for the year in question have been delivered to the Registrar; and

(c) whether the auditors have made a report on the statutory accounts, and if so whether or not it was qualified (s.240(3)).

A company which is obliged to prepare group accounts must not publish its individual accounts without also publishing its group accounts (s.240(2)).

A company which contravenes these requirements and any defaulting officers are liable to be fined.

Summary financial statements

Under s.251 and SI 1995/2092, a listed company can send its members a summary financial statement instead of the full accounts, although those wishing to receive the latter must be sent them. The summary financial statement must be derived from the company's annual accounts and the directors' report, and it must include statements:

(a) indicating that it only contains summarised financial information;

(b) by the auditors as to whether the information given is consistent with the full accounts and the directors' report;

(c) whether the full auditors' report is qualified, and if so include that full report; and

---

[21] Above, pp.418–419.

[22] Non-statutory accounts include preliminary announcements made by listed companies and simplified statements circulated to employees, but not summary financial statements (see below).

(d) whether the full auditors' report contains a statement concerning the accounting records and/or the adequacy of the information and explanations received, and if so include such statements in full.

Failure to observe these conditions renders the company and every defaulting officer liable to a fine.

Under SI 2004/2947, the Secretary of State has power to extend the summary financial statement provisions to all companies.

THE ANNUAL ACCOUNTS

The traditional view is that annual accounts represent an historical stewardship record of a company's financial affairs. Unfortunately, however, the only objective historical record of this type is afforded by a company's cash account. Any attempt to measure profit inevitably involves valuation, either of the business itself as a going concern, or (more usually) of the individual net assets it owns. Yet what potential users want above all seems to be a measure of profit, even though this must inevitably involve an element of subjectivity in its calculation. The traditional accounting approach has been to value the net assets according to a reasonably flexible set of conservatively biased rules, the overall effect of which is to delay the recognition of profit through time. However, inflation can defeat the accountants' aim to exercise prudence in determining income.

In practice, most users of financial statements are well aware of the shortcomings of conventional accounts and refer to other information to help them assess a business's current position and likely future prospects. Where accounting figures are used not as one of a number of signals of likely future performance, but rather as the basis of a particular calculation (such as a share of profits, the liability to corporation tax, or a restriction under a debt covenant), the interested parties must specify more carefully the exact accounting conventions that are to be adopted in preparing the company's relevant annual financial statements. A framework justifying the use of particular accounting conventions is provided by the Statement of Principles published by the Accounting Standards Board.

It is against this background that the statutory disclosure requirements contained in the Companies Acts should be seen. They establish a basic minimum of information which must be disclosed and be subjected to audit, thus increasing its credibility in the eyes of the reader and so hopefully reducing his uncertainty about future likely outcomes. Many companies will disclose more, either in the statutory accounts themselves and in supplementary statements demanded by the ASB and by other regulatory authorities; or by other means (*e.g.* for quoted companies through the chairman's report, press releases, or news leaked onto the market via stockbrokers' reports; and for unquoted companies by disclosing relevant information directly to bank managers, other major creditors and employee representatives).

Basic principles

Sections 226, 226A and 226B require the directors of a company to prepare for each financial year its "individual accounts" (*i.e.* its end-year balance sheet and a profit and loss account) applying national or international accounting standards, as appropriate. Likewise, ss 227, 227A, 227B and 227C require the directors of a company which is a parent company to prepare "group accounts" (below, p.444 *et seq.*) applying international or national accounting standards, as appropriate.[23] These sections establish two basic principles with regard to a company's or group's financial statements: first, that insofar as they are prepared under these sections of the Act they must comply as to their form and content with the provisions of Schs 4 and 4A to the Act; and, secondly, that the balance sheets and profit and loss account and notes thereto must give a true and fair view of the company's or group's financial position and its profit or loss for a given period.

Since the responsibility for preparing the accounts falls on the directors, a shareholder is not entitled to bring proceedings to require certain information to be included in the accounts.[24]

For the purpose of determining whether group accounts should be prepared, a parent undertaking is essentially defined in relation to a subsidiary if:

(a) it holds a majority of the voting rights;

(b) it is a member of the subsidiary and has power to appoint or remove a majority of its directors; or

(c) it can exert a dominant influence over the subsidiary (*e.g.* by virtue of a contract) or the companies are managed on a unified basis (s.258 and Sch. 10A).

Where a group relationship exists, the parent company must prepare group as well as individual company accounts, and they will generally be in the form of consolidated accounts comprising:

(a) a consolidated balance sheet dealing with the state of affairs of the parent company and its subsidiary undertakings, and

(b) a consolidated profit and loss account dealing with the profit or loss of the parent company and its subsidiary undertakings (s.227A(1)).

However, where a parent undertaking prepares a consolidated profit and loss account, it need not publish a separate individual profit and loss account as long as it discloses how much of the consolidated profit or loss has been dealt with in the company's individual accounts and that it is taking advantage of this exemption (s.230).

The requirement for the individual and group financial statements to give a true and fair view is an overriding one, so where information additional to the minimum specified in the Acts is necessary for the financial statements to give a true and fair view, such extra information must be included in those statements. Likewise, where the circumstances are such that strict compliance with a

---

[23] s.226B requires that where the financial statements have been prepared applying international accounting standards (IASs), this should stated in a note to the accounts.
[24] *Devlin v Slough Estates Ltd.*, (1982) 126 S.J. 623.

requirement of the Act would not result in a true and fair view, the company must depart from that requirement, full particulars of the reasons for the departure and its effect being disclosed in the notes to the accounts (ss 226A(4)–(6) and 227A(4)–(6); Sch. 4, para.15).

The exact meaning of the phrase "a true and fair view" is unfortunately far from clear, but it seems that adherence to normal accounting practice would be *prima facie* evidence of giving such a view. Thus the claim that accounts were misleading because they included property at original cost rather than at current market value was rejected by the courts because normal practice had been followed.[25] More recently, the status of accounting standards in helping to clarify the meaning of the phrase has been examined in the case of *Lloyd Cheyham and Co. Ltd v Littlejohn and Co.*[26] There Woolf J. held that "while they are not conclusive . . . and they are not . . . rigid rules, they are very strong evidence as to what is the proper standard which should be adopted . . ." Nevertheless, it is clear that the "true and fair view override" cannot be used without proper justification, as was demonstrated in the *Argyll Foods* case.[27] There the company wished, with the agreement of its auditor, to record "economic substance" at the expense of "legal form". The magistrates who heard the case decided that the accounts did not show a true and fair view, and subsequently the DTI (which had brought the prosecution) issued a statement interpreting the decision as confirming its view that the "true and fair view override" is confined to the disclosure requirements of the Companies Acts and that it does not enable companies to depart from the other provisions (*e.g.* definitions) in the Acts. In such circumstances it would seem appropriate where necessary to indicate the underlying economic substance in notes to the accounts or in supplementary *pro forma* statements.

The figures included in the annual accounts have been given added significance since 1980 as the Companies Acts now prescribe that distributable profit is generally the aggregate of accumulated realised net profits as reported in the latest audited (or, if relevant, interim) accounts (ss 263–281). Moreover, a public company can only pay a dividend if the net assets (after payment of the dividend) at least equal its capital plus any reserves not available for distribution (below, Ch.22).

Large, medium, and small-sized companies

Although the directors of private companies have always had to prepare statutory accounts to lay before their shareholders in general meeting, prior to 1967 most were exempted from the need to file these financial statements with the Registrar of Companies. From then until 1981, however, the only concessions were that companies below a certain size did not have to disclose details of turnover and directors' remuneration, nor in their directors' reports the value of exports, the average number of employees and their aggregate remuneration, and turnover

---

[25] *Re Press Caps Ltd.* [1949] Ch. 434.
[26] [1986] P.C.C. 389.
[27] Unreported, but see Ashton, R.K., "The Argyll Foods Case: A Legal Analysis" (1986), *Accounting and Business Research*, Vol. 17, no. 65, pp. 3–12.

and pretax profit or loss by each class of business. It was the view of the Bolton committee of enquiry on small firms that these concessions did not seriously prejudice the work of credit assessment agencies and the interests of unsecured creditors.[28]

Since 1981, while all limited companies have had to prepare and lay detailed accounts before their members in general meeting in accordance with one or other of a set of prescribed forms of financial statement now given in Sch. 4 to the 1985 Act (s.241),[29] medium and small-sized companies can avail themselves of concessions whereby they need only *file* "abbreviated" accounts (above, p.418–419). In order to qualify for this exemption, small or medium-sized companies or groups must neither be nor include public companies, banks, insurance companies or authorised persons under the Financial Services Act 1986 (s.247A).

A company qualifies as medium or small sized where it meets specified criteria: (1) in its first financial year; or (2) subsequently in the current and previous years; or (3) it was so qualified in the previous financial year (s.247). The criteria are that it should meet at least two of three conditions concerning annualised turnover, balance sheet totals and the average weekly number of employees as follows:

		Small-sized	*Medium-sized*
(1)	annualised turnover	≤£5.6m	≤£22.8m
(2)	balance sheet total	≤£2.8m	≤£ 11.4m
(3)	average weekly number of employees	≤50	≤250

The concessions available to qualifying medium and small-sized private companies are summarised below on pp.427–428, 437, 450. However, a parent company will not qualify unless it meets the conditions necessary to exempt it from the need to prepare group accounts under s.248, described below.

In order to *file abbreviated accounts*, a qualifying medium or small sized company must:

(a) append to the filed accounts a statement indicating that advantage is being taken of the exemptions and the grounds for doing so (s.246(8)); and

(b) if the directors have not taken advantage of the provisions of s.249A(1)–(2) exempting the company from the requirement to have an audit,[30] attach a signed special auditors' report stating that in their opinion the company is entitled to the exemptions and that the accounts have been properly prepared in accordance with the provisions of Sch.8A. Included in this report will be the audit report required under s.235, which refers to the full accounts, if such a report is qualified (s.247B).

[28] (1972) Cmnd. 4811, Ch.17.
[29] Small companies may however present "shortened" accounts to shareholders (above, pp.418–419), in which case they must be accompanied by a statement indicating that they are prepared according to the provisions of Sch.8: ss 246 and 248A.
[30] See pp.418–419, 460, 472.

A parent company of a group which qualifies as a medium or small-sized group need not *present* or *file group accounts*. However, a group is not eligible if any of its members are public companies, banks, insurance companies or authorised persons under the Financial Services Act 1986 (s.248).

To qualify as a medium or small-sized group, and thus be eligible not to prepare group accounts under the provisions of s.249, the parent company must meet specified criteria: (1) in its first financial year; or (2) subsequently in the current and previous years; or (3) it was so qualified in the previous financial year.

The qualifying criteria under s.249 of the 1985 Act are that it should meet at least two of the conditions concerning annualised turnover, balance sheet totals and the average weekly number of employees as follows[31]:

		Small-sized		Medium-sized	
		Net	Gross	Net	Gross
(1)	annualised turnover	≤£2.8m	≤£3.36m	≤£11.2m	≤£13.44m
(2)	balance sheet total	≤£1.4m	≤£1.68m	≤£ 5.6m	≤ £6.72m
(3)	average weekly number of employees	≤50		≤250	

Form and content of accounts[32]

Schedule 4 to the 1985 Act[33] implements the EU's prescriptive Fourth Council Directive on company law harmonisation. Section A of Pt I of the Schedule establishes the *general rules* in relation to the form and content of full individual company accounts. It requires that one of the prescribed formats (four for the profit and loss account and two for the balance sheet) should be used (para.1) and be adhered to year by year unless there are special reasons justifying a change (para.2). However, some flexibility is allowed (para.3). Comparative figures for the previous accounting period are to be shown (para.4), and individual items may not be set off against each other (para.5). In determining how amounts are presented in the profit and loss account and balance sheet, the directors must also have regard to the substance of the reported transaction or arrangement in accordance with generally accepted accounting principles (GAAP) (para.5A, as inserted by SI 2004/2947).

Section B of Pt I of Sch.4 to the 1985 Act sets out two alternative formats of *balance sheet*, the contents of which are in fact identical. The first (see Appendix, pp.465–468) equates net assets to the aggregate of the share capital and reserves, and is the most widely used layout in the UK. The second format equates assets against claims, a method of presentation more commonly used in continental European countries.

---

[31] Net means after set-offs required by Sch. 4A when consolidated accounts are being prepared, and gross means before those set-offs.

[32] In the remainder of this chapter, paragraph references are to Sch.4 to the 1985 Act, unless otherwise indicated.

[33] Schs 4A, 8, 8A, 9 and 9A contain the corresponding requirements respectively for group accounts, "shortened" accounts, small companies' abbreviated accounts, banks' accounts, and insurance companies' accounts.

In the balance sheets there are three tiers of headings, identified by capital letters, Roman numerals and Arabic numbers. The latter may be combined if it facilitates assessment of a company's performance or position (para.3). With regard to specific headings, various requirements are specified. Thus preliminary expenses, issuing expenses and commissions, and research expenditure are not permitted to be treated as assets in a company's balance sheet (para.3(2)). Intangible assets, such as patents and trademarks, can however be included if they were either acquired for valuable consideration or were created by the company itself. Similarly, only goodwill acquired for valuable consideration can be shown as an asset in a balance sheet, but its cost must be written off systematically over a period which must not exceed its estimated useful economic life (para.21). The amount of each item to be shown under the head "debtors" must be split between those amounts receivable within one year of the balance sheet date and those receivable later than that; and in determining the amount to be shown under "net current assets", amounts shown as "prepayments and accrued income" have to be taken into account.

As regards claims, where there are debenture loans these have to be split between convertible and non-convertible loans; and the amounts of allotted and paid-up share capital have also to be shown separately. Payments received on account for orders must be shown under creditors unless disclosed as a deduction from stocks of finished goods. The amount of each item to be shown under the head "creditors" and in aggregate must be split between those amounts payable within one year of the balance sheet date and those receivable later than that.

A "participating interest" is an interest held by an undertaking in the shares of another undertaking which it holds on a long-term basis. Normally a holding of 20 per cent of a company's shares, including convertibles and options, will give rise to the presumption of there being a "participating interest" unless the contrary is shown (s.260).

A provision is "any amount retained as reasonably necessary for the purpose of providing for any liability or loss which is either likely to be incurred, or certain to be incurred but uncertain as to amount or as to the date on which it will arise" (para.89).

A company will normally only hold its own shares where it has acquired them by forfeiture or surrender. Where it purchases or redeems its own shares they must be cancelled (ss 146 and 160(4)).[34]

Under the provisions of s.246, small companies need only file an *abbreviated balance sheet* which complies with the provisions of Sch.8A to the Act. Effectively this means that items can be aggregated under each of the main balance sheet headings (see Appendix, pp.455–458), although the aggregate amounts of debtors and creditors have to be divided between amounts receivable or payable within one year and those receivable or payable beyond that period. Small companies may also present to shareholders "shortened" financial statements under Sch.8, comprising a full profit and loss account and a balance sheet in which certain items are combined together (see Appendix, pp.455–458).

---

[34] The rules relating to share premium and capital redemption reserve accounts are dealt with in Chs 9 and 10, above.

Of the four *profit and loss account* formats given in Sch.4, the first two are presented in a vertical form (and are therefore probably the most likely to be used in the UK), while the third and fourth show expenses on the left and income on the right. Formats 1 and 3 classify some 20 expense categories by function, whereas formats 2 and 4 classify them by type. Format 1 is the layout most commonly used by large UK companies.

Where the format classifies expenses by function, the amounts to be shown under cost of sales, distribution costs and administrative expenses are to include depreciation charges and provisions for diminution in the value of assets. However, the amounts of any such charges or provisions for both tangible and intangible fixed assets must be disclosed separately in the notes to the financial statements. In addition, any interest or similar charges payable to group companies must be shown separately.

Apart from the above, whichever format is adopted the profit or loss on ordinary activities before taxation must be disclosed separately in the profit and loss account(para. 3(6)). In addition, the notes to the accounts must disclose:

(a) movements to or from reserves;

(b) dividends paid in the year (other than those for which a liability existed at the immediately preceding balance sheet date):

(c) the dividends that the company is liable to pay at the balance sheet date: and

(d) the aggregate amount of dividends that are proposed before the date of approval of the accounts and are not otherwise disclosed (para.35A, as inserted by SI 2004/2947).

Large-sized companies have to file a full profit and loss account, but medium-sized companies are permitted to file an abbreviated statement which combines a number of items (s.246A(3)(a)) (see Appendix, pp.455–458). A small-sized company is exempted from having to file a profit and loss account (s.246(5)(a)). However, there are no concessions in the regulations relating to "shortened" accounts with respect to profit and loss account disclosures.

Various accounting standards affect the calculation and presentation of items in the profit and loss account, and they can be accommodated either in the notes or in the body of the statement as supplementary disclosures. These standards are either those published by the Accounting Standards Board (ASB), referred to as Financial Reporting Standards (FRSs); or those which it inherited from its predecessor body, the Accounting Standards Committee (ASC) and which it has yet to replace, referred to as Statements of Standard Accounting Practice (SSAPs).[35]

---

[35] Until the ASB issues equivalent standards, listed companies will have to apply IASs in 2005 when preparing their consolidated group accounts (see above, p.413). In order to facilitate this, the IASB established what it terms "a stable platform" of standards in April 2004. This comprises five of its own IFRSs and 32 IASs that it inherited from the IASC (although many of the latter have now been amended by the IASB). The main differences will affect the way listed companies account for business combinations, amortise goodwill and report financial instruments in their balance sheets, applying "fair-value principles" (see p.443–444, 448, below).

With respect to the profit and loss account, the most important innovation is probably that a further "primary" statement has to be presented of equal prominence to the usual financial statements, showing the total of recognised gains and losses and their components. Moreover, where there is a material difference between the result as disclosed in the profit and loss account and the result on an unmodified historical cost basis, a note of the historical cost profit or loss for the period is to be presented.[36] Further, a note should be given reconciling the opening and closing totals of the shareholders' funds over the period under review.

Accounting standards have also been published on: earnings per share, which requires listed companies to show such a figure on the face of the profit and loss account; associated companies, which requires partial consolidation of associated companies' profits; accounting for subsidiary undertakings, which deals with the methods of consolidation; reporting financial performance, which *inter alia* indicates the restricted circumstances when extraordinary items arise and how and where they should be disclosed; taxation, which indicates how current and deferred tax charges should be disclosed; foreign currency translation; accounting for leases and hire purchase contracts (including the use of "fair-value" accounting); segmental reporting; related party disclosures; accounting for acquisitions and mergers; accounting for goodwill; the impairment of fixed assets and goodwill; disclosures relating to derivatives and other financial instruments; and provisions and contingencies. In addition, all except the smallest companies are required to publish a supplementary cash flow statement (below, p.444). Other standards deal with accounting policies; accounting for capital instruments (such as deep discount bonds, convertible debt, participating preference shares, stepped interest bonds and minority interests); reporting the substance of transactions (*e.g.* how "off balance sheet financing" should be reflected in financial statements, and how revenue should be recognised); financial reporting in hyperinflationary economies; the measurement, disclosure and presentation of financial instruments; and accounting for government grants, VAT, depreciation, research and development, stocks and work in progress, retirement benefits, investment properties, events after the balance sheet date, and share based payments.[37] There is also a standard which indicates the extent to which the various requirements should be applied when preparing the accounts of smaller entities.

Notes to the financial statements

Information which cannot be accommodated in Sch.4's model formats has to be given in notes to the financial statements. These notes may be contained in the accounts themselves or in a separate document annexed to the accounts (s.261).

---

[36] The application of historical cost and "alternative" accounting valuation rules are discussed below, pp.439–443.

[37] International accounting standards that will soon be adopted by the ASB and for which there is currently no British equivalent cover the following topics: insurance contracts; non-current assets held for resale and discontinued operations; presentation in financial statements; construction contracts; property, plant and equipment; borrowing costs; interim financial reporting; and agriculture.

Most of the details of items which are to be disclosed in note form are given in Sch.4, paras 35–58, and in Schs 5 and 6. However, items in the model statements required by Sch.4 which are preceded by Arabic numerals can also be relegated to a note (para.3(4)). Conversely, items required to be shown in notes may, where feasible, be shown on the face of the accounts (paras 3(1) and 35).

By way of *general notes*, the accounting policies used by a company must be disclosed, in particular indicating the depreciation and foreign currency translation methods employed (paras 36 and 58(1)). There must also be a statement indicating whether the accounts have been prepared in accordance with applicable accounting standards[38] and giving particulars of any material departure from such standards and the reasons for it (para.36A).

Corresponding amounts for the previous financial year (adjusted if necessary to make them comparable) have to be given for all items disclosed in the notes, except for movements on reserves, provisions, fixed asset and depreciation accounts; loans and other transactions with directors and officers of the company; details of the accounting treatment of acquisitions; and information on subsidiaries and significant shareholdings (para.58(2),(3)).

The following details must be disclosed by way of *notes to the balance sheet*:

(A) *Share capital and loan stock*

  (a) Authorised share capital and the number and nominal value of each class of shares allotted (para.38).

  (b) Where redeemable shares (either preference or equity) have been allotted, the notes must disclose the earliest and latest dates of redemption, whether the company is obliged to redeem them or merely has the option to do so, and whether any premium is payable on redemption, and if so the amount (para.38).

  (c) Where shares or debentures have been allotted during the year, the classes of securities involved and the amount/number issued or allotted, and the aggregate nominal value and the consideration received for each class. Moreover, in respect of debentures particulars must be disclosed of the nominal amount and book value of any debentures held by a nominee or trustee of the company (paras 39, 41).

  (d) Where an option or similar right exists in relation to shares, the number, description and amount of the shares involved, the period during which the right is exercisable, and the price payable have to be disclosed (para.40).

(B) *Reserves, provisions and deferred tax*[39]

The aggregate amounts of each reserve and provision at the beginning and end of the financial year must be disclosed, together with details of movements to and

---

[38] Above, pp.428–429; and below, pp.437–438.
[39] "Provisions" are defined in Sch.4, paras 88–89, above, p.427.

from such reserves and provisions during the year (para.46). In addition, the amount of any provision for deferred taxation other than the amount of any provision for other taxation must be disclosed separately (para.47).

(C) *Fixed assets*[40]

For each item under this heading, both tangible and intangible assets, and also for long-term investments, the notes must disclose in respect of cost or valuation the aggregate amounts at the beginning and end of the year, the amounts of any acquisitions, disposals and transfers, and the effect of applying the "alternative accounting valuation rules"[41] (paras 17–21 and 27). In addition, details must be given of the cumulative amounts of provisions for depreciation or for the diminution in the value of assets at both the beginning and end of the financial year, and the amounts of any additions, reductions through asset disposals, and any other adjustments to such provisions made during the year (para.42).

Where a fixed asset (other than listed investments) has been revalued, the notes must disclose the years in which the assets were severally valued and the several values; and in the years of each valuation the names or qualifications of the valuers and the bases of valuation (para.43). Land and buildings must be divided among freeholds, long leaseholds (*i.e.* those with more than 50 years of lease unexpired at the year end) and short leaseholds (paras 44, 83).

(D) *Investments*

Certain details of investments must be disclosed, regardless of whether they are shown as fixed or current assets.

The following information must be shown with respect to *listed investments*: their amount, together with their quoted value (and estimated market value where this is higher) if it (or they) differ from the value(s) shown in the balance sheet; and unlisted investments (paras 45 and 84).

For companies required to prepare group accounts, the following information must be disclosed in respect of all *subsidiary undertakings* of the parent company at its year end: their names; the countries in which they are incorporated or, if they are unincorporated, their principal places of business; whether they are included in consolidated group accounts and, if not, the reasons why not; how they qualify as subsidiaries under s.258 of the Act, except where this is a result of majority holdings of voting shares; and the proportions of each class of a subsidiary's shares held by the parent company and by the group as a whole (Sch.5, para.15).

With respect to each subsidiary not included in consolidated accounts, the aggregate of its year end capital and reserves and the profit or loss as shown in its last accounts must be disclosed, except where: the investment is dealt with by the equity consolidation method (below, p.449); the investee company is not required by the Act to deliver a copy of its accounts and does not publish them elsewhere;

[40] "Fixed assets" are defined in s.262(1).
[41] Below, pp.442–443.

the holding is less than half the nominal value of the subsidiary's shares; or it is immaterial (Sch.5, para.17). Details must also be disclosed of shares and debentures in the parent company held by subsidiary undertakings (Sch.5, para.20).

Similar disclosures must be made by a company which has subsidiary undertakings but is not required to prepare group accounts (Sch.5, paras 1–6). However, in such circumstances the company has to disclose the reason why it is not preparing group accounts and, if the reason is that all the subsidiaries fall within the exemptions specified in s.229, a statement for each subsidiary indicating which exclusion applies; and, if a subsidiary's reporting period does not coincide with that of the parent, its last year-end date (Sch.5, paras 1(4)–(5) and 4).

A company which is required to prepare group accounts, and which accounts for an undertaking as a *joint venture* using the method of *pro rata* proportional consolidation (below, p.449), must disclose: the undertaking's name; its principal place of business; the basis of its joint management; the proportion of its capital held by undertakings included in the consolidation; and, where its financial year does not coincide with that of the company, its most recent year end (Sch.5, para.21).

A company which is required to prepare group accounts, and which has an undertaking included in the consolidation that has an interest in an *associated undertaking* (below, p.449), must disclose the following in respect of such an associated undertaking: its name; the country in which it is incorporated or, if it is unincorporated, its principal place of business; and the proportions of each class of the associate's shares held by the parent company and by the group as a whole (Sch.5, para.22).

With respect to *other significant holdings*, companies, whether required to prepare group accounts or not, must disclose the following information (if not otherwise given) with respect to companies in which:

(1)   they hold more than 20 per cent of the nominal value of any class of share; or

(2)   the amount invested, as shown in the investor company's individual accounts, exceeds 20 per cent of its assets:

their names; the countries in which they are incorporated or, if they are unincorporated, their principal places of business; and the proportions of each class of the investee company's shares held (Sch.5, paras 7–8, 23–24).

The aggregate amount of the investee company's year end capital and reserves and of its annual profit or loss must also be disclosed, except where: the investment is dealt with by the equity consolidation method (below, p.449); the investee company is not obliged to deliver a copy of its accounts and does not publish them elsewhere; the holding is less than half the nominal value of the subsidiary's shares; it is immaterial; or the investor company is exempt from preparing group accounts as its accounts are included in the financial statements of a larger group (Sch.5, paras 9 and 25). Similar criteria are to be applied in respect of a group (rather than just the parent company) where this is relevant (Sch.5, paragraphs 26–28).

(E) *Creditors*

Reference has already been made to the fact that each item under the headings "debtors" and "creditors" has to be divided between amounts receivable or payable within one year and those receivable or payable beyond that period (above, p.427). In addition, for each category of creditor due for payment after more than one year, the following must be disclosed: the aggregate amount payable (other than by instalments) more than five years hence; the aggregate amount of any instalments payable five or more years hence; the terms of payment and any applicable rate of interest; the aggregate figure for secured creditors and the nature of securities given; and the amount and period of any arrears of fixed cumulative dividends (paras 48, 49, 85):

(F) *Guarantees and financial commitments*[42]

Under para.50, the following items must be disclosed: the amount of third-party liabilities secured by charges on the company's assets; the amount, nature and security provided (if any) in relation to any contingent liability; the aggregate amount of contracted capital expenditure, so far as not provided for; pension commitments (a) provided for, and (b) not provided for; and any other commitments not provided for which are relevant to a proper understanding of the company's affairs. Under para.59A, commitments undertaken on behalf of subsidiaries of the company and parent or fellow subsidiary undertakings must be stated separately both from each other and from the company's other commitments.

(G) *Loans made for the purchase of a company's shares*

Details of any outstanding loan made for the purpose of acquiring the company's shares under ss 153(4) or 155 (above, Ch.11) must be disclosed in aggregate for each item in which they are included (para.51).

(H) *Credit transactions with directors and officers of the company*

Under Pts II and III of Sch.6 to the Act, particulars must be disclosed in notes to the accounts of any material credit transaction or arrangement with a director, shadow director, connected person or officer other than a director which are permitted under ss 330–338 (above, pp.291–292). Under paras 22 and 29 of Sch.6, the information to be disclosed is generally: the fact that the transaction, loan, arrangement or agreement was made or existed during the financial year; and the name of the director or connected person and/or the number of officers concerned.

With regard to directors and connected persons, the value of credit transactions has to be disclosed, as well as the nature of any material interest; while for loans and similar arrangements the following details must be given: principal

---

[42] Further guidance on these matters is given in accounting standards.

and interest at the beginning and end of the financial year, the maximum amount of the liability during the year, interest due but not paid, and related bad debt provisions; and the liability of the company or its subsidiaries under guarantees or security and other similar arrangements at the beginning and end of the year, the maximum potential liability, and expenses or liabilities incurred in discharging the guarantee or security arrangement (Sch.6, para.22(2)).

With regard to officers other than directors, disclosure must be made of loans and other equivalent arrangements in terms of the aggregate amounts outstanding at the end of the year, together with the number of persons concerned, under the following headings: loans or security therefor and similar arrangements; quasi-loans or security therefore and similar arrangements; and credit transactions or security therefore and similar arrangements (Sch.6, para.29; and, for recognised banks, Sch.9, Pt IV).

Exemptions from the disclosure requirements for directors, connected persons and officers of the company are permitted on a number of grounds, most notably in relation to service contracts and where the values of the items or interest are small (Sch.6, paras 17–21, 23–26, 29(2)).

In addition to the above requirements, directors' interests in shares of group companies and in material contracts with the company or its subsidiaries have to be disclosed in the directors' report, either as a result of statutory requirements or in order to comply with the *Listing Rules*.

(I) *Derivatives and other financial instruments*

Accounting standards require certain disclosures with respect to derivatives and other financial instruments (including hedged items), and Sch.4, para.34A (inserted by SI 2004/2947) provides for their statement at "fair value" (below, p.443–444). Guidelines for determining such values are given in paras 34B and 34C, while paras 34E and 34F indicate that changes in such values should be credited or debited to either the profit and loss account or to a "fair value reserve", depending on the circumstances.

The following details must be disclosed by way of *notes to the profit and loss account*:

(A) *Segmental analysis*

    (a)   Where, in the opinion of the directors, a company has carried on two or more classes of business which differ substantially, the notes must show the turnover for each class. In this context turnover means revenues from ordinary activities, net of trade discounts, VAT and other duties. In determining the source of turnover the directors are to have regard to the way in which the company's activities are organised (para.55 and s.262(1)).

    (b)   Where, in the opinion of the directors, a company has supplied goods and services to two or more geographical *markets* the turnover must be disaggregated by *destination* (para.55). Accounting standards also require a geographical analysis of turnover and contribution to trading results by *origin*.

(c) Segmental information need not be disclosed if the directors are of the opinion that its publication would be detrimental to the company's best interests, but if this is the case the fact that such an analysis is being withheld must be stated (para.55(5)).

(d) Accounting standards also require that the pre-tax profit or loss and assets employed should be disclosed for each segment.

(B) *Extraordinary items*

Particulars must be disclosed of prior year transactions included in the profit and loss account; extraordinary items (gross and net of associated tax); and exceptional items (*i.e.* those which arise as a result of the ordinary activities of the business but are abnormal by virtue of their size or incidence) (para.57). Further guidance on the treatment and presentation of extraordinary items is given in accounting standards.

(C) *Taxation*

The notes must disclose the amounts of the charges to UK corporation and income taxes, together with a note of the gross amount of the former before any double taxation relief, and details of any overseas taxation borne. Moreover, the tax associated with any extraordinary item must also be shown separately. In addition, details of special circumstances that affect any liability to taxation must be disclosed (para.54). Further requirements concerning the calculation and disclosure of taxation are given in accounting standards.

(D) *Specific charges against income*

The following charges against income must be disclosed:

(a) Interest on loans outside the group, analysed between (i) bank loans and overdrafts; and (ii) any other loans (para.53).

(b) Auditors' remuneration, including expenses, distinguishing between amounts payable for audit and non-audit work, and the nature of services provided by them and their associates (ss 390A and 390B, as amended and substituted by the Companies (Audit, Investigations and Community Enterprise) Act 2004, s.7: below, p.468).

(c) Dividends paid in the year (other than those for which a liability existed at the immediately preceding balance sheet date); the dividends that the company is liable to pay at the balance sheet date; and the aggregate amount of dividends that are proposed before the date of approval of the accounts and are not otherwise disclosed (para 35A, as inserted by SI 2004/2947).

(d) Disclosure of hire charges for plant and machinery is required by an accounting standard.

(E) *Employees and their remuneration*

Details must be disclosed of the following

(a) The monthly average number of employees in the financial year, broken down into such categories of employee as the directors select, having regard to the company's organisation (s.231A(1)–(3), (5), as inserted by SI 2004/2947).

(b) In so far as they are not disclosed in the profit and loss account, the aggregate amount of each of the following: wages and salaries payable; social security costs, including contributions to state run pension schemes; and other pension costs (s.231A(4), (6)–(7), as inserted by SI 2004/2947).

(c) Under s.232 and Sch.6, para.1, the aggregate of: directors' emoluments (*i.e.* basic salary and annual bonuses); gains made by directors on the exercise of share options (listed companies only); gains made by directors under long term incentive schemes; and company contributions to both money purchase and defined benefit pension schemes. Under Sch.6, paras 7–9, companies must also disclose excess retirement benefits of directors; compensation payable to directors for loss of office; and sums payable to third parties in respect of directors' services.

(d) Under s.232 and para.2 of Sch.6, where the total emoluments of all the directors exceed £200,000 in the year in question, the emoluments of the highest paid director, together with pension contributions made on his behalf.

(e) The *Listing Rules* also require that particulars of any arrangement whereby a director has waived or agreed to waive emoluments should be disclosed.

"Emoluments" are defined in Sch.6, para.1(3).

Under SI 2002/1986, which amended s.241 and inserted ss 234B, 234C, 235(4)–(5) and Sch.7A into the 1985 Act (see p.287), listed companies are required to disclose all aspects of directors' remuneration in a report, which (so far as possible) is subject to audit and then has to be approved by shareholders at the AGM. The contents of this report are specified in Sch.7A to the 1985 Act (*e.g.* details of individual director's pay packages, an explanation of how directors' pay is assessed, membership of the remuneration committee, names of any pay consultants used, the company's future policy on directors' remuneration (including the use of incentive schemes and the award of share options), and a graph showing the company's share price performance against an appropriate market index).

Certain other information, including that on government grants, has to be disclosed in notes to the financial statements (or sometimes on the face of the accounts themselves) in order to comply both with the provisions of the Companies Act 1985 on accounting principles and rules (discussed below) and with provisions of various accounting standards and (for quoted companies) the *Listing Rules*. Moreover, as indicated above (pp.423–424), where there is a departure from strict compliance with a requirement of the Act to ensure the financial statements reflect a true and fair view, the reasons for the departure and its effect have to be disclosed in a note to the accounts (para.15). The accountancy profession also suggests that a material difference between reported and distributable profits should be disclosed in a note (below, Ch.22).

Under paras 11 and 30–31 of Sch.5, a company which is a subsidiary must state the name and country of incorporation of its ultimate parent company.

With respect to *abbreviated financial statements* under s.246A, the directors of a *medium-sized*[43] private company may omit from their filed accounts the statement indicating that they have been prepared in accordance with applicable accounting standards,[44] as well as detailed information concerning their trading operations (above, p.428) and turnover by line of business and geographical market.

Under paras 4–9 of Sch.8A, *small-sized*[45] private companies need only disclose the following: *General notes*: accounting policies, in particular indicating the depreciation and foreign currency translation methods employed. *Balance sheet notes*[46]: (A) Share capital and loan stock: items (a) and (b), and in so far as it relates to shares (but not to loan stock) (c); (C) Fixed assets, but only in respect of categories in Sch.8A preceded by letters and Roman numerals, and excluding disclosure of the effect of applying "alternative accounting rules"; (E) Creditors: amounts payable in aggregate within and after one year must be shown separately; and similarly the aggregate amount payable within and after five years, but in the latter context drawing a distinction between debts repayable by instalments and those which are not; and the aggregate figure for each item under "creditors" the amounts secured and the nature of securities given; (H) Transactions with directors and officers of the company. *Profit and loss account*: None. *Other notes*: None of those required by Sch.4 (*e.g.* relating to accounting principles and rules, except in so far as they can be interpreted as accounting policies), nor those required under Sch.6 Pt I, disclosing the remuneration of directors, nor some of the details required under Sch.5 concerning subsidiary companies.

Comparative amounts for previous years must still be given where appropriate for such items as are disclosed in notes.

ACCOUNTING PRINCIPLES AND RULES

Prior to 1981, successive Companies Acts gave little guidance as to what

---

[43] Above, pp.418–419, 424–426 and below, 449–452.
[44] Above, pp.428–429; and below, p.438 *et seq.*
[45] Above, pp.418–419, 424–426, and below, pp.449–452.
[46] The letters and Roman numbers correspond to the items referred to above on pp.430–436. The disclosures referred to here are in addition to the requirement to show the aggregate amounts of debtors and creditors divided between amounts receivable or payable within one year and those receivable or payable beyond that period (above, p.427).

accounting principles and rules should be followed in preparing the annual accounts of companies. The generally accepted view was that the traditional historical cost convention used by accountants was appropriate. However, following a number of celebrated debacles in the City, the Accounting Standards Committee (ASC) was established in 1969, with the aim of codifying different practices and narrowing choice between them. While the ASC's pronouncements provided a useful framework for standardising conventions and forms of presentation, it did not greatly change the substance of accounting practice. Only in relation to current cost accounting, on which its hand was forced by the government, did it take a new initiative, requiring that listed companies should publish supplementary current cost financial statements from 1980 onwards. However, even this standard was effectively withdrawn in 1986.

In the circumstances, it was widely argued that a more broadly based body was needed to promulgate and monitor accounting standards. The result was the creation of the Financial Reporting Council in 1989, which under s.256 of the 1985 Act now sets and polices standards via three subsidiary bodies (above, p.412). Its authority is reinforced by s.257, which empowers the Secretary of State to alter the regulations concerning the contents of annual accounts and the directors' report by statutory instrument.[47]

While the ASC was developing standards in the 1970s, the EU was identifying accounting procedures which could be consistently applied within the Common Market, and its ideas were included in its Fourth Council Directive of 1978. For the most part these related to the historical cost convention, but it was necessary to accommodate current (replacement) cost accounting, used by major companies in the Netherlands, and also the practice whereby many listed companies in the UK periodically revalued all or some of their fixed assets. The result was that Pt II of Sch.1 to the 1981 Act was divided into three sections: accounting principles; historical cost accounting rules; and alternative accounting rules. This now constitutes Pt II of Sch.4 to the 1985 Act.

1. Accounting principles and conventions

Paragraphs 10–15 of Sch.4 to the 1985 Act identify four so-called concepts which, so long as they are consistent with the statements presenting a true and fair view, underlie the preparation of annual accounts: going concern concept, consistency concept, accruals concept, and prudence doctrine. The *going concern concept* implies that the net realisable values of fixed assets will not normally be the relevant values to use in the accounts—indeed, they will only be appropriate where liquidation is envisaged. *Consistent application of accounting policies*, both within a set of accounts and over time, is necessary to try and ensure comparability from year to year and reduce opportunities to manipulate results. The *accruals concept* requires that revenues and expenses reported should relate

---

[47] s.14 of the Companies (Audit, Investigations and Community Enterprise) Act 2004 empowers the Secretary of State for Trade and Industry to appoint a body (likely to be the FRRP) to examine interim and non-company accounts. ss 16–18 further empower the Secretary of State to make grants to a body carrying out supervisory functions relating to auditing and accounting (*i.e.* the FRC) and to impose levies on its behalf to help meet its operating costs.

to the financial year in question, regardless of when cash is actually received or spent. In practice, however, accountants rarely take the accruals principle to its logical conclusion, preferring to apply the *prudence doctrine*, which an accounting standard indicates should prevail under conditions of uncertainty.

Paragraph 12 of Sch.4 specifies two rules in relation to the prudence doctrine: (a) that only realised profits should be included in the income statement (though s.262(3) of the 1985 Act defines such profits only in terms of best accounting practice at the time); and (b) that all liabilities and losses that have arisen and are likely to arise should be taken into account. Moreover, they must be included even when they only become apparent after the end of the accounting year.

Paragraph 14 indicates that each asset and liability must be valued separately. Since an asset is undefined this might technically cause problems—for instance, where a machine is owned, is it the machine itself or its component parts that constitute(s) the asset(s)? However, the main purpose of the requirement seems to be to try to ensure that assets which may reasonably be regarded as separate (such as different lines of stock) are valued on an individual rather than a group basis.[48]

Paragraph 15 permits directors to depart from any of the principles referred to above if their application is inconsistent with the overriding requirement of ss 226A and 227A to present a true and fair view. However, particulars of such a departure, the reasons and the effect must be disclosed.

2. Historical cost accounting rules

Section 262(1) defines *fixed assets* as those assets intended for use on a continuing basis, and the basic rule is that they should be shown at either the purchase price or production cost, net of any depreciation or diminution in value (para.17). The latter applies where a fixed asset is wasting in nature and has a limited useful economic life, the cost (net of estimated scrap value) being written off "systematically" over such life (para.18). Additional depreciation *may* be provided for fixed asset investments in respect of a decline in value (para.19(1)), and *must* be for any fixed asset (including a fixed asset investment) where such decline in value is expected to be permanent (para.19(2)). The basis of such valuation is not defined, but under the going concern concept it will presumably normally be current value in use. Charges for additional depreciation, and amounts written back if such provisions are deemed no longer necessary, must be separately disclosed in the profit and loss account itself or in the notes thereto. Moreover, as regards the former, a distinction must be drawn between charges made under para.19(1) and those under para.19(2).

With respect to *intangible fixed assets*, the original amount at which acquired *goodwill* is shown in the accounts must be written off "systematically" over a period chosen by the directors which must not exceed its useful economic life. The period of, and the reasons for choosing, such period must be disclosed in a note (para.21). Moreover, the amount written off goodwill year-by-year has to be

---

[48] For tax purposes, however, it is permissable to value stocks on a group basis: *IRC v Cock, Russell and Co.* [1949] 29 T.C. 387.

disclosed in the profit and loss account; and para.14 of Sch.4A further requires that movements in goodwill must be shown in a note to a group's consolidated accounts (below, pp.445–449). Accounting standards offer further guidance on the value that should be attributed to purchased goodwill (including brands); how impairments in its value should be recognised; how its cost should be amortised; and how it should be treated on the disposal of a subsidiary undertaking.

Paragraph 20 permits *development costs* to be "capitalised" (a term defined in s.262(1)) and be shown in the balance sheet, but only in "special circumstances". Where this is done, notes must disclose the reasons for capitalising such development costs and the period over which they are being written off. Development expenditure is defined in an accounting standard but not in the Act. It is essentially identifiable expenditure, related to a specific project, which can reasonably be expected to be recovered in the future. Upon capitalisation it is to be amortised on a systematic basis. Where such expenditure is capitalised a further note to the accounts will generally be required by s.269 and para.20 to indicate that such unamortised expenditure is not being treated as a realised loss in calculating distributable profits and the justification for such treatment (which under s.262(3) is likely to be that it is consistent with accepted accounting principles and practice).

The Act does not specifically refer to *research expenditure*, which is distinguished from development expenditure in the relevant accounting standard as expenditure which cannot be related to a specific project and cannot reasonably be expected to be recovered in the future. Such expenditure should be written off immediately against revenues in the profit and loss account, which would appear to be consistent with the intention of the Act, given its specific use of the word "development".[49]

Current assets are defined in s.262(1) as any assets not intended for use on a continuing basis in the company's activities.

The first step with such assets is to establish their *ownership*, particularly in the case of *stocks*, which are sometimes the subject of a reservation of title clause: *i.e.* ownership of the goods remains with the supplier until a given event occurs. If there is doubt about ownership, the "economic substance" will be reflected by recording the goods as stock, but showing in the accounts either a provision against the liability or (if the likelihood of having to return the goods is remote) a note of the contingent liability.[50]

Generally, current assets are to be *valued* at the lower of, on the one hand, purchase price or production cost; and, on the other, net realisable value (paras 22–23). This rule is applied not only to stocks[51] but also to debtors, which are

---

[49] The reason for such interest in the treatment of intangible assets is partly because debt covenants frequently contain clauses which specifically refer to a maximum ratio of debt to assets so as to provide the lender with a margin of security. This seems to encourage companies to engage on the one hand in off balance sheet financing to reduce the face value of debt; and on the other to capitalise spending by creating or maintaining intangible assets, such as goodwill.

[50] The key distinction is between "mixed" and "unmixed" goods: see *Aluminium Industrie Vasser BV v Romalpa Aluminium Ltd.* [1976] 2 All E.R. 552; *Re Peachdart Ltd.* [1983] 3 All E.R. 204; and *Modelboard Ltd. v Outer Box Ltd. (in liquidation)* [1993] B.C.L.C. 623.

[51] For tax purposes, the replacement cost of stocks rather than net realisable value is a permitted alternative interpretation of "market value": *B.S.C. Footwear Ltd. v Ridgway* [1971] T.R. 121.

generally shown net of a bad debts provision. Small companies normally determine such provisions in relation to specific debts, as is required for calculating the company's liability to corporation tax.[52] However, larger companies usually make general bad debt provisions for financial reporting purposes.

Where the going concern assumption is reasonable, accounting practice is generally to value *work-in-progress* at cost, since net realisable value (which would usually be far lower) is irrelevant in such circumstances. Moreover, it is also common practice, in line with the terms of the relevant accounting standard, for profits to be recognised gradually over the period of long-term contracts, although so as to ensure these are "realised" they have to be included in the turnover and debtors figures.

Paragraph 23 of Sch.4 indicates that where an asset has been written down to net realisable value, but such value has subsequently risen, even if not fully up to cost again, the amount of the provision so made and no longer required must be written back.

Under para.27 of Sch.4, the *purchase price* or *production cost* of each class of stocks and similar fungible items (*i.e.* assets where individual units—such as shares held—are indistinguishable from each other), may be determined using the most appropriate of any one of four methods: first-in first-out (FIFO), last-in first-out (LIFO), weighted average cost, and any similar method. In addition, para.25 (referred to below) effectively permits use of the base stock method for stocks of raw materials and consumables. LIFO and base stock methods are not acceptable for tax purposes in the UK,[53] and in such circumstances, because of the need to keep a second set of stock records, it is generally impractical to use the former for financial reporting purposes.

As discussed below, where stocks and work-in-progress are valued at *production cost*, the latter *may* include a reasonable proportion of manufacturing overheads. Presumably these can comprise either just variable or both variable and fixed overhead costs. Tax law is fairly flexible on this matter,[54] but the relevant accounting standard *requires* that for financial reporting purposes a reasonable proportion of manufacturing overheads (including a proportion of fixed costs) should be included in the valuation of stocks and work-in-progress.

Whatever method of stock valuation is used, any *material difference* between the purchase price or production cost and the "relevant alternative amount" must be shown in a note to the accounts. Such "relative alternative amount" will normally be replacement cost at the balance sheet date, but an acceptable approximation very often will be a value based on the most recent purchase price or production cost (paras 27(3), (4), (5)).

The 1985 Act defines *purchase price* and *production cost*. Under para.26(1) of Sch.4 and s.262(1), the former is identified as the actual price paid for an asset, including expenses incidental to its acquisition; whereas production cost is the sum of (a) the purchase price of raw materials and consumables used; and (b) direct production costs incurred (but, in the case of current assets, excluding

[52] Income and Corporation Taxes Act 1988, s.74.
[53] The relevant cases are, respectively: *Minister of National Revenue v Anaconda American Brass Ltd.* [1956] A.C. 85; and *Patrick v Broadstone Mills* [1953] 33 T.C. 44.
[54] *Ostime v Duple Motor Bodies* [1961] 39 T.C. 537.

distribution costs); plus (c) other costs that *may* be included, being a reasonable proportion of indirect costs in so far as they relate to the period of production. Such indirect costs may include interest on borrowed capital, where appropriate, but if this is the case, the fact and the amount involved must be disclosed in a note (para.26).

Where there is no record for an asset of its original purchase price or production cost, or of related expenditure, the earliest value ascribed to it may be used instead, but this fact must be disclosed in the accounts or the notes thereto (paras 28 and 51(1)).

Paragraph 25 permits *tangible fixed assets* and *stocks* of raw materials and consumables to be shown at a fixed quantity and fixed value where they are constantly being replaced and (a) their overall value is not material to the assessment of the company's state of affairs; and (b) their quantity, value and composition is not subject to material variation.

Under para.24, where an amount owed to a creditor is greater than the value of the asset received, the difference may be treated as an asset rather than an expense, analogous to acquired goodwill. However, it must be written off by "reasonable amounts" each year and must be completely written off before repayment of the debt. Any such asset in the balance sheet must be disclosed either in the statement or in the notes thereto. There is no reference to systematic amortisation in these provisions, as there is in relation to acquired goodwill, nor apparently is it necessary to indicate the period over which the asset is being written off.

3. Alternative accounting rules

Companies may adopt any of the "alternative accounting rules" outlined in Section C of Pt II of Sch.4. Such rules only apply to the main financial statements, which as a result can be prepared not only in terms of the historical cost convention, but can instead be modified to take into account selective revaluations or be completely re-stated in current cost terms.

The ASC introduced a standard on current cost accounting in 1980 (finally withdrawn in 1988), which permitted the listed and very large companies to which it applied to present current cost accounts either as supplementary statements (which became the usual practice) or as the main financial statements. Only in the latter case did the alternative accounting rules apply. Currently only utility companies (*e.g.* in the electricity industry) publish supplementary current cost statements. These *regulatory accounts* better reflect underlying economic costs and thus give some indication whether the companies' monopoly power is being exploited to earn abnormally high profits.

The alternative rules outlined in Sch.4 (paras 31–34) are as follows:

(a) Intangible assets, other than goodwill, may be shown at current cost.

(b) Goodwill (for which current cost has no clear meaning) should be shown at its cost of acquisition, less amortisation, unless it is written off immediately.

(c) Tangible fixed assets may be stated either at their market values on the dates they were last valued or at current cost. (The latter could either be the second-hand value or the current cost new less notional depreciation.)

(d) Fixed asset investments may be stated either at their market values on the dates they were last valued or at a value determined on an appropriate basis given the company's circumstances, in which case the method and reasons for using it must be disclosed.

(e) Current asset investments and stocks may be stated at their current costs.

(f) As regards wasting fixed assets, depreciation should be based on the revalued amounts, not the purchase price or production cost. The charge to the profit and loss account can either be that based on the current value or just be the historical cost charge. However, in the latter case, the difference between the two must be disclosed either in the accounts or in the notes thereto. This would appear to allow such differences to be debited or credited direct to the revaluation reserve.

(g) Accumulated unrealised holding gains arising from revaluations which result from application of the alternative accounting rules must be credited to a revaluation reserve, and this must be shown separately in the balance sheet. Amounts can only be transferred from the revaluation reserve to the profit and loss account where the amount in question: (i) was previously charged to the profit and loss account; (ii) represents a realised profit; or (iii) is applied wholly or partly in paying up bonus shares allotted to members of the company. In addition, amounts can be transferred to or from the revaluation reserve in respect of taxation relating to any profit or loss credited or debited to the reserve. Overall, however, the balance of the reserve has to be reduced where there is no longer any justification for its existence (*e.g.* where there has been a subsequent decline in the value of an asset previously revalued upwards). An explanation of the tax effects of increases or reductions in the revaluation reserve (such as the tax that would be payable if the asset were sold at its revalued amount) must be disclosed in a note to the accounts.

(h) Where alternative rules are applied, the notes must state the items affected, the basis of valuation of each balance sheet item, and (with the exception of stocks) for each of the latter items, including provisions separately, either the corresponding amount under the historical cost convention or the differences between the two sets of figures. Alternatively the basis of valuation, and the corresponding amount or differences, can be disclosed on the face of the balance sheet rather than in notes.

4. *Fair value accounting*

Although current cost accounting is no longer employed by UK companies, except for utilities in their regulatory accounts (above, p.442), UK and international accounting standards have in recent years been adopting current cost principles on a piecemeal basis. The principle is now termed "fair value accounting", and SI 2004/2947 has inserted a new section, D, in Pt II of Sch.4. Para. 34B indicates that such "fair values" should be market values, but these may if necessary be approximated using financial models. Amongst the assets and liabilities that can be stated at fair value are: financial instruments (including derivatives, defined in para.76A), hedged items, investment property (defined in para.82A), and living animals and plants (paras 34A, 34C and 34D). Changes in fair value are to be credited or debited as appropriate to the profit and loss account or to the fair value reserve (paras 34E and 34F). Full disclosure of the valuation procedures used for each category of asset and liability is required, including details of any model used to determine fair values (paras 45A—45D).

Non-statutory requirements

The most important additional disclosure required by the ASB is a cash flow statement, although this does not apply to small companies eligible to file abbreviated accounts. Other additional disclosures required by accounting standards include earnings per share statistics for listed companies; the basis of currency translation; and a separate statement of realised gains and losses (above, p.429).

The *Listing Rules inter alia* require quoted companies to publish half-yearly interim and preliminary profit announcements. The former may be important in terms of the requirement of s.272 that for a public company the declaration of an interim dividend should be related to accumulated realised profits, determined if necessary in interim accounts. These should be prepared on a basis consistent with the requirements of the Act with regard to a company's statutory annual accounts (below, Ch.22). In addition, various other matters have to be disclosed by quoted companies under the *Listing Rules* (below, p.452).

GROUP ACCOUNTS

While some users of accounting statements (*e.g.* creditors) may focus on the financial affairs of a *legal entity*, others (such as existing and potential shareholders) may instead be rather more interested in the affairs on an *economic entity*. Such an entity can extend as far as a colluding group of companies, or where companies are tied together economically in a joint venture arrangement[55] or even sometimes by the existence of a long-term contract. This latter notion of a group, where undertakings are managed on a central and unified basis, is the view taken in the EU's Seventh Council Directive on company law harmonisation. The traditional British view is somewhat narrower, s.736 determining the existence of a group where the holding company either controls the composition of the board of directors of a subsidiary, or controls more than half its voting rights. However, under s.258 of the 1985 Act (inserted in 1989) new criteria were

---

[55] *e.g.* until recently Unilever and Royal Dutch-Shell have published joint venture accounts as their main financial statements, as well as the strictly legal accounts for their British participant companies.

introduced for determining whether a company should prepare group accounts. Essentially this adopts the broader view taken in the EU's Seventh Directive, the critical element being whether "a parent company" has the power to exercise, or actually exercises, a dominant influence (above, pp.422–423).[56]

The advantage of having access to a set of group accounts is that the statements can be prepared so as to eliminate the often sizeable internal, intra-group transactions and show a more complete picture of the group financial structure. However, the price of consolidation is that potentially interesting information will be lost (*e.g.* the fact that a particular subsidiary has been operating at a loss). Nevertheless, the significance of group accounts has long been recognised, many large public companies in the UK voluntarily publishing them before a legal requirement to do so was introduced in the 1948 Companies Act.

General requirements

As indicated above (pp.422–423), a *parent company* must prepare its individual accounts for its shareholders,[57] and to facilitate this the Sch.4 balance sheet formats include various headings which are appropriate for individual parent and subsidiary companies. In addition, SI 2004/2947 has amended s.227 and inserted new ss 227A, 227B, 227C and 228A to facilitate the adoption of international accounting standards (IASs) by listed companies in their consolidated accounts (above, p.413–414).

By ss 227 and 227A, where at the end of its financial year a company is a parent company, its directors must prepare *group accounts* comprising a consolidated profit and loss account and balance sheet. Such accounts must give a true and fair view of the group's position and profit or loss, so far as concerns the members of the company, and comply with the provisions of Sch.4A concerning the form and content of group accounts. However, if there is a conflict, either sufficient additional information must be disclosed to ensure a true and fair view is given, or there must be departure from the requirements of Sch.4A, explaining the reasons for such action and its effect. Sections 227B and 227C require that where a group prepares consolidated accounts applying IASs, this should be stated in notes to the accounts, and that normally the accounts of the parent and subsidiary undertakings should also be prepared applying those standards.

Under s.228, as amended, *sub-groups* need not prepare group accounts if the immediate parent undertaking of the sub-group prepares audited group accounts under the law of an EEA state and the subsidiary undertaking is wholly owned by the sub-group parent, or it holds more than 50 per cent of the shares and there is no request by a minority holding either half the remaining shares or 5 per cent of the total shares for such sub-group accounts to be prepared. However, exemption from the obligation to prepare group accounts is conditional also on the company indicating that it is taking advantage of the concession; stating the name of the parent and its country of incorporation (or, if it is unincorporated, its principal

---

[56] See Ch.2, above, for further discussion of the contents of ss 736, 736A and 736B.
[57] One reason for this is that the dividend declared by a parent company must be based on these accounts and not on the group accounts (below, pp.483–484).

place of business); delivering copies of the group accounts and auditors' report (if necessary with an English translation) to the Registrar; and not having securities listed on a stock exchange within an EEA state.[58]

Under s.229, subsidiary undertakings *may* be excluded from consolidation where: (a) their inclusion individually or collectively would not be material in giving a true and fair view; (b) long term restrictions hinder the parent's right to manage; (c) the information required for the preparation of group accounts cannot be obtained without disproportionate expense or undue delay; and (d) the interest of the parent is only temporary. In addition, they must be excluded from consolidation where their activities are so fundamentally different that such accounts would not give a true and fair view. In such circumstances, they should be included in the consolidated financial statements using the *equity method*[59] (Sch.4A, para.18).

Accounting standards go further than s.229 and *require* exclusion from consolidation in cases (b) and (d) above. Further, under (b) they require that the investment should be carried at its original cost if the restriction existed at its acquisition date; or at the equity value at the date at which the restriction arises if that is subsequent to acquisition. With respect to exclusions on ground (d), they require that the investment should be treated as a current asset and be valued accordingly at the lower of cost and net realisable value. They further require (1) that subsidiary undertakings excluded because of the fundamentally different nature of their activities should be recorded in the consolidated financial statements using the *equity method*[60]; and (2) that various disclosures should also be made for subsidiary undertakings excluded from consolidation.

Under Sch.4A, group accounts must be prepared so far as possible to comply with the provisions of Sch.4 as if the undertakings included in the consolidation were a single company (Sch.4A, para.1(1)), with the formats for accounts under Sch.4 being modified to include an item for "minority interests" (Sch.4A, para.17).

For the purpose of consolidation, the accounts must incorporate in full the information contained in the individual accounts of the undertakings included in the consolidation. However, if the financial year of a subsidiary does not coincide with that of the parent, the group must deal with the subsidiary's state of affairs at the end of its financial year ending last before that of the parent company's, providing it is within three months of the latter. Otherwise, interim accounts must be used. Moreover, the parent company should try to apply standard accounting rules when undertaking a consolidation. If it does not, it should disclose this in a note. Likewise, any differences between the accounting rules used in preparing a parent company's individual accounts and its group accounts should be disclosed in a note (Sch.4A, paras 2-4).

---

[58] SI 2004/2947 substituted "EEA" for "EU" in s.228. The European Economic Area (EEA) comprises the EU plus Iceland, Norway, Switzerland and Liechtenstein, but the concession that sub-groups need not prepare group accounts only applies if the ultimate parent company complies with the requirements of the EU's Seventh Directive on company law harmonisation. SI 2004/2947 also inserted s.228A, which offers a similar exemption for sub-groups where the parent is not established under the law of a state in the EEA, but where the group accounts comply with the requirements of the EU's Seventh Directive.

[59] Below, p.449.

[60] *ibid.*

Where an acquisition takes place in a financial year, the name of the undertaking acquired must be disclosed in a note, stating whether the combination has been accounted for using the acquisition or merger methods of accounting (see below). In addition, details of the fair value of the consideration given must be disclosed, giving details in the case of an acquisition of the book values and fair values of the assets and claims and of the goodwill. Similarly, details of any adjustments made, in particular to the consolidated reserves, must be given where the merger method is used. The parent company must also show movements in the goodwill figure shown in the group accounts. Where there has been a disposal of an undertaking in the year that significantly affects the figures shown in the group accounts, the name of the undertaking and the amount of profit or loss attributable to it must also be disclosed in a note (Sch.4A, paras 13–15). Additional guidance on how those provisions should be implemented is given in accounting standards.

Methods of consolidation

Consolidated accounts can be prepared in three main ways: (a) the acquisition method; (b) the merger method; and (c) proprietary methods. However, listed companies applying international accounting standards (above, p.413–414) have from 2005 not had the option to apply merger accounting following the publication of International Financial Reporting Standard (IFRS) 3, "Business Combinations", in March 2004.

The *acquisition method* is used where a majority of the equity shares of a subsidiary is acquired for cash. Where the entire share capital is purchased, the difference between the cash paid and the fair value of the net assets acquired as recorded in the books constitutes "goodwill". On consolidation, the net assets of the constituent companies in the group are added together line-by-line in the group balance sheet. The latter will also include as an asset the goodwill, which represents the difference between the market going concern value of the business acquired and its net assets at the date of its purchase. The retained profits in the consolidated balance sheet will just be those of the parent company, not including those of the subsidiary. It will only be in subsequent years that the post-acquisition profits of the subsidiary will be added to the parent company's pre- and post-acquisition profits in the consolidated balance sheet.

Where the parent company acquires less than the entire share capital of a subsidiary, but more than 50 per cent, goodwill is calculated as the difference between the cash paid and the *pro rata* share of the net assets of the subsidiary at the date of purchase. The remaining share of the net assets is attributed to a minority interest claim. Post-acquisition profits of the subsidiary after the takeover will be split *pro rata* between the group and the minority interest.

Where consideration for an acquisition is in the form of new shares issued by the parent company, such shares will need to be valued. Where they are attributed a cash-equivalent market value, the acquisition method of consolidation will again be applied. However, it is possible to argue in certain circumstances that what is really happening is that two continuing businesses are voluntarily fusing their operations. It would therefore be more appropriate to apply the *merger method* of consolidation, whereby the value of consideration paid is the nominal rather than the market value of the new shares issued. The effect on the consolidated balance sheet will on the one hand be that no goodwill will be raised; and on the other that most, if not all, of the technical subsidiary's pre-acquisition profits will be added to the parent company's.

The most commonly used procedure for consolidation where a parent controls a subsidiary has always been the acquisition method. This continues to be the case as Sch.4A, paras 7–9, indicate that it is the acquisition method of consolidation (as there described, applying fair values) which must generally be applied under the 1985 Act. The only circumstances where the merger method is to be applied are where certain specific conditions (described below) exist.

It can be argued that the merger method of accounting more closely reflects the "economic entity" group concept than the acquisition method. Some British listed companies therefore applied it from the late 1960s onwards, although there was doubt about its validity in view of the decision in *Head (Henry) & Co., Ltd. v Ropner Holdings Ltd.*,[61] concerning the need to establish a share premium account (above, Ch.9). However, the 1981 Companies Act provided relief to *individual companies* from what is now s.130 in the 1985 Act in ss 131–134, making it legitimate to use the approach as long as the necessary conditions are met—(the main one is that the acquiring company should secure at least 90 per cent in nominal value of each class of the share capital of the company being taken over (above, Ch.9).

With respect to *groups* opting to prepare consolidated accounts using the merger method (as there described), paras 10–11 of Sch.4A prescribe that the parent company must hold at least 90 per cent of the relevant shares as a result of offering its or its subsidiaries' equity shares; and that the fair value of consideration other than equity shares given does not exceed 10 per cent of the value of the shares issued. Accounting standards set rather tighter criteria to determine whether or not a true "pooling of interests" has taken place. Where these are met the merger method *must* be applied when preparing consolidated accounts.

As mentioned above, listed companies have from 2005 no longer had the option of applying merger accounting. Moreover, the relevant international accounting standard, IFRS 3, not only requires that net assets acquired should be valued at their fair values, but that any goodwill arising should be tested annually for impairment rather than be amortised on a systematic basis. Further, it does not permit reversals of impairment losses on goodwill, while negative goodwill has to be recognised immediately in the profit and loss account as a gain. Separately identified intangible assets other than goodwill should also be tested annually for impairment.

The third approach to consolidation is the *proprietary approach*, which is usually applied where the ownership stake is 50 per cent or less. This eliminates recognition of the outside interest in both the balance sheet and the profit and loss account, and the concept can be implemented in one of two ways: (a) by

---

[61] [1952] Ch. 124. The decision in that case was confirmed in *Shearer v Bercain Ltd* [1980] 3 All E.R. 295.

proportional consolidation, where income, assets and liabilities are separately added in to the holding company's accounts on a *pro rata* basis item-by-item; or (b) by the *equity method of consolidation*, where an investment is shown in the group balance sheet *pro rata* to its current net asset value, the net changes each year usually being dealt with in the profit and loss account.

Proportional consolidation has rarely been practised by British companies, but the equity method has been applied to account for associated companies (*i.e.* basically those in which a 20–50 per cent stake is held) since the early 1970s. Paragraph 19 of Sch.4A indicates that where an undertaking is jointly managed with one or more independent third parties, it is a *joint venture* and may be accounted for by the method of proportional consolidation.

Paragraphs 20–22 define an *associated company* as one in which an undertaking has a participating interest and exercises a significant influence, and this is normally presumed if it holds over 20 per cent of the voting rights. In such circumstances, the equity method of accounting is to be used, with the standard format of accounts modified accordingly and with goodwill being treated as under the acquisition method. Further guidance is given in accounting standards on the appropriate treatment, with pro rata consolidation being restricted to joint arrangements that are not entities and the equity method for associates. However, for joint ventures which are separate entities a variant of the equity method (the "gross equity method") should be used, which goes some way towards the pro rata consolidation procedure.

Unrealised intra-group profits

One further point relating to consolidated accounts, which is of some relevance in relation to distributable profits as defined in ss 263-281, concerns the treatment of unrealised inter-company profits. Briefly, if one member of a group sells goods to another, such goods as are in stock at the balance sheet date will potentially include an element of unrealised profit. This can logically be eliminated in one of two ways: (a) adopting a "single entity" approach and treating the transactions as though they had never taken place: this means writing back the unrealised profit against the company which sold the goods, with the minority interest in the selling company bearing its appropriate share; or, (b) adopting a "separate entity" approach, in which case any unrealised profit must be written back against the company which holds the goods, with the minority interest in that company (if any) again bearing its appropriate share.

Paragraph 6 of Sch.4A merely states that intra-group debts and claims and intra-group transactions should be eliminated when group accounts are prepared; and that unrealised profits may be eliminated "in proportion to the group's interest in the shares of the undertakings". However, accounting standards require elimination in full.

DIRECTORS' REPORT

The intention of the EU's Fourth Council Directive was that the directors' report should merely supplement the financial details given in the accounts with certain narrative information about the company's activities and its future prospects. However, the report's role has grown in importance, and the ASB, with the backing of the London Stock Exchange, issued a statement in 1993 recommending that large companies should include in their annual reports an "Operating and Financial Review" (OFR). This could helpfully identify factors which have affected past performance and which are likely to affect future trading; aspects which are particularly subject to uncertainty; the impact of exchange rates on profitability; discuss a business's capital structure; summarise investment plans; and so on. In 2003 the ASB published revised guidelines, at much the same time as the EU issued a directive, which require medium and large companies to report on the principal risks and uncertainties facing their business and to publish relevant key performance indicators. In order to implement the directive, the DTI published draft regulations in May 2004 that will require some 1,300 listed companies to publish statutory OFRs from 2005 onwards. The contents of these reports will be determined by standards issued by the ASB.

Small-sized companies (above, pp.424–426) do not have to *file* a directors' report with the Registrar, and certain concessions are available to them under Sch.8 to the 1985 Act reducing the amount of detail that has to be included in *reports submitted to shareholders*. Failure to comply with the statutory requirements makes the offending directors liable to a fine, although it is a defence to prove that all reasonable steps were taken to secure compliance.

Briefly, the items requiring *disclosure* in the directors' report may be summarised as follows:

(a) A fair review of the development of the business of the company and its subsidiaries during the financial year ending with the balance sheet date and of their position at the end of it (s.234(1)(a)).

(b) The amount recommended to be paid by way of dividend (s.234(1)(b)).

(c) Names of directors at any time during the year under review (s.234(2)).

(d) Principal activities of the company and its subsidiaries and significant changes in those activities (s.234(2)).

(e) An indication of the difference between the book amount and the market values of land and buildings if, in the opinion of the directors, the difference is of such significance that it should be drawn to the attention of the members or debenture holders (Sch.7, para.1(2)).

(f) Interests of directors and their immediate families at the beginning and end of each year in shares or debentures of the company or its group undertakings, if such information is not shown in a note to the accounts. Details of options granted or exercised are also to be disclosed (Sch.7, paras 2, 2A, 2B).[62]

(g) Details for a company or group of its UK charitable donations and political contributions, as defined, where in aggregate they exceed £200. For political purposes, contributions to any party or person which exceed £200 must also be separately disclosed (Sch.7, paras 3–5).

---

[62] Additional disclosures are required by the *Listing Rules*.

(h) In relation to the use of financial instruments by a group, an indication of its financial risk management objectives and policies, including hedging; and, where material, the exposure to price risk, credit risk, liquidity risk and cash flow risk (Sch.7, para.5A).

(i) Particulars of any important events affecting the company which have occurred since the end of the year (Sch.7, para.6(a)). Accounting standards additionally require disclosure of events which require adjustment to the accounting figures and those which do not.

(j) An indication of future likely developments in the business of the company and of its subsidiaries (Sch.7, para.6(b)).

(k) An indication of the activities (if any) of the company and its subsidiaries in the field of research and development (Sch.7, para.6(c)). Accounting standards also require disclosure of deferred development expenditure at the beginning and end of the year, movements during the year, and the accounting policy adopted (above, p.440).

(l) An indication of the existence of branches outside the UK (Sch.7, para.6(d)).

(m) In respect of purchases of its own shares during the year by the company, the number and nominal value of the shares; the percentage of called-up capital so purchased; the aggregate consideration paid; and the reasons for such purchase. Further disclosures are required in respect of other acquisitions of a company's shares (*e.g.* indirectly by persons with financial assistance from the company) (Sch.7, paras 7–8).

(n) For companies where the weekly average number of employees in the UK during the financial year exceeded 250, a statement of the company's policy in respect of applications for employment from disabled persons; employees who have become disabled; and training, career development and promotion of disabled persons (Sch.7, para.9).

(o) Where during the year a company has had on average more than 250 employees in the UK, a statement describing action taken to introduce, maintain or develop arrangements aimed at providing relevant information to those employees, consulting them or their representatives on a regular basis, encouraging their involvement in the business, and making them more aware of the financial and economic factors affecting its performance (Sch.7, para.11).

(p) If the company is a public company, or a large private company that is a subsidiary of a public company, its policy and practice with respect to the payment of creditors in the current year. Such a statement should *inter alia* show the ratio of end year trade creditors to invoiced purchases from suppliers for the previous year (*i.e.* as covered by the annual accounts) (Sch.7, para.12).

(q) Where a company is subject to a statutory audit, the directors' report must contain a statement that none of the directors is aware that information relevant for their work has not been brought to the attention of the auditors (s.234ZA).[63]

(r) Disclosure of third party indemnity provision for the benefit of a director of the company or its associated companies (s.309C).

Under s.234A, the directors' report must be *approved* by the board, and both it and the copy *filed* with the Registrar must be signed on the board's behalf by a director or the secretary. Moreover, the name of such a person must appear on each copy laid before the company in general meeting or otherwise circulated or published. Failure either to sign the report or to show the name of the signatory on circulated copies renders the company and its defaulting officers liable to a fine.

Under s.235(3) the *auditor* has a statutory duty to consider whether or not the information contained in the directors' report is consistent with the financial statements. Moreover, he is required to draw attention in his report to any inconsistency between the two for the year in question.

Under the *Listing Rules* the following information not directly relating to items disclosed elsewhere in the financial statements has to be detailed by a quoted company's directors: explanations of significant differences (*i.e.* 10 per cent or more) between outcomes and any forecasts made; interest capitalised during the year and the amount and treatment of related tax relief; particulars regarding equity shares issued for cash other than *pro rata* to existing equity shareholdings, unless specifically authorised; details of any participation by a parent company in any vendor consideration placing; substantial holdings (*i.e.* 3 per cent or more) in the company's shares, etc., and indicating if there is no such interest; particulars of any agreement to waive dividends; directors' interests in contracts with the company; contracts between the company and substantial shareholders; a statement indicating compliance with the Code of Best Practice on Corporate Governance (below, pp.461);[64] and related party transactions.

AUDITORS' REPORT[65]

Section 235 of the 1985 Act requires that, where a company is required to have a statutory audit,[66] its auditors should make a report to its members on all accounts laid before the company in general meeting, identifying the financial reporting framework applied in their preparation and the auditing standards in accordance with which the audit was conducted. The report must also state whether the financial statements comply with the Companies Act and, where appropriate, international accounting standards, sufficient to give a true and fair

---

[63] Inserted by the Companies (Audit, Investigations and Community Enterprise) Act 2004.

[64] The Code *inter alia* requires that directors should state in their report that the business is a going concern and the assumptions on which that judgement is based; and a report on the effectiveness of the company's system of internal control for further discussion of the code, see Ch.18.

[65] This topic is dealt with in more detail on pp.460 and 472.

[66] For exemption from the requirement to have a statutory audit, see pp.418–419.

view. In addition, the auditors must state the fact if: information relating to the year given in the directors' report is inconsistent with the financial statements; proper accounting records have not been kept and branch returns have not been obtained; the financial statements are not in agreement with the accounting records; full information and explanations regarded as necessary for the audit have not been obtained; and/or companies have taken advantage of the exemption to prepare group accounts under s.248 on the grounds that they qualify as small or medium sized groups but are not entitled to do so (ss 235(3) and 237(1)–(3),4A). The report should also include details of directors' emoluments and loans if not disclosed as required by Sch.6 to the 1985 Act (s.237(4)); and, if the report is qualified, indicate whether the qualification is material in determining whether a distribution can lawfully be made (s.271(3),(5)). Auditors belonging to the main professional accountancy bodies in the UK are also required by those bodies to refer in their reports to any breaches of accounting standards.

Auditors are also required to make special reports when listed companies circulate summary financial statements; where a parent company is exempted from the obligation to prepare group accounts; and (where appointed and the directors have not taken advantage of the provisions of s.249A(1)–(2) exempting the company from the obligation to have an audit) when abbreviated accounts are filed by medium or small sized companies.

Under s.240, the auditors' report must not be published with non-statutory accounts, although the latter must be accompanied by a statement indicating that such a report has been made on the statutory accounts and whether or not it is qualified.

Special Classes of Company

Dormant companies

Under s.249AA of the 1985 Act a dormant company—which is one in which no significant accounting transaction occurred during the period in question—need not have its accounts audited. To qualify for such exemption the company must meet the following three conditions: (a) it was not required to prepare group accounts during the previous financial year; (b) it was classed as a small company during the previous financial year; and (c) it has been dormant since the end of the previous financial year.

Investment companies[67]

Companies qualify for special treatment if they are investment companies within the meaning of s.266 of the 1985 Act and were not during the year prohibited from making a distribution under s.265 (Sch.4, para.73: below, p.488).[68]

---

[67] "Open-ended investment companies" (OEICs) are subject to separate regulations (SI 1996/2827; and the Securities and Investments Board (SIB) Regulations 1997). The requirements with respect to their financial statements are very similar to those demanded by the Department of Trade and Industry of unit trusts and are not dealt with here.

[68] Under s.267 the Secretary of State can extend the provisions of ss 265–266 to other investment companies, including those whose asset holdings are in the form of land, although this power has yet to be used.

An investment company is defined under s.266 as being a public company which has given notice to the Registrar of its intention to carry on business as an investment company and meets the following conditions: (a) it invests its funds in a portfolio of securities for the benefit of, and to spread risk for, its shareholders; (b) none of its individual investments exceeds 15 per cent in value of its total investments; (c) its memorandum and articles prohibit a distribution of capital profits; and (d) it retains no more than 15 per cent of its income available for distribution in an accounting reference period. In addition, under s.351(1)(c) an investment company must indicate its status on its letter heads and on its order forms; while under paras 71–73 of Sch.4 and, for a group where the parent is an investment company, under para.1(3) of Sch.4A, the requirements with regard to the contents of the accounts are subject to modification from those generally applicable to other companies.

The above conditions substantially coincide with those demanded of an approved investment trust if it is to secure tax and other privileges, although it would for these purposes also have to be resident in the UK and have its shares listed on a recognised stock exchange. It would then be subject to various other conditions contained in the *Listing Rules*—*e.g.* no more than 20 per cent of the group's assets could be invested in any one company; and it would have to disclose supplementary information with its accounts, including a summary of its 10 largest investments and an analysis of realised and unrealised surpluses, with a separate statement of profits and losses analysed between listed and unlisted investments.

The provisions of the 1985 Act are adapted in three ways for investment companies: (a) revaluations of investments need not be credited or debited to the revaluation reserve; (b) where the value of fixed asset investments is written down, such a debit need not be passed through the profit and loss account if it is either charged against a reserve to which investment revaluations have been credited, or shown as a separate item under "other reserves"; (c) disclosure must be made in a note of any distribution reducing the company's net assets to less than the aggregate of its called-up capital and undistributable reserves (Sch.4, paras 71–72).[69]

Banking and insurance companies

Between 1948 and 1991, banks and insurance companies did not have to prepare and publish financial statements in the full form required of other companies by the Companies Acts.[70] The broad effect was to enable qualifying companies to conceal movements on reserve and fixed asset accounts, the justification being that it was desirable not to undermine public confidence in such financial institutions. However, the concessions were effectively removed between 1991 and 1993 to implement EU directives, new ss 255 and 255A–D and Schs 9 and 9A being inserted into the 1985 Act.

In the meantime, successive governments have developed ways of monitoring the financial viability of banks and insurance companies. In the case of the

---

[69] The latter can arise if the company applies the asset ratio test for distribution rather than the capital maintenance criterion: s.264.

[70] In fact, many of the privileges were removed from the large clearing banks in 1970.

former, the Bank of England and the FSA exercise control under provisions of the Banking Act 1987, requiring certain returns to be submitted on a regular basis.[71] Similar monitoring procedures have evolved for the insurance industry, where—under the Insurance Companies Act 1982, as amended—very detailed returns have to be made to the FSA. These include statements which are more important in many respects than the conventional accounts (*e.g.* the actuarial report for long term business, such as life assurance[72]; and individual fund accounts for short term business, such as that covered by fire, theft, and motor policies).[73]

Acknowledgment of Debts

In *Jones v Bellgrove Properties Ltd*[74] it was held that the inclusion of a sundry creditors figure in a balance sheet signed by the company's agents, a firm of chartered accountants, was an acknowledgment of a debt included in that figure. However, this decision was not followed in *Re Transplanters (Holding Co.) Ltd*,[75] where the directors had made the acknowledgment in favour of one of themselves; while in *Good v Parry*[76] it was decided that to be acknowledged a debt must be quantified in figures and be ascertainable by calculation or external evidence.

In *Consolidated Agencies Ltd. v Bertram Ltd*,[77] it was decided that acknowledgment only extended to a debt existing at the date of signature on a balance sheet and not to a debt at the date of a balance sheet. However, it was held in *Re Gee & Co. (Woolwich) Ltd*[78] that a balance sheet, duly signed by the directors, is capable of being an effective acknowledgment of the state of the company's indebtedness at the balance sheet date, so that the cause of action should be deemed to have accrued at that date, being the date to which the signature of the directors relates. Moreover, on the facts of the *Gee* case, the acknowledgment was effective, even though it was made by the directors in favour of one of themselves, because it was sanctioned by every member of the company.

Appendix

Reproduced below are Format 1 of the full balance sheet and Format 1 of the profit and loss account, as given in Sch.4 to the 1985 Act. Such statements must be presented to its shareholders by a company which does not qualify as "small sized" under s.246.

---

[71] The monitoring procedures undertaken by the FSA are described in *The FSA Handbook, Interim Prudential Sourcebook: Banks* (*www.fsa.gov.uk/handbook/ipru_bank.pdf*)

[72] The significance of this report is acknowledged in s.268, which recognises actuarial surpluses or deficits as the appropriate measure of realised profits or losses available for distribution (below, pp.487–489).

[73] See *The FSA Handbook, Interim Prudential Sourcebook: Insurers: Vol.2: Appendices to the Rules* (*www.fsa.gov.uk/handbook/ipru_ins.pdf*), which supersedes *The Insurance Companies (Accounts and Statements) Regulations 1983*, as amended.

[74] [1949] 2 K.B. 700 (C.A.).

[75] [1958] 1 W.L.R. 822.

[76] [1963] 2 Q.B. 418 (C.A.).

[77] [1965] A.C. 470 (P.C.).

[78] [1975] Ch. 52.

Under Sch.8, small sized companies must present the full profit and loss account to members, but in "shortened" accounts certain items in the balance sheet can be aggregated together: namely, in the format below — *B I* 1, 2 and 4; *B II* 2, 3 and 4; *B III* 1 and 3; 2 and 4; 6 and 7; *C I* 1, 2 and 3; *C II* 2 and 3; 4, 5 and 6; *C III* 2 and 3; *E* 6 and 7; 1, 3, 5, 8 and 9; *H* 6 and 7; 1, 3, 5, 8 and 9; *I* 1, 2 and 3; *K IV* 1, 2, 3 and 4.

Under Sch.8A, statements to be lodged with the Registrar by a small sized company can be further "abbreviated" to include only a balance sheet including the items marked with an asterisk.

Under s.246A, medium sized companies must file a full balance sheet but may combine various heads in the profit and loss account. In Format 1 (below) these are items 1, 2, 3 and 6, giving rise to a "gross profit or loss" figure.

Balance sheet—Format 1

A   *Called up share capital not paid**
B   *Fixed assets**
   I Intangible assets*
      1 Development costs
      2 Concessions, patents, licences, trade marks and similar rights and assets
      3 Goodwill
      4 Payments on account
   II Tangible assets*
      1 Land and buildings
      2 Plant and machinery
      3 Fixtures, fittings, tools and equipment
      4 Payments on account and assets in course of construction
   III Investments*[79]
      1 Shares in group undertakings
      2 Loans to group undertakings
      3 Participating interests
      4 Loans to undertakings in which the company has a participating interest
      5 Other investments other than loans
      6 Other loans
      7 Own shares
C   *Current assets**
   I Stocks*
      1 Raw materials and consumables
      2 Work in progress
      3 Finished goods and goods for resale
      4 Payments on account

---

[79] Small companies delivering abbreviated accounts to the Registrar must disclose the fair values of any financial fixed assets where those assets are shown in the accounts at amounts in excess of fair value (Sch.8A, para.7A).

  II Debtors*
    1 Trade debtors
    2 Amounts owed by group undertakings
    3 Amounts owed by undertakings in which the company has a participating interest
    4 Other debtors
    5 Called up share capital not paid
    6 Prepayments and accrued income
  III Investments*
    1 Shares in group undertakings
    2 Own shares
    3 Other investments
  IV Cash at bank and in hand*

D *Prepayments and accrued income**

E *Creditors: amounts falling due within one year**
    1 Debenture loans
    2 Bank loans and overdrafts
    3 Payments received on account
    4 Trade creditors
    5 Bills of exchange payable
    6 Amounts owed to group undertakings
    7 Amounts owed to undertakings in which the company has a participating interest
    8 Other creditors including taxation and social security
    9 Accruals and deferred income

F *Net current assets (liabilities)**

G *Total assets less current liabilities**

H *Creditors: amounts falling due after more than one year**
    1 Debenture loans
    2 Bank loans and overdrafts
    3 Payments received on account
    4 Trade creditors
    5 Bills of exchange payable
    6 Amounts owed to group undertakings
    7 Amounts owed to undertakings in which the company has a participating interest
    8 Other creditors including taxation and social security
    9 Accruals and deferred income

I *Provisions for liabilities**
    1 Pensions and similar obligations
    2 Taxation, including deferred taxation
    3 Other provisions

J *Accruals and deferred income**

K *Capital and reserves**
  I Called up share capital*
  II Share premium account*
  III Revaluation reserve*

    IV Other reserves*
        1 Capital redemption reserve
        2 Reserve for own shares
        3 Reserves provided for by the articles of association
        4 Other reserves
    V Profit and loss account*

Profit and loss accounts—Format 1

1	Turnover
2	Cost of sales
3	Gross profit or loss
4	Distribution costs
5	Administrative expenses
6	Other operating income
7	Income from shares in group undertakings
8	Income from participating interest
9	Income from other fixed asset investments
10	Other interest receivable and similar income
11	Amounts written off investments
12	Interest payable and similar charges
13	Tax on profit or loss on ordinary activities
14	Profit or loss on ordinary activities after taxation
15	Extraordinary income
16	Extraordinary charges
17	Extraordinary profit or loss
18	Tax on extraordinary profit or loss
19	Other taxes not shown under the above items
20	Profit or loss for the financial year

Chapter 21

AUDITORS

INTRODUCTION

The justification for having a statutory audit

Where there is inequality of information between parties, it is desirable, not only between the parties concerned, but also from a wider social perspective that the accounts should be attested by an independent third party. This is necessary to avoid a breakdown in the market mechanism in two sets of circumstances.

First, a prospective purchaser of a company's shares will require information before he commits himself to the transaction. Economists have demonstrated that, in the absence of reliable information, the market will become unstable and at the limit no trading will take place. There are various ways to combat this—*e.g.* by offering guarantees and warranties; or by having an independent third party validate information. It is for this reason that disclosure of attested "due diligence" information is required in the primary share markets when a prospectus or listing particulars are published. But a prospective purchaser of a company's shares in the secondary markets will also want similar, reliable information.

The second situation arises where a "principal" (*e.g.* a shareholder) attempts to assess the performance of his "agent" (*e.g.* a manager) but has to rely on information given to him by the latter. The manager is clearly in a position to manipulate the data, and it is largely to counteract this that the device of a statutory audit has been developed. As will be described below, the auditor is given wide powers by ss 389A, 391A, 392, 392A, and 394 of the 1985 Act, being able to enforce them by qualifying his report and, in an extreme case, by refusing to certify the accounts. But just as it is important for readers of financial statements to have a guarantee that they have been properly prepared under an accepted set of conventions, it is also necessary for them to be able to rely on the word of those persons who certify them as having been so produced. This means that auditors should be recognised as fit and proper persons to carry out the duties of their office. Traditionally, the market response to situations where the public wishes to purchase quality services (*e.g.* in medicine, architecture, law or accountancy) is for practitioners to organise themselves into professional bodies, which then set minimum standards for members. Self-regulation along these lines can be very successful, but the position of professional bodies frequently enables them to restrict entry and exploit their monopoly power, making it necessary for governments to intervene to try to redress the balance.

Prior to the Companies Act 1989 a person could only be appointed as an auditor of a company if he was a member of a professional body recognised by the Secretary of State. Part II of the 1989 Act, concerned with eligibility for company auditors, has introduced the provisions of the EU's Eighth Council Directive on company law harmonisation into British legislation. However, these have not greatly altered the position, except to impose a more elaborate regulatory framework. This in turn has imposed greater compliance costs on those involved—directly on auditors and indirectly on the customers for their services—while at the same time the authorities are continuing for the most part to rely on competition in the market place to ensure that professional bodies do not over-exploit their monopoly power.

Abolishing the statutory audit for small companies

The reporting-to-shareholder function is effectively redundant for two thirds or more of the 1.5 million companies on the register where the entire share capital is owned by the directors. The 1989 Act partly addressed this matter by introducing an "elective regime" for private companies so that under a revised s.252 of the 1985 Act they can by unanimous resolution dispense with the holding of annual general meetings and the laying of accounts and reports before such meetings (above, pp.419–420). However, this concession did little to reduce the administrative burden on small companies, and it was for this reason that legislation was introduced in 1994 to exempt about half of all companies from having to have a statutory audit (below, p.472). Instead, only the largest "small" companies had to have their accounts attested, and then frequently by means of a less demanding examination culminating in a *compilation report*. Further concessions were introduced in 1997, when the need even to have a compilation report was abolished. Yet despite this, attested accounts still have to be prepared to reassure lending bankers and the Inland Revenue. Moreover, if companies do not publish reliable information, they are also likely to find suppliers will be less prepared to advance credit. Nevertheless, around two thirds of companies took advantage of the audit exemption concession in 2003–2004.

Closing the "expectation gap"

At the other end of the scale, there has been increasing concern, both amongst institutional investors and the general public, that the largest companies are not being run by directors in the best interests of either their shareholders or society in general. This has caused concern amongst the accountancy professional bodies as the public often seems to expect more from the audit than is legally required (*e.g.* identifying risks, reviewing future prospects, detecting fraud, controlling directors' actions, and establishing effective internal control systems). Moreover, the audit report is often seen as uninformative, failing to disclose material issues and concerns arising from the audit. There are also misgivings about the independence of auditors, especially when faced with the threat of litigation— important when the number and size of claims for negligence has mushroomed since the early 1980s. The profession has attempted to address these problems by elaborating the audit report and by revising the guidelines for conducting audits (below, pp.470–471).

However, these initiatives came to be regarded as inadequate following a succession of financial reporting debacles in the US and Europe in 2001–2003 (*e.g.* Enron, WorldCom and Parmalat). This put pressure on the US regulatory authority, the Securities and Exchange Commission, and the EU Commission to make the adoption of international accounting and auditing standards compulsory and to introduce tighter corporate governance rules (*e.g.* culminating in the Sarbanes-Oxley Act in the US).

Corporate governance

Public concern has also been expressed since the mid 1970s at a perceived lack of accountability of the directors of the largest public companies, both to their shareholders and to society in general. In an attempt to improve the situation a Code of Best Practice on Corporate Governance was developed in 1992 and endorsed by the London Stock Exchange. The "Combined Code" was revised and expanded in 1998 and 2003 and is now issued by the FSA (see Ch.18). Its provisions deal with: the board of directors; non-executive directors; executive directors; directors' remuneration; and reporting and controls.

In terms of financial reporting, the Code requires that all listed companies should have audit committees, the aim of which is to strengthen the independence of the external auditor and reinforce the position of internal auditors. The Combined Code and its predecessors also affect the position of the auditors in a number of other respects, including the following: interim announcements should be subject to review by a company's auditors; the accountancy profession should draw up guidelines for the rotation of audit partners; directors should report on the effectiveness of their system of internal financial control; directors should state in their report that the business is a going concern, indicating the assumptions on which they base their judgement, and the auditors should report on such a statement; and companies should publish a statement indicating that they have complied with the Code, but only after it has been the subject of review by the auditors.

The auditor's statement of compliance with the Code is separate from the audit of financial statements, and this should be made clear in their report to shareholders.

PROFESSIONAL QUALIFICATIONS OF AUDITORS

Supervisory bodies

A *Recognised Supervisory Body*[1] (RSB) is a body established in the UK which maintains and enforces rules concerning:

(a) the eligibility of persons seeking appointment or acting as company auditors; and

---

[1] So far the three institutes of chartered accountants in the British Isles, the Chartered Association of Certified Accountants, and two much smaller professional bodies have been recognised as RSBs.

(b) the conduct of company audit work,

which are binding on persons seeking appointment or acting as company auditors, either because they are members of that body, or because they are otherwise subject to its control (s.30(1) of the Companies Act 1989). Bodies wishing to become RSBs have to apply to the Secretary of State for recognition, and the conditions for granting or revoking recognition are specified in Sch.11[2] to the 1989 Act, paras 1–3. RSBs have to ensure that only individuals with appropriate qualifications and firms controlled by qualified persons are eligible for appointment as company auditors (paras 4–6).

An RSB's rules are required to ensure that company audit work is conducted properly and with integrity and independence; that certain technical standards are applied; and that procedures exist for ensuring eligible persons maintain an appropriate level of competence (paras 6–9). To this end the Auditing Practices Board (APB), whose aim is to establish standards that can be adopted by RSBs, published 30 Statements of Auditing Standards (SASs), together with two Statements of Investment Circular Reporting Standards (SIRs), as well as various Practice Notes and Bulletins.

The APB is now under the supervision of the Financial Reporting Council (FRC) (above, p.412), but from 2005 onwards, following the introduction of a Regulation by the European Commission in 2002 (above, p.413), listed companies have to comply with international auditing standards published the International Auditing and Assurance Standards Board (IAASB). As a result, the APB issued 30 new International Standards on Auditing (ISAs) in December 2004, which replace SASs for audits of financial statements for periods commencing on or after December 15, 2004.

Legislation further requires that an RSB's rules should deal with monitoring and enforcement of compliance with its rules; admission and expulsion of members; the grant and withdrawal of eligibility for appointment as company auditors; disciplinary procedures; the investigation of complaints against its members and the body itself; and the provision by eligible persons of indemnity insurance and similar arrangements to meet claims arising from company audit work (paras 10–13). The Councils of the three Institutes of Chartered Accountants in the British Isles published a "Guide to Professional Ethics" in 1992, which deals with a number of these matters. The amended version of this Guide was superseded by the publication of five Ethical Standards (ESs) by the APB in December 2004, which take account of EU requirements and IAASB statements on ethics. Amongst the matters covered by the ESs are: procedures to be adopted by auditing firms to ensure independence; rotation of partners involved with an audit after a period of five years; prohibiting firms from undertaking audits on a contingent fee basis; and ensuring that no client's fees account for more than 10 per cent of the auditing firm's revenues.

RSBs must also have rules requiring eligible persons to comply with ss 35 and 36 of the 1989 Act, respectively dealing with disclosure of auditors' names in a

---

[2] The Companies (Audit, Investigations and Community Enterprise) Act 2004, ss1–2, amended Sch.11 to the 1989 Act to require RSBs to comply with independent auditing standards, monitoring and disciplinary procedures.

register and information about firms eligible for appointment as company auditors; have satisfactory arrangements for meeting the costs of complying with their rules; and be able and willing to promote higher standards of integrity in company audit work.

Under s.47 of the 1989 Act and Sch.14, an RSB's rules and other guidance have to be submitted to the Director General of Fair Trading before recognition is granted so that he can assess whether they will restrict or prevent competition.

Professional qualifications

Effectively, the 1989 Act requires that auditors should hold an appropriate qualification granted by a *Recognised Qualifying Body* (RQB), approved by the Secretary of State under s.32 of the Companies Act 1989. The procedure for recognition is similar to that for an RSB (Sch.12 to the Act, paras 1–3). Basically, the qualification must only be open to persons who have attained university entrance level or have at least seven years of professional experience; and who have passed an examination and have completed at least three years' practical training (Sch.12, paras 4–9).[3]

The Secretary of State's powers and penalties for offences

The Secretary of State has powers under the 1989 Act with respect to RSBs and RQBs to provide for the payment of fees (s.45); to otherwise regulate them (ss 37–40); and to delegate his powers to a separate body (ss 46 and 46A and Sch.13).[4] Moreover, penalties are specified in the Act for giving false or misleading information (ss 41–44).

Eligibility of partnerships

Prior to the 1989 Act, partnerships and corporate bodies could not be appointed as auditors, only individuals. However, the Act now specifically provides that a firm may be appointed as a company auditor and that the liability of individuals (though not of firms) in professional indemnity claims can be limited (ss 25–26 and Sch.11, paras 4–5 and 7).

Ineligibility to act as an auditor

Section 27 of the Companies Act 1989 defines the circumstances in which a person is ineligible for appointment as a statutory auditor on the grounds of lack of independence—namely, if he is an officer or employee of the company or a parent or subsidiary undertaking, or a partner or employee of such a person; or if there is a connection between him or any associate of his and the group of companies. Further guidance on these matters is given in APB's Ethical Standards (above, p.462).

Acting as a statutory auditor when ineligible is an offence, and under s.28 the guilty party is liable to a fine on conviction. However, it is a defence to show that

---

[3] The Companies (Audit, Investigations and Community Enterprise) Act 2004, s.6, amended s.33 of the 1989 Act providing greater flexibility with respect to the recognition and removal of recognition of overseas auditing qualifications.

[4] The Companies (Audit, Investigations and Community Enterprise) Act 2004, ss 3–5, inserted s.46A into the 1989 Act and amended Sch.13 to empower the Secretary of State to delegate various supervisory functions to an independent regulator, such as the FRC (above, p.412).

there was no knowledge and no reason to believe that the person concerned was ineligible. When a person becomes ineligible, he should vacate office and give notice in writing to the company that he has resigned.

Where a company audit has been carried out by an ineligible person, the Secretary of State may under s.29 direct that an eligible person be appointed, either to undertake a second audit or to review the first audit and report whether a second audit is needed. The company must comply within 21 days or face being fined. The company is entitled to recover costs incurred complying with these provisions if the ineligible person knew he was ineligible.

APPOINTMENT OF AUDITORS

Except where a company:

(a) is dormant;

(b) is a private company electing to dispense with the laying of accounts; or

(c) is exempt from having to have a statutory audit (below, p.472)

auditors will be appointed at a general meeting where the company's accounts are laid (s.384 of the 1985 Act). Moreover, except again where a private company elects to dispense with the laying of accounts, a company must appoint an auditor at each general meeting where accounts are laid until the next such meeting. However, the first auditors may be appointed by the directors before the first general meeting at which accounts are laid, or—failing action by them—by the company in general meeting (s.385).

Where a private company has elected in accordance with s.252 to dispense with the laying of accounts[5] and is not exempt from statutory audit requirements, auditors must be appointed by the company at a general meeting held within four weeks of accounts for the previous year being sent to members under s.238[6]; or, where such a meeting was held, the conclusion of a general meeting at which accounts for the previous year were laid. Such auditors hold office until the next date at which an appointment falls due. In the case of the first auditors of a private company taking advantage of an election under s.252, the directors (rather than the company in general meeting) can exercise the power of appointment, failing which the company in general meeting will appoint (s.385A).

Private companies may by elective resolution under s.379A opt to dispense with the obligation to appoint auditors annually, in which case the existing auditors will, so long as the election continues, be deemed to have been reappointed unless either the company is a dormant company or a resolution is passed ending the appointment (s.386).

Where no auditors are appointed, a company shall within a week of the term of such an appointment elapsing give notice to the Secretary of State so that he

---

[5] Above, pp.419–420.
[6] Above, pp.420–421.

can fill the vacancy. Failure to give such notice renders the defaulting company and its officers liable to be fined (s.387).

A company's directors or the company in general meeting are empowered to fill a casual vacancy for the office of auditor. Where this is done by the company in general meeting, special notice is required, as it is when an auditor appointed to fill a casual vacancy by the directors is subject to reappointment by the company in general meeting. Copies of such notice have to be sent to the auditor concerned and to his predecessor if he resigned (s.388).

A company which is *dormant* under the provisions of s.250 of the 1985 Act[7] is exempt from the obligation to appoint auditors (s.388A(1)). To qualify as dormant, a company must either have been dormant since its formation or have been dormant since the end of the previous financial year. In the latter case it must also meet the following conditions: (i) it is classed as a small company; and (ii) it is not required to prepare group accounts (s.249AA(1)–(2)). It must additionally not have engaged in any significant accounting transaction other than the receipt of monies for its shares from subscribers to the memorandum of association during the period in question (s.249AA (4)–(7)). Dormant companies are subject to the provisions of s.249B(2)–(5), which give members holding 10 per cent or more in nominal value terms of the company's share capital the right to demand an audit.

Where a company ceases to be dormant, the directors may appoint auditors to hold office until the next meeting at which accounts are to be laid. Alternatively, if the company elects under s.252 to dispense with laying accounts, they may either appoint auditors within 28 days of the annual accounts being sent to members under s.238; or, if a shareholder gives notice requiring the laying of accounts at a general meeting, at the beginning of that meeting. If the directors fail to exercise such powers, they may be exercised by the company in general meeting (s.388A(2)–(5)).

VACATION OF OFFICE BY AUDITORS

Removal and resignation of auditors

A company may, by ordinary resolution, *remove* an auditor before his period of office has expired and notwithstanding any agreement with him. Where he is so removed, the company must give notice in a prescribed form within two weeks, failing which both it and the defaulting officers are liable to a fine. An auditor so removed retains his rights to compensation or damages in respect of the termination of his appointment; and he is also entitled under s.390 of the 1985 Act to receive all communications relating to general meetings when his term of office would normally expire or at which it is proposed to appoint his successor, and to attend and be heard at such meetings (s.391).

Special notice is required for a resolution removing an auditor or appointing his successor, and such notice must be forwarded to the parties concerned. The auditor who is being removed or who is resigning may make representations of

---

[7] See above, p.453, for the necessary conditions.

reasonable length to the company which, if requested, must circulate them with the resolution, failing which the auditor may require them to be read out at the meeting. However, application may be made to the court by the company or other aggrieved party, and if such representations are deemed to be needlessly defamatory they need not be circulated or be read out at the meeting. In such circumstances, the court may require the auditor to pay some or all of the costs involved (s.391A).

An auditor may *resign* by depositing notice in writing at a company's registered office, but under s.394 it must be accompanied by a statement indicating whether or not there are any special circumstances leading to such action. The auditor's period of office ends when such notice is lodged, unless it specifies another date. The company must deliver a copy of the notice to the Registrar within a fortnight of its being lodged at the registered office, failing which the company and its defaulting officers are liable to a fine (s.392).

When an auditor's resignation letter is accompanied by a statement of circumstances leading to such action, as required by s.394, he may deposit a signed requisition calling on the directors to convene an extraordinary general meeting to receive such a statement and other explanations he may wish to give. He may also request the company to circulate a written explanation of reasonable length concerning the circumstances before such a meeting is convened, or before a meeting at which his term of office would normally have expired. The company must indicate in the notice of the meeting that such a statement has been made and circulate it to members of the company. The directors must convene a meeting within three weeks of the requisition being lodged, and it must be held within four weeks of the date of the notice of the meeting being given. Failure to do so renders every director who did not take reasonable steps to secure compliance liable to a fine. If the statement is not circulated, the auditor may require it to be read out at the meeting. However, application may be made to the court by the company or other aggrieved party, and if such representations are deemed to be needlessly defamatory they need not be circulated or be read out at the meeting. In such circumstances, the court may require the auditor to pay some or all of the costs involved (s.392A).

Where a private company by s.386 has elected to dispense with the annual appointment of an auditor, any member can deposit up to one notice in writing in each financial year at its registered office proposing that the appointment shall be terminated. The directors must then hold a general meeting within four weeks at which a resolution shall be put concerning the termination of the auditor's appointment. If the decision is to end the appointment, the auditor shall be deemed not to be reappointed when next he would be. Moreover, if notice was lodged within a fortnight of the accounts being circulated, any deemed reappointment that has taken place will be invalid. Where the directors fail to take steps to convene a general meeting within a fortnight of a member depositing notice, he may himself convene such a meeting, being reimbursed by the company for his expenses. The company in turn may then recoup them from the defaulting directors. However, no compensation or damages are payable directly as a result of such termination of appointment, although an agreement between the company and the auditor may still provide for compensation for loss of office (s.393).

Statement by a person ceasing to hold office as auditor

A person who for any reason has ceased to hold office as auditor is required to deposit at the company's registered office within specified periods a statement detailing any circumstances connected with his departure which he considers should be brought to members' or creditors' attention. Where the auditor considers there are no such circumstances, the statement should indicate that fact. However, where there are such circumstances, the company must either send copies of the statement to those persons entitled to receive copies of the accounts under s.238[8] or alternatively apply to the court, in which case the auditor must be informed. For his part, the auditor must send a copy of his statement to the Registrar within four weeks of depositing it with the company, unless he receives notice within three weeks that the company has applied to the court. If the court is satisfied that the auditor is needlessly using his statement for defamatory purposes, it will direct that copies of it should not be circulated and may order the auditor to pay some or all of the costs involved. Moreover, the company will have to circulate another statement indicating the effect of the court's order. If, however, the court is not satisfied that the auditor's statement is vexatious, the company must circulate it within 14 days and notify the auditor, who will then send a copy to the Registrar within a week of being so informed (s.394).[9]

The specified periods within which a statement under s.394 should be deposited at a company's registered office are as follows:

- resignation: to be deposited together with the notice of resignation forwarded to the company under s.392.

- failure to seek reappointment: to be deposited not less than 14 days before the end of the time allowed for next appointing auditors.

- in any other case: to be deposited within 14 days of the auditor ceasing to hold office (s.394(2)).

An individual auditor or a partnership acting as auditors are guilty of an offence if they breach the provisions of s.394, although it is a defence to show all reasonable steps were taken to comply. For its part, the company and every defaulting officer is liable to a fine.

THE LEGAL POSITION OF AUDITORS

The auditor is not a person included in the definition of "officer" in s.744 of the 1985 Act. However, he is an officer of the company for the purpose of a misfeasance summons under s.212 of the Insolvency Act 1986[10] and for the

---

[8] Above, pp.420–421.

[9] Whether such a statement is defamatory has been considered in *Jarvis plc v Pricewaterhouse Coopers (a firm)* (2000) *New Law Journal* 1109.

[10] *Re London and General Bank* [1895] 2 Ch. 166 (C.A.). s.212 of the Insolvency Act 1986 replaces s.631 of the 1985 Companies Act; it is dealt with above, p.320.

purpose of offences under ss 206–211 and 218 of that same Act[11] (which are also concerned with offences by officers of companies in liquidation). An auditor is presumably an officer for the purpose of the Theft Act 1968, s.19,[12] which is concerned with false statements by an officer of a body corporate, but an auditor appointed *ad hoc* for a limited purpose (*e.g.* appointed by the directors for a private audit) is not an officer.[13]

Under s.434(4) an auditor is specifically identified as an agent of the company for the purpose of an investigation into its affairs,[14] and he may be examined on oath by an inspector. Otherwise the auditor is not (in the absence of a special contract) an agent of the company, and his normal certificate as to whether the accounts represent a true and fair view of the company's affairs under s.235 cannot constitute an acknowledgement by an agent for the purposes of the Limitation Act 1980.[15]

An auditor is treated in the same way as an officer by ss 310 (provisions relieving officers and auditors from liability) and 727 (relief of officers and auditors).[16]

REMUNERATION OF AUDITORS

The remuneration of the auditor of a company appointed by the directors or by the Secretary of State is fixed by the directors or by the Secretary of State, as the case may be. In any other case it is fixed by the company in general meeting or as the company in general meeting may determine. "Remuneration" includes sums paid by the company in respect of his expenses (s.390A).

The auditor's remuneration (including expenses paid by the company) must be separately disclosed in the profit and loss account or in a note thereto (s.390A(3)–(4)).[17]

A company is also required under s.390B and SI 1991/2128 to disclose in a note to the accounts remuneration received by its auditors for non-audit work, including benefits in kind and expenses. Such disclosures relate not only to the company's auditor but to his associates; and to associated undertakings of the company. The auditors are also obliged to supply the company's directors with the necessary information for inclusion in the note to the accounts.

The Companies (Audit, Investigations and Community Enterprise) Act 2004, s.7, has amended s.390A and substituted s.390B, empowering the Secretary of State to make regulations which require disclosure not only of remuneration for audit and non-audit services, but also of the nature of those services.

---

[11] ss 206–211 and 218 of the Insolvency Act 1986 replace ss 624–629 and 632 of the 1985 Companies Act.
[12] Not applicable to Scotland. See below, p.480.
[13] *R. v Shacter* [1960] 2 Q.B. 252 (C.C.A.).
[14] Above, pp.382, 386.
[15] *Re Transplanters (Holding Co.) Ltd.* [1958] 1 W.L.R. 822.
[16] Above, pp.314–315; and below, p.477.
[17] Above, p.345.

THE AUDITORS' REPORT[18]

1. Report addressed to the members

The auditors must report *to the members*[19] on the annual accounts to be laid before the company in general meeting during their terms of office (s.235(1) of the 1985 Act).

2. Content of the report

The report must state[20]:

(a) whether in the auditors' opinion the annual accounts have been properly prepared in accordance with the Companies Act 1985;

(b) whether in their opinion a true and fair view is given:

  (i) in the case of an individual balance sheet, of the state of affairs of the company at the end of its financial year;

  (ii) in the case of an individual profit and loss account, of the profit or loss of the company for the financial year; and

  (iii) in the case of group accounts, of the state of affairs at the end of the financial year, and the profit and loss for the financial year, of the undertakings included in the consolidation as a whole, so far as concerns the members of the company (s.235(2)).

(c) whether they are of the opinion that the information given in the directors' report for the financial year for which the annual accounts are prepared is consistent with those accounts (s.235(3)).

If the auditors think that proper accounting records or returns have not been kept or received, or that the balance sheet and (unless framed as a consolidated profit and loss account) the profit and loss account are not in agreement with the accounting records and returns, they must state that fact in the report (s.237(2)). Further, if auditors fail to obtain all the information and explanations which, to the best of their knowledge and belief, are necessary for their audit, they must state that fact in the report (s.237(3)). The auditors are also required to make statements in their report if they believe information given in the directors' report is inconsistent with that given in the accounts (s.253(3)); and where directors have taken advantage of the provisions of s.248 exempting a small or

---

[18] See also pp.452–453, above.

[19] The exact terms would normally be established in formal engagement letters, on the form of which professional guidance is available. Following the decision in *Royal Bank of Scotland v Bannerman Johnstone Maclay (a firm) and Another* (2002), *Times Law Reports*, August 1 2002, auditors have altered the wording of their reports to make it clear that third parties (such as lending bankers) should not rely on the audit opinion.

[20] In the case of banking and insurance companies, the auditor has to ensure that the accounts comply with, and reflect a true and fair view with respect to, the provisions of Schs 9 and 9A rather than Sch.4. See ss 255 and 255A, above, pp.454–455.

medium-sized group from preparing group accounts when not entitled to do so (s.237(4A)).

If the requirements of Sch.6 are not complied with in the accounts (*i.e.* concerning directors' emoluments; and details of loans and other credit transactions favouring directors and officers), it is the auditors' duty to include in their report, so far as they are reasonably able to do so, a statement giving the required information (s.237(4)). The APB also issued guidance in 2002 indicating that auditors of listed companies should include in their report an opinion as to whether the "auditable part" of the directors' remuneration report required by SI 2002/1986 (above, pp.287 and 436) has been properly prepared in accordance with legislative requirements.

3. Signing of the auditors' report

The auditors' report and the copy delivered to the Registrar must state the names of the auditors and be signed by them and be dated. Similarly, all copies of the report laid before the company in general meeting or otherwise circulated must state the names of the auditors, and the penalty for default of these provisions is a fine (s.236, as amended by SI 2004/2947).

4. The duties of auditors in relation to the audit report

In preparing their report the auditors must carry out certain investigations, namely those which will enable them to form an opinion as to:

(a) whether proper accounting records have been kept by the company and proper returns adequate for their audit have been received from branches not visited by them;
(b) whether the company's individual accounts are in agreement with the records and returns (s.237(1)).

Guidance on how such investigations should be undertaken is given in the APB's Statements of Auditing Standards (SASs) and the corresponding ISAs (see p.462). These deal with matters including: the general principles of auditing; fraud and error; going concern; engagement letters; subsequent events; materiality; audit risk assessment; audit evidence; analytical procedures; audit of accounting estimates; audit sampling; management representations; overall review of financial statements; considering the work of internal auditors; the relationship between principal auditors and other auditors; auditors' report on financial statements; imposed limitation of scope; reports to directors and management; and the auditors' right and duty to report to regulators in the financial sector. Further advice is available concerning the verification of debts; stocks and work in-progress; the implications where goods have been sold subject to reservation of title; and ascertaining contingent liabilities.

The standard audit report required in the SAS "Auditors' reports on financial statements" and the corresponding ISA describe the respective responsibilities of directors and auditors; and the basis of the opinion expressed and the key features of the audit process. In addition, it indicates that auditors should draw attention to the inherent uncertainties that they consider to be fundamental. The SAS and the corresponding ISA also give a number of examples of model audit reports, the wording of which is now normally followed.

The auditors perform their duty to the members by forwarding their report to the secretary. They are not responsible if the report is not put before the members.[21] However, in an Australian case it was held that they must pay due regard to the possibility of fraud and must warn the appropriate level of management promptly and without waiting for the general meeting to report to the shareholders.[22]

The articles cannot preclude the auditors from availing themselves of all the information to which they are entitled as material for their report.[23]

5. Qualified reports

Section 235(2A) and 240(3) (as substituted and amended by SI 2004/2947) indicate that an auditors' report must be either qualified or unqualified; and it must also refer to any matters to which the auditors wish to draw attention by way of emphasis without going so far as to qualify their report.

The SAS on "Auditors' reports on financial statements" and the corresponding ISA indicate that such reports should contain a clear expression of opinion on the financial statements and on any further matters required by statute or other requirements applicable to the particular engagement. A qualified opinion should be issued either when there is a limitation on the scope of the auditors' examination; or when the auditors disagree with the treatment or disclosure of a matter in the financial statements. However, in either case, in order to give a qualified opinion the effect of the matter should be material so that the financial statements do not give a true and fair view of the matters on which the auditors are required to report or do not comply with relevant accounting or other requirements.

An *adverse opinion*, stating that the accounts do not give a true and fair view, should be issued when the effect of a disagreement is so material or pervasive that the auditors conclude that the financial statements are seriously misleading. Where the effect of a disagreement is not so significant as to require an adverse opinion, an opinion should be expressed that is qualified by stating that the financial statements give a true and fair view except for the effects of the matter giving rise to disagreement.

A *disclaimer of opinion* should be expressed when the possible effect of a limitation on scope is so material or pervasive that the auditors have been unable to obtain sufficient evidence to support an opinion on the financial statements. However, where the auditors conclude that the possible effect of the limitation is not so significant to require a disclaimer, they should issue an opinion that is qualified by stating that the financial statements give a true and fair view except for the effects of any adjustments that might have been found necessary had the limitation not affected the evidence available to them.

[21] *Re Allen, Craig & Co (London) Ltd.* [1934] Ch. 483.
[22] *Pacific Acceptance Corpn. Ltd. v Forsyth* (1970) 92 W.N. (N.S.W) 29.
[23] *Newton v Birmingham Small Arms Co. Ltd.* [1906] 2 Ch. 378.

6. Special audit reports

(A) Banking and insurance companies

Banking and insurance companies prepare their accounts under the special provisions of Schs 9 and 9A.[24] However, the auditors of banks and insurance companies have a wider responsibility than in an audit of an ordinary commercial company, and under ss 39 and 47 of the Banking Act 1987 and 21A of the Insurance Companies Act 1982 they have a duty, not only to report to members, but to the relevant regulators as well (*i.e.* the Bank of England and the FSA respectively). This may include vetting specific returns that have to be made to the regulatory authorities.

(B) Small and medium-sized companies

If the company qualifies as a small or medium sized company, the directors may choose to file abbreviated accounts (above, pp.418–419, 424–426). In such circumstances, unless the company is exempt from having to have a statutory audit (see below) or is dormant (above, pp.483), the auditors must attach to the filed accounts a signed special report stating that the company is entitled to deliver abbreviated accounts and that such accounts have been properly prepared. The auditors' report required under s.235 (*i.e.* for the full accounts to be presented to shareholders in general meeting) need not be filed. However, if it is qualified or includes a statement that the accounting records or explanations given are inadequate, such a report must be included within the special report (s.247B).

(C) Small company exemption from having a statutory audit

Under s.249A a company (other than a charitable company) which qualifies as small under s.246 (above, pp.418–419, 424–426) and whose annual turnover and balance sheet totals respectively do not exceed £5.6m and £2.8m is exempt from the statutory audit requirement. The exemption applies to around two thirds of companies preparing annual accounts.[25] However, a small company is not exempt if 10 per cent or more of its members demand a full statutory audit (s.249B(2)). Where a company takes advantage of the exemption, its directors have to make a statement on its balance sheet which *inter alia* acknowledges the directors' responsibility for ensuring that proper accounting records are kept; and for preparing accounts which comply with the Companies Act 1985 and which give a true and fair view of the state of affairs of the company at the end of its financial year and of its profit or loss for that period (s.249B(4)(5)).

---

[24] Above, pp.454–455.
[25] Small charitable companies with annual turnovers over £90,000 but below £250,000 have to have a *compilation report* prepared by an independent accountant if they choose not to have a statutory audit. The compilation report has to state whether, in the independent accountant's opinion, the accounts agree with the accounting records; and whether, on the basis of the information in the accounting records, they have been drawn up in accordance with the provisions of the Companies Act 1985: ss 249A(3A)(4); 249C; 249D.

(D) Summary financial statements

Another special report must be made when a summary financial statement is circulated by a listed company under the provisions of s.251. This should indicate:

(i)   whether in the auditors' opinion such statement

    (a)   is consistent with its full accounts and the directors' report; and

    (b)   complies with the requirements of s.251 and the regulations relating to summary financial statements; and

(ii) whether the auditors' report on the full accounts was qualified, and if so setting out that report together with further material necessary to understand the qualification (s.251(4)).[26]

(E) Profits available for distribution

Under s.270(2) of the 1985 Act, in order to determine whether a company has profits available for distribution,[27] and (if it is a public company) under s.264(1) to confirm that a distribution will not reduce the amount of the company's net assets below the aggregate of its called-up share capital plus its undistributable reserves, reference must be made to certain items in the company's *relevant accounts*. Under s.270(3) such accounts will normally be the company's latest audited financial statements laid before the company in general meeting, but where necessary interim accounts or initial accounts must be prepared.[28]

With respect to the auditors, the annual accounts (where used as the relevant accounts) must be accompanied by the auditors' report required under s.235 (s.271(3)); while any initial accounts, where used, must be accompanied by a report of the auditors in which they state whether in their opinion they have been properly prepared (s.273(4)). Interim accounts, where used, need not be subjected to an audit. With regard to the annual or initial accounts, where the auditors' report is qualified, it must be stated in writing whether the qualification is material in determining the legality of the proposed distribution (ss 271(3),(4); 273(4),(5)).

In the case where the annual accounts are used as the relevant accounts, the statement will be laid before the shareholders in general meeting; whereas in the case where the initial accounts are used as the relevant accounts, the statement together with the accounts and audit report will merely have to be filed with the Registrar of Companies. It should be noted, incidentally, that a material qualification in this context can be either favourable or unfavourable in terms of the proposed distribution.

In the case of an insurance company with long term business covered by s.268 of the Act (*e.g.* a life insurance company) the amount of distributable profits is effectively determined by an actuarial valuation.[29]

---

[26] However, if the full report is unqualified it must not be published with non-statutory accounts.
[27] Below, Ch.22.
[28] See below, pp.489–490, for further discussion of the *relevant accounts*.
[29] Above, pp.453–454, and below, pp.487–489.

(F) Accountants' reports for creditors

As mentioned above, the audit report is addressed to members of the company (*i.e.* its shareholders), for whose benefit indeed the statutory accounts are basically prepared. It is therefore the case that, except in specific circumstances where they are with the auditors' knowledge referring to the accounts and the auditors' report for a specific purpose (below, pp.479–480), third parties cannot rely on them in helping to reach a particular decision. As was made clear in an investigation into the affairs of an Australian company,[30] this is even true of creditors, including debenture stock holders. It may therefore be necessary for such parties, with the company's approval, to commission their own audit (if necessary by different accountants from those employed by the company to undertake the statutory audit).

(G) Accountants' reports to management

A company's statutory auditors may similarly undertake specific investigations which exceed their responsibilities in respect of a company's statutory accounts and their report on them to the shareholders under s.235—for example, with respect to the records, systems and internal control that have been examined in the course of the statutory audit. In such circumstances, the letters of engagement should clearly specify the extent of such supplementary investigations.

(H) Reports for prospectuses and on bid forecasts

Accountants will also be commissioned to write reports in connection with the issue of listing particulars or a prospectus (above, Ch.7), and professional guidance on the conduct of such investigations has been issued, including two Statements of Investment Circular Reporting Standards (SIRs) by the Auditing Practices Board (APB, with more due to be published in the future).

(I) Special reports under the Companies Acts

Special reports are also required from auditors under company legislation in the following circumstances:

	Companies Act 1985
• Re-registration of a private company as a public company	s.43(3)(b)
• Allotment of shares by a public company otherwise than for cash	s.103(1)
• Transfer of non-cash assets to a public company by a member of the company	s.104(4)(b)

[30] See E. Stamp, "The Reid Murray Affair", *Accountancy* (August 1964).

- Redemption or purchase by a private company of its own shares out of capital   s.173(5)

- Financial assistance for acquisition of a private company's own shares   s.156(4)

(J) Agreed valuations of private companies

As explained in Ch.13, articles of private companies often provide that a member who wants to sell his shares must first offer them to the existing members at a price to be fixed by the auditors. Similar provisions are often applicable in the case of a member's death. In such circumstances case law has established grounds under which the valuation can be set aside and/or the auditors may be liable in negligence.

(K) Preliminary announcements and interim reports

The *Listing Rules* require that preliminary announcements of quoted companies' annual results should be agreed with their auditors. The APB has therefore issued guidance for auditors dealing with such announcements and with interim reports.

Powers of Auditors

(A) Rights to inspect books and receive explanations

The auditors have a right of access at all times to the books and accounts and vouchers of the company, and they are entitled to require from the officers and employees of the company and its subsidiaries such information and explanations as they think necessary for the performance of their duties as auditors (s.389A).[31] However, they cannot require the information to be furnished in any particular form or that it should be certified in some way, as by the board of directors. There is no power to require the information to be supplied in writing, but auditors can reasonably say that they are not in a position to perform their duties without making further inquiries if they are asked to act on unrecorded oral statements. If proper information is not given, the auditors' remedy is to qualify their report.

If an officer or employee of the company or any of its UK subsidiaries makes a misleading or false statement to the auditors, he is liable to imprisonment and/or a fine (s.389B, as substituted by the Companies (Audit, Investigations and Community Enterprise Act 2004, s.8).

---

[31] s.389A was substituted by the Companies (Audit, Investigations and Community Enterprise) Act 2004, s.8. The right to seek information and explanations is in part necessary to enable auditors to obtain particulars of the directors' emoluments, including expenses charged to tax and benefits in kind, which may not be ascertainable from an examination of the books: above, pp.436, 453.

(B) Rights to attend general meetings

Auditors have the right to attend any general meeting of the company and to receive the same notices of general meetings as the members, and to be heard at any general meeting on any part of the business which concerns them as auditors (s.390).

Where for a private company those entitled to attend and vote at a meeting agree under s.381A a resolution in writing without holding a meeting, the auditors are entitled to receive all relevant communications (s.381B(1)).

(C) Reliance on the work of subsidiary companies' auditors

The APB has published a Statement of Auditing Standards (SAS) and an International Standard on Auditing (ISA) concerning the reliance that can be placed on the work of other auditors in respect of group financial statements.

British subsidiaries and their auditors are required to give the parent company's auditors relevant information and explanations, in default of which they will be liable to a fine and possible criminal proceedings. Parent companies are equally required to obtain relevant information and explanations from overseas subsidiaries for the benefit of their auditors (s.389A). In practice, the consolidation of an overseas subsidiary's accounts may necessitate a formal qualification in the auditors' report (*e.g.* where it has complied with local rather than UK accounting requirements).

DUTIES OF AUDITORS

General duties

The duties of auditors depend on the terms of the articles as well as on the statutory provisions. They may be summarised as follows:

(1) They must acquaint themselves with their duties under the articles and the Act.[32]

(2) They must carry out their duties with respect to the auditors' report as outlined above. They must also ascertain and state the true financial position of the company by an examination of the books. This examination must be not merely to ascertain what the books show, but also to ascertain that the books show the true financial position.[33]

This is exemplified in the following judgements:

"The duty of the auditor . . . [is] . . .not to confine himself merely to the task of verifying the arithmetical accuracy of the balance sheet, but to inquire into its substantial accuracy, and to ascertain that it . . . was properly drawn up, so as to contain a true and correct representation of the state of the company's affairs": *per* Stirling J. in *Leeds Estate Co. v Shepherd* (1887) 36 Ch.D. 787 at p. 802.

---

[32] *Re Republic of Bolivia Exploration Syndicate Ltd.* [1914] 1 Ch. 139.
[33] *Per* Lindley L.J. in *Re London and General Bank (No. 2)* [1895] 2 Ch. 673 (C.A.) at pp. 682 *et seq.*

An auditor "is not to be written off as a professional 'adder-upper and subtractor'. His vital task is to take care to see that errors are not made, be they errors of computation, or errors of omission or commission, or downright untruths. To perform this task properly he must come to it with an inquiring mind—not suspicious of dishonesty, I agree—but suspecting that someone may have made a mistake somewhere and that a check must be made to ensure that there has been none": *per* Lord Denning in *Fomento (Sterling Area) Ltd. v Selsdon Fountain Pen Co. Ltd.* [1958] 1 W.L.R. 45 (H.L.) at p. 61.

The statutory duty of an auditor (*e.g.* to state whether in his opinion a true and fair view is given by the balance sheet and the profit and loss account) is a personal one, and if he adopts the opinion of the company's accountant, and he is sued by the company for wrongly stating that a true and fair view is given, it has been held in Australia that he has no cause of action against the accountant.[34]

(3) They must act honestly, and with reasonable care and skill, as the following observations make clear:

"An auditor is not bound to be a detective, or . . . to approach his work . . . with a foregone conclusion that there is something wrong. He is a watchdog, but not a bloodhound. He is justified in believing tried servants of the company in whom confidence is placed by the company . . . If there is anything calculated to excite suspicion he should probe it to the bottom; but in the absence of anything of that kind he is only bound to be reasonably cautious and careful": *per* Lopes L.J. in *Re Kingston Cotton Mill Co. (No. 2)* [1896] 2 Ch. 279 (C.A.) at p. 288.

"It is the duty of an auditor to bring to bear on the work he has to perform that skill, care and caution which a reasonably competent, careful, and cautious auditor would use. What is reasonable skill, care and caution must depend on the particular circumstances of each case. An auditor . . . is not bound to do more than exercise reasonable care and skill in making inquiries . . . He is not an insurer; he does not guarantee that the books do correctly show the true position of the company's affairs . . . he must be honest . . Where there is nothing to excite suspicion very little inquiry will be reasonably sufficient . . . Where suspicion is aroused more care is obviously necessary; but, still, an auditor is not bound to exercise more than reasonable care and skill, even in a case of suspicion . . ." : *per* Lindley L.J. in *Re London and General Bank (No. 2)* [1895] 2 Ch. 673 (C.A.) at p. 683.

If directors do not allow auditors time to conduct such investigations as are necessary in order to make the statements required to be contained in their report, the auditors must either refuse to make a report or make an appropriately qualified report. They are not justified in making a report containing a statement the truth of which they have not had an opportunity of ascertaining.[35]

Auditors cannot be relieved from liability for any breach of duty by any provision in the articles or any contract (s.310), but in certain circumstances they may obtain relief from the court (s.727).[36]

---

[34] *Dominion Freeholders Ltd. v Aird* [1966] 2 N.S.W.R. 293 (C.A.), distinguishing *Hedley Byrne & Co. Ltd. v Heller & Partners Ltd.* [1964] A.C. 465.

[35] *Per* Pennycuick J. in *Re Thomas Gerrard* [1968] Ch. 455, at p. 477.

[36] Above, pp.314–315, 468.

Specific duties

(A) Grounds for suspicion

It may be that entries in or omissions from the books ought to make the auditors suspicious. In such a case they must make full investigations into the suspicious circumstances, but they are not liable for "not tracking out ingenious and carefully laid schemes of fraud when there is nothing to arouse their suspicion".[37]

(B) Unauthorised borrowing

If payments are made or sums borrowed by the company, the auditors should see that they are authorised and made in accordance with the articles and the Act.[38]

(C) Existence of Securities

Auditors must satisfy themselves that securities owned by a company in fact exist and are in safe custody. This duty is discharged by their making a personal inspection of the securities in question. If, however, the securities are in the possession of a person who in the ordinary course of his business keeps securities for his customers (e.g. a banker) and that person is regarded as trustworthy, the auditors may safely accept his certificate that the securities are in his custody.[39]

(D) Existence of cash balances

Auditors must check the cash in hand and also the balance at the bank, by inspecting the pass book (or bank statement) or obtaining a certificate from the bank.[40]

(E) Stocks and work-in-progress

Auditors are under no duty to take stock,[41] but this is part of the wider question of the auditors' duty as to the value of the assets. However, the auditor must consider the effect of a reservation of title clause, where it exists, particularly where the stocks are unmixed goods (above, p.440).

Auditors are entitled to take the values of stocks and work-in-progress from the manager or other responsible official of the company, unless they have any reason to suppose them inaccurate.[42]

---

[37] per Lopes L.J. in Re Kingston Cotton Mill Co. (No. 2) [1896] 2 Ch. 279 (C.A.) at p. 290. However, in Re City Equitable Fire Insurance Co. Ltd. [1925] Ch. 407 (C.A.) it was held that there was no negligence on the part of the auditors because, although the transactions in question, when isolated, should have led them to conclude that fraud had taken place, they only formed only one item in a large audit.

[38] Thomas v Devonport Corpn. [1900] 1 Q.B. 16 (C.A.); and Re Republic of Bolivia Exploration Syndicate Ltd. [1914] 1 Ch. 139 at p. 171.

[39] Re City Equitable Fire Insurance Co. Ltd. [1925] Ch. 407.

[40] Fox & Son v Morrish, Grant & Co. (1918) 35 T.L.R. 126.

[41] Re Kingston Cotton Mill Co. (No. 2) [1896] Ch. 279 (C.A.).

[42] In Re Kingston Cotton Mill Co. (No. 2) [1896] Ch. 279 (C.A.) it was held that the auditors were entitled to rely on a certificate; but not in Re Thomas Gerrard & Son Ltd. [1968] Ch. 455, where the circumstances were not dissimilar, Pennycuick J. commenting (at p. 475): "The standards of reasonable care and skill are, upon the expert evidence, more exacting today than those which prevailed in 1896".

(F) Fixed assets

The duty of the auditors as to the value to be placed on fixed assets has previously been discussed (pp.439–440, 442). Apart from complying with the requirements of Sch.4 to the 1985 Act, if the auditors have formed an opinion that the assets are overvalued, they are bound to report it to the shareholders.[43]

(G) Policies of the company

Auditors are not concerned with the policy of the company or whether the company is well or ill managed.[44]

Liability to third parties

Apart from the auditor's contractual duty of care to the company, he owes a duty of care to third persons with whom he is not in contractual or fiduciary relationship if, as a reasonable man, he knows that he is being trusted or that his skill and judgment are being relied on, and he does not make it clear that he accepts no responsibility for information or advice which he gives.[45] For breach of this duty an action for negligence lies if damage results from the negligence.

The scope of this duty was originally defined by Lord Denning in *Candler v Crane, Christmas & Co.*[46] In subsequent cases on professional negligence three principles emerged. Thus in order for a claim by a third party to succeed, the event leading to a loss should be *foreseeable*; there should be *proximity* between the two parties (*i.e.* the third party should not be so remote that his interests would not reasonably have been considered at the time the supposedly negligent statement was made); and the supposedly defective advice had to be given as a normal part of the expert's business.

The question of proximity was left open. Should liability just extend to persons to whom auditors show the accounts and those to whom they knew the company would show them? Or should it also extend to a general class of persons whom the auditors ought reasonably to have foreseen at the time the accounts were prepared might rely on the accounts? In two cases involving takeovers the latter, broader view of proximity was taken (*JEB Fasteners Ltd. v Marks, Bloom, & Co.*[47] and *Twomax Ltd. v Dickson, McFarlane and Robinson*[48]), although it was held that the auditors would only be liable if reliance on the accounts caused loss to the other party. However, this view was rejected in another, landmark case (which also involved a takeover), *Caparo Industries plc v Dickman*,[49] where in a

---

[43] *Re London and General Bank (No. 2)* [1895] 2 Ch. 673 (C.A.).

[44] *Per* Lindley L.J. in *Re London and General Bank (No. 2)* [1895] 2 Ch. 673 (C.A.) at p. 682.

[45] *Hedley Byrne & Co. Ltd. v Heller & Partners Ltd.* [1964] A.C. 465, disapproving *Candler v Crane, Christmas & Co.* [1951] 2 K.B. 164 (C.A.). See also *Esso Petroleum Co. Ltd. v Mardon* [1976] 2 All E.R. 5 (C.A.), *Yianni v Edwin Evans & Sons* [1981] 3 All E.R. 592 and *Electra Private Equity Partners v KPMG Peat Marwick* [1998] P.N.L.R. 135.

[46] [1951] 2 K.B. 164 (C.A.) at p. 180.

[47] [1981] 3 All E.R. 289, affirmed [1983] 1 All E.R. 583.

[48] [1982] S.C. 113.

[49] [1990] 2 W.L.R. 358. The case also failed on grounds of foreseeability.

House of Lords decision the court preferred the narrow view of proximity as determining liability to third parties. Moreover, in a number of subsequent cases it is the narrow view that has prevailed.

Since then the court has also narrowed the potential third party liability of auditors by addressing the issue of *causation*. Thus in another case involving a takeover, *Galoo Ltd. v Bright, Grahame and Murray*,[50] it was held that negligence was not the dominant cause of the plaintiffs' loss, so consequently their case could not succeed.

What constitutes professional skill and judgment where a reporting accountant or auditor is potentially liable is an interesting point. For instance, it is quite possible—even likely, perhaps—that over time as a result of inflation, the conventional historical cost accounts of many companies might show an upward trend in profits, whereas under current cost accounting principles the trend might instead be downwards, which arguably could give a misleading impression to an interested party.[51] However, it would seem likely that adherence to generally accepted principles, as codified by the accountancy profession, would provide a reasonable defence in such circumstances—though in view of the jury's attitude in the Royal Mail case in relation to a prospectus, where accounting principles acceptable at that time were properly followed, it is not clear that this would be adequate defence in a criminal prosecution.[52]

More generally, legislation enacted in 1999 has enabled large firms of auditors to become "limited liability partnerships" (LLPs). This followed developments in the US where, however, state laws had also been altered to make liability proportional to blame. The effect has been to reduce drastically the number of negligence law suits filed against the Big Five (now the Big Four) multinational accounting firms, widely perceived as having "deep pockets". In a competitive environment this should be matched by a reduction in fees as the auditors' exposure to risk is reduced—but (perhaps unsurprisingly!) there has been no evidence of this.

---

[50] [1994] 1 All E.R. 16.
[51] For historical and current cost accounting rules, see p.439 *et seq.*, above.
[52] *R. v Kylsant* [1932] 1 K.B. 442 (C.C.A.). Potential criminal liability for auditors arises under ss 17-20 of the Theft Act 1968 (not applicable in Scotland).

Chapter 22

DIVIDENDS

INTRODUCTION

From an economic perspective, a listed company's distribution policy should be determined by the directors' investment strategy, since it should only retain those funds which will yield a risk-adjusted return greater than can be earned elsewhere by shareholders. At one extreme, therefore, a company which has identified many profitable investment projects would make no distributions at all.[1] Shareholders wishing to secure a cash income for a particular year would be able to sell off part of their holdings in order to realise some of the capital gain that will be reflected in the increasing value of their shares. At the other extreme, a company which has identified no profitable projects to justify reinvestment should logically distribute all its funds, including capital invested in the past. It can also be demonstrated that even the potential distortions introduced by the differential incidence of taxation can be substantially neutralised in the market, since certain types of investor prefer capital gains, while others will prefer dividend income.

There are, however, a number of complicating factors. Thus, for instance, listed companies seem to use the time trend of dividends as a signal of future likely prospects—*e.g.* a cut in dividend may reflect the directors' pessimism, and an increase their optimism.[2] Another factor is that many investors can only hold shares carrying trustee investment status, a condition of which is that dividends must be paid regularly.

The distribution policy for unlisted companies must take into account the fact that their shares are not readily marketable, and for private companies it may be preferable for tax purposes to distribute profits as directors' fees and salaries. However, for closely held companies (*i.e.* those whose shares are owned or controlled by a small group of persons), revenue law even deems that a certain amount of profits may be treated as distributed to shareholders, regardless of whether or not such dividend payments have been made.

But whatever the economic rationale may be, the law also has to take account of the existence of limited liability. Effectively this means the doctrine of (money) capital maintenance (above, Ch.9) must be applied so as to try to ensure a company's resources are not distributed so as to prejudice the interests of unsecured creditors. In fact, it is not possible to provide fully effective protection

---

[1] In so doing, it would also avoid the not insignificant costs of raising capital. This partly explains the popularity amongst listed companies of offering shareholders the option of taking dividends in cash or as scrip.

[2] For a readable discussion of the economic rationale for dividend payout policies, see Brealey, R. and Myers, S., *Principles of Corporate Finance* (7th ed.), McGraw-Hill, London, 2002.

to creditors in this way, but the general philosophy of money capital maintenance has nevertheless been behind the development of the law relating to the distribution of dividends as it has evolved over the past 150 years. However, in many of the cases around the turn of the century judges went out of their way not to impose unreasonable restrictions which might potentially lead to a misallocation of resources within the economy.[3]

In view of the underlying rationale behind the law in this area, the realised profits test introduced by the Companies Act 1980 can be viewed as a retrograde step. However, in practice it is unlikely to prove an effective constraint. In the rare cases in which companies might wish to distribute more than their accumulated realised profits, they could always convert unrealised gains into realised income by selling off assets (and, if necessary, buying or leasing them back); purchase their own shares under s.162 (above, Ch.10)[4]; or, as has happened on a number of occasions in recent years, apply to the court for a reduction of capital under s.135.

THE NATURE OF A DIVIDEND

Technically a dividend is the portion, received by a shareholder, of the company's profits legally available for dividend and divided among the members.[5] No express power to pay dividends is required in the memorandum or the articles, but under s.281 provisions in the articles or memorandum may restrict either the amounts available for distribution or the circumstances in which a distribution may be made. Sections 263(3) and 270(2) of the 1985 Act state that dividends must only be paid out of *accumulated realised profits* as reported in the statutory accounts.

Dividends should be distinguished from interest. Interest is a debt which, like all debts, is payable out of the company's assets generally. A dividend, however, is not a debt until it has been declared by the company.

Profits Available for Dividend

As mentioned above and in Ch.9, it is a fundamental principle of company law that a company's subscribed money capital (*i.e.* issued share capital plus share premium) be maintained. Paid-up capital must not be paid to the shareholders except by leave of the court or under strictly defined circumstances. It must be spent only upon the objects defined in the memorandum. Any other expenditure is *ultra vires* and reduces the fund available for the company's creditors in satisfaction of their claims.[6]

---

[3] See French, E. A., "The Evolution of the Dividend Law of England," in *Studies in Accounting* (3rd. ed., 1977), ed. Baxter, W. T., and Davidson, S., Institute of Chartered Accountants in England and Wales, London (pp. 306–331*)*.

[4] SI 2003/1116 inserted ss 162A—162G and 169A into the 1985 Act, allowing listed and AIM companies to hold and resell their own shares up to a limit of 10 per cent of the total number of the relevant class in issue. This enables a listed company to repurchase shares on the market and hold them in its "treasury".

[5] Under s.30(3)(b)(ii) of the Act, a company may be prohibited from paying a dividend.

[6] See, *per* Jessel M.R., in *Flitcroft's Case* (1882) 21 Ch.D. 519 (C.A.) at p. 533; and *Re Walters' Deed of Guarantee* [1933] Ch. 321. However, in *Quayle Munro Limited Petitioners*, 1991 G.W.D. 35–2104, [1994] B.C.L.C. 410, the Court approved a scheme for the cancellation of a company's share premium account which had the effect of converting the account into "distributable profits".

Prior to the 1980 Companies Act, in fact, there were no statutory provisions governing the funds available for distribution to the shareholders as dividend. The courts generally took the view that they should not interfere in the business decision making process unless there were good grounds for believing that the rights of certain interested parties were prejudiced. Unfortunately the decisions in a number of cases were often regarded as determining specific rules for distinguishing between on the one hand income, which could be applied for distributions, and on the other capital, which could not.[7] In the circumstances, accountants tended to follow a conservative interpretation of the law and for the most part took the view that only accumulated realised profits should be regarded as available for distribution.

The situation was clarified by the Companies Act 1980,[8] which included provisions (now ss 263–281 of the 1985 Act) requiring that the fund from which distributions can be made should be the accumulated *realised* profits of a company, and that these should be the profits shown in its statutory accounts. This effectively requires that a company's statutory accounts should only report realised profits as income, even though it might well be that to reflect its performance properly the income figure reported in the financial statements should include unrealised gains.

Under s.263(2) of the 1985 Act, the rules outlined below apply to all *distributions* made by a company; and a distribution is defined there as any payment of a company's assets to members of the company except:

(a)   an issue of bonus shares[9];

(b)   the redemption or purchase by a company of its own shares[10];

(c)   an authorised reduction of capital under s.135[11]; and

(d)   distributions on a winding up.

Under s.263(1) such *distributions* may only be made out of the profits available for that purpose.[11a] In fact, there are two tests to ascertain such profits. The first, the *realised profits test*, applies to all companies; the second, the *net assets test*, only to public companies.

It should be noted that with regard to a group, it is only the accumulated realised profits of the holding company that are available for distribution to shareholders of that company. Profits of a subsidiary can be transferred to the

---

[7] *e.g.* the "rules" that before 1980 in England it was neither necessary to charge depreciation nor to make good past trading losses when determining distributable profits. In fact, the judgements in the main supporting cases (*Lee v Neuchatel Asphalte Co.* (1889) 41 Ch.D. 1 (C.A.), and *Ammonia Soda Co. v Chamberlain* (1918) 1 Ch. 266 (C.A.) respectively) seem to have been very much dependent on the particular circumstances of the cases. For a general discussion of this point, see French, *op. cit.*

[8] Sections 39–45 of this Act implemented recommendations of the Jenkins Committee (1962, Cmnd., 1749, paras 335–350) and the EU's Second Council Directive on company law harmonisation.

[9] Below, p.493 *et seq.*

[10] Above, Ch.10.

[11] Above, Ch.9.

[11a] See *Clydebank Football Club Ltd v Steedman* 2002 S.L.T. 109, O.H.

holding company by declaration of dividends by that subsidiary. However, any part of such revenues receivable by the holding company cannot be regarded by it as available for distribution to its shareholders if it represents a return of part of the purchase price shown in the accounts as being the consideration paid for the subsidiary. Under the acquisition method of consolidating the group accounts, this effectively means that only the subsidiary's post-acquisition profits may be transferred for distribution, but under the merger method (where it is available— see pp.146–147 and Ch.20), all or some of the preacquisition profits may also be transferred for this purpose, depending respectively on whether the nominal value of shares issued by the holding company is less than or equal to the nominal value of the subsidiary company's shares acquired; or whether the nominal value of the shares issued is greater than the par value of shares acquired.

THE REALISED PROFITS TEST

A company's profits available for distribution are its accumulated realised profits (so far as not already distributed or capitalised[12]) less its accumulated realised losses (so far as not already written off by a proper reduction of capital) (s.263(3)). There is no attempt to distinguish between income and capital profits or losses—the only criterion is whether they are *realised*. Unrealised profits (*e.g.* on a revaluation upwards of an asset in the accounts which produces a gain) cannot be used: the gain must be realised (*i.e.* the asset must effectively be sold at arm's length).

Prior to 1980 a decision in a Scottish case[13] was in line with this principle, but one in a case in England was not.[14] Similarly under the provisions of the 1985 Act, realised losses (*e.g.* previous trading losses) must be deducted before a dividend can be declared (again in line with the decision in a Scottish case,[15] but not with that in an English one.[16] Unrealised profits cannot be used to pay up debentures or any amounts unpaid on issued shares (s.263(4)).

The notion of what is and is not a *realised* profit is specifically referred to in s.263(3) and defined in s.262(3) in the following terms:

> "references to 'realised profits' and 'realised losses' . . . are to such profits or losses . . . as fall to be treated as realised profits, in accordance with principles generally accepted, at the time when the accounts are prepared, with respect to the determination for accounting purposes of realised profits or losses."

This is hardly illuminating, and the few cases in tax law dealing with the question of realisation are not necessarily relevant in this context. Given that the notion of what is and is not a realised profit is a subtle one, which has caused some controversy amongst accountants, the professional accountancy bodies in

---

[12] Below, p.493.
[13] *Westburn Sugar Refineries Ltd. v Inland Revenue*, 1960 S.L.T. 297.
[14] *Dimbula Valley (Ceylon) Tea Co. Ltd. v Laurie* (1961) Ch. 353, 373.
[15] *Niddrie etc. Coal Co. Ltd. v Hurll* (1891) 18 R. 805.
[16] *Ammonia Soda Co. Ltd. v Chamberlain* (1918) 1 Ch. 266 (C.A.).

the British Isles issued guidance on the matter in March 2003.[17] Essentially this endorses guidance given previously in September 1982, reaching three conclusions:

(i) Accounting standards[18] would constitute evidence of generally accepted accounting principles and the profits calculated applying such standards should in general be regarded as "realised profits," even where the usual criteria for establishing "realisation" (such as receipt of cash, or the creation of a contractual obligation to pay a specific sum of money) are not met. This would mean, for instance, that the procedures of gradually recognising profits on long term contracts (above, p.441) and the inclusion in the profit and loss account of foreign currency translation gains and losses on net monetary items would both give rise to "realised profits".

(ii) Where no accounting standard is applicable a profit can be regarded as "realised" where the policy followed is consistent with the accruals concept and prudence doctrine outlined in Sch.4 to the Act.

(iii) Where necessary a company must, in order for its accounts to show a true and fair view of its financial performance and position, depart from accepted accounting principles and include an unrealised profit in its income statement. However, where this is done, para.15 of Sch.4 requires that a note should be given with the accounts indicating the nature of the departure, the reasons for it, and the effect.

Apart from these general considerations, realised profits and losses are, under s.280(3), all profits and losses, whether revenue (*i.e.* income) or capital, which are deemed to have been realised. It follows that when a company sells an undepreciated fixed asset (such as freehold land) which has been revalued in the accounts for consideration above its original cost, and the revaluation has been credited direct to reserves, the relevant part of the revaluation reserve has to be regarded as realised profit, even though it has never been credited to the profit and loss account.

Similar considerations relate to wasting fixed assets, although the provisions are more complex. Thus s.275 refers specifically to the question of depreciation provisions for such assets. Section 275(1) indicates that charges made to create or increase a depreciation provision in any one year are to be treated as realised losses, but under s.275(2) any additional depreciation charges made against an upward revaluation of the cost new of a similar asset do not have to be so treated, even though they will be reflected in the lower reported profit figure.

---

[17] "Guidance on the determination of realised profits and losses in the context of distributions under the Companies Act 1985". The March 2003 statement gives specific guidance with respect to a number of issues: *e.g.* the translation of foreign currencies, valuing securities at their current market values ("marking to market"), payments in kind ("top slicing"), and the treatment of positive and negative goodwill.

[18] The status of accounting standards has been examined in terms of clarifying the meaning of the phrase "a true and fair view" in the case of *Lloyd Cheyham and Co. Ltd. v Littlejohn and Co.* [1986] P.C.C. 389: above, pp.424 and 437 *et seq.*

In applying this latter provision, when there is no record of the original cost of an asset, or it cannot be obtained without unreasonable expense or delay, the calculations of any loss or gain in respect of that asset may be based on the earliest available record of its value since its acquisition by the company (s.275(3)). However, under s.275(1) a provision for a loss in value of one fixed asset cannot be offset against revaluation gains on other fixed assets unless *all* the company's fixed assets (other than goodwill) are revalued at the same time. Moreover, under s.275(4),(5) the valuation does not have to be formal: it is sufficient that the directors are satisfied, after *considering* the value of a fixed asset against the value of all the company's fixed assets; and that the aggregate value is not less than the aggregate value at which such fixed assets are stated in the accounts. But where the directors take advantage of such a procedure, they must disclose in the notes to the accounts:

(i) that they have considered the value of some of the company's fixed assets, without actually revaluing those assets;

(ii) that they are satisfied that the aggregate value of the fixed assets whose value has been considered is not less than their value as stated in the accounts; and

(iii) that the asset that has diminished in value is recorded in the accounts after providing for that decline in value (s.275(6)).

With regard to development costs, s.269 specifically requires that where they are capitalised and shown as assets in a company's accounts, they should nevertheless be treated as a realised loss for the purpose of calculating distributable profits, unless there are special circumstances, and the note required by para.20 of Sch.4 gives the reasons for treating such an item as an asset.

Under s.263(5), where a company's directors are unable to determine whether a profit or loss made before December 22, 1980, is realised or unrealised, they may treat the profit as realised and the loss as unrealised.

Finally, when a company makes a distribution of a non-cash asset (*e.g.* part of its undertaking on a demerger) any element of unrealised profits (*e.g.* on a revaluation) represented by those assets may be regarded as a realised profit (s.276). However, to make such a distribution the company has to be so empowered by its articles.[19] Moreover, the value attributed to the asset that is being distributed will have to be a fair value—*i.e.* generally its open market value in a transaction at arm's length.

THE NET ASSETS TEST

The realised profits test applies to all companies. A public company, however, is subject to a second, net assets, test. This means that even if it has profits available under the realised profits test, a public company may only make a distribution if, first, at the time the amount of its net assets is not less than the aggregate of its

---

[19] The current Table A contains such a power in Art.105: below, p.492.

called-up share capital and its undistributable reserves; and, secondly, the amount of the proposed distribution will not lower the amount of those assets to less than that aggregate (s.264(1)).

The effect of the net assets test is that, whereas a private company can make a distribution provided only that it has sufficient realised profits available, a public company can do so only if it has sufficient profits available after it has provided for any net unrealised losses.

A public company's *net assets* for this purpose are the aggregate of its assets less the aggregate of its liabilities, including any provision for liabilities or charges in the accounts (s.264(2)). Uncalled share capital[20] may not, however, be used as an asset for this purpose (s.264(4)).

The net assets must be measured against the *called-up share capital and undistributable reserves* of the company. The called up share capital is the aggregate amount of the calls made on its shares, whether or not they have been paid; any amount paid without being called; and any instalments due on the shares.[21] It is therefore more than the amount necessarily received by the company (s.737).

The undistributable reserves are those set out in s.264(3) of the 1985 Act:

(a) the share premium account[22];

(b) the capital redemption reserve[23];

(c) the excess of its accumulated unrealised profits over its accumulated unrealised losses, inasmuch as they have not previously been capitalised or written off, the only exception being a capitalisation resulting from a transfer of profits to capital redemption reserve on or after December 22, 1980; and

(d) any other reserve which cannot be distributed either by law (*e.g.* a revaluation reserve created under the alternative accounting rules: Sch.4, para.34[24]) or by the company's memorandum and articles.

INVESTMENT AND INSURANCE COMPANIES

It would be inappropriate to apply the rules outlined above to certain types of company, and this is recognised in ss 265–268 of the 1985 Act, which relate to investment companies and insurance companies with long-term (generally life assurance) business. Thus in the case of the former, it might well be that the value of the portfolio of an investment company has fallen and is below the aggregate of its called-up share capital and undistributable reserves, yet still be well in excess of its liabilities to third parties. In such circumstances the Act provides alternative rules for determining distributable profits to the two generally available to public companies described above.

[20] Above, p.140.
[21] Above, p.140.
[22] Above, p.145 *et seq.*
[23] Above, p.166.
[24] Above, Ch.20.

With regard to insurance companies, the natural time horizon of long-term insurance business stretches over a period of anything up to 40 years rather than 12 months, and the appropriate valuation to determine profits and surplus is therefore determined by actuaries. When valuing the assets of a particular insurance "fund", they use either current market values or compound interest to discount projected streams of premium and investment income to a present value. From their valuation of the assets they then deduct the corresponding discounted present value of projected payments to meet anticipated claims, thus deriving a "surplus" or "deficit". Increases in a surplus over time can be regarded as "profits" and decreases as "losses".

Investment companies

A company which qualifies under s.266 as an investment company (above, pp.453–454) can take advantage of the alternative test for assessing profits available for distribution outlined in s.265(1) and described below, but it must also satisfy the following conditions:

(a) its shares must be listed on a recognised stock exchange (s.265(4)(a));

(b) during the previous accounting reference period the company must not have distributed any of its capital profits, nor must it have applied any unrealised profits or any capital profits in paying up debentures or amounts unpaid on its issued shares (s.265(4)(a),(5)); and

(c) it must have given the necessary notice to the Registrar to qualify as an investment company under s.266 (s.265(6)).

Where these conditions are met, the alternative test of distributable profits prescribed under s.265(1) may be applied. This involves a realised profits test which, however, only applies to revenue and not to capital profits or losses; capital profits are thus excluded from the funds available for distribution. Moreover, for this purpose accumulated realised revenue profits are calculated as realised revenue profits less realised and unrealised revenue losses. The corresponding net assets test requires that the value of the assets must be at least 1.5 times the aggregate of the company's liabilities (including provisions) both before and after the proposed distribution. However, where a distribution by an investment company reduces the amount of its net assets below the aggregate of its called-up share capital and undistributable reserves, this fact must be disclosed in the notes to its financial statements (Sch.4, para.72(1)).[25]

Insurance companies

For an insurance company which qualifies as such under the provisions of the Insurance Companies Act 1982, and which carries on long term business, the profits and losses to be used in applying the general realised profits test described

[25] Above, Ch.20.

above on pp.484–486 are to be the result of amounts properly transferred to the profit and loss account of the company from surpluses or deficits on actuarial valuations. Moreover, any other profits or losses included in the company's profit and loss accounts are to be left out of account in applying the realised profits test (s.268).

RELEVANT ACCOUNTS

In deciding whether a company has distributable profits, reference must be made to its accounts. Moreover, in assessing whether a proposed dividend can properly be made, its effect on such accounts must be evaluated. For this purpose, where successive distributions are to be made by reference to one set of accounts, the amounts of the distributions, paid and proposed, must be accumulated (s.274). Under s.270(2) the items to be referred to in the relevant accounts are:

(a) profits, losses and liabilities;

(b) provisions (including those for depreciation); and

(c) share capital and reserves (including undistributable reserves).

Section 270(3), (4) of the Act identifies the relevant accounts for this purpose. The general rule is that they are the company's *last annual accounts* prepared in respect of the last preceding accounting reference period[26] (s.270(3)). However, in two cases other accounts may be used: first, such accounts as are necessary to enable a reasonable judgment to be made to determine distributable profits— these are referred to as *interim accounts;* and secondly, if the distribution is proposed during the company's first year before any annual accounts are prepared, such accounts as are necessary for a reasonable judgment to be made. These are referred to as *initial accounts* (s.270(4)).

The requirement that the *last annual accounts* must have been properly prepared in all material respects and in accordance with the Companies Act applies to all companies (*i.e.* including banking and insurance companies) (s.271(2)). The auditors must have prepared either an unqualified report[27] on the accounts or, if it is qualified, they must state in writing whether their qualification is relevant to the question of distributable profits. Finally a copy of any such statement must be laid before the company in general meeting (s.271(3)–(5)).

A public company may only use *interim accounts* if they have been properly prepared in compliance with the format of accounts set out in ss 226A and 226B[28] and Sch.4 to the Act in all material respects and have been signed by the directors as required under s.233 (s.272(2),(3)). A copy must be sent to the Registrar with a certified English translation if appropriate (s.272(4),(5)). Section 272 does not apply to private companies, which may therefore use any interim accounts.

---

[26] Above, Ch.20.

[27] Above, Ch.21.

[28] Above, Ch.20. The reference in ss 270(2) and 273(3) is only to ss 226A and 226B, relating to individual company accounts, and not to s.227, relating to group accounts, since only the holding company and not the group can declare dividends.

A public company may only use *initial accounts* if they have been properly prepared in compliance with the format of accounts set out in ss 226A and 226B[29] and Sch.4 to the Act in all material respects and have been signed by the directors as required under s.233 (s.273(2),(3)). Further, there must be an auditors' report that the accounts have been so prepared and which is either unqualified, or, if qualified, accompanied by a statement that the qualification is irrelevant to the question of distributable profits (s.273(4),(5)). A copy of the accounts and the auditors' report must be sent to the Registrar with a certified English translation if appropriate (s.273(6),(7)). Section 273 does not apply to private companies, which may therefore use any initial accounts.

The rules under ss 274–275 relating to distributions are modified for *banking and insurance companies* (in particular with respect to relevant accounts) by s.279 and Sch.11.

The consequences of an unlawful distribution

Under s.270(5), a breach of the requirements of ss 270–273 relating to the relevant accounts for determining distributable profits constitutes a breach of the test of distributability.[30] Section 277(1) further provides that any shareholder who receives a distribution which he knows, or has reasonable grounds to believe, has been paid in breach of the 1985 Act rules, must repay that amount to the company. This is expressly made an addition to the shareholders' existing liabilities set out below, but it does not apply in relation either to financial assistance given by a company to a person to help him purchase its shares in contravention of s.151; or to any payment made by a company in respect of the redemption or purchase by the company of shares in itself (s.277(2)).

With regard to payments of dividends out of capital, it was established prior to the 1980 Act that directors who are knowingly parties to such payments are jointly and severally liable to the company to replace the amounts of dividends so paid, with interest, and ratification is impossible so as to bind the company.[31] In such a case they are entitled to be indemnified by each shareholder who received dividends, knowing them to be paid out of capital, to the extent of the dividends received.[32] A shareholder who has knowingly received a dividend paid out of capital cannot individually, or on behalf of the company, maintain an action against the directors to replace the dividends so paid, at any rate until he has repaid the money he has received.[33]

PAYMENT OF DIVIDENDS

Dividends are paid in the manner laid down in the articles. The current Table A

---

[29] *ibid.*

[30] Shareholders cannot agree to waive these requirements: *Precision Dippings Ltd. v Precision Dippings Marketing Ltd.* [1985] B.C.L.C. 385 (C.A.).

[31] *e.g.* where debts known to be bad were entered as assets in reports and balance sheets, so that an apparent profit was shown, and the shareholders, relying on these documents, declared dividends: *Flitcroft's Case* (1882) 21 Ch. D 519 (C.A.). See also *Liquidators of City of Glasgow Bank v Mackinnon* (1881) 9 R. 535. Directors who authorise dividend payments other than out of distributable profits may be personally liable to reimburse the company: *Bairstow v Queens Moat Houses plc* [2000] 1 B.C.L.C. 549, QBD.

[32] *Moxham v Grant* [1900] 1 Q.B. 88 (C.A.).

[33] *Towers v African Tug Co.* (1904) 1 Ch. 558 (C.A.); *Liquidators of City of Glasgow Bank v Mackinnon* (1881) 9. R. 535.

(SI 1985/805), Art.102, provides that the company may declare a final dividend by ordinary resolution at the annual general meeting "but no dividend shall exceed the amount recommended by the directors." An interim dividend is a dividend paid on some date between two annual general meetings of the company,[34] and Art.103 provides *inter alia* that the directors may pay such a dividend if it appears to be justified by the profits available for distribution.

Before recommending a dividend, directors should have a complete and detailed list of the company's assets and investments prepared for their information, and they should not rely for their value merely on the opinion of the chairman or the auditors.[35]

In the absence of anything to the contrary in the articles,[36] a company cannot be compelled to declare a dividend and no action can be brought for its recovery until it has been declared.[37] In England the declaration of a dividend creates a simple contract debt due from the company to the shareholder which will be barred in six years from the date of declaration.[38] In Scotland the period of prescription is five years.[39] However, the current Table A, Art.108, provides that a dividend unclaimed for 12 years can be forfeited by resolution of the directors.[40]

When preference shares entitle the holder to receive out of the profits of the company for each year a fixed dividend, the "profits of the company" are the profits available for dividend after setting aside such reserves as the directors think fit. If the whole of the profits are transferred to reserve the preference shareholders are not entitled to any dividend.[41]

More generally, the rights of holders of preference and other special shares must be observed, since infringement of such rights will give aggrieved members the right to apply for an injunction or other relief. Moreover, if dividends are paid infringing such rights, any class of members which suffers will be able to take legal action against the company, while the directors who wrongly paid the dividends will be liable to replace the sum involved.

When the articles (*e.g.* the current Table A, Art.103) give the directors power to pay interim dividends, a resolution by the company in general meeting requiring the directors to declare an interim dividend is inoperative.[42]

In English law, unless the articles otherwise provide, dividends are payable to the shareholders in proportion to the nominal amounts of their shares, irrespective of the amounts paid up.[43] Section 119(c) of the Act, however, permits a

---

[34] *per* Lawrence J. in *Re Jowitt* [1922] 2 Ch. 442, at p. 447.

[35] *per* Romer J. in *Re City Equitable Fire Insurance Co. Ltd.* (1925) Ch. 407 at pp. 471, 474.

[36] For articles which were interpreted as requiring whole profits to be divided, see *Paterson v R. Paterson & Sons Ltd.*, 1917 S.C. (H.L.) 13; 1916 S.C. 452.

[37] *Bond v Barrow Haematite Steel Co.* [1902] 1 Ch. 353.

[38] *Re Compania de Electricidad de la Provincia de Buenos Aires Ltd.* [1978] 3 All E.R. 668.

[39] Prescription and Limitation (Scotland) Act 1973, s.6.

[40] This was originally supported by a requirement of the *Listing Rules*.

[41] *Re Buenos Ayres Great Southern Railway Co. Ltd.* [1947] Ch. 384; *cf.* the Scottish case *Wemyss Collieries Trust Ltd. v Melville* (1905) 8 F. 143, in which transfer of a sum to reserve was, on an interpretation of the articles, held to be valid, although preference shareholders were thereby deprived of an additional non-cumulative dividend.

[42] *Scott v Scott* [1943] 1 All E.R. 582.

[43] *Birch v Cropper* (1889) 14 App.Cas.525.

company, if so authorised by its articles,[44] to pay dividend in proportion to the amount paid up on each share where a larger amount is paid up on some shares than on others.

In Scots law, if articles provide that "the directors may . . . declare a dividend to be paid to the members in proportion to their shares" and define "shares" as shares in the nominal capital, dividends fall to be declared according to the nominal amounts of the shares, irrespective of the amounts paid up.[45] Where, however, there is no provision in the articles as to how dividends are to be paid, the common law principle applicable is that they are payable in proportion to the amounts paid up on the shares.[46] The articles usually provide (as does the current Table A, Art.106) that dividends payable in cash may be paid by a cheque sent through the post to the registered address of the shareholder, or to such persons and to such address as the shareholder may in writing direct. In the absence of such a provision in the articles, the company will have to issue a fresh dividend cheque to the shareholder should the cheque first sent be lost in the post.[47]

Unless power is given in the articles, dividends declared must be paid in cash, and a shareholder can restrain the company from paying them in any other way.[48] Accordingly, if it is desired to have the power to pay dividends otherwise than in cash, the articles should give such power (as does the current Table A, Art.105).

CREATION OF A RESERVE

Section 234 of the Act requires that the directors should state in their report the amount, if any, which they recommend should be paid as dividend. Prior to 1996, they were also required to state the amount, if any, which they proposed to carry to reserves. Consequently companies' articles often contain provisions dealing with the creation of a reserve. Indeed, there was an article to this effect in Table A to the 1948 Act, although no corresponding article exists in the current Table A. Yet even where no power to create a reserve is included in its articles, a company may nevertheless create one as this is a business matter to be decided by the company itself.[49] "The general practice of companies certainly is not to divide the total available profits, but to carry forward a part to make provision for meeting current liabilities."[50] Moreover, a reserve may at any time be distributed as dividend or be employed in any other way authorised by the articles.[51] The fact that it has been used in the business does not show that it has been capitalised so as not to be available for dividend.[52]

---

[44] Authorisation is given in the current Table A, Art.104.

[45] *Oakbank Oil Co. Ltd. v Crum* (1882) 10 R. (H.L.) 11; (1881) 9 R. 198.

[46] *Hoggan v Tharsis Sulphur etc. Co. Ltd.* (1882) 9 R. 1191.

[47] *Thairlwall v Great Northern Railway* [1910] 2 K.B. 509.

[48] *Wood v Odessa Waterworks Co.* (1889) 42 Ch.D. 636.

[49] *Burland v Earle* [1902] A.C. 83 (P.C.). Scottish cases decided on the interpretation of articles were *Cadell v Scottish Investment Trust Co. Ltd.* (1901) 9 S.L.T. 299, affirming (1901) 8 S.L.T. 480 (O.H.) (power to carry forward profits to the next year instead of paying a larger dividend on deferred shares); and *Wemyss Collieries Trust Ltd. v Melville* (1905) 8 F. 143 (transfer of profits to reserve fund instead of paying additional dividend on preference shares).

[50] *Per* Lord M'Laren in *Cadell v Scottish Investment Trust Co. Ltd.* (1901) 9 S.L.T. 299 at p. 300.

[51] *e.g. Blyth's Trustees v Milne* (1905) 7 F. 799.

[52] *Re Hoare & Co. Ltd.* [1904] 2 Ch. 208 (C.A.).

CAPITALISATION OF RESERVES

Capitalisation of a company's profits is defined in s.280 as relating either to the creation of bonus shares; or to the transfer of profits to capital redemption reserve. However, to be able to issue so-called "bonus" shares credited as fully or partly paid, a company has to be so empowered by its articles.[53]

Scrip dividends have become increasingly popular amongst listed companies over the past 15 years, originally because many had unrelieved Advance Corporation Tax as a result of substantial overseas earnings. The tax advantages were effectively removed by 1993 Finance Act, but offering scrip dividends still enables companies to retain funds and thus avoid the not insignificant costs of raising capital. Consequently listed companies now frequently offer shareholders the option of taking dividends in cash or as scrip.

When a company capitalises its *distributable reserves*, it reduces at a stroke its accumulated realised profits available for dividend and issues in their place to existing ordinary shareholders in proportion to their holdings shares or loan stock credited as fully paid up. From an accounting viewpoint, the distributable reserves figure in the balance sheet is reduced and the share or loan capital accounts increased by an equivalent offsetting amount. As a result, other things being equal, the net effect on the value of an individual's holding in the company remains unchanged. The term "bonus" used to describe such issues is therefore misleading, and more appropriate descriptions are "capitalisation-", "scrip-" or "script-issues".

In practice, other things are not usually equal, and the effect will generally be to increase the value of a holding. Thus one reason for engaging in such an exercise is to provide more security for creditors (particularly to existing or prospective holders of loan stock), which alters the balance of risk bearing between them and the company's shareholders. Another is to achieve a subdivision of the equity capital, similar to that permitted under s.121 (above, pp. 147–149): this can make the company's shares more marketable. Thus, for instance, if the market value per share of a company has risen to £20 as a result of its retention of profits over time to finance growth, it may be preferable to reduce this to nearer £5 per unit. Moreover, in practice listed companies tend to use capitalisation issues as a means of signalling to the investing public that the company's future prospects are encouraging, often indicating specifically that it is not the directors' intention to reduce the dividend per share *pro rata* to the increase in the number of share units in issue, and there is empirical evidence which confirms that this news content is appreciated by the market.[54] Capitalisation issues can also be used to credit partly-paid shares with a further amount paid up.

With respect to capitalising *undistributable reserves*, a company which by its articles, prior to the 1980 Act, could use a reserve resulting from the revaluation of capital assets to pay for bonus shares, may continue to do so (s.278 of the 1985

---

[53] The current Table A, Art.110, gives the directors such powers if authorised by an ordinary resolution.

[54] *e.g.* M. A. Firth, "An Empirical Investigation of the Announcement of Capitalisation Issues on Share Prices," *Journal of Business Finance and Accounting*, Spring 1977, pp. 47–60.

Act). Such a reserve could arise on a revaluation of fixed assets made in good faith by competent valuers and not being likely to fluctuate in the short term.[55] Moreover, by ss 130(2) and 170(4) of the 1985 Act respectively (above, pp.145–146 and p.166), a share premium account and a capital redemption reserve can be used to pay for unissued shares of the company to be allotted to members as fully paid bonus shares.

If bonus shares are to be issued:

(1) There must be authority in the company's articles.[56]

(2) The company's nominal share capital must be sufficient.

(3) The members must resolve by ordinary resolution to capitalise profits or to apply the share premium account or the capital redemption reserve fund, and to issue bonus shares.[57]

(4) The shares must be allotted by the board in the proportions specified in the articles, usually the same proportions as those in which the members would have received a cash dividend.[58]

(5) A return of allotments and a contract between the members and the company (which may be signed on the members' behalf by the person authorised by the articles) must be delivered to the Registrar within one month after the allotment.[59]

[55] *Dimbula Valley (Ceylon) Tea Co. Ltd v Laurie* [1961] Ch. 353.
[56] *Wood v Odessa Waterworks Co.* (1889) 42 Ch.D. 636. Also see the current Table A, Art.110.
[57] See the current Table A, Art.110.
[58] *ibid.*
[59] Above, Ch.8.

Chapter 23

DEBENTURES

This chapter is concerned with the borrowing of money by a company where the borrowing is on debentures or on debenture stock, and with fixed and floating charges which a company may create over its property in order to secure the principal sum borrowed and interest thereon until re-payment. Thus the chapter deals with the relationship between a company and its creditors, which is also central to the following chapters up to Chapter 29.

The most important part of the chapter is that with regard to charges and the registration of charges, particularly registration with the Registrar of Companies under. s.395 or, in Scotland, s.410. This system is currently being reviewed by the Law Commission as part of a series of consultations.[1] The Law Commission is in favour of reform of the registration system so as to replicate, at least to some extent, Art.9 of the Uniform Commercial Code of the United States. A brief outline of main planks of the Law Commission's recommendations will be provided at the end of this Chapter[2] after the unmodified provisions have been considered.

A Company's Power to Borrow Money

Prior to the substantial changes to corporate transactions contained in ss 35 and 35A and 322A of the 1985 Act as substituted by the 1989 Act,[3] it was important to decide whether or not the company had the capacity, *i.e.* by virtue of an express or implied power, to borrow money, and it was possible for a loan to be *ultra vires* the company and so void.[4]

Following those changes, however, any borrowing is simply one type of transaction by a company and so its validity is now governed, as with all other corporate transactions, by the new provisions. It follows that unless the lender is either not acting in good faith[5] or is a director of the borrowing company[6] no question of invalidity can arise as a result of the company's constitution. Even if the lender is not acting in good faith or is a director, the transaction may still be ratified by the appropriate resolution. Ratification is also possible if the defect

---

[1] See Law Com Consultation Paper 164, *Registration of Security Interests: Company Charges and Property other than Land* (TSO, 2002); Law Com Consultation Paper 176, *Company Security Interests* (TSO, 2004). See too Scot Law Com Rep No.197, *Registration of Rights in Security by Companies* (TSO, 2004).

[2] Below, p.527.

[3] Ch.6, above.

[4] For the position prior to the 1989 Act changes see the 13th edition of this work at pp.607–11.

[5] So that s.35A cannot apply.

[6] Thus applying s.322A.

arises from a lack of authority on the part of those negotiating the loan on behalf of the company, if it arises under the general law of agency rather than from the company's constitution.[7]

DEBENTURES AND DEBENTURE STOCK

A debenture is a document which creates or acknowledges a debt due from a company. Such document need not be, although it usually is, under seal,[8] it need not give, although it usually does give, a charge on the assets of the company by way of security, and it may or may not be one of a series.[9] Thus debentures may be either secured or unsecured. As will be seen, debentures may be collaterally secured by a trust deed.[10] Convertible debentures, *i.e.* debentures which the holder has the right to convert, at stated times, into shares in the company, have already been mentioned.[11]

It may be helpful to mention here that some of the differences between shares and debentures are:

(1) the holder of a debenture is a creditor, not a member, of the company; a shareholder is a member[12];

(2) debentures may be issued at a discount; shares, in general, may not be[13];

(3) a company may purchase its own debentures since that would amount to repaying a debt; it must not purchase its own shares except in accordance with specific procedures[14];

(4) interest at the specified rate on debentures may be paid out of capital; dividends on shares must be paid only out of distributable profits.[15]

Section 744 defines "debenture" as including debenture stock, bonds, and any other securities[16] of a company whether constituting a charge on the assets of the company or not. A mortgage of land by a company is a debenture.[17] Debentures, including debenture stock, loan stock, bonds and certificates of deposit are investments for the purposes of Pt V of the Criminal Justice Act 1993[18]: see Chapter 19, above.

Debenture stock is borrowed money consolidated into one mass for the sake of convenience. This is normally done by a trust deed,[19] which may give the trustees

---

[7] *i.e.* because the agent has no authority to bind the company.
[8] N.B. the provisions relating to the sealing of documents in ss 36A and 36B, above, p.90.
[9] See *Lemon v Austin Friars Investment Trust Ltd* [1926] Ch. 1, CA.
[10] Below. p.497.
[11] See *Mosely v Koffyfontein Mines* [1904] 2 Ch. 108, above p.142.
[12] Above, p.186.
[13] Above, p.142.
[14] Above, Ch.10.
[15] Above, Ch.22.
[16] "Securities", as used in s.744, does not include shares.
[17] *Knightsbridge Estates Trust Ltd v Byrne* [1940] A.C. 613.
[18] Criminal Justice Act 1993, Sched. 2.
[19] See n.10, above.

a charge on the company's property. Where there is no charge, debenture stock is commonly called unsecured loan stock. The main advantage of debenture stock is that, unlike a single debenture it is transferable in fractional amounts, although the trust deed may specify the minimum fractional amount which can be transferred. Again, the debenture stockholders will be given simple debenture stock certificates instead of debentures.

ISSUES OF DEBENTURES

Debentures are issued in accordance with the provisions of the articles, usually by a resolution of the board of directors.

When debentures have been issued, the prospectus[20] cannot be looked at to ascertain the contract, but if the contract was intended to be contained in the prospectus and the debenture together, or if the prospectus contains a collateral contract the consideration for which was the taking up of the debentures, the prospectus can be looked at.[21]

Debentures or debentures stock certificates must be completed and ready for delivery within two months after allotment or after the lodging of a transfer, unless the conditions of issue otherwise provide: s.185.

There is no objection to the issue of debentures at a discount but when any commission, allowance or discount has been paid or made to any person in consideration of his subscribing or procuring subscriptions for debentures, particulars of the amount or rate of the commission or discount must be sent to the Registrar within 21 days. The omission to do this does not, however, affect the validity of the debentures. The deposit of debentures as security for a debt of the company does not, for this purpose, amount to the issue of debentures at a discount: ss 397(3) and 413(3).

A contract to take up debentures may be enforced by specific performance: s.195. This section provides an exception to the rule, laid down in *South African Territories Ltd v Wallington*,[22] that specific performance will not be granted of a contract to lend money since damages are an adequate remedy for breach of such contract.

Apart from the section, an agreement to issue debentures made in consideration of an actual balance of money has the effect in English law of putting the lender in equity in the same position as if the debentures had actually been issued.

A syndicate agreed to sell goods to a company on the terms that, as part payment, £3,000 debentures charged upon all the company's assets were issued. On this agreement the syndicate allowed the company to remove the goods, which were subsequently taken in execution by F. *Held*, although no debentures were actually issued, the syndicate was in the same position as if they had been and so F was entitled subject to the charge: *Simultaneous Colour Printing Syndicate v Foweraker* [1901] 1 K.B. 771.

TRUST DEEDS

Debentures and particularly debenture stock are usually secured by a trust deed.

---

[20] This presumably also applies to listing particulars.
[21] *Jacobs v Batavia and General Plantations Trust Ltd* [1924] 2 Ch. 329, CA.
[22] [1898] A.C. 309.

Contents of a trust deed

The main terms of a *debenture trust deed* are:

(1) a covenant by the company for payment to the debenture holders of the principal moneys and interest;

(2) clauses giving the trustees a legal mortgage by demise of the company's freeholds and leaseholds, which are specified,[23] and a floating charge over the rest of the undertaking and property[24];

(3) a clause specifying the events on which the security is to become enforceable, *e.g.* default in the payment of interest or principal moneys, order made or resolution passed for winding-up, appointment of a receiver, cessation of business, breach of covenant by the company;

(4) a clause giving the trustees power to take possession of the property charged when the security becomes enforceable, to carry on the business and to sell the property charged and to apply the net sale moneys in payment of the principal and interest and to pay the balance to the company;

(5) power for the trustees to concur with the company in dealings with the property charged;

(6) covenants by the company to keep a register of debenture holders, to insure and to keep in repair the property charged;

(7) provision for meetings of debenture holders;

(8) power for the trustees to appoint a receiver when the security becomes enforceable;

(9) provision for serving notices on the debenture holders by post.

A *debenture stock trust deed*, in addition to containing the foregoing terms, constitutes a stock by acknowledging that the company is indebted to the trustees in a specified sum and provides for the issue of debenture stock certificates.

A trust deed usually contains a clause providing that the rights of the debenture holders against the company or any property charged by the deed may be modified or compromised by extra-ordinary resolution of the debenture holders.

Liability of trustees

Trustees for debenture holders are in the same position towards their beneficiaries as any other trustees, and cannot purchase the debentures, the subject of the deed, without making full disclosure of all the information relating to them

---

[23] In Scotland, security over specified heritable property would be created by the execution of a standard security which would be referred to in the trust deed.

[24] Fixed charges may also be taken over other assets, *e.g.* book debts of a company. See p.608, below.

which is in their possession.[25] Any provision in a trust deed, or in a contract with the holders of debentures secured by a trust deed, for exempting the trustees from, or indemnifying them against, liability for breach of trust where they fail to show the degree of care and diligence required of them as trustees, is void, except that the trustees may be released from liability by a release given after the liability has arisen; and a provision in a trust deed for the giving of such a release by a majority of not less than three-fourths in value of the debenture holders present and voting in person or by proxy at a meeting summoned for the purpose is not void: s.192. (Contrast s.310, above,[26] as regards officers and auditors.)

Section 727 (power of court to grant relief), above,[27] does not apply to the trustees although the Trustee Act 1925, s.61, and the Trusts (Scotland) Act 1921, s.32, do, and so in an appropriate case the court may relieve the trustees from liability.

Right to copy of trust deed

A debenture holder is entitled to require a copy of the trust deed on payment of the prescribed fee: ss 191, 356.

REGISTERED DEBENTURES

Debentures or debenture stock may be payable to either (1) the registered holder; or (2) the bearer.

Contents of a registered debenture

Where there is a trust deed the usual form of debenture payable to the registered holder is a document issued under the seal of the company and containing two clauses. The clauses are as follows:

(a) the company, for valuable consideration received, covenants to pay the registered holder the principal sum on a specified day or on such earlier day as it becomes payable under the indorsed conditions, and in the meantime to pay interest by equal half-yearly payments on specified dates at a specified rate;

(b) the debenture is said to be issued subject to and with the benefit of the conditions indorsed thereon.

The indorsed conditions usually include the following:

(i) the debenture is said to be one of a series, each for securing a specified sum;

(ii) the registered holders of all the debentures of the issue are said to be entitled *pari passu* to the benefit and subject to the provisions of the trust deed, the date of execution of which the parties to which are specified, and the charges conferred by the trust deed are recited.

[25] *Re Magadi Soda Co.* (1925) 41 T.L.R. 297.
[26] p.314.
[27] p.315.

This has the effect of putting all the debentures of the issue on an equal footing; in the absence of such a clause the debentures would rank according to the order in which they were executed[28]:

(iii)   the company is empowered, at any time after a specified date, by giving not less than a specified number of months' notice, to pay off the principal moneys secured with interest to the date of payment;

(iv)   provision is made for keeping a register of debenture holders at the registered office. We shall see that this will comply with s.190 and that a right of inspection is given by s.191[29];

(v)   the company is not to be bound to recognise anyone as having any title to the debenture except the registered holder, or his personal representative, and is not to be bound to enter notice of any trust in the register.

Section 360, which provides that trusts are not to be entered on the register of members in England and Wales, does not apply to the register of debenture holders, and consequently such a clause is necessary. If the company does receive notice of a trust, the clause relieves it from the obligation of entering it on the register, but if it deals with the debentures as a trader, *e.g.* by advancing money on them, after notice of a trust, it will be bound by that trust[30];

(vi)   transfer of the debenture is provided for. Every transfer must be in writing, as will be explained later;

(vii)   equities or, in Scots law, rights of compensation, between the company and any person other than the registered holder are excluded. This will be explained later[31];

(viii)   the principal moneys and interest are made payable at the company's registered office or at its bankers.

If this clause is not inserted it is the company's duty to follow the usual rule and seek out its creditor and pay him.

F held 18 £100 debentures repayable in June, 1913, in the M Corporation. Before the date of redemption F died, and her executors neglected to present the debentures to the company for payment. In June, 1916, the company was sued for principal and interest. *Held*, as the debentures contained no clause to the effect set out above, it was the company's duty to seek out the debenture holder and pay her; as this had not been done, the company was liable to pay the principal with interest until the date of actual payment: *Fowler v Midland Electric Corpn.* [1917] 1 Ch. 656 CA;

(ix)   the company is empowered to purchase any of the debentures of the issue at any time;

---

[28] *Gartside v Silkstone and Dodworth Coal, etc., Co.* (1882) 21 Ch.D. 762.
[29] Below, p.444.
[30] *Bradford Banking Co. v Briggs & Co.* (1886) 12 App.Cas.29; *Mackereth v Wigan Coal Co. Ltd* [1916] 2 Ch. 293.
[31] Below, p.502.

(x) interest is made payable by warrant on the company's bank payable to the order of the registered holder and sent by post to his registered address;

(xi) the principal moneys are made immediately payable if the company defaults in the payment of interest for a specified number of months, or if a winding up order is made or resolution passed, or if the security constituted by the trust deed becomes enforceable and the trustees enforce it.

The debenture holder is entitled to repayment of his principal on the company's going into liquidation, whether or not the date fixed for repayment has arrived.[32]

Transfer of registered debentures

The following account does not apply to transfers of debentures held in electronic form under the CREST system which operates in respect of some listed companies.[33]

Registered debentures are transferred in the manner laid down in the indorsed conditions (which usually require a transfer to be in writing under the hand of the registered holder or of his personal representatives) or by a stock transfer under the Stock Transfer Act 1963. As in the case of a transfer of shares[34] it is unlawful for a company to register a transfer of debentures unless a "proper instrument of transfer" has been delivered to the company: s.183(1).

The company must have the debenture or debenture stock certificate ready for delivery within two months of the lodging of the instrument of transfer unless the conditions of issue otherwise provide: s.185. If registration of a transfer is refused, notice of refusal must be given to the transferee within two months: s.183(5).

Registered debentures are in England choses in action, and in Scotland incorporeal moveable property to the assignation of which the rule *assignatus utitur jure auctoris* ('the assignee acquires no higher right than his cedent had") applies. They are not negotiable instruments, and consequently a transferee takes them subject to all claims which the company may have against prior holders at the date of the transfer.

After a receiver had been appointed and a winding up petitions had been presented, P, a debenture stockholder, transferred £10,000 debenture stock to X, who was registered as the owner. P, was also a director of the company and a claim was made against him for money had and received by him while a director. *Held*, X was not entitled to payment until the amount due from P to the company had been ascertained and deducted: *Re Rhodesia Goldfields Ltd* [1910] 1 Ch. 239.

To avoid this result, the indorsed conditions usually provide that the principal and interest shall be paid to the registered holder without regard to any equities

---

[32] *Hodson v Tea Co.* (1880) 14 Ch.D. 859.
[33] See p.213, above.
[34] Above, pp.213 *et seq.*

or rights of compensation existing between the company and any prior holder of the debenture. Such a clause amounts to a contract by the company that it will not rely on equities or rights of compensation, and its effect is to make the debentures more marketable.

A company was in liquidation. C, who had been a director of the company, transferred debentures to R as security for a loan. The debentures contained a clause similar to that set out above. It was then discovered that C had been guilty of misfeasance and he was ordered to pay a sum of money to the liquidator in respect thereof. The liquidator refused to register R's transfer. *Held*, the right to transfer and to have the transfer registered was not affected by the winding up, and R was entitled to payment without regard to C's debt to the company: *Re Goy & Co. Ltd* [1900] 2 Ch. 149.

A transferee cannot claim the benefit of such a clause unless either he is registered or the conditions specifically allow the holder to transfer the debenture free of equities.

B held debentures containing a clause similar to that set out above. After a resolution for winding up had been passed he transferred them for value to C, who took without notice of any defect in B's title. Notice of transfer but no request for registration was given to the liquidator. C claimed payment but the court found that B had paid nothing for the debentures and had obtained them by misrepresentation. *Held*, notwithstanding the clause, C took subject to the company's claim against B. *Re Goy & Co.*, above, was distinguished on the ground that when the transfer in that case was sent for registration the company was not aware of and was not setting up any equities between itself and the transferor: *Re Palmer's Decoration and Furnishing Co.* [1904] 2 Ch. 743. Where the actual agreement specifically allowed the holder to transfer free of all equities it has been held that following such a transfer the issuing company is bound to register the transfer: *Hilger Analytical Ltd v Rank Precision Industries Ltd* [1984] B.C.L.C. 301.

Section 184 (certification of transfers) above[35] applies to transfers of debentures as well as to transfers of shares.

Register of debenture holders

A company is not required to keep a register of debenture holders but there are provisions regulating those companies which do. A company registered in England must not keep its register of debenture holders in Scotland, and vice versa. The register must be kept at the registered office or at any other office of the company where it is made up or, if it is made up by an agent, it may be kept at the agent's office: s.190. Debenture holders and shareholders in the company may, without fee, inspect the register of debenture holders within limits laid down by the Secretary of State. Other persons may inspect the register on payment of a prescribed fee. A copy may be demanded on payment of the prescribed fee: s.191.[36] A computer may be used to keep the register of debenture holders: s.723.

BEARER DEBENTURES

Debentures payable to bearer are in the same form as registered debentures

---

[35] p.214.
[36] For the relevant limits and fees see the Companies (Inspection and Copying of Registers, Indices and Documents) Regulations 1991 (SI 1991/1998).

except that they are expressed to be made payable to bearer and coupons for the interest are attached. The indorsed conditions are also in the same form with the necessary modifications for bearer, instead of registered, instruments.

Bearer debentures are negotiable instruments and consequently a transferee in good faith and for value takes them free from any defects in the title of a prior holder.

> The B Company owned some bearer debentures and kept them in a safe. The secretary fraudulently took them from the safe and deposited them with the bank, who took them in good faith and as security for advances to the secretary. *Held*, the debentures were negotiable instruments transferable by delivery and the bank was entitled to them as against the B Company: *Bechuanaland Exploration Co. v London Trading Bank* [1898] 2 Q.B. 658.

Bearer debentures are transferable by delivery and no stamp duty is payable on transfer. Interest is payable by means of the coupons which are cut off and presented for payment to the company's bankers when the date of payment arrives.

REDEEMABLE DEBENTURES

Debentures may be (1) redeemable at the option of the company, or (2) irredeemable or perpetual.

Sometimes debentures are issued on the terms that the company is bound to redeem a certain number each year by "drawings" (in which case, in effect, the numbers of the debentures to be redeemable are drawn out of a hat),[37] or that it may purchase, *e.g.* on the Stock Exchange, or that it is bound to set aside a sinking fund for redemption purposes on a specified date. When debentures have been so redeemed, s.194 empowers the company to reissue them or issue other debentures in their place, unless:

(a) the company, in its articles or otherwise, has contracted not to reissue them; or

(b) the company has shown an intention to cancel the debentures by passing a resolution to that effect, or by some other act.

On a reissue of redeemed debentures, the person entitled to them has the same priorities as if the debentures had never been redeemed: s.194. The date of redemption of the reissued debentures cannot be later than that of the original debentures.[38]

Reissued debentures are treated as new debentures for the purpose of stamp duty: s.194.

PERPETUAL DEBENTURES

Debentures are not invalid merely because they are made irredeemable, or

---

[37] For difficulties which may arise from the company's inability to trace the holders to whom repayment is due, see *United Collieries Ltd v Lord Advocate*, 1950 S.C. 458.

[38] *Re Antofagasta (Chile) and Bolivia Ry. Co.'s Trust Deed* [1939] Ch. 732.

redeemable on the happening of a contingency, however remote, *e.g.* the winding up of the company, or on the expiration of a period, however long, *e.g.* 100 years after the issue of the debenture, *i.e.* the legal or contractual date for redemption may be postponed, despite any rule of equity to the contrary: s.193.

In Scotland, the Conveyancing and Feudal Reform (Scotland) Act 1970, ss 11 and 18, conferred on the debtor in a standard security the right, which could not be varied by agreement, to redeem the security on giving two months' notice. The Redemption of Standard Securities (Scotland) Act 1971, however, amended the 1970 Act on this point by providing that the condition relating to the debtor's right of redemption might be varied by agreement. The 1971 Act also, for the avoidance of doubt, declared that the provisions of the 1970 Act relating to the standard security do not affect the operation of s.193.

CHARGES SECURING DEBENTURES

A charge on the assets of a company given by a debenture or a trust deed in order to secure money borrowed by the company may be either (1) a specific or fixed charge, or (2) a floating charge.

In practice many debentures are secured by both a fixed and a floating charge. Such charges are usually drafted to cover "all moneys" due by the company to the lender including contingent and future liabilities. In *Re Quest Cae, Ltd*[39] it was held that such wording only covered debts arising as a result of transactions between the company and the lender so that where the lender subsequently acquired loan stock issued by the company to a third party it was not protected by the charge. The debt had not arisen by virtue of a transaction between the company and the lender.

Fixed charges (English law)

A fixed charge is a mortgage of ascertained and definite property, *e.g.* a legal or an equitable mortgage of a specified factory, and prevents the company from realising that property, *i.e.* disposing of it free from the charge, without the consent of the holders of the charge. It has been said in one case,[40] however, that a limited licence for the company to deal with the charged property may not be inconsistent with a fixed charge, depending upon the nature of the property charged and the degree of the licence to deal. But in *Re Cosslett (Contractors) Ltd*[41] the Court of Appeal made it clear that the essence of a fixed charge is that the company cannot deal with the assets without the consent of the chargee. Whether or not a charge is a fixed or floating charge does not depend upon the intention of the parties but upon the wording of the charge.[42] Where a charge is on fixed plant and machinery it will only apply to those items physically attached to the company's premises and not to all a company's fixed, *i.e.* capital, assets.[43]

---

[39] [1985] B.C.L.C. 266.
[40] *Re Cimex Tissues Ltd* [1995] 1 B.C.L.C. 409.
[41] [1997] B.C.C. 724, CA.
[42] *Re G.E. Tunbridge Ltd* [1995] 1 B.C.L.C. 34.; *Agnew v Inland Revenue Commissioner [2001]* 2 A.C. 710.
[43] *Re Hi-Fi Equipment (Cabinets) Ltd* (1987) 3 B.C.C. 478, not following *Tudor Heights Ltd v United Dominions Corporation Finance Ltd* [1977] 1 N.Z.L.R. 532.

The question of creating a fixed charge over the book debts or other moneys due to the company is considered below.[44]

Floating charges (English law)

In *Re Yorkshire Woolcombers Association Ltd*[45] Romer L.J. said that if a charge has the three characteristics set out below it is a floating charge:

(1) it is a charge on a class of assets of a company, present and future;

(2) which class is, in the ordinary course of the company's business, changing from time to time;

(3) it is contemplated by the charge that, until the holders of the charge take steps to enforce it, the company may carry on business in the ordinary way as far as concerns the class of assets charged.

Thus a floating charge is an equitable charge on some or all of the present and future property of a company, *e.g.* the company's undertaking, *i.e.* all its property, present and future.[46] It is effective as to future property only when that property is acquired by the company. It is not necessary for the existence of a floating charge that the company has complete unfettered freedom to deal with the charged assets; the distinction between a fixed and floating charge is whether the chargee is in control of those assets. In a floating charge the company retains control of the assets and may withdraw them from the charge.[47] A floating charge will be valid even if the assets covered do not yet exist.[48]

However, when the security is enforceable, *e.g.* there is default with regard to payment of interest or repayment of the principal sum, and the debenture holders or the trustees enforce it, *e.g.* they appoint an administrative receiver of the property charged, the floating charge is said to crystallise; *i.e.* it becomes a fixed charge on the assets in the class charged at the time of crystallisation or, where the floating charge so provides, assets which come to the company after crystallisation.[49]

Crystallisation also occurs on the commencement of the winding up of the company, even if it is a voluntary winding up for the purpose of reconstruction,[50] or when the company ceases business.[51] The latter, which is a form of "implied automatic crystallisation" in that it needs no act or specific event to bring it about and so may be difficult for other creditors to judge, was disputed until 1986. In coming to his decision on this point, Nourse J. pointed out that cessation of

---

[44] Below, p.508.
[45] [1903] 2 Ch. 284, CA at p.295.
[46] *Re Panama, etc., Royal Mail Co.* (1870) L.R. 5 Ch. App. 318.
[47] *Re Cosslett (Contractors) Ltd* [1997] B.C.C. 724; *Agnew v Inland Revenue Commissioner* [2001] 2 A.C. 710; *Re Spectrum Plus Ltd (In Liquidation)* [2004] EWCA Civ 670.
[48] *Re Croftbell Ltd* [1990] B.C.C. 781.
[49] *N. W. Robbie & Co. Ltd v Whitney Warehouse Co. Ltd* [1963] 1 W.L.R. 1324, CA; *Ferrier v Bottomer* (1972) 126 C.L.R. 597.
[50] *Re Crompton & Co.* [1914] 1 Ch. 954.
[51] *Re Woodroffes (Musical Instruments) Ltd* [1986] Ch. 366.

business prevents a company from dealing with its assets and so there is no reason why the charge should not crystallise. Being an implied term it may be excluded by express terms in the agreement but this will only be the case where there is no doubt that that was the intention.[52] Nourse J., however, rejected another such ground for implied crystallisation, *i.e.* on the crystallisation of a second floating charge which is postponed to the relevant floating charge.[53]

It is possible that the charging deed may provide for crystallisation on a certain event, *e.g.* an attempt by the company to create another charge over the assets in the class charged, or simply by the giving of a notice to that effect. Such "express automatic crystallisation" is valid under English law following the decision of Hoffmann J. in *Re Brightlife Ltd*[54] The judge pointed out that floating charges were developed to enable companies to raise money without inhibiting their ability to trade, but this involved potential prejudice to other creditors who could suddenly find assets becoming subject to a charge on crystallisation without anyone else being aware. The appointment of an administrative receiver, administrator or liquidator were public acts, but the giving of a notice or the happening of an event would not be. The judge, however, considered that any restrictions on the contractual freedom of parties to a floating charge were matters for Parliament, and it would be "wholly inappropriate" for the courts to impose restrictions on the ground of public policy. The judge followed a decision of the New Zealand courts to a similar effect,[55] but noted that very clear language would be required to demonstrate the parties' intention to automatically crystallise a floating charge. This was because such crystallisation would, in many cases, be commercially inconvenient, so much so that there existed a strong presumption that the parties did not intend it.[55a]

The characteristics of a floating charge are therefore:

(1)   it is an equitable charge on assets for the time being of the company[56];

(2)   it attaches to the class of assets charged in the varying condition in which they happen to be from time to time,[57] *i.e.* it does not fasten on any definite property but is a charge on property which is constantly changing;

(3)   it remains dormant, subject to any automatic crystallisation until the undertaking charged ceases to be a going concern, or until the person in whose favour it is created intervenes. His right to intervene may be suspended by agreement but if there is no agreement for suspension he may intervene whenever he pleases after default.[58] When this happens the charge is said to "crystallise" and becomes fixed[59];

---

[52] *Re The Real Meat Co. Ltd* [1996] B.C.C. 254.
[53] But see as to priority *Re H & K Medway Ltd* [1997] B.C.C. 853.
[54] [1987] Ch. 200.
[55] *Re Manurewa Transport Ltd.* [1971] N.Z.L.R. 909; *cf. R. v Consolidated Churchill Copper Corpn. Ltd* [1978] 5 W.W.R. 652. See also the Australian case of *Deputy Commissioner of Taxation v Horsburgh* [1984] V.R. 773.
[55a] [1987] Ch. 200, p.213.
[56] *per* Lord MacNaghten in *Governments Stock Investment Co. Ltd v Manila Ry. Co. Ltd* [1897] A.C. 81, at p.86. See *Re G. E. Tunbridge Ltd* [1994] B.C.C. 563.
[57] *ibid.*
[58] See n.49, above.
[59] *Evans v Rival Granite Quarries Ltd* [1910] 2 K.B. 979, CA.

(4) although it is an immediate and continuing charge, until it becomes fixed the company can, without consent,[60] control the assets, including taking them outside the scope of the charge, *e.g.* it has been held that a company can sell all or any of its business or property for shares or debentures of another company if the memorandum gives it power to do so, and the debenture holders cannot prevent such a sale if the company remains a going concern[61]; similarly, a company with three businesses may sell one of the three.[62]

Where, before crystallisation of a floating charge over all the company's assets and undertaking, the company contracted to sell goods to a buyer to whom it owed money under a previous contract, and the goods were delivered after crystallisation, the company's right to sue for the debt due to it was embraced, when it arose, by the floating charge, but the debenture holder could not be in a better position to assert the rights under the previous contract than the company.[63]

The advantage of a floating charge from the *company's* point of view is that the company can give security for a loan to it by charging property which changes in the course of business and over which it is impracticable to create a fixed charge, *e.g.* the company's stock-in-trade. Further, until crystallisation the company can carry on business in the ordinary way.

A floating charge can be created only by a registered company not by a partnership or a sole trader. One reason is that such a charge created by a firm over chattels would be a bill of sale within the Bills of Sale Acts 1878 and 1882, and would have to be registered and, as a mortgage bill, would have to be in the statutory form and specify the chattels, which is impossible.[64]

From the *chargee's* point of view, an important advantage is that, upon crystallisation of the floating charge, the chargee obtains priority in the payment of debts over the ordinary unsecured creditors and the existence of such a charge entitles the chargee to appoint an administrator or, in certain circumstances, an administrative receiver.[65] However, there are a number of disadvantages attached to a floating charge from the chargee's point of view. For example:

(1) As will be seen, a floating charge is postponed to certain other interests.[66]

---

[60] Limited restrictions on the company's power of disposal do not, however, convert a floating charge into a fixed charge: *Re G. E. Tunbridge Ltd* [1995] 1 B.C.L.C. 34; see also *Re Cosslett (Contractors) Ltd*, above n.47, where the company could remove charged plant from a site only with the permission of an architect. The charge was held to be a floating charge.

[61] *Re Borax Co.* [1901] 3 Ch. 326.

[61] *Re H. H. Vivian & Co. Ltd* [1900] 2 Ch. 654.

[63] *Rother Iron Works Ltd v Canterbury Precision Engines Ltd* [1974] Q.B. 1, CA applied in *George Barker (Transport) Ltd v Eynon* [1974] 1 W.L.R. 462, CA.

[64] The Law Commission is recommending that the law be changed to allow unincorporated organisations to create such security over personal property under a notice filing system, a recommendation which will require the repeal and replacement of the Bills of Sale Acts: see Law Commission Consultation Paper No. 176 (above, n.1), para.1.3.

[65] See Ch.26, below.

[66] Below, pp.511–512.

(2) A floating charge may be invalidated under s.245 of the Insolvency Act 1986, below.[67]

Charges over book debts

Creditors, aware of these drawbacks to a floating charge, yet wishing to give the company the maximum flexibility in dealing with its assets, have faced a difficult problem in relation to using the company's book debts as security for a loan. Book debts are moneys owed to the company, which by their nature are constantly being created and paid off. Creditors have therefore attempted to create fixed charges over the company's book debts and this was accepted as a possibility by Slade J. in *Siebe Gorman & Co. Ltd v Barclays Bank Ltd*[68] where the terms of the charge required the chargor to pay the proceeds of book debts (*i.e.*, the cash or cheques collected by the chargor company) into an account with the chargee bank.

The significance of this requirement was taken to be that it restricted the company's freedom to deal with the proceeds of the debts, such freedom being the hallmark of a floating charge and inconsistent with a fixed charge. Thus, where a charge over book debts expressed in the debenture to be fixed nevertheless allowed the company to collect and pay the proceeds into its current account (which was not with the chargee) it was held to be a floating charge.[69] Moreover, in *Re Keenan Bros Ltd*,[70] the Supreme Court of Ireland placed emphasis on the fact that the charged debts had to be paid into an account with the chargee bank over which significant restrictions on withdrawals existed. These were sufficient to support the parties' denomination of the charge as fixed.

The possibility of creating a genuine fixed charge over book debts which nevertheless allowed the company to use the proceeds in the ordinary course of its business was further tested in *Re New Bullas Trading Ltd*.[71] In that case, the chargee was granted a fixed charge over the company's uncollected book debts. The charge went on to provide that, in the absence of instructions from the chargee, the company could collect the debts and that the proceeds would be subject to a separate floating charge. No instructions were ever given. At first instance the charge was construed as a floating charge, but the Court of Appeal considered that it was fixed, giving effect to the parties' terms as they stood.

The reasoning of the Court of Appeal was rejected in *Agnew v Inland Revenue Commissioner*,[72] where the Privy Council exhaustively reviewed the authorities on the fixed/floating charge dichotomy. The charge in *Agnew* was in virtually identical terms to that in *New Bullas*, and here it was held to be a floating charge. According to Lord Millett, the critical question in determining the nature of a charge is whether the company "should be free to deal with the charged assets and to withdraw them from the security without the consent of the holder of the

---

[67] Below, p.516.
[68] [1979] 2 Lloyds Rep. 142.
[69] *Re Brightlife Ltd* [1987] Ch. 200. See also *Re G.E. Tunbridge Ltd* [1995] 1 B.C.L.C. 34.
[70] [1986] B.C.L.C. 242 (Ir).
[71] [1994] 1 B.C.L.C. 485, CA.
[72] [2001] 2 A.C. 710.

charge." If control of the charged assets lies with the chargor the charge is a floating charge, if it lies with the chargee then it is fixed. The *Bullas* debenture gave the chargor rights of disposal of the debts that were inherently inconsistent with the charge being fixed, and the case was wrongly decided.

The decision in *Agnew* seemed also to have implications for standard form debentures requiring a chargee to pay the proceeds of book debts into a nominated bank account (most often with the chargee). Lord Millett supported the reasoning in *Re Keenan Bros*[73] and suggested that where the chargor was free to draw on the nominated account the charge would be floating: the requirement of payment into the nominated account would not be an adequate restriction, of itself, on the company's freedom to deal with the charged debts.

This dicta was followed at first instance in *Re Spectrum Plus Ltd*[74] in relation to a charge, similar to that seen in *Siebe Gorman & Co. Ltd*,[75] requiring the company to pay the proceeds of its book debts into an account with the chargee bank but allowing the company to draw on that account. The judge categorised the charge as floating. However, the Court of Appeal[76] overruled the judge and held the charge to be fixed. This was because, as a matter of banking law, moneys paid into a bank account cease to be the property of the payer and become that of the bank,[77] although the bank may give the account holder a contractual right to make withdrawals from the account. Thus, the chargee bank could be said to have imposed adequate controls on the proceeds of the debt for the charge to be fixed, notwithstanding that the chargee retained a contractual right to draw on the account.

Further, in *Re Spectrum Plus Ltd*[78] the Court of Appeal held that, according to the doctrine of precedent, it was bound to follow *Re New Bullas Trading Ltd Ltd*.[79] That decision therefore remains good law, notwithstanding the opinion of the Privy Council in *Agnew v Inland Revenue Commissioner*[80] that it was wrongly decided. Unless and until the House of Lords has the opportunity to consider this area of law, it appears that the issue of fixed charges over book debts remains a troubled one.[81]

Retention of title clauses

Sellers, particularly of raw materials, frequently protect themselves by inserting into the contract of sale a retention of title or *"Romalpa"* clause whereby they seek to retain title to the materials supplied until the buyer has paid for them. There have been many cases since the original decision in *Aluminium Industrie Vaassen BV v Romalpa Aluminium Ltd*[82] that such a clause could have the effect

---

[73] [1986] B.C.L.C 242 (Ir).
[74] [2004] EWHC 9.
[75] [1979] 2 Lloyd's Rep. 142.
[76] [2004] EWCA 607.
[77] *Foley v Hill* (1848) 2 HLC 28.
[78] [2004] EWCA 607.
[79] [1994] 1 B.C.L.C. 485, CA.
[80] [2001] 2 A.C. 710.
[81] At the time of writing, leave has been given to appeal against the decision of the Court of Appeal in *Re Spectrum Plus Ltd*.
[82] [1978] 1 W.L.R. 676, CA.

of retaining the legal title to the goods. Some clauses have failed, *e.g.* because the raw materials have ceased to exist,[83] or because they have created a floating charge which has thus been declared void for non-registration under the Companies Act[84] or because they have created a charge over the book debts of the company, which again is void for non-registration.[85] The distinction is always one of construction of the particular clause—is the buyer conferring a charge on *his* goods or the proceeds of sale of those goods[86] in favour of the seller,[87] or is the seller retaining title to *his* goods to provide himself with a security.[88] It may be indicative of the former if the seller attempts to retain title to the goods into which the raw materials have been incorporated.[89]

A seller supplied yarn to some fabric manufacturers. He included a clause whereby the ownership of the yarn was to remain with the seller and if it was incorporated into other goods the ownership of these other goods was to remain with the seller, in either case until payment. The Court of Appeal held that the first part of the clause was a valid retention of title clause whereas the second created a floating charge. Since only the unused yarn was claimed the seller was allowed to succeed: *Clough Mill Ltd v Geoffrey Martin* [1985] 1 W.L.R. 111, CA.

If there is a valid retention of title clause and the purchaser sells on the goods, to a sub-purchaser also subject to such a clause, the original seller can claim title in the goods until the sub-purchaser pays the purchaser.[90] A valid clause can retain the seller's title until *all* debts due from the buyer have been discharged.[91]

Priority of charges (English law)

Whilst fixed charges over the same assets rank in the order of creation, a company which has created a floating charge cannot later create another floating charge over some of the same assets ranking in priority to or *pari passu* with the original charge unless the provisions of the original charge allow this.[92]

On the other hand, since a company which has created a floating charge can, without the consent of the holders of the charge, deal with the class of assets in the ordinary course of business, it follows that the company can, in the ordinary course of business, create a later fixed charge, legal or equitable, over specific assets and with priority over the floating charge,[93] unless the floating charge

---

[83] *Borden (U.K.) Ltd v Scottish Timber Products Ltd* [1981] Ch. 25; *Chaigley Farms Ltd v Crawford Kaye & Grayshire Ltd* [1996] B.C.C. 957.

[84] *Re Bond Worth Ltd* [1980] Ch. 228; *Stroud Architectural Systems Ltd v John Laing Construction Ltd* [1994] 2 B.C.L.C. 276.

[85] *E. Pfeiffer Weinkellerei-Weineinkauf GmbH & Co. v Arbuthnot Factors Ltd* [1988] 1 W.L.R. 150; *Re Weldtech Equipment Ltd* [1991] B.C.L.C. 393.

[86] *Tatung (U.K.) Ltd v Galex Telesure Ltd* (1989) 5 B.C.C. 325.

[87] *Re Peachdart Ltd* [1984] Ch. 131; *Specialist Plant Services Ltd v Braithwaite Ltd* (1987) 3 B.C.C. 119, CA.

[88] *Hendy Lennox (Industrial Engines) Ltd v Grahame Puttick Ltd* [1984] 1 W.L.R. 485; *Re Andrabell Ltd* [1984] B.C.L.C. 522.

[89] *John Snow & Co. Ltd v D. B. G. Woodcroft & Co. Ltd* [1985] B.C.L.C. 54.

[90] *Re Highway Foods International Ltd* [1995] 1 B.C.L.C. 209.

[91] *Armour v Thyssen Edelstahlwerke AG* [1991] 2 A.C. 339.

[92] *Re Automatic Bottle Makers Ltd* [1926] Ch. 412, CA.

[93] *Wheatley v Silkstone, etc., Coal Co.* (1885) 29 Ch.D. 715.

provides that the company is not to create any mortgage or charge ranking *pari passu* with or in priority to the floating charge, known as a negative pledge clause, in which case any fixed chargee taking *with notice of this provision*[94] will be postponed to the floating charge. In spite of such a provision the holder of a specific charge will obtain priority over a floating charge on all the company's property if:

(1) taking a legal charge, he obtains his charge without notice of the provision, even though he has notice of the debentures[95]—the maxim "where the equities are equal the law prevails" will apply; or

(2) taking an equitable fixed charge, he obtains the title deeds without notice of the debentures[96]—the maxim "where the equities are otherwise equal the earlier in time has priority" will not apply since the debenture holders left the title deeds with the company so as to enable it to deal with its property as if it was unincumbered so that the equities are not equal.

Further, registration of a floating charge under the Companies Act, below,[97] although constructive notice under certain circumstances of the charge, is not notice that the charge contains a provision prohibiting the creation of subsequent charges with priority over the floating charge.[98]

A floating charge is also postponed to an earlier fixed charge, including an earlier floating charge which has crystallised prior to the creation of the second charge.[99]

The following also have priority over a floating charge:

(1) an execution creditor if the goods are sold by the sheriff,[1] or the company pays out the sheriff to avoid a sale,[2] or the creditor obtains a garnishee order absolute[3] (not a garnishee order nisi),[4] *before* crystallisation of the floating charge;

(2) a landlord's distress for rent or a local authority's distress for unpaid business rates levied before crystallisation[5];

---

[94] But see n.95, below.
[95] *English and Scottish Mercantile etc. Co. Ltd v Brunton* [1892] 2 Q.B. 700, CA.
[96] *Re Castell & Brown Ltd* [1898] 1 Ch. 315.
[97] pp.519, *et seq.*
[98] *per* Eve J. in *Wilson v Kelland* [1910] 2 Ch. 306 at p.313; *Dempsey v Traders' Finance Corpn.* [1933] N.Z.L.R. 1258, CA; but see *Ian Chisholm Textiles Ltd v Griffiths* [1994] 2 B.C.L.C. 291.
[99] *Re The Real Meat Co. Ltd* [1996] B.C.C. 254, [1997] B.C.C. 537, CA.
[1] *Re Standard Manufacturing Co.* [1891] 1 Ch. 627, CA.
[2] *Heaton and Dugard Ltd v Cutting Bros. Ltd* [1925] 1 K.B. 655.
[3] *Evans v Rival Granite Quarries Ltd* [1910] 2 K.B. 979, CA.
[4] *Norton v Yates* [1906] 1 K.B. 112.
[5] *Re Roundwood Colliery Co.* [1897] 1 Ch. 373, CA; *Re ELS Ltd* [1994] B.C.C. 449. It follows that where distress is levied after crystallisation the floating charge takes priority. However, where a floating charge crystallised before the company's landlord served a distress notice on the company's tenants which assigned their rents to the landlord, the chargee still took priority over the landlord, since the latter had notice of the crystallisation, which was an earlier assignment by the company to the chargee: *Rhodes v Allied Dunbar Pension Services Ltd* [1988] B.C.L.C. 186.

(3) the rights of persons such as one who has sold goods to the company under a hire-purchase agreement by which the goods are still the property of such person[6];

(4) the rights of certain statutorily preferred creditors: ss 40, 175, 176A I.A. 1986.[7]

On the other hand a floating charge may not be postponed to the holder of a *Mareva* injunction over the assets. Such an injunction prohibits the company from removing its assets outside the United Kingdom. The holder of the floating charge may apply to have the injunction set aside and will succeed if the holders of the injunction are unsecured creditors.[8]

Fixed securities and floating charges (Scots law)

Before 1961, any attempt by a Scottish company to create a floating charge was of no effect, since such a charge violated the principle of the common law expressed in the maxim *"traditionibus, non nudis pactis, dominia rerum transferuntur,"* *i.e.* "delivery, and not mere agreement, is required for the transfer of real rights."

> "There is no principle more deeply rooted in the law than this, that in order to create a good security over subjects delivery must be given. If possession be retained no effectual security can be granted"; *per* Lord Shand in *Clark v West Calder Oil Co. Ltd* (1882) 9 R. 1017 at p.1033 (a case in which trustees for debenture holders to whom the company had assigned certain leasehold and moveable property in security were held to have no preference over the ordinary trade creditors of the company since no possession had followed on the assignation).

"The whole method of creating a floating charge . . . is absolutely foreign to our law": *per* Lord President Dunedin in *The Ballachulish Slate Quarries Co. Ltd v Bruce* (1908) 16 S.L.T. 48 at p.51 (an attempt to create a floating charge in English form on the uncalled capital and other assets of a company was held to give a debenture holder no valid security).

A company registered in Scotland and having a place of business and assets in England borrowed money under debentures which were in English form and by which the company purported to create a floating charge over its whole undertakings, property and assets. *Held*, that no valid and effectual floating charge had been created even over the company's assets in England: *Carse v Coppen*, 1951 S.C. 233.

> "It is clear in principle and amply supported by authority that a floating charge is utterly repugnant to the principles of Scots law and is not recognised by us as creating a security at all. In Scotland the term 'equitable security' is meaningless. Putting aside the rare and exceptional cases of hypothec, we require for the constitution of a security which will confer upon the holder rights over and above those which he enjoys in common with the general body of unsecured creditors of a debtor, (a) the transfer to the creditor of a real right in specific subjects by the method appropriate for the constitution of such rights in the particular classes of property in question, or (b) the creation of a nexus over specific property by the due use of the appropriate

---

[6] See *Re Morrison, Jones and Taylor Ltd* [1914] 1 Ch. 50, CA.
[7] Below, Chs 25, 26, 27.
[8] *Cretanor Maritime Co. Ltd v Irish Marine Management Ltd* [1978] 1 W.L.R. 966, CA.

form of diligence. A floating charge, even after appointment of a receiver, satisfies none of these requirements": *per* Lord President Cooper at p.239.

Floating charges were introduced to Scots law by the Companies (Floating Charges) (Scotland) Act 1961, but there was no power under that Act to appoint receivers. Subsequently, on the recommendation of the Scottish Law Commission,[9] the Companies (Floating Charges and Receivers) (Scotland) Act 1972 was passed with the twofold purpose of:

(1) re–enacting with substantial modification the provisions of the Act of 1961; and

(2) making it competent under Scots law for receivers to be appointed.

The 1972 Act was subsequently repealed and appeared as ss 462 to 487 of the 1985 Act. Of these sections the first five (*i.e.* ss 462 to 466) relate to floating charges and are still applicable, but the remaining sections (*i.e.* ss 467 to 487) relating to receivers were amended by the Insolvency Act 1985 and in their amended form have now been consolidated by the Insolvency Act 1986, where they appear as ss 50 to 71.

Scottish floating charges and receivers have statutory definitions and statutory incidents which distinguish them in some respects from their English common law originals. The term "fixed security" is used in the statutory provisions to denote a security other than a floating charge.[10]

Floating charges (Scots law)

The main characteristics of the Scottish floating charge are:

(1) It is a charge created by an incorporated company[11] over all or any part of the property (including uncalled capital) which may from time to time be comprised in its property and undertaking.

(2) It may be created for the purpose of securing any debt or other obligation (including a cautionary obligation) incurred or to be incurred by, or binding upon, the company or any other person. It is therefore possible, for instance, for a subsidiary company to create a floating charge over its own property to secure a debt due by its parent company (another person), or for a subsidiary company to guarantee a debt due by its parent company and create a floating charge over its own property to secure its liability under the guarantee.

(3) It can be created by a Scottish company only by words in a bond or other written acknowledgment of a debt or obligation which purports to create a floating charge. There is no longer any statutory form as there

---

[9] *Report on the Companies (Floating Charges) (Scotland) Act 1961*, (1970) Cmnd. 4336.

[10] s.486.

[11] Floating charges may also be created by industrial and provident societies registered in Scotland: Industrial and Provident Societies Act 1967, as amended by the Companies (Floating Charges and Receivers) (Scotland) Act 1972, s.10. See now the Financial Services and Markets Act 2000 (Mutual Societies) Order 2001 (SI 2001/2617).

was under the 1961 Act. An alternative to execution by the company itself is execution by an attorney who has been authorised for that purpose by writing under the company's common seal. Where the floating charge relates to heritable property in Scotland, it takes effect on that property even although the instrument creating it has not been recorded in the Register of Sasines or registered under the Land Registration (Scotland) Act 1979: s.462.

(4) On the commencement of the winding up or on the appointment of a receiver it attaches (provided it is not invalid under s.410 of the 1985 Act[12] or s.245 of the Insolvency Act 1986[13]) to the property then comprised in the company's property and undertaking. Where heritable property had been disponed by a company and the disposition had been delivered to the purchaser but had not yet been recorded before the appointment of a receiver, the property was held to be no longer beneficially owned by the company and was not therefore attached by the floating charge.[14]

References in the Act to the crystallisation of a floating charge are, in relation to a Scottish floating charge, construed as references to the attachment of the charge.[15]

(5) Once attached it has the same effect as if it were a fixed security over the property for the principal of, and any interest due or to become due on, the debt or obligation to which it relates. The security extends to interest stipulated for from the date of attachment until payment.[16]

(6) It is postponed to the rights of certain creditors[17]: s.463.

The instrument creating a floating charge may contain:

(a) provisions prohibiting or restricting the creation of any fixed security or any other floating charge having priority over, or ranking equally with, the floating charge[18]; or

(b) with the consent of the holder of any subsisting floating charge or fixed security which would be adversely affected, provisions regulating the order in which the floating charge is to rank with any other subsisting or future floating charges or fixed securities over the property or part of it: s.464.[19]

---

[12] Below, p.524.

[13] Below, p.516.

[14] *Sharp v Thomson* 1997 S.C. HL 66.

[15] ss 419(4) and 420, inserted by C.A. 1989, s.104.

[16] *National Commercial Bank of Scotland Ltd v Liquidators of Telford Grier Mackay & Co. Ltd*, 1969 S.C. 181, followed in *Royal Bank of Scotland Ltd v Williamson*, 1972 S.L.T. (Sh.Ct.) 45, and given statutory force by s.463(4).

[17] Below, Ch.29.

[18] For an example see *AIB Finance Ltd v Bank of Scotland* 1993 S.C. 588 (clause in floating charge prohibiting creation of subsequent standard securities gave the holder of the floating charge and the receiver priority over the holder of the standard security).

[19] As amended by s.140 Companies Act 1989.

A floating charge may be altered by an instrument of alteration: s.466.

The advantage of a floating charge from the *company's* point of view is that the company can give security for a loan to it by charging property such as stock-in-trade and other moveables which it would be impracticable to deliver to the lender. Until the floating charge has attached to the property the company can, in the ordinary course of business, realise any of its assets without the consent of the creditor who is entitled to the benefit of the floating charge.

From the *creditor's* point of view, the two disadvantages exemplified on p.507, above, in relation to English law, apply also in Scots law, but for the protection of the creditor it is provided that a Scots company may be wound up by the court "if there is subsisting a floating charge over property comprised in the company's property and undertaking and the court is satisfied that the security of the creditor entitled to the benefit of the floating charge is in jeopardy". The security of the creditor is deemed to be in jeopardy "if the court is satisfied that events have occurred or are about to occur which render it unreasonable in the creditor's interests that the company should retain power to dispose of the property which is subject to the floating charge": Insolvency Act 1986, s.122(2).

Priority of charges (Scots law)

Where all or any part of a company's property is subject both to a fixed security and to a floating charge, the fixed security has as a general rule priority over the floating charge. This is always so if the fixed security is one arising by operation of law (*e.g.* by a statutory provision). If the fixed security is not of that nature (*e.g.* is a standard security over heritable property under the Conveyancing and Feudal Reform (Scotland) Act 1970),[19a] the order of ranking may be regulated by provisions in the document which creates the floating charge or in any instrument of alteration. Where the right to a fixed security has become a real right before a floating charge has attached, the fixed security has priority of ranking over the floating charge.

Where there are two or more floating charges, the charges as a general rule rank with one another according to the time of their registration with the Registrar,[20] and if received by the Registrar by the same postal delivery they rank equally with one another. Here again the order of ranking may be regulated by provisions in the document creating a floating charge or in any instrument of alteration. There is, however, the following statutory restriction on the priority which may be obtained: where the holder of a floating charge which has been registered receives a written intimation of the subsequent registration of another floating charge over the same property or part of it, the preference in ranking of the first floating charge is restricted to security for:

(a)   the holder's present advances;

(b)   future advances which he may be required to make;

(c)   interest due or to become due on advances within (a) and (b), above; and

---

[19a] See now the Abolition of Feudal Tenure etc. (Scotland) Act 2000.
[20] Below, p.521.

(d) expenses or outlays reasonably incurred by the holder: s.464.

The following have priority over a floating charge:

(1) the rights of any person who has effectually executed diligence on the property or any part of it: s.463.[20a] The meaning of the phrase "effectually executed diligence" is uncertain: in *Lord Advocate v Royal Bank of Scotland Ltd*, 1977 S.C. 177, it was suggested that arrestment only became "effectually executed diligence" when completed by an action of furthcoming and in *Armour and Mycroft, Petitioners*, 1983 S.L.T. 453 (O.H.), the creditor conceded without argument that an inhibition laid after the granting of a floating charge but not followed by adjudication before the appointment of receivers was ineffectual;

(2) the rights of persons such as one who has sold goods to the company under a hire-purchase agreement by which the goods are still the property of such person;

(3) certain *un*secured but preferential debts: Insolvency Act 1986, s.175.[21]

Avoidance of floating charges

To prevent those in control of insolvent companies from creating floating charges to secure past debts so as to gain priority over other unsecured creditors, s.245 of the Insolvency Act 1986 provides that floating charges created within 12 months prior to the presentation of a successful petition for a winding up[22] or for an administration order[23] are invalid unless the company was solvent immediately after the charge was created, except insofar as money was paid or goods or services supplied to the company or a debt of the company was reduced or discharged, in consideration of and at the same time as or after the creation of the charge, with interest if appropriate.

The position is different if the floating charge is created in favour of a person who is connected with the company. In such cases the ambit of the section is widened to catch floating charges created within two years prior to the winding-up or administration petition, as appropriate, and it is of no consequence that the company was solvent immediately after granting the charge.

The difficulty therefore is to establish whether money was paid, goods or services supplied or a debt reduced or discharged in consideration of the charge and whether that was at the same time as the creation of the charge. The value of any goods or services so supplied are to be valued at the cost which could reasonably be expected to be paid for goods or services supplied at that time in the ordinary course of business and on the same terms (apart from the granting

---

[20a] See *Commissioners of Customs and Excise v John D Reid Joinery Ltd* 2001 S.L.T. 588, O.H., where a bank's floating charge of 1994 was held to confer on it rights and preference of a holder of a fixed security, but not to otherwise alter the effect of insolvency on diligence.

[21] Below, Ch.27.

[22] This, and not the date of the winding-up order is the relevant date: *Power v Sharp Investments Ltd* [1994] 1 B.C.L.C. 111, CA.

[23] Below, Ch.26.

of a floating charge) as those on which they were supplied to the company. Section 245 replaced s.617 of the Companies Act 1985 which invalidated floating charges created within a year of a winding up except to the amount of any cash paid to the company in consideration and at the time of the charge (unless the company was solvent immediately after granting the charge).

Whether cash was paid at the time when the charge was created was a question of fact for s.617, and "a payment made on account of the consideration for the security, in anticipation of its creation and in reliance on a promise to execute it, although made some days before its execution, [was] made at the time of its creation within the meaning of the section."[24] Section 245, on the other hand, expressly requires it to be paid *at the same time as or after the creation of the charge*.

The question arises, therefore, as to whether the relaxed attitude of the courts under the former section has been preserved.

In *Re Fairway Magazines Ltd*,[25] Mummery J. considered that it had and that the advancing of the cash and the creation of the charge should be regarded as a matter of substance rather than form so that a month's gap between the two did not prevent the cash being paid to the company at the same time as the charge. In *Re Shoe Lace Ltd*,[26] on the other hand, Hoffmann J. considered that the wording between the old and new sections was sufficiently different to justify a new approach which he considered should be whether a reasonable businessman, having knowledge of the statute, would regard the money as having been paid at the same time as the charge.

The reasoning of both judges was, however, rejected by the Court of Appeal in the *Shoe Lace* case.[27] The Court of Appeal decided that the difference in wording was insufficient to justify a distinction from the old cases but that they had been wrongly decided in the first place. It followed that any gap between the advancement of the cash and the creation of the charge would invoke s.245.[28] A mere agreement to create a charge at the time when the money was advanced would not be enough unless that agreement itself created an equitable charge. The words "in consideration for the charge" in s.617 meant "in consideration of the fact that the charge exists".

A company created a floating charge to secure its overdrawn current account with its bank. *Held*: (1) Every payment made by the bank to the company after the creation of the charge was "cash paid to the company" and was made in consideration of the charge. Consequently the charge was not invalid against the liquidator, and the bank was a secured creditor as to such payments. (2) The rule in *Clayton's Case*[29] applied. Each payment by the bank after the date of the charge was a provision of "new money" and there was nothing to displace the presumption that payments in by the company after the charge should be set in the first instance against the company's debt to the bank at the date of the charge: *Re Yeovil Glove Co. Ltd* [1965] Ch.148, CA.

[24] *per* Neville J. in *Re Columbian Fireproofing Co. Ltd* [1910] 1 Ch. 758, at p.765; *Re F. & E. Stanton Ltd* [1928] 1 Ch. 180.
[25] [1992] B.C.C. 924.
[26] [1992] B.C.L.C. 636.
[27] Reported as *Power v Sharp Investments Ltd* [1994] 1 B.C.L.C. 111, CA.
[28] Although they did concede that a short break for coffee might not count!
[29] (1816) 1 Mer. 572.

Section 245 of the Insolvency Act uses the phrase "so much of the consideration as consists of". *Quaere* whether *Re Yeovil Glove Co. Ltd* is still valid?

In *Mace Builders (Glasgow) Ltd v Lunn*[30] it was held that the effect of s.617 was
simply to render the charge invalid from the date of the winding up so that where
the charge was repaid prior to the winding up the section had no effect.[31] The
wording of s.245 is not identical, however, and it may be that the position is now
different.

Payments made direct to the company's creditors, though made on the
company's behalf, have been held not to be within the phrase "Cash paid to the
company".[32] The question is one of substance, however.

D. was a director of the company and a partner in the firm of D. & Co. who supplied
goods to the company. The company owed D. & Co. £1,954 and D. & Co. refused to
supply any more goods until this debt was paid. In March D., who wished to save the
company, agreed to lend the company £3,000 on the security of a floating charge if the
company would, out of this sum, pay £1,954 to D. & Co. This was done. The company was
insolvent at the time. In July the company went into liquidation. *Held*, the floating charge
was valid, the whole £3,000 being cash paid to the company: *Re Matthew Ellis Ltd* [1933] 1
Ch. 458.

On the other hand, the cash must have been intended to benefit the company
and not certain creditors or the directors.[33]

An insolvent company granted a floating charge to Z to secure £900. The money was
provided by D, for whom Z was a nominee, and the same day as it was paid to the
company the company paid £350 each to B and S for directors' fees and £200 to D, the
amount guaranteed by D in respect of the company's overdraft. Within 12 months, the
company went into liquidation. *Held*, the charge was invalid, as its object was to benefit B,
S and D and not the company—in substance, no cash was paid to the company: *Re
Destone Fabrics Ltd* [1941] Ch.319, CA.

Cash was held not to be paid to the company where the substance of the
transaction was the substitition of a better security for the company's debts.[34] It
was also said that the section would apply irrespective of the motives of the
chargee.[35] These decisions on whether cash has been paid to the company have
been applied to s.245.[36]

Preferences and transactions at an undervalue

Any charge made by a company within *six* months[37] before the commencement of
winding up, or presentation of a successful administration petition is void if it is a
preference of any of the company's creditors, or, within a two year period, if it is
part of a transaction of an undervalue, or within a three year period, if it is part

[30] (1986) 130 S.J. 839, CA.
[31] See also *Re Parkes Garage* [1929] 1 Ch. 139.
[32] *Libertas-Kommerz GmbH v Johnston*, 1977 S.C. 191 (O.H.).
[33] *Re Orleans Motor Co. Ltd* [1911] 2 Ch. 41.
[34] *Re G. T. Whyte & Co. Ltd* [1983] B.C.L.C. 311.
[35] *ibid., per* Nourse J., p.317.
[36] *Re Fairway Magazines Ltd* [1992] B.C.C. 924.
[37] Two years for persons connected with the company.

of an extortionate credit transaction: Insolvency Act 1986, ss 238–244, ch. 29, below.

REGISTRATION OF CHARGES

Charges created by a company are required to be registered (1) in the company's own register of charges, and (2) with the Registrar of Companies.

Registration in company's own register of charges

Section 407, applicable in England, provides that every *limited* company must keep at its registered office a register of *all* charges specifically affecting the property of the company and *all* floating charges on the undertaking or any property of the company. The register must give:

(a) a short description of the property charged;

(b) the amount of the charge;

(c) the names of the persons entitled thereto, except in the case of bearer securities.

There is a corresponding provision for Scotland in s.422 but that section applies to *every* company and is not restricted to *limited* companies.

The omission to comply with s.407 or s.422 merely results in a fine on every officer who is knowingly a party to the omission. The validity of the charge is *not* affected.

Every company must keep a copy of every instrument creating a charge required to be registered under s.407, s.422, or under ss 395 and 400 (for Scotland, ss 410 and 416), below, at the registered office of the company. In the case of a series of uniform debentures a copy of one of the series is sufficient: ss 406 and 421.

These copies, and also the company's register of charges, are open to the inspection of any creditor or member of the company without fee for at least two hours each day during business hours. The register of charges *only* is similarly open to the general public on payment of a fee not exceeding five pence: ss 408 and 423.

Registration with Registrar

There are some differences between the registration requirements imposed on English companies by the Act and those imposed on Scottish companies originally by the, now consolidated, Companies (Floating Charges and Receivers) (Scotland) Act 1972.[37a]

[37a] This Act was subsequently repealed by the Companies Consolidation (Consequential Receivers) Act 1985.

Registration in England

Section 395 provides that prescribed particulars of certain specified charges *created* by companies registered in England, together with the instrument, if any, creating them, must be delivered to the Registrar within 21 days after their creation. The object of registration is to protect the grantee of the charge.[38]

The charges to which s.395 applies are specified in s.396:

(a) a charge to secure an issue of debentures;

(b) a charge on uncalled share capital;

(c) a charge created or evidenced by an instrument which, if executed by an individual, would require registration as a bill of sale[39];

(d) a charge on any land or any interest therein;

The general rule is that a deposit of title deeds by a company to secure a debt, whether owed by the company or a third party creates an equitable charge on the land,[40] and not just a naked lien on the documents themselves, which charge is registrable under s.395 since it is contractual in nature even though created as a result of a presumption of law.[41]

(e) a charge on book debts of the company;

If a company which has entered into hire-purchase agreements for the disposal of its products deposits the agreements as security for advances, there is a charge on the company's book debts.[42] Whether a particular agreement amounts to a charge on book debts is a question of construction.[43] In *Morris v Rayners Enterprises Inc*[44] the House of Lords held that it was possible for a creditor to grant a charge-back to the debtor on the debt but left open the question of whether such a charge was registerable as a book debt.

A charge on future book debts is registrable under s.395. However, where the subject-matter of a charge at the date of its creation is the benefit of a contract which does not then comprehend a book debt, *e.g.* a contract of insurance, the contract cannot be brought within s.395 merely because it might ultimately result in a book debt.[45] The test is whether there is a charge on future book debts as

---

[38] *Per* Bankes L.J. in *National Provincial Bank v Charnley* [1924] 1 K.B. 431, CA at p.442.

[39] See *Stoneleigh Finance Ltd v Phillips* [1965] 2 Q.B. 537, CA. The transfer of goods by way of security is caught by this head: *Welsh Development Agency v Export Finance Co. Ltd* [1991] B.C.L.C. 936, reversed on other grounds [1992] B.C.L.C. 148.

[40] But see *Re Alton Corporation* [1985] B.C.L.C. 27.

[41] *Re Wallis & Simmonds (Builders) Ltd* [1974] 1 W.L.R. 391, distinguishing *London and Cheshire Insce. Co. Ltd v Laplagrene Property Co. Ltd* [1971] Ch. 499 (unpaid vendor's lien created by law not registrable). In *Wallis & Simmonds* there was no lien on the title deeds having a separate existence and the charge was void for non-registration.

[42] *Independent Automatic Sales Ltd v Knowles & Foster* [1962] 1 W.L.R. 974.

[43] *Carreras Rothmans Ltd v Freeman Matthews Treasure Ltd* [1985] 1 All E.R. 155; *Re Welsh Irish Ferries Ltd* [1985] 3 W.L.R. 610; *Orion Finance Ltd v Crown Financial Management Ltd* [1996] 2 B.C.L.C. 78.

[44] [1998] A.C. 214.

[45] *Paul & Frank Ltd v Discount Bank (Overseas) Ltd* [1967] Ch. 348.

and when they arise or there is simply an assignment of a contingent contractual right[46];

(f) a floating charge on the undertaking or property of the company;

There is no requirement to register a possessory lien over certain assets of a company. The fact that the lien includes a power of sale does not convert it into a floating charge. The distinction is that a lien depends upon possession, whereas a floating charge does not.[47]

(g) a charge on calls made but not paid;

(h) a charge on a ship or aircraft;

(i) a charge on goodwill, on a patent or a licence under a patent, on a trademark or on a copyright or a licence under a copyright.

Registration in Scotland[47a]

For Scotland s.410, corresponding to ss 395–396, requires registration of prescribed particulars of certain specified charges created by companies, together with *certified copies* of any instruments creating the charges.

The section applies to the following charges:

(a) A charge on land wherever situated or any interest therein. Hence registration with the Registrar in Scotland is required of a charge created by a Scottish company over heritable property in England.[48]

(b) A security over the uncalled share capital of the company.

(c) A security over incorporeal moveable property of any of the following categories—

   (i) the book debts of the company;
   (ii) calls made but not paid;
   (iii) goodwill;
   (iv) a patent or a licence under a patent;
   (v) a trademark;
   (vi) a copyright or a licence under a copyright;
   (vii) a registered design or a licence of respect of such a design;
   (viii) a design or a licence under a design right.

(d) A security over a ship or aircraft.

(e) A floating charge.

A security over incorporeal moveable property not falling within any of the categories specified (*e.g.* shares in other companies) does not require registration,

---

[46] *Re Brush Aggregates* [1986] B.C.L.C. 320.
[47] *Re Hamlet International plc* [1999] 2 B.C.L.C. 506 (CA).
[47a] Recently reviewed by the Scottish Law Commission in its report, *Registration of Rights in Security by Companies*, No.197 (TSO, 2004).
[48] *Amalgamated Securites Ltd, Petitioners*, 1967 S.C. 56.

and if particulars of such a charge have been registered the court will order their deletion from the register.[49]

It is to be observed that a charge to secure an issue of debentures which is the first in the English list is absent from the Scottish list. "For some inscrutable reason no corresponding provision has been made in regard to Scotland."[50]

In the Companies (Floating Charges) (Scotland) Act 1961 no provision was made for re-registration of any instrument creating a charge,[51] or for registration of an instrument increasing the amount secured.[52] Consequently, if at a later date the amount secured by a fixed charge was to be increased, the security had to be re-created from the beginning, a "cumbersome and expensive" practice for which the Scottish Law Commission suggested a remedy.[53] The 1972 Act accordingly provided that where the amount secured by a fixed charge was increased, a further charge was to be held to have been created, and that the registration provisions applied to that further charge. The provision is now in s.414(2) of the 1985 Act.

A fixed charge on land cannot now be created in any form other than a "standard security" under the Conveyancing and Feudal Reform (Scotland) Act 1970. For the creation of a real right the standard security must be recorded in the Register of Sasines or registered in the Land Register of Scotland: 1970 Act, ss 9, 11; Land Registration (Scotland) Act 1979, ss 2, 3 as amended by the Abolition of Feudal Tenure etc. (Scotland) Act 2000.

Section 410(5) provides that the date of creation of a floating charge is the date on which the instrument creating the floating charge is executed by the company, and the date of creation of any other charge is the date on which the right of the person entitled to the benefit of the charge becomes a real right, *e.g.* in the case of a standard security, the date of recording in the Register of Sasines.[54]

The registration provisions extend to any instrument of alteration under s.466(4) if the instrument:

(a) prohibits or restricts the creation of any fixed security or any other floating charge having priority over, or ranking equally with, the floating charge; or

(b) varies, or otherwise regulates the order of, the ranking of the floating charge in relation to fixed securities or to other floating charges; or

(c) releases property from the floating charge; or

(d) increases the amount secured by the floating charge.

Registration in England and Scotland

In the case of a series of debentures containing, or giving by reference to another instrument, a charge to the benefit of which the debenture holders are entitled *pari passu*, it is sufficient if the following particulars are registered:

---

[49] *Scottish Homes Investment Co. Ltd, Petitioners,* 1968 S.C. 244.
[50] *per* Lord President Clyde in the *Scottish Homes* case, above, at p.248 (shares in other companies assigned to trustees in security for an issue of debenture stock).
[51] *Archibald Campbell, Hope & King Ltd, Petitioners,* 1967 S.C. 21.
[52] *Scottish and Newcastle Breweries Ltd v Liquidator of Rathburne Hotel Co. Ltd,* 1970 S.C. 215 (O.H.).
[53] (1970) Cmnd. 4336, paras 17, 18.
[54] See n.51, above.

   (a) the total amount secured by the series;

   (b) the dates of the resolutions authorising the issue of the series and the date of the covering deed, if any, by which the security is created;

   (c) a general description of the property charged;

   (d) the names of the trustees, if any, for the debenture holders; and

   (e) in the case of a Scottish floating charge, a statement of the restrictions, if any, on the company's power to grant further securities ranking prior to or equally with the floating charge;

together with the deed (or in Scotland a copy of the deed) creating the charge or, if there is no deed, one of the debentures (or in Scotland a copy of one of the debentures) of the series: ss 397, 413. The sections also require registration of the date and amount of each issue in the series but failure to do so does not affect the validity of the debentures.

Particulars of the amount, or rate per cent, of the commission, allowance or discount on an issue of debentures must be registered: ss 397, 413(3).

The register contains the following particulars:

   (a) in the case of a series of debentures, the particulars set out above;

   (b) in other cases—

      (i) the date of the creation of the charge;
      (ii) the amount secured by the charge;
      (iii) short particulars of the property charged;
      (iv) the persons entitled to the charge; and
      (v) in the case of a Scottish floating charge, a statement of the restrictions, if any, on the company's power to grant further securities ranking prior to or equally with the floating charge: ss 401, 417(3).

It is the duty of the company to register the particulars required by s.395 or s.410. Registration, however, may be effected by any person interested in the charge and the registration fees may be recovered from the company: ss 399, 415.

On the registration of a charge the Registrar gives a certificate of registration which is conclusive evidence that the requirements of the Act as to registration have been complied with: ss 401(2)(b), 418(2)(c). The particulars delivered to the Registrar may incorrectly state the property charged, or the amount or date of the charge, but if a certificate is given, the grantee of the charge is protected.[55]

---

[55] This is equally true where the particulars are delivered late with the consent of the court under s.404, below: *Exeter Trust Ltd v Screenways Ltd* [1991] B.C.L.C. 888.

The certificate is conclusive evidence that the Registrar has entered the particulars in the register and that the prescribed, *i.e.* accurate, particulars have been presented to him.[56]

> In the course of its business in 1960 a company bought properties. R., a shareholder, advanced money for each purchase and the company undertook to execute formal mortgages on demand. In 1961 the directors and R. agreed that the company should implement its undertakings, and memoranda of deposit of title deeds purporting to charge some of the properties with payments to R. of certain sums on demand were signed but not dated on June 5, 1961. On July 11, the memoranda were registered with the Registrar, the date of execution being given as June 23. On August 4, the company went into voluntary winding-up. *Held*, the charges were not void since the certificate of registration was conclusive that all the requirements of the Act had been complied with within 21 days of execution, although the particulars submitted for registration incorrectly stated the date of the charges: *Re Eric Holmes (Property) Ltd* [1965] Ch.1052, applied in *Re C. L. Nye Ltd* [1971] Ch 442, CA.

The Registrar used to adopt the practice whereby if incorrect particulars of a charge were delivered for registration within the 21-day period he would register the charge after the 21-day period on the delivery of amended particulars. This practice was challenged in the courts and disapproved of by the Court of Appeal, who nevertheless refused to allow the Registrar's certificate to be challenged. No evidence could be adduced to challenge the correctness of his decision—he has jurisdiction finally and conclusively to determine any question of law or fact as to whether the requirements for registration have been complied with. Only the Attorney-General can challenge registration by means of judicial review since the Crown is not bound by the section.[57] Following that decision, however, the Registrar has changed his practice so that unless correct forms are submitted within the 21 day period registration will not be allowed without the court's permission under s.404 (or 420).[58]

To discover the exact terms of a charge one has to look at the document creating it (which document, or in Scotland a copy of which document, will have been filed), and not at the register.[59]

In England, a copy of the certificate of registration must be indorsed on every debenture or debenture stock certificate issued by the company and the payment of which is secured by the charge registered. The penalty of neglect is a fine: s.402. There is no corresponding provision for Scotland.

When the debt for which any registered charge was given is satisfied, in whole or in part, or part of the property charged is released or ceases to form part of the company's property, the Registrar enters a memorandum of satisfaction or release on the register. The company is entitled to a copy of the memorandum: ss 403, 419.[60] A statement of satisfaction may be made to the Registrar electronically: s.403(1A), 419(1A).

---

[56] *Re C. L. Nye Ltd* [1971] Ch. 442, CA.
[57] *R. v Registrar of Companies, ex p. Central Bank of India* [1986] Q.B. 1114, CA.
[58] Below, p.525.
[59] *Re Mechanisation (Eaglescliffe) Ltd* [1966] Ch. 20, following *National Provincial Bank v Charnley* [1924] 1 K.B. 431, CA.
[60] See, *e.g. Scottish & Newcastle plc v Ascot Inns Ltd (in receivership)*, 1994 S.L.T. 1140.

In Scotland the Registrar must not enter any such memorandum on the register unless either:

(a) the creditor entitled to the benefit of the floating charge, or a person authorised by the creditor, certifies as correct the particulars submitted to the Registrar with respect to the entry; or

(b) the court, on being satisfied that such certificate cannot readily be obtained, directs the Registrar to make the entry: s.419(3).

The register is open to public inspection: ss 401, 417(4).

Effect of non-registration

If a charge which ought to be registered under s.395 or s.410 is not so registered:

(a) the company and every officer who is knowingly a party to the default, is liable to a default fine (ss 399, 415(3));

(b) the charge is, so far as any security on the company's property is concerned, void against the liquidator or administrator and any creditor of the company; but without prejudice to the contract to repay the money secured, which becomes immediately repayable (ss 395, 410(3)). The result is that the holder of the charge is reduced to the level of an *unsecured* creditor.

In March the company gave T, a legal mortgage of specific land to secure £500. The mortgage was not restricted. In December the company issued debentures secured by a floating charge on its undertaking and assets to J to secure another £500. This charge was registered. *Held*, although J, when he took his security, had actual notice of T's mortgage, he nevertheless had priority over T: *Re Monolithic Building Co.* [1915] 1 Ch. 643, CA.

A council loaned money to a company to purchase plant to be used on the council's land. The loan granted rights to the council which were construed as creating a floating charge over the plant. This charge was not registered. The company defaulted on making the loan repayments and the council sold the plant: *held*, the floating charge was void against the administrator of the company and the council was liable in damages to the company for conversion of the plant: *Smith (Administrator of Cosslett (Contractors) Ltd v Bridgend CBC* [2002] 1 A.C. 336.

Rectification of register

Under s.404 for England and s.420 for Scotland the court may, on application by the company or any person interested, extend the time for registration or rectify the register if:

(a) the omission to register a charge within the required time or the omission or mis-statement of a particular with respect to a charge is:
    (i) accidental; or

(ii)   due to inadvertence[61] or some other sufficient cause; or

(iii)   not of a nature to prejudice the creditor or shareholders; or

(b)   on other grounds it is just and equitable to grant relief.[62]

Sections 404 and 420 require the court to be satisfied with respect to certain matters before it orders an extension of time and, therefore, if serious issues of fact are involved it should arm itself with the best information and evidence available.[63] The section does not empower the court to grant interim relief.

If, on an application for late registration, it is shown either that a liquidation of the company is imminent or has actually occurred, the court is unlikely to order an extension of time. This was held to be a factor against the applicant in *Re Telomatic Ltd*[64] and in *Re Barrow Borough Transport Ltd*,[65] where the court refused an application where the company was in administration for the purpose of ensuring the company's survival but that had proved to be incapable of achievement. The company's liquidation was not merely imminent, it was inevitable. The court indicated that the same would apply if the administration had not included the survival of the company as one of its purposes. On the other hand, the imminence of a liquidation is not an absolute bar to a late registration order if there are other circumstances which justify it. Thus in *Re Braemar Investments Ltd*[66] the court made an order on the basis that the fault was that of the chargee's solicitors and the chargee had acted promptly on discovering the non-registration.

That case also shows that when a chargee discovers that, by mistake, he is unregistered he must apply without delay for an extension of time and not deliberately defer his application in order to see which course would be to his best advantage. Failure to do so will prejudice his application: *Victoria Housing Estates Ltd v Ashpurton Estates Ltd*.[67]

It has been argued that the court will allow late registration where to do so would prevent one of its officers invoking the non-registration so as to benefit the other creditors unfairly. In *Re John Bateson*,[68] Harman J. regarded such a rule as strange and that in any event it could only apply if the court officer had acted in an unworthy manner. He also doubted whether a voluntary liquidator was an officer for this purpose.

Relief will usually only be granted "without prejudice to the rights of parties acquired prior to the time when [the charge is] actually registered".[69] This

---

[61] See, *e.g. Re Chantry House Developments plc* [1990] B.C.L.C. 813.

[62] See, *e.g. Re Fablehill Ltd* [1991] B.C.L.C. 830, where the directors registered their own charge during the period of non-registration of the applicant's charge.

[63] *Re Heathstar Properties Ltd* [1966] 1 W.L.R. 993. In *Re Heathstar Properties Ltd (No. 2)* [1966] 1 W.L.R. 999, it was found that the omission to register was due to inadvertence and the time for registration was extended notwithstanding that an action was proceeding in which the validity of the charge was in issue.

[64] [1994] 1 B.C.L.C. 90.

[65] [1989] B.C.L.C. 653.

[66] [1989] Ch. 54.

[67] [1983] 3 All E.R. 665, CA. See also *Re Telomatic Ltd* [1994] 1 B.C.L.C. 90.

[68] [1985] B.C.L.C. 259.

[69] *Re Joplin Brewery Co. Ltd* [1902] 1 Ch. 79.

proviso protects rights acquired *against the company's property in the extension of time*,[70] so that a secured creditor whose charge is created and registered in such time will not lose priority.[71] This is equally true if the later chargee knew of the existence of the unregistered charge at the date of registration of the later charge since the system is based on registration and not upon the actual notice of the chargee.[72] The court always has a discretion in these matters, however, so that in *Re Fablehill Ltd*[73] the court applied the proviso to give priority to one later registered charge but not another, since the latter had been created by the directors of the company in their own favour with full knowledge that the applicant's charge was unregistered.

The effect of the proviso is different where the second charge is created and registered within the 21-day period allowed by s.395 for registration of the first charge, *e.g.* the second chargee's rights do not gain priority by reason of the proviso—such rights are acquired at the date of execution of the second charge.

On January 22, a company created two floating charges on its undertaking and property by issuing a first debenture to X to secure £10,000 lent by him to the company and a second debenture to Y to secure £5,000. The second debenture was registered on January 28, but, by mistake, the first was returned to X unregistered. On October 20, X applied under s.101 of the 1948 Act for an extension of the time allowed for registration and on October 28, the court ordered an extention to November 11, with a proviso that the order was "without prejudice to the rights of any parties acquired prior to the time when the said debenture is to be registered." Also on October 28, Y appointed a receiver under the second debenture. The first debenture was registered on November 5, and a receiver appointed thereunder on November 8. On November 9, the company went into a creditors' voluntary liquidation.

Held, (1) Y's rights under the second debenture were acquired at the date of its execution and not at the expiration of the 21 days allowed by s.395 for registration of the first debenture (February 12), when the first debenture being then unregistered became void, nor in the ensuing period, during which it remained void, between the expiration of the 21 days and the date of its actual registration, and accordingly such rights did not gain priority over the first debenture by reason of the proviso to the court order; (2) although the appointment by Y of a receiver crystallised his floating charge, Y did not thereby acquire rights but merely exercised a power acquired when the debenture was executed (*Watson v Duff, Morgan and Vermont (Holdings) Limited* [1974] 1 W.L.R. 450).

Unsecured creditors with no charge on the company's property do not qualify for the purposes of the proviso. However, if the company has gone into liquidation there will be, as a general rule, no benefit in obtaining an extension of time, as the unsecured creditors will then have acquired rights against the property of the company.[74]

A clear case for the exercise of the court's power was held to have been made out where a Scottish company had failed to register a charge created over heritable property in England.[75] In a sheriff court case an extension of time was

---

[70] *Re Ehrmann Bros. Ltd* [1906] 2 Ch. 697, CA.

[71] *Re Monolithic Building Co.* [1915] 1 Ch. 643, CA, above.

[72] *Re Telomatic Ltd* [1994] 1 B.C.L.C. 90.

[73] [1991] B.C.L.C. 830.

[74] *Re S. Abrahams & Sons* [1902] 1 Ch. 695.

[75] *Amalgamated Securities Ltd, Petitioners*, 1967 S.C. 56; contrast *Archibald Campbell, Hope & King Ltd, Petitioners*, 1967 S.C. 21, in which a prayer for extension was held inept under the 1961 Act where the instrument creating the charge had already been registered and the company was seeking to re-register it for the purpose of securing an additional sum; see now s.414.

granted where there had been a misunderstanding as to which party was to effect registration.[76]

Registration of charges existing on property acquired

If a company acquires any property which is already subject to a charge which, if created by the company, would have required registration under s.395 or 410, *the company* must register particulars of the charge and a copy of the instrument creating or evidencing it within 21 days after the acquisition is completed. Default renders the company and every officer in default liable to a default fine (ss 400, 416) but the validity of the charge is not affected.

Reform

The Law Commission[76a] has recently reviewed the operation of the system of registration of company charges and made recommendations for root and branch reform.[77] The system preferred by the Law Commission is based on Art.9 U.C.C., a model which has been widely adopted in relation to security over personal property generally.

In essence, if enacted, the Law Commission's recommendations will see the introduction of "notice-filing" to replace the current system of registration under s.395 Companies Act. This will allow the security holder to file (electronically) a notice of the grant to him of a security interest *or* an agreement to grant a security interest. Questions of priority will be determined by the date of filing rather than the date of creation of the security interest.

The Law Commission envisages that this scheme will apply to a much wider range of devices which, functionally if not formally, operate as security interests. Thus it will apply to "traditional" forms of security such as mortgages and charges, but also to title retention devices. If filing does not take place, the holder of the security interest will lose priority in a way similar to that seen above in relation to the non-registration of company charges under s.395. For a more detailed exposition of the proposed scheme, the reader is referred to the Law Commission's Consultation Papers 164 and 176.

REMEDIES OF DEBENTURE HOLDERS

1. If a debenture confers no charge, a debenture holder is an ordinary unsecured creditor. Thus, if there is default in the payment of principal or interest he may (a) sue for the principal or interest and, after obtaining judgment, levy execution against the company,[78] or (b), as will be explained later,[79] petition either for an

---

[76] *M. Milne Ltd, Petitioners* (1963) 79 Sh. Ct. Rep. 105.
[76a] See too Scot Law Com Report No.197, *Registration of Rights in Security by Companies* (TSO, 2004).
[77] See Law Com Consultation Paper 164, *Registration of Security Interests: Company Charges and Property other than Land* (TSO, 2002); Law Com Consultation Paper 176, *Company Security Interests* (TSO, 2004).
[78] The Scots equivalent is "do diligence on the decree obtained".
[79] Below, Chs 26 and 27.

administration order or for the winding-up of the company by the court on the ground that the company is unable to pay its debts.

2. When a charge is conferred on the company's assets by way of security, and default is made in the payment of principal or interest, a debenture holder, or the trustees where there is a trust deed, may:

(a) sue for the principal or interest; or

(b) if the charge is a "qualifying floating charge", appoint an administrator of the company[81]; or

(c) present a petition for the winding up of the company; or

(d) if the charge was created prior to September 15, 2003,[82] exercise any powers conferred by the debenture or the trust deed, *e.g.* of appointing a receiver or administrative receiver of the assets charged, of selling the assets charged or of taking possession of the assets and carrying on the business; or

(e) if the debenture or the trust deed does not contain powers in that behalf, apply to the court for:
   (i) the appointment of a receiver or a receiver and manager; or
   (ii) an order for sale or foreclosure.

A debenture or trust deed will normally contain an express power to appoint a receiver or administrative receiver of, or to sell, the company's assets charged by way of security. If there is no express power there will be an implied power under the Law of Property Act 1925, s.101,[83] if the debenture or trust deed is under seal. Failing an express or an implied power, an application may be made to the court for the appointment of a receiver or an order for sale. A company's inability to pay its debts for the purpose of appointing a receiver is to be assessed at the date of appointment. Further, where the receiver is to be appointed by a deed, his appointment is not invalidated by an appointment in another manner— that operates as an agreement to perfect the power if necessary.[84]

Where the debenture is an "all moneys" debenture (*e.g.* one for all sums owed to a bank) the demand for payment need not specify the exact sum due and a receiver may be appointed once reasonable time to effect payment has passed.[85] Similarly a demand for an amount less than the full amount due will be sufficient for the appointment of a receiver, although there is no authority if the demand is excessive, *i.e.* for more than the amount due.[86]

In England, where there are numerous debentures of the same class, a *debenture holders' action* is usually brought. This is brought by one debenture holder on behalf of himself and all other debenture holders of the same class as himself. In it a claim may be made for:

[81] Below, Ch.26.
[82] Below, Ch.25.
[83] Not applicable to Scotland.
[84] *Byblos Bank S.A.L. v Al Khudhairy, Financial Times*, November 7, 1986.
[85] *Bank of Baroda v Panessar*, [1987] Ch. 335.
[86] *N.R.G. Vision Ltd v Churchfield Leasing Ltd* (1988) 4 B.C.C. 56.

(1) a declaration that the debenture holders are entitled to a (first) charge
     on the property of the company;

(2) if there is a trust deed, the enforcement of the trust;

(3) an account of what is due to the debenture holders;

(4) the enforcement of the charge by sale or foreclosure;

(5) the appointment of a receiver and manager.

An order for foreclosure will only be made if all the debenture holders of the same class as the plaintiff are before the court. If the assets require immediate protection an application for the appointment of a receiver is made.[87]

In Scotland, prior to the Companies (Floating Charges and Receivers) (Scotland) Act 1972, there was no provision for the appointment of receivers, and this constituted a major difference between Scots and English law in the remedies available to the holder of a floating charge and in the procedure for enforcing the security. On the recommendation of the Scottish Law Commission[88] receiverships were introduced to Scotland by the Act of 1972.[88a] Though based in general on the English model, the Scottish provisions form a distinct self-contained code and are given separate consideration below.

The various remedies are discussed in Chapter 25, below.

---

[87] *Re Continental Oxygen Co.* [1897] 1 Ch. 511.
[88] *Report on the Companies (Floating Charges) (Scotland) Act 1961*, (1970) Cmnd. 4336, para. 38.
[88a] Itself since repealed by the Companies Consolidation (Consequential Receivers) Act 1985.

Chapter 24

CORPORATE INSOLVENCY

The Insolvency Act 1985 enacted major changes to the legal regulation of both corporate and personal insolvencies.[1] It introduced new concepts and controls and also amended (or repealed) several sections of the Companies Act 1985 concerned with corporate insolvency. The interaction of the two Acts led to the consolidation of Parts XIX, XX and XXI of the Companies Act 1985 and the Insolvency Act 1985 into the Insolvency Act 1986.

The Insolvency Act 1986 is thus the major Act[2] which applies to this and the next five chapters. However, the Insolvency Act 1986 itself has been subject to significant modification by the Enterprise Act 2002, and these chapters incorporate those changes. Chapter 25 deals with receivers and the concept, introduced by the Insolvency Act 1985, of an administrative receiver, usually appointed by a debenture holder as the most efficient way of protecting his security in the face of possible insolvency. The entitlement to appoint an administrative receiver has been substantially restricted by the Enterprise Act 2002.[3] Such appointments may or may not lead to the ultimate liquidation of the company. Chapter 26 deals with one alternative to the liquidation of an insolvent company—the making of an administration order. Such orders were also introduced by the Insolvency Act 1985. The administration procedure has been streamlined by the Enterprise Act 2002. Chapters 27 to 29 are, on the other hand, concerned with liquidations, that is to say the effective demise of the company, which may in fact arise otherwise than on an insolvency. The majority of liquidations, however, are caused by such an eventuality. We have already discussed, in Chapter 15, one other aspect of insolvency law introduced by the 1985 Insolvency Act, *i.e.* that in relation to the disqualification of directors of insolvent companies.[4]

The present chapter is concerned with three general matters. The new framework for corporate insolvency, the controls on insolvency practitioners involved in the various aspects of insolvency, *e.g.* as administrative receivers, liquidators, administrators etc., and a second alternative to the liquidation of an insolvent company—a voluntary arrangement, *i.e.* a composition with creditors.[5]

THE NEW FRAMEWORK FOR INSOLVENCY

One of the two main themes of the Insolvency Act 1986 was to update a system

---

[1] On the background to these changes, see *Final Report of the Insolvency Review Committee (Cork Report)* 1982, Cmnd. 8558; *A Revised Framework of Insolvency Law*, 1984 Cmnd. 9175. In Scotland major changes to personal insolvencies were made by the Bankruptcy (Scotland) Act 1985.
[2] See also the Insolvency Act 1994 and the Insolvency (No. 2) Act 1994, above, p.546. The latter Act does not apply to Scotland.
[3] Below, Ch.25.
[4] Above, p.321.
[5] For the other alternative see Ch.26, below.

which had its origins in the Bankruptcy Act 1914 (in Scotland the Bankruptcy (Scotland) Act 1913) and was inadequate to deal with unscrupulous liquidators and directors who allowed companies which were hopelessly insolvent to continue to trade. The second aim of the legislation was to provide alternative and less drastic remedies than liquidation for an insolvent company, where such remedies would provide a better opportunity for the creditors to recover their debts and for the companies concerned to remain in existence. Measures designed to assist in the first aim include the regulation of insolvency practitioners,[6] the disqualification of directors' provisions (including the concept of wrongful trading)[7] and the many amendments to the laws relating to receiverships and liquidations, including the new statutory concept of an administrative receiver. To achieve the second aim the Act introduced the new administration procedure[8] and a simplified procedure for a composition with creditors.[9] The use of these "rescue" procedures has been low as compared to the number of insolvencies. The Insolvency Act 2002 and the Enterprise Act 2002 contains provisions intended to make them more attractive to both corporate debtors and their creditors.[10] These statutory provisions are supplemented by many rules and regulations.[11] In particular, the Insolvency Rules 1986[12] and the rules relating to Qualified Insolvency Practitioners.[13]

The Insolvency Act 1986 also retained and redefined the role of Official Receivers for England and Wales in all types of corporate proceedings.[14] In effect, although they are civil servants under the control of the Secretary of State, Official Receivers are also officers of the court and are attached to the High Court or to one or more county court having insolvency jurisdiction. They assume the functions and responsibilities specified in the Act or the Rules in those cases falling within the jurisdiction of the court to which they are attached. Deputy Official Receivers can be appointed and have the same status and functions as an Official Receiver.

By virtue of s.426 of the Insolvency Act 1986, the courts in each part of the United Kingdom are required to recognise and enforce orders made by the courts of all other parts of the United Kingdom in relation to insolvency law. Thus where property exists *e.g.* in Scotland, but the insolvency proceedings are taking place in London, all such property can be protected and claimed for the benefit of creditors.[15] The European Council Regulation on Insolvency Proceedings[15a] also provides for the recognition of insolvency proceedings commenced in a Member State on a Europe-wide basis, and for the enforcement of judgments thereunder.

---

[6] Below.
[7] Above, pp.317 and 321.
[8] Below, Ch.26.
[9] Below, p.534.
[10] Below, pp.534–539 and Ch.26.
[11] I.A. 1986, ss 411–413, 419.
[12] SI 1986/1925 as amended. For Scotland see the Insolvency (Scotland) Rules 1986 (SI 1986/1915, s.139) as amended.
[13] See Insolvency Practitioners Regulations 1990, SI 1990/439 as amended.
[14] I.A. 1986, ss 399–401.
[15] The United Kingdom courts are also required to assist the courts of other designated jursidictions: see s.426(4); also *Hughes v Hannover Ruckversicherungs-Aktiengesellschaft* [1997] B.C.C. 921, CA.
[15a] (EC) No.1346/2000.

INSOLVENCY PRACTITIONERS

Part XIII of the Insolvency Act 1986 subjects insolvency practitioners to proper regulation by ensuring that they are "qualified" within the terms of s.390. To act as an insolvency practitioner in relation to a company when not qualified to do so is a criminal offence under s.389. For this purpose "acting as an insolvency practitioner" means acting either as a liquidator,[16] administrator,[17] administrative receiver[18] or as the supervisor of a composition with creditors,[19] s.388,[20] although such a supervisor is subjected to use less stringent provisions of s.389A. This offence is one of strict liability—the knowledge of the person concerned is irrelevant. It does not, however, apply to the Official Receiver. The Official Receiver does not come within the terms of s.388 and therefore escapes the qualification requirements of s.390 and the criminal penalty in s.389; the control exercised over such public officials within the Department of Trade and Industry is deemed sufficient safeguard.

Section 390 sets out the requirements for qualification. Only an individual can be qualified to act as an insolvency practitioner.[21] He must be currently authorised to act as an insolvency practitioner either by virtue of membership of a professional body recognised under s.391[22] or by a direct authorisation granted by a competent authority,[23] and must have provided the requisite security (or, in Scotland, caution) for the proper performance of his functions.[24]

Even if a person is so qualified to act he may be disqualified if (a) he is an undischarged bankrupt,[25] or (b) he is subject to a disqualification order under the Company Directors Disqualification Act 1986[26] or (c) he is a patient under the Mental Health Act 1983 or the Mental Health (Scotland) Act 1984.[27] This is subject to s.389A, Insolvency Act 1986.

Most individuals will qualify by virtue of being members[28] of a recognised professional body who are permitted to act as such by the rules of that body. The bodies currently recognised by the Secretary of State include the established accountancy bodies, the Law Society and the Insolvency Practitioners Association. The intention is that the control exercised by such bodies over their members shall be equivalent to that exercised by the competent authority over

---

[16] Below, p.602.

[17] Below, Ch.26.

[18] Below, Ch.25.

[19] Below, p.535.

[20] In relation to insolvent partnerships, see s.388(2A) inserted by the Insolvent Partnerships Order 1994 (SI 1994/2421).

[21] I.A. 1986, s.390(1).

[22] See Insolvency Practitioners (Recognised Professional Bodies) Order 1986, SI 1986/1764.

[23] *ibid.*, s.390(2)(b). The Secretary of State or a body designated by him.

[24] s.390(3); by means of a fidelity bond in the amount of £250,000 plus an additional sum varying with the value of the assets in relation to which he is to act in the particular case: Insolvency Practitioners Regulations 1990, r.12.

[25] See I.A. 1986, ss 278–282, and Bankruptcy (Scotland) Act 1985, ss 54–56.

[26] See above, p.321.

[27] *i.e.* someone who has been judicially assessed to be mentally incapable of managing and administering his affairs.

[28] This includes those who, although not members, are subject to the rules of a recognised body in the practice of their profession: I.A., s.391.

those directly authorised by that body under ss 392 to 398 of the Insolvency Act 1986. For those who cannot qualify as qualified insolvency practitioners by virtue of membership of a recognised professional body, those sections of the Act allow a direct application to the competent authority appointed to deal with such matters. Currently the Secretary of State is the competent authority for this purpose and he must grant the application if satisfied that the applicant is a fit and proper person to be an insolvency practitioner and satisfies prescribed educational and experience requirements: s.393.[29] Such authorisation is for a maximum of three years and may be withdrawn earlier on his ceasing to comply with the s.393 requirements or where he was authorised by virtue of false, misleading or inaccurate information. There is a right to make representations before a refusal or withdrawal of authorisation and a right to appeal against an adverse decision to the Insolvency Practitioners Tribunal.[30] Withdrawal of authorisation results in automatic vacation of office.

P was acting as liquidator in relation to a number of companies when his authorisation was withdrawn. It was held that, though no longer a liquidator, he was a proper person to apply to the court under s.108 of the Insolvency Act 1986 for a compendious appointment in relation to all the companies with which he had been concerned: *Re A. J. Adams (Builders) Ltd* [1991] B.C.C. 62.[31]

The appointment of an insolvency practitioner as officeholder is a personal appointment not an appointment of his firm. On retirement meetings of creditors should normally be convened to approve a change of officeholder.[32] An insolvency practitioner's firm can apply to the court for his removal.[32a]

VOLUNTARY ARRANGEMENTS—COMPOSITIONS WITH CREDITORS

Sections 1 to 7 of the Insolvency Act 1986 introduced a new procedure which enables an insolvent or potentially insolvent company to come to a legally binding arrangement with its creditors. If the procedure is complied with it binds creditors, even those who have not agreed to it[33] (I.A. 1986, s.5(2)) and so perhaps will avoid a liquidation. There are alternative methods of effecting such a scheme under ss 425 to 427[34] of the Companies Act 1985 or s.110 of the Insolvency Act 1986[35] but these procedures were not designed expressly for the purpose of enabling an insolvent company to rationalise its affairs and proved to be cumbersome in practice for such a purpose. Schemes of arrangement under ss 425 to 427 require the court's involvement at every stage and the court's ultimate consent. Schemes of reconstruction under s.110 do not bind dissentient

---

[29] *ibid.* regs 4–8.
[30] I.A. 1986, ss 395, 396. This Tribunal is governed by Schedule 7 to I.A. 1986, and by the Insolvency Practitioners Tribunal (Conduct of Investigations) Rules 1986 (SI 1986/952).
[31] In some circumstances the application may be by the recognised professional body: see *Re Stella Metals Ltd* [1997] B.C.C. 626.
[32] *Re Sankey Furniture Ltd* [1995] B.C.L.C. 594.
[32a] *Re A. & C. Supplies Ltd* [1998] B.C.C. 708; see also *Cork v Ralph* (2001) 98(7) L.S.G. 40.
[33] See below; p.537.
[34] See below, Ch.30.
[35] *ibid.* See also administration orders, below, Ch.26.

creditors.[36] The essence of the Insolvency Act scheme is to simplify both the procedure and the court's involvement whilst maintaining the ability to bind creditors to the scheme if the requisite procedure is complied with.

Implementing a voluntary arrangement

Section 1 of the Insolvency Act 1986 allows either a liquidator or administrator of a company (if it is in liquidation[37] or administration[38]) or, if there is no liquidator or administrator, the directors, to make a proposal to the company and to its creditors for a composition in satisfaction of its debts or a scheme of arrangement of its affairs, to be known as a voluntary arrangement.[39] This proposal must provide for some person who is qualified to act as an insolvency practitioner in relation to the company[40] to act as the *nominee* of the scheme, *i.e.* as trustee or otherwise for the purpose of implementing the scheme. Under s.389A of the I.A., a wider range of practitioners may act as nominees and supervisors of voluntary arrangements, and in particular turnaround specialists authorised by the Secretary of State are able to act. It is a criminal offence for an unqualified person to act as a nominee.[41]

Where the nominee is not the liquidator or administrator, he must observe the formalities in s.2 of the Insolvency Act 1986 which involve the scrutiny by him of the soundness of the proposed arrangement and the submission of a report to the court stating whether in his opinion meetings of the company and of its creditors should be summoned to consider the proposal, and, if so, the date, time and place he proposes the meetings should be held. In effect he is required to state that the scheme is worth pursuing.

No such report is needed where the nominee is the liquidator or administrator; proper scrutiny by such office holders is assumed. In such a case the liquidator or administrator may proceed directly by virtue of s.3(2) of the Insolvency Act 1986 to summon meetings of the company and its creditors to consider the proposal for such a time, date and place as he shall think fit. Following a positive report by a nominee other than a liquidator or administrator, under s.2 of the Insolvency Act, that nominee should call the meetings as stated in that report unless the court orders otherwise: I.A. 1986 s.3(1). Section 3(3) requires every creditor of the company of whose claim and address the nominee is aware to be given notice of the creditors' meeting. There is no requirement to hold separate meetings for separate classes of creditors[42] which is a feature of schemes of arrangements under ss 425 to 427 of the Companies Act 1985.[43]

Voluntary arrangement with moratorium

One of the perceived weaknesses of the voluntary arrangement was that it remained possible for creditors to undermine it in its early stages by instituting

[36] I.A. 1986, s.111.
[37] See below, Ch.27.
[38] See below, Ch.26.
[39] For a discussion of the meaning of "scheme of arrangement" see below, Ch.30.
[40] This is someone qualified by virtue of s.390 of the I.A. 1986 and not connected with the company so as to be in breach of the professional or regulatory rules.
[41] I.A. 1986, ss 388, 389.
[42] See below, p.536, 655.
[43] See below, Ch.30.

enforcement actions against the company. This could be avoided by implementing the arrangement under the umbrella of an administration order, during the course of which an automatic moratorium would be in place, but such a step was seen as complex and expensive. Therefore, following a series of consultations,[44] the Insolvency Act 2000 introduced s.1A and Sch.A1 into the Insolvency Act 1986. These provisions came into force on January 1, 2003.

Only the directors of "eligible" companies may take steps to obtain a moratorium during a voluntary arrangement: s.1A(1). The criteria for eligibility is found in Sch.A1 paras 2–5, and are primarily concerned with whether the company satisfies two or more of the requirements for being a "small company" in s.247(3) of the Companies Act 1985. Such small companies are *prima facie* eligible companies, unless they are subject to some other form of insolvency procedure or are otherwise excluded from eligibility under paras 4A-4J of Sch.A1.

The procedure for obtaining a moratorium is contained in paras 6-11 of Schedule A1. The directors of an eligible company must submit to the nominee[45] a document setting out the terms of the proposed arrangement and a statement of the company's affairs: Sch.A1, para.6(1). The nominee must then submit to the directors a statement that, in his opinion, the proposed voluntary arrangement has a reasonable prospect of being approved and implemented, that the company is likely to have sufficient funds during the moratorium to enable it to carry on business, and that meetings of the company should be summoned to approve the arrangement: para.6(2). The directors must then file with the court documents setting out the terms of the proposed arrangement, a statement of the company's affairs and the nominee's statement: para.7. The moratorium comes into force at the time the documents are filed with the court and lasts for 28 days or until meetings of the company and its creditors to approve the arrangement are held, whichever is the sooner: para.8.

Whilst the moratorium is in force, no petition or resolution for winding up may be presented or passed and no administrator or administrative receiver of the company may be appointed and creditors may not take steps to enforce security over the company's property without leave of the court: para.12. There are restrictions on the amount of credit a company can obtain during the moratorium and on disposals and payments it may make: paras 16, 17. Property subject to a charge may only be disposed of with the consent of the chargee or leave of the court, and the chargee has the same priority over the proceeds of disposals as he had over the charged property itself: para.20. The nominee is required to monitor the company's affairs during the moratorium: para.24.

Consideration of a voluntary arrangement

It is for the two meetings convened by the nominee to decide whether to approve the proposed composition or scheme, with or without modifications. Any such modification is allowed, including a change in the nominee, subject to three

---

[44] *CVAs and Administration Orders* (DTI, 1993); *Revised Proposals for a New CVA Procedure* (DTI, 1995); *A Review of Company Rescue and Business Reconstruction Mechanisms* (DTI, 2000).
[45] See above as to the nominee.

limitations. First no modification is allowed if the proposal would thereby cease to comply with the terms of s.1 of the Insolvency Act, *i.e.* it would no longer be a voluntary arrangement as there defined. Secondly no modification can affect a secured creditor's[46] rights to enforce his security without his consent. Third no modification can interfere with the rights of a preferred creditor, either as against ordinary creditors or other preferred creditors, without his consent.[47] The Insolvency Rules 1986[48] regulate the conduct of the meetings and it is for the chairman to make a report of the result to the court and other prescribed persons: I.A. 1986, s.4.

If both the company and creditors' meetings approve the proposal in identical terms, the scheme or composition "takes effect as if made by the company at the creditors' meeting," and binds every person who in accordance with the rules had notice of,[49] and was entitled to vote at, that meeting (whether or not he was present or represented at the meeting) as if he were a party to the voluntary arrangement": I.A. 1986, s.5(1), (2). Where there is disagreement between the meetings of creditors on the one hand, and members on the other, the decision of creditors' meetings prevails s.4A.[50]

Creditors vote in accordance with the amount of their debt.[51] The Rules provide that a creditor is not entitled to vote in relation to an unliquidated amount except where the chairman agrees to put upon the debt an estimated minimum value.[52] The creditor's consent is not required.

L sought to vote in respect of total future rent arising under a lease. The chairman, bearing in mind the likelihood that L would terminate the lease by forfeiture in the near future, valued L's claim at a minimum of one year's rent. L did not agree and did not vote. L later claimed not to be bound by the arrangement in respect of the future rent. *Held*: The chairman had agreed to put a minimum value on the claim and had done so. Therefore L had been entitled to vote and was bound. *Doorbar v. Alltime Securities Ltd* [1995] B.C.C. 1149, CA.[53]

The position is otherwise where a creditor claims a liquidated debt but the company disputes the amount or claims a set off. Here the creditor is entitled to vote in respect of the whole debt subject to his votes subsequently being declared invalid.[54] The chairman's decision on a creditor's entitlement to vote can be challenged by a creditor or member.[55]

---

[46] Defined in s.248. See also *Re Naeem* [1990] 1 W.L.R. 48; *Peck v Craighead* [1995] B.C.C. 525; and below, p.567 where the term is considered in the context of administration orders.

[47] Preferred creditors are defined in the same way as for a liquidation except that they are calculated by reference to the date of the approval of the proposal if there is no liquidation or administration order in force: I.A. 1986, s.387.

[48] For Scotland, the Insolvency (Scotland) Rules 1986 (hereafter I.(S.)R.).

[49] On notice by post, see I.R., r.12.10 and *Beverley Group plc v McClue* [1995] B.C.C. 751. For Scotland, see I.(S.)R. r.7.22.

[50] In the case of a company registered as a social landlord, the arrangement cannot take effect without the prior consent of the Housing Corporation: Housing Act 1996, Sch.1, para.13(5).

[51] Insolvency Rules 1986 (hereafter I.R. 1986), r.1.17(2). For Scotland I.(S.)R. rr.4.15 and 4.16.

[52] I.R. r.1.17(3). A token value will not do: *Doorbar v Alltime Securities Ltd* [1994] B.C.C. 1007 (Knox J.).

[53] This related to an individual voluntary arrangement but the position was said to be the same for a company voluntary arrangement: at p.1155; and see *Re Sweatfield Ltd* [1997] B.C.C. 744; *cp. Re Cranley Mansions Ltd* [1994] B.C.C. 576.

[54] r.1.17A(4). I.(S.)R., rr.4.15 and 4.16. *Re A debtor (No. 222 of 1990)*, [1992] B.C.L.C. 137 (individual voluntary arrangements).

[55] I.R. 1986, r.1.17A(3).

While the creditors bound by the arrangement cannot assert claims against the company which are inconsistent with it, they may still be able to sue any co-debtors of the company (unless the scheme has the additional effect of releasing all co-debtors)[56] Payment by a co-debtor may result in an indemnity claim by such co-debtor against the company thus undermining the arrangement. A consequential claim of this sort may perhaps be avoided by ensuring that a co-debtor has notice of the arrangement and is bound by it.[57] Where, under the terms of the arrangement, a particular claim is not brought within it that claim can still be pursued by a credit bound by the other terms of the arrangement.[58]

Once the arrangement is duly approved a supplier of gas, electricity and other public utilities cannot make it a precondition of any further supply that outstanding charges in respect of earlier supplies are met.[59]

If a proposal is approved while the company is in liquidation or subject to an administration order the court may stay the winding-up proceedings or discharge the administration order or give such directions as to their future conduct as will facilitate the scheme. No such order can be made within 28 days from the date when the court received the reports of the meeting since that is the period allowed for the meetings' approval to be challenged in the court,[60] or at any time when such a challenge is under consideration by the court: I.A. 1986, s.5(3), (4).

Challenge to a voluntary arrangement

Within 28 days of the report of the meeting having been made to the court, anyone who was entitled to vote at either meeting, the nominee or his replacement or the liquidator or administrator (if any) can challenge the approval of the scheme by an application to the court. This challenge can, however, only be made on one of two grounds: either that the scheme will unfairly prejudice[61] the interests of a creditor, member or contributory[62] of the company, or there has been some material irregularity at or in relation to either of the meetings: I.A. 1986, s.6(1), (2), (3).[63]

Section 6 is not concerned with the conduct of an approved arrangement, but with the process of approval itself. There may be an irregularity at a meeting of the company or its creditors, but that irregularity must still be shown to be material.

At a meeting of creditors to approve a voluntary arrangement, offers to purchase the company's business were not disclosed by the administrators of the company. *Held*, whilst

---

[56] By its express or implied terms or the effect of action taken under it: *Johnson v Davies* [1998] 2 All E.R 649, CA (individual voluntary arrangement); *R.A. Securities Ltd v Mercantile Credit Co Ltd* [1995] 3 All E.R. 581.

[57] *Mytre Investments Ltd v Reynolds* [1995] 3 All E.R. 588; *March Estates plc v Gunmark* [1996] 2 B.C.L.C. 1.

[58] *Alman v Approach Housing Ltd* [2001] B.P.I.R. 203.

[59] S.233 I.A. 1986 and see below, p.550, 604.

[60] See below.

[61] There is no definition of this but the words are used in s.459 of the Companies Act 1985 in relation to the protection of a minority shareholder generally, see above, p.359. And see *Re Primlaks (U.K.) Ltd (No. 2)* [1990] B.C.L.C. 234; *Inland Revenue Commissioners v Wimbledon Football Club Ltd* [2004] EWHC 1020.

[62] This is the term used for a member once the company has gone into liquidation.

[63] Irregularities not challenged within 28 days cannot invalidate the approval: I.A. 1986, s.6(7).

the non-disclosure amounted to an irregularity, it was not material as there was no real prospect that disclosure would have affected the approval of the arrangement: *Re Trident Fashions plc* [2004] EWHC 293.

Supervising an approved voluntary arrangement

An approved scheme which is not subject to a challenge is then put into effect. At this stage the person carrying out the nominee's functions is known as the *supervisor*. The supervisor is under the control of the court and any interested party, including the company,[64] may apply to the court if his conduct is unsatisfactory and the court may make an order to give him directions as it thinks fit. In return the supervisor himself may apply to the court for directions and can petition for a winding-up or the making of an administration order. *In extremis* the court can replace the supervisor or appoint an additional one: I.A. 1986, s.7. Under the Insolvency Rules 1986[65] the supervisor must keep accounts and records and must report annually upon the progress of the arrangement. A voluntary arrangement is not automatically terminated on a subsequent winding-up. It depends on the terms of the arrangement and the nature of the petition. If it is terminated, the liquidator is not automatically entitled to claim funds already held in trust for creditors under the terms of the arrangement.[66]

---

[64] *County Bookshops Ltd v Grove* [2002] EWHC 1160.
[65] For Scotland, the Insolvency (Scotland) Rules 1986.
[66] *Re Halson Packaging Ltd* [1997] B.C.C. 993; *Re Leisure Study Group Ltd* [1994] 2 B.C.L.C. 65. Cp. *Davis v Martin-Sklan* [1995] B.C.C. 1122 (individual voluntary arrangement) and *Re Arthur Rathbone* [1997] 2 B.C.L.C. 280 and [1998] B.C.C. 450; *Re NT Gallagher & Sons Ltd* [2002] 1 B.C.L.C. 224 (CA).

Chapter 25

RECEIVERS AND ADMINISTRATIVE RECEIVERS

English and Scots law

The law relating to receivers has developed quite separately in England and Scotland, and for that reason this chapter is divided into two parts, the first dealing with English law and the second with Scots law. The relevant statute law is also quite separate: ss 28 to 49 of the Insolvency Act 1986 apply only to English law and ss 50 to 71 of that Act apply only to Scotland. The two sets of provisions are mutually exclusive.[1] On the other hand, s.72 of the Insolvency Act 1986 provides that a receiver appointed under a floating charge in one jurisdiction may exercise his powers in the other "so far as their exercise is not inconsistent with the law applicable there."

In *Norfolk House plc (in receivership) v Repsol Petroleum Ltd*, 1992 S.L.T. 235 (O.H.), a receiver of an English company with heritable property in Scotland was enabled by s.72 to grant a valid disposition to purchasers; the effect of s.72 was said to bridge the transaction from the original English crystallisation of the floating charge to the appointment of the receiver in order to ensure that the receiver could exercise his powers under Sch.1 to the Act in relation to Scottish heritable property untrammelled by Scottish conveyancing and property law.

The Enterprise Act 2002, by inserting s.72A into the Insolvency Act 1986, significantly restricts the right to privately appoint an administrative receiver in both England and Scotland.[2] However, this provision is only applicable to holders of floating charges granted on or after September 15, 2003. It is therefore likely that the appointment of receivers as administrative receivers will continue for some time into the future and that what follows will remain relevant law whilst ever there remain in existence floating charges pre-dating September 15, 2003.

ENGLISH LAW

Receivers and other officeholders

A receiver takes possession of the property of the company over which he is appointed and realises it for the benefit of the debenture holder(s). Where the charged property includes a business, a *receiver and manager* is usually appointed to preserve the goodwill pending sale or the resumption of control by the company on discharge of the debt. A receiver should not be confused either with

---

[1] See I.A. 1986, ss 28 and 50.
[2] On administrative receivers generally, see below, pp.548 *et seq.*

a liquidator or an administrator. A liquidator is appointed with the object of winding up the company and terminating its existence. An administrator is appointed with the object of saving a company from a winding up or obtaining a more advantageous realisation of its assets, and acts for the benefit of the company's creditors and shareholders generally,[3] whereas a receiver is usually appointed by a specific debenture holder to protect his security under a fixed or floating charge.[4] A receiver may take possession of only part of a company's property[5] (*e.g.* of a specific asset secured by a fixed charge) but if he takes possession of the whole (or substantially the whole) of the company's property and was appointed by the holders of a charge which, as created, was a floating charge, he is known as an *administrative receiver*, as long as the charge in question was granted before September 15, 2003.[6] Most receivers will in fact be administrative receivers since the major creditors appointing them, *e.g.* the banks, usually take extensive fixed and floating charges as a security. Administrative receivers are subject to special rules and given special powers by the Insolvency Act 1986.

As mentioned in Chapter 23, a receiver can be appointed: (1) under an express power[7] contained in the debenture or trust deed; or (2) by an order of the court where there is no such power.[7a]

Receiver appointed by the court

While the Insolvency Act refers to receivers appointed by the court, and certain of its provisions,[8] applicable to all receiverships, would seem to apply to them, it has little to say about them. It is accepted that the court may appoint a receiver when:

(1) the principal or interest is in arrear[9]; or

(2) the company is being wound up[10]; or

(3) the security is in jeopardy.

A creditor obtained judgment against the company and was in a position to issue execution. There was no default in payment of debenture principal or interest. *Held*, the debenture holders with a floating charge on the undertaking and property of the company

---

[3] See below, Ch.26.

[4] Although it is now possible for the debentive holder to appoint an administrator to realise his security.

[5] I.A. 1986, s.29(1)(a).

[6] *ibid.*, s.29(2)(a). So long as his security extends to the whole or substantially the whole of the company's property, the fact that some other person has previously been appointed receiver of the part of the company's property under a charge having priority to the floating charge and that consequently he does not in fact have possession of the whole or substantially the whole of the company's property, does not prevent him from coming within the definition of an administrative receiver: s.29(2)(b).

[7] The court will not imply a term entitling a debenture holder to appoint a receiver on the basis of business efficacy: *Cryne v Barclays Bank plc* [1987] B.C.L.C. 548.

[7a] Where it appears just and convenient to do so: s.37(1) Supreme Court Act 1981.

[8] *e.g.* I.A. 1986, ss 30, 39, 40 and 41; C.A. 1985, s.405(1), see above.

[9] *Bissill v Bradford Tramways* [1891] W.N. 51.

[10] *Wallace v Universal Automatic Machines Co.* [1894] 2 Ch. 547, CA.

were entitled to the appointment of a receiver because the security was in jeopardy: *Re London Pressed Hinge Co. Ltd* [1905] 1 Ch. 576.

The security is in jeopardy when there is a risk of its being seized and taken to pay claims which are really not prior to the debenture holders' claims. Accordingly a receiver was appointed where the company's works were closed and creditors were threatening actions,[11] where execution was actually levied by a judgment creditor,[12] where a creditor's winding up petition was pending and compulsory liquidation was imminent,[13] where the company proposed to distribute its reserve fund, which was its only asset, among its members[14] and where there was a real risk that assets would be "switched from one shadowy hand to another in breach of a *Mareva* order".[15] Mere insufficiency of security is not jeopardy where the company is a going concern, is not being pressed by its creditors and there is no risk of its assets being seized by its creditors.[16]

or (4) the creditor is unlikely to obtain payment of a judgment debt by the process of legal execution.

A defendant company's assets consisted of payments to become due under a supply contract with a Guernsey company. The ability of the defendant company to manipulate the supply contract and the inability of the plaintiff to ascertain payments due under it made it unlikely that the plaintiff would obtain satisfaction by a garnishee order. *Held*: A receiver should be appointed by the court. *Soinco v Novokuznetsk Aluminium Plant* [1998] Q.B. 406[17]

Appointments by the court are infrequent[18] and usually occur because there is no adequate power of appointment in the instrument of charge or there is some doubt as to the validity of the instrument or the appointment under it.[19] The appointment is made on the application of the debenture holders. It is uncertain whether a receiver appointed by the court can fall within the definition of an administrative receiver.[20] Where the company is being wound up by the court, the court can appoint the Official Receiver as receiver: I.A. 1986, s.32. A receiver appointed by the court is an officer of the court, not an agent of the company or of the debenture holders.[21] He is personally liable on contracts he enters into.[22]

---

[11] *McMahon v North Kent Ironworks* [1891] 2 Ch. 148.

[12] *Edwards v Standard Rolling Stock Syndicate* [1893] 1 Ch. 574.

[13] *Re Victoria Steamboats Ltd* [1897] 1 Ch. 158.

[14] *Re Tilt Cove Copper Co.* [1913] 2 Ch. 588.

[15] *per* Robert Walker J. in *International Credit and Investment Co. (Overseas) Ltd v Adham* [1998] B.C.C. 134, at p.137.

[16] *Re New York Taxicab Co.* [1913] 1 Ch. 1.

[17] The court accepted that the receiver should be able to execute future, as well as existing, debts.

[18] And have disadvantages, see Lightman & Moss, *The Law Relating to Receivers of Companies*, 1994 2nd ed., para.22.06.

[19] As in *B.C.C.I. S.A. v B.R.S. Kumar Bros. Ltd* [1994] B.C.L.C. 211 (where a receiver was appointed over the assets of a company to which the chargor company had transferred its assets).

[20] See Crabb, "Receivers" in Ian F. Fletcher, *Law of Insolvency* (1996 2nd ed.), p.368.

[21] See I.A. 1986, s.29(2).

[22] But not on pre-receivership contracts unless he novates. In some circumstances he may have a duty to perform such contracts: see *Re Newdigate Colliery Ltd* [1912] 1 Ch. 468.

B was appointed receiver and manager by the court. He gave a signed order for goods, with the words "receiver and manager" appended to his signature. *Held*, he was personally liable to pay for the goods: *Burt, Boulton and Hayward v Bull* [1895] 1 Q.B. 276, CA.

However, he is entitled to an indemnity out of the assets in respect of which he is appointed[23] for liabilities properly incurred.[24] He "supersedes the company which becomes incapable of making contracts on its own behalf."[25]

His appointment causes floating charges to crystallise and thus prevents the company from dealing with assets without his consent. To enable him to carry on the business of the company or to preserve the property of the company, the court can authorise the receiver to borrow money ranking in priority to the debentures.[26] The company's servants are automatically dismissed[27] (but they may be entitled to damages for breach of contract) although they may be employed by the receiver.[28] As an officer of the court he cannot sue or be sued without leave of the court[29] but such leave may be given to enable an action to be brought against him by a person at whose instance he was appointed.[30] Officers of the court have a duty to act not merely lawfully, but in accordance with the principles of justice and honest dealing.[31] His remuneration is fixed by the court. The criteria relevant to determine the level of remuneration have been set out by Ferris J. in *Mirror Group Newspapers plc v Maxwell*.[32] The task is to reward value rather than indemnify cost. Remuneration is not a "cost" of the receivership.[33]

Notice of his appointment must appear on invoices, business letters, orders for goods, etc.: I.A. 1986, s.39.

Receivers appointed out of court

A body corporate is disqualified for appointment as receiver[34]: I.A. 1986, s.30. Also, an undischarged bankrupt is disqualified from acting as receiver or manager, unless he is appointed by the court: I.A. 1986, s.31. Persons subject to the various disqualification orders under the Company Directors Disqualification Act 1986[35] cannot act as receivers.

Since an administrative receiver, but not an ordinary receiver, is acting as an insolvency practitioner within s.388 of the Insolvency Act 1986, only a qualified

---

[23] *Mellor v Mellor* [1992] 4 All E.R. 10.
[24] *ibid.* Where he is appointed manager of the business pending its sale within a limited time, unless the time is extended, expenditure incurred outside that time will be disallowed: *Re Wood Green Steam Laundry* [1918] 1 Ch. 423.
[25] *Moss S.S. Co. Ltd v Whinney* [1912] A.C. 254, 260.
[26] *Greenwood v Algesiras Rly. Co.* [1894] 2 Ch. 205, CA.
[27] The tenure of directors and other officers is unaffected: *Re South Western of Venezuela Ry.* [1902] 1 Ch. 701.
[28] *Reid v Explosives Co. Ltd* (1887) 19 Q.B. 264, CA.
[29] *Viola v Anglo American Cold Storage Co.* [1912] 2 Ch. 305; *Searle v Choat* [1884] 25 Ch. 723, CA.
[30] *L. P. Arthur Insurance Ltd v Sisson* [1966] 1 W.L.R. 1384.
[31] *Re Tyler* [1907] 1 KB 865. *cp. Re John Bateson Co. Ltd* [1985] B.C.L.C. 259.
[32] [1998] B.C.C. 324. See also the report of Ferris J.'s working party on the remuneration of office holders (July 31, 1998).
[33] *Mirror Group Newspapers plc v Maxwell (No. 2)* [2001] B.C.C. 488.
[34] An attempted appointment of a body corporate is a nullity, and the body corporate does not thereby become an agent for the purpose of the Law of Property Act 1925, s.109, and the Limitation Act 1980: *Portman Building Society v Gallwey* [1955] 1 All E.R. 227.
[35] Above, p.321.

insolvency practitioner may be appointed as such[36] and it is a criminal offence for anyone else so to act.[37]

Time of appointment and defects in appointment

A receiver or manager is appointed when the document of appointment is handed to him or his agent provided that he accepts such an appointment by the end of the next business day after such receipt[38]; I.A. 1986, s.33. The person delivering the document to the receiver or his agent must be a person having authority to appoint and the circumstances must be such that it could fairly be said that he was appointing the receiver.[39]

If the appointment of a receiver is discovered to be invalid (*e.g.* the document of appointment was defective[40] or the charge has been set aside for non-registration) the court can order the person appointing the receiver to indemnify him against any liability which arises solely by reason of that invalidity: I.A. 1986, s.34. This section will not protect a receiver from liability arising from other causes, *e.g.* his negligence in managing the company's affairs, simply because his appointment was also invalid. The court has a complete discretion in cases where the section applies and it may well seek to establish where the blame for the invalidity lies.

Effect of appointment of receiver

When a receiver is appointed:

(1) Floating charges crystallise and become fixed. This prevents the company from dealing with the assets charged, without the receiver's consent.[41]

(2) When a receiver of the undertaking of the company is appointed, the directors' power of controlling the company is suspended[42] but they may have a residual role to play. Thus, where a receiver decides not to get in or realise an asset, which it would be in the interests of the company and its other creditors to get in or realise, the directors have power to act on the company's behalf, so long as the interests of the debenture holders, *qua* debenture holders, are not threatened.

The assets in respect of which a receiver was appointed included an action for damages against the debentureholders who had appointed him. It was alleged that they had, in breach of contract, refused further finance causing the company to forfeit its interest in, and profit from, a joint venture. The receivers having refused to sue the debentureholders, the action was initiated by the directors on behalf of the company. *Held*, the action could continue: *Newhart Developments v Co-operative Commercial Bank.*[43]

---

[36] Above, p.533.

[37] I.A. 1986, s.389.

[38] Administrative receivers must confirm in writing within seven days: Insolvency Rules 1986, r.3.1.

[39] *A. Cripps & Sons Ltd v Wickenden* [1973] 1 W.L.R. 944, applying *Windsor Refrigerator Co. Ltd v Branch Nominees Ltd* [1961] Ch. 375, CA.

[40] But see *Byblos Bank S.A.L. v Rushingdale S.A.* [1987] B.C.L.C. 232.

[41] Above, p.550.

[42] *Gomba Holdings UK Ltd v Homan* [1986] 3 All E.R. 94.

[43] [1978] 2 All E.R. 896. See also *Lascomme Ltd v United Dominion Trusts* [1994] I.L.R.M. 227 (High Court of Ireland); *cf. Tudor Grange Holdings Ltd v Citibank N.A.* [1991] 4 All E.R. 1.

The directors cannot claim fees from the receiver unless he employs them, but they can still claim from the company any fees to which they are entitled.[44]

(3) On the appointment of a receiver by the court the company's employees are dismissed.[45] The company ceases to employ them because it is no longer carrying on business: the receiver may carry on the business but he is not the company's agent. In the case of a receiver appointed by the debenture holders and acting as the company's agent,[46] "the business is still the company's business carried on by the company's agent"[47] and therefore there will generally be no automatic dismissal of company employees.Automatic dismissal will however occur if, exceptionally, the receiver is acting as agent for the debenture holders or if the receiver, having transferred the business to a third party, ceases to act as the company's agent in that regard.[48] Further, a particular employee may be subject to automatic dismissal if continuance of his contract of employment is inconsistent with the receiver's role and functions.[49] Where employees are automatically dismissed, the company is liable for breach of contract. Where they are not dismissed, the company remains liable for remuneration, etc., arising. The receiver will not be liable[50] in the absence of novation or adoption.[51]

(4) Every invoice, order for goods or business letter which is issued by or on behalf of the company or the receiver and on which the company's name appears must contain a statement that a receiver has been appointed: I.A. 1986, s.39.

(5) Within seven days after the appointment, the person who made or obtained the appointment must give notice of the fact to the Registrar who must enter it in his register of charges: Companies Act 1985, s.405(1).

(6) When a receiver appointed under a power in an instrument ceases to act, he must give notice to the Registrar: Companies Act 1985, s.405(2).

(7) A receiver appointed under a power in a debenture has his remuneration fixed by agreement. The court may, however, on the application of the liquidator, fix the receiver's remuneration. Under this power the remuneration may be fixed retrospectively, and any excess paid before the making of the order must be accounted for: I.A. 1986, s.36. This power does not entitle the court to interfere with the receiver's right to be indemnified for disbursements which have been properly incurred.[52]

Position of receiver other than administrative receiver

In the case of a receiver appointed under a power in a debenture or a trust deed the debenture usually provides[53] that he is to be the agent of the company.

[44] *Re South Western of Venezuela etc. Rly.* [1902] 1 Ch. 701.
[45] Above, p.548.
[46] Most debentures will provide that the receiver is to be the agent of the company and, as to administrative receivers, statute so provides: I.A. 1986, s.44 (1)(a); See, however, *Silven Properties Ltd v Royal Bank of Scotland plc* [2003] EWCA Civ. 1409.
[47] *per* Dillon L.J. in *Nicoll v Cutts* [1985] B.C.L.C. 322, CA.
[48] *Re Foster Clark's Indenture Trusts* [1966] 1 W.L.R. 125.
[49] *Griffiths v Secretary of State for Social Security* [1974] Q.B. 468.
[50] *Nicoll v Cutts*, above.
[51] See below, I.A. 1986, ss 37, 44.
[52] *Re Potters Oils* [1986] 1 W.L.R. 201.
[53] If it does not, he is agent of the debentureholders who are answerable for his faults and omissions: *Re Vimbos* [1900] 1 Ch. 470.

Consequently the debenture holder(s) or the trustees are not liable for his acts, though the company is.Through this agency the company can claim documents brought into existence in the course of the receivership in discharge of the receiver's duties to the company but not otherwise.[54]

Contracts made by the company and current at the date of his appointment are not binding on the receiver personally, unless they become binding by novation,[55] or, in the case of contracts of employment, adoption: I.A. 1986, s.37(1), (2).[56] The receiver must, however, carry out the company's current contracts if not to do so would injure the company's goodwill,[57] but if the contracts can only be carried out by borrowing money ranking in priority to the debenture holders and are unprofitable, he need not carry them out.[58] As agent of the company, he is immune from personal liability for breach of such contracts or for inducing a breach of contract so long as his decision not to carry out the contract is bona fide and within his authority.[59]

Under s.37(1), (3) of the Insolvency Act 1986, a receiver appointed under a power in an instrument (other than an administrative receiver) is, to the same extent as if he had been appointed by the court, personally liable on contracts made by him in the performance of his functions except so far as they otherwise provide[60] and on any contract of employment adopted by him in the performance of his functions.Nothing he does or does not do within 14 days of his appointment can be regarded as his adopting such a contract of employment. S.37(1)(a) was in part a response to *Nicoll v Cutts*[61] which decided that a receiver who merely continued a contract of employment on behalf of the company did not incur personal liability. The employee, in relation to post-receivership remuneration, had the status of an unsecured creditor. Now causing the company to continue the contract of employment amounts to adoption and results in personal liability.[62] The receiver is unable to avoid personal liability unilaterally, as by service of a notice.[63] The liability is restricted to liabilities incurred on the contract while he was receiver.[64] In respect of it he enjoys a right of indemnity against the company's assets under s.37(1)(b). The Insolvency Act 1994, which qualifies the liability of administrative receivers and administrators,[65] is not applicable to ordinary receivers within s.37. It may be that the liability could be

---

[54] *Gomba Holdings UK Ltd v Minories Finance Ltd* [1989] B.C.L.C., CA.

[55] *Parsons v Sovereign Bank of Canada* [1913] A.C. 160, PC.

[56] See below.

[57] *Re Newdigate Colliery Ltd* [1912] 1 Ch. 468, CA, and see *Airlines Airspares Ltd v Handley Page Ltd* [1970] Ch. 193, and *Freevale v Metrostore Holdings* [1984] Ch. 199; See also *Astor Chemical v Synthetic Technology Ltd* [1990] B.C.C. 97.

[58] *Re Thames Ironworks Co. Ltd* (1912) 106 L.T. 674.

[59] *Lathia v Dronsfield Bros. Ltd* [1987] B.C.L.C. 321.

[60] Where liability is excluded the receiver may in appropriate circumstances be exposed to a claim under s.213 for fraudulent trading: *Re Leyland Daf Ltd: Re Ferranti Ltd* [1994] B.C.C. 658, 668.

[61] [1985] B.C.L.C. 322, CA.

[62] See *Powdrill v Watson, Re Leyland Daf Ltd, Re Ferranti International plc,* [1995] 2 All E.R. 65 HL (relating to s.19 (administrators) and s.44 (administrative receivers)).

[63] *ibid. cf. Re Specialised Mouldings Ltd*, February 13, 1987 (unreported) which gave rise to the practice, now known to be ineffective, of sending "Specialised Mouldings" letters opting out of personal liability.

[64] *Powdrill v Watson*, above.

[65] See below, Ch.26.

excluded or modified by a contract with the employees but such a contract will not readily be implied.[66] On the commencement of a winding up of the company the receiver ceases to be the company's agent and his authority to bind the company ceases[67] but his powers with regard to the property charged are unaffected[68] so that he may continue to use the company's name for the purpose of the realisation of its assets.[69] On a liquidation the receiver may well become the agent of the debenture holder who will then be liable for his acts.[70] Where the appointing debenture holder "intermeddles" with the receiver's performance of his functions (*e.g.*, by giving him instructions) the receiver may also become the agent of the debenture holder rather than that of the company.[71]

A debenture holder or mortgagee must exercise his power to appoint a receiver in good faith for the propose of obtaining repayment.[72] If he complies with this rule, it is irrelevant that the appointment of a receiver is disadvantageous to the company and its other creditors, because, for example, it causes unnecessary expense[73] or frustrates negotiations with a third party for additional funding.[74] Once appointed, a receiver owes a duty of good faith to the company but it is qualified by the recognition that the primary function of the charge is repayment of the debt. Thus, where he is appointed manager of a business, he manages in order to discharge the debt and not, as would its directors, in order to benefit the company.[75] Where he exercises a power of sale, he can give preference to the interests of the debenture holders regarding the time of sale[76] but he does owe a duty of reasonable care to obtain the true value of the property at the time he chooses to sell it.[77] This may include a duty to pursue a sale of the property and the business as a going concern.[78] This duty has been equated with a duty of care in negligence[79] but it is now accepted that it is an equitable duty only[80] and it is owed to a limited class, namely, the company, subsequent encumbrancers and guarantors.[81]

Where a receiver decides to continue the business of the company he owes an equitable duty of care to do so with reasonable competence.

---

[66] *Re Leyland Daf Ltd* [1994] B.C.C. 658.
[67] *Gosling v Gaskell* [1897] A.C. 575; *Thomas v Todd* [1926] 2 K.B. 511.
[68] *Gough's Garages Ltd v Pugsley* [1930] 1 K.B. 615.
[69] *Sowman v David Samuel Trust Ltd* [1978] 1 W.L.R. 22.
[70] *American Express International Banking Corp. v Hurley* [1985] 3 All E.R. 564.
[71] *American Express International Banking Corp. v Hurley* [1985] 3 All E.R. 564; *Royal Bank of Scotland plc v Binnell* [1996] B.P.I.R 352.
[72] *cf. Downsview Nominees Ltd v First City Corpn. Ltd* [1993] 3 All E.R. 626, PC, where the appointment was made to prevent a subsequent encumbrancer enforcing his security.
[73] *Re Potter Oils Ltd (No. 2)* [1986] 1 All E.R. 890.
[74] *Shamji v Johnson Matthey Bankers Ltd* [1991] B.C.L.C. 36.
[75] *Re B. Johnson & Co. (Builders) Ltd* [1955] 2 All E.R. 775, 790–91.
[76] *Cuckmere Brick Co. Ltd v Mutual Finance Ltd* [1971] 2 All E.R. 633, CA, even if redemption is imminent so long as there has been no valid tender of the redemption price: see *Routestone Ltd v Minories Finance Ltd* [1997] B.C.C. 180, 187. See also *Cohen v TSB Bank plc* [2002] 2 B.C.L.C. 32, *Silven Properties Ltd v Royal Bank of Scotland plc* [2003] EWCA Civ. 1409.
[77] *ibid.* And see *Downsview*, above.
[78] Unless the business has previously ceased: see *A.I.B. Ltd v Debtors (Alsop & Another)* [1998] B.C.C. 780, CA.
[79] *e.g. in Knight v Lawrence* [1991] 01 E.G. 105.
[80] *China & South Sea Bank Ltd v Tan* [1980] 3 All E.R. 839, PC; *Parker—Tweedale v Dunbar Bank, plc (No. 1)* [1990] 2 All E.R. 577, CA; *Downsview*, above.
[81] *American Express International Banking Corp. v Hurley* [1985] 3 All E.R. 564; *Parker—Tweedale*, above.

Receivers appointed over a pig-farming business were advised that discounts on orders of feed were available. The receivers failed to request such discounts. *Held*, the receivers were liable to compensate the mortgagor in respect of the discounts, as these were lost as a result of their breach of an equitable duty of skill and care: *Medforth v Blake* [2000] Ch.86

This duty is owed to the company and to subsequent encumbrancers and guarantors.[82] The duty does not compel the receiver to continue to operate the business where it is not in the interests of the debenture holder to do so,[83] but it will be a breach of duty for a receiver to remain passive where to do so damages the interests of the debenture holder or the company.[84]

A company in receivership cannot interfere with the receiver in the proper exercise of his powers but, in *Watts v Midland Bank plc*,[85] Peter Gibson J. thought that it could maintain an action against him for the proper performance of his duties and so refused to allow a minority shareholder to bring a derivative action[86] against him.

A receiver appointed out of court, or the person who appointed him, may apply to the court for directions in any matter concerning the performance of his functions: I.A. 1986, s.35.[87] The court's jurisdiction is not limited to giving guidance and instruction; it may also make an order enforcing a contract of indemnity between the receivers and the debenture holders who appointed them.[88] He must within one month of his first year of appointment, every subsequent period of six months and on ceasing to act, deliver to the Registrar the requisite accounts of his receipts and payments: I.A. 1986, s.38. Since the receiver is usually the agent of the company he must produce full accounts to the company when required to do so.[89] The court may order the receiver to make any returns or give any notices which he is by law required to give or make: I.A. 1986, s.41.[90]

Administrative receivers

The right to appoint a receiver who qualifies as an administrative receiver has been restricted by s.72A of the Insolvency Act 1986. The legislative purpose behind this provision is to promote the use of the new, streamlined administration procedure,[91] as this regime is seen as fairer, more inclusive for *all* creditors and, most importantly, as more likely to result in the rescue of the company or its business.[92] Section 72A, however, applies only to the entitlement of the holders of a 'qualifying floating charge'[93] to make such an appointment, and is not retrospec-

---

[82] *Medforth v Blake* [2000] Ch. 86.
[83] *ibid.*
[84] *Silven Properties Ltd v Royal Bank of Scotland plc* [2003] EWCA Civ. 1409.
[85] [1986] B.C.L.C. 15.
[86] Above, p.343.
[87] This section also applies to administrative receivers.
[88] *Re Therm-a-Stor Ltd* [1996] 3 All E.R. 228.
[89] *Smiths Ltd v Middleton* [1979] 3 All E.R. 843.
[90] This section also applies to administrative receivers.
[91] Below, Ch.26.
[92] See *Productivity and Enterprise: Insolvency—A Second Chance* (DTI: Cm 5234: HMSO: July 2001), para.2.2.
[93] See Insolvency Act 1986 Sch.B1, para.14.

tive in effect: s.72A(4). Therefore, holders of charges granted prior to September 15, 2003 will still be entitled to appoint an administrative receiver and the following exposition of the law will remain of relevance for some time to come.

The prohibition in s.72A is also subject to a number of exceptions found in s.72B-72GA, although these exceptions relate to rather specialist financing transactions. Moreover, it does not prevent a debenture holder from appointing a receiver over the fixed charge element of the secured property, although such a receiver would not be an administrative receiver.

S.44 of the Insolvency Act 1986 provides that an administrative receiver is deemed to be the agent of the company unless and until it goes into liquidation[94] so that the company remains liable as principal on all contracts made by him.[95] The section also provides that an administrative receiver is personally liable on all contracts he makes in carrying out his functions and on any contract of employment he adopts (*i.e.* allows to continue for more than 14 days after his appointment).[96] In respect of contracts of employment adopted on or after March 15, 1994, the administrative receiver's personal liability is limited to liabilities arising under the contract of employment[97] which fall within the definition of a "qualifying liability" (I.A. 1986, s.44, as amended by I.A. 1994, s.2)[98] being:

(a) a liability to pay a sum by way of wages or salary[99] or contribution to an occupational pension scheme,

(b) incurred while the administrative receiver is in office, and

(c) in respect of services rendered wholly or partly after adoption of the contract.[1]

Where the liability arises in respect of services rendered partly before and partly after the adoption, it is provided that only so much of it as relates to the post-adoption period qualifies.[2]

In respect of the s.44 liability, the administrative receiver is entitled to an indemnity out of the assets of the company and this is without prejudice to any indemnity he can claim under any express clause in his appointment or in an order of the court under s.34 of the Act.

An administrative receiver has the powers set out in Schedule 1 to the Insolvency Act 1986, subject to any contrary express terms in the relevant debenture; Insolvency Act 1986, s.42(1). Schedule 1 in fact states the powers

---

[94] *American Express Banking Corp. v Hurley* [1985] 3 All E.R. 564.

[95] A contract within s.320 C.A. 1985 (see above p.257) is liable to be avoided: *Demite Ltd v Protec Health Ltd* [1998] B.C.C. 638 (Park J.).

[96] In respect of liabilities incurred while he was receiver. See *Powdrill v Watson, Re Leyland Daf Ltd, Re Ferranti International plc* [1995] 2 All E.R. 65, HL. See above, p.674.

[97] *cf.* liabilities arising by virtue of statute in relation to redundancy or unfair dismissal.

[98] See Current Law Statutes Annotated (David Milman).

[99] s.2(3) of the I.A. 1994 inserts into s.44 I.A. 1986 a new subsection, (2C), which includes within the definition of wages or salary amounts payable in periods of absence due to holidays and sickness and also amounts payable in lieu of holidays.

[1] s.2(3) of the I.A. 1994 inserting a new subsection, (2A), into s.44 I.A. 1986.

[2] s.2(3) of the I.A. 1994 adding a new section (2B) to s.44 of the I.A. 1986.

given to an administrator appointed under an administration order and they are set out in the following chapter of this book. S.42(2) of the Act adapts those powers to an administrative receiver.[3] S.42(3) of the Insolvency Act 1986 provides that a person dealing with an administrative receiver in good faith and for value does not need to inquire whether the receiver is acting within his powers.

By virtue of s.43(1) of the Insolvency Act an administrative receiver can sell property[4] which is subject to a security having priority over the security of his appointor[5] free of that security if the court is satisfied that such a sale is likely to promote a more advantageous realisation of the company's assets.[6] The secured creditor whose security is thus overturned is protected by s.43(3) so that the net proceeds of sale must be used to discharge his debt together with, if the court regards such proceeds as less than the open market value of the property, such additional sums as are necessary to make good the deficiency.[7] The receiver must send an office copy of any court order under this section to the registrar within 14 days, with a fine in default.

Supplies to administrative receivers

Supplies of gas, electricity, water and telecommunications requested by an administrative receiver are protected: I.A. 1986, s.233.[8] Supplies of other goods and services are not protected,[9] and the supplier is entitled at common law to stipulate for payment in full of pre-receivership arrears before making further supplies.[10] Such a demand is not a breach of Art.86 of the Treaty of Rome which prohibits abuse of a dominant position.[11]

Where an administrative receiver himself contracts for post-receivership supplies, he will incur personal liability and will be entitled in respect of it to an indemnity out of the company's assets.[12] Where he merely continues the company's contract, he incurs no personal liability.[13] Thus he is not personally liable to pay rent or hire charges under an existing lease or hire-purchase agreement, even where he uses the land or goods. Such amounts are a company

---

[3] Note also that I.A. 1986, ss 233, 234, 235, 236 and 237 apply to administrative receivers. See below.
[4] Being property in relation to which he is the receiver or would be the receiver but for the appointment of a receiver by a prior chargee: I.A. 1986, s.43(7).
[5] I.A., s.43(2).
[6] Following a recommendation of the *Cork Report* paras.1510–1513; *cf.* I.A. below, p.508. Sch.B1, para.70, below, p.573.
[7] If there is more than one charge on the property they are to be repaid in order of priority: I.A. 1986, s.43(4).
[8] See, below p.604.
[9] Whether requested by an administrative receiver or an ordinary receiver.
[10] *Leyland Daf Ltd v Automotive Products, plc* [1993] B.C.C. 389.
[11] *ibid.*
[12] I.A. 1986, s.44. Such indemnity, together with his renumeration and any expenses properly incurred by him is charged on any property of the company in his custody or under his control at the time he vacates office in priority to any security held by the person who appointed him: I.A. 1986, s.45. Similar provisions apply to ordinary receivers: I.A. 1986, s.37.
[13] In the absence of novation.

liability and "it is to the company that, along with other creditors, the lessor and the owner of the goods must look for payment".[14]

Where goods are hired or leased to the company under a hire purchase or chattel lease agreement, and the appointment of the receiver terminates that agreement that receiver may apply for equitable relief against forfeiture of the subject matter of the agreement.[15] In such circumstances, a receiver should make such an application speedily, rather than pay a premium to the owner of the goods in question and then attempt to avoid that payment on the grounds of economic duress.[16]

Duties of administrative receiver

On appointment an administrative receiver must forthwith inform the company of his appointment and publish that fact in the *Gazette* and a newspaper appropriate for ensuring that it comes to the notice of the companies creditors: Insolvency Rules 1986, r.3.2(3). Within 28 days of his appointment he must send a notice of his appointment to all the creditors of the company[17] so far as he is aware of their addresses. There are fines in default: I.A. 1986, s.46.

He must also obtain "forthwith" a statement of the company's affairs from some or all of the officers of the company (past or present), its promoters (if they acted within the year prior to his appointment), its employees (if they are in his opinion capable of giving the information required and are either current employees or have been employed within the preceding year) and the officers of any company which is (or has been within the previous year) an officer of the company concerned. Such a statement must be made within 21 days of being asked for, with a fine in default. Such persons are entitled to be paid their reasonable expenses by the administrative receiver.[18] The receiver may excuse any person from the obligation or extend the time limits although the court may intervene and exercise the power on his behalf: I.A. 1986, s.47.

Statements submitted under s.47 must be verified by affidavit and contain particulars of the company's assets, debts and liabilities, the names and addresses of its creditors, any securities held by them and when they were given and such further information as may be prescribed. Similar statements are required to be given to an administrator.[19]

Within three months of his appointment, unless the court allows an extension, an administrative receiver must report to the Registrar, the trustees for secured creditors and all secured creditors of whose addresses he is aware; I.A. 1986, s.48(1). This report must include details of the events leading up to his

---

[14] *per* Nicholls L.J. in *Re Atlantic Computer Systems plc* [1992] 1 All E.R. 476 at p.486. Unlike in the case of an administration or liquidation, such amounts are not treated as a prior charge on the assets, but, if not paid, the lessor or owner is free to take legal proceedings. *cf.* I.A. 1986, ss 11, 130. As to liability for rates, see *Re Sobam B.V.* [1996] B.C.C. 351.

[15] *Transag Haulage Ltd v Leyland DAF Finance Plc* [1994] B.C.C. 356, *On Demand Information Plc v Michael Gerson (Finance) Plc* [2000] 4 All E.R. 734.

[16] *Alf Vaughan & Co Ltd v Royscot Trust plc* [1999] 1 All E.R. (Comm) 856.

[17] Unless the court otherwise directs, not to the shareholders.

[18] Insolvency Rules 1986, r.3.7(1).

[19] Below, Ch.26.

appointment, any dealings of his with company property and his carrying on of the company's business, the amounts of principal and interest payable to those debenture holders who appointed him and the amounts payable to preferential creditors, and the amount (if any) likely to be available for the payment of other creditors. It must also include a summary of the statements of affairs submitted to him under s.47 together his comments: I.A. 1986, s.48(5). It need not include anything "which would seriously prejudice the carrying out by the administrative receiver of his functions": I.A. 1986, s.48(6).

In addition, within three months an administrative receiver must also either send a copy of his report to all the company's unsecured creditors (of whose addresses he is aware) or publish an address to which they may write for copies to be sent to them free of charge. In either case he must also summon a meeting of the unsecured creditors on not less than 14 days' notice, before which he must lay a copy of the report. The court may dispense with such a meeting if the report states that the receiver intends to apply for such an order and the other requirements as to publicity are complied with at least 14 days before the application: I.A. 1986, s.48(2), (3). Such a meeting may appoint a committee, which may summon the receiver to attend before it and to give it such information as is reasonable, provided it gives him 7 days' notice: I.A. 1986, s.49. If the receivership is overtaken by a winding up, the report must be sent to the liquidator within 7 days: I.A. 1986, s.48(4). The administrative receiver must provide annual and final accounts of his receipts and payments to the Registrar of Companies, the company, the person who appointed him and each member of the creditors' committee (where there is one).[20]

These provisions replaced more limited ones in the Companies Act 1985 and reflect the Cork Committee's intention that creditors should be more aware and receivers more accountable.

Preferential payments

A receiver appointed to enforce a charge which, as created, was a floating charge, must pay the preferential debts[21] in priority to any claims for principal and interest in respect of the debentures.[22] This obligation applies even if the charge had crystallised prior to the appointment of a receiver, but it does not apply to a charge which as created was fixed. Creditors relying on a floating charge are thus deferred to the preferential debts but they are entitled to have the consequent depletion of assets made good out of assets available for the payment of general creditors: I.A. 1986, s.40.[23]

A receiver who pays floating charge funds to his debenture holder in the knowledge that preferential creditors have not been paid is liable in the tort of breach of statutory duty, and liable to the preferential creditors.[24]

---

[20] *Gomba Holdings UK Ltd v Homan* [1986] 1 W.L.R. 1301; I.R. 1986, r.3.32(1).

[21] See s.386 and Sch.6, I.A. 1986. Below, p.508. In this case the periods mentioned in Sch.6 run from the appointment of the receiver or the taking of possession. The duty does not cease on the claim of the appointor being met: *Re Pearl Maintenance Services Ltd* [1995] B.C.C. 657.

[22] Both the debentures in respect of, and those having priority to, the debentures under which he has been appointed: see *H. & K. (Medway) Ltd* [1997] B.C.C. 853.

[23] See also s.196 Companies Act 1985.

[24] *Inland Revenue Commissioners v Goldblatt* [1972] Ch. 498.

Share of assets for unsecured creditors

An administrative receiver must make available for the satisfaction of unsecured debts a "prescribed part of the company's property": s.176A(2) IA.[25] The company's net property is the amount that would have been available to floating charge holders but for s.176A: s.176A(6). The duty does not apply where the company's net property is less than the 'prescribed minimum' *and* the receiver thinks that the cost of making a distribution to unsecured creditors is disproportionate to the benefits.[26]

The prescribed part is calculated as a percentage of the company's property subject to a floating charge (but not a fixed charge). Where such property does not exceed £10,000 in value, the prescribed part is 50 per cent of that value, where it exceeds £10,000 the prescribed part is 50 per cent of the first £10,000 and 20 per cent of property exceeding £10,000, subject to a maximum of £600,000: SI 2003/2097, para.3. Only floating charges granted on or after September 15, 2003 are affected: s.176A(9).

Vacation of office by receiver

An administrative receiver may only be removed from office by an order of the court although he may resign on giving due notice. In addition he must vacate his office if he ceases to be a qualified insolvency practitioner. When he does give up office he must inform the registrar within 14 days and is subject to a fine in default: I.A. 1986, s.45. Any administrative receiver must also vacate his office.

When any receiver vacates office any remuneration, expenses or indemnity to which he is entitled at that time take priority over any security held by the person who appointed him: I.A. 1986. Where the expenses of a receiver appointed by the court exceed the assets in his hands, he is not entitled to recover them from the person who appointed him or the company.[27]

SCOTS LAW

The reasons for the introduction of the office of receiver to Scotland by the Companies (Floating Charges and Receivers) (Scotland) Act 1972[28] were:

---

[25] As inserted by s.252 Enterprise Act 2002.

[26] Section 176A(3)(a). The prescribed minimum is £10,000: The Insolvency Act 1986 (Prescribed Part) Order 2003 (SI 2003/2097, paragraph 2). If the company's net property exceeds the prescribed minimum and the receiver thinks that the cost of making a distribution to unsecured creditors is disproportionate to the benefits, he must apply to court for an order disapplying s.176A(2): s.176A(5).

[27] *Evans v Clayhope Ltd* [1988] B.C.L.C. 238, CA.

[28] A petition for the appointment of a judicial factor *ad interim* on the affairs of a limited company is competent at common law: *Fraser, Petitioner,* 1971 S.L.T. 146. (O.H.) (appointment made in a "position of chaos requiring urgently to be dealt with"). In *Weir v Rees,* 1991 S.L.T. 345 (O.H.), a judicial factor *ad interim* was appointed where all the directors had been removed and the company was controlled by the secretary and the manager who were amongst the directors who had been removed, and who did not have the confidence of the majority of the members of the company. Where both a liquidator and a receiver were appointed, the receiver was held (*i*) to be entitled to take control of the property to satisfy the debt of the holder of the floating charge and (*ii*) to be primarily liable for the payment of the fixed securities and preferential debts of the company: *Manley, Petitioner,* 1985 S.L.T. 42 (O.H.). In *McGuinness v Black (No. 2),* 1990 S.C. 21 (O.H.), there were circumstances in which, following *Fraser, Petitioner*, above, the appointment of an interim judicial factor was preferred to the appointment of a provisional liquidator.

(a) to enable the fortunes of a company to be revived and thus prevent unnecessary liquidation;

(b) to strengthen the rights of a holder of a floating charge by making it possible for him to take possession of and realise the security without liquidation; and

(c) to lessen the difficulties which could arise from the difference between Scots and English law where a group of companies included both Scottish and English companies.[29]

This Act was consolidated into the Companies Act 1985 and then, after amendments made by the Insolvency Act 1985 the general purpose of which was to standardise the English and Scottish provisions, into the Insolvency Act 1986. References are to sections of the 1986 Act, except when there is a statement to the contrary.

A receiver may be appointed by either the holder of a floating charge or the court on the application of the holder of a floating charge: s.51. The term "holder of the floating charge" is sufficiently widely defined as to include, in the case of a series of debentures, the trustees acting for the debenture holders under a trust deed, or, if there are no such trustees, specified majorities of the debenture holders: s.70(2).

Appointment by holder of floating charge

A receiver may be appointed by the holder of the floating charge on the occurrence of any event which, by the instrument creating the charge, entitles the holder to make that appointment, and, in so far as the instrument does not provide otherwise, on the occurrence of any of the following:

(a) expiry of 21 days after the making of a demand—which is unsatisfied— for payment of the whole or part of the principal sum secured;

(b) expiry of two months during which interest has been in arrears;

(c) making of an order or passing of a resolution to wind up the company;

(d) appointment of a receiver by virtue of any other floating charge created by the company: s.52(1).[29a]

The appointment is made by means of an "instrument of appointment," validly executed by the holder of the charge or by a person having his written authority. A copy, certified in the manner prescribed by the Receivers (Scotland) Regulations 1986 (SI 1986/1917) to be a correct copy, must be delivered by the person making the appointment to the Registrar within seven days of its execution, and

---

[29] *Report on the Companies (Floating Charges) (Scotland) Act 1961*, (1970) Cmnd. 4336, paras.37, 38.
[29a] But *cf.* now s.72A(2)(2), which provides that the holder of a qualifying floating charge in respect of a company's property may not appoint or apply to the court for the appointment of a receiver who on appointment would be an administrative receiver of property of the company. See too, above, p.540.

the Registrar enters particulars of the appointment in the register of charges. The receiver is regarded as having been appointed on the date and at the time when the instrument of appointment is received by him provided he accepts the appointment by the end of the business day next after such receipt (either by him or on his behalf).[30] A docquet signed by the receiver stating when he received the instrument of appointment is conclusive evidence of that fact.[31] As from the date of the receiver's appointment the floating charge, subject to ss 410 to 414 of the Companies Act 1985 and s.245 of the 1986 Act, attaches to the property and takes effect as if it were a fixed security. Failure without reasonable excuse duly to register the certified copy of the instrument of appointment attracts a fine but does not affect the validity of the appointment: s.53(2).

In the case of a floating charge which covers the whole of the property from time to time comprised in the company's undertaking (an "all-assets" floating charge), any property which comes into the company's hands after the receiver's appointment will be attached and be available, if need be, for realisation by the receiver.

A receiver appointed to a company under an "all-assets" floating charge discovered that, before his appointment, the company had sold part of its stock-in-trade to a loan creditor and that the purchase price had been set off against the amount then due to that creditor. The receiver persuaded the creditor to return the stock to the company and allowed the debt to be correspondingly reinstated. The receiver then realised the assets of the company, including the restored stock. A liquidator was thereafter appointed, and he contended that the repurchased stock should not have been regarded as attached by the charge under what is now s.53. Held, it was not relevant to inquire whether particular assets were or were not comprised in the company's undertaking at the date of the receiver's appointment; the question was whether the instrument creating the floating charge covered the assets in question, and as the instrument in this case was expressed to cover assets whenever they came to be comprised in the company's undertaking, the reacquired stock was attached and available for realisation by the receiver: Ross v Taylor, 1985 S.C. 156.

The interpretation of the phrase "as if the charge was a fixed security" in s.53(7) must take into account the definition of "fixed security" in s.70. The definition provides that "fixed security" means any security, other than a floating charge, which on the winding up of the company in Scotland would be treated as an effective security over the property.

Joint receivers were appointed by a bank over the whole of a company's property. The following day another creditor of the company purported to arrest in the hands of a third party a sum owing to the company. Held, because, by the appointment of the receivers, the floating charge had attached to, inter alia, the debt purported to be arrested, that debt had to be treated as if it had been attached as a fixed security, i.e. as if there had been an assignation of the debt in security in favour of the holders of the floating charge, followed by due intimation of the assignation to the third party; the liability of the third party to pay the debt to the company had therefore disappeared and the debt could not be effectively arrested: Forth & Clyde Construction Co. Ltd v Trinity Timber & Plywood Co. Ltd, 1984 S.C. 1.

[30] The Regulations make special provision for joint receivers.
[31] Secretary of State for Trade and Industry v Houston, 1994 S.L.T. 775 (O.H.).

Appointment by court

The circumstances in which a receiver may be appointed by the court are the same as those for an appointment by the holder of the floating charge (above, p.554) except that for paragraph (d) there must be substituted:

> (d)   where the court is satisfied that the position of the holder of the charge is likely to be prejudiced if no appointment is made: s.52(2)(a).

The application to the court for the appointment is by petition, which must be served on the company. A certified copy of the court's interlocutor making the appointment must be delivered by or on behalf of the petitioner to the Registrar within seven days of the date of the interlocutor or such longer period as the court may allow, and the Registrar enters particulars of the appointment in the register of charges. The receiver is regarded as having been appointed on the date of the interlocutor, and as from that date the floating charge attaches to the property and takes effect as if it were a fixed security. Failure without reasonable excuse duly to register the certified copy of the interlocutor attracts a fine but does not affect the validity of the appointment: s.54(3).

Who can be appointed receiver

The following are disqualified from being appointed as receiver:

> (a)   a body corporate;
>
> (b)   an undischarged bankrupt; and
>
> (c)   a Scottish firm: s.51(3).

It is permissible to have joint receivers: s.51(6).

Where there are two or more floating charges, the same person may be appointed receiver by virtue of both or all of them: s.56(7).

Powers of receiver

A receiver has the powers, if any, conferred on him by the instrument creating the floating charge, and in addition he has the extensive powers listed in Sch.2 to the Act in so far as these are not inconsistent with any provision contained in the instrument creating the charge: s.55(1), (2). The statutory powers are such as to place the receiver in a position corresponding to that of an administrative receiver in England, and include the following powers:

> (a)   to take possession[32] and dispose of the company's property;

---

[32] It is a matter of controversy whether this empowers a receiver to take proceedings in his own name against debtors to the company without having acquired an assignation of the debts from the company: *McPhail v Lothian Regional Council*, 1981 S.C. 119 (O.H.), not followed in *Taylor, Petitioner*, 1982 S.L.T. 172 (O.H.). Funds consigned in court as a condition of recall of arrestment and inhibition on the dependence were held not to fall within the company's property in *Hawking v. Hafton House Ltd*, 1990 S.C. 198 (O.H.).

(b)   to raise or borrow money and grant security over the property;

(c)   to appoint agents and professional persons such as a solicitor and an accountant and to employ and dismiss employees;

(d)   to bring or defend legal proceedings in the name and on behalf of the company,[33]

(e)   to refer questions to arbitration;

(f)   to insure the company's business and property;

(g)   to use the company's seal and execute documents, including bills of exchange and promissory notes, in the name and on behalf of the company;

(h)   to carry on the company's business or any part of it;

(i)   to grant or accept a surrender of a lease and to take on leases;

(j)   to make any arrangement or compromise on behalf of the company;

(k)   to call up any uncalled capital of the company;

(l)   to establish subsidiaries of the company and to transfer to subsidiaries the business of the company or any part of it or any of the property;

(m)   to change the situation of the company's registered office;

(n)   to present or defend a petition for the winding up of the company; and

(o)   to do all other things incidental to the exercise of his other powers.

The receiver may require to exercise only some of these wide statutory powers of management. It is a matter for his discretion as to which powers he will exercise and when he will exercise them. The company, through its directors, cannot normally interfere with the exercise by the receiver of his discretion by, for instance, raising actions which the receiver considers should not be raised but, where a receiver in the exercise of his discretion does not pursue an asset such as a claim for damages, the directors are entitled, and may be bound by their duty to other creditors, to vindicate the asset.[34]

The receiver has a duty of care to beneficiaries of the company's pension scheme, which he must not terminate without first giving adequate notice. Failure to do so may make him liable in damages to the beneficiaries.[35]

---

[33] In *Imperial Hotel (Aberdeen) Ltd v Vaux Breweries Ltd,* 1978 S.C. 86 (O.H.), it was held not competent for the directors to raise actions in connection with the property which was within the receivership, but in *Shanks v Central Regional Council,* 1987 S.L.T. 410 (O.H.), it was observed that, while the *Imperial* case was applicable to *most* situations, it did not mean that an action brought by a company in receivership was inherently incompetent or necessarily a fundamental nullity: it could not be held that directors were not empowered in any circumstances to deal in any way, including the raising of proceedings, with assets which were the subject of the floating charge. *Shanks* was doubted in *Independent Pension Trustee Ltd v LAW Construction Co. Ltd,* 1997 S.L.T. 1105 (where company's assets included its powers under an occupational pension scheme, directors were held to have lost their power of appointment of trustees when the company went into receivership). A receiver has no title to sue in his own name: the action must be raised in the name of the company: *Ritchie v EFT Industrial Ltd,* 1997 G.W.D. 24–1400 (Sh. Ct.).

[34] *Imperial Hotel (Aberdeen) Ltd v Vaux Breweries Ltd,* and *Shanks v Central Regional Council,* above.

[35] *Larson's Executrix v Henderson,* 1990 S.L.T. 498 (O.H.), a case in which the receiver was held to have given adequate notice.

The exercise by the receiver of his powers is subject to the rights of persons who have effectually executed diligence[36] before his appointment and to the rights of persons who hold a fixed security or floating charge with prior or equal ranking: s.55(3).

A person dealing with a receiver in good faith and for value is not concerned to inquire whether the receiver is acting within his powers: s.55(4).

Precedence among receivers

Where there are two or more floating charges, a receiver may be appointed by virtue of each charge, but the receiver whose charge has priority of ranking is entitled to exercise the statutory powers to the exclusion of any other receiver: s.56(1). Where two or more floating charges rank equally and two or more receivers have been appointed by virtue of these charges, the receivers are deemed to be joint receivers: s.56(2). The powers of a receiver whose charge has a ranking postponed to that of another charge by virtue of which a receiver has later been appointed are, from the date of the later appointment, suspended so far as is necessary to enable the second-mentioned receiver to exercise his statutory powers, and they revive when the prior floating charge ceases to attach to the property: s.56(4).

Agency and liability of receiver for contracts

A receiver is deemed to be the agent of the company in relation to the property attached by the floating charge[37] and in relation to any contract of employment adopted by him in the carrying out of his functions: s.57(1) and (1A) (inserted by Insolvency Act 1994, s.3(1) (2)).

He is personally liable on any contract entered into by him in the performance of his functions, except in so far as the contract otherwise provides, and, to the extent of any qualifying liability, on any contract of employment adopted by him in the carrying out of those functions: s.57(2) as amended by Insolvency Act 1994, s.3(1) (3).

A contract of employment is, by s.57(2A), inserted by Insolvency Act 1994, s.3(1) (4), a "qualifying liability" if:

    (a)   it is a liability to pay a sum by way of wages or salary or contribution to an occupational pension scheme,

---

[36] An arrestment which has not been followed by a decree of furthcoming is not an "effectually executed diligence" for this purpose: *Lord Advocate v Royal Bank of Scotland Ltd*, 1977 S.C. 155; nor is a landlord's hypothec for rent: *Cumberland Development Corporation v Mustone*, 1983 S.L.T. (Sh. Ct.) 55. The *Royal Bank* case was distinguished in *Iona Hotels Ltd (in receivership) v Craig*, 1990 S.C. 330 (an arrestment had made sums litigious in December 1987 and arrester's advantage could not be defeated by a subsequent voluntary act of the debtor, namely the granting of a floating charge in January 1988). The *Cumberland* case was not followed in *Grampian Regional Council v Drill Stem (Inspection Services) Ltd (in receivership)* 1994 S.C.L.R. 36 (Sh. Ct.).

[37] This presumption was held to be rebuttable in *Inverness District Council v Highland Universal Fabrications*, 1986 S.L.T. 556 (O.H.) (landlords seeking payment from receiver personally for occupation of premises after his appointment). In an application of this statutory provision receivers who carried on the company's business in licensed premises owned by the company were held not liable for rates since it was the company which remained in rateable occupation of the premises during the receivership: *McKillop, Petitioner*, 1995 S.L.T. 216 (O.H.).

(b) it is incurred while the receiver is in office, and

(c) it is in respect of services rendered wholly or partly after the adoption of the contract.

However, where the sum payable as a qualifying liability is payable for services rendered partly before and partly after the adoption of the contract, the liability extends only to the sum payable for services rendered after the adoption of the contract: s.57(2B), inserted by Insolvency Act 1994, s.3(1) (4).

A receiver who is personally liable under s.57(2) is entitled to be indemnified out of the property in respect of which he was appointed: s.57(3).

As regards contracts of employment, nothing which is done or omitted within 14 days after his appointment is to be taken as an adoption of the contract by the receiver: s.57(5).

Contracts entered into by or on behalf of the company before the receiver's appointment continue in force, subject to the terms of the contract, after the appointment: s.57(4)[38]; but the receiver does not, merely by his appointment, incur personal liability on such contracts.

The provisions of s.57 do not limit any right to indemnity which the receiver would have apart from them, nor do they limit his liability on contracts made or adopted without authority: s.57(6).[39]

Contracts entered into by a receiver whose powers are later suspended under s.56, above, continue in force, subject to the terms of the contract, after that suspension; s.57(7).[40]

A receiver has been held to be a joint occupier with the company of the company's premises for the purposes of the Explosives Act 1875, s.23, which requires the occupier of every factory to take precautions against accidents by fire or explosion.[41]

Remuneration of receiver

The remuneration to be paid to a receiver is fixed by agreement between the receiver and the holder of the floating charge, but where there has been no such agreement or the remuneration fixed is disputed by the receiver, the holder of any floating charge or fixed security, the company or the liquidator, it may be fixed instead by the Auditor of the Court of Session: s.58(1)(2).

Preferential payments and distribution of moneys

The Act provides that where a company is not at the time of the receiver's appointment in course of being wound up the debts which would be preferential

---

[38] See *Myles J. Callaghan Ltd v City of Glasgow District Council*, 1988 S.L.T. 227 (O.H.).

[39] In *Hill Samuel & Co. Ltd v Laing*, 1988 S.L.T. 452 (affirmed 1989 S.L.T. 760), a receiver who had recommenced business was held not to be exempted from personal liability by a clause in the debenture, that being a contract between the chargeholder and the company to which the receiver was not a party.

[40] See *Macleod v Alexander Sutherland Ltd*, 1977 S.L.T. (Notes) 44 (O.H.) (decree of implement refused). For judicial comment on the receiver's position in general and on the distinction between receivership and liquidation, see *Lord Advocate v Royal Bank of Scotland Ltd*, 1977 S.C. 155, and *Taylor, Petitioner*, 1982 S.L.T. 172 (O.H.).

[41] *Lord Advocate v Aero Technologies Ltd (in receivership)*, 1991 S.L.T. 134 (O.H.).

payments in winding up[42] must be paid out of any assets coming into the receiver's hands in priority to claims of the holder of the floating charge: s.59(1). This applies only to debts which have been intimated to the receiver or have become known to him within six months after he has advertised for claims in the *Edinburgh Gazette*[42a] and in a local newspaper: s.59(2). Payments made in accordance with these provisions must be recouped as far as may be out of the assets available for ordinary creditors: s.59(3).

The moneys received by the receiver are distributed in the following order:

(a) to the holder of any fixed security which ranks prior to or equally with the floating charge, persons who have effectually executed diligence on any part of the property, creditors to whom the receiver has incurred liability, the receiver himself in respect of his liabilities, expenses and remuneration, and preferential creditors entitled to payment under s.59, above (s.60(1));

(b) to the holder of the floating charge in or towards satisfaction of the debt secured by the floating charge (s.60(1)); and

(c) to any other receiver, to the holder of a fixed security over the property, and to the company or its liquidator, according to their respective rights and interests (s.60(3)).

Where there is doubt as to the persons entitled to a payment, or where a receipt or discharge of a security cannot be obtained for a payment, the receiver must consign the amount in a bank of issue in Scotland in name of the Accountant of Court for behoof of the person entitled to it: s.60(3).

Cessation of appointment

A receiver may, on application to the court by the holder of the floating charge, be removed from office by the court on cause shown. He may resign his office on giving the prescribed notice: s.62(1). In addition he must vacate office if he ceases to be a qualified insolvency practitioner: s.62(2).

Where at any time a receiver vacates office, his remuneration, any expenses properly incurred by him and any indemnity to which he is entitled out of the company's property must be paid out of the property which is subject to the floating charge and has the priority provided for in s.60, above: s.62(4).

Except where the cessation of a receiver's appointment is due to his death or removal by the court, he must give notice of the cessation to the Registrar within 14 days.Where the receiver has been removed by the court, the duty to give such notice lies on the holder of the floating charge. The Registrar enters the notice in the register of charges.Default in complying with the requirement as to notice makes the receiver or the holder of the charge as the case may be liable to a fine: s.62(5).

---

[42] See n.7, above.
[42a] See *www.gazettes-online.co.uk*.

If, on the expiry of one month after cessation of a receiver's appointment, no other receiver has been appointed, the charge then ceases to attach to the property and becomes again a floating charge: s.62(6).

Powers of court

Under the Act the court may exercise certain powers in relation to receiverships, whether the receiver has been appointed by the holder of the floating charge or by the court:

(a) The court may give directions in connection with the performance by the receiver of his functions.The application to the court may be made either by the receiver or by the holder of the floating charge: s.63(1).[43]

(b) The court may, on the application of the holder of the floating charge, remove the receiver on cause shown: s.62(1), above.

(c) Where the property which is subject to the floating charge is also subject to another security or burden or is affected by diligence, and the receiver wishes to sell or dispose of the property but is unable to obtain the necessary consent of the other parties, the court may, on the application of the receiver, authorise the sale or disposal of the property free of the security or burden or diligence: s.61(1).

However, where there is a fixed security over the property ranking prior to the floating charge, the court must not authorise the sale or disposal unless it is satisfied that this would be likely to provide a more advantageous realisation of the company's assets than would otherwise be effected: s.61(3). In such a case the court must impose the condition that the net proceeds of the disposal be applied to discharge the sums secured by the fixed security, together with, if the court regards such proceeds as less than the open market value of the property, such additional sums as are necessary to make good the deficiency: s.61(4).

Within 14 days of the granting of the authorisation the receiver must send a certified copy of the authorisation to the Registrar, and if without reasonable excuse he fails to comply with that provision he is liable to a default fine: s.61(7).

Where a sale or disposal has taken place under such court authorisation, the receiver must grant to the purchaser or disponee an appropriate document of transfer or conveyance, which, when recorded, intimated or registered as the case may be, has the effect of disencumbering the property of the security affecting it, and freeing the property from the diligence executed upon it: s.61(8).[44]

---

[43] *Jamieson and Others, Petitioners*, 1997 S.C. 195: A number of receivers petitioned for direction to facilitate the administration of claims arising as a result of the English House of Lords case *Powdrill v Watson* [1995] 2 A.C. 394; petition dismissed as incompetent because it sought to impose requirements (a questionnaires to be completed by claimants) on persons other than the receivers and was therefore outwith s.63(1).

[44] An example of a sale authorised by the court where inhibiting creditors had refused consent occurred, under the 1972 Act, in *Armour and Mycroft, Petitioners*, 1983 S.L.T. 43 (O.H.).

These provisions do not prejudice the right of any creditor of the company to rank for his debt in the winding up of the company: s.61(9).

(d) Where the appointment of a person as a receiver by the holder of a floating charge is discovered to be invalid (whether because of the invalidity of the instrument or otherwise), the court may order the holder to indemnify the person appointed against any liability which arises solely on account of the invalidity of the appointment: s.63(2).

(e) If the receiver makes default in delivering the documents or giving the notices which are required of him, below, the court may order him to make good the default within a specified time: s.69(1)(a). Application to the court for this purpose may be made by any member or creditor of the company or by the Registrar: s.69(2). Similarly, if the receiver fails, on the liquidator's request, to render proper accounts of receipts and payments and to pay over the proper amount to the liquidator, the court may, on the liquidator's application, order the receiver to make good the default within a specified time: s.69(1)(b).

Requirements as to notification and information

When a receiver is appointed:

(a) Every invoice, order for goods or business letter which is issued by or on behalf of the company or the receiver or the liquidator and on which the company's name appears must contain a statement that a receiver has been appointed: s.64(1).

(b) The receiver must forthwith send to the company and publish notice of his appointment: s.65(1).

(c) The receiver must forthwith require a statement of the company's affairs to be submitted to him by some or all of the officers of the company (past or present), its promoters (if they acted within the year prior to his appointment), its employees (if they are in his opinion capable of giving the information required and are either present employees or have been employed within the preceding year) and the officers of any company which is (or has been within the previous year) an officer of or in the employment of the company concerned: s.66(1)(3). Such a statement must be submitted within 21 days of its being asked for, with a fine in default: s.66(4). The receiver may excuse any person from this obligation or extend the time limit, and if the receiver has refused to exercise such powers, the court may do so: s.66(5).

A statement submitted under these provisions must be verified by affidavit and show particulars of the company's assets, debts and liabilities, the names and addresses of its creditors, the securities held by them and the date when they were given and such further information as may be prescribed: s.66(2).

(d) Within three months of his appointment, unless the court allows an extension, a receiver must send to the Registrar, the holder of the floating charge by virtue of which he was appointed and to any trustees for secured creditors of the company and (so far as he is aware of their addresses) to all secured creditors a report as to the events leading up to his appointment, his disposal of any property of the company and the carrying on by him of any business of the company, the amounts of principal and interest payable to the holder of the floating charge by virtue of which he was appointed and the amounts payable to preferential creditors, and the amount, if any, likely to be available for the payment of other creditors: s.67(1). The report also includes a summary of the statement of affairs submitted to the receiver under s.66 and of his comments, if any, on it: s.67(5).

The receiver must also, within three months (or longer if the court allows) after his appointment either send a copy of the report to all unsecured creditors of whose addresses he is aware, or publish a notice stating an address to which unsecured creditors should write for copies of the report to be sent to them free of charge. In either case he must summon a meeting of the unsecured creditors on not less than 14 days' notice and must lay a copy of the report before that meeting: s.67(2). The court may dispense with such a meeting if the report states that the receiver intends to apply for such an order and the other requirements as to publicity are complied with at least 14 days before the application: s.67(3).

If the company has gone or goes into liquidation, the receiver must send a copy of the report to the liquidator, at latest within seven days after the liquidator's appointment: s.67(4).

(e) The meeting of creditors summoned under s.67 may establish a committee ("the creditors' committee"), and that committee may, on giving at least seven days' notice, require the receiver to attend before it and furnish it with such information as to the carrying out by him of his functions as it may reasonably require: s.68.

Penalties are imposed for failure to comply with the requirements of ss 64 to 67: ss 64(2), 65(4), 66(6), and 67(8).

Chapter 26

THE ADMINISTRATION PROCEDURE

The Insolvency Act 1985 introduced an entirely new concept into UK company law—the administration order.[1] It was intended to provide an alternative to liquidation for companies where no administrative receiver could be appointed because no suitably secured creditor existed to make such an appointment. It was hoped that the administration regime would prove to be an effective form of "company rescue". However, the use of administration orders in the years following the introduction of the procedure was disappointingly low and so, after a series of Consultations and Reports,[2] the Enterprise Act 2002 made a number of significant changes to the law, all intended to promote the use of administration and, as a result, to increase the incidence of rescue amongst financially troubled companies. These apply to Scotland as well as England and Wales.

One method of achieving this aim was to restrict the power of a floating charge holder to appoint an administrative receiver,[3] but it was also hoped to persuade such creditors that the administration procedure would serve their interests equally well. Therefore, Pt 10 of the Enterprise Act 2002 contained provisions designed to "streamline" that procedure. Section 248 of the Enterprise Act substitutes a "new" Sch.B1 to the Insolvency Act 1986 for the "old" Pt II of that Act. This chapter will focus on the "new" administration regime, although it should be noted that for administration orders pre-dating September 15, 2003,[4] the "old" Pt II will continue to apply. The reader is referred to the 16th Edition of this work for a full exposition of the old law.

Whilst Sch.B1 makes some significant changes to the administration procedure, an equally significant number of its provisions mirror those contained in Pt II of the Insolvency Act. Therefore, authorities decided in relation to Pt II will remain of relevance to similarly (or identically) worded provisions of Sch.B1 and will be referred to as appropriate in this chapter. References to paragraphs in the following are to the paragraphs of Sch.B1 unless the contrary is indicated.

The emphasis of the administration regime.

"The recognition of administration as an important tool in providing a company in financial difficulties with a breathing space in which to put together a rescue plan or,

---

[1] See the *Cork Report*, Ch.9.

[2] See *A Review of Company Rescue and Business Reconstruction Mechanisms, The Insolvency Service* (1999); *A Review of Company Rescue and Business Reconstruction Mechanisms: Report by the Review Group, The Insolvency Service* (2000); *Productivity and Enterprise: Insolvency—A Second Chance, The Insolvency Service*, Cm 5234 (2001).

[3] Enterprise Act 2002 s.250, inserting s.72A Insolvency Act 1986. See Ch.25, p.548.

[4] The date on which Pt 10 Enterprise Act 2002 was brought into force: SI 2003/2093.

alternatively, in providing a better return to creditors than would be likely in a liquidation, has increased steadily in recent years. Nonetheless, if administration is to become a fully efficient procedure in all circumstances, it will need to be streamlined."[5]

In order to promote administration as a rescue-orientated regime Sch.B1 provides for a hierarchy of objectives in any administration. The pivotal provision is para.3:

"3(1) The administrator of a company must perform his functions with the objective of—

(a) rescuing the company as a going concern, or
(b) achieving a better result for the company's creditors as a whole than would be likely if the company were wound up (without first being in administration), or,
(c) realising property in order to make a distribution to one or more secured or preferential creditors."

The objective of rescuing the company as a going concern must be pursued unless the administrator thinks that it is not reasonably practicable to achieve that objective *or* that the company's creditors as a whole would be better served by the pursuit of the objective in para.3(1)(b): para.3(3). The administrator may only realise property in order to make a distribution to secured or preferential creditors if he thinks that it is not reasonably practicable to achieve either of the other objectives and, in any event, he must not unnecessarily harm the interests of the company's creditors as a whole: para.3(4). Subject to this, an administrator must perform his functions in the interests of the company's creditors as a whole,[6] and as quickly and efficiently as is reasonably practicable: para.4. Moreover, where the administrator thinks that the objectives of rescuing the company or achieving a better result for the company's creditors as a whole cannot be achieved he must, in his statement of proposals,[7] explain his reasons for so thinking: para.49(2)(b).

Taken together, these provisions are intended to ensure that, where reasonably practicable, some attempt will be made to devise a rescue strategy in relation to the company, *or* that the interests of the company's creditors *as a whole* will be prioritised. The interests of secured creditors, which are seen as the main concern in administrative receivership, are relegated to the lowest rung of this hierarchy.

Entering administration

Prior to the coming into force of Sch.B1 the administration procedure was exclusively available through an application to the court. This involved a petition for an administration order and was seen as unduly cumbersome and expensive. Sch.B1 now provides three ways for a company to enter administration, thus streamlining the entry procedure. In all cases an administrator has to be qualified

---

[5] Productivity and Enterprise (above n.2), para.2.7.
[6] Para.3(2).
[7] Below.

to act as an insolvency practitioner in relation to a company and so has to satisfy the requirements of s.390 of the Insolvency Act: para.6.[8] An administrator, whether appointed by the court or not, is an officer of the court: para.5.

There are certain general restrictions on the appointment (whether or not by the court) of an administrator. Most obviously, no appointment may be made where a company is already in administration: para.7.[9] An administrator may not be appointed of the company is in liquidation,[10] *unless* an administration application[11] is made by a qualifying floating charge holder[12] (in the case of a court-ordered winding-up) *or* the company's liquidator[13] (in the case of both a voluntary and court-ordered winding-up), and the court sees fit to make an administration order. In either case the court shall then discharge the winding-up.

Appointment by the court following administration application

Paragraphs 10–13 relate to the appointment of an administrator by the court. It is a pre-condition to any court order appointing an administrator that the court is satisfied that the company is or is likely to become unable to pay its debts and that the administration order is reasonably likely to achieve the purpose of the administration: para.11. As to the first requirement, the statutory wording is identical to that of its predecessor,[14] in relation to which it has been held that the court must be satisfied that it is more probable than not that the company will become unable to pay its debts: *Re Colt Telecom Group plc* [2002] EWHC 2815.[15] As to the second, it would appear that the particular purpose out of the para.3 hierarchy must be specified in the application.

In a case described as "unusual" an administration order was granted in respect of a company that had not traded for some time and had no assets except for potential claims against its own directors. The purpose for which the order was sought was to achieve a better result for the creditors than would be likely on a winding up (during which such claims could also be pursued). The applicant had offered to provide funding towards the claim. *Held*, the administration order would be granted. Whilst liquidation was an alternative to administration, the provision of funding, which might not be available in liquidation, suggested that the specified purpose was reasonably likely to be achieved: *Re Logitext UK Ltd* [2004] EWHC 2899.[16]

An administration order is acquired by an application to the court (an "administration application": para.12(1)). Such an application may be made by the company, its directors or any one or more of its creditors.[17] The applicant is

---

[8] As to s.390 see p.533.
[9] Subject to certain qualifications: see below.
[10] Para.8.
[11] Below.
[12] Para. 37. See below as to the definition of a qualifying floating charge holder.
[13] Para.38.
[14] Insolvency Act 1986 s.8(1).
[15] And see *Re AMCD (Property Holdings) Ltd* [2004] All E.R. (D) 125.
[16] See also *Re Redman Construction Ltd* [2004] All E.R. D 146, *Re MCA Coffee Shops Ltd* [2004] All E.R. (D) 320.
[17] Para.12(1). An application may also be made by the justices' chief executive for a magistrates' court under s.87A Magistrates' Courts Act 1980, or by the supervisor of a company voluntary arrangement (para.12(5)).

under a duty to notify any person who has appointed or is entitled to appoint an administrative receiver or an administrator: para.12(2). An application made by directors may be made by a majority of the company's directors: para.105. A creditor, for these purposes, includes a contingent or prospective creditor: para.12(4).[18] The court's powers on hearing an administration application are listed in para.13, which is subject to para.39, whereby the court must dismiss the application if an administrative receiver is in office and the receiver's appointor does not consent to the making of the administration order unless the court "thinks" the security under which the receiver was appointed may be vulnerable.[19] Paragraph 39 applies whether the administrative receiver is appointed before or after the making of the administration application, so that the notification requirement in para.12(2) allows a person entitled to appoint an administrative receiver to "pre-empt" the administration applicant by making such an appointment.

Appointment by qualifying floating charge holder

A qualifying floating charge holder may appoint an administrator of the company: para.14(1). Prior to the Enterprise Act 2002, such a charge holder would be entitled to appoint an administrative receiver. Where the charge was granted on or after September 15, 2003, such an appointment is now prohibited by s.72A of the Insolvency Act,[20] and it is clearly envisaged that the appointment of an administrator will serve as a substitute method of enforcing the security.[21] However, such an appointment may also be made in order to achieve either of the other two statutory purposes in para.3(1), and as an alternative to the appointment of an administrative receiver in the case of a charge granted prior to September 15, 2003.

A qualifying floating charge is defined in para.14(2) as one which states that para.14 applies to a floating charge, or purports to empower its holder to appoint an administrator or a receiver who would be an administrative receiver within the meaning of s.29(2) Insolvency Act 1986. These are alternatives. A qualifying floating charge holder is defined in para.14(3). No appointment may be made under para.14 unless two business days' written notice has been given to the holder of a prior floating charge or that holder consents to the making of an appointment: para.15.[22] No appointment may be made if the floating charge is not enforceable (if, for example, no default has been made by the company or the charge has not been registered in accordance with s.395 Companies Act 1985[23]) or if a provisional liquidator or administrative receiver has been appointed: paras 16, 17.

By para.18, the appointor of an administrator under para.14 must file a notice of appointment with the court which must include a statutory declaration that he

---

[18] And see *Thunderbird Industries LLC v Simico Digital UK Ltd* [2004] EWHC 209.
[19] i.e., open to challenge under ss 238. 239 or 245, as to which see pp.640–647.
[20] See above p.548
[21] The enforcement of security is included in the hierarchy of objectives in administration: para.3(1)(c), above.
[22] Priority is determined, for these purposes, by the test in para.15(2), (3).
[23] See above, pp.524–525.

holds an enforceable qualifying floating charge in relation to the company's property. The notice must identify the administrator and be accompanied by his statement that he consents to the appointment and that in his opinion the purpose of administration is reasonably likely to be achieved. It is only when the requirements of this paragraph have been complied with that the appointment takes effect: para.19.

The appointment of administrators who were proposing to accept the surrender of leases granted by the company was challenged on the grounds of invalidity. The chargee made the appointment on November 20, at which time the company had not defaulted on its obligations under the charge. Notice of the appointment was filed on November 24, by which time default had taken place and the charge had become enforceable. *Held*, the appointment was valid. According to para.19, it could not take effect until the requirements of para.18 had been satisfied and this had not occurred until November 24. Therefore the appointment had been made at a time when the charge was enforceable: *Fliptex v Hogg* [2004] EWHC 1280.

When the para.18 requirements have been satisfied, the appointor must notify the administrator as soon as reasonably practicable: para.20. If the appointment subsequently turns out to be invalid, the court may order the appointor to indemnify the appointee against any liability arising by reason of the invalidity: para.21. It is worth noting that where a qualifying floating charge holder makes an administration appointment there is no requirement that the company is or is likely to become unable to pay its debts. This may well allow a rescue attempt through administration to be commenced at a time when a company is experiencing financial difficulties but has not yet reached the point of insolvency (perhaps at the request of the company's directors). Such an attempt very likely stands a better chance of success.

Appointment by company/directors

Paragraph 22 empowers the company or its directors[24] to appoint an administrator, but not if such an appointment has been made before and less than 12 months have elapsed since the earlier appointment ceased to have effect: para.23. Nor may a para.22 appointment be made where a petition for winding up or an administration application under para.12 has been presented and remains undisposed of, or an administrative receiver is in office: para.25. Where it is proposed to appoint under para.22 the prospective appointor must give five business days' written notice to any person entitled to appoint an administrative receiver or an administrator under para.14, that notice specifying the proposed administrator: para.26. This will allow such a person to appoint an administrative receiver or the administrator of his choice if he wishes. Such a notice must be filed with the court and be accompanied by a statement that the company is or is unlikely to become unable to pay its debts: para.27.[25] Once the notice of intention to appoint has been filed the company or its directors have 10 days within which to make the appointment: para.28.

---

[24] Or a majority of them: para.105.
[25] *c.f.* on an appointment under para.14, where no such requirement is imposed.

Notice of a para.22 appointment must be filed with the court and accompanied by a statutory declaration that the person making the appointment is entitled to make it. The notice must identify the administrator and be accompanied by his statement that he consents to the appointment and that, in his opinion, the purpose of administration is reasonably likely to be achieved: para.29. The appointment takes effect when the requirements of para.29 are complied with and the appointor must notify the administrator as soon as reasonably practicable thereafter: paras 31, 32. If an appointment by a qualifying floating charge holder is made under para.14 *prior* to the para.29 requirements being satisfied the para.22 appointment shall not take effect: para.33. If the para.22 appointment turns out to be invalid the court may order the appointor to indemnify the administrator against any liability arising by reason of the appointment's invalidity: para.34.

The effect of an administration order or appointment

If an administration order or appointment under any of the preceding provisions is made certain consequences follow, all of which are intended to allow the administrator to assume control of the company's property and affairs and to provide him with a certain "breathing space" within which to attempt to achieve the objective of the administration. Paragraphs 40–43 are in similar or identical terms to provisions of Pt II Insolvency Act 1986, and therefore case law relating to the latter is likely to be highly persuasive as regards interpretation of the former. The consequences are as follows:

(1) any winding-up petition is dismissed, except for a petition under s.124A Insolvency Act 1986 (public interest) or s.367 Financial Services and Markets Act 2000: para.40.

(2) Any administrative receiver shall vacate office: para.41.[26]

(3) No resolution may be passed or order made for the company's winding up, except under s.124A Insolvency Act 1986 (public interest) or s.367 Financial Services and Markets Act 2000: para.42.

(4) No steps may be taken to enforce security over the company's property, to repossess goods in the company's possession under a hire purchase-agreement,[27] or to forfeit a lease be peaceable re-entry[28] except with the consent of the administrator or permission of the court: para.43. In *Bristol Airport v Powdrill*[29] it was held that the right of an airport under s.88 of the Civil Aviation Act 1982 to detain an aircraft for non-

---

[26] The receiver's remuneration (including his expenses and any indemnity to which he is entitled) become payable out of the company's property under his control immediately prior to vacation of office: para.41(3), (4).

[27] Which includes a conditional sale agreement, a chattel leasing agreement or a retention of title agreement: para.111.

[28] Overturning case law under the old administration regime which held that forfeiture by peaceable re-entry did not amount to an enforcement of security and therefore did not require the administrator's consent or the court's permission.

[29] [1990] 2.All E.R. 493.

payment of airport charges is a security (the enforcement of which therefore requires consent or permission) within s.11 Insolvency Act 1986, and there would appear to be no change of substance in the wording of the provisions in Sch.B1. A contractual lien arising *after* the commencement of an administration is also a security requiring consent or permission to enforce: *London Flight Centre (Stansted) Ltd v Osprey Aviation* [2002] B.P.I.R. 1115.[30] Goods subject to a hire-purchase or leasing agreement are in the possession of the company even if it has sublet them[31] or the agreement has been terminated prior to the commencement of the administration.[32] The substantive rights of a security holder are not affected by this provision but rather rendered subject to a moratorium on enforcement.[33] On an application for leave to enforce the court has a wide discretion. The principles upon which the court will determine the issue were extensively considered by the Court of Appeal in *Re Atlantic Computer Systems plc*,[34] and are likely to remain relevant to applications under Sch.B1. The Court of Appeal considered that it is for the person seeking leave to make out a case, and that the court should have regard to the purpose of the moratorium, which is to enable the company, through its administrator, to achieve the objective of the administration, and to balance that purpose against the legitimate interests of the security holder in enforcing his security. In general, great importance is usually attached to the proprietary rights of the security holder, which should not be prejudiced purely in the interests of unsecured creditors. The court will, however, seek to achieve proportionality: if a substantially greater loss would be caused to others by a grant of leave than would be suffered by the security holder by a refusal to grant leave, the latter course may be appropriate.[35] Leave may be granted, or refused, subject to conditions.[36] Where an administrator wrongfully refuses consent, as where he seeks to use the goods as a bargaining chip against the owner, he may be liable in conversion and, additionally, the court may require him to pay rental and compensation to the owner.[37]

(5) No legal process (including legal proceedings, execution, distress or diligence) may be instituted or continued against the company or its property without the administrator's consent or the leave of the court: para.43(6). The meaning of "legal process" has been considered in a number of contexts in relation to this provision's predecessor (s.11(3)(d) Insolvency Act 1986). In *Re Olympia & York Canary Wharf Ltd*[38] Millett J. considered that the phrase suggested a process which

---

[30] So too is a solicitor's lien: *Re Carter Commercial Developments Ltd* [2002] B.C.C. 803.
[31] *Re Atlantic Computer Systems plc* [1992] 1 All E.R. 476 CA.
[32] *Re David Meek Access Ltd* [1993] B.C.C. 175.
[33] *Barclays Mercantile Business Finance Ltd v Sibec Developments Ltd* [1992] 1 W.L.R. 1253.
[34] [1992] Ch. 505.
[35] *ibid.* pp.542–544.
[36] *ibid.*
[37] *Barclays Mercantile Business Finance Ltd v Sibec Developments Ltd* [1992] 1 W.L.R. 1253
[38] [1993] B.C.C. 154.

required the assistance of the court, and so did not include the serving of a contractual notice making time of the essence or the acceptance of a repudiatory breach of contract which would terminate the contract itself. The bringing of criminal proceedings against the company has been held to require leave,[39] as does a claim for unfair dismissal,[40] and the reference of a contractual dispute to a statutory adjudication procedure.[41] An application to court seeking an extension of time for the registration of a floating charge is not a proceeding against the company or its property and therefore does not require leave: *Re Barrow Borough Transport Ltd* [1989] B.C.C. 646.

(6) No appointment of an administrative receiver may be made: para.43(6A).

(7) All business documents[42] issued by or on behalf of the company must state the name of the administrator and that the company's affairs, business and property are being managed by him: para.45

(8) Suppliers of utilities cannot make it a precondition of further supplies that pre-administration debts be paid: s.233 Insolvency Act 1986.[43]

A similar, interim moratorium exists where an administration application has been made and not yet granted, or granted but has yet to take effect: para.44.

Powers of an administrator

General powers

In general, an administrator will manage the company's business and property with a view to achieving one of the para.3 purposes of administration. He is given extensive powers in this regard. First, he may do anything necessary or expedient for the management of the affairs, business and property of the company, and any person dealing with the administrator in good faith and for value need not enquire whether he is acting within his powers: para.59. He may summon a meeting of shareholders[44] or of creditors,[45] and may apply to the court for directions.[46] An administrator may remove or appoint a director of the company[47] and the company, or any of its officers, may not exercise management powers (meaning any power the exercise of which could interfere with the exercise of the administrator's powers) without the administrator's consent: para.64.

The administrator is also given the specific powers in Sch.1 of the Insolvency Act 1986: para.60.[48] These are as follows:

---

[39] *Re Rhondda Waste Disposal Ltd* [2001] Ch. 57.
[40] *Carr v British Intl Helicopters Ltd* [1993] B.C.C. 855, although leave should rarely be refused, given the emphasis of employment protection legislation.
[41] *Straume (UK) Ltd v Bradlor Developments Ltd* [2000] B.C.C. 333.
[42] Meaning invoices, orders for goods or services or business letters: para.45(3).
[43] See below, p.604.
[44] Insolvency Rules, r.2.49.
[45] Para.62.
[46] Para.63.
[47] Para.61.
[48] As is an administrative receiver.

(1) Power to take possession of, collect and get in the property of the company and, for that purpose, to take such proceedings as may seem to him expedient.

(2) Power to sell or otherwise dispose of the property of the company by public auction or private contract or, in Scotland, to sell, feu, hire out or otherwise dispose of the property of the company by public roup or private bargain.

(3) Power to raise or borrow money and grant security therefore over the property of the company.

(4) Power to appoint a solicitor or accountant or other professionally qualified person to assist him in the performance of his functions.

(5) Power to bring or defend any action or other legal proceedings in the name and on behalf of the company.

(6) Power to refer to arbitration any question affecting the company.

(7) Power to effect and maintain insurances in respect of the business and property of the company.

(8) Power to use the company's seal.

(9) Power to do all acts and to execute in the name and on behalf of the company any deed, receipt or other document.

(10) Power to draw, accept, make and endorse any bill of exchange or promissory note in the name and on behalf of the company.

(11) Power to appoint any agent to do any business that he is unable to do himself or which can more conveniently be done by an agent and power to employ and dismiss employees.[49]

(12) Power to do all such things (including the carrying out of works) as may be necessary for the realisation of the property of the company.

(13) Power to make any payment that is necessary or incidental to the performance of his functions.

This power has been held to apply to the payment of a distribution to creditors who might otherwise insist on a liquidation[50] and to the payment of pre-administration debts where it is necessary to the survival of the company as a going concern.[51] However, a distribution to preferential creditors was not included in the purpose of the administration order and so was not "necessary or incidental" to the performance of the administrator's functions.[52] The position as to the payment of pre-administration debts and the making of distributions is now expressly covered in Sch.B1.[53]

---

[49] Compliance with the consultation requirements of s.188 Trade Union and Labour Relations (Consolidation) Act 1992 is required: *Re Hartlebury Printers Ltd* [1993] 1 All E.R. 470.
[50] *Re W.B.S.L Realisations 1992 Ltd* [1995] B.C.C. 1118.
[51] *Re John Slack Ltd* [1995] B.C.C. 1116.
[52] *Re The Designer Room Ltd* [2004] EWHC 720.
[53] Below p.580.

(14) Power to carry on the business of the company.

(15) Power to establish subsidiaries of the company.

(16) Power to transfer to subsidiaries of the company the whole or any part of the business and property of the company.

(17) Power to grant or accept a surrender of a lease or tenancy of any of the property of the company, and to take a lease or tenancy of any property required or convenient for the business of the company.

(18) Power to make any arrangement or compromise on behalf of the company.

(19) Power to call up any uncalled capital of the company.

(20) Power to rank and claim in the bankruptcy, insolvency, sequestration or liquidation of any person indebted to the company and to receive dividends, and to accede to trust deeds for the creditors of any such person.

(21) Power to present of defend a petition for the winding up of the company.

(22) Power to change the situation of the company's registered office.

(23) Power to do all other things incidental to the exercise of the foregoing powers.

Sch.B1 explicitly adds the power to make distributions to creditors of the company: para.65. Preferential debts of the company are given priority to the claims of floating charge holders in much the same way as in liquidation and administrative receivership by para.65(2), but no distribution may be made to ordinary unsecured creditors unless the court gives permission: para.65(3). However, a payment may be made otherwise than in accordance with para.65 if the administrator thinks it likely to assist achievement of the purpose of the administration: para.66.

Any exercise of powers by the administrator is as agent of the company: para.69.

Powers to deal with charged property

In order that the achievement of the purpose of administration (especially where that purpose is to rescue the company or achieve a better result for its creditors than on liquidation) is facilitated, administrators are given powers to deal with charged property as though it were not subject to the charge. In the case of property subject to a floating charge, the administrator may dispose of it or take action in relation to it without leave of the court. The charge-holder retains his priority in respect of any acquired property which directly or indirectly represents the property disposed of: para.70.

In relation to property which is subject to a security other than a floating charge, the court may make an order enabling the administrator to dispose of such property. Such an order is subject to the condition that the court thinks that such disposal would be likely to promote the purpose of the administration and that the net proceeds of disposal (and any additional sum required to produce the amount which would be realised on a sale of the property at market value) be applied towards discharging the sums secured by the security: para.71. A similar provision applies in relate to the disposal of goods in the company's possession under a hire-purchase agreement: para.72.[54]

Duties of an administrator

General duties

As an officer of the court,[55] an administrator is under a duty to act "honourably" in accordance with the rule in *Ex p. James*[56]. Thus, where he is found liable to pay over an amount as an expense of the administration, and he has that amount invested pending the outcome of the dispute, he is liable to pay the amount together with the interest it has earned: *Powdrill v Watson, Re Paramount Airways Ltd (No. 3)* [1994] B.C.C. 172, 182, CA. An administrator need not, however, advise a creditor on what steps he should take to enforce his security.[57]

On appointment the administrator must take custody or control or all property to which he thinks the company is entitled: para.67. He owes a duty to take reasonable care to obtain a proper price for the company's property and in choosing the time to sell,[58] although it appears that he owes no general duty of care to the company's unsecured creditors absent an assumption of responsibility towards them.[59] This proposition must now be read subject to the provisions of Sch.B1, which impose upon the administrator a duty to perform his functions as quickly and efficiently as is reasonably practicable,[60] and in the interests of the creditors as a whole.[61]

An administrator will also be under a duty to meet preferential claims, to be calculated according to the date at which the company enters administration: para.65(2), s.387 Insolvency Act 1986. Furthermore, he is subject to the s.176A Insolvency Act 1986 duty to set aside a "prescribed part" of the company's net property for distribution to unsecured creditors.[62] Moreover, as soon as is reasonably practicable after appointment, the administrator should require one or more "relevant persons"[63] to provide him with a statement of affairs of the

---

[54] Which would include goods subject to a chattel lease, a conditional sale agree or a retention of title clause: para.111.

[55] Para.5.

[56] (1874) 9 Ch. App 609. See Dawson, *The Administrator, Morality and the Court* [1996] J.B.L 437.

[57] *Re Sabre International Products* [1991] B.C.L.C. 470.

[58] *Re Charnley Davies (No. 2) Ltd* [1990] B.C.L.C. 760

[59] *Kyrris v Oldham* [2003] EWCA Civ. 1506.

[60] Para.4

[61] Para.3(2), subject to para.3(4) (administrator realising property in order to make a distribution to secured or preferential creditors). In this event the administrator must not unnecessarily harm the interests of the company's general creditors: para.3(4)(b). As to creditors' actions against the administrator, see below.

[62] This duty applies *mutatis mutandi* to administrative receivers and liquidators. For details of the workings of s.176A see above, p.553.

[63] Defined in para.47(3).

company: para.47. The statement must show, *inter alia*, the company's assets and liabilities, the names and addresses of its creditors, details of security held by those making it and any other prescribed information: para.47(2). It must be provided within 11 days of the administrator's request and there are fines on default: para.48.

The administrator and creditors

Notwithstanding the breadth of an administrator's powers, he does not have *carte blanche* to do as he sees fit. One of the central planks of administration is that it is inclusive in nature, so that the company's creditors have a real stake in its outcome. In order to achieve this the administrator is required to formulate proposals for achieving the purpose of the administration, a copy of which must be sent to the registrar of companies, every creditor of whom the administrator is aware and every member[64] of the company as soon as reasonably practicable after his appointment, and in any event within eight weeks of it: para.49.[65]

The statement of proposals must be accompanied by an invitation to an "initial" creditors' meeting, which must be scheduled as soon as reasonably practicable after the company enters administration and, in any event, within 10 weeks of that time: para.51.[66] Notice of this meeting should normally be advertised in accordance with the Insolvency Rules 1986[67] and be sent to past or present directors of the company whose presence the administrator thinks is required.[68] The initial creditors meeting need not be called where the administrator thinks that the company has sufficient property to enable each creditor to be paid in full, that the company has insufficient property to enable a distribution to be made other than by virtue of s.176A(2),[69] or where he thinks that neither of the objectives in para.3(1)(a) or (b) can be achieved: para.52(1). Such a meeting must be summoned, however, if requested by creditors whose debts amount to at least 10 per cent of the total debts of the company; para.52(2).[70]

The administrator must present a statement of his proposals at the initial creditors' meeting[71] and the meeting may approve them without modification or with any modification to which the administrator consents. The decision of the initial creditors' meeting must be reported to the court and the registrar of companies, and there are penalties for non-compliance: para.53. Should the proposals be approved (with or without modification), and should the administra-

---

[64] The duty to members is complied with if the administrator publishes a notice undertaking to provide a copy of his proposals to any member applying in writing to a specified address: para.49(6).

[65] Notices by email have been held not to be in compliance with the requirements of paras 46 and 49: *Re Sporting Options plc* [2004] All E.R. D 30.

[66] The periods specified in this paragraph may be varied in accordance with para.107.

[67] Rule 2.34(1).

[68] Insolvency Rules, r.2.34(2).

[69] See above, p.553.

[70] It would appear that the administrator appointed under paras 14 or 22 may dispense with the calling of an initial creditors meeting where he thinks that the purpose of the administration has been sufficiently achieved or where he proposes to move straight from administration to dissolution: para.80, Insolvency Rules, r.2.33(4), para.84.

[71] Para.51(3).

tor wish to revise them in a manner which he thinks is substantial, he should summon a further creditors' meeting and send a statement of the proposed revision to each creditor and member of the company.[72] A statement of the proposed revision must be presented to the creditors' meeting which may approve it without modification or with such modification as the administrator consents to: para.54. As with the initial creditors' meeting, its decision must be notified to the court and registrar of companies and there are penalties for non-compliance.[73]

Should the initial creditors' meeting, or a creditors' meeting called to approve revised proposals, fail to approve the original or revised proposals (as the case may be) the administrator must report this to the court, which can then provide that his appointment shall cease to have effect from a specified time, adjourn the hearing, make an interim order, make an order on a petition for winding up suspended under para.49 or make any order it thinks appropriate: para.55. It seems likely that if a meeting has failed to approve *revised* proposals the administrator is free to continue to act in accordance with the approved original proposals. Further creditors' meetings are to be called if requested in the prescribed manner[74] by creditors whose debts amount to not less than 10 per cent of the total debts of the company, or if the court so directs: para.56. The important issue of entitlement to vote at creditors' meetings is governed by the Insolvency Rules 1986.[75] Finally, creditors' meetings may now be conducted by "correspondence"[76], which includes correspondence by telephone or other electronic means.[77]

A creditors' meeting may establish a creditors' committee: para.57(1).[78] The committee may require the administrator to attend on it and provide it with information: para.57.

A question that has arisen in relation to the above provisions is whether an administrator may exercise his powers prior to the approval of any proposals by the creditors meeting. There may be good reasons why an administrator might wish to do so: in particular, if he is seeking to dispose of assets, or even the entire undertaking of the company, in order to achieve a better result for creditors as a whole it may well be the case that speed is of the essence, and that a purchaser is unwilling to wait until the meeting has approved this course of action. It would, of course, be open to an administrator to apply to the court for directions in this respect under para.63, but, again, this may prove costly in terms of time.

Under the "old" Pt II of the Insolvency Act 1986, a note of caution was sounded in *Re Consumer & Industrial Press Ltd (No. 2)*[79] where it was considered that such a course of action would frustrate the statutory purposes of administration. Later authorities suggested that that an administrator need not seek the

---

[72] Members may be notified in the manner described in n.64, above.
[73] Para.54(6), (7).
[74] See Insolvency Rules, r.2.37.
[75] See, in particular, rr 2.38–2.43.
[76] Para.58, and see Insolvency Rules, r.2.48.
[77] Para.111.
[78] For the constitution and procedural aspects of the creditors' committee see Insolvency Rules, rr 2.50–2.65.
[79] (1988) B.C.C. 72.

court's approval to dispose of the company's property or undertaking in advance of the creditors' meeting sanctioning such a course.[80] In *Re T & D Industries plc*,[81] Neuberger J. opined that, in cases of extreme urgency, the administrator should be free to proceed without the sanction of the court or creditors' committee, although he noted that it might be expedient to informally consult the company's major creditors (where there are only a few). An administrator was only required to act in accordance with the court's directions where such had been given.

This approach has been adopted in relate to the "new" administration regime under Sch.B1.

Administrators applied to the court for directions as to whether they required a court order to sell the undertaking of the company prior to obtaining the approval of the creditors' meeting. *Held*, no such order was required. The wording of para.68(2) appeared to mirror the authority of *Re T & D Industries*, reflecting a policy of non-interference by the courts in commercial decisions of administrators: *Re Transbus International* [2004] EWCA 932.

Notwithstanding the above, creditors are given power to challenge the administrator's conduct of the company by application to court. By para.74, any creditor or member may apply to court claiming that the administrator has acted or is acting in such a way as to "unfairly harm the interests of the applicant" (whether alone or in common with some or all other creditors or members).[82] An application may also be made on the grounds that an administrator is proposing to act in such a way.[83] Creditors and members may also make an application based on an allegation that the administrator is not performing his functions as quickly or efficiently as is reasonably practicable: para.74(2). The court, on hearing such an application, may grant relief, dismiss it, adjourn the hearing, make an interim order or make any order it thinks appropriate,[84] and in particular may regulate the administrator's exercise of his functions, require him to do or not to do a specified thing, require creditors' meeting to be held or provide for the administrator's appointment to cease to have effect.[85] No order may be made where it would impede or prevent the implantation of a voluntary arrangement, a scheme of arrangement or proposals (original or revised) approved more than 28 days before the application: para.74(6).

This provision is worded slightly differently to its predecessor, s.27 Insolvency Act 1986, in that it refers to conduct which would "unfairly harm" the interests of the applicant, rather than "unfairly prejudice" those interests. There was, perhaps surprisingly, little authority on s.27, save that holding that it did not apply where the allegation was that the administrator had been negligent.[86] In general, the courts have been reluctant to interfere with commercial decisions taken by administrators and have thus discouraged the use of s.27 to attempt to

---

[80] *Re NS Distribution Ltd* [1990] B.C.L.C. 169 (single asset); *Re Charnley Davies Ltd* [1990] B.C.C. 605 (entire undertaking).

[81] [2000] 1 W.L.R. 646.

[82] Para.74(1)(a).

[83] Para.74(1)(b).

[84] Para. 74(3).

[85] Para.74(4).

[86] *Re Charnley Davies* [1990] B.C.C. 605, *per* Millett J. at p.624.

persuade them to second guess his judgment.[87] Whether the same approach will be followed in relation to para.74 remains to be seen.

Paragraph 75 provides that the court may examine the conduct of an administrator on the grounds of misfeasance. An application may be made under this paragraph by the official receiver, an administrator[88], the liquidator of the company, a creditor of the company or a contributory of the company[89] and must allege that the administrator has misapplied or retained money or other property of the company, has become accountable for such money or property, has breached a fiduciary or other duty owed to the company or has been guilty of misfeasance.[90] On an examination under para.75, the court may order the administrator to repay, restore or account for money or other property of the company, to pay interest, or to contribute a sum of money to the company's property by way of compensation for breach of duty or misfeasance.[91] Where the administrator in question has been discharged under para.98[92] an application may only be made with the permission of the court: para.75(6).

Ending administration

An administration appointment automatically ceases to have effect one year after the date on which it took effect: para.76(1). However, the administrator may apply to court to have his term of office extended for a specified period *or* that term may be extended by consent for a specified period not exceeding six months: para.76(2). In the latter case, consent means the consent of each secured creditor of the company and that of at least 50 per cent of the company's unsecured creditors: para.78(1). A court extension may be made where there has already been an extension by consent, but not after the expiry of the administrator's term of office: para.77. The registrar of companies must be notified of any order made under para.76: para.77(3).

An administrator's term of office may be extended by consent only once, and not after an extension by the court or after expiry: para.78(4). The court and the registrar of companies must be notified of any extension by consent and there are penalties for non-compliance: para.78(5), (6).

An administration appointment may also come to an end where the administrator applies to the court if he thinks the purpose of the administration cannot be achieved, that the company should not have entered administration or where a creditors' meeting requires him to make an application: para.79. Further, where the appointment was made by court order, the administrator must make an application if he thinks the purpose of the administration has been sufficiently achieved: para.79(3). A similar provision applies where the administrator was appointed out-of-court[93] and the administrator thinks the purpose of the

---

[87] See, e.g., *MTI Trading Systems Ltd v Winter* [1998] B.C.C. 591.
[88] Obviously, a subsequent administrator!
[89] Para.75(2).
[90] Para.75(3). This paragraph is now a substitute for s.212 Insolvency Act 1986, from which all references to an administrator have been removed. Case law on s.212 may still be of relevance, however, given the close similarity between the wording of the two provisions.
[91] Para. 75(4).
[92] Below.
[93] *i.e.*, under paras 14 or 22.

administration has been sufficiently achieved: para.80. In this latter case the administrator may file a notice in the prescribed form with the court and the registrar of companies, at which point his appointment ceases to have effect: para.80(2), (3).

The court may end an administration on the application of a creditor of the company under para.81. Such an application must allege an improper motive on the part of the person making an administration application (in the case of a court-ordered administration) or the administrator's appointor (in the case of an appointment under paras 14 or 22): para.81. Where a winding-up order is made in the public interest[94] or under s.367 Financial Services and Markets Act the court may order that the appointment of an administrator shall cease to have effect *or* that it shall continue to have effect: para.82.

It is now possible, under Sch.B1, to move the company from administration to creditors' voluntary liquidation or to dissolution. Where an administrator thinks that the total amount payable to secured creditors has been paid or set aside and that a distribution will be made to unsecured creditors he may send a notice to the registrar of companies stating that para.83 applies: para.83(1), (2) (in Scotland), (3). Such notice should also be sent to the court and creditors: para.83(5). On the registration of the notice the appointment of the administrator ceases to have effect and the company is wound up as though a resolution for voluntary winding up had been passed. The liquidator may be a person nominated by the creditors or, if no nomination is made, the administrator: para.83(6)(7).

If the administrator thinks that there will be no property to distribute to creditors he may send a notice to this effect to the registrar and, on registration of the notice, his appointment ceases to have effect and the company proceeds to dissolution: para.84. It has been held that nothing in either paras 83 or 84 requires the administrator to obtain a court order for a move to a creditors' voluntary liquidation or dissolution. The appointment is brought to an end by the registration of the notice and it is a matter for the administrator whether to send the notice. These provisions are designed to produce administrative efficiency and costs savings: *Re Ballast plc* [2004] EWHC 2356.

An administrator may resign in circumstances prescribed by the Insolvency Rules 1986, r.2.119[95] and only by giving written notice to the person who appointed him (*i.e.*, the court, a qualifying floating charge holder, the company or its directors): para.87. He must vacate office if he ceases to be qualified to act as an insolvency practitioner: para.89. The court is also given power under para.88 to remove an administrator from office. In any of the above cases, and in the case of the death of the administrator, paras 91–95 have effect to fill the vacancy left by the administrator. Depending upon the mode of appointment, the court, a qualifying floating charge holder, the company or its directors may replace the administrator. Where the company or its directors propose to replace the administrator they may only do so with the consent of any qualifying floating charge holder or permission of the court: para.94.

---

[94] Under s.124A Insolvency Act 1986.
[95] Intention to cease practice as an insolvency practitioner, conflict of interest, change in personal circumstances or, on other grounds, with the permission of the court.

Vacation of office: charges and liabilities

Where a person ceases to be administrator of a company his remuneration and expenses shall be charged on and payable property over which he had custody or control immediately before cessation and in priority to any security to which para.70 applies: para.99(3). This provision elevates the administrator's remuneration and expenses above the claims of floating charge holders, in sharp contrast to the position in liquidation as held by the House of Lords in *Buchler v Talbot*.[96] The expenses of the administration are payable in the order listed in the Insolvency Rules 1986 r.2.67, and it is likely that the ruling in *Re Toshoku Finance UK plc*[97] will apply in this regard. The charge referred to in para.99(3) is deferred to any liability arising under a contract of employment adopted by him or his predecessor to the extent that sum sums constitute "qualifying liabilities". An administrator adopts a contract of employment if he causes the company to continue the employment for mare than fourteen days after his appointment: para.99(5). No adoption will take place where no positive action is taken by the administrator.

Administrators were appointed and continued to use the services of employees they believed to be employed by the company's subsidiary. In fact these employees were employed by the company in administration. This fact was discovered 16 days after the administrators' appointment, at which point steps were taken to terminate the employment. *Held*, the administrators had not adopted the contracts of employment. Adoption involved a choice on the part of the administrators to adopt the contracts in question: *Re Antal International Ltd* [2003] B.C.L.C. 406.

Qualifying liabilities are defined in terms similar to those applicable to administrative receivers.[98]

Where a person ceases to be administrator of a company he is discharged from liability in respect of any action of his as administrator: para.98(1). This does not prevent a challenge to the conduct of the administrator on the grounds of misfeasance under para.75: para.98(4).[99]

Adjustment of prior transactions

In administration, certain charges and other transactions may be liable to be set aside under ss 238 to 246 of the Insolvency Act 1986. These sections also apply on a liquidation and are dealt with in Chapter 29 below.

---

[96] [2004] UKHL 9. See below, p.647.
[97] [2002] UKHL 6. See below, p.649.
[98] See above, p.549.
[99] For misfeasance, see above, p.578.

Chapter 27

WINDING UP BY THE COURT

[*N.B. References in this chapter are to sections of the Insolvency Act 1986 unless otherwise specified.*]

THIS chapter and the following three chapters deal with the winding up of a company, which is governed by the Insolvency Act 1986. That Act is a consolidation of parts of the Companies Act 1985 (itself a consolidation) and the Insolvency Act 1985. A winding up may be:

(1) by the court; or

(2) voluntary; (s.73).[1]

and there are two kinds of voluntary winding up, namely:

(a) a members' voluntary winding up; and

(b) a creditors' voluntary winding up (s.90).

It will be recalled that winding up by the court on the "just and equitable ground" was explained in Chapter 18. Chapter 29 (Contributories and Creditors; Completion of the Winding Up) is partly concerned with winding up by the court, as well as the present chapter. Chapter 28 is concerned with voluntary winding up.

Section 652 of the Companies Act 1985, which is explained in Chapter 29,[2] provides a method of dissolving a defunct company by striking it off the register without a winding up, and under s.427 of the Companies Act 1985, below,[3] the court may order dissolution without winding up where there is a compromise or an arrangement to facilitate a reconstruction or an amalgamation.

A company cannot in Scotland be sequestrated.[4]

In addition to the statutory provisions, s.11 of the 1986 Act provides for the making of rules governing the conduct of company liquidation (the Insolvency

---

[1] A third form, winding up subject to supervision of the court, was abolished by the Insolvency Act 1985. In practice that form was not used.

[2] Below, p.653.

[3] p.652.

[4] *Standard Property Investment Co. Ltd v Dunblane Hydropathic Co. Ltd* (1884) 12 R. 328; Bankruptcy (Scotland) Act 1985, s.6(2). A Scottish company could, however, be made notour bankrupt for the purpose of the statutory provisions relating to equalisation of diligences: *Clarke v Hinde, Milne & Co.* (1884) 12 R. 347; see now s.185 of the Insolvency Act 1986, applying s.37(1) to (6) of the Bankruptcy (Scotland) Act 1985.

Rules 1986).[5] The Rules are made by the Lord Chancellor with the concurrence of the Secretary of State. In relation to Scotland, rules can be made by the Secretary of State.[6]

Section 414 governs the fixing of fees.[7]

JURISDICTION TO WIND UP COMPANIES

In England

To obtain a winding up by the court, a petition must be presented to the court having the necessary jurisdiction. Section 117 provides that the courts having jurisdiction are:

(1) the High Court, *i.e.* the Companies Court,[8] in the case of all companies registered in England;

(2) Where the paid-up share capital does not exceed £120,000,[9] the county court of the district in which the registered office is situated, provided that such county court has winding up jurisdiction.[10]

In Scotland

The courts having jurisdiction are:

(1) the Court of Session, in the case of all companies registered in Scotland: s.120(1);

(2) where the paid-up share capital does not exceed £120,000,[11] the sheriff court of the sheriffdom in which the registered office is situated: s.120(3).

GROUNDS FOR WINDING UP BY THE COURT

S.122 provides that a company[12] may be wound up by the court if:

(1) the company has by special resolution resolved to be wound up by the court[13]; or

---

[5] SI 1986/1925.

[6] See SI 1986/1915 (S.139).

[7] Insolvency Fees Order 1986 (SI 1986/2030) as amended by SI 2004/593.

[8] *Eastern Holdings v Singer & Friedlander Ltd* [1967] 1 W.L.R. 1017.

[9] This amount can be varied by order.

[10] See Civil Courts Order 1983 (SI 1983/713) as amended; s.117(4).

[11] See n.9. The sheriff court has no jurisdiction to wind up a company limited by guarantee and not having a share capital: *Pearce, Petitioner*, 1991 S.C.L.R. 861 (Sh. Ct.)

[12] *i.e.* one formed or registered under the Companies Act 1985 or a former Companies Act: C.A. 1985, s.735, I.A. 1986, s.73.

[13] *cf.* s.84, below, p.554, which is more commonly resorted to, under which a company may pass a special resolution to be wound up voluntarily.

(2) in the case of a public company first registered as such, no certificate of entitlement to commence business has been issued and the company has been registered for more than one year[14]; or

(3) the company does not commence business within a year after its incorporation, or suspends business for a whole year[15]; or

(4) the number of members is reduced below two; or

(5) the company is unable to pay its debts; or

(6) the time for a moratorium under s.1A has come to an end without the approval of a voluntary arrangement; or

(7) the court is of opinion that it is just and equitable that the company should be wound up. This part of the section was explained in connection with statutory protection of the minority.[16] It should be added that the power to wind up a company under this part is not confined to cases in which there are grounds analogous to those mentioned earlier in the section[17]; or

(8) in the case of a Scottish company, there is subsisting a floating charge over property comprised in the company's property and undertaking and the court is satisfied that the security of the creditor entitled to the benefit of the floating charge is in jeopardy.[18]

There is another, transitional, ground, namely that the company is an old public company, *i.e.* a pre-1981 public company which does not comply with the criteria for such a company[19] and did not re-register as a private company in 1981.[20]

Ground (3): Company not carrying on business

The period of a year is fixed by s.122, above, so as to give the company a reasonable time in which to commence or resume business, as the case may be.

A winding-up order will only be made on this ground if the company has no intention of carrying on business.[21]

A company was formed to build and use assembly rooms. Owing to a depression in trade in the neighbourhood, building was suspended for more than three years although the company intended to continue its operations when trade prospects improved. A shareholder presented a winding-up petition which was opposed by four-fifths of the share-

---

[14] Above, p.138.
[15] *cf.* C. A. 1985, s.652, below, p.586, under which a defunct company may be struck off the register and so dissolved without being wound up.
[16] Above, p.353.
[17] *Loch v John Blackwood Ltd* [1924] A.C. 783, PC; *Symington v Symingtons' Quarries Ltd* (1905) 8 F. 121; *Baird v Lees*, 1924 S.C. 83; *Ebrahimi v Westbourne Galleries Ltd* [1973] A.C. 360.
[18] s.122(2), for the meaning of "in jeopardy" see above, p.542.
[19] Above, p.42.
[20] See the Companies (Consequential Provisions) Act 1985, ss 1–9.
[21] *Re Metropolitan Rlwy. Warehousing Co.* (1867) 36 L.J. Ch.827.

holders. *Held*, the petition should be dismissed. Since the conduct of the majority was not unreasonable or something of which the minority had a right to complain, the wishes of the majority were not to be disregarded. It would have been different if business could not have been carried on or there was an intention to abandon the undertaking: *Re Middlesborough Assembly Rooms Co.* (1880) 14 Ch.D. 104, CA.

If a company is formed to carry on business in England and abroad and has carried on business abroad, it will not be wound up merely on the ground that it has not started its business in England within the year if it intends to do so as soon as possible.[22] There is no need to wait a year if it is apparent within the year that the company cannot carry out the objects for which it was formed.[23]

Ground (5): Company unable to pay its debts

This is the ground on which a petition for a compulsory winding up is usually presented.

A company is *deemed* to be unable to pay its debts if:

(a) a creditor, by assignment or otherwise, to whom the company is indebted in a sum exceeding £750[24] then due has served on the company, by leaving it at the registered office,[25] a demand in the prescribed form[26] requiring the company to pay the sum so due, and the company has for three weeks thereafter neglected to pay the sum due or to secure[27] or compound for it to the creditor's satisfaction; or

(b) in England and Wales, execution issued on a judgment in favour of a creditor is returned unsatisfied in whole or in part; or

(c) in Scotland, the induciae of a charge for payment on an extract decree have expired without payment being made; or

(d) it is proved to the satisfaction of the court that the company is unable to pay its debts as they fall due; or

(e) if it is proved to the satisfaction of the court that, taking the company's contingent and prospective liabilities into account, the value of its assets is less than the amount of its liabilities: s.123.

---

[22] *Re Capital Fire Insurance Association* (1882) 21 Ch.D. 209.

[23] *Re German Date Coffee Co.* (1882) 20 Ch.D. 169, CA. (petition on the "just and equitable" ground).

[24] This sum may be increased by order.

[25] The demand need not be served by an officer of the court (*Lord Advocate v Traprain*, 1989 S.L.T. (Sh. Ct.) 99), but, if it is not, the court must have evidence that the person who served the statutory demand was duly authorised by the creditor (*Lord Advocate v Blairwest Investment Ltd*, 1989 S.L.T. (Sh. Ct.) 97). A statutory demand by a person bearing to act for and on behalf of the creditor is sufficient service: *Lord Advocate, Petitioner*, 1993 S.L.T. 1324 (O.H.).

[26] See I.R. 1986, rr 4.4–4.6; Form 4.1; and I.(S.)R. 1986, Sch.5, Form 4.1(Scot), as amended by I.(S.) Amendment Rules 1987 (SI 1987/1921 (s.132)).

[27] The security must be a marketable security covering the amount of the debt: *Commercial Bank of Scotland Ltd v Lanark Oil Co. Ltd* (1986) 14 R. 147.

A company has not neglected to pay a debt within (a), above, if it bona fide and upon substantial grounds disputes the debt.[28] Winding up proceedings are not appropriate for the adjudication of the question whether the petitioner is a creditor or not.[29] The creditor must prove that the demand was left at the company's registered office; if this can be proved, it does not matter whether it was left by the creditor personally or by an agent or employee. If it is put in the post, it is properly served if delivery is accepted or proved.[30]

The period of three weeks' neglect required in (a) above, has been held to be a period of three clear weeks, excluding the day of service of the demand for payment and the day of presentation of the petition.[31] A creditor will not rely upon a statutory demand where there is a risk of dissipation of the assets in the three-week interval. If available, he may use (b), (c) or (e) above; otherwise he can employ the more general ground in (d)—that the company is unable to pay its debts as they fall due. Thus in *Taylor's Industrial Flooring Ltd v M. H. Plant Hire Manchester Ltd*[32] it was held that if a debt was due and unpaid and could not be disputed on some substantial ground, the presentation of a petition under ground (d), above, was amply warranted even in the absence of a statutory demand. The Court of Appeal commented that the practice of prevaricating in the payment of due debts was to be discouraged. A company is also unable to pay its debts if its acceptances have been dishonoured[33] or it has informed a judgment creditor that it has no assets on which to levy execution,[34] or the petitioner has demanded the sum due to him without success,[35] or the company disputes a comparatively small amount but fails to pay a much larger outstanding balance due to the same creditor.[36] A company is not unable to pay its debts just because it is carrying on a losing business, if its assets exceed its liabilities.[37] However, a company may be unable to pay its debts under (d) where its assets exceed its liabilities if its assets are not presently available to meet its current liabilities. Where a company persistently fails or neglects to pay its debts until forced to do

---

[28] *Re London and Paris Banking Corporation* (1874) L.R. 19 Eq. 444; *Cunninghame v Walkinshaw Oil Co. Ltd* (1866) 14 R. 87; *W. & J.C. Pollok v Gaeta Pioneer Mining Co. Ltd*, 1907 S.C. 182. Where it is doubtful whether there is a bona fide dispute, the Scots court may sist the petition in order that the petitioners may constitute their debt: *Landauer & Co. v Alexander & Co. Ltd*, 1919 S.C. 492. There were held to be substantial grounds for dispute in *Walter L. Jacob & Co. v FIMBRA*, 1988 S.C.L.R. 184 (Sh. Ct.). In *Craig v Iona Hotels*, 1988 S.C.L.R. 130 (Sh. Ct.), the sheriff held that (1) where a company was in bona fide doubt as to the identity of a creditor, liquidation proceedings were not a legitimate means of enforcing payment and (2) the statutory demand for payment was defective because it was sent by recorded delivery post to, and not left at, the company's registered office.

[29] *Stonegate Securities Ltd v Gregory* [1980] 1 All E.R. 241, *per* Buckley L.J. at p. 243; *Re Richbell Strategic Holdings Ltd* [1997] 2 B.C.L.C. 429; *Customs and Excise v Broomco (1984) Ltd* [2000] B.T.C. 8035.

[30] *Re A Company, (No 008790 of 1990)* [1992] B.C.C. 11; *cf. Re A Company* [1985] B.C.L.C. 37.

[31] See *Re Lympne Investments Ltd* [1972] 1 W.L.R. 523.

[32] [1990] B.C.L.C. 216.

[33] *Re Globe, etc., Steel Co.* (1875) L.R. 20 Eq. 337; *Gandy, Petitioner*, 1912 2 S.L.T. 276.

[34] *Re Flagstaff etc. Co. of Utah* (1875) L.R. 20 Eq. 268; *Re Douglas Griggs Engineering Ltd* [1963] Ch. 19.

[35] *Stephen, Petitioner* (1884) 21 S.L.R. 764.

[36] *Blue Star Security Services (Scotland) Ltd, Petitioners*, 1992 S.L.T. (Sh. Ct.) 80.

[37] *Re Joint Stock Coal Company* (1869) L.R. 8 Eq. 146.

so,[38] the court may find that it is unable to pay its debts under (d): *Re A Company* [1986] B.C.L.C. 261. Where a petition is dismissed by consent on the company making late payment, costs may be awarded against the company.[39]

While grounds (b)–(d), above, do not require the petitioner's debt to be £750 or more, in practice, an order will not usually be made unless this condition is complied with, since there must be circumstances which justify an inference that the company is insolvent.[40] On the other hand, where a company refused to pay a debt of £35 on the ground that it was too small to be the foundation of a petition, an order was made.[41] The Scottish practice has been to apply the rule that "any creditor, whatever the amount of his debt, is entitled to a winding-up order, unless special circumstances exist for refusing it."[42]

PERSONS WHO MAY PETITION FOR WINDING UP BY THE COURT

Subject as below, a winding-up petition may be presented by any of the following parties:

(1) the company or its directors[43];

(2) a creditor or creditors (including contingent and prospective creditors);

(3) a contributory: s.124(1);

(4) in England, where the company is already being wound up voluntarily, the official receiver (s.124(5));

(5) the Secretary of State for Trade and Industry (Insolvency Act 1986, s.124(4)[44]; Insurance Companies Act 1982, ss 53–54;[45] Financial Services Act 1986, s.72); or

(6) in England, in the case of a charitable company, the Attorney-General (Charities Act 1993, s.63); and in Scotland the Lord Advocate (Law Reform (Miscellaneous Provisions) (Scotland) Act 1990, s.14(3));

(7) In England, in the case of a banking company, the Bank of England (Banking Act 1987, s.92.[46])

A creditor

A compulsory liquidation is usually initiated by a creditor's petition. A secured creditor may petition but will normally rely on his security so that the petitioner

---

[38] Public companies and their large private subsidiaries must include in the Directors' Report information on their policy and practice on payment of creditors: see Companies Act 1985, s.235 and Sch.7, para.12. See also the Late Payment of Commercial Debts (Interest) Act 1998 which implies a term into contracts for the supply of goods and services, where both parties are acting in the course of a business, entitling the supplier to statutory interest in the event of late payment.

[39] *Re Nowmost Co. Ltd* [1997] B.C.C. 105.

[40] *Re Industrial Assurance Association* [1910] W.N. 245.

[41] *Re World Industrial Bank* [1909] W.N. 148.

[42] *Per* Lord Johnston in *Speirs & Co. v Central Building Co. Ltd,* 1911 S.C. 330 at p.333.

[43] All: see *Re Instrumentation Electrical Services* (1988) 4 B.C.L.C. 550—some or a majority will not do.

[44] If the case falls within s.122(1)(b) or (c), or 124A.

[45] See *Re a Company (No. 007816 of 1994)* [1995] 2 B.C.L.C. 539.

[46] Petitions can also be presented, in appropriate circumstances, by the Building Societies Commission (Building Societies Act 1997, s.15) and the Housing Corporation (Housing Act 1996, s.7 and Sch.1, para.14).

is almost always an unsecured creditor. Where a petitioning creditor's debt is disputed on a substantial ground the court will usually restrain the prosecution of the petition as an abuse of the process of the court, even if the company appears to be insolvent.[47] On the other hand, even if the company is solvent, a creditor whose debt is clearly established can present a petition if there is a persistent refusal to pay the debt,[48] and no bona fide defence.[49]

A creditor whose debt is presently due and who cannot obtain payment normally has a right as between himself and the company *ex debito justitiae* to a winding-up order,[50] even if the company is being wound up voluntarily[51] or is in receivership.[52] This is not displaced merely by showing that the company has appealed against the judgment giving rise to the debt,[53] or has a disputed claim against the petitioning judgment creditor which is the subject of litigation in other proceedings.[54] Where there is a cross-claim the matter is one for the discretion of the judge.[55] If the company has a serious claim for an amount exceeding that of the petitioning creditors debt which it has been unable to litigate, the petition should be dismissed or stayed, unless there are special circumstances.[55a] It is, however, an improper use of the court to present a petition on the basis of a debt which has never been demanded and for which no opportunity to repay has been given.[56] It is an abuse of the process of the court to maximise pressure on the company by simultaneously serving the petition on the company and faxing notice to its bankers precipitating the disruption of the company's bank account and depriving it of the opportunity to consider its position.[57] The re-presentation of a dishonoured cheque suspends the creditor's right to payment and the presentation of a petition to wind up is in these circumstances an abuse of the process of the court.[58] A petitioning creditor's solicitor may be ordered to pay the company's costs where the petition was filed improperly, unreasonably or negligently.[59]

The *ex debito justitiae* rule applies only between the petitioning creditor and the company. As between the petitioning creditor and the other creditors he is

---

[47] *Mann v Goldstein* [1968] 1 W.L.R. 1091. A creditor must show an interest in the winding up; a petitioner who has been paid in full after the presentation of petition no longer has such an interest: *Furmston, Petitioner*, 1987 S.L.T. (Sh. Ct.) 10.

[48] *Cornhill Insurance plc v Improvement Services Ltd* [1986] 1 W.L.R. 114.

[49] *Re A Company (No. 0012209 of 1991)* [1992] 2 All E.R. 797; *Re A Compay (No. 0160 of 2004)* [2004] EWHC 380.

[50] See *Re Chapel House Colliery Co.* (1883) 24 Ch.D. 259, CA; *Gardner & Co. v Link* (1894) 21 R. 967.

[51] *Re James Millward & Co. Ltd* [1940] Ch. 333, CA; *Smyth & Co. v The Salem (Oregon) Capitol Flour Mills Co. Ltd* (1887) 14 R. 441.

[52] *Foxhall & Gyle (Nurseries) Ltd, Petitioners*, 1978 S.L.T. (Notes) 29 (O.H.).

[53] *Re Amalgamated Properties of Rhodesia (1913) Ltd* [1917] 2 Ch. 115, CA.

[54] *Re Douglas Griggs Engineering Ltd* [1963] Ch. 19; *cf. Re Fitness Centre (South East) Ltd* [1986] B.C.L.C. 518.

[55] *Re L. H. F. Wools Ltd* [1969] 3 All E.R. 882, CA; *Re A Company (No. 006273 of 1992)* [1992] B.C.C. 794.

[55a] *Re Bayoil, S.A.* [1998] B.C.C. 988. CA; *Alexander Sheridan Ltd v Beaujersey Ltd* [2004] EWHC 2072.

[56] *Re A Company* [1983] B.C.L.C. 492.

[57] *Re Bill Hennessey Associates Ltd* [1992] B.C.C. 386.

[58] *Ex. P. Medialite* [1991] B.C.L.C. 594.

[59] *Ridehalgh v Horsefield* [1994] 3 All E.R. 848, CA; *Re a Company (No. 006798 of 1995)* [1996] 2 All E.R. 417.

invoking a class right and so it is improper for him to present a petition for some private purpose. On the other hand if the petition is genuinely for the benefit of the class of creditors, malice on his part will not make the petition improper.[60] As with all matters relating to winding up, the court may have regard to the wishes of the creditors or contributories of the company, as proved by sufficient evidence, and may, for the purpose of ascertaining those wishes, direct meetings to be called, and in the case of creditors regard must be had to the value of each creditor's debt: s.195.[61] This gives the judge a wide unfettered discretion to decide whether to make the order or not. Once an administrator has been appointed, however, no winding-up order can be made and any such petition must be dismissed.[62]

Where the company is insolvent the views of the creditors alone, as the only persons interested, are considered. In other cases the views of the contributories are considered.[63] Where there are different classes of creditors the wishes of those particularly interested will be given most weight and, in particular, where the company's assets are not entirely charged in favour of debenture holders the wishes of the unsecured creditors will be primarily considered. Where the assets are entirely charged in favour of debenture holders, if the petition of an unsecured creditor is opposed by the debenture holders the petitioner is entitled to a winding-up order unless the opposing creditors can show that there is no reasonable possibility of the unsecured creditors obtaining a benefit from a winding up.[64] The court must not refuse a winding-up order just because the assets of the company have been mortgaged to an amount in excess of those assets or there are no assets: s.125(1).

If the petition of an unsecured creditor is opposed by the majority in value of the unsecured creditors, although the court has a complete discretion under s.125(1), above, to make or refuse an order and the fact of the majority opposition is not conclusive, if they oppose for good reason (*e.g.* because the assets exceed the liabilities and there are prospects of the company being able to continue business) their wishes will prevail in the absence of special circumstances making winding up desirable.[65] Similarly if the petition is opposed by a minority of creditors this will normally not prevent the order being made although the wishes of the minority may prevail in special cases.[66]

If a company is being wound up voluntarily a compulsory order will not usually be made if the majority of the creditors want the voluntary liquidation to

---

[60] *ibid.*
[61] If there is a real prospect of formulating a voluntary arrangement (above p.474) which will command majority support a petition may be dismissed or suspended: *Re Dollar Land (Feltham) Ltd* [1995] B.C.C. 740.
[62] Above, p.569.
[63] If only a contributory opposes a petition it will usually be granted: *Re Camburn Petroleum Products Ltd* [1979] 1 W.L.R. 86, but see *Allso v Secretary of State for Trade and Industry* [2004] EWHC 862.
[64] *Re Crigglestone Coal Co. Ltd* [1906] 2 Ch. 327, CA; *Gardner's case*, above.
[65] *Re Vuma Ltd* [1960] 1 W.L.R. 1283, CA; *Re P & J Macrae Ltd* [1961] 1 W.L.R. 229, CA. See also *Re A. B. C. Coupler Co.* [1961] 1 W.L.R. 243, *Re Fitness Centre (South East) Ltd* [1986] B.C.L.C. 518.
[66] *Re Southard & Co. Ltd* [1979] 1 W.L.R. 1198, CA.

continue.[67] Where there are special circumstances the court may give effect to the wishes of the minority.[68]

Any assignee of a debt or a definite part of a debt can petition,[69] even if a petition was presented in respect of the debt before the assignment.[70] A secured creditor can petition, and his security will not be prejudiced; the holder of bearer debentures can also petition.[71] It has been held that the holder of debenture stock secured by a normal trust deed cannot present a petition as he is not a creditor of the company,[72] the trustees being the proper persons to present the petition in such case.[73]

It has been held in England that a garnishor of a debt due from the company cannot petition, because he is not a creditor, a garnishee order only giving him a lien on the debt and not operating as a transfer of the debt,[74] and that a petition cannot be presented by a person with a claim against the company for unliquidated damages.[75] However, it may be that such persons can petition as "contingent or prospective creditors."[76]

A contributory

The term "contributory" means every person liable to contribute to the assets of the company in the event of its being wound up. As we shall see, it includes the present members and certain past members of the company: I.A. 1986, s.79.[77] A holder of fully paid-up shares in a limited company is a contributory.[78]

By s.124(2), the right of a contributory to present a petition is limited to cases where:

(1) the number of members is reduced below two[79]; or

---

[67] Re Home Remedies Ltd [1943] Ch. 1; Re B. Karsberg Ltd [1956] 1 W.L.R. 57, CA; Re J. D. Swain Ltd [1965] 1 W.L.R. 909, CA; cf. Pattisons Ltd v Kinnear (1899) 1 F. 551, Elsmie & Son v The Tomatin etc. Distillery Ltd (1906) 8 F. 434 and Re Fitness Centre (South East) Ltd [1986] B.C.L.C. 518.

[68] Bell's Trustees v The Holmes Oil Co. Ltd (1900) 3 F. 23; Bouboulis v Mann, Macneal & Co. Ltd, 1926 S.C. 637; Re Southard & Co. Ltd [1979] 1 W.L.R. 1198, CA; Re H.J. Tomkins & Son [1990] B.C.L.C. 76.

[69] See Re Steel Wing Co. [1921] 1 Ch. 349.

[70] Perak Pioneer Ltd v Petroleum National Bhd [1986] 3 W.L.R. 105, PC; cf. Re Paris Skating Rink (1877) 5 Ch.D. 959.

[71] Re Olathe Silver Mining Co. (1884) 27 Ch.D. 278.

[72] Re Dunderland Iron Ore Co. Ltd [1909] 1 Ch. 446.

[73] But see Palmer's Company Law, para.14.312, n.45.

[74] Re Combined Weighing Machine Co. (1889) 43 Ch.D. 99, CA.

[75] Re Pen-y-Van Colliery Co. (1877) 6 Ch.D. 477.

[76] In Re A Company [1973] 1 W.L.R. 1566 it was pointed out by Megarry J. at p.1571 that the Pen-y-Van case was decided on s.82 of the 1862 Act which, unlike the present section, says nothing about contingent or prospective creditors and it is very doubtful whether it is an authority for the proposition that a claim for unliquidated damages will not support a petition. See also Re Dollar Land Holdings plc [1993] B.C.C. 823.

[77] Below, p.634.

[78] Re National Savings Bank Association (1866) L.R. 1 Ch. App. 547; Walker and Others, Petitioners (1894) 2 S.L.T. 230 and 397 (O.H.).

[79] The section does not apply where the company has always only had one shareholders. Re Pimlico Capital Ltd [2002] EWHC 878.

(2) his shares, or some of them, were originally allotted to him or have been held by him, and registered in his name, for at least six months[80] during the 18 months before the commencement of the winding up, or have devolved on him through the death of a former holder.

The object of the latter provision is to prevent a person acquiring shares to qualify himself to present a petition to wreck the company.[81]

A shareholder whose calls are in arrear can petition, but he must first pay the amount of the call into court.[82] A person to whom shares have been allotted can petition even though the shares have not been registered in his name, unless there is a bona fide dispute as to the allotment.[83] A person who is not an original allottee cannot petition unless he has been registered as a shareholder.[84] A registered shareholder has *locus standi* to petition notwithstanding that he is disputing the beneficial ownership of other shares. However, the court may order that the petition should not be advertised until the dispute has been settled.[85]

In the case of the holder of a share warrant the shares are not "registered in his name", so that unless, *e.g.* he is an original allottee, he cannot petition.[86]

The trustee in bankruptcy of a bankrupt shareholder, where the trustee is not on the register of members, is not a contributory and cannot petition.[87] It seems that the personal representative of a deceased shareholder is a contributory.[88]

A person who may be required to repay an amount to an insolvent private company following a payment out of capital by that company for the purchase or redemption of its own shares under s.76,[89] may petition to wind up the company on either the just and equitable or insolvency grounds, but no others: s.124(3).

---

[80] See *Re Gattopardo Ltd* [1969] 1 W.L.R. 619, CA, where an order was made that a name be entered on the register of members but the company was not a party to the proceedings and therefore was not bound to register the individual as a shareholder, and so the six months' period did not commence when the order was made.

[81] Where the *locus standi* of a petitioner is disputed the court will consider all the circumstances, including the likelihood of damage to the company if the petition is not dismissed, in deciding whether to require the petitioner to seek the determination of his status outside the petition: *Alipour v Ary (Re a Company (No. 002180 of 1996)* [1997] 1 B.C.L.C. 557, CA.

[82] *Re Diamond Fuel Co.* (1879) 13 Ch.D. 499, CA.

[83] *Re J.N. 2* [1978] 1 W.L.R. 183.

[84] *Re Quickdome* (1988) B.C.L.C. 370 (mere agreement to acquire shares).

[85] *Re Garage Door Associates Ltd* [1984] 1 W.L.R. 35.

[86] *Re* Chitty J. in *Re Wala Wynaad India Gold Mining Co.* (1882) 21 Ch.D. 849, at p.853.

[87] *Re H. L. Bolton Engineering Co. Ltd* [1956] Ch. 577 (s.82(2), by which the trustee represents the bankrupt shareholder, does not come into effect until a winding-up order is made.) In the Scottish case *Ker, Petitioner* (1897) 5 S.L.T. 126 (O.H.), a trustee in bankruptcy was held entitled as a contributory to petition for the removal of a liquidator and for a supervision order. The trustee on a sequestrated estate in Scotland can present a petition without registering his title to the shares since the whole estate, including the capacity to take proceedings, vests in the permanent trustee by virtue of the act and warrant: Bankruptcy (Scotland) Act 1985, s.31(1), (8) and *Cumming's Tr. v Glennrinnes Farms Ltd*, 1993 S.L.T. 904 (O.H.).

[88] See *Re Norwich Yarn Co.* (1850) 12 Beav. 366; *Re Cuthbert Cooper & Sons Ltd* [1937] Ch. 392, at p.399, where Simonds J. assumed, without deciding, that such a personal representative is a contributory, *per* Wynn-Parry J. in *Re H. L. Bolton Engineering Co. Ltd* [1956] Ch. 577, at p.582; and *Re Meyer Douglas Pty. Ltd* [1965] V.R. 638, where Gowans J. pointed out at p.655 that in *Re Norwich Yarn Co.* the statutory definition of "contributory" included not only every member, but also every other person liable to contribute, whether as an heir, devisee, executor or administrator of a deceased member. See also *Re Bayswater Trading Co. Ltd* [1970] 1 W.L.R. 343, and *Howling's Trustees v Smith* (1905) 7 F. 390.

[89] Above, p.170, below, p.634.

The court will not, as a rule, make an order on a contributory's petition unless the contributory alleges and proves a financial interest in the winding up. A member's liability to contribute to the assets of the company on a winding up will suffice for this purpose. A holder of fully paid shares however will have to show, at least to the extent of a *prima facie* case, that there will be assets for distribution among the shareholders,[90] or that the affairs of the company require investigation in respects which are likely to produce a surplus of assets available for such distribution.[91] However, where a contributory's petition is based on the just and equitable ground[92] and alleges a failure by the company to supply accounts and information about its affairs, so that he cannot tell whether there will be a surplus for contributories,[93] a surplus need not be shown. The jurisdiction of the court to order the winding up of a company on the just and equitable ground on a contributory's petition is very wide and depends upon a full investigation of the facts at the hearing. A contributory may rely on a report by Department of Trade and Industry inspectors to support his petition.[94]

A petition by a contributory is uncommon. Such a petition which is opposed by the majority of the contributories will not be granted except where the conduct of the majority is something of which the minority have a right to complain.[95]

The right of a contributory to petition cannot be excluded or limited by the articles.

The articles provided that no winding-up petition could be presented without the consent of two directors, or unless a resolution to wind up was passed at a general meeting, or unless the petitioner held one-fifth of the share capital. None of these conditions was fulfilled. *Held*, the restrictions were invalid and a petition could be presented: *Re Peveril Gold Mines Ltd* [1898] 1 Ch. 122, CA.

The Official Receiver

The official receiver can petition for a winding up by the court when a company is already in voluntary liquidation in England. An order will only be made if the court is satisfied on a balance of probabilities,[96] that the existing liquidation cannot be continued with due regard to the interests of the creditors or contributories: s.124(5). The fact that a liquidator must now be a qualified insolvency practitioner and, in a creditors' voluntary winding up, his powers are restricted prior to the creditors' meeting, may reduce the occasions upon which this can be shown. However, the court may be disposed to grant an order where there is suspicion of "sharp practice" that calls for independent and impartial investigation.[97]

[90] *Re Rica Gold Washing Co.* (1879) 11 Ch.D. 36, CA; followed in *Re Expanded Plugs Ltd* [1966] 1 W.L.R. 514; *Black v United Collieries Ltd* (1904) 7 F. 18, *per* Lord Trayner at p.20. *O'Connor v Atlantis Fisheries Ltd*, 1998 G.W.D. 8–359 (Sh. Ct.).

[91] *Re Othery Construction Ltd* [1966] 1 W.L.R. 69, considering *Re Haycraft Gold etc., Co* [1900] 2 Ch. 230 and *Re Newman and Howard*, below.

[92] Above, p.353.

[93] *Re Newman and Howard Ltd* [1962] Ch. 257.

[94] *Re St. Piran Ltd* [1981] 3 All E.R. 270.

[95] *Re Middlesborough Assembly Rooms Co.* (1880) 14 Ch.D. 104, CA, above, p.516; *Galbraith v Merito Shpg. Co. Ltd*, 1947 S.C. 446; *Re Tivoli Freeholds Ltd* [1972] V.R. 445; *Re St. Piran Ltd* [1981] 3 All E.R. 270.

[96] *Re J. Russell Electronics Ltd* [1968] 1 W.L.R. 1252.

[97] *Re Gordon & Breach Science Publishers Ltd* [1995] B.C.C. 261.

The Secretary of State for Trade and Industry

Where a petition for compulsory winding up is presented by the Secretary of State after he has reached the conclusion (which need not to be based on evidence of illegality[98]) that it is expedient in the public interest to wind up the company compulsorily,[98a] it is for the court to decide on the material before it whether it is just and equitable to make the winding-up order.[99] Where there are circumstances of suspicion it is highly desirable that the winding up be by the court[1]; and the passing of a resolution for voluntary winding up shortly before the petition is presented ought not to be allowed to put the voluntary winding up in an entrenched position which can only be demolished if the Secretary of State can show that voluntary winding up would be markedly inferior to compulsory winding up.[2]

A report of inspectors appointed by him is prima facie evidence on which the court may act in deciding to make a winding-up order on a petition by the Secretary of State.[3] The Secretary of State's petition is in his own capacity and not that of a notional creditor.[4] Where the petition is subsequently withdrawn, the company is liable for the costs if the petition was properly presented.[5] In certain circumstances, on the presentation of a successful petition, the courts have ordered directors of the company to personally meet the applicant's *and the company's costs: Secretary of State for Trade and Industry v Aurum Marketing Ltd* [2002] B.C.C. 31.

PETITION FOR WINDING UP BY THE COURT

In England the winding-up petition must be in one of the forms specified in the Insolvency Rules 1986.[6]

Unless the court otherwise directs, the petition must be advertised in accordance with the rules.[7] The rules require the advertisement[8] to appear not less than seven clear days after the petition has been served on the company and not less than seven clear days before the day fixed for the hearing.[9] This gives the company the opportunity to discharge, or dispute, the debt or apply for validation of its transactions under s.127 before the advertisement appears.[10] The

---

[98] *Re S.H.V. Senator Hanseatische Verwaltungs Gesellschaft mbH* [1997] B.C.C. 112 (lottery).
[98a] See I.A. 1986, s.124A and p.336, above.
[99] *Re Walter L Jacob & Co Ltd* [1989] B.C.L.C. 345.
[1] See, *e.g.*, *Re Equity & Provident Ltd* [2002] EWHC 186.
[2] *Re Lubin, Rosen and Associates* [1975] 1 W.L.R. 122.
[3] *Re Armvent Ltd* [1975] 3 All E.R. 441.
[4] *Re Highfield Commodities Ltd* [1985] 1 W.L.R. 149.
[5] *Re XYLLYX (No. 2)* [1992] B.C.L.C. 378; *cf. Re Secure & Provide plc* [1992] B.C.C. 405.
[6] SI 1986/1925, r. 12.7(1); forms 4.2 & 4.3. For Scotland see SI 1986/1915 (s.139), I(S.)R., rr. 4.1–4.82.
[7] Unless the court otherwise directs, in the *Gazette*: I.R. 1986, r.4.11.
[8] The advertisement which the rule itself requires to be made: see *Secretary of State for Trade & Industry v North West Holdings plc* [1998] B.C.C. 997, at 1005, CA (press notice).
[9] r.4.11(2)(b). This rule is mandatory. It is designed to ensure that the class remedy of winding-up is made available to all creditors and is not used merely as a means of putting pressure on the company to pay the petitioner's debt: Practice Direction (No. 1 of 1996) Ch.D. (Companies Court) [1996] B.C.C. 677.
[10] *Re Bill Hennessey Associates Ltd,* [1992] B.C.C. 506.

court will restrain the issue of the advertisement if the detriment to the petitioner from an injunction is outweighed by the potential harm caused to the company from the advertisement,[11] if the petition is an abuse of the process of the court,[12] or if the debt is bona fide disputed.[13] Premature advertisement is an abuse of the process of the court:

T and L formed a company but their relationship broke down and L began telephoning the company's creditors informing them that she intended to have the company wound up. Serious damage to the company resulted. *Held:* L's petition should be struck out: *Re Doreen Boards Ltd* [1996] 1 B.C.L.C. 501.

In England, it has been held (in a case where the Secretary of State presented the petition on the ground that winding up was expedient by reason of matters referred to in a report of inspectors appointed to investigate the affairs of the company) that when grave charges are levelled against individuals in a petition, the court will not be satisfied with merely prima facie evidence. The petitioner must, if practicable, prove facts by the evidence of witnesses who have first-hand knowledge of the matters on which they give evidence.[14] However, in a later case it was held that the report of inspectors stands in a wholly different position from the ordinary affidavit evidence and represents the conclusions of a statutory fact-finding body, after hearing oral evidence and examination of books.The court is entitled to look at the report and accept it not as hearsay evidence but as material of a different character. At least where the report is not challenged by the company, the court does not have to be satisfied anew by evidence of the ordinary nature as to the facts found in the report.[15]

After the presentation of a petition (which has not been struck out or dismissed[16]) an application may be made to the court for the appointment of a *provisional liquidator*: I.A. 1986, s.135.[17] The applicant must provide a deposit or security for the appointee's remuneration.[18] In England the appointment may be made at any time before the making of a winding-up order, and the person usually appointed is the official receiver. In Scotland the appointment may be made at any time before the first appointment of liquidators: s.135(1). An

[11] *Re A Company (No. 009080 of 1992)* [1993] B.C.L.C. 269. See also *Re A Company (No. 0079239 of 1994)* [1995] B.C.C. 634 (an advertisement liable to cause serious damage to the reputation and financial stability of the company was restrained).

[12] *Re A Company (No. 0012209 of 1991)* [1992] 2 All E.R. 797.

[13] *Ex p. Avocet Aviation* [1992] B.C.L.C. 869 (costs awarded against petitioner on an indemnity basis).

[14] *Re A. B. C. Coupler Co. (No. 2)* [1962] 1 W.L.R. 1236; not followed in *Re Travel & Holiday Clubs Ltd*, below.

[15] *Re Travel & Holidays Clubs Ltd* [1967] 1 W.L.R. 711, where it was said (at p.716c) that it is undesirable that inspectors who have conducted an enquiry should have to give evidence of their findings upon which they would be liable to be cross-examined. This case was followed in *Re S.B.A. Properties Ltd* [1967] 1 W.L.R. 799. And see *Re Allied Produce* [1967] 1 W.L.R. 1469.

[16] *Re A Company* [1973] 1 W.L.R. 1566.

[17] Directors who improperly oppose the application may be ordered to pay the costs thrown away personally: *Gamelstaden plc v Brackland Magazines Ltd* [1993] B.C.C. 194. The application may be heard *in camera*: Practice Direction (No. 3 of 1996) [1997] 1 W.L.R. 3.

[18] I.R. 1986, rr 4.27 & 4.28, I.(S.)R., rr 4.3 and 4.4.

appointment is made if the assets are in jeopardy,[19] or to avoid possible prejudice.[20]

The provisional liquidator takes all the company's property into his custody or under his control (s.144), and after his appointment no legal proceedings can be commenced or continued against the company without leave of the court: s.130(2). An interpleader summons to which the company is made respondent is a proceeding against the company[21]; so also is distress levied on the company's property by the Commissioners of Customs and Excise for non-payment of VAT.[22] In one case the court gave leave to proceed to a person who had an unimpugnable right to a claim for specific performance of an agreement to sell property belonging to the company.[23] Leave will be given to enable a person to enforce a debt against the company under an existing contract which the liquidator chose to continue for the benefit of the liquidation or a debt under a new contract with the liquidator entered into for the purposes of the liquidation.[24] The appointment of a provisional liquidator has the same result as the making of a winding-up order in that the board of directors of the company becomes *functus officio* and its powers are assumed by the liquidator,[25] but notwithstanding the appointment the board has some residuary powers, *e.g.* it can instruct solicitors and counsel to oppose the petition and, if a winding-up order is made, to appeal against it.[26] The board can also act in interlocutory proceedings, including a motion to discharge the provisional liquidator.

The court may also, after the presentation of a petition (which is still subsisting[27]) and before a winding-up order has been made, on the application of the company or of any creditor or contributory, stay or restrain any pending legal proceedings against the company: s.126. s.126 is an exception to the rule that proceedings pending in the Supreme Court cannot be restrained by injunction. The object of ss 126 and 130(2) is "to put all unsecured creditors upon an equality, and to pay them *pari passu.*"[28]

Withdrawal of petition

A petitioner can apply to the court for leave to withdraw his petition so long as he does so at least five days prior to the hearing and satisfies the court that the petition has not been advertised, that no notices (whether in support or in

---

[19] *e.g. Levy v Napier*, 1962 S.C. 468, in which a deferred shareholder whose petition was opposed by the controlling ordinary shareholders averred that he was apprehensive that the proceeds of the sale of the company's business and assets were being depleted to his prejudice. See also, *Ex p. Nyckeln Finance Co.* [1991] B.C.L.C. 539 (where there was a real chance of assets being dissipated by being distributed otherwise than rateably between the creditors).

[20] *e.g. McCabe v Andrew Middleton (Enterprises) Ltd*, 1969 S.L.T. (Sh. Ct.) 29.

[21] *Eastern Holdings v Singer & Friedlander Ltd* [1967] 1 W.L.R. 1017.

[22] *Re Memco Engineering Ltd* [1986] Ch. 86.

[23] *Re Coregrange Ltd* [1984] B.C.L.C. 453.

[24] *Re Atlantic Computer Systems plc* [1992] 1 All E.R. 476, CA.

[25] Below, p.600. The authority of agents appointed on behalf of a company by the directors is revoked: see *Pacific & General Insurance Co. Ltd v Home & Overseas Insurance Co. Ltd* [1997] B.C.C. 400.

[26] *Re Union Accident Insce. Co. Ltd* [1972] 1 W.L.R. 640.

[27] See n.13, above.

[28] *per* Lindley L.J. in *Re Oak Pits Colliery Co.* (1882) Ch.D. 322, CA at p.329.

opposition) have been received by him with reference to the petition, and that the company consents to an order being made.[29]

Hearing of petition

The company and any creditor or contributory may attend the hearing of the petition. For this purpose a person is a creditor if he is a creditor for a present debt, a prospective debt or a contingent debt. Whether a person is a contingent creditor depends on circumstances existing at the date of the hearing.[30]

On the hearing of a petition the court may dismiss it, or adjourn the hearing conditionally or unconditionally, or make any interim order, or any other order that it thinks it fit: s.125(1).[31] The court may have regard to the wishes of the creditors or contributories: s.195.[32] When exercising its discretion to adjourn the hearing of a petition for the winding up of an international bank, the court had to consider the interests of the creditors worldwide rather than the interests of one class of creditor within the jurisdiction; English law does not permit the court to erect a ring fence around assets or creditors in any one jurisdiction.[33]

When a judgment creditor[34] is deprived of the right *ex debito justitiae* to a winding-up order because his petition is opposed by the majority of the creditors, the fair practice is to make no order as to costs.[35] The same is true where the petitioning creditor is not a judgment creditor but his debt is undisputed.[36] *Aliter* if the petitioning creditor acted unreasonably in presenting or prosecuting his petition,[37] or the company is being wound up voluntarily and no evidence is filed on behalf of the petitioner beyond an affidavit verifying the petition.[38] In special circumstances costs may be awarded against one party, *e.g.* where the company failed to defend an action so that the plaintiff petitioned to wind up the company, on the petition being dismissed and the action set aside, the company was held liable for the costs of the petition.[39] However, where a petitioner was paid in full by the company, apart from his costs, the petitioner was unable to recover his costs because he had not complied with the rules as to advertisement of the petition.[40]

When a winding-up order is made, it is usual to order the costs of (1) the petitioner, (2) the company, and (3) one set of creditors and one set of contributories, to be paid out of the assets. Any other creditor who wishes to

---

[29] I.R. 1986, r. 4.15 and see Practice Direction: Insolvency Proceedings [2000] B.C.C. 927.
[30] *Re S.B.A. Properties Ltd* [1967] 1 W.L.R. 799.
[31] Above.
[32] See also *Re Middlesborough Assembly Rooms Co.* (1880) 14 Ch.D. 104, CA, and *Galbraith v Merito Shpg. Co. Ltd*, 1947 S.C. 446.
[33] *Re Bank of Credit & Commerce International S.A.* [1992] B.C.C. 83.
[34] Scots equivalent, a creditor who has obtained a decree.
[35] *Re R. W. Sharman Ltd* [1957] 1 W.L.R. 774; *Re A. B. C. Coupler Co.* [1961] 1 W.L.R. 243.
[36] *Re Sklan Ltd* [1961] 1 W.L.R. 1013.
[37] *Re A. E. Hayter & Sons (Porchester) Ltd* [1961] 1 W.L.R. 1008.
[38] *Re Riviera Pearls Ltd* [1962] 1 W.L.R. 722.
[39] *Re Lanaghan Bros. Ltd* [1977] 1 All E.R. 265. See also *Re M. McCarthy & Co. (Builders) Ltd (No. 2)* [1976] 2 All E.R. 339 and *Re Arrow Leeds Ltd* [1986] B.C.L.C. 538.
[40] *The Shusella Ltd* (1982) 126 S.J. 577.

appear does so at his own expense. As a general rule no order for costs will be made in favour of one creditor against another.[41]

A copy of the order must be sent by the company to the Registrar of Companies: s.130(1).

Section 711 of the Companies Act 1985 provides that the Registrar must cause notice of the receipt by him of the copy of the order to be published in the *Gazette.* The notice must state the company's name, a description of the document received and the date of receipt.

The court has power to stay (in Scots law, "sist") a winding-up order either altogether or for a limited time,[42] on such terms and conditions as it thinks fit, if an application is made to it by the liquidator or (in England) the official receiver or any creditor or contributory. In England the court may require the official receiver to furnish a report on matters relevant to the application. A copy of any order made by the court under this provision must be sent to the Registrar: s.147. Such an order is not usually made unless all the creditors are paid or satisfied, but the court will have regard to commercial morality and not just to the interests of the creditors.[43] As a matter of practice a stay is almost never granted, for good reasons,[44] but there may be circumstances when a court will do so.[44a]

An appeal from the making of a winding-up order in England may be brought within four weeks: R.S.C., Ord. 59, r. 4.[45] An order made by a Lord Ordinary in Scotland may be reviewed by the Inner House if a reclaiming motion is enrolled within 14 days: s.162.[46]

Where an order winding up a solvent company was made on a contributory's petition opposed by the company and another contributory, and the company appealed against the order, the company had to provide security for the costs of the appeal otherwise than from the company's assets.It would have been wrong, if the appeal failed, for the petitioner to be liable to bear any proportion of the costs of the appeal or of a liquidation. An order was made that security be provided by the directors or shareholders promoting the appeal: *Re E. K. Wilson & Sons Ltd* [1972] 1 W.L.R. 791, CA.

CONSEQUENCES OF A WINDING-UP ORDER

The consequences of the making of a winding-up order date back to an earlier date than that on which the order was actually made. This date is called the *commencement of the winding up* and is:

(1) the time of the presentation of the petition; or

(2) where, before the presentation of the petition, the company was in voluntary liquidation, the time of the passing of the resolution for voluntary winding up.

---

[41] *Re Esal (Commodities) Ltd* [1985] B.C.L.C. 450. This case also provides guidance for costs where an alternative scheme of arrangement under s.425 of the Companies Act 1985, below p.660 is under consideration.

[42] See *Re Boston Timber Fabrications Ltd* [1984] B.C.L.C. 328.

[43] *Re Telescriptor Ltd* [1903] 2 Ch. 174; See also for general principles *Re Lowston Ltd* [1991] B.C.L.C. 570.

[44] See, *per* Plowman J. in *Re A & B.C. Chewing Gum Ltd* [1975] 1 W.L.R. 579, at p.592.

[44a] As in *McGruther v James Scott Ltd* 2004 S.C. 514, E.D.

[45] See I.R. 1986, r.7.47.

[46] *e.g. Levy, Petitioner*, 1963 S.C. 46.

(3) the date on which the court makes an order for winding up on the hearing of an administration application under para.13(1)(c) of Sch.B1 (s.125).

The consequences of a winding-up order are:

(1) Any disposition of the property of the company, and any transfer of shares or alteration in the status of the members, after the commencement of the winding up, is void unless the court otherwise orders: s.127. The company is divested of beneficial ownership of its assets.[47]

The object of s.127 is to prevent, during the period which must elapse before a petition can be heard, the improper alienation and dissipation of the property of a company *in extremis.* However, where a company is trading, the court can sanction transactions in the ordinary course of business—otherwise the presentation of a petition, whether well- or ill-founded, would paralyse the company's trade.[48] Thus the court may sanction the continued operation of the company's bank account in the ordinary course of business, so long as there is no serious doubt as to the company's solvency.[49] Further in the case of a solvent company the court will normally sanction a disposition which the directors consider to be necessary or expedient in the interests of the company for reasons which an intelligent and honest man could reasonably hold.[50]

Between the date of the presentation of the petition and the making of a winding-up order X advanced £1,200 to the company to enable it to pay wages due to the staff and took a debenture as security. X knew, at the time of the issue of the debenture, of the presentation of the petition. *Held,* the debenture was valid: *Re Park, Ward & Co. Ltd* [1926] Ch.828.

The court may order that a debenture taken after the commencement of the winding up is not void if the money is advanced, not for the payment of wages, but for the company's benefit to enable it to carry out its contracts and the lender has acted in good faith and with the honest intention of benefiting the company.[51] If however the disposition was made with a view to assisting the company's creditors, it will not be validated.[52]

Payments into or out of the company's bank account were held to fall within the section in *Re Gray's Inn Contruction Co. Ltd.*[53] This proposition has since been held to be too broad. Payments *into* an account in credit were held not to be a disposition of the company's property in *Re Barn Crown Ltd,*[54] and in *Bank*

[47] *Ayerst v C & K (Construction) Ltd* [1976] A.C. 167.
[48] *per* Lord Cairns in *Re Wiltshire Iron Co.* (1868) L.R. 3 Ch. App. 443, at p.447; see also *United Dominions Trust Ltd, Noters,* 1977 S.L.T. (Notes) 56 (O.H.) (warrant to sell security subjects valid).
[49] *Re A Company (No. 007532 of 1986)* [1987] B.C.L.C. 200.
[50] *Re Burton & Deakin Ltd* [1977] 1 W.L.R. 390.
[51] *Re Steane's (Bournemouth) Ltd* [1950] 1 All E.R. 21, applied in *Re Clifton Place Garage Ltd* [1970] 1 All E.R. 352, CA.
[52] *Re Webb's Electrical* [1988] B.C.L.C. 332.
[53] [1980] 1 W.L.R. 711, C.A.
[54] [1994] 1 W.L.R. 147.

of Ireland v Hollicourt (Contractors) Ltd[55] Court of Appeal held that a payment made by cheque *out* of an account, whether in credit or overdrawn, similarly would not be such a disposition by the bank.

After the presentation of a petition property may safely be transferred or payment made *to* the company,[56] but payments made *by* the company in respect of debts previously incurred must be refunded by the recipient,[57] and property transferred is held by the recipient on trust for the company, unless an order under s.127 is obtained.[58]

After the commencement of winding up, a company paid for petrol delivered prior to that date. The payments, which were made in good faith, in ignorance of the petition and were beneficial to the company and the unsecured creditors in that they were necessary to ensure further supplies, were validated by the court: *Denny v John Hudson & Co. Ltd*.[59]

The word "disposition" in s.127 includes dispositions of a company's property whether made by the company or by a third party, or whether made directly or indirectly.[60] However where, prior to the petition, the company has entered into an unconditional contract capable of specific performance to sell its property the completion of the contract after the presentation of the petition is not a disposition of its property within s.127 because whatever interest the company has at that time gives it no control over the property. Leave is therefore not required: *Re French's Wine Bar*.[61]

The court may, under the section, authorise a disposition of a company's property after presentation of the petition notwithstanding that a winding-up order has not yet been made and will do so if the disposition will benefit creditors of the company if an order is made.[62]

Section 127 contains no express provision as to who can apply for the validation of dispositions. However, an applicant must have some discernible interest in the matter. The company can apply under the section. A shareholder has a sufficient *locus standi* to apply. A director may have a sufficient *locus standi*.[63]

The rule which makes transfers of shares and alterations in the status of members void operates for the benefit of the company and its creditors, not for the benefit of third parties, and so, in Scotland, an assignation of shares, if duly intimated to the company, cuts out a subsequent arrestment of the shares.[64]

---

[55] [2001] Ch. 555.
[56] *Mersey Steel Co. v Naylor, Benzon & Co.* (1882) 9 Q.B.D. 648, CA; (1884) 9 App.Cas.434; *Millar v The National Bank of Scotland Ltd* (1891) 28 S.L.R. 884 (O.H.).
[57] *Re Civil Service and General Store Ltd* (1888) 57 L.J.Ch. 119; *McLintock v Lithauer*, 1924 S.L.T. 755 (O.H.).
[58] *Re French's Wine Bar* [1987] B.C.L.C. 499.
[59] [1992] B.C.C. 110.
[60] *Re Leslie Engineers Co. Ltd* [1976] 1 W.L.R. 292. But see *Re Mal Bower's Macquarie Electrical Centre Pty. Ltd (in Liqdn.) etc.* [1974] 1 N.S.W.L.R. 254 (to the effect that the section does not affect agencies such as a bank interposing between a company, as disponor, and the recipient of the property, as disponee) and also *Re Barn Crown Ltd* [1994] B.C.C. 381.
[61] *ibid.* In *Site Preparations v Buchan Developments Co.*, 1983 S.L.T. 317 (O.H.), a floating charge created after the presentation of a petition was held to be a disposition.
[62] *Re A. I. Levy (Holdings) Ltd* [1964] Ch. 19; See also *Re Newport County Association Football Club* (1987) 3 B.C.C. 635.
[63] *Re Argentum Reductions (U.K.) Ltd* [1975] 1 W.L.R. 186.
[64] *Jackson v Elphick* (1902) 10 S.L.T. 146 (O.H.).

By s.27(2), the paragraph does not apply in respect of anything done by an administrator of a company while a winding-up petition is suspended under para.40 of Sch.B1.

(2) As regards English companies and such property of Scottish companies as is situated in England, any attachment, sequestration, distress or execution put in force against the estate or effects of the company after the commencement of the winding up is void: s.128.[65] As regards Scottish companies and such property of English companies as is situated in Scotland, any winding up is, as at the date of its commencement, equivalent to an arrestment in execution and decree of furthcoming, and to a completed poinding, and also to a decree of adjudication of the heritable property of the company for payment of the whole of its debts: s.185.

In spite of its plain words, s.128 is subject to the provisions of s.126, above, and s.130(2), below, the combined effect of which is that a creditor who wishes validly to proceed to execution can apply to the court for leave.[66]

In relation to Scotland, the effect of s.185 is to equalise diligence by depriving any creditor who does diligence after the commencement of winding up (or within 60 days before that date) of the benefit which his diligence would otherwise have given him. The section is not restricted by the provisions of s.130(2), below. Accordingly the court could not under s.130(2) sanction diligence contrary to section 155.[67] Section 185 has been held not to render ineffectual an arrestment executed within 60 days before the commencement of winding up but superseded, owing to payment of the debt, before that date.[68]

(3) After a winding-up order has been made or a provisional liquidator has been appointed, no action can be proceeded with or commenced against the company except by leave of the court: s.130(2).

The purpose of s.130(2) is to ensure that when a company goes into liquidation the assets are administered for the benefit of all the creditors.[69] An action commenced without leave is a nullity and cannot be retrospectively authorised.[70]

Notwithstanding the section, if a company in liquidation brings an action the defendant may, without leave of the court, set up a cross-demand for liquidated or unliquidated damages, but only as a set-off to reduce or extinguish the plaintiff's claim.[71]

---

[65] A prior charging order nisi will not be confirmed after a liquidation: *Roberts Petroleum Ltd v Bernard Kenny Ltd* [1983] A.C. 192.

[66] *Re Lancashire Cotton Spinning Co.* (1887) 35 Ch.D. 656, CA; *The Constellation* [1966] 1 W.L.R. 272.

[67] *Allan v Cowan* (1892) 20 R. 36; see also opinion of Lord Trayner in *Radford & Bright Ltd v D. M. Stevenson & Co.* (1904) 6 F. 429 at p.431.

[68] *Johnston v Cluny Trustees*, 1957 S.C. 184.

[69] *per* Widgery L.J. in *Langley Constructions (Brixham) Ltd v Wells* [1969] 1 W.L.R. 503, CA at p.508; *cf.* the effects of an administration order, above, p.565.

[70] See *Re National Employers Mutual General Insurance Association* [1995] B.C.C. 774. But *cp. Re Linkrealm Ltd* [1998] B.C.C. 478 and *Palmer's Company Law*, Vol. 3, para.15.443.

[71] *Langley Constructions (Brixham) Ltd v Wells*, above.

Since "the court" is defined as "the court having jurisdiction to wind up the company" (Companies Act 1985, s.744), an action brought in a Scottish court against a company registered in England requires to be sisted until leave of the English court has been obtained.[72]

(4) On a winding-up order being made in England, the official receiver becomes the liquidator, and he continues to act until another person becomes liquidator. He also acts as liquidator during any vacancy: s.136(2), (3).

(5) On a winding-up order being made, the powers of the directors cease,[73] and are assumed by the liquidator. Some of the duties of the directors cease, too, *e.g.* as to the mode of keeping the company's accounting records under ss 221 to 223 of the Companies Act 1985.[74] One of the duties which remains after the making of a winding-up order is the duty not to disclose confidential information.[75]

(6) On a winding-up order being made, the employees of the company are *ipso facto,* dismissed,[76] and may be able to sue for damages for breach of contract, but an employee who continues to discharge the same duties and receive the same wages as before may be held to have entered by tacit relocation into a contract of service with the liquidator.[77] Where a liquidator re-engaged employees in order to complete certain contracts and thereafter dismissed them on the ground of redundancy, the employees were held, for the purposes of the Redundancy Payments Act 1965, to have been continuously employed by one employer (*i.e.* the company) from the dates of their initial engagement by the company down to the dates of their dismissal by the liquidator.[78]

Every invoice, order for goods or business letter issued by or on behalf of the company or the liquidator, on which the company's name appears, must contain a statement that the company is being wound up: s.188.

Appointment of special manager

Where either a company has gone into liquidation or a provisional liquidator has been appointed, the liquidator or provisional liquidator, as appropriate, may apply to the court for the appointment of a special manager of the company's business or property if the nature of that business or property or the interests of the creditors, members or contributories require it. The court may give the special manager such powers as it thinks fit. Such a person need not, however, be

[72] *Martin v Port of Manchester Insce. Co. Ltd*, 1934 S.C. 143. And see *Coclas v Bruce Peebles & Co. Ltd* (1908) 16 S.L.T. 7 (O.H.).
[73] *Fowler v Broad's Patent Night Light Co.* [1893] 1 Ch. 724.
[74] Above, Ch.20.
[75] *Re Country Traders Distributors Ltd etc.* [1974] 2 N.S.W.L.R. 135.
[76] *Chapman's Case* (1866) L.R. 1 Eq. 346; *Laing v Gowans* (1902) 10 S.L.T. 461 (O.H.).
[77] *Day v Tait* (1900) 8 S.L.T. 40 (O.H.).
[78] *Smith v Lord Advocate*, 1978 S.C. 259.

a qualified insolvency practitioner but must give such security (or in Scotland, caution) as is prescribed[79]: s.177. This power applies to all kinds of liquidation.

Proceedings After a Winding-Up

Statement of company's affairs and investigation by the official receiver

Where the court has made a winding-up order or appointed a provisional liquidator the official receiver[80] may require a statement of affairs to be produced. The persons who may be required to make such a statement, its contents and the procedural aspects are the same as those on the appointment of an administrative receiver[81] or administrator[82]: s.131.

In England, it is the duty of the official receiver after a winding-up order has been made to carry out two investigations: (1) if the company has failed, into the causes of the failure, and (2), in any case, into the promotion, formation, business dealing and affairs of the company. Consequently, he may make a report to the court, which is prima facie evidence of the facts stated in it in any proceedings: s.132. The official receiver is therefore bound under (2) to investigate all compulsory liquidations and not just those concerned with insolvency, but he need only make a report to the court if he thinks fit.

If the company has insufficient assets to cover the expenses of the liquidation and the official receiver is satisfied that no further investigation is required he may apply for an early dissolution, in which case his responsibilities cease. This procedure is dealt with in Chapter 29, below.[83]

Public examination of officers

Section 133(1) provides that the official receiver[84] may at any time before the dissolution of the company apply to the court for the public examination of (a) anyone who is or has been an officer of the company; (b) has acted as liquidator, administrator, receiver, or manager of its property; or (c) anyone else who has been concerned or has taken part in the promotion, formation or management of the company.[85] A public examination serves to expose serious misconduct and to promote a higher standard of commercial morality.[86]

The official receiver must apply for a public examination if he is requested to do so by either one half of the creditors or three quarters of the contributories: s.133(2). Failure to attend without a reasonable excuse is a contempt of court: s.134. Questions as to the company's formation, promotion, management or as to

---

[79] I.R. 1986, rr.4.206–4.210, I.(S.)R. 1986, rr.4.69–4.73.
[80] In Scotland, the liquidator, or provisional liquidator, as appropriate.
[81] Above, Ch.25.
[82] Above, Ch.26.
[83] p.651.
[84] In Scotland, the liquidator.
[85] The jurisdiction is not confined to British subjects or to persons within the jurisdiction at the relevant time: *Re Seagull Manufacturing Co. (In liquidation)* [1993] B.C.C. 241, CA; *Re Casterbridge Properties Ltd* [2002] B.C.C. 453 *cf.*, below, private examinations.
[86] Cork Report (1982), Cmnd. 8558, para.656.

the person's conduct of its affairs or dealings with that company may be put by the official receiver, liquidator, special manager,[87] any creditor who has tendered a claim or any contributory: s.133(3), (4). The person examined is not entitled to refuse to reply on the ground of self-incrimination.[88]

Appointment of a liquidator

In England the official receiver becomes the first liquidator until another person is appointed. There are two ways in which such a successor may be appointed:

(1) Within 12 weeks of the winding-up order the official receiver must decide whether or not to summon separate meetings of the company's creditors and contributories so that they might choose a liquidator in his place. If he decides not to do so he must notify the court, creditors and contributories to that effect but he must summon the meetings if requested by one quarter in value of the creditors, and any notice to the creditors of his refusal to summon the meetings must refer to that obligation: s.136.

If such meetings are held, each meeting may nominate a liquidator and, in the event of a disagreement, the creditors' nominee is to be the liquidator of the company subject to an application by any creditor or contributory to the court for the appointment of the contributories' nominee or some other person: s.139. This is similar to the appointment of a liquidator in a creditors' voluntary winding up except that the directors as such cannot apply to the court.[89] If no person is chosen as liquidator by the meetings, the official receiver must decide whether to refer the question of the appointment to the Secretary of State: s.137(2).

(2) The official receiver always has the alternative of applying to the Secretary of State for the appointment of a liquidator rather than summoning the meetings of creditors and contributories.The Secretary of State has complete discretion whether to appoint a liquidator but if he does so, the liquidator must give notice of his appointment to the creditors or advertise his appointment as directed by the court: s.137(3), (4).

Where a winding-up order either follows the cessation of effect of the appointment of an administrator[90] or is made at the time of a voluntary arrangement,[91] the court may appoint the administrator or supervisor, as appropriate, as liquidator. In such cases the official receiver does not become the liquidator at all: s.140.

The liquidator is to be known by the style of "the liquidator" of the particular company unless he is also the official receiver, where he is to be known as "the official receiver and liquidator" of the company: s.163.

In Scotland, a liquidator, referred to as the "interim liquidator" is appointed by the court at the time when the winding-up order is made. He must, within 28

---

[87] Above, p.600.
[88] *Re Paget* [1927] 2 Ch. 85; *Bishopsgate Investment Management Ltd v Maxwell* [1992] 2 All E.R. 856, 869–871, CA.
[89] Below, p.627.
[90] Above, p.579.
[91] Above, p.534.

days of the winding-up order, summon separate meetings of creditors and contributories to choose another person or himself to be liquidator, except that, if the ground for winding up is inability to pay debts, the interim liquidator need summon only a meeting of creditors.If at the meeting or meetings no person is appointed liquidator, the interim liquidator reports that fact to the court which makes the appointment: s.138.

The provisions of ss 139 and 140 apply to Scotland as in England.

Liquidation committees

If meetings of creditors and contributories are summoned to choose a liquidator, they may also, in England, appoint a committee (of creditors and contributories) to be known as the liquidation committee. This committee then fulfils several functions in the liquidation procedure the main one being to sanction certain actions of the liquidator.[92] Its exact composition and functions are governed by the Rules.[93] Such a committee may alternatively be appointed by general meetings of creditors and contributories summoned by the liquidator (not the official receiver). The liquidator must summon such meetings if requested to do so by one tenth in value of the creditors.If there is no liquidation committee or the liquidator is the official receiver the functions of the committee are vested in the Secretary of State: s.141.

In Scotland a liquidation committee may be established by the meetings of creditors and contributories (or of creditors only) summoned under s.138: s.142.[94] The provisions of s.142 are the same as those of s.141 applicable to England except that where there is no liquidation committee, the functions of the committee are vested in the court, and that a liquidation committee may have conferred on it the powers and duties of commissioners in a sequestration.

THE LIQUIDATOR AS OFFICE HOLDER

Office holders

The Insolvency Act applies certain basic rules and gives certain common powers to office holders. These are an administrator,[95] an administrative receiver,[96] a liquidator and a provisional liquidator (in any form of winding up). All such persons must be qualified insolvency practitioners[97]: s.230, Sch.B1, para.6. If any joint appointment is made the terms of the appointment must specify whether they are required to act together or may operate individually: s.231, Sch.B1, para.100(2). The acts of an office holder are valid despite any defect in his appointment, nomination or qualifications[98]: s.232, Sch.B1, para.104.

---

[92] See *e.g.* s.167, I.A. 1986.
[93] I.R. 1986, rr4.151–4.172A. As to its constitution and rights, see *Re W & A Glaser Ltd* [1994] B.C.C. 199.
[94] For the committee's exact composition and functions, see I.(S.)R. 1986, rr4.40-4.59A.
[95] Above, Ch.26.
[96] Above, p.548.
[97] Above, p.533.
[98] *cf.* C.A. 1985, s.285; above, p.103.

Administrative receivers and administrators have been the subject of Chapters 25 and 26 but it is convenient to deal with the provisions applicable to all office holders in one place. The following provisions apply therefore to both those earlier Chapters, this Chapter and Chapter 28 on voluntary winding up.

Supplies by public utilities

Although the utilities, such as gas, water and electricity are unsecured creditors, they could exercise considerable power against an office holder by refusing to continue supplies unless their debts from the company were paid in full. If the company's business was continuing this would be a potent threat. The Cork Committee therefore recommended[99] that an office holder must be treated as a new customer with a statutory right to receive supplies independently of the company whose account is in arrears.This recommendation was accepted and is contained in s.233.

The supplies affected are a public supply of gas, public supply of electricity, a supply of water by a water undertaker, or, in Scotland, a water authority and a supply of telecommunications services by a public telecommunications operator.[1]

Although they may not require outstanding bills of the company to be paid[2] before supplying the office holder, they may require a personal guarantee from him for any subsequent supplies.

This section also applies to the supervisor of a voluntary arrangement who is not an office holder for any other purpose.[3]

Getting in the company's property

The court may order any person who possesses any property, books, papers or records apparently belonging to the company to transfer them to the office holder. If the office holder[4] seizes or disposes of property which does not belong to the company but which he reasonably believes he is entitled to take or deal with, he is not liable for any loss or damage except that caused by his own negligence and is entitled to a lien on the property to recover any expenses: s.234.

Co-operation with the office holder—private examination

Any person who may be asked to furnish a statement of affairs[5] to an office holder (including the official receiver) must on request give such information concerning the company's affairs as the office holder may reasonably require and must attend on him when required to do so: s.235. Such private examinations are designed to assist the office holder to carry out his task quickly and effectively.

---

[99] Paras 1451–1462.
[1] I.A. 1986, s.233(5).
[2] Directly or indirectly, *e.g.* by insisting on a coin-operated meter supply so calibrated as to recoup the previous unpaid amounts.
[3] Above, p.538.
[4] This includes the Official Receiver.
[5] Above. Basically insiders.

Private examinations

The office holder[6] is given powers to apply to the court if there is insufficient co-operation under the provisions detailed above. The application[7] is lodged with a confidential report, parts of which may be made available to the proposed examinee.[8] On such an application the court may summon any officer of the company, any person known or suspected of possessing company property or supposed to be indebted to the company, or any person it thinks capable of giving information about the company's affairs,[9] to appear before it and to submit an affidavit detailing his dealings with the company, or to produce any relevant documents: s.236.[10]

The principles upon which the court exercises its discretion under s.236 were set out in *British & Commonwealth Holdings plc v Spicer & Oppenheimer*.[11] A balance must be struck between the requirements of the office holder and oppression of the examinee.

> "An application is not necessarily unreasonable because it is inconvenient for the addressee or causes him a lot of work or may make him vulnerable to future claims or is addressed to a person who not an officer or employee of, or contractor with, the company . . ., but all these factors will be relevant, together no doubt with many others."[12]

While the court can exercise its power to enable the office-holder to reconstitute the state of knowledge which the company should possess, the discretion is broader and may be exercised to provide the office-holder with any information he reasonably requires to carry out his functions.[13]

B.C. plc had taken over A. Ltd for £420 million and subsequently invested a further £117 million in it. Two years later A. Ltd became insolvent with a deficiency of £279 million. B.C. plc itself went into administration and its administrator sought an order under s.236 requiring the auditors of A. Ltd to produce books and papers relating to certain audits and to the takeover. The House of Lords granted the order even though B.C. plc would not have been entitled to such information when solvent: *British & Commonwealth Holdings plc v Spicer & Oppenheimer*.[14]

---

[6] Including at any time, the official receiver.

[7] Which may be made *ex parte* if there is good reason: see *Re Maxwell Communications Corporation plc, Homan v Vogel* [1994] B.C.C. 741, 747.

[8] *Re British & Commonwealth Holdings plc* [1992] B.C.L.C. 641, CA; *Re Bishopsgate Investment Management Ltd (No. 2)* [1994] B.C.C. 732.

[9] In some cases, notwithstanding legal professional privilege: *cp. Barclays Bank plc v Eustice* [1995] B.C.C. 978, CA; *Royscott Spa Leasing Ltd v Lovett* [1995] B.C.C. 502, CA.

[10] The jurisdiction is subject to territorial limitations: see s.237(3); *Re Seagull Manufacturing Co. Ltd* [1993] B.C.C. 241, CA. The section applies to the Crown: see *Soden v Burns* [1996] 3 All E.R. 967 (disclosure by the DTI of witness statements given to inspectors appointed under s.432 Companies Act 1985).

[11] [1992] 3 W.L.R. 853, HL, followed in *McIsaac and Wilson, Petitioners*, 1995 S.L.T. 498 (O.H.) (reference to "any person" in s.236 indicated that the provisions were not confined to persons resident in the jurisdiction of the court; in this case the order was limited to the production of documents by a firm of accountants). In relation to solvent companies, see *Re Galileo Ltd* [1998] B.C.C. 228.

[12] Lord Slynn, *ibid.*, p.885. See also *Re Sasea Finance Ltd (in liq.)* [1998] 1 B.C.L.C. 559.

[13] Compare *Joint Administrators of Cloverbay v Bank of Credit & Commerce International S.A.* [1991] Ch. 90. See also *First Tokyo Index Trust Ltd v Gould* [1993] G.W.D. 36-2298 (O.H.).

[14] [1992] 3 W.L.R. 853, HL.

The court[15] may examine a person on oath and he may be ordered to hand over property, or to pay amounts due, to the company: I.A. 1986, s.237. A person being examined under these provisions is not entitled to remain silent: the privilege against self-incrimination is impliedly abrogated by the statute in the interests of enabling the office holder more effectively to perform his investigative functions.[16] However, the use of statements obtained under compulsion in later criminal proceedings was held to be contrary to the European Convention on Human Rights in *Saunders v United Kingdom*.[17] The court is less inclined to make an order where proceedings have been commenced and pursued against the proposed examinee or where he is suspected of wrongdoing,[18] although the House of Lords has held that an order may be made where the purpose is to obtain information with a view to instituting disqualification proceedings against the director in question.[19] It was recognised in *Re Barlow Clowes Gilt Managers Ltd*[20] that the confidentiality of a private examination is important for the efficient functioning of the investigation, encouraging speedy, voluntary disclosure to the office holder. However, the ability of the office holder to ensure confidentiality is impaired by s.433 of the Insolvency Act 1986 which provides that a statement made, *inter alia*, under s.236 can be used in evidence against the person making it and also by s.2(3) of the Criminal Justice Act 1987 which authorises the Director of the Serious Fraud Office to request transcripts from the office holder (notwithstanding any assurances of confidence which may have been given and notwithstanding a direction of the court under s.168(3)[21] that access should be denied as being prejudicial to the conduct of the investigation: *Re Arrows Ltd (No. 4))*.[22] However, the use against the examinee, in a criminal trial, of statements acquired in this way may violate the right under Art.6 of the European Convention for the Protection of Human Rights and Fundamental Freedoms.[23]

THE PROPERTY OF THE COMPANY IN A WINDING UP BY THE COURT

Custody of company's property

When a winding-up order has been made, or a provisional liquidator appointed,

---

[15] Usually acting through the office holder: see *Re Kingscroft Insurance Co. Ltd* [1994] B.C.C. 343 (effect of the lapse of the office holder's appointment); *Re Maxwell Communications Corporation plc (No. 3)* [1995] 1 B.C.L.C. 521 (non-office holders).

[16] *Bishopsgate Investment Management Ltd v Maxwell* [1992] B.C.C. 214, CA; an order made in favour of a company in the course of an action for an account of assets is outside the scope of the statutory exception and the director can claim the right to silence (*ibid.*); see also *Re Jeffrey S. Levett* [1992] B.C.C. 137 (Vinelott J.); *Re Brook Martin & Co.* [1993] B.C.L.C. 328. The privilege against self-incrimination is not available to persons examined by the Director of the Serious Fraud Office exercising powers under s.2 of the Criminal Justice Act 1987; *Smith v Director of the Serious Fraud Office* [1992] 3 W.L.R. 66, HL.

[17] [1997] B.C.C. 872.

[18] *Re Bank of Credit & Commerce International S.A., Morris v Bank of America* [1997] B.C.C. 561, 572; *Re James McHale Automobiles Ltd* [1997] B.C.C. 202.

[19] *Re Pantmaenog Timber Co Ltd* [2003] UKHL 49.

[20] [1991] 4 All E.R. 385.

[21] and I.R. 1986, r.9.5(4).

[22] [1993] B.C.C. 473, CA; [1994] 3 All E.R. 814, HL. The liquidator does not, at the same time, have to disclose to the person charged: *Re Headington Investments Ltd*, CA [1993] B.C.C. 500.

[23] See *Saunders v United Kingdom* (Case 43/1994/490/572). On civil proceedings, see *R. v Secretary of State for Trade & Industry, ex p. McCormick* [1998] B.C.C. 379.

the liquidator must take into his custody or under his control all the property to which the company is or appears to be entitled. In Scotland, if and so long as there is no liquidator, all the company's property is deemed to be in the custody of the court: s.144.

Winding up does not, as does bankruptcy or sequestration, operate as a *cessio bonorum* or transfer of property; the company's property remains vested in it as before[24] unless, under s.145, the court makes an order vesting it in him in his official name. Section 234[25] and s.160[26] also contain wide powers to enable the liquidator to get the company's property into his custody.

Restriction of rights of creditor as to execution or attachment where company being wound up in England

In the case of a company being wound up in England, s.183 provides that where a creditor has issued execution against the goods or lands of a company or has attached any debt due to it, and the company is subsequently wound up, he is not entitled to retain the benefit of the execution or attachment against the liquidator unless he completed the execution or attachment before the commencement of the winding up[27] or, if he had notice of a meeting at which a resolution for voluntary winding up was to be proposed, before such notice. A purchaser in good faith, under a sale by the sheriff, of goods on which execution has been levied acquires a good title to them against the liquidator. The section does not apply to a distress for rent by a landlord.[28]

An execution against goods is taken to be completed either by seizure and sale or by the making of a charging order,[29] and an attachment of a debt by receipt of the debt, and an execution against land by seizure, the appointment of a receiver or by the making of a charging order: s.183(3)

Where a judgment creditor issued a writ of *fi. fa.* in respect of the judgment and the sheriff seized the company's goods and, after a petition for a compulsory winding up had been presented (although this was unknown to the sheriff), sold them, when an order for winding up was made the sheriff had to hand over the proceeds to the liquidator[30]

The phrase "the benefit of the execution" does not refer to "the fruits of the execution" but to the charge conferred on the creditor by the issue of execution.

Where a creditor has issued a writ of *fi. fa.* against a company, money paid to the sheriff or his officers in order to avoid a sale and which remains in their hands at the commencement of the winding up is outside "the benefit of the execution" so that the liquidator is not entitled to such money as against the creditor.[31]

---

[24] *Per* Warrington L.J. in *Re H. J. Webb & Co. (Smithfield, London) Ltd* [1922] 2 Ch. 369, CA, at p.388; *per* Lord President Inglis in *Queensland Mercantile etc. Co. Ltd v Australasian Investment Co. Ltd* (1888) 15 R. 935 at p.939; *per* Lord Hailsham in *Alexander Ward & Co. Ltd v Samyang Navigation Co. Ltd*, 1975 S.C. HL 26 at p.47.
[25] Above.
[26] Applies to England only.
[27] Above, p.596.
[28] *Re Bellaglade Ltd* [1977] 1 All E.R. 319.
[29] Under s.1 of the Charging Orders Act 1979.
[30] *Bluston & Bramley Ltd v Leigh* [1950] 2 K.B. 548.
[31] *Re Walkden Sheet Metal Co. Ltd* [1960] Ch. 170.

"The benefit of the attachment" means the right to take the necessary steps to complete it.

If a judgment creditor who has obtained a garnishee order obtains payment after receipt by him of notice of a meeting called for the winding up of the company, he must, subject to the court's discretion under s.183(2)(c), below, account to the liquidator for the money.[32]

By s.183(2)(c), the rights conferred by s.183(1), above, on the liquidator may be set aside by the court in favour of the creditor. The basic scheme of the Insolvency Act is that in a winding up unsecured creditors rank *pari passu* and an execution creditor who has not completed his execution at the commencement of the winding up is for this purpose in the same position as any other unsecured creditor. s.183(2)(c) gives the court a free hand to do what is right and fair according to the circumstances of the case,[33] but weighty reasons are necessary to justify the court in exercising its discretion.[34]

Where a judgment creditor of a company refrained from levying immediate execution because of a promise of payment by a director, there being no dishonesty by the director, and the execution was not completed before the commencement of the winding up, the court refused to set the liquidator's rights aside. To allow the creditor to retain the benefit of the execution would have been contrary to the basic scheme of the Acts and unfair to the other creditors.During the year before the winding up the company was keeping its general body of trade creditors at bay and there was no reason why one execution creditor who had not completed execution should be preferred to the other creditors whether or not they had obtained judgment or commenced execution.[35]

On the other hand, where before the action the company stalled the creditors' claims by promises and defended the action by disputing a debt already admitted, the liquidator's rights were set aside.[36]

Duties of sheriff as to goods taken in execution

Section 184 provides that where goods are taken in execution in England and Wales and, before their sale or the completion of the execution, notice of the appointment of a provisional liquidator, of a winding-up order or resolution for voluntary winding up, is served upon the sheriff, he must, if required, deliver up the goods to the liquidator. The costs of execution are however a first charge upon them. Where goods are seized in respect of a judgment exceeding £500 the sheriff must deduct the costs of execution and retain the balance for 14 days and pay it to the liquidator if so required. The rights of the liquidator may be set aside in favour of the creditor as the court thinks fit.

---

[32] *Re Caribbean Products (Yam Importers) Ltd* [1966] Ch. 331, CA; overruling *Re Rainbow Tours Ltd* [1964] Ch. 66.
[33] *Re Redman (Builders) Ltd* [1964] 1 W.L.R. 541.
[34] *Re Caribbean Products (Yam Importers) Ltd*, above.
[35] See n.26, above.
[36] *Re Suidair International Airways Ltd* [1951] Ch. 165.

Scottish companies, and property of English companies in Scotland

As regards Scottish companies and such property of English companies as is situated in Scotland, s.185 applies s.37(1) to (6) of the Bankruptcy (Scotland) Act 1985 with the following effect:[37]

(a) The winding up is, as at the date of commencement, equivalent to an arrestment in execution and decree of furthcoming, and to a completed poinding, and no arrestment or poinding of the funds or effects of the company executed on or after the sixtieth day before that date is effectual as against the liquidator except to the limited extent that an arrester or poinder who is thus deprived of the benefit of his diligence is entitled to a preference for the expense bona fide incurred by him in his diligence.

C brought an action of payment against a company and arrested the sum sued for in the hands of S, a debtor of the company. On the instructions of the company, S paid the sum arrested to C with the result that the arrestment was superseded. Later, but less than 60 days after the execution of the arrestment, an order was made for the winding up of the company, and the liquidator brought an action to recover the amount paid to C *Held*, the only arrestments made ineffectual by s.185 were those which, but for it, would have been effectual at the commencement of winding up, and therefore the section did not apply to arrestments which had been withdrawn or superseded by payment of the debt before that date: *Johnston v Cluny Trustees*, 1957 S.C. 184.

In *Commercial Aluminium Windows Ltd v Cumbernauld Development Corporation*, 1987 S.L.T. (Sh. Ct.) 91, where an arrestment had been executed more than 60 days before the winding up, the liquidator defended an action of furthcoming made during the winding up. *Held*, that the arrestment was effectual, because the liquidator had by this statutory provision the equivalent of an arrestment *and decree of furthcoming*. Contrast *Lord Advocate v Royal Bank of Scotland Ltd*, 1977 S.C. 155: in receivership, an arrestment by itself was not "effectually executed diligence."[37a]

(b) The winding up is, as at the date of its commencement, also equivalent to a decree of adjudication of the heritable estates of the company for payment of the whole debts of the company, subject to any preferable heritable rights and securities which are valid and unchallengeable and subject to the limited right to poind the ground provided for in (c).[38]

(c) A poinding of the ground which has not been carried into execution by sale of the effects 60 days before the commencement of winding up is of no effect in a question with the liquidator unless the poinder holds a heritable security which is preferable to the right of the liquidator, in

---

[37] The phrase "date of commencement" in the following provisions in (a), (b) and (c) means the day on which the winding-up order *was made*. (In other contexts it is the date of presentation of the petition.) See *Morrison v Integer Systems Control Ltd*, 1989 S.C.L.R. 495 (Sh.Ct.) (refusal of recall of arrestments because outwith the 60-day period before the winding-up order).

[37a] See now *Commissioners of Customs and Excise v John D Reid Joinery Ltd* 2001 S.L.T. 588, O.H.

[38] For an instance of the application of provision (b), see *Turnbull v Liquidator of Scottish County Investments Co. Ltd*, 1939 S.C. 5; on the interrelation of this provision and The Conveyancing and Feudal Reform (Scotland) Act 1970, s.24 (application to court for warrant to sell), see *United Dominions Trust Ltd, Noters*, 1977 S.L.T. (Notes) 56 (O.H.).

which case the poinding is available for the interest for the current half-year and for the arrears of interest for the preceding year, but for no more.

Attendance of officers at meetings in Scotland

While the public examination which may be required in sequestration[39] has no place in the liquidation of a company, the court in the compulsory winding up of a Scottish company has power to require any officer of the company to attend any meeting of creditors or of contributories or of a liquidation committee for the purpose of giving information as to the trade, dealings, affairs or property of the company: s.157.

Fraudulent trading

Section 213 provides that if in the winding up of a company it appears that business has been carried on with intent to defraud creditors or for any fraudulent purpose, the court, on the application of the liquidator, may declare that any persons who were knowingly parties to the fraudulent trading shall make such contributions to the company's assets as the court thinks proper.[40]

Fraudulent trading (so defined) is also a criminal offence under s.458 of the Companies Act 1985.[41] The criminal offence, unlike the civil penalties in the Insolvency Act, however, is not linked to a winding up.

In general it may be properly inferred that there is an intent to defraud creditors if a company carries on business and incurs debts when, to the knowledge of the directors, there is no reasonable prospect of the company being able to pay them.[42] It is not necessary to show that there was no prospect of the creditors *ever* being paid. It is enough that there is no reason for thinking that they will be paid as the debts fall due or shortly thereafter.[43] In general, the courts have used the benchmark of "actual dishonesty" in determining whether the requirements of the section are made out.[44]

The expression "parties to" the fraudulent trading in s.213(2) indicates no more than "take part in" or "concur in" and involves some positive steps. Mere omission by the secretary to give certain advice (that the company is insolvent and should cease to trade) is not being a party to carrying on the business in a fraudulent manner.[45] However, a creditor who, knowing of the circumstances, accepts money fraudulently obtained by the company may be liable to repay it even if he took no part in the fraudulent trading itself.[46]

---

[39] Bankruptcy (Scotland) Act 1985, s.45.
[40] Any order is in favour of the liquidator not an individual shareholder: *Re Esal (Commodities) Ltd* [1997] 1 B.C.L.C. 705, CA.
[41] There must be a finding of dishonesty for the criminal offence to be committed: *R. v Cox* [1983] B.C.L.C. 169. For the purposes of s.458, "creditors" have been held to include future creditors: *R. v Smith* [1996] 2 B.C.L.C. 109, CA.
[42] *Re William C. Leitch Bros. Ltd* [1932] 2 Ch. 71.
[43] *R. v Grantham* [1984] Q.B. 675.
[44] *Re Patrick and Lyon Ltd* [1933] Ch 786; *Bernasconi v Nicholas Bennett & Co* [2000] B.C.C. 921.
[45] *Re Maidstone Buildings Provisions Ltd* [1971] 1 W.L.R. 1085, *R. v Miles* [1992] Crim.L.R. 657.
[46] *Re Gerald Cooper Chemicals Ltd* [1978] Ch. 262.

It is not fraudulent trading for a parent company to give promises of support to a subsidiary which are not implemented. The fraud of the parent company cannot be linked to the subsidiary, since to establish liability the fraudulent trading must be committed by someone carrying on the business, *i.e.* the subsidiary. In any event such general statements would not be sufficient to prove fraud.[47]

It is not fraudulent trading to intend to prefer one creditor to another even if all could not be paid in full,[48] nor to sell goods which prove to be defective knowing that liability for such defects might not be met.[49]

The court may charge the liability of a person declared liable under s.213 on any debt due to him from the company, or on any charge on any assets of the company held by him, or any company or person on his behalf, or certain assignees from him or such a company or person: s.215.

Wrongful trading

The difficulties of establishing the "fraudulent" element of fraudulent trading led to many directors who had carried on the business recklessly being exempt. The Insolvency Act introduced another concept, that of wrongful trading which is designed to apply to such cases.Wrongful trading, which applies only to directors and to insolvent liquidations, has been dealt with in Chapter 15, above.[50] As far as directors are concerned wrongful trading will largely replace fraudulent trading. Fraudulent trading, however, remains for other persons and as a criminal offence for serious cases (wrongful trading is not a criminal offence).

Summary remedy against delinquent directors, etc.

This was explained in the chapter on directors.[51]

Disclaimer in case of company wound up in England

Where any part of the property of a company which is being wound up is onerous property, the liquidator may on giving notice disclaim that property. Onerous property for this purpose is (a) any unprofitable contract; or (b) any other property of the company which is unsaleable or not readily saleable or is such that may give rise to a liability to pay money or perform any other onerous act: s.178(1)–(3). A waste management licence has been held to be "property" or a right incidental to property for the purposes of the section: *Celtic Extraction Ltd & Bluestone Chemicals Ltd v Environment Agency* [2001] Ch.475, CA.

A disclaimer operates to determine the rights and liabilities of the company in respect of the property disclaimed but does not, except for the purpose of

---

[47] *Re Augustus Barnett & Son Ltd* [1986] B.C.L.C. 170.
[48] *Re Sarflax Ltd* [1979] Ch. 592.
[49] *Norcross Ltd v Amos* (1981) 131 N.L.J. 1213. See also *Rossleigh Ltd v Carlaw*, 1986 S.L.T. 204 in Scotland as to the knowledge required of the intent to defraud.
[50] Above, p.317.
[51] Above, p.320.

releasing the company from liability, affect the rights or liabilities of any other person: s.178(4).[52]

Thus, where an insolvent company is the tenant under a lease, a disclaimer by the liquidator releases the future rent liability of the company but not that of its surety or of former tenants.[53] Furthermore, payment by a surety or former tenant gives rise to no right of indemnity against the company: see *Hindcastle Ltd v Barbara Attenborough Associates Ltd* [1996] 1 All E.R. 737, HL.[54] The liquidator cannot disclaim any property if notice in writing is served on him by a person interested in the property, requiring him to decide whether he will disclaim or not, and he does not, within 28 days, or any longer period allowed by the court, give notice of disclaimer: s.178(5).

Any person injured by a disclaimer is deemed a creditor of the company to the extent of his loss or damage and may prove for that amount in the winding up: s.178(6).[55]

Where the property is a leasehold, no disclaimer can take effect unless the liquidator has served a notice on every person claiming under the company as underlessee or mortgagee and either no application for a vesting order (see below) has been made by such a person within 14 days or, if such application has been made, the court nevertheless directs that the disclaimer shall take effect: s.179.

The court may, on the application of any person interested in the property,[56] or who is under an undischarged liability in respect of the disclaimed property,[57] make an order for the vesting or delivery of the property to that person or his trustee on such terms as it thinks fit.[58] The effect of any such order must be taken into account in assessing any loss subsequently provable in the winding up: s.181. Where the property is a leasehold, such a vesting order cannot be made in favour of an underlessee or mortgagee, unless it is either (a) subject to the same liabilities and obligations as those to which the company was subject under the lease at the commencement of the winding up, or (b), if the court thinks fit, subject only to the same liabilities and obligations as if the lease had been assigned to that person at that date: s.182.

Any person who is, as against the liquidator, entitled to the benefit or subject to the burden of a contract with the company may apply to the court for an order rescinding the contract. The court may grant rescission on such terms as it thinks fit, including the payment of damages for breach of contract. Any damages

---

[52] See *Capital Prime Properties plc v Worthgate Ltd* [2000] B.C.C. 525.

[53] In relation to pre-1996 leases the liability of former tenants is contractual; in relation to leases granted on or after January 1, 1996 liability may arise under an authorised guarantee agreement: see Landlord & Tenant (Covenants) Act 1995, s.16.

[54] Overruling *Stacey v Hill* [1901] 1 Q.B. 660.

[55] In relation to the disclaimer of a lease, the landlord can claim the difference between the aggregate of the rent and other amounts which it was entitled to be paid by the tenant for the residue of the lease subject to a discount for accelerated receipt and the income which it could obtain from another tenant entering into the same lease (save as to rent) for a term equivalent to the residue of the term: *Re Park Air Services plc* [2000] 2 A.C. 172.

[56] This includes a statutory tenant: *Re Vedmay* [1994] 10 E.G. 108.

[57] *e.g.* the tenant-company's surety, see *Re A.E. Realisations* (1985) [1987] B.C.L.C. 486. Compare *Re Spirit Motorsport Ltd* [1996] 1 B.C.L.C. 684.

[58] For example that on sale the surplus should be repaid to the liquidator for the benefit of the other creditors: *cp. In Re Lee (a Bankrupt), The Times*, February 24, 1998.

payable to such a person under the order may be proved for in the liquidation: s.186.

The Insolvency Act widened the former disclaimer provisions in two major respects. First the consent of the court is no longer required. The discretion previously vested in the court is now vested in the liquidator and its exercise can only be challenged[59] on the grounds of *mala fides* or perversity.[60] Second the definition of onerous property has been widened to include unsaleable property.[61]

Repudiation in case of company wound up in Scotland

By the common law of Scotland the liquidator may either adopt or repudiate current contracts, and if he repudiates them the company is liable in damages for breach of contract. If the liquidator does not within a reasonable time declare his intention to adopt a contract, he will be held to have abandoned it and to be liable in damages.[62]

Where the company is bound under two separate contracts with the same party, the liquidator is entitled to adopt one and repudiate the other, and the other party to the contracts is not entitled to retain a sum due to the company under the contract adopted, either in security for the proper fulfilment of that contract by the company or in security for a claim for damages in respect of the contract repudiated.[63]

The main criticism of the common law in this connection was the possible uncertainty of the other contracting party as to his position. Following a recommendation of the Scottish Law Commission,[64] the Bankruptcy (Scotland) Act 1985, s.42, enables the other contracting party to require the permanent trustee to reach a decision within 28 days of receiving written notice. By s.169 of the Insolvency Act 1986 the liquidator has the same powers, subject to the rules, as a trustee on a bankrupt estate.

THE LIQUIDATOR IN A WINDING-UP BY THE COURT

The liquidator in a winding up by the court is an officer of the court.[65]

---

[59] See I.A. 1986, s.168(5).
[60] *Re Hans Place Ltd* [1992] B.C.C. 737; *Cavendish Offices & Houses Investments Ltd v Adams* [1992] E.G. 107.
[61] *cf. Re Potters Oils Ltd* [1986] 1 W.L.R. 201 decided on the old law.
[62] *Crown Estate Commissioners v Liquidators of Highland Engineering Ltd*, 1975 S.L.T. 58 (O.H.).
[63] *Asphaltic Limestone Concrete Co. Ltd v Glasgow Corpn.*, 1907 S.C. 463; see also *Gray's Trustees v Benhar Coal Co. Ltd* (1881) 9 R. 225.
[64] *Report on Bankruptcy and Related Aspects of Insolvency and Liquidation*, 1982 Scot. Law Com. No. 68, para.10.26.
[65] *per* Megarry J. in *Re Rolls Razor Ltd (No. 2)* [1970] Ch. 576, 586. In *International Factors Ltd v Ves Voltech Electronic Services Ltd*, 1995 S.L.T. (Sh.Ct.) 40, it was observed that a provisional liquidator was an officer of the court and was required to comply with an order of the court and the statutory regulations governing his appointment; should advertisement of his appointment not be appropriate, he should immediately apply to the court for dispensation from the requirement to advertise; as the provisional liquidator had not done so in this case, the sheriff refused payment of his fees and expenses out of the property of the company.

Appointment

The liquidator is appointed in the manner already discussed.[66] He is an office holder[67] and as such must be a qualified insolvency practitioner.[68]

The court has appointed as liquidator a person resident beyond the jurisdiction of the court but such an appointment was only made where there was an adequate reason.[69]

Any person who gives, or agrees or offers to give, any member or creditor of the company any valuable consideration with a view to securing his own appointment or nomination, or to securing or preventing the appointment or nomination of someone else, as the liquidator, is liable to a fine: s.164.

Resignation and removal

A liquidator may resign by giving notice to the court before the completion of the liquidation: s.172(6).

In Scotland leave to resign was granted to an official liquidator where it was stated that there was nothing to recover from the estate, and the liquidator's application was concurred in by substantially all the creditors and was unopposed.[70]

A liquidator must vacate his office on ceasing to be a qualified insolvency practitioner[71] and on the holding of the final meeting of creditors[72]: s.172(5), (8).

A liquidator may be removed either by the court or by a meeting of the creditors: s.172(2). Grounds on which a liquidator has been removed by the court include personal unfitness (due to, *e.g.* his character, his residence,[73] or his personal interest or involvement,[74]) insanity,[75] prosecuting a claim against the wishes of a majority of the creditors where the company is insolvent,[76] or failing to carry out his duties with sufficient vigour and displaying a relaxed and complacent attitude towards wrongdoing by the directors.[77] On the other hand the court has refused to remove a liquidator merely because he is a shareholder and former director,[78] or because the majority of the creditors or of the contributories desire it[79] or because the liquidator has made a serious mistake.[80]

---

[66] p.602.

[67] Above, p.603.

[68] Above, p.533.

[69] *Brightwen & Co. v City of Glasgow Bank* (1878) 6 R. 244 (appointment as joint liquidator of accountant resident in London refused); see also *Barberton Development etc. Ltd, Petitioners* (1898) 25 R. 654, and contrast *Liquidators of Bruce Peebles & Co. Ltd v Shiells*, 1908 S.C. 692.

[70] *Jamieson, Petitioner* (1877) 14 S.L.R. 667.

[71] Above, p.533.

[72] Below, p.651.

[73] *Skinner, Petitioner* (1899) 6 S.L.T. 388 (O.H.) (residence in England of sole liquidator).

[74] *Lysons v Liquidator of the Miraflores Gold Syndicate Ltd* (1895) 22 R. 605; *Re Corbenstoke (No. 2)* [1990] B.C.L.C. 60 (liquidator was the company's debtor).

[75] *Re The North Molton Mining Co. Ltd* (1886) 54 L.T. 602.

[76] *Re Tavistock Ironworks Co.* (1871) 24 L.T. 605.

[77] *Re Keypack Homecare* [1987] B.C.L.C. 409.

[78] *M'Knight & Co. Ltd v Montgomerie* (1892) 19 R. 501; but see *Re Corbenstoke, ibid.*, where Harman J. considered it unlikely that a director would ever be a suitable person to act as liquidator.

[79] *Ker, Petitioner* (1897) 5 S.L.T. 126 (O.H.).

[80] *Re Edennote Ltd* [1996] B.C.C. 718.

The conduct of the liquidator must give rise to a reasonable loss of confidence on the part of the creditors.[81]

The meeting of the creditors to replace a liquidator may be called by the liquidator himself, the court or one quarter in value of the creditors. If the liquidator was appointed by the Secretary of State only the Secretary of State may remove him.

A vacancy in the office of the liquidator appointed by the court is filled in England by the official receiver: s.136(3).

Duties

The functions of a liquidator are to secure that the assets of the company are got in, realised and distributed to the company's creditors and, if there is a surplus, to the persons entitled to it: s.143(1).

A liquidator must:

(1) in England, give all information, assistance and documents to the official receiver as he may reasonably require: s.143(2);

(2) take all the property of the company into his custody as soon as possible: s.144;

(3) in England, as soon as may be, settle a list of contributories,[82] collect the company's assets, apply them in discharge of its liabilities and distribute any surplus among the members according to their rights and interests in the company: ss 148, 154, 160.

In Scotland, he must perform such duties as will enable the court to exercise the functions mentioned: ss 148, 154.

The word "liabilities" excludes claims which are not legally enforceable. Thus it does not include arrears of tax claimed by a foreign state, even one which adheres to the Commonwealth.[83]

If the liquidator distributes the assets without making provision for the liabilities he is liable to pay damages to the unpaid creditors.

The company had a lease of premises expiring in 1938 at a yearly rent of £1,217 10s.The lease was assigned to M, and in 1933 the company went into voluntary liquidation. M was insolvent and unable to pay the rent. The liquidator distributed the assets without making any provision for the company's liabilities under the lease. *Held,* the liquidator had committed a breach of his duty and was liable in damages to the lessor: *James Smith & Sons (Norwood) Ltd v Goodman* [1936] Ch.216, CA.

(4) In England, summon meetings of the creditors or contributories when directed by resolution of the creditors or contributories or requested in writing by one-tenth in value of the creditors or contributories: s.168(2).

---

[81] *ibid.*
[82] But see below, p.635.
[83] *Government of India v Taylor* [1955] A.C. 491; *cf. Clyde Marine Insurance Co. Ltd v Renwick & Co.,* 1924 S.C. 113.

He may summon meetings on his own initiative whenever he wants to ascertain the wishes of the creditors or contributories: s.168(2).

In Scotland, the committee or any member of it may apply to the court for an order on the liquidator to summon a meeting of creditors or contributories or both: R.C.S. r.74.32 (Court of Session) and Sheriff Court Company Insolvency Rules 1986, Rule 30.

(5) Summon a final meeting in accordance with s.146.[84]

(6) In common with administrative receivers and administrators,[85] a liquidator must set aside a prescribed part of the company's property to be made available to the company's unsecured creditors: s.176A.

Powers of the liquidator

S.167[86] provides that:

(1) The liquidator (including a provisional liquidator[87]) in a winding up by the court has power, *with the sanction of the court or of the liquidation committee:*

(a) To bring or defend actions and legal proceedings in the name and on behalf of the company.

It is a matter for his discretion whether he should litigate or not and so the court will not give guidance as to whether he should appeal to a higher court.[88] If the liquidator brings an unsuccessful action, only in exceptional circumstances (involving impropriety) will he be ordered to pay the costs personally.[89] Where the company has insufficient funds to meet the costs, the defendant should seek an order for security of costs.[90] An agreement between a liquidator and third parties that the latter would fund an action brought by the company in return for half of the amount recovered contravenes the law of maintenance and champerty and the action will be stayed.[91]

(b) To carry on the business of the company so far as may be necessary for beneficial winding up.

In *Liquidator of Burntisland Oil Co. Ltd v Dawson* (1892) 20 R. 180, the court refused the liquidator's application to carry on the business for an indefinite

---

[84] Below, p.651.
[85] See Chs 25 and 26, pp.553 and 574 respectively.
[86] and Schedule 4.
[87] *Wilsons (Glasgow and Trinidad) Ltd, Petitioners*, 1912 2 S.L.T. 330.
[88] *Note for Liquidator in Liquidation of S.S. "Camelot" Ltd* (1893) 1 S.L.T. 358 (O.H.).
[89] See *Metalloy Supplies Ltd v M.A. (U.K.) Ltd* [1997] B.C.C. 165, CA; *Roods of Queensferry Ltd v Shand Construction Ltd* (costs) [2002] EWCA Civ. 918. Compare where he brings an action in his own name: *Re Wilson Lovatt & Sons Ltd* [1977] 1 All E.R. 274.
[90] *Mettaloy*, above.
[91] See *Grovewood Holdings plc v James Capel & Co. Ltd* [1995] B.C.C. 760. A liquidator can sell a bare cause of action on terms providing for the division of recoveries (*ibid.*) and the validity of the assignment is not impaired by the fact that its purpose was to enable the litigation to be conducted with the benefit of Legal Aid: *Norglen Ltd v Reeds Rains Prudential Ltd* [1998] B.C.C. 44, HL.

period on the ground that the company's property could not then be sold except on ruinous terms but granted power to carry on for six weeks while the property was advertised for sale. However, in *McIntyre, Petitioner* (1893) 30 S.L.R. 386 (O.H.) power was granted to carry on business until the time of the year when the company's property, which consisted of a hall let for public entertainments, could be sold to best advantage.

When a liquidator carries on the business of the company he does so as the company's agent[92] and is not personally liable on contracts which he enters into as liquidator.[93]

    (c) To pay any classes of creditors in full.

    (d) To make any compromise or arrangement with creditors.[94]

    (e) To compromise all calls and liabilities to calls and other debts and liabilities.

If a liquidator does any of the acts listed without the necessary sanction of the court or the liquidation committee he is personally liable although the court may retrospectively sanction such an act.[95]

(2) On his own responsibility and *without obtaining any sanction,* the liquidator can;

    (a) Sell the property of the company.[96]

    (b) Do all acts and execute, in the name and on behalf of the company, all deeds and documents, and use the company's seal therefor.

    (c) Prove, rank and claim in the bankruptcy, insolvency or sequestration of any contributory.

    (d) Draw, accept, make and indorse any bill of exchange or promissory note in the name and on behalf of the company.

    (e) Raise money on the security of the company's assets.

    (f) Take out letters of administration to any deceased contributory and do any other act necessary for obtaining payment of money due from a contributory or his estate.

    (g) Appoint an agent to do business which he cannot do himself.

    (h) Do all such other things as are necessary for winding up the affairs of the company and distributing its assets.

---

[92] See *Smith v Lord Advocate*, 1978 S.C. 259.

[93] *Stead, Hazel & Co. v Cooper* [1933] 1 K.B. 840; *Stewart v Engel* [2000] B.C.C. 741.

[94] This was held, in *Taylor, Noter*, 1993 S.L.T. 375, to extend to entering into a compromise with the trustee on the sequestrated estate of a director where the director's own assets and those of his two companies were so confused that it was impossible to identify the assets of each.

[95] *Re Associated Travel Leisure and Services Ltd (in Liquidation)* [1978] 1 W.L.R. 547.

[96] This includes a bare cause of action (*Norglen Ltd v Reeds Rains Prudential Ltd, supra*) but not the fruits of wrongful or fraudulent trading litigation under ss 213 and 214: *Re Oasis Merchandising Services Ltd* [1997] B.C.C. 282, CA.

The exercise of these powers is subject to the control of the court and any creditor or contributory[97] may apply to the court with respect to such exercise: s.167(3). If, in England, any person is aggrieved by any act or decision of the liquidator, that person may apply to the court, which may make such order as it thinks just: s.168(5).

The liquidator assigned the company's cause of action to V for £7,000 plus 10 per cent of the proceeds of the action without considering whether others would have made a higher offer. *Held:* The liquidator's act was utterly unreasonable and absurd and the assignment should be set aside. *Re Edennote Ltd* [1996] B.C.C. 718, CA.]

Aside from creditors and contributories, persons who may apply to the court under this section are restricted to those directly affected by the exercise of a specific power: *Mahomed v Morris (No. 2)* [2001] B.C.C. 233.

In England, the liquidator may apply to the court for directions in relation to any particular matter arising under the winding up: s.168(3). The right should be exercised in every case of serious doubt or difficulty in relation to the performance by the liquidator of his statutory duties.The omission to exercise it may lead the liquidator into serious liabilities.[98]

Subject to the various statutory provisions the liquidator may use his own discretion as to the management and distribution of the company's assets: s.168(4).

In Scotland, the liquidator has (subject to the rules) the same powers as a trustee on a bankrupt estate: s.169(2).

Liability

A liquidator is not strictly speaking a trustee for the individual creditors or contributories, his position being that of agent of the company.

During a liquidation a claim was made by a contributory for damages for delay in handing over to the contributory his proportion of the surplus assets of the company. *Held,* in the absence of fraud, bad faith or personal misconduct, an action for damages would not lie against the liquidator at the suit of a creditor or contributory, the proper remedy being an application to the court to control the liquidator in the exercise of his powers: *Knowles v Scott* [1891] 1 Ch. 717.[99]

On the other hand, for breach of any of his statutory duties the liquidator will be liable in damages to a creditor or contributory for injury caused to them.

A liquidator distributed the assets of the company without paying X, a creditor, who had no notice of the liquidation. The books of the company showed X to be a creditor but

---

[97] With a prospect of substantial return: *Re Greenhaven Motors Ltd* [1997] B.C.C. 547.

[98] See *Re Windsor Steam Coal Co. (1901) Ltd* [1929] 1 Ch. 151, and *Re Home and Colonial Insurance Co. Ltd* [1930] 1 Ch. 102, *post.* The opinion was expressed in *Ross v Smith*, 1986 S.L.T. (Sh. Ct.) 59, that the liquidator in Scotland was entitled to seek directions from the court in appropriate circumstances. The test to be applied was the same as that which applied to applications to the court by a liquidator in a voluntary winding up, *i.e.* the court had to be satisfied that the determination of the question would be "just and beneficial".

[99] *cf. Liquidator of Upper Clyde Shipbuilders Ltd*, 1975 S.L.T. 39 (O.H.), *per* Lord Grieve (Ordinary), p.40.

the liquidator made no attempt to communicate with X beyond issuing an insufficient advertisement for creditors.The company was dissolved. *Held*, the liquidator was liable in damages to X. The duty of the liquidator was not merely to advertise for creditors but to write to those of whom he knew and who did not send in claims: *Pulsford v Devenish* [1903] 2 Ch. 625.

A liquidator should make provision for contingent claims of which he has notice, *e.g.* where the company, having assigned a lease, remains liable for the rent,[1] or where he knows of possible claims by workmen for injuries not covered by insurance.[2]

If a liquidator applies the company's assets in paying a doubtful claim, which turns out to be unfounded, without taking proper legal advice or applying to the court for directions, he will be liable to refund the amount paid on a misfeasance summons taken out by a creditor or contributory.[3]

A liquidator, however, is not liable for admitting a proof of debt which is ill-founded, provided he exercises all due care beforehand. But a "high standard of care and diligence is required from a liquidator in a . . . winding up. He is of course paid for his services; he is able to obtain wherever it is expedient the assistance of solicitors and counsel; and, which is a most important consideration, he is entitled, in every serious case of doubt or difficulty . . . to submit the matter to the Court and to obtain its guidance".[4]

H Co. made a reinsurance agreement with L Co. which was invalid. On H going into liquidation, L tendered a proof which the liquidator ultimately accepted for £89,100, on which £38,000 was paid to L in dividends.On learning that he should have disallowed the claim, the liquidator sued L but the claim was dismissed, as no mistake of fact on the part of the liquidator was made. A creditor took out a misfeasance summons.*Held*, the liquidator was negligent in admitting so large a proof without taking legal advice or applying for directions, and was liable to pay compensation to the company: *Re Home and Colonial Insurance Co. Ltd* [1930] 1 Ch. 102.

Where a liquidator has paid money to shareholders under an error in law, caused, *e.g.* by an underestimation of tax liability, he is not entitled to recover it under the *condictio indebiti*, there being no special relationship between the liquidator and the shareholders such as to take the situation outside the general rule.[5]

Release (England)

When a liquidator ceases to hold office, the question is whether and when he can be released from his obligations. If the liquidator is the official receiver he can be

---

[1] *James Smith & Sons (Norwood) Ltd v Goodman* [1936] Ch. 216, CA; *cf. Lord Elphinstone v Monkland Iron etc. Co. Ltd* (1886) 13 R. HL 98. See now Landlord and Tenant (Covenants) Act 1995.

[2] *Re Armstrong Whitworth Securities Co. Ltd* [1947] Ch. 673.

[3] *Re Windsor Steam Coal Co. (1901) Ltd* [1929] 1 Ch. 151, CA; where the court refused to grant him relief under s.61 of the Trustee Act 1925 (s.32 Trusts (Scotland) Act 1921).

[4] *per* Maugham J. in *Re Home and Colonial Insurance Co. Ltd* [1930] 1 Ch. 102 at p. 125. In *Macrae v Henderson,* 1989 S.L.T. 523 (O.H.), the question was whether the liquidator owed a duty to guarantors or cautioners to take reasonable care in realising assets to maximum advantage. *Held,* the liquidator did owe the duty, but on the evidence the offer which the liquidator had refused was not a reasonable one, and the liquidator was assoilzied.

[5] *Taylor v Wilson's Trustees,* 1975 S.C. 146.

released either by notifying the Secretary of State that the winding up is for all practical purposes complete or, if he is replaced by another liquidator, on giving notice to the court that he has been so replaced. If he is replaced by a liquidator appointed by the court, it is for the court to determine his release: s.174(2)(3).

If the liquidator is someone other than the official receiver his release takes effect as follows:

(a) if he was removed by the creditors' meeting which did not resolve against his release, or if he has died, at the time when notice of removal or death is given to the court;

(b) if the creditors' meeting voted against his release but removed him from office, or he ceases to be a qualified insolvency practitioner he must apply to the Secretary of State for his release;

(c) on resignation his release is governed by the rules[6];

(d) if he has vacated office having called the final meeting of creditors he is released at that time unless the meeting votes to the contrary, in which case (b) applies: s.174(4).

The effect of a release is to discharge the liquidator from all liability in respect of his acts or omissions as such: s.174(6).

Release (Scotland)

Section 174 applies to Scotland with the following modifications:

(a) the provisions relating to the official receiver have no application;

(b) for references to the Secretary of State substitute references to the Accountant of Court: s.174(7).

WINDING UP OF UNREGISTERED COMPANIES

Section 221(5) provides that an unregistered company may be wound up by the court[7] if:

(i) it is dissolved, or has ceased business, or is carrying on business only for the purpose of winding up its affairs; or

(ii) it is unable to pay its debts[8]; or

(iii) the court is of the opinion that it is just and equitable that the company should be wound up.

---

[6] I.R. 1986, r. 4.121. For Scotland, see I.(S.)R., rr 4.29 and 4.30.
[7] Such a company cannot be wound up voluntarily: I.A. 1986, s.221(4). For a petition by a member of an incorporated association for the appointment of a judicial factor, see *Munro v Edinburgh District Trades Council Social Club*, 1989 G.W.D. 6–240 (O.H.).
[8] This will be deemed in the circumstances set out in ss 222–224.

The expression "unregistered company" includes any association or company[9] with the exception of a company registered in any part of the UK under the Joint Stock Companies Acts or under legislation (past or present) relating to companies in Great Britain (s.220(1)). Examples include companies incorporated by special Act or Royal Charter and certain foreign companies.[10] Investment Companies with Variable Capital[11] and an European Economic Interest Group may also be wound up under these provisions.[12]

Section 227 extends s.126[13] (stay of proceedings against company) to proceedings against a contributory where the application to stay is by a creditor, and s.228 provides that where an order has been made for winding up an unregistered company, no action or proceeding shall be proceeded with or commenced against any contributory of the company in respect of any debt of the company, except by leave of the court.

The provisions of Pt V of the Act (ss 220 to 229) with respect to unregistered companies are in addition to and not in restriction of the provisions with respect to the winding up of companies by the court, and the court or liquidator has the same powers in the case of unregistered companies as in the case of the winding up of companies formed and registered under the Act: s.229.

---

[9] While these words are very wide, they do not include an association which Parliament could not reasonably have intended should be subject to the winding-up process: *Re International Tin Council* [1988] 3 All E.R. 257, 361 C.A. approving *Re St. James Club* (1852) 2 D & GM & G 383; see also *Re Witney Town Football & Social Club* [1993] B.C.C. 874. The word "company" includes those incorporated elsewhere than in Great Britain: *Re Normandy Marketing Ltd* [1993] B.C.C. 879 (Northern Ireland). A limited partnership was included in the definition of an unregistered company in s.665 of the 1985 Act but was removed by the Insolvency Act 1985 and the Bankruptcy (Scotland) Act 1985; as the 1986 Act was a consolidating Act which was not intended to alter the existing law, a limited partnership was not an unregistered company which could be wound up under s.220: *Smith v Smith*, 1998 G.W.D. 26–1341.

[10] See *Palmer's Company Law*, Vol. 3, 15.222.

[11] See Open-Ended Investment Companies (Investment Companies with Variable Capital) Regs 1996 (SI 1996/2827), regs 25–27.

[12] E.C. Council Regulations EEIG, reg. 2137/85, O.J. 1985 L199/1, Art. 35.2.

[13] Above, p.594.

Chapter 28

VOLUNTARY WINDING UP

[*N.B. All references in this chapter are to the Insolvency Act 1986 unless otherwise stated.*]

FROM the point of view of the company itself, a voluntary winding up has many advantages over a compulsory winding up, the chief being that there are not so many formalities to be complied with. In consequence the great majority of liquidations are voluntary liquidations. The Cork Committee, however, made several recommendations to prevent abuses in the system of voluntary liquidation and some of these were adopted by the Insolvency Act 1985, since consolidated into the Insolvency Act 1986.

Initiation of voluntary winding up

S.84 provides that a company may be wound up voluntarily:

(1) When the period, if any, fixed for its duration by the articles expires, or the event, if any, occurs, on the occurrence of which the articles provide that it is to be dissolved, and the company in general meeting passes a resolution (*i.e.* an *ordinary resolution*) to be wound up voluntarily.

(2) If it resolves by *special resolution*[1] to be wound up voluntarily.

A company can be wound up by special resolution without any reason being assigned.

(3) If the company resolves by *extraordinary resolution* that it cannot by reason of its liabilities continue its business and that it is advisable to wind up.

An extraordinary resolution is allowed here because time is of the essence since the company is insolvent and a special resolution would normally require a longer period of notice.[2]

Before any resolution is passed for voluntary winding up, the company must give notice of the resolution to the holder of a qualifying floating charge[3] to

---

[1] Above, p.259. In the case of a company registered as a social landlord under the Housing Act 1996, such a resolution has no effect unless the Housing Corporation gives its prior consent: see Housing Act 1996. Sch.1, para.13(6).
[2] Above, p.259.
[3] For the meaning of qualifying floating charge, see Sch.B1, para.14.

which s.72A applies: s.84(2A). This is to allow the holder of such a charge to appoint an administrator[4] under para.14 of Sch.B1 if he sees fit. Once notice has been given, no resolution for voluntary winding up may be passed unless the qualifying floating charge holder consents or until after five business days have elapsed without the appointment of an administrator having been made.

A resolution for voluntary winding up must be advertised in the *Gazette* within 14 days after it is passed: s.85.[5] In Scotland, where failure to make timeous advertisement was due to inadvertence and no prejudice had been suffered as a result of the failure, the Court of Session, in the exercise of its *nobile officium,* authorised the liquidator to make a belated advertisement, the expenses of the proceedings to be borne by the liquidator personally.[6]

A voluntary winding up commences at the time of the passing of the resolution: s.86.

Kinds of voluntary winding up

A voluntary winding up may be either (1) a members' voluntary winding up; or (2) a creditors' voluntary winding up: s.90.

MEMBERS' VOLUNTARY WINDING UP

A members' voluntary winding up takes place only when the company is solvent. It is entirely managed by the members, and the liquidator is appointed by them. No meeting of creditors is held and no liquidation committee is appointed. To obtain the benefit of this form of winding up, a declaration of solvency must be filed: s.89.

Declaration of solvency

This is a statutory declaration made by the directors or, if there are more than two of them, by the majority, at a board meeting, that they have made a full inquiry into the company's affairs and, having done so, they have formed the opinion that the company will be able to pay its debts in full together with interest at the official rate[7] within a specified period not exceeding 12 months from the commencement of the winding up.[8] The declaration has no effect unless it is made within the five weeks immediately preceding the date of the passing of the winding-up resolution. It may even be made on that date providing that it precedes the resolution.

The declaration must be filed with the Registrar within 15 days of the passing of the resolution. Further, the declaration has no effect unless it embodies a statement of the company's assets and liabilities as at the latest practicable date before it is made: s.89. If there is something which can reasonably be described as

---

[4] See, generally, Ch.26, above.
[5] A copy must be forwarded to the Registrar of Companies within 15 days.
[6] *Liquidator of Nairn Public Hall Co. Ltd, Petitioner*, 1946 S.C. 395.
[7] See s.251.
[8] See above.

"a statement of the company's assets and liabilities," then, even if it subsequently appears that there were errors and omissions, these will not prevent it from being a statement within s.89.[9]

A director making a declaration of solvency without reasonable grounds is liable to imprisonment or a fine or both.[10] If the debts plus interest are not paid or provided for within the period stated, he is presumed not to have had reasonable grounds: s.89(5).

If a declaration is made in accordance with the section the winding up is a members' voluntary winding up: s.90.

The liquidator

Unlike the liquidator in a winding up by the court, a liquidator in a voluntary winding up is not an officer of the court.[11] He is the agent of the company, but not of the individual members.[12] He is appointed, by the company in general meeting (s.91), and within 14 days he must give notice of his appointment to the registrar of companies and publish it in the *Gazette*: s.109.[13] He may be appointed at the meeting at which the resolution for voluntary winding up is passed. If there is no liquidator acting, the court may appoint one. The court may also, on cause shown, remove a liquidator and appoint another: s.108[14] Where a person had been appointed liquidator without his knowledge and he declined to act, it was held that the appointment was invalid and there was therefore no need to remove him.[15] Anyone subject to a disqualification order under the Company Directors Disqualification Act 1986 cannot act as a liquidator.[16] The liquidator is also an office holder under the Insolvency Act.[17] He must be a qualified insolvency practitioner[18] and has the powers and duties of an office holder.

If a liquidator appointed by the company vacates office, whether by death, resignation or otherwise, the company at a general meeting, summoned by any contributory or by a continuing liquidator, may, subject to any arrangement with creditors, fill the vacancy: s.92.

In the period before the appointment of a liquidator the directors cannot exercise their powers without the sanction of the court, except to dispose of perishable goods or goods which are likely to fall in value if not disposed of immediately and to do anything necessary for the protection of the company's assets: s.114. This provision was introduced following a recommendation of the Cork Committee to prevent dissipation of the company's assets prior to the

---

[9] *De Courcy v Clement* [1971] Ch. 693.
[10] See Sch.10.
[11] *per* Megarry J. in *Re Rolls Razor Ltd (No. 2)* [1970] Ch. 576, 586.
[12] See *Taylor v Wilson's Trustees*, 1975 S.C. 146.
[13] This provision applies to all voluntary liquidations. The powers of the directors cease unless the general meeting or the liquidator sanction their continuance: see s.91(2).
[14] This provision applies to all voluntary liquidations.
[15] *Liquidator of Highland etc. Dairy Farms Ltd and Another, Petitioners*, 1964 S.C. 1.
[16] Above, p.321.
[17] Above, p.613.
[18] Above, p.533.

appointment of a liquidator. Failure to comply with s.114 is a criminal offence[19] on the part of the directors and transactions effected are invalid.[20]

A special manager may also be appointed under s.177.[21]

Vacation of office by or removal of a liquidator

Being an office holder, a liquidator must vacate office if he ceases to be a qualified insolvency practitioner.[22] He may resign in accordance with the rules.[23] He vacates office on giving notice to the Registrar of the final meetings held under s.94.[24]

He may be removed at any time by a general meeting of the company summoned for that purpose or by the court. If the liquidator has been appointed by the court (*e.g.* to fill a vacancy) he may be removed and replaced by a meeting of members holding not less than one half of the total voting rights, or by a general meeting of the company summoned by the liquidator or the court: s.171.

Release of a liquidator

The liquidator is released at the time of the final meeting. If he has been removed from office by a general meeting of the company his release operates from the date at which notice was given to the Registrar in accordance with the rules. If he has been removed by the court he must apply to the Secretary of State for his release. If the liquidator has resigned he is released in accordance with the rules: s.173[25] Such a release absolves him from all liability in relation to the winding up except for proceedings against him under s.212.[26]

Conduct of liquidation

Subject to s.96,[27] within three months after the end of the first and every succeeding year of the liquidation, the liquidator must summon a general meeting of the company and lay before it an account of his acts and dealings and of the conduct of the winding up during the preceding year: s.93.

As soon as the affairs of the company are fully wound up the liquidator must call a general meeting of the company. This is done by advertisement in the *Gazette* at least one month before the meeting. At the meeting the liquidator must present an account of the winding up, showing how the winding up has

---

[19] s.114(4).
[20] *Re A Company (No. 006341 of 1992), ex p. B Ltd* [1994] B.C.L.C. 225. Where a third party deals in good faith with the directors, in circumstances where he does not, and could not be expected to, know of the limitation on the directors' authority (as where the resolution to wind up has been neither registered nor advertised) the transaction may be binding on the company by virtue of ostensible authority. Judge Paul Baker, QC *ibid.*
[21] Above, p.600.
[22] Above, p.533.
[23] I.R. 1986, r.4.142; I.(S.)R., r.4.28.
[24] Below.
[25] I.R. 1986, r.4.144; I.(S.)R. 1986, r.4.28A (inserted by Sch.2).
[26] *ibid.*
[27] Above, p.616.

been conducted and how the company's property has been disposed of. A copy of this account, together with a return of the holding of meeting, must be sent to the Registrar within a week after the meeting: s.94. It is not necessary for the affairs of the company to be fully wound up before the liquidator can validly make his return, only that they should be fully wound up so far as the liquidator is aware.[28]

If a quorum is not present at the final meeting, the liquidator must make a return that the meeting was summoned but no quorum was present, and this has the same effect as a return of the holding of the meeting: s.94(5).

The Registrar must publish in the *Gazette* notice of the receipt of the return (Companies Act 1985, s.711).

Effect of insolvency on a members' voluntary winding up

If the liquidator is of the opinion that the company will in fact be unable to pay its debts in full (including interest) within the time specified by the directors in their declaration of solvency he must call a creditors' meeting within 28 days, giving them at least seven days' notice by post and advertising it in the *Gazette* and two local newspapers.[29] He must also supply the creditors with any information they might reasonably require in that period: s.95(1), (2).

The liquidator must lay before the meeting a statement of affairs set out in accordance with the rules,[30] showing, in particular, the company's assets, debts and liabilities, its creditors and their securities, together with the dates on which they were created: s.95(3), (4).

The effect of holding such a meeting is that the winding up proceeds as if the declaration of solvency had never been made; *i.e.* as a creditors' voluntary winding up: s.96.

CREDITORS' VOLUNTARY WINDING UP

If no declaration of solvency is filed with the Registrar, a voluntary winding up is a creditors' voluntary winding up: s.90.

In such a case the company must summon a meeting of creditors[31] for a date not later than 14 days after the passing of the resolution to wind up the company. Notices of the meeting must be sent to the creditors at least seven days before the meeting. Notice of the meeting must also be advertised in the *Gazette* and two local newspapers.[32] The notice must also state either the name and address of a person qualified to act as an insolvency practitioner in relation to the company who will provide such information as the creditors may reasonably request prior to the meeting or a place in the locality where on two business days prior to the meeting a list of the creditors' names and addresses will be available free of charge: s.98.

---

[28] *Re Cornish Manures Ltd* [1967] 1 W.L.R. 807.
[29] *i.e.* within the location of its principal place of business during the preceding six months.
[30] I.R. 1986, r.4.34—CVL; I.(S.)R. 1986, r.4.7 as substituted by Sch.1.
[31] If the winding up has been converted to a creditors' winding up the creditors' meeting making such a decision under s.95, above, is the creditors' meeting for this purpose: s.102.
[32] See n.27 above.

Management of such a winding up is shared by the members and creditors but in all cases the creditors have the ultimate control by virtue of the following provisions.

Meeting of creditors

The meeting of creditors is presided over by one of the directors nominated for that purpose by the directors: s.99. The business of the meeting is:

(1) To receive a full statement by the directors as to the company's affairs, together with a list of the creditors, and details of any securities and other information required by the rules[33]: s.99.

(2) To appoint a liquidator: s.100, below.

(3) To appoint a liquidation committee: s.101, below.

The liquidator

The creditors and the company at their respective meetings may nominate a liquidator and, if different persons are nominated, the person nominated by the creditors is the liquidator, subject to any order made by the court. If the creditors make no nomination the company's nominee is the liquidator. If different persons are nominated, any director, member or creditor of the company may, within seven days after the creditors' nomination, apply to the court for an order that the company's nominee be liquidator instead of or jointly with the creditors' nominee, or that some other person be liquidator: s.100. A liquidator appointed under this section is not an officer of the court: *Re T H Knitwear (Wholesale) Ltd* [1988] Ch.275.

Under this system of appointing a liquidator it is still possible for the company to appoint a liquidator elect for the 14 days before a creditors' meeting is required to be held. Prior to the Insolvency Act it was possible to delay the creditors' meeting for several weeks because of the decision in *Re Centrebind Ltd*[34] to the effect that whilst failure to call the meeting was a criminal offence, it did not invalidate the appointment of the nominated liquidator or his actions. This abuse, known as "centre-binding", whereby the company's assets were in fact unprotected and beyond the creditors' control, has been countered by many provisions, following recommendations of the Cork Committee.[35] These include the requirement that any liquidator be a qualified insolvency practitioner,[36] that until any liquidator is appointed the directors' powers are subject to the court's control[37] and the 14 day time limit within which the creditors' meeting must now be held.[38]

---

[33] I.R. 1986, r.4.34—CVL; I.(S.)R. 1986, r.7.30 and Sch.5.
[34] [1967] 1 W.L.R. 377.
[35] Paras 667–673.
[36] Above, p.533.
[37] s.114.
[38] Below.

In addition where the company nominates a liquidator prior to the creditors' meeting his powers can only be exercised with the court's consent. He may, however, assume custody of the company's property, dispose of perishable goods and those likely to diminish in value unless disposed of, and protect the company's assets. He must attend the creditors' meeting and report to that meeting on the exercise of any of his powers in the meantime. He is also charged with the duty to apply to the court if the company or the directors fail to comply with the requirement *vis-à-vis* the creditors' meeting: s.166. This effectively prevents "centre-binding" since any liquidator acting in default can be fined and will be liable under s.212.[39]

Any vacancy, by reason of death, resignation or otherwise, in the office of a liquidator, other than a liquidator appointed by the court may be filled by the creditors: s.104.

A liquidator may vacate office by removal and be released from liability in the same way as a liquidator in a members' voluntary winding up, except that the function of the members' meetings are carried out by a meeting of creditors: ss 171, 173, above.[40]

Liquidation committee

The creditors, at their first or any subsequent meeting, may appoint a liquidation committee of not more than five persons to act with the liquidator.[41] If they do so, the company in general meeting may appoint not more than five persons to act as members of the committee, but the creditors may resolve that these persons ought not to be members of the committee, and thereupon, unless the court otherwise directs, they cannot act on the committee: s.101.

Conduct of liquidation

Within three months after the end of the first and every succeeding year of the liquidation the liquidator must summon a general meeting of the company and a meeting of creditors, and lay before the meetings an account of his acts and dealings and of the conduct of the winding up during the preceding year: s.105.

When the liquidation is complete, the liquidator must, by at least one month's notice in the *Gazette,* call final meetings of the company and the creditors, and present his account. Within a week after these meetings, a copy of the account and a return of the holding of the meetings or a return that no quorum was present thereat must be filed with the Registrar, who must publish it in the *Gazette* (Companies Act 1985, s.711).

CONSEQUENCES OF ANY VOLUNTARY WINDING UP

The commencement of a voluntary winding up is the date of the passing of the resolution for voluntary winding up: s.86. Even if the company is subsequently

[39] Above, p.320.
[40] p.625.
[41] Below, p.631.

wound up by the court, the commencement of the winding up is the date of the passing of the resolution: s.129.

The consequences of a voluntary winding up are:

(1) As from the commencement of the winding up the company must cease to carry on business except so far as is required for its beneficial winding up, although the corporate state and powers continue until the company is dissolved: s.87. Notification that the company is in liquidation must be given on the company's documents on which its name appears: s.188.[42]

(2) No transfer of shares can be made without the sanction of the liquidator and any alteration in the status of the members is void: s.88. A transfer of debentures can, however, be made.[43]

(3) On the appointment of a liquidator the powers of the directors cease except so far as the company in general meeting or the liquidator (in a members' voluntary winding up), or the liquidation committee or, if there is no such committee, the creditors (in a creditors' voluntary winding up), sanction their continuance: ss 91(2) and 103.

A voluntary winding up does not automatically operate as a discharge of the company's employees.[44] However, the liquidator has power to terminate contracts of employment and may do so by his conduct.[45] The liquidator may equally continue the employment of the company's employees if required to ensure a more beneficial winding up of the company.[46]

In England there is no statutory provision for the stay of actions and other proceedings against the company in the case of a voluntary winding up (*cf.* ss 126, 128, 130, above[47]), but on an application under s.112, below,[48] the court has a discretion to stay proceedings.[49] Executions will usually be stayed when it is necessary to ensure the distribution of assets among the creditors *pari passu*,[50] but actions will not be stayed when there is a dispute as to liability, or when no advantage will be gained, *e.g.* no expense will be saved, by a stay.[51]

In Scotland, the provision now in s.112 had been interpreted as not giving the court power to stay proceedings against the company,[52] and s.113 provides that, on the application of the liquidator of a Scottish company, the court may direct that no action or proceeding shall be proceeded with against the company except

---

[42] Above, p.598.
[43] *Re Goy & Co. Ltd* [1900] 2 Ch. 149.
[44] Compare a winding up by the court; above, p.597.
[45] *Fowler v Commercial Timber Co. Ltd* [1930] 2 K.B. 1, CA. See generally *Totty & Moss*, Vol. 2, H. 15.04.
[46] *cf. Day v Tait* (1900) 8 S.L.T. 40 (O.H.).
[47] Ch.27, pp.597, 599.
[48] p.631.
[49] *Currie v Consolidated Kent Collieries Corpn. Ltd* [1906] 1 K.B. 134, CA.
[50] *Anglo-Baltic Bank v Barber & Co.* [1924] 2 K.B. 410, CA.
[51] *Cook v "X" Chair Patents Co. Ltd* [1960] 1 W.L.R. 60.
[52] *Sdeuard v Gardner* (1876) 3 R. 577.

by leave of the court. Section 185 (relating to diligence in Scotland)[53] applies to voluntary, as well as to compulsory, winding up.

Distribution of the Property of the Company in a Voluntary Winding-Up

The costs, charges and expenses properly incurred in a voluntary winding up, including the remuneration of the liquidator, are payable in priority to all other claims: s.115. The pre-liquidation expenses of a person who expected to be liquidator but was not, in the event, appointed, can be paid but only in so far as they were incurred to enable the company to pass the winding-up resolution. Expense incurred in collecting the assets was not recoverable: *Re Sandwell Copiers*.[54] The liquidator must then apply the property[55] of the company first in paying the preferential debts[56] and then in discharging the liabilities of the company *pari passu*. The liquidator has a duty to inquire into all claims against the company.[57] Even where the company is solvent, statute-barred debts cannot be paid unless the contributories consent.[58] Any surplus must then be distributed amongst the members according to their rights and interests in the company: I.A. 1986, s.107. A distribution which fails to take a creditor's claim into account exposes the liquidator to liability for breach of statutory duty.[59]

Provision may be made for employees on the cessation of business if it is approved by the members or otherwise in accordance with the articles either before or during the liquidation. Such payment must be made out of the assets available to the members: Companies Act 1985, s.719. Any exercise of this power is not subject to s.107: s.187.

A contracting out of the provisions of s.107 is contrary to public policy.[60] Section 107 does not, however, affect contracts which bona fide deprive the company of ownership prior to the winding up, *e.g.* the creation of a trust fund.[61] Such contracts may, however, be invalid under alternative provisions.[62]

---

[53] Above, p.609.
[54] [1988] B.C.L.C. 209.
[55] Below, Ch.29.
[56] See s.175, below, p.647.
[57] *Austin Securities Ltd v Northgate and English Stores Ltd* [1969] 1 W.L.R. 529 CA applying *Pulsford v Devenish* and *Re Armstrong Whitworth Securities Co. Ltd.* See also *Royton Industries Ltd v Lawrence* (1994) *The Independent*, February 28, 1994 (rent liability on a lease which the company has assigned).
[58] *Re Art Reproduction Co. Ltd* [1952] Ch. 89. The Scottish equivalent of "statute-barred" is "prescribed."
[59] *AMF International Ltd v Ellis* [1995] B.C.C. 439; [1996] B.C.C. 335.
[60] *British Eagle International Air Lines Ltd v Compagnie Nationale Air France* [1975] 1 W.L.R. 758, HL, where the rules of the general liquidation prevailed over the International Air Transport Association clearing house arrangements and, despite such arrangements, the plaintiff company was entitled to recover the sums payable to it by other airlines for services rendered by it and not cleared through the I.A.T.A. system and vice versa. See also *Money Markets International Stockbrokers Ltd (In Liquidation) v London Stock Exchange Ltd* [2002] 1 W.L.R. 1150; *Fraser v Oystertec plc* [2004] B.C.C. 233.
[61] *Carreras Rothmans Ltd v Freeman Matthews Treasure Ltd* [1985] Ch. 207.
[62] Below, Ch.29.

Powers and Duties of the Liquidator in a Voluntary Winding-Up

In every voluntary winding up it is the duty of the liquidator to pay the debts of the company and adjust the rights of the contributories among themselves.[63]

To enable him to do this, s.165[64] and Sch.4 provide that he may *without sanction*:

(1)   commence or defend legal proceedings on behalf of the company;

(2)   carry on the company's business so far as it is beneficial for the winding up;

He may carry on the business of the company, if he reasonably thinks it is necessary for the beneficial winding up of the company. If he does so, those to whom he incurs obligations are entitled to be paid in priority to the creditors at the commencement of the winding up: *Re Great Eastern Electric Co. Ltd* [1941] Ch. 241.[65]

(3)   exercise all the general powers of a liquidator listed in Pt III of Sch.4, I.A 1986.

In a members' voluntary winding up, *with the sanction* of an extraordinary resolution of the company, and in a creditors' voluntary winding up, *with the sanction* of the court or the liquidation committee or (if there is no such committee) a meeting of the creditors, the liquidator may:

(1)   pay any classes of creditors in full;

(2)   make any compromise or arrangement with creditors;

(3)   compromise all calls and liabilities to calls and other debts and liabilities: s.165, Sch.4.

Power to apply to court

In a voluntary winding up the liquidator, or any contributory or creditor, may apply to the court to determine any question arising in the winding up or to exercise any of the powers which the court could exercise if the company were being wound up by the court: s.112.[66] This gives the liquidator in a voluntary winding up the same right to the guidance of the court as in a compulsory

---

[63] The duty to pay the company's debts is a fiduciary one and the liquidator of a Scottish company, no matter where he resides, can be called to account before the Court of Session; his duty continues despite the dissolution of the company, and the jurisdiction of the court is not brought to an end by dissolution: *Lamey v Winram*, 1987 S.L.T. 635 (O.H.).

[64] Subject to s.166.

[65] *cf. Day v Tait* (1900) 8 S.L.T. 40 (O.H.).

[66] For examples of applications under s.112, see *Liquidators of North British Locomotive Co. Ltd v Lord Advocate*, 1963 S.C. 272 (O.H.), *Smith and Another, Petitioners*, 1969 S.L.T. (Notes) 94 (O.H.) (as to exercise of directors' discretionary powers under pension scheme) and *Liquidators of Highland Engineering Ltd v Thomson*, 1972 S.C. 87 (O.H.) (as to provisional liquidator's right to retain funds to pay his remuneration and expenses).

liquidation. For example, in England, if he is of opinion that fraud has been committed in the formation or promotion of the company or in relation to the company since its formation, he can obtain an order of the court for the public examination[67] of any promoter, director or other officer of the company concerned. Again, he can apply for an order for private examination.[68]

In 1971, a company went into voluntary liquidation. In 1976, it became apparent that it might be liable for claims in tort for negligence during its operations. In 1979, after the liquidators had started preparing the final accounts, solicitors warned the liquidators of the possible claims. The liquidators applied for an order that they should distribute the final dividend to the members without regard to the claims on the basis of delay. Alternatively they sought an order that the claimants should bear the costs of the delay in distribution. Megarry V.-C. held that the test was whether in all the circumstances it was just to make either of the orders sought. Default or lack of diligence by either party was relevant and the court was less likely to facilitate a distribution among the members than among the creditors. In the circumstances, both orders would be refused: *Re R-R Realisations Ltd* [1980] 1 All E.R. 1019.

Duty to report criminal offences

If the liquidator thinks that any past or present officer, or any member, of the company has committed a criminal offence in relation to the company, he must report the matter, in an English winding up, to the Director of Public Prosecutions, and in a Scottish winding up, to the Lord Advocate. The matter may then be referred to the Department of Trade and Industry, who have the same powers of investigating the company's affairs as in an investigation into the affairs of a company under ss 431 or 432 of the Companies Act 1985: s.218.

COMPULSORY LIQUIDATION AFTER COMMENCEMENT OF VOLUNTARY LIQUIDATION

A voluntary liquidation does not bar the right of any creditor or contributory to have the company wound up by the court: s.116. A creditor of a company in voluntary liquidation is not entitled *ex debito justitiae* as between himself and the company to a compulsory winding-up order and the views of the contributories must be taken into consideration,[69] unless the company is insolvent.[70] Even in such a case it had been said that the court will require reasons as to why the voluntary winding up is inappropriate: it is not inappropriate merely because the petitioner would prefer a different liquidator.[71] However, more recently it has been stated that a compulsory order should be made wherever the creditors would otherwise be left with a justifiable feeling of grievance that they had been prevented from having the company's affairs investigated by a liquidator who was

---

[67] *Re Campbell Coverings Ltd (No. 2)* [1954] Ch. 225 and see above p.601 (Public Examination of Officers) and p.604 (Private Examination).
[68] As in *Re Rolls Razor Ltd (No. 2)* [1970] Ch. 576. Despite the wording of s.112(1), it seems that a creditor cannot apply: *Re James McHale Automobiles Ltd* [1997] B.C.C. 202.
[69] *Re Surplus Properties (Huddersfield) Ltd* [1984] B.C.L.C. 89.
[70] *ibid.*, *Re James Millward & Co. Ltd* [1940] Ch. 333, CA.
[71] *Re Medisco Equipment Ltd* [1983] B.C.L.C. 305, *per* Harman J.

not appointed by the directors.[72] There is no rule that the probity or competence of the liquidator must be attacked[73] but he must not only be independent but must be seen to be independent.[74] Further, the court is bound to have regard to the wishes of all the creditors,[75] and if the majority favour the continuance of the voluntary liquidation an order will not be made unless the petitioner can show special circumstances.[76] The court can, however, examine the motives of the creditors,[77] and, in particular, of those creditors who are also members.[78] Considerations of fairness and commercial morality should also be taken into account.[79] In the case of a financial company, the wish of the regulatory authority, based upon reasonable material, to have the sort of investigation which would follow on from a compulsory winding up may outweigh factors like inconvenience and expense.[80] A contributory must satisfy the court that the rights of the contributories will be prejudiced by a voluntary winding up: s.116. What the Secretary of State must show when he is the petitioner has been dealt with already.[81]

When a voluntary winding up is superseded by a compulsory winding up, all proceedings in the voluntary winding up are deemed to have been validly taken unless the court, on proof of fraud or mistake, thinks fit to direct otherwise: s.129, above.

[72] Re M.C.H. Services [1987] B.C.L.C. 535, Vinelott J.; Re Pinstripe Farming Co. Ltd. [1996] B.C.C. 913.

[73] Re Palmer Marine Services Ltd [1986] 1 W.L.R. 573.

[74] Re Lowestoft Traffic Services Ltd [1986] B.C.L.C. 81: and see H.J. Tomkins & Son [1990] B.C.L.C. 76.

[75] Re Home Remedies Ltd [1943] Ch. 1; Re Lowestoft Traffic Services Ltd [1986] B.C.L.C. 81; cf. Pattisons Ltd v Kinnear (1899) 1 F. 551 and Elsmie & Son v The Tomatin etc. Distillery Ltd (1906) 8 F. 434.

[76] Re B. Karsberg Ltd [1956] 1 W.L.R. 57, CA; Re J.D. Swain Ltd [1965] 1 W.L.R. 909, CA; for special circumstances, see Bouboulis v Mann, Macneal & Co. Ltd, 1926 S.C. 637: and see Re H.J. Tomkins, ibid., where the court followed the wishes of creditors representing a majority in value, though not in number; Re Magnus Consultants Ltd [1995] 1 B.C.L.C. 203.

[77] Re Falcon (R.J.) Developments [1987] B.C.L.C. 437.

[78] Re Palmer Marine Surveys Ltd [1986] 1 W.L.R. 573.

[79] ibid. See also Re Gordon & Breach Science Publishers Ltd [1995] B.C.C. 261.

[80] Securities & Investments Board v Lancashire and Yorkshire Portfolio Management Ltd [1992] B.C.C. 381.

[81] Above, p.592; and see Re Pinstripe Farming, above n.70.

Chapter 29

CONTRIBUTORIES AND CREDITORS: COMPLETION OF THE WINDING UP

[N.B. References in this chapter are to sections of the Insolvency Act 1986 unless otherwise stated].

As soon as may be after a winding-up order is made, it is the duty of the liquidator in England to:

    (1)   settle a list of contributories;

    (2)   collect the company's assets and apply them in discharge of its liabilities: ss 148, 160.

   In Scotland it is for the court to settle a list of contributories and to cause the assets of the company to be collected and applied in discharge of the company's liabilities; s.148. Section 160, which provides for delegation of the court's power to the liquidator, does not apply to Scotland.

CONTRIBUTORIES

A contributory is a person liable to contribute to the assets of a company in the event of its being wound up: s.79. A fully paid-up shareholder in a company limited by shares falls within this definition.[1] Section 74 provides that on a winding up every present and past member is liable to contribute to the assets of the company to an amount sufficient for payment of its debts and liabilities, and the expenses of the winding up, and for the adjustment of the rights of the contributories among themselves. This is subject to certain qualifications, below, *e.g.* a past member is not liable to contribute if he ceased to be a member one year or more before the commencement of the winding up[2]: s.74(2)(a).

   Where a private company which has purchased or redeemed its own shares out of capital under s.173 of the Companies Act 1985 goes into liquidation within one year of such payment, and is found to be insolvent, the directors and the recipient are liable to contribute up to the amount of the payment to cover any insufficiency: s.76.[3]

---

[1] *Re Anglesea Colliery Co.* (1866) L.R. 1 Ch. App. 555, followed, *e.g.* in *Paterson v M'Farlane* (1875) 2 R. 490.

[2] Above, p.589, this qualification does not apply to the winding up of an unlimited company which has re-registered as limited, see s.77.

[3] Above, p.170. However, their liability falls outside ss 74 & 75 (s.76(5)) and they are not true contributories (s.79(3)).

The list of contributories

The list of contributories is in two parts, the A list and the B list. The A list consists of the members of the company at the commencement of the winding up, *i.e.* present members. The B list consists of persons who were members within a year before the commencement of the winding up. The B list is often not settled at all, and is never settled unless it appears that the A contributories are unable to satisfy their contributions.[4] The list must distinguish between contributories who are liable in their own right and those liable as representatives of others[5]: s.148(3).

The court may dispense with the settlement of a list of contributories where it appears that it will not be necessary to make calls on or adjust the rights of contributories: s.148(2). The distribution of surplus assets among the contributories does not of itself involve an adjustment of the rights of the contributories among themselves and therefore no list need be settled.[6] The court should not exercise its discretion to dispense with a list of contributories if the company has a large number of shares held by a large number of shareholders.[7]

Liability of contributories

The liability of a contributory in a company limited by shares[8] is qualified as follows:

(1) The liability of a contributory, whether on the A list or the B list, is limited to the amount unpaid on his shares: s.74(2)(d). Where shares are partly paid, a past member only has to contribute if the existing member has not paid up in full. Where there are several past members in the year before the winding up, all will appear on the B list but the primary liability will be on the latest transferor.[9] The fact that all debts have been paid does not necessarily absolve the holder of partly paid shares from his liability: a contribution may still be required to adjust the rights of the contributories amongst themselves.[10]

(2) B contributories are not liable to contribute in respect of any debt or liability of the company contracted *after* he ceased to be a member: s.74(2)(b).

The assets of the company, including the amount received from A contributories, are first applied *pari passu* in payment of the debts of the company, irrespective of the time when they were contracted.[11] The liability of the B

---

[4] See s.74(2)(c) IA 1986.
[5] See below.
[6] *Re Phoenix Oil, etc., Co.* [1958] Ch. 560.
[7] *Re Paragon Holdings Ltd* [1961] Ch. 346.
[8] See s.74(3) for companies limited by guarantee.
[9] *Humby's Case* (1872) 26 L.T. 936.
[10] *Re Anglesea Colliery Co.* (1866) L.R. 1 Ch. 555.
[11] *Morris' Case* (1871) L.R. 7 Ch. App. 200.

contributories is therefore further restricted, because they are liable only for such of the company's debts contracted before they ceased to be members as have not been satisfied by the distribution of the company's other assets among the creditors generally. The B contributories may therefore not be fully called upon although the creditors are not paid in full.

The liquidator made calls on the B contributories of 5p a share in 1925, and 7¹/₂p a share in 1927. The amount so realised exceeded by about £10,000 the debts of the company contracted while the B contributories were members but the total of all the calls did not suffice to pay the creditors in full. The liquidator asked to retain the full amount of the calls on the B contributories as assets available for the creditors. *Held*, he could not retain the full amount, but must return the £10,000 to the B contributories: *Re City of London Insce. Co. Ltd* [1932] 1 Ch. 226.

B contributions are part of the general assets of the company, and are not to be applied, preferentially or exclusively, to the payment of debts incurred before the B shareholders ceased to be members.[12]

    (3) B contributories are not liable to contribute unless it appears to the court that the existing members are unable to satisfy their contributions: s.74(2)(c).

Example: C and D are holders of £1 shares, 37¹/₂p. paid. C transfers his shares to X and D transfers to Y. Within a year the company is wound up, and is insolvent. X pays up his shares in full, but Y pays nothing. No contribution will be required from C. A contribution will be required from D.

A member[13] cannot claim a sum due to him in his character of member (*e.g.* by way of dividend, profits or otherwise) in competition with any other creditor not a member of the company: s.74(2)(f). A sum is so due if it arises under the statutory contract between the members and the company constituted by s.14(1) of the Companies Act 1985[14] Such debts are deferred as the price members pay for limited liability:

B & C plc purchased all the shares in A plc for £434m. Both companies later went into administration. The administrators of B & C plc brought an action against A plc for damages for negligent misrepresentation inducing the purchase. The administrator of A plc sought directions as to whether any damages recoverable by B & C plc were due to them in their character of a member of A plc. *Held*: They were not so due and should not be deferred: *Soden v British & Commonwealth Holdings plc* [1997] 4 All E.R. 353, HL.[15]

This provision has been held in Scotland not to apply to dividends which have been carried to an account current between the company and a member.[16] In England the section has been applied to dividends due to a holding company but

---

[12] *Webb v Whiffin* (1872) L.R. 5 H.L. 711.
[13] Includes past members, see *Re Consolidated Goldfields of New Zealand Ltd* [1953] Ch. 689.
[14] Above, pp.67–68.
[15] The House of Lords left open the status of a damages claim arising from a contract to subscribe for shares.
[16] *Liquidator of Wilsons (Glasgow and Trinidad) Ltd v Wilson's Trustees*, 1915 1 S.L.T. 424 (O.H.).

retained by the subsidiary for use in its business. The judge decided that the onus of proving that such sums were not due as dividends to a member in his capacity of a member was on the holding company. This could be done by an express or implied agreement which created a loan by the holding company of the money involved or recognition of that fact with the passage of time, but there was no such evidence in that case.[17]

The liability of a contributory creates a debt (in England of the nature of a speciality) accruing at the time when his liability commenced, but payable when a call is made: s.80.

If a contributory dies either before or after he has been placed on the list of contributories, his personal representatives are liable. They are not personally liable; they are liable in their representative character. In England, if they make a default in payment, proceedings may be taken for administering the estate of the deceased: s.81.

If a contributory becomes bankrupt, his trustee in bankruptcy represents him for all the purposes of the winding up and is a contributory accordingly. Calls already made and the estimated value of the bankrupt's liability to future calls may be proved against the estate.[18]

There are special provisions as to the liability of B contributories where a company has re-registered under s.49 or 51 of the Companies Act[19]: ss 77, 78.

Calls on contributories

In England calls on contributories are made by the liquidator with the leave of the court or the sanction of the liquidation committee: s.160. In Scotland calls are made by the court: s.150.

Calls may be made either before or after the insufficiency of the assets has been ascertained. They are made for an amount necessary to satisfy the debts and liabilities of the company, and the costs of winding up, and for adjustment of the rights of the contributories among themselves. In fixing the amount regard is had to the probability that some contributories may fail to pay the call: s.150.

A debt due from the company to a contributory cannot be set off against calls, whether made before or after the winding up,[20] except:

(1) where all the creditors have been paid in full (s.149); or

(2) in the case of an unlimited company, where the debt is due to him on an independent dealing with the company and not due to him as a member in respect of dividend or profit (s.149); or

(3) where the contributory is bankrupt.[21]

---

[17] *Re L. B. Holliday & Co. Ltd* [1986] 2 All E.R. 367.
[18] s.82.
[19] Above, Ch.2.
[20] *Grissell's Case* (1866) L.R. 1 Ch. App. 528; *Cowan v Gowans* (1878) 5 R. 581; this has been held to be so where a shareholder deposited money with the company against calls: *Millar v Aikman* (1891) 28 S.L.R. 955 (O.H.).
[21] *Re Duckworth* (1867) L.R. 2 Ch. App. 578. On s.149, see *Penningtons Corporate Insolvency Law* (1997) 2nd ed. pp. 159 & 276.

A contributory on the list may be ordered by the court, at any time after the making of a winding-up order, to pay any money due from him to the company: s.149.[22] The court can also order the arrest of, and seizure of the movable personal property of, a contributory believed to be about to abscond or to remove his property with the object of evading payment of calls: s.158.

CREDITORS

The rules apply with regard to (1) the respective rights of secured and unsecured creditors, (2) debts provable, and (3) the valuation of annuities and future and contingent liabilities.

Secured creditors

A secured creditor is one who holds some security for a debt due to him from the company, such as a mortgage, charge or lien. He must give credit for the realised or estimated value of his security unless he surrenders it. Thus he may:

(1)   realise his security and prove,[23] as an unsecured creditor, for any balance due to him after deducting the amount realised; or

(2)   value his security and prove, as an unsecured creditor, for any balance due after deducting the value of the security; or

(3)   surrender his security and prove, as an unsecured creditor, for the whole debt; or

(4)   where he is fully secured, rely on his security and not prove at all.

A secured creditor who has realised his security for less than the total amount of his debt, part of which is preferential,[24] can appropriate the proceeds of sale to that part of his debt which is not preferential, so that he can prove for the preferential part.[25]

If the creditor has made a mistake in the valuation of his security, he may amend it by application to the court. If he subsequently realises his security, the amount realised must be substituted for the amount in the proof.

Proof of debts

The debts which are provable on a winding up, and the manner of proof, are governed by the Insolvency Rules 1986.[26] The liability must exist at the commencement of the winding up[27] but, subject to that, it may be present or future, certain or contingent, ascertained or sounding only in damages. Where

---

[22] The effect of s.149 dies with the company when it is dissolved: *Butler v Broadhead* [1975] Ch.D. 97.
[23] The term used in Scotland is "claim".
[24] Below, pp.647, *et seq.*
[25] *Re William Hall (Contractors) Ltd* [1967] 1 W.L.R. 948.
[26] r.12.3 and rr.4.73–4.99; I.(S.)R. 1986, r.7.30 and Sch.5.
[27] *Re Oriental Commercial Bank* (1871) 7 Ch. App. 99, 103–4.

two creditors lodge proof in respect of what is, in substance, the same debt only one dividend can be paid (the rule against double proof)[27] notwithstanding the existence of two contracts.[28] The liquidator can estimate the value of any debt of uncertain amount[29] or, in difficult cases, he can apply to the court for directions: s.168(3).[30] It is no longer the case that in an insolvent winding up unliquidated claims in tort are excluded. Some claims can only be proved when those of all other creditors have been paid in full, with interest, *e.g.* those arising by virtue of restitution orders under ss 6 and 61 of the Financial Services Act 1986.[31] Statute-barred debts cannot be proved.[32]

If a debt is owed in foreign currency it must be paid at the rate of exchange prevailing at the commencement of the liquidation and not at the date of payment.[33]

Where there have been mutual credits, mutual debts or other mutual dealings between the company and one of its creditors, an account is taken of what is due from one to the other, and the balance of that account and no more can be claimed or paid.[34]

A Co. borrowed money from B Co. on the security of bills of sale charging some machinery and providing for its insurance against fire. The policies were in the name of B, and A paid the premiums. The machinery was destroyed by fire and the insurance amounting to £1,600 paid to B. A then went into liquidation. £744 was owing to B on the bills of sale at the date of the fire, so that B had £856 in hand, but A owed B £2,009 unsecured book debts. *Held*, B could set off the £856 against the £2,009: *Re H. E. Thorne & Son Ltd* [1914] 2 Ch. 438.

The holder of a life policy in an assurance company mortgaged the policy to the issuing company. On the company's going into liquidation the policy holder claimed to set off the value of the policy against his mortgage debt. *Held,* he was entitled to do so: *Re City Life Assurance Co. Ltd* [1926] Ch.191.

This statutory set-off cannot be excluded by agreement between the parties.[35] It applies automatically, irrespective of the wishes of the parties, wherever there are mutual debts (or provable claims) between the company and a creditor, so that the liquidator cannot deal with the subject of such mutual cross-claims free of the right of set-off.[36] Where the company is entitled to set-off a claim against a

---

[27] *Re Oriental Commercial Bank* (1871) 7 Ch. App. 99, 103–4.
[28] For example, in a suretyship situation, between the creditor and the debtor and between the creditor and the surety. The rule is explained in *Re Polly Peck International plc (in administration)* [1996] B.C.C. 486, *per* Robert Walker J. at p.492.
[29] I.R. 1986, r.4.86; I.(S.)R. 1986, rr.4.15, 4.16.
[30] Any person aggrieved can also apply: s.168(5).
[31] Scotland I.R. 1986, r.12.3(2A).
[32] *Re Art Reproduction Co. Ltd* [1952] Ch. 89; *Re Overmark Smith Warden Ltd, The Times,* March 22, 1982. In a compulsory winding up the limitation period is ascertained by reference to the date of the winding-up order not the petition: *Re Case of Taffs Well* [1991] 3 W.L.R. 731.
[33] *Re Lines Brothers Ltd* [1983] Ch. 1, CA.
[34] I.R. 1986, r.4.90; I.(S.)R., r.4.16; on mutuality see I. F. Fletcher. *The Law of Insolvency,* 2nd ed. 1996, pp.272–279, 599 and *Palmer's Company Law,* Vol. 3, paras 15.415–15.417. Note also *Re Norman Holdings Co. Ltd* [1990] 3 All E.R. 757 (a secured creditor who opts to rely upon his security rather than prove is not subject to r.4.90).
[35] *National Westminster Bank Ltd v Halesowen Presswork & Assemblies Ltd* [1972] A.C. 785.
[36] *Farley v Housing and Commercial Development Ltd* [1984] B.C.L.C. 442; *Stein v Blake* [1996] A.C. 243 HL (Bankruptcy).

preferential creditor[37] who is also a non-preferential creditor, the company's claim must be set-off rateably in proportion to the amounts of the preferential and non-preferential claims.[38] It has been held that directors who had guaranteed a loan to their company, had constituted themselves principal debtors with their company,[39] and had lodged deposits with the lender as further security, could, when the lender went into liquidation, set-off the amount of the deposits against both their own and the company's debt.[40]

Interest is payable on all debts provable in the winding up, including interest which has accrued under the contract rate prior to the winding up. Post-winding-up interest is only payable, however, if there is a surplus after paying all debts (including pre-winding-up interest), and is paid before any surplus is returned to the contributories. The rate of post-winding-up interest is that specified by order made under s.17 of the Judgments Act 1838[41] on the commencement of the winding up, unless the contract itself provided for a higher rate of interest[42]: s.189. If interest is payable on a foreign currency debt it should be calculated with respect to the exchange rate at the date of winding up and not when it is paid.[43]

Adjustment of prior transactions

The Insolvency Act contains provisions which enable the liquidator to apply to the court to set aside certain prior transactions which are disadvantageous to the general body of creditors. These provisions also apply where an administration order has been made.[44]

Transactions at an undervalue and preferences in England

A transaction at an undervalue entered into by a company is a transaction whereby a company makes a gift to another person or enters into a transaction on terms which provide that the company either receives no consideration or significantly less consideration than the value of the consideration it provides, measured in money or money's worth: s.238(4).[45] In valuing the consideration received by the company for the purposes of s.238(4), the court should have regard to the reality of the situation, and this may require viewing the impugned transaction with hindsight:

The consideration for a sale of the company's business included an agreement that the purchaser would pay four annual instalments of £312,500 for sub-rental of the company's

---

[37] Below, p.647.
[38] *Re Unit 2 Windows Ltd* [1986] B.C.L.C. 31.
[39] It may be otherwise where such a liability has not been assumed: see *Morris v Rayners Enterprises Inc.* [1997] B.C.C. 965, HL.
[40] *High Street Services Ltd v Bank of Credit and Commerce International S.A.* [1993] B.C.C. 360, CA.
[41] In Scotland see the Insolvency (Scotland) Rules 1986 (SI 1986 No. 1915 (S. 139)), r.4.66.
[42] Such a rate may be challenged by the liquidator under s.244, below, p.578.
[43] *Re Lines Brothers Ltd (No. 2)* [1984] Ch. 438.
[44] Above, Ch.26.
[45] The creation of a security over the company's assets has been held not to be a transaction at an undervalue: *Re M.C. Bacon Ltd* [1990] B.C.C. 78. In determining whether there is an undervalue the court will look at the transaction as a whole not merely a discrete part of it: see *Agricultural Mortgage Corporation plc v Woodward* [1994] B.C.C. 688, CA.

leased computer equipment. The head lease contained a prohibition against sub-leasing which, when breached, entitled the lessor to repossess the equipment. This occurred before any instalments had been paid and the purchaser terminated the agreement. *Held*: The instalments should be ignored for the purpose of determining the value received by the company. The court should, when an agreement provided for a consideration that was speculative, have regard to circumstances after the agreement was entered into. *Phillips (Liquidator of AJ Bekhor & Co) v Brewin Dolphin Bell Lawrie* [2001] UKHL 2.

However, this does not include transactions entered into by the company in good faith for the purpose of carrying on its business and at the time there were reasonable grounds for believing that the transaction would benefit the company: s.238(5). Further such a transaction must have taken place at a time when the company was unable to pay its debts[46] (or became unable to pay them as a result of the transaction) and also within two years prior to the commencement of the winding up.[47] If the transaction is with a person connected with the company the company is assumed to have been insolvent at the time unless the contrary is shown: s.240.

A company gives a preference to a creditor[48] if it does anything or suffers anything to be done which has the effect of putting the creditor into a position which, in the event of the company going into insolvent liquidation, would be better than the position he would have been in if that thing had not been done,[49] and the company in doing that was influenced by a desire to produce that effect. Such a motive is presumed if the creditor is connected with the company; s.239.[50] The preference must have been given at a time when the company was unable to pay its debts[51] (or became unable to do so as a result of the preference) and also within six months of the commencement of the winding up. The time limit is extended to two years if the creditor is connected with the company: s.240. The relevant time for considering the company's motive is not when it decides to pay the creditor but when it does so.[52]

Both transactions at an undervalue and preferences may be challenged by the liquidator who can apply for a court order to return the position to what it would have been if the company had not entered into the transaction or given the preference: ss 238, 239. The court can make any order it thinks fit[53] and s.241 gives it wide powers relating to the transfer of property, return of benefits received and release of any security. A charge may therefore be set aside under these provisions.[54] An order under s.238 or 239 may affect the property of, or impose an obligation on, any person whether or not he is the person with whom the company entered the transaction or to whom the preference was given.

---

[46] As defined in s.123, above p.584.

[47] Or on the date an administration application is made or an administrator is appointed under paras 14 or 22 of Sch.B1.

[48] Including a surety or guarantor for any of its debts or liabilities.

[49] If a payment intended to be preferential does not, in the event, have that effect it cannot be impugned: *cp. Lewis v Hyde* [1997] B.C.C. 976, PC.

[50] See, *e.g. Re Exchange Travel (Holdings) Ltd* [1996] B.C.C. 933; *Weisgard v Pilkington* [1995] B.C.C. 1108.

[51] See n.46.

[52] *Wills v Corfe Joinery Ltd* [1997] B.C.C. 511.

[53] Even against a person resident abroad: *Re Paramount Airways Ltd* [1992] 3 All E.R. 7, CA.

[54] A floating charge may also be attacked under s.245, above, p.516.

However, the position of such third parties is protected by s.241 (as amended by s.1 of the Insolvency (No. 2) Act 1994) which limits the orders which the court can make where a person has acted in good faith and for value. Lack of good faith is presumed if, at the time of the acquisition of the property or the receipt of the benefit, the person had notice of the relevant surrounding circumstances and the relevant proceedings[55] or was connected with, or an associate of, either the company, the person with whom the company entered the transaction or the person to whom the company gave the preference. The relevant surrounding circumstances are the fact that the transaction was at an undervalue or the circumstances which amounted to the giving of the preference.

In relation to preferences, in the past, a liquidator had to prove that the giving of the preference was accompanied by a dominant intention to prefer on the part of the company. Section 239(5) requires merely that the company be influenced by a desire to prefer, even if there was no dominant intention to do so. If, however, the company has no positive desire to prefer at all and the preference was given solely as a result of commercial pressure (*e.g.* to avoid the appointment of a receiver by the bank) or for proper commercial considerations, it is not subject to avoidance.[56] Where several parties to a transaction are found to have been preferred, an order can only be made against those which the company desired to prefer:

A company hired machinery from CAF. S, a director, gave a personal guarantee for the rental. When the company was on the brink of liquidation, CAF threatened to repossess unless rental arrears were cleared. S caused the company to pay CAF. *Held*: CAF had to repay. The company (through S) was influenced by a desire to improve the position of CAF because only by such improvement could it achieve its desire to protect its director, S. *Re Agriplant Services Ltd* [1997] B.C.C. 842.

Transactions in fraud of creditors

These are transactions at an undervalue (defined as in s.238, above entered into for the purpose of putting assets beyond the reach of creditors or otherwise prejudicing their interests:[57] s.423. A wide meaning has been given to "transaction":

D owned a farm which was mortgaged to P. D was unable to keep up the re-payments and P was likely to re-possess the farm and sell it. D leased the farm, at full market rent, to his wife, W, with the result that the proceeds of any sale by P would be insufficient to meet the mortgage debt. *Held*: While D received a full market rent for the lease, the transaction as a whole was at an undervalue taking into account that it placed W in a position to secure payment from P for the surrender of the lease. *Agricultural Mortgage Corporation plc v Woodward* [1994] B.C.C. 688, CA.[57a]

---

[55] See s.241(3A) to 241(3C).

[56] *Re M. C. Bacon Ltd* [1990] B.C.C. 78; *Re Fairway Magazines Ltd* [1992] B.C.C. 924; *Re Beacon Leisure Ltd* [1991] B.C.C. 213; *cf. Re D.K.G. Contractors Ltd* [1990] B.C.C. 903.

[57] Such need not be the sole purpose: *Chohan v Saggar* [1992] B.C.C. 306, 321; see also *Inland Revenue Commissioners v Hashmir* [2002] EWCA Civ. 981. To provide evidence of purpose, the court may order discovery of documents passing between a defendant and his legal advisor in connection with structuring a transaction: *Barclays Bank plc v Eustice* [1995] B.C.C. 978, CA.

[57a] See also *National Westminster Bank plc v Jones* [2001] EWCA Civ. 1541.

The relevant purpose can be established in relation to future and unknown creditors as where assets are transferred to protect them from the consequences of a possible failure of a new business venture.[58] An order can be made, on the application of the liquidator,[59] restoring the position to what it would have been had the transaction not been entered into and protecting the interests of persons who are victims of the transaction. The court does not have to set aside the transaction but should seek both to restore the position and protect the victims so far as practicable. Unlike s.238, s.423 operates independently of insolvency and is subject to no time limits.[60]

Gratuitous alienations and unfair preferences (Scots law)

In Scotland, ss 242 and 243 relate, respectively, to the challenge of gratuitous alienations and unfair preferences.[61]

By s.242(1), once a winding up has commenced an alienation to which the section applies may be challenged by:

(a) any creditor the debt to whom was incurred on or before the date of the commencement of the winding up; or

(b) the liquidator.[62]

The section covers any alienation by which any part of the company's property is transferred or by which any claim or right of the company is discharged or renounced, provided the alienation has become completely effectual:

(a) if it favours an "associate", on a day not earlier than five years before the commencement of the winding up; or

(b) if it favours any other person, on a day not earlier than two years before such commencement.[62a]

The definition of "associate" is incorporated from s.74 of the Bankruptcy (Scotland) Act 1985, a section which may be altered by regulations. By that section the term "associate" extends to husband, wife, relative (*i.e.* brother, sister, uncle, aunt, nephew, niece, lineal ancestor or lineal descendant), partner,

---

[58] *Midland Bank plc v Wyatt* [1997] 1 B.C.L.C. 242.
[59] Or the administrator or victim (a person who is or is capable of being prejudiced: s.423(5); *cf Pinewood Joinery v Starelm Properties Ltd* [1994] B.C.C. 569).
[60] *Arbuthnot Leasing International Ltd v Havelet Leasing Ltd (No. 2)* [1990] B.C.C. 636; *Chohan v Saggar* [1994] B.C.C. 134.
[61] Formerly governed by the Bankruptcy Acts of 1621 and 1696, respectively. *Bank of Scotland, Petitioners*, 1988 S.L.T. 690, made it clear that gratuitous alienations by companies can be challenged at common law; the common law right had not been taken away but had been extended by ss 242 and 243. In this case there was held to be a prima facie case for an interim interdict. In *Bob Gray (Access) v T.M. Standard Scaffolding*, 1987 S.C.L.R. 720 (Sh. Ct.) the liquidator was entitled to recover £6,000 paid by the debtor to a particular creditor under the 1696 Act.
[62] The liquidator does not require the sanction of the court to bring such an action, since s.167 and Sch.4, para.4 (see p.618, above) relate to actions in the name and on behalf of the company, which an action under s.242 is not: *Dyer v Hislop* 1994 S.C.L.R. 171 (Sh.Ct.).
[62a] s.242(3). See *Jackson v The Royal Bank of Scotland plc* 2002 S.L.T. 1123, O.H.

employer, employee (any director or other officer of a company being treated as an employee of the company for this purpose), and the section has been amended by the Bankruptcy (Scotland) Regulations 1985 (SI 1985/1925, para.11) to provide for circumstances in which a company is an "associate" of another company.

On a challenge being brought within these provisions, the court must grant decree of reduction or for such restoration of property to the company's assets or other redress as may be appropriate, unless the person seeking to uphold the alienation establishes:

(a) that immediately, or at any other time, after the alienation the company's assets were greater than its liabilities; or

(b) that the alienation was made for adequate consideration[63]; or

(c) that the alienation was a reasonable alienation by way of a birthday, Christmas or other conventional gift or by way of a gift for a charitable purpose to a person other than an associate of the company.

A reduction under s.242 was granted in *McLuckie Brothers Ltd v Newhouse Contracts Ltd*, 1993 S.L.T. 641 (O.H.). The company in question had disponed a partially completed housing development to N. Ltd for £300,000. At no time after the disposition did the company's assets exceed its liabilities. The issue was whether the price paid represented adequate consideration. The evidence showed that N. Ltd.'s director, who was a brother of the company's director, had purchased the site without its having been advertised and that the company's director had not checked the sum offered.

A challenge does not prejudice any right or interest acquired in good faith and for value from or through the transferee in the alienation.

Further, a liquidator has the same right to challenge a gratuitous alienation as a creditor has at common law. For a successful challenge at common law the challenger would require to prove that the company was absolutely insolvent at the date of the transaction (or was made so by the transaction) and continued to be absolutely insolvent at the date of the challenge, as well as that the transaction was gratuitous and to the prejudice of lawful creditors. While proof of these points would make a common law challenge more difficult, such a challenge is not restricted to alienations made to associates nor is it restricted to alienations made within two years prior to the commencement of winding up. For an example see *Stuart Eves Ltd (in liquidation) v Smiths Gore*, 1993 S.L.T. 1274 (O.H.).

Section 243(1) applies to transactions entered into by a company which have the effect of creating a preference in favour of a creditor to the prejudice of the

---

[63] "Adequate" is to be judged from an objective standpoint: *Lafferty Construction Ltd v McCombe*, 1994 S.L.T. 858 (O.H.) and must be determined at the time of transaction (*Nova Glaze Replacement Windows Ltd v Clark Thomson and Co* 2001 S.C. 815, O.H.). Thus, a gratuitous discharge by the company of a security would be for "adequate consideration", if the company had not made any advances to the debtor: *Rankin v Meek*, 1995 S.L.T. 526 (O.H.). Similarly, the promise of an entitlement to future income might well, in commercial terms, constitute an adequate consideration (*Nova Glaze Replacement Windows Ltd v Clark Thomson and Co* 2001 S.C. 815, O.H.).

general body of creditors, provided the preference has become completely effectual not earlier than six months before the commencement of the winding up.

There are the following exceptions to the right of challenge under s.243(2):

(a) a transaction in the ordinary course of trade or business;

(b) a payment in cash[64] of debts due, unless the transaction was collusive with the purpose of prejudicing the general body of creditors;

(c) a transaction by which the parties to it undertake reciprocal obligations[65] unless the transaction was collusive as under (b), above;

(d) any mandate granted by the company authorising an arrestee to pay over arrested funds to an arrester, where:

(i) there has been a decree for payment or a warrant for summary diligence; and

(ii) the decree or warrant has been preceded by an arrestment on the dependence of the action or followed by an arrestment in execution.

The challenge may be brought by:

(a) any creditor the debt to whom was incurred on or before the date of commencement of the winding up; or

(b) the liquidator (s.243(4)).

On a challenge being brought, the court, if satisfied that the transaction challenged is one to which s.243 applies, must grant decree of reduction or for such restoration of property to the company's assets or other redress as may be appropriate: s.243(5).

A challenge does not prejudice any right or interest acquired in good faith and for value from or through the creditor in whose favour the preference was created.

---

[64] In an action by a company for a sum consigned on deposit receipt six months before the winding up, the sum consigned was held to have the character of a cash payment: *Craiglaw Development Ltd v. Wilson*, 1997 S.C. 356. "The crucial question is whether the debtor has been completely divested of the funds, and of power or control over them": *per* Lord Prosser, delivering the opinion of the court, at p.361. In *R. Gaffney & Son Ltd (in liquidation) v Davidson*, 1996 S.L.T. (Sh. Ct.) 36, a payment was made to the defender by a third party, a few days before liquidation, in exchange for withdrawal of arrestments in an action which had been raised by the defender. *Held*: that the payment was an unfair preference, arrestment was not a transaction in the ordinary course of business and the payment was in effect an assignation of the debt owed by the third party and not a payment in cash.

[65] The consideration given must not be less than full value: *Nicoll v Steel Press (Supplies) Ltd*, 1992 S.C. 119 (payment of £5,071 made by company in order to obtain the release of supplies worth £584). There was held to be an unfair preference in *Dumbarton Building and Civil Engineering Co. Ltd (in liquidation) v Devoy* 1996 G.W.D. 9–469 (when £30,000 was due by a company for contracts carried out for it, the company agreed to transfer three motor vehicles supposed to be in security for the commencement of new contracts; the liquidator was successful in proving that the vehicles were actually security for the company's existing indebtedness).

As with gratuitous alienations, the liquidator has the same right to challenge a preference created by the debtor company as a creditor has at common law: s.243(6).

At common law the challenger must prove that:

(a) the debtor was insolvent at the date of the transaction and continuously thereafter down to the date of the challenge;

(b) the debtor was aware at the date of the transaction that he was insolvent;

(c) the transaction was voluntary and in satisfaction or further security of a prior debt; and

(d) the transaction was to the prejudice of the debtor's other creditors.[66]

At common law the following are recognised as exceptions and are not reducible unless there is proof of fraudulent contrivance between debtor and creditor[67]—(i) cash payments of debts actually due, (ii) transactions in the ordinary course of trade[68] and (iii) *nova debita*, namely, new debts arising out of new transactions.

A transaction is not "voluntary" if the debtor is doing "the very thing which he is bound to do",[69] such as implementing a prior obligation to grant a specific security provided that obligation is part of the original contract.[70]

The preference is equally challengeable whether conferred directly (*e.g.* where security is given to a creditor previously unsecured) or directly.[71]

An isolated and unprecedented assignation by an insolvent company cannot claim the protection afforded to transactions "in the ordinary course of trade", and is therefore reducible.[72]

Avoidance of certain floating charges

As we have seen s.245 provides that certain floating charges created within 12 months prior to the liquidation are voidable unless new consideration was supplied by the creditor.[73] This provision operates in addition to ss 238 to 244 detailed above.

Extortionate credit transactions

A transaction is an extortionate credit transaction if credit has been supplied to a company on terms which are extortionate (grossly exorbitant) having regard to

---

[66] For a comprehensive review of the authorities see *Nordic Travel Ltd v Scotprint Ltd*, 1980 S.C. 1.

[67] Mere knowledge on the creditor's part of the debtor's absolute and irretrievable insolvency at the time of payment is not enough: *Nordic Travel Ltd v Scotprint Ltd*, above.

[68] See *Nordic Travel Ltd v Scotprint Ltd*, above.

[69] *Taylor v Farrie* (1855) 17 D. 639 at p. 649 (joint opinion).

[70] *T. v L.*, 1970 S.L.T. 243 (O.H.).

[71] *Walkraft Paint Co. v Lovelock*, 1964 S.L.T. 103 (O.H.) (mandates given by the company to certain of its debtors to pay the favoured creditor); *Walkraft Paint Co. Ltd v James H. Kinsey Ltd*, 1964 S.L.T. 104 (O.H.) (cheque from company's debtor endorsed by company to the favoured creditor).

[72] *Walkraft Paint Co. Ltd v James H. Kinsey Ltd*, above.

[73] Above, p.516.

the risk involved or it otherwise grossly contravenes the ordinary principles of fair dealing.[74] All credit transactions are presumed to be extortionate until the contrary is proved. The transaction must have been entered into within three years prior to the commencement of the winding up.

In such cases the liquidator may apply to the court for an order setting aside the transaction, varying its terms, for repayment of money or property held as security to the company or for the taking of accounts. This power may be used concurrently with the power to avoid a transaction at an undervalue: s.244.

Unenforceability of liens

Under s.246, a liquidator can override any lien or other right to retain possession of any books, papers or records of the company in order to gain possession of them. The only exception is a lien on documents which give a title to property and are held as such.

Order of application of assets

The effect of ss, 175, 176 and the rules is that in a winding up the assets of the company are applicable in the following order:

(1) costs, charges and expenses properly incurred in the winding up,[75] including the remuneration of the liquidator;

(2) the preferential debts;

(3) debts secured by a charge which as created was a floating charge[76];

(4) the ordinary unsecured debts;

(5) post insolvency interest on debts;

(6) deferred debts;

(7) the balance (if any) to be returned to the contributories.

It should be noted that whilst preferential debts are payable out of the proceeds of floating charge realisations,[77] the House of Lords has recently held that the expenses of the liquidation are not to be paid out those proceeds. Liquidation expenses are thus payable *only* out of the company's uncharged assets.[78]

All liabilities belonging to a higher category must be paid for or provided for in full before any payment can be made in respect of liabilities of a lower

---

[74] *cf.* Consumer Credit Act 1974, ss 137–139.

[75] For example liabilities under contracts made or continued by the liquidator for the purposes of the winding-up: *Re Atlantic Computer Systems plc* [1992] 1 All E.R. 476.

[76] s.175(2)(b) and s.251; where necessary the property subject to the charge can be used to pay liabilities in categories (1) and (2). For the position where a fixed charge is made subject to a floating charge see: *Re Portbase Clothing Ltd* [1993] 3 All E.R. 829.

[77] Below, p.649.

[78] *Buchler v Talbot* [2004] UKHL 9, overruling *Re Barleycorn Enterprises Ltd* [1970] Ch. 465. *c.f.* the position in administration, above, p.580.

category. None of this will affect creditors with a fixed charge (so long as it is valid and properly registered): they may simply pay themselves out of their security. In relation to any balance remaining unpaid, they rank as ordinary or preferential unsecured creditors.[79]

In the event of the assets being insufficient to satisfy the costs, charges and expenses incurred in the winding up, there is an internal order of priority: s.156 and Insolvency Rules 1986, rule 4.218.[80] Unless the court orders otherwise, the order of priority is[81]:

(a) Fees and expenses properly incurred in preserving, realising or getting in the assets. These can include costs relating to the bringing of legal proceedings under ss 214, 238, 239, etc.[82] The cost of employing a shorthand writer appointed by the court to conduct an examination is included here.[83]

(b) Costs of the *petition*[84] including costs of those appearing on the petition whose costs are allowed by the court.[85]

(c) Remuneration of the special manager (if any).

(d) Costs and expenses of any person who makes the company's statement of affairs.

(e) Charges of a shorthand writer appointed by the court.

(f) Disbursements of the liquidator including expenses of the liquidation committee.

(g) Costs of any person properly employed by the liquidator.

(h) Remuneration of the liquidator.[86]

Where the company is a lessee rent accrued due after the winding-up order is an expense of the liquidation if the liquidator retained the lease solely for the benefit of the liquidation, and not for the joint benefit of himself and the

---

[79] See, *e.g. Re Mesco Properties* [1980] 1 W.L.R. 96.

[80] For Scotland, see I.(S.)R. 1986, r.4.5(3) and (4); the words in r.4.5(3) "without prejudice to any order of the court as to expenses" give the court a wide discretion: *Graham v John Tullis & Son (Plastics) Ltd*, 1991 S.C. 302 (held unreasonable in the circumstances for the company to be required to bear the outlays and remuneration of the provisional liquidator). In *Cleghorn, Noter* 1996 G.W.D. 18–1029 (Sh. Ct.), where the assets were insufficient to meet the expenses of both the provisional and interim liquidator (C.) and the liquidator (G.), the court ordered the fees to be paid pro rata, with the provisional and interim liquidator having no priority.

[81] For a detailed list, see I.R. 1986, r.4.218.

[82] The provision was amended by SI 2002/2712 so as to bring such proceedings within the category of liquidation expenses and effectively overrules a line of cases deciding otherwise: see, *e.g., Re M. C. Bacon Ltd (No 2)* [1991] Ch. 127, *Re Floor Fourteen Ltd* [2001] 3 All E.R. 499.

[83] r.4.218(2) & (3).

[84] See *Re Bostels* [1968] Ch. 346.

[85] In *Re Bathampton Properties Ltd* [1976] 1 W.L.R. 168 the company's costs were increased by its unsuccessful and unjustifiable opposition to the petition, and only its costs down to and including the first hearing, when it could have consented were paid out of the assets.

[86] As for priority between successive liquidators, see r.4.219 and *Re Salters Hall School Ltd (in liquidation)* [1998] B.C.C. 503.

lessors.[87] Instalments of non-domestic rates, for which the company had been billed before liquidation but which were payable after liquidation, in respect of property of which the liquidator retained possession for the purposes of the company, should be paid as a liquidation expenses.[88]

Rule 4.218(1) is a definitive statement of what constitutes a liquidation expense and is not subject to any implied qualification: *Re Toshoku Finance UK plc* [2002] UKHL 6.

The *preferential debts* rank equally among themselves and must be paid in full, after the expenses of winding up, unless the assets are insufficient to meet them, in which case the preferential debts abate in equal proportions: s.175(2)(a). The Enterprise Act 2002 abolished the preferential status of debts due to Inland Revenue (generally, arrears of employees' PAYE contributions), debts due to Customs and Excise (arrears of Value Added Tax) and arrears of social security contributions due under the Social Security Contributions & Benefits Act 1992: Enterprise Act 2002 s.251.[88a] The remaining categories of preferential debts are found in Sch.6 Insolvency Act 1986: s.386(1). They include:

(a) Remuneration owed to an employee in respect of services rendered to the company within four months next before the relevant date, not exceeding £800 per claimant.[89]

The expression "the relevant date" means, when the company is being wound up compulsorily, the date of the appointment of a provisional liquidator or, if no such appointment was made, the date of the winding up-order; if the company is or was being wound up voluntarily, it means the date of the passing of the resolution for winding-up. If the winding-up follows a conversion from administration to winding up, the relevant date is that on which the company entered administrator: s.387. There are equivalent rules for voluntary arrangements, administrations and receiverships: s.387.

In England a full-time company secretary is probably an employee,[90] but in Scotland there may be more doubt.[91] A managing director[92] is not an employee nor is a director as such. However, a director may, under power in the articles, be employed in a salaried position with the company and so be an employee. Thus, where a director could be, and was, employed as editor of a periodical, he was a preferential creditor.[93]

---

[87] *Re A.B.C. Coupler & Engineering Co. Ltd (No. 3)* [1970] 1 W.L.R. 702; and see *Re Downer Enterprises Ltd* [1974] 1 W.L.R. 1460, where an intermediate lessee paid the arrears of rent and was held entitled to the lessor's rights by way of subrogation; such rent does not however fall within the para. (a) but para. (f), see *Re Linda Marie* [1989] B.C.L.C. 46.

[88] *Re Noltan Business Centre Ltd* [1996] B.C.C. 500 (presumably, under para. (f)).

[88a] *cf. Jackson and Long, Notes*, 2004 S.C. 474, O.H.

[89] This includes other sums payable to employees by virtue of s.121 of the Employment Protection (Consolidation) Act 1978 and various other statutory benefits: see Sch.6, para.13. See also the Employment Rights Act 1996 Pts XI & XII.

[90] *Cairney v Back* [1906] 2 K.G. 746. The former wording was "clerk or servant".

[91] *Scottish Poultry Journal Co.* (1896) 4 S.L.T. 167 (O.H.) (secretary and manager); *Clyde Football etc. Co. Ltd* (1900) 8 S.L.T. 167 (O.H.); *Laing v Gowans* (1902) 10 S.L.T. 461 (O.H.). *Quaere* whether these still apply to the changed wording.

[92] *Re Newspaper Proprietary Syndicate Ltd* [1900] 2 Ch. 349.

[93] *Re Beeton & Co. Ltd* (1913) 2 Ch. 279.

A chemist engaged two days a week at a salary to work on formulae for perfumiers is an employee.[94] A contributor, even a regular contributor, to a newspaper, although paid by a fixed salary, is not.[95]

(b) Accrued holiday remuneration in respect of any period of employment before the relevant date payable to an employee whose employment has been terminated before, on, or after that date.

(c) Debts due under Sch.4 of the Pension Schemes Act 1993.

(d) Debts in respect of levies on the production of coal and steel, or any surcharge for delay, as imposed under the European Coal and Steel Treaty.[96]

In England, if a landlord or other person has distrained on the company's goods within three months next before a winding-up order, the preferential debts are a first charge on the goods or the proceeds of the distress. The landlord or other person, however, has the same priority as the persons paid out of the proceeds: s.176. This section applies to anyone who has seized goods and is holding them for the purpose of sale at the time of the winding-up order.[97]

The ordinary debts rank and abate equally *inter se*.[98]

It may be mentioned here that a sum of money paid into a company's bank account for behoof of the company's employees and which is at the date of the liquidation "clearly distinguishable and capable of being disentangled from the company's own funds" do not form part of the company's assets but must be paid to the employees.[99]

Where a company fails to implement an agreement to purchase its shares under s.162 of the Companies Act 1985[1] or to redeem its shares under s.159 of that Act,[2] and the company subsequently goes into liquidation the vendor/shareholder may enforce the agreement as a creditor. This will not apply if at any time between the date for purchase or redemption and the commencement of the winding up the company could not have fulfilled its obligation out of distributable profits: Companies Act 1985, s.178.[3]

COMPLETION OF WINDING UP BY THE COURT

When the liquidator has collected the assets and received the proofs of the creditors, he proceeds to divide the assets among the creditors.

---

[94] *Re G. H. Morison & Co. Ltd* (1912) 106 L.T. 731.

[95] See n.93, above.

[96] See SI 1987/2093.

[97] *Re Memco Engineering Ltd* [1986] Ch. 86. The position is different in a voluntary winding up: *Re Herbert Berry Associates Ltd* [1977] 1 W.L.R. 1437, CA.

[98] *per* Lord Selbourne in *Black & Co.'s case* (1872) L.R. 8 Ch. 254 at p.262. There is, however, no objection to an agreement whereby a creditor agrees to subordinate his debt and such agreements are accordingly valid: *Re Maxwell Communications Corp. plc (No. 2)* 1994 1 All E.R. 737.

[99] *Smith v Liquidator of James Birrell Ltd*, 1968 S.L.T. 174 (O.H.).

[1] Above, Ch.10.

[2] *ibid.*

[3] Above, Ch.10.

If there is any surplus after the costs of the liquidation and the company's debts have been paid, the court must adjust the rights of the contributories among themselves and distribute any surplus among the persons entitled thereto: s.154.[3a] The section requires a court order before the liquidator can distribute surplus assets, whether or not an adjustment has to be made[4] among the contributories. It will be remembered that under normal articles preference shareholders are entitled to priority over ordinary shareholders in the return of capital.[5] Persons not registered as members but in possession of share certificates as collectors or scriptophilists are not beneficially entitled to the shares to which the certificates relate and have been excluded from a distribution of surplus assets.[6]

If the liquidation is not completed within a year after its commencement, the liquidator must send to the Registrar of Companies, at such intervals as may be prescribed, a statement in the prescribed form and giving prescribed particulars as to the position of the liquidation: s.192.[7]

Final meetings and release of the liquidator

The holding of final meetings of the company or its creditors as appropriate in the case of a voluntary winding up has been dealt with already,[8] together with the release of the liquidator consequential upon such a meeting.[9]

In a compulsory winding up the liquidator, other than the official receiver, if he is satisfied that the liquidation is for practical purposes complete, must call a final general meeting of the creditors. The liquidator will then make his report to that meeting which must then decide whether to release him. He may also give notice of any final distribution of the company's property at the same time. If he cannot do so the meeting must be adjourned until he can do so. The costs of the final meeting must be covered by the company's assets and so the liquidator must retain sufficient for this purpose: s.146. The release of a liquidator consequential on this meeting has been dealt with above.[10]

Early dissolution of company in England

If the company is in compulsory liquidation and the official receiver, who is automatically the first liquidator,[11] discovers that the realisable assets of the company will be insufficient to cover even the expenses of the winding up he may apply to the Registrar of Companies for an early dissolution of the company. Before he can do this, however, he must be satisfied that the company's affairs do

---

[3a] In Scotland, the liquidator must also lodge in an appropriate bank, in the name of the Accountant of the Court, unclaimed dividends and unapplied or undistributable balances. See *Joint Liquidators of Automatic Oil Tools Ltd, Noters* 2001 S.L.T. 279, O.H.

[4] As where shares are unequally paid up, *see Re Phoenix Oil, etc., Co. Ltd* [1958] Ch. 560.

[5] Above, Ch.12.

[6] In *Re Baku Consolidated Oilfields Ltd* [1993] B.C.C. 653.

[7] See I.R. 1986, r.4.223.

[8] Above, p.628.

[9] *ibid.*

[10] Above, p.625.

[11] p.602.

not require any further investigation and he must give 28 days' notice of his intention to the creditors, contributories and any administrative receiver. Once such a notice is given the official receiver's duties are at an end, although any creditor, contributory, administrative receiver or even the official receiver himself, may apply to the Secretary of State for directions within three months on the grounds either that the assets are sufficient to cover the expenses, the company's affairs do merit further investigation or that an early dissolution would be inappropriate: ss 202, 203.

If no such application is made the company is automatically dissolved three months after the Registrar receives the application. If the Secretary of State does give directions, those would be that the winding up should proceed as if no notice of early dissolution had been given and he may defer the date of dissolution as he thinks fit. Notice of such directions must be given to the Registrar of Companies by the applicant within seven days. There is an appeal from the Secretary of State's decision to the court: ss 202, 203.

This procedure was adopted on the recommendation of the Cork Committee.[12] Up to one-third of companies in compulsory liquidation are likely to be subject to these provisions.

Early dissolution of company in Scotland

If after a meeting or meetings under s.138 (which deals with appointment of a liquidator in a compulsory winding up in Scotland) it appears to the liquidator that the realisable assets of the company are insufficient to cover the expenses of the winding up, he may apply to the court for an order that the company be dissolved, and the court then makes an order for early dissolution under s.204 if it appears to the court appropriate to do so: s.204(2)(3).

Within 14 days from the date of the order, the liquidator must forward a copy of the order to the Registrar of Companies, who immediately registers it, and, at the end of the period of three months from the day of that registration, the company is dissolved: s.204(4).

The court may, however, on an application made to it by any person who appears to the court to have an interest, order that the date of dissolution be deferred for such period as the court thinks fit: s.204(5). If such an order for deferment is made, the person who applied for it must, within seven days of the making of the order, deliver a copy of it to the Registrar of Companies: s.204(6).

Dissolution of company

In the case of a compulsory winding up where either the liquidator gives notice to the Registrar that the final meeting has been held and that he has vacated office,[13] or the official receiver gives notice that the winding up is complete, the registration of that notice begins a period of three months at the end of which the company will be automatically dissolved unless on the application of an

[12] Paras 649–651.
[13] Above, Ch.27.

interested party the Secretary of State defers that date.[14] There is an appeal to the court from any such decision: s.205.

In a voluntary winding up the three months' period ending with the automatic dissolution of the company begins with the registration of the liquidator's final account and return under either s.94 or s.106.[15] Otherwise the procedure is the same as on a compulsory winding up: s.201.

Subject to any order which may at any time be made by the court under ss 651 or 652 of the Companies Act 1985, any property vested in or held on trust for a company immediately before its dissolution (excluding property held by the company on trust for any other person) vests in the Crown as *bona vacantia*: s.654 of the Companies Act 1985. The Crown may disclaim such property by a notice signed in the case of property in England by the Treasury Solicitor (and in the case of property in Scotland by the Queen's and Lord Treasurer's Remembrancer): s.656 of the Companies Act 1985. The effect of such disclaimer is much the same as if the property had been disclaimed under s.178, above.[16] The notice of disclaimer must be executed within 12 months after the vesting of the property came to the notice of the Crown representative or, where any person interested in the property applies in writing to the Crown representative requiring him to decide whether he will disclaim, usually within three months after the application. The notice of disclaimer must be delivered to the Registrar of Companies and registered by him, and copies must be published in the *Gazette* and sent to persons who have given the Crown representative notice of their interest in the property: ss 656, 657 of the Companies Act 1985.

Where a company has been dissolved the court may make an order declaring the dissolution void. Such an order may be made on the application of the liquidator or of any other person who appears to the court to be interested: s.651 of the Companies Act 1985. A solicitor acting on behalf of a client with a claim against the dissolved company, and having neither a financial nor a proprietary interest, is not a "person . . . interested" within s.651.[17] A liquidator de son tort, *i.e.* a person who has never been a duly appointed liquidator of the company but who has, without lawful authority, been carrying on the liquidation of the company, is.[18] So is a contributory in the liquidation.[19] The Inland Revenue may apply where an assessment for taxes has been made but the assessments were under appeal when the company was struck off the register under s.652 of the Companies Act 1985, below.[20]

As a general rule, the application cannot be made more than two years after the date of the dissolution.[21] This has caused some hardship, *e.g.* to employees who contract an industrial disease which becomes apparent in later years, and

---

[14] In Scotland there can be no application to the Secretary of State to defer the date of dissolution if the winding-up order was made by the court, but the court can itself defer the date.
[15] Above, Ch.28.
[16] Ch.27. See also *Allied Dunbar Assurance plc v Fowle*, (1994) B.C.C. 422.
[17] *Roehampton Swimming Pool Ltd* [1968] 1 W.L.R. 1693.
[18] *Re Wood and Martin (Bricklaying Contractors) Ltd* [1971] 1 W.L.R. 293.
[19] *Re Thompson and Riches Ltd* [1981] 2 All E.R. 477.
[20] *Re Belmont and Co. Ltd* [1952] Ch. 10; followed in *Re Test Holdings (Clifton) Ltd* [1970] Ch. 285. As may the Secretary of State in performance of his statutory duties: *Re Townreach Ltd (No. 002081 of 1994)* [1994] 3 W.L.R. 983.
[21] s.651(4).

special provision has now been made for such cases.[22] An application for the purpose of bringing proceedings against the company for damages for death, personal injuries or funeral expenses can now be made at any time. No order will be made if the limitation period for such action under the Limitation Act 1980 (or the Prescription and Limitation (Scotland) Act 1973 and 1984) has already expired but the court has power to extend such limitation period by the period between the dissolution and the order declaring the dissolution void: s.651(5) and (6) of the Companies Act 1985.[23]

When a dissolution is declared void, any property of the company which vested in the Crown under s.654 of the Companies Act 1985 remains the Crown's property. Instead the company will receive a cash payment equivalent to those assets. This payment will be either the sum the Crown received or the value of any property which has since been disposed of by the Crown. This provision allows the Crown to dispose of such property without fear of a revival of the company: s.655 of the Companies Act 1985. An office copy of the order declaring the dissolution void must be delivered to the Registrar of Companies within seven days: s.651 of the Companies Act 1985. Such an order does not validate proceedings taken on behalf of the company between the dissolution and its avoidance.[24] Thus it does not revive a misfeasance summons issued, but not served, before dissolution.[25]

It is incompetent for the court to declare the dissolution void for a limited purpose only.[26]

The court has an absolute discretion whether to declare a dissolution void and the petition may be opposed, *e.g.* by the Official Receiver, the Treasury Solicitor or a third party whose position would be directly affected thereby.[27] The delay between the dissolution and the petition is a factor the court will take into account.[28] It is sufficient ground for the exercise of his discretion that some liability of the company may otherwise remain unpaid.

The company was the original tenant under a lease which it had assigned prior to its dissolution. The lease ultimately became vested in B.C.C.I. which became insolvent. The landlord sought therefore to have the company's dissolution declared void to enable the company to meet its contractual liability for rent (probably by making a claim against its immediate assignee under an indemnity covenant). *Held,* the company should be restored to the register. *Re Forte's Manufacturing Ltd* [1994] B.C.C. 84.[29]

The discretion is also exercised to enable a liquidator to distribute overlooked assets, *e.g.* money wrongly paid to the Inland Revenue.[30] It was not exercised

---

[22] As from November 16, 1989.

[23] See *e.g. Re Philip Powis Ltd* [1998] B.C.C. 756; *Scottish Lion Engineering v Benson* 2001 S.L.T. 1037, O.H.

[24] *Morris v Harris* [1927] A.C. 252.

[25] *Re Lewis and Smart Ltd* [1954] 1 W.L.R. 755.

[26] *Champdany Jute Co. Ltd, Petitioners*, 1924 S.C. 209 (for the purpose of receiving a repayment from the Inland Revenue).

[27] *Re Forte Manufacturing Ltd* [1994] B.C.C. 84.

[28] *per* Slade J. in *Re Thompson and Riches Ltd* [1981] 2 All E.R. 477, 488.

[29] See also *Re Spottiswoode, Dixon and Hunting Ltd* [1912] 1 Ch. 410.

[30] *Champdany case*, above. And to enable a liquidator to grant a title to property of the company sold since dissolution: *McCall and Stephen Ltd, Petitioners* (1920) 57 S.L.R. 480.

where the application had nothing to do with unpaid liabilities or undistributed assets but was "an attempt to play ontological ducks and drakes with the law relating to legacies"[31]:

A testatrix by her will gave a share of her residuary estate to a company but the company was dissolved before she died. An order was refused because the share of residue did not belong to the company before dissolution. The next of kin therefore took the lapsed share as on a partial intestacy: *Re Servers of the Blind League* [1960] 1 W.L.R. 564.

The discretion may be exercised even where the utility of reviving the company depends upon the successful outcome of other legal proceedings.[32]

In very special circumstances the Court of Session in the exercise of its *nobile officium* may declare a dissolution void, although the application has not been made within the two years.[33]

DEFUNCT COMPANIES

By s.652 of the Companies Act 1985, if the Registrar of Companies has reasonable cause to believe that a company is not carrying on business or is not in operation, he may, after carrying out a specified procedure, strike the company's name off the register, after which it is dissolved and ss 654 to 657, above, apply.

The procedure under s.652 is:

(1) The Registrar sends to the company by post a letter asking whether the company is carrying on business.

(2) If no answer is received within one month, he sends within the next 14 days a registered letter, stating that if no reply is received within one month a notice will be published in the *Gazette* with a view to striking the company's name off the register.

(3) If no satisfactory reply is received he sends to the company by post and publishes in the *Gazette* a notice, stating that unless cause is shown to the contrary the company will be struck off after three months.

(4) If cause is not shown to the contrary, he strikes the company off and publishes notice thereof in the *Gazette*, whereupon the company is dissolved.

Companies have, in the past, by inviting the Registrar to exercise his powers, used s.652 as a form of voluntary dissolution. There is now a statutory procedure for voluntary dissolution of private companies: Companies Act 1985, ss 652A–652F.[34] It applies where the company has not traded, and otherwise complies with s.652B, in the three months prior to the application.

---

[31] *per* Hoffmann, L.J. in *Re Forte Manufacturing Ltd*, above at p.87.
[32] *Re Oakleague Ltd* [1995] B.C.C. 921.
[33] *Collins Brothers and Co. Ltd, Petitioners*, 1916 S.C. 620. Contrast *Kerr (Lord Macdonald's Curator Bonis) and Another, Petitioners*, 1924 S.C. 163, and *Forth Shipbreaking Co. Ltd, Petitioners*, 1924 S.C. 489.
[34] Inserted by the *Deregulation & Contracting Out Act* 1994, s.13 & Sch.5.

Striking the company's name off the register does not affect the liability of any director or member of the company, and the company may still be wound up by the court. If the company is to be wound up, it should first be restored to the register under s.653 of the Companies Act 1985.[35]

Section 653 provides that if the company, or any member or creditor[36] thereof, feels aggrieved[36a] by the striking off the register, it or he may within 20 years, apply[37] to the court which, if satisfied that the company was carrying on business or in operation at the time of the striking off or otherwise that it is just that the company be revived, may order that the name of the company be restored to the register.[38] A petition for restoration under the section should contain an outline explanation of why the company was struck off.[39] Upon an office copy of the order being delivered to the Registrar the company is deemed to have continued in existence as if its name had not been struck off.[40] The court may, by the order, give directions for placing the company and all other persons in the same position as nearly as may be as if the company had not been struck off. This provision should be compared with s.651, above, as to the persons who may apply for a court order. A contributory may apply under either section although the time limits are different; 20 years under s.653 and two years under s.651.[41] The word "creditor" in s.653 extends to a plaintiff claiming damages under the Fatal Accidents Acts 1846 to 1959 and having therefore an unquantified claim against the company.[42]

To qualify as a "member or creditor" within s.653 an applicant for restoration must have been a member or creditor of the company at the date when it was struck off the register. However, the personal representative of a deceased shareholder has been held entitled to apply for restoration of a company's name to the register, and then for its winding up, even though he is not registered as a shareholder.[43]

On an application for restoration to the register, the court may only restore or refuse to restore and cannot, *e.g.*, impose a penalty (beyond costs) as a condition of restoration.[44] Nor may it attach terms protecting the position of a particular

---

[35] *Re Cambridge Coffee Room Association Ltd* [1952] All E.R. 112. *Alliance Heritable Security Co. Ltd, Petitioners* (1886) 14 R. 34; *Beith Unionist Association Trustees, Petitioners*, 1950 S.C. 1.

[36] Even in respect of a liability which was merely contingent at the date of the striking off: *City of Westminster Assurance Co. Ltd v Registrar of Companies* [1997] B.C.C. 960, 963, CA.

[36a] As to which, see now *Conti v AIP Private Bank Ltd* 2000 S.L.T. 1015, E.D.

[37] By petition: RSC, O. 102, r.5; R.C.S. 14.2.

[38] S.653(2A)–(2D).

[39] Practice Note (Companies Court) [1974] 1 W.L.R. 1459.

[40] Thus, where the company's interest in a lease had vested in the Crown as *bona vacantia* and, the Crown having disclaimed it, the surety's liability for future rent had terminated, the effect of restoring the company to the register was that none of these events were deemed to have occurred: *Allied Dunbar Assurance plc v Fowle* [1994] B.C.C. 422. *Re Thompson and Riches Ltd* [1981] 2 All E.R. 477.

[41] *Re Harvest Lane Motor Bodies Ltd* [1969] 1 Ch. 457. In *Percy v Garwyn Ltd* 1991 G.W.D. 2–80 (O.H.) P.'s petition for restoration of a dissolved company was granted since P. had demonstrated an interest in having the company restored, *i.e.* to enable him to pursue a claim of damages for injuries suffered while employed by the company.

[42] *Re New Timbiqui Gold Mines Ltd* [1961] Ch. 319; *Re Aga Estate Agencies* [1986] B.C.L.C. 346.

[43] *Re Bayswater Trading Co. Ltd* [1970] 1 W.L.R. 343.

[44] *Re Brown Bayley's Steel Works Ltd* (1905) 21 T.L.R. 374; *Re Moses and Cohen Ltd* [1957] 1 W.L.R. 1007.

individual.[45] It may, however, make the restoration conditional on the company's filing such statutory returns with the Registrar as are necessary to bring the company's file up to date.[46] A company has been restored to enable a landlord to serve a rent review notice on it, thus increasing the liability of an original tenant for the company's defaults[47] and also to enable a landlord, on default by an assignee of the lease, to recover from the surety of the original tenant company.[48] Where an application to restore is pending, the court should adjourn proceedings mistakenly brought on behalf of the dissolved company rather than give judgment for the defendant.[49]

The restoration of the company to the register under s.653 validates retrospectively all acts done on behalf of the company between its dissolution and its restoration.[50] In one English case, where the petition was that of a contributory and there were assets available for the shareholders or creditors, as the case might be, the court directed that, as regards creditors whose debts were not statute-barred at the date of dissolution, the period between dissolution and restoration to the register was not to be counted for the purposes of any Statute of Limitations.[51] Where, *e.g.*, a creditor petitions and there is no indication that other creditors might be unfairly affected by an order not containing a special provision as to the limitation of actions, no such provision will be inserted in the order.[52] In so far as the property of the company has passed to the Crown under s.654, above, the provisions of s.655 apply and the Crown may validly dispose of those assets paying a cash sum in lieu on the company's revival, above.

Where the company is in breach of its statutory obligations and at least one applicant is guilty of some default, the normal order for taxation of costs should be on a common fund basis (instead of the usual order on a party and party basis).[53]

---

[45] *Re Priceland Ltd* [1997] B.C.C. 207.

[46] *Healy, Petitioner* (1903) 5 F. 644, followed in *Charles Dale Ltd, Petitioners*, 1927 S.C. 130.

[47] *Re Priceland Ltd, ibid.*

[48] *City of Westminster Assurance Co. Ltd v Registrar of Companies* [1997] B.C.C. 960, CA.

[49] *Steans Fashions Ltd v Legal & General Assurance Society Ltd* [1995] B.C.C. 510, CA.

[50] *Tymans Ltd v Craven* [1952] 2 Q.B. 100, C.A., applied in *Re Boxco Ltd* [1970] Ch. 442 (Legal charge created by a company after being struck off. Order for restoration made. Company put in same position retrospectively as if charge duly created and registered).

[51] *Re Donald Kenyon Ltd* [1956] 1 W.L.R. 1397. *Aliter* where the company is already in liquidation: *Re Vickers and Bott Ltd* [1968] 2 All E.R. 264.

[52] *Re Huntington Poultry Ltd* [1969] 1 W.L.R. 204, distinguished *Re Donald Kenyon*, above.

[53] *Re Court Lodge Developments Co. Ltd* [1973] 1 W.L.R. 1097.

Chapter 30

MERGERS AND DIVISIONS

NEITHER of the words "merger" or "division" has any definite general legal meaning.[1] A division is where a company transfers its assets to one or more new companies with substantially the same shareholders. The latter case is also known as a demerger or a reconstruction. A merger is the amalgamation of two or more companies into one. This occurs, *e.g.* where a company acquires the assets of, or the shares in, one or more companies whose shareholders are issued with the appropriate number of shares in the new company. In this chapter the formal procedures which are available to achieve such divisions and agreed mergers, *i.e.* where all the companies, but not necessarily all the shareholders and creditors, concerned are in agreement, are set out. The alternative, an often contested form of merger, is usually referred to as a "takeover", *i.e.* the acquisition of a controlling interest in the shares in one company as the consequence of an offer to acquire those shares by another company. Such takeovers are the subject of Chapter 31, below.

Both a merger and division in the sense used in this chapter may be effected (1) under s.110 of the Insolvency Act 1986, or (2) by a scheme at arrangement under ss 425 to 427A of the Companies Act 1985.[2] The latter procedure becomes more complex in certain mergers and divisions involving public companies, as a result of the implementation of the third and sixth EC directives[3] by Schedule 15B.

A scheme of arrangement under s.425 can also be used for purposes other than mergers and divisions, *e.g.* to effect a re-organisation of share capital, a composition with creditors or a variation of class rights.

MERGERS OR DIVISIONS UNDER SECTION 110 OF THE INSOLVENCY ACT 1986

Under s.110, a company (1) which is in voluntary winding up; (2) may transfer or sell the whole or part of its business or property to another company, whether a company within the meaning of the Act or not; and (3) may, in the case of a members' voluntary winding up, pass a special resolution authorising the

---

[1] There is a definition for some mergers and divisions of public companies as the result of the implementation of two EC directives. See p.669, below.
[2] For examples of agreed mergers see *Head (Henry) & Co. Ltd v Ropner Holdings Ltd* [1952] Ch. 124. *Government Stock etc. Investment Co. Ltd v Christopher* [1956] 1 W.L.R. 237; *Rights and Issues Investment Trust Ltd v Stylo Shoes Ltd* [1965] Ch. 250; and *Re BTR plc* [2000] 1 B.C.L.C. 740.
[3] Adopted on October 9, 1978 [1978] O.J. L295/36, and December 17, 1982 [1982] O.J. L378/47, respectively.

liquidator to receive as consideration cash or shares, policies or other like interests in the transferee company for distribution among the members of the transferor company according to their rights and interests in that company. The sanction of the court is unnecessary in a members' voluntary winding up. In the case of a creditors' winding up the liquidator's authority for (3) must come either from the court, or from the liquidation committee.

The sale may be to a foreign company.[4] However, it must be to a company and not to a speculator who hopes to form a company to take over the assets.[5]

Procedure

The following procedure might be adopted under s.110 if a members' voluntary winding up is involved. A meeting of the transferor company is summoned in order to pass resolutions for reconstruction or amalgamation. At the meeting, resolutions are passed for the voluntary winding up of the company, the appointment of a liquidator, and giving authority to the liquidator to enter into an agreement with the transferee company on the terms of a draft submitted to the meeting.

The agreement typically provides that the transferee company shall purchase the assets of the transferor company, except a sum retained by the liquidator to discharge its liabilities, that the consideration shall be the allotment by the transferee company to the liquidator or his nominees of shares, fully or partly paid up, in the transferee company, that the liquidator shall give notice to the shareholders of the transferor company of the number of shares to which they are entitled, and the time within which they must apply, and that failure to apply for shares within that time shall preclude their rights to any shares.

A reconstruction scheme provided that shareholders in the old company should apply for shares in the new company within 10 days after being given notice requiring them to apply, and that the liquidator should dispose of all shares not applied for. On June 12, the liquidator sent out notices requiring application for shares in the new company to be made before June 25. P, a shareholder in the old company, applied on August 24. *Held*, P was not entitled to an allotment of shares in the new company, or to any other relief: *Postlethwaite v Port Philip, etc., Gold Mining Co.* (1889) 43 Ch.D. 452.

In the case of a creditors' winding up the necessary authority would come either from the court or from the liquidation committee.[6]

Instead of the liquidator being authorised to dispose of all shares not applied for by the members of the transferor company, an underwriting agreement may be made in respect to such shares.[7] If the agreement is silent as to the disposal of the proceeds of sale of the shares not applied for, the proceeds must be distributed among the members of the transferor company who have not applied for shares in the transferee company.[8]

Shares may be given directly to the members of the transferor company instead of being applied for in the manner explained above.

---

[4] *Re Irrigation Co. of France* (1871) L.R. 6 Ch. App. 176.
[5] *Bird v Bird's Patent, etc., Sewage Co.* (1874) L.R. 9 Ch. App. 358.
[6] Above, Ch.28.
[7] *Barrow v Paringo Mines (1909) Ltd* (1909) 2 Ch. 658.
[8] *Re Lake View Extended Gold Mine Co.* [1900] W.N. 44.

Protection of dissentient members

A sale or arrangement under s.110 of the Insolvency Act 1986 is binding on all members of the transferor company, whether they agree to it or not: s.110(5). However, a member who (1) did not vote in favour of the special resolution, and (2) expressed his dissent from it in writing addressed to the liquidator and left at the registered office within seven days after the passing of the resolution, may require the liquidator either to abstain from carrying the resolution into effect or to purchase his interest at a price to be determined by agreement or arbitration: s.111 of the Insolvency Act 1986. Subs.111(3) below shows that the election is that of the liquidator.

A transferee of shares whose transfer was not registered when the special resolution was passed may be entitled to have the register of members rectified and to dissent from the resolution.[9]

If the liquidator elects to purchase the member's interest, the purchase money must be paid before the transferor company is dissolved, and be raised by the liquidator as is determined by special resolution: s.111(3). The agreement usually provides for the retention by the liquidator out of the assets of the transferor company of a sum to cover the interests of the dissentient shareholders.

The articles cannot deprive a member of his statutory right to the value of his shareholding if he dissents.[10]

Protection of dissentient creditors

The liquidator must pay the creditors of the transferor company in the usual way in a winding up. If, however, the creditors conceive that they will be prejudiced by the transfer of all the company's assets to the transferee company, they may petition for a compulsory winding-up order. Section 110(6) of the Insolvency Act 1986 provides that the special resolution for reconstruction shall not be valid if, within a year, an order is made for winding up the company by the court, unless the court sanctions the resolution.

Sale under power in memorandum

The memorandum of association may give power to a company to sell its undertaking for shares in another company. If, however, the whole of the undertaking is to be sold and the proceeds are to be distributed among the shareholders, the procedure laid down in s.110 of the Insolvency Act 1986, including the provisions for the protection of dissentient shareholders and creditors, cannot be excluded.[11]

SCHEME OF ARRANGEMENT UNDER SECTION 425 OF THE COMPANIES ACT 1985

Scope of the section

The Insolvency Act contains provisions whereby the administrator or liquidator

---

[9] *Re Sussex Brick Co.* [1904] 1 Ch. 598, CA.

[10] *Payne v The Cork Co. Ltd* [1900] 1 Ch. 308.

[11] *Bisgood v Henderson's Transvaal Estates Ltd* [1908] 1 Ch. 743, CA; *cf. Waverley Hydropathic Co. Ltd, Petitioners*, 1948 S.C. 59.

may make an arrangement with a company's creditors.[12] Those are not suitable for mergers or divisions, however. But under s.425 of the Companies Act 1985 a company can also enter into a compromise or arrangement with its creditors, and also its members, or any class thereof, without going into liquidation. Schemes of arrangement under s.425 have a wider potential than voluntary arrangements under the Insolvency Act and can be used for an agreed merger or division of two or more companies subject to the requirements of the section as to consent of the members and the court.

The proper way to distribute the assets of a company otherwise than strictly in accordance with creditors' rights has been held to be by a scheme of arrangement under s.425 which binds all creditors, and not by an agreement or compromise under s.167 of the Insolvency Act which would deprive non-assenting creditors of the court's protection and prevent them from expressing their views.[13] Under s.425 the court may approve a scheme which differs from the statutory scheme on a liquidator.[14]

Although this chapter is concerned primarily with mergers and divisions, since schemes of arrangement can be used for many other purposes, especially in relation to creditors, the following discussion therefore involves all aspects of the procedure.

Statutory requirements

Section 425 provides that a compromise or arrangement will be binding on the company and the creditors or class of creditors or the members or class of members, as the case may be, if:

(1) The court, on the application in a summary way of the company or of any creditor or member of the company (or, if the company is being wound up, of the liquidator), orders a meeting of the creditors[15] or class of creditors, or of the members or class of members[16], to be summoned.

(2) The compromise or arrangement is agreed to by a majority in number representing three-fourths in value[17] of those present and voting either in person or by proxy at the meeting.

(3) It is sanctioned by the court.

If the scheme involves the merger or division of one of more public companies additional requirements are imposed.[18]

---

[12] ss 1–7A and 167. Above Ch.24.

[13] *Re Trix Ltd* [1970] 1 W.L.R. 1421.

[14] *Re Anglo American Insurance Ltd* [2001] 1 B.C.L.C. 755.

[15] Creditors who cannot possibly benefit, *e.g.* because the company's assets are too low, need not be involved in the scheme: *Re British & Commonwealth Holdings plc (No. 3)* [1992] B.C.C. 58; *Re Maxwell Communications Corp. plc* [1994] 1 B.C.L.C. 1.

[16] Members who could not benefit from the scheme have no right to object: *Re RAC Motoring Services Ltd* [2000] 1 B.C.L.C. 307.

[17] In the case of creditors the value of their debt is the relevant criterion; see, *e.g. Re Exchange Securities and Commodities Ltd* (1987) 3 B.C.C. 48.

[18] See p.669, below.

To effect a merger or division under this section, the scheme, involving a transfer of one company's assets to another in return for shares in that company, must therefore be approved by at least 75 per cent of the members and creditors of the transferor company, and by the court. The benefit is that, if the scheme is approved, dissenting shareholders and creditors are bound by it.[19] This is not possible under s.110 of the Insolvency Act, above.

The word "company" in ss 425 and 426[20] means any company liable to be wound up under the Act: s.425(6). Thus it includes a company formed and registered under the 1985 Act, an existing company (in effect, a company formed and registered under a previous Companies Act), or an unregistered company.[21]

Compromise or arrangement

The word "arrangement" has a very wide meaning, and is wider than the word "compromise".[22] An arrangement may involve debenture holders giving an extension of time for payment, accepting a cash payment less than the face value of their debentures,[23] giving up their security in whole or in part, exchanging their debentures for shares in the company[24] or in a new company[25] or having the rights attached to their debentures varied in some other respect.[26] Creditors may take cash in part payment of their claims and the balance in shares or debentures in the company; preference shareholders may give up their rights to arrears of dividends,[27] agree to accept a reduced rate of dividend in the future, or have their class rights otherwise varied[28] (the use of s.425 to vary class rights has already been dealt with[29]). The section is also widely used for compromises with policy holders by insurance companies.[30] Or the members of a company in liquidation may agree with the company to seek or not to oppose a stay of the winding up, whereunder the members will give up their existing right to have all the proceeds of the company's assets distributed among them and instead be remitted to their contractual rights under the articles.[31] It even includes a scheme whereby the shareholders transfer their shares to another company, since that affects the contractual arrangements between the shareholders and their company so that there is an arrangement between them.[32]

Section 425 itself provides that the expression "arrangement" includes a reorganisation of the share capital of the company by the consolidation of shares

---

[19] s.425(2). For examples of the effect of such approval see *Barclays Bank plc v British & Commonwealth Holdings plc* [1995] B.C.C. 19 and *Re Waste Recycling Group plc* [2004] B.C.C. 328.
[20] Below.
[21] Which the court has power to wind up under s.221 of the I.A. 1986. This can include companies incorporated abroad: See *e.g. Re Drax Holdings Ltd* [2004] B.C.C. 334.
[22] *Re Guardian Assce. Co.* [1917] 1 Ch. 431, CA.
[23] *e.g. The Philadelphia Securities Co. v The Realisation etc. Corpn. of Scotland Ltd* (1903) 11 S.L.T. 217 (O.H.).
[24] *e.g. Re Telewest Communications plc* [2005] B.C.C. 36.
[25] *Re Empire Mining Co.* (1890) 44 Ch.D.402.
[26] *e.g. Wright & Greig Ltd, Petitioners* 1911 1 S.L.T. 353.
[27] *e.g. Balmenach-Glenlivet Distillery Ltd, Petitioners*, 1916 S.C. 639.
[28] *City etc., Trust Corporation Ltd, Petitioners*, 1951 S.C. 570.
[29] Above, p.209.
[30] See *e.g. Re Equitable Life Assurance Society* [2002] 2 B.C.L.C. 510.
[31] *Per* Megarry J. in *Re Calgary and Edmonton Land Co. Ltd* [1975] 1 W.L.R. 355 at p.363.
[32] *Re N.F.U. Development Trust* [1972] 1 W.L.R. 1548.

of different classes or by the division of shares into shares of different classes. The word "compromise" implies some element of accommodation on each side. It is not apt to describe a total surrender. Similarly, the word "arrangement" implies some element of give and take.[33]

Where an arrangement under s.425 is essentially a scheme for the purchase by an outsider of all the issued shares of a company the scheme will not be sanctioned unless that company consents. Such consent may be expressed by the members in general meeting or by the board of directors.[34] It cannot be used therefore for a contested take-over or merger. Even if the takeover or merger is an agreed one, one judge has said that the court will not allow the provisions of ss 428 to 430F, which require the outside purchaser to acquire 90 per cent of the shares before he may compulsorily acquire the remainder,[35] to be circumvented by the use of s.425 where the necessary resolution under s.425 can only be passed with the assistance of votes of the wholly-owned subsidiary of the offeror company.[36] But there is no general principle that s.425 is subordinate to the rights of minority shareholders under ss 428 to 430F. The lower majority required is balanced by the need for the court's approval.[37]

Summoning the class meetings

The first stage in effecting a scheme of arrangement is to ask the court to summon the appropriate meetings of shareholders or creditors. This requires identification of the different classes (if any) of shareholders or creditors, since each class must meet and vote separately. Until recently, the court would simply act on the company's proposals and would not consider the issue as to whether the classes were properly constituted until it came to approve the scheme after the meetings had been held. The problem was that this sometimes meant that a scheme would be turned down at that late stage because of incorrect class identification even if there were no objections, when the issue could have been dealt with at the beginning, thus saving a great deal of expense. The courts finally began to appreciate this anomaly,[38] and the procedure was changed by a Practice Statement in 2002.[39] Thus, if there is a potential problem as to the identity of the classes, the matter is now considered at the initial stage.[40] The onus is on the company to draw the court's attention to any potential problems and to notify those affected so that they can raise objections. It is still possible for there to be objections on this point at the final stage but the court will want to know why those objections were not raised earlier.

---

[33] *Re Savoy Hotel Ltd* [1961] 3 All E.R. 646.
[34] *ibid.* But not all such cases will fail, see *Re National Bank Ltd* [1966] 1 W.L.R. 819; *The Singer Manufacturing Co. Ltd v Robinow*, 1971 S.C. 11 (scheme to enable parent company to acquire remaining 7·3 per cent shareholding in subsidiary held competent).
[35] Ch.31, below.
[36] *Re Hellenic & General Trust Ltd* [1976] 1 W.L.R. 123.
[37] *Re BTR plc* [2000] 1 B.C.L.C. 740 (CA).
[38] *Re Hawk Insurance Co Ltd* [2001] 2 B.C.L.C. 480 at 513, *per* Chadwick L.J.; *Re Equitable Life Assurance Society* [2002] B.C.L.C. 510.
[39] See [2002] 3 All E.R. 96.
[40] See eg *Re Telewest Communications plc* [2004] B.C.C. 342, affmd [2005] B.C.C. 29 CA.

Identifying the correct classes

The litigation concerning the correct classes which require separate meetings has involved both members and creditors. The classic test is that propounded by Bowen L.J. in *Sovereign Life Assurance Co v Dodd*:[41]

> "It must be confined to those whose rights are not so dissimilar as to make it impossible for them to consult together with a view to their common interest."

Thus it is a question of looking at the rights of those involved and not their personal interests. Members or creditors with the same legal rights may well have different or even conflicting interests, but that is an issue to be looked at in the context of fairness, at the final approval stage. Otherwise there would be a plethora of classes.[42] Further, even the existence of different rights does not always require separate class meetings. Chadwick L.J. in *Re Hawk Insurance Co Ltd*,[43] said that, having looked at the rights to be released and those to be gained, the court should ask whether those rights are really so dissimilar that they cannot consult together. Too zealous an application could give a minority an inappropriate veto. Their rights would be better considered at the sanction stage. Thus in *Re Telewest Communications plc*,[44] bondholders who had different rights on an insolvency, since some were denominated in sterling whilst others were in US dollars, were nevertheless held to constitute a single class for the purpose of agreeing to the scheme. This was because there was a single scheme whereby they would all be credited with shares in a new holding company, pro rata to their claims, in place of their bonds. It was a single scheme with all the bondholders. The difference would come in the conversion rate to be applied, which it was argued would unfairly discriminate against the sterling bondholders and would be different from that applied on a liquidation. That issue could be considered as a matter of the overall fairness of the scheme at the approval stage.[45] Shareholders or creditors with no interest in the company, *e.g.* because the company is insolvent and they would not be entitled to anything on a winding-up, need not be included.[46]

Other jurisdictional issues

At the preliminary hearing the court will also decide other jurisdictional issues, *i.e.* those as to whether the court would have the power to approve the scheme if were to be approved by the class meetings. One example is where the scheme

---

[41] [1892] 2 Q.B. 573 at 583.

[42] *Re BTR plc* [1999] 2 B.C.L.C. 675, affmd [2000] 1 B.C.L.C. 740 (CA) (where even the objectors could not identify all the classes on that basis); *Re Anglo American Insurance Ltd* [2001] 1 B.C.L.C. 755; *Re Waste Recycling Group plc* [2004] B.C.C. 328; *Re Telewest Communications plc* [2004] B.C.C. 342 affmd [2005] B.C.C. 29 CA; c.f. *Re Hellenic and General Trust Ltd* [1976] 1 W.L.R. 123 , explained on other grounds in *Re BTR plc*.

[43] [2001] 2 B.C.L.C. 480 at 519. See also *Re Equitable Life Assurance Co* [2002] 2 B.C.L.C. 510, *per* Lloyd J. where the concept of "consulting together" was said to be an outdated idea.

[44] [2004] B.C.C. 342 affmd [2005] B.C.C. 29 CA.

[45] See [2005] B.C.C. 36 where the scheme was held to be inherently fair.

[46] *Re Mytravel plc* [2004] EWHC 2741 (Ch).

required an order to be made by the court under s.427 and the court would have had no power to make such an order. In those circumstances, holding the meetings would have been pointless and so the court refused to summon the meetings.[47]

Holding the class meetings

Where a meeting of creditors or members is summoned under s.425, with every notice of the meeting there must be sent a statement explaining the effect of the compromise or arrangement and, in particular, stating any material interests of the directors in any capacity and the effect thereon of the compromise or arrangement in so far as it is different from the effect on the like interest of other persons. If the meeting is summoned by advertisement, a similar statement, or a notification of the place where such a statement may be obtained, must be included. Where the compromise or arrangement affects the rights of debenture holders the statement must give the like explanation as respects the trustees of a deed for securing the issue of debentures as it is required to give as respects the directors: s.426.

Section 426 must be faithfully complied with; the court "has no discretionary power to dispense with the procedural requirements of section [426]."[48] Thus a scheme will not be sanctioned if the explanatory statement, while stating that the company's assets have been revalued, does not give the amount of the revaluation,[49] or if a copy of the petition[50] or a copy of the scheme[51] has been sent without any further explanation.[52] Material interests of directors must always be stated, even although those interests are in no way differently affected by the scheme from the interests of other persons.[53] In deciding whether the members of the class have been properly informed, the notice summoning the meeting and the circular can be read together.[54]

Where there is a change in the material interests of the directors or of any other material circumstances between the issue of the statement and the meetings to consider the scheme the court will nevertheless sanction the scheme, even though the meetings are not informed of the change, if it is satisfied that no reasonable shareholder would have altered his decision as to the scheme had he known of the changes.[55] The test is whether all material changes of circumstances which have come to the attention of the board between the issuing of the circular and the meeting have been disclosed to those entitled to vote at the meeting. A material change for this purpose is one which would be likely to affect a reasonable shareholder's voting intentions.[56]

---

[47] ibid. The matter was not raised before the CA in that case.
[48] Per Lord Guthrie in *The Scottish Eastern etc. Trust Ltd, Petitioners*, 1966 S.L.T. 285 at p.288.
[49] *Re Dorman, Long & Co. Ltd* [1934] Ch. 635.
[50] *Rankin & Blackmore Ltd, Petitioners*, 1950 S.C. 218.
[51] *Peter Scott & Co. Ltd, Petitioners*, 1950 S.C. 507.
[52] The fact that some creditors have more background information than others is not fatal, however: *Re Heron International NV* [1994] 1 B.C.L.C. 667.
[53] *Coltness Iron Co. Ltd, Petitioners*, 1951 S.C. 476; contrast *Second Scottish Investment Trust etc., Petitioners*, 1962 S.L.T. 392.
[54] *Re RAC Motoring Services Ltd* [2000] 1 B.C.L.C. 307.
[55] *Re Jessel Trust Ltd* [1985] B.C.L.C. 119; *Re Minster Assets plc* [1985] B.C.L.C. 200; *Re Allied Domecq plc* [2000] 1 B.C.L.C. 134.
[56] *Re MB Group plc* (1989) 5 B.C.C. 584.

As to (2) above, "three-fourths in value of the members or class of members" in s.425 refers to the size of the stake which each member has in the company. "The purpose is to prevent a numerical majority with a small stake outvoting a minority with a large stake, *e.g.* to prevent 51 members with one share each outvoting 49 members with 10 shares each."[57]

Any proper form of proxy may be used and it is not necessary to its validity that it should be sent to the company's offices before the meeting.[58] Directors who, pursuant to the court's order, receive proxies must use them whether they are for or against the scheme.[59]

The sanction of the court

Before giving its sanction to a scheme of arrangement the court will see "First, that the provisions of the statute have been complied with. Secondly, that the class was fairly represented by those who attended the meeting and that the statutory majority are acting bona fide and are not coercing the minority in order to promote interests adverse to those of the class whom they purport to represent; and, thirdly, that the arrangement is such as a man of business would reasonably approve."[60] That judgment is to be made assuming that the intelligent and honest person was acting as a member of the class concerned and in respect of his interests as such.

Whilst the courts are concerned to state that approving a scheme is not merely a matter of checking that all the procedural requirements of the sections have been met with,[61] they are reluctant to interfere if the scheme has been approved by the correct majority, and typically the majority is usually far in excess of that required. Thus, for example, in *Re Waste Recycling Group*,[62] the judge was impressed by the facts that the scheme (a merger) was approved by 99.7 per cent in value of the shares voted and that those votes came principally from the smaller shareholders. That was so even though the number of shareholders who actually voted was small and only 74 per cent of the potential votes were actually exercised. In *Re Telewest Communications plc (No. 2)*,[63] the scheme (to convert bonds into shares) was approved by 88 per cent of the bondholders. The dissenters were some of those who held only bonds denominated in sterling and who complained as to the unfairness of the proposed exchange rate vis a vis the dollar bondholders. Again the judge was impressed by the strength of the majority[64] and by the fact that some of those who owned only sterling bonds had

---

[57] *per* Brightman J. in *Re N.F.U. Development Trust Ltd* [1972] 1 W.L.R. 1548 at p.1553.

[58] *Re Dorman, Long & Co. Ltd* [1934] Ch. 635; *La Lainière de Roubaix v Glen Glove etc. Co. Ltd*, 1926 S.C. 91.

[59] See n.53, above.

[60] *per* Astbury J. in *Re Anglo-Continental Supply Co. Ltd* [1922] 2 Ch. 723 at p.736. CA at p.238. For adoption in Scotland, see *per* Lord President Dunedin in *Shandon Hydropathic Co. Ltd, Petitioners*, 1911 S.C. 1153 at p.1155. This statement is always applied.

[61] The important point as to establishing the correct identity of the classes is now mainly dealt with at the earlier stage: see above.

[62] [2004] B.C.C. 328. See also eg *Re Equitable Life Assurance Society* [2002] 2 B.C.L.C. 510.

[63] [2005] B.C.C. 36.

[64] Although this was inevitable once it had been decided that all the bondholders could meet as a single class: *Re Telewest Communications plc* [2004] B.C.C. 342, affmd [2005] B.C.C. 29 CA, above.

voted for the scheme. In any event, the scheme apart from the exchange rate was very much in the bondholders' interests and the exchange rate proposals were not inherently unfair.

In *Re Allied Domecq plc*,[65] the judge also relied on the fact that the scheme (for the disposal of a subsidiary) had been recommended by the board. In that case the intended and named buyer dropped out after the approval by the meeting but before the court's sanction was obtained. The court nevertheless approved the scheme since the mechanics of the sale were not dependent on any particular buyer.[66] But the approval was made on terms that no actual sale could proceed without a special resolution as required by the original scheme. In another unusual case, *Re BAT Industries plc*,[67] the judge considered that contingent creditors (*i.e.* those with a potential tort action against the company) had the right to object at this stage, although on the facts he rejected their objections.

The court cannot alter the scheme and impose one that the relevant classes have not agreed to,[68] but it would be prepared to set aside a scheme where the court's consent has been obtained by fraud, even if that means unravelling the scheme. But not if the result would have been the same without the fraud[69] or if it would not assist the objectors.[70]

An order sanctioning a compromise or arrangement under s.425 has no effect until an office copy has been delivered to the Registrar of Companies. A copy of the order must also be annexed to every copy of the memorandum issued after the making of the order: s.425(3).

The costs of the scheme may be borne by the company and there may be one set of costs for opposing creditors but not for any supporting creditors. In general, costs should be kept to a minimum and one set of creditors should not be ordered to pay the costs of another set of creditors.[71]

Human rights issues

The argument has been made that the procedure under s.425 by which, as we have seen, dissenting shareholders or creditors can be compelled to accept a scheme which changes their rights, is contrary to Art.1 of the First Protocol to the European Convention on Human Rights, now part of UK law by virtue of the Human Rights Act 1998. That article provides that;

> "Every natural and legal person is entitled to the peaceful enjoyment of his possessions. No one shall be deprived of his possessions except in the public interest and subject to the conditions provided for by law and by the general principles of international law. The preceding provisions shall not, however, in any way impair the right of a State to enforce such laws as it deems necessary to control the use of property in accordance with the general interest . . ."

---

[65] [2000] 1 B.C.L.C. 134.
[66] And that this would have been clear to those voting at the meeting, and even, if not, it would not have affected the way a reasonable shareholder would have cast his vote.
[67] September 3, 1998.
[68] *Kempe v Ambassador Insurance Co* [1998] 1 B.C.L.C. 234, PC.
[69] There are other sanctions available to the court against the fraudsters.
[70] *Fletcher v Royal Automobile Club Ltd* [2000] 1 B.C.L.C. 331.
[71] *Re Esal (Commodities) Ltd* [1985] B.C.L.C. 450.

In *Re Equitable Life Assurance Society*,[72] Lloyd J. rejected that argument on two grounds. First, he relied on a decision of the European Commission of Human Rights,[73] that provisions such as s.425 are only caught by Art.1 of the First Protocol if the law creates such inequality that one person could be arbitrarily and unjustly deprived of property in favour of another. The terms of s.425 and the case law made it clear that that was not the case. Second, that it did not amount to a confiscation of property since all schemes require some exchange of rights. No scheme capable of being confirmed could amount to a confiscation in breach of Art.1. The same judge heard the case of *Re Waste Recycling Group plc*,[74] where the objector argued that, since he had bought his shares on environmental grounds, being deprived of those shares under the scheme meant that he would no longer be able to influence the company's policies on that issue at meetings, etc. That interest, being non-financial, invoked Art.1 since it could not be compensated for by a financial exchange. The judge said that s.425 took account of rights but not interests and that Art.1, in its operation in relation to s.425, did not distinguish between shareholders as to why they purchased their shares, be it for financial or public benefit reasons.

A different issue arose in *Re Pan Atlantic Insurance Co Ltd*,[75] where a scheme which involved claims being settled by an independent adjudicator was challenged as being contrary to Art.6(1) of the Convention itself. That Article provides for a fair and public hearing of any dispute as to civil rights by an independent and impartial tribunal established by law. Lloyd J., again, heard the case and, after reviewing the case law on Art.6(1),[76] decided that the right of access to the courts was not absolute and could be subject to limitations, provided they do not go to the very essence of the right but pursue a legitimate and proportional aim. On the facts the scheme did exactly that since the arbitrator's decision was final and binding only insofar as the law allowed and was proportional in the context of the scheme (an alternative to a winding up).

Facilitating a division or a merger

In order to facilitate schemes which can be classified as a reconstruction,[77] or amalgamation, s.427 provides that when an application is made to the court under s.425 for the sanctioning of a compromise or arrangement, where the compromise or arrangement is for the purposes of a scheme for the division of a company or the merger of two or more companies and the scheme involves the transfer of the whole or part of the undertaking or property of a company (called "a transferor company") to another company (called "the transferee company"), the court may make an order providing for the following matters:

---

[72] [2002] 2 B.C.L.C. 510 at 535–7.
[73] *Bamelid and Malström v Sweden* (1982) 29 D.R. 64.
[74] [2004] B.C.C. 328.
[75] [2003] B.C.C. 847.
[76] *Ashingdane v United Kingdom* (1985) E.H.R.R. 528.
[77] A reconstruction has been held to require that the members of the old and new company are the same: *Re Mytravel plc* [2004] E.W.H.C. 2741 (Ch). The CA was not concerned with this point.

(1) The transfer to the transferee company of the whole or part of the undertaking and of the property or liabilities of a transferor company. This cannot apply to non-assignable rights,[78] nor can it transfer the office of executor from one bank to another; such an office of personal trust is incapable of assignment.[78a] But contracts of employment are transferred under the Transfer of Undertaking, (Protection of Employment) Regulations 1981.[79]

(2) The allotting by the transferee company of any shares, debentures, policies or other similar interests in such company to the appropriate persons.

(3) The continuation by or against the transferee company of any legal proceedings pending by or against a transferor company.

(4) The dissolution, without winding up, of a transferor company.

(5) The provision to be made for persons who dissent from the scheme.

(6) Any incidental matters.

An office copy of an order made under s.427 must be registered with the Registrar of Companies within seven days.

Mergers and divisions of public companies—additional requirements

Following the implementation of the third and sixth EC directives on company law[80] by the Companies (Mergers and Divisions) Regulations 1987,[81] additional requirements to those already required by ss 425 to 427 are imposed where the scheme of arrangement falls within one of the following three categories as defined in s.427A.

Case 1—Mergers by acquisition

Where a public company proposes to transfer all of its undertaking, property and liabilities to another public company (which has not been formed for that purpose) in return for shares in the transferee company to be held by the transferor shareholders.

Case 2—Mergers by formation of a new company

Where two or more public companies propose to transfer all their undertakings, etc. to any type of company formed for that purpose, members of the transferor company receiving shares in the new company by way of total or part consideration.

[78] *Re L Hotel Co Ltd* [1946] 1 All E.R. 319.
[78a] *In the Estate of Skinner (Decd.)* [1958] 1 W.L.R. 1043.
[79] SI 1981/794.
[80] Dir. 78/885 [1978] O.J. L295/36 and Dir. 82/891, [1982] O.J. L378/47.
[81] SI 1987/1991.

Note that case 1 does not apply where the transferee company is specially formed to receive the assets, etc., of the transferor and that case 2 applies where the transferee company is a private company provided it was set up for the purpose of the merger.

Case 3—Divisions

Where a public company proposes to divide all its undertaking, etc. between two or more companies which are either public companies or companies formed for the purpose of the division, members of the transferor company receiving shares in the transferee companies by way of total or part consideration.

In all these cases there is therefore an agreed arrangement involving a share exchange by the transferee company's shareholders. It is envisaged that the transferor company or companies will be dissolved after the scheme has gone through.[82]

Where s.427A applies the court cannot sanction a scheme unless the additional requirements specified in Sch.15B have been complied with. These are somewhat complex since there are eight additional requirements for specified mergers and divisions with a further two for divisions alone, whilst at the same time there are seven different exemptions from some or all of these additional requirements. As a final complication, in three of these exemptions additional exemptions from parts of ss 425 and 426 are also included.

The following is a summary of the additional requirements and exemptions:

The additional requirements

    (i)   In a case 1 or case 3 scheme there must be a meeting of each class of members of any transferee company not formed for the purpose of the merger or division. Section 425 already requires a meeting of the transferor company.

   (ii)   The directors of all transferor and transferee companies[83] must draw up draft terms of the merger or division. These must include details of the companies involved, the share exchange ratio, the allotment of the new shares, the directors' benefits, and, in a division, the allocation of the shares.

 (iii)   The draft terms must be delivered to the Registrar who will publish a notice of receipt in the Gazette. This gives official notification of that receipt.[84]

 (iv)   There must be at least one month's gap between such publication and the holding of any meeting[85] to consider the scheme.

---

[82] These requirements do not apply if the transferor company is already in liquidation and so do not apply to reconstructions under s.110 of the Insolvency Act 1986, above.
[83] Except those formed specifically for the purpose of the scheme.
[84] Above, p.61.
[85] Including one under s.425.

(v) The directors[86] must draw up a report consisting of the explanatory statement already required by s.426[87] together with the legal and economic grounds for the draft terms including the share exchange ratio, and in a division, the allocation arrangements.

(vi) An expert's report must be drawn up for each transferor and transferee[88] company involved, dealing in particular with the share exchange ratio and any valuation problems. A statement as to the reasonableness of these must be included.

(vii) The draft terms, directors' report, experts' report and the previous three years' accounts must be available for inspection for at least one month prior to any meeting required under s.425 or (i) above.

(viii) The memorandum and articles of any transferee company set up for the purpose of the scheme must be approved by an ordinary resolution of each transferor company involved.

(ix) In a division the directors of the transferor company must report any material changes between the time when draft terms were adopted and any meeting, to that meeting and to the directors of the transferee company.

(x) Following receipt of a report under (ix) the transferee directors must notify the change to any meetings of the transferee companies or send a notice to every member entitled to attend such meetings.

Exceptions to the additional requirements

(a) The requirement to hold a meeting of the transferee company may be dispensed with if five per cent. of the transferee members could have required such a meeting and no such meeting has been requested, provided requirement (vii) has been complied with.

(b) There need be no directors' or experts' reports in a case 3 scheme if all the relevant shareholders agree.

(c) The court may decide that no meetings at all need be held (including ones held under s.425) in a case 3 scheme.

(d) In a case 1 scheme where the transferor is wholly owned by the transferee company, the draft terms of the merger can omit all references to share exchange ratios, etc., the directors' and experts' reports can be omitted and no explanatory circular under s.426 need be given.

(e) Where exemption (d) applies the court may order that no meetings of either company be held, even under s.425.

---

[86] Of all the companies.
[87] Above.
[88] Except those formed specifically for the purpose of the scheme.

(f) In a division, where the transferor is wholly-owned by the transferee companies the court may dispense with the need for a meeting of the transferor company under s.425.

(g) In a case 1 scheme, where the transferor is an 80 per cent. or more but not wholly owned subsidiary of the transferee company the court may dispense with a meeting of the transferee company.

Chapter 31

TAKEOVERS

The majority of mergers or takeovers, take place without a scheme of arrangement under s.425 or a reconstruction under s.110 of the Insolvency Act 1986, but by the simple method of one company acquiring a majority or the whole of the shares of another company from its shareholders. In such a case it is usual for the acquiring company (the offeror company) to make an offer (called a takeover bid) to the shareholders in the other company (the target or offeree company) to purchase their shares at a stated price and to fix a time within which the offer is to be accepted, with a condition that if a named percentage of the shareholders do not accept the offer, the offer is to be void. The offer is usually at a higher price than the current market price of the shares as quoted on the Stock Exchange and it may be in cash (*e.g.* £2 per share) or in kind (*e.g.* two of the offeror company's shares for each of the target company's shares). There are many economic reasons why such an offer is made. Sometimes more than one takeover bid is made for the same company so that there are rival bidders. As has already been seen[1] this form of merger is the only practical form where the two companies do not agree to the merger although it can also be used for agreed mergers by way of an agreed bid.

Statutory and other provisions

There is currently little in the Companies Act of specific relevance to such takeovers. Section 428–430F are an exception to this in that they allow an offeror who has received 90 per cent or more acceptances to purchase the remaining shares compulsorily. Those sections are considered in detail at the end of this chapter. Other parts of the Act which are relevant include: the restrictions on a company acquiring its own shares[2]; the restrictions on companies giving financial assistance for the acquisition of their shares[3]; the rules on merger accounting relating to the share premium account[4]; and disclosure of interests by directors.[5] The public controls of mergers to avoid monopoly situations arising, which is outside the scope of this book, are contained in legislation both domestic and from the European Union. The most important controls on the conduct of takeovers are those set out in the City Code on Takeovers and Mergers and administered by the City Panel. At present, this is a "voluntary" self-regulatory

[1] Above, p.663.
[2] See p.160, above.
[3] See p.172, above.
[4] See p.145, above.
[5] See p.273, above.

code to which all who deal in shares in public companies are subject. The City Code is dealt with below. The distinction between the legal and self-regulatory controls will largely disappear when the UK implements the 13th Directive on takeover bids in 2006.[6] The considerable effects of that Directive on the current situation are discussed below.

Other relevant legal provisions

Various common law and equitable rules also play a part in the legal regulation of takeovers. The directors of both the offeror and target companies will continue to owe fiduciary duties to their companies.[7] The impact of these duties in a takeover situation has arisen where the target directors have entered into an agreement with an offeror company whereby they agree to recommend the bid to their shareholders but subsequently decide that a better offer has been made by another offeror and they recommend that bid instead.

In *Dawson International plc v Coats Patons plc*,[8] the directors sought to excuse their breach of contract by claiming that to adhere to it would breach their fiduciary duty to their shareholders to act in their best interests. That proposition was rejected by the Scottish court on the basis that their duties were owed to the company and not to the shareholders as sellers of their shares. The two were not necessarily the same. If the directors take it upon themselves to give advice to current shareholders they have a duty not to mislead and to give good advice but that is not a pre-existing duty which prevents them from entering into such an agreement. In a subsequent hearing[9] the Court decided that there was no such agreement partly because their statements had been made subject to the City Code and thus could not amount to a legal agreement.

In England, the impact of the directors' fiduciary duties on agreements by directors has been considered generally. Initially it was held that if they broke such agreements because not to do so would be contrary to their duties to the company at the time of breach (*e.g.* because of subsequent events) then they would have a defence[10], but in *Fulham Football Club Ltd v Cabra Estates plc*[11] the Court of Appeal decided that the test should be whether at the time of the agreement the directors were acting bona fide for the benefit of the company. If they were then the agreement would be binding on them even if they now considered that to implement it would be contrary to the company's interests.

The ordinary law of contract also applies to takeovers and there have been occasions where parties have resorted to the law of tort. Thus in *Lonrho plc v Fayed*[12] claims were made involving the torts of conspiracy and wrongful interference with trade, alleging that false information was given by one potential offeror to the Secretary of State causing him not to refer that offer to the

---

[6] Dir. 2004/25/EC, OJ 142/12.

[7] See Ch.15, above.

[8] 1988 S.L.T. 854 (O.H.); (1989) 5 B.C.C. 405.

[9] 1989 S.L.T. 155; [1991] B.C.C. 276.

[10] *John Crowther Group plc v Carpets International plc* [1990] B.C.L.C. 460; *Rackam v Peek Foods Ltd* [1990] B.C.L.C. 895.

[11] [1992] B.C.L.C. 863.

[12] [1991] B.C.L.C. 779, HL.

Monopolies and Mergers Commission which prejudiced the chances of a rival offeror. Similarly, in *Lonrho plc v Tebbit*[13] the Secretary of State was held to owe a potential duty of care to that second offeror in deciding whether or not to release them from a monopolies' restriction. In *Partco Group Ltd v Wragg*,[14] it was said that the mere supply of information by the directors of a target company as required by the City Code did not necessarily make them liable to an action for negligent misstatement. There had to be some assumption of personal responsibility but this could be judged in the light of the obligations imposed upon them.

CITY CODE ON TAKEOVERS AND MERGERS

The latest edition of the City Code was published in May 2005. Unlike the early editions, this edition is in loose leaf form and can be regularly amended.[14a] It is administered by the City Panel which was instituted by the Bank of England and contains representatives of all the major City institutions, so that anyone in breach of its provisions is liable to fall foul of his own professional organisation and may suffer penalties in consequence. In particular the Stock Exchange is represented, and withdrawal of a licence to deal on the Exchange is a potent threat against those dealing in shares on a takeover. The City Panel is currently an autonomous body, although it is backed by the Financial Services Authority which has statutory powers under the Financial Services and Markets Act 2000. It also administers the Rules governing Substantial Acquisitions of Shares. Those Rules, dealt with below,[15] relate to the build-up of shares prior to a bid. The Panel also has a full-time executive, under a full time Director General, which is available for advice at any time during the course of the bid, not as to the merits of the offer but as to procedure and conduct. It is founded largely by a levy on takeover transactions. There is also a separate Code Committee which makes detailed recommendations as to the wording of the Code.

Current Administration of the Code

The Panel and the executive have the joint responsibility for the administration of the Code. In *R. v Panel on Takeovers and Mergers, ex Parte Guinness plc* Watkins L.J. expressed the function of the executive as follows[16]:

> "It is the executive which takes the lead in examining the circumstances of takeover bids and, if thought necessary, referring them to the Panel for consideration and adjudication according to the rules. Almost daily it is called upon to give advice and rulings, which mostly are accepted. . . . It acts as a sort of fire brigade to extinguish quickly the flames of unacceptable and unfair practice."[17]

If the executive or either of the parties considers that the matter is serious enough it will be referred to the Panel for a full hearing. This is a quasi-judicial

---

[13] [1993] B.C.L.C. 96.
[14] [2004] BCC 782, CA. No such restriction would apply to an action for deceit.
[14a] This replaced the amended 2002 edition.
[15] p. 607.
[16] (1988) 4 B.C.C. 325, DC.
[17] See *e.g.* Panel statement on *British Coal Pension Funds/Globe Investment Trust plc* [1991] J.B.L. 67.

affair and at the end the Panel may give a definitive ruling imposing either disciplinary sanctions or a course of action which the parties must adhere to. These vary from private reprimands, through public censures to "cold-shouldering" *i.e.* withdrawing market rights.

There is only an automatic right of appeal from a decision of the Panel if disciplinary action is taken[18] or the dispute is as to the Panel's jurisdiction. In other cases there is only a right of appeal with the Panel's consent. Any appeal lies to the Appeals Committee with an independent chairman. That Committee will only interfere if it concludes that the Panel was wrong or, where the Panel's exercise of a discretion is being challenged, if either that power has been wrongly exercised or the Panel has misdirected itself.[19]

Impact of the 13th Directive—new legal framework underpinning the Panel

The UK must implement the terms of the EC 13th Directive on takeover bids[20] by May 2006. To that end, the Government has published a Consultative Document indicating its intentions with regard to the Directive's implementation.[21] At the same time, the Panel has issued an explanatory statement on the changes to its constitution and rules consequent on the Government's proposals.[22] Many of the substantive provisions of the Directive, which are minimum standards only, are derived from the City Code and the impact of the Directive on the actual rules will, on the whole, be fairly minimal. Where there will be changes these are noted below. There will, however, be changes to the jurisdiction of the Code (see below). But above all there will be a change to the nature and constitution of the Panel itself. The Panel will continue as the regulator of all takeover activity, whether covered by the Directive or not,[23] but it will be placed into a legal framework by a new Act.

The legislation will therefore designate the Panel as the competent authority for the Directive. The Panel will retain considerable autonomy as to its constitution but, whilst the executive will continue as at present, there will have to be a clear separation between the rule-making and judicial functions of the Panel, with an independent appellate committee in respect of appeals from the latter. To this end, the Panel has indicated that the Code Committee (rule making) will continue as at present except that its members will be members of the full Panel. In making its rules, the Panel will have to comply with the Directive and its general principles. There will be a new Hearings Committee (for judicial matters) and the membership of the two will be mutually exclusive.[24] Appointments to the Panel will be made, as now, by its member organisations. The independent members (to be increased by one representing employees'

---

[18] Including a ruling as to exempt principal trader or market maker status, below, p.691.
[19] Appeal statement on *BAT Industries plc* [1990] J.B.L. 67.
[20] Dir 2004/25/EC, OJ L142/12.
[21] January 20, 2005. Available on *www.dti.gov.uk/cld/current.htm*
[22] Panel Statement 2003/10, 20/1/05.
[23] The alternatives of the DTI or the FSA were rejected. Schemes of arrangement and unquoted public companies are not covered by the Directive.
[24] And a former member of the Code Committee can never be a member of the Hearings Committee.

interests) will be appointed by the Panel on a recommendation from a new Nominations Committee. There will also be a Remunerations Committee[25] and the Appeal Committee will become the Appeal Tribunal which will have only non-Panel members appointed by the Master of the Rolls. It will be able to hear appeals against any decision of the Hearings Committee.[26] The Panel will continue to publish an annual report, which will become a statutory obligation. In general terms its funding arrangements will remain as they are.

The Government is also proposing that the Panel be given a number of statutory enforcement powers, in effect as a back up to its current de facto powers. These will include powers to obtain information or documents, subject to legal privilege,[27] to order compensation consequent on a breach, and to follow or refrain from a course of action. The Panel will also be able to apply to the court for an enforcement order.[28] The Panel has indicated that such an order would be very much a last resort. Sanctions will remain as they are. The need for confidentiality under the Directive and the need to co-operate with other financial regulators (especially the FSA) will be balanced by the introduction of a number of "gateways" provided for by secondary legislation.

The City Panel and the Law—the Current Position

In 1987 a Canadian-based company, Datafin, became the first party to challenge a Panel decision in the courts by way of an application for judicial review. In the Court of Appeal it was established that the Panel was subject to the process of judicial review.[29] Lord Donaldson M.R., however, stressed that an application for judicial review should not be used as a ploy to hinder a bid and that in general the Panel's decisions would remain binding until otherwise directed. He considered that a challenge could be made against the Panel acting as legislator if it made a rule contrary to its own terms of reference; as interpreter of the Code; and as a disciplinary body, but in that case the internal appeals procedure should be used first.

The dispute in *Datafin* was as to the Panel's interpretation of a particular rule. The Court of Appeal rejected the application on the basis that a challenge would have to show that the Panel's view was so far removed from the natural and ordinary meaning of the words that no ordinary user of the market could reasonably be misled. In the case of an exercise of the Panel's discretion the Court would only interfere in a totally inequitable case.

A second challenge to the Panel by way of judicial review was mounted by Guinness plc on the basis of a breach of natural justice in the Panel's proceedings. This too failed, the Court finding that although the Panel had been inconsiderate and harsh there was no procedural impropriety and no breach of

---

[25] The Bank of England will still be involved by nominating one member of the Nominations and Remunerations Committee.

[26] At present the decisions appealable are limited.

[27] The Panel also intends to include an obligation of disclosure of relevant information and a duty not to mislead the Panel.

[28] The Government perhaps optimistically considers that the court will not go into the merits of the ruling.

[29] *R. v Panel on Takeovers and Mergers, Ex P. Datafin* [1987] Q.B. 815, CA.

the rules of natural justice.[30] The Court of Appeal accepted again, however, that judicial review could apply and Lord Donaldson M.R. suggested the test as being whether something had gone wrong of a nature and degree which required the intervention of the court.

The third challenge mounted against the Panel by way of judicial review concerned a Panel executive's ruling that there had been a breach of the Code and a proposed hearing of the Panel to investigate this. This was challenged by the Fayed brothers on two grounds. First, that the ruling would be prejudicial to civil litigation then in progress relating to the same matter, and second that the hearing would rely on the report of DTI inspectors which was hearsay evidence. This challenge was rejected by the Court of Appeal.[31] There was no general risk of prejudice to the civil litigation and the judge in that trial would not be unduly influenced by any decision of the Panel. Further, the Panel would be aware that the evidence before them was hearsay and take that factor into account.

That decision also raises the issue as to how the Code is viewed in legal proceedings in which it is raised.

In *Dunford & Elliott Ltd v Johnson & Firth Brown Ltd*[32] one party to a bid sought an injunction to prevent the abuse of alleged confidential information in a takeover situation. Both Lord Denning M.R. and Roskill L.J. quoted the Code and used it as a guide to good commercial practice in an area where the court had a discretion. Again in *Re St. Piran Ltd*[33] the Court said that when considering whether to wind up a company on the just and equitable ground[34] the fact that the directors of a public company chose to flout the City Code or to ignore, without good reason, the consequent directions of the City Panel so that the minority shareholders were hurt by a withdrawal of the company's Stock Exchange quotation,[35] would be strong evidence in favour of granting the petition. Conversely in *Re Astec (BSR) plc*,[36] it was held that the provisions of the Code could not give rise to any legitimate expectations for the shareholders for the purposes of a petition for unfairly prejudicial conduct. It did not form part of the company's constitution.

In *R. v Spens*[37] the question arose in a criminal trial as to whether the Code was a document which should be left to the jury to consider or quasi-legislation which was a matter for the judge to interpret for the benefit of the jury. The Court of Appeal had no doubt:

> "As to the present case, our view is that the code sufficiently resembles legislation as to be likewise regarded as demanding construction of its provisions by a judge. Moreover, the code is a form of consensual agreement between the affected parties with penal consequences."

Further, as we have seen,[38] the court has held that statements made during the course of a bid did not amount to a binding legal agreement because they were

[30] *R. v Panel on Takeovers and Mergers, Ex P. Guinness plc* [1990] Q.B. 147, CA.
[31] *R. v Panel on Takeovers and Mergers, ex p. Fayed* [1992] B.C.L.C. 938.
[32] [1977] 1 Lloyd's Rep. 505, CA.
[33] [1981] 3 All E.R. 270.
[34] Above, p.353.
[35] This effectively prevents the shares being sold.
[36] [1998] 2 B.C.L.C. 556.
[37] [1991] B.C.C. 140.
[38] p.674, above.

made in the context of the operation of the Code to that bid.[39] On the other hand where a shareholder agreed to accept an offer unless a higher offer was announced by midnight on a certain date, the provisions of the Code were used to determine whether such an announcement had been so made,[40] and in considering the concepts of "control" and "acting in concert" in a contract.[41]

In earlier times, however, the Court awarded injunctions preventing the Panel from issuing statements,[42] and the Panel had, on one occasion, a battle of words with the Department of Trade and Industry following an inspectors' report under s.432.[43]

Avoiding tactical litigation under the proposed statutory framework

The limits of an application for judicial review have effectively prevented tactical litigation designed to hamper or frustrate a bid or a defence to a bid. This is seen as a great advantage of the current regulatory system and the Government has indicated that it wishes to preserve that advantage.[44] It has indicated that the new takeovers legislation to implement the Directive will neither undermine nor be inconsistent with the *Datafin* principles.[45] With regard to other types of litigation, *e.g.* civil litigation between parties to a bid on the interpretation of the Code, which would become possible since the Code will become a legal document, the Government is proposing to enact three specific measures. The first is that there should be no action against any person for breach of statutory duty as a result of the Code's new status. Second, to promote certainty, transactions will not be set aside simply because of a breach of the Code or failure to comply with a Panel ruling, and third, parties to Panel hearings will not be able to challenge their rulings apart from before the Panel's own Appeal Tribunal or under the limited current judicial review process.

Scope of the code

The Code is currently applicable to all mergers and takeover transactions involving resident public companies and not just listed companies[46] and applies to all those involved whether as directors, advisers, offerors, offerees or in any other capacity. Implementing the 13th Directive will replace, for takeovers covered by the Directive only, the residence[47] of a company as a parameter, by making a distinction (if there is one) between the country of incorporation and that of the market where its shares are quoted. Where the UK is both then the Panel will

---

[39] *Dawson International plc v Coats Patons plc* 1989 S.L.T. 655; [1991] B.C.C. 276.

[40] *Hasbro U.K. Ltd v Harris* [1994] B.C.C. 839.

[41] *Philip Morris Products Inc v Rothmans International Enterprises Ltd* [2002] B.C.C. 265.

[42] Panel statement on *Sandstar Ltd v Graff Diamonds Ltd* [1979] J.B.L. 274.

[43] Panel statement of May 14, 1979 [1979] J.B.L. 364.

[44] Consultative Document on Implementing the 13th Directive, January 20, 2005. The Directive itself expressly allows Member States to preserve these limitations in Art. 4.6.

[45] Para.2.38 of the Consultative Document.

[46] Panel statement on *Chez Nico Restaurants Ltd* [1991] J.B.L. 352. See also *Re Astec (BSR) plc* [1998] 2 B.C.L.C. 556.

[47] Which requires incorporation and control in the UK. This may continue to apply to unquoted public companies which are not subject to the directive.

have full jurisdiction.[48] In other cases the Panel will have a shared jurisdiction. If the company is incorporated here but listed elsewhere, the Panel will only have responsibility for the company law aspects of a takeover (*e.g.* information provision to employees, frustrating action, mandatory bids etc). Conversely where the company is not incorporated here but has its sole or primary listing here,[49] the Panel will only have jurisdiction for matters relating to the bid procedure and timetable. The Code will continue to apply to all takeover transactions, except in the case of a shared jurisdiction where it will limit itself to those covered by the Directive (thus excluding *e.g.* unquoted companies and schemes of arrangement). It will discuss the shared jurisdiction position for non-Directive transactions with other EU regulatory authorities.[50] However, the Code only applies where a merger or takeover bid is concerned.[51] The Panel does not see itself as being concerned with the merits of a bid but as an instrument of investor protection.

The Code itself is divided into General Principles and Rules. The following is a summary of some of the more important parts of the Code. The references in this chapter to Panel decisions and statements are to *The Journal of Business Law* which monitors the Panel on a regular basis.

General principles

There are currently 10 general principles concerned with the provision of adequate and timely information to the shareholders so that all are to be treated equally, and with the general responsibilities of the boards of directors of both the offeror and the offeree companies. The introduction to the general principles emphasises that the spirit as well as the precise wording of the Code must be observed. This enables the Panel to find that there has been a breach of the Code even though no specific provision was involved.[52]

The boards of both companies are required to act in the best interests of their respective shareholders. The offeree board should seek competent independent advice on receiving an offer and must not do anything to frustrate the offer without the general meeting's approval. In particular, rights of control must be exercised in good faith—minority oppression is "wholly unacceptable" (G.P.s.1, 7 and 8).[53]

General Principle 3 provides that no offer should be announced unless the offeror has every reason to believe that it can, and will continue to be able to, implement the offer. This responsibility also applies to the offeror's financial advisers.[54]

---

[48] Even if it is controlled elsewhere.

[49] Or, if there are more than one equal listing, the company chooses to be regulated by the Panel.

[50] Panel Statement 2005/10, 20/1/05.

[51] Panel statement on *N.F.U. Development Trust* [1976] J.B.L. 162; *cf.* Panel statement on *Chaddesley Investments Ltd* [1979] J.B.L. 271. The Code does not apply to offers for non-voting non-equity capital.

[52] Panel statement on *Mount Charlotte Investments v Gale Lister & Co. Ltd* [1974] J.B.L. 310: *cf.* Panel statement on *Swiss Bank Corporation/Trafalgar House plc/Northern Electric plc* [1995] J.B.L. 409.

[53] Thus the offeree must not take any action to frustrate a bid or to prevent their shareholders considering it on its merits without shareholder consent. This includes taking legal action. See, *e.g.* Appeal Committee Statement on *BAT Industries plc* [1990] J.B.L. 67. But that prohibition does not extend beyond the offeree board: Panel statement 1996/17 [1998] J.B.L. 71–72.

[54] Panel statement on *Luirc Corp/Merlin International Properties Ltd* [1992] J.B.L. 105.

General Principle 4 requires that the shareholders be put in possession of all the facts necessary for an informed judgment as to the merits of an offer and must have sufficient time to make an assessment and decision. No relevant information is to be withheld from them. No false market in shares is to be created—this can cause problems in relation to the disclosure of information about preliminary negotiations.[55] Rumour and speculation can drastically affect the quoted share price of a company so that misleading statements must not be made (G.P. 6).[56] The Panel have indicated that a false market usually involves an element of contrivance but it may also be caused by any step which results in a market price which is manifestly unrealistic.[57] It was, however, held not to include the use of derivatives linked to the relevant shares (*i.e.* investments which depend upon the value of those shares, but do not carry any rights to those shares).[58] As a result the detailed rules of the Code were changed.

General Principle 9 relates to the responsibilities of the directors of the companies involved, in effect reminding them of their fiduciary duties to their company and warning them against entering into binding commitments which could restrict their freedom to advise shareholders.[59]

The Panel has decided that, following the implementation of the 13th Directive, it will use the Directive's principles. There are two main reasons for this. First, all dispensations given by the Panel must be taken in the light of the Directive's principles and, second, the Directive's principles incorporate GPs 1, 3, 4, 6 and 9. The other existing principles can be transformed into rules, and the only new principle in the Directive, prohibiting frustrating action, is currently in the rules.[60]

The rules

There are 38 rules currently in the Code. However, many of these are subdivided and are further amplified by notes. In addition the executive has begun issuing non-binding practice statements on its understanding of the operation of some of the rules.

(1) *The approach, announcements and independent advice (Rules 1–3)*

An offer should be made first to the board of the offeree company or its advisers. The identify of the offeror if it is not the person making the bid should be disclosed at the outset and the offeree board is entitled to be satisfied that the offeror company will be in a position to implement its offer (either in cash or by

---

[55] Panel statement on *Rockwell International Corporation v Wilmot Breedon (Holdings) Ltd* [1979] J.B.L. 387. Dealings in derivatives linked to the offeree company's shares must be approved in advance by the Panel: Statement on *Swiss Bank Corporation/Trafalgar House plc/Northern Electric plc*, March 3, 1995.
[56] See the Panel statements on *Rentokil Group plc/BET plc* [1996] J.B.L. 611 and *Redland Cement plc/Ennemix plc* [1996] J.B.L. 613.
[57] Panel statement on *Gateway plc* [1990] J.B.L. 72.
[58] Panel statement on *Swiss Bank Corporation plc* [1995] J.B.L. 409.
[59] See p.674. above.
[60] Panel statement 2005/10, 20/1/05.

shares) in full. The offeree board must circulate the independent advice it is required to obtain, usually from a merchant bank, to its shareholders. This independent advice must come from outside any financial conglomerate involved in the bid.[61]

When a firm intention to make an offer is notified from a serious source a press notice must be issued immediately followed by a circular to the shareholders. More difficult is the announcement of approaches which may or may not lead to an offer. Too early an announcement may kill the offer, too late and the market will have reacted in advance with all the possibilities of insider dealing by those with insider information.[62] Accordingly, an announcement, together with a temporary halt in dealings on the Stock Exchange, is normally expected either when negotiations have reached a point at which a company is reasonably confident that an offer will be made for its shares or when negotiations are about to be extended to embrace more than a small group of people. The responsibility is on the offeree company to make the announcement.[63] However, the Code requires a statement from the potential offeror company where, prior to an approach, the offeree company is the subject of rumours and speculations or an untoward price movement,[64] and there are reasonable grounds for concluding that it is the potential offeror's actions which have led to the situation.[65] Consultation with the Panel on whether or not an announcement is needed is encouraged. An announcement that a block of shares carrying over 30 per cent of the voting rights or that the board is seeking offers for the company will be treated as an announcement of a possible offer for the purposes of the Code. Offerors will usually be bound by so-called denial statements, *i.e.* that no bid is intended, for six months after making the statement. Such statements must be clear and unambiguous.[66]

If there is still no intention to make a firm offer, an announcement that talks are taking place or that an offer is under consideration will suffice, although if any possible terms are mentioned, the offeror may be bound to them. The target company can request that the Panel impose a time limit within which the offeror must clarify its position (so-called "put up or shut up" rulings).[67] Pre-conditions to the making of an offer are carefully monitored.[68]

The formal announcement of an intention to make an offer must include details of existing shareholdings and connected derivatives and any conditions to which the offer is subject including the conditions as to acceptance levels, the ability to achieve a quotation for the new shares and the authority to issue those

---

[61] Panel statement on *Carter Allen Holdings plc* [1998] J.B.L. 67; *WPP Group/Tempo Group* [2003] J.B.L. 328.

[62] Above, Ch.19.

[63] See Panel statement on *Dickinson Robinson Group Ltd/Royal Sovereign Group Ltd* [1978] J.B.L. 66; *Teachers (Distillers) Ltd/Allied Breweries Ltd* [1978] J.B.L. 67; and *Balfour Ltd/Aurora Holdings Ltd* [1979] J.B.L. 366.

[64] This is defined in the rule as being approximately ten per cent. See Panel statement 1997/3 [1998] J.B.L. 70–71.

[65] Panel statement on *Argyll Group plc/Distillers Group plc* [1986] J.B.L. 233.

[66] Panel statement on *Storehouse plc* [1989] J.B.L. 518.

[67] See *e.g.* Panel Statement on *Manchester United plc/Malcolm Glazer Family Limited Partnership*, 2005/26.

[68] Panel statement on *Corporate Services Group plc* [1999] J.B.L. 565.

new shares if a share for share offer is being made. Thus where a requirement as to the giving of a proxy vote was included in the offer documents but not in the original announcement the former were held to be void.[69] If a formal offer is not forthcoming within 28 days after the announcement the offeror must be prepared to justify this to the Panel.[70] If necessary the Panel will take steps to enforce completion of the offer, *e.g.* by freezing the voting rights of shares already obtained.[71]

(2) *Dealings and restrictions on the acquisition of shares and rights over shares (Rules 4–8)*

Rule 4 provides that no person, other than the offeror, may deal in the offeree company's shares, including options and derivatives referenced to such shares,[72] if he is privy to confidential price-sensitive information[73] relating to the offer, between the time when there is reason to suppose that an approach or offer is contemplated and the public announcement. Nor should such persons make any recommendations to any other person as to dealing in the relevant securities. Together with Rule 2 relating to the announcement of a prospective offer, this provision is an attempt to inhibit insider trading by preventing both the leakage of information and dealings by the "informed". Despite this, prior to the criminalisation of insider dealing, a pattern emerged. There was a substantial price movement in the market price of shares in a company the reason for which became apparent when a takeover bid involving the company was subsequently announced. Subsequent investigations rarely brought to light any dealings by actual "insiders".[74]

A similar prohibition applies to purchases of offeree shares by the advisers of the offeree company during the offer period. The ban applies to derivatives, options, loans or indemnities relating to those shares.[75]

If the offeror, potential offeror, or anyone acting in concert[76] with him purchases shares at above the offer price,[77] then that price must be increased to the highest price, excluding stamp duty and commission, so paid. If 15 per cent or more of the shares of a class are acquired for cash, the offer must include a cash alternative, being the highest price paid for such shares. A cash alternative may

---

[69] Panel statement on *Bassishaw Investments Ltd/UDS Group plc* [1982] J.B.L. 329.

[70] Panel statement on *Combined English Stores Ltd/David Grieg Ltd* [1974] J.B.L. 312; *WPP Group plc/Tempus Group plc* [2003] J.B.L. 327.

[71] Panel statements on *St. Martins Property Ltd/Hays Wharf Ltd* [1974] J.B.L. 312; *B.S.Q. Securities Ltd/Court Hotels (London) Ltd* [1976] J.B.L. 162.

[72] See [1996] J.B.L. 613. The Code Committee have proposed detailed changes in this respect.

[73] As defined by the Code. See also the Panel statement on *Johnson & Firth Brown Ltd/Dunsford & Elliott Ltd* [1977] J.B.L. 161.

[74] See the Panel statements on *United Drapery Stores Ltd/William Timpson Ltd* [1973] J.B.L. 37; Panel statement on *G.K.N. Ltd/Miles Drew & Co. Ltd* [1974] J.B.L. 309; Panel statement on *Boots Co. Ltd* and *House of Fraser Ltd* [1975] J.B.L. 43; *cf.* the Panel decision on *P. R. Grimshawe & Co. Ltd, Grimshawe-Windsor Merger* [1973] J.B.L. 46 and *D. R. Lyons Co. Ltd* [1973] J.B.L. 451.

[75] Thus reversing the position explained in [1998] J.B.L. 71.

[76] As defined in the Code. See Panel statements on *United Newspapers plc/Fleet Holidays plc* [1986] J.B.L. 230 and *Chiltern Radio plc* [1995] J.B.L. 87.

[77] For a non-cash offer see Panel statement on *Six Continents plc/Capital Management and Investment plc* 2003/7.

also be required if the offeror cannot fulfil the paper offer.[78] When a revised offer is announced it should "whenever practicable" disclose the number of securities purchased and the price paid. Purchases by a financial adviser for discretionary clients must be cleared by the Panel unless he is an exempt fund manager (see below).

Voting rights are defined in the City Code as all voting rights attributable to the share capital of a company currently exercisable at a general meeting. This will include preference shareholders whose shares have acquired temporary voting rights through their dividends being in arrears during the entire course of an offer. It is not clear how this will operate if the preference shareholders lose their votes during the course of a bid. Since treasury shares have no rights, they are excluded for this purpose.

Rule 8 requires dealings in all relevant shares, options and derivatives by parties to the offer and their associates either for themselves or for discretionary or non-discretionary clients, to be disclosed daily. This applies to dealings whereby an associate indemnifies a third party who has acquired relevant shares against any loss on the resale of those shares.[79] Such disclosure must now reveal the true identity of the person dealing, and in the case of an associate why such disclosure was necessary. Disclosure of dealings must also be made by a holder of one per cent of the shares in either company.[80] Further, any type of inducement to deal or refrain from dealing or for any connected person to bear any investment risk[81] must be disclosed if a party to the bid is involved. Disclosure is also required of any irrevocable commitments to accept or reject an offer but not of any stock borrowing or lending.

In 1981 Rules governing Substantial Acquisitions of Shares were published.[82] These were originally framed for "dawn raids" of the type experienced in 1980 and apply to acquisitions giving a holding of between 15 and 30 per cent. The Rules, which are dealt with below, basically provide a seven day freeze on all offers to acquire more than a 15 per cent but less than a 30 per cent holding.[83]

At the same time the City Code was amended by what is now Rule 5. Anyone who owns 30 per cent of the voting rights of a company may not increase his holding above 30 per cent prior to the first closing day[84] of an offer. Anyone who owns 30 per cent already, but less than 50 per cent, may not acquire any more voting rights prior to that time. There are four exceptions: acquisitions which immediately precede and are conditional on the announcement of an agreed bid; acquisitions from a single shareholder; where the offer has been recommended by the offeree board or declared unconditional; and where it is by way of acceptance of an offer. In one case the Panel has excused a breach of Rule 5 where the breach was due to inaccurate professional advice.[85]

---

[78] To avoid the problems such as those raised in the Panel statement on *St. Martins Property Ltd/Hays Wharf Ltd* [1974] J.B.L. 312.

[79] Panel statement on *Turner and Newall plc/AE plc* [1987] J.B.L. 140.

[80] Excluding any treasury shares.

[81] Following the Guinness plc revelations. See [1989] J.B.L. 520.

[82] These were revised in 1985 and 1988. See below, p.693.

[83] All these figures exclude any treasury shares.

[84] The time limits in these Rules relate to midnight on the day in question and not to 3.00 p.m. as had been previously thought. Panel statement on *Arthur Bell & Sons plc/Gleneagles Hotels plc* [1984] J.B.L. 421.

[85] Panel statement on *Glanfield Lawrence plc/Gregory Securities Ltd* [1985] J.B.L. 47.

Following the ending of single capacity on the Stock Exchange Rule 38 was added to deal with the problems of multi-service financial organisations: see below.[86]

(3) *The mandatory offer and its terms (Rule 9)*

Since January 1972 the Code has contained rules which require a compulsory bid to be made by a purchaser of shares who has amassed a significant holding of the shares without making a formal offer. This concept has now been applied throughout the European Union by virtue of Art. 5 of the 13th directive. This presented problems of enforcement, particularly in times of economic recession, and the present position, set out in Rule 9, is that anyone who, together with persons acting in concert,[87] has acquired 30 per cent or more of the voting rights by a series of transactions or who, owning between 30 and 50 per cent of such rights acquires any additional rights within a period of a year, shall make an offer. The rule is activated by a relevant purchase by any one member of a group who have previously "come together" to obtain control of a company. The obligation extends to each of the principal members of a consortium if the facts so warrant. The Panel has drawn a distinction between a group acting to obtain control of a company (a "wide concert party") and those dealing with a community of interest in the purchase of a dealing profit. The latter, known as a "fan club," do not fall within this Rule but it may well be difficult to distinguish between them.[88]

The requirement to make a mandatory offer can extend to a situation whereby as the result of a successful offer, the offeror company has effected a change of control in another company owned in part by the target company. This is known as the "chain principle." An offer will be required if either the second company is financially significant with regard to the first or one of the main purposes was to obtain control of the second company. It has been held not to apply to a joint venture company where the target company's holding in that company was deadlocked.[89]

If the implementation of such an offer would require a resolution, then no purchases which would give rise to the offer shall be made.[90] The offer must be in cash of at least the highest price paid by the offeror in the previous year or have a cash alternative. The offer must be conditional on acceptances carrying 50 per cent of the voting rights and, if it does not become conditional, then no further shares may be purchased.[91] In certain circumstances the Panel may grant a

---

[86] p.691.
[87] See notes 1–5 on rule 9:1 and *e.g.* Panel statement on *St. Martins Property Ltd/Hays Wharf Ltd* [1974] J.B.L. 312; *Ashbourne Investments Ltd* [1975] J.B.L. 44; *St. Piran Ltd (No. 1)* [1980] J.B.L. 270; *St. Piran Ltd (No. 2)* [1980] J.B.L. 358; *cf.* Panel statement on *Inoco plc/Petranol plc* [1986] J.B.L. 409. See also *Philip Morris Products Inc v Rothmans International Enterprises Ltd* [2002] B.C.C. 265, CA.
[88] Panel statement on *Glanfield Lawrence plc/Bajou Ltd* [1985] J.B.L. 47.
[89] Panel statement on the *British Land Company plc/Stanhope Properties plc* [1995] J.B.L. 411.
[90] Panel statement on *Manx & Overseas Investments Ltd* [1978] J.B.L. 184. See also Panel statement on *Rothmans International Ltd* [1981] J.B.L. 373.
[91] See [1980] J.B.L. 270; J.B.L. 358; Panel statement on *Westminster Property Group plc* [1983] J.B.L. 358; Panel statements on *Westminster Property Group plc* [1983] J.B.L. 491, and [1983] J.B.L. 492; and Panel statement on *Gilgate Holdings Ltd* [1980] J.B.L. 269.

dispensation from this rule—the main one is known as the whitewash procedure.[92]

(4) *The voluntary offer and its terms (Rules 10–13)*

No offer which, if accepted in full, would result in the offeror having voting control can be declared unconditional unless acceptances are received or promised amounting to a total of 50 per cent of the voting rights of the equity share capital.[92a] If any of the shares of any class under offer are purchased for cash by the offeror during the offer period or within 12 months prior to its commencement a cash alternative must be included in the offer of at least the highest price paid for those shares during that period, excluding stamp duty and commission, unless the Panel agrees to the contrary.[93] Failure to make such a cash alternative will make the offeror liable to compensate those who have suffered as a result.[94] A similar rule applies where the shares were purchased by exchange of securities. The alternative offer required is of the same number of securities or their cash value of the time of the purchase.[95] Further if there is a possibility of a reference to the Monopolies and Mergers Commission or the European Commission then the offer must be subject to withdrawal on such a reference. Where there is a delay in deciding whether such a reference is to be made, the Panel has decided that the time limits for the bid[96] are suspended until after the decision not to make a reference has been announced.[97] Any conditions which allow the offer to lapse must not be subjective or within the control of the offeror company.

(5) *Provisions applicable to all offers (Rules 14–18)*

Rule 14 requires comparable offers where there is more than one class of share capital involved[98] and Rule 15 states the appropriate offer for convertible securities etc. Rule 16 prohibits an offeror from entering into arrangements to make purchases of shares in the offeree company if such arrangements have attached thereto favourable conditions which are not extended to all shareholders. The Panel does, however, allow an exception if the payments can be justified commercially.[99]

Rule 17 is concerned with the announcement or failure to announce acceptance levels at critical times during the offer period.[1]

---

[92] See Appendix 1 and Panel statement on *Alexander Holdings plc/Orb Estate plc* [2003] J.B.L. 329.

[92a] As to what can be counted as acceptances see [1986] J.B.L. 317 and [1990] J.B.L. 71. For the counting of acceptances under the CREST system of dematerialised shares see [1996] J.B.L. 616. For difficulties in the counting process see Panel statement on *Blue Circle Industries plc/Britoil Qualcast plc* [1988] J.B.L. 323, and [1989] J.B.L. 69.

[93] See *e.g.* Panel statements on *Hillsdown Holdings plc/S & W Beresford plc* [1986] J.B.L. 407; and *International Marine Systems Ltd/Benjamin Priest Group plc* [1991] J.B.L. 351.

[94] Panel statement on *Guinness plc/Distillers Company plc* [1989] J.B.L. 520.

[95] Where the purchase is a mixed one of cash and securities the Panel must be consulted.

[96] Rules 30–34, below.

[97] See [1992] J.B.L. 314.

[98] See Panel statement on their usual practice in *Stead & Simpson plc* [1990] J.B.L. 72.

[99] Panel statement on *Mooloya Investments Ltd/Customagic Manufacturing Co. Ltd* [1979] J.B.L. 49.

[1] For an interesting example of the crucial importance of such announcements see the Panel statement on *Burton Group plc/Debenhams plc* [1985] J.B.L. 231.

(6) Conduct during the offer (Rules 19–22)

Rule 19 relates to the quality of and responsibility for information issued during the course of an offer, together with its distribution. In addition to the imposing of a standard of care equivalent to that required in preparing a prospectus (see Ch.7, above), it prohibits statements which whilst not factually inaccurate may mislead shareholders and the market or may create uncertainty.[2] In particular, an offeror should not make a statement to the effect that it may improve its offer without committing itself to doing so and specifying the improvement.[3] There are special requirements attached to "merger benefit" statements, *e.g.* as to the expected financial benefits of a merger.[4] Following an increase in newspaper advertisements made in connection with takeovers and the nature of the material used, Rule 19 restricts such advertisements to nine specific types, seven of which require Panel clearance in advance.[5] Special attention is paid to organised telephone campaigns,[6] including cold-calling, and media interviews and debates.

Copies of all documents must be sent at the time of release to the press to the Panel and the advisers to all the other parties involved in the offer, even outside office hours.[7] Statements made whilst an offer is being referred to the Monopolies and Mergers Commission or the European Commission must be capable of being substantiated if the offer is subsequently revived.

Rule 20 applies to the equality of the supply of the information subject to Rule 19 to all shareholders. In addition all competing offerors are entitled to receive information given to one, favoured offeror, at least where there has been a public announcement of that offeror's existence.[8] A less welcome offeror is required to specify the questions to which it requires answers.

Rule 21 currently provides that in the case of an actual or imminent offer, the offeree board must not, without approval of the members, issue shares, sell or transfer treasury shares, grant options create any convertible securities, or sell or otherwise dispose of material assets except under a pre-existing obligation or enter into contracts except in the ordinary course of business.[9] Inducement or break fees (fees payable by the target company to the offerer if specified events occur) are prohibited unless less than 1 per cent of the offer value.

(6a) Post and pre-bid defences—the effect of the 13th Directive

The impact of the 13th Directive on the operation of the substantive rules of the Code is in general minimal but there is one exception to this. In relation to actions by the target board *after* a bid is announced, (*i.e.* post-bid defences) there

---

[2] See, *e.g.* Panel statement on *Enterprise Oil plc/LASMO plc* [1995] J.B.L. 86.

[3] See [1984] J.B.L. 422.

[4] *cf.* Panel statement 1997/5 [1998] J.B.L. 64.

[5] See Panel statements on *Imperial Group Ltd* [1986] J.B.L. 315 and on advertisements [1986] J.B.L. 318. See also Panel statement on graphs and diagrams [1985] J.B.L. 476.

[6] Following the Panel statements on *B.P.C.C. plc/John Waddingtons plc* [1983] J.B.L. 491.

[7] Panel statement on *European Leisure plc/Midsummer Leisure plc* [1991] J.B.L. 66.

[8] See *e.g.* Panel statement 1997/2 [1998] J.B.L. 70.

[9] See, *e.g.* Panel statements on *W. Henshall & Sons (Addlestone) Ltd/Bovbourne Ltd* [1979] J.B.L. 46; *Burton Group plc/Debenhams plc* [1985] J.B.L. 231; *IMI plc./Birmingham Mint Group plc* [1991] J.B.L. 178; 1996/17, 1996/18; and 1997/4 [1998] J.B.L. 71.

are already restrictions in place in Rule 21 and General Principle 7. Art.9 of the directive contains similar requirements but there are two differences. That article requires shareholder approval for any target board decision which is outside the ordinary course of business and which could result in the bid being frustrated, whereas Rule 21 currently applies to particular actions only. Second, Art.9 applies even if (unlike the current rule) the action was taken before the bid but has not been fully implemented at the time when the bid is made.

On the other hand there is no current equivalent of Art.11, the so-called breakthrough rule, which relates to arrangements in place in the target company before any bid is announced but which are intended to make a successful bid very difficult (*i.e.* pre-bid defences). These could include restrictions on share ownership, multiple voting rights or restrictions on transfer or a limit on voting rights in a bid situation, not uncommon in other Member States. Article 11 provides that any such restrictions on transfer are not to apply during the offer period and that any multiple voting rights or restrictions on voting rights shall not apply in deciding whether to approve any post-bid defences (*e.g.* under Rule 21). The article also provides that if the offeror obtains 75 per cent of the target's capital carrying voting rights, (the breakthrough threshold) such multiple voting rights, or any extraordinary rights to appoint or dismiss directors, shall not apply to any meeting called by the offeror (*e.g.* to remove such rights).

These two articles were among the most controversial parts of the directive and delayed its implementation.[10] The ensuing compromise is found in Art.12 which allows Member States a choice as to whether to implement both or either of Arts 9 and 11. If the UK were to do this then the position would be relatively simple,[11] but the Government has indicated that whilst it will adopt Art.9 (with very few consequences except the changes to Rule 21 of the Code noted above[12]) it will opt out of Art.11.[13] There are very few companies in the UK which have any form of pre-bid defence and Art.11 would discourage flexibility. The position then becomes more complex. Under Art.12 the Government must nevertheless allow companies incorporated in the UK the chance to voluntarily opt in to the terms of Art.11. The Government proposal is that this should be achieved by existing mechanisms. Thus it would be made by a resolution of the company in general meeting[14] and so subject to the current protection for holders of class rights and minorities. The Government has listed the matters which would be covered by Art.11 and also deals with any compensation which may become payable to anyone who loses a contractual right as a result.[15]

In any event, Art.10 requires disclosure of a number of things, including all such pre-bid defences, in the company's annual report. The Government is anxious to absorb these new disclosure requirements into existing disclosure regimes. Art.10 also requires an explanatory report on these matters to be

---

[10] The final proposal was made by the Commission in October 2002, the previous one being rejected after 12 years of negotiations.

[11] The mandatory bid provision was another major disagreement.

[12] But see the discussion of the reciprocity rule below.

[13] GP 7 will disappear but will be incorporated in the amended Rule 21 to comply with the directive: Panel statement 2005/10, 20/1/05.

[14] Consultative Document January 20, 2005.

[15] This would be have to be a special resolution if the articles have to be altered.

presented to the general meeting, but this could be by way of additional text to the annual report.

There is a further complication in that if, as seems likely, the UK opts out of Art.11 but a particular British company opts in to it, the UK (and not the opted-in company) may further choose to allow such opted-in companies to opt out again if they are the subject of a bid by an opted-out company. This is known as the *reciprocity rule*. The practical effect of this may be to make companies opt in so that if they make an offer an opted-in target company will not be able to opt out. It is a matter of debate whether this reciprocity opt out rule is available if the company is opted in not by its own choice but by the state's decision to adopt Art.11. In the event the Government has indicated that it does not propose to adopt the reciprocity rule. They do not believe in ring-fencing British companies from third-country takeovers for fear of retaliation. They also add that to adopt it would complicate the new law considerably!

(7) Documents from the offeror and the offeree board (Rules 23–27)

The rules elaborate General Principal 5 that all documents, etc. falling within these headings must be treated with the same standard of care as if they were prospectuses.[16] Amongst the minimum content of the information to be disclosed must be the social and employment consequences of the projected takeover, including the offeror's intention with regard to the continuance of the business. Rule 24 sets out the required contents of offer documents in some detail. The 13th Directive will require communications to be made to the employees according to the low of the place of incorporation.

Rule 25 sets out the contents of the target company's response. In particular it requires that documents sent to shareholders of the offeree company recommending acceptance or rejection of offers must contain particulars of all service contracts over 12 months of any director or proposed director with the offeree company or any of its subsidiaries. Further, any amendment to such contract within six months of the date of the document must be stated; if there are no such amendments that should be stated. Rule 26 concerns the availability of documents for inspection and Rule 27 concerns the need to inform shareholders of material changes to the published information during a bid.

(8) Profit forecasts (Rule 28)

This rule, together with its note occupies seven pages of the Code, which reflects the many problems encountered by the Panel in the area. Despite the hazard of forecasting, profit forecasts must be compiled with "care and objectivity" by the directors and checked on that basis by their financial advisers. It is now mandatory to include in a forecast: taxation, extraordinary items, the assumptions on which it is based and minority interests where these are expected to be significant. The Rule also defines a profit forecast for its own purposes.[17]

---

[16] Panel statement on *York Trust Ltd/Greenword and Batley Ltd* [1978] J.B.L. 68.
[17] See Panel statements on *Guinness Peat/The Distillers Company* [1986] J.B.L. 316; *TI Group plc/Dowty Group plc* [1992] J.B.L. 599. An "earning enhancement statement" which is not intended to be a profit forecast must be expressly stated as such: c/f [1998] J.B.L. 64.

In one statement the Panel condemned the publication by an offeror of a profit forecast produced by the offeree company and sent to the offeror in confidence. This was based on the facts that the Panel did not feel it right to require the offeree to publish the forecast, that publication here was in breach of confidence and that what was made public was the profit forecast of another company on which the offeror was not in a position to obtain the reports acquired by the Code.[18]

(9) *Asset valuations (Rule 29)*

This rule requires valuations to be supported by a named independent valuer (as defined) and lays down criteria for the valuer. It applies wherever a valuation is given "in connection with an offer" although this will not normally include the usual estimates for accounting purposes. The basis of valuation must be stated; in general this is to be open market value and there are special rules for land with development value.[19]

(10) *Timing and revision (Rules 30–34)*

Rule 30 relates to the timing of the offer document and the offeree circular, 28 days from an announcement in the first case and 14 days from the offer document in the second. Rule 31 is concerned with the timing of the offer, specification of further closing dates and the well established rule that an offer must remain open for 14 days after being declared unconditional as to acceptances. No offer may be declared so unconditional after midnight on the 60th day after the posting of the offer based on acceptance up to 1.00 p.m. on that day.[20] The effect of this is to limit any changes in an offer to the first 46 days since all revised offers must be kept open for 14 days. This includes the making of a "no increase" statement by the offeror.[21] Since no offer may be open for more than 60 days all such amendments are restricted to the first 46 days, including any purchase of shares which would trigger a mandatory bid under rule 9 since that would amount to a revised offer. This has caused many problems, in particular where there are competing offers still extant at the end of the 46 day period and an auction situation has in effect arisen.[22] As a result an "auctions procedure" was introduced by the Panel in 2002.[23] The Panel can vary the time limits in other circumstances.[24] Rule 34 gives the acceptor of an offer the right to withdraw his acceptance within 21 days of the first closing date of the offer unless it has then become unconditional.

---

[18] Panel statement on *Yule Catto & Co. plc/Donald Macpherson Group plc* [1984] J.B.L. 425.
[19] The Panel cannot, however, prevent genuine disputes, *e.g.* as to property valuations: Panel statements on *BS Group plc/Scott's Restaurant plc* [1991] J.B.L. 350.
[20] See Panel statement on *Burton Group plc/Debenhams plc* [1986] J.B.L. 231.
[21] Panel statement on *Siebe Gorman/Telecamit* [1984] J.B.L. 159.
[22] Panel statements on *Allianz Verischerungs A.G./Bat Industries plc/Eagle Star Holdings plc* [1984] J.B.L. 158 and *Texas Utilities Company/Pacificorp/The Energy Group plc* 29/4/98.
[23] See [2003] J.B.L. 320 and Panel statements on *Laragrove Ltd/Baroness Retail Ltd* 2003/23 and *Canary Wharf Group* 2004/11.
[24] Panel statements on *Woolworth Holdings plc/Dixons plc; Emess Lighting plc/Rotaflex plc* [1986] J.B.L. 410; *Service Corporation International plc/Great Southern Group plc* [1995] J.B.L. 89; [1995] J.B.L. 90; 1996/17, 1996/18, 1997/4 [1998] J.B.L. 71.

(11) *Restrictions following offers (Rule 35)*

Rule 35 provides that where an offer has not become unconditional in all respects the offeror (and persons acting in concert) may not within 12 months from the offer's withdrawal or lapse make a further offer or purchase shares if the offeror either falls within the mandatory bid rules or, if it holds 49 per cent but less than 50 per cent of the offeree shares. There are exceptions to this rule, *e.g.* where the subsequent offer is an agreed offer,[25] or the original offer was referred to the Monopolies and Mergers Commission or the European Commission[26] and the Panel has a general power of dispensation.[27] The rule will be applied, however, even if there has been no formal offer but the target company has been subjected to a state of siege by a threatened offer.[28] If the offeror holds over 50 per cent of the offeree shares it cannot purchase shares at above the offer price for six months. Nor may it conclude special deals with favourable conditions during that period.

(12) *Partial offers (Rule 36)*

The Panel's consent is required for a partial offer. There are complex provisions governing these offers, *e.g.* an offer for 30 per cent or more requires 50 per cent approval. Tender offers may be allowed as an alternative.[29]

(13) *Redemption or purchase by a company of its own voting shares (Rule 37)*

Following the provisions of the Companies Act allowing companies to purchase their own shares the Code is concerned with the position whereby a shareholder will, as a result of such a purchase or redemption, come to hold shares which carry more than 30 per cent or more of the voting rights of that company, or to have increased the percentage of his holding by more than two per cent in the relevant 12 months period if he already holds 30 per cent or more. Rule 37 states that such a shareholder will not be obliged to make a mandatory bid if he only votes in favour of a resolution authorising the board to exercise the powers of purchase or redemption. However, when the board actually exercises the power, the Panel will examine the relationship between the board and the shareholder concerned.

(14) *Dealings by connected exempt market makers (Rule 38)*

Multi-service financial organisations—acting in concert. With the repeal of the existing single capacity on the Stock Exchange, *i.e.* the separation of jobbers, brokers and corporate advisers, etc., it is now perfectly allowable for one financial

---

[25] *i.e.* agreed by the offeree board. See Panel statement on *Trafalgar House plc/Northern Electric plc* (No. 2) [1995] J.B.L. 413.
[26] Panel statement on *GC & C Brands/Irish Distillers Group plc* [1989] J.B.L. 150.
[27] Panel statement on *Severn Trent plc/Caird Group plc* [1991] J.B.L. 177.
[28] Panel statement on *Storehouse plc* [1989] J.B.L. 518.
[29] See p.693, below.

organisation to perform all those functions, *i.e.* it can act as a market-maker, broker, investment adviser and corporate finance adviser. This has clear implications for the City Code since the same organisation may be acting as adviser to the offeror (or offeree), making investment decisions for its discretionary clients, providing information as brokers to other clients and making a market in the offeree company's shares. Opportunities to influence an offer clearly abound— for example, an adviser to an offeror may acquire offeree shares as a market maker, deal in those shares for it discretionary clients and influence others to deal.

Market-making and other dealings as a principal. The basic rule is that where one arm of a multi-service financial organisation is advising an offeror, any dealings by that organisation as principal (*i.e.* not as agent for its clients) in the offeree's securities will be presumed to be acting in concert with the offeror. This will affect the price to be paid, the mandatory bid rule and the possible obligation to make a cash offer, etc.

However, there is an exception to this presumption in the case of market-making only (and not for other dealings as principal) if the market maker arm of the organisation achieves the status of an *exempt principal trader, i.e.* one which is recognised as such by the Panel who must be satisfied that an effective "Chinese Wall" system operates within the whole organisation, in particular separating the market making division from the corporate finance division.

Exempt principal traders will, however, be subject to Rule 38 of the Code. Rule 38.1 provides that if they are connected with an offeror or offeree company they must not carry out any dealings with the purpose of assisting the offeror or offeree, as appropriate. Nor can they accept or vote on any offer from a connected offeror until the offer has been declared unconditional. An exempt principal trader will be so connected if it is controlled by, controls or is under the same control as, the offeror, offeree, or any bank, broker, financial or other professional adviser to the offeree or offeror company. The sanction for a breach of this rule will be loss of exempt status—which may amount to exclusion from the market in practical terms.[30]

Rules 38.2 to 4 provide three restrictions on dealings with an exempt principal trader where it is connected with the offeror or offeree.[31] These are: (i) a ban on dealings by the connected offeror (or concert parties) with the principal trader during the offer period; (ii) a ban on assents of shares owned by the principal trader to the offeror until the offeror has become or been declared unconditional as to acceptances; and (iii) the exempt principal trader must not vote with shares in the connected offeror or offeree in the context of a takeover or possible takeover. Liability under (i) is on the offeror, under (ii) and (iii) on the principal trader.

Finally rule 38.5 requires disclosure to the Panel and the Company Announcements Office of the Stock Exchange by the exempt principal trader of dealings in relevant shares, including derivatives referenced to those shares, where there is a connected offeree or offeror company by noon on the next business day. This

---

[30] Panel statement on *Raine Industries plc/Tarmac plc* [1989] J.B.L. 67.

[31] See Panel statement on *Peachey Property Corporation plc/Estates Property Investment Co. plc* [1988] J.B.L. 325; *Canary Wharf Group plc* 2004/12.

must include details as to amount, price, the nature of the connection and, if appropriate, the relevant overseas location.

There is no presumption of acting in concert between fund managers and connected offerors before the involvement of the corporate finance arm has become public (although that situation may of course exist in fact). However, such fund managers may now apply for exemption from certain Code consequences which would otherwise follow once the connection with the offeror/offeree is public knowledge. Exemption is achieved by application to the Panel, the criteria being the existence of a "Chinese Wall" as with exempt market-makers. Rule 7.2 provides that the presumption is that a fund manager will be acting in concert with a connected offeror or offeree unless he is an exempt fund manager, thus bringing into play the consideration, mandatory bid and partial offer rules. No such presumption will apply to an exempt fund manager.

Where the exempt fund manager is associated with a party to a takeover it will not have to disclose its dealings in the relevant securities except privately to the Panel. One exception to this will arise where the associate status arises because the fund manager holds five per cent or more of the issued equity capital of an offeror or offeree company (*i.e.* under paragraph (6) of the definition of an associate in the Code).

RULES GOVERNING SUBSTANTIAL ACQUISITIONS OF SHARES

The City Code on Takeovers only operates in a takeover situation and this effectively commences either on an offer being made or a 30 per cent holding of shares being amassed by one person or consortium.[32] In 1980, however, there was a series of "dawn raids" on the Stock Exchange whereby one person would acquire, in a matter of minutes, less than 30 per cent of the shares of a public company but nevertheless a significant amount. Such practices were considered undesirable for two reasons. First, the identity of the acquirer would often be disguised, *e.g.* by several linked companies each acquiring five per cent of the shares on behalf of an unnamed person, and, second, it was obvious that only a few shareholders benefited from being able to dispose of their shares on a "dawn raid" at above market value. This opportunity was not available to the other shareholders.

The first problem was countered by pressure on the Government which led to the rules on share disclosures by shareholders or groups owning originally five per cent, now three per cent, or more of the shares of a public company introduced by the 1981 Act.[33] The second problem, that of equal opportunity, was to be the subject of another self-regulatory code, the Rules Governing the Substantial Acquisition of Shares.[34] The City Panel[35] is responsible for administering these Rules, which have no application to an offeror who has announced a firm intention to make an offer with no pre-conditions. The implementation of the 13th Directive will place the Panel's supervision of the SARS on the same legal foundation as the Code. But there are no changes to the rules themselves.[36]

---

[32] Rule 9, above.
[33] Above, p.197.
[34] Introduced on December 11, 1980.
[35] Above, p.675.
[36] Consultative Document, January 20, 2005.

The Rules apply to acquisitions of listed shares in United Kingdom resident companies[37] within seven days amounting to 10 per cent or more of the voting rights in any one company and which take the purchaser's holding to 15 per cent or more of that company's voting rights but less than 30 per cent, at which stage the City Code will come into operation.[38] Purchase by two or more persons acting together by agreement or understanding are regarded as purchases by a single purchaser, including those held on a discretionary basis by a non-exempt fund manager (for the purposes of the City Code).[39] There are exceptions for purchasers from a single shareholder[40] if that is the only one in a seven day period and purchased in advance of an agreed bid.

Any acquisition caught by the Rules must now either follow the strict rules for partial bids set out in the City Code on Takeovers[41] or be acquired by means of a tender offer.[42] Under this procedure the buyer makes a firm offer to buy a specified number of shares for cash only either at a fixed price or up to a maximum price. Shareholders then offer their shares by tender, in the latter case at any price up to the maximum specified. Shareholders are bound by their tenders and the purchaser and his associates must not deal in the shares during the tender period of at least seven days. Tenders are to be advertised in two national newspapers and sent to the company and the Stock Exchange.

The effect of these rules is to check advances in shareholdings between 10 per cent and 30 per cent.

POWER TO ACQUIRE SHARES OF SHAREHOLDERS NOT ACCEPTING TAKE-OVER OFFER ACCEPTED BY MAJORITY

Sections 428 to 430F were substituted by the Financial Services Act 1986, replacing the original ss 428 to 430 which dated from the 1948 Act. The purpose of the sections is the same, however, to tidy up after a successful takeover offer, so that if an offeror has achieved a 90 per cent acceptance it may compulsorily acquire the remaining shares, or, alternatively, the minority may require such an offeror to buy them out. These "squeeze-out" and "sell-out" provisions were also covered by the 13th EC Directive on takeovers,[43] implementation of which[44] will require three changes to the existing legislation. The Government has indicated that in addition to those changes it is proposing, with one exception which would conflict with the Directive, to enact at the same time the changes suggested by the Company Law Review.[45] All these changes will apply to all companies and not just those covered by the Directive. Those changes were technical rather than substantive in nature and are mentioned in the text below. At the same time the European Commission has proposed introducing similar rights where a person

---

[37] Thus not to all public companies.
[38] Rule 9, above.
[39] See, *e.g.* Panel statement on the *Norton Group plc* [1991] J.B.L. 352.
[40] See, *e.g.* Panel statement on *Timpson plc/Automagic Holdings plc* [1991] J.B.L. 65.
[41] Rule 36.
[42] See Panel statement on *Norton Opax plc* [1989] J.B.L. 148.
[43] Dir 2004/25/EC, OJ L 142/12.
[44] By May 2006. The Government has indicated that this will be by primary legislation.
[45] Consultative Document January 20, 2005.

acquires 90 per cent or more of the shares in a company other than on a takeover.[46]

Scope of ss 428 to 430F

Before the powers conferred by these sections can be used there must be a takeover offer made by an offeror to acquire all the shares (or all of a class of shares) of a company on the same terms,[47] except for those shares already owned by the offeror[48] at the date of the offer: s.428(1). The offer must be for all the shares (or class of shares) allotted on the date of the offer but it may also include shares allotted subsequently to the offer before a date specified by or determined in accordance with the offer: s.428(2). Where shareholders are invited to offer their shares to a person, that person is not making a takeover offer for the purposes of the sections and so cannot invoke the powers conferred by them.[49]

There is no need, however, to show that the offer was actually communicated to each shareholder in the strict contractual sense—the requirement is that there must be an offer to acquire all the shares which has been said to mean that there must be a sufficiently widely distributed and notified offer so that anyone with the relevant shares can provide the offeror with an acceptance. This can be achieved by individual offers, general advertisement[50] or notification. If one or more shareholders are simply unaware of such an offer then the sections may still be used.[51] The Company Law Review recommended that where a shareholder has not provided an address to which the offer can be posted, then an advertisement, indicating where a copy of the offer document might be accessed, should be put in the London or Edinburgh Gazette as appropriate.[52]

Treasury shares, including those shares which become treasury shares during the offer period, are presumed to be excluded from the offer (and therefore the thresholds) unless the offer is extended to them, in which case they will count.[53]

Any revised offer is not a new offer for the purpose of the timetable laid down in the sections provided that the original offer made provision for such a revised offer. If it did not, each revision counts as a fresh offer and the acceptances cannot be added together to achieve the 90 per cent threshold[54]: s.428(6).

---

[46] COM 04, Oct 2004.

[47] A variation is allowed if it is necessary to comply with any foreign laws as to what consideration must be provided under the offer to shareholders resident abroad (*e.g.* in the USA): s.428(3), (4). The Company Law Review recommended that it should be made clear that an offer is on the same terms irrespective of the ability of offerees to accept, or if some offerees are prepared to accept more onerous terms.

[48] These include shares he has contracted to buy but not those which he has contracted to buy in consideration of making the offer: s.428(5). The Company Law Review recommended that this should include shares which he has conditionally contracted to acquire: *Final Report* Vol. 1 (2002) para.13.28.

[49] *Re Chez Nico (Restaurants) Ltd* [1992] B.C.L.C. 192. That was not intended to be a general definition of a take-over for other purposes, however.

[50] Usually in the *Financial Times* or the London *Evening Standard*.

[51] *Re Joseph Holt plc* [2001] 2 B.C.L.C. 604.

[52] *Final Report* Vol. I (2002) para 13.44.

[53] s.428 (2) (2A). Treasury shares cannot be assented to an offer otherwise than for cash and under the City Code no treasury shares can accept a cash offer until it has been declared unconditional.

[54] *ibid.*

The sections apply not only to an offeror but also to its associates, *i.e.* its nominees, members of the same group of companies or a company which is de facto controlled by the offeror or part of a consortium: s.430E(4)–(8). Thus in deciding whether an offer has been made for *all* the shares (or class of shares) the following are to be discounted:

    (i)   shares already owned by the offeror at the date of the offer (s.428(1));

   (ii)   shares which the offeror has contracted to buy at the date of the offer except for acquisitions without consideration[55] and, in England, by deed or when the consideration is the promise to make the offer (s.428(5)); and

  (iii)   shares already owned or contracted to an associate of the offeror at the date of the offer (s.430E(1)).

Joint offerors

Section 430D allows joint offerors to take advantage of (or be subject to) the sections, provided they acquire the shares jointly and accept joint or several liability for other purposes. In general their rights under the sections are joint rights whereas their obligations are joint and several (*i.e.* each is liable for the whole). Offeror is so construed unless the particular provision expressly states to the contrary.

Convertible securities

Problems arose with the original sections over convertible securities, *e.g.* debentures which can be converted into shares on a takeover offer being made. In *Re Simo Securities Trust Ltd*[56] some such debentures were converted into shares in the name of the offeror, others were converted into shares and then transferred to the offeror, and others were not converted at all. The Judge decided that those debentures which were converted could be counted towards the 90 per cent acceptance—those not converted were ignored. Now s.430F provides that all securities which are convertible into shares or entitle the holder to subscribe for shares are shares for the purposes of the sections but they are to be treated as a separate class of shares separate from other shares. The effect of this is that such securities have a 90 per cent threshold of their own since each class of shares is treated separately by the new sections.[57]

Compulsory purchases by the offeror

If the offeror achieves a 90 per cent (in value)[58] acceptance figure[59] he can serve a notice on those who have not accepted the offer that he desires to acquire their

---

[55] The Company Law Review recommended that this should be changed to "consideration of a material value": *Final Report* Vol. 1 (2002) para.13.41.

[56] [1971] 1 W.L.R. 1455.

[57] See the next paragraph.

[58] The Thirteenth Directive requires that this must also give the offeror 90 per cent of the voting rights: Dir 2004/25/EC, Art.15.2

[59] *i.e.* acquired or contracted to acquire by offeror (plus associates). The Company Law Review recommended that this should be clarified to include only those which it has unconditionally contracted to require *Final Report* Vol. 1 (2002) para.13.29.

shares. The 90 per cent threshold applies to each class of shares separately so that each class is subject to a separate offer for this purpose: s.429(1), (2). Once a s.424 *notice has been served*, it cannot be unilaterally withdrawn by the offeror.[60]

The 90 per cent threshold is calculated excluding those shares to which the offer does not relate (*i.e.* shares already held or contracted to an offeror or his associates at the date of the offer). However, the offeror can count shares acquired by the offeror or his associates during the course of the offer otherwise than by acceptance of the offer (*e.g.* by market purchase) provided either that they have been so acquired for less than the offer price or that the offer price is revised upwards to the price paid[61]: ss 429(8), 430E(2).

To take advantage of the compulsory purchase power the 90 per cent threshold must be acquired within four months of the date of offer and the notice served in the prescribed manner within two months of achieving the threshold: s.429.

Under the 13th Directive, the 90 per cent value and voting threshold must be met within three months from the time when the offer closed for acceptances. The Company Law Review recommended a different time span which is inconsistent with this and so will not be implemented. But the two-month period from achieving the threshold within which notices may be issued will remain. The Review also recommended that if further shares are issued during the offer, and the offer extends to them, the threshold should apply to those in issue at the time. Further if shares are issued more than two months but less than 18 months after the threshold has been reached, then the offerer may, if he still has the requisite threshold, issue notices in respect of them or any other shares in issue. Shares issued after notices have been validly sent out and which reduce the threshold do not invalidate those notices. Finally, if shares are issued shortly before the end of the offer period so as to prevent the threshold being reached in time, the period for obtaining the threshold will be extended by one month.

Provided that the notice has been validly served,[62] the offeror "shall be entitled and bound to acquire" the non-acceptor's shares "on the terms of the offer": s.430(2). If the offer provided for alternative consideration, *e.g.* cash or shares in the offeror company, the offeror must give the non-acceptors the same choice with six weeks in which to choose. Any notice must specify this choice, the time limit and which will be paid if no choice is initiated: s.430(3).[63] If the non-cash consideration is no longer available[64] the cash equivalent must be paid[65]: s.430(4).

The mechanics of the acquisition are that six weeks after the notice has been issued,[66] the offeror sends a copy to the offeree company and pays it the consideration due (or allots the shares, as appropriate) together with an instrument of transfer executed by a person nominated by the offeror. The

---

[60] *Re Greythorn Ltd* [2002] BCC 559.

[61] This adopts the principles of r.4 of the City Code. Under the Company Law Review proposals, this would only include unconditional acquisitions: *Final Report* Vol.1 (2002), para.13.30.

[62] The notice can be signed by a solicitor and a copy must be sent to the offeree company at the same time, together with a statutory declaration that the requisite conditions for its issue have been met. See *Re Chez Nico (Restaurants) Ltd* [1992] B.C.L.C. 192.

[63] The Company Law Review recommended that where an offer is partly in cash and partly in shares, the same proportion should be offered: *Final Report* Vol.1 (2002), para.13.60.

[64] From any of the joint offerors.

[65] This confirms the decision in *Re Carlton Holdings Ltd* [1971] 1 W.L.R. 918.

[66] Unless there is an application to the court by the dissentients—see below.

offeree company must then register the offeror as owner of the shares. The offeree company must keep the consideration so received in a separate bank account on trust for the former shareholders. If they cannot be traced within 12 years after reasonable enquiries have been made at reasonable intervals, the money, etc., is to be paid into court: s.430(5)–(15).

If the offeror fails to achieve the necessary number of acceptances the court, on its application, may nevertheless allow it to acquire the remaining shares if the reason is that some shareholders have proved to be untraceable. The court can only do this, however, if the total acceptances[67] plus untraceable shareholders amount to the 90 per cent figure and the consideration is fair and reasonable. In making its decision the court must decide that it is just and equitable to allow such an acquisition having regard to the number of known shareholders who have rejected the offer: s.430C(5).

Minority right to apply to the court to prevent acquisition

The offeror's right to acquire the non-acceptor's shares under s.429 is subject to the latters' right to apply to the court under s.430C. Within six weeks of receiving a notice of intent to acquire, any non-acceptor can apply to the court for an order (a) preventing the compulsory acquisition or (b) specifying different acquisition terms: s.430C(1). The effect of such an application is to freeze the compulsory acquisition process until the application has been disposed of: s.430C(2). No order for costs or expenses may be made against an applicant unless the application was improper or vexatious, or there has been unreasonable delay or conduct on his part: s.430C(4).[68]

In *Re Britoil plc.*[69] the Court of Appeal ruled that an application will not be vexatious (and so will not incur a penalty in costs) if there is evidence justifying the court's looking at the offer to make sure it is fair. The fact that, of necessity, only a small minority of shareholders have not accepted the offer will not preclude the operation of s.430C(4).

The minority had a similar right to petition under the former sections although only to prevent an acquisition and not to specify different terms. The cases decided on the former sections are therefore of relevance as to whether to prevent the acquisition altogether.

Under the former sections the court decided that it would only make such an order if it was satisfied that the scheme was unfair to the general body of shareholders in the transferor company. There was normally a heavy burden of proof on the dissentients[70]—since the scheme has been approved by nine-tenths of the shareholders, *prima facie* it must be taken to be a fair one.[71] The test was

---

[67] The Company Law Review recommended that this should not include conditionally contracted shares: *Final Report* Vol 1 (2000) para.13.32

[68] The Review also recommended in para.13.62 that the applicant should be required to notify the offeror promptly, who must then notify the other shareholders.

[69] [1990] B.C.C. 70, CA.

[70] *Re Sussex Brick Co. Ltd* [1961] Ch. 289: *Nidditch v The Calico Printers' Association Ltd*, 1961 S.L.T. 282.

[71] The onus is the other way round under s.425, above: *per* Templeman J. in *Re Hellenic & General Trust Ltd* [1976] 1 W.L.R. 123, at pp. 130, 131.

one of fairness to the body of shareholders as a whole and not to individual shareholders, and it was not enough merely to prove that the scheme was open to criticism or capable of improvements.[72] It was not enough that the materials put before the shareholders were inadequate to enable them to form a just conclusion as to the acceptance or refusal of the offer.[73] Where there was a Stock Exchange quotation for the shares, prima facie that could be taken as the value of the shares.[74] The element of control of the transferor company, which would accrue to the transferee company from the acquisition of all the shares in the transferor company, was not taken into account in determining the value of the shares of a minority shareholder.[75] It was also held, however, that dissentient shareholders, who were not satisfied with the price offered, could not obtain an order for discovery so as to enable them to carry out an investigation into the value of the shares, unless there were special circumstances[76] but a more recent decision has established that discovery will apply unless the court is satisfied that it is unnecessary.[77]

However, if the dissentient shareholders showed that in substance the transferee company was the same as the majority holding in the transferor company the onus was on the majority to satisfy the court that the scheme was one which the minority ought reasonably to be compelled to fall in with.

A and B were the two shareholders, each holding 50 shares, in the transferee company which offered to purchase the shares in the transferor company in which there were three shareholders, A and B, who each held 4,500 shares and who accepted the offer, and C, who held 1,000 shares and who dissented. *Held*, that C, by showing that the transferee company was, for practical purposes, equivalent to the holders of nine-tenths of the shares in the transferor company who accepted the offer, had, prima facie, shown that the case was one in which the circumstances were special and the court ought to "order otherwise" within the meaning of s.[430C], and the majority had not shown that there was some good reason in the interests of the company (*e.g.* the minority shareholder was acting in a manner highly damaging to the interests of the company) for allowing the section to be invoked for the purposes of enabling the majority to expropriate the minority: *Re Bugle Press Ltd* [196] Ch. 270, CA.

The general attitude of the courts on the former section has been followed in two decisions on s.430C(1)(a). In *Re Lifecare International plc*,[78] the dissentients were said to have a heavy burden of proof to discharge, especially where their directors took independent advice and recommended acceptance of the bid. In *Re Chez Nico (Restaurants) Ltd*,[79] on the other hand, where the offeror was an insider, as in the *Bugle Press* case, it was held that the burden of proof would be reversed, so that the offeror would need to show that the offer was fair. Since there had been breaches of the City Code in that case, that had not been discharged.

[72] *Re Grierson, Oldham & Adams Ltd* [1968] Ch. 17.
[73] *Re Evertite Locknuts Ltd* [1945] Ch. 220.
[74] See *Re Press Caps Ltd* [1949] Ch. 434, CA.
[75] See n.71 above.
[76] *Re Press Caps Ltd* [1948] 2 All E.R. 638.
[77] *Re Lifecare International plc* [1990] B.C.L.C. 222.
[78] [1990] B.C.L.C. 222.
[79] [1992] B.C.L.C. 192.

There have also been two decisions on the new right to apply for the terms of the acquisition to be varied under s.430C(1)(b). In *Re Greythorn plc*, [80] the offeror was seeking to withdraw its compulsory offer altogether. The claimant, having originally sought an order to prevent the acquisition under s.430C(1)(a), now sought to hold the offeror to the acquisition but on different terms from the offer under s.430C(1)(b). The judge said, but did not decide, that it was perfectly possible for the court to make such an order against the offeror even though the claimant had originally specified a different remedy and the offeror no longer wished to acquire the shares at all.[81] If the offeror, however, still wishes to proceed with the acquisition, there is no doubt that the court may vary the terms of the acquisition. Such an order was made in *Fiske Nominees Ltd v Dwyka Diamonds Ltd*,[82] where the claimant successfully argued that not enough information had been given to them (as distinct minority shareholders) as to the valuation of the offer[83] so that they were unable to make an informed decision. Their shares would be valued by an independent expert and then acquired by the offeror.

Non-acceptor's right to be bought out by offeror

If the offeror has acquired 90 per cent in value[84] of all the shares in a company (or all the shares of a class)[85] any non-acceptor can require the offeror to acquire his shares: s.430A(1), (2). Note that this is not 90 per cent of shares subject to the offer but of all the shares, so that shares held by the offeror etc. at the date of the offer or contracted to him are included both in the total and the 90 per cent threshold.[86] This is different from the threshold which enables the offeror to acquire the shares under s.429.

If the offer is still open for acceptances the shareholder can apply to be bought out by a written communication to the offeror.[87] Otherwise within one month[88] of gaining the 90 per cent threshold (and not necessarily that for a compulsory purchase) the offeror must inform the non-acceptors of their rights to be bought out—unless it has already served a compulsory purchase notice: s.430A(3), (5). The offeror must give non-acceptors at least three months from the end of the offer period in which to apply to be bought out: s.430(4).

If a non-acceptor sends such a written communication the offeror is then "entitled and bound" to acquire the shares on the terms of the offer or such other terms as may be agreed: s.430B(1), (2). The provisions relating to

---

[80] [2002] B.C.C. 559.

[81] The wording in s.430C(3) (see below) is much clearer in allowing the court to impose terms on an unwilling offeror.

[82] [2002] B.C.C. 707.

[83] Although the City Code was not in issue, its Rules were cited as good practice as to what the acquisition documents should contain.

[84] This must also amount to 90 per cent at the voting rights under the 13th Directive.

[85] The Company Law Review recommended that this should only include those which the offeror has unconditionally contracted to acquire: *Final Report* Vol 1 (2002) para.13.31.

[86] Associates are counted in for this purpose: s.430E(3).

[87] To one of two or more joint offerors will suffice.

[88] The Company Law Review recommended that this be extended to two months: *Final Report* Vol 1 (2002) para.13.54.

alternative consideration under the offer are the same as for a compulsory purchase: s.430B(3), (4).[89]

In the case of any dispute any non-acceptor who has applied to be bought out can apply to the court to set the terms for the acquisition: s.430(3). Again such an applicant is protected as to costs: s.430C(4).

[89] Above, p.697.

Chapter 32

CROSS-BORDER MERGERS AND MIGRATION—THE EUROPEAN COMPANY

Problems of migration and cross-border mergers

Companies, like individuals, need to have a domicile, *i.e.* a country whose laws govern their existence and internal affairs. In Britain, we regard that as being the country where the company has its registered office,[1] irrespective of where its head office or major activities are located. At present, it is impossible for a British company to move its registered office as between the two British jurisdictions, let alone to another country altogether. The only practical way is to form a new company in another state and then effectively sell the British company to it. That raises very difficult tax issues as well as concerns as to the protection of creditors and members of the British company. The Government has recently rejected proposals from the Company Law Review to facilitate such migration, even with safeguards for creditors etc., for fear of loss of tax revenue.[2]

It follows, however, that nothing in our company law prevents a company from moving its operations and control to another country—it will still be a British company so far as British law is concerned. The complication in such a case is that many other countries, including most Member States of the European Community, apply a different test to determine a company's domicile—they apply the *siège réel* (real seat) theory—*i.e.* the law where a company's central management is located. Thus a company incorporated in London but whose head office is in Paris would be regarded as an English company here and as a French company in France, which since it would not be registered there presents problems as to whether it even has legal personality under French law. This clash of legal systems has been recognised by the EC from its earliest days, but a convention for the mutual recognition of each other's companies was never ratified, even by the original six Member States, and the position is still unresolved. The issue has, however, since come before the European Court of Justice on a few occasions in connection with the freedom of establishment.

In *Centros Ltd v Erhverus-og Selkabsstyrelsen*,[3] the Court upheld the right of a English registered company to operate as a branch in Denmark. The Danish authorities had refused to allow it to do so on the basis that this was, in reality, a Danish company, which had simply registered in London to avoid the minimum capital rules applied to Danish private companies. In *Überseering BV v Nordic Construction Company Baumanagement GmbH*,[4] a Dutch company transferred its

---

[1] We even distinguish in this way between England and Wales and Scotland: s.2(1).
[2] *Final Report* Vol 1 (2002) para.14.12. *Modernising Company Law* (2003) pp.54–55.
[3] [1999] E.C.R. 1–1458
[4] [2002] E.C.R. 1–9919

head office to Germany. Under Dutch law, which uses the place of registration or the incorporation theory, as we do, it still remained a Dutch company. Under German law (which uses the real-seat theory), it was held to be subject to German law and accordingly it was refused legal personality there. The European Court held that although there should be some controls on migration, denial of legal personality was a clear breach of the freedom of establishment. The basic problems on migration remain, however, although there is a draft proposal for a 14th Directive in an attempt to solve some these issues. This is discussed at the end of this chapter.

A different, but related issue concerns the lack of any mechanism for cross-border mergers between companies. Although the domestic merger procedures within the Community were harmonised by the Third Directive,[5] none of them works well if companies from more than one jurisdiction are involved. Complex arrangements are needed to get round the problem. There are also tax and administrative problems, and difficulties arising from non-harmonised areas of company law, especially in the area of worker participation, which differ as between Member States. These issues are also in the minds of the Community, and there is a draft 10th Directive on this issue in circulation at the moment which is discussed at the end of this chapter. This is less of a problem for British companies which generally use the takeover rather than the scheme of arrangement as a means of achieving cross-border mergers.

The European Company

All these problems of cross-border migration and mergers are clearly concerns with which the Community is bound to be involved. As long ago as 1959, a very radical solution was put forward, to have a totally separate entity, which would not belong to any Member State but would be domiciled in the Community. This European Company would have its own complete code of company law and allow such companies to operate throughout the Community free of national restrictions. That ideal proved, however, to be illusory. Proposals made in 1970 and 1975 were in effect abandoned in 1982. But in 1988, the idea, on a less grand scale, was revived. After prolonged negotiation and consultation, drafting and redrafting, the EC Regulation establishing the European Company Statute was adopted in 2001 and automatically became law throughout the Community on October 8, 2004.[6] The contentious issue of employee participation was dealt with in a separate directive which had to be implemented into national law on the same day.[7]

Although the Regulation is free-standing and needs no implementation in Britain, it did need some enabling changes to be made to British law and it did allow for some its articles to be optional so that choices had to be made. These changes and options have been made by the European Public Limited Liability Company Regulations 2004,[8] (the enabling Regulations), which also implemented the employee participation directive.

---

[5] See Ch.30 (schemes of arrangement) above.
[6] 2001/2157 [2001] O.J. L294/1 (the EC Reg). This has been passed under Art.308 of the Treaty.
[7] 2001/86/EC.
[8] SI 2004/2326, effective from October 8, 2004.

But this European Company is far removed from the original concept. It must be registered in one Member State and much of the law applicable to it will be the public company law of that state.[9] In addition, each Member State can decide whether to choose some or all of the options in the EC Regulation. Thus there will be as many variants of the European Company as there are Member States of the Community. We can therefore speak of a British or a French European Company, which ought to be a contradiction in terms. It does, however, retain one aspect of the original proposal, its name, which will end with the abbreviation SE rather than the domestic LLP. SE is the abbreviation for the Latin *Societas Europea* and will be used in the remainder of this chapter.

Whether the SE will ever be more than a political flagship exercise is far too early to tell. There has been little enthusiasm shown in Britain in the various consultation exercises. Given the incredible complexity of the employee participation provisions, the difficulty in divining the applicable laws (from the EC Regulation, the enabling regulations and parts of existing British company law) and the still apparently intransigent tax issues, the future does not look too promising. On the other hand, it may prove to be rather more popular in some other Member States and so involve British employees of a non-British SE, and British companies wishing to participate in the formation of a non-British SE. It may well also be the forerunner of more realistic and genuine attempts to promote cross-border migration and mergers within the Community in the shape of the proposed 10th and 14th Directives. As such it is therefore worth noting the more important aspects of the SE, 2004-style.

Laws applicable to an SE

Article 9 of the EC Regulation provides that there is a distinct order of priority as to which law is applicable to an SE. This is: (i) the provisions of the Regulation; (ii) those areas specified by the Regulation as being a matter for the company's constitution; (iii) the harmonised domestic company law applicable to LLPs; (iv) other domestic LLP law; and (v) the SE's constitution. The SE is domiciled in the state in which it has its registered office and in which it must also have its head office.[10]

Forming an SE

Art.2 of the Regulation provides for four methods of formation. The common theme is that it involves companies from more than one Member State.[11] The four methods are:

(i) merger (in Britain by a scheme of arrangement) of two or more EC public companies from at least two Member States.[12] The cross-border issues[13] are dealt with by requiring the law of each Member State to be

---

[9] See Art.10 of the EC Reg.

[10] EC Reg Art.7. This allows the real-seat theory to operate.

[11] A British SE can also include a company with a head office outside the EC to be involved provide it is registered in a Member State and has a real and continuous link with a Member State's economy: reg.55, EPLLC Regs 2004.

[12] This will be in accordance with the existing mergers by acquisition and by the formation of a new company procedures in the 3rd Directive and which are now part of ss 425–427A (see Ch.30 above).

[13] Of some interest in connection with cross-border mergers generally: see below.

applied, taking into account the cross-border protection of creditors, etc. The pre-merger procedure must be certified by the appropriate authority of each relevant Member State but the final scrutiny of the merger will be by the court of the intended state of registration. Other provisions are similar to those applicable to mergers of public companies subject to s.427A. Britain has taken up the option of being able to object to a merger on public interest grounds;[14]

(ii) formation of an SE as a holding company with subsidiaries[15] in at least two Member States. The draft terms must be identical from each participating company, none of which can have a controlling interest in the SE. Otherwise the procedure is that laid down by the third directive;

(iii) formation as a joint[16] subsidiary of two or more EC companies from at least two Member States under the law applicable to forming a subsidiary under the national law of each participating company; and

(iv) transformation of an existing EC public company provided it has had a subsidiary in another Member State for at least two years. There is no winding up of the old company and no new legal person is created. Terms of the conversion must be drawn up and approved by the general meeting. The company's net assets must also be equivalent to its capital and undistributable reserves.

Once formed, an SE has both legal personality and limited liability.[17] A British SE can express its share capital in either Euros or sterling.[18] Otherwise British law applies to its share and loan capital, accounts and insolvency.[19] Registration is the same as for a British plc, but no SE can be registered unless it has in place arrangements for worker participation in accordance with the directive.[20] The management of British SEs will be able to change the constitution to comply with any new arrangements for worker participation in the directive without a general meeting.[21] An SE can also form an SE as a subsidiary of itself.

Migration of an SE

An SE may move from one Member State to another. Art.8 of the EC Regulation provides the necessary safeguards for employees, creditors and shareholders but does not mention tax.[22] There must be a transfer proposal

---

[14] EPLLC Regs, reg. 60.
[15] These may be public or private companies.
[16] But not necessarily equal.
[17] Art.1 EC Reg. In Britain it is a body corporate—EPLLC Regs, reg.81.
[18] This is the combined effect of Arts 4 and 67 of the EC Reg and reg.67 of the EPLLC Regs 2004.
[19] Arts 5, 61 and 63, EC Reg. The existing domestic sanctions have been applied to SEs by the EPLLC Regs.
[20] See below.
[21] EPLLC Regs, reg.59.
[22] These formed the basis for the CLR's proposals for migration generally (above) which were rejected by the British government.

giving details of the proposed safeguards for those rights, and approval by a special resolution after a delay of at least two months. Further, the outgoing Member State must certify to the new Member State that the interests of creditors arising prior to the transfer[23] have been adequately protected. In the case of a British SE, it will have to produce a statement of solvency.[24] The proposal must be filed and officially notified. The British Government has also taken advantage of options to strengthen the rights of creditors and shareholders to examine the proposal prior to the meeting[25] and for it to be able to oppose a transfer of an SE from Britain on public interest grounds.[26]

Structure of an SE

Article 38 of the EC Regulation provides that an SE shall comprise a general meeting of shareholders and either a one tier system with a single management/administrative organ or a two tier system with separate supervisory and management organs. This reflects the two management systems which are in place in the EC.

With regard to meetings, there must be one each year.[27] In addition to the members of the management board(s), the holders of 10 per cent of the shares can request that a meeting be convened and 5 per cent can ask for additional items to be placed on the agenda.[28] The Secretary of State can convene a meeting in default. Ordinary and special resolutions are the same as for domestic companies. A quorum is to be half the members.[29]

At first sight the requirement that all SEs be allowed the choice of the two-tier management/supervisory board system would seem to be difficult for British law which has only a unitary system of the board of directors. But the Government has taken the view that the British structure, allowing virtually complete freedom to companies to provide any form of management structure they like in their articles, is flexible enough to provide for the prescribed two-tier system as a practical proposition without the need for any specially enabling legislation.[30]

That prescribed two-tier system requires that no one can be a member of both the management and supervisory boards. The managers must be appointed by the supervisory board, the function of which is supervise the work of the management board. Its membership is in turn appointed by the general meeting and under any worker participation arrangements made under the directive. The management board must make quarterly reports to the supervisory board on

---

[23] Britain has exercised its option to extend this from liabilities prior to the publication of the transfer proposal; EPLLC Regs, reg.57.

[24] EPLLC Regs, reg.73.

[25] EPLLC Regs, reg.56.

[26] EPLLC Regs, reg.58.

[27] Although the first one may be within 18 months of the company's formation: EPLLC Regs, reg.65.

[28] EPLLC Regs, reg.66.

[29] EC Reg, Art.50.

[30] It is arguable that many existing large companies with executive and non-executive directors have a *de facto* two-tier board system anyway. The existing rules in the Companies Act as to directors duties, disclosure etc are to apply to all members of either the one tier or two tier boards (but separately in the latter case) and there is to be a register of members of the supervisory board kept by the SE and open for inspection: EPLLC Regs, regs.77–79.

progress and foreseeable developments and provide "any information on events likely to have an appreciable effect on the SE". For a British SE, the minimum number of members of the management and supervisory board is two in each case. In the case of a single-tier system there must be at least two directors of a British SE.[31]

No manager or supervisor can be appointed for more than six years but can be re-appointed. The SE's constitution is to set out the categories of transactions which require authorisation by the board(s).[32] Persons disqualified as directors of British companies cannot be a member of any of the boards of an SE and conduct as a director/manager/supervisor of an SE could lead to disqualification proceedings under the 1986 Directors Disqualification Act.[33]

Conversion of an SE into a plc

Article 66 of the EC Regulation allows for an SE to convert back into a domestic public company but not within the first two years of registration or before at least two sets of accounts have been approved. There is no winding up or creation of a new legal entity. Draft terms of the conversion must be drawn up and approved by a special resolution and an independent expert must confirm that the company has net assets equivalent to its capital. The draft constitution of the plc must also be approved. The enabling Regulations provide all the necessary formal registration and notification requirements for the conversion.[34]

Employee involvement in the SE

One of the most fundamental differences within the EC is the extent and form of employee involvement in the affairs and management of companies. The German system of co-determination (equality of employees and shareholders representatives on the supervisory board) is the most formalistic. Britain has arguably the most flexible system. Agreeing a formula for the SE was therefore a major stumbling block, which was only resolved when the matter was hived off to a Directive[35] which requires implementation by national law. In Britain this has been done by Pt 3 of the enabling Regulations. We have already seen that no SE can be registered unless it has in place arrangements for employee participation as required by the directive. As a minimum, these will cover information and consultation but may also include employee involvement in the management structure itself.

Part 3 of the enabling regulations has transposed these requirements into British law. They apply to all British SEs and in some cases to British employees of non-British SEs. They set out the composition and appointment of the special negotiating body (SNB) which is to be set up to negotiate the arrangements with the participating companies of the proposed SE.[36] They also set out the

---

[31] EPLLC Regs, reg.62. This must be three if worker participation is involved: EC Reg, Art.43.
[32] EC Reg, Art.48.
[33] EC Reg, Art.47 and 9.1(c)(ii).
[34] Regs 85–89.
[35] 2001/86/EC.
[36] These apply to all British employees of an SE.

consequences of the various possibilities arising from those negotiations, the default arrangements if there is no agreement and it is still proposed to set up an SE, and, finally, rules to ensure the compliance, enforcement, confidentiality and protection of the members of the SNB.[37]

The structure, as envisaged by the Directive, is in essence as follows:

(i) the participating companies in the proposed SE provide employee representatives with information for the purpose of calculating the number and allocation of members of the SNB;

(ii) the SNB members are elected either by ballot of the employees or appointed by consultative committee and the six-month negotiating period begins;[38]

(iii) if an agreement is reached within that period the SE may be registered. This agreement may be (a) to rely on the national information and consultation rules,[39] (b) for some other employee involvement arrangement; or (c) to implement the default or standard rules as set out in the Annex to the Directive.

(iv) if no agreement is reached but the participating companies wish to continue to set up an SE then the standard rules will be automatically applied and the SE can be registered.

The default or standard rules for employee involvement are reproduced in Sch.3 to the enabling regulations. There must be a representative body of the employees of an SE and its subsidiaries and establishments elected or appointed by the members of the SNB. Such a body must after four years decide whether to open negotiations for a specific agreement or continue to rely on the standard rules. It may elect a select committee, be assisted by experts and is to be funded by the SE.[40]

With regard to information and consultation, the management of any SE is required to give the representative body regular reports on the progress and prospects for the SE's business, provide it with copies of the agenda for management meetings[41] and general meetings, and inform it of "any exceptional circumstances affecting the employees' interests to a considerable extent". If requested, there must be a meeting between the representative body and the management at least once a year to discuss those reports.[42] The representative body is entitled to a pre-meeting on its own. If there are "exceptional circumstances" (as above), then the select committee may meet with the top

---

[37] These latter apply if any British company or employee is involved in the special negotiating body.
[38] This can be extended by a further six months if the parties agree.
[39] This can be decided by a two-thirds majority of the SNB.
[40] But only for one expert.
[41] Including, where appropriate, of the supervisory board.
[42] In particular those meetings are to look at "the structure, economic and financial situation, the probable development of business and of production and sales, the situation and probable trends of employment, investments and substantial changes concerning organisation, introduction of new working methods or production processes, transfers of production, mergers, cut-backs or closures of undertakings, establishments or important parts thereof and collective redundancies."

management; although any member of the representative body who represents workers directly affected may attend. If, after the meeting, the management has not acted in accordance with the opinion of the representative body, the latter may request another meeting. After the meetings etc the representative body must inform the employees or their representatives of the content and results of the process.

In the more divisive area of direct employee participation in the management structure of the SE, the directive draws a distinction between an SE formed by transformation from an existing national LLP and the other methods of formation. In the first case any existing rules as to employee participation in the management (or supervisory boards) will be continued into the SE. In the case of a British company there are none. In other cases, where in at least one of the participating companies there were employee participation rights, the representative body will be able to appoint[43] members to the appropriate board. The number of such members is to be the highest proportion (of the board) in force in the participating companies at the time of registration. Thus employees in any participating company will be protected as to their existing rights on the formation of an SE. For example, if a German and a British company decide to form a British SE, the pre-existing co-determination rights of the German employees will be applicable to the SE.

Membership of the board(s) will in all cases be allocated as between employees in different Member States according to the ratio of employees in each state, but with at least one member from each Member State involved. Employee members of the board(s) are to be treated as full members of the relevant board and with full voting rights.

Proposed 10th Directive on cross-border mergers

The current proposal for a 10th Directive on cross-border mergers dates from 2003,[44] inspired by the proposals for the formation of an SE by merger. The proposal is that each merging company is to be subject to its own existing domestic merger procedure (in Britain a scheme of arrangement) but that there will be a common merger plan, etc., drawn up by all the merging companies. At the end, the merged (or surviving) company will acquire the assets and liabilities of the merging companies in the state chosen by the merging parties. The mechanics as set out in the draft reflect those of the third directive which are already part of British law.[45] The only significant impact would be that those apply only to domestic mergers of public companies whereas under the proposal they will be applied to cross-border mergers of private companies as well.

The proposals for employee participation are similar but not identical to those adopted for the SE. The major difference is that if the law of the state of the merged company has any form of employee participation then that will apply, irrespective of any rights in the states of the merging companies. In the SE the "fullest" system of rights of the participating companies prevails—no one loses

---

[43] The wording is elect, appoint, recommend or oppose.
[44] COM(2003) 703, 18.11.03. This replaced an earlier proposal from 1985.
[45] See Ch.30, above.

their rights. Thus, if we accept that Germany has the most advanced system and that, say, Italy has a less advanced system, if a German company and an Italian company wish to merge into at Italian domestic company under the Directive, the Italian system of employee rights will apply and the German employees' rights will be accordingly reduced. If, however, they set up an Italian SE, the German system would apply to it.

But if the jurisdiction of the merged company has no employee participation rights (*e.g.* Britain) and the law of any one of the merging companies does contain such rights (*e.g.* Germany) then the employee participation rights as set out in the SE directive[46] are to apply to the merged company.[47] There will have to be a special negotiating body, subsequent negotiation with the management of the merging companies, and if there is no agreement, the standard or default rules in the annex to the directive will apply, just as they would to an SE. Once these rights are agreed or imposed they will apply to all employees of the merged company wherever they are employed.

The British Government has expressed its support in principle for this 10th Directive,[48] and it was formally agreed by the Council of Ministers on November 25, 2004. It is now before the European Parliament for its comments/approval under the co-determination procedure. There is already a Directive providing for tax neutrality on such mergers.[49]

Draft proposal for a 14th Directive on company migration

There is as yet no formal proposal for a 14th Directive. An informal draft relating to transfers of both the registered and head offices was published in 1997,[50] and there was support for it in principle.[51] The concept was also endorsed by the Commission's own "High Level Group" of company law experts as being a priority since there is a perceived demand for greater mobility of companies within the EC.[52] The problems, as ever, were identified as being those of tax neutrality and the protection of employees, creditors and shareholders. Given the success of the SE statute it would seem that, of those, only tax will be a major stumbling block. But there is also the major problem of the clash between the incorporation and real seat theories, identified at the beginning of this chapter.[53]

As we have seen, the European Court has to some extent partially solved the problem of moving a company's registered office within the Community, but it has not yet had to deal with the transfer of a company between two countries which both operate the real seat theory. The High Level Group considered that the real seat theory was a disproportionate measure and possibly, as such,

---

[46] 2001/86/EC, above.

[47] It follows that if none of the merged companies have such rights then the merged company will not be subject to any employee participation rights.

[48] DTI, Draft Directive on Cross-Border Mergers: A Consultation Document, URN 04/595, June 2004.

[49] Dir 90/434/EEC, [1990] O.J. L225.

[50] XV/6002/97-EN.

[51] Responses to the Commissions Consultation Document on Company Law in 1997.

[52] A modern Regulatory Framework for Company Law in Europe (Brussels 2002).

[53] The Government consulted on the draft proposal in March 2005. Their response will follow.

contrary to EC law. They also thought that the SE statute could be a model for dealing with structure and employee participation issues but that it should not be followed on the real-seat problem.[54]

The High Level Group put forward the following recommendations on the real-seat problem to the Commission;

(i) there should be no sanction when a company moves its real-seat between Member States;

(ii) if a company's real-seat is transferred into a real-seat state (*e.g.* France) then that host state can apply its law over that of the state of that company's incorporation (*e.g.* Britain), but only within the limits imposed by the EC legal principles of legitimate interest, proportionality, minimum intervention, non-discrimination and transparency;

(iii) in particular, host states (France in the above example) should not interfere in the internal governance of the company;

(iv) where a company transfers its real seat out of a real-seat state, that home state should only impose sanctions in accordance with EC legal principles; any other problems as to domicile should be solved between the states by reciprocity; and

(v) if a third state is involved with a company which has moved its real seat, it should apply the law of the company's incorporation.[55]

In the event the Commission decided to carry out a consultation exercise in 2004 but only on a proposal to cover the transfer of a company's registered office. It considered it wise to leave the transfer of the head office to a separate directive at some later, unspecified, date. If there is to be a 14th Directive therefore it will be a much watered down version of the original concept.

In its consultation exercise the Commission laid down the principles it was considering including in the directive. These would be:

(i) a recognition of the right of a company to transfer its registered office to and so acquire legal personality in another Member State and that it would not lose its legal personality in the original Member State[56] until it acquired legal personality in the new state;

(ii) the decision must be taken by a special resolution of the general meeting[57] and this should include any necessary amendments to the company's constitution so as to make it recognisable by the new state. It would be for the new state (and not the old state) to decide whether all its requirements as to registration had been complied with. If the new

---

[54] The SE is required to have both its registered and head offices in the same Member State.
[55] This may lead to a circular application and under the conflict of laws doctrine of *renvoi* in that case the host state's law will apply.
[56] By virtue of initiating the transfer procedure.
[57] There would be publication of this, presumably in the company's file at Companies House and in the Gazette.

state required that a company's head office be in the same jurisdiction as its registered office then that would also have to be complied with prior to registration in the new state.

(iii) if the company has complied with the transfer formalities and made the necessary amendments to its constitution, the new state cannot insist on new incorporation documents;

(iv) the roles of the old and new states in the transfer process should be co-ordinated. The old state should attest to the validity of the decision to transfer and the process of altering the constitution. Verification of those changes would be for the new state;

(v) registration in the new state would automatically result in the company being removed from the register in the old state; the transfer being recorded in the registers of both countries;

(vi) the transfer should not result in any winding up or affect any third party liabilities or transactions;

(vii) special rights for minority shareholders and/or creditors could be protected along the lines of the protection for them in the third directive on a domestic mergers, the proposed 10th Directive on cross-border mergers and the SE statute;

(viii) the transfer should be tax neutral along the lines already provided for on cross-border mergers;[58] and

(ix) employee protection rights should be governed by the laws of the new Member State but subject to the proviso that if the laws of the old state are "more firmly enshrined" they should be maintained or negotiated under a procedure laid down by the old state.

The results of the Commission's consultation were that there was a substantial majority in favour of all these principles with the exception of the last one on employee protection where the majority in favour was quite small. It may be that a better solution would be to use the SE machinery to break any deadlock in this area.

---

[58] Dir 90/434/EEC; O.J. L225. This would have to be amended accordingly.

INDEX